The Developing Labor Law

Third Edition

Other BNA Books Authored by the ABA Section of Labor & Employment Law

Covenants Not to Compete: A State-by-State Survey

Employee Benefits Law

Employment Discrimination Law

How Arbitration Works (Supplement)

Labor Arbitration: A Practical Guide for Advocates

Labor Arbitrator Development: A Handbook

Occupational Safety and Health Law

The Developing Labor Law

The Board, the Courts, and the National Labor Relations Act

Third Edition

Volume I

Editor in Chief
Patrick Hardin
Professor of Law
The University of Tennessee
Knoxville

Editors

James R. LaVaute
Attorney at Law
Syracuse, NY

Timothy P. O'Reilly
Attorney at Law
Philadelphia, PA

Editor in Chief, First and Second Editions
Charles J. Morris
Committee on the Development of the Law
Under the National Labor Relations Act

Section of Labor and Employment Law
American Bar Association

BNA BOOKS

The Bureau of National Affairs, Inc., Washington, D.C.

Library of Congress Cataloging-in-Publication Data

The Developing labor law : the board, the courts, and the National
Labor Relations Act / editor in chief, Patrick Hardin ; editors,
James R. LaVaute, Timothy F. O'Reilly.
p. cm.
"Committee on the Development of the Law Under the National Labor
Relations Act, Section of Labor and Employment Law, American Bar
Association."
ISBN 0-87179-665-1 (hard cover set). — ISBN 0-87179-663-5 (v. 1).
— ISBN 0-87179-664-3 (v. 2)
1. Labor laws and legislation—United States. I. Hardin,
Patrick. II. LaVaute, James R. III. O'Reilly, Timothy P.
IV. American Bar Association. Committee on Development of the Law
Under National Labor Relations Act.
KF3369.D48 1992
344.73'01—dc20
[347.3041] 92-16326
CIP

Printed in the United States of America

31

ROBERT A. BUSH
Burbank, CA

RICHARD S. CLEARY
Louisville, KY

CHARLES I. COHEN
Washington, D.C.

DAVID DUNN
New York, NY

GARY M. EBY
Cincinnati, Ohio

THEODORE T. GREEN
Washington, D.C.

KEVIN H. HARREN
Albany, NY

ROBERT J. HENRY
Washington, D.C.

CHRISTOPHER T. HEXTER
St. Louis, MI

MARK F. KELLY
Tampa, FL

G. ROGER KING
Columbus, OH

JOHN C. LOMBARD
Dayton, OH

JOHN T. NEIGHBOURS
Indianapolis, IN

WARREN H. PYLE
Boston, MA

BERNARD W. RUBENSTEIN
Lutherville, MD

LEONARD SINGER
Kansas City, MO

PATRICIA C. SLOVAK
New York, NY

ARTHUR B. SMITH, JR.
Chicago, IL

JESSE H. STRAUSS
Newark, NJ

MARTIN WALD
Philadelphia, PA

IRA H. WEINSTOCK
Harrisburg, PA

PETER W. ZINOBER
Tampa, FL

CONTRIBUTING EDITORS

Charles A. Edwards
John W. Edwards
Kathleen Edwards
Leon Ehrlich
William J. Emanuel
Sheldon Engelhard
Mark Epstein
Howard C. Equitz

Edward J. Fahy
Zachary D. Fasman
Nicholas R. Femia
Donald W. Fisher
Steven J. Fishman
James Fox
Carl B. Frankel
Gary D. Frey
Terence M. Fruth

Janet Y. Gadient
Charles V. Gagliardi
Joseph G. Galagaza
Michael Geffner
William Patton Getty
Brent M. Giddens
Kenneth R. Gilberg
Charles W. Gilligan
Thomas S. Giotto
David F. Girard-diCarlo
E. Joseph Giroux, Jr.
Dennis Alfred Gladwell
Gail E. Glick
Deborah Godwin
James R. Goldberg
Janet E. Goldberg
Franklin H. Goldberger
David Goldman
Perry L. Goorman
Robert F. Gore
Eugene B. Granof
Lewis C. Green
Brian S. Greig
Martin Gringer
Harold Edward Grotta
Daniel F. Gruender
Craig Gumpel
Russell M. Guttshall III

W. Melvin Haas III
Lewis R. Hagood
Robert S. Halagan
Donald M. Hall
Frank E. Hamilton III
Jonathan R. Harkavy
Janet G. Harner
Michael T. Harren
Damon W. Harrison, Jr.
Jeffrey E. Hartnett
Gerald T. Hathaway
R. Kent Henslee
Wayne A. Hersh
H. W. Heunemann
Jerald A. Hochsztein
Harold L. Hoffman
Herbert L. Holtz
Norman Holtz
Daniel L. Hornbeck
Alan R. Howe
Mark A. Hutcheson
Melvin R. Hutson

Scott F. Innes

Cynthia L. Jackson
Joseph Jacobs
Neil H. Jacobs
Beth A. Jacobson
Peter A. Janus
Mark L. Juster

Raymond L. Kalmans
Steven Kaminshine
Alvin I. Kaplan
Bruce J. Kasten
Nathan L. Katz
Barry J. Kearney
Herbert G. Keene, Jr.
Joel Ibert Keiler
Estelle M. Kelley
Thomas J. Kennedy
David B. Kern
David E. Khorey
Patricia R. King
Paul J. Kingston
Alfred Klein
Ronald J. Klepetar
Linda S. Klibanow
Richard M. Kobdish, Jr.
Stephen D. Kort
David Koskinen
Michael Kota
Lester Kushner

William M. Lamoreaux
Robert J. Landsman
David W. Larrison
M. Jane Lawhon
Charles R. Leech, Jr.
Alan S. Levins
Jay J. Levit

Mark E. Levitt
Dennis G. Lindner
D. Michael Linihan
Richard J. Loftus
R. Michael Lowenbaum
W. F. Lubersky
Gerald R. Lucey
Stephen W. Lyman
Raymond F. Lynch
Paul V. Lyons

Joseph Mack III
Ernest R. Malone, Jr.
Frank T. Mamat
James J.P. Manning
Marcus Manoff
Robert D. Mariani
John Markle, Jr.
Barry W. Marr
Gary A. Marsack
John D. Marshall
William Martin
Francis A. Mastro
John P. McCarthy
David C. McDonald
John W. McKendree
Thomas W. McLane
Charles W. McManigal
Arthur P. Menard
Ronald J. Mendrick
Frank L. Merrill
Michael P. Merrill
Michael E. Meyer
A. David Mikesell
James M. Miles
John Stonewall Miller, Jr.
Robert H. Miller
Robert T. Miller
Paul Oscar Miller III
Thorley C. Mills, Jr.
Karen Milner
Robert B. Mitchell
Armin J. Moeller, Jr.
Glenn L. Moller
J. Mark Montobbio
Stanley C. Moore III
Robert Wayne Morgan
Russ R. Mueller
Michelle A. Murphy

Patrick A. Nagel
John J. Naun
Clifford Howard Nelson
John Bernard Nelson, Jr.
Kevin Nelson
Luella E. Nelson
Frank A. Nemia
Stuart L. Newman
John W. Noble, Jr.
Richard William Noble
Edwin O. Norris
Manuel A. Nunez
Peter D. Nussbaum

James R. O'Connell
Donald T. O'Connor
Nancy M. O'Connor
Thomas L.P. O'Donnell
Gary John Okey
Ernest B. Orsatti
Marlin Osthus
Paul M. Ostroff
Loyd E. Owen, Jr.
Jeffrey W. Pagano
Frank Paiva, Jr.
Al Palewicz
Mario J. Palumbo
Peter M. Panken
Patty L. Parsons
Robert E. Paul
John W. Pelino
John J. Pendergast III
Russell L. Perisho
Alan R. Peterman
John J. Pierano, Jr.
Bertrand B. Pogrebin
Michael Poprik III
John W. Prager, Jr.
E. Frederick Preis, Jr.
Emanuel N. Psarkis

William R. Radford
Douglas E. Ray
Brent Douglas Rector
Denis Y. Reed
Richard Jay Reibstein
Kathleen A. Reimer
Richard M. Resnick
J. David Richeson
Stephen Drexel Ridley
Kenneth E. Ristau, Jr.
David B. Ritter
Daniel J. Riviera
Marianne Goldstein Robbins
Michael A. Robbins

Barton W. Robertson
Susan Salitan Robfogel
John W. Robinson IV
William J. Rodgers
Lawrence Rosenbluth
Robert S. Rosenfeld
Louis Rosner
Alan Gilbert Ross
Jeffrey K. Ross
Nelson G. Ross
William L.S. Ross
Curtis L. Roy
Ivan C. Rutledge
David Ryan
Timothy F. Ryan

Theodore Sachs
Frank J. Saibert
Richard L. Samson
Marc L. Sandman
Stanley M. Saunier, Jr.
Richard C. Scheidt
Glenn H. Schlabs
Lorraine Schmall
Mark William Schneider
Mark M. Schorr
Glen Schultz
Stephen J. Schultz
Ann Marie Sferra
Mark A. Shank
Ron Sharp
Robert E. Sheahan
William J. Sichko, Jr.
M. V. Siebert
Arthur F. Silbergeld
Stephen M. Silvestri
Kenneth M. Simon
Howard S. Simonoff
Douglas L. Skor
Henry W. Sledz, Jr.
Lafe E. Solomon
Joel Spivak
Stephen B. Spolar
Laurence D. Steinsapir
John H. Stephens
J. Hamilton Stewart III
Marc L. Sussman

Michael J. Tannler
Eric A. Taussig
David M. Thomas II
George Joseph Tichy II
William C. Tidwell III
Robert P. Tinnin, Jr.
David Charles Toomey
Regis J. Trenda
John C. Truesdale
John Francis Tully
Ronald Turner
Herbert L. Turney

Carol L. Van Hal
Judith P. Vladeck
Paul S. Vogel
Thomas M. Vogt

Robert E. Wachs
Frank M. Wagner, Jr.
Gerard M. Waites
Henry Jared Wallace, Jr.
Thomas E. Walsh, Jr.
Thomas John Walter
James M. Walters
Clay Warner
Mark A. Wasserman
William Wardlaw Watkins
Charles B. Waud
Mark A. Weintraub
Priscilla Wheeler
Dermott J. White
Norman I. White
William A. Whiteside, Jr.
Barry R. Whitman
Robert A. Wiesen
Howard I. Wilgoren
James R. Willard
Brent Lawrence Wilson
David W. Wolf
Donald F. Woodcock
Edwin V. Woodsome
John C. Wright, Jr.
John Francis Wymer III

Carl S. Yaller
Ted M. Yeiser, Jr.
Jacqueline A. Young

Andrew E. Zelman
Don A. Zimmerman
Lawrence T. Zimmerman
Edgar Alan Zingman
Bennet D. Zurofsky

FOREWORD

Since 1945 the ABA Section of Labor and Employment Law has had as its stated purposes (1) to study and report upon continuing developments in the law affecting labor relations, (2) to assist the professional growth and development of practitioners in the field of employment and labor relations law, and (3) to promote justice, human welfare, industrial peace, and the recognition of the supremacy of law in labor-management relations.

Through the publication of books such as *The Developing Labor Law,* and through annual and committee meeting programs designed to provide a forum for the exchange of ideas, the Section has pursued these stated goals. Gradually, the Section has built a library of comprehensive legal works intended for the use of the Section membership as well as the Bar generally.

The Section of Labor and Employment Law is pleased to provide this third edition of its classic treatise on the National Labor Relations Act as part of its library of books published by BNA Books, a Division of The Bureau of National Affairs, Inc. As was the case with the first two editions and their supplements, the combined efforts of many individual authors from the Committee on Development of the Law under the National Labor Relations Act of the Section are reflected in this supplement.

The Section wishes to express its appreciation to the Committee members, and in particular to the editor-in-chief, Patrick Hardin; the editors, James R. LaVaute and Timothy P. O'Reilly; and the associate editors. This group has tried to accomplish two primary objectives: (1) to be equally balanced and nonpartisan in their viewpoints, and (2) to ensure the book is of significant value to the practitioner, student, and sophisticated nonlawyer. A thank-you is also due to the University of Tennessee College of Law for making Professor Hardin and its facilities available to the Section for this project.

The views expressed herein do not necessarily represent the views of the American Bar Association, or its Section of Labor and Employment Law, or any other organization, but are simply the collective, but not necessarily the individual, views of the authors.

DONALD J. CAPUANO
Chair

VINCENT J. APRUZZESE
Chair-Elect

Section of Labor
and Employment Law
American Bar Association

April 1992

PREFACE

The work of editing the Third Edition has resembled the work of a curator at the Louvre: the decisions about what to add have been much simpler than the decisions about which of the abundant treasures already in place to rearrange or retire from view. This Third Edition is built entirely on the sturdy foundation of the First and Second Editions. All of us who have contributed to this edition are indebted beyond easy description to Professor Charles J. Morris and his collaborators. Their achievements in those volumes were monumental.

The major purposes of our work on this Edition have been to bring the volumes up to date and to continue to make the body of rules of law and practice under the National Labor Relations Act readily accessible to a broad range of users in the legal and labor relations communities. This new edition provides coverage through December 1989 with important developments through April 1, 1992, including major Supreme Court decisions. That the work be accessible seems more important now than at any time since the earliest days of the Wagner Act. The advent of legally enforceable individual rights in America's workplaces presents new challenges to the regimen of collective representation contemplated by the Act. Those challenges come, moreover, at a time when other forces in our politics, and in the domestic and global economies, raise doubts whether a system of vigorous collective bargaining will remain the centerpiece of national employment policy. Yet, the regimen under the Act offers the Nation many advantages, including greater fairness and efficiency, when compared to any system based upon the enforcement of individual employees' legal rights through litigation. The Third Edition has been prepared in the hope of promoting a wider understanding of those advantages.

There are not means to thank all who have helped me prepare for and execute this work, but my special indebtedness to some compels me to single them out. Years ago, Bernie Meltzer, Ed Miller, and Bill Ryza awakened me to the satisfactions to be had from a career in labor law. Later, Burt Subrin and Nort Come taught me much about the Act, often under highly exigent circumstances. More immediately, the University of Tennessee College of Law was as generous as possible in its support of this undertaking, and I am grateful to Deans Marilyn Yarbrough and Dick Wirtz on that account. I was also much assisted in the work by my students, including Alan Pritchard, Paul Stanley, and especially Brad Mokros. Throughout the work, Jim LaVaute and Tim O'Reilly, my principal editor partners from the Labor and Employment Law Section, and Tim Darby, Acquisitions Manager from BNA Books, were unfailingly helpful, encouraging, and understanding. Finally, Jean Moore here in Knoxville and Anne Scott, Senior Editor at BNA Books, have done wondrous work in cleaning up the manuscript and proofs: the book would be a far poorer one if I had not had their constant, cheerful, help. Of course, I alone am responsible for the errors that persist.

I have dedicated my work on the book to my entire family, all of whom have endured my absence and neglect, and especially to Julie, who so lovingly helped me through all the months and chapters.

PATRICK HARDIN

Knoxville, Tennesee
May 1992

SUMMARY TABLE OF CONTENTS

VOLUMES I AND II

PART I

HISTORY OF THE NATIONAL LABOR RELATIONS ACT

PART II

PROTECTED EMPLOYEE ACTIVITY

PART III

THE REPRESENTATION PROCESS AND UNION RECOGNITION

PART IV

THE COLLECTIVE BARGAINING PROCESS

PART V

ARBITRATION AND THE ACT

PART VI

ECONOMIC ACTION

PART VII

RELATIONS BETWEEN EMPLOYEE AND UNION

PART VIII

ADMINISTRATION OF THE ACT

DETAILED TABLE OF CONTENTS

VOLUME I

PART II

PROTECTED EMPLOYEE ACTIVITY

PART III

THE REPRESENTATION PROCESS AND UNION RECOGNITION

PART IV

THE COLLECTIVE BARGAINING PROCESS

PART I

HISTORY OF THE NATIONAL LABOR RELATIONS ACT

Chapter 1

HISTORICAL BACKGROUND OF THE WAGNER ACT

By the early 1930s organized labor had been a part of the American scene for over a century.[1] It had been a century rich in crises and governmental countermeasures. From the informing perspective of six decades later, three major themes can easily be identified:

1. The case law demonstrated that the courts were not institutionally capable of formulating or implementing a workable labor policy.
2. The course of legislative and judicial action revealed increasing awareness that the role of organized labor presented a question of national proportions that no state was capable of answering definitively.
3. Two mutually incompatible national policies towards organized labor had emerged: one regarding it as creating market restraints inimical to the national economy, and the other regarding it as necessary to a regime of industrial peace based upon a balanced bargaining relationship between employers wielding the combined power of incorporated capital wealth and unions wielding the power of organized labor.

I. The Inadequacies of Judicial Regulation

The inability of the courts to provide viable solutions to the problems presented by the labor movement was twofold. First,

[1]The "first" American labor case, known as the Philadelphia Cordwainer's case, was decided in 1806. *See* C. Gregory, Labor and the Law 22 (3rd ed., 1979). For a detailed account of the trial, *see* Lieberman, Unions Before the Bar 1-15 (rev. ed., 1960); Nelles, *The First American Labor Case*, 41 Yale L.J. 165 (1931). *See generally* Witte, *Early American Labor Cases*, 35 Yale L.J. 825 (1926).

the process of case-by-case adjudication was an inadequate instrument for the formulation of a cohesive policy or rational substantive norms of conduct. The industrial revolution, and the combinations of capital and of labor that it called to life, presented problems that called for broad legislative solutions. The courts were unable to develop any workable standards for governing concerted employee conduct; they did not even try to establish any standard to regulate the behavior of employers towards labor organizations. Second, court procedures proved too cumbersome, and judicial remedies too inflexible, to effectuate whatever substantive standards the courts announced.

American courts engaged in an early flirtation with the proposition that any concerted employee action, even to raise wages, was indictable as criminal conspiracy, even though the motivating purpose and the means utilized would be legal if similar action were taken by individuals. During the first 40 years of the 19th century, numerous convictions were upheld ostensibly upon the conspiracy theory, although many of the decisions in fact involved violence or coercion, or contained language suggesting that the crime in question required either a motivating purpose or resort to means that would be illegal under some established category of common law.[2] Chief Justice Shaw of Massachusetts drew these threads together in his 1842 opinion in *Commonwealth v. Hunt*,[3] in which the conspiracy doctrine was narrowed and rationalized as requiring either an illegal purpose or resort to illegal means.

The *Hunt* decision also provided a bridge between declining use of the conspiracy doctrine, whose criminal sanctions produced overwhelmingly adverse public reaction,[4] and judicial use of civil remedies to regulate union activity. Since *Hunt*, "American legal history is a steady accumulation of instances where the line has been drawn between purposes and acts permitted, and purposes and acts forbidden."[5] But after *Hunt*, the evolution of these standards occurred primarily in the context of civil proceedings for damages or injunctions, rather than in criminal prosecutions.

---

[2]The Philadelpha Cordwainers' case, *see* F. FRANKFURTER & N. GREENE, THE LABOR INJUNCTION 2-3 (1930).

[3]4 Met. 111 (1842). *See* Nelles, Commonwealth v. Hunt, 32 COLUM. L. REV. 1128 (1932).

[4]GREGORY, *supra* note 1, at 27.

[5]FRANKFURTER & GREENE, *supra* note 2, at 4-5.

Even this basic analytical division into purposes and means was not without its difficulties. In many instances, it merely provided alternative avenues for judicial condemnation of union activity. Inducing a strike against *A* to discourage *A* from doing business with *B* may have been condemned upon the theory that its secondary purpose was illegal or, quite as easily, upon the theory that the secondary boycott was an illegal means.[6] Similarly, federal courts were inclined to make the legality of an organizational strike depend upon the manner in which it was conducted, while "in Massachusetts, the rationale for decision [shifted] almost completely to an emphasis upon the issue of justifiable ends."[7]

Aside from the ambiguity inherent in the easy interchangeability of the two tests of "ends" and "means," in the administration of each test serious problems were encountered. Even when the means test was utilized to condemn such clearly reprehensible conduct as threatening physical injury to person or property, there was a tendency toward judicial subjectivity. As late as 1900, for example, the Supreme Court of Massachusetts suggested that a threat to strike was illegal because it necessarily implied accompanying violence and injury, "however mild the language or suave the manner in which the threat to strike is made."[8]

It was in judging the legality of purposes of labor activity that the gravest difficulties were encountered. Although a few courts briefly entertained contentions to the contrary,[9] the view quickly and overwhelmingly prevailed that intentional infliction of economic harm, even by means that were not illegal, was actionable unless justified by some legitimate purpose creating a defense of privilege.[10] The difficulty was that judges were unable to agree as to what purposes were sufficient to justify the infliction of harm. Some adopted the position that any economic self-interest

---

[6]The "objectives" test was adopted in Massachusetts under the persuasive aegis of Holmes, C.J., in Plant v. Woods, 176 Mass 492 (1900) (although Holmes himself dissented in this case); the "means" test found favor in certain federal courts, *e.g.*, Atchison, Topeka & Sante Fe Ry. v. Gee, 139 F 582 (SD Iowa, 1905) (peaceful picketing compared with chaste vulgarity); FRANKFURTER & GREENE, *supra* note 2, at 24-46.

[7]FRANKFURTER & GREENE, *supra* note 2, at 27.

[8]Plant v. Woods, 176 Mass 492, 497 (1900).

[9]GREGORY, *supra* note 1, at 76-82, in which this minority view is called the "civil rights" view.

[10]Vegelahn v. Guntner, 167 Mass 92, 105 (1896) (Holmes, J., dissenting); *see* RESTATEMENT OF TORTS §775 (1939).

was an adequate justification. Their thesis was that competition was worth more to society than it cost, or at any rate that this was a basic value judgment of the common law, the alteration of which was the proper business of legislators but not of judges.[11] Other judges undertook to assess the importance of the union's asserted interest and to weigh it against competing interests of other segments of society, and frequently found organized labor on the light side of the scales.[12]

Needless to say, the economic sophistication and bias of an individual judge were often pivotal when such balancing was undertaken. Between the pure bargaining strike by employees against their own employer, which came to be quite generally accepted,[13] and the many forms of secondary pressure, which were condemned with equal generality on a wide variety of rationales,[14] there was a diversity of judicial opinion as to the legitimacy of almost all peaceful forms of concerted employee conduct.[15] Thus, one judge might conclude that a concerted refusal to work for the purpose of expanding union membership was not justified by any legitimate purpose; another judge, attributing greater weight to the importance to the union of a strong bargaining position, might find that the same strike was for the ultimate purpose of raising wages, and therefore privileged.[16]

On the remedial side, other institutional shortcomings of judicial regulation became evident. Broad use of criminal sanctions imposed for peaceful labor activity quickly proved unacceptable to the public at large and was abandoned. Money damages, the standard remedy in actions at law, imposed an inordinately heavy sanction for peaceful conduct condemned upon such unreliable criteria as those just discussed, especially since a business enterprise's capacity for economic injury so far exceeds the usual employee's ability to pay damages.[17] Because of the uncertain legality of much proposed union action under the substan-

---

[11]Vegelahn v. Guntner, *supra* note 10, at 106 (Holmes, J., dissenting); Duplex Printing Press Co. v. Deering, 254 US 443, 488 (1921) (Brandeis, J., dissenting).

[12]Vegelahn v. Guntner, *supra* note 10; Plant v. Woods, *supra* note 8.

[13]GREGORY, *supra* note 1, at 60.

[14]FRANKFURTER & GREENE, *supra* note 2, at 43.

[15]*Id.* at 26-27.

[16]*Compare* the majority opinion by Hammond, J., in Plant v. Woods, *supra* note 6, *with* the dissent by Chief Justice Holmes in the same case, *id.* at 504.

[17]*E.g.*, in Loewe v. Lawlor, 208 US 274 (1908), plaintiffs were seeking $80,000 in damages from union members. *See* Chapter 30, "Accommodations to Other Federal Enactments," at notes 6–7.

tive law, the deterrent effect of either criminal penalties or damages was too undiscriminating; in close cases, deterrence operated with equal effect whether the proposed concerted action would ultimately be determined to have been permissible or not. The only traditionally judicial remedy that transcended these limitations was the equitable remedy of injunction, and American courts turned increasingly to its use during the last two decades of the nineteenth century.[18]

The injunction was used in the labor field almost exclusively at the behest of employers to prevent injury by restraining concerted labor activity.[19] It easily lent itself to this role, since it provided prompt provisional restraint of the activity complained of, unlike criminal and common-law sanctions. But where the substantive law was uncertain, the availability of temporary injunctive relief became more important as a practical matter than the substantive law ultimately applied, since the momentum of a temporarily enjoined strike could not normally be regained even if the injunction ultimately was vacated.[20] There were other objectionable features of labor injunctions. They were frequently so vaguely worded as to be unintelligible. Contempt sanctions enabled courts to punish violations by criminal penalties without the intercession of a jury or even of a judge, other than the author of the prohibition. And all this coercive machinery could be set in motion by an ex parte application for provisional relief supported only by affidavits of interested parties.[21] The resulting "government by injunction" became a national political issue as early as 1896.[22]

By the 1930s, it had been clear for some time that the courts could not be expected to provide answers to the problems presented by the labor movement. They were not the appropriate institution to formulate a rational basis for discriminating between tolerable and intolerable concerted employee activity, with the single exception of nonpeaceful conduct. Although they had extrapolated from precedent in an attempt to regulate

---

[18] In re Debs, 158 US 564 (1895); FRANKFURTER & GREENE, *supra* note 2, at 17-18, 23. *See* FRANKFURTER & GREENE, *Injunctions in American Labor Controversies*, 44 LAW Q. REV. 164 (1928).

[19] On rare occasion a union successfully obtained injunctive relief; *see* FRANKFURTER & GREENE, *supra* note 2, at 108.

[20] *See* In re Debs, *supra* note 18; FRANKFURTER & GREENE, *supra* note 2, at 17.

[21] A. COX & D. BOK, LABOR LAW CASES AND MATERIALS 100-101 (6th ed., 1965); FRANKFURTER & GREENE, *supra* note 2, at 53-60.

[22] FRANKFURTER & GREENE, *supra* note 2, at 1.

union activity, it would probably have been preferable had they not done so, and certainly no one had ever expected them to make a similar effort in order to formulate norms for employer conduct. Thus, by the time a controversy reached the courts, industrial strife usually already had occurred, and the remedies available limited the range of judicial decision to whether the union activity in question should be punished or suppressed, and, if so, by what sanction.

II. THE RISE OF FEDERAL REGULATION

Federal courts played two roles in regulating labor disputes before the Wagner Act. In exercising their diversity-of-citizenship jurisdiction, they were major participants in the unsuccessful attempt to make common-law precedents answer the challenge of organized labor. In exercising federal-question jurisdiction under several federal statutes, for a time they imported much of this unfortunate common-law precedent into national policy, and they marked out—in what proved to be a tentative fashion—the permissible limits of federal governmental action to regulate labor disputes.

Under the doctrine of *Swift v. Tyson*,[23] federal courts deciding questions of state common law were not bound to follow decisions of state courts as precedents. Federal judges, enjoying tenure for life as a practical matter,[24] were on the whole far less sensitive to the demands of organized labor than their brothers on the state bench whose tenure frequently was less secure. Thus in many instances an employer might expect a more favorable result in federal than in state court. And employers, as plaintiffs, were able to manipulate the matter of citizenship with considerable success to enable themselves to maintain suit in federal court. Consequently there grew a large body of federal "common law" applicable to labor disputes. Further, federal equity practice, which had always been independent of state law, provided fertile soil for the development of labor injunctions.[25]

As late as 1930, it appears, a majority of the labor cases in federal courts were there because of diversity jurisdiction.[26] But

---

[23]41 US 1 (1842).
[24]U.S. CONST. art. III, §1.
[25]FRANKFURTER & GREENE, *supra* note 2, at 5-17.
[26]*Id.* at 210.

beginning before 1900, an increasing number of cases—many of them extremely influential—were brought into federal court by virtue of federal legislation. In 1895, in the landmark case of *In re Debs*,[27] the Supreme Court upheld the jurisdiction of a federal court to enjoin labor violence in a railroad strike, at the instance of the United States, on the basis of statutes prohibiting obstruction of the mails and regulating interstate commerce. The latter of these, the Interstate Commerce Act,[28] was used as the basis of federal intervention in a number of labor cases marked by uncertainty as to the applicability of the common-law tests of illegal means and illegal ends.[29]

This problem never had to be resolved; even before the *Debs* case, lower federal courts had commenced to use another statute as a basis for federal-question jurisdiction to intervene in labor disputes.[30] This was the Sherman Act,[31] enacted in 1890. Section 1 of the Act rendered illegal "every contract, combination in the form of trust or otherwise, or conspiracy, in restraint of trade or commerce among the several states." The Act created a cause of action for treble damages for persons injured by violations, authorized injunctions and criminal prosecution of violations, at the instance of the United States, and created federal jurisdiction over all such proceedings.

The Supreme Court avoided the question of the Sherman Act's role in labor cases in the *Debs* litigation, but ultimately faced it in a series of decisions beginning in 1908 with *Loewe v. Lawlor*,[32] the celebrated *Danbury Hatters'* case. A threshold question that has been extensively and acrimoniously debated was whether the Sherman Act was applicable to labor unions at all.[33] The Act was intended primarily "as a safeguard against the social and economic consequences of massed capital,"[34] but its substantive provisions are worded broadly enough to encompass violations by labor organizations, and a proposed amendment to exempt them specifically was advanced in the Senate but never

---

[27]158 US 564 (1895).

[28]24 Stat. 379 (1887), 49 USC §§10501 & passim (1988).

[29]Toledo, A.A. & N.M. Ry. v. Pennsylvania Co., 54 F 730 (ND Ohio, 1893); Knudson v. Benn, 123 F 636 (D Minn, 1903).

[30]United States v. Debs, 64 F 724 (ND Ill, 1894).

[31]26 Stat. 209 (1890), 15 USC §§1-7 (1988). *See generally* Chapter 30, "Accommodations to Other Federal Enactments."

[32]208 US 274 (1908); *see* Blumrosen, *Group Interests in Labor Law*, 13 RUTGERS L. REV. 432, 446 (1959).

[33]*See* H. MILLIS & E. BROWN, FROM THE WAGNER ACT TO TAFT-HARTLEY 9 (1949).

[34]FRANKFURTER & GREENE, *supra* note 2, at 8.

incorporated into the statute. In any event, the question was resolved in favor of applicability in the *Danbury Hatters'* decision.

Without more, the Supreme Court's decision that labor organizations were not excluded from the category of potential violators of the Sherman Act meant merely that it would be possible for an employer to state a claim for treble damages against a union and its adherents "arising under" the Act and thus within the jurisdiction of federal courts, and that there similarly would be judicial cognizance of government proceedings to impose injunctive or penal sanctions. But deciding this did not decide what ingredients were essential to a violation of the statute in a labor dispute.

As muddy as the common law was in its application to labor activity, it seems clear that Congress intended the Court to turn to the common law to determine the scope of the Sherman Act's prohibitions.[35] It thus seems odd that the Court did not accept this invitation to indulge its own economic and social ideas in determining what purposes and means of concerted action should or should not render such action prohibited under the Act. Several decisions by the Court, and further action by Congress, were required for the Court to reach something approximating this result. In its first application of the Sherman Act to organized labor in the *Danbury Hatters'* case, the Court indicated that it would be enough to establish a violation if the employees' concerted action obstructed the flow of the employer's product in interstate commerce.[36] The activity actually before the Court in the case could for the most part have been condemned on narrower grounds; in an attempt to insulate its gains from price competition by nonunion products, the union was utilizing primary and secondary consumer boycotts to organize a nonunion manufacturer. All this pressure might have been condemned under the means and objectives tests at common law; but the rule adopted by the Court was much broader.

A degree of flexibility was added to the rule in two decisions in 1921 and 1922, with the result that federal regulation of union activity under the Sherman Act conformed somewhat more closely with the results reached at common law. The first of these involved the Clayton Act,[37] which, as a result of union lobbying

---

[35]GREGORY, *supra* note 1, at 205.
[36]Loewe v. Lawlor, *supra* note 32, at 292-93.
[37]38 Stat. 730 (1914), 15 USC §§12-27 (1988). *See* notes 39 and 40, *infra*, for cases.

in response to the *Danbury Hatters'* decision, contained two provisions that were widely thought to relieve the strictures that case had imposed upon union activity. These provisions, Sections 6 and 20 of the Clayton Act, are discussed subsequently.[38] It is enough here to say that they were very narrowly construed by the Supreme Court in *Duplex Printing Press Co. v. Deering*[39] and held to exempt only concerted activity already regarded as lawful at common law, and then only when engaged in by employees in an effort to settle a labor dispute with their own employer. With this exception, any concerted action was a violation of the Sherman Act if it produced a disruption in the flow of goods in interstate commerce. The activity involved in *Duplex* was a secondary labor boycott: the union induced its members not to work for those who purchased or used Duplex's products. The Court might have condemned the boycott on the narrower ground that it would have been illegal under the means or objectives tests at common law. As it was, the *Duplex* decision imported into the Sherman Act a line of distinction—between pressure upon one's employer and pressure exerted upon others—closely akin to the distinction utilized by common law to condemn secondary boycotts.

A closer conformity between the Sherman Act and the common law was achieved one year later in *Mine Workers v. Coronado Coal Co.*[40] As in the two boycott cases, the union ultimately was concerned with eliminating price competition from nonunion-produced commodities. The concerted action took the form of a strike accompanied by violence and property destruction, the effect of which was to halt the mining of coal, and thereby, of course, to disrupt the flow of the employer's product in interstate commerce. The Court chose to differentiate between this kind of disruption, caused by interference with manufacturing or mining the product, and the disruptions caused by boycotts which inhibited demand for the product. The former was characterized as an "indirect" obstruction to interstate commerce; the Court took the view that such an indirect restraint would violate the Sherman Act only if used to further an intention to create a market restraint or monopoly in interstate commerce.[41] This was in fact the ultimate purpose in the two boycott cases as

---

[38] *See* Chapter 30, "Accommodations to Other Federal Enactments," at notes 9–10.
[39] 254 US 443 (1921).
[40] 259 US 344 (1922).
[41] *Id.* at 410-11.

well as in the *Coronado* case. But in the latter, since the obstruction to interstate commerce was "indirect," proving the purpose became crucial. This meant that, given adequate proof of this subjective purpose, the federal courts had a means of condemning organizational strikes while leaving purely bargaining strikes uncondemned by the Sherman Act.[42]

Thus the Supreme Court ultimately embraced an application of the Sherman Act to organized labor not greatly different from the pattern reached by many courts at common law. The major differences, aside from the requirement of a disruption of interstate commerce, were (1) that the Sherman Act, as amended by the Clayton Act, gave to employers the remedy of treble damages as well as the injunction and (2) that the United States was empowered to sue for injunctions and to institute criminal prosecutions for violations of the Sherman Act.

At best, all this amounted to in terms of substantive law was a step backward. Partially counterbalancing this, however, is the consideration that some degree of federal power to regulate labor disputes under the Commerce Clause was thoroughly established. Indeed, even an "indirect" obstruction caused by a cessation of mining or manufacturing had been recognized as a sufficient link to validate regulation by Congress. From this it was only a step—albeit not an easy one—to recognition of Congress' power to regulate labor policies of employers engaged in interstate commerce, as well as organized employee activities.

III. AN AFFIRMATIVE NATIONAL LABOR POLICY: THE ANCESTRY OF THE WAGNER ACT

While the federal courts were pursuing their unsuccessful quest for an answer to the challenge posed by the labor movement, the two other branches of the federal government became increasingly sensitive to the same challenge and slowly began to articulate their own policies toward organized labor. The judicial policy in essence was one of selective suppression of organized labor's activities whenever they trenched too heavily upon the interests of any other segment of society. Commercial interests must not be injured by disruption of the interstate flow of

---

[42]Coronado Coal Co. v. Mine Workers, 268 US 295 (1925). The "fink" had been discovered. *See* GREGORY, *supra* note 1, at 216.

goods; consumers and unorganized laborers must not be injured by wage standardization; employers and the public at large must not be injured by expansion of labor disputes through secondary boycotts. Save for the bargaining strike and accompanying picketing, very little indulgence was given to the claims of organized labor to an institutional role in the nation's economy.

The rival policy that was developed by the executive and legislative branches of government assigned an important function to organized labor in the operation of the national economy and sought to protect this function in two ways: by eliminating judicial interference with the operation of labor organizations and by affording some of these operations affirmative legal protection.

A. The Erdman Act

The history of this governmental second front on labor policy begins with the 1894 Pullman strike, which gave rise to the *Debs* case.[43] The United States Strike Commission, appointed by President Cleveland to inquire into the matter, filed a report adopting ideas that are now a part of our national labor policy. The commission concluded that the judicial approach to labor organization was inappropriate in the light of "the rapid concentration of power and wealth, under stimulating legislative conditions, in persons, corporations, and monopolies."[44] It suggested that organization of employees was beneficial to the employment relationship because organization tended to reduce failures of communication and promote rational and responsible settlement of labor disputes by peaceful means. At least some of the courts were nonetheless "still poring over the law reports of antiquity in order to construe conspiracy out of labor unions."[45]

The commission's central conclusion was that employers should recognize and deal with labor organizations: If employers "take labor into consultation at proper times, much of the severity of strikes can be tempered and their number

---

[43]In re Debs, 158 US 564 (1895).

[44]UNITED STATES STRIKE COMMISSION, REPORT ON THE CHICAGO STRIKE OF JUNE-JULY 1894 XLVII (1894).

[45]*Id.*

reduced."[46] "Yellow dog" contracts obligating employees to abstain from union membership should be made illegal. In response to the railway strike that had occasioned its inquiry, the commission recommended a permanent federal commission to investigate, conciliate, and if necessary decide railway labor disputes with judicial enforcement power. The parties to each dispute—employees through their unions if they so chose—should be entitled to representation in the hearing body. While proceedings were pending, and for six months thereafter, a moratorium should be imposed upon concerted union activity against the employer and upon employer discrimination against adherents of the union. More broadly, the presidential commission's report recommended that the states establish agencies to mediate and conciliate labor disputes and to encourage and facilitate arbitration, and that the states give labor organizations "standing before the law."[47]

This report became the basis of the Erdman Act, enacted by Congress in 1898.[48] Though limited to employees engaged in the operation of interstate trains, the Act suggested what was to become the basis for future legislation relating to organized labor. It imposed criminal penalties for the discharge or threatened discharge of employees for union membership, and, utilizing unions as representatives of employees, provided procedures for mediation and conciliation of railway labor disputes. The mediators were directed to encourage submission of unsettled disputes to arbitration.

The mediation provisions of the Erdman Act operated with moderate success until World War I, when the government took over the railroads.[49] The prohibition in Section 10 of the Act against antiunion discrimination, however, was held unconstitutional by the Supreme Court in *Adair v. United States*,[50] decided one week before the *Danbury Hatters*'[51] case in early 1908. The Court concluded that Section 10 of the Act deprived the railroads and their agents, as well as railroad employees, of liberty of contract without due process of law, in violation of the Fifth Amendment, and, further, that the commerce power did not

---

[46]*Id.* at LIV.
[47]*Id.*
[48]30 Stat. 424 (1898).
[49]COX & BOK, *supra* note 21, at 70.
[50]208 US 161 (1908).
[51]Loewe v. Lawlor, *supra* note 32.

authorize Congress to make this regulation of contractual relations. A railroad employees' membership in a labor organization, the Court said,

> cannot have, *in itself* and in the eye of the law, any bearing upon the commerce with which the employé is connected by his labor and services. . . . One who engages in the service of an interstate carrier will, it must be assumed, faithfully perform his duty, whether he be a member or not a member of a labor organization.[52]

Thus, in *Adair* the Court disagreed with the factual conclusions reached by President Cleveland's commission, and by Congress as well, that disruptions in interstate transportation were traceable directly to the railroads' refusal to deal with labor organizations. A majority of the Justices could conceive of only one national policy toward organized labor, which they attributed to Congress a week later in the *Danbury Hatters'* case. Symptomatic relief of commercial disruptions was deemed a legitimate exercise of federal power, but Congress could not root out the cause by regulating the employment relationships out of which commercial disruptions arose. State legislation implementing the recommendations of the commission's report met a similar fate by application of the Due-Process Clause of the Fourteenth Amendment.[53]

B. The Clayton Act

Sections 6 and 20 of the Clayton Act,[54] which deal expressly with organized labor, may best be regarded historically as a response to the Supreme Court's *Adair* and *Danbury Hatters'* decisions. In those two cases, the Court had told Congress: first, that it had no power to protect interstate commerce against labor disruptions by regulating employers' hiring and firing practices to promote the growth of unions; and second, that Congress had, in the Sherman Act, adopted a contrary policy of suppressing the activities of organized labor when they interfered with the flow of goods in interstate commerce. On the first of these points, Congress recognized that the Supreme Court has the final say because of its power to determine the constitutionality

---

[52]Adair v. United States, *supra* note 50, at 178.

[53]Coppage v. Kansas, 236 US 1 (1915).

[54]38 Stat. 731 (1914), 15 USC §17 (1988); 38 Stat. 738 (1914), 29 USC §52 (1988). For general discussion of the applicability of the antitrust laws to labor union activity, see Chapter 30, "Accommodations to Other Federal Enactments."

of federal legislation. On the second, however, Congress recognized that it had the power to alter the policy attributed to it by the Court's interpretation of the Sherman Act in the *Danbury Hatters'* decision. This is what Congress sought to do in the labor provisions of the Clayton Act. Accepting the Court's admonition that affirmative promotion of unionism by regulation of employer conduct was beyond its constitutional power, Congress sought to advance the same policy in a negative fashion by limiting narrowly the circumstances in which the courts might intervene to assist an employer in resisting the organizational efforts of labor unions.

There appears to have been some fear after the *Danbury Hatters'* decision that the Supreme Court might resurrect ancient law under the Sherman Act to conclude that *all* organized labor activity interfering with the flow of goods in interstate commerce was in violation of the Act, since the basic principle of labor organization is combination to control the supply, and thereby the price, of labor in a given market.[55] Section 6 of the Clayton Act was designed to eliminate the possibility of any such judicial action by providing that labor itself is not "an article of commerce" and that the antitrust laws do not prohibit the existence of labor organizations or their "lawfully carrying out" their "legitimate objectives."

The full meaning of section 6 standing alone is quite nebulous; in order to determine what concerted employee activity is exempted from the antitrust laws, it is necessary to give some content to the phrase "lawfully carrying out . . . legitimate objectives." The operative words "lawfully" and "legitimate" suggest, of course, the two-part formulation of the common law: The concerted activity must not itself be an illegal means, and it must be justified by a legitimate purpose. But the content that the common law gave to these two tests was itself amorphous. Further light is cast upon the scope of the section 6 exemption by section 20.

Section 20 of the Clayton Act consists of two paragraphs. The first of these sought to eliminate the broad-scale use of labor injunctions by revitalizing the classical requirement of equity jurisdiction that there must be actual or threatened injury and no adequate remedy at law before an injunction will issue—a requirement that had fallen by the wayside with the growth of

---

[55]GREGORY, *supra* note 1, at 205, 208.

labor-injunction practice prior to the turn of the century.[56] In this paragraph Congress referred to the cases it was dealing with as those "between an employer and employees, or between persons employed and persons seeking employment, involving, or growing out of, a dispute concerning terms or conditions of employment."

The second paragraph of section 20 limits labor injunctions by a different technique. It describes several basic categories of concerted labor activity, and provides that none of these activities shall "be considered or held to be violations of any law of the United States," and that even if there is injury and no adequate remedy at law, so that an injunction might issue under the first paragraph of section 20, "no such . . . injunction shall prohibit" any of the described activities. Needless to say, Congress did not intend to legitimate violent acts, physical injury to persons or property, threats of such conduct, or similar illegal means. The categories of activity legalized by the second paragraph of section 20 reflect this at several points. Persuading others to strike must be "by peaceful means"; proselytizing for a union is limited to "any place where any such person or persons may lawfully be," and the persuasion must be exercised "peacefully." One may persuade others to cease to patronize "by peaceful and lawful means." Groups may "peaceably" assemble, "in a peaceful manner, and for lawful purposes." With the sole exception of the last-quoted phrase, section 20 makes no reference to legality of purpose. To the contrary, the final category of activity legitimated by the section indicates that Congress intended to extend immunity without regard to the objective of the activity, so long as the activity did not fall within any established, non-labor-oriented category of illegality at common law: No one, singly or in concert, is to be restrained "from doing any act or thing which might lawfully be done in the absence of such [labor] dispute by any party thereto." The section thus appeared to remove all limitations upon the permissible purposes of concerted labor activity. Not even economic self-interest was required. The Act appeared to adopt a "civil rights" labor philosophy that had found only temporary acceptance in even the most liberal state courts.[57]

---

[56]*Id.* at 98-99; FRANKFURTER & GREENE, *supra* note 2, at 23, 60, 200-201.
[57]GREGORY, *supra* note 1, at 76-82.

The Clayton Act also amended the Sherman Act by authorizing private injunction suits to restrain violations.[58] It was such a suit that brought sections 6 and 20 of the Clayton Act before the Supreme Court in *Duplex Printing Press Co. v. Deering*.[59] The defendants had imposed a secondary labor boycott in an effort to complete the organization of the newpaper-press manufacturing industry and thereby protect union gains already made in that industry against price competition from Duplex's nonunion-made presses. The boycott successfully halted the movement of some Duplex presses in interstate commerce, and so violated section 1 of the Sherman Act as interpreted in the *Danbury Hatters'* case, unless the Clayton Act had changed the law.

The Supreme Court concluded that if the Clayton Act had changed the law, it had done so only to a very slight extent. The Court read the first paragraph of section 20, requiring the absence of an adequate remedy at law, as an approval of existing practice rather than an attempt to resurrect a fallen barrier to the issuance of injunctions in labor cases. The only significance attributed to the paragraph was the restriction found to be imposed upon the second paragraph. The first paragraph's reference to cases "between an employer and employees" was read to mean between an employer and *his* employees. The second paragraph was read as legalizing the described categories of concerted activity only in such cases, since it afforded protection against injunctions issued subject to the requirements of the first paragraph. This restrictive reading was reinforced, the Court found, by the emphasis in the second paragraph "on the words 'lawful' and 'lawfully,' 'peaceful' and 'peacefully,'" in describing the activities to be afforded protection. The Court found in this emphasis legislative approval and adoption of the common law's unmanageable tests for the legality of concerted employee action, rather than a legislative command not to interfere with such action in the absence of violence or similar misconduct. Since secondary boycotts were illegal at common law, the Court reasoned that the second paragraph of section 20 did not mean to legalize them. This reinforced the conclusion that section 20 applied only to cases between an employer and its own employees.[60]

---

[58]38 Stat. 737 (1915), 15 USC §26 (1988).

[59]254 US 443 (1921). *See* Chapter 30, "Accommodations to Other Federal Enactments," at notes 9–10.

[60]254 US at 470-74.

Two incompatible policies toward organized labor thus were fairly well crystallized by the Clayton Act and the *Duplex* decision. The polarity of these policies should not be obscured by the fact that the Supreme Court managed to read one policy into legislation designed to promulgate the other,[61] a distortion facilitated by the remarkable turgidity of Congress' language in sections 6 and 20. It remained for Congress to design and enact legislation that would effectuate its policy of fostering collective bargaining in the face of opposition, not only from employers, but from the Supreme Court as well.

C. The Railway Labor Act

In *Adair v. United States*,[62] the Supreme Court had invalidated only section 10 of the Erdman Act, and the statutory machinery for settlement of railway labor disputes remained intact. The report of President Cleveland's United States Strike Commission was joined by others in 1902 and 1915 making similar recommendations for the fostering of labor relations based upon collective bargaining between employers and labor organizations.[63] The Wilson Administration, under which Congress had enacted the Clayton Act provisions that Samuel Gompers had hopefully dubbed "labor's charter of freedom," extended more effective protection to the labor movement when, in 1917, government intervention to prevent labor disputes became necessary to maintain the production of war materiel. President Wilson established the War Labor Conference Board in early 1918, and upon its recommendations established the National War Labor Board.

The fundamental policy adopted by the new Board was as follows:

> The right of workers to organize in trade unions and to bargain collectively, through chosen representatives, is recognized and affirmed. This right shall not be denied, abridged, or interfered with by the employers in any manner whatsoever.[64]

---

[61] *Id.* at 484-86 (Brandeis, J., dissenting).

[62] 208 US 161 (1908).

[63] ANTHRACITE COAL STRIKE COMM. REP., S. DOC. NO. 6, 58th Cong. Spec. Sess., 63 (1902); UNITED STATES COMM. ON INDUSTRIAL RELATIONS REPORT, published in 1915, is carefully analyzed in ADAMS, AGE OF INDUSTRIAL VIOLENCE 1910–15 (1966).

[64] NATIONAL WAR LABOR BOARD, PRINCIPLES AND RULES OF PROCEDURE 4 (1919); COX & BOK, *supra* note 21, at 81.

Employers who persisted, in defiance of orders of the Board, in tactics designed to discourage organization of their employees—such as discharge for union activities, espionage, and interrogation of employees—in several cases found their businesses seized and operated by the government.[65]

Although business and government repudiated the collective bargaining policy as a general proposition when the crisis of war was past, the Railway Shopmen's strike in 1922 ultimately produced, in 1926, a statute that successfully established the collective bargaining policy on the railroads: the Railway Labor Act.[66] In addition to machinery for settlement of minor disputes, i.e., employee grievances arising under collective agreements, the Act established a presidentially appointed board with authority to mediate contract-negotiation disputes, implementing a statutory duty imposed upon both sides to make "every reasonable effort to make and maintain agreements concerning rates of pay, rules, and working conditions." Should mediation fail and the parties be unwilling to submit to arbitration, the Board was to notify the President if the dispute threatened a disruption of interstate commerce sufficient to deprive any section of the country of essential transportation services. The President might then appoint an "emergency" board with power to investigate and report upon the dispute. During this process, the statute imposed a moratorium for up to 60 days upon any change in the status quo by either party to the dispute.

The provisions of the Railway Labor Act had been largely negotiated in advance by the railroads and the railroad brotherhoods.[67] The 60-day embargo had been conceded by labor in exchange for provisions protecting union organizational efforts. The Act provided that "collective action, without interference, influence or coercion exercised by either party over the self-organization or designation of representatives by the other" was to be the manner in which representatives of parties to labor disputes under the Act should be selected.

The Railway Labor Act was challenged in *Texas & New Orleans Railroad v. Railway, Airlines & S.S. Clerks*,[68] which reached the Supreme Court in 1930. The railroad had sought to establish a company-dominated union and in so doing had engaged in a

---

[65]COX & BOK, *supra* note 21, at 81.
[66]44 Stat. 577 (1926), 45 USC §§151-63 (1988).
[67]COX & BOK, *supra* note 21, at 113.
[68]281 US 548 (1930).

campaign of discharges for union activity and other forms of coercion. Since the Act did not provide any means of enforcement of the employees' right to select their representatives without "interference, influence or coercion" by the employer, the union brought suit in federal court to enjoin the employer's antiunion activities. The Supreme Court upheld the suit, and in doing so removed major obstacles to further legislative implementation of the policy fostering collective bargaining.

Specifically, the Court recognized that Congress, in exercising its power to regulate commerce,

> may facilitate the amicable settlements of disputes which threaten the service of the necessary agencies of interstate transportation. In shaping its legislation to this end, Congress was entitled to take cognizance of actual conditions and to address itself to practicable measures. The legality of collective action on the part of employees in order to safeguard their proper interests is not to be disputed. . . . Congress was not required to ignore this right of the employees but could safeguard it and seek to make their appropriate collective action an instrument of peace rather than of strife.[69]

Adair v. United States[70] was distinguished upon the unconvincing basis that, unlike the Erdman Act, the Railway Labor Act "does not interfere with the normal exercise of the right of the carrier to select its employees or to discharge them," but is aimed rather "at the interference with the right of employees to have representatives of their own choosing."[71] Freedom to engage in such interference was not a right protected by the Constitution.

D. The Norris-LaGuardia Act

The last piece of major labor legislation enacted before the advent of the New Deal was the Norris-LaGuardia Act.[72] The Supreme Court's decisions upholding the constitutionality of the Railway Labor Act as an exercise of the national power to regulate interstate commerce had not overturned the Court's established view that this power did not extend to local businesses such as manufacturing and mining, and this limited vision of the commerce power was a major factor in the shaping of the new legislation. It sought not to regulate labor relations under

---

[69] *Id.* at 570.
[70] 208 US 161 (1908).
[71] Texas & New Orleans R.R. v. Railway, Airlines & S.S. Clerks, *supra* note 68, at 571.
[72] 47 Stat. 70 (1932), 29 USC §§101-15 (1988).

the commerce power, but to further the policy of collective bargaining by preventing judicial interference with labor activities in an exercise of Congress' power, under article I, section 8, of the Constitution, to regulate the jurisdiction of the lower federal courts under Article III.

Two important sections of the statute—sections 4[73] and 7[74]—are reminiscent of section 20 of the Clayton Act, with these exceptions:

(1) They are phrased as denials of jurisdiction, rather than as prohibitions against the issuance of injunctions;
(2) Section 7 imposes more rigid restrictions upon the issuance of labor injunctions than the mere absence of an adequate remedy at law;
(3) There is no provision giving substantive legitimacy to the activities that are thus exempted from injunction; and
(4) Primarily by a broad definition of "labor dispute" in section 13(c), the provisions of sections 4 and 7 are made applicable "whether or not the disputants stand in the proximate relation of employer and employee," thus avoiding possible judicial emasculation such as that suffered by the Clayton Act provisions in the *Duplex* case.

Because the Norris-LaGuardia Act operated solely to restrict federal judicial intervention in labor disputes, it has been said that the point of the Act "is not what it does for organized labor but what it permits organized labor to do for itself without judicial interference."[75] Notwithstanding this laissez-faire approach, it would be inaccurate to attribute to Congress a neutral attitude toward labor disputes in the enactment of the statute. Through the medium of eliminating judicial interference, the statute was designed to promote employer recognition of unions and thus foster the practice of collective bargaining as an institution in the conduct of labor relations. It was primarily because of limitations upon its power to regulate employer conduct under the Commerce Clause, as then construed by the Supreme Court, that Congress limited itself to this

---

[73]47 Stat. 70 (1932), 29 USC §104 (1988).
[74]47 Stat. 71 (1932), 29 USC §107 (1988).
[75]GREGORY, *supra* note 1, at 186. For a discussion of judicial adaptation of the Norris-LaGuardia Act to enforcement of collective bargaining agreements, see Chapter 17, "Relation of Board Action to Enforcement of Agreements Under Section 301."

method of effectuating its policy. Section 2 of the Act contains a statement of the national policy the Act was designed to advance:

> Whereas under prevailing economic conditions, developed with the aid of governmental authority for owners of property to organize in the corporate and other forms of ownership association, the individual unorganized worker is commonly helpless to exercise actual liberty of contract and to protect his freedom of labor, and thereby to obtain acceptable terms and conditions of employment, wherefore, though he should be free to decline to associate with his fellows, it is necessary that he have full freedom of association, self-organization, and designation of representatives of his own choosing, to negotiate the terms and conditions of his employment, and that he shall be free from the interference, restraint, or coercion of employers of labor, or their agents, in the designation of such representatives or in self-organization or in other concerted activities for the purpose of collective bargaining or other mutual aid or protection. . . .[76]

Additional provisions of the Act, in furtherance of this policy, render unenforceable in federal courts the "yellow-dog" contract, by which employees obligated themselves to refrain from union membership; limit the imposition of vicarious liability upon union officials and members for acts of other agents of the union; deny injunctive relief to any party who has not attempted to settle the dispute by negotiation or resort to available governmental machinery for mediation or voluntary arbitration; and impose procedural safeguards for litigants against whom contempt sanctions are sought.

The length to which Congress went to promote union organization in the Norris-LaGuardia Act is perhaps most vividly evident in the scope given the Act by the definitional provisions in section 13.[77] The Act was made applicable to any case involving or growing out of a labor dispute. Such a case was defined as one involving "persons who are engaged in the same industry, trade, craft, or occupation; or have direct or indirect interests therein," and labor dispute was broadly defined to include "any controversy concerning terms or conditions of employment, or concerning the association or representation of persons in negotiating, fixing, maintaining, changing, or seeking to arrange terms or conditions of employment, regardless of

[76] 47 Stat. 70 (1932), 29 USC §102 (1988).
[77] 47 Stat. 73 (1932), 29 USC §113 (1988).

whether or not the disputants stand in the proximate relation of employer and employee." The "allowable area of economic conflict"[78] had been enlarged, for purposes of avoiding federal injunctive action, as much as organized labor had any reason to wish.[79]

[78]FRANKFURTER & GREENE, *supra* note 2, at Chap. I.

[79]GREGORY, *supra* note 1, at 190. For an account of American labor history during the era preceding the New Deal, see I. BERNSTEIN, THE LEAN YEARS—A HISTORY OF THE AMERICAN WORKER 1920-1933 (1960).

Chapter 2

THE WAGNER ACT PERIOD

I. The Political Climate

The Great Depression and the advent of the New Deal spawned a political climate that was favorable to—or at least tolerant of—the major federal legislation thought necessary at the time to promote the growth of organized labor. This growth was considered by many to be essential if employees in American industry were to acquire sufficient economic leverage to bargain effectively with management. It was hoped that the end result of these concurrent developments would be an equitable division between labor and management of the wealth generated by private enterprise and, coincidentally, an important impetus to the revitalization of the economy. The economic conditions prevailing during the early 1930s focused attention on the plight of the worker, and economists were quick to point out that low spending power among the employees of American business would prolong the depression. The infallibility of industry management was disproved by post-1929 events, and the political influence that management could marshal against pro-union legislation was considerably diminished by the abrupt change from a boom to a bust economy.

The Norris-LaGuardia Act[1] had given organized labor a shield against judicial interference with the tools of union self-help. But by itself the Act was in fact of little value in promoting the growth of organized labor and the development of collective bargaining in American industry. Similarly, section 7(a) of the National Industrial Recovery Act (NIRA),[2] passed by Congress

---

[1] 47 Stat. 70 (1932), 29 USC §§101-115 (1988). *See* Chapter 1, "Historical Background of the Wagner Act."

[2] 48 Stat. 198 (1933).

in 1933, had attempted to persuade industry to recognize employee rights to organize and to bargain collectively, but the absence of any power to enforce these "rights" rendered them virtually useless in the face of management's understandable hesitancy to aid the growth of organized labor. Most employers rebuffed union efforts and refused recognition and collective bargaining; in the alternative, employers created company unions and agreed to bargain with those unions, but with no others.[3] In this way an employer was able to go through the motions of recognizing and cooperating with organized labor, but was able to avoid the danger inherent in the recognition of a union that had a mind of its own. Also, while employees had a "right" to organize into labor unions, employers had a commensurate "right" to inflict serious injury—in particular, discharge—upon employees brash enough to exercise their organizational "right."[4]

II. THE ROLE OF SENATOR WAGNER

These, then, were the conditions prevailing in 1934, when Senator Robert Wagner introduced a far-reaching bill that he felt would give the needed federal support to employee organization and to collective bargaining.[5] In particular, Senator Wagner stressed the failure of mere persuasion under section 7(a) of the NIRA and proposed in his bill the creation of a quasi-judicial tribunal with defined legal authority and the power to have its orders enforced by court decree. In the face of well-organized industry opposition, Wagner's bill had little chance of success; however, on June 19, 1934, Congress did enact a compromise measure, Resolution 44, authorizing the President's appointment of a board with the power to order and conduct elections and the power to investigate labor controversies "arising under" section 7(a) of the NIRA or burdening the "free flow of interstate commerce."[6] But neither Senator

---

[3]A. LINK & W. CATTON, AMERICAN EPOCH 416 (1963).

[4]For a general discussion of the failure of §7(a) of the NIRA, see I. BERNSTEIN, TURBULENT YEARS 172-85 (1970); J. GROSS, THE MAKING OF THE NATIONAL LABOR RELATIONS BOARD: 1933-1937 at 23-39, 122-30 (1974).

[5]*See* H. MILLIS & E. BROWN, FROM THE WAGNER ACT TO TAFT-HARTLEY 24 (1950).

[6]48 Stat. 1183 (1934). For a more complete discussion of Resolution 44 and its place in the legislative developments of the early 1930s, see Madden, *The Origin and Early History of the National Labor Relations Board,* 29 GEO. WASH. L. REV. 234, 237-38 (1960).

Wagner nor others of the same view were placated by this compromise measure, and in 1935 Wagner introduced another bill, similar to his 1934 bill.

As in 1934, Senator Wagner's bill met with vigorous opposition from industry, but in 1935 this opposition was unable to create in Congress a climate incompatible with the bill's passage. But another potential obstacle arose as the Administration refused to support the Wagner bill when it was first introduced.[7] Although President Roosevelt eventually joined the Wagner camp, he delayed until after the bill had been passed by the Senate and passage by the House was a certainty. In short, the bill's passage was largely dependent upon Senator Wagner's talent for coordinating the support of his colleagues and upon the sentiment of the times. Unlike other major New Deal legislation, the Wagner Act thus was the product of a single man's efforts; and, although the political circumstances of 1935 may have been favorable to these efforts, it required Wagner's energy and expertise as a legislative midwife to bring forth the origin of modern American labor law—the Wagner Act.[8]

III. THE NATIONAL LABOR RELATIONS ACT: THE BEGINNING OF AN ERA

From the outset, Wagner considered the National Labor Relations Act to be more than a weapon against the disruption of industry by labor-management disputes. This was, of course, an important function of the Act, but in the Senator's eyes its reach was far broader.[9] As was implicit in his recurrent statements on the Senate floor in support of the bill, he envisioned the pro-

---

[7]In addition to Administration neutrality, there was active opposition to the Wagner bill among several high-ranking members of the Roosevelt Administration. *See* Keyserling, *The Wagner Act: Its Origin and Current Significance,* 29 GEO. WASH. L. REV. 199, 203-204 (1960); GROSS, *supra* note 4, at 148.

[8]*See* Address by Judge J. Warren Madden, Section on Labor Relations Law of the ABA, Luncheon Meeting, Aug. 9, 1966, in 1966 SECTION OF LABOR RELATIONS LAW PROCEEDINGS, MONTREAL, CANADA 24 (1967).

[9]The broad reach desired by Senator Wagner was, in fact, embodied in the final version of his bill as enacted. Despite the language of §1, which described the purpose of the Act almost exclusively in terms of "industrial strife" and "burdening or obstructing commerce," the provisions of the Act created the substantive rights and federal machinery that Senator Wagner believed would produce economic and social progress. The actual language of §1 seems to have been designed primarily to give the Act a jurisdictional basis under the Commerce Clause and did not indicate a failure by Senator Wagner to achieve the broad reach that he sought. *See* GROSS *supra* note 4, at 144.

posed legislation as an "affirmative vehicle"[10] for economic and social progress.

> Caught in the labyrinth of modern industrialism and dwarfed by the size of corporate enterprise, [the employee] can attain freedom and dignity only by cooperation with others of his group.[11]

To accomplish this broad purpose, the Act created a right for employees to organize and, unlike the earlier provisions of the NIRA, made this right legally enforceable.[12] The Act also gave meaning to this organizational right by requiring employers to bargain collectively with employees[13] through representatives chosen by the employees.[14] The cornerstone of the Act was section 7, which originally provided:

> Employees shall have the right to self-organization, to form, join or assist labor organizations, to bargain collectively through representatives of their own choosing, and to engage in concerted activities for the purpose of collective bargaining or other mutual aid or protection.

This triad of rights—(1) the right to organize, (2) the right to bargain collectively, and (3) the right to engage in strikes, picketing, and other concerted activities—was considered essential to establish a balance of bargaining power between employer and employee and thereby to avoid the pitfalls and inadequacies which had characterized earlier labor legislation.

To enforce the substantive rights given employees by section 7 and the specific provisions implementing those rights—particularly the provisions of section 8 defining employer unfair labor practices—the Wagner Act established the type of administrative agency which had become a hallmark for much of the New Deal legislation. Sections 3 through 6 created the National Labor Relations Board (NLRB) and set out the essential details of its operation. Section 9, in addition to introducing into labor relations the principle of majority rule, gave the NLRB exclusive jurisdiction over questions of employee representation. Sec-

---

[10]Keyserling, *supra* note 7, at 218.

[11]79 CONG. REC. 7565 (1935) (remarks of Senator Wagner).

[12]*See* Chapter 32, "NLRB Orders and Remedies."

[13]*See* Chapters 13, "The Duty to Bargain," 14, "Effect of Change in Bargaining Representation During the Term of a Collective Bargaining Agreement," 15, "Effect of Change in the Employing Unit: Successorship," and 16, "Subjects of Bargaining."

[14]*See* Chapters 10, "Representation Proceedings and Elections," 11, "Appropriate Bargaining Units," and 12, "Recognition and Withdrawal of Recognition Without an Election."

tion 10 accorded the Board exclusive jurisdiction over the unfair labor practices defined by section 8 and also set forth the broad outlines for NLRB procedure,[15] including provisions for judicial review and court enforcement of Board orders.[16]

A conspicuous characteristic of the Wagner Act, when set in the context of the shield given employee activities by the Norris-LaGuardia Act, was its one-sided nature. The prime function of the Act was to protect employees against employer tactics designed either to obstruct organizational efforts or to withhold the fruits of those efforts. Management was given no corresponding protection against union actions, and little attention was paid to the protection of employee interests against abuse by unions.[17] The Act was focused on the creation of a meaningful—that is, enforceable—right to organize and to bargain collectively; and, in fulfilling this primary function, Senator Wagner and Congress had looked no farther than the needs of the employee who was bent on organizing. But Congress' narrow vision could not have been fairly criticized at the time, for in 1935 it was generally believed that the shortcomings of federal labor law arose primarily from the inability of employees to join together into units having sufficient economic leverage to bargain with their employers. Management could and did frustrate attempts at organization with its arsenal of self-help devices; the threat of discharge, in particular, was a formidable weapon during the depression, when jobs were few and far between. And in 1935 the one-sided nature of the Wagner Act did not seem a conspicuous deficiency, for labor unions then were a force of less than awesome proportions.[18] Furthermore, one-sided legislation may have been deliberately chosen by Senator Wagner and Congress as the best means to ensure that organizational rights were, in fact, respected and enforced. If the Wagner Act had included express restrictions on union

---

[15] *See* Chapters 29, "Federal Preemption of State Regulation," 30, "Accommodations to Other Federal Enactments," and 31, "NLRB Procedures."

[16] *See* Chapters 32, "NLRB Orders and Remedies," and 33, "Judicial Review and Enforcement."

[17] The §9 provision for majority rule afforded some protection to the employee—at least in the initial stage when employees chose their bargaining representative. And a proviso in §9(a) seemed to guard against union inaction by extending to each employee the "right" to present grievances to the employer.

[18] *See* I. BERNSTEIN, *supra* note 4, at 318-51, for a colorful description of the passage of the Act. For a discussion of union membership trends during the 1930s, see H. MILLIS & R. MONTGOMERY, ORGANIZED LABOR 192-201 (1945); *see generally* Magruder, *A Half Century of Legal Influence on the Development of Collective Bargaining*, 50 HARV. L. REV. 1071 (1937).

activities, the attainment of its principal goal—protecting organizational efforts—might have been jeopardized.

Today, when critics of the Wagner Act have before them evidence of almost 60 years of operation and 2 major enactments that have emphasized the fallibilities of the Act,[19] it may be easy to criticize Congress' action in 1935. But whatever criticism may be fair in retrospect, it is certain that the Act was the starting point for contemporary American labor law. Whatever the justification, the Wagner Act, set against the Norris-LaGuardia backdrop, was the statute by which the national government intended to give labor unions the power to become an important force in American industry.

IV. CRITICISM OF THE ACT: ONE-SIDED LEGISLATION

Critics of the Wagner Act set to work immediately following its passage by Congress in 1935. Their first step was to urge the unconstitutionality of the Act in the hope that the judiciary would be less receptive to Senator Wagner's efforts than Congress had been. In 1935, a group of 58 prominent lawyers and public figures published the "Report on the Constitutionality of the National Labor Relations Act," which was essentially a brief pro bono publico, setting forth the opinion that the Wagner Act was unconstitutional. This Liberty League Brief, as it was called, marshaled forces along two fronts: the Due Process Clause and the Commerce Clause. It argued that section 9(a) and its provision for majority rule deprived minority groups and individual employees of their right to negotiate with their employers, thereby infringing the constitutional requirement of due process. More basically, the brief claimed that Congress was without jurisdiction to impose the Wagner Act's provisions upon employers and employees; the Commerce Clause, it was urged, did not give Congress the plenary authority over private economic activity necessary for the enactment of this legislation. The Supreme Court, apparently by coincidence, lent considerable support to the arguments offered by the brief when *United*

---

[19]The Taft-Hartley amendments, discussed in Chapter 3, "The Taft-Hartley Changes," and the Landrum-Griffin amendments, discussed in Chapter 4, "The Landrum-Griffin Changes."

States v. Butler[20] and *Carter* v. *Carter Coal Co.*[21] were handed down in 1936.

The NLRB was not oblivious to the constitutional threat posed by the Liberty League Brief and by the precedents of the Supreme Court; it was thus careful not to allow the constitutional issue to be presented to the Court in an unfavorable posture. Considerable effort was made to have insignificant cases settled or terminated before court action;[22] and the Board was successful in delaying adjudication of the constitutional issues until 1937, when five cases presenting these issues, in what the agency believed was a satisfactory context, were brought to the Court. On April 12, 1937, in *Jones & Laughlin Steel Corp.*,[23] the Court rejected the argument of the critics of the Wagner Act and held the Act constitutional. Concluding that the Commerce Clause issue was pivotal, the Court adopted a more liberal definition of the commerce power than it had accepted in its earlier opinions—for example, in *Carter Coal Co.* The constitutional criterion, the Court said, was not the locus of the actions and conditions which Congress sought to regulate; rather, it was whether or not those actions and conditions were the *source* of burdens and obstructions to the free flow of commerce. In the light of the Wagner Act's purpose and effect, which relied on the statutory phrase "affecting commerce," the Act clearly fell within the scope of congressional powers.

With the constitutional issue settled, the critics of the Act changed their tack and concentrated upon particular revisions of the statutory scheme which they considered desirable. Although some continued to press for outright repeal of the Act, most believed that any chance for its complete demise was lost when the Supreme Court handed down its decision in *Jones & Laughlin.* Numerous bills were introduced in Congress to amend the regulatory scheme created by the Norris-LaGuardia and Wagner Acts. In 1940, and again in 1941, Representative Howard W. Smith of Virginia introduced bills to amend the Wagner Act, and in each instance the bill was passed by the

---

[20] 297 US 1 (1936) (holding the Agriculture Adjustment Act, 1933, unconstitutional).

[21] 298 US 238 (1936) (holding the Bituminous Coal Conservation Act of 1935 unconstitutional).

[22] *See* Madden, *supra* note 8; GROSS, *supra* note 4, at 183-88.

[23] NLRB v. Jones & Laughlin Steel Corp., 301 US 1 (1937). See further discussion of the Act's constitutionality in Chapter 28, "Jurisdiction: Coverage of the Act."

House but thereafter failed to be reported out of committee in the Senate.[24]

Critics took the view that the Act was one-sided legislation, slanted heavily in favor of organized labor; therefore a number of "equalizing" amendments were needed. The primary spokesmen of the campaign to equalize the Act were the United States Chamber of Commerce and the National Association of Manufacturers (NAM). The American Federation of Labor (AFL) was also in favor of limited amendments during this period;[25] it was disturbed over certain Board decisions which it felt showed favoritism toward the emerging Congress of Industrial Organizations (CIO) unions.[26]

The drive for amendment faltered as the nation busied itself with the problems of World War II. However, a series of work stoppages in the coal industry in 1943 focused public attention on the problem of labor relations. These stoppages were especially unpopular since unions were operating under a no-strike pledge for the duration of the war. The displeasure of Congress over the strikes was reflected in the passage, over the veto of President Roosevelt, of the Smith-Connally War Labor Disputes Act.[27]

When World War II ended, a renewed campaign to amend the Wagner Act gained momentum as a result of certain well-publicized activities of some labor unions. The wartime strikes of the United Mine Workers had aroused public feeling that unions were becoming irresponsible. A union tactic which received considerable news-media coverage was mass picketing during strikes. Certain types of secondary boycotts also came under close scrutiny, as, for example, the practice of picketing or boycotting small retail outlets rather than directly organizing the workers.[28] In addition, both employers and the general public were disturbed over friction and division within the labor move-

---

[24]*See* Reilly, *The Legislative History of the Taft-Hartley Act*, 29 GEO. WASH. L. REV. 285, 287 (1960).

[25]MILLIS & BROWN, *supra* note 5, at 284.

[26]*See, e.g.*, the *American Can* case, 13 NLRB 1252, 4 LRRM 392 (1939).

[27]The Smith-Connally Act gave the President authority to seize and operate struck plants, made instigating a strike subject to criminal penalties, and required 30 days' notice of any labor dispute that might interrupt production. On the 30th day the NLRB was required to conduct a secret strike vote. Act of June 25, 1943, ch. 144, §§1-11, 57 Stat. 163, appendix, 50 USC §§1501-11 (1982). Sec. 8 of the War Labor Disputes Act, 57 Stat. 167, §1508 of appendix, 50 USC, dealing with the function of the NLRB to take secret ballots of employees on the question of an interruption of war production, was abolished by 5 USC §133y-16, Reorg. Plan of 1946, No. 3, Part VII, 701 (1988).

[28]H. MILLIS & E. BROWN, FROM THE WAGNER ACT TO TAFT-HARTLEY 24, 279 (1950).

ment. These controversies often resulted not only in "raiding" rivalries between unions competing to represent certain units, but also in jurisdictional disputes which caught the employer in the middle. Finally, there were isolated instances of glaring abuses in the conduct of the internal affairs of some unions. These included the imposition of exorbitant dues under closed-shop conditions and cases of outright racketeering. Certain unions were said to practice discrimination in choosing their membership and to expel members under vague and undemocratic circumstances.[29]

In 1946 both Houses passed the Case bill, aimed at curbing abuse of union power under the existent statutory scheme; but the bill was vetoed, and the House was unable to muster the necessary two-thirds vote to override the veto.[30]

The publicizing of union misconduct, however random, coupled with the effective campaign still being waged by the Chamber of Commerce and the NAM, led to continued legislative activity. Indeed, prior to 1947 most of the major provisions of the Taft-Hartley Act had been introduced in Congress in one or more forms. Professors Millis and Brown have pointed out that 230 major bills dealing with amendment of the Wagner Act were introduced from 1936 to the passage of Taft-Hartley, excluding the Taft-Hartley proposals.[31] They divide these bills into several distinct categories reflecting the major criticisms of the Wagner Act in the 12-year period:

(1) *NLRB organization and procedures:* One of the most common complaints was that the NLRB combined the functions of investigation, prosecution, and adjudication. Other dissatisfactions with the Board stemmed from its handling of evidence, its treatment of employers' rights of speech in organizational campaigns, and its use of subpoena powers. Another complaint was that there was inadequate court review provided for the Board's decisions. Proposed bills in this area ranged from changing the size of the Board to removing its unfair labor practice jurisdiction.

(2) *Representation problems:* There was much criticism of the Board's determination of appropriate bargaining units, and there were various proposals to amend the majority-rule con-

---

[29]*Id.* at 280.
[30]H.R. 4908, 79th Cong., 2d Sess. (1946).
[31]MILLIS & BROWN, *supra* note 5, at 333.

cept of section 9(a). Much of this controversy was directly attributable to the craft-unit versus industrial-unit question arising out of the disputes between the AFL and the CIO.

(3) *The scope and procedures of collective bargaining:* Of particular concern was the growing union practice of bargaining for the closed shop. Some of the proposals would have placed unions under the antitrust laws.

(4) *Union or employee unfair labor practices:* The one-sided nature of legislation that prohibited only employer unfair labor practices became a growing issue.

(5) *Stricter controls of unions and disputes:* Other proposals were offered to place restrictions on certain types of concerted activities, to place stricter legal obligations and responsibilities on unions and employers, and to provide better methods of dispute settlement.

The large number of such bills introduced in Congress in the first 12 years of the Wagner Act reflected the increasing pressure to amend the law.[32] Although no proposal was ultimately successful, except the extraordinary Smith-Connally Act, the problem areas were being explored and the foundation was being laid for legislative action in 1947.

---

[32]Developments on the state level also reflected a growing mood of disillusionment with major portions of the Wagner Act. Although a few states had passed legislation after 1937 modeled after the Wagner Act, an overall trend of restrictive legislation was established in the late forties. By 1947, only three states still had legislation modeled after the Wagner Act. *See* MILLIS & BROWN, *supra* note 28, at 316-32.

Chapter 3

THE TAFT-HARTLEY CHANGES

I. Industrial Unrest and Congressional Response

A. Union Growth

While earlier attempts to revise the Wagner Act had not met with tangible success, such efforts did make an important contribution to the political atmosphere in 1947. When the Eightieth Congress convened in January, it was apparent that the status quo was no longer assured. Between 1935 and 1947 unions had flourished in the climate provided by the Norris-LaGuardia Act[1] and the Wagner Act.[2] Union membership had expanded from 3 to 15 million.[3] In some industries, such as coal mining, construction, railroading, and trucking, four-fifths of the employees were working under collective bargaining agreements.[4] Under government policy prevailing during World War II, union leaders had assumed important and prestigious positions and were often consulted by the Administration in an obvious attempt to maintain internal industrial peace. This growing image of union power led one commentator to conclude in 1947 that the labor movement in the United States was the "largest," the most powerful, and the most aggressive that the world has ever seen; and the strongest unions . . . are the most powerful private economic organizations in the country."[5] Moreover, organized labor was not at all hesitant to exercise this burgeoning power to obtain the benefits it wanted.

---

[1]47 Stat. 70 (1932), 29 USC §§101-115 (1988).
[2]*See* Chapter 2, "The Wagner Act Period."
[3]A. Cox & D. Bok, Labor Law Cases and Materials 130 (6th ed., 1965).
[4]*Id.*
[5]S. Slichter, The Challenge of Industrial Relations 154 (1947).

Perhaps the most notorious example of the exercise of this power occurred during the Second World War when the United Mine Workers under John L. Lewis conducted two prolonged and crippling strikes in which the coal miners returned to work only after the government had made substantial concessions.[6] And following the war, in 1946 a wave of strikes shut down steel mills, seaports, automobile assembly plants, and many other industries critical to the post-war conversion of the American economy.[7]

B. A Republican Congress

1. Response to President Truman's Proposals. The disorderly state of industrial relations and resulting public indignation toward union strike activity created important issues for the mid-term political campaign of 1946, when the elections established Republican majorities in both houses of Congress for the first time since 1930. On the first day of the new congressional session, 17 bills[8] dealing with labor relations were introduced, and by the end of the first week no fewer than 200 bills on the subject had been offered.[9] Additional labor bills continued to pour in during the next few weeks; added momentum was provided by President Truman's State of the Union Message, in which he proposed a limited revision of the nation's labor laws. His proposals included: (1) prevention of jurisdictional disputes, (2) prohibition of certain secondary boycotts, (3) establishment of machinery to help solve disputes arising under existing collective bargaining agreements, and (4) creation of a temporary commission to investigate the entire field of labor-management relations.[10]

When the hearings opened in the House and Senate, however, it soon became obvious that Congress had stronger legislation in mind than the President had proposed. The Senate and House committee hearings on the numerous bills did much to marshal

---

[6]COX & BOK, *supra* note 3, at 130.

[7]*See* Reilly, *The Legislative History of the Taft-Hartley Act,* 29 GEO. WASH. L. REV. 285, 288 (1960).

[8]Perhaps the most outspoken advocate of change was Senator Joseph Ball of Minnesota, who had presented four bills, including S. 360, which was to become the skeleton for Title 1 of the Taft-Hartley Act, the title which amended the basic Wagner Act. *See* Reilly, *supra* note 7, at 289-91.

[9]*See* H. MILLIS & E. BROWN, FROM THE WAGNER ACT TO TAFT-HARTLEY 363 (1950).

[10]*Id.* at 364.

support for statutory revision. The emphasis in the House hearings was an investigation of abuse by labor of its power; the emphasis in the Senate hearings was on the accumulation of testimony from all sides on the merits and demerits of the proposed reforms. Although major labor legislation was by no means a foregone conclusion in January, as the session progressed it became increasingly clear that such legislation was likely.

2. Problem Areas. Attention focused upon several problem areas that had come to prominence during and just after the war. These were spotlighted by the hearings: (1) the secondary boycott, which had proved to be a potent tool in the hands of some unions, injuring not only the immediate parties to the labor dispute, but disinterested third parties as well, (2) closed- and union-shop agreements, which in many instances had led to abuse and certainly contributed to labor's political and economic strength, (3) strikes and picketing, which had often turned into violence when unions were unable to achieve their goals by peaceful means, (4) corruption, which had appeared in some unions, although it was not as conspicuous during the 1940s as it later became during the 1957 McClellan Committee investigation, and (5) frequent jurisdictional disputes between unions in the construction industry, which had halted many large projects for long periods as unions bickered about the rights of different employees to various job assignments.[11]

The committee hearings were extensive. Opinions differed as to their objectivity, although it was generally conceded that the Senate hearings were conducted fairly.[12] Senator Taft noted that no bill with which he had ever been concerned had ever "been considered in more detail and more thoroughly studied."[13] But as to the House proceedings, professors Millis and Brown concluded that they "did not do credit to that body in terms of adequate and relevant analysis of the important issues

[11]*See* H. REP. NO. 245 on H.R. 3020, 80th Cong., 1st Sess. (1947), 1 LEGISLATIVE HISTORY OF THE LMRA 292-354; S. REP. NO. 105 on S. 1126, 80th Cong., 1ST SESS. (1947), 1 LEGISLATIVE HISTORY OF THE LMRA 407-62.

[12]Senator Morse, who opposed the majority bill, stated that "the bill represents a fine example of committee work in which men devoted to the public welfare did their best to resolve their differences on a basis of fair compromise." 93 CONG. REC. 3786 (Apr. 17, 1947); *see also* 1 LEGISLATIVE HISTORY OF THE LMRA 1000.

[13]93 CONG. REC. 3786-87 (Apr. 17, 1947); *see also* 1 LEGISLATIVE HISTORY OF THE LMRA 1001.

presented,"[14] and even the Senate debate, in their view, "did not match the difficulty of the subject or the needs of the times."[15]

3. Differences Between Senate and House Bills. The Senate and House each passed a version of a labor reform bill, with the House bill being broader in scope and more restrictive on unions. The Conference Committee was faced with the following provisions in the House bill which differed substantially from the Senate version:

(1) The NLRB was abolished, and a new board to hear cases and an agency to prosecute cases were created.

(2) A long and detailed list of concerted activities by unions was declared unlawful, and unions were placed under the antitrust laws.

(3) Employers were permitted to seek injunctions against unions' unlawful concerted activities.

(4) Economic strikes were permitted only after any employee vote of approval and after notice and a "cooling-off" period.

(5) Mass picketing was made unlawful.

(6) Employer payments to joint health and welfare funds were outlawed.

(7) Industry-wide bargaining was severely limited.

(8) Detailed regulation of internal union activity was provided.

(9) Strikes by government employees were banned.

(10) Political contributions or expenditures in national elections were banned.[16]

On the following points, the two bills were similar though not identical:

(1) Certain union unfair labor practices were specified.
(2) "Free speech" rights were extended to employers.
(3) The closed shop was outlawed.
(4) Involuntary checkoff was prohibited.
(5) Supervisors were removed from coverge of the NLRA.

---

[14]MILLIS & BROWN, *supra* note 9, at 374. The authors commented on the minority charge, that the bill was "one-sided" and that the "wishes of employers expressed during the hearings had been given full satisfaction while labor appeals were ignored" by noting that labor representatives had failed to propose any suggested legislation of their own and would not admit that there were any abuses which would stand legislative treatment. *Id.* at 372.

[15]*Id.* at 381.

[16]*Id.* at 383.

(6) Bargaining rights were denied to unions having Communist officers.

(7) The government was empowered to seek injunctions in "national emergency" disputes.

(8) An independent agency for mediation and conciliation was established outside the Department of Labor.

(9) Provision was made for damage suits in federal district courts for violation of collective bargaining agreements and for certain unlawful concerted activities.[17]

C. Presidential Veto

When the Conference Committee had completed its work, the resulting bill reflected the fact that the Senate Taft bill had served as the model for the final draft.[18] The conference report was passed by the House 320 to 79 and by the Senate 54 to 17. However, President Truman vetoed the bill, stating that, in his view:

> The bill taken as a whole would reverse the basic direction of our national labor policy, inject the Government into private economic affairs on an unprecedented scale, and conflict with important principles of our democratic society. Its provisions would cause more strikes, not fewer. It would contribute neither to industrial peace nor to economic stability and progress. It would be a dangerous stride in the direction of a totally managed economy. It contains seeds of discord which would plague this Nation for years to come.[19]

Congress was willing to risk the test of history.[20] The veto was overridden by a vote of 68 to 25 in the Senate and 331 to 83 in the House, and the bill became law on August 22, 1947.

II. THE NEW AMENDMENTS

The new statute, named the Labor Management Relations Act of 1947, shifted the emphasis of federal labor law. From an

---

[17]*Id.*

[18]S. 1126, 80th Cong., 1st Sess. (1947). The only two major provisions on which the Senate yielded were the sections dealing with strikes by government employees and political contributions by unions.

[19]President's Message on Veto of Taft-Hartley Bill (June 20, 1947), 20 LRRM 22 (1947).

[20]According to Gerard Reilly, who served as special counsel to the Senate Labor Committee and assisted in the drafting of the bill, President Truman, in his veto message, "relied upon a staff memorandum of the N.L.R.B. attacking the conference bill in the same extreme and irrational terms that characterized the C.I.O. literature on the subject. . . . Senator Taft . . . on the networks that same evening was able to make an effective rebuttal." Reilly, *supra* note 7, at 300. *But see* MILLIS & BROWN, *supra* note 9, at 389-90, regarding the President's study of the legislation and the preparation of the veto message.

attitude of federal protection for the rights of employees to organize into unions and to engage in concerted economic activity and collective bargaining, the emphasis shifted to a more balanced[21] statutory scheme that added restrictions on unions and also guaranteed certain freedoms of speech and conduct to employers and individual employees.[22]

A. Employee Rights

The change was reflected in the amended section 1 "Findings and Policy" and in the amended section 7 "Rights of Employees." Whereas section 1 in the Wagner Act spoke of "denial by some employers of the right of employees to organize . . ." and "inequality of bargaining power between employees . . . and employers . . . ," the amended section 1 was directed equally at labor organizations:

> [C]ertain practices by some labor organizations . . . have the intent or the necessary effect of burdening or obstructing commerce . . . through strikes . . . or concerted activities. . . . The elimination of such practices is a necessary condition to the assurance of the rights herein guaranteed.

It should be noted, however, that Congress left unchanged the original commitment in the final paragraph of section 1, which declares the policy of the United States to be that of

> encouraging the process and procedure of collective bargaining and . . . protecting the exercise of full freedom of association, self-organization, and designation of representatives of their own choosing. . . .

The amended section 7 gave employees the right to *refrain* from engaging in activities protected in the original section 7:[23]

> [Employees] . . . shall also have the right to refrain from any or all such activities except to the extent that such right may be affected by an agreement requiring membership in a labor organization as a condition of employment as authorized in section 8(a)(3).

---

[21]Organized labor contended that the new statute was overbalanced in favor of employers and dubbed the legislation a "slave labor" law. MILLIS & BROWN, *supra* note 9, at 389. *See* notes 47-48 and accompanying text, *infra*.

[22]The entire Labor Management Relations Act contains five titles, but only Title I is treated here because the scope of this book is limited to the National Labor Relations Act, which Title I amended.

[23]See Chapter 6, "Interference With Protected Rights," at notes 3–4, for a detailed comparison of the original §7 to the amended version.

B. Structural Changes in Board Administration

Some of the earlier criticisms of the Wagner Act had been directed at the procedure and structure of the NLRB itself.[24] Several changes were designed to meet those criticisms. Section 3(a) increased the size of the Board from three to five members. Section 3(d) separated the office of General Counsel from the Board proper, making the General Counsel an independent officer appointed by the president and confirmed by the Senate. The General Counsel was given supervision over the attorneys employed by the Board and over the officers and employees in the regional offices. The General Counsel was also given final authority over investigating charges, issuing complaints, and prosecuting them before the Board. The function of adjudication was thus separated from investigation and prosecution.[25]

C. Union Unfair Labor Practices

Section 8(b), which creates six union unfair labor practices, was added in its entirety. Section 8(b)(1) forbids restraint or coercion of employees "in the exercise of the rights guaranteed in Section 7."[26] Section 8(b)(2) makes it an unfair labor practice for a union "to cause . . . an employer to discriminate against an employee in violation of subsection (a)(3). . . ."[27] Section 8(b)(3) places an affirmative duty on employee representatives to bargain collectively with their employer.[28]

Sections 8(b)(4)(A), (B), and (C) outlaw various secondary boycotts.[29] Section 8(b)(4)(D) makes it an unfair labor practice for a union to force or require assignment of work in a jurisdictional dispute.[30]

Section 8(b)(5) forbids a union to charge excessive or discriminatory initiation fees.[31] Section 8(b)(6) is directed at the practice

---

[24] *See* Chapter 2, "The Wagner Act Period."

[25] *See* Chapter 31, "NLRB Procedures."

[26] *See* Chapter 6, "Interference With Protected Rights."

[27] *See* Chapter 7, "Discrimination in Employment." The "closed shop" was made unlawful, but a "Union Shop" was allowed in those states where it was lawful under state law. *See* §8(a)(3) *proviso* and §14(b) and Chapter 27, "Union Security."

[28] *See* Chapters 13, "The Duty to Bargain," 14, "Effect of Change in Bargaining Representative During the Term of a Collective Bargaining Agreement," 15, "Effect of Change in the Employing Unit," and 16, "Subjects of Bargaining."

[29] *See* Chapter 23, "Handbilling and Consumer Picketing."

[30] *See* Chapter 25, "Jurisdictional Disputes and 'Featherbedding.'"

[31] *See* Chapter 27, "Union Security."

of "featherbedding," i.e., causing or attempting to cause an employer to pay for services not performed.[32]

D. "Free Speech" Proviso

Section 8(c), the "free speech" proviso, was added as a guarantee for both employers and unions:

> The expressing of any views, argument, or opinion, or the dissemination thereof, whether in written, graphic, or visual form, shall not constitute or be evidence of an unfair labor practice under any of the provisions of this Act, if such expression contains no threat of reprisal or force or promise of benefit.

E. Collective Bargaining Duties

Section 8(d) sets out in rudimentary form the duties of the parties in collective bargaining:

> To bargain collectively is the performance of the mutual obligation of the employer and the representative of the employees to meet at reasonable times and confer in good faith with respect to wages, hours, and other terms and conditions of employment . . . [but] . . . such obligation does not compel either party to agree to a proposal or require the making of a concession.[33]

Section 8(d) also provides that either party to a collective bargaining contract desiring termination or modification of the contract must (1) serve a 60-day written notice prior to the expiration date of the contract, (2) offer to meet and confer, (3) notify the Federal Mediation and Conciliation Service (and any comparable state mediation agency) within 30 days, and (4) continue all the terms of the agreement in full force and effect,

> without resorting to strike or lockout . . . for a period of sixty days after such notice is given or until the expiration date of such contract, whichever occurs later. . . . Any employee who engages in a strike within the sixty-day period specified in this subsection shall lose his status as an employee . . . for the purposes of sections 8, 9, and 10. . . .[34]

---

[32]*See* Chapter 25, "Jurisdictional Disputes and 'Featherbedding.'"
[33]*See* Chapter 13, "The Duty to Bargain."
[34]*See* Chapters 13, "The Duty to Bargain," and 19, "The Primary Strike."

F. Representation Under Section 9

Section 9 also underwent important changes. Section 9(a) gives individual employees the right to present grievances to their employer "and to have such grievances adjusted, without the intervention of the bargaining representative, as long as the adjustment is not inconsistent with the . . . collective bargaining contract" and if the "bargaining representative has been given an opportunity to be present. . . . "[35]

Section 9(b) provides that the Board shall not: (1) combine professional and nonprofessional employees in the same unit unless a majority of the professional employees vote for inclusion; (2) decide that any craft unit is inappropriate on the ground that a different unit has been established by a prior Board determination, unless a majority in the proposed craft-unit vote against separate representation; or (3) include plant guards in a unit with other employees.[36]

Section 9(c) made changes in the area of representation questions. It gives the employer the right to file a representation petition and employees the right to file a petition to decertify a union. It forbids the Board to treat unions affiliated with a national labor organization differently from unaffiliated unions. Section 9(c)(3) was also added:

> No election shall be directed in any bargaining unit . . . within which, in the preceding twelve-month period, a valid election shall have been held. Employees on strike . . . not entitled to reinstatement shall not be eligible to vote. . . . In any election where none of the choices . . . receives a majority, a run-off shall be conducted . . . between the two choices receiving the largest and second largest number of valid votes. . . .[37]

Section 9(e) established a procedure whereby 30 percent of the employees in a bargaining unit could request an election to rescind a union-security agreement.[38]

G. Regulation of Internal Union Affairs

Section 9(f) was directed at regulating internal affairs of unions and required any union that desired coverage or protec-

---

[35]*See* Chapter 26, "The Duty of Fair Representation."
[36]*See* Chapter 11, "Appropriate Bargaining Units."
[37]*See* Chapter 10, "Representation Proceedings and Elections."
[38]*See* Chapter 27, "Union Security."

tion under the Act to file with the Secretary of Labor copies of its constitution and bylaws and a report showing:

(1) The name of the organization and its principal place of business.
(2) The name and title of, and compensation paid to, any officer or agent who was paid more than $5,000 in the preceding year.
(3) The manner in which these officers were selected.
(4) Initiation fees for new members.
(5) Dues of regular members.
(6) A detailed statement of the procedure followed with respect to qualifications for membership, election of officers and stewards, calling of meetings, levying of assessments, imposition of fines, authorization of bargaining demands, ratification of contract terms, authorization for strikes, authorization for disbursement of union funds, audit of union financial transactions, participation in insurance or other benefit plans, and grounds for expulsion of members.

Also required was a report showing union receipts and their sources, total union assets and liabilities, and a list of disbursements made and their purposes.

Section 9(g) provided that any union failing to meet these new filing requirements would not be certified under the Act and no complaint would be issued on a charge filed by it. Section 9(h) provided for the filing of non-Communist affidavits. No benefits of the Act would be accorded to any labor organization whose officers had not submitted affidavits within the preceding 12 months showing that they were free from Communist Party affiliation or belief.[39]

H. Procedural Changes

Section 10(a) gives the Board authority to cede jurisdiction to state agencies in certain cases, even though the dispute might affect commerce, where the applicable state law is consistent with the NLRA.[40] Section 10(b) provides that no complaint may

---

[39]Secs. 9(f), (g), and (h) were repealed by the Landrum-Griffin Act in 1959. *See* Chapter 4, "The Landrum-Griffin Changes."

[40]*See* Chapters 28, "Jurisdiction: Coverage of the Act," and 29, "Accommodations to Other Federal Enactments."

issue where the unfair labor practice occurred more than six months prior to the filing of the charge.[41]

Section 10(e) provides that "findings of the Board with respect to questions of fact if supported by substantial evidence on the record considered as a whole shall be conclusive."[42]

I. Injunctions

Section 10(j), the "discretionary injunction" section, was added. It provides that when the Board has issued a complaint charging that any person has engaged or is engaged in an unfair labor practice, it may petition a district court for appropriate temporary relief or restraining order as the court deems "just and proper."[43] Section 10(k) relates to section 8(b)(4)(D). It requires the Board to hear and determine cases involving jurisdictional strikes unless the parties are able to show within 10 days that they have settled the dispute themselves.[44] Section 10(l), the "mandatory injunction" section, requires the Board to give priority over all other cases to any charge of an unfair labor practice under sections 8(b)(4)(A), (B), and (C)—the secondary boycott provisions. If there are reasonable grounds for believing the charge to be true, the Board officer or regional attorney is required to petition a district court for injunctive relief pending Board determination.[45]

J. "Right to Work" Laws

Finally, section 14(b) was added to give state "right to work" laws precedence over the new union-shop proviso in section 8(a)(3):

> Nothing in this Act shall be construed as authorizing the execution or application of agreements requiring membership in a labor organization as a condition of employment in any State or Territory where such . . . is prohibited. . . .[46]

---

[41]*See* Chapter 31, "NLRB Procedures."

[42]*See* Chapter 33, "Judicial Review and Enforcement," at notes 59–81.

[43]*See* Chapters 31, "NLRB Procedures," and 32, "NLRB Orders and Remedies."

[44]*See* Chapter 25, "Jurisdictional Disputes and 'Featherbedding.'"

[45]*See* Chapters 23, "Secondary Strikes and Picketing," and 32, "NLRB Orders and Remedies." With respect to §8(b)(4)(D) jurisdictional dispute cases, "where appropriate," §10(l) injunctions are also made available (but are not mandatory). *See* Chapter 25, "Jurisdictional Disputes and 'Featherbedding.'"

[46]*See* Chapter 27, "Union Security."

III. THE REACTION

A. Labor Response

American labor policy had undergone its second sweeping revision in 12 years. The initial response of organized labor to passage of the Taft-Hartley Act was to publicize its opposition to what it called the "slave labor law." Labor leaders of all unions resolved to work steadfastly for repeal.[47] This response was not surprising, for it was consistent with the position that organized labor had taken throughout the legislative proceedings. In the face of some recognized shortcomings within the labor movement, and even in the light of President Truman's limited call for labor legislation, the unions had decided to oppose any and all revision of the Wagner Act. In adopting that intransigent position, labor virtually destroyed any chance that it might have had of exerting significant influence on the final outcome of Taft-Hartley. The result was a statute on which union views had no measurable impact. Consequently, labor's critics were able to exert the most influential pressures on the 1947 legislation. As professors Archibald Cox and Derek Bok explain:

> [T]he Taft-Hartley Act was the product of diverse forces—the offspring, a critic might say, of an unhappy union between the opponents of all collective bargaining and the critics of the unions' abuses of power. The former group was probably the more influential of the two in writing the Taft-Hartley amendments, for organized labor's unfortunate decision to oppose all legislation left its sympathetic critics in a dilemma.[48]

Union leadership continued to hold to this "all or nothing at all" attitude in the period immediately following passage of the Act. Its aim was not to amend but to repeal. The first manifestation of this approach was seen in 1948, when union leaders—erroneously assessing the upset victory of President Truman—thought the time had come to wipe Taft-Hartley off the books. In the words of one commentator, labor viewed the election as a "popular mandate" to "return to the good old days of the Wagner Act."[49] Leaders of both the AFL and the CIO publicly urged Congress to follow a "two-package approach" toward

---

[47] A. MCADAMS, POWER AND POLITICS IN LABOR LEGISLATION 29 (1964).

[48] COX & BOK, *supra* note 3, at 133.

[49] Aaron, *Amending the Taft-Hartley Act: A Decade of Frustration,* 11 INDUS. & LABOR REL. REV. 327, 329 (1958).

labor legislation: It should immediately repeal Taft-Hartley and restore the status quo ante of the Wagner Act; only then should it consider the Administration's proposed amendments.[50]

B. Congressional Response

The House response was to pass a bill which substantially reenacted Taft-Hartley. In the Senate, a substitute bill sponsored by Senator Taft was passed in place of an Administration bill. At this point, the Administration chose to drop the fight, and Taft-Hartley was left on the books unchanged. The tactics of organized labor had been proved unrealistic:

> Their "all or nothing" demands seemed arrogant and unreasonable, especially when contrasted with the deceptively conciliatory proposals of Taft to discuss and, if need be, amend or eliminate any provision of the existing law that was demonstrably unworkable or prejudicial to labor's legitimate interests. Whatever slight hope there might have been for popular support of substantial revision of Taft-Hartley was shattered by the unions' intransigent position.[51]

C. Stalemate Years

The years 1949 to 1952 were marked by a general stalemate in attempts to revise Taft-Hartley. This was a period of intense internal rivalry within the labor movement. Individual unions embarked on a program of pursuing their individual interests, opposing any suggestions from rival unions which might threaten their own positions.[52]

In the early 1950s both management and labor began developing programs of proposed legislation to amend the National Labor Relations Act. Management groups had two primary goals: to close "loopholes" in section 8(b)(4), which still permitted certain types of secondary activities (such as "hot cargo" agreements and "roving picketing") and to establish strict regulations for organizational picketing. As they had done in 1937, management interests set up an informal organization, known as the Secondary Boycott Committee, to further these goals. Its first move was to undertake a broad program aimed at informing the business community, the public, and Congress of man-

---

[50] *Id.*
[51] *Id.* at 330.
[52] McADAMS, *supra* note 47, at 32.

agement's views. Two subcommittees were formed, one concentrating on drafting legislation and presenting it to Congress, and the other providing materials aimed at the general public.[53] In contrast to labor, management was able to put aside other differences and present a generally united front on matters pertaining to labor legislation.[54]

Certain labor unions did develop specific proposals that they wished to see enacted. For example, the building and construction trades desired a provision allowing "prehire" agreements. Since the employers in the building industry depend heavily on transient labor, each union wanted to be allowed to negotiate a contract with a contractor before the union's status as a representative had been certified by the time-consuming process of an NLRB election, or even before the workers were hired for the job. Such an arrangement was an unfair labor practice under Taft-Hartley.

Although both management and labor groups had in mind definite amendments to the NLRA during the early 1950s, neither side was able to generate much support for its proposals. It was not until 1957 that the issue of labor legislation again came to the forefront.

---

[53]*Id.* at 68-69.
[54]*Id.* at 71.

Chapter 4

THE LANDRUM-GRIFFIN CHANGES

I. The Impetus of Legislative Investigation

The attention of the nation was focused once again on labor problems in 1957 when the Senate Committee on Improper Activities in Labor-Management Relations, chaired by Senator McClellan (D—Ark), opened hearings to investigate alleged wrongdoings in the labor-management field.[1] As the hearings progressed, they gradually began to center on corruption in several strong unions. Testimony indicated that certain high officials within these unions were engaged in misconduct "ranging from embezzlement to illicit secret profits."[2] Much public feeling was aroused by the disclosures, and one commentator concluded that the activity of the committee "was clearly the motivating force in bringing about the passage of legislation in 1959."[3]

The public clamor and legislative interest in corrective labor legislation were directed primarily at achieving internal union democracy, a subject not theretofore effectively covered by the national labor laws.[4] At the same time, the labor unions

---

[1]*See* A. McAdams, Power and Politics in Labor Legislation 36–40 (1964), for a discussion of the political make-up of the McClellan Committee. *See also* The Labor Reform Law (Washington: BNA Books, 1959).

[2]A. Cox, Law and the National Labor Policy 18 (1960).

[3]McAdams, *supra* note 1, at 39.

[4]As Professor Benjamin Aaron pointed out, "[T]he Labor Management Relations (Taft-Hartley) Act of 1947 included only a few provisions purporting to regulate the conduct of union government." Aaron, *The Labor-Management Reporting and Disclosure Act of 1959*, 73 Harv. L. Rev. 851 (1960). During passage of Taft-Hartley a campaign had begun to strengthen, through federal lesiglation, internal union democracy. It was "formally launched by the American Civil Liberties Union, which submitted a Trade Union Democracy bill to the Congress during the 1947 hearings on new labor legislation." *Id. See* Chapter 3, "The Taft-Hartley Changes." *See also* Aaron & Komaroff, *Statutory Regulation of Internal Union Affairs—II*, 44 Ill. L. Rev. 631, 636-72 (1949).

attempted to turn congressional attention to amending the Taft-Hartley Act.

In 1958 Congress made its first unsuccessful response to the McClellan Committee disclosures when the Senate passed the bipartisan Kennedy-Ives bill[5] by a vote of 88-to-1. This bill had five titles directed at abuses that had been spotlighted by the McClellan Committee and a sixth title containing limited amendments to the Labor Management Relations Act of 1947. The sixth title had been added as a "sweetener" for certain unions in return for their support of the bill.[6] The union strategy was to oppose any labor legislation that did not also include several desired amendments to the 1947 Act.

Despite its overwhelming passage in the Senate, the bill had received only lukewarm backing of most of the senators, and it was doomed to failure in the House. The sweeteners had not succeeded in stimulating enthusiastic labor support for the bill. The AFL-CIO ostensibly supported it, but George Meany's comment, "God save us from our friends,"[7] reflected labor's true attitude.

II. THE POLITICAL CLIMATE

The national elections in the fall of 1958 had a misleading effect on efforts to pass labor legislation in 1959. The Republican party, attempting to capitalize on the public resentment raised by the McClellan disclosures, chose to make "right to work" laws a major issue in a number of states.[8] Fearing widespread enactment of new right-to-work legislation, organized labor threw all the opposition it could muster into these campaigns. As a result, all the right-to-work laws but one were defeated and 70 percent of the AFL-CIO-supported candidates for Congress won.[9] The Republican response bordered on despair, and "union bosses" were generally credited with the Democratic sweep.[10] Conversely, the Democrats were elated; however, the Democratic leadership was convinced that it was necessary to pass a labor reform bill, plus certain amendments to

---

[5]S. 3974, 85th Cong., 2d Sess. (1958).
[6]McAdams, *supra* note 1, at 45.
[7]*Id.*, at 46.
[8]*Id.*, at 2.
[9]*Id.*, at 48.
[10]N.Y. Times, Dec. 6, 1958,, at 1, col. 7.

the Taft-Hartley Act, in order to demonstrate the "responsibility" of the Democratic party in the area of union regulation.[11] A combination of factors—McClellan Committee publicity, confidence given labor by the success of the 1958 elections, Democratic determination to pass a bill, and public endorsement of legislation by President Eisenhower—resulted in passage of the Landrum-Griffin Act, a statute which many have considered to be less favorable to labor than the political climate of 1958 would have indicated.[12]

III. SENATE ACTION

Early in the 1959 session, Senator John F. Kennedy found himself uncomfortably situated in his relations with organized labor. The Democratic leadership in Congress had concluded that the Kennedy-Ives bill, a package of modest reforms which had been passed by the Senate, had failed in the House in 1958 because of the Title VI sweeteners added to garner union support. They therefore wanted to pursue a two-package approach by splitting the reform measures and the amendments to the 1947 Act into separate bills. They intended first to secure passage of a reform measure, then proceed with the amendments.[13] Influential labor leaders, however, made it known to Kennedy that they would not support any reform bill that did not also contain the sweeteners. Labor's refusal to compromise proved a major tactical error. The labor demand for Taft-Hartley amendments had opened a Pandora's box, and now labor was unable to control the cumulative response of a national demand for more restrictive Taft-Hartley amendments.

Acceding to union wishes, Senator Kennedy introduced the Kennedy-Ervin bill.[14] It was closely modeled upon the 1958 bill and, like its predecessor, contained the sweeteners.[15] Other bills,

---

[11]McAdams, *supra* note 1, at 9.

[12]For treatment of the legislative background of the Landrum-Griffin Act, see THE LABOR REFORM LAW, *supra* note 1; LEGISLATIVE HISTORY OF THE LABOR-MANAGEMENT REPORTING AND DISCLOSURE ACT OF 1959 (GPO, 1959).

[13]McAdams, *supra* note 1, at 49.

[14]S. 505, 86th Cong., 1st Sess. (1959) (drafted in major part by Professor Archibald Cox and union attorney Arthur Goldberg).

[15]The sweeteners were found in S. 505, Title VI, which amended the 1947 Act. They included §603(a) (authorizing prehire agreements in the building and construction industry), §604 (amending §9(c)(3) to permit voting by economic strikers), and §605 (restricting the definition of "supervisor" in §2(11)).

including the McClellan bill[16] and the Administration bill,[17] also were introduced.

When the Labor Subcommittee, chaired by Senator Kennedy, began its hearings, it became apparent that management would not support a bill that included sweeteners only for labor and not for management.[18] Organized employers thus demanded further statutory restrictions on union activities, especially picketing and boycotts.[19] Nevertheless, the Administration bill, which contained the desired management sweeteners, was defeated in subcommittee; and the Kennedy-Ervin bill, after referral to the full committee, was reported out with no management sweeteners.[20]

Senators McClellan and Ervin asked Senator Kennedy to drop the Title VI sweeteners in return for full support of the reform measures and aid in defeating any amendments offered from the floor that were unfavorable to labor. The labor leadership, again misreading the temper of Congress, refused to support the bill without the Title VI provisions.[21] As a result, Senator McClellan introduced a floor amendment which became known as the McClellan "Bill of Rights of Members of Labor Organizations."[22] This amendment provided for more extensive regulation of internal union affairs than did the Kennedy bill. Following an impassioned speech by Senator McClellan, the amendment passed by the slim margin of 47 to 46.[23]

After the passage of the McClellan amendment, several other amendments which had previously been expected to meet with rejection, also were passed, further changing the complexion of the original bill. Added were provisions dealing with economic strikers, "hot cargo" agreements, the "no man's land" jurisdictional question, and organizational picketing. After some modification of the Bill of Rights section, the bill (now with seven titles)[24] was passed and sent to the House.

---

[16]S. 1137, 86th Cong., 1st Sess. (1959) (containing no Taft-Hartley amendments).

[17]S. 748, 86th Cong., 1st Sess. (1959) (sponsored by Senator Goldwater and containing revisions to Taft-Hartley desired by both labor and management).

[18]*Hearings on Labor-Management Reform Legislation Before the Subcomm. on Labor of the Senate Comm. on Labor and Public Welfare*, 86th Cong., 1st Sess. 145-48 (1959).

[19]*See* Aaron, *supra* note 4, at 1088.

[20]S. 1555, 86th Cong., 1st Sess. (1959).

[21]McAdams, *supra* note 1, at 87-88.

[22]105 CONG. REC. 5810 (daily ed., Apr. 22, 1959).

[23]*Id.*, at 5827.

[24]McClellan's Bill of Rights amendment became Title I of the seven titles of S. 1555.

IV. STRUGGLE IN THE HOUSE

During the interim before House consideration of the Senate bill, the AFL-CIO developed a strategy that it would follow in the House. It was decided that no further support would be given to the Kennedy bill because of distaste for the Title I Bill of Rights section and the Title VII provisions dealing with hot-cargo agreements and organizational picketing.[25] However, at the same time labor intended to continue to press for its desirable Title VII provisions amending Taft-Hartley.

When hearings began in the House Labor Committee, the AFL-CIO felt it had enough votes to bottle up the Kennedy bill in committee. Again, labor miscalculated its strength. The House was under the same pressure to pass a bill as the Senate had been. When it finally became obvious that a bill was, indeed, emerging from committee, union leaders adopted the strategy of supporting a straight reform bill without any amendments to the LMRA.[26] But this concession had come too late. The Administration and many influential congressmen were now pressing for the restrictive amendments dealing with hot-cargo agreements, secondary boycotts, and organizational picketing. Title VII remained intact. After several weeks of wrangling, the committee reported out the Elliott bill,[27] which was, nevertheless, more favorable to labor than the Senate bill.[28]

Once the Elliott bill had been reported out of committee, other bills were introduced. The most important were the Shelley[29] and the Landrum-Griffin bills.[30] The Shelley bill was substantially the same as the Elliott bill except that it deleted the Title VII provisions offensive to labor. The Landrum-Griffin proposals were also substantially identical to the Eliott bill but included stringent provisions in Title VII relating to hot-cargo agreements, secondary boycotts, and recognitional and organizational picketing. The AFL-CIO supported the Shelley bill, though it obviously stood no chance of passing.[31]

---

[25]A. MCADAMS, POWER AND POLITICS IN LABOR LEGISLATION at 123.

[26]*Id.*, at 148. This was the approach originally suggested by the Democratic leadership.

[27]H.R. 8342, 86th Cong., 1st Sess. (1959).

[28]Levitan, *Union Lobbyists' Contributions to Tough Labor Legislation*, 10 LAB. L.J. 675, 678 (1959).

[29]H.R. 8490, 86th Cong., 1st Sess. (1959).

[30]H.R. 8400, 8401, 86th Cong., 1st Sess. (1959).

[31]*See* Levitan, *supra* note 28, at 678.

Once the Landrum-Griffin bill had been unveiled, management groups throughout the country launched a massive campaign of support for it. The campaign reached its peak when President Eisenhower appeared on national television and radio to plead for public support for the measure.[32] After his address, Congress was deluged with mail supporting the bill. Backers of the moderate Elliott bill, primarily the House Democratic leadership, were left in a precarious position: Labor supported the Shelley bill, but widespread public support was growing for the Landrum-Griffin bill. When debate began in the House, the Landrum-Griffin bill was substituted for the committee's Elliott bill,[33] and the Landrum-Griffin bill passed by a vote of 303 to 125.[34] The House then requested that a House-Senate conference committee be appointed to resolve the differences between it and the Senate bill.

V. Reconciling Title VII

The conference committee had little trouble reconciling the first six titles of the Senate and House bills and came to agreement on these provisions in a little more than three days.[35] The real struggle was to come over the Title VII provisions.

An examination of the pertinent Title VII provisions of the two bills illustrates the major differences that had to be resolved by the committee.

A. A Jurisdictional Problem: "No-Man's Land"

The first major discrepancy in the two bills concerned the "no-man's-land" question. The Senate bill provided that state agen-

---

[32]McAdams, *supra* note 25, at 193-98.

[33]In commenting on the procedures employed in the House in adopting the LMRDA, Goldberg and Meiklejohn concluded:

"It is, of course, unusual for either body of Congress to adopt a bill on the floor without prior consideration by the appropriate committee. This is true of nearly all legislation, let alone legislation of the importance and far-reaching effect of that here involved.

"Yet, the Landrum-Griffin Bill was adopted by the House in precisely this unorthodox manner. The House Education and Labor Committee . . . reported out the Elliott Bill. Although the Landrum-Griffin Bill was substantially different from the Elliott Bill in major respects, it was substituted for this bill directly on the House floor and adopted without referral to the Labor Committee for study and calm consideration." Goldberg & Meiklejohn, *Title VII: Taft-Hartley Amendments, with Emphasis on the Legislative History*, 54 Nw. U.L. Rev. 747, 780 (1960).

[34]105 Cong. Rec. 14540-14541 (daily ed., Aug. 14, 1959).

[35]McAdams, *supra* note 25, at 249-51.

cies but *not* courts could assert jurisdiction over cases that the NLRB had declined to accept.[36] The Senate version further provided that when the state agencies took such jurisdiction, they had to apply federal law and enforcement and appeal would be through the federal courts. The Landrum-Griffin bill provided that state agencies *and* courts could take jurisdiction over cases that the NLRB had declined to handle. The Board was empowered to decline jurisdiction "over any labor dispute involving any class or category of employers, where, in the opinion of the Board, the effect of such labor dispute on commerce is not sufficiently substantial to warrant the exercise of its jurisdiction."[37] The House bill made no mention of which law was to be applied in such cases.

When the conference committee met, a modified version of the Landrum-Griffin "no-man's-land" provision was accepted. The Board was forbidden to decline jurisdiction of those disputes that were within its jurisdictional standards on August 1, 1959.

B. The "Hot-Cargo" Provision

A second amendment to Taft-Hartley dealt with "hot-cargo" agreements. The Senate bill made it an unfair labor practice to make a hot-cargo agreement with a *common carrier*. The House bill made it an unfair labor practice to make a hot-cargo agreement with *any employer*. The House bill also made it an unfair labor practice for a union to induce individuals employed by any person to refuse to handle goods in order to force any person to

---

[36]This provision, Section 701 of Title VII, was oiginally a product of the McClellan Committee. This committee had recommended that states assume jurisdiction over those labor disputes that the Board refused to hear. SENATE SELECT COMM. ON IMPROPER ACTIVITES IN THE LABOR AND MANAGEMENT FIELD, INTERIM REPORT, S. DOC. NO. 1417, 85th Cong., 2d Sess. 453 (1958) (41 LRRM 54). During the First Session of the 86th Congress, the Senate Labor Committee had included in the Kennedy-Ervin bill a proposal that the Board be required to assert jurisdiction over all disputes arising under the National Labor Relations Act. Goldberg & Meiklejohn, *supra* note 33. This proposal was rejected by the Senate, and thus the Senate bill provided that state agencies but not courts could assert jurisdiction over such cases. See discussion of Guss v. Utah L.R.B., 353 US 1, 38 LRRM 2567 (1957), and the jurisdictional "no man's land" which precipitated this legislative drive, Chapters 28, "Jurisdiction: Coverage of the Act," and 29, "Federal Preemption of State Regulation."

[37]S. 1555, as passed by the House of Representatives Aug. 14, 1959, 86th Cong., 1st Sess. §701. The House version of §701 was also modified to provide for a procedural change amending §3(b) of the Act and empowering the Board to refer representation cases to its regional directors for a final determination, subject to the Board's review. *See* Goldberg & Meiklejohn, *supra* note 33, at 750.

cease doing business with another person. The House bill further made it unlawful for a union to "threaten" any person to force any person to cease doing business with another.[38]

C. Restrictions on Organizational and Recognitional Picketing

There were differences in the two bills concerning organizational and recognitional picketing.[39] The Senate bill provided that organizational picketing was an unfair labor practice if the employer had recognized another union, or if a valid representation election had been held in the preceding nine months without the picketing union being certified as the bargaining representative. The Senate version also provided that an employer unfair labor practice was a defense to a charge of unlawful picketing.

The House version provided that such picketing was an unfair labor practice if

(1) another union had been recognized by the employer or,
(2) a valid election had been held in the preceding 12 months without the picketing union being certified or,
(3) the union could not show "sufficient interest" on the part of the employees or,
(4) the picketing had continued for 30 days without the filing of an election petition.

The House bill had no provision making an employer unfair labor practice a defense to the charge of unlawful picketing.

D. Prehire Agreements

The Senate bill permitted prehire agreements in the construction industry requiring union membership after seven days' employment. Landrum-Griffin allowed such agreements only

---

[38]*See* Chapter 24, "Section 8(e): The 'Hot-Cargo' Agreement."

[39]These provisions were to be the most bitterly opposed provisions in the Act. Organized labor asserted such provisions were designed to undermine legitimate labor activities rather than smoke out "racketeers." Business and management groups argued that the provisions were necessary to cope with the corrupt and improper activities within the unions. Goldberg & Meiklejohn, *supra* note 33, at 762. *See* Chapter 21, "Picketing for Organization and Recognition."

where there had been a prior history of collective bargaining and left the time limit for union membership at 30 days.[40]

E. Voting Rights for Economic Strikers

The Senate bill provided that economic strikers could vote subject to regulations prescribed by the NLRB. The House bill contained no provisions at all on this subject.[41]

VI. THE COMPLETED VERSION

A. The Changes

The final bill hammered out by the conference committee made several important changes in the NLRA:

1. Recognitional and Organizational Picketing. Section 8(b)(7) was added to deal with the issue of recognitional or organizational picketing.[42] Such picketing was made unlawful if

(a) another union had been recognized and a question of representation could not be raised or,
(b) a valid election had been held within the preceding 12 months or,
(c) the picketing continued without the filing of an election petition within a reasonable time, not to exceed 30 days.

Expedited investigations are required under this provision, and when a petition is filed under (c) an election must be directed forthwith without regard to the 30-percent showing of interest. A proviso to (c) permits truthful "publicity" picketing not having the effect of inducing individuals employed by other persons "not to pick up, deliver or transport any goods or not to perform any services."

2. Secondary-Boycott Changes. Section 8(b)(4) was amended to tighten up "loopholes" in the secondary-boycott provisions of Taft-Hartley.[43] Taft-Hartley had made it an unfair labor practice for a union to "engage in, or to induce or encourage the employees of any employer to engage in, a strike

---

[40]*See* Chapters 13, "The Duty to Bargain," and 27, "Union Security."
[41]*See* Chapters 10, "Representation Proceedings and Elections," and 19, "The Primary Strike."
[42]*See* Chapter 21, "Picketing for Organization and Recognition."
[43]*See* Chapter 22, "Secondary Strikes and Picketing."

or a concerted refusal in the course of their employment" for the proscribed objects enumerated in 8(b)(4). This provision had been interpreted not to extend to direct pressure on neutral employers.[44] The section was amended to provide that "threatening, coercing or restraining any person" for the proscribed objects constitutes an unfair labor practice.

A proviso to section 8(b)(4) exempts from the secondary-boycott ban the publicizing of a labor dispute (other than by picketing) for the purpose of truthfully advising the public that a primary dispute exists with an employer and that the employer's products are being distributed by another employer. The proviso requires, however, that such publicity shall not result in inducing any individual employed by any person other than the primary employer to refuse to pick up, deliver, or transport any goods or to fail to perform any services at the establishment of the employer engaged in such distribution.

3. "Employer" and "Employee" Redefined. The categories of "employer" and "employee" were amended to include "any individual employed by any person."[45] Under the old definitions, agricultural laborers, family employees, employees covered by the Railway Labor Act, government employees, supervisors, and independent contractors had not been included.[46] Taft-Hartley had banned the inducement or encouragement of employees engaged in a *concerted* refusal to perform a service. To prohibit appeals to individual employees or neutral employers, the Landrum-Griffin amendment deleted the word "concerted."

4. Hot-Cargo Restrictions. Section 8(e), dealing with the hot-cargo issue,[47] was added in full. This amendment made it an unfair labor practice "for any labor organization and any employer to enter into any contract or agreement, express or implied, whereby such employer ceases or refrains . . . from handling . . . any of the products of any other employer. . . ." Thus, if any such agreement is made, it is unenforceable. Exempted from this provision are such agreements in the construction industry (if the work is to be performed at the site) and in the apparel and clothing industry.

---

[44]See discussion of the 1959 amendments in Chapter 22, "Secondary Strikes and Picketing," and discussion of "person" in Chapter 28, "Jurisdiction: Coverage of the Act."

[45]Section 8(b)(4)(i).

[46]*See* Chapter 28, "Jurisdiction: Coverage of the Act."

[47]*See* Chapter 24, "Section 8(e): The 'Hot-Cargo' Agreement."

5. Prehire Agreements. Section 8(f) was added to permit the execution of prehire agreements in the building and construction industry.[48]

6. Voting Rights for Economic Strikers. Taft-Hartley had provided in section 9(c)(3) that "[e]mployees on strike who are not entitled to reinstatement shall not be eligible to vote."[49] This provision was interpreted to mean that a replaced economic striker was ineligible to vote. It was amended to read as follows:

> Employees engaged in an economic strike who are not entitled to reinstatement shall be eligible to vote under such regulations as the Board shall find are consistent with the purposes and provisions of this Act in any election conducted within twelve months after the commencement of the strike.

7. Delegation of Board Authority Authorized. Section 3(b) was amended to change certain internal operations of the Board. The Board was empowered to delegate to regional directors its section 9 powers of determining the appropriate bargaining unit, of investigating and providing for hearings, and of determining whether questions of representation exist.[50]

8. Taft-Hartley Provisions Repealed. Finally, sections 9(f), (g), and (h) of the Taft-Hartley Act were repealed by section 201(d) of the LMRDA.[51]

B. Enactment

The bill containing the Title VII amendments to the NLRA was signed into law by President Eisenhower on September 14, 1959. The national labor policy had undergone another important and, in this case, unexpected change. The change was the culmination of campaigns launched by both labor and management groups in 1947 to amend the Taft-Hartley Act. As long as the political strength of these two groups remained balanced, no effort to amend that Act had been successful. The equilibrium was upset in 1959 by two factors: (1) the McClellan Committee and its attendant publicity and (2) labor's unwillingness to support any legislation unless its demands for Taft-Hartley changes

---

[48] *See* Chapters 13, "The Duty to Bargain," and 27, "Union Security."

[49] *See* Chapters 10, "Representation Proceedings and Elections," and 31, "NLRB Procedures."

[50] *See* Chapter 31, "NLRB Procedures."

[51] *See* note 4 *supra*. Titles I through VI of the LMRDA pertain to internal union affairs and are outside the scope of the present work.

were met.[52] Once the drive for Taft-Hartley amendments had been launched, labor was unable to control its course. The outcome for organized labor was a hard lesson in the politics of legislation.

[52] *See* Aaron, *The Labor-Management Reporting and Disclosure Act of 1959,* 73 HARV. L. REV. 851 (1960); Levitan, *Union Lobbyists' Contributions to Tough Labor Legislation,* 10 LAB. L.J. 675, 678 (1959).

CHAPTER 5

THE POST–LANDRUM-GRIFFIN PERIOD

The most significant development in the years since enactment of the Landrum-Griffin amendments in 1959 is that the Act has remained essentially unchanged. There have been minor amendments, however, and these comprise the principal subject matter of this chapter.

I. JURISDICTION OVER UNITED STATES POSTAL SERVICE

Without formally amending the National Labor Relations Act, Congress in 1970 incorporated the provisions of that Act, with certain modifications, into the Postal Reorganization Act of 1970 (PRA)[1] and thereby granted enforceable collective bargaining rights to rank-and-file postal employees.[2] This was the first time this private sector statute was given application to public employment.[3] In section 1208(b) of the PRA, Congress also incorporated the language of section 301 of the LMRA. Accordingly, the body of law concerning the enforcement of collective bar-

---

[1]84 Stat. 720, 39 USC §101 *et seq.* (1988).

[2]*See* U.S. Postal Serv., 208 NLRB 948, 85 LRRM 1212 (1974); Postal Employees v. Klassen, 369 F Supp 747, 85 LRRM 2609 (D DC, 1974), *aff'd*, 514 F2d 189, 85 LRRM 2558 (CA DC), *cert. denied*, 423 US 1037 (1975) (exclusive jurisdiction to investigate unfair labor practice charges and to issue unfair labor practice complaints vested in Board). Excluded from collective bargaining rights under the PRA are (1) any management official or supervisor and (2) any employee engaged in personnel work in other than a purely nonconfidential clerical capacity. 39 USC §1202.

[3]In the administration of its postal jurisdiction, the Board has applied "private sector" criteria in many situations. *E.g.*, U.S. Postal Serv., 208 NLRB 145, 85 LRRM 1577 (1974) (processing of grievances by a minority union); U.S. Postal Serv., 221 NLRB 735, 90 LRRM 1679 (1975) (application of deferral policies to grievance-arbitration procedures); *see also* Malone v. U.S. Postal Serv., 526 F2d 1099, 90 LRRM 3287 (CA 6, 1975) (employees may not bypass the collective bargaining representative in grievance-arbitration proceedings). *Accord* 39 USC §1208(b). *But see* U.S. Postal Serv., 208 NLRB 948, 85 LRRM 1212 (1974) (determination of appropriate bargaining units); Chapter 11, "Appropriate Bargaining Units," at notes 306–326.

gaining agreements developed under section 301 has been held to be pertinent to the interpretation of section 1208.[4]

II. SECTION 302 AMENDMENTS AND ADDITIONAL BARGAINING SUBJECTS

Although not amendments to the National Labor Relations Act itself, three of the several amendments to section 302(c)[5] of the Taft-Hartley Act (LMRA) have broadened the scope of matters which may be negotiated under the Act. Each amendment relates to the purposes for which employers may contribute funds to joint employer-union managed trust funds without being in violation of statutory prohibitions relating to employer contributions.[6]

The first amendment, adopted in 1969, allows contributions to trust funds for (1) scholarships for the benefit of employees, their families, and dependents for study at educational institutions, and (2) child care centers for preschool and school-age dependents of employees.[7] The amendment provides, however, that no labor organization or employer may be required to bargain over the establishment of any such trust fund and that refusal to do so will not constitute an unfair labor practice. The subject is thus statutorily determined to be a permissive rather than a mandatory subject of bargaining.[8]

The second amendment,[9] enacted in 1973, permits payments to trust funds established for the purpose of defraying the costs of legal services for employees, their families, and dependents for legal counsel or a legal-service plan of their choice. The use of such legal services is precluded (1) in matters involving the specific employer and union which have negotiated the plan, (2) in matters arising under the National Labor Relations Act and the Labor Management Relations Act, and (3) in any proceeding in which a labor organization would be precluded from

---

[4]Postal Workers v. U.S. Postal Serv., 356 F Supp 335, 83 LRRM 3032 (ED Tex, 1972); Laborers Local 317 v. Post Office Mailhandlers, 100 LRRM 2949 (D Ala, 1979), *aff'd*, 696 F2d 1300, 112 LRRM 2668 (CA 11 1983). *See generally* Chapter 17, "Relation of Board Action to Enforcement of Agreements Under Section 301."

[5]29 USC §186(c) (1978).

[6]§302(a), 29 USC §186(a) (1978).

[7]83 Stat. 133, 29 USC §186(c)(7) (1978).

[8]*See generally* Chapter 15, "Effect of Change in the Employing Unit: Successorship."

[9]87 Stat. 314, 29 USC §186(c)(8) (1978).

defraying the cost of legal services under the Labor-Management Reporting and Disclosure Landrum-Griffin Act.

In 1978 section 302(c) was again amended to authorize employer contributions to a plant, area, or industrywide labor-management committee.[10] Employer payments are permissible if the committee is established for one or more of the purposes prescribed by the Labor Management Cooperation Act of 1978.[11] These purposes, set forth in section 6(b) of that Act,[12] are the following: (1) to improve communication between representatives of labor and management; (2) to provide workers and employers with opportunities to study and explore new and innovative joint approaches to achieving organizational effectiveness; (3) to assist workers and employers in solving problems of mutual concern not susceptible to resolution within the collective bargaining process; (4) to study and explore ways of eliminating potential problems which reduce the competitiveness and inhibit the economic development of the plant, area, or industry; (5) to enhance the involvement of workers in making decisions that affect their working lives; (6) to expand and improve working relationships between workers and managers; and (7) to encourage free collective bargaining by establishing continuing mechanisms for communication between employers and their employees through federal assistance to the formation and operation of labor-management committees.[13]

At one time, the Board's position was that it did not have jurisdiction to determine whether a particular contractual provision violated section 302 of the Act.[14] However, the Board mod-

---

[10]92 Stat. 2021, 29 USC §186(c)(8) (1978).

[11]29 USC §173(e), 175a. The Labor Management Cooperation Act of 1978 authorizes and directs the Federal Mediation and Conciliation Service to encourage and support the establishment and operation of joint labor-management activities conducted by plant, area, and industrywide committees designed to improve labor-management relationships—including improving communications with respect to subjects of mutual interest and concern, job security, and organizational effectiveness—enhancing economic development or involving workers in decisions affecting their jobs.

[12]Section 6(b), Pub. L. No. 95-524, 92 Stat. 2020, 29 USC §175a (1978). The amendment to §302(c) states that employer payments are permitted to be made to labor-management committees established for one or more of the purposes set forth in "Section 5(b)" of the Labor Management Cooperation Act of 1978. The compiler's note following 29 USCA §186 states that this reference to §5(b) "probably means Section 6(b) of Pub. L. No. 95-524. . . ."

[13]*Cf.* Chapter 8, "Employer Domination and Assistance to Labor Organizations," at notes 13–46.

[14]Central Fla. Sheet Metal Contractors Ass'n, 234 NLRB 1238, 97 LRRM 1476 (1978), *aff'd*, 664 F2d 489 (CA 5, 1981).

ified that position in *BASF Wyandotte Corp.*,[15] ruling that even though it does not have authority to enforce section 302, it is not barred from considering arguments concerning section 302 to the extent they support, or raise possible defenses, in an unfair labor practice allegation. The Board noted that its refusal to consider violations of section 302 caused a dilemma: a party had either to adhere to a contractual provision, and possibly violate section 302, or to cease to honor the contract provision and violate section 8(a)(5) or 8(b)(5).

The content of collective bargaining was also affected by the Health Maintenance Organization Act of 1973 ("HMO Act"),[16] which was enacted to foster the development of health maintenance organizations (HMOs). HMOs are organizations formed to provide a broad range of basic and supplemental health services to their members. Under the HMO Act, covered employers[17] must include in any health benefit plan offered to their employees the option of membership in a qualified HMO.[18] The HMO Act provides that employers are not required to pay more for health benefits under the HMO Act than is required by prevailing collective bargaining agreements.[19]

III. HEALTH CARE INSTITUTION AMENDMENTS

Prior to 1974, although the Board has asserted jurisdiction over proprietary hospitals and nursing homes which otherwise

---

[15]274 NLRB 978, 119 LRRM 1035 (1985), *enforced*, 798 F2d 849, 123 LRRM 2320 (CA 5, 1986). *See also* BASF Wyandotte Corp., 278 NLRB 173, 122 LRRM 1152 (1986), *enf'd sub nom.* BASF Wyandotte Corp. v. Chemical Workers Local 227, 791 F2d 1046, 122 LRRM 2750 (CA 2, 1986); Independent Stave Co., 278 NLRB 593, 122 LRRM 1104 (1986).

[16]87 Stat. 914 et seq., 42 USC §300e et seq. (1988).

[17]Any employer who is required to pay minimum wages in any calendar quarter under the Fair Labor Standards Act and who also employs in that quarter an average number of not less than 25 employees. 42 USC §300e-9 (1988).

[18]An employer's obligation to offer his employees the HMO option does not arise, however, unless a qualified HMO has requested inclusion in the employer's health benefits plan, 42 CFR §110.802(a)(2)(ii) (1976).

[19]42 USC §300e-9(c) (1988). Regulations issued by the Department of Health, Education and Welfare (now the Department of Health and Human Services) in 1975 provided that the employer's offer of the HMO option to his employees "shall be carried out consistently with the obligations imposed on such employer . . . under the National Labor Relations Act and the Railway Labor Act. . . ." 40 CFR §110.808. In 1976 Congress adopted this interpretation by providing that an employer must first offer the HMO option to the bargaining agent, and thereafter to its employees on an individual basis only if the option is accepted by the collective bargaining agent. 90 Stat. 1950, 42 USC §300e-9(a)(1) (1976). In 1978, Congress also added a provision requiring employers, upon the consent of the employee, to arrange for the deduction of HMO membership payments from the employee's salary. 92 Stat. 2135, 2140, 42 USC §300e-9(c) (1988).

met its jurisdictional standards for institutions of those types, it was precluded by statute from asserting jurisdiction over nonprofit hospitals.[20] In 1974 the Act was amended to eliminate the exclusion of nonprofit hospitals and to create a new category of employer, denominated "health care institution," which was broadly defined to include "any hospital, convalescent hospital, health maintenance organization, health clinic, nursing home, extended care facility, or other institution devoted to the care of sick, infirm or aged person(s)."[21]

Related amendments designed to meet perceived special problems of health care institutions were also adopted. Section 8(d) of the Act defines the duty to bargain collectively and sets forth certain procedures the bargaining parties must exhaust before terminating or modifying their agreements. That section was amended to provide more stringent notice requirements in the health care industry than are prescribed for other industries.[22] A new section 8(g) was added, setting forth special notice requirements to be met before a union may strike or picket at a health care institution;[23] section 8(d) was modified regarding the loss of employee status of those striking in violation of the notice requirements of sections 8(d) and 8(g); and although the language of section 9 concerning appropriate bargaining units was not changed or supplemented, the report of the Senate Committee specifically admonished the Board to give due consideration to avoid proliferation of bargaining units in the industry.[24]

IV. RELIGIOUS CONSCIENTIOUS OBJECTORS EXEMPTED FROM UNION-SECURITY COVERAGE

In the closing days of the Carter Administration, the Congress passed and the President signed a religious conscientious objec-

---

[20]Section 2(2) had read: "The term 'employer' . . . shall not include . . . any corporation or association operating a hospital, if no part of the net earnings inures to the benefit of any private shareholder or individual." 49 Stat 449, 29 USC §152(2) (1947).

[21]88 Stat. 395, 29 USC §152(14) (1974). *See* Chapter 28, "Jurisdiction: Coverage of the Act," at notes 87–112.

[22]88 Stat. 395, 396, 29 USC §158(d) (1974).

[23]*See* Chapters 13, "The Duty to Bargain," at notes 893–909, and 19, "The Primary Strike," at notes 52–57.

[24]S. REP. NO. 93-766, 93rd Cong., 2d Sess., *reprinted in* 1974 U.S. CODE CONG. & ADMIN. NEWS 3950. *See* Chapter 11, "Appropriate Bargaining Units," at notes 133–225.

tor amendment to the union-security requirements of the Act.[25] The amendment expands section 19, which had previously applied only to employees of health care institutions, to exempt all employees belonging to a "bona fide religion, body, or sect which historically has held conscientious objections to joining or financially supporting labor organizations" from compulsory union membership. However, such employees may be required, through a collective bargaining agreement, to contribute a sum equal to dues and initiation fees to a nonreligious charity. The provision also requires such employees to reimburse the union bargaining agent for the cost of representation in a grievance or arbitration procedure.[26] [*See* **Editor's Note,** below.]

V. UNSUCCESSFUL EFFORTS TO AMEND THE BASIC ACT

As the paucity of these changes indicates, legislative stability has been the prevailing rule in the development of the Act since 1959. This is not to say that there have not been many proposals to amend the Act. Numerous bills have been proposed, most never emerging from committee. But until the latter half of the 1970s, no major effort to amend the Act in any fundamental manner was attempted. In the latter half of the 1970s, however, unions and their political allies made three major efforts, two of which came within a hair's breadth of success.

The first, which almost succeeded, involved an attempt by the construction unions to change the law regarding "common-situs" picketing at construction sites,[27] to make picketing of the whole site legal whenever a union had a dispute with a contractor or subcontractor at the site. A bill to that effect, introduced in 1975,[28] was passed by both the House and the Senate[29] only to be vetoed by President Ford.[30] The Senate overrode the veto,

---

[25]Pub. L. No. 96-593, 94 Stat. 3452 (1980). *See* LRX 3770.

[26]*See* Chapter 27, "Union Security," at notes 28–29 and 472–476. [**Editor's Note:** In Wilson v. NLRB, 920 F2d 1282, 135 LRRM 3177 (CA 6, 1990), the Sixth Circuit held this provision unconstitutional because it is in conflict with the Second Amendment's Establishment Clause.]

[27]*See generally* Chapter 22, "Secondary Strikes and Picketing."

[28]H.R. 5900, 94th Cong., 1st Sess., 121 CONG. REC. 10012 (1975).

[29]*Id.*, at 24844 (House passage); *id.*, at 37462 (Senate passage); *id.*, at 40067 (House agreement to Conference Committee Report); *id*, at 40553 (Senate agreement to Conference Committee Report).

[30]*Id.*, at 42015.

but the House did not.[31] Following the election of President Carter in 1977, a second effort was made.[32] This time, however, the bill was defeated in the House, never reaching the Senate.[33]

Undeterred by these two defeats, and with hopes buoyed by the accession of President Carter to the Executive Office, organized labor made another effort to achieve major changes in the statute. In July 1977, a far-reaching bill, supported by the President, was introduced in the House. That bill, entitled the Labor Law Reform Bill,[34] proposed to streamline the procedures of the Board and provide more effective means of enforcement. This was to be achieved primarily by the following devices: speeding up schedules for conducting union representation elections and processing complaints; substituting rule making for most hearings in representation cases; providing for mandatory section 10(1) injunctions in discharge cases; making Board orders self-enforcing; and stiffening penalties for employers who oppose union organizing by illegal means, by requiring awards of double back pay to employees fired for union activities and by barring flagrant labor law violators from receiving government contracts.[35] In October 1977, the bill passed the House by a vote of 257 to 163.[36]

The Senate Human Resources Committee held hearings on a companion bill and, in January 1978, reported out its version by a 13-to-2 vote. The Senate bill added to the House version provisions expanding the membership of the National Labor Relations Board to seven, giving union organizers "equal access" to the work place under certain circumstances, reducing election time limits, and providing for a make-whole remedy when an employer was responsible for an unreasonable delay in negotiations.[37]

A five-week Senate filibuster blocked congressional approval of the legislation. On June 22, 1978, after six unsuccessful

---

[31] The House neither overrode nor sustained the veto. Instead, it committed the bill to Committee. H.R. 5900, 94th Cong., 2nd Sess., 122 CONG. REC. 145 (1976).

[32] H.R. 4250, 95th Cong., 1st Sess., 123 CONG. REC. H1657 (daily ed. March 2, 1977).

[33] House Roll Call Vote No. 98, H.R. 4250, 95th Cong., 1st Sess., March 23, 1977, 123 CONG. REC. 8713 (1977).

[34] H.R. 8410, 95th Cong., 1st Sess., 123 CONG. REC. H10714 (daily ed. July 19, 1977). A companion bill was introduced in the Senate on the same day. S. 1883, 95th Cong., 1st Sess., 123 CONG. REC. S12266 (daily ed. July 19, 1977).

[35] *See* 1977 CQ ALMANAC 144-46, 95th Cong., 1st Sess. (1977).

[36] H.R. 8410, 95th Cong., 1st Sess., 123 CONG. REC. H10714 (daily ed. October 6, 1977). *See* note 33, *supra*.

[37] *See* 1978 CQ ALMANAC 285, 95th Cong., 2nd Sess. (1978).

attempts at invoking cloture, the bill was recommitted to the Senate Human Resources Committee.[38] There the bill languished and died.[39]

Since late 1979, despite extended debate concerning the adequacy of major features of the law, no proposal for amendment has attracted sufficient political support to become viable. The debate, centered largely in the academy, has addressed broad questions of the adequacy of the legal standards and remedies provided by a law now more than half a century old.[40] In contrast, the few concrete proposals introduced as legislation have been specific responses to specific perceived problems rather than comprehensive adjustments of the statutory scheme. Legislation proposed in late 1979, for example, would have extended coverage of the Act to interns and residents in health care institutions, overruling a contrary decision of the Board.[41] Similarly, in 1989 legislation was proposed to restrict the option of employers to hire permanent replacements for employees engaged in an economic strike.[42] When social and political developments will alter this state of legislative repose cannot be predicted.

---

[38]S. 1883, 95th Cong., 2nd Sess., 124 CONG. REC. S9411 (daily ed. June 22, 1978).

[39]Following recommittal, the Senate Human Resources Labor Subcommittee held hearings and drafted a "barebones" bill which eliminated certain controversial provisions of earlier proposals, but that bill was never reported out of the Subcommittee.

[40]*See, e.g., Special Project: Labor-Management Cooperation*, 41 VAND. L. REV. 537 (1988); Epstein, *A Common Law for Labor Relations: A Critique of the New Deal Labor Legislation*, 92 YALE L.J. 1357 (1983); Getman & Kohler, *The Common Law, Labor Law, and Reality: A Response to Professor Epstein, id.* at 1415; Weiler, *Promises to Keep: Securing Workers' Rights to Self-Organization Under the NLRA*, 96 HARV. L. REV. 1769 (1983).

[41]In November 1979, the House rejected a bill that would have amended the Act so as to overrule the decision in Cedars-Sinai Medical Center, 223 NLRB 251, 91 LRRM 1398 (1976). H.R. 2222 96th Cong., 1st Sess., 125 CONG. REC. H11,295 (daily ed. November 28, 1979. *See* Chapter 28, "Jurisdiction: Coverage of the Act," at notes 362–367.

[42]H.R. 1383, 101st Cong., 1st Sess. (1979).

Part II

PROTECTED EMPLOYEE ACTIVITY

CHAPTER 6

INTERFERENCE WITH PROTECTED RIGHTS

I. OVERVIEW

A. Introduction

In regulating organizational activities, the Board's primary concern is to protect the statutory rights of employees, but in doing so it must also balance those rights against the rights of the employer and, to a lesser extent, those of the union.[1] The

---

[1]For scholarly comment on many of the topics in this chapter, *see* J. ATELSON, VALUES AND ASSUMPTIONS IN AMERICAN LABOR LAW (1983); J. GETMAN, S. GOLDBERG & J. HERMAN, UNION REPRESENTATION ELECTIONS: LAW AND REALITY (1976); R. WILLIAMS, P. JANUS & K. HUHN, NLRB REGULATION OF ELECTION CONDUCT (1974); King, *Pre-Election Conduct—Expanding Rights and Some New and Renewed Perspectives*, 2 IND. L.J. 185 (1977); Wellington, *Union Fines and Worker Rights*, 85 YALE L. J. 1022 (1976); Barksdale, *Employer Speech During Union Organizational Campaigns*, 46 MISS. L.J. 401 (1975), Cantor, *Dissident Worker Action, After The Emporium*, 29 RUTGERS L. REV. 35 (1975); Fanning, *Union Solicitation and Distribution of Literature on the Job—Balancing the Rights of Employers and Employees*, 9 GA. L. REV. 367 (1975); Helm, *Union Waiver of Initiation Fees During the Organizational Campaign*, 63 KY. L. J. 841 (1975); Millian, *Disciplinary Developments Under §8(b)(1)(A) of the National Labor Relations Act*, 20 LOYOLA L. REV. 245 (1974); Craver, *The* Boeing *Decision: A Blow to Federalism, Individual Rights and Stare Decises*, 122 U. PA. L. REV. 556 (1974); Zimny, *Access of Union Organizers to "Private" Property*, 25 LAB. L.J. 618 (1974); Jarvis, *Organizational Campaigns: Private Rights v. Public Rights*, NYU TWENTY-SIXTH ANNUAL CONFERENCE ON LABOR 3 (1973); Seham, *Limitations Upon and Directions of a Union's Right to Discipline Its Members*, NYU TWENTY-FIFTH ANNUAL CONFERENCE ON LABOR 191 (1973); Swift, *NLRB Overkill: Predictions of Plant Relocation and Closure and Employer Free Speech*, 8 GA. L. REV. 77 (1973); Shaffer, *Some Gray Areas in Employer Free Speech*, 6 CREIGHTON L. REV. 39 (1972); Dereshinsky, *The Solicitation and Distribution Rules of the NLRB*, 40 U. CIN. L. REV. 417 (1971); Lubin & Schlossberg, *Union Fines and Union Discipline Under the National Labor Relations Act*, NYU TWENTY-THIRD CONFERENCE ON LABOR 207 (1971); Coleman, *Union Discipline Under 8(b)(1)(A) of the National Labor Relations Act: The Emergence of a New Trilogy*, 45 ST. JOHN'S L. REV. 219 (1970); Pokempner, *Employer Free Speech Under the National Labor Relations Act*, 25 MD. L. REV. 111 (1965); Bok, *The Regulation of Campaign Tactics in Representation Elections Under the National Labor Relations Act*, 78 HARV. L. REV. 38 (1964); Christensen, *Free Speech Propaganda and the National Labor Relations Act*, 38 N.Y.U. L. REV. 213 (1963); Aaron, *Employer Free Speech: The Search for Policy*, in PUBLIC POLICY AND COLLECTIVE BARGAINING 28 (Shister, Aaron, & Summers, eds., 1962);

various sections of the Act bearing on organizational activities and some of the Board's preelection rules will be examined in this chapter, and their application to particular kinds of conduct will be discussed. Additional material on preelection rules and conduct, particularly conduct that might violate "laboratory conditions" without the commission of unfair labor practices, is treated elsewhere.[2]

B. Section 7—Rights of Employees

1. To Form, Join, or Assist Labor Organizations. Since its inception in 1935, the Act has had as its primary concern the rights of employees, both individually and collectively:

> It is hereby declared to be the policy of the United States . . . [to protect] the exercise by workers of full freedom of association, self-organization, and designation of representatives of their own choosing, for the purpose of negotiating the terms and conditions of their employment or other mutual aid or protection.[3]

Section 7 was fashioned to implement this policy. The 1935 statute provided that the rights of employees shall include the rights to "self-organization, to form, join, or assist labor organizations" and to engage in "other concerted activities for the purpose of collective bargaining or other mutual aid or protection." The Act made it an unfair labor practice for an employer "to interfere with, restrain or coerce employees" in the exercise of those guaranteed rights.

2. To Refrain From Such Activities. In 1947 the protection of section 7 was expanded by the Taft-Hartley Act. Section 7 was amended to guarantee employees the right "to refrain from any and all of such activities." To protect this right, further amendments made it an unfair labor practice for a union to restrain or coerce employees in the exercise of their section 7 rights. The amendments were rooted in the statute's amended declaration of policy "to protect the rights of individual employees in their relations with labor organizations. . . ."[4]

Brown, *Free Speech in NLRB Representation Proceedings*, 50 LRRM 72 (1962); Koretz, *Employer Interference With Union Organization Versus Employer Free Speech*, 29 GEO. WASH. L. REV. 399 (1960).

[2]Chapter 9, "Restrictions of Preelection Activity: 'Laboratory Conditions.'"

[3]Section 1.

[4]Section 1(b), Short Title and Declaration of Policy, Labor-Management Relations Act of 1947, Pub. L. No. 101, 80th Cong., 1st Sess.; 29 U.S.C. §141 et seq. (1976). *See* Chapter 3, "The Taft-Hartley Changes."

3. Other Concerted Activities.[5] The protection extended to employees by section 7 is not limited to the right to join or assist labor organizations or to refrain from such activities; it also includes activity engaged in for "other mutual aid or protection," and section 7 has been invoked to protect concerted employee activity unrelated to union organization.[6] Interference, restraint, or coercion in the exercise of these additional rights is an unfair labor practice under section 8(a)(1); discrimination against employees engaging in such concerted activities may also violate section 8(a)(3).

The ambit of section 7 is extremely broad, though limits have been defined. To be protected, employee activity must be "concerted," that is, undertaken together by two or more employees, or by one on behalf of others.[7] But even a conversation, "although it involves only a speaker and a listener," may constitute concerted activity if it has some relation to group action in the interests of employees.[8] The Supreme Court has agreed with the Board, moreover, that an individual employee's action to enforce the terms of a collective bargaining agreement, even though pursued singly, is concerted activity because it is a continuation of the concerted activity of negotiating the agreement.[9]

---

[5]For detailed treatment of this subject, see Part III, *infra*.

[6]*E.g.*, Redwing Carriers, 137 NLRB 1545, 50 LRRM 1449 (1962), *aff'd sub nom.*, Teamsters Local 79 v. NLRB, 325 F2d 1011, 54 LRRM 2707 (CA DC, 1963), *cert. denied*, 377 US 905, 55 LRRM 3023 (1964) (refusing, in the course of employment, to cross a picket line located at another employer's place of business). Brown & Root, Inc. v. NLRB, 634 F2d 816, 106 LRRM 2391 (CA 5, 1981) (refusal to work in the face of dangerous working conditions); Wheeling-Pittsburgh Steel Corp. v. NLRB, 618 F2d 1009, 104 LRRM 2054 (CA 3, 1980) (expressing concern for safety of fellow employees and refusal to work in the face of dangerous working conditions); Jim Causley Pontiac v. NLRB, 620 F2d 122, 104 LRRM 2190 (CA 6, 1980), *on remand*, 253 NLRB 695, 105 LRRM 1683 (1980) (discussing excessive paint fumes in work area with fellow employees and filing of complaint with state public health department); Walls Mfg. Co. v. NLRB, 321 F2d 753, 53 LRRM 2428 (CA DC, 1963), *cert. denied*, 375 US 923, 54 LRRM 2596 (1963) (writing a letter complaining of sanitary conditions on behalf of fellow employees); Salt River Valley Water Users' Ass'n v. NLRB, 206 F2d 325, 32 LRRM 2598 (CA 9, 1953) (circulating a petition to authorize an individual to collect wages allegedly due under the Fair Labor Standards Act); *see also* Lewittes Furniture Enters., 244 NLRB 810, 102 LRRM 1266 (1979) (nonunion employees banding together and requesting wage increase).

[7]Esco Elevators, 276 NLRB 1245, 120 LRRM 1214 (1985), *enforced*, 794 F2d 1078, 122 LRRM 3178 (CA 5, 1986) (safety complaint by individual employee concerted activity because employee was union officer and inspected job site for safety as duty of office).

[8]Mushroom Transp. Co. v. NLRB, 330 F2d 683, 685, 56 LRRM 2034 (CA 3, 1964); Supreme Optical Co. v. NLRB, 628 F2d 1262, 105 LRRM 3022 (CA 6, 1980); Self Cycle & Marine Distributor Co., 237 NLRB 75, 98 LRRM 1517 (1978); Owens-Corning Fiberglas Corp. v. NLRB, 407 F2d 1357, 70 LRRM 3065 (CA 4, 1969); Interboro Contractors, 157 NLRB 1295, 61 LRRM 1537 (1966), *enforced*, 388 F2d 495, 67 LRRM 2083 (CA 2, 1967).

[9]NLRB v. City Disposal Sys., 465 US 822, 115 LRRM 3193 (1984), *on remand*, 766 F2d 969, 119 LRRM 3200 (CA 6, 1985); *see* notes 387–392, *infra*, and accompanying text.

Apart from action to claim or enforce a right under a collective bargaining agreement, the Board has ruled, in recent years, that activity by a single employee for her or his own personal benefit is not concerted activity.[10] This is so, the Board held in *Meyers Industries,*[11] even when the solitary employee asserts a right enjoyed by fellow employees, such as a right under a state statute establishing equipment safety standards. But where an individual employee's action was a "logical outgrowth" of earlier protest by other employees, the Board has found concerted activity present. In *Every Woman's Place,*[12] for example, a social worker who was discharged after calling the Labor Department to question her employer's holiday pay practices was engaged in concerted and protected activity because other employees had raised the question of overtime pay with the employer on prior occasions and the telephone call was therefore a logical outgrowth of the original protest by all three of the affected employees.

---

[10]Adelphi Inst., 287 NLRB 1073, 127 LRRM 1161 (1988) (employee placed on probation who asked co-worker if co-worker had ever been placed on probation was not engaged in concerted activity because employee did not seek to initiate, induce, or prepare for group action); Herbert F. Darling, Inc., 267 NLRB 476, 114 LRRM 1048 (1983), (I), *rev'd sub nom.* Ewing v. NLRB, 732 F2d 1117, 116 LRRM 2050 (CA 2, 1984), (II), *decision on remand,* 273 NLRB 346, 118 LRRM 1060 (1984), *rev'd* (Ewing II), 768 F2d 51, 119 LRRM 3273 (CA 2, 1985), *decision on remand,* 287 NLRB 1356, 127 LRRM 1241, *affirmed* (Ewing III), 861 F2d 353, 129 LRRM 2853 (CA 2, 1988) (no concerted activity where employee discharged on mistaken belief that employee filed OSHA charge); Pelton Casteel, Inc. v. NLRB, 627 F2d 23, 105 LRRM 2124 (CA 7, 1980), *denying enforcement to* 246 NLRB 310, 102 LRRM 1493 (public venting of a personal grievance is not a concerted activity); Kohls v. NLRB, 629 F2d 173, 104 LRRM 3049 (CA DC, 1980) (individual protest against work assignment is not a concerted activity); Krispy Kreme Doughnut Corp. v. NLRB, 635 F2d 304, 105 LRRM 3407 (CA 4, 1980) (discharge of an individual for refusing to forgo worker's compensation claim is not interference with a protected "concerted" activity); NLRB v. Adams Delivery Serv., 623 F2d 96, 104 LRRM 3093 (CA 9, 1980) (individual "griping" about disputed overtime pay is not a concerted activity); National Wax Co., 251 NLRB 1064, 105 LRRM 1371 (1980) (individual's pursuit of personal merit pay increase held not a concerted activity); Air Surrey Corp. v. NLRB, 601 F2d 256, 102 LRRM 2599 (CA 6, 1979) (employee seeking information about amount of funds in employer's payroll checking account held not protected because employer was unaware that employee was acting in concert). *But see* Whittaker Corp., Kettenburg Marine Div., 289 NLRB 933, 130 LRRM 1247 (1988) (employee's protest, at earliest opportunity, in presence of other employees, of change in an employment term affecting all employees was protected, concerted activity, even if the protesting employee never actually tried to enlist group support before, during, or after the meeting).

[11]268 NLRB 493, 115 LRRM 1025 (1984), *rev'd sub nom.* Prill v. NLRB, 755 F2d 941, 118 LRRM 2649 (CA DC), *cert. denied,* 474 US 971, 120 LRRM 3392 (1985), *decision on remand,* 281 NLRB 882, 123 LRRM 1137 (1986), *aff'd,* 835 F2d 1481, 127 LRRM 2415 (CA DC, 1987), *cert. denied sub nom.* Meyers Indus. v. NLRB, 487 US 1205, 128 LRRM 2664 (1988); *see* notes 519–553, *infra,* and accompanying text.

[12]282 NLRB 413, 124 LRRM 1001 (1986), *enforced,* 833 F2d 1012, 128 LRRM 2296 (CA 6, 1987).

Activity for "mutual aid and protection" embraces expressions of "common cause," including common cause with workers employed elsewhere.[13] Furthermore, employees do not lose their protection under the "mutual aid and protection" clause "when they seek to improve terms and conditions of employment or otherwise improve their lot as employees through channels outside the immediate employee-employer relationship."[14] The protective umbrella of section 7, however, will not shelter concerted activity that is violent, unlawful, in breach of contract, or "indefensibly disloyal."[15] Similarly, the Act does not protect concerted activity that has an object inimical to the fundamental purpose of the statute, such as action intended to supplant a recognized union as the exclusive bargaining representative.[16]

C. Employer Interference With Section 7 Rights: Section 8(a)(1)

Section 8(a)(1), which forbids employers to "interfere with, restrain or coerce" employees in the exercise of section 7 rights, is the broadest of the subdivisions of section 8(a). Violations of section 8(a)(1) are either *derivative* or *independent.*

1. Derivative Violations. The Board has noted since its earliest days that "a violation by an employer of any of the four subdivisions of section 8, other than subdivision one, is also a violation of subdivision one."[17] Derivative 8(a)(1) violations are treated elsewhere in this work in connection with the primary unfair labor practices to which they are attached.

2. Independent Violations. Some acts infringe upon section 8(a)(1) only and are not incidental to the violation of any other subdivision of section 8. Acts constituting general inter-

---

[13]*See* Yellow Cab, 210 NLRB 568, 86 LRRM 1145 (1974); Serv. Employees, Washington State Council No. 18, Local 6 (Severn), 188 NLRB 957, 76 LRRM 1467 (1971); General Elec. Co., 169 NLRB 1101, 67 LRRM 1326 (1968); NLRB v. Peter Cailler Kohler Swiss Chocolate Co., 130 F2d 503, 10 LRRM 852 (CA 2, 1942); Fort Wayne Corrugated Paper Co. v. NLRB, 111 F2d 869, 6 LRRM 888 (CA 7, 1940).

[14]Eastex, Inc. v. NLRB, 437 US 556, 565, 98 LRRM 2717, 2720 (1978); NLRB v. Washington Aluminum Co., 370 US 9, 50 LRRM 2235 (1962); NLRB v. Electrical Workers (IBEW) Local 1229 (Jefferson Standard Broadcasting Co.), 346 US 464, 33 LRRM 2183 (1953); *see* notes 420–443 *infra* and accompanying text.

[15]*See* notes 519–553 *infra* and accompanying text.

[16]Emporium Capwell Co. v. Western Addition Community Org., 420 US 50, 88 LRRM 2660 (1975), *rev'g* 485 F2d 917, 83 LRRM 2738 (CA DC, 1973), *rev'g sub nom.* The Emporium, 192 NLRB 173, 77 LRRM 1669 (1971).

[17]1938 NLRB ANN. REP. 52 (1939).

ference with section 7 rights, but not specifically prohibited by other subdivisions of section 8(a), fall within this category and are treated in this chapter.

3. Motive Not an Essential Element of Section 8(a)(1) Violations. Motive, in the NLRB's view, is not the critical element of a section 8(a)(1) violation. The Board's "well settled" test has been that

> interference, restraint, and coercion under Section 8(a)(1) of the Act does not turn on the employer's motive or on whether the coercion succeeded or failed. The test is whether the employer engaged in conduct which, it may reasonably be said, tends to interfere with the free exercise of employee rights under the Act.[18]

The view of the Supreme Court has been generally supportive but not nearly so clear.[19] In *Burnup & Sims*,[20] the Court upheld the Board's position in the context of a good-faith discharge of employees engaged in protected activity. The employer's good-faith but mistaken belief as to the employee's conduct was held not to be a defense to the resultant interference with the employees' section 7 rights. Justice Harlan wrote in a separate opinion, however, that only in a "rare situation" might the Board ignore motive. But a year later Justice Harlan asserted in his opinion for the Court in *Darlington*[21] that "a violation of Section 8(a)(1) alone . . . presupposes an act which is unlawful even absent a discriminatory motive."[22] Justice Harlan's citations of *Republic Aviation Corp.*[23] and *Nutone*[24] in this connection bolster the conclusion that motive is not an essential element, but this seemingly clear picture has been somewhat blurred by succeeding cases.[25]

---

[18]American Freightways Co., 124 NLRB 146, 147, 44 LRRM 1302 (1959); *see also* Roadway Express, 250 NLRB 393, 104 LRRM 1349 (1980); Cooper Thermometer Co., 154 NLRB 502, 503 n.2, 59 LRRM 1767 (1965); NLRB v. Illinois Tool Works, 153 F2d 811, 17 LRRM 841 (CA 7, 1946).

[19]For a detailed analysis of this problem, see Christensen & Svanoe, *Motive and Intent in the Commission of Unfair Labor Practices: The Supreme Court and the Fictive Formality*, 77 YALE L.J. 1269 (1968); Oberer, *The Scienter Factor in Sections 8(a)(1) and (3) of the Labor Act: Of Balancing Hostile Motive, Dogs and Tails*, 52 CORNELL L.Q. 491 (1967).

[20]NLRB v. Burnup & Sims, 379 US 21, 57 LRRM 2385 (1964).

[21]Textile Workers v. Darlington Mfg. Co., 380 US 263, 58 LRRM 2657 (1965). *See* Chapter 7, "Discrimination in Employment," at notes 261–264.

[22]380 US at 269.

[23]Republic Aviation Corp. v. NLRB, 324 US 793, 16 LRRM 620 (1945). *See* notes 95–101 and 148 *infra* and accompanying text.

[24]NLRB v. Steelworkers (Nutone, Inc.), 357 US 357, 42 LRRM 2324 (1958).

[25]*See* NLRB v. Brown, 380 US 278, 58 LRRM 2663 (1965) and American Ship Bldg. Co. v. NLRB, 380 US 300, 58 LRRM 2672 (1965), in both of which the Court emphasized motive in finding no violation of §8(a)(1). The Court did not classify employers' lockouts

After the Court's 1967 decisions in *Fleetwood Trailer*[26] and *Great Dane*,[27] a clear analysis still remained elusive. Those cases involved rights of striking employees and were decided in the context of section 8(a)(3) violations. Presence or absence of unlawful motivation was not relied upon by the Court in upholding the finding of a section 8(a)(3) violation. A fortiori, scienter would not seem to be essential in section 8(a)(1) cases.

Despite the Board's finding of section 8(a)(1) and (3) violations in *Burnup & Sims*,[28] the Court rested its decision solely on section 8(a)(1). Conversely, the Court's decision in *Darlington* was grounded solely upon section 8(a)(3), whereas the Board had also found a violation of section 8(a)(1). The extent to which a section 8(a)(1) violation overlaps a section 8(a)(3) violation may be relevant. One commentator[29] has suggested that in overlapping situations it may make sense to engraft a hostile-motive requirement but that this should not normally be done in the case of independent section 8(a)(1) violations. He further suggests a rough "rule of thumb" that motive should be "presumptively irrelevant" in cases of independent section 8(a)(1) violations and "presumptively relevant" in section 8(a)(3) violations.[30]

D. Union Restraint and Coercion—Section 8(b)(1)(A)

Section 8(b)(1)(A) is concerned with the rights of individual employees in their relations with labor organizations.[31] This provision makes it an unfair labor practice for a union to "restrain or coerce employees in the exercise of the rights guaranteed in Section 7: Provided, that this paragraph shall not impair the right of a labor organization to prescribe its own rules with respect to the acquisition or retention of membership therein. . . ."

---

of employees as either inherently discriminatory or unlawful per se, within the meaning given those terms in NLRB v. Erie Resistor Corp., 373 US 221, 53 LRRM 2121 (1963). Thus, *American Ship* and *Brown* can be read as turning on lack of hostile motive.

[26]NLRB v. Fleetwood Trailer Co., 389 US 375, 66 LRRM 2737 (1967). *See* Chapter 19, "Relation of Board Action to Enforcement of Agreements Under Section 301," at note 90.

[27]NLRB v. Great Dane Trailers, 388 US 26, 65 LRRM 2465 (1967). *See* Chapter 7, "Discrimination in Employment," at note 95.

[28]*Supra* note 20.

[29]*See* Oberer, *supra* note 19, at 516.

[30]*Id.* See generally Chapter 7, "Discrimination in Employment," for a discussion of discrimination under §8(a)(3).

[31]For detailed treatment of §8(b)(1)(A) see notes 554–626 *infra* and accompanying text.

1. Not a Derivative Counterpart of Section 8(a)(1). Although section 8(b)(1)(A) may be thought of generally as a counterpart of section 8(a)(1), the Board from the outset has taken the position that "Congress did not intend that Section 8(b)(1)(A) be given the broad application accorded Section 8(a)(1)."[32] Thus, in *National Maritime Union (Texas Co.)*,[33] its earliest decision under the provision, the Board concluded that violations of other parts of section 8(b) did not give rise to derivative violations of section 8(b)(1)(A):

> Nothing in this legislative history indicates that a union which refuses to bargain is to be considered as having per se "restrained" or "coerced" employees in the exercise of their rights guaranteed in Section 7. . . . Nor is there any suggestion in the legislative history of Section 8(b)(1)(A) that "coercion" and "restraint" may be found to flow automatically from a union's violation of Section 8(b)(2). . . .[34]

This relatively narrow scope of section 8(b)(1)(A) was given specific approval by the Supreme Court in *Curtis Bros.*[35] The Court cited with approval the Board's decision in *National Maritime Union*[36] that

> Section 8(b)(1)(A) is a grant of power to the Board limited to authority to proceed against union tactics involving violence, intimidation, and reprisal or threats thereof—conduct involving more than the general pressures upon persons employed by the affected employers implicit in economic strikes.[37]

2. Nature of the Violation. Violence or threats of violence constitute coercion and restraint within the meaning of section 8(b)(1)(A). Thus, threatening an employee with bodily harm may constitute an unfair labor practice. Restraint and coercion may also be found in cases where nonviolent physical force is used to prevent employees from exercising their section 7 rights, for example, mass picketing by a union preventing employees from gaining entrance to the employer's premises.[38]

Although the Act literally proscribes only restraint and coercion of "employees" in section 8(b)(1)(A), violent conduct

---

[32] 1949 NLRB ANN. REP. 81 (1950).

[33] 78 NLRB 971, 22 LRRM 1289 (1948), *enforced*, 175 F2d 686, 24 LRRM 2268 (CA 2, 1949), *cert. denied*, 338 US 954, 25 LRRM 2395 (1950).

[34] 78 NLRB at 985.

[35] NLRB v. Drivers Local 639 (Curtis Bros.), 362 US 274, 45 LRRM 2975 (1960). *See* Chapter 21, "Picketing for Organization and Recognition," at notes 4–9.

[36] *Supra* note 33.

[37] 362 US at 290. *See* Chapter 26, "The Duty of Fair Representation," for treatment of §8(b)(1)(A) conduct that constitutes a breach of a union's duty of fair representation.

[38] *E.g.*, Mid-States Metal Prods., 156 NLRB 872, 61 LRRM 1159 (1966), *enforced*, 403 F2d 702, 69 LRRM 2656 (CA 5, 1968); Longshoremen (ILWU) Local 6 (Sunset Line & Twine Co.), 79 NLRB 1487, 23 LRRM 1001 (1948).

directed at nonemployees has been held violative of the section when it is substantially certain that employees will hear about it[39] or when the violence is committed in their presence.[40]

Resort to the Board is not the exclusive remedy for such conduct. States, under their criminal laws, may punish violence that constitutes an unfair labor practice.[41] State courts may also enjoin such violence[42] and grant compensatory and punitive damages in common-law tort actions involving intimidation or violence.[43]

The bulk of the cases concerning violations of section 8(b)(1)(A) do not involve violence; they most often concern threats of loss of employment,[44] improper use of union discipline,[45] or discriminatory or other improper conduct practiced by a union in violation of its duty of fair representation[46] or its obligations under hiring-hall or union-shop procedures.[47] These cases are treated in detail elsewhere.[48]

3. Motive Not an Essential Element of Section 8(b)(1)(A) Violations. The Board does not require evidence of unlawful intent to support a finding of violation of 8(b)(1)(A).[49] As in the

---

[39]Brooklyn Spring Corp., 113 NLRB 815, 36 LRRM 1372 (1955), *enforced*, 233 F2d 539, 38 LRRM 2134 (CA 2, 1956).

[40]Retail, Wholesale & Dept. Store Employees (B. Brown Assocs.), 157 NLRB 615, 61 LRRM 1382 (1966), *enforced*, 375 F2d 745, 64 LRRM 2750 (CA 2, 1967); Retail, Wholesale & Dep't Store Employees (I. Posner, Inc.), 133 NLRB 1555, 49 LRRM 1066 (1961). Threats of *future* picket-line violence made during an election campaign have not, however, been held to violate §8(b)(1)(A) or to constitute grounds for setting aside an election. Hickory Springs Mfg. Co., 239 NLRB 641, 99 LRRM 1715 (1978).

[41]Auto Workers (Kohler Co.) v. Wisconsin Employment Relations Bd., 351 US 266, 38 LRRM 2165 (1956). *See generally* Chapter 29, "Federal Preemption of State Regulations," for discussion of federal preemption and its exceptions.

[42]Auto Workers (Kohler Co.) v. Wisconsin Employment Relations Bd., *supra* note 41.

[43]*See* Construction Workers v. Laburnum Constr. Corp., 347 US 656, 34 LRRM 2229 (1954). *See also* Auto Workers v. Russell, 356 US 634, 42 LRRM 2142 (1958).

[44]Armco, Eastern Steel Div., Ashland Works v. NLRB, 832 F2d 357, 126 LRRM 2961 (CA 6, 1987), *enforcing in part* 279 NLRB 1184, 123 LRRM 1335 (1986), *cert. denied*, 486 US 1042, 130 LRRM 2800 (1988).

[45]Pattern Makers v. NLRB (Rockford-Beloit Pattern Jobbers), 473 US 95, 119 LRRM 2928 (1985).

[46]*E.g.*, NLRB v. Carpenters Local 608 (John Harte), 811 F2d 149, 124 LRRM 2766 (CA 2, 1987), *enforcing* 279 NLRB 747, 123 LRRM 1253 (1986), *cert. denied*, 484 US 817, 126 LRRM 2495 (1987).

[47]Theatrical Stage Employees Local 7 (Universal City Studios), 254 NLRB 1139, 106 LRRM 1228 (1981).

[48]*See* Part IV *infra*; *also* Chapters 26, "The Duty of Fair Representation," and 27, "Union Security."

[49]Ladies' Garment Workers (Bernhard-Altmann Tex. Corp.) v. NLRB, 366 US 731, 48 LRRM 2251 (1961); Painters Local 798 (Master Painters Ass'n), 212 NLRB 615, 86 LRRM 1728 (1974), *enforced*, 91 LRRM 2924 (CA 7, 1976). The Board has, however, ruled that evidence of legitimate motivation will exonerate a union from a §8(b)(1)(A) violation. Ashley, Hickham-Uhr Co., 210 NLRB 32, 86 LRRM 1024 (1974).

case of section 8(a)(1), however, there is some uncertainty on this point in the courts.[50]

E. "Freedom of Speech"—Section 8(c) in General

The enactment of section 8(c) in the Taft-Hartley amendments resulted from a line of early Board decisions severely limiting an employer's freedom of speech. The Board had insisted that the employer maintain strict impartiality in matters pertaining to unions, holding that statements concerning unionism constituted interference with section 7 rights of employees.[51] However, in 1941, the Supreme Court, in *NLRB v. Virginia Electric & Power Co.*,[52] held that employers had a constitutional right to express opinions that were noncoercive in nature. The Board thereafter developed a less restrictive approach toward employer speeches but otherwise continued to limit employer expression.[53] Prior to the passage of Taft-Hartley, there was some indication that the Board had changed its position and was according more latitude to employer speeches;[54] the shift, however, came too late to prevent passage of section 8(c). As stated in the Senate Report:[55] "The committee believes these [Board] decisions to be too restrictive and . . . provides that if, under all the circumstances, there is neither an express or [sic] implied threat of reprisal, force, or offer of benefit, the Board shall not predicate any finding of unfair labor practice upon the statement." The House version was more restrictive: "[A] statement may not be used against the person making it unless it, standing alone, is unfair within the express terms of Section 7 and 8 of the amended act."[56]

---

[50]*E.g.*, NLRB v. Teamsters Local 294 (August Bohl Contracting Co.), 470 F2d 57, 81 LRRM 2920 (CA 2, 1972).

[51]*E.g.*, Schult Trailers, 28 NLRB 975, 7 LRRM 162 (1941); Ford Motor Co., 23 NLRB 732, 6 LRRM 310 (1940); Southern Colo. Power Co., 13 NLRB 699, 4 LRRM 341 (1939), *enforced*, 111 F2d 539, 6 LRRM 1011 (CA 10, 1940).

[52]314 US 469, 9 LRRM 405 (1941). *See also* NLRB v. American Tube Bending Co., 134 F2d 993, 12 LRRM 615 (CA 2, 1943), *cert. denied*, 320 US 768, 13 LRRM 850 (1943).

[53]*See, e.g.*, Monumental Life Ins., 69 NLRB 247, 18 LRRM 1206 (1946) (holding speech coercive where coupled with other unfair labor practices); Clark Bros. Co., 70 NLRB 802, 18 LRRM 1360 (1946), *enforced*, 163 F2d 373, 20 LRRM 2436 (CA 2, 1947) (speech during working time on plant premises held to be unfair labor practice).

[54]*See* Herzog, *Words and Acts: Free Speech and the NLRB*, 18 LRRM 147 (1946).

[55]S. REP. NO. 105 on S. 1126, 1 LEGISLATIVE HISTORY OF THE LABOR MANAGEMENT RELATIONS ACT 1947, 429–30 (1948).

[56]H.R. REP. NO. 345 on H.R. 3020, 1 LEGISLATIVE HISTORY OF THE LABOR MANAGEMENT RELATIONS ACT 1947, 299, 324.

The final version of section 8(c) as passed by Congress was the House version, with only minor changes:

> The expressing of any views, argument, or opinion, or the dissemination thereof, whether in written, printed, graphic, or visual form, shall not constitute or be evidence of an unfair labor practice under any of the provisions of this Act, if such expression contains no threat of reprisal or force or promise of benefit.[57]

This language, according to the Supreme Court's decision in *NLRB v. Gissel Packing Co.*,[58] "merely implements the First Amendment," but the Court also made clear that the protections afforded to speech by section 8(c) are not absolute. "Any assessment of the precise scope of employer expression," the Court noted, "must be made in the context of its labor relations setting. Thus, an employer's rights cannot outweigh the equal rights of the employees to associate freely, as those rights are embodied in §7 and protected by §8(a)(1) and the proviso to §8(c)."[59] The evaluation of employer speech under this standard thus requires, according to the Court, an approach markedly different from the tolerance for "robust debate"[60] required by the First Amendment in the context of political elections. "What is basically at stake" in an NLRB election, the Court concluded, "is the establishment of a nonpermanent, limited relationship between the employee and his union agent, not the election of legislators or the enactment of legislation whereby that relationship is ultimately defined and where the independent voter may be freer to listen more objectively and employers as a class freer to talk."[61]

Since the passage of section 8(c), the Board has engaged in a continuing effort to balance the right of free speech and the prohibition of interference, restraint, or coercion of employees in their exercise of section 7 rights.[62] The character of threats or promises found unlawful spans the range of human expression. A sampling of one year's decisions discloses Board condemnation of

---

[57]Section 8(c). *See* H.R. REP. NO. 510, 80th Cong. 1st Sess. 15 (1947).

[58]395 US 575, 71 LRRM 2481 (1969). *See* note 215 *infra*.

[59]395 US at 617.

[60]*See* New York Times Co. v. Sullivan, 376 US 254 (1964). *Cf.* Linn v. Plant Guard Workers Local 114, 383 US 53, 61 LRRM 2345 (1966), discussed in Chapter 29, "Federal Preemption of State Regulation," at notes 192–203.

[61]NLRB v. Gissel Packing Co., *supra* note 58, at 617–18.

[62]*See* Bok, *The Regulation of Campaign Tactics in Representation Elections Under the National Labor Relations Act*, 78 HARV. L. REV. 38 (1964); Koretz, *Employer Interference With Union Organization Versus Employer Free Speech*, 29 GEO. WASH. L. REV. 399 (1960).

> threatened loss of employment, threatened closing of plant or going out of business, threatened moving of plant to new location, threatened unfavorable reply concerning credit rating, threatened loss or reduction in pay or overtime, threatened loss of promotion, and threatened violence.[63]

During the same year the Board found unlawful, promises

> to "take care" of employees who voted against the union, to give paid holidays, to assist in securing Air Force approval for additional benefit, to grant raises if the pay scale rose in the area, or to "get a raise next week" for the employee who affirmed he was on the employer's side.[64]

1. Threat or Prophecy? The most troublesome element in employer-speech cases has been the difficulty of distinguishing between illegal threats and legitimate prophecies. The Supreme Court's opinion in *Gissel* provided a guideline for evaluating employer speech by declaring that any balancing of the employer rights of free speech and the rights of employees to be free from coercion, restraint, and interference "must take into account the economic dependence of the employees on their employers, and the necessary tendency of the former, because of that relationship, to pick up intended implications of the latter that might be more readily dismissed by a more disinterested ear."[65] In distinguishing "threats" from "predictions" in the context of employer statements about plant closings, the Court indicated that

> [a] prediction must be carefully phrased on the basis of objective fact to convey an employer's belief as to demonstrably probable consequences beyond his control. . . . If there is an implication that an employer may or may not take action solely on his own initiative for reasons unrelated to economic necessities and known only to him, the statement is no longer a reasonable prediction based on available facts but a threat of retaliation based on misrepresentation and coercion, and as such without the protection of the First Amendment.[66]

Because the employer has control over the employment relationship and knows it best, the Court concluded that the em-

---

[63]1962 NLRB ANN. REP. 89 (1963).

[64]*Id.*

[65]*Supra* note 58 at 617.

[66]*Supra* note 58 at 618. The seeds of the Court's distinction between "threats" and "predictions" could be found in earlier Board and court decisions, but the line of demarcation was less than rigid. For example, in 1953 the Board stated that a "prophecy that unionization might ultimately lead to loss of employment is not coercive where there is no threat that the employer will use its economic power to make its prophecy come true." Chicopee Mfg. Co., 107 NLRB 106, 107, 33 LRRM 1064 (1953).

ployer "can easily make his views known without engaging in brinkmanship. . . . At least he can avoid conscious overstatements he has reason to believe will mislead his employees."[67]

In distinguishing between *threat* and *prophecy*, the Board and the courts have long been concerned with the effect to be given circumstances surrounding employer speech. *Virginia Electric*,[68] a pre-section 8(c) case, suggested that the "totality of conduct" be considered so the Board might "look at what the Company has said, as well as what it has done."[69] Decisions during the Eisenhower Administration, after the passage of section 8(c), "tended to view each contested statement in isolation from other comments or conduct of the employer."[70] During the 1960s, the Board began placing greater emphasis on surrounding conduct so that the existence of a violation turned not upon the express words used but upon their meaning in the context in which they were uttered.[71] The Board continued to evaluate employer statements in the light of surrounding conduct and circumstances during the 1970s and 1980s.[72]

2. The Outer Limit of Employer Speech. The countervailing pressures of sections 8(c) and 8(a)(1) yield an unquiet standard. Either of two formulations may be proposed: Speech that is coercive under section 8(a)(1) is not protected by section 8(c); or, speech that is protected under section 8(c) does not violate section 8(a)(1). The outer limit of permissible employer speech thus varies depending on which section is given primacy. A

[67]*Supra* note 58, at 620. The Seventh Circuit, prior to *Gissel*, had announced a rule of caution, stating that "one who engages in 'brinkmanship' may easily overstep and tumble into the brink." Wausau Steel Corp. v NLRB, 377 F2d 369, 372, 65 LRRM 2001 (CA 7, 1967).

[68]*Supra* note 52.

[69]314 US at 478; *see* NLRB v. Eastern Oil Co., 340 F2d 607, 58 LRRM 2255 (CA 1), *cert. denied*, 381 US 951, 59 LRRM 2432 (1965); *see also* International Harvester Co., 258 NLRB 1162, 108 LRRM 1179 (1981).

[70]Christensen, *Free Speech Propaganda and the National Labor Relations Act*, 38 N.Y.U. L. REV. 213, 258 (1963).

[71]*See* Lord Baltimore Press, 142 NLRB 328, 53 LRRM 1019 (1963); Lake Catherine Footwear, 133 NLRB 443, 48 LRRM 1683 (1961); *see also* Dal-Tex Optical Co., 137 NLRB 1782, 50 LRRM 1489 (1962).

[72]*E.g.*, Chambers Dev. Co., 267 NLRB 611, 114 LRRM 1138 (1983) (statement that union "will never be here" lawful in view of fact that commonly owned and controlled company had agreement with same union); NLRB v. Creative Food Design ta Broker, 852 F2d 1295, 128 LRRM 3089 (CA DC, 1988), *enforcing* 282 NLRB 1265, 124 LRRM 1273 (1987) (unlawful to tell employees it was possible restaurant would close if unionized: statement not "purely social" and not dissipated by later statement that restaurant would run as normally). According to some commentators the Board often produced inconsistent results when deciding whether the same words amounted to a threat or prediction. *See* J. GETMAN, S. GOLDBERG, & J. HERMAN, UNION REPRESENTATION ELECTIONS: LAW AND REALITY, at 21 (1976).

comparison of two often-cited circuit court decisions illustrates the problem. In *NLRB v. TRW-Semiconductors*,[73] the Board had found that a series of electioneering communications amounted to a violation of section 8(a)(1). It did not specifically refer to section 8(c). On review, the Ninth Circuit held that the "broad language of Section 8(a)(1) is not the test of whether election propaganda violates the Act." Rather, it "must first be found that it contains a threat of force or reprisal or promise of benefit."[74] Finding none, the court declared that section 8(c) determined the outer limit, whereas the trial examiner, relying on the Supreme Court's decision in *Exchange Parts*,[75] had considered the surrounding circumstances in which the statements were made and also their impact upon the employees. The Ninth Circuit indicated that whatever the impact and intent of the propaganda, they did not deprive the employer of the protection of section 8(c).

In direct contrast to the Ninth Circuit's approach was that of the First Circuit in the 1968 *Sinclair* case,[76] which later formed the basis of the Supreme Court's *Gissel* ruling.[77] The employer contended that since each of a series of statements was lawful in itself, the statements in combination could not be unlawful. In upholding the Board's order, which rejected that argument, the First Circuit stated that in considering coercive effect, the test must include the totality of the circumstances; and whether language is coercive in its effect is for the Board to resolve on the basis of its specialized experience. On review of *Sinclair* (as part of its *Gissel*[78] decision), the Supreme Court affirmed the approach taken by the Board and the First Circuit, holding that any assessment of the precise scope of employer expression must be made in the context of its setting and with due regard for the economic dependence of the employees on their employers.

---

[73]385 F2d 753, 66 LRRM 2707 (CA 9, 1967), *denying enforcement to* 159 NLRB 415, 62 LRRM 1469 (1966).

[74]*Id.* at 758.

[75]NLRB v. Exchange Parts, 375 US 405, 55 LRRM 2098 (1964) (lawfulness of preelection wage increase dependent upon lawful motive).

[76]Sinclair Co., 164 NLRB 261, 65 LRRM 1087 (1967), *enforced*, 397 F2d 157, 68 LRRM 2720 (CA 1, 1968), *aff'd sub nom.* NLRB v. Gissel Packing Co., 395 US 575, 71 LRRM 2481 (1969). *See* Chapter 12, "Recognition and Withdrawal of Recognition Without an Election," for the portion of the *Gissel* opinion concerning union recognition without an election; *see also* note 215 *infra*.

[77]*Supra* note 58.

[78]*Supra* note 58. *See* further discussion at notes 214–215 *infra*.

II. ORGANIZATIONAL AND PREELECTION ACTIVITY

A. In General: Relation of Unfair Labor Practices to "Laboratory Conditions" Required for Elections

An employer may violate the Board's restrictions on preelection activity in either of two ways. Some violations comprise unfair labor practices—these generally take the form of independent violations of section 8(a)(1). Other violations may breach preelection rules or disturb "laboratory conditions" without contravening any statutory unfair labor practice provision. In cases of the former type, the Board is authorized to find unfair labor practices and to remedy them by appropriate means,[79] including setting aside the result of the election,[80] ordering a new election,[81] and, in extreme cases, issuing a bargaining order without an election.[82] In the latter type case, the Board's sanctions are limited to setting aside the results of the election and rerunning the election at an appropriate time.[83] The legal distinction between the two types of conduct is important, although from the pragmatic standpoint of what actually happens during an election campaign the difference relates primarily to the remedial sanctions that will be available.

The distinction between the two types of conduct provides the basis for separating the material relating to preelection conduct in this treatise. The material on preelection conduct contained in this chapter relates primarily to unfair labor practices, whereas Chapter 9 addresses violations of laboratory conditions and preelection rules that do not rest on unfair labor practice prohibitions. To ascertain the full range of rules applicable to union elections, related portions of both chapters must be read together.

The protection of employer speech contained in section 8(c) applies by its terms only to unfair labor practice cases. The Board has made extensive use of this distinction in regulating elections. In its 1948 *General Shoe Corp.*[84] decision the Board

---

[79]*See* Chapter 31, "NLRB Procedures."
[80]*See* Chapter 10, "Representation Proceedings and Elections."
[81]*Id.*
[82]*See* Chapter 12, "Recognition and Withdrawal of Recognition Without an Election."
[83]See Chapter 31, "NLRB Procedures," at notes 8–13.
[84]77 NLRB 124, 21 LRRM 1337 (1948).

defined the "laboratory conditions" required for the conduct of elections under section 9:

> [T]he criteria applied . . . in a representation proceeding . . . need not necessarily be identical to those employed in testing whether an unfair labor practice was committed. . . . In election proceedings, it is the Board's function to provide a laboratory in which an experiment may be conducted, under conditions as nearly ideal as possible, to determine the uninhibited desires of the employees. . . .[85]

Under this doctrine, fault is not an issue. When conduct affecting the election drops below acceptable standards, the requisite "laboratory conditions" are not present and the "experiment" must be conducted again.

During the period of the Eisenhower Board the *General Shoe* doctrine was eclipsed by section 8(c) as the outer limit of employer speech in election cases.[86] In some instances, section 8(c) was applied more restrictively in employer unfair labor practice cases than were the Board's rules for employer conduct during an election campaign.[87] With the advent of new Board members in 1961, the criterion applied to employer speeches changed dramatically. In *Dal-Tex Optical Co.*,[88] the Board announced a per se rule applicable to unfair labor practices committed during election campaigns:

> Conduct violative of Section 8(a)(1) is, *a fortiori*, conduct which interferes with the exercise of a free and untrammeled choice in an election. This is so because the test of conduct which may interfere with the "laboratory conditions" for an election is considerably more restrictive than the test of conduct which amounts to interference, restraint, or coercion which violates Section 8(a)(1).[89]

During the 1970s, the Board qualified its *Dal-Tex* approach; it is no longer a per se requirement that an election be automatically set aside whenever section 8(a)(1) conduct has occurred during the preelection period. The Board has ruled that de minimis employer misconduct affecting the results of an election, even though amounting to an unfair labor practice, will not

---

[85] *Id.* at 127. As to how realistic this objective is, *see* Bok, *The Regulation of Campaign Tactics in Representation Elections Under the National Labor Relations Act*, 78 HARV. L. REV. 38, 45–47 (1964); J. Getman, S. Goldberg, & J. Herman, *supra* note 72.

[86] *See* National Furniture Co., 119 NLRB 1, 40 LRRM 1442 (1957); Lux Clock Mfg. Co., 113 NLRB 1194, 36 LRRM 1432 (1955); Esquire, Inc., 107 NLRB 1238, 33 LRRM 1367 (1954); American Laundry Mach. Co., 107 NLRB 511, 33 LRRM 1181 (1953).

[87] Wirtz, *The New National Labor Relations Board; Herein of "Employer Persuasion,"* 49 NW. U.L. REV. 594 (1954).

[88] 137 NLRB 1782, 50 LRRM 1489 (1962). The Board expressly overruled the cases cited in note 86 *supra*.

[89] 137 NLRB at 1786–87.

be grounds for setting an election aside.[90] Accordingly, in evaluating the impact of misconduct to determine whether it is de minimis, "the Board [now] takes into consideration the number of violations, their severity, the extent of dissemination and other relevant factors."[91] Section 8(a)(1) "violations as to which it is virtually impossible to conclude that they would have affected the results of the election" do not require that it be set aside.[92]

B. Unlawful Employer Conduct

1. Employer's Restrictions on Union and Employee Activity on Employer's Property. Access or nonaccess to employees at the workplace is frequently a threshold concern in an organizing campaign. The Board and the courts have therefore long been engaged in "working out an adjustment between the undisputed right of self-organization assured to employees . . . and the equally undisputed right of employers to maintain discipline in their establishments."[93] Because "reasonable men can and do differ in striking this adjustment,"[94] strong reliance has been placed on presumptions to facilitate the decision-making process.

a. Basic Presumptions. In its early landmark decision in *Republic Aviation*,[95] the Supreme Court adopted the presumption that the enforcement and promulgation of a rule prohibiting union solicitation by employees outside working time, although on company property, "is an unreasonable impediment to self-organization and therefore discriminatory in the absence of evidence that special circumstances make the rule necessary" for maintaining "production and discipline."[96] The genesis of this

---

[90]Caron Int'l, 246 NLRB 1120, 103 LRRM 1066 (1979); Super Thrift Mkts., 233 NLRB 409, 96 LRRM 1523 (1977); *see also* Coca Cola Bottling Co. Consol., 232 NLRB 717, 96 LRRM 1289 (1977).

[91]Caron Int'l, *supra* note 90, 103 LRRM at 1067.

[92]Super Thrift Mkts., *supra* note 90, 96 LRRM at 1523. *Accord* Custom Trim Prods., 255 NLRB 787, 107 LRRM 1198 (1981).

[93]Republic Aviation Corp. v. NLRB, 324 US 793, 16 LRRM 620, 797–98 (1945).

[94]Stoddard-Quirk Mfg. Co., 138 NLRB 615, 616 n.2, 51 LRRM 1110 (1962).

[95]*Supra* note 93. *See generally* Dereshinsky, *The Solicitation and Distribution Rules of the NLRB*, 40 U. CIN. L. REV. 417 (1971).

[96]324 US at 803 n.10 (citing Peyton Packing Co., 49 NLRB 828, 843–44, 12 LRRM 183 (1943), *enforced*, 142 F2d 1009, 14 LRRM 792 (CA 5), *cert. denied*, 323 US 730, 15 LRRM 973 (1944)). For application of the "special circumstances" exception in the context of structured large group meetings in a lunchroom with potential for disturbance and disruption, see National Vendors v. NLRB, 630 F2d 1265, 105 LRRM 2281 (CA 8, 1980). In American Cast Iron Pipe Co. v. NLRB, 600 F2d 132, 101 LRRM 2522 (CA 8,

presumption was the Board's 1943 decision in *Peyton Packing Co.*, where the Board formulated the corollary presumption that the promulgation and enforcement of a no-solicitation rule for working hours "must be presumed to be valid in the absence of evidence that it was adopted for a discriminatory purpose." The Board's rationale was that "working time is for work," but the time outside working hours "is an employee's time to use as he wishes without unreasonable restraint although the employee is on company property."[97] In *Our Way*,[98] the Board reaffirmed the view that rules prohibiting solicitation during working time are lawful because such rules imply that solicitation is permitted during nonworking time.[99] However, bans on solicitation during "company time"[100] remain presumptively invalid.

b. Rights of Employees Over Nonemployees. A distinction is made between rules of law applicable to employees and those applicable to nonemployees (i.e., union organizers); and "the distinction is one of substance."[101] Consequently, in *Babcock & Wilcox*[102] the Supreme Court held that an employer may prohibit the distribution of union literature on the employer's premises by nonemployee union organizers if (1) "reasonable efforts . . . through other available channels of communication will enable it to reach the employees," and (2) the employer does

---

1979), the court held that rules barring written or verbal "false, vicious, or malicious" statements about the company on or off company property were overly broad, reasoning that the company would only be justified in prohibiting "maliciously false or disloyal" statements under the special circumstances exception; *see also* Great Lakes Steel v. NLRB, 625 F2d 131, 104 LRRM 3156 (CA 6, 1980); Wheeling-Pittsburgh Steel Corp., 244 NLRB No. 166, 102 LRRM 1386 (1979).

[97] *Supra* note 93, at 843–44.

[98] 268 NLRB 394, 115 LRRM 1009 (1983).

[99] In so holding, the Board overruled its earlier decision in T.R.W., Inc., Bearings Div., 257 NLRB 442, 107 LRRM 1481 (1981) to the extent that *T.R.W.* held that rules prohibiting employees from engaging in organizational activity during "working time" were presumptively unlawful. The Board's view that rules banning solicitation during "working hours" are presumptively invalid has not wavered. The *Our Way* decision marked a return to the view expressed in Essex Int'l, 211 NLRB 749, 86 LRRM 1411 (1974) (holding that rules banning solicitation during "working time" are presumptively valid). *See also* Beverly Enters, dba Provincial House Total Living Center, 287 NLRB 158, 127 LRRM 1237 (1987) (employer lawfully administered rule that forbade solicitation or distribution during "work time" rather than "work hours").

[100] NLRB v. Chicago Metallic Corp., 794 F2d 527, 122 LRRM 3163 (CA 9, 1986), *enforcing in part* 273 NLRB 1677, 118 LRRM 1294 (1985) and 275 NLRB 871, 119 LRRM 1288 (1985). *But see* Hawkins-Hawkins Co., 289 NLRB No. 158, 129 LRRM 1269 (1988) ("company time" rule valid where employer refined rule to make clear that employees could solicit on breaks, lunch, and before and after work).

[101] NLRB v. Babcock & Wilcox, 351 US 105, 113, 38 LRRM 2001 (1956).

[102] *Id.*

not discriminate against the union by allowing distribution of items by other nonemployees.[103]

The Court also took cognizance of the location of the plant and the residences of the employees, noting that if employees lived beyond the reach of reasonable union efforts to reach them, the employer's property must be made available even though the public is normally excluded from the property.[104] For the most part, the *Babcock & Wilcox* right of access by nonemployees has been recognized in cases in which employees are working at remote locations, such as lumber camps,[105] or are housed on employer property in "company towns"[106] or at self-contained, often seasonal, workplaces such as fish canneries[107] and resort hotels.[108] [*See* **Editor's Note**, below.]

c. No-Solicitation and No-Distribution Rules Generally. The differences between oral solicitation and the distribution of literature have caused the Board to apply somewhat different rules to employer efforts to restrict the two activities. Since *Republic Aviation*,[109] which dealt specifically with oral solicitations, the Board has maintained the position that oral solicitations by employees may be prohibited only during working time.[110] But the Board has generally allowed employers to forbid distribution of literature by employees both during working time and in work-

---

[103]In Sabine Towing & Transp. Co. v. NLRB, 599 F2d 663, 101 LRRM 2956 (CA 5, 1979), the court held that the union bears the affirmative obligation of showing that no other reasonable means exist for communicating its organizational message. *See also* Belcher Towing Co. v. NLRB, 614 F2d 88, 103 LRRM 2939 (CA 5, 1980), *on remand*, 256 NLRB 666, 107 LRRM 1300 (1981), *enforcement denied*, 683 F2d 418, 111 LRRM 2137 (CA 11, 1982). For an example of the distinction between rules applicable to employees and union organizers, see G.C. Murphy Co., 171 NLRB 370, 68 LRRM 1108 (1968), *enforced*, 422 F2d 685, 71 LRRM 2397 (CA DC, 1969). [**Editor's Note:** In Lechmere, Inc. v. NLRB, ___ US ___, 139 LRRM 2225 (1992), relying on *Babcock & Wilcox*, the Supreme Court overturned a Board ruling allowing nonemployee organizers to handbill in a shopping mall parking lot.]

[104]NLRB v. Babcock & Wilcox, *supra* note 101. Employer efforts to prevent protected activity on property that is normally open to the public are dealt with below. See text at note 173 and following.

[105]NLRB v. Lake Superior Lumber Corp., 167 F2d 147, 21 LRRM 2707 (CA 6, 1948); Husky Oil NPR Operations, 245 NLRB No. 68, 102 LRRM 1450 (1979), *enforced*, 669 F2d 643, 109 LRRM 2548 (CA 10, 1982) (petroleum exploration camp).

[106]NLRB v. Stowe Spinning Co., 336 US 226, 23 LRRM 2371 (1949).

[107]Chugach Alaska Fisheries, 295 NLRB No. 8, 132 LRRM 1197 (1989); Trident Seafoods Corp., 293 NLRB 1016, 131 LRRM 1247 (1989).

[108]NLRB v. S&H Grossinger's, Inc., 372 F2d 26, 64 LRRM 2295 (CA 2, 1967), *enforcing in part* 156 NLRB 233, 61 LRRM 1025 (1965). *See* note 167 *infra*.

[109]Republic Aviation Corp. v. NLRB, 324 US 793, 16 LRRM 620 (1945).

[110]Fruehauf Corp., Paceco Div. v. NLRB, 601 F2d 180, 102 LRRM 2146 (CA 5, 1979); Keystone Resources v. NLRB, 597 F2d 1041, 101 LRRM 2784 (CA 5, 1979), *on remand*, 245 NLRB 512, 102 LRRM 1320 (1979); Stoddard-Quirk Mfg. Co., *supra* note 94.

ing areas.[111] The difference reflects the Board's view that solicitation can only occur when both the soliciting and the solicited employee have an opportunity for the exchange of views and must presumptively be allowed at any location where both employees simultaneously find that opportunity, that is, when neither employee is on working time. Distribution of literature from employee to employee, however, can be done in an instant and the message preserved for later consideration. But it involves a hazard to employer interests absent from oral solicitation, the threat of litter and other risks to productive order, and may on that account be prohibited in work areas.[112] For purposes of the distinction, the Board has consistently treated the solicitation to sign an authorization card as a solicitation, and not a distribution of literature.[113]

(1) Presumptions of validity. To be presumptively valid, a rule prohibiting union solicitation must incorporate a clear statement of its scope and limitations.[114] However, a rule that is presumptively valid may still be unlawful if it is promulgated or enforced in a discriminatory manner.[115] In *J.C. Penney Co.*,[116] the Board held the absence of evidence that an invalid rule was enforced does not preclude a remedial order based on the unlawful maintenance of the rule. In another case, however, an employer averted a remedial order for unlawfully promulgating

---

[111]Stoddard-Quirk Mfg. Co., *supra* note 94. In the absence of a no-solicitation rule, an employer may not seize union literature placed on workers' desks prior to the start of working hours. F.W. Woolworth Co. v. NLRB, 530 F2d 1245, 92 LRRM 2240 (CA 2), *cert. denied*, 429 US 1023, 93 LRRM 3019 (1976); *see also* United Aircraft Corp., 139 NLRB 39, 51 LRRM 1259 (1962), *enforced*, 324 F2d 128, 54 LRRM 2492 (CA 2, 1963), *cert. denied*, 376 US 951, 55 LRRM 2769 (1964).

[112]Stoddard-Quirk Mfg. Co., *supra* note 94. *See* Bok, *The Regulation of Campaign Tactics in Representation Elections Under the National Labor Relations Act*, 78 HARV. L. REV. 38, 93 (1964).

[113]Stoddard-Quirk Mfg. Co., *supra* note 94 at 619 n.5; *see also* Rose Co., 154 NLRB 228, 229 n.1, 59 LRRM 1738 (1965).

[114]Head Div., AMF, Inc. v. NLRB, 593 F2d 972, 100 LRRM 3035 (CA 10, 1979). *See also* note 135 *infra*.

[115]Marathon LeTourneau Co., Longview Div. v. NLRB, 699 F2d 248, 112 LRRM 3129 (CA 5, 1983), *enforcing* 256 NLRB 350, 107 LRRM 1432 (1981); Lawson Co., 267 NLRB 463, 114 LRRM 1173 (1983), *modified and enforced*, 753 F2d 471, 118 LRRM 2505 (CA 6, 1985); St. Vincent's Hosp., 265 NLRB 38, 111 LRRM 1349 (1982), *enforced in part and denied in part*, 729 F2d 730, 115 LRRM 3656 (CA 11, 1984); United States Indus., Hammary Mfg. Corp. Div., 265 NLRB 57, 111 LRRM 1346 (1982), *amending* 258 NLRB 1319, 108 LRRM 1200 (1981). *But see* Hawkins-Hawkins Co., 289 NLRB 1423, 129 LRRM 1269 (1988) (promulgation of no-solicitation rule during union campaign held not discriminatory where no evidence that employer tolerated nonunion solicitation).

[116]266 NLRB 1223, 113 LRRM 1117 (1983).

an invalid rule by effectively communicating a change in policy to its employees.[117]

(2) Facial validity of rule. No-solicitation rules drawn so broadly as to encompass nonworking time are presumptively unlawful,[118] although the Board has reformulated the precise language of an allowable rule from time to time.[119] An exception to this presumption is made for retail department stores, which may prohibit employee solicitation on the selling floor even during nonworking time because of the nature of their business.[120]

Another exception to the basic presumption has been applied in health care facilities. The Board's general approach has been to permit a health care facility to ban employee solicitation as well as distribution in "immediate patient care areas," such as operating rooms, patients' rooms, and patients' lounges, and to require the health care institution to carry the burden of justifying any greater restrictions as being necessary to avoid disruption of patient care or disturbance of patients. This approach was endorsed by the Supreme Court in *Beth Israel Hospital*[121] and

---

[117]East Bay Newspapers, 263 NLRB 566, 111 LRRM 1044 (1982).

[118]For an exhaustive collection of such cases, *see* Gould, *The Question of Union Activity on Company Property*, 18 VAND. L. REV. 73, 75-76 n.10 (1964); *see also* Fanning, *Union Solicitation and Distribution of Literature on the Job—Balancing the Rights of Employers and Employees*, 9 GA. L. REV. 367 (1975); Dereshinsky, *The Solicitation and Distribution Rules of the NLRB*, 40 U. CIN. L. REV. 417 (1971).

[119]Our Way, 268 NLRB 394, 115 LRRM 1009 (1983).

[120]Goldblatt Bros., 77 NLRB 1262, 22 LRRM 1153 (1948); Meier & Frank Co., 89 NLRB 1016, 26 LRRM 1081 (1950); Marshall Field & Co., 34 NLRB 1, 8 LRRM 325 (1941), *enforced*, 129 F2d 169, 10 LRRM 753 (CA 7, 1942), *aff'd*, 318 US 253, 12 LRRM 519 (1943); *see also* Marriott Corp., 223 NLRB 978, 92 LRRM 1028 (1976); McDonald's Corp., 205 NLRB 404, 84 LRRM 1316 (1973); Maxam Buffalo, Inc., 139 NLRB 1040, 51 LRRM 1459 (1962). In Times Publishing Co. v. NLRB, 605 F2d 847, 102 LRRM 2710 (CA 5, 1979), it was determined the lobby of a building that housed the newspaper publisher employer's offices, although a work area, was not sufficiently like the selling areas of a retail establishment to be entitled to the retail department-store exception. *See also* notes 163–167 and accompanying text.

[121]Beth Israel Hosp. v. NLRB, 437 US 483, 98 LRRM 2727 (1978). The Court upheld the Board's ruling that it was unlawful for the hospital to prohibit solicitation and distribution of literature in its cafeteria, which was operated primarily for employees and infrequently used by patients or their families. *See also* Eastern Me. Medical Center, 253 NLRB 224, 105 LRRM 1665 (1980) (rule banning solicitation in second floor waiting room lobby held unlawful); Los Angeles New Hosp., 244 NLRB 960, 102 LRRM 1189 (1979), *enforced*, 640 F2d 1017, 106 LRRM 2855 (CA 9, 1981) (ban on solicitation and distribution in employee break area adjacent to an operating room held unlawful); Vassar Bros. Hosp., 243 NLRB 1142, 102 LRRM 1024 (1979) (ban on solicitation in corridor adjacent to employee cafeteria held unlawful). In NLRB v. Baylor Medical Center, 439 US 9, 99 LRRM 2953 (1978), the Supreme Court, per curiam, vacated a Court of Appeals for the District of Columbia Circuit decision, 578 F2d 351, 97 LRRM 2669 (CA DC, 1978), holding that a hospital's rule banning solicitation in its cafeteria did

in *Baptist Hospital.*[122]

The Court and the Board have disagreed, however, as to which parts of a health care institution are "immediate patient care areas." In *Baptist Hospital,* the Court determined, contrary to the Board, that corridors and sitting rooms on floors of a hospital housing either patients' rooms or operating and therapy rooms were "immediate patient use areas" where solicitation could be banned; but it agreed with the Board that solicitation in the cafeteria, gift shop, and lobbies on the first floor of the hospital could not be lawfully prohibited where there was no showing by the hospital that the needs of essential patient care would be adversely affected.[123] In *Beth Israel Hospital,* the Court had admonished the Board that it " '[bears] a heavy continuing responsibility to review its policies concerning organizational activities in various parts of hospitals.' "[124] In *Baptist Hospital,* the Court observed that "the experience to date raises serious doubts as to whether the Board's interpretation of its present

---

not violate §8(a)(1) and remanded the issue for reconsideration in light of *Beth Israel.* The Court left intact the lower court's holding that union solicitation could be barred in the hospital's corridors, noting that *Beth Israel* had not considered this issue. On remand, the Board reaffirmed its prior holding that the rule prohibiting solicitation in the cafeteria violated §8(a)(1) because the employer had not established that the total ban on solicitation by employees in the cafeteria was necessary to fulfill its mission as a health care facility. Baylor Univ. Medical Center, 247 NLRB 1323, 103 LRRM 1311 (1980), *enforcement denied,* 662 F2d 56, 108 LRRM 2041 (CA DC, 1981). *See also* Albert Einstein Medical Center, 245 NLRB 140, 102 LRRM 1508 (1979). *But see* Baptist Medical Sys. v. NLRB, 876 F2d 661, 131 LRRM 2565 (CA 8, 1989), *denying enforcement to* 288 NLRB No. 97, 130 LRRM 1272 (1988), where the court held that when an employer chooses not to allow any solicitation or promotional activity by nonemployees in its public facility and union organizers attempt to use that facility for such activities, the principles of *Babcock & Wilcox* contemplate that the union activities may validly be prohibited, even where the activity is not disruptive. The court thus refused to enforce a Board order that held so long as a union organizer's activity is not disruptive, the employer must grant the organizer access to the employer's public restaurant, and stated that the Board standard did not afford "an adequate accommodation of the employer's private property rights." *Id.*

[122]NLRB v. Baptist Hosp., 442 US 773, 101 LRRM 2556 (1979). *See also* NLRB v. National Jewish Hosp., 593 F2d 911, 99 LRRM 3141 (CA 10, 1978), *vacated,* 443 US 903, 101 LRRM 2628 (1979) (hospital could not demonstrate distribution of union literature in cafeteria affected patient care); NLRB v. St. Joseph's Hosp., 587 F2d 1060, 99 LRRM 3404 (CA 10, 1978); Medical Center Hosp., 244 NLRB 742, 102 LRRM 1105 (1979) (hospital could not prohibit solicitation and distribution in walkways and driveways leading to front entrance of hospital when conducted at times designed to coincide with periods in which a majority of employees arrive or leave hospital); NLRB v. Presbyterian Medical Center, 586 F2d 165, 99 LRRM 3137 (CA 10, 1978) (hospital could not prohibit distribution of union literature outside the hospital building).

[123]101 LRRM at 2561. The Board, on remand for a determination of the outstanding issues remaining after the Supreme Court's decision, determined that the hospital also violated §8(a)(1) by prohibiting solicitation in the snack bar adjacent to the cafeteria and in locker rooms on the hospital's first floor. Baptist Hosp., 246 NLRB 149, 102 LRRM 1418 (1979).

[124]437 US at 508.

presumption adequately takes into account the medical practices and methods of treatment incident to the delivery of patient care services in a modern hospital."[125]

The wording of a no-solicitation rule may be significant, and where the rule is susceptible of differing interpretations, the risk of ambiguity must be borne by the employer.[126] For example, a rule in a retail establishment prohibiting solicitation "on store premises during working hours by any persons" was held invalid because it could be read as prohibiting employee activity in nonselling areas during employees' nonworking time.[127] Also deemed ambiguous and invalid was a rule prohibiting unauthorized solicitation "except such solicitation during the employees' nonworking time as is protected by the National Labor Relation Act"; likewise invalid was the prohibition of unauthorized distribution of literature "except such distribution during nonworking time in nonworking areas as is protected by the National Labor Relations Act."[128] A rule prohibiting solicitation or distribution in a "working area" may be subject to varying interpretation depending on the circumstances of its application.[129] The Board's position regarding ambiguous rules is aptly summed up in the Second Circuit's declaration that "the risk of ambiguity must be held against the promulgator of the rule rather than the employees who are supposed to abide by it."[130]

---

[125]101 LRRM at 2562. *See also* NLRB Gen. Counsel Guidelines for Handling No-Solicitation, No-Distribution Rules in Health-Care Facilities, Memorandum 79-76 (October 5, 1979).

[126]St. Joseph's Hosp., 263 NLRB 375, 111 LRRM 1053 (1982). *Accord* Presbyterian/St. Luke's Medical Center v. NLRB, 723 F2d 1468, 115 LRRM 2306 (CA 10, 1983). *See also* James F. Stanford, Inc., 249 NLRB 623, 104 LRRM 1449 (1980).

[127]G.C. Murphy Co., 171 NLRB 370, 68 LRRM 1108 (1968), *enforced*, 422 F2d 685, 71 LRRM 2397 (CA DC, 1969). *See* T.R.W., Bearings Div., 257 NLRB 442, 107 LRRM 1481 (1981). *See also* Lyman Steel Co., 249 NLRB 296, 104 LRRM 1323 (1980). Prohibitions phrased in terms of "company time" have also been ruled ambiguous and invalid. *See* Birmingham Iron Co. v. NLRB, 615 F2d 661, 104 LRRM 2132 (CA 5, 1980) (prohibition on solicitation "at any time" ruled unlawful); Fruehauf Corp., Paceco Div. v. NLRB, *supra* note 110; General Motors Corp., Frigidaire Div., 240 NLRB 168, 100 LRRM 1283 (1979). *See also* Pepsi Cola Bottlers of Miami, 155 NLRB 527, 60 LRRM 1357 (1965), where a prohibition against solicitation "on the job" was held valid on its face.

[128]Westinghouse Elec. Corp., 240 NLRB 905, 100 LRRM 1391, *aff'd*, 612 F2d 1072, 103 LRRM 2171 (CA 8, 1979); McDonnell Douglas Corp., 240 NLRB 794, 100 LRRM 1483 (1979); Chrysler Corp., 227 NLRB 1256, 95 LRRM 1448 (1977), *enforcement denied*, 595 F2d 364, 101 LRRM 2837 (CA 6, 1979). *See also* Baldor Elec. Co., 245 NLRB 614, 102 LRRM 1261 (1979) (rule prohibiting solicitation in working areas without company approval held invalid).

[129]Thermo Elec. Co., 222 NLRB 358, 91 LRRM 1310 (1976), *enforced*, 547 F2d 1162, 94 LRRM 2947 (CA 3, 1977), defined work areas as including space near a time clock and permitted enforcement of a no-solicitation rule there. *See also* Times Publishing Co. v. NLRB, *supra* note 120 (lobby of a building housing employer's business offices held to be a "work area").

[130]NLRB v. Miller Charles & Co., 341 F2d 870, 874, 58 LRRM 2507 (CA 2, 1965).

Clarifications of ambiguous rules or narrowing interpretations of overly broad rules must be effectively communicated to an employer's work force before the Board will conclude that the impact of facially illegal rules has been eliminated.[131] However, the Board has allowed the ambiguity of an otherwise invalid rule prohibiting "non-job related activities during working hours" to be cured by an oral clarification that the rule did not apply to lunch periods.[132]

No-solicitation rules will not be deemed invalid merely because they specify a charity as the sole exception to restrictions on solicitation.[133] However, the level and nature of solicitations under such an exception can be the basis for finding that the employer applied its rule in a disparate manner.[134]

(3) Unlawful promulgation or enforcement. A rule presumptively valid on its face is also presumptively valid as to its promulgation and enforcement. But these presumptions can be rebutted by evidence establishing a discriminatory purpose in the adoption or application of the rule.[135] Discriminatory enforcement to stifle employee criticism of union leadership or of management action may also rebut the presumptive validity of a rule.[136]

Since its 1964 decision in *Wm. H. Block Co.*,[137] in which it abandoned a less restrictive, but short-lived, approach,[138] the Board has considered the extent to which the promulgation of a no-solicitation rule coincided with the ebb and flow of union activity and other evidence of union animus in the adoption or enforce-

---

[131]Chicago Magnesium Castings Co., 240 NLRB 400, 100 LRRM 1267 (1979), *aff'd*, 612 F2d 1028, 103 LRRM 2241 (CA 7, 1980); Essex Int'l, 211 NLRB 749, 86 LRRM 1411 (1974). *But see* American Safety Equip. Corp. v. NLRB, 643 F2d 693, 106 LRRM 2836 (CA 10, 1981).

[132]Standard Motor Prods., 265 NLRB 482, 112 LRRM 1383 (1982).

[133]*See* South Nassau Communities Hosp., 274 NLRB 1181, 118 LRRM 1590 (1985).

[134]*See* United States Indus., Hammary Mfg. Corp. Div., 265 NLRB 57, 111 LRRM 1346 (1982), *amending* 258 NLRB 1319, 108 LRRM 1200 (1981).

[135]AMF, Inc., Head Ski Div., 228 NLRB 1406, 95 LRRM 1027 (1977), *enforced*, 593 F2d 972, 100 LRRM 3035 (CA 10, 1979); Top Sec. Patrol, 226 NLRB 46, 93 LRRM 1280 (1976); Walton Mfg. Co., 126 NLRB 697, 45 LRRM 1370 (1960), *enforced*, 289 F2d 177, 47 LRRM 2794 (CA 5, 1961).

[136]NLRB v. Transcon Lines, 599 F2d 719, 101 LRRM 3031 (CA 5, 1979); American Hosp. Ass'n, 230 NLRB 54, 95 LRRM 1266 (1977), *enforced*, 582 F2d 1283 (CA 7, 1978); United Parcel Serv., 230 NLRB 1147, 95 LRRM 1520 (1977); Dreis & Krump Mfg. Co. v. NLRB, 544 F2d 320, 93 LRRM 2739 (CA 7, 1976).

[137]150 NLRB 341, 57 LRRM 1531 (1964).

[138]The Board overruled Star-Brite Indus., 127 NLRB 1008, 56 LRRM 1139 (1960), in which a rule had been upheld as valid despite evidence that it was promulgated after the onset of organizing and was applied only to union activities because, as the Board said, it would be anomalous to forbid the adoption of a rule "when the occasion for its use arises." *Id.* at 1011.

ment of the rule. In 1981, in *Friendly Ice Cream Corp.*,[139] the Board ruled a prima facie case rebutting the presumption of validity was established by evidence that the employer: (1) promulgated the rule at a time of "intensive union activity" and applied it in the first instance to a leading union adherent; (2) permitted solicitations of other kinds during working time; and (3) disclosed hostility to organizational efforts by a pattern of violations of sections 8(a)(1) and (3). Although the Board's findings concerning the employer's conduct were rejected by the First Circuit, and the order was not enforced,[140] the Board's general approach has been upheld in the courts.[141]

d. Implementation of Rules: Timing as an Element of Legality. The timing of implementation of a no-solicitation or no-distribution rule remains an important consideration in assessing its validity.[142] Timing the implementation of an otherwise lawful rule to coincide with union organizational activity does not automatically result in illegality where "the surrounding context is devoid of unlawful activity."[143] Strict enforcement of an existing rule, or promulgation of a new one during a union organizing campaign, has been regarded as evidence of illegal conduct, unless a showing is made that an objectively observable decline in productivity was caused by solicitation or by the campaign.[144]

---

[139]254 NLRB 1206, 106 LRRM 1300 (1981), *enforcement denied*, 677 F2d 170, 110 LRRM 2352 (CA 1, 1982). *See also* State Chem. Co., 166 NLRB 455, 65 LRRM 1612 (1967).

[140]NLRB v. Friendly Ice Cream Corp., *supra* note 139.

[141]*See* Restaurant Corp. of Am. v. NLRB, 827 F2d 799, 126 LRRM 2129 (CA DC, 1987), *vacating* 801 F2d 1390, 123 LRRM 2513 (CA DC, 1986), *enforcing in part and denying in part* 271 NLRB 1080, 117 LRRM 1094 (1984); NLRB v. S.E. Nichols, Inc., 862 F2d 952, 129 LRRM 3098 (CA 2, 1988), *enforcing as modified* 284 NLRB 556, 127 LRRM 1298 (1987), *cert. denied*, 490 US 1108, 131 LRRM 2528 (1989) (employer discriminatorily enforced no-solicitation rule where no evidence that any employee was ever reprimanded for or told to cease solicitation or distribution for nonunion purposes and there was testimony that employees constantly solicited for other kinds of organizations).

[142]*See* Ward Mfg., 152 NLRB 1270, 59 LRRM 1325 (1965), where the rule was promulgated one day after the first union meeting; *see also* Elmendorf & Fort Richardson Barber Concessions, 247 NLRB 667, 103 LRRM 1236 (1980).

[143]Brigadier Indus. Corp., 271 NLRB 656, 117 LRRM 1033 (1984), *review denied sub nom.* Clothing & Textile Workers v. NLRB, 776 F2d 365, 121 LRRM 2120 (CA DC, 1985). *See also* Westinghouse Elec. Corp., 277 NLRB 136, 120 LRRM 1295 (1985). *Cf.* Cadiz Convalescent Center, 258 NLRB 559, 108 LRRM 1233 (1981) (implementation of rule during union campaign was not unlawful where employer replaced facially unlawful rule by presumptively lawful rule; NLRB v. Roney Plaza Apts., 597 F2d 1046, 101 LRRM 2794 (CA 5, 1979); F.P. Adams Co., 166 NLRB 967, 968, 65 LRRM 1695 (1967).

[144]*See* note 143 *supra*; Bankers Club, 218 NLRB 22, 89 LRRM 1812 (1975); North Am. Rockwell Corp., 195 NLRB 1046, 79 LRRM 1593 (1972).

e. Union Buttons and Insignia. In *Republic Aviation*,[145] the Supreme Court upheld, as a protected activity, the right of employees to wear union buttons while at work. This general rule also encompasses the right to wear other emblems, such as badges and T-shirts, demonstrating union support.[146] This right must be balanced against the right of the employer to manage its business in an orderly fashion. Striking that balance, the Board allows an employer to promulgate and enforce a rule prohibiting the wearing of union emblems only where the prohibition is necessary because of "special circumstances," such as maintenance of production and discipline,[147] safety,[148] preventing alienation of customers,[149] or a possible adverse effect on patients in a health care institution.[150] Thus, for example, where friction and animosity exist between groups of employees

---

[145]Republic Aviation Corp. v. NLRB, 324 US 793, 16 LRRM 620 (1945). *See also* Han-Dee Pak, Inc., 249 NLRB 725, 104 LRRM 1009 (1980); Dixie Mach. Rebuilders, 248 NLRB 881, 104 LRRM 1094 (1980); Carbonex Coal Co., 248 NLRB 779, 104 LRRM 1009 (1980), *enforced*, 679 F2d 200, 110 LRRM 2566 (CA 10, 1982); Regal Tube Co., 245 NLRB 968, 102 LRRM 1531 (1979); Pepsi-Cola Bottling Co., 242 NLRB 265, 101 LRRM 1141 (1979); Laredo Packing Co., 241 NLRB 184, 100 LRRM 1573 (1979), *enforced*, 625 F2d 593, 105 LRRM 2551 (CA 5, 1980), *cert. denied*, 449 US 1080, 106 LRRM 2137 (1981); Dependable Lists, 239 NLRB 1304, 100 LRRM 1148 (1979).

[146]Publishers Printing Co., 246 NLRB 206, 102 LRRM 1628 (1979), *enforced*, 650 F2d 859, 107 LRRM 3349 (CA 6, 1981); De Vilbiss Co., 102 NLRB 1317, 31 LRRM 1374 (1953).

[147]Midstate Tel. Corp. v. NLRB, 706 F2d 401, 113 LRRM 2213 (CA 2, 1983), *enforcing in part and denying in part* 262 NLRB 1291, 110 LRRM 1533 (1982) (employer could prohibit wearing of T-shirts saying "I survived the Midstate strike of 1971-75-79" to preserve discipline and improve labor-management relations). Fabric-Tek, Inc. v. NLRB, 352 F2d 577, 60 LRRM 2376 (CA 8, 1965); Standard Fittings Co., 133 NLRB 928, 48 LRRM 1808 (1964); Floridan Hotel of Tampa, 137 NLRB 1484, 50 LRRM 1433 (1962), *enforced as modified*, 318 F2d 545, 53 LRRM 2420 (CA 2, 1963). *See also* May Dep't Stores Co., 174 NLRB 770, 70 LRRM 1307 (1969). The fact that an employer maintains a dress code does not alone justify prohibitions on wearing union insignia. Woonsocket Health Centre, 245 NLRB 652, 102 LRRM 1494 and 245 NLRB 668, 102 LRRM 1385 (1979). *But see* Burger King Corp. v. NLRB, 725 F2d 1053, 115 LRRM 2387 (CA 6, 1984), *enforcing in part and denying in part* 265 NLRB 1507, 112 LRRM 1185 (1982) (no violation for employer to ban union button from uniform of employees who had contact with public).

[148]Fluid Packaging Co., 247 NLRB 1469, 103 LRRM 1415 (1980); Andrews Wire Corp., 189 NLRB 108, 76 LRRM 1568 (1971). *See* Mack's Supermarkets, 288 NLRB 1082, 130 LRRM 1439 (1988).

[149]Rooney's at the Mart, 247 NLRB 1004, 103 LRRM 1291 (1980), *enforcement denied*, 677 F2d 44, 110 LRRM 2426 (CA 9, 1982). *See also* Davison-Paxon Co. v. NLRB, 462 F2d 364, 80 LRRM 2673 (CA 5, 1972); NLRB v. Harrah's Club, 337 F2d 177, 57 LRRM 2198 (CA 9, 1964). Buttons that are not provocative and do not serve to alienate customers, particularly when worn by employees not in contact with the public, may not be prohibited. Floridan Hotel of Tampa, *supra* note 147. *Accord* Nordstrom, Inc., 264 NLRB 698, 111 LRRM 1344 (1982) (employer could not forbid wearing of "tasteful and inconspicuous" union insignia by department store salespersons).

[150]George J. London Memorial Hosp., 238 NLRB 704, 99 LRRM 1680 (1978).

because of a strike, prohibition of union insignias may prove to be a legitimate precaution against discord and violence.[151]

A rule based on "special circumstances" must be narrowly drawn to restrict the wearing of union insignia only in areas or under circumstances that justify the rule.[152] Enforcement of a valid rule prohibiting the wearing of certain objects, including union insignia, is unlawful if it is applied strictly to union insignia while other breaches of the rule are permitted.[153]

The Act does not protect the wearing of badges or symbols that fail to express participation in union or other protected activity. Thus, an employer could lawfully prohibit department store employees from wearing flowers that were distributed by union representatives.[154] The wearing of employer-supplied campaign badges, though expressive, is subject to different regulatory considerations altogether because providing such badges can amount to an interrogation that interferes with or coerces employees in the exercise of their rights.[155]

f. "Captive Audience" Speeches, Conferences, and Interviews. Prior to the advent of section 8(c), the Board adopted a rule of absolute prohibition of captive-audience speeches, that is, speeches on employer premises during working time.[156] In 1948 this rule was repudiated as inconsistent with section 8(c).[157] Nonetheless,

---

[151]United Aircraft Corp., 134 NLRB 1632, 49 LRRM 1384 (1961) (involving pins worn by employees who had not crossed the picket line during a bitter strike); Caterpillar Tractor Co. v. NLRB, 230 F2d 357, 37 LRRM 2619 (CA 7, 1956) (involving "scab buttons"); Boeing Airplane Co. v. NLRB, 217 F2d 369, 34 LRRM 2821 (CA 9, 1954) (involving rival unions in a violent strike). The Board's citation of all three cases for the same proposition in Floridan Hotel of Tampa, *supra* note 147, at 1486 n.6, may indicate an adoption of the Seventh and Ninth Circuit decisions consistent with *United Aircraft.*

[152]George J. London Memorial Hosp., *supra* note 150, where a psychiatric hospital's rule prohibiting the wearing of insignia other than of a professional nature was ruled unlawfully broad because it was not restricted to patient care areas. *Accord* Asociacion Hosp. del Maestro, 283 NLRB 419, 125 LRRM 1095 (1987), *enforced,* 842 F2d 575, 127 LRRM 3178 (CA 1, 1988).

[153]Nestle Co., 248 NLRB 732, 103 LRRM 1567 (1980), *enforced,* 659 F2d 252, 108 LRRM 2175 (CA DC, 1981). *See also* Pay 'n Save Corp., 247 NLRB 1346, 103 LRRM 1334 (1980), *enforced,* 641 F2d 697, 106 LRRM 3040 (CA 9, 1981); C. Markus Hardware, Inc., 243 NLRB 903, 102 LRRM 1353 (1979); St. Joseph's Hosp., 225 NLRB 348, 93 LRRM 1179 (1976).

[154]Gimbel Bros., 147 NLRB 500, 505, 56 LRRM 1287 (1964). *See also* Pillowtex Corp., 234 NLRB 560, 97 LRRM 1369 (1978).

[155]Chas. V. Weise Co., 133 NLRB 765, 48 LRRM 1709 (1961). See discussion of unlawful interrogation *infra* at notes 271–315.

[156]Clark Bros. Co., 70 NLRB 802, 18 LRRM 1360 (1946), *enforced,* 163 F2d 373, 20 LRRM 2436 (CA 2, 1947). For a general discussion of captive-audience speeches, see Note, *NLRB Regulation of Employer's Pre-Election Captive Audience Speeches,* 65 Mich. L. Rev. 1236 (1967).

[157]Babcock & Wilcox Co., 77 NLRB 577, 578, 22 LRRM 1057 (1948).

the Board attempted to control captive-audience speeches to some degree by formulating its *Bonwit-Teller*[158] doctrine of equal opportunity. That doctrine held that captive-audience speeches by the employer, when coupled with a no-solicitation rule, constituted a discriminatory application of the rule. The Board sought to avoid conflict with section 8(c) by emphasizing the employer's refusal to permit a reply under similar conditions, rather than its delivery of a noncoercive speech. Two years later, in 1953, a Board reconstituted during the Eisenhower Administration rejected the equal-opportunity doctrine. In *Livingston Shirt Corp.*,[159] the Board held that "an employer does not commit an unfair labor practice if he makes a preelection speech on company time and premises to his employees and denies the union's request for an opportunity to reply."[160] In *Nutone*,[161] the Supreme Court apparently approved this rule, at least where the union has other means to carry its message to the employees.

As a companion to *Livingston Shirt*, the Board decided *Peerless Plywood*,[162] which formulated the still-current "24-hour rule" prohibiting both unions and employers from delivering captive-audience speeches to massed groups of employees within 24 hours of an election. Conflict with section 8(c) was said to be avoided because an infringement of the rule is not deemed an unfair labor practice but merely a basis for setting aside the election.

In 1962, in *May Department Stores*,[163] a Board reconstituted during the Kennedy Administration distinguished *Livingston Shirt* on the ground that the *Livingston* no-solicitation rule was presumptively valid and inapplicable to nonworking hours. But use of a broad, privileged no-solicitation rule, coupled with antiunion speeches, was deemed to create "a glaring 'imbalance in opportunities for organizational communication' "[164] within the *Nutone* doctrine, thus violating section 8(a)(1). The Sixth Circuit, however, refused enforcement, charging that the Board had failed to give adequate consideration to various other means of

---

[158]Bonwit-Teller, Inc., 96 NLRB 608, 28 LRRM 1547 (1951), *modified*, 104 NLRB 497, 32 LRRM 1102 (1953).

[159]Livingston Shirt Co., 107 NLRB 400, 33 LRRM 1156 (1953).

[160]*Id.* at 409.

[161]NLRB v. Steelworkers (Nutone, Inc.), 357 US 357, 42 LRRM 2324 (1958).

[162]Peerless Plywood Co., 107 NLRB 427, 33 LRRM 1151 (1953). *See* Chapter 9, "Restrictions of Preelection Activity: 'Laboratory Conditions,'" at note 39.

[163]May Dep't Stores Co., 136 NLRB 797, 49 LRRM 1862 (1962), *enforcement denied*, 316 F2d 797, 53 LRRM 2172 (CA 6, 1963).

[164]*Id.*, 49 LRRM at 1864.

communication available to the union.[165] But the Board adhered to its position and in *Montgomery Ward & Co.*[166] found a violation where an unlawful no-solicitation rule, which banned union solicitation in nonworking areas during nonworking time, prevented a response to antiunion speeches delivered to massed employees during working time. The Board found the speeches coercive and unprotected by section 8(c); and that, when coupled with a no-solicitation rule, they created a "glaring imbalance" in organizational communication. This time the Sixth Circuit enforced the Board's order, distinguishing its *May* decision on the ground that the no-solicitation rule in *May* had been valid and the speeches noncoercive.[167]

In *General Electric Co.*,[168] the employer made speeches on company time to massed employees who were informed that attendance was not mandatory. The union was denied equal time. In a petition to set aside the election, the union urged the Board to overrule *Livingston Shirt* and reactivate and extend *Bonwit-Teller* as a substantive rule of preelection conduct. The Board refused, preferring to postpone any reconsideration of Board doctrine in the area of plant access until after it had the benefit of experience with the rule adopted in *Excelsior Underwear.*[169] To date the Board has not reassessed its rule on union

---

[165]May Dep't Stores v. NLRB, 316 F2d 797, 53 LRRM 2172 (CA 6, 1963).

[166]Montgomery Ward & Co., 145 NLRB 846, 55 LRRM 1063 (1964), *enforced as modified*, 339 F2d 889, 58 LRRM 2115 (CA 6, 1965).

[167]*Id. See also* S&H Grossinger's, Inc., 372 F2d 26, 64 LRRM 2295 (CA 2, 1967), *enforcing in part* 156 NLRB 233, 61 LRRM 1025 (1965), in which the Board conditioned validity of employer's continual antiunion speeches during working time upon the granting of a similar opportunity to the union. Since many employees lived on premises of the resort hotel involved, meaningful outside communication was blocked. The Second Circuit held that an equal-opportunity requirement could be imposed only when the employer is enforcing its no-solicitation rule; but because it also upheld the Board's invalidation of the employer's rule excluding union organizers from the employer's property, the court found there was no need to order the employer to provide the union with an equal opportunity to address the employees.

[168]156 NLRB 1247, 61 LRRM 1222 (1966).

[169]156 NLRB 1236, 61 LRRM 1217 (1966), holding that parties to a pending election may have access to a list of the names and addresses of all employees eligible to vote; the *Excelsior* rule, though not the means of its promulgation, was approved by the Supreme Court in NLRB v. Wyman-Gordon Co., 394 US 759, 70 LRRM 3345 (1969). *See* Chapter 10, "Representation Proceedings and Elections," at notes 239–251, and Chapter 31, "NLRB Procedures," at notes 236–258. *See also* Bok, *The Regulation of Campaign Tactics in Representation Elections Under the National Labor Relations Act*, 78 HARV. L. REV. 38 (1964).

One of the provisions of the Labor Law Reform Bill, which failed of enactment in 1978, would have required the Board to develop rules and regulations involving equal access by unions to employer premises whenever an employer delivered a captive-audience speech. *See* H. R. 8410, 95th Cong., 1st Sess. (1977); S. 2467, 95th Cong., 1st Sess. (1977). *See* Chapter 5, "The Post–Landrum-Griffin Period."

access to employer facilities.[170]

g. No-Access Rules. In defining the right of off-duty employees to enter or remain on plant premises for purposes of engaging in union activities, the Board balances employee self-organizational rights against the employer's interest in its property and productivity, and considers whether an alternative means of communication is available to the labor organization and employees it seeks to represent.

In *GTE Lenkurt*,[171] a nondiscriminatory rule prohibiting off-duty employees from entering or remaining on the plant premises for *any* purpose was found valid. The Board reasoned that the status of an off-duty employee is more nearly analogous to that of a nonemployee, in that both are invitees or trespassers to the same extent and thus neither is entitled more than the other to admission to the premises. An off-duty employee, it was noted, might still engage in union solicitation during nonworking time within the employer's premises while on-the-clock.

The Board has since emphasized, however, that *GTE Lenkurt* is to be narrowly construed and confined to its precise facts. The Board adopted that view in *Tri-County Medical Center*,[172] where it declared that a rule denying off-duty employees access to the employer's premises is presumptively valid only if (1) it limits access solely with respect to the interior of the plant and other working areas; (2) it is clearly disseminated to all employees; and (3) it applies to off-duty employees seeking access to the plant for any purpose and not just to those employees engaged in union activity. Thus, a rule that denies off-duty employees entry to parking lots, gates, and other outside nonworking areas will be invalid unless justified by specific business reasons.[173]

---

[170]For a full account of the Board's regulation of captive audience and related issues in the election setting, *see* Chapter 9, "Restrictions of Preelection Activity: 'Laboratory Conditions.'"

[171]204 NLRB 921, 83 LRRM 1684 (1973).

[172]222 NLRB 1089, 91 LRRM 1323 (1976).

[173]For application of this rule in varying contexts, see NLRB v. Ohio Masonic Home, 892 F2d 449, 133 LRRM 2179 (CA 6, 1989), *enforcing* 290 NLRB No. 122, 129 LRRM 1153 (1988); NLRB v. Pizza Crust Co. of Pa., 862 F2d 49, 129 LRRM 3002 (CA 3, 1988), *enforcing* 286 NLRB 490, 129 LRRM 1281 (1987); NLRB v. Roney Plaza Apts., 597 F2d 1046, 101 LRRM 2794 (CA 5, 1979); Stein Seal Co. v. NLRB, 605 F2d 703, 102 LRRM 2297 (CA 3, 1979); NLRB v. Presbyterian Medical Center, 586 F2d 165, 99 LRRM 3137 (CA 10, 1978); Northeastern Univ., 235 NLRB 858, 98 LRRM 1347 (1978), *enforced in part*, 601 F2d 1208, 101 LRRM 2767(CA 1, 1979); Sparks Nugget, Inc., 230 NLRB 275, 95 LRRM 1298 (1977); East Bay Newspapers, 228 NLRB 692, 96 LRRM 1019 (1977); Carda Hotels dba Holiday Hotel & Casino, 228 NLRB 926, 94 LRRM 1702 (1977), *enforced*, 604 F2d 605, 102 NLRB 2484 (CA 9, 1979); East Bay Newspapers, 225 NLRB 1148, 93 LRRM 1102 (1976); Continental Bus Sys., 229 NLRB 1262, 95 LRRM 1307

h. Prohibiting Protected Activity on Private Property Open to Public. In its 1968 *Logan Valley* decision,[174] the Supreme Court ruled that property rights must yield to a union's constitutionally protected right to picket and handbill on a privately owned shopping center parking lot. Such private property, the Court said, had taken on a "quasi-public" character.[175] In *Central Hardware,*[176] however, the Court refused to extend the "quasi-public" doctrine to nonemployee solicitation on retail store customer parking lots, noting that every retail and service establishment in the United States was open to the public and thus could be deemed to be "quasi-public." Subsequently, in *Hudgens v. NLRB,*[177] the Supreme Court effectively overruled *Logan Valley* and rejected application of constitutional principles to disputes over nonemployee access to private property normally open to the public. The Court held that in deciding whether prohibitions on nonemployee access to private, "quasi-public" property were reasonable, only the balancing standards under the Act, as established in *Babcock & Wilcox,*[178] would govern.

In applying the *Babcock & Wilcox* standards to activity carried out on private property open to the public, the Board, on remand of *Hudgens,*[179] reached results similar to those produced under the Supreme Court's *Logan Valley* decision but without relying on the discredited constitutional underpinnings of that decision. Thus, picketing on shopping mall property in support of an economic strike against a warehouse of one of the retail stores leasing premises on the mall was deemed protected activity. The Board said that the distinction between economic activities and the organizational activities in *Babcock & Wilcox* might "require a different application of the accommodation principle because of the different purposes sought to be

(1971). *See also* Sahara Tahoe Hotel Corp. dba Sahara Tahoe Hotel, 292 NLRB 812, 131 LRRM 1021 (1989) (mistaken belief, in good faith, that employees are nonemployees is no defense to allegation of unlawful refusal of access).

[174]Food Employees Local 590 v. Logan Valley Plaza, 391 US 308, 68 LRRM 2209 (1968).

[175]See Chapter 19, "The Primary Strike," at notes 22–27, for further discussion of the constitutional aspects of *Logan Valley*.

[176]Central Hardware Co. v. NLRB, 407 US 539, 80 LRRM 2769 (1972). *See* Chapter 19, "The Primary Strike," at notes 197–198.

[177]424 US 507, 91 LRRM 2489 (1976). *See* Chapter 19, "The Primary Strike," at notes 199–201.

[178]NLRB v. Babcock & Wilcox, 351 US 105, 38 LRRM 2001 (1956).

[179]Scott Hudgens, 230 NLRB 414, 95 LRRM 1351 (1977), *on remand from* Hudgens v. NLRB, 424 US 507, 91 LRRM 2489 (1976), *reaff'g* 192 NLRB 671, 77 LRRM 1872 (1971). *See also* note 182 *infra*.

served."[180] It ruled, nevertheless, that the mall owner's threat to arrest the picketers violated section 8(a)(1) because the message sought to be conveyed by the picketing would have been too greatly diluted if the picketers had been forced to use alternative channels of communication and because

> safety considerations, the likelihood of enmeshing neutral employers, and the fact that many people become members of the pickets' intended audience on impulse all weigh against requiring the pickets to remove to public property, or even to the sidewalks surrounding the mall.[181]

In reaching that conclusion, the Board held that section 8(a)(1) had been violated even though the property rights impinged upon were those of the shopping mall owner rather than those of the employer against whom the union activity was directed. It relied on the facts that the mall owner was protecting its own interests as well as acting as the retail store owner's agent in policing the mall and removing picketers.[182]

The Board has followed and refined that approach in later cases. In *Fairmont Hotel Co.*,[183] officers of a union that had an area standards dispute with an unorganized bakery handbilled at the entrance of a large hotel that the bakery supplied. The handbills asked members of the public not to patronize the hotel until it stopped doing business with the bakery. Hotel management ordered the handbillers to leave its premises, requiring them to handbill on the less accessible public sidewalk. The Board dismissed the complaint against the hotel. It observed that *Babcock & Wilcox* requires it to accommodate section 7 and

---

[180]230 NLRB at 416.

[181]*Id.* at 417.

[182]*But see* Giant Foods Mkts. v. NLRB, 633 F2d 18, 105 LRRM 2916 (CA 6, 1980). Finding an absence of substantial evidence as to whether alternative channels of communication were available to the union, and as to whether neutral employers were "enmeshed" in the union's dispute by its "area standards" picketing in a shopping center, the Sixth Circuit refused enforcement and remanded the Board's order; the Board had determined that a peaceful demand, by the employer store owner (against whom the union was picketing on shopping center property) and by another store owner conducting business there, that pickets leave the shopping center property violated §8(a)(1), 241 NLRB 727, 100 LRRM 1598 (1979). However, in Seattle-First Nat'l Bank, 243 NLRB 898, 101 LRRM 1537 (1979), *enforcement denied in part and remanded*, 651 F2d 1272, 105 LRRM 3411 (CA 9, 1980), a demand by the owner of a bank building that union representatives who were handbilling on the 46th floor of the building near the premises of a restaurant with which the union was engaged in a labor dispute leave the building or be arrested was held to violate §8(a)(1) (the Ninth Circuit remanded for revision of the order to ensure that the number of union representatives on the floor and their behavior be properly restricted.) *See also* Meijer, Inc., NLRB Gen. Counsel Advice Memo., Case No. 7-CA-16237, 101 LRRM 1529 (1979), for discussion of *Hudgens* principles in context of stranger picketing on shopping center property.

[183]282 NLRB 139, 123 LRRM 1257 (1986).

property rights with "as little destruction of one as is consistent with the other."[184] This required that the relative strength of the competing rights must be weighed and that where one clearly predominated, it should prevail.[185] A plurality of the Board announced that it would consider the effectiveness of the union's alternative means of communication to be determinative only where the competing rights were relatively equal.

The Board concluded that the hotel's property rights were clearly stronger than the union's section 7 rights. The hotel generally reserved its front entrance for patrons of the hotel; employees and suppliers were required to use other entrances. The hotel had never previously permitted handbilling on its private property. Moreover, it had a valid interest by reason of its innkeeper's duty of care to prohibit handbilling in order to maintain decorum at its entrance and to minimize congestion, litter, and the possibility of theft of luggage. By contrast, the union's section 7 right to handbill had limited significance. The union did not have a primary dispute with the hotel. The union was not trying to represent the hotel's employees who were organized, and those employees stood to derive no benefit, not even an incidental one, from the union's activities. Because the property and section 7 rights asserted were not relatively equal in strength, the Board did not consider whether the union had reasonable, alternative means to communicate its message.[186]

---

[184]*Supra* note 178, at 112.

[185]The Board said factors that may affect the relative strength or weakness of a property right "include, but are not limited to, the use to which the property in question is put; the restrictions, if any, that are imposed on public access to the property or to the facility located on the property; and the size and location of the private facility." 123 LRRM at 1259–60. Factors that may affect the strength of a §7 right "include, but are not limited to, the nature of the right asserted, the purpose for which it is being asserted, the employer that is the target of the activity, the situs of the activity, the relationship of the situs to the target, the intended audience of the activity, and, possibly, the manner in which the right is being asserted." *Id.* at 1260.

[186]Fairmont Hotel Co., *supra* note 183, at 1261. The Board attempted to apply this "balance of the rights" test in a variety of factual settings. In some cases, the Board decided that the employer's property rights prevailed. *See, e.g.*, Sisters Int'l, 285 NLRB 796, 126 LRRM 1148 (1987). In other cases, the Board concluded that the employees' §7 rights prevailed. *See* Center St. Mkt. dba Medina Super Duper, 286 NLRB 728, 126 LRRM 1212 (1987); Schwab Foods dba Mooresville IGA Foodliner, 284 NLRB 1055, 125 LRRM 1225 (1987), *enforced*, 858 F2d 1285, 129 LRRM 2601 (CA 7, 1988). In still other cases, the Board concluded, or at least assumed, that the strength of the competing rights was comparatively equal. In those cases, the Board then considered whether the party seeking access had reasonable alternative means of communicating its message. *See* 40-41 Realty Assocs., 288 NLRB 200, 128 LRRM 1001 (1988), *enforced sub nom.* Dental Union Local 38A v. NLRB, 132 LRRM 2528 (CA 6, 1988); L & L Shop Rite, 285 NLRB 1036, 126 LRRM 1151 (1987). *See* Emery Realty v. NLRB, 863 F2d 1259, 1263, 130 LRRM 2154, 2157 (CA 6, 1988), *enforcing* 286 NLRB 372, 126 LRRM 1241 (1987), the Sixth

In *Jean Country*,[187] the Board reevaluated the analytical approach it developed in *Fairmont Hotel* for resolving conflicts between section 7 and private property rights and concluded that the availability of reasonable alternative means is a factor "that must be considered in every access [to private property] case."[188] Accordingly, the Board overruled *Fairmont Hotel* in so far as it held that alternative means of communication were to be considered only if neither property rights nor section 7 rights predominated.[189] In *Jean Country*, a shopping mall manager and an employer that leased a store in the mall demanded that nonemployee union picketers cease informational picketing in front of the store or be arrested for trespassing. The union was told that it would only be allowed to picket on public roads beyond the mall property. Taking into account the quasi-public nature of the property at issue, the Board found that the property rights of the owner were weak; in contrast, the union's section 7 rights were strong and would have been destroyed absent entry onto the mall property. Despite the fact that section 7 rights predominated, the Board departed from its *Fairmont Hotel* policy and considered the availability of reasonable alternative means of communicating the union's message. The Board found that communication of the union's message from public property at the mall entrances was not an effective alternative and thus held that the union was entitled to picket in front of the store.[190] The Board has applied *Jean Country* in subsequent

---

Circuit rejected the *Fairmont Hotel* standard because it "erroneously subordinates the issue of reasonable alternative means of access . . . to other factors." To the Sixth Circuit, "the existence of such alternatives is a threshold question, not something to be considered only when all other factors balance out." *Id.* at 1264, 130 LRRM at 2158.

[187]291 NLRB 11, 129 LRRM 1201 (1988).

[188]*Id.*, 129 LRRM at 1203.

[189]*Id.* at n.2.

[190]"Factors that may be relevant to the assessment of alternative means include, but are not limited to the desirability of avoiding the enmeshment of neutrals in labor disputes, the safety of attempting communications at alternative public sites, the burden and expense of nontrespassory communication alternatives and, most significant, the extent to which exclusive use of nontrespassory alternatives would dilute the effectiveness of the message." Jean Country, *supra* note 187, 129 LRRM at 1204–1205. The General Counsel need not "show that the party engaging in the §7 conduct actually attempted those means and found them futile." *Id.* at 1204. "What is required is simply a clear showing, based on objective considerations, rather than subjective impressions, that reasonably effective alternative means were unavailable in the circumstances." *Id.* This is the view held by most circuits that have addressed the issue. National Maritime Union v. NLRB (SCNO Barge Lines), 867 F2d 767, 130 LRRM 2641 (CA 2, 1989); Emery Realty, *supra* note 186; Husky Oil, N.P.R. Operations v. NLRB, 669 F2d 643, 109 LRRM 2548 (CA 10, 1982), *enforcing* 245 NLRB 353, 102 LRRM 1450 (1979); Hutzler Bros. Co. v. NLRB, 630 F2d 1012, 105 LRRM 2473 (CA 4, 1980), *denying enforcement to* 241 NLRB 914, 101 LRRM 1062 (1979); Belcher Towing Co. v. NLRB, 614 F2d 88, 103 LRRM 2939

cases.[191] [*See* **Editor's Note**, below.]

i. Prohibiting Distribution of Political Materials. The rights of employees to distribute material of a "political" nature on company property were considered by the Supreme Court in *Eastex, Inc. v. NLRB*.[192] The Court adopted the Board's ruling that a company violated section 8(a)(1) by prohibiting distribution of a newsletter that urged employees to write their legislators to oppose incorporation of the state "right-to-work" statute into a revised state constitution, criticized a Presidential veto of an increase in the federal minimum wage, and urged employees to register to vote to "defeat our enemies and elect our friends." The subject matter of the newsletter, in the Court's judgment, "bears such a relation to employees' interests as to come within the guarantee"[193] of section 7 and "fairly is characterized as concerted activity for the 'mutual aid or protection'"[194] of the employer's employees and of employees generally. The Court stopped short, however, of adopting a general rule governing every in-plant distribution of "political" literature, noting that "[t]here may well be types of conduct or speech that are so purely political or so remotely connected to the concerns of employees as employees as to be beyond the protection of [Section 7]."[195] The

---

(CA 5, 1980), *denying enforcement in part, remanding in part*, 238 NLRB 446, 99 LRRM 1566 (1978). *But see* NLRB v. Tamiment, Inc., 451 F2d 794, 78 LRRM 2726 (CA 3, 1971), *cert. denied*, 409 US 1012, 81 LRRM 2672 (1972) (Board should consider total effectiveness of alternative channels of communication only after union has shown that it used "reasonable efforts" to utilize these channels).

[191]Little & Co., 296 NLRB No. 89, 132 LRRM 1173 (1989); Sentry Mkts., 296 NLRB No. 5, 132 LRRM 1001 (1989); Chugach Alaska Fisheries, 295 NLRB No. 8, 132 LRRM 1197 (1989); Red Food Stores, 296 NLRB No. 62, 132 LRRM 1164 (1989); Granco, Inc. dba Thriftway Supermarket, 294 NLRB No. 7, 131 LRRM 1325 (1989); Federated Dep't Stores, Richway Div., 294 NLRB No. 49, 131 LRRM 1362 (1989); Trident Seafoods Corp., 293 NLRB 1016, 131 LRRM 1247 (1989); Tecumseh Foodland, 294 NLRB No. 37, 131 LRRM 1365 (1989); Lechmere, Inc., 295 NLRB No. 15, 131 LRRM 1480 (1989) (employer violated §8(a)(1) by excluding nonemployee organizers from shopping center parking lot in urban community) [**Editor's Note:** *aff'd*, 914 F2d 313, 135 LRRM 2329 (CA 1, 1990), *rev'd*, ___ US ___, 139 LRRM 2225 (1992). In *Lechmere* the Supreme Court rejected *Jean Country*. *See* **Editor's Note**, *supra* note 103.] Mountain Country Food Stores, 292 NLRB 967, 130 LRRM 1329 (1989).

[192]437 US 556, 98 LRRM 2717 (1978).

[193]*Id.* at 569. *See also* Hesse Corp., 244 NLRB 985, 102 LRRM 1340 (1979) (ban on employees' wearing of stickers protesting "right to work" laws held illegal).

[194]437 US at 570.

[195]*Id.* at 570 n.20. *See* Firestone Steel Prods. Co., 244 NLRB 826, 102 LRRM 1172 (1979) (employer lawfully prohibited distribution of literature supporting candidates in a statewide election for supreme court justice, governor, and United States Senator); Ford Motor Co., 221 NLRB 663, 666, 90 LRRM 1731 (1975), *enforced*, 546 F2d 418, 93 LRRM 2570 (CA 3, 1976) (distributing a "purely political tract" calling for independent workers' party and workers' government on employer's premises held unprotected even though "the election of any political candidate may have an ultimate effect on employment conditions").

Court specifically confined its holding in *Eastex* to its precise facts, leaving development of more general policy to case-by-case consideration.

Adopting the tenets set forth in Eastex, the Circuit Court for the District of Columbia in *Auto Workers Local 174 v. NLRB (Firestone Steel Products Co.)*[196] upheld a Board decision that denied section 7 protection for the distribution of a leaflet featuring union-endorsed candidates for public office. The court distinguished the leaflet from the newsletter considered in *Eastex* because "the principal thrust of the leaflet was to induce employees to vote for specific candidates, not to educate them on political issues relevant to their employment conditions."[197] However, in *Union Carbide Corp.-Nuclear Division v. NLRB*,[198] the Sixth Circuit upheld the Board in ruling that the employer, a federal contractor, violated the Act by confiscating a "Taxpayer Petition" posted by a union steward.

j. Effect of Contractual Waiver of Right to Solicit or Distribute. Collective bargaining agreements sometimes contain otherwise invalid rules prohibiting solicitation and distribution, purporting thereby to waive employee section 7 rights. Board decisions on the legal effect of such waivers have been inconsistent. The Board's initial position was that unions could not use collectively bargained clauses to waive distribution and solicitation rights of employees who were seeking to criticize or to oppose the union's leadership.[199] Later, the Board expanded its interpretation of section 7 to strike down contract provisions restricting the rights of employees seeking to support the union as well.[200]

The 1974 Supreme Court *Magnavox* decision[201] resolved a disagreement between the circuits and the Board. It held that employee section 7 rights to solicit and to distribute literature advocating support of or opposition to an incumbent union may not be contractually waived in the absence of production considerations that may make special restrictions necessary. "The place of work is a place uniquely appropriate for dissemination of

---

[196] 645 F2d 1151, 106 LRRM 2561 (CA DC, 1981), *denying review of* 244 NLRB 826, 102 LRRM 1172 (1979).

[197] *Id.*, 106 LRRM at 2563.

[198] 714 F2d 657, 114 LRRM 2129 (CA 6, 1983), *enforcing in part and denying in part* 259 NLRB 974, 109 LRRM 1062 (1982).

[199] Gale Prods. Div. of Outboard Marine Corp., 142 NLRB 1246, 53 LRRM 1242 (1963), *enforcement denied*, 337 F2d 390, 57 LRRM 2164 (CA 7, 1964).

[200] *See* Magnavox Co., 195 NLRB 265, 79 LRRM 1283 (1972), *enforcement denied*, 474 F2d 1269, 82 LRRM 2852 (CA 6, 1973), *rev'd*, 415 US 322, 85 LRRM 2475 (1974).

[201] NLRB v. Magnavox Co., 415 US 322, 85 LRRM 2475 (1974).

views concerning the bargaining representative and the various options open to the employees," the Court said, and "[s]o long as the distribution is by employees to employees and so long as the in-plant solicitation is on nonworking time, banning of that solicitation might seriously dilute §7 rights."[202] The Court's decision did not, however, specifically deal with the Board's position that a union may lawfully waive any right employees might have to distribute union "institutional literature."[203]

The Board has applied the *Magnavox* decision in a wide variety of situations, most of which have involved enforcement of contractual restrictions on solicitation and distribution of matters critical of the incumbent union.[204] In *United Technologies Corp.*,[205] the Board applied *Magnavox* to invalidate a contractual provision that prohibited solicitation during paid nonworking time. The Second Circuit rejected this reading of *Magnavox* noting it saw no indication that the Supreme Court intended to limit an incumbent union's power to bargain with respect to mere limitations on the time and place of union solicitation, as contrasted with the complete elimination of such solicitation,[206] so long as the time and place restriction did not favor a particular union.[207]

2. Specific Conduct Violative of Section 8(a)(1). A wide assortment of traditional and imaginative techniques have been employed either to frustrate or to further union organizational efforts. Usually these have been utilized during election campaigns and have been evaluated by the Board in terms of election interference. In some instances, however, they have been employed at other stages of employer-employee relationships and

---

[202]*Id.* at 325.

[203]*Id.* at 329. The Board has subsequently ruled that whatever right an employee has to post union literature on a bulletin board may be lawfully waived by a restriction in a collective bargaining agreement. General Motors Corp., Frigidaire Div., 240 NLRB 168, 100 LRRM 1283 (1979). *See also* Special Mach. & Eng'g, 247 NLRB 884, 103 LRRM 1209 (1980).

[204]*E.g.*, Ford Motor Co., 233 NLRB 698, 96 LRRM 1513 (1977); General Motors Corp., 211 NLRB 986, 87 LRRM 1167 (1974), *enforced in relevant part*, 512 F2d 447, 89 LRRM 2431 (CA 6, 1975). *See* Chapter 18, "Accommodation of Board Action to the Arbitration Process," at notes 153–156, for a discussion of cases involving the Board's application of *Magnavox* to contract provisions limiting unit employees' rights to distribute literature.

[205]260 NLRB 68, 109 LRRM 1129 (1982), *enforcement denied*, 706 F2d 1254, 113 LRRM 2326 (CA 2, 1983).

[206]NLRB v. United Technologies Corp., 706 F2d 1254, 113 LRRM 2326 (CA 2, 1983).

[207]*See* Metropolitan Edison Co. v. NLRB, 460 US 693, 112 LRRM 3265 (1983) (citing *Magnavox* for the proposition that a union may bargain away its members' "economic rights," but confirming that a waiver that impairs the employees' choice of bargaining representatives will be invalidated).

have been evaluated in the broader context of interference with section 7 rights. In the discussion that follows, various techniques are considered in terms of their legality or illegality, regardless of setting.

a. Threats and Withdrawals of Benefits. Employer election campaigns and antiunion activity generally have sometimes been marked by withdrawals of benefits or by threats of withdrawals, both express and implied. The discontinuance of benefits, such as coffee breaks and discount privileges on employee purchases, are unlawful reprisals.[208] Exclusion of unionized employees from an employee stock plan is a violation of section 8(a)(1).[209] Direct threats to close a plant[210] or to discharge union adherents[211] as a means of combating an organizational drive constitute unlawful interference.

More troublesome are implied threats. Certain campaign themes have become familiar in the election arena. Employers seeking to inform employees of unfavorable consequences of unionization may develop their themes in a number of written or oral messages. The Board and courts have long evaluated the messages, not in isolation from each other but in their "total context."[212] If the overall effect of the messages creates an atmosphere of fear by portraying the selection of a bargaining agent as "futile" and the "economic hazards" as "inevitable," free choice may be rendered impossible.[213] The conveyance of a

---

[208]Davis Wholesale Co., 165 NLRB 271, 65 LRRM 1494 (1967), *enforced*, 413 F2d 407, 70 LRRM 3436 (CA DC, 1969); Buddy Schoellkopf Prods., 164 NLRB 660, 65 LRRM 1231 (1967), *enforced*, 410 F2d 82, 71 LRRM 2089 (CA 5, 1969).

[209]Bendix-Westinghouse Automatic Air Brake Co., 185 NLRB 375, 75 LRRM 1079 (1970), *enforced*, 443 F2d 106, 77 LRRM 2368 (CA 6, 1971). *But see* Goodyear Tire & Rubber Co. v. NLRB, 413 F2d 158, 71 LRRM 2977 (CA 6, 1969).

[210]*Cf.* Textile Workers v. Darlington Mfg. Co., 380 US 263, 274 n.20, 58 LRRM 2657 (1965), where the Court distinguished a termination of a business from the unjustifiable threat to do so. *See* Chapter 7, "Discrimination in Employment," at notes 261–285. *See also* Nebraska Bulk Transp., 240 NLRB 135, 100 LRRM 1340, *modified*, 608 F2d 311, 104 LRRM 2384 (CA 8, 1979).

[211]NLRB v. Neuhoff Bros., Packers, 375 F2d 372, 64 LRRM 2673 (CA 5, 1967), where Judge Brown provides a lively discussion on flagrant election campaign violations. *See also* Donald E. Hernly, Inc., 240 NLRB 840, 100 LRRM 1368 (1979), *enforcement denied*, 613 F2d 457, 103 LRRM 2347 (CA 2, 1980).

[212]TRW, Inc. v. NLRB, 654 F2d 307, 108 LRRM 2641 (CA 5, 1981), *denying enforcement to* 245 NLRB 1158, 102 LRRM 1544 (1979). Madison Kipp Co., 240 NLRB 879, 100 LRRM 1381 (1979); Arch Beverage Corp., 140 NLRB 1385, 52 LRRM 1251 (1963); *see* notes 73-78 *supra* and accompanying text; *see also* Kleeb, *Taft-Hartley Rules During Union Organizing Campaigns*, 55 LRRM 115, 117 (1964); Bok, *The Regulation of Campaign Tactics in Representation Elections Under the National Labor Relations Act*, 78 HARV. L. REV. 38 (1964).

[213]Oak Mfg. Co., 141 NLRB 1323, 52 LRRM 1502 (1963); Storkline Corp., 142 NLRB 875, 53 LRRM 1160 (1963).

"clear message" to employees "that it was futile for them to select [the union] as their bargaining representative for the purpose of improving their conditions of employment, and that selection . . . could only bring strikes, violence and loss of jobs" has been held unlawful interference and cause for invalidation of an election.[214]

(1) Permissible predictions and prohibited threats. In *Gissel,* the Supreme Court established the following guidelines for making the elusive distinction between permissible preelection predictions and unlawful threats of reprisal:

> [A]n employer is free to communicate to his employees any of his general views about unionism or any of his specific views about a particular union, so long as the communications do not contain a "threat of reprisal or force or promise of benefit." He may even make a prediction as to the precise effects he believes unionization will have on his company. In such a case, however, the prediction must be carefully phrased on the basis of objective fact to convey an employer's belief as to demonstrably probable consequences beyond his control or to convey a management decision already arrived at to close the plant in case of unionization. . . . If there is any implication that an employer may or may not take action solely on his own initiative for reasons unrelated to economic necessities and known only to him, the statement is no longer a reasonable prediction based on available facts but a threat of retaliation based on misrepresentation and coercion, and as such without the protection of the First Amendment. We therefore agree with the court below that "conveyance of the employer's belief, even though sincere, that unionization will or may result in the closing of the plant is not a statement of fact unless, which is most improbable, the eventuality of closing is capable of proof." . . . [A]n employer is free only to tell "what he reasonably believes will be the likely economic consequences of unionization that are outside his control," and not "threats of economic reprisal to be taken solely on his own volition."[215]

The efforts of the Board and courts to find a consistent line separating threats from predictions reveal both the difficulty of the task and the inescapable elasticity of the *Gissel* guidelines, especially the one concerning the foundation of statements upon "the basis of objective fact." Thus, an employer's predic-

---

[214]Garry Mfg. Co., 242 NLRB 539, 101 LRRM 1197 (1979), *enforced in part,* 630 F2d 934, 105 LRRM 2113 (CA 3, 1980); General Dynamics Corp., 250 NLRB 719, 104 LRRM 1438 (1980); General Indus. Elec. Co., 146 NLRB 1139, 1141, 56 LRRM 1015 (1964).

[215]NLRB v. Gissel Packing Co., 395 US 575, 618-19, 71 LRRM 2481 (1969). The Court cited Textile Workers v. Darlington Mfg. Co., *supra* note 210 and NLRB v. River Togs, Inc., 382 F2d 198, 202, 65 LRRM 2987 (CA 2, 1967). *See supra* notes 58–78, and accompanying text.

tion that unionization would result in the loss of the employees' bonuses because the union's contract with other dealerships did not include bonus payments was found not to be a prediction based on objective facts.[216] Similarly, in *Crown Cork & Seal Co.*,[217] the Board held that the employer had not met its burden of proving an objective factual basis for its prediction that unionization at the plant involved would result in a shutdown because a master agreement with the union would automatically increase wages 30 to 40 percent.[218] However, an employer's comments that a unionized restaurant in the state was not doing well and that two other unionized restaurants had closed were found by the Board to be lawful statements of fact rather than unlawful threats to close the business where the employer expressly stated that he did not know whether the problems with these restaurants were related to unionization, he did not refer to the effect, if any, unionization would have on his restaurant, and he told the employees he would try to negotiate a three-year contract if the union won the election.[219]

(2) Futility of organizing. That it would be futile to select a bargaining agent has been conveyed, for example, by an explanation that the employer's wage policies would continue to be determined unilaterally, "union or no union."[220] A sense of

---

[216]Ed Chandler Ford, Inc., 254 NLRB 851, 107 LRRM 1101 (1981), *enforced in pertinent part*, 718 F2d 892, 115 LRRM 2543 (CA 9, 1983).

[217]255 NLRB 14, 107 LRRM 1195 (1981), *enforced mem.*, 691 F2d 506, 111 LRRM 2650 (CA 9, 1982).

[218]*See also* Palmas Del Mar Co. v. NLRB, 797 F2d 39, 123 LRRM 2060 (CA 1, 1986), *enforcing* 277 NLRB 71, 120 LRRM 1270 (1985) (employer unlawfully made "repeated, high powered, and undocumented assertions of . . . [its] 'critical' financial condition" and "equally unsupported panic-inducing predictions" as to union's bargaining demands): Consani Co. dba Pioneer Concrete Co., 282 NLRB 749, 124 LRRM 1394 (1987) (employer unlawfully threatened plant closure in event of unionization in absence of evidence of any valid economic or other factors beyond employer's control); TVA Terminals, 270 NLRB 284, 116 LRRM 1088 (1984) (employer unlawfully told employees that there would be less work if union won election because shippers would not use unionized warehouse since statement was not grounded on any objective appraisal made known to employees).

[219]Bo-Ed dba Golden Fan Inn, 281 NLRB 226, 123 LRRM 1116 (1986). *See also* NLRB v. Village IX dba Shenanigans, 723 F2d 1360, 115 LRRM 2297 (CA 7, 1983), *enforcing in part and remanding in part* 264 NLRB 908, 112 LRRM 1096 (1982) (no violation where employer said restaurant would close if union voted in: employer conveyed only the message that the business was too fragile to survive if union wage scales were paid); Patsy Bee, Inc. v. NLRB, 654 F2d 515, 107 LRRM 3155 (CA 8, 1981), *denying enforcement and remanding* 249 NLRB 976, 104 LRRM 1285 (1980) (no violation where employer said unionization would cause loss of business of two customers and might force closure of plant: withdrawal of customers was reasonably foreseeable and no threats were made).

[220]Trane Co., 137 NLRB 1506, 50 LRRM 1434 (1962). *See also* American Telecommunications Corp., Electromechanical Div., 249 NLRB 1135, 104 LRRM 1282 (1980) ("uniform benefits" regardless of existence of union representation at any of employer plants held to be unlawful statement).

futility was imported in blunter terms when an employer indicated that it would abide by its present policies "even if Jesus Christ were representing" the employees.[221] But ordinarily conveyance of a sense of futility may not be sufficient to set aside an election unless the employer has stated "either expressly, or by clear implication that it would not bargain in good faith with a union even if it were selected by the employees."[222] An employer's warning, for example, that "he could make negotiations last a year and therefore another election would be necessary" was ground for setting aside an election.[223] Promises of "future litigation," however, will not necessarily be treated in the same manner, particularly if the surrounding circumstances are devoid of coercive conduct.[224]

(3) Inevitability of strikes or violence. Depicting strikes, violence, and loss of jobs as the inevitable consequence of unionization can be ground for setting aside an election.[225] The tactic of showing the classic propaganda film "And Women Must Weep," which purported to depict violence during a 1956 strike at Potter-Brumfield Co. and emphasized enactments of picket line vandalism, telephone threats, a house bombing, and a night gunfire attack on a dissenting worker's home, frequently resulted in findings of unfair labor practices and objectionable election conduct.[226] But the Board's 1974 *Litho Press* decision overruled prior inconsistent decisions and held that presenting the movie was not violative of the Act.[227]

---

[221]Metropolitan Life Ins. Co., 142 NLRB 929, 53 LRRM 1187 (1963).

[222]American Greetings Corp., 146 NLRB 1440, 1445 n.4, 56 LRRM 1064 (1964). *See* American Telecommunications Corp., *supra* note 220; Dal-Tex Optical Co., 137 NLRB 1782, 1783, 50 LRRM 1489 (1962) (statement by the employer that the election process "will not mean a thing if the union wins" because the employer would take a "couple of years" to litigate it). *See also* Fry Foods, 241 NLRB 76, 100 LRRM 1513, *enforced*, 609 F2d 267, 102 LRRM 2894 (CA 6, 1979) (employer stated that it would not bargain with the union even if the union won the election and "four years" would be needed to get a union into the plant). For other decisions suggesting that a sense of futility may be conveyed in the absence of express employer statements indicating it would not bargain in good faith, see Pacific Tel. Co., 256 NLRB 449, 107 LRRM 1269 (1981); North Am. Car Corp., 253 NLRB 958, 106 LRRM 1036 (1980); Piezo Technology, 253 NLRB 900, 106 LRRM 1276 (1980).

[223]Wall Colmonoy Corp., 173 NLRB 40, 69 LRRM 1205 (1968).

[224]W.T. Grant Co., 147 NLRB 420, 56 LRRM 1231 (1964).

[225]Louis Gallet, Inc., 247 NLRB 63, 103 LRRM 1125 (1980); Storkline Corp., *supra* note 213.

[226]*E.g.*, Storkline Corp., *supra* note 213 (employer's warning that economic injury would befall employees, intensified by showing the film "And Women Must Weep," held to have created an impression of "unreasoning fear" that impaired free choice). A filmed rebuttal entitled "Anatomy of a Lie" has frequently been used by unions as a counteraction to the employer's use of "And Women Must Weep."

[227]Litho Press, 211 NLRB 1014, 86 LRRM 1471 (1974), *enforced*, 512 F2d 73, 89

Stressing the likelihood of strikes is not necessarily improper if it is germane to the strike record and claims of job security of the union in issue and is not simply raised as a "straw man" to create unwarranted fear.[228] Depending on their context, employer statements as to the possibility of strikes have been found to be "rhetoric" or "opinion" and, as such, permissible campaign techniques.[229] Similarly, the lawfulness of predicting loss of customer patronage and resulting employment reductions depends on whether the loss is portrayed as an inevitable or as a possible result of unionizing.[230]

(4) Assessing recurrent phrases and themes. The Board's attempt to assess an employer's statements in the context of its pattern of conduct is illustrated in its treatment of recurrent phrases used in election campaigns. Whether or not such a phrase is legally objectionable will depend upon the reading of the statement as a whole and any "evidence of accompanying unfair labor practices that might reasonably color an employee's view of the statement."[231] These assessments are difficult and unanimity is not always attainable, as the Board has acknowledged:

> [I]n all cases such as this one, where one must attempt to fathom the meaning of another's words and assess the impress of such words on employees, reasonable men may differ . . . .[232]

The following are examples of frequently employed campaign phrases that the Board has evaluated in various settings.

(a) "Serious harm." Statements to the effect that "[i]f this union were to get in here, it would not work to your benefit but to your

---

LRRM 2171 (CA 5, 1975) (the Board held that showing "And Women Must Weep" was not violative of the Act regardless of the circumstances of the campaign). *See also* Sab Harmon Indus., 252 NLRB 953, 105 LRRM 1353 (1980) (showing the movie "The Springfield Gun" held unobjectionable on the basis of *Litho Press*).

[228]Morristown Foam & Fibre Corp., 211 NLRB 52, 86 LRRM 1420 (1974); Universal Elec. Co., 156 NLRB 1101, 61 LRRM 1189 (1966); Coors Porcelain Co., 158 NLRB 1108, 62 LRRM 1158 (1966); American Greetings Corp., 146 NLRB 1440, 56 LRRM 1064 (1964).

[229]*See, e.g.*, NLRB v. Eastern Smelting Corp., 598 F2d 666, 101 LRRM 2328 (CA 4, 1979); TRW-United Greenfield Div., 245 NLRB 1135, 102 LRRM 1520 (1979), *enforced*, 637 F2d 410, 106 LRRM 2768 (CA 5, 1981).

[230]*Compare* Haynes Stellite Co., 136 NLRB 95, 49 LRRM 1711 (1962), *enforcement denied sub nom.* Union Carbide Corp. v. NLRB, 310 F2d 844, 52 LRRM 2001 (CA 6, 1962) *and* R.D. Cole Mfg. Co., 133 NLRB 1455, 49 LRRM 1033 (1961) *with* Freeman Mfg. Co., 148 NLRB 577, 57 LRRM 1047 (1964). *See also* Jasta Mfg. Co., 246 NLRB 48, 102 LRRM 1610 (1979); First Data Resources, 241 NLRB 713, 100 LRRM 1587 (1979).

[231]*Compare* Trent Tube Co., 147 NLRB 538, 56 LRRM 1251 (1964) *with* Marsh Supermarkets, 140 NLRB 899, 52 LRRM 1134, *enforced*, 327 F2d 109, 55 LRRM 2017 (CA 7, 1963), *cert. denied*, 377 US 944, 56 LRRM 2288 (1964) *and* Astronautics Corp., 164 NLRB 623, 624 n.2, 65 LRRM 1161 (1967).

[232]Allied/Egry Business Sys., 169 NLRB 514, 514, 67 LRRM 1195 (1968).

serious harm" are evaluated by the Board under the standard of *Greensboro Hosiery Mills:*

> We have not ordinarily found such notices to be illegal in and of themselves, for the bare words, in the absence of conduct or other circumstances supplying a particular connotation, can be given a noncoercive and nonthreatening meaning.[233]

Reference to the adverse economic impact unionization might have on the company, such as "bringing a union into our plant at this time could be the straw that broke the camel's back," may or may not be objectionable depending on whether the employer is in fact experiencing substantial economic hardships unrelated to union activity.[234]

(b) "Bargaining will start from scratch." "Bargaining from scratch" or "bargaining begins with a clean table" campaign messages may imply that existing benefits may be diminished or discontinued if the employer is forced to negotiate with the union, for the duty to bargain ordinarily forecloses unilateral changes, and bargaining begins with existing wages and conditions.[235] But, depending on the context, such phrases might

---

[233]162 NLRB 1275, 1276, 64 LRRM 1164 (1967), *enforced in part*, 398 F2d 414, 68 LRRM 2702 (CA 4, 1968); Ohmite Mfg. Co., Subsidiary of N. Am. Philips Co., 217 NLRB 435, 89 LRRM 1530 (1975), *enforced*, 557 F2d 577, 95 LRRM 2766 (CA 7, 1979). "Serious harm" notices and statements were found to violate §8(a)(1) in Holly Farms Poultry Indus., 194 NLRB 952, 79 LRRM 1127, *enforced in part*, 470 F2d 983, 82 LRRM 2110 (CA 4, 1972); Serv-Air, Inc., 161 NLRB 382, 63 LRRM 1270 (1966), *enforced in part*, 395 F2d 557, 67 LRRM 2337 (CA 10, 1968). *Compare* NLRB v. Greensboro Hosiery Mills, 398 F2d 414, 68 LRRM 2702 (CA 4, 1968) *and* Suprenant Mfg. Co. v. NLRB, 341 F2d 756, 58 LRRM 2484 (CA 6, 1964) (no violation) *with* J.P. Stevens & Co. v. NLRB, 380 F2d 292, 65 LRRM 2829 (CA 2), *cert. denied*, 389 US 1005, 66 LRRM 2728 (1967) *and* Serv-Air, Inc. v. NLRB, 395 F2d 557, 67 LRRM 2337 (CA 10), *cert. denied*, 393 US 840, 69 LRRM 2435 (1968). *See also* Dillingham Marine & Mfg. Co., 239 NLRB 904, 100 LRRM 1109 (1978), *enforced*, 610 F2d 319, 103 LRRM 2430 (CA 5, 1980) (statement that signing union cards "would follow employees for the rest of their lives" held a violation); J.P. Stevens & Co., 245 NLRB 198, 102 LRRM 1437 (1979) (violation when employees told that identity of card signers would "become public knowledge" and that signing cards would have "serious consequences"). But in Howard Johnson Co., 242 NLRB 386, 101 LRRM 1165 (1979), employer's statement that a union "would only make things more difficult for us all" was held not to be the equivalent of a "serious harm" message.

[234]Chrysler Airtemp S. C., Inc., 224 NLRB 427, 92 LRRM 1636 (1976) (no violation); NLRB v. Four Winds Indus., 530 F2d 75, 91 LRRM 2460 (CA 9, 1976) (violation); Honeywell, Inc., 225 NLRB 617, 92 LRRM 1426 (1976) (statement that new marketing approaches involving recall of 10 or more employees and designed to improve company's economic recovery would be hindered by labor organization held objectionable); Rospatch Corp., 193 NLRB 772, 78 LRRM 1360 (1971) (no violation where employer in preelection statement told employees that if union won election, it would result in considerable legal expense that would reduce profits and employer's contributions to existing profit-sharing plan). *See also* NLRB v. Intertherm, 596 F2d 267, 100 LRRM 3016 (CA 8, 1979) (statement that employer had previously closed plants or moved them elsewhere when a union would not agree to the company's position held to be a statement of the employer's opinion as to the consequences of unionization protected by §8(c)).

[235]*See* Chapter 13, "The Duty to Bargain," at notes 68–104.

simply be a reminder that the selection of a union will not automatically produce any improved benefits. The Board has held both that "bargaining from scratch" statements have interfered with a representation election, and that they have not, the difference in result depending upon the "totality of circumstances" in which the message was conveyed.[236] Moreover, an employer statement that a possible consequence of collective bargaining will be a loss of benefits was lawful when made in response to union claims that employees could "only gain and . . . get better things from collective bargaining."[237]

(c) Statements regarding plant closing. Employer statements regarding plant closing that might result from unionization are also evaluated within the "total context" in which they appear, in accordance with the standards established by the Supreme Court's *Gissel* decision. Such statements have seldom been found to be predictions "based on objective fact," rather than coercive threats.[238] In *Sertafilm, Atlas Microfilming Division,*[239] for example, the Board found a violation where a supervisor told all the employees in her department that the plant would close if the employees selected the union. The Board rejected the em

---

[236]*Finding objectionable conduct:* TRW-United Greenfield Div., *supra* note 229; Taylor Dunn Mfg. Co., 252 NLRB 799, 105 LRRM 1548 (1980); BRK Elec., 248 NLRB 1275, 104 LRRM 1039 (1980); Centre Eng'g, 246 NLRB 632, 102 LRRM 1660 (1979); Dominican Santa Cruz Hosp., 242 NLRB 1107, 101 LRRM 1303 (1979); Madison Kipp Co., 240 NLRB 879, 100 LRRM 1381 (1979); Plastronics, Inc., 233 NLRB 155, 96 LRRM 1422 (1977); Coach & Equip. Sales Corp., 228 NLRB 440, 94 LRRM 1391 (1977); North Elec. Co., 225 NLRB 1114, 93 LRRM 1203 (1976), *enforced,* 588 F2d 213, 100 LRRM 3004 (CA 6, 1978); Saunders Leasing Sys., 204 NLRB 448, 83 LRRM 1626 (1973), *enforced in relevant part,* 497 F2d 453, 86 LRRM 2345 (CA 8, 1974); Cargill, Inc., Nutrena Mills Div., 172 NLRB 183, 69 LRRM 1293 (1968). *Finding no objectionable conduct:* Donn Prods. v. NLRB, 613 F2d 162, 103 LRRM 2338 (CA 6, 1980); NLRB v. Interstate Eng'g, 583 F2d 1087, 99 LRRM 3245 (CA 9, 1978); Checker Motors Corp., 232 NLRB 1077, 96 LRRM 1386 (1977); Campbell Soup Co., 225 NLRB 222, 93 LRRM 1046 (1976); Computer Peripherals, 215 NLRB 293, 88 LRRM 1027 (1974); Wagner Indus. Prods. Co., 170 NLRB 1413, 67 LRRM 1581 (1968).

[237]Ludwig Motor Corp., 222 NLRB 635, 91 LRRM 1199 (1976).

[238]Patsy Bee, Inc., 249 NLRB 976, 104 LRRM 1285 (1980), *enforcement denied,* 654 F2d 515, 107 LRRM 3155 (CA 8, 1981); Nebraska Bulk Transp. v. NLRB, 608 F2d 311, 104 LRRM 2384 (CA 8, 1979); Anderson Cottonwood Concrete Prods., 246 NLRB 1090, 103 LRRM 1077 (1979); Continental Kitchen Corp., 246 NLRB 611, 102 LRRM 1659 (1979); American Spring Wire Corp., 237 NLRB 1551, 99 LRRM 1127 (1978); El Rancho Mkt., 235 NLRB 468, 98 LRRM 1153 (1978); Paoli Chair Co., 231 NLRB 539, 96 LRRM 1115 (1977); Hanover House Indus., 233 NLRB 164, 96 LRRM 1463 (1977); Willow Mfg. Co., 232 NLRB 344, 96 LRRM 1272 (1977); Florida-Texas Freight, 230 NLRB 952, 95 LRRM 1426 (1977); Yellow Cab Co., 229 NLRB 643, 95 LRRM 1124 (1977); W.A. Kruger Co., 224 NLRB 1066, 93 LRRM 1129 (1976); Hedstrom Co., 223 NLRB 1409, 92 LRRM 1297 (1976), *enforced in relevant part,* 558 F2d 1137, 95 LRRM 3069 (CA 3, 1977); May Dep't Stores Co., 211 NLRB 150, 86 LRRM 1423 (1974), *enforced,* 514 F2d 894, 90 LRRM 2844 (CA DC, 1975).

[239]267 NLRB 682, 114 NLRB 1120 (1983), *enforced,* 753 F2d 313, 118 LRRM 2628 (CA 3, 1985).

ployer's contention that the coercive effects of the threat were cured by a later retraction because there was no evidence that every employee who heard the threat also heard the retraction.

In its *Mount Ida Footwear Co.*[240] decision, a Board majority concluded that the employer did not violate section 8(a)(1) when its president told its assembled employees not to sign "any cards" because "they can be fatal to a business." In the Board's view, the employer's statements "merely expressed respondent's position that the employees would be better served . . . by rejecting the union." The use of the word "fatal" was not deemed a threat to plant closure but rather "was a reference to the possibility that unionization could lead to difficulties if the union were to strike to obtain unreasonable demands." In a sharp dissent, two members of the Board called the statement "a management directive to employees not to sign cards,"[241] and therefore unlawful under settled authority that distinguishes such "directives" or "instructions"[242] from noncoercive expressions of "views" or "opinion."[243]

b. Promises and Grants of Benefits. Organizational campaigns have been met with promises of benefits as well as threats. But "interference is no less interference because it is accomplished through allurement rather than coercion."[244] The promise or grant of benefits to stifle, or in some circumstances to further, an organizational campaign may be unlawful interference even though no strings are explicitly attached. As the Supreme Court said in *Medo Photo Supply*:[245] "The action of employees with respect to the choice of their bargaining agents may be induced by favors bestowed by the employer as well as by his threats or

---

[240]217 NLRB 1011, 89 LRRM 1169 (1975). Members Fanning and Jenkins dissented.

[241]*Id.* at 1014, 89 LRRM at 1172.

[242]Colony Printing & Labeling, 249 NLRB 223, 104 LRRM 1108 (1980), *enforced*, 651 F2d 502, 107 LRRM 3049 (CA 7, 1981). Emphasis in original. Airporter Inn Hotel, 215 NLRB 824, 88 LRRM 1032 (1974) (overruling Trojan Battery Co., 207 NLRB 425, 84 LRRM 1619 (1973)).

[243]Carrom Div., Affiliated Hosp. Prods., 245 NLRB 703, 102 LRRM 1462 (1979); R.J. Reynolds Tobacco Co., 240 NLRB 620, 100 LRRM 1350 (1979) *Cf.*, Producers Rice Mill, 222 NLRB 875, 91 LRRM 1414 (1976); *see also* Fayette Cotton Mill, 245 NLRB 428, 102 LRRM 1485 (1979).

[244]NLRB v. Crown Can Co., 138 F2d 263, 267, 13 LRRM 568 (CA 8, 1943), *cert. denied*, 321 US 769, 13 LRRM 850 (1944) (citing Western Cartridge Co. v. NLRB, 134 F2d 240, 244, 12 LRRM 541, *cert. denied*, 320 US 746, 13 LRRM 851 (1943)). *See also* NLRB v. General Tel. Directory Co., 602 F2d 912, 102 LRRM 2487 (CA 9, 1980) (statement that wage increases had been "budgeted" ruled vague and innocuous and not an unlawful promise).

[245]Medo Photo Supply Corp. v. NLRB, 321 US 678, 686, 14 LRRM 581 (1944).

domination." In *Exchange Parts*,[246] the Court explained the impact of a grant of benefit:

> The danger inherent in well-timed increases in benefits is the suggestion of a fist inside a velvet glove. The employees are not likely to miss the inference that the source of benefits now conferred is also the source from which future benefits must flow and which may dry up if it is not obliged.[247]

The infringement may stem from timing and impact. The fact that the benefits are not conditioned upon voting against the union is not controlling if the employer's purpose is one of "impinging upon . . . freedom of choice for or against unionization, and is reasonably calculated to have that effect."[248]

Conferral of employment benefits during an organizing campaign is not per se, unlawful, but the Board presumes that such action is objectionable "unless the Employer establishes that the timing of the action was governed by factors other than the pendency of the election."[249]

(1) Employer inducements. In some cases, the employer's action is clearly unlawful. An offer of money accompanied by an urging to vote a particular way will be treated as interference.[250] A bribe to work against the union will have the same result.[251] In

---

[246]NLRB v. Exchange Parts Co., 375 US 405, 55 LRRM 2098 (1964).

[247]*Id.* at 409. Shortly before the election, the employer sent the employees a letter announcing certain new employee benefits—a birthday holiday, a more favorable system for holiday overtime, and a more favorable vacation schedule. The employer asserted that the policy behind the benefits had been established earlier, but the first general announcement was contained in the preelection letter. *See also* Honolulu Sporting Goods Co., 239 NLRB 1277, 100 LRRM 1172, 1979, *enforced*, 620 F2d 310, 105 LRRM 2896 (CA 9, 1980). For a critique of this analysis, *see* Bok, *The Regulation of Campaign Tactics in Representation Elections Under the National Labor Relations Act*, 78 HARV. L. REV. 38, 113 (1964).

[248]375 US 6 at 409. In an early case, the Supreme Court said: "There could be no more obvious way of interfering with these rights of employees than by grants of wage increases upon the understanding that they would leave the union in return." Medo Photo Supply Corp. v. NLRB, *supra* note 245, at 686.

[249]American Sunroof Corp., 248 NLRB 748, 104 LRRM 1157 (1980), *enforced in part*, 667 F2d 20, 109 LRRM 2862 (CA 6, 1981); Honolulu Sporting Goods Co., *supra* note 247; Micro Measurements, 233 NLRB 76, 96 LRRM 1402 (1977). *See also* Drug Fair-Community Drug Co., 162 NLRB 843, 64 LRRM 1079 (1967); Champion Pneumatic Mach. Co., 152 NLRB 300, 306, 59 LRRM 1089 (1965); International Shoe Co., 123 NLRB 682, 43 LRRM 1520 (1959). *See also* Simpson Elec. Co. v. NLRB, 654 F2d 15, 107 LRRM 3197 (CA 7, 1981), *denying enforcement to* 249 NLRB 1481, 104 LRRM 1187 (1980).

[250]Coca Cola Bottling Co., 132 NLRB 481, 48 LRRM 1370 (1961). *See also* NLRB v. Del Rey Tortilleria, 787 F2d 1118, 122 LRRM 2111 (CA 7, 1986), *enforcing* 272 NLRB 1106, 117 LRRM 1449 (1984) (promise of wage increase in return for rejection of union).

[251]Wesselman's Enters., 248 NLRB 1017, 104 LRRM 1069 (1980). *See also* Maid in New York, 289 NLRB 524, 130 LRRM 1462 (1988) (offer of management position if employee would cease supporting union).

cases not so clearly drawn, the Board has condemned increases where they (1) were given in the context of repeated references to the union;[252] (2) were made effective just before an election;[253] (3) conformed to an earlier request made by one of the union rivals in an organizing campaign;[254] (4) were announced before an election when they could reasonably have been delayed until afterward[255] or were otherwise introduced in a manner calculated to influence the employees' choice;[256] (5) were given to employees in fulfillment of illegal promises of benefits made by the employer during the campaign;[257] or (6) were granted to women employees after the union had filed a petition for an election, even though the increase ended a company practice in violation of the Equal Pay Act.[258]

Whether to implement improvements decided upon prior to the advent of a union may present a dilemma for an employer, since failure to proceed may appear to be a reprisal. A factor that will weigh heavily with the Board is whether the employer had previously told the employees of its decision to make the improvements.[259] Other important factors are (1) whether the

---

[252]In St. Francis Fed'n of Nurses & Health Professionals v. NLRB, 729 F2d 844, 115 LRRM 3352 (CA DC, 1984), *enforcing* 263 NLRB 834, 111 LRRM 1153 (1982), the court agreed with the Board's finding that the employer violated the Act by making implied promises of future benefits through numerous statements urging employees to give the new administrator "one year" to take care of the problems and suggesting that employees could get things faster by working with the new administration. *But see* Hyatt Hotels Corp., 296 NLRB No. 36, 132 LRRM 1130 (1989) (no violation where employer asked employees to give new manager a chance). NLRB v. Colonial Haven Nursing Home, 542 F2d 691, 93 LRRM 2241 (CA 7, 1976); Allegheny Mining Corp., 167 NLRB 81, 65 LRRM 1751 (1967), *enforced*, 406 F2d 1330, 70 LRRM 2880 (CA 4, 1969).

[253]NLRB v. Exchange Parts Co., *supra* note 246. *See also* World Wide Press, 242 NLRB 346, 101 LRRM 1205 (1979); Frito Lay, Inc. v. NLRB, 585 F2d 62, 99 LRRM 2658 (CA 3, 1978); D'Youville Manor Nursing Home, 217 NLRB 173, 89 LRRM 1060, *enforced*, 526 F2d 3, 90 LRRM 3100 (CA 1, 1975); NLRB v. Tommy's Spanish Foods, 463 F2d 116, 80 LRRM 3039 (CA 9, 1972). *But see* American Sunroof Corp., *supra* note 249.

[254]Seneca Plastics, 149 NLRB 320, 57 LRRM 1314 (1964).

[255]NLRB v. Arrow Elastic Corp., 573 F2d 702, 98 LRRM 2004 (CA 1, 1978) (enforcing Board decision that an employer violated §8(a)(1) when two days before an election it announced a pension plan for the employees that it did not become legally committed to provide until seven months after the election); International Shoe Co., *supra* note 249. *See also* Coronet Instructional Media, Div. of Esquire, Inc., 250 NLRB 940, 104 LRRM 1470 (1980). *Compare* American Sunroof Corp., *supra* note 249 (no violation) *with* Faith Garment Co., Div. of Dunhall Pharmaceutical, 246 NLRB 299, 102 LRRM 1515 (1979), enforced, 630 F2d 630, 105 LRRM 2568 (CA 8, 1980) (violation).

[256]NLRB v. Rich's of Plymouth, 578 F2d 880, 98 LRRM 2684, 2687 (CA 1, 1978).

[257]Tipton Elec. Co., 242 NLRB 202, 101 LRRM 1154 (1979), *enforced*, 621 F2d 890, 104 LRRM 2073 (CA 8, 1980).

[258]Rupp Indus., 217 NLRB 385, 88 LRRM 1603 (1975).

[259]Crown Tar & Chem. Works v. NLRB, 365 F2d 588, 63 LRRM 2067 (CA 10, 1966). *See also* Louisiana Plastics, 173 NLRB 1427, 70 LRRM 1019 (1968). In *Exchange Parts*, *supra* note 246, the employer vainly asserted that the "policy" behind the announcement of benefits had been established earlier, but in Litton Dental Prods. v. NLRB, 543 F2d 1085, 93 LRRM 2714 (CA 4, 1976), the employer prevailed on that point.

benefit increase during the campaign is consistent with an established past practice of announcing changes in employment terms at the same time every year; (2) whether the benefit improvements are excessive, compared with past practice;[260] (3) whether the benefit changes apply to other employer facilities or to employees not involved in the organizing campaign;[261] and (4) whether the benefit improvements were essential to remain competitive with other employers in the same industry regarding the attraction and retention of a stable work force.[262]

(2) *Withholding benefits during an election campaign.* The Board's general rule is that an employer's legal duty during a preelection campaign period is to proceed with the granting of benefits that would otherwise have been granted to employees in the normal course of the employer's business, just as it would have done had the union not been on the scene.[263] The Second[264] and Fifth[265] Circuits, however, have disagreed with Board applications of

---

[260]In Automated Prods., 242 NLRB 424, 101 LRRM 1208 (1979), although the employer gave a larger wage increase than was its past practice, no violation was found since (1) the employer was undergoing a period of rapid expansion; (2) the purpose of the increase was to improve the employer's hiring prospects; (3) the change in the wage structure had been previously announced; and (4) the timing of the increase was accelerated due to bookkeeping problems.

[261]Town & Country Supermarkets, 244 NLRB 303, 102 LRRM 1275 (1979), *enforced,* 666 F2d 1294, 109 LRRM 2116 (CA 10, 1981); Hayes-Albion Corp., Tiffin Div., 237 NLRB 20, 99 LRRM 1020 (1978); Centralia Fireside Health, Inc., 233 NLRB 139, 96 LRRM 1471 (1977); Villa Sancta Anna Home, 228 NLRB 571, 94 LRRM 1449 (1977); Medline Indus., 218 NLRB 1404, 89 LRRM 1829 (1975); Essex Int'l, 216 NLRB 575, 88 LRRM 1346 (1975). *See also* Delchamps, Inc. v. NLRB, 588 F2d 476, 100 LRRM 2555 (CA 5, 1979), *denying enforcement to* 234 NLRB 262, 97 LRRM 1363 (1978).

[262]NLRB v. Circo Resorts, 646 F2d 403, 107 LRRM 2608 (CA 9, 1981), *enforcing as modified* 244 NLRB 880, 102 LRRM 1262 (1979); Delchamps, Inc. v. NLRB, *supra* note 261; NLRB v. Gotham Indus., 406 F2d 1306, 70 LRRM 2289 (CA 1, 1969); Springfield Jewish Nursing Home for Aged, 292 NLRB No. 138, 130 LRRM 1431 (1989); Town & Country Supermarkets., *supra* note 261; Schulte's IGA Foodliner, 241 NLRB 855, 101 LRRM 1048 (1979); Poultry Packers, 237 NLRB 250, 99 LRRM 1027 (1978).

[263]*See, e.g.,* Abbey's Transp. Servs. v. NLRB, 837 F2d 575, 127 LRRM 2437 (CA 2, 1988), *enforcing* 284 NLRB 696, 125 LRRM 1242 (1987); Martin Indus., Huntsville Div., 290 NLRB 857, 130 LRRM 1150 (1988) (employer violated Act by withholding annual wage increases during union organizing campaign without giving employees any explanation for its abrupt departure from its wage policy, leading employees to infer that wage increases were withheld as punishment for past union activities); Associated Milk Producers, 255 NLRB 750, 106 LRRM 1459 (1981) (violation to withhold system-wide increase from employees at facility where organizing campaign in progress); American Telecommunications Corp., Electromechanical Div., 249 NLRB 1135, 104 LRRM 1282 (1980) (emphasizing that Board applies this rule not only to preelection period, but also to period subsequent to the election but before certification and to period after certification has issued). Sourdough Sales, Inc., 246 NLRB 106, 102 LRRM 1633 (1979); Travis Meat & Seafood Co., 237 NLRB 213, 98 LRRM 1574 (1978); Signal Knitting Mills, 237 NLRB 360, 98 LRRM 1580 (1978).

[264]Newberry Co. v. NLRB, 442 F2d 897, 77 LRRM 2097 (CA 2, 1971).

[265]NLRB v. Big Three Indus. Gas & Equip. Co., 441 F2d 774, 77 LRRM 2120 (CA 5, 1971).

this rule. The First Circuit has suggested that section 8(a)(1) is violated by withholding benefits during a union organizing campaign: "[1] if the increase was promised by the employer prior to the union's appearance; [2] if it normally would be granted as part of a schedule of increases established by the employer's past practice; or [3] if the employer attempts to blame the union for the withholding."[266] Illegality occurs, the Court opined, "only if the employer is found to be manipulating benefits in order to influence his employees' decision during the union's organizing campaign."[267]

Where an employer declares that benefits granted to its other (unorganized) employees will be withheld from a group of employees being organized, on the ground that the benefits may be subject to further negotiations, the Board may find a violation; but this type of statement is allowable "[i]n a context of good faith bargaining and absent other proof of unlawful motive."[268] Thus, an attempt by the employer's declaration to disparage the union by placing on it the onus for the withholding of benefits will be deemed a violation of section 8(a)(1).[269] Promising a benefit solely for the purpose of withholding its actual grant, although assertedly to avoid the commission of an unfair labor practice, has been characterized as the "carrot on the stick" and held to be interference.[270]

c. Interrogation and Polling. An employer's interrogation of employees as to union sympathy and affiliation may violate sec

---

[266]NLRB v. Otis Hosp., 545 F2d 252, 254-55, 93 LRRM 2778 (CA 1, 1976) (enforcing Board order finding §8(a)(1) violation); *see also* NLRB v. Marine World USA, 611 F2d 1274, 103 LRRM 2272 (CA 9, 1980), *remanded*, 251 NLRB 1211, 105 LRRM 1158 (1980); Convalescent Home, 585 F2d 79, 99 LRRM 2985 (CA 3, 1978); G. C. Murphy Co. v. NLRB, 550 F2d 1004, 94 LRRM 3040 (CA 4, 1977) (enforcing Board order finding §8(a)(1) violation in employer's cancelling planned wage increases and annual wage review procedure during union organizing campaign, where union had notified employer that unfair labor practice charges would not be filed if wage increases were granted).

[267]NLRB v. Otis Hosp., *supra* note 266, at 255. *See also* Marine World USA, *supra* note 266.

[268]Shell Oil Co., 77 NLRB 1306, 22 LRRM 1158 (1948); Chevron Oil Co., Standard Oil Co. of Tex. Div., 182 NLRB 445, 74 LRRM 1323 (1970); McGraw-Edison Co., 172 NLRB 1604, 69 LRRM 1023 (1968), *enforced*, 419 F2d 67, 72 LRRM 2918 (CA 8, 1969).

[269]American Telecommunications Corp., Electromechanical Div., *supra* note 263; J.P. Stevens & Co., 239 NLRB 738, 100 LRRM 1052 (1978); Baker Brush Co., 233 NLRB 561, 96 LRRM 1566 (1977); Florida Steel Corp., 220 NLRB 1201, 90 LRRM 1329 (1975), *enforced*, 538 F2d 324, 92 LRRM 3424 (CA 4, 1976).

[270]Goodyear Tire & Rubber Co., 170 NLRB 539, 67 LRRM 1555 (1968), *enforced as modified*, 413 F2d 158, 71 LRRM 2977 (CA 6, 1969); Cadillac Overall Supply Co., 148 NLRB 1133, 1136, 57 LRRM 1136 (1964); Interstate Smelting & Ref. Co., 148 NLRB 219, 221, 56 LRRM 1489 (1964). *See also* Staco, Inc., 244 NLRB 461, 102 LRRM 1223 (1979).

tion 8(a)(1) "because of its natural tendency to instill in the minds of employees fear of discrimination on the basis of the information the employer has obtained."[271] Employers "cannot discriminate against union adherents without first ascertaining who they are."[272] Questioning employees as to their union sympathies is not treated as an expression of views or opinions within the meaning of section 8(c) because the "purpose of an inquiry is not to express views but to ascertain those of the persons questioned."[273] The prohibition against interrogation also extends to laid-off employees or discharged union adherents when they have an expectation of reemployment.[274]

The Board originally viewed all interrogation by an employer as unlawful per se.[275] In 1954, in *Blue Flash*,[276] the Board responded to judicial disapproval by abandoning the per se test and adopting a more permissive test. The Board held that it would find interrogation unlawful only when it was coercive in the light of surrounding circumstances, adding that "the time, place, personnel involved, information sought and . . . the employer's known preference must be considered."[277] Preelection distribution of "Vote No" buttons to employees by a supervisor, for example, constituted illegal interrogation since the offer of the button by the supervisor and the acceptance or refusal by the employee required the employee to make an observable choice in the presence of the supervisor.[278]

(1) Polling. Blue Flash involved the validity of a poll conducted by the employer to determine the extent of the employees' support for the union. The Board found the poll lawful, apply-

---

[271]NLRB v. West Coast Casket Co., 205 F2d 902, 904, 32 LRRM 2353 (CA 9, 1953). *See generally* Craver, *The Inquisitorial Process in Private Employment*, 63 CORNELL L. REV. 1 (1977).

[272]Cannon Elec. Co., 151 NLRB 1465, 58 LRRM 1629 (1965).

[273]Struksnes Constr. Co., 165 NLRB 1062, 65 LRRM 1385 (1967). *See also* NLRB v. Lorben Corp., 345 F2d 346, 59 LRRM 2184 (CA 2, 1965).

[274]H.C. Nutting Co., 219 NLRB 224, 90 LRRM 1125 (1975), *enforced*, 535 F2d 357, 92 LRRM 3648 (CA 6, 1976); Chesterfield Chrome Co., 203 NLRB 36, 82 LRRM 1764 (1973).

[275]Standard-Coosa-Thatcher Co., 85 NLRB 1358, 24 LRRM 1575 (1949).

[276]Blue Flash Express, 109 NLRB 591, 34 LRRM 1384 (1954).

[277]*Id.* as *quoted in* Struksnes Constr. Co., *supra* note 273.

[278]Kurz-Kasch, Inc., 239 NLRB 1044, 100 LRRM 1118 (1978); Pillowtex Corp., 234 NLRB 560, 97 LRRM 1369 (1978); York Div., Borg-Warner, 229 NLRB 1149, 95 LRRM 1283 (1977); Kellwood Co., 206 NLRB 665, 84 LRRM 1573 (1973); Bancroft Mfg. Co., 189 NLRB 619, 77 LRRM 1366 (1971); Beiser Aviation Corp., 135 NLRB 399, 49 LRRM 1508 (1962); *see also* Sterling Faucet Co., 203 NLRB 1031, 83 LRRM 1530 (1973) (employer's having "made available" buttons with company insignia held not objectionable conduct where there was no evidence that employees had been required to wear them); *see* note 155 *supra* and accompanying text.

ing these guidelines: (1) that the employer's sole purpose was to ascertain whether the union demanding recognition actually represented a majority of the employees, (2) that the employees were so informed, (3) that assurances against reprisal were given, and (4) that the questioning occurred in a background free from employer hostility to union organization.[279]

The Board encountered judicial opposition in applying the *Blue Flash* rule because of disagreement by the circuit courts as to the proper weight to be given the circumstances surrounding the interrogation.[280] The Second Circuit, for example, held in *Bourne v. NLRB*[281] that interrogation that is not threatening in itself will not be an unfair labor practice unless it "meets certain fairly severe standards."[282] In setting aside the Board finding of unlawful interrogation, that Circuit based its holding on five criteria: (1) background of employer hostility, (2) the identity of the interrogator (i.e., rank in the employer hierarchy), (3) the place of the interrogation, (4) the method used, and (5) the truthfulness of the employee's response.

The use of differing criteria by the circuits and the Board in applying the *Blue Flash* rule created "considerable uncertainty in this area of labor-management relations."[283] The Board finally concluded that the rule did not operate to discourage intimidation of employees by employer polls.[284] Therefore, pursuant to a suggestion by the Circuit Court for the District of Columbia that it "come to grips with this constantly recurring problem,"[285] the Board in *Struksnes Construction Co.*,[286] revised the *Blue Flash* criteria as follows:

> Absent unusual circumstances, the polling of employees by an employer will be violative of Section 8(a)(1) of the Act unless the following safeguards are observed: (1) the purpose of the poll is to determine the truth of a union's claim of majority, (2) this purpose is communicated to the employees, (3) assurances against reprisal are

---

[279]Struksnes Constr. Co., *supra* note 273.

[280]*Id.* at n.10.

[281]332 F2d 47, 56 LRRM 2241 (CA 2, 1964), *enforcing as modified* 144 NLRB 805, 54 LRRM 1158 (1963).

[282]*Id.* at 48.

[283]Struksnes Constr. Co., *supra* note 273, at 1063.

[284]*Id.*

[285]Operating Eng'rs Local 49 v. NLRB (Struksnes Constr. Co.), 353 F2d 852, 856, 60 LRRM 2353 (CA DC, 1965).

[286]*Supra* note 273. *See also* Tom Wood Pontiac, Inc., 179 NLRB 581, 72 LRRM 1494 (1969), *enforced*, 447 F2d 383, 77 LRRM 2968 (CA 7, 1971); Wm. Walters, Inc. aka Computronics, 179 NLRB 709, 72 LRRM 1504 (1969), *enforced*, 76 LRRM 2815 (CA 7, 1971).

> given, (4) the employees are polled by secret ballot, and (5) the employer has not engaged in unfair labor practices or otherwise created a coercive atmosphere.[287]

The new element in the revision was the requirement that polls be conducted by secret ballot. The Board cautioned against the use of polls while a petition for a Board election is pending, because it would not "serve any legitimate interest of the employer that would not be better served by the forthcoming Board election."[288] The *Struksnes* decision, however, did not provide any specific ground rules for conducting a secret ballot.[289]

Polls designed to elicit union sympathies indirectly, rather than by direct inquiry, have also run afoul of section 8(a)(1). Thus, a poll on the issue of whether temporary employees should be permitted to vote in the upcoming representation election violated section 8(a)(1) because only the union favored inclusion of temporary employees; the poll was therefore viewed as a means of revealing union sympathies.[290]

The Board, however, recognized the right of an employer in the health care industry to submit questionnaires to its employees asking their intent to report for work, after the employer had received from the union the 10-day notice of intent to strike required by section 8(g) of the Act.[291] Approval, however, was conditioned on the employer's clear conveyance to the employees (1) that the purpose of the questionnaire was to assist in planning for staff requirements in the event of a strike, (2) that they were free to make their own decisions and (3) that no reprisals would be taken.[292]

---

[287]165 NLRB at 1063.

[288]*Id. See also* Fontana Bros., 169 NLRB 368, 67 LRRM 1210 (1968).

[289]*See* Oleson's Food Stores, 167 NLRB 543, 66 LRRM 1108 (1967), where the ballots were privately counted by the employer in the absence of any observers.

[290]Clothing Workers v. NLRB (AMF, Inc.), 564 F2d 434, 95 LRRM 2821 (CA DC, 1977). *See also* Burns Int'l Sec. Serv., 225 NLRB 271, 92 LRRM 1439 (1976), *enforcement denied*, 567 F2d 945, 97 LRRM 2350 (CA 10, 1977).

[291]*See* Chapter 19, "The Primary Strike," at notes 50–52.

[292]Preterm, Inc., 240 NLRB 654, 100 LRRM 1344 (1979). The Board did rule illegal the employer's individual questioning of 11 employees in this case and stressed that the safeguards outlined in Johnnie's Poultry Co., 146 NLRB 770, 55 LRRM 1403 (1964), *enforcement denied*, 334 F2d 617, 59 LRRM 2117 (CA 8, 1965) and Struksnes Constr. Co., *supra* note 273, still regulate the manner of a health care employer's interrogation. *See* Commercial Mgmt., 233 NLRB 665, 97 LRRM 1247 (1977). *But see* W.A. Sheaffer Pen Co. v. NLRB, 486 F2d 180, 84 LRRM 2456 (CA 8, 1973) (poll, in absence of *Struksnes* safeguards, asking job applicants whether they would cross a picket line, conducted by employer facing strike deadline, ruled coercive). *See also* notes 316–318 *infra* and accompanying text.

Not all preelection polls to elicit union sympathies conducted in the absence of *Struksnes* safeguards violate section 8(a)(1). The Board has dispensed with the *Struksnes* requirements where (1) employees have volunteered their sentiments to the employer, and the employer seeks to verify those previously announced preferences; (2) other safeguards are present at the time of the poll, such as the presence of union representatives when the poll is taken or a clearly manifested solidarity of the employees is demonstrated.[293]

An employer's poll of employees who are already represented by a union to determine whether they desire continued representation raises different considerations. The Board has held that such a poll violates section 8(a)(1) if it is conducted at a time when the employer lacks sufficient objective evidence to support a reasonable doubt of the union's continued majority support, evidence, that is, that would justify the lawful withdrawal of recognition.[294] In *Thomas Industries v. NLRB*,[295] however, the Sixth Circuit refused to enforce an order of the Board that applied that rule. The court ruled that such a poll is lawful if the employer "has substantial objective evidence of a loss of union support, even if that evidence is insufficient in itself to justify withdrawal."[296] Although two other circuits have adopted the view of the Sixth Circuit on this question,[297] the Board has explicitly declined to relax its standard of legality, saying "it is only through the application of such a . . . stringent standard for polling that the dual goals of collective-bargaining stability and employee free choice can be protected."[298]

---

[293]Bushnell's Kitchens, 222 NLRB 110, 91 LRRM 1113 (1976); *see also* Jerome J. Jacomet, 222 NLRB 899, 91 LRRM 1370 (1976) (questioning found noncoercive where employees requested a meeting at which an employee spokesman informed the employer that they did not want to join the union, and the employer then inquired, "Nobody wants to join the union?"—to which all nodded "Yes").

[294]Jackson Sportswear Corp., 211 NLRB 891, 87 LRRM 1254 (1974). *See generally* Chapter 12, "Recognition and Withdrawal of Recognition Without an Election," at notes 227–250 and 342.

[295]687 F2d 863, 111 LRRM 2233 (CA 6, 1982), *enforcing in part and denying in part* 255 NLRB 646, 107 LRRM 1070 (1981).

[296]*Id.*, 111 LRRM at 2236.

[297]NLRB v. A.W. Thompson, Inc., 651 F2d 1141, 107 LRRM 3245, *enforcing as modified*, 108 LRRM 2336 (CA 5, 1981); Mingtree Restaurant dba Forbidden City Restaurant v. NLRB, 736 F2d 1295, 116 LRRM 3089 (CA 9, 1984). The Third Circuit expressly declined to decide this question in Hajoca Corp. v. NLRB, 872 F2d 1169, 131 LRRM 2447 (CA 3, 1989), *enforcing* 291 NLRB 104, 129 LRRM 1296 (1988).

[298]Texas Petrochemicals Corp., 296 NLRB No. 136, 132 LRRM 1279, 1283 (1989).

(2) Individual or isolated questioning. The criteria for determining the validity of interrogation by means other than polling are not altogether clear,[299] although the Second Circuit's *Bourne*[300] test has gained some judicial acceptance.[301] Where interrogation is sufficiently isolated and occurs in an atmosphere free of coercive conduct, an election will not be set aside;[302] nor will a remedial order issue in an unfair labor practice case.[303] On the other hand, interrogation accompanied by threats has been held to interfere with an election even though only one percent of the employees were threatened.[304] Generally, the Board has used the approach it adopted in *Blue Flash*, of evaluating interrogation in the light of all the surrounding circumstances, including the time, place, personnel involved, and known position of the employer.[305] Where employers seek to force employees to disclose their union sentiments without communicating a valid purpose and an assurance against reprisal, questioning will typically be held coercive.[306] Questioning that places employees in the position of acting as informers regarding the union activities of their fellow employees is likewise unlawful.[307] But where the

---

[299] *See* Bok, *The Regulation of Campaign Tactics in Representation Elections Under the National Labor Relations Act*, 78 HARV. L. REV. 38, 107 (1964), and *compare* West Tex. Equip. Co., 142 NLRB 1358, 53 LRRM 1249 (1963) *with* Zayre Corp., 154 NLRB 1372, 60 LRRM 1222 (1965), where the trial examiner noted that tests applicable to systematic polling do not necessarily apply to other types of interrogation but considered the Second Circuit's test an outer limit in finding a violation. *See also* Gruber's Food Center, 159 NLRB 629, 62 LRRM 1271 (1966).

[300] *Supra* notes 281–282 and accompanying text.

[301] *See* NLRB v. Roney Plaza Apts., 597 F2d 1046, 101 LRRM 2794 (CA 5, 1979); NLRB v. Intertherm, 596 F2d 267, 100 LRRM 3016 (CA 8, 1979). *See also* Teamsters Local 633 (Bulk Haulers) v. NLRB, 509 F2d 490, 88 LRRM 2072 (CA DC, 1974) (criticizing Board for inadequate inquiry into *Bourne* factors).

[302] West Tex. Equip. Co., *supra* note 299; Alley Constr. Co., 210 NLRB 999, 86 LRRM 1316 (1974).

[303] Dieckbrader Express, 168 NLRB 867, 67 LRRM 1081 (1967).

[304] Huntsville Mfg. Co., 211 NLRB 54, 86 LRRM 1587 (1974), *enforcement denied*, 514 F2d 723, 89 LRRM 2592 (CA 5, 1972) (union lost election by large majority); Super Thrift Mkts., 233 NLRB 409, 96 LRRM 1523 (1977).

[305] In Sunnyvale Medical Clinic, 277 NLRB 1217, 121 LRRM 1025 (1985), the Board expressly noted its longstanding reliance on *Blue Flash*. *See* Camvac Int'l v. NLRB, 877 F2d 62 (CA 6, 1989), *remanding* 288 NLRB 816, 130 LRRM 1447 (1988). *See* Bok, *supra* note 299, at 107; Gruber's Food Center, *supra* note 299.

[306] NLRB v. Solboro Knitting Mills, 572 F2d 936, 97 LRRM 3047 (CA 2, 1978), *cert. denied*, 439 US 864, 99 LRRM 2601 (1978); Teamsters Local 633 (Bulk Haulers) v. NLRB, *supra* note 301; Monroe Mfg. Co., 200 NLRB 62, 82 LRRM 1042 (1972); Mississippi Extended Care Center, 202 NLRB 1065, 82 LRRM 1738 (1973), *enforced*, 496 F2d 862, 86 LRRM 3120 (CA 6, 1974).

[307] Hanover Concrete Co., 241 NLRB 936, 101 LRRM 1016 (1979); Abex Corp., 162 NLRB 328, 64 LRRM 1004 (1966). This rule has been held applicable to an employer's interrogation of a supervisor to determine which employees had union sympathies. Dependable Lists, 239 NLRB 1304, 100 LRRM 1148 (1979); *see also* Burns Elec. Sec. Serv., 245 NLRB 742, 102 LRRM 1553 (1979) ("who is filing these ridiculous unfair labor

inquiry is "innocuous,"[308] is part of a normal response to a conversation initiated by an employee,[309] or is conducted in a joking atmosphere where employees do not feel compelled to answer,[310] it does not rise to the level of coercion.

Interrogation, not accompanied by threats or other coercion, of an employee who has openly and voluntarily disclosed support for the union offers conflicting possibilities. On the one hand, such an employee might be thought more than normally resistant to the coercive influence of employer questions about the employee's preferences. On the other hand, the action of an employer in asking questions about the already known views of such an employee might be thought more than normally ominous—an expression of "displeasure"[311]—and, therefore, more likely to be coercive. The Board has favored each view at different times. The former view influenced the Board's 1973 decision in *B.F. Goodrich Footwear Co.*[312] In that case, the Board considered the employee's known support for the union to be a relevant circumstance that diminished the coercive tendency of the interrogation. In *PPG Industries,*[313] however, the Board concluded that the interrogations of known union supporters had been, under the circumstances, a coercive "probing into employees' union sentiments." In that case, the Board explicitly overruled *B.F. Goodrich* "to the extent that" it held an employer could "lawfully initiate questioning about . . . union sentiments" of a known union adherent.[314]

More recently, in *Rossmore House Hotel,*[315] the Board repaired to its former view and found no violation of the Act in the interrogation of an avowed union supporter. The Board overruled

---

practice charges"); Pelton Casteel, Inc. v. NLRB, 627 F2d 23, 105 LRRM 2124 (CA 7, 1980).

[308]Sandy's Stores, 163 NLRB 728, 65 LRRM 1034 (1967), *enforcement denied on other grounds*, 398 F2d 268, 68 LRRM 2800 (CA 1, 1968); Madison Kipp Co., 240 NLRB 879, 100 LRRM 1381 (1979); Pelton Casteel, Inc., *supra* note 307.

[309]Phillips-Van Heusen Corp., 165 NLRB 1, 65 LRRM 1355 (1967).

[310]NLRB v. Scott & Fetzer Co., 570 F2d 742, 97 LRRM 2881 (CA 8, 1978). For extensive discussion of the factual setting in which interrogations are evaluated, see the trial examiner's decision in Campbell Soup Co., 170 NLRB 1547, 68 LRRM 1036 (1968).

[311]PPG Indus., 251 NLRB 1146, 105 LRRM 1434, 1436 (1980).

[312]201 NLRB 353, 82 LRRM 1262 (1973). *See also* Stumpf Motor Co., 208 NLRB 431, 85 LRRM 1113 (1974).

[313]*Supra* note 311.

[314]*Id.*

[315]269 NLRB 1176, 116 LRRM 1025 (1984), *aff'd sub nom.* Hotel Employees Local 11 v. NLRB, 760 F2d 1006, 119 LRRM 2624 (CA 9, 1985). *See also* Hunter Douglas, Inc. v. NLRB, 804 F2d 808, 123 LRRM 2912 (CA 3, 1986), *cert. denied*, 481 US 1069, 125 LRRM 2440 (1987).

PPG Industries which, it said, had erroneously established a per se rule inconsistent with time-worn *Blue Flash* principles.

(3) Preparation of defense for trial of unfair labor practice case. Despite the "inherent danger of coercion," an employer may exercise a limited privilege of interrogating employees in the "investigation of facts concerning issues raised in a complaint" where this is necessary to the preparation of its defense for the pending trial.[316] To minimize the coercive impact and to strike a balance between conflicting interests, the Board in *Johnnie's Poultry*[317] enunciated a number of safeguards: (1) The purpose of the questioning must be communicated to the employee. (2) An assurance of no reprisal must be given. (3) The employee's participation must be obtained on a voluntary basis. (4) The questioning must take place in an atmosphere free from union animus. (5) The questioning itself must not be coercive in nature. (6) The questions must be relevant to the issues involved in the complaint. (7) The employee's subjective state of mind must not be probed. (8) The questions must not "otherwise interfere with the statutory rights of employees."[318]

When the employer or its attorney fails to follow these safeguards in employee interviews in preparation for an unfair labor practice hearing, the Board has been quick to find that section 8(a)(1) has been violated.[319] It is the Board's position that "[c]ompliance with all the *Johnnie's Poultry* safeguards is the minimum required"[320] to dissipate the potential of coercion and that "failure to adhere strictly to the rules set forth in *Johnnie's Poultry* constitutes a per se violation of §8(a)(1)."[321]

---

[316]Johnnie's Poultry Co., 146 NLRB 770, 55 LRRM 1403 (1964), *enforcement denied*, 344 F2d 617, 59 LRRM 2117 (CA 8, 1965).

[317]*Id.*

[318]*Id.* The Eighth Circuit's denial of enforcement did not express disagreement with the standards but held that the factual determinations were "not supported by substantial evidence." 344 F2d at 619.

[319]*See, e.g.*, Kyle & Stephen, Inc., 259 NLRB 731, 109 LRRM 1009 (1981) (*Johnnie's Poultry* safeguards apply regardless of employer intent to coerce or extent of questioning); A&R Transp., 237 NLRB 1084, 99 LRRM 1108 (1978), *enforced in part*, 601 F2d 311, 101 LRRM 2856 (CA 7, 1979); Anserphone, Inc., 236 NLRB 931, 98 LRRM 1385 (1978), *enforced in part*, 632 F2d 4, 105 LRRM 2753 (CA 6, 1980); Jack August Enters., 232 NLRB 881, 97 LRRM 1560 (1977), *enforced*, 583 F2d 575, 99 LRRM 2582 (CA 1, 1978); Mr. F's Beef & Bourbon, 212 NLRB 462, 87 LRRM 1601 (1974), *enforced*, 96 LRRM 2107 (CA 6, 1975); Tamper, Inc., 207 NLRB 907, 85 LRRM 1375 (1973), *enforced in part*, 522 F2d 781, 89 LRRM 3034 (CA 4, 1975); Hedison Mfg. Co., 260 NLRB 1037, 109 LRRM 1258 (1982).

[320]Roadway Express, 239 NLRB 653, 100 LRRM 1046 (1978) (no assurances given to employee that no reprisals would be taken as a result of the interview; the Board held that §8(a)(1) was violated even though the employer's good faith was not questioned).

[321]A&R Transp. v. NLRB, *supra* note 319 (court found that interview was not coercive and denied enforcement of that portion of the order dealing with coercive interroga-

The courts, by and large, have considered the *Johnnie's Poultry* standards appropriate in determining whether questioning of employees is coercive,[322] but except for the Fourth Circuit[323] they have declined to apply the rules in a per se fashion.[324] Several circuits have applied a "totality of the circumstances" test to determine coercion.[325]

The Board has not clarified what role *Johnnie's Poultry* standards play in employer interrogation of employees in preparation for arbitration hearings[326] or in investigatory interviews of employees about plant rule violations.[327]

d. Surveillance and Photographing. Since the earliest days of the Act, surveillance of employees by an employer, whether with supervisors, rank-and-file employees, or outsiders, has consistently been held to violate section 8(a)(1).[328] The Board has

---

tion). Limitations on this *per se* approach are suggested in two cases. Lammert Indus., 229 NLRB 895, 96 LRRM 1557 (1977), *enforced*, 578 F2d 1223, 98 LRRM 2992 (CA 7, 1978) (Board found that attorney made it clear that no reprisals would be taken against employee being interviewed, even though the word "reprisals" was not used); Salina Concrete Prods., 218 NLRB 496, 89 LRRM 1734 (1975) (Board found no §8(a)(1) violation even though company attorney did not use the word "voluntary" in telling employees that they were not compelled to participate).

[322]*See* Auto Workers (Preston Prods. Co.), v. NLRB, 392 F2d 801, 66 LRRM 2548 (CA DC, 1967), *cert. denied*, 392 US 906, 68 LRRM 2408 (1968); Montgomery Ward & Co. v. NLRB, 377 F2d 452, 65 LRRM 2285 (CA 6, 1967); NLRB v. Neuhoff Bros. Packers, 375 F2d 372, 64 LRRM 2673 (CA 5, 1967).

[323]Standard-Coosa-Thatcher, Carpet Yarn Div. v. NLRB, 691 F2d 1133, 111 LRRM 2987 (CA 4, 1982), *enforcing* 257 NLRB 304, 107 LRRM 1506 (1981), *cert. denied*, 460 US 1083, 113 LRRM 2112 (1983).

[324]*See* NLRB v. Neuhoff Bros. Packers, *supra* note 322; A&R Transp., *supra* note 319. The Court of Appeals for the District of Columbia Circuit has also applied the *Johnnie's Poultry* interrogation safeguards, but it is not clear whether it has adopted a per se approach. *See* Auto Workers (Preston Prods. Co.) v. NLRB, *supra* note 322.

[325]*See, e.g.*, NLRB v. Complas Indus., 714 F2d 279, 114 LRRM 2028 (CA 7, 1983), *denying enforcement to* 255 NLRB 1416, 107 LRRM 1152 (1981); Retired Persons Pharmacy v. NLRB, 519 F2d 486, 89 LRRM 2879 (CA 2, 1975).

[326]*Compare* Pacific Sw. Airlines, 242 NLRB 1169, 101 LRRM 1366 (1979) (Board agreed with ALJ that the *Johnnie's Poultry* safeguards are not relevant to prearbitration interviews) *with* Cook Paint & Varnish Co., 246 NLRB 646, 102 LRRM 1680 (1979), *enforcement denied and remanded*, 648 F2d 712, 106 LRRM 3016 (CA DC, 1981), *decision on remand*, 258 NLRB 1230, 108 LRRM 1150 (1981) (ALJ applied *Johnnie's Poultry* safeguards to prearbitration interviews; Board affirmed ALJ's finding of illegal interrogation but made no mention of the *Johnnie's Poultry* rationale).

[327]*See* Levingston Shipbuilding Co., 249 NLRB 1, 104 LRRM 1058 (1980) (ALJ found that the *Johnnie's Poultry* safeguards apply to the interrogation of employees about possible plant rule violations; Board did not specifically embrace ALJ's reasoning).

[328]Consolidated Edison Co. v. NLRB, 305 US 197, 3 LRRM 645 (1938). In Elder-Beerman Stores Corp. v. NLRB, 415 F2d 1375, 72 LRRM 2510 (CA 6, 1969), *cert. denied*, 397 US 1009, 73 LRRM 2849 (1970), an employer violated §8(a)(1) by instructing a supervisor to engage in surveillance of employees' union activity and by discharging him for failure to comply. The conduct was deemed unlawful regardless of whether the employees had knowledge of the instruction or the reason for the discharge. Impact Indus., 285 NLRB 5, 128 LRRM 1122 (1987), *remanded*, 847 F2d 379, 128 LRRM 2455 (CA 7, 1988) ("well-nigh continuous scrutiny of employee handbilling"). For general commen-

successfully maintained that surveillance is unlawful regardless of whether the employees know of it.[329] Under this principle the surreptitious electronic surveillance of a union organizer's motel room by two management employees was ruled unlawful.[330]

The law is equally clear that an employer violates section 8(a)(1) if it creates the impression among employees that it is engaged in surveillance,[331] for by thus highlighting its "anxiety" concerning union activities it tends to inhibit an employee's future union activities.[332] The Board has also found a section 8(a)(1) violation in surveillance of union activities by supervisors who were motivated solely by their own curiosity and who were subsequently forbidden by the employer to continue such surveillance.[333] An employer violates the Act by encouraging employees to engage in surveillance of union activities.[334]

---

tary on the principles discussed in this section, *see* Craver, *The Inquisitorial Process in Private Employment,* 63 CORNELL L. REV. 1 (1977).

[329]NLRB v. Grower-Shipper Vegetable Ass'n, 122 F2d 368, 8 LRRM 891 (CA 9, 1941); Bethlehem Steel Co. v. NLRB, 120 F2d 641, 8 LRRM 962 (CA DC, 1941).

[330]NLRB v. J.P. Stevens & Co., 563 F2d 8, 96 LRRM 2150 (CA 2, 1977), *cert. denied,* 434 US 1064, 97 LRRM 2747 (1978). The employer's subsequent disclaimer "disapproving" surveillance and announcing suspension of the management personnel did not absolve it of culpability. The court ruled that in light of J.P. Stevens' antiunion history, it should at the very least have assured employees that it would ignore any information obtained by the surveillance.

[331]In NLRB v. Simplex Time Recorder Co., 401 F2d 547, 69 LRRM 2465 (CA 1, 1968), because of the unusually broad, and perhaps vague, conduct forbidden by a cease-and-desist order directed against creating the "impression" of surveillance, the First Circuit added a limitation to the Board's order. It enforced an order that it interpreted as meaning "willful conduct and a justifiable impression." *See,* finding an impression of surveillance: Link Mfg. Co., 281 NLRB 294, 123 LRRM 1084 (1986), *enforced mem.,* 840 F2d 17, 129 LRRM 2600 (CA 6, 1988), *cert. denied,* 488 US 854, 129 LRRM 2600 (1988). Dillingham Marine & Mfg. Co., 239 NLRB 904, 100 LRRM 1109 (1978), *enforced,* 610 F2d 319, 103 LRRM 2430 (CA 5, 1980); Hamilton Avnet Elec., 240 NLRB 781, 100 LRRM 1502 (1979); J.P. Stevens & Co., 244 NLRB 407, 102 LRRM 1039 (1979); J.P. Stevens & Co., 245 NLRB 198, 102 LRRM 1437 (1979); NLRB v. Rybold Heater Co., 408 F2d 888, 70 LRRM 3159 (CA 6, 1969). *See,* finding no impression of surveillance: Checker, Inc., 247 NLRB 835, 103 LRRM 1111 (1980); Tartan Marine Co., 247 NLRB 646, 103 LRRM 1247 (1980), *enforced in part,* 644 F2d 882, 106 LRRM 3076 (CA 4, 1981); NLRB v. Pilgrim Food, 591 F2d 110, 100 LRRM 2494 (CA 1, 1978).

[332]NLRB v. Prince Macaroni Mfg. Co., 329 F2d 803, 55 LRRM 2852 (CA 1, 1964); Hendrix Mfg. Co. v. NLRB, 321 F2d 100, 53 LRRM 2831 (CA 5, 1963). In CBS Records Div., 223 NLRB 709, 91 LRRM 1564 (1976), the Board ruled that the employer's focusing of a closed circuit camera on a building used for a union headquarters during an organizing campaign violated §8(a)(1) even though no actual surveillance was ever conducted.

[333]Intertype Co. v. NLRB, 371 F2d 787, 64 LRRM 2257 (CA 4, 1967). *See also* NLRB v. J.P. Stevens & Co., *supra* note 330.

[334]NLRB v. National Garment Co., 614 F2d 623, 104 LRRM 2069 (CA 8, 1980); Saginaw Furniture Shops v. NLRB, 343 F2d 515, 58 LRRM 2417 (CA 7, 1965); NLRB v. Saxe-Glassman Shoe Corp., 201 F2d 238, 31 LRRM 2271 (CA 1, 1953). *But see* Beverly Enters. dba Provincial House Total Living Center, 287 NLRB 158, 127 LRRM 1237 (1987) (no violation where employer told employees to summon her if nonemployee organizer returned to employer premises: employer uniformly enforced a lawful no-solicitation rule excluding nonemployees).

The Board has not condemned employer observation of employee activity, such as picketing and handbilling, that has occurred on or near the employer property, where the observation was consistent with the protection of legitimate employer interests in good order and productivity.[335] Similarly, enhanced surveillance of employees at the workplace that coincides with organizing activity does not violate the Act if instituted for and justified by legitimate concerns for security, product integrity, or quality control.[336] The random or isolated viewing of a union gathering by an employer agent is not prohibited surveillance.[337] Neither is the limited attendance at union meetings of a supervisor present as an invited guest.[338]

An employer that photographs or videotapes employees engaged in concerted activities may engage in prohibited surveillance, or may unlawfully create the impression of surveillance, or both. In general, the Board has analyzed this problem by presuming that the photographing of peaceful protected activity violates section 8(a)(1), but it allows the employer to rebut the presumption by proof of specific justifying circumstances.[339] The Board's application of this presumption has often been upheld in the courts, especially in cases involving unlawful employer response to organizing activity or other employer animus toward protected rights.[340] The Board has allowed such photographing, however, where the employee

---

[335]Key Food Stores Coop., 286 NLRB 1056, 129 LRRM 1172 (1987); Baton Rouge Gen. Hosp., 283 NLRB 192, 126 LRRM 1071 (1987); Porta Sys. Corp., 238 NLRB 192, 99 LRRM 1251 (1978), *enforced*, 625 F2d 399, 104 LRRM 2918 (CA 2, 1980). *But see* Crown Cork & Seal Co., 254 NLRB 1340, 106 LRRM 1270 (1981) (note-taking by plant personnel manager during otherwise lawful observation of union activity violated §8(a)(1)).

[336]Lechmere, Inc., 295 NLRB No. 15, 131 LRRM 1480 (1989); Liberty Nursing Homes, 245 NLRB 1194, 102 LRRM 1517 (1979); Lebanon Apparel Corp., 243 NLRB 1024, 102 LRRM 1022 (1979); *see also* Pacific Intermountain Express Co., 250 NLRB 1451, 104 LRRM 1532 (1980), *aff'd*, 672 F2d 893, 109 LRRM 2360 (CA DC, 1981); American Ship Bldg. Co., 240 NLRB 1, 100 LRRM 1269 (1979).

[337]Stead Indus. dba Hoyt Water Heater Co., 282 NLRB 1348, 124 LRRM 1314 (1987).

[338]Osco Drug, Inc., 237 NLRB 231, 99 LRRM 1150 (1978). *See also* Nice-Pak Prods., 248 NLRB 1278, 104 LRRM 1127 (1980).

[339]Larand Leisurelies, Inc., 213 NLRB 197, 197 n.1, 87 LRRM 1129 (1974), *enforced*, 523 F2d 814, 90 LRRM 2631 (CA 6, 1975). *See also* Love's Barbeque Restaurant No. 62, 245 NLRB 78, 102 LRRM 1546 (1979); Faith Garment Co., 246 NLRB 299, 102 LRRM 1515 (1979); Hotel Employees Local 19, 240 NLRB 240, 100 LRRM 1354 (1979), *enforcement denied*, 628 F2d 1357, 111 LRRM 2515 (CA 9, 1980).

[340]*See* United States Steel Corp. v. NLRB, 682 F2d 98, 110 LRRM 2902 (CA 3, 1982), *denying enforcement to* 255 NLRB 1338, 107 LRRM 1097 (1981) (presumption not warranted where employer photographed protest march by represented employees where employer and union had long history of good relations). *See also* NLRB v. Colonial Haven Nursing Home, 542 F2d 691, 93 LRRM 2241 (CA 7, 1976) (presumption approved).

activity involved violence, or where the employer plausibly sought to make a record of unlawful conduct by the union[341] or unprotected activity by the employees.[342]

e. Soliciting or Remedying Employee Grievances. An employer who solicits grievances or complaints from employees during a period of organizing activity may be deemed to have made an implied promise that complaints elicited will be favorably resolved. Such an implied promise, if made for the purpose of influencing employee choice, is unlawful for reasons described above.[343] However, an employer that has an established practice of soliciting and resolving employee grievances may continue that practice during the organizing activity,[344] if the past practice is not significantly altered.[345] The Board has applied these principles to a broad array of employer practices including the installation of a "grievance hot line" telephone[346] and the use of questionnaires and attitude surveys.[347]

---

[341]Berton Kirshner, Inc., 209 NLRB 1081, 85 LRRM 1548 (1974), *enforced*, 523 F2d 1046, 90 LRRM 2958 (CA 9, 1975). The Board's decision relied heavily on the fact that subsequent handbilling by the union occurred without incident and no photographs of this later occasion were taken.

[342]Concord Metal, Inc., 295 NLRB No. 94, 131 LRRM 1703 (1989); Roadway Express, 271 NLRB 1238, 117 LRRM 1089 (1984).

[343]*See* text at notes 244–249, *supra*. *See also* Color Tech Corp., 286 NLRB 476, 126 LRRM 1289 (1987); Electric Hose & Rubber Co., 267 NLRB 488, 114 LRRM 1058 (1983). *But see*, Idaho Falls Consol. Hosps., 257 NLRB 1045, 108 LRRM 1017 (1981), *enforcement denied on this point*, 731 F2d 1384, 116 LRRM 2390 (CA 9, 1984); where the court refused enforcement because the circumstances of the solicitation carried no implication of a promise of remedy. *Accord* Hayes-Albion Corp., Tiffin Div., 237 NLRB 20, 99 LRRM 1020 (1978); El Rancho Mkt., 235 NLRB 468, 98 LRRM 1153 (1978); NLRB v. Broyhill Co., 514 F2d 655, 89 LRRM 2203 (CA 8, 1975); Lasco Indus., 217 NLRB 527, 89 LRRM 1058 (1975).

[344]Bell Halter, Inc., 276 NLRB 1208, 120 LRRM 1322 (1985); Williams Litho Serv., 260 NLRB 773, 109 LRRM 1261 (1982).

[345]Carbonneau Indus., 228 NLRB 597, 94 LRRM 1502 (1977). The objectionable conduct by the employer included the following: (1) replacing an old suggestion box with a new one in a more convenient location; (2) failing to limit questions at employee meetings initiated by the employer to subjects other than employee grievances; and (3) distributing paper and pencils to employees at group meetings and asking them to submit questions. The Board also found that the employer had interfered with the election by posting employee suggestions with employer responses such as "checking into," "done," "finished," or "forthcoming," and by otherwise indicating that certain grievances would be corrected. *See also* S.E. Nichols, Inc., 284 NLRB 556, 127 LRRM 1298 (1987), *modified and enforced*, 862 F2d 952, 129 LRRM 3098 (CA 2, 1988), *cert. denied*, 490 US 1108, 131 LRRM 2528 (1989).

[346]Garry Mfg. Co., 242 NLRB 539, 101 LRRM 1197 (1979), *enforced in pertinent part*, 630 F2d 934, 105 LRRM 2113 (CA 3, 1980).

[347]Bell Halter, Inc., *supra* note 344 (attitude survey allowed as continuation of past practice); Leland Stanford, Jr. Univ. & Stanford Univ. Hosp., 240 NLRB 1138, 100 LRRM 1391 (1979) (attitude survey for legitimate business reasons allowed); St. Joseph's Hosp., 247 NLRB 869, 103 LRRM 1315 (1980) (survey not allowed where promise of benefit was implicit). *See also* Camvac Int'l, 288 NLRB 816, 130 LRRM 1447 (1988) (survey violated §8(a)(1)).

f. Employer's Responsibility for Third-Party Conduct. Objectionable third-party conduct during an organizational campaign may be a basis for setting aside an election regardless of employer complicity.[348] But where the employer is charged with an unfair labor practice, rather than with objectionable preelection conduct, considerations of agency are more significant. Coercive conduct must be attributable to an employer before an unfair labor practice will be found.[349] For example, in a small, nonindustrial community where the employer actively influenced community opinion against the union, it was held responsible for third-party distribution of a leaflet containing a threat that union representation would result in plant closure.[350] The Board has applied the principle of apparent agency in determining whether rank-and-file employees, or others associated with the employing enterprise, are agents of the employer for purposes of the Act.[351]

g. Employer Violence. An employer that uses[352] or threatens[353] violence against employees because of their union or other protected activities, or that causes others to use or threaten such violence,[354] violates section 8(a)(1). However, an employer's violence need not be aimed at employees to be unlawful. Physical assaults by employers on nonemployee union organizers violate section 8(a)(1) by inhibiting employees' exercise of rights.[355]

---

[348]*See* Chapter 9, "Restrictions of Preelection Activity: 'Laboratory Conditions,'" at notes 137–147.

[349]Dean Indus., 162 NLRB 1078, 64 LRRM 1193 (1967); *see also* Cagle's, Inc., 234 NLRB 1148, 98 LRRM 1117 (1978), *enforced in part*, 588 F2d 943, 100 LRRM 2590 (CA 5, 1979) (agency relationship found in part because employer failed to disavow actions of third party); Hyster Co. v. NLRB, 480 F2d 1081, 83 LRRM 2801 (CA 5, 1973), *enforcing in part* 198 NLRB 192, 80 LRRM 1603 (1972) (agency relationship); Panama-Williams, Inc., 226 NLRB 315, 93 LRRM 1286 (1976) (no agency relationship); Salant Corp. dba Carrizo Mfg. Co., 214 NLRB 171, 88 LRRM 1314 (1974) (same).

[350]Star Kist Samoa, 237 NLRB 238, 98 LRRM 1558 (1978).

[351]*See* Chapter 28, "Jurisdiction: Coverage of the Act," at notes 170–181.

[352]Yolo Transp., 286 NLRB 1087, 128 LRRM 1055 (1987); S.M.C. Restaurant Corp. dba Poletti's Restaurant, 261 NLRB 313, 110 LRRM 1092 (1982), *enforced mem.*, 718 F2d 1086, 116 LRRM 2191 (CA 2, 1983).

[353]Ford Bros., 294 NLRB No. 10, 132 LRRM 1346 (1989) (threat to strikers by display of holstered handgun); Lord Jim's, 259 NLRB 1162, 109 LRRM 1095 (1982).

[354]Sunshine Mining Co., 7 NLRB 1252, 2 LRRM 415 (1938), *modified and enforced*, 110 F2d 780, 6 LRRM 981 (CA 9, 1940), *cert. denied*, 312 US 678, 7 LRRM 326 (1941) (employer induced and condoned violence by nonstrikers against strikers).

[355]*See* NLRB v. Village IX dba Shenanigans, 723 F2d 1360, 115 LRRM 2297 (CA 7, 1983), *enforcing in part and remanding in part*, 264 NLRB 908, 112 LRRM 1096 (1982); McLane/Western v. NLRB, 723 F2d 1454, 115 LRRM 2112 (CA 10, 1983), *on remand*, 276 NLRB 579, 120 LRRM 1109 (1985), *enforced*, 827 F2d 1423, 126 LRRM 2285 (CA 10, 1987).

h. Discipline and Discharge of Supervisors. Supervisors are excluded from the Act's definition of "employee"[356] because they are agents of the employer. Accordingly, supervisors do not enjoy the protection of the Act and are subject to other discipline for engaging in union or concerted activity. Thus, when an employer has disciplined or discharged a supervisor out of a legitimate desire to assure the loyalty of its management personnel and its action was "reasonably adapted" to that end, the Board has found such conduct permissible even if an incidental effect was to instill in employees the fear that the same fate would befall them for engaging in protected activity.[357]

For many years, however, the Board has held that the discipline or discharge of a supervisor violates section 8(a)(1) "when it interferes with the . . . exercise [by employees of] their rights under Section 7 of the Act."[358] Thus, an employer may not discipline or discharge a supervisor for giving testimony adverse to an employer's interests,[359] for refusing to commit unfair labor practices,[360] or for failing to prevent unionization.[361] Similarly,

---

[356]Section 2(11). *See, e.g.,* Long Beach Youth Center, 230 NLRB 648, 95 LRRM 1451 (1977), *enforced,* 591 F2d 1276, 101 LRRM 2501 (CA 9, 1979); Sibilio's Golden Grill, 227 NLRB 1688, 94 LRRM 1439 (1977).

[357]Stop & Go Foods, 246 NLRB 1076, 103 LRRM 1046 (1979).

[358]Parker-Robb Chevrolet, Inc., 262 NLRB 402, 404, 110 LRRM 1289 (1982), *review denied sub nom.* Auto Salesmen's Local 1095 v. NLRB, 711 F2d 383, 113 LRRM 3175 (CA DC, 1983).

[359]Kessel Food Mkts. v. NLRB, 868 F2d 881, 130 LRRM 2761 (CA 6, 1989), *enforcing* 287 NLRB 426, 130 LRRM 1165 (1987), *cert. denied,* 493 US 820, 132 LRRM 2624 (1989) (employer unlawfully discharged two supervisors allegedly for repeated acts of disloyalty where real reason was supervisors' testimony against employer at NLRB hearing); Rohr Indus., 220 NLRB 1029, 90 LRRM 1541 (1975); Ebasco Servs., 181 NLRB 768, 73 LRRM 1518 (1970); Leas & McVitty, Inc., 155 NLRB 389, 60 LRRM 1333 (1965), *enforcement denied,* 384 F2d 165, 66 LRRM 2353 (CA 4, 1967); Oil City Brass Works, 147 NLRB 627, 56 LRRM 1262 (1964), *enforced,* 357 F2d 466, 61 LRRM 2318 (CA 5, 1966); Dal-Tex Optical Co., 131 NLRB 715, 48 LRRM 1143 (1961), *enforced,* 310 F2d 58, 51 LRRM 2608 (CA 5, 1962); Better Monkey Grip Co., 115 NLRB 1170, 38 LRRM 1025 (1956), *enforced,* 243 F2d 836, 40 LRRM 2027 (CA 5), *cert. denied,* 355 US 864, 41 LRRM 2007 (1957).

[360]Country Boy Mr. "D" Corp. dba Country Boy Mkts., 283 NLRB 122, 124 LRRM 1355 (1987), *enforced sub nom.* Delling v. NLRB, 869 F2d 1397, 130 LRRM 2909 (CA 10, 1989). *See also* Phoenix Newspapers, 294 NLRB No. 3, 132 LRRM 1342 (1989); Miami Coca Cola Bottling Co., 140 NLRB 1359, 52 LRRM 1242 (1963), *enforced in part,* 341 F2d 524, 58 LRRM 2458 (CA 5, 1965); General Eng'g, 131 NLRB 648, 48 LRRM 1105 (1961), *enforced in part,* 311 F2d 570, 52 LRRM 2277 (CA 9, 1962); Jackson Tile Mfg. Co., 122 NLRB 764, 43 LRRM 1195 (1958), *enforced,* 272 F2d 181, 45 LRRM 2239 (CA 5, 1959); Inter-City Advertising Co., 89 NLRB 1103, 26 LRRM 1065 (1950), *enforced as modified,* 190 F2d 420, 28 LRRM 2321 (CA 4, 1951), *cert. denied,* 342 US 908, 29 LRRM 2285 (1952); Vail Mfg. Co., 61 NLRB 181, 16 LRRM 85 (1945), *enforced,* 158 F2d 664, 19 LRRM 2177 (CA 7), *cert. denied,* 331 US 835, 20 LRRM 2185 (1947).

[361]Talladega Cotton Factory, 106 NLRB 295, 32 LRRM 1479 (1953), *enforced,* 213 F2d 309, 34 LRRM 2196 (CA 5, 1954). *See also* Howard Johnson Motor Lodge, 261 NLRB 866, 110 LRRM 1135 (1982), *enforced,* 702 F2d 1, 112 LRRM 2904 (CA 1, 1983).

an employer violates section 8(a)(1) by discharging a supervisor because of the union activity of the supervisor's spouse[362] or child.[363]

In a second line of analysis, now abandoned, the Board formerly held that an employer violated section 8(a)(1) by discharging a supervisor when that discharge was an "integral part" of a pattern of misconduct undertaken for the purpose of discouraging union support among employees generally.[364] In *Parker-Robb Chevrolet*,[365] the Board repudiated that analysis, overruling earlier contrary decisions. Applying *Parker-Robb*, the Board has found no violation in the discharge of a supervisor even though it occurred in a pattern of other conduct found to be unlawful,[366] nor in the discharge of a supervisor because he insisted that the employer adhere to a collective bargaining agreement.[367]

3. Other Unlawful Employer Interference. *a. Bonuses or Benefits to Nonstrikers and Strike Replacements.* When an employer assigns to strike replacements or nonstrikers a benefit that is withheld from strikers, or withholds from nonstrikers a burden that is imposed on strikers, the action ordinarily raises an issue of discrimination under section 8(a)(3) of the Act.[368] In some instances, however, the Board has considered whether such differentiations, regardless of discriminatory motive or impact, are interference prohibited by section 8(a)(1). In *Aero-Motive Manufacturing Co.*,[369] for example, the Board overruled prior inconsistent cases and held that an employer violated section 8(a)(1)

---

[362]Consolidated Foods Corp., 165 NLRB 953, 65 LRRM 1470 (1967), *enforced in part*, 403 F2d 662, 69 LRRM 2729 (CA 6, 1968).

[363]Advertiser's Mfg. Co., 280 NLRB 1185, 124 LRRM 1017 (1986), *enforced*, 823 F2d 1086, 125 LRRM 3024 (CA 7, 1987).

[364]Brothers Three Cabinets, 248 NLRB 828, 829, 103 LRRM 1506 (1980). *See also* Nevis Indus., 246 NLRB 1053, 103 LRRM 1035 (1979), *enforcement denied*, 647 F2d 905, 107 LRRM 2890 (CA 5, 1981); Downslope Indus., 246 NLRB 948, 103 LRRM 1041 (1979). *But cf.* Sheraton P.R. Corp. v. NLRB, 651 F2d 49, 107 LRRM 2735 (CA 1, 1981).

[365]*Supra* note 358. *See* Chapter 28, "The Duty of Fair Representation," at notes 241–245.

[366]*See* Jack Welsh Co., 284 NLRB 378, 125 LRRM 1222 (1987); Sahara-Reno Corp., 262 NLRB 824, 110 LRRM 1544 (1982), *enforced mem.*, 722 F2d 734, 115 LRRM 2359 (CA 3, 1983).

[367]Wer-Coy Fabrication Co., 268 NLRB 907, 115 LRRM 1124 (1984).

[368]*E.g.*, NLRB v. Erie Resistor Corp., 373 US 221, 53 LRRM 2121 (1963). *See* Chapter 7, "Discrimination in Employment," at notes 110–111.

[369]195 NLRB 790, 79 LRRM 1496 (1972), *enforced*, 475 F2d 27, 82 LRRM 3052 (CA 6, 1973). *See also* S&W Motor Lines, 236 NLRB 938, 98 LRRM 1488 (1978), *enforced in part*, 621 F2d 598, 104 LRRM 2310 (CA 4, 1980); Portland Williamette Co., 212 NLRB 272, 86 LRRM 1677 (1974), *enforcement denied*, 534 F2d 1331, 92 LRRM 2113 (CA 9, 1976) (retroactive pay to nonstrikers held unlawful).

by paying a $100 bonus to employees who worked during an economic strike, while denying the bonus to strikers, even though the bonus was not announced or paid until after the strike had ended. The Board held that regardless of the employer's motives, its action interfered with the employees' right to strike by effectively conveying the message that nonstrikers had received, and could expect, special benefits that had been denied to strikers. Changes in work-scheduling practices during a strike, which were continued in effect after the strike to the advantage of nonstriking employees, have also been ruled in violation of section 8(a)(1).[370] However, the Board has also held that legitimate business considerations can justify disparate treatment of strikers and nonstrikers.[371]

The continued vitality of this line of analysis has been placed in doubt. In 1979, in *Emerson Electric*,[372] the Board held that an employer engaged in prohibited discrimination and, independently, in prohibited interference when, during a strike, the employer terminated the disability benefits of employees who had been unable to work when the strike began. The Board held that the employer violated section 8(a)(1) by terminating the benefits of the recipients based on the strike actions of others, and by inviting the disabled employees to disavow the strike as a condition of continued benefits. Although the Board's order was enforced by the Third Circuit, the court relied only on the conclusion that the employer had engaged in discrimination.[373] In its later decision in *Texaco, Inc.*[374] the Board embraced the analysis employed by the Third Circuit and announced its abandonment of the interference rationale on which *Emerson Electric* rested.

b. Requests for Employee Statements to the NLRB. The Board follows the rule that an employer's request to an employee for a copy of a written statement given by the employee to the Board "is a *per se* violation of Section 8(a)(1) in the absence of assurances to the employee that there will be no retaliation for

---

[370]Moore Business Forms, 224 NLRB 393, 93 LRRM 1437 (1976), *enforced in part*, 574 F2d 835, 98 LRRM 2773 (CA 5, 1978); Mercy-Memorial Hosp., 231 NLRB 1108, 96 LRRM 1239 (1977).

[371]Pilot Freight Carriers, 223 NLRB 286, 92 LRRM 1246 (1976).

[372]Emerson Elec. Co., E.L. Wiegand Div., 246 NLRB 1143, 103 LRRM 1073 (1979), *enforced as modified*, 650 F2d 463, 107 LRRM 2112, *amended*, 107 LRRM 3303 (CA 3, 1981), *cert. denied*, 455 US 939, 109 LRRM 2778 (1982).

[373]*Id.*, 107 LRRM at 2115.

[374]285 NLRB 241, 126 LRRM 1001 (1987).

refusal and a showing by the employer that the statement is needed for the employer's trial preparation."[375] The Board reasons that such a request in most circumstances "would naturally inhibit its employee's desire to cooperate with the Board's investigative efforts and deter others from so cooperating."[376] Some circuit courts have expressed their preference for a more flexible approach under which the propriety of requests for statements of this type is to be determined in light of the "voluntary nature of the compliance and the employer's need for the information."[377]

In applying its rule, however, the Board has sometimes found no unlawful conduct where the employees' answers were voluntary and the inquiry was being legitimately used in the preparation of a defense in an unfair labor practice case.[378]

c. Employer Conduct Relating to Authorization Cards. The Board applies a per se rule in holding that employer encouragement and assistance to employees in withdrawing authorization cards is a violation of section 8(a)(1).[379] If the employer's assistance is deemed "too minimal,"[380] however, or has simply informed employees of their right to withdraw from the union without solicit

---

[375]NLRB v. Maxwell, 637 F2d 698, 701, 106 LRRM 2387 (CA 9, 1981), *enforcing sub nom.* Pioneer Concrete Co., 241 NLRB 264, 101 LRRM 1012 (1979).

[376]Martin A. Gleason, Inc., 215 NLRB 340, 88 LRRM 1344 (1975), *enforcement denied,* 531 F2d 166, 91 LRRM 2682 (CA 2, 1976); S&M Grocers, 236 NLRB 1594, 98 LRRM 1471 (1978); John Dory Boat Works, 229 NLRB 844, 96 LRRM 1079 (1977); S.E. Nichols Marcy Corp., 229 NLRB 75, 95 LRRM 1110 (1977). For discussion of the potential misuse of such statements by employers, see NLRB v. Robbins Tire & Rubber Co., 437 US 214, 98 LRRM 2617 (1978), holding the statements exempt from disclosure requirements of the Freedom of Information Act.

[377]*Compare* Dayton Typographic Serv. v. NLRB, 778 F2d 1188, 121 LRRM 2001 (CA 6, 1985), *enforcing in part and denying in part* 273 NLRB 1205, 118 LRRM 1232 (1984) (violation found) *with* Anserphone v. NLRB, 632 F2d 4, 105 LRRM 2753 (CA 6, 1980), *enforcing in part and denying in part* 236 NLRB 931, 98 LRRM 1385 (1978) (no violation found). *See also* NLRB v. Martin A. Gleason, Inc., *supra* note 376. *See also* Robertshaw Controls Co. v. NLRB, 483 F2d 762, 84 LRRM 2156 (CA 4, 1973) (Fourth Circuit refused to enforce a Board order finding a §8(a)(1) violation where the employer requested the employees to give it copies of statements given to Board agent).

[378]*See* 299 Lincoln St., 292 NLRB 172, 130 LRRM 1065 (1988); Daniels Cadillac, 270 NLRB 466, 117 LRRM 1110 (1984). *But see* Hedison Mfg. Co., 260 NLRB 1037, 109 LRRM 1258 (1982) (violation to post and publish in newspaper request to employees who had given statements to identify themselves).

[379]American Linen Supply Co., 297 NLRB No. 18, 132 LRRM 1313 (1989); Arkansas Lighthouse for the Blind, 284 NLRB 1214, 126 LRRM 1060 (1987), *enforcement denied,* 851 F2d 180, 128 LRRM 2819 (CA 8, 1988); Fugazy Continental Corp., 265 NLRB 1301, 112 LRRM 1203 (1982), *enforced,* 725 F2d 1416, 115 LRRM 2571 (CA DC, 1984); International Mfg. Co., 238 NLRB 1361, 99 LRRM 1328 (1978). *See also* NLRB v. Monroe Tube Co., 545 F2d 1320, 94 LRRM 2020 (CA 2, 1976), *denying enforcement to* 220 NLRB 302, 90 LRRM 1526 (1975).

[380]Poly Ultra Plastics, 231 NLRB 787, 96 LRRM 1147 (1977) (employer did not initiate, sponsor, or assist in the circulation of a withdrawal petition but only gave assistance to the employees in its phrasing).

ing or encouraging withdrawal,[381] the Board's per se rule does not require that a violation of section 8(a)(1) be found.

d. Suits and Threats of Suits Against Employees. The Board applies the general rule that "the filing of a civil suit, as opposed to the threat to file a civil suit, does not constitute an unfair labor practice."[382] Applying this rule, the Board has held that the threat to file a lawsuit against employees engaged in protected activity is interference or restraint prohibited by section 8(a)(1).[383] The Board has also held that the filing of a civil suit in bad faith—for the purpose, for example, of retaliating against those who exercise statutory rights, is prohibited.[384] In *Bill Johnson's Restaurants v. NLRB*,[385] the Supreme Court affirmed part of the Board's rationale: the filing in bad faith of a nonmeritorious state law civil action is an unfair labor practice. In such instances, upon its determination that the employer's suit also lacks a reasonable basis, the Board may direct the employer to cease the violation, effectively halting prosecution of the state court action, and to reimburse the employees for the costs of their defense. However, the Court rejected the position of the Board that the prosecution of a meritorious state law action violates the Act if motivated by animus toward the exercise of statutory rights. If meritorious, the Court held, such actions cannot violate the Act regardless of the employer's motivation.[386]

---

[381]Ace Hardware Corp., 271 NLRB 1174, 117 NLRB 1096 (1984). *But see* Cordin Transp., 296 NLRB No. 34, 132 LRRM 1128 (1989) (solicitation or encouragement of withdrawal); Hancock Fabrics, 294 NLRB No. 4, 131 LRRM 1306 (1989), *enforced*, 902 F2d 28, 134 LRRM 2064 (CA 4, 1990) (same); Rose Printing Co., 289 NLRB 252, 131 LRRM 1420 (1988) (same).

[382]S.E. Nichols Marcy Corp., *supra* note 376, at 75.

[383]United Aircraft Corp., 192 NLRB 382, 77 LRRM 1785 (1971), *enforced in part*, 534 F2d 422, 90 LRRM 2272 (CA 2, 1975), *cert. denied*, 429 US 825, 92 LRRM 2501 (1976); Frank Visceglia, 203 NLRB 265, 83 LRRM 1066 (1973), *enforcement denied*, 498 F2d 43, 86 LRRM 2541 (CA 3, 1974); Clyde Taylor Co., 127 NLRB 103, 45 LRRM 1514 (1960). The Board's reasoning is that it "should accommodate its enforcement of the Act to the right of all persons to litigate their claims in court rather than condemn the exercise of such right as an unfair labor practice." Clyde Taylor Co., *id.* at 109.

[384]Power Sys., 239 NLRB 445, 99 LRRM 1652 (1978), *enforcement denied*, 601 F2d 936, 101 LRRM 2978 (CA 7, 1979); George A. Angle, 242 NLRB 744, 101 LRRM 1209 (1979), *enforced*, 683 F2d 1296, 111 LRRM 2191 (CA 10, 1982); United Credit Bureau of Am., 242 NLRB 921, 101 LRRM 1277 (1979), *enforced*, 643 F2d 1017, 106 LRRM 2751 (CA 4, 1981), *cert. denied*, 454 US 994, 108 LRRM 2823 (1981); *see also* Food & Commercial Workers Local 227 (Kroger Co.), 247 NLRB 195, 103 LRRM 1140 (1980).

[385]461 US 731, 113 LRRM 2647 (1983).

[386]*See* Sure Tan v. NLRB, 467 US 883, 116 LRRM 2857 (1984) (violation to report undocumented alien employees to Immigration Service). *But see* Dahl Fish Co., 279 NLRB 1084, 123 LRRM 1322 (1986), *enforced*, 813 F2d 1254, 125 LRRM 3063 (CA DC, 1987).

III. OTHER CONCERTED ACTIVITY

Protected concerted activity under the Act is usually associated with union activity. But section 7 broadly protects "concerted" activity, not merely union activity. Thus, concerted activity that is not specifically union oriented may also be protected by section 7. Such conduct is the principal subject of this part of the chapter. Additionally, this part covers certain other forms of concerted employee activity which, though union oriented, may not be directly related to organizational activity.

A. Protected Concerted Activity: In General

1. Individual vs. Concerted Activity: The *City Disposal* Rule. Under the Act, employee concerted activities fall into three categories—those prohibited by section 8, those protected by section 7, and those that are neither prohibited nor protected—often referred to as unprotected activities. Protected concerted activities are those pursued by employees in a peaceful manner in the exercise of their section 7 rights. These include certain peaceful economic strikes, sympathy strikes,[387] and other conduct such as dissident activity in resistance or opposition to the union's leadership.[388] Many other examples of protected conduct will be discussed below. Unprotected concerted activities may include activities that are unlawful, violent, in breach of contract, or indefensibly disloyal.[389]

To be protected under section 7, employee activity must be both "concerted" in nature and pursued either for union-related purposes aimed at collective bargaining or for other "mutual aid and protection." These statutory prerequisites have been

---

[387]Russell Sportswear Corp., 197 NLRB 1116, 80 LRRM 1495 (1972), *enforcement denied sub nom.* S.W. Noggle Co. v. NLRB, 478 F2d 1144, 83 LRRM 2225 (CA 8, 1973) (sympathy strike to protest employer's unfair labor practice at another plant); General Tire & Rubber Co., 190 NLRB 227, 77 LRRM 1215 (1971), *enforced*, 451 F2d 257, 78 LRRM 2836 (CA 1, 1971) (refusal of nonunit employee to cross picket line and work during strike).

[388]Red Cab, 194 NLRB 279, 78 LRRM 1699 (1971).

[389]*See* NLRB v. Electrical Workers Local 1229 (Jefferson Standard Broadcasting Co.), 346 US 464, 33 LRRM 2183 (1953) (disloyalty); Southern S.S. Co. v. NLRB, 316 US 31, 10 LRRM 544 (1942) (unlawful activity); NLRB v. Fansteel Metallurgical Corp., 306 US 240, 4 LRRM 515 (1939) (violence); NLRB v. Sands Mfg. Co., 306 US 332, 4 LRRM 530 (1939) (breach of contract); *see* Chapter 7, "Discrimination in Employment," for detailed treatment of employment discrimination relating to union activity. *See also* Gregory, *Unprotected Activity and the NLRA*, 39 VA. L. REV. 421 (1953); Note, *Unprotected Activity Under the National Labor Relations Act*, 3 UTAH L. REV. 358 (1953).

broadly construed by the Board and the courts.[390] Thus, the concert requirement of section 7 has not been literally construed to provide protection solely to employee activity involving group action directly. For example, an individual protagonist will be deemed to have engaged in "concerted activities" if a group of employees designates that individual to act on their behalf.[391] In determining whether activity by a single employee is concerted, the Board will look to the purpose and effect of the employee's actions. Applying the rule of *Interboro Contractors*,[392] the Board has repeatedly ruled that individual activity involving attempts to enforce the provisions of an existing collective bargaining agreement is concerted activity. Individual action taken to implement a collective bargaining agreement is "but an extension of the concerted activity that gave rise to the Agreement."[393] Such activity is deemed concerted, regardless of whether the employee's understanding of the contract is correct.[394]

In *NLRB v. City Disposal Systems*,[395] the Supreme Court endorsed the Board's *Interboro* rule that action by an individual to enforce a provision of an existing collective bargaining agreement is concerted activity and protected by section 7. In *City Disposal*, an employee was discharged when he refused to drive a truck that he believed to be unsafe because of faulty brakes. The collective bargaining agreement provided that the employer could not require employees to operate any vehicle that was not in safe operating condition. The Supreme Court, agreeing with the Board, held that an employee's invocation of a right rooted in the collective bargaining agreement is an integral part of the

---

[390]*See* NLRB v. Washington Aluminum Co., 370 US 9, 50 LRRM 2235 (1962), and discussion at notes 439–441 *infra*. For a treatment of the historical development of the concept of concerted activity, *see* Note, Cox, *The Right to Engage in Concerted Activities*, 26 IND. L.J. 319 (1951); Comment, *Constructive Concerted Activity and Individual Rights: The Northern Metal-Interboro Split*, 121 U. PA. L. REV. 152 (1972); *The Requirement of "Concerted" Action Under the NLRA*, 53 COLUM. L. REV. 514 (1953).

[391]*See* Fotomat Corp., 207 NLRB 461, 463, 84 LRRM 1487 (1973), *enforced*, 497 F2d 901, 87 LRRM 2256 (CA 6, 1974); Pacific Electricord Co., 153 NLRB 521, 59 LRRM 1507 (1965), *enforced*, 361 F2d 310, 63 LRRM 2064 (CA 9, 1966).

[392]Interboro Contractors, 157 NLRB 1295, 61 LRRM 1537 (1966) *enforced*, 388 F2d 495, 67 LRRM 2083 (CA 2, 1967); *see also* G.W. Wilson, 240 NLRB 333, 100 LRRM 1276 (1979); Alleluia Cushion Co., 221 NLRB 999, 91 LRRM 1131 (1975); Roadway Express, 217 NLRB 278, 88 LRRM 1503 (1975), *enforced per curiam*, 532 F2d 751, 91 LRRM 2239 (CA 4, 1976); B&M Excavating, 155 NLRB 1152, 60 LRRM 1466 (1965); Bunney Bros. Constr. Co., 139 NLRB 1516, 51 LRRM 1532 (1962).

[393]Bunney Bros. Constr. Co., *supra* note 392.

[394]Interboro Contractors, *supra* note 392.

[395]465 US 822, 115 LRRM 3193 (1984).

collective bargaining process and is therefore a "concerted" activity, even though the individual employee may not have cited the collective bargaining agreement or stated that he or she was acting on behalf of himself or herself as well as other employees. Since the Court's decision in *City Disposal*, the Board has held that an employee may forfeit the protections of the Act by asserting a contract right if by so asserting the right the employee's actions amount to insubordination.[396] Nonetheless, a minor infraction will not necessarily remove the protection of the Act.[397]

2. Individual vs. Concerted Activity: *Meyers Industries*. Until 1975, the Board confined the *Interboro* analysis essentially to situations where there was a collective bargaining agreement in existence. In that setting, an individual employee's action to enforce the agreement was viewed as merely an extension of the initial concerted activity that had culminated in the collective bargaining agreement. In 1975, however, the Board extended the *Interboro* rule to situations where there was no collective bargaining agreement in effect and where the employee making the protest was not represented by a collective bargaining agent.

In *Alleluia Cushion Co.*,[398] a nonunion employer discharged an employee for writing a letter to the California Occupational Safety and Health Administration complaining about alleged safety problems. The Board reversed its ALJ and held that the employee's action had been concerted. While it conceded that the employee had acted alone and in the "absence of any outward manifestation of support for his efforts" by his fellow employees, the Board said that he was nonetheless engaged in protected concerted activity. The Board reasoned that "consent and concert of action emanates from the mere assertion" of statutory rights declared in California's occupational safety and health laws and that, "in the absence of any evidence that fellow employees disavow such representation," there was an "implied consent."[399] Such activity was therefore deemed concerted.

---

[396]Carolina Freight Carriers Corp., 295 NLRB No. 124, 131 LRRM 1762 (1989) (employer lawfully discharged employee who, insisting on contractual entitlement to 6 hours' pay, persistently challenged supervisor's direct order to clock out).

[397]Great Dane Trailers Ind., 293 NLRB 384, 131 LRRM 1789 (1989) (employer violated Act in suspending employee for using obscene language in response to supervisor's refusal to provide assistance even though employer had disciplined its employees in the past for using obscene language towards foremen).

[398]221 NLRB 999, 91 LRRM 1131 (1975).

[399]*Id.*, 91 LRRM at 1133.

The Board applied the rationale of *Alleluia Cushion Co.* to other situations where, in the absence of a collective bargaining agreement, individual employees have resorted to administrative agencies or complained to their employer about working conditions. Thus, in *Triangle Tool & Engineering Co.*,[400] the Board found a section 8(a)(1) violation where an employee had been disciplined for making a complaint to the federal Wage and Hour Division regarding a claimed overtime payment. The concert requirement of section 7 was held to be satisfied even though the employee had acted alone, with no labor agreement in effect.[401]

While *Alleluia Cushion Co.* was not reviewed directly by a court of appeals, the Board's extension of the *Interboro* rule to nonunion and noncollective bargaining situations was rejected in other cases by the Fourth, Fifth, Eighth, and Ninth circuits.[402]

In 1984, as the *City Disposal* case awaited decision in the Supreme Court, the Board overruled *Alleluia Cushion*. In *Meyers Industries (Meyers I)*,[403] the Board considered the discharge of a truck driver who had complained to his employer about safety defects in his truck, had complained to a state transportation

[400]226 NLRB 1354, 94 LRRM 1108 (1976).

[401]The rationale of *Alleluia Cushion Co.* was also applied in Hitchiner Mfg. Co., 238 NLRB 1253, 99 LRRM 1645 (1978) (employee letter to employer complaining about supervisor's abusive conduct); Bighorn Beverage, 236 NLRB 736, 98 LRRM 1396 (1978), *vacated in pertinent part*, 614 F2d 1238, 103 LRRM 3008, 3011 (CA 9, 1980) (complaint made about safety conditions at state agency); Air Surrey Co., 229 NLRB 1064, 95 LRRM 1212 (1977), *enforcement denied*, 601 F2d 256, 102 LRRM 2599 (CA 6, 1979) (employee inquiry at employer's bank to determine whether employer had sufficient funds to meet upcoming payroll); Dawson Cabinet Co., 228 NLRB 290, 96 LRRM 1373, *enforcement denied*, 566 F2d 1079, 97 LRRM 2075 (CA 8, 1977) (employee seeking to vindicate rights under Title VII of the Civil Rights Act of 1964 refused to work on machine unless paid the same rate as the men who were doing same work); Ambulance Serv. of New Bedford, 229 NLRB 106, 95 LRRM 1239 (1977) (employee filed criminal charges against his employer because of "bouncing" paychecks); P&L Cedar Prods., 224 NLRB 244, 93 LRRM 1341 (1976) (employee complained to employer of alleged safety violations).

[402]Krispy Kreme Doughnut Corp. v. NLRB, 635 F2d 304, 105 LRRM 3407 (CA 4, 1980); NLRB v. Bighorn Beverage, *supra* note 401; NLRB v. Buddie Supermarkets, 481 F2d 714, 83 LRRM 2625 (CA 5, 1979); NLRB v. Dawson Cabinet Co., *supra* note 401. The First Circuit distinguished *Alleluia Cushion Co.* in NLRB v. Wilson Freight Co., 604 F2d 712, 102 LRRM 2269 (CA 1, 1979), *cert. denied*, 445 US 962, 103 LRRM 3082 (1980), on the ground that the case before it involved a union steward filing various unauthorized complaints with government agencies against the employer in defiance of contract limitations on his powers. The Sixth Circuit refused to rely on the *Alleluia Cushion* doctrine in Jim Causley Pontiac v. NLRB, 620 F2d 122, 104 LRRM 2190 (CA 6, 1980), enforcing the Board's order instead with other rationales.

[403]268 NLRB 493, 115 LRRM 1025 (1984), *rev'd sub nom.* Prill v. NLRB, 755 F2d 941, 118 LRRM 2649 (CA DC), *cert. denied*, 474 US 971, 120 LRRM 3392 (1985), *decision on remand sub nom.* Meyers Indus., 281 NLRB 882, 123 LRRM 1137 (1986), *aff'd*, 835 F2d 1481, 127 LRRM 2415 (CA DC, 1987), *cert. denied*, 487 US 1205, 128 LRRM 2664 (1988).

agency about the employer's failure to repair the alleged defects, and, following an accident, had refused to drive the truck thereby defying a direct order from the employer. The Board concluded that the driver's conduct had not been concerted because all of his actions had been in pursuit of personal interests and he had neither acted nor claimed or intended to act on behalf of other employees. Further, the Board concluded, the statutory language required that there be some such concert in fact and the *Alleluia Cushion* rationale imputing such concert to the acts of solitary employees was not a permissible reading of the statute. Accordingly, *Alleluia Cushion* was expressly overruled. The Board distinguished *Interboro*, and implicitly *City Disposal*, on the ground that those cases involved collective bargaining agreements.[404]

The Court of Appeals for the District of Columbia Circuit set aside the Board's order because the Board had mistakenly assumed that its definition of "concerted activity" was mandated by section 7.[405] In the court's view, there were other reasonable definitions of that term and the Board was empowered to choose among them. The court remanded so that the Board could reexamine its definition of concerted activity in light of those alternatives.

On remand, the Board in *Meyers II* reaffirmed its initial ruling that individual employees must act "with or on the authority of" their fellow workers and not solely on their own behalf in order to engage in concerted activity.[406] The Board asserted that the Supreme Court's *City Disposal* decision was consistent with its definition of concerted activity in *Meyers I* and held that a nonunion employee's decision to assert a statutory right is not an extension of collective action in the sense described in *City Disposal*.[407] According to the Board, the Court's decision in *City Disposal* indicated that concerted activity can include some, but not all, individual activity by employees, that an essential component of concerted activity is its collective nature, and that the definition of concerted activity is separate from the concept of "mutual aid and protection."[408]

---

[404]*Id.*, 115 LRRM at 1028.
[405]Prill v. NLRB, *supra* note 403.
[406]*Supra* note 403.
[407]123 LRRM at 1143.
[408]*Id.*

The Board reiterated that its definition of concerted activity encompasses the lone employee who is acting for or on behalf of other workers, who has discussed the matter with his or her fellow workers, or who is acting alone to initiate group action such as bringing group complaints to the attention of management.[409] The Board emphasized that "in construing Section 7, we are not holding that employee contract rights are more appropriate subjects for joint employee action than are rights granted by Federal and state legislation concerning such matters as employee safety."[410] However, the Board stated that in *Meyers*, the link between group activity and the individual employees asserting their rights under a state safety law was so attenuated that the individual employee's action simply could not be considered concerted for purposes of section 7. In sum, the Board held that the "invocation of employee contract rights is a continuation of an ongoing process of employee concerted activity, whereas employee invocation of statutory rights is not."[411]

On review, the Court of Appeals for the District of Columbia Circuit held that the Board adequately responded to the court's objections to *Meyers I* and found that in *Meyers II* the Board "has adopted a reasonable—but by no means the only reasonable—interpretation of Section 7."[412]

Since *Meyers I*, activities undertaken by individual employees on their own behalf generally have not been found to be "concerted" activity. For example, in *Goodyear Tire & Rubber Co.*,[413] an employee's refusal to perform an assignment based on his belief that the equipment was unsafe was held not to be protected concerted activity where none of the other employees had complained.[414]

---

[409]*Id.* at 1142.

[410]*Id.* at 1143.

[411]*Id.*

[412]Prill v. NLRB, 835 F2d 1481, 127 LRRM 2415 (CA DC, 1987), *aff'g sub nom.* Meyers Indus., 281 NLRB 882, 123 LRRM 1137 (1986). *See also* Ewing v. NLRB (III), 861 F2d 353, 129 LRRM 2853 (CA 2), *aff'g sub nom.* Herbert F. Darling, Inc., 287 NLRB 1356, 127 LRRM 1241 (1988) (*Meyers* rule represents reasonable interpretation of NLRA).

[413]269 NLRB 881, 115 LRRM 1333 (1984).

[414]*See also* Adelphi Inst., 287 NLRB 1073, 127 LRRM 1161 (1988) (employee placed on probation who asked co-worker if co-worker had ever been placed on probation was not engaged in concerted activity because employee did not seek to initiate, induce, or prepare for group action); Herbert F. Darling, Inc., 267 NLRB 476, 114 LRRM 1048 (1983), (I) *rev'd sub nom.* Ewing v. NLRB, 732 F2d 1117, 116 LRRM 2050 (CA 2, 1984), (II), *decision on remand*, 273 NLRB 346, 118 LRRM 1060 (1984), *rev'd* (Ewing II), 768 F2d 51, 119 LRRM 3273 (CA 2, 1985), *decision on remand*, 287 NLRB 1356, 127 LRRM 1241,

The Board has applied the "logical outgrowth" doctrine, however. In *Salisbury Hotel*,[415] the Board held that an employee who called the Department of Labor regarding her employer's lunch-hour policy without explicitly consulting her co-workers was engaged in concerted activity because the call was a continuation of efforts initiated by a group of employees to protest the new lunch-hour policy. The Board explained that "[a]lthough there is no evidence that respondent's employees agreed to act together to change the respondent's new lunch hour policy, they did at least tacitly agree that they had a grievance and that they should take it up with management."[416]

Nor is it necessary for the other employees to be in agreement with the protesting employee for the action to be considered concerted. For example, in *NLRB v. Jasper Seating Co.*,[417] two

---

affirmed (Ewing III), 861 F2d 353, 129 LRRM 2853 (CA 2, 1988) (no concerted activity where employee discharged on mistaken belief that employee filed OSHA charge); Barmet of Ind., 284 NLRB 1024, 125 LRRM 1338 (1987) (two employees questioned during an OSHA investigation about use of safety equipment held not engaged in concerted activity despite presence of clause in collective bargaining agreement obligating employer to provide such equipment, where employees did not initiate investigation, were questioned individually, and acted neither on authority of each other nor of any other employees); Bearden & Co., 272 NLRB 931, 117 LRRM 1417 (1984) (employee not engaged in concerted activity when he filed individual unemployment compensation claim); ABF Freight Sys., 271 NLRB 35, 116 LRRM 1330 (1984) (employee who acted alone when he complained of tractor-trailer's safety and refused to drive it held not to be engaged in concerted activity); Central Ga. Elec. Membership Corp., 269 NLRB 635, 115 LRRM 1311 (1984) (filing of workers' compensation claim held not to be protected concerted activity). *But see* Wheeling-Pittsburgh Steel Corp. v. NLRB, 821 F2d 342, 125 LRRM 2824 (CA 6, 1987), *enforcing* 277 NLRB 1388, 121 LRRM 1101 (1985) (employee who refused to operate crane with missing bolts and frayed cables held engaged in protected concerted activity under collective bargaining agreement with safety clause); Hoytuck Corp., 285 NLRB 904, 126 LRRM 1319 (1987) (employee who circulated petition complaining about supervisor's alleged harassment of workers and seeking his discharge was held engaged in protected concerted activity on ground that supervisor's conduct had impact on working conditions); Esco Elevators, 276 NLRB 1245, 120 LRRM 1214 (1985), *enforced*, 794 F2d 1078, 122 LRRM 3178 (CA 5, 1986) (safety complaint by individual employee deemed protected concerted activity because employee was local union president and inspected job site for safety conditions as part of his job as union official); NLRB v. McEver Eng'g, 784 F2d 634, 121 LRRM 3125 (CA 5, 1986), *enforcing* 275 NLRB 921, 119 LRRM 1219 (1985) (seven employees who walked off job to protest unsafe working conditions were engaged in protected concerted activity since employees had acted together after discussing their common grievance); Churchill's Catering Corp. dba Churchill's Restaurant, 276 NLRB 775, 120 LRRM 1233 (1985) (employee who acted on his own in criticizing employer's allegedly discriminatory treatment of Hispanic employees held to have engaged in protected concerted activity since it was "engaged in with or on the authority of other employees").

[415]283 NLRB 685, 125 LRRM 1020 (1987).

[416]*Id.*, 125 LRRM at 1021–22. *See also* Jhirmack Enters., 283 NLRB 609, 125 LRRM 1010 (1987) (employee who relayed performance complaints of other employees to fellow worker to encourage him to take corrective action to preserve his job held protected under logical outgrowth doctrine as well as under actual concerted activity line of authority).

[417]857 F2d 419, 129 LRRM 2337 (CA 7, 1988), *enforcing* 285 NLRB 550, 127 LRRM 1119 (1987).

workers walked out in protest over the cold and drafty working condition created by having a door near their workplace left open. The other employees, however, had complained of the heat when the door was left shut. Despite the fact that none of the other employees agreed with the protesting employees' demand to have the door closed, the Seventh Circuit upheld the Board's determination that the protest was protected activity because it was directed toward a continuing dispute over working conditions.[418]

3. Employee Activity for "Other Mutual Aid or Protection." Concerted activity, to be protected, must satisfy the section 7 requirement that it be for the purpose of collective bargaining or for "other mutual aid or protection."[419] The Supreme Court in *Eastex, Inc. v. NLRB*[420] recognized that Congress intended in the "mutual aid and protection" clause to extend and broaden the ambit of protected employee activity beyond concerted activities associated with grievance settlement, collective bargaining, and self-organization. The reach of section 7 encompasses concerted activities of employees "in support of employees of employers other than their own."[421] It also extends to employee efforts "to improve terms and conditions of employment or

---

[418]*Id. See also* Rockwell Int'l Corp. v. NLRB, 814 F2d 1530, 125 LRRM 2132 (CA 11, 1987), *enforcing* 278 NLRB 55, 122 LRRM 1285 (1986) (lack of specific authorization held no bar to find protected concerted activity where employee voiced objections to management at employee meeting on grounds that she expressed concerns common to employees in attendance, co-workers were generally aware of her actions by their presence at meeting, and employer knew she spoke on their behalf).

[419]The words "concerted activities" in §7 are "limited in meaning by the words with which they are associated." Joanna Cotton Mills Co. v. NLRB, 176 F2d 749, 24 LRRM 2416 (CA 4, 1949). Thus, protection of concerted activities under §7 is "expressly limited" to activities pursued for the specific purposes stated therein. *Id.* at 752.

[420]437 US 556, 565, 98 LRRM 2717, 2720 (1978). *See* note 511 *infra* and accompanying text.

[421]*Id.* at 565, 98 LRRM at 2720 (citing Phelps Dodge Corp. v. NLRB, 313 US 177, 191-92, 8 LRRM 439 (1941)). *See, e.g.,* Yellow Cab, Inc., 210 NLRB 568, 569, 86 LRRM 1145 (1974) (right to distribute literature in support of another employer's employees); Service Employees, Washington State Council No. 18, Local 6 (Severn), 188 NLRB 957, 959, 76 LRRM 1467 (1971) (right to demonstrate in support of another employer's employees); General Elec. Co., 169 NLRB 1101, 67 LRRM 1326 (1968) (right to solicit funds for benefit of agricultural laborers employed elsewhere); Redwing Carriers, 137 NLRB 1545, 1546-47, 50 LRRM 1449 (1962), *enforced sub nom.* Teamsters Local 79 v. NLRB, 325 F2d 1011, 54 LRRM 2707 (CA DC, 1963), *cert. denied,* 377 US 905, 55 LRRM 3023 (1964) (right to honor picket line of another employer's employees); NLRB v. J.G. Boswell Co., 136 F2d 585, 595, 12 LRRM 776 (CA 9, 1943) (right to express sympathy for striking employees of another employer); NLRB v. Peter Cailler Kohler Swiss Chocolate Co., 130 F2d 503, 10 LRRM 852 (CA 2, 1942) (right to publish support for a cooperative association of dairy farmers that had called a milk strike); Fort Wayne Corrugated Paper Co. v. NLRB, 111 F2d 869, 874 (CA 7, 1940) (right to assist in organizing another employer's employees).

otherwise improve their lot as employees through channels outside the immediate employee-employer relationship."[422] Thus, protection is afforded employees when they seek to improve working conditions through "resort to administrative and judicial forums" and through "appeals to legislators to protect their interests as employees."[423]

Although the Court in *Eastex* indicated that "some concerted activity bears a less immediate relationship to employees' interests as employees than other such activity," and "at some point the relationship becomes so attentuated" that an activity cannot fairly be viewed as within the meaning of "mutual aid and protection," it emphasized that the task of delineating the boundaries of the "mutual aid and protection" clause was for the Board to perform in the first instance.[424]

In *Kaiser Engineers*,[425] the Board broadly construed the clause to protect a group of engineers who wrote a series of letters to several legislators in which they opposed any relaxation of immigration laws that would allow immigration into the United States of foreign-educated engineers. That position was contrary to that of their employer, who was heavily engaged in overseas engineering projects. When the employer learned of the letters, it constructively discharged the principal author. Although the employees' activity did not concern a matter over which their employer had any control and, indeed, was outside the confines

---

[422]437 US at 565, 98 LRRM at 2720 (1978). The employee activity that the employer sought to prohibit was the distribution of a union newsletter on company property in nonworking areas during nonworking time. The newsletter, among other things, urged employees to oppose inclusion of a right-to-work provision in the state constitution and criticized a presidential veto of an increase in the federal minimum wage.

[423]*Id. See, e.g.*, Kaiser Eng'rs v. NLRB, 538 F2d 1379, 92 LRRM 3153 (CA 9, 1976), *enforcing* 213 NLRB 752, 87 LRRM 1447 (1975); Altex Ready Mixed Concrete Corp. v. NLRB, 542 F2d 295, 297, 93 LRRM 2940 (CA 5), *enforcing* 223 NLRB 696, 91 LRRM 1591 (1976); Socony Mobil Oil Co., 153 NLRB 1244, 59 LRRM 1619 (1965), *enforced*, 357 F2d 662 (CA 2, 1966); Walls Mfg. Co., 137 NLRB 1317, 50 LRRM 1376 (1962), *enforced*, 321 F2d 753, 53 LRRM 2428 (CA DC), *cert. denied*, 375 US 923, 54 LRRM 2576 (1963).

[424]437 US at 567, 98 LRRM at 2721. The "mutual aid and protection" clause has also been broadly construed by the Board, but with only limited approval by the courts, to encompass certain employee protests over changes in supervisory personnel. Puerto Rico Food Prods. Corp. v. NLRB, 619 F2d 153, 104 LRRM 2304 (CA 1, 1980); Bide-A-Wee Home Ass'n, 248 NLRB 853, 104 LRRM 1036 (1980); Abilities & Goodwill, Inc. v. NLRB, 612 F2d 6, 103 LRRM 2029 (CA 1, 1979); NLRB v. Okla-Inn, 488 F2d 498, 503, 84 LRRM 2585 (CA 10, 1973); American Art Clay Co. v. NLRB, 328 F2d 88, 55 LRRM 2502 (CA 7, 1964); Dobbs Houses, Inc. v. NLRB, 325 F2d 531, 538-39, 54 LRRM 2726 (CA 5, 1963); NLRB v. Guernsey-Muskingum Elec. Coop., 285 F2d 8, 47 LRRM 2260 (CA 6, 1960); NLRB v. Phoenix Mut. Life Ins. Co., 167 F2d 983, 22 LRRM 2089 (CA 7, 1948), *cert. denied*, 335 US 845, 22 LRRM 2590 (1948).

[425]*Supra* note 423.

of the employment relationship, the Board held, with approval of the Ninth Circuit, that it was protected concerted activity.[426]

4. Limits on Protection of Concerted Activity. *a. Employer Property and Business Interests.* Enforcement of section 7 requires the balancing of an employee's right to engage in concerted activities against the employer's right to maintain order and control in the plant. The Board in one case held that an employee who gave a pro-union speech at the plant with company permission could not be discharged for refusing to lower his voice when ordered to do so several times by his supervisor, since the employee's conduct did not disturb plant business and operations.[427] Similarly, an employer hospital violated the Act by denying union employees the use of the workplace cafeteria for election of a negotiating team after allowing its use for comparable purposes by nonrepresented employees.[428] The employer's right to maintain discipline in the plant, however, was adjudged the overriding consideration in a Board decision upholding the employer's right to discharge 22 employees who disrupted a meeting that had been planned by the employer for presentation of antiunion views on the eve of an election.[429]

---

[426]In enforcing the Board's order, the Ninth Circuit concluded that "the concerted activity of employees, lobbying legislators regarding changes in national policy which affect their job security, can be action taken for 'mutual aid or protection' within the meaning of §7." *Id.* at 1385.

[427]Farah Mfg. Co., 202 NLRB 666, 82 LRRM 1623 (1973). *See* F.W. Woolworth Co., 251 NLRB 1111, 105 LRRM 1374 (1980), *enforced*, 655 F2d 151, 107 LRRM 3261 (CA 8, 1981), *cert. denied*, 455 US 989, 109 LRRM 2779 (1982) (employee asking question at captive-audience meeting before election held protected notwithstanding company policy against such questions); AMC Air Conditioning Co., 232 NLRB 283, 97 LRRM 1146 (1977) (discharge of employee for creating commotion in plant held unlawful where commotion was generated by employer's suppression of employee's speech during lunch period); Bob Henry Dodge, Inc., 203 NLRB 78, 83 LRRM 1077 (1973) (employee's defiance in grievance procedure protected since his words did not go beyond permissible bounds of free speech and open discussion contemplated by the Act); Prescott Indus. Prods. Co., 205 NLRB 51, 83 LRRM 1500 (1973), *enforcement denied*, 500 F2d 6, 86 LRRM 2963 (CA 8, 1974) (employee insistence in questioning his employer following the latter's anti-union "24-hour" speech held protected by Board, but court of appeals disagreed, stating that a deliberate defiance of the employer in front of assembled employees is not protected).

[428]Methodist Hosp. of Gary, 263 NLRB 411, 111 LRRM 1150 (1982), *enforced*, 733 F2d 43, 116 LRRM 2327 (CA 7, 1984); *see also* St. Joseph Medical Center, 276 NLRB 456, 120 LRRM 1116 (1985) (nondisruptive meetings in operating room lounge).

[429]J.P. Stevens & Co., 219 NLRB 850, 89 LRRM 1814 (1975), *enforced*, 547 F2d 792, 93 LRRM 2262 (CA 4, 1976). *See* Clark Equip. Co., 250 NLRB 1333, 105 LRRM 1071 (1980) (5-day suspension upheld for union adherent who called employer's official a "bastard" at meeting at which official attempted to persuade employees they did not need the union). *But see* Howell Metal Co., 243 NLRB 1136, 102 LRRM 1031 (1979) (employee's profanity at meeting was merely "animal exuberance" of the moment and not a part of a scheme to disrupt meeting; employee's conduct held protected).

The difficulty in balancing employer and employee rights in this area is illustrated by employee protests that take the form of sit-in demonstrations conducted after the end of the employees' shift. In *Overhead Door Corp.*,[430] the Board found a violation in the employer's discharge of employees who engaged in a sit-in after the end of their shift. A different result, however, was reached in *Peck, Inc.*,[431] where the Board upheld the discharge of employees for engaging in a sit-in and preventing the employer from closing the plant. The immediacy of the situation that the employees were protesting in *Overhead Door*, in contrast to the absence of "any necessary immediacy of action" in the protestor's conduct in *Peck*, was said to be the distinguishing factor.[432]

b. Exclusive Union Representation. In *Emporium Capwell*,[433] the Supreme Court ruled that concerted activities by union-represented employees may be denied the protection of section 7, to which they might otherwise be entitled, where the activity is in derogation of the union's statutory role as exclusive representative of all employees in the bargaining unit.

The employees involved had claimed that their department-store employer was discriminating against them by failing to give qualified minority employees assignments and promotions. Spurning the union's invocation of the grievance-arbitration procedure, two employees sought to circumvent their elected bargaining representative and deal directly with the employer. In support of their demand, they picketed the employer's premises and distributed handbills urging a consumer boycott. Reversing the lower court and affirming the Board, the Supreme Court upheld the ensuing discharges of the two, concluding that the principle of majority rule and exclusivity expressed in section 9(a) of the Act mandated that minority employees not bypass their collective bargaining agent. The Court reasoned that to permit subgroups within the bargaining unit to enforce their conflicting demands for direct dealings would be

---

[430] 220 NLRB 431, 90 LRRM 1257 (1975), *enforcement denied in part*, 540 F2d 878, 93 LRRM 2147 (CA 7, 1976). *See* notes 520–523 *infra* and accompanying text.

[431] 226 NLRB 1174, 93 LRRM 1434 (1976). *See* notes 524–525 *infra* and accompanying text.

[432] *Id.*, 93 LRRM at 1435.

[433] Emporium Capwell Co. v. Western Addition Community Org., 420 US 50, 88 LRRM 2660 (1975), *rev'g* 485 F2d 917, 83 LRRM 2738 (CA DC, 1973), *rev'g sub nom.* The Emporium, 192 NLRB 173, 77 LRRM 1669 (1971).

counterproductive, for it would dissipate the union's collective strength for combating discrimination, pit one minority group against another, and create a situation where the "probability of strife and deadlock is high" and the "likelihood of making headway against discriminatory practices would be minimal."[434]

In *Dreis & Krump Manufacturing Co. v. NLRB*,[435] the Board and Seventh Circuit, distinguishing *Emporium Capwell*, held that the employer violated section 8(a)(3) when it discharged an employee who had distributed fliers derogatory of the employer's supervisors. Unlike the protesting employees in *Emporium Capwell*, the employee in *Dreis & Krump* had filed a grievance under the established grievance procedure and was pursuing it.[436] In contrast, the First Circuit in a later case applied the principles of *Emporium Capwell* to various employee complaints that had been raised in opposition to positions taken by the union itself. That court declared that such conduct, "being contrary to the principle of exclusive representation," would "not seem entitled to the protection of §7."[437]

B. Protected Concerted Activity: Specific Conduct

1. Work Stoppages. A primary strike is concerted, but may be protected or unprotected, depending upon the circumstances. Where the strike is protected, discipline or discharge of the strikers will usually violate section 8(a)(1). Conversely, where

---

[434] *Id.* at 68. For a discussion of *Emporium Capwell* and the relationship between national policy under §7 of the NLRA and Title VII of the Civil Rights Act of 1964, *see* Lopatka, *Protection Under the National Labor Relations Act and Title VII of the Civil Rights Act for Employees Who Protest Discrimination in Private Employment*, 50 N.Y.U. L. REV. 1179, 1187–95 (1975). *See generally* 1973-1974 *Annual Survey of Labor Relations Law*, 15 B.C. IND. & COM. L. REV. 1105, 1198-1203 (1974); 87 HARV. L. REV. 656 (1974); Meltzer, *The National Labor Relations Act and Racial Discrimination: The More Remedies, the Better?*, 42 U. CHI. L. REV. 1, 26-38 (1975); Note, *Racial Discrimination in Employment and the Remedy of Self-Help: An Unwarranted Addition*, 15 WM. & MARY L. REV. 615 (1974); Lynd, *The Right to Engage in Concerted Activity After Union Recognition: A Study of Legislative History*, 50 IND. L.J. 720 (1975); 25 DE PAUL L. REV. 179 (1976).

[435] 544 F2d 320, 93 LRRM 2739 (CA 7, 1976). *See* Chapter 19, "The Primary Strike," at note 167.

[436] Also distinguishing *Emporium Capwell*, the Sixth Circuit, in Richardson Paint Co. v. NLRB, 574 F2d 1195, 1205-1207, 98 LRRM 2951 (CA 5, 1978), agreed with the Board that an employee who merely circulated a petition during nonwork time concerning the layoff of fellow members of his work crew was protected, because nothing in the employee's activity "would undermine the Union's status as the bargaining representative or pose any serious threat to stable relations." And the Board majority in Armco Steel Corp., 232 NLRB 696, 96 LRRM 1325 (1977), distinguished *Emporium Capwell* on the ground that the employee circulating the petition was requesting that the employer and union renegotiate their agreement and was not seeking to bypass the union and bargain directly with the employer.

[437] NLRB v. Wilson Freight Co., 604 F2d 712, 725 n.17, 102 LRRM 2269, 2278 n.17 (CA 1, 1979).

the primary strike is not protected, discharging or disciplining the strikers ordinarily does not violate section 8(a)(1).[438]

In *NLRB v. Washington Aluminum Co.*,[439] the Supreme Court enforced a Board order reinstating with backpay seven employees discharged for walking off their jobs without permission when they claimed it was too cold to work in the shop. The Fourth Circuit had refused to enforce the Board's order[440] because the workers (who were unorganized) had left without affording the company an opportunity to avoid the work stoppage by presenting a specific demand to remedy the objectionable condition. Reversing, the Supreme Court saw the language of section 7 as "broad enough to protect concerted activities whether they take place before, after, or at the same time . . . a demand is made."[441]

While legally striking employees are entitled to enlist the support of the public for their cause, "they may not elicit that support by force, trickery or guile, nor may they deliberately inflict on the employer economic harm unnecessary to the legitimate concerted activities."[442] When strikers stray over these boundaries, they will be deemed to forfeit the Act's coverage of their otherwise protected activity.[443]

2. Honoring Picket Lines. In the absence of a contractual or other waiver, employees who refuse to cross another union's lawful picket line are generally engaging in protected activity and may not be discharged unless the discharge is "justified by legitimate business considerations of an overriding nature."[444]

---

[438]*See generally* Chapter 19, "The Primary Strike," at notes 110–164.

[439]370 US 9, 50 LRRM 2235 (1962).

[440]128 NLRB 643, 46 LRRM 1385 (1960), *enforcement denied*, 291 F2d 869, 48 LRRM 2558 (CA 4, 1961).

[441]370 US at 14. *See also* Vic Tanny Int'l v. NLRB, 622 F2d 237, 104 LRRM 2395 (CA 6, 1980) (unorganized employees who walked off job to present job-related grievances held protected). *But see* NLRB v. Marsden, 701 F2d 238, 112 LRRM 2945 (CA 2, 1983), *denying enforcement to* 259 NLRB 909, 109 LRRM 1047 (1982) (employees who left job site during rain without disclosing any complaint or demand not protected).

[442]Montefiore Hosp. v. NLRB, 621 F2d 510, 104 LRRM 2160, 2165 (CA 2, 1980) (citing NLRB v. Washington Aluminum Co., *supra* note 439); NLRB v. A. Lasaponara & Sons, 541 F2d 992, 998, 93 LRRM 2314 (CA 2, 1976), *cert. denied*, 430 US 914, 94 LRRM 2798 (1977).

[443]Montefiore Hosp. v. NLRB, 104 LRRM at 2166 (deceptive appeals to public by picketing doctors to turn persons away from using clinic operated by struck employer held unprotected). *See also* Can-Tex Indus. v. NLRB, 683 F2d 1183, 110 LRRM 3196 (CA 8, 1982), *denying enforcement in part to* 256 NLRB 863, 107 LRRM 1422 (1981) (employees who turned off equipment vital to production of plant for purpose of halting production not protected). For general treatment of unprotected concerted activity, *see infra* at notes 519–553.

[444]Cooper Thermometer, 154 NLRB 502, 59 LRRM 1767 (1965). *See also* Business Servs. by Manpower, 272 NLRB 827, 117 LRRM 1345 (1984), *enforcement denied*, 784 F2d

The right to cross picket lines may be waived by the employee's collective bargaining representative by negotiation of no-strike provisions or picket line clauses. But such waivers must be expressed in "clear and unmistakable language."[445]

3. Filing or Processing of Grievances. The discharge or discipline of employees for filing or processing grievances in concert, whether pursuant to a formal contractual grievance procedure or informally in the absence of such a procedure, is generally held to be a violation of section 8(a)(1).[446]

Assembling employees to present grievances,[447] filing of grievances by employees in a manner that bypasses the union,[448] grieving under a collective bargaining agreement by probationary employees,[449] and filing of numerous grievances[450] have all been viewed by the Board as concerted activity protected by section 7.[451]

442, 121 LRRM 2827 (CA 2, 1986) (court rejected determination by Board that employees of temporary services employer were protected in refusing to cross picket line at location of temporary employment and in failing to report their refusal to their employer promptly). *See generally* Chapter 19, "The Primary Strike," at notes 168–184.

[445]Gary-Hobart Water Co., 210 NLRB 742, 86 LRRM 1210 (1974), *enforced*, 511 F2d 284, 88 LRRM 2830 (CA 7), *cert. denied*, 423 US 925, 90 LRRM 2921 (1975). In Indianapolis Power & Light Co., 273 NLRB 1715, 118 LRRM 1201 (1985), *remanded sub nom.* Electrical Workers (IBEW) Local 1395 v. NLRB, 797 F2d 1027, 122 LRRM 3265 (CA DC, 1986) the Board held that a broad no-strike clause prohibits sympathy strikes, unless the contract or extrinsic evidence demonstrates that the parties intended to allow sympathy strikes. The Court of Appeals for the District of Columbia Circuit agreed with this approach but remanded for the Board to consider extrinsic evidence. On remand, the Board clarified its earlier decision to emphasize that "careful consideration be accorded extrinsic evidence" and to caution that the earlier decision "must not be applied as if it established an irrebutable presumption that a broad no-strike clause bars sympathy strikes." Upon finding that the negotiating history showed an "agreement to disagree," the Board concluded that there was no waiver of the right to honor stranger picket lines. Indianapolis Power & Light Co., 291 NLRB 1039, 130 LRRM 1001 (1988). *Accord* Electrical Workers (IBEW) Local 803 v. NLRB (Metropolitan Edison Co.), 826 F2d 1283, 126 LRRM 2065 (CA 2, 1987), *enforcing* 279 NLRB 313, 122 LRRM 1069 (1986). *See generally* Chapter 19, "The Primary Strike."

[446]Columbia Univ., 236 NLRB 793, 98 LRRM 1353 (1978); John Sexton & Co., 217 NLRB 80, 88 LRRM 1502 (1975); Ernst Steel Corp., 212 NLRB 78, 87 LRRM 1508 (1974); Southwestern Bell Tel. Co., 212 NLRB 43, 87 LRRM 1446 (1974).

[447]Shell Oil Co. v. NLRB, 561 F2d 1196, 96 LRRM 2789 (CA 5, 1977), *enforcing* 226 NLRB 1193, 93 LRRM 1512 (1976).

[448]Crown Wrecking Co., 222 NLRB 958, 91 LRRM 1319 (1976).

[449]Seven-Up Bottling Co. of Detroit, 223 NLRB 911, 92 LRRM 1001 (1976); R&S Steel Corp., 222 NLRB 69, 91 LRRM 1137 (1976).

[450]Ad Art, Inc., 238 NLRB 1124, 99 LRRM 1626 (1978), *enforced*, 645 F2d 669, 106 LRRM 2010 (CA 9, 1980).

[451]For discussion of other protected activity arising out of the presentation of grievances, see Caterpillar Tractor Co. v. NLRB, 638 F2d 140, 106 LRRM 2853 (CA 9, 1981), *enforcing* 242 NLRB 523, 101 LRRM 1207 (1979); High Performance Tube, 251 NLRB 1362, 105 LRRM 1145 (1980); Greyhound Taxi Co., 234 NLRB 865, 97 LRRM 1385 (1978); May Dep't Stores Co. v. NLRB, 555 F2d 1338, 95 LRRM 2657 (CA 6, 1977), *enforcing* 220 NLRB 1096, 90 LRRM 1444 (1975); Clara Barton Terrace Convalescent Center, 225 NLRB 1028, 92 LRRM 1621 (1976).

The Board has also held that union stewards and employees, when filing and processing grievances, are protected by the Act even if they "'exceed the bounds of contract language, unless the excess is extraordinary, obnoxious, wholly unjustified, and departs from the res gestae of the grievance procedure.'"[452] While there is a line beyond which a grievant or a union steward may not go with impunity in pursuit of protected activities, the protections of the Act are not lost merely because their concerted activities "'exceed the bounds of lawful conduct in a moment of animal exuberance or in a manner not motivated by improper motives. . . .'"[453]

4. Employee Insistence on Union Representation: The *Weingarten* Rule. In its 1975 companion decisions in *NLRB v. Weingarten, Inc.*,[454] and *Ladies' Garment Workers v. Quality Manufacturing Co.*,[455] the Supreme Court, in agreement with the Board, ruled that employee insistence upon union representation at an employer's investigatory interview, which the employee reasonably believes might result in disciplinary action, is protected concerted activity. Accordingly, the discipline or discharge of an employee for refusal to cooperate in such an investigatory interview without union representation is a violation of section 8(a)(1).[456]

In its discussion of the source, "contours," and "limits" of the *Weingarten* rule, the Supreme Court explained that (1) the right to union representation "inheres in §7's guarantee of the right of employees to act in concert for mutual aid and protection";[457] (2) the right arises "only in situations where the employee re-

---

[452]Union Fork & Hoe Co., 241 NLRB 907, 101 LRRM 1014, 1015 (1979) (the steward had walked out with a grievant's time sheet during a discussion of the grievance with a supervisor) (quoting Clara Barton Terrace Convalescent Center, *supra* note 451).

[453]Union Fork & Hoe Co., *supra* note 452, at 1015 (quoting Prescott Indus. Prods. Co., 205 NLRB 51, 51-52, 83 LRRM 1500 (1973)). *See* Acme-Arsena Co. v. NLRB, 804 F2d 359, 123 LRRM 2995 (CA 6, 1986), *enforcing* 276 NLRB 1291, 120 LRRM 1156 (1985) (steward's threat made during grievance discussion to "drop-a-dime," believed by employer to be threat to call IRS, is protected); Illinois Bell Tel. Co., 259 NLRB 1240, 109 LRRM 1111 (1982) (employee did not lose the Act's protection even though she uttered obscenity during grievance meeting); U.S. Postal Serv., 250 NLRB 1195, 105 LRRM 1014 (1980).

[454]420 US 251, 88 LRRM 2689 (1975).

[455]420 US 276, 88 LRRM 2698 (1975).

[456]*See generally* Note, *Union Pressure in Disciplinary Meetings*, 41 U. CHI. L. REV. 329 (1974); 12 HOUS. L. REV. 1179 (1975); 7 U. TOL. L. REV. 298 (1976); Note, 6 SETON HALL L. REV. 514 (1975); 14 DUQ. L. REV. 257 (1969). A threat of discipline if employees exercise their rights to union representation during an investigatory interview is a violation of §8(a)(1) under the *Weingarten* rule. Southwestern Bell Tel. Co., 227 NLRB 1223, 94 LRRM 1305 (1977).

[457]*Supra* note 454, at 256–57.

quests representation";[458] (3) the employee's right to request representation as a condition to participation in the interview "is limited to situations where the employee reasonably believes the investigation will result in disciplinary action";[459] (4) exercise of the right may not interfere with "legitimate employer prerogatives"; (5) the employer may carry on its inquiry without interviewing the employee, thus leaving to the employee "the choice between having an interview unaccompanied by his representative, or having no interview and foregoing any benefits that might be derived from one";[460] and (6) the employer has no duty to bargain with any union representative who may be permitted to attend the investigatory interview.[461]

While it may be clear that the rule of *Weingarten* is inapplicable to "such run-of-the-mill shop-floor conversations as, for example, the giving of instructions or training or needed corrections of work techniques,"[462] the Board and the courts have had difficulty in determining under what circumstances a reasonable basis exists for believing that the investigatory interview will result in disciplinary action.[463] The Supreme Court's instruction

---

[458]*Id.* at 257. *See* Kohl's Food Co., 249 NLRB 75, 104 LRRM 1063 (1980); Lennox Indus., 244 NLRB 607, 102 LRRM 1298 (1979).

[459]420 US at 257-58.

[460]*Id.* at 258-59.

[461]*Id.* at 259-60. Although the employer has no duty to bargain with the union representative, the representative must be accorded an opportunity to speak, for the rule contemplates meaningful representation. In Southwestern Bell Tel. Co., 251 NLRB 612, 105 LRRM 1246 (1980), *enforcement denied*, 667 F2d 470, 109 LRRM 2602 (CA 5, 1982) the employer demanded that the union steward remain silent during the interview—conduct that the Board found unlawful: "It is clear from the Supreme Court's decision that the role of the statutory representative at the investigative interview is to provide 'assistance' and 'counsel' to the employee being interrogated." *Id.*, 105 LRRM at 1247. *See also* Texaco, Inc., 251 NLRB 633, 105 LRRM 1239 (1980), *enforced*, 659 F2d 124, 108 LRRM 2850 (CA 9, 1981).

[462]*Supra* note 454 at 257-58 (quoting Quality Mfg. Co., 195 NLRB 197, 199, 79 LRRM 1269, 1271 (1972)). *See* General Elec. Co., 240 NLRB 479, 100 LRRM 1248 (1979).

[463]AAA Equip. Serv. Co., 238 NLRB 390, 99 LRRM 1262 (1978), *enforcement denied*, 598 F2d 1142, 101 LRRM 2381 (CA 8, 1979); Spartan Stores, Inc., 235 NLRB 522, 100 LRRM 1181 (1978), *enforcement denied*, 628 F2d 953, 105 LRRM 2293 (CA 6, 1980); Mt. Vernon Tanker Co. v. NLRB, 218 NLRB 1423, 89 LRRM 1793 (1975), *enforcement denied*, 549 F2d 571, 94 LRRM 3054 (CA 9, 1977). The Board and Ninth Circuit, however, have agreed that employer counseling sessions deemed by management to be a "preliminary step to the imposition of discipline," fall within the ambit of the *Weingarten* rule. Alfred M. Lewis, Inc. v. NLRB, 587 F2d 403, 410, 99 LRRM 2841 (CA 9, 1978), *enforcing in part* 229 NLRB 757, 95 LRRM 1216 (1977). But counseling sessions for absenteeism conducted under management assurances that the sessions were not disciplinary meetings and would not be recorded in the employees' personnel files were deemed by the Board to be unprotected by the *Weingarten* rule. Amoco Chem. Corp., 237 NLRB 394, 99 LRRM 1017 (1978). *See also* Newton Sheet Metal v. NLRB, 598 F2d 478, 101 LRRM 2422 (CA 8, 1979); Good Hope Refiners v. NLRB, 620 F2d 57, 104 LRRM 2883 (CA 5, 1979), *cert. denied*, 449 US 1012, 105 LRRM 3327 (1980).

that the inquiry must be based on "objective standards"[464] and upon a reasonable evaluation of "all the circumstances," rather than upon the subjective reaction of the employee, has not eliminated all ambiguity.

In *Certified Grocers of California*,[465] the Board found *Weingarten* applicable not only to investigatory interviews but also to noninvestigatory interviews about which a reasonable basis exists for believing disciplinary action will result. The employee was required to meet with the plant manager without union representation and was given a disciplinary layoff for low production. The Ninth Circuit denied enforcement of the Board's order,[466] concluding that *Weingarten* was not controlling since the purpose of the meeting was "'to deliver the warning notice,' not to investigate."[467]

After the Ninth Circuit's decision, the Board concluded that *Certified Grocers* "was wrongly decided on the facts" and overruled it to the extent that it read *Weingarten* to require union representation at an interview called merely to inform an employee of disciplinary action already decided upon.[468] The full panoply of *Weingarten* protections might become applicable even at a disciplinary interview, however, if the employer engages in any conduct "beyond merely informing the employee of a previously made disciplinary decision."[469]

The statutory predicate for the right recognized in *Weingarten* is the guarantee of section 7 that employees may act in concert for "mutual aid or protection." Although the *Weingarten* case involved a represented employee, the protections of section 7 are not confined to such employees. Thus, the Board soon faced the vexing question whether the *Weingarten* right is enjoyed by unrepresented employees. In its first assay of that question, in *Materials Research Corp.*,[470] the Board held that unrepresented em-

---

[464]*Supra* note 454, at 257 n.5. *See* Alfred M. Lewis, Inc. v. NLRB, *supra* note 463.

[465]227 NLRB 1211, 94 LRRM 1279 (1977).

[466]587 F2d 449, 100 LRRM 3029 (CA 9, 1978).

[467]*Id.*, 100 LRRM at 3030. *See also* Mobil Oil Corp., 196 NLRB 1052, 80 LRRM 1188 (1972) in which the Board, before *Weingarten*, distinguished meetings for imposition of discipline from those for investigatory purposes.

[468]Baton Rouge Water Works Co., 246 NLRB 995, 103 LRRM 1056 (1979). *Accord* Barmet of Ind., 284 NLRB 1024, 125 LRRM 1338 (1987); Port Plastics, 279 NLRB 362, 123 LRRM 1320 (1986); San Antonio Portland Cement Co., 277 NLRB 338, 121 LRRM 1234 (1985).

[469]103 LRRM at 1058.

[470]262 NLRB 1010, 110 LRRM 1401 (1982).

ployees enjoy the right under *Weingarten* to request the assistance of a fellow employee in the appropriate situations, and the employer is bound to accede to the request or forego the interview. The result was based on the language of section 7 and on the Board's conclusion that the beneficial purposes of *Weingarten* could be equally well served in the absence of a recognized bargaining representative by the presence of a fellow employee. The Board explained that the presence of a fellow employee might deter employer overreaching and relieve the interrogated employee of needless apprehension and disserving reticence.[471]

Just three years later, after changes in membership, the Board reconsidered the matter and overruled *Materials Research.* In *Sears, Roebuck & Co.*,[472] the Board concluded that it had misread the Act and that section 7 does not confer the *Weingarten* right where there is no recognized exclusive bargaining representative. The Board declared that its decision was required by the Act: "[w]e view the result rendered as one the Act compels."[473]

The Board revisited the issue in *E.I. du Pont de Nemours & Co.*[474] (*du Pont III*). In *du Pont,* the Board initially applied *Materials Research* and its order (*du Pont I*) was enforced by the Third Circuit.[475] However, at the Board's request, the court vacated its decision and remanded the case to the Board.[476] The Board then issued a supplemental decision (*du Pont II*) in which it held, in reliance on *Sears,* that the Act required a finding that unrepresented employees are not entitled to the presence of a co-employee at an investigatory interview.[477] Again, the Third Circuit remanded the case this time on the ground that the Board erred in holding that the Act compelled such a conclusion.[478] On remand *(du Pont III)* the Board, pursuant to the court's order, overruled *Sears'* holding that the Act *compels* a finding that unrepresented employees are not entitled to *Weingarten* rights.[479] The Board nonetheless determined that denying such rights represented the proper balance between the conflicting interests of labor and management. The Board noted

[471]*Id.*, 110 LRRM at 1405.
[472]274 NLRB 230, 118 LRRM 1329 (1985).
[473]*Id.* n.5.
[474]289 NLRB 627, 128 LRRM 1233 (1988).
[475]262 NLRB 1028, 110 LRRM 1417 (1982), *enforced*, 724 F2d 1061, 115 LRRM 2153 (CA 3, 1983).
[476]733 F2d 296, 116 LRRM 2343 (CA 3, 1984).
[477]274 NLRB 1104, 118 LRRM 1555 (1985).
[478]794 F2d 120, 122 LRRM 2867 (CA 3, 1986).
[479]*Supra* note 474.

that the objectives served by providing *Weingarten* rights to union employees, that is, having the presence of a knowledgeable union representative who could assist the employee and heading off formal grievance procedures, are not similarly served in a nonunion setting.[480] The Third Circuit then denied the employee's petition for review, citing the deferential standard of review.[481]

Despite the outcome of *Sears*, the Board has held that an employee's request for the presence of a fellow employee other than a representative of a recognized union is a request to engage in protected activity.[482] Thus, the *request* is protected activity and insulated against reprisal, even though the employer has no obligation to grant the request or alter its intended conduct.[483] The Board also has held that an employer's unlawful refusal to recognize or bargain with a majority union cannot defeat the *Weingarten* right of the employees.[484] Likewise, an employee's request for the assistance of a representative from a newly elected but not yet certified union must be honored by the employer under *Weingarten*.[485]

Once an employee makes a valid request for union representation, the employer is permitted one of three options:[486] (1) grant the request; (2) dispense with or discontinue the interview;[487] or (3) offer the employee the choice of continuing the interview unaccompanied by a union representative or of having no interview at all and thereby dispensing with any benefits that the interview might have conferred on the employee.[488] The

---

[480] *Id.*, 128 LRRM at 1235-36.

[481] Slaughter v. NLRB, 876 F2d 11, 131 LRRM 2546 (CA 3), *amended*, 132 LRRM 2221 (1989).

[482] Chromalloy Am. Corp., L.A. Water Treatment Div., 263 NLRB 244, 110 LRRM 1506 (1982). *See* Sears, Roebuck & Co., *supra* note 472, at 1330, n.8 (Member Dennis concurring). The request for assistance of an attorney, however, appears to be unprotected. *See* TCC Center Cos., 275 NLRB 604, 119 LRRM 1195 (1985).

[483] U.S. Postal Serv., 277 NLRB 1382, 121 LRRM 1103 (1985).

[484] Glomac Plastics, 234 NLRB 1309, 97 LRRM 1441 (1978), *enforced*, 600 F2d 3, 101 LRRM 2456 (CA 2, 1979); Anchortank, Inc., 239 NLRB 430, 99 LRRM 1622 (1978), *enforcement granted in part and denied in part*, 618 F2d 1153, 104 LRRM 2689 (CA 5, 1980).

[485] ITT Corp., Lighting Fixtures Div., 261 NLRB 229, 110 LRRM 1025 (1982), *enforcement granted in part and denied in part*, 719 F2d 851, 114 LRRM 2777 (CA 6, 1983).

[486] Roadway Express, 246 NLRB 1127, 103 LRRM 1050, 1052–53 (1979). These options had been discussed by the Board in its earlier decision in U.S. Postal Serv., 241 NLRB 141, 100 LRRM 1520 (1979). *See* Amoco Oil Co., 238 NLRB 551, 99 LRRM 1250, 1251 (1978).

[487] The employer, when faced with a request for union representation, may dispense with the interview and inform the employee of any previously determined disciplinary decision. Amoco Oil Co., *supra* note 486; Chrysler Corp., 241 NLRB 1050, 101 LRRM 1020 (1979).

[488] *See* Meharry Medical College, 236 NLRB 1396, 99 LRRM 1002 (1978).

employer, however, may not continue the interview without granting the requested union representation unless the employee "voluntarily agrees to remain unrepresented *after* having been presented by the employer with the choices" just described or "is otherwise made aware of these choices."[489]

When an employer merely requests an employee to leave the production area and proceed to an office or some other location where further discussion is contemplated, then the employee "acts at his or her peril if he or she declines to do so";[490] in such a case the employee is not privileged to ignore the employer's directions.

Once the employer has scheduled the interview, the employer is under no obligation to accord the employee "consultation with his union representative on company time if the interview date otherwise provides the employee adequate opportunity to consult with union representatives on his own time prior to the interview."[491] If the employer insists that the interview take place immediately, however, it must permit the employee and his or her union representative to confer in private in advance.[492] *Weingarten* does not require an employer to postpone an interview because the specific union representative the employee requests is absent, so long as another union representative is available at the time set for the interview. Nor is the employer obliged to suggest or secure alternative representation for the employee.[493]

In *Consolidated Casinos Corp., Sahara Div.*,[494] the Board held that *Weingarten* protection applies to prepolygraph interviews, to the administration of polygraph tests, and to postpolygraph interviews.

---

[489]U.S. Postal Serv., *supra* note 486, at 142 (emphasis in original); Penn Dixie Steel Corp., 253 NLRB 91, 105 LRRM 1470 (1980).

[490]Roadway Express, *supra* note 486, at 1052. However, in discussing Glomac Plastics, *supra* note 484, the Board found an employee may be so privileged where it is clear that the employer intends solely to discuss the merits of the matter which might result in discipline *and* will not permit a *Weingarten* representative to be present; an employee need not attend an illegal interview. *Id.*, 103 LRRM at 1051 n.4. *See also* Joseph F. Whelan Co., 273 NLRB 340, 118 LRRM 1040 (1984) (discharge lawful where employee refused to leave shop floor for discussion with supervisor).

[491]Climax Molybdenum Co. v. NLRB, 584 F2d 360, 365, 99 LRRM 2471 (CA 10, 1978), *denying enforcement to* 227 NLRB 1189, 94 LRRM 1177 (1977).

[492]U.S. Postal Serv., 288 NLRB No. 93, 130 LRRM 1184 (1988).

[493]Pacific Gas & Elec. Co., 253 NLRB 1143, 106 LRRM 1077 (1981); Roadway Express, *supra* note 486; Coca-Cola Bottling Co., 227 NLRB 1276, 94 LRRM 1200 (1977).

[494]266 NLRB 988, 113 LRRM 1081 (1983).

The *Weingarten* rights of a representative at a disciplinary meeting can be waived by the employees' collective bargaining representative, but a waiver will not be lightly inferred.[495] Waivers must not be ambiguous; they must be clear and unmistakable.[496] The Board has held that the mere signing of a form permitting the interview is not necessarily a waiver of *Weingarten* rights.[497]

The Board's first attempt to formulate a comprehensive policy on *remedies* for violation of the *Weingarten* rule was revealed in *Kraft Foods*:[498]

> Initially, we determine whether the General Counsel has made a prima facie showing that a make-whole remedy such as reinstatement, backpay, and expungement of all disciplinary records is warranted. The General Counsel can make this showing by proving that respondent conducted an investigatory interview in violation of *Weingarten* and that the employee whose rights were violated was subsequently disciplined for the conduct which was the subject of the unlawful interview.
>
> In the face of such a showing, the burden shifts to the respondent. Thus, in order to negate the prima facie showing of the appropriateness of a make-whole remedy, the respondent must demonstrate that its decision to discipline the employee in question was not based on information obtained at the unlawful interview. Where the respondent meets its burden, a make-whole remedy will not be ordered. Instead, we will provide our traditional cease-and-desist order in remedy of the 8(a)(1) violation.[499]

The *Kraft Foods* remedial policy was short-lived. In *Taracorp Industries*,[500] the Board overruled *Kraft Foods* and held that reinstatement and backpay are inappropriate remedies for

---

[495] *See* Prudential Ins. Co., 275 NLRB 208, 119 LRRM 1073 (1985), *on remand from* 661 F2d 398, 108 LRRM 3041 (CA 5, 1981), *denying enforcement to* 251 NLRB 1591, 105 LRRM 1159 (1980).

[496] NLRB v. U.S. Postal Serv., 689 F2d 835, 111 LRRM 2621 (CA 9, 1982), *denying enforcement in part to* 256 NLRB 78, 107 LRRM 1172 (1981).

[497] Montgomery Ward & Co., 273 NLRB 1226, 118 LRRM 1025 (1984), *enforced*, 785 F2d 316, 122 LRRM 2368 (CA 9, 1986).

[498] Kraft Foods, 251 NLRB 598, 105 LRRM 1233 (1980). *See also* Coyne Cylinder Co., 251 NLRB 1503, 105 LRRM 1270 (1980); Consolidated Food Co., 253 NLRB 25, 105 LRRM 1407 (1980); NLRB v. Potter Signal Co., 600 F2d 120, 101 LRRM 2378 (CA 8, 1979); NLRB v. Illinois Bell Tel. Co., 674 F2d 618, 109 LRRM 3244 (CA 7, 1982), *enforcing in part and denying in part* 251 NLRB 932, 105 LRRM 1236 (1980).

[499] 251 NLRB at 598.

[500] 273 NLRB 221, 117 LRRM 1497 (1984). *See also* Massillon Hosp. Ass'n dba Massillon Community Hosp., 282 NLRB 675, 124 LRRM 1125 (1987) (denial of make-whole award in light of just-cause discharge); Greyhound Lines, 273 NLRB 1443, 118 LRRM 1199 (1985) (same).

Weingarten violations if the employee was disciplined for just cause. Unless the discipline was the direct result of an employee's assertion of *Weingarten* rights, the Board cannot order "make-whole" remedies nor can it make punitive awards. Even blatant violations of *Weingarten* rights do not give rise to make-whole remedies when discipline is for just cause. The Board's decision in *Taracorp* adopted the view of the Eighth and Ninth circuits.[501] Prior to *Taracorp*, the Sixth and Seventh Circuits had held that a make-whole remedy is not appropriate if some other independent evidence, not obtained in the unlawful interview, demonstrates that the discharge was for good cause.[502] The Seventh Circuit has since upheld the Board's *Taracorp* doctrine as a permissible exercise of discretion.[503]

5. Safety-Related Protests. Cases involving alleged unsafe working conditions have raised questions concerning the scope of protected concerted activity. Concerted employee conduct and protests involving safety strikes, refusals to accept job assignments claimed unsafe, filing of complaints at government occupational safety and health agencies, and complaining to the employer about job safety conditions have been held protected under section 7.[504] But lack of any great or immediate danger

---

[501]*See* Pacific Tel. & Tel. Co. v. NLRB, 711 F2d 134, 113 LRRM 3529 (CA 9, 1983), *enforcing in part and denying in part* 262 NLRB 1034, 110 LRRM 1416 and 262 NLRB 1048, 110 LRRM 1411 (1982); Montgomery Ward & Co. v. NLRB, 664 F2d 1095, 109 LRRM 2005 (CA 8), *enforcing in part and denying in part* 254 NLRB 826, 106 LRRM 1148 (1981).

[502]*See* General Motors Corp. v. NLRB, 674 F2d 576, 109 LRRM 3345 (CA 6, 1982), *enforcing in part and denying in part* 251 NLRB 850, 105 LRRM 1439 (1980); NLRB v. Illinois Bell Tel. Co., *supra* note 498.

[503]Communications Workers Local 5008 v. NLRB (Illinois Bell Tel. Co.), 784 F2d 847, 121 LRRM 3078 (CA 7, 1986), *enforcing* 275 NLRB 148, 118 LRRM 1645 (1985).

[504]*Compare* NLRB v. City Disposal Sys., 465 US 822, 115 LRRM 3193 (1984) (safety complaint by lone employee invoking claim of right under collective bargaining agreement held concerted) *with* Meyers Indus., 281 NLRB 882, 123 LRRM 1137 (1986), *aff'd sub nom.* Prill v. NLRB, 835 F2d 1481, 127 LRRM 2415 (CA DC, 1987) (safety complaint by lone employee invoking claim of right under state statute held not concerted). *See* Lenape Prods., 283 NLRB 178, 125 LRRM 1002 (1987) (protest of employer's failure to control excessive fumes and rat infestation held protected); Leslie Metal Arts Co., 208 NLRB 323, 85 LRRM 1314 (1974), *enforced,* 509 F2d 811, 88 LRRM 2437 (CA 6, 1975) (refusal to work, protesting failure of supervisor to protect employees from aggressions of other workers, held protected). *See also* Kiechler Mfg. Co., 238 NLRB 398, 99 LRRM 1578 (1978); Anheuser-Busch, Inc., 239 NLRB 207, 99 LRRM 1548 (1978); Alleluia Cushion Co., 221 NLRB 999, 91 LRRM 1131 (1975); Fry Roofing Co., 237 NLRB 1005, 99 LRRM 1544 (1978); Modern Carpet Indus., 236 NLRB 1014, 98 LRRM 1426 (1978), *enforced,* 611 F2d 811, 103 LRRM 2167 (CA 10, 1979); Empire Steel Mfg. Co., 234 NLRB 530, 97 LRRM 1304 (1978); Tappan Co., 228 NLRB 1389, 95 LRRM 1035 (1977), *enforced,* 607 F2d 764 (CA 6, 1979); P & L Cedar Prods., 224 NLRB 244, 93 LRRM 1341 (1976). Where, however, an employee protest concerning the presence of containers of combustible material at the job site went to the extreme of closing the entrance to the employer's operation, the Board sustained the discharge of three employees on the ground

may render an employee's refusal to work to protest safety conditions unprotected.[505]

Concerted refusal to work because of unsafe working conditions may be protected even in the face of a no-strike agreement. Thus, in *Combustion Engineering*,[506] the Board held that a concerted walkout of employees from a job site was not prohibited by a contractual no-strike provision, since the presence of two belligerent, partly inebriated intruders on the site created an "abnormally dangerous" condition within the meaning of section 502 of the LMRA.[507] Since the employer had not provided adequate protection, the discharges for engaging in the work stoppage constituted a violation of the Act.[508]

6. Protests Relating to Employment Discrimination. Conduct protesting alleged discrimination in employment on racial and other grounds protected by antidiscrimination legislation has been held entitled to section 7 protection. Thus, in *Vought Corp.-MLRS Systems Division*,[509] the Board held, and the Eighth Circuit agreed, that an employee who informed other employees of potential race discrimination in a recent promotion decision had engaged in protected activity.

---

that such serious misconduct was unprotected by the NLRA. Mal Landfill Corp., 210 NLRB 167, 86 LRRM 1304 (1974).

[505]A refusal to operate certain equipment to protest safety hazards was held unprotected by the Board where the refusal continued after the equipment had been repaired and the hazards eliminated. Pyro Mining Co., 230 NLRB 782, 96 LRRM 1175 (1977).

[506]224 NLRB 542, 93 LRRM 1049 (1976).

[507]Section 502 provides:

"Nothing in this Act shall be construed to require an individual employee to render labor or service without his consent, nor shall anything in this Act be construed to make the quitting of his labor by an individual employee an illegal act; nor shall any court issue any process to compel the performance by an individual employee of such labor or service, without his consent; nor shall the quitting of labor by an employee or employees in good faith because of abnormally dangerous conditions for work at the place of employment of such employee or employees be deemed a strike under this Act."

[508]In Gateway Coal Co. v. Mine Workers, 414 US 368, 85 LRRM 2049 (1974), the Supreme Court recognized that §502 provides an exception to the general rule that strikes in violation of no-strike provisions are unprotected, but characterized the exception as a "limited" one that must be supported by "ascertainable, objective evidence." *See* Chapter 17, "Relation of Board Action to Enforcement of Agreements Under Section 301," at notes 176–177. *Cf.* Whirlpool Corp. v. Marshall, 445 US 1, 8 OSHC 1001 (1980), approving an Occupational Safety and Health regulation, 29 CFR §1977 12(b), which protects an employee's right to refuse work because of reasonable apprehension of death or serious injury.

[509]273 NLRB 1290, 118 LRRM 1271 (1984), *enforced*, 788 F2d 1378, 122 LRRM 2168 (CA 8, 1986). *See also* NLRB v. Magnetics Int'l, 699 F2d 806, 112 LRRM 2658 (CA 6, 1983), *enforcing* 254 NLRB 520, 106 LRRM 1133 (1981) (filing and pursuing Title VII claim protected activity). *See generally* Chapter 7, "Discrimination in Employment," at notes 364–376.

The protection of section 7 may be denied, however, where employee protests against employment discrimination are in derogation of the collective bargaining representative's role as exclusive representation of all of the employees in the bargaining unit.[510]

7. Appeals to Agencies and Filing of Court Actions. The Supreme Court in *Eastex, Inc. v. NLRB*[511] construed the "mutual aid and protection" clause of section 7 as extending protection to concerted activities by employees "to improve terms and conditions of employment or otherwise improve their lot as employees through channels outside the immediate employee-employer relationship."[512] Thus, protection is afforded employees when they seek to improve working conditions through "resort to administrative and judicial forums" and through "appeals to legislators to protect their interests as employees."[513] Since the decisions in *Meyers Industries*,[514] however, the Board has required that such protests be concerted within the meaning of *Meyers*.[515]

Concerted employee appeals and complaints lodged with governmental agencies and officials in the areas of occupational safety, employment discrimination, and labor standards[516] have been held to constitute protected concerted activities. Resort to a judicial forum by employees to further their interests as employees have similarly been afforded protection of section 7. Thus,

---

[510]Emporium Capwell Co. v. Western Addition Community Org., 420 US 50, 88 LRRM 2660 (1975), *rev'g* 485 F2d 917, 83 LRRM 2738 (CA DC, 1973), *rev'g sub nom.* The Emporium, 192 NLRB 173, 77 LRRM 1669 (1971), and text accompanying notes 433-434 *supra.*

[511]437 US 556, 565, 98 LRRM 2717, 2720 (1978).

[512]*Id.*

[513]*Id. See also* cases cited in note 423 *supra.*

[514]*Supra* note 504.

[515]*E.g.*, Katy Indus., Oakes Mach. Corp., 288 NLRB No. 52, 128 LRRM 1065 (1988) (protest to county health official not in concert with other employees); Litton Sys., Jefferson Elec. Co. Div., 271 NLRB 1089, 117 LRRM 1092 (1984) (individual filing of OSHA safety claim not concerted).

[516]*See* Salisbury Hotel, 283 NLRB 685, 125 LRRM 1020 (1987) (telephone call to Department of Labor regarding employer's modification of lunch policy protected); Squier Distrib. Co. v. Teamsters Local 7, 801 F2d 238, 123 LRRM 2460 (CA 6, 1986), *enforcing* 276 NLRB 1195, 120 LRRM 1155 (1985) (employees giving sworn statements to sheriff's department protected); Aztec Concrete, 277 NLRB 1244, 121 LRRM 1087 (1985), *enforced*, 805 F2d 1039 (CA 9, 1986) (employees complaining to federal government concerning alleged violations of Davis-Bacon Act protected); Pet O'Dell & Sons Steel Erectors, 277 NLRB 1358, 121 LRRM 1115 (1985) (employee's meeting with US Army Corps to discuss employer's compliance with Davis-Bacon Act protected activity, where union filed charge); Wolfkill Feed & Fertilizer Corp., 277 NLRB 635, 120 LRRM 1307 (1985) (employees complaining to state agency regarding access to restrooms protected); Cristy Janitorial Serv., 271 NLRB 857, 117 LRRM 1028 (1984) (employees complaining about their wages to Wage-Hour Division protected).

the filing of a labor-related lawsuit by a group of employees against their employer seeking actual and punitive damages is treated as protected activity, unless prompted by malice or bad faith.[517] If the lawsuit is filed in good faith, "the fact that it may have been groundless or that it was later dismissed on the pleadings would not in itself make the activity unprotected. . . ."[518]

C. Unprotected Concerted Activities

1. Sit-Down Strikes. The so-called sit-down strike, in which the strikers remain on the employer's premises during the strike, taking possession of the property and excluding others from entry, is a method of striking that the Supreme Court condemned as unprotected conduct shortly after passage of the Wagner Act because of the trespass on and interference with private property that the conduct entailed.[519] Employees engaging in sit-down strikes have thus historically been deprived of the protections of the Act and have been subject to discharge by their employer.

As the Board and the courts expanded the scope of protected concerted activity, however, they also reduced and limited the types of activities that may be deemed unprotected; thus, in two decisions issued in the mid-1970s, the Board read the Supreme Court's condemnation of sit-down strikes narrowly, indicating that sit-down strike activities under certain circumstances may be protected.

In *Overhead Door Corp.*,[520] five employees protested a change in their shift by engaging in a "work-in" after the scheduled hour

---

[517]Trinity Trucking & Materials Corp., 221 NLRB 364, 90 LRRM 1499, 1500 (1975), *supplemented*, 227 NLRB 792, 94 LRRM 1223, *enforced*, 96 LRRM 3413 (CA 7, 1977) (not officially published).

[518]221 NLRB at 365. All Brite Window Cleaning & Maintenance Serv., 235 NLRB 596, 98 LRRM 1297 (1978) (employee activity in retaining attorney in order to obtain back pay owed under collective bargaining agreement ruled protected). *See also* Kaiser Eng'rs v. NLRB, 538 F2d 1379, 92 LRRM 3153 (CA 9, 1976), *enforcing* 213 NLRB 752, 87 LRRM 1447 (1975), where the Ninth Circuit upheld a Board decision that the lobbying efforts of a group of engineers in opposition to changes in national immigration policy concerning importation of alien engineers was "for mutual aid or protection" and that the constructive discharge of the engineer principally responsible for the lobbying effort was therefore violative of the Act; *see* discussion at notes 425–426 *supra.*

[519]Apex Hosiery Co. v. Leader, 310 US 469, 6 LRRM 647 (1940); NLRB v. Fansteel Metallurgical Corp., 306 US 240, 4 LRRM 515 (1939); *see* Cone Mills Corp. v. NLRB, 413 F2d 445, 71 LRRM 2916 (CA 4, 1969). For commentary supportive of the sit-down strike concept, *see* Green, *The Case for the Sit-Down Strike*, 90 NEW REPUBLIC 199 (1937).

[520]220 NLRB 431, 90 LRRM 1257 (1975), *enforcement denied in part*, 540 F2d 878, 93 LRRM 2147 (CA 7, 1976).

of plant closing. After they defied the employer and police directives to leave the premises, the protesting employees were removed from the plant under arrest. The Board found the employee conduct protected, but the Seventh Circuit refused to enforce this aspect of the Board's decision.[521] Quoting a dissenting Board member, the court described the "result reached by the [Board] majority and the proposition of law for which it stands" as "wholly repugnant to the purposes of the Act."[522] In the court's view, that other avenues of protest were open to the employees in the form of a grievance procedure "shifted the locus of the accommodation between employees' rights and private property rights in favor of the employer."[523]

In *Peck, Inc.*,[524] however, the Board found a sit-down strike to be unprotected. In *Peck*, a group of employees remained on the employer's premises after the end of the shift, "to prove a point" to their supervisor who had refused to allow them to leave early in the face of an impending snowstorm. The Board affirmed its approach in *Overhead Door*, but distinguished the contrary result because the employees in *Overhead Door* were protesting "an immediate situation," whereas in *Peck* the sit-down was not "predicated on any necessary immediacy of action."[525]

The Board has affirmed that not every refusal by employees to leave the premises amounts to a sit-down strike. In *City Dodge Center*,[526] a few employees remained on the premises after a work stoppage, despite being asked to leave. The employees left two hours later after being told by the company president that they would be terminated if they remained. In finding that the discharge of these employees was unlawful, the Board stated that the employees' actions did not "rise to the level of the

---

[521]*Id.*

[522]*Id.*, 540 F2d at 885.

[523]*Id.*

[524]226 NLRB 1174, 93 LRRM 1434 (1976).

[525]*See* Meilman Food Indus., 234 NLRB 698, 97 LRRM 1372 (1978), where the immediacy of the situation and the fact that the employee's work stoppage and refusal to leave the plant had been prompted by employer unfair labor practices were factors relied upon by the Board in finding the employees' activity protected. For further discussion of sit-down strikes, *see* Chapter 19, "The Primary Strike," at notes 110–113.

[526]289 NLRB 194, 130 LRRM 1396 (1988). *See also* NLRB v. Pepsi-Cola Bottling Co. of Miami, 449 F2d 824, 78 LRRM 2481 (CA 5, 1971), *cert. denied*, 407 US 910, 80 LRRM 2665 (1972), *enforcing* 186 NLRB 477, 75 LRRM 1367 (1970) (sit-down strike of "a few hours" during normal work hours protected where strikers did not impair employer access to strike area).

disregard of property rights and defiance of law associated with an unprotected sit-down strike."[527]

2. Other Unprotected Activity. The concept of "disloyalty" has been used to deny the protection of section 7 to certain concerted activities. The leading case on the point is the Supreme Court's *Jefferson Standard Broadcasting*[528] decision. A technicians' union had a collective bargaining dispute with a television station. While remaining on the job, but during their off hours, some of the technicians distributed handbills severely criticizing the quality of programming, suggesting that the city was being treated as "second class." The handbills made no reference to the union, collective bargaining, or the current labor dispute. The Court ruled that the employer had cause for discharging the employees who had distributed the handbills, for while employees continue at work they owe a duty not to disparage the product or services of their employer.[529] This duty may persist even during a strike, since strikers intend to return to work and have certain rights to reinstatement.[530] The Court stated that "there is no more elemental cause for discharge of an employee than disloyalty to his employer. . . ."[531]

In cases presenting the issue of whether particular employee conduct is sufficiently "disloyal" to remove it from the protection of section 7, the Board has progressively narrowed the area of unprotected activity. The courts have not always agreed. These "disloyalty" cases have involved (a) breach of confidentiality, (b) false allegations or affidavits concerning the employer, and (c) disparagement of the employer's business activities.

a. Breach of Confidentiality. Employees who divulge wage or salary information to one another in violation of their employer's rule requiring that salaries be treated as confidential are deemed to be engaged in protected activity.[532]

---

[527]*Id.*

[528]NLRB v. Electrical Workers (IBEW) Local 1229 (Jefferson Standard Broadcasting Co.), 346 US 464, 33 LRRM 2183 (1953).

[529]*See* Boeing Airplane Co. v. NLRB, 238 F2d 188, 38 LRRM 2276 (CA 9, 1956); Hoover Co. v. NLRB, 191 F2d 380, 28 LRRM 2353 (CA 6, 1951).

[530]*See* Patterson-Sargent Co., 115 NLRB 1627, 38 LRRM 1134 (1956).

[531]346 US at 472.

[532]Waco, Inc., 273 NLRB 746, 118 LRRM 1163 (1984) (wage discussions). *See also* Scientific-Atlanta, 278 NLRB 622, 122 LRRM 1263 (1986) (merit increase discussions); Jeannette Corp., 217 NLRB 653, 89 LRRM 1224 (1975), *enforced*, 532 F2d 916, 91 LRRM 2968 (CA 3, 1976). *See also* Blue Cross-Blue Shield of Ala., 225 NLRB 1217, 93 LRRM 1281 (1976) (rule barring employees from discussing their salaries with other employees

The Board in *International Business Machines Corp.*,[533] found a valid business justification for the employer's rule regarding distribution of wage data that it had compiled and classified as confidential. While the rule did not preclude employees from discussing their own wages with each other, they could not have access to or distribution of company-compiled information. In upholding the discharge of an employee who disclosed wage information in violation of the rule, the Board refused to hold categorically that a company could enforce a confidentiality policy by discharging any employee who disseminated confidential wage information regardless of the circumstances. Here, the discharge was not unlawful because the employee knew that the documents had been classified as confidential, he was aware of the company's rule prohibiting their distribution, and he had not obtained the information under circumstances that would lead him reasonably to believe that his possession and dissemination of the material was authorized. The Board distinguished *Texas Instruments*,[534] where the company had not established legitimate and substantial business justification in support of a rule prohibiting dissemination of a wage survey and where the company had released to competitors the information claimed to be confidential.

In *Bell Federal Savings & Loan Ass'n*,[535] however, the Board refused to find protected a switchboard operator's disclosure to the union of the number of times the company president had talked with the company's labor counsel, even though the operator had never been instructed that her work was confidential. The employer, in the Board's view, had the right to expect an

---

held to be violative of the Act). In Texas Instruments, 236 NLRB 68, 98 LRRM 1299 (1978), *modified and remanded*, 599 F2d 1067, 102 LRRM 2292 (CA 1, 1979), the Board had concluded that the employer violated §§8(a)(1) and (3) when it discharged employees during a union organizing drive for publishing confidential industry wage information in disregard of the employer's internal security regulations. The First Circuit modified and remanded the decision. On remand, the Board reaffirmed its earlier order. Texas Instruments, 247 NLRB 253, 103 LRRM 1144 (1980). On review, the First Circuit reversed the Board and upheld the discharges on the ground that the confidential information disclosure was unprotected activity. "While the NLRA protects against retaliation on account of union activities, it does not license activists to violate valid company rules with impunity." Texas Instruments v. NLRB, 637 F2d 822, 106 LRRM 2137, 2144 (CA 1, 1981).

[533]265 NLRB 638, 111 LRRM 1665 (1982).

[534]*Supra* note 532. *See also* L.G. Williams Oil Co., 285 NLRB 418, 126 LRRM 1081 (1987) (employer violated the Act by maintaining blanket rule prohibiting all salary discussions among employees and by discharging clerical employee who discussed salary offer conveyed to prospective employee in correspondence typed by clerical employee).

[535]214 NLRB 75, 87 LRRM 1415 (1974).

operator not to reveal information about telephone calls. The Board distinguished this type of information from information such as addresses of employees on time cards, which employees would have a right to use for organizational purposes.

In *Knuth Brothers,*[536] the Board and the Seventh Circuit disagreed on whether an employee's avowed purpose of aiding a union organizational campaign was sufficient, under the circumstances, to protect him from the effects of his disclosure of confidential information to the employer's customers. Since the information was sensitive and might have jeopardized some customer relationships, the court found that the employee had "acted in reckless disregard of his employer's business interests, and that revealing the information "was an act of disloyalty" which constituted cause for discharge.[537]

b. False Allegations or Affidavits Concerning the Employer. It has long been the rule that employees do not forfeit the protection of the Act by making false or inaccurate allegations concerning their employer in connection with appeals or complaints to government agencies, provided the allegations are not "deliberately or maliciously" false.[538] But in *Altex Ready Mix Concrete Corp. v. NLRB*[539] the Board, with Fifth Circuit approval, may have extended the rule. Two employees signed false affidavits that were filed in support of the union's lawsuit. Both subsequently admitted that they knew the affidavits were inaccurate, but claimed they had not read or understood them. Their conduct was deemed protected activity, and their discharge for making the false affidavits was accordingly ruled unlawful.[540]

c. Disparagement of the Employer or Its Business Activities. Employee conduct disparaging management officials or the employer's business may be protected activity if the remarks or

---

[536]218 NLRB 869, 89 LRRM 1422 (1975), *enforcement denied,* 537 F2d 950, 92 LRRM 3275 (CA 7, 1976). *See* Comment, NLRB v. Knuth Brothers: *The Boundaries of Unprotected "Disloyalty" When a Non-Striking Employee's Section 7 Concerted Activity Threatens Employee-Customer Relations,* 125 U. PA. L. REV. 1339 (1977).

[537]537 F2d at 956. Similarly, a union activist's efforts to obtain a restricted list of employees and their telephone numbers were considered grounds for discharge by the Fifth Circuit, also in disagreement with the Board. NLRB v. Florida Steel Corp., 544 F2d 896, 94 LRRM 2237 (CA 5, 1977).

[538]Walls Mfg. Co., 137 NLRB 1317, 50 LRRM 1376 (1962), *enforced,* 321 F2d 753, 53 LRRM 2428 (CA DC), *cert. denied,* 375 US 923, 54 LRRM 2576 (1963).

[539]542 F2d 295, 93 LRRM 2940 (CA 5), *enforcing* 223 NLRB 696, 91 LRRM 1591 (1976).

[540]*See also* Big Three Indus. Gas & Equip. Co., 212 NLRB 800, 87 LRRM 1543 (1974), *enforced,* 512 F2d 1404, 93 LRRM 2842 (CA 5, 1975) (discharge of employee for giving "inaccurate" testimony at NLRB hearing held unlawful where employee did not "knowingly and willfully testify falsely").

conduct relate to employee interests or working conditions and are not egregious in nature. In *Community Hospital of Roanoke Valley v. NLRB*,[541] the Fourth Circuit, in a divided opinion, agreed with the Board's finding that a nurse's statement on a television broadcast protesting wages and staffing conditions at the hospital at which she was employed were protected, notwithstanding the hospital's contention that the statements were disparaging and disloyal. The court concluded that the statements were distinguishable from those found unprotected in the *Jefferson Standard* case,[542] because they were "directly related to protected concerted activity in progress."[543]

The Board's general approach, which was followed in *Community Hospital*, is that an employee may properly engage in communications with a third party in an effort to obtain the third party's assistance "in circumstances where the communication [is] related to a legitimate, ongoing labor dispute between the employees and their employer, and where the communication [does] not constitute a disparagement or vilification of the employer's product or its reputation."[544] But care must be taken to distinguish between public disparagement of an employer's products or services and the mere "airing of what may be highly sensitive issues."[545] In *Allied Aviation Service Co. of New Jersey*,[546] two letters sent by employees to airline customers concerning safety issues, while raising "sensitive" and "delicate" issues, did not rise, in the Board's view, "to the level of public disparage-

---

[541]538 F2d 607, 92 LRRM 3158 (CA 4, 1976), *enforcing* 220 NLRB 217, 90 LRRM 1449 (1975).

[542]*See* text at note 528 *supra*.

[543]538 F2d at 610. *See also* Great Lakes Steel Div., 236 NLRB 1033, 98 LRRM 1551 (1978), *enforced*, 625 F2d 131, 104 LRRM 3156 (CA 6, 1980) (publication of leaflet seeking improvement of employer's medical and ambulance policy held protected); Automobile Club of Mich., 231 NLRB 1179, 96 LRRM 1267 (1977), *enforced*, 610 F2d 438, 104 LRRM 2632 (CA 6, 1979) (issuance of press release describing lawsuit employees had filed against employer held protected); Springfield Library & Museum, 239 NLRB 1623, 99 LRRM 1380 (1978); Firestone Tire & Rubber Co., 238 NLRB 1323, 99 LRRM 1429 (1978).

[544]Allied Aviation Serv. Co. of N.J., 248 NLRB 229, 103 LRRM 1454, 1455, *enforced*, 636 F2d 1210, 108 LRRM 2279 (CA 3, 1980). *See* Pareco, Inc., 269 NLRB 1027, 116 LRRM 1191 (1984) (protected activity to urge employees to boycott employers adjacent restaurant in dispute over meal-ticket benefit); Greyhound Lines, 251 NLRB 1638, 105 LRRM 1232 (1980); Automobile Club of Mich. v. NLRB, *supra* note 543.

[545]Allied Aviation Service Co. of N.J., *supra* note 544, 103 LRRM at 1456. "[A]bsent a malicious motive, [an employee's] right to appeal to the public is not dependent on the sensitivity of [the employer] to his choice of forum." Richboro Community Mental Health Council, 242 NLRB 1267, 101 LRRM 1319, 1320 (1979).

[546]*Supra* note 544.

ment necessary to deprive otherwise protected activities of the protections of the Act."[547] The Board declared:

> [I]t is not the Board's function to appraise the potential effectiveness of the tactics utilized by employees in their disputes with management. At what point the employees determine that third-party assistance will be of more benefit than private talks with their employer is a tactical decision. Thus, if the communication is related to the dispute, the employee sending the communication is equally protected whether such a step is taken early on in the dispute, or at a later date after all internal avenues have been exhausted.[548]

The Ninth Circuit approved a similarly narrow definition of "disloyalty" in *Sierra Publishing Co. v. NLRB*.[549] In that case, employees of a newspaper were involved in an ongoing labor dispute. Some of the employees sent a letter to 50 of the paper's main retail advertisers stating that the union was trying to get a fair contract, that the employees could not live with a 15 percent to 20 percent pay cut, that circulation had plummeted, and that the newspaper was "speeding downhill." In enforcing the Board's order finding the employees' discharge unlawful, the court stated that "first and most important" the letter was related to the labor dispute and to the employees' efforts to improve their working conditions. Although the court recognized the charge that "circulation has plummeted" may be considered product disparagement since the letter was sent to advertisers, the court stated that "the effect of *Jefferson Standard* was not to equate every critical comment with unprotected disloyalty."[550] The court also held that effective third party appeals will interfere in some way with an employer's business, and this alone is insufficient to remove the Act's protection.

In comparison, in *Washington Adventist Hospital*,[551] the Board concluded that the employer lawfully fired an employee who sent a systemwide computer message protesting impending layoffs and criticizing management where the message disrupted the work of over 100 terminal users and was in violation

---

[547] *Id.*, 103 LRRM at 1456.

[548] *Id. See* Emarco, Inc., 284 NLRB 832, 125 LRRM 1311 (1987) (protected activity for strikers to tell third-party contractor that employer did not pay its bills and could not finish job: comment related to dispute and not reckless).

[549] 889 F2d 210, 132 LRRM 2961 (CA 9, 1989), *enforcing* 291 NLRB 540, 131 LRRM 1338 (1988).

[550] *Id.*, 132 LRRM at 2965.

[551] 291 NLRB 95, 131 LRRM 1276 (1988).

of a computer security agreement that had been signed by the employee. Likewise, in *Crystal Linen & Uniform Service*,[552] the Board found that striking employees who worked for the employer's competitor and solicited the employer's customers to transfer their business to the competitor engaged in unprotected disloyal conduct. Thus, the employer did not violate the Act when it issued written warnings to the strikers and threatened further discipline upon noncompliance.[553]

IV. UNION RESTRAINT AND COERCION

A. Section 8(b)(1)(A): Restraint and Coercion of Employees

Section 8(b)(1)(A) is concerned with the rights of individual employees in their relations with labor organizations. This section makes it an unfair labor practice for a union to "restrain or coerce employees in the exercise of the rights guaranteed in Section 7." Under section 7 employees are guaranteed both the right to engage in concerted activities and the "right to refrain from any or all such activities. . . ." However, the proviso to section 8(b)(1)(A) states that the section "shall not impair the right of a labor organization to prescribe its own rules with respect to the acquisition or retention of membership therein. . . ."[554]

1. Not a Derivative Counterpart of Section 8(a)(1). As previously noted,[555] while section 8(b)(1)(A) may appear to be a counterpart of section 8(a)(1), it has always been the Board's position that section 8(b)(1)(A) was not intended to have the same broad application as section 8(a)(1). In *National Maritime Union*,[556] the Board and the Second Circuit concluded that violations of other provisions of section 8(b) do not give rise to derivative violations of section 8(b)(1)(A). The Supreme Court,

---

[552]274 NLRB 946, 118 LRRM 1625 (1985).

[553]*See also* Lapeer Foundry & Mach., 289 NLRB 952, 129 LRRM 1001 (1988) (lawful to deny recall to employee who advised customers to purchase products elsewhere); Giant Open Air Mkt., 231 NLRB 945, 96 LRRM 1227 (1977) (lawful to discharge employee who irritated and alienated customers).

[554]For detailed treatment of the closely related §8(b)(2), which prohibits a union from causing or attempting to cause an employer to discriminate in violation of §8(a)(3), see Chapter 7, "Discrimination in Employment."

[555]*Supra* at note 32.

[556]78 NLRB 971, 22 LRRM 1289 (1948), *enforced*, 175 F2d 686, 24 LRRM 2268 (CA 2, 1949), *cert. denied*, 338 US 954, 25 LRRM 2395 (1950).

in *Curtis Brothers*,[557] approved the Board's decision in *National Maritime Union* and noted that section 8(b)(1)(A) provides only a limited prohibition relating to "union tactics involving violence, intimidation, and reprisals or threats thereof."[558]

This important distinction between sections 8(a)(1) and 8(b)(1) was reiterated by the Board in 1980 in a dismissal of a complaint against a union for interfering with the dissemination of information by an employee. The Board stated:

> The cases relied on by the Administrative Law Judge, although similar, differ critically in the material fact that they involved employee action and an employer respondent and thus a different section of the Act. Section 8(a)(1) makes it an unfair labor practice for an employer to interfere with, restrain, or coerce employees in the exercise of the rights guaranteed in Section 7. Section 8(b)(1)(A), however, makes it an unfair labor practice for a labor organization to restrain or coerce employees in the exercise of Section 7 rights.[559]

Although union unfair labor practices involving provisions other than section 8(b)(1)(A) generally do not automatically result in derivative violations of section 8(b)(1)(A), an exception typically occurs when the unfair labor practice is a violation of section 8(b)(2). Thus, in superseniority,[560] hiring hall,[561] and unfair representation cases,[562] a violation of section 8(b)(2) will usually be deemed a violation of section 8(b)(1)(A) as well. These cases are treated elsewhere in connection with the specific subject areas in which they occur. Also treated elsewhere are the actions of minority unions when involved in employer violations of section 8(a)(2); for example, a union that is a party to a "sweetheart" contract violates section 8(b)(1)(A). Such cases are treated in the chapter on employer domination of and assistance to labor organizations.[563]

2. Fines and Discipline of Union Members. A union may fine or discipline a member without violating section 8(b)(1)(A) so long as the fine or discipline is not imposed on the basis of conduct protected under section 7. Congress intended for disci-

---

[557]NLRB v. Drivers Local 639 (Curtis Bros.), 362 US 274, 45 LRRM 2975 (1960). *See* Chapter 21, "Picketing for Organization and Recognition," at notes 4–9.

[558]362 US at 290.

[559]Teamsters Local 515 (Roadway Express), 248 NLRB 83, 103 LRRM 1318 (1980).

[560]*See* Chapter 7, "Discrimination in Employment," at notes 369–376 and 431–458.

[561]*See* Chapter 27, "Union Security," at notes 252–349.

[562]*See* Chapter 26, "Section 8(e): The 'Hot-Cargo' Agreement."

[563]*See* Chapter 8, "Employer Domination and Assistance to Labor Organizations,"at notes 9–12 and 203–213.

pline to remain essentially an internal union matter as reflected by the proviso to section 8(b)(1)(A), that the section "shall not impair the right of a labor organization to prescribe its own rules with respect to the acquisition or retention of membership therein. . . ."[564] This proviso has been interpreted broadly by both the Board and the courts in cases where only union membership is at stake. Consequently, expulsion alone is not restraint or coercion under section 8(b)(1)(A).[565] Similarly, subject to the exceptions noted below, unions may suspend membership[566] and impose fines for breaches of internal union rules without restraining or coercing employees within the meaning of the Act. The Supreme Court held in *NLRB v. Allis-Chalmers Manufacturing Co.*[567] that a union may seek enforcement in state court of such fines in cases where the employee enjoys "full membership" in the union. "Full membership" is to be distinguished from the mere tender of periodic dues and initiation fees for the purpose of compliance with a union-security clause.[568]

In 1969 the Supreme Court decided *Scofield v. NLRB*,[569] upholding the legality of fines of members. The union promulgated a rule designed to discourage employees engaged in piecework operations from exceeding a production ceiling. Members who demanded full payment when they exceeded the production ceiling were subject to a fine. The Board found no violation of section 8(b)(1)(A), and the Seventh Circuit affirmed.[570] The Supreme Court agreed, listing four requirements for lawful imposition of union fines under the Act:

> §8(b)(1)(A) leaves a union free to enforce [1] a properly adopted rule which [2] reflects a legitimate union interest, [3] impairs no policy which Congress has imbedded in the labor laws, and [4] is

---

[564]The argument has been advanced that "indeed within the National Labor Relations Act itself an inherent contradiction between the Union's rights and the union member's rights exists." Meyerhofer, *The Inherent Conflict between Sections 7 and 8(b)(1)(A) of the National Labor Relations Act*, 1978 WISC. L. REV. 859 (1978).

[565]American Newspaper Publishers Ass'n v. NLRB, 193 F2d 782, 29 LRRM 2230 (CA 7, 1951), *enforcing* 86 NLRB 951, 25 LRRM 1002 (1949).

[566]NLRB Gen. Counsel Admin. Ruling F-862, 44 LRRM 1113 (1959).

[567]388 US 175, 65 LRRM 2449 (1967).

[568]*Id.* at 197. For a discussion of some of the implications of this distinction, see Hanley, *Labor Law Decisions of the Supreme Court, 1966-67 Term*, LABOR RELATIONS YEARBOOK—1967 at 131 (1968). *See also* Chapter 27, "Union Security," at notes 30–46.

[569]394 US 423, 70 LRRM 3105 (1969).

[570]Auto Workers Local 283 (Wisconsin Motor Corp.), 145 NLRB 1097, 55 LRRM 1085 (1964) (1964), *enforced sub nom.* Scofield v. NLRB, 393 F2d 49, 67 LRRM 2673 (CA 7, 1968).

reasonably enforced against union members who are free to leave the union and escape the rule.[571]

a. Impact of Discipline on Employee Relationship. Application of section 8(b)(1)(A) to the enforcement of union rules requires a dual approach. The use of external enforcement of a union rule, that is, attempting to affect a member's employment status, is proscribed by section 8(b)(1)(A). On the other hand, a union rule is ordinarily legally enforceable against a member by internal means (i.e., by expulsion or fine). Union discipline of members may not adversely affect an employee's employment status and may not otherwise further illegal objectives. A union thus violates section 8(b)(1)(A) by refusing to refer a member for employment,[572] or by causing an employer to reduce the seniority[573] or attempting to cause the discharge[574] of an employee. Even under a valid union-security clause a union has an affirmative duty to specifically inform employees of their obligations and to afford them a reasonable opportunity to satisfy them before seeking an employee's discharge.[575]

b. The Effect of Resignation on Legality of Discipline. In two decisions in the early 1970s,[576] the Supreme Court made clear that a union may not fine employees who are no longer union mem-

[571]394 US at 430.

[572]Longshoremen (ILA) Local 1408 v. NLRB (Jacksonville Maritime Ass'n), 705 F2d 1549, 113 LRRM 2799 (CA 11, 1983), *enforcing* 258 NLRB 132, 108 LRRM 1262 (1981). *See also* Glass & Pottery Workers Locals 185 & 128 (Liberty Glass Co.), 273 NLRB 198, 118 LRRM 1091 (1984) (violation for union to threaten impairment of future employment opportunities); M.W. Kellogg Constructors, 273 NLRB 1049, 118 LRRM 1616 (1984), *enforcement denied*, 806 F2d 1435, 124 LRRM 2288 (CA 9, 1986), *on remand*, 284 NLRB 507, 125 LRRM 1195 (1987), *enforcement denied*, 867 F2d 498, 130 LRRM 2648 (CA 9, 1989).

[573]Auto Workers (Pitt Processing Co.), 208 NLRB 736, 85 LRRM 1185 (1974), *supplemented*, 217 NLRB 320, 89 LRRM 1031 (1975); Red Ball Motor Freight, 157 NLRB 1237, 61 LRRM 1522 (1966), *enforced*, 379 F2d 137, 65 LRRM 2309 (CA DC, 1967).

[574]Communications Workers Local 1104 (New York Tel. Co.) v. NLRB, 520 F2d 411, 89 LRRM 3028 (CA 2, 1975), *enforcing* 211 NLRB 114, 87 LRRM 1253 (1974), *cert. denied*, 423 US 1051, 91 LRRM 2099 (1976). *See also* Auto Workers Local 594 v. NLRB (General Motors Corp.), 776 F2d 1310, 120 LRRM 3289 (CA 6, 1985), *enforcing* 272 NLRB 705, 117 LRRM 1391 (1984); Communications Workers Local 1127 & 1125 (New York Tel. Co.), 208 NLRB 258, 85 LRRM 1102 (1974).

[575]Teamsters Local 572 (Ralph's Grocery), 247 NLRB 934, 103 LRRM 1268 (1980). Only uniformly required dues and fees may be compelled. Teamsters Local 439 (Leandro), 281 NLRB 255, 124 LRRM 1143 (1986), *enforced*, 838 F2d 1217 (CA 9, 1988) (violation of §8(b)(2) to compel payment of transfer fee which included fair share and building assessment components). *See also* NLRB v. Teamsters Local 291 (Kaiser Indus.), 633 F2d 1295, 105 LRRM 3458 (CA 9, 1980). *See generally* Chapter 27, "Union Security," and also Chapter 7, "Discrimination in Employment," at notes 459–498.

[576]NLRB v. Textile Workers Local 1029, Granite State Joint Bd. (International Paper Box Mach. Co.), 409 US 213, 81 LRRM 2853 (1972); Machinists Booster Lodge 405 v. NLRB (Boeing Co.), 412 US 84, 83 LRRM 2189 (1973).

bers. According to the Court, "when there is a lawful dissolution of a union-member relationship the union has no more control over the former member than it has over the man in the street."[577]

In *Granite State*,[578] the Court upheld the Board's determination that a union violated section 8(b)(1)(A) by fining members who had engaged in strikebreaking activities *after* they had resigned from the union. Giving "little weight" to the fact that the resigning members had voted in favor of the strike, the Court concluded that "the vitality of §7 requires that the member be free to refrain in November from the actions he endorsed in May and that his §7 rights are not lost by a union's plea for solidarity or by its pressures for conformity and submission to its regime."[579]

Consistent with this rationale, and notwithstanding a union constitutional provision prohibiting member involvement in strikebreaking activity, the Court also found a violation in *Machinists Booster Lodge 405*,[580] where a union sought enforcement of fines imposed upon strikebreaking members who had resigned from the union.

Discipline, other than fines, may be allowable even though the "strikebreaker" has resigned from the union. The First Circuit denied enforcement of a Board order finding illegal a union's five-year suspension from membership of members who had resigned from the union during a strike and engaged in strikebreaking activity.[581] The Court distinguished *Granite State*, concluding that a union may "bar membership to employees who have engaged in strikebreaking after having resigned from the union," which it contrasted with imposing and seeking judicial enforcement of fines.[582] In a similar case in which former members were expelled from a union for crossing picket lines following their effective resignations, the Board held such discipline to be privileged by the section 8(b)(1) provisio.[583]

---

[577]NLRB v. Textile Workers Local 1029, Granite State Joint Bd. (International Paper Box Mach. Co.), *supra* note 576 at 217.

[578]*Supra* note 576. *See also* Graphic Communications Locals 32B & 88L (George Banta Co.), 250 NLRB 850, 105 LRRM 1073 (1980) (union violated §8(b)(1)(A) by threatening to fine former members for conduct occurring after the former members had effectively resigned).

[579]409 US 217–18.

[580]Machinists Booster Lodge 405 v. NLRB (Boeing Co.), *supra* note 576.

[581]NLRB v. Machinists Dist. Lodges 99 & 2139 (General Elec. Co.), 489 F2d 769, 85 LRRM 2145 (CA 1, 1974), *denying enforcement to* 194 NLRB 938, 79 LRRM 1208 (1972).

[582]*Id.*, 85 LRRM at 2145.

[583]Pattern Makers (Lietzau Pattern Co.), 199 NLRB 96, 81 LRRM 1177 (1972).

The decision of the Supreme Court in *Scofield* upheld a union rule allowing discipline of members who worked behind a picket line provided that the members were "free to leave the union and escape the rule."[584] *Allis-Chalmers* and *Machinists Booster Lodge 405*, which invalidated discipline of *former* members, were followed by a series of cases at the Board raising the legality of union constitutional provisions, or other rules, abolishing or restricting the right of a member to resign when a strike was imminent or occurring. Although the union's legitimate interest in enhancing solidarity by such restrictions could not be gainsaid,[585] such restrictions undoubtedly cast shadows on the section 7 right of individual choice, as contemplated by the Court in *Scofield*. The Board first adopted the approach that such restrictions were valid so long as they did not amount to a withdrawal of the right, even during a strike, to resign "and escape the rule."[586] By the time the legality of such restrictions reached the Supreme Court, however, the Board had shifted ground and embraced the view that any such restriction was an invalid restraint on section 7 rights.[587]

In *Pattern Makers*,[588] the Supreme Court accepted the Board's reading of the statute. In that case, the union adopted a rule providing that "No resignation . . . from [the union] shall be accepted during a strike or lockout, or at a time when a strike or lockout appears imminent."[589] Members who attempted to resign during a strike were fined when the strike ended. The Board held that the fines violated section 8(b)(1)(A) and the Seventh Circuit enforced the Board's order, holding that the union rule "frustrate[d] the overriding policy of labor law that

---

[584] *See* text at *supra* note 571.

[585] " 'Integral to this federal labor policy has been the power in the chosen union to protect against erosion of its status under that policy through reasonable discipline of members who violate rules and regulations governing membership. That power is particularly vital when the members engage in strikes.' " NLRB v. Allis-Chalmers Mfg. Co., 388 US 175, 181, 65 LRRM 2449 (1967) (quoted in Machinists Local 1327, Dist. 115 (Dalmo Victor II), 263 NLRB 984, 111 LRRM 1115, 1117 (1982)).

[586] Electrical Workers (IUE) Local 444 (Sperry Rand Corp.), 235 NLRB 98, 98 LRRM 1526 (1978); Machinists Local 1327 (Dalmo Victor), 231 NLRB 719, 96 LRRM 1160 (1977), *enforcement denied and remanded*, 608 F2d 1219, 102 LRRM 2583 (CA 9, 1979), *on remand* (Dalmo Victor II), 263 NLRB 984, 111 LRRM 1115 (1982), *enforcement denied*, 725 F2d 1212, 115 LRRM 2972 (CA 9, 1984), *vacated and remanded*, 473 US 901, 119 LRRM 2992, *enforced on remand*, 773 F2d 1070, 120 LRRM 2864 (CA 9, 1985).

[587] Machinists Local Lodge 1414 (Neufeld Porsche-Audi), 270 NLRB 1330, 116 LRRM 1257 (1984).

[588] Pattern Makers v. NLRB (Rockford-Beloit Pattern Jobbers), 473 US 95, 119 LRRM 2928 (1985).

[589] *Id.* at 97.

employees be free to choose whether to engage in concerted activities."[590] In reviewing the lower court's judgment, however, the Supreme Court noted the deference owed the Board and narrowed the question to whether the Board's construction of section 8(b)(1)(A) was a reasonable one. Finding it so, the Court affirmed.

As a remedial measure, the Board has ordered both local unions and international unions to expunge unlawful resignation provisions from their bylaws and/or constitutions.[591] The Board has explained that such expungement is required because mere posting of a notice to members, stating that the union will cease to maintain and enforce unlawful restrictions on resignation, is insufficient to erase the coercive effects of such provisions.[592] However, provisions mandating that a member's resignation be in writing and sent to a designated office of the local union are lawful. They serve the legitimate purpose of enabling the union to maintain accurate membership rolls and are not unduly restrictive or burdensome.[593] As a part of its remedy the Board has ordered unions to make employees whole for any loss of earnings, benefits, travel expenses, or any other expenses incurred as a result of defending against internal charges brought pursuant to an unlawfully maintained rule, including any such losses that resulted from union-initiated state court actions to collect unlawfully imposed fines.[594]

c. Discipline for Refusal to Engage in Unlawful or Unprotected Activity. Discipline for refusal by union members to engage in unlawful or unprotected activity pursued by a union violates section 8(b)(1)(A). Although, as a general proposition, a union is free to discipline a member by internal means without violation of the Act,[595] such sanctions are subject to a basic exception: "[I]f

---

[590]NLRB v. Pattern Makers (Rockford-Beloit Pattern Jobbers), 724 F2d 57, 60, 115 LRRM 2264 (CA 7, 1983), *enforcing* 265 NLRB 1332, 112 LRRM 1030, 112 LRRM 1116 (concurring and dissenting opinions) (1982).

[591]Machinists Local Lodge 1374 (Columbia Mach.), 274 NLRB 123, 119 LRRM 1047 (1985).

[592]Auto Workers Locals 73 & 1093 (McDonnell Douglas Corp.), 282 NLRB 466, 124 LRRM 1025 (1986).

[593]Auto Workers Local 449 v. NLRB (National Metalcrafters), 865 F2d 791, 125 LRRM 1042 (CA 6, 1989).

[594]Machinists Dist. 94, Local Lodge 575 (McDonnell Douglas Corp.), 283 NLRB 881, 125 LRRM 1091 (1987). *See also* Food & Commercial Workers Local 1439 (Allied Employers), 275 NLRB 995, 119 LRRM 1226 (1985).

[595]Although the NLRA may not be applicable to all such discipline, the Labor Management Reporting and Disclosure Act of 1959 (Landrum-Griffin Act), 29 USC §§401-531 (1970), particularly Title I thereof, does provide extensive regulation of union disciplinary procedures.

the [union] rule invades or frustrates any overriding policy of the labor laws the rule may not be enforced, even by fine or expulsion, without violating Section 8(b)(1)(A)."[596] Thus, a union violates section 8(b)(1)(A) when it levies a fine in furtherance of unlawful secondary boycott activity[597] or of strike action taken in the face of a valid no-strike clause.[598]

A union fine that invades or frustrates an overriding policy of the labor laws may also be held violative of section 8(b)(1)(A), even though it is not imposed in furtherance of unlawful union activity. Thus the Board held that a union violated the Act by fining members for refusing to honor a lawful picket line established by a sister union, where the union's collective bargaining agreement contained a promise not to discipline members who worked behind such a picket line.[599] A union also violated section 8(b)(1)(A) when it brought charges against members who refused to participate in conduct that the Board subsequently found to be unlawful.[600]

The Board has invalidated union discipline under section 8(b)(1)(A) where the discipline was imposed to support a sympathy strike at a health care facility and where the strike was unprotected because the union had not given notice required under section 8(g).[601] Similarly, the Board has struck down

---

[596]Scofield v. NLRB, 394 US 423, 429, 70 LRRM 3105 (1969); Theatrical Stage Employees (RKO Gen.), 223 NLRB 959, 92 LRRM 1031, 1032 (1976).

[597]Plumbers Local 388 (Daily Heating & Air Conditioning), 280 NLRB 1260, 124 LRRM 1137 (1986) (fines of members who crossed picket lines that violated §§8(e) and 8(b)(4)(B); Plumbers & Pipe Fitters Local 444 (T.S. Hanson Plumbing), 277 NLRB 1231, 121 LRRM 1090 (1985), *enforced*, 827 F2d 579, 126 LRRM 2395 (CA 9, 1987) (fines revealed secondary object of refusal to cross another union's primary picket line); Carpenter's Dist. Council Local 362 (Pace Constr. Co.), 222 NLRB 613, 91 LRRM 1205 (1976); Longshoremen (ILWU) Local 30 (United States Borax & Chem. Corp.), 223 NLRB 1257, 92 LRRM 1282 (1976).

[598]Laborers Local 135 (Bechtel Power Corp.), 271 NLRB 777, 117 LRRM 1213 (1984); Building & Constr. Trades Council (Roy C. Anderson, Jr., Inc.), 222 NLRB 649, 91 LRRM 1215, *enforced*, 542 F2d 573, 93 LRRM 2943 (CA 5, 1976).

[599]Food & Commercial Workers Local 1439 (Rosauer's Supermarkets), 275 NLRB 30, 118 LRRM 1637 (1985). *See* Theatrical Stage Employees (RKO Gen.), *supra* note 596 (where union continued to discipline members after a federal court issued an injunction enjoining sister union's picketing). *See also* Verville v. Machinists, 520 F2d 615, 89 LRRM 3206 (CA 6, 1975) (sympathy strike in violation of no-strike clause in collective bargaining agreement); Communications Workers Local 1104 (New York Tel. Co.) v. NLRB, 520 F2d 411, 89 LRRM 3028 (CA 2, 1975), *enforcing* 211 NLRB 114, 87 LRRM 1253 (1974), *cert. denied*, 423 US 1051, 91 LRRM 2099 (1976) (illegal secondary boycott); Mine Workers Dist. 50, Local 12419 (National Grinding Wheel Co.), 176 NLRB 628, 71 LRRM 1311 (1969). *But see* Operating Eng'rs Local 18 (Davis-McKee, Inc.), 238 NLRB 652, 99 LRRM 1307 (1978), where the Board stated that *National Grinding Wheel* had been overruled sub silentio by subsequent decisions.

[600]NLRB v. Communications Workers Local 1170 (Rochester Tel. Corp.), 474 F2d 778, 82 LRRM 2101 (CA 2), *enforcing* 194 NLRB 872, 79 LRRM 1113 (1972).

[601]Operating Eng'rs Local 39 (Kaiser Found. Hosps.), 268 NLRB 115, 114 LRRM 1244 (1983), *enforced*, 746 F2d 530, 117 LRRM 2956 (CA 9, 1984).

union discipline that was imposed to support an unprotected partial strike.[602]

d. Discipline for Intraunion Activity. A similar principle has been applied to discipline for wholly internal activity. Although section 8(b)(1)(A) "leaves a union free to enforce a properly adopted rule which reflects a legitimate union interest and impairs no policy Congress has imbedded in the labor laws," it does not permit enforcement by fine or expulsion of a rule that invades or frustrates an overriding policy of the labor laws.[603] A union may not, under the guise of enforcing internal discipline, deprive its members of the right to participate fully and freely in the internal affairs of their own union.[604] Thus, a union fine levied on a member because of his intraunion activities in opposition to incumbent union officials was held to be a violation of section 8(b)(1)(A).[605] In another case, a local union that brought charges against and fined a member who circulated a newsletter critical of the local's leadership was found to have violated the Act notwithstanding that the union's international executive board reversed the conviction and fine.[606] The internal union charge was held to be an element in a pattern of harassment of a union dissident that continued after the appeal to the international was sustained.

e. Discipline for Activity Deemed Disloyal (Including the Filing of NLRB Petitions and Charges). It is well settled that a union's attempt to fine or expel a member for filing unfair labor practice charges violates section 8(b)(1)(A), for such action frustrates Congress' basic policy of free and uncoerced access to the Board.[607] Thus, a local union violated section 8(b)(1)(A) by fil-

---

[602]Graphic Communication Local 229 (Daily Printing), 272 NLRB 1088, 117 LRRM 1448 (1984).

[603]*See* text at *supra* note 571.

[604]Carpenters Local 22 (Graziano Constr. Co.), 195 NLRB 1, 79 LRRM 1194 (1972).

[605]*Id. See also* Helton v. NLRB, 656 F2d 883, 107 LRRM 2819 (CA DC, 1981), *granting review to* 248 NLRB 83, 103 LRRM 1318 (1980).

[606]Operating Eng'rs Local 139 (Associated Gen. Contractors of Am., Wisconsin Chapter), 273 NLRB 992, 118 LRRM 1396 (1984), *enforced*, 796 F2d 985, 123 LRRM 2021 (CA 7, 1986); *see also* Machinists Dist. 91, Local Lodge 707 (United Technologies Corp., Pratt & Whitney Div.), 278 NLRB 39, 122 LRRM 1336 (1986), *enforced*, 817 F2d 235, 125 LRRM 2335 (CA 2, 1987).

[607]Auto Workers Local 2017 (Federal Mogul Corp.), 283 NLRB 799, 125 LRRM 1044 (1987) (violation to reprimand members who filed unfair labor practice charges); Operating Eng'rs Local 825 (Building Contractors Ass'n of N.J.), 284 NLRB 188, 125 LRRM 1176 (1987) (violation to threaten reprisal against member for filing unfair labor practice charges); Laborers Local 308, Mail Handler Div. (U.S. Postal Serv.), 281 NLRB 1074, 124 LRRM 1243 (1986) (violation to remove member from shop steward position for filing unfair labor practice charge); Iron Workers (Walker Constr. Co.), 277 NLRB 1071, 121 LRRM 1001 (1985), *enforced*, 864 F2d 1225, 130 LRRM 2585 (CA 5, 1989) (violation for

ing internal disciplinary charges against members who filed unfair labor practice charges with the Board.[608] Moreover, the district council organization with which the local was affiliated violated the Act by scheduling internal trials of the members. To remedy the violations, the Board overruled prior decisions and ordered the union, inter alia, to reimburse the members for their costs of appearing at the trials.[609] However, the Fifth Circuit[610] has held that the right of access to the Board is not absolute and union regulations that impinge on such access may be lawful if they comply with the standards for internal union affairs established by the Supreme Court in *NLRB v. Marine & Shipbuilding Workers Local 22 (United States Lines Co.)*.[611] The Ninth Circuit has held that a union's civil suit against a member who had filed charges with the Board is not unlawful under the Act unless, as required by analogy to *Bill Johnson's Restaurants*,[612] the action is both lacking a reasonable basis in fact and pursued in bad faith.[613] It was not a per se violation for a union to expel a member based upon conduct that was proscribed by the union's international constitution but that had been revealed through his testimony in an unfair labor practice proceeding.[614] And although a union may legally *expel* a member for filing a decertification petition, it is a violation of section 8(b)(1)(A) for a union to *fine* a member for filing such a petition, because unlike expulsion, a fine does not serve any union "defense" purpose.[615]

---

union to discipline local union president who, in name of local, filed charge against international union). NLRB v. Marine & Shipbuilding Workers (United States Lines Co.), 391 US 418, 68 NLRB 2257 (1968). *See also* Transport Workers, 249 NLRB 1171, 104 LRRM 1304 (1980); Painters Local 1555 (Alaska Constructors), 241 NLRB 741, 100 LRRM 1578 (1979); Graphic Arts Local 96B (Williams Printing Co.), 235 NLRB 1153, 98 LRRM 1096 (1978); Teamsters Local 294 (August Bohl Contracting Co.), 193 NLRB 920, 78 LRRM 1479 (1971), *enforced,* 470 F2d 57, 81 LRRM 2920 (CA 2, 1972).

[608]Laborers Local 294, Northern Cal. Dist. Council (Hayward Baker Co.), 275 NLRB 278, 119 LRRM 1033 (1985).

[609]The Board reversed Transit Union Div. 825 (Robert Meier), 240 NLRB 1267, 100 LRRM 1441 (1979) and Television Wis., 224 NLRB 722, 93 LRRM 1494 (1976). The Board has applied the same remedies in strike resignation cases. *See* Machinists Dist. 94, Local Lodge 575 (McDonnell Douglas Corp.), *supra* note 594.

[610]NLRB v. Iron Workers (Walker Constr. Co.), 864 F2d 1225, 130 LRRM 2585, 2589 (CA 5, 1989).

[611]391 US 418, 68 LRRM 2257 (1968).

[612]461 US 731, 113 LRRM 2647 (1983). *See* text at *supra* note 595.

[613]Sheet Metal Workers Local 355 v. NLRB (Zinsco Elec. Prods.), 716 F2d 1249, 114 LRRM 2569 (CA 9, 1983), *enforcing in part, vacating and remanding in part,* 254 NLRB 773, 106 LRRM 1137 (1981).

[614]Carpenters Dist. Council (Hughes Helicopters), 224 NLRB 350, 92 LRRM 1341 (1976).

[615]Service Employees Local 1-J (I. Shor Co.), 273 NLRB 929, 118 LRRM 1227 (1984) (threat to expel and expulsion of member from health and welfare fund); NLRB v.

A union also violates the Act by threatening members with intraunion charges in the event they testify against other members in an arbitration proceeding.[616] But a union does not violate the Act by maintaining provisions in its constitution requiring members to exhaust internal remedies before resorting to court or administrative proceedings.[617]

f. Reasonableness of Fines Imposed. The Board has refused to examine in section 8(b)(1)(A) proceedings the reasonableness of otherwise legally imposed union fines. Such refusal was approved by the Supreme Court in *NLRB v. Boeing Co.*,[618] where the Court relied on legislative history that indicated Congress did not intend to regulate the internal affairs of unions through section 8(b)(1)(A); it reasoned that inquiry by the Board into the "multiplicity of factors" bearing on the reasonableness issue would "necessarily lead the Board to a substantial involvement in strictly internal union affairs." Recognizing that the reasonableness issue "must be decided upon the basis of the law of contract, voluntary associations," or other principles of law to be applied in a competent forum, the Court asserted that "State Courts will be wholly free to apply state law to such issue at the suit of either the union or the member fined."[619]

3. Violence and Threats. Violence or threats of violence constitute coercion and restraint within the meaning of section 8(b)(1)(A). Thus, threatening an employee with bodily harm may be an unfair labor practice.[620] A violation was found

---

Molders Local 125, 442 F2d 92, 77 LRRM 2067 (CA 7, 1971). *See also* Teamsters Local 165 (Goodyear Tire & Rubber Co.), 211 NLRB 707, 86 LRRM 1433 (1974) (whereas a fine of a member is a violation of §8(b)(1)(A), expulsion is not, since a union constitution may lawfully include disciplinary provisions which serve to foster its own existence).

[616]NLRB v. Electrical Workers (IUE) Local 745 (McGraw-Edison, Nat'l Elec. Coil Div.), 759 F2d 533, 118 LRRM 3407 (CA 6, 1985), *enforcing* 268 NLRB 308, 114 LRRM 1269 (1983); Steelworkers Local 5550 (Redfield Co.), 223 NLRB 854, 92 LRRM 1062 (1976).

[617]Plasterers & Cement Masons Local 521 (McKee & Co.), 189 NLRB 553, 77 LRRM 1149 (1971) where the Board held that such a clause was not per se unlawful. However, the Board has also held that such clauses may not be invoked against a member for filing an NLRB charge without exhausting intraunion remedies over a discriminatory referral practice. J. Willis & Son Masonry, 191 NLRB 872, 77 LRRM 1693 (1971).

[618]412 US 67, 74, 83 LRRM 2183 (1973).

[619]*Id.* In Carpenters Local 720 v. NLRB (UMC of La.), 798 F2d 781, 123 LRRM 2299 (CA 5, 1986), *vacating and remanding* 276 NLRB 59, 120 LRRM 1071 (1985), the union enforced a new rule against a member who lacked notice of the rule. The Board found a violation of §8(b)(1)(A) because the rule was not duly promulgated. The circuit court refused enforcement on the ground that the Board had intruded into internal union matters without sufficient statutory warrant. The Board dismissed the complaint on remand, Carpenters Local 720 (UMC of La.), 287 NLRB 545, 127 LRRM 1166 (1987).

[620]*E.g.*, Operating Eng'rs Local 450 (Associated Gen. Contractors of Am., Houston Chapter), 267 NLRB 775, 114 LRRM 1201 (1983) (threats and physical assaults by union

where a union had coerced employees into crossing a rival union's picket line.[621] Restraint and coercion have also been found in cases where nonviolent physical force was used to prevent employees from exercising their section 7 rights—for example, mass picketing by a union that prevented employees from gaining entrance to the employer's premises.[622]

Although the Act literally proscribes only restraint and coercion of "employees" in section 8(b)(1)(A), violent conduct directed at nonemployees has been held violative of the section when it was substantially certain that employees would hear about it[623] or when the violence was committed in their presence.[624] It is also a violation of the Act to threaten nonstrikers and supervisory personnel with physical violence.[625]

A union restrains and coerces an employee when its threats cause an employer to refrain from hiring a prospective employee. Thus section 8(b)(1)(A) was violated when a union threatened to "take some kind of action" if a nonunion employee was hired.[626]

B. Sections 8(b)(1)(B) and 8(b)(4)(A): Restraint and Coercion in Selection of Employer Representatives

1. Interference With the Employer's Choice of Representatives. Section 8(b)(1)(B) prohibits a union from interfering with an employer's choice of representatives for collective bargaining or the adjustment of grievances, and section 8(b)(4)(A) makes it unlawful for a union to force an employer or self-employed person to join any labor or employer organization. Each party to

---

agents against employees). *See also* Boilermakers Local 27 (Daniel Constr. Co.), 266 NLRB 602, 113 LRRM 1014 (1983); Rockville Nursing Center, 193 NLRB 959, 78 LRRM 1519 (1971); Teamsters Local 5 v. NLRB (Altex Ready-Mixed Concrete Corp.), 406 F2d 439, 70 LRRM 2226 (1969); Chemical Workers Local 738 (Midstates Metal Prods.), 156 NLRB 872, 61 LRRM 1159 (1966).

[621]Teamsters Local 729 (Penntruck Co.), 189 NLRB 696, 76 LRRM 1753 (1971).

[622]Longshoremen (ILWU) Local 6 (Sunset Line & Twine Co.), 79 NLRB 1487, 23 LRRM 1001 (1948).

[623]Furniture Workers Local 140 (Brooklyn Spring Corp.), 113 NLRB 815, 36 LRRM 1372 (1955), *enforced*, 233 F2d 539, 38 LRRM 2134 (CA 2, 1956).

[624]Retail, Wholesale & Dep't Store Union Dist. 65, (B. Brown Assocs.), 157 NLRB 615, 61 LRRM 1382 (1966), *enforced*, 375 F2d 745, 64 LRRM 2750 (CA 2, 1967); Retail, Wholesale & Dep't Store Union Dist. 65, (I. Posner, Inc.), 133 NLRB 1555, 49 LRRM 1066 (1961).

[625]Teamsters Local 298 (Schumacher Elec. Corp.), 236 NLRB 428, 98 LRRM 1486 (1978); Congreso de Uniones Industriales de P.R. (National Packing Co.), 237 NLRB 1406, 99 LRRM 1110 (1978).

[626]Theatrical Stage Employees Local 52 (Michael Levee Prods), 238 NLRB 19, 99 LRRM 1645 (1978), *enforced*, 593 F2d 197, 100 LRRM 2766 (CA 2, 1979).

a collective bargaining relationship has both the right to select its representatives for bargaining and the duty to deal with the chosen representative of the other party.[627]

It is a violation of section 8(b)(1)(B) for a union to engage in a course of conduct that coerces the employer into discharging or demoting its grievance-adjustment representative, whether or not the union expressly demands such action.[628]

The Board has recognized, however, that if the presence of a particular representative in negotiations makes collective bargaining impossible or futile, then the party's right to choose its own representative may be limited and the other party may be relieved of its duty to deal with that particular representative.[629] The test is whether there is "*persuasive evidence* that the presence of the particular individual would create ill will and make good-faith bargaining impossible."[630]

The Board found no violation of section 8(b)(1)(B) where a union picketed with the aim of forcing the employer to hire an additional third mate;[631] nor was there a violation where a union struck to force an employer to conform its contract to a multiemployer contract.[632]

---

[627]Under §8(b)(1)(B) it is "an unfair labor practice for a labor organization or its agent . . . to restrain or coerce . . . an employer in the selection of his representatives for the purposes of collective bargaining or the adjustments of grievances." *See* Chapters 22, "Secondary Strikes and Picketing," and 24, "Section 8(e): The 'Hot-Cargo' Agreement." A union that threatened to strike to force multi-employer bargaining violated §§8(b)(1)(A) and 8(b)(4)(A). Mine Workers Local 1854 (Amax Coal Co.), 238 NLRB 1583, *enforced in pertinent part sub nom.* Amax, Inc. v. NLRB, 614 F2d 872, 103 LRRM 2482 (CA 3, 1980). *See also* Frito-Lay, Inc. v. Teamsters Local 137, 623 F2d 1354, 104 LRRM 2931 (CA 9, 1980), *cert. denied*, 449 US 1112, 106 LRRM 2200 (1981); Longshoremen (ILWU) (General Ore., Inc.), 126 NLRB 172, 45 LRRM 1296 (1960). *But cf.* Teamsters Local 901 (Jaime Andino Trucking), 240 NLRB 925, 100 LRRM 1377 (1979), *aff'd*, 619 F2d 147, 104 LRRM 2183 (CA 1, 1980). The Supreme Court also held, in NLRB v. Amax Coal Co., 453 US 322, 107 LRRM 2769 (1981), that employer-selected trustees under §302(c)(5) of the LMRA are not employer representatives under §8(b)(1)(B).

[628]Longshoremen (ILWU) Local 10 (Pacific Maritime Ass'n), 254 NLRB 540, 106 LRRM 1342 (1981); Union Independiente de Empleados de Servicios Legales de P.R. 249 NLRB 1044, 104 LRRM 1433 (1980); Teamsters Local 610 (Bianco Mfg. Co.) v. NLRB, 100 LRRM 3123 (1979); Auto Workers Local 259 (Atherton Cadillac, Inc.) v. NLRB, 562 F2d 38, 95 LRRM 3011 (CA 2, 1977), *enforcing* 225 NLRB 421, 92 LRRM 1417 (1976); ITO Corp., 246 NLRB 810, 102 LRRM 1682 (1979).

[629]Fitzsimons Mfg. Co., 251 NLRB 375, 105 LRRM 1083 (1980).

[630]KDEN Broadcasting Co., subsidiary of North Am. Broadcasting Co., 225 NLRB 25, 35, 93 LRRM 1022 (1976) (emphasis in original). *See also* Teamsters Local 70 (Kockos Bros.), 183 NLRB 1330, 74 LRRM 1401 (1970).

[631]Masters, Mates & Pilots (Newport Tankers Corp.), 233 NLRB 245, 96 LRRM 1498 (1977) ("because the employer retained absolute control in its selection of bargaining representatives").

[632]Typographical Union No. 6 (New York) (Clark & Fritts), 236 NLRB 317, 98 LRRM 1279 (1978) (since the employer had signed a memorandum agreement which bound it to future contracts negotiated by the union and the multi-employer association). *See generally* Chapter 11, "Appropriate Bargaining Units," at notes 327–398.

2. Union Discipline of Supervisor-Members. Union discipline of a supervisor-member violates section 8(b)(1)(B) if it has the effect of restraining or coercing the employer in the selection of its representatives for the purpose of collective bargaining or the adjustment of grievances. Restraint or coercion exists if the discipline may affect the conduct of the supervisor in the performance of his grievance adjusting or collective bargaining duties.

In 1968, in *Typographical Union No. 18 (Northwest Publications)*,[633] the Board departed from its past practice of finding a violation of 8(b)(1)(B) only if the conduct clearly fell within the statutory prohibition. In that case, three union-member foremen were expelled from the union for assigning bargaining-unit work allegedly in violation of the collective agreement. Despite the absence of union pressure or coercion aimed at securing the replacement of the foremen, the Board held that by seeking to influence the manner in which the foremen interpreted the contract, the union violated section 8(b)(1)(B).

The Board thus extended section 8(b)(1)(B) to protect employers in the selection of their collective bargaining representatives.[634] The Board declared that "[i]n enacting Section 8(b)(1)(B) Congress sought to prevent union interference with an employer's control over its own representatives."[635]

The Board has found violations of section 8(b)(1)(B) where a union fined and suspended a supervisor-member for assigning another member to unpleasant tasks and for allegedly breaching a contractual provision relating to overtime work,[636] where a union went on strike to coerce the employer into signing an interim agreement designating a certain multiemployer organization as its bargaining representative,[637] and where a union refused to recognize the employer's selection of a nonmember as an assistant foreman.[638]

---

[633] 172 NLRB 2173, 69 LRRM 1157 (1968).

[634] In the course of the Senate's consideration of §8(b)(1)(B), Senator Ellender stated: "[Q]uite a few unions forced employers to change foremen. They have been taking it upon themselves to say that management should not appoint any representative who is too strict with the membership of the union. This amendment seeks to prescribe a remedy in order to prevent such interferences." 93 CONG. REC. 4266 (1947); LEGISLATIVE HISTORY OF THE LMRA 1077. *See* Teamsters Local 986 (Tak-Teak, Inc.), 145 NLRB 1511, 55 LRRM 1205 (1964); Ladies' Garment Workers (Helen Rose Co.), 127 NLRB 1543, 46 LRRM 1235 (1960).

[635] 172 NLRB at 2173.

[636] Longshoremen (ILA) Local 333, United Marine Div. (Morania Oil Tankers), 233 NLRB 387, 96 LRRM 1609 (1977).

[637] Retail Clerks Local 770 (Fine's Food Co.), 228 NLRB 1166, 95 LRRM 1062 (1977).

[638] Typographical Union No. 6 (New York News), 237 NLRB 1241, 99 LRRM 1111 (1978).

In *Florida Power & Light Co.*,[639] the Supreme Court retarded the expansion of section 8(b)(1)(B) by holding that a union does not violate section 8(b)(1)(B) by disciplining its supervisor-members for performing rank-and-file bargaining-unit work during a lawful strike. Reviewing applicable legislative history, the Court found the conclusion

> inescapable that a union's discipline of one of its members who is a supervisory employee can constitute a violation of Section 8(b)(1)(B) only when that discipline may adversely affect the supervisor's conduct in performing the duties of, and acting in his capacity as, grievance adjuster or collective bargainer on behalf of the employer.[640]

The Court rejected the Board's argument that the statutory language encompasses "any situation in which the union's actions are likely to deprive the employer of the undivided loyalty of his supervisory employees."[641] In the Court's view, the "divided loyalty" problem was not addressed by Congress through section 8(b)(1)(B) but, rather, through other provisions in the Act that permit the employer to refuse to hire union members as supervisors, to discharge supervisors because of union activities or membership, and to refuse to engage in collective bargaining with them.

Subsequently, the Board directed its attention to the question of whether the union's discipline could adversely affect the supervisor's conduct in performing his grievance-adjustment or collective bargaining duties on behalf of the employer. This approach resulted in the Board's limiting the application of *Florida Power* only to supervisors who perform rank-and-file work during a strike.[642] The Board held that it is an unfair practice under section 8(b)(1)(B) for a union to discipline supervisor-members for crossing a picket line to perform their regular functions during a strike if their regular duties include the adjustment of grievances.[643] This holding rested on the Board's conclusion

---

[639]Florida Power & Light Co. v. Electrical Workers (IBEW), 417 US 790, 86 LRRM 2689 (1974). *See* Grissom, *Union Discipline of Supervisor Members Under Section 8(b)(1)(B) of the National Labor Relations Act: Drawing the Line After* Florida Power, 27 ALA. L. REV. 575 (1975); Abraham, *Changing Interpretation of NLRB Section 8(b)(1)(B)—Union Discipline of Supervisors in the Aftermath of* Florida Power and Light, 10 JOHN MARSHALL J. OF PRAC. & PROC. 117 (1976).

[640]417 US at 804.

[641]*Id.* at 806.

[642]Typographical Union No. 6 (New York) (Triangle Publications), 216 NLRB 896, 88 LRRM 1384 (1975).

[643]Typographical Union No. 16 (Chicago) (Hammond Publishers), 216 NLRB 903, 88 LRRM 1378 (1975), *enforced*, 539 F2d 242, 98 LRRM 2740 (1976).

that such discipline imposed on the supervisor would have a "carry-over" effect and would influence the supervisor in the performance of his or her adjustment functions after the strike, thereby interfering with and coercing the employer in the choice of its grievance representative.[644]

Although the Board restricted the application of *Florida Power* to supervisors performing rank-and-file work during a strike, the Federal courts were divided over the application of *Florida Power* to supervisors who were fined for exercising both supervisory and rank-and-file work or the performance of only supervisory work during a strike.[645] The Supreme Court addressed this issue in *American Broadcasting Cos. v. Writers Guild W.*[646]

In *Writers Guild*, the union had argued that it is never an unfair labor practice for unions to discipline supervisor-members for working during a strike, regardless of the type of work they may perform behind the picket line. The Supreme Court disagreed; in a five-to-four decision reversing the Second Circuit, the Court reasoned that discipline of a supervisor may have a "carry over" effect on his or her capacity as a grievance adjuster or collective bargainer. In such situations, therefore, the employer would be restrained and coerced in its selection of those representatives. The Court stated that the Board correctly understood *Florida Power* to mean the following:

> In ruling upon a §8(b)(1)(B) charge growing out of union discipline of a supervisory member who elects to work during a strike, it may—

---

[644]Longshoremen (ILWU) Local 6 (Associated Food Stores), 220 NLRB 809, 90 LRRM 1363 (1975); Carpenters Wis. Dist. Council (Skippy Enters.), 218 NLRB 1063, 89 LRRM 1477 (1975), *enforced*, 532 F2d 47, 91 LRRM 2961 (CA 7, 1976).

[645]*Compare* American Broadcasting Co. v. NLRB, 547 F2d 159, 93 LRRM 2958 (CA 2, 1976), *denying enforcement to* 217 NLRB 957, 89 LRRM 1221 (1975) (the Second Circuit denied enforcement of a Board order finding a §8(b)(1)(B) violation where the union fined and disciplined supervisor-members who had crossed a picket line and performed only managerial working during a strike); NLRB v. Musicians Local 66 (Civic Music Ass'n), 514 F2d 988, 89 LRRM 2193 (CA 2, 1975) (the Second Circuit held that a fine of a supervisor engaged only in supervisory work and not in grievance adjustment or collective bargaining was not a violation of §8(b)(1)(B); *with* Typographical Union No. 16 (Chicago) v. NLRB (Hammond Publishers), 539 F2d 242, 98 LRRM 2740 (CA DC, 1976), *enforcing* 216 NLRB 903, 88 LRRM 1378 (1975) (the Court of Appeals for the District of Columbia Circuit affirmed the Board's finding that the union violated §8(b)(1)(B) by fining and expelling two supervisor-members who had crossed the union picket line during a strike and performed only a minimal amount of rank-and-file work in addition to their supervisory duties, which included grievance adjustment); Carpenters Wis. Dist. Council v. NLRB (Skippy Enters.), *supra* note 644 (the Seventh Circuit enforced the Board's finding of §8(b)(1)(B) violation where the union fined a supervisor-member and subsequently instituted legal action against him to collect the fine; the supervisor had spent 30% of his time performing rank-and-file work before the strike, and that amount did not increase after the strike began).

[646]437 US 411, 98 LRRM 2705 (1978), *rev'g* 547 F2d 159, 93 LRRM 2958 (CA 2, 1976).

> indeed it must—inquire whether the sanction may adversely affect the supervisor's performance of his collective bargaining or grievance adjustment tasks and thereby coerce or restrain the employer contrary to §8(b)(1)(B).[647]

After *American Broadcasting Cos.*, the Board continued to give an expansive reading to section 8(b)(1)(B). In particular, the Board adhered to the "reservoir doctrine," which treated all of an employer's supervisors as a pool, or reservoir, from which the employer should be free to draw uncoerced grievance adjusters and collective bargainers as need might dictate.[648] The Board's reading of section 8(b)(1)(B) in this regard was rejected by the Supreme Court in *NLRB v. Electrical Workers (IBEW) Local 340 (Harold E. Nutter, Inc.)*.[649] In that case, the Board held that a union violated section 8(b)(1)(B) by disciplining member-supervisors employed by an employer with whom the union neither had nor sought any collective bargaining relationship.[650] The Court, disagreeing with the Board, rejected the "reservoir" rationale:

> Although both . . . were supervisors within the meaning of Section 2(11), neither had grievance-adjustment or collective-bargaining responsibilities protected by Section 8(b)(1)(B). The possibility that a Section 2(11) supervisor might someday perform Section 8(b)(1)(B) functions and that past discipline might then have an adverse effect on the performance of such duties is simply too speculative to support a finding [of violation].[651]

The Court thus emphasized that the protection of section 8(b)(1)(B) extends only to the subclass of section 2(11) supervisors who represent the employer in the adjustment of grievances and in collective bargaining.

---

[647] *Id.* at 430.

[648] In Teamsters Local 296 (Northwest Publications), 263 NLRB 778, 111 LRRM 1076 (1982), the Board affirmed its adherence to the "reservoir doctrine" and to its view that all supervisors within the definition of §2(11) are "representatives" within the scope of §8(b)(1)(B).

[649] 481 US 573, 125 LRRM 2305 (1987).

[650] Electrical Workers (IBEW) Local 340 (Harold E. Nutter, Inc.), 271 NLRB 995, 117 LRRM 1056 (1984), *enforcement denied*, 780 F2d 1489, 121 LRRM 2563 (CA 9, 1986).

[651] 125 LRRM at 2311.

Chapter 7

DISCRIMINATION IN EMPLOYMENT

I. Discrimination as an Unfair Labor Practice

The most frequently filed unfair labor practice charges are those that allege discrimination in employment.[1] This chapter addresses the general problem of employment discrimination relating to union activity.[2] Discrimination as it specifically relates to strikes,[3] lockouts,[4] union-security agreements,[5] and a union's

---

[1]1987 NLRB Ann. Rep. 6 (1989).

[2]For scholarly comment on the subject of discrimination under the Act, see the following: Lieb, *Constructive Discharge Under Section 8(a)(3) of the National Labor Relations Act: A Study in Undue Concern Over Motives*, 7 Indus. Rel. L. J. 143 (1985); Coleman, *Clear Thinking,* Clear Pine, *and Strike Misconduct Discharges*, 15 Cum. L. Rev. 23 (1984); Goore, *Discriminatory Discharge in a Sports Context: A Reassessment of the Burden of Proof and Remedies Under the National Labor Relations Act,* 53 Fordham L. Rev. 615 (1984); Remar, *Climbing* Mt. Healthy*: In Search of the "Wright Line" on Mixed-Motive Discharges Under Section 8(a)(3)*, 1 Indus. Rel. L. J. 636 (1982); Cole, *Discriminatory Discipline of Union Representatives for Breach of Their "Higher Duty" in Illegal Strikes*, 1982 Duke L. J. 900 (1982); Dagley, *Discharge of Supervisors for Union Related Activity: An Examination of "Pattern of Conduct" Analysis*, 34 Vand. L. Rev. 361 (1981); Moss, *Plant Removal—Labor Law Issues*, 54 Cal. S. B.J. 42 (1979); Kaplan & Yates, *Plant Relocation: Management Solution to Labor Problems*, 34 Mo. B.J. 416 (1978); Jennings & Wolters, *Discharge Cases Reconsidered*, 31 Arb. J. 164 (1976); Swift, *Plant Relocation: Catching Up With The Runaway Shop*, 14 B. C. Ind. & Comm. L. Rev. 1135 (1973); Bernhardt, *Lockouts: An Analysis of Board and Court Decisions Since* Brown *and* American Ship, 57 Cornell L.Q. 211 (1972); Shieber, *Section 8(a)(3) of the National Labor Relations Act: A Rationale—Part I, Discrimination*, 29 La. L. Rev. 46 (1968); Shieber & Moore, *Section 8(a)(3) of the National Labor Relations Act: A Rationale—Part II, Encouragement or Discouragement of Membership in Any Labor Organization and the Significance of Employer Motive*, 33 La. L. Rev. 1 (1972); Christensen & Svanoe, *Motive and Intent in the Commission of Unfair Labor Practices: The Supreme Court and the Fictive Formality*, 77 Yale L. J. 1269 (1968); Cox, *The Right to Engage in Concerted Activities*, 26 Ind. L. J. 319 (1951); Getman, *Section 8(a)(3) of the NLRA and the Effort to Insulate Free Employee Choice*, 32 U. Chi. L. Rev. 735 (1965); Janofsky, *New Concepts in Interference and Discrimination Under the NLRA: The Legacy of* American Ship Building *and* Great Dane Trailers, 70 Colum. L. Rev. 81 (1970); Oberer, *The Scienter Factor in Section 8(a)(1) and (3) of the Labor Act: Of Balancing, Hostile Motive, Dogs and Tails*, 52 Cornell L.Q. 491 (1967); Schatzki, *Some Observations and Suggestions Concerning a Misnomer—"Protected" Concerted Activities*, 47 Tex. L. Rev. 378 (1969).

[3]*See* Chapter 19, "The Primary Strike."

[4]*See* Chapter 20, "The Lockout."

[5]*See* Chapter 27, "Union Security."

duty of fair representation[6] will be treated in detail in subsequent chapters.

Discrimination for certain specified reasons is expressly prohibited by three provisions of the National Labor Relations Act.

Under section 8(a)(3) of the Act it is unlawful for an employer "by discrimination in regard to hire or tenure of employment to encourage or discourage membership in any labor organization." The provision does not, however, proscribe all types of employment discrimination. As the Supreme Court has stated, section 8(a)(3) does not "outlaw discrimination in employment as such; only such discrimination as encourages or discourages membership in a labor organization is proscribed."[7] The statutory ban against such discrimination is qualified by two provisos. The first proviso permits an employer and a labor organization to enter into a union-shop agreement if the labor organization represents the employer's employees and the employees have not voted to prohibit a union-shop agreement in an election held within one year prior to the date of such agreement.[8] The second proviso, however, prohibits an employer from discriminating against an employee for nonmembership in a labor organization if the employer "has reasonable grounds for believing . . . that membership was not available to the employee on the same terms and conditions generally applicable to other members," or if it "has reasonable grounds for believing that membership was denied or terminated for reasons other than failure . . . to tender the periodic dues and initiation fees uniformly required as a condition of acquiring or retaining membership."[9]

Discrimination by unions is prohibited by section 8(b)(2).[10] That provision makes it an unfair labor practice for a labor organization or its agents "to cause or attempt to cause an employer to discriminate against an employee in violation of subsection (a)(3) or to discriminate against an employee with

---

[6]*See* Chapter 26, "The Duty of Fair Representation."

[7]Radio Officers v. NLRB (A.H. Bull S.S. Co.), 347 US 17, 43, 33 LRRM 2417 (1954).

[8]This "first" proviso modifies an original Wagner Act provision that permitted a closed shop. Union-shop agreements are unlawful in "right to work" states by virtue of §14(b) of the Act, which provides that an agreement requiring membership in a labor organization as a condition of employment may be prohibited by state or territorial law. *See generally* Chapter 27, "Union Security."

[9]The "second" proviso was enacted in 1947. *See* Chapter 27, "Union Security."

[10]Section 8(b)(2) was enacted in 1947.

respect to whom membership in such organization has been denied or terminated on some ground other than failure to tender the periodic dues and initiation fees uniformly required as a condition of acquiring or retaining membership."

The third prohibition against employment discrimination is in section 8(a)(4). Section 8(a)(4), enacted as section 8(4) with the passage of the Wagner Act in 1935, makes it unlawful for an employer "to discharge or otherwise discriminate against an employee because he has filed charges or given testimony under this Act." Although section 8(b) of the Act does not specifically address the subject of union discrimination for filing charges or testifying in NLRB proceedings, reprisals by labor organizations for such conduct violate section 8(b)(1)(A).[11] Thus, a union violates section 8(b)(1)(A) if it expels, fines, or otherwise disciplines a member or officer,[12] refuses to process a grievance,[13] refuses to refer individuals for employment opportunities,[14] or threatens them with physical harm[15] because they have filed charges or given testimony under the Act.[16]

---

[11]This section of the Act makes it unlawful for a labor organization "to restrain or coerce employees in the exercise of the rights guaranteed" by §7 of the Act. *See* Chapter 6, "Interference With Protected Rights."

[12]Sheet Metal Workers Local 204 (Majestic Co.), 246 NLRB 318, 102 LRRM 1503 (1979); NLRB v. Teamsters Local 294 (August Bohl Contracting Co.), 470 F2d 57, 81 LRRM 2920 (CA 2, 1972); NLRB v. Operating Eng'rs Local 825 (Tarantino), 420 F2d 961, 73 LRRM 2419 (CA 3, 1970); NLRB v. Marine & Shipbuilding Workers Local 22 (United States Lines), 391 US 418, 68 LRRM 2257 (1968). *Cf.* NLRB v. Boilermakers (General Am. Transp. Corp.), 581 F2d 473, 99 LRRM 2855 (CA 5, 1978) (union did not violate §8(b)(1)(A) when it removed steward from office because of his failure to pursue his discharge grievance under collective bargaining agreement before filing unfair labor practice charges).

[13]Graphic Arts Local 96B (Williams Printing Co.), 235 NLRB 1153, 98 LRRM 1096 (1978); Penn Indus., 233 NLRB 928, 97 LRRM 1299 (1977); NLRB v. Teamsters Local 703 (Dominick's Finer Foods), 81 LRRM 2488 (CA 7, 1972), *enforcing* 188 NLRB 873, 76 LRRM 1607 (1971); Packers & Drivers (Guy's Foods), 188 NLRB 608, 76 LRRM 1380 (1971); Selwyn Shoe Mfg. Corp., 172 NLRB 674, 68 LRRM 1417, *modified on other grounds,* 428 F2d 217, 74 LRRM 2474 (CA 8, 1970).

[14]Painters Local 1555 (Alaska Constructors), 241 NLRB 741, 100 LRRM 1578 (1979); Plumbers & Pipe Fitters Local 195 (Stone & Webster Eng'g Corp.), 240 NLRB 504, 100 LRRM 1460 (1979); Laborers Local 663 (Robert A. Treuner Constr. Co.), 205 NLRB 455, 84 LRRM 1314 (1973); Iron Workers Local 577 (Tri-State Steel Erectors), 199 NLRB 37, 81 LRRM 1275 (1972).

[15]Electrical Workers (IBEW) Local 3 (Welsbach Elec. Corp.), 236 NLRB 503, 99 LRRM 1271 (1978); NLRB v. Union Nacional de Trabajadores, 540 F2d 1, 92 LRRM 3425 (CA 1, 1976), *cert. denied,* 429 US 1039, 94 LRRM 2201 (1977), *enforcing* 219 NLRB 429, 89 LRRM 1746 (1975); Teamsters Local 705 (Associated Transp.), 209 NLRB 292, 86 LRRM 1119 (1974).

[16]*See* Chapter 6, "Interference With Protected Rights," at notes 607–617.

II. EMPLOYER DISCRIMINATION

A. Persons Within the Protection of Section 8(a)(3)

The protection of section 8(a)(3) extends to applicants for employment as well as to individuals who are already employed. In the landmark case of *Phelps Dodge Corp. v. NLRB*,[17] the Supreme Court ruled that an employer violated section 8(a)(3) by refusing to hire job applicants who were union members. Thereafter, relying on the broad definition of "employee" contained in section 2(3), the Board frequently stated that the Act protects "members of the working class generally."[18] Thus, the protection of section 8(a)(3) extends to employees who are not union members,[19] to foreign nationals,[20] and even to professional organizers who obtain employment solely for the purpose of organizing the employer's work force.[21] Section 8(a)(3) also forbids discrimination against employees based upon the union activities of their relatives.[22]

Certain confidential employees[23] and managerial employ-

---

[17]313 US 177, 8 LRRM 439 (1941). *Accord* Gatliff Business Prods., 276 NLRB 543, 120 LRRM 1262 (1985); Hutchens Trucking Co., 268 NLRB 509, 115 LRRM 1048 (1984), *enforced*, 749 F2d 32, 117 LRRM 3336 (CA 4, 1984); Consolidated Freightways Corp., 242 NLRB 770, 101 LRRM 1454 (1979); Mack Trucks, 242 NLRB 651, 101 LRRM 1249 (1979); Alexander Dawson, Inc. v. NLRB, 586 F2d 1300, 99 LRRM 3105 (CA 9, 1978); Atlantic Maintenance Co. v. NLRB, 305 F2d 604, 50 LRRM 2494 (CA 3, 1962).

[18]*E.g*, Giant Food Mkts., 241 NLRB 727, 100 LRRM 1598, 1599 n.5 (1979); Little Rock Crate & Basket Co., 227 NLRB 1406, 94 LRRM 1385 (1977); Oak Apparel, 218 NLRB 701, 89 LRRM 1381 (1975); Briggs Mfg. Co., 75 NLRB 569, 21 LRRM 1056 (1947).

[19]NLRB v. Electrical Workers (IBEW) Local 322 (Bechtel Power Corp.), 597 F2d 1326, 101 LRRM 2157 (CA 10, 1979); Narragansett Restaurant Corp., 243 NLRB 125, 101 LRRM 1579 (1979); Schorr Stern Food Corp., 227 NLRB 1650, 94 LRRM 1331 (1977).

[20]Sure Tan, Inc. v. NLRB, 467 US 883, 116 LRRM 2857 (1984); Amay's Bakery & Noodle Co., 227 NLRB 214, 94 LRRM 1165 (1976); Handling Equip. Corp., 209 NLRB 64, 85 LRRM 1603 (1974).

[21]Pilliod of Miss., 275 NLRB 799, 119 LRRM 1279 (1985) (Board rejected employer's defense that employee is unprotected by §8(a)(3) because he was union organizer at time of hire); Anthony Forest Prods. Co., 231 NLRB 976, 97 LRRM 1014 (1977); Oak Apparel, *supra* note 18.

[22]Advertisers Mfg. Co., 280 NLRB 1185, 124 LRRM 1017 (1986), *enforced*, 823 F2d 1086, 125 LRRM 3024 (CA 7, 1987) (discharge of supervisor because of union activities of son was unlawful); Consolidation Coal Co., 266 NLRB 670, 113 LRRM 1022 (1983) (retired grandfather of employee enjoyed §8(a)(3) protection while picketing at request of his grandson); Shawnee Milling, 265 NLRB 710, 112 LRRM 1072 (1982). *Compare* NLRB v. Village IX dba Shenanigans, 723 F2d 1360, 115 LRRM 2297 (CA 7, 1983) (employer found to have lawfully barred employee's husband from entering restaurant where, during working time, he would solicit employees to join union). *See also* Mission Valley Mills, 225 NLRB 442, 93 LRRM 1227 (1976).

[23]Lucky Stores, 269 NLRB 942, 116 LRRM 1463 (1984) (termination of secretary to manager of labor relations did not violate §8(a)(3) because individual was "confidential" employee, and because discharge was based on reasonable suspicion that employee had and would divulge confidential labor relations material to union). *See also* Crest Mark Packing Co., 283 NLRB 999, 125 LRRM 1139 (1987) (Board held that bookkeeper, whose

ees[24] are not protected by the Act and may be discharged for their union activity or for their failure to lawfully assist an employer in its efforts to combat a union-organizing drive.[25]

Supervisors are generally not protected by section 8(a)(3), and their demotion or discharge because of union activities usually is not unlawful.[26] However, a supervisor's discharge may violate section 8(a)(1) if it results from a supervisor's refusal to commit unfair labor practices, or the supervisor's unfavorable testimony at a Board or arbitration hearing.[27] In the past, the Board also held it unlawful to discharge supervisors as an integral part of an overall plan to discourage employees from engaging in protected activity.[28]

---

only involvement in labor relations matters was typing two labor-related proposals, was not a confidential employee); Intermountain Rural Elec. Ass'n, 277 NLRB 1, 120 LRRM 1245 (1985), *aff'd*, 112 Lab. Cas. ¶11,269 (CA 10, 1988), *cert. denied*, 490 US 1046, 112 Lab. Cas. ¶11,270 (1989) ("[a] single instance of notetaking at a management meeting and typing three memos of uncertain labor policy content simply are inadequate to provide a basis for finding that [a secretary] served in a confidential capacity"); NLRB v. Hendricks County Rural Elec. Membership Corp., 454 US 170, 108 LRRM 3105 (1981), *rev'g* 627 F2d 766, 104 LRRM 3158 (CA 7, 1980), *denying enforcement to* 247 NLRB 498, 103 LRRM 1129 (1980), *supplementing* 236 NLRB 1616, 98 LRRM 1526 (1978). *See* Chapter 28, "Jurisdiction: Coverage of the Act," at notes 269–278, for discussion of *Hendricks* and NLRB coverage regarding confidential employees.

[24]NLRB v. North Ark. Elec. Coop., 446 F2d 602, 77 LRRM 3114 (CA 8, 1971), *denying enforcement to* 185 NLRB 550, 75 LRRM 1068 (1970), *supplementing* 168 NLRB 921, 67 LRRM 1193 (1967); *see* NLRB v. Bell Aerospace, 416 US 267, 85 LRRM 2945 (1974), and Chapter 28, "Jurisdiction: Coverage of the Act," notes 246–268.

[25]Western Sample Book & Printing Co., 209 NLRB 384, 86 LRRM 1171 (1974); *cf.* P. R. Mallory & Co., 175 NLRB 308, 70 LRRM 1574 (1969); Florida Builders, 111 NLRB 786, 35 LRRM 1575 (1955).

[26]*See* Parker-Robb Chevrolet, 262 NLRB 402, 110 LRRM 1289 (1982), *review denied sub nom.* Auto Salesmen's Local 1095 v. NLRB, 711 F2d 383, 113 LRRM 3175 (CA DC, 1983) (Board overrules prior cases holding discharge of supervisor violation of §8(a)(1) if part of "pattern" of unlawful conduct). *See also* ARA Leisure Servs. v. NLRB, 782 F2d 456, 121 LRRM 2598 (CA 4, 1986), *enforcing* 272 NLRB 1300, 118 LRRM 1103 (1984); Purolator Prods., 270 NLRB 694, 117 LRRM 1036 (1984), *enforced*, 121 LRRM 2120 (CA 4, 1985); Hunter Douglas, Inc., 277 NLRB 1179, 121 LRRM 1064 (1985), *enforcement granted*, 804 F2d 808, 123 LRRM 2912 (CA 3, 1986), *cert. denied*, 481 US 1069, 125 LRRM 2440 (1987); Carl H. Newman dba Newman Nursing Home, 270 NLRB 663, 116 LRRM 1447 (1984); Wer-Coy Fabrication Co., 268 NLRB 907, 115 LRRM 1124 (1984). *But see* Cooper Indus., Crouse-Hines Co. Div., 273 NLRB 333, 118 LRRM 1063 (1984) (employer violated §8(a)(1) by terminating supervisor for maintaining part-time outside business relationship with union organizer).

[27]*See, e.g.*, Glover Bottled Gas Corp., 275 NLRB 658, 119 LRRM 1177 (1985), *enforced mem.*, 801 F2d 391, 124 LRRM 2424 (CA 2, 1986), *cert. denied*, 479 US 1085, 124 LRRM 3272 (1987) (supervisors unlawfully terminated for their anticipated and actual testimony at unfair labor practice hearing); Orkin Exterminating Co., 270 NLRB 404, 116 LRRM 1089 (1984) (supervisor unlawfully terminated for announced intention to testify before Board).

[28]The Board abandoned this analysis in Parker-Robb Chevrolet, *supra* note 26. For development of the earlier law, see Empire Gas, 254 NLRB 626, 106 LRRM 1163 (1981); Nevis Indus., 246 NLRB 1053, 103 LRRM 1035 (1979), *modified on other grounds*, 647 F2d 905, 107 LRRM 2890 (CA 9, 1981); Downslope Indus., 246 NLRB 948, 103 LRRM 1041 (1979), *modified on other grounds*, 676 F2d 1114, 110 LRRM 2261 (CA 6, 1982); Fairview

Finally, the Supreme Court in *Sure Tan, Inc. v. NLRB*[29] endorsed the Board's view[30] that the Act's protection is available to undocumented alien employees. Following an election that resulted in the certification of a union, the company president alerted the Immigration and Naturalization Service (INS) to the presence of undocumented aliens among its employees. The INS arrested five of the seven bargaining unit members who had been eligible voters in the election and returned them to Mexico. The employer argued that undocumented aliens were not "employees" within the meaning of the Act, but the Supreme Court disagreed and affirmed the Board's holding that the employer constructively discharged the employees in violation of section 8(a)(3).[31]

B. Purpose of the Discrimination

As stated previously, not all discrimination is unlawful under section 8(a)(3). In *Radio Officers v. NLRB (A.H. Bull Steamship Co.)*,[32] the Supreme Court explained:

> The language of §8(a)(3) is not ambiguous. The unfair labor practice is for an employer to encourage or discourage membership by means of discrimination. Thus this section does not outlaw all encouragement or discouragement of membership in labor organizations; only such as is accomplished by discrimination is prohibited. Nor does this section outlaw discrimination in employment as such; only such discrimination as encourages or discourages membership in a labor organization is proscribed.[33]

Thus, in most cases, the employer's reason for discriminating will determine whether it has committed an unfair labor practice. If the discrimination is motivated by an antiunion purpose and has the foreseeable effect of either encouraging or discouraging union membership, it violates section 8(a)(3).[34]

Nursing Home, 202 NLRB 318, 82 LRRM 1566 (1973), *enforced*, 486 F2d 1400, 84 LRRM 3010 (CA 5, 1973), *cert. denied*, 419 US 827, 87 LRRM 2397 (1974). For a fuller discussion of this matter, *see* Chapter 6, "Interference With Protected Rights," at notes 375–386.

[29]467 US 883, 116 LRRM 2857 (1984).

[30]*See* Sure Tan, Inc., 234 NLRB 1187, 97 LRRM 1439 (1978), *enforced*, 672 F2d 592, 109 LRRM 2995 (CA 7, 1982), *aff'd in part, rev'd and remanded in part*, 467 US 883, 116 LRRM 2857 (1984).

[31]*Id.*, 467 US at 894, 116 LRRM at 2860-61.

[32]347 US 17, 33 LRRM 2417 (1954).

[33]*Id.* at 42-43.

[34]Retail Clerks Local 770 (Carl A. Palmer), 208 NLRB 356, 85 LRRM 1082 (1974).

A showing of actual encouragement or discouragement, however, is unnecessary. The Board is empowered to draw reasonable inferences from the evidence presented. If the employer's action could naturally and foreseeably have an adverse effect on employee rights, either at the time or in the future, the Board may infer encouragement or discouragement of union membership.[35]

Proving a specific antiunion purpose is also unnecessary where the employer's conduct is found to be "inherently destructive" of section 7 rights.[36] In such cases, the Board and the courts will not require an affirmative showing of the employer's unlawful motive. Rather, they will presume the unlawful motive to exist, even when the employer introduces evidence of a legitimate business purpose. In *Radio Officers*, the Supreme Court explained:

> [S]pecific evidence of intent to encourage or discourage is not an indispensable element of proof of violation of Section 8(a)(3) . . . . [A]n employer's protestation that he did not intend to encourage or discourage must be unavailing where a natural consequence of his action was such encouragement or discouragement. Concluding that encouragement or discouragement will result, it is presumed that he intended such consequence. In such circumstances intent to encourage is sufficiently established . . . .[37]

On the other hand, where the conduct in issue has only a "comparatively slight" adverse effect on employee rights and the employer has come forward with evidence of legitimate and substantial business ends, antiunion motivation must be proved in order to sustain a section 8(a)(3) violation.[38]

Although the statute literally prohibits only discrimination "to encourage or discourage [union] membership," the courts have long maintained that Congress intended section 8(a)(3) to protect more than "bare membership" and have long held that discrimination generally designed to encourage or discourage union activities or support is unlawful.[39] The term "membership" thus refers to all types of indicia of union support.

---

[35]*Supra* note 32, at 48-52. *See* Republic Aviation Corp. v. NLRB, 324 US 793, 16 LRRM 620 (1945).

[36]See discussion of conduct that carries its own indicia of intent to discriminate, at notes 88-109 *infra*.

[37]347 US at 44-45; *cf.* NLRB v. Burnup & Sims, 379 US 21, 57 LRRM 2385 (1964); Chapter 6, "Interference With Protected Rights," notes 18–30.

[38]NLRB v. Great Dane Trailers, 388 US 26, 65 LRRM 2465 (1967). *See* discussion at notes 95-102 *infra*.

[39]Radio Officers v. NLRB, *supra* note 32. *Cf.* Lunsford v. City of Bryan, 297 SW2d 115, 39 LRRM 2306 (Tex., 1957).

1. Conduct Requiring Proof of Union Animus: The *Wright Line* Rule. The great majority of section 8(a)(3) cases do not involve conduct "inherently destructive of employees rights." Most claims of unlawful discrimination arise out of employer decisions concerning whom to hire and fire, and what terms and conditions of employment to offer. Such conduct does not violate section 8(a)(3) so long as it is motivated by legitimate and substantial business reasons and not by a desire to penalize or reward employees for union activity or the lack of it. In cases of this type, the employer's motive is determinative.[40]

If an unlawful purpose is not present or cannot be implied as a matter of law, "discrimination" does not violate the Act, even if the employer's conduct is deemed unjustified or unfair.[41] Where a prohibited motive is found, it is not controlling that the employer may have been mistaken in determining whether the individual was engaged in protected activity or was a union supporter.[42] Moreover, a dismissal may violate section 8(a)(3) even though the dismissed employee is not a union adherent. When an employer discharges uncommitted or antiunion employees together with union adherents in an effort to disguise its unlawful intent, the discharge of both groups violates section 8(a)(3).[43]

Because only discriminatory conduct that is motivated by union animus[44] violates section 8(a)(3), establishing the employer's unlawful motivation is a precondition to finding a

---

[40]Laidlaw Corp., 171 NLRB 1366, 68 LRRM 1252 (1968), *enforced*, 414 F2d 99, 71 LRRM 3054 (CA 7, 1969), *cert. denied*, 397 US 920, 73 LRRM 2537 (1970); Wellington Mill Div. v. NLRB, 330 F2d 579, 55 LRRM 2914 (CA 4), *cert. denied*, 379 US 882, 57 LRRM 2276 (1964), *denying enforcement to* 141 NLRB 819, 52 LRRM 1445 (1963); Edward G. Budd Mfg. Co. v. NLRB, 138 F2d 86, 13 LRRM 512 (CA 3, 1943); NLRB v. Jones & Laughlin Steel Corp., 301 US 1, 1 LRRM 703 (1937). *But cf.* NLRB v. Burnup & Sims, *supra* note 37. In discharge and discipline cases, the Board is expressly prohibited by §10(c) of the Act from issuing orders of reinstatement or backpay where an employee has been "suspended or discharged for cause"; implicit in the notion of "cause" is that it motivated the disciplinary action. *See* notes 162-179 *infra* and accompanying text.

[41]Indeed, an employer may discharge for poor cause or no cause, and there is no violation of §8(a)(3) unless the employer's purpose is to encourage or discourage union membership. Borin Packing Co., 208 NLRB 280, 85 LRRM 1062 (1974); NLRB v. McGahey, 233 F2d 406, 38 LRRM 2142 (CA 5, 1956); Indiana Metal Prods. v. NLRB, 202 F2d 613, 31 LRRM 2490 (CA 7, 1953); NLRB v. Montgomery Ward & Co., 157 F2d 486, 19 LRRM 2008 (CA 8, 1946); NLRB v. Condenser Corp., 128 F2d 67, 10 LRRM 483 (CA 3, 1942); Associated Press v. NLRB, 301 US 103, 1 LRRM 732 (1937).

[42]Pleasant View Rest Home, 194 NLRB 426, 78 LRRM 1683 (1971); Link-Belt Co., 311 US 584, 7 LRRM 297 (1941). *But see* Lucky Stores, *supra* note 23 (discharge based on employer's good faith but "more than conjectural" mistaken view that employee would disclose confidential information to union did not violate §8(a)(3)).

[43]Howard Johnson Co., 209 NLRB 1122, 86 LRRM 1148 (1974).

[44]*See* notes 38-39 *supra*. *But see infra* at notes 87-105.

violation of section 8(a)(3). An employer has the right to take disciplinary action for good cause related to the maintenance of order and efficiency in its plant.[45] Section 10(c) recognizes this right by prohibiting Board orders of reinstatement and backpay orders where the employee was "suspended or discharged for cause." Implicit in the notion of "cause" is that the "cause" motivated (or at least was the primary reason for) the disciplinary action. Where the employer's conduct is challenged, the issue becomes: What was the employer's real motive for the action taken?[46]

Initially, the various circuits were divided on the issue of the "quantum of animus" necessary to find a violation of section 8(a)(3).[47] For example, the First[48] and Ninth[49] circuits required that the discriminatory motive be the primary, or controlling, factor promoting the employer's conduct. On the other hand, the Fifth Circuit upheld a Board finding of a section 8(a)(3) violation where the force of the antiunion motive was "reasonably equal" to the lawful motive asserted in defense by an employer.[50] Other circuits simply required a showing that the employer's decision was "partly" motivated by union animus[51] or merely "a factor" in the employer's decision.[52]

---

[45]*See* notes 40-41 *supra*.

[46]*E.g.*, Laidlaw Corp., *supra* note 40; Wellington Mill Div. v. NLRB, *supra* note 40; Edward G. Budd Mfg. Co. v. NLRB, *supra* note 40.

[47]*See, e.g.*, NLRB v. Montgomery Ward & Co., 554 F2d 996, 1002, 95 LRRM 2433 (CA 10, 1977) ("partially motivated"); Neptune Water Meter Co. v. NLRB, 551 F2d 568, 570, 94 LRRM 2513 (CA 4, 1977) (no discharge "except for"); Oil Workers v. NLRB (Kansas Refined Helium Co.), 547 F2d 575, 590, 92 LRRM 3059 (CA DC, 1976), *cert. denied*, 431 US 966, 95 LRRM 2642 (1977) ("motivated in any part"); NLRB v. Townhouse TV & Appliances, 531 F2d 826, 828, 91 LRRM 2636 (CA 7, 1976) ("motivated at least in part"); NLRB v. Gentithes, 463 F2d 557, 560, 80 LRRM 3057 (CA 3, 1972) ("substantial or motivating cause"); NLRB v. Fibers Int'l Corp., 439 F2d 1311, 76 LRRM 2798 (CA 1, 1971) ("dominant motive"); NLRB v. Gladding Keystone Corp., 435 F2d 129, 131, 76 LRRM 2099 (CA 2, 1970) ("partially motivated"); Frosty Morn Meats v. NLRB, 296 F2d 617, 621, 49 LRRM 2159 (CA 5, 1961) ("moving cause"). *See* note 167 *infra*.

[48]Coletti's Furniture v. NLRB, 550 F2d 1292, 94 LRRM 3071 (CA 1, 1977), *enforcing per curiam* 224 NLRB 1547, 92 LRRM 1585 (1976) (Board must find affirmatively that discharge would not have occurred but for improper reason). *See also* Hubbard Regional Hosp. v. NLRB, 579 F2d 1251, 98 LRRM 2891 (CA 1, 1978).

[49]Polynesian Cultural Center v. NLRB, 582 F2d 467, 99 LRRM 3416 (CA 9, 1978) (improper motive must be dominant and "moving cause" of employer's conduct). *See also* Stephenson v. NLRB, 614 F2d 1210, 103 LRRM 2238 (CA 9, 1980); NLRB v. South Shore Hosp., 571 F2d 677, 97 LRRM 3004 (CA 1, 1978); NLRB v. West Coast Casket Co., 469 F2d 871, 81 LRRM 2857 (CA 9, 1972).

[50]NLRB v. Aero Corp., 581 F2d 511, 99 LRRM 2800 (CA 5, 1978), *enforcing* 233 NLRB 401, 96 LRRM 1539 (1977).

[51]*See, e.g.*, Edgewood Nursing Center v. NLRB, 581 F2d 363, 99 LRRM 2036 (CA 3, 1978); NLRB v. Gogin, 575 F2d 596, 98 LRRM 2250 (CA 7, 1978).

[52]*E.g.*, Neptune Water Meter Co. v. NLRB, *supra* note 47; M.S.P. Indus. v. NLRB, 568 F2d 166, 97 LRRM 2403 (CA 10, 1977), *enforcing in part* 222 NLRB 220, 91 LRRM 1379 (1976).

In its 1980 decision of *Wright Line*,[53] the Board undertook to eliminate this uncertainty among the courts of appeals and between the courts and the Board regarding causation in cases alleging unlawful discrimination. The Board there adopted, in essence, the analysis used by the Supreme Court in *Mt. Healthy City School District Board of Education v. Doyle*,[54] a case involving a discharge motivated in part by constitutionally protected activity. The Board's approach in *Wright Line*, which was approved by the Supreme Court,[55] is applied in all cases alleging violations of section 8(a)(3) that turn on employer motivation.[56] The initial focus is on the elements of the General Counsel's prima facie case, that is, the existence of protected activity,[57] knowledge of that activity by the employer,[58] and union animus. Proof of these elements by the General Counsel warrants at least an inference that the employee's protected conduct was a moti-

---

[53]Wright Line, Wright Line Div., 251 NLRB 1083, 105 LRRM 1169 (1980), *enforced*, 662 F2d 899, 108 LRRM 2513 (CA 1, 1981), *cert. denied*, 455 US 989, 109 LRRM 2779 (1982).

[54]429 US 274 (1977). *See also* Village of Arlington Heights v. Metropolitan Housing Dev. Corp., 429 US 252 (1977).

[55]NLRB v. Transportation Mgmt. Corp., 462 US 393, 113 LRRM 2857 (1983), *rev'g* 674 F2d 130, 109 LRRM 3921 (CA 1, 1982).

[56]*See, e.g.*, HS Healthcare, 295 NLRB No. 2, n.2, 133 LRRM 1105 (1989); Bridgeway Oldsmobile, 281 NLRB 1246, 123 LRRM 1267 (1986); Frank Black Mechanical Servs., 271 NLRB 1302, n.2, 117 LRRM 1183 (1984). The *Wright Line* analysis also applies to §§8(a)(1) and 8(a)(4) cases where motive is an issue. *See* Taylor and Gaskin, 277 NLRB 563, 120 LRRM 1302 (1985). Wright Line, Wright Line Div., *supra* note 53, at 1089, 105 LRRM at 1174-75. The Board also has purported to apply *Wright Line* in a §8(a)(3) and §8(b)(2) case where the defense was a preference permitted by §8(f)(4), but affirmative proof was not clearly required from the employer or the union. M.W. Kellogg Constructors, 273 NLRB 1049, 118 LRRM 1616 (1984), *enforcement denied*, 806 F2d 1435, 124 LRRM 2288 (CA 9, 1986), *supplemented*, 284 NLRB 507, 125 LRRM 1195 (1987), *enforcement denied*, 867 F2d 498, 130 LRRM 2648 (CA 9, 1989). *But see* Northern Wire Corp., 291 NLRB 727, 131 LRRM 1372, *enforced*, 887 F2d 1313, 132 LRRM 2818 (CA 7, 1989) (Board refused to apply *Wright Line* analysis to determination of whether strike was caused in whole or in part by unfair labor practices.)

[57]Although it appears that discrimination based on "protected" activity is a prerequisite in §8(a)(3) cases, the decisions on this issue are not entirely consistent. *Compare*, Hanlon & Wilson Co. v. NLRB, 738 F2d 606, 612, 116 LRRM 3014, 3018 (CA 3, 1984) ("since protected activities were not found to have been a motivating factor in the discharge, we conclude that the ALJ's finding [of illegality] is not supported by substantial evidence") *with* JMC Transp. v. NLRB, 776 F2d 612, 120 LRRM 3217 (CA 6, 1985), *enforcing* 272 NLRB 545, 117 LRRM 1271 (1984) (employee's termination held to be unlawful under §8(a)(3) notwithstanding dissenting opinions in Board and court decisions based on assertion that employee's activities were not "protected" under the Act). The protected activity element can be supplied by an employer's belief that the employee engaged in such activity. *E.g.*, F&E Erection Co., 292 NLRB 587, 130 LRRM 1264 (1989); BMD Sportswear Corp., 283 NLRB 142, 124 LRRM 1268 (1987).

[58]Knowledge of such activity is often found by drawing inferences from other aspects of the prima facie case, the size of the unit, or other unfair labor practices. *See, e.g.*, Active Transp., 296 NLRB No. 58, 132 LRRM 1194 (1989) (employer knowledge was based on occurrence of interrogation—not the answers—timing of discharges, and pretextual evidence); Clark & Wilkins Indus., 290 NLRB 106, 130 LRRM 1362 (1988), *enforced*, 887 F2d 308, 132 LRRM 2758 (CA DC, 1989).

vating factor in the adverse personnel action and that a violation of the Act has occurred.[59] The General Counsel is not required to prove any particular degree of unlawful motivation as part of the prima facie case. A showing that unlawful motivation played a role suffices.[60] The employer may rebut the General Counsel's prima facie case by showing that prohibited motivations played no part in its actions.[61] If the employer cannot rebut the prima facie case, it must demonstrate that the same personnel action would have taken place for legitimate reasons regardless of the employee's protected activity.[62] In this regard, the employer has both the burden of going forward with the evidence *and* the burden of persuasion.[63] It is not enough to articulate a legitimate nondiscriminatory reason. The employer must affirmatively introduce enough evidence to persuade the Board that the

---

[59]For cases where the General Counsel failed to establish a prima facie case, see Verland, 296 NLRB No. 61, 132 LRRM 1149 (1989); Hemisphere Broadcasting Corp. (WBCN), 290 NLRB 394, 129 LRRM 1239 (1988); Geo. V. Hamilton, Inc., 289 NLRB 1335, 129 LRRM 1067 (1988); Dresser Aggregates Corp., 276 NLRB 71, 120 LRRM 1066 (1985); Eagle Discount Supermarkets., 275 NLRB 874, 119 LRRM 1231 (1985).

[60]Nordstrom dba Seattle Seahawks, 292 NLRB 899, 130 LRRM 1249 (1989).

[61]Such a defense does not involve shifting the burdens of production and persuasion to the employer under *Wright Line*. NKC of Am., 291 NLRB 683, n.4, 130 LRRM 1408 (1988). The employer's obligation to establish a cause other than prohibited discrimination arises only after the General Counsel establishes a prima facie case. *E.g.*, Mistletoe Express Serv., 295 NLRB No. 33, 132 LRRM 1099 (1989); Hyatt Hotels Corp. dba Hyatt Regency Memphis, 296 NLRB No. 36, 132 LRRM 1130 (1989).

[62]For cases where the employer discharged its burden of demonstrating that the action would have occurred independently of any unlawful motivation, see GHR Energy Corp., 294 NLRB No. 76, 133 LRRM 1069 (1989); Verland, *supra* note 59; Ruff Elec. Constr. Co., 296 NLRB No. 71, 132 LRRM 1156 (1989); California Coop. Creamery, 290 NLRB 355, 129 LRRM 1045 (1988) (§8(a)(1) refusal to hire case); Centre Property Mgmt. v. NLRB, 807 F2d 1264, 125 LRRM 2409 (CA 5, 1987); Kona 60 Minute Photo, 277 NLRB 867, 120 LRRM 1313 (1985); Wignall dba Lovilia Coal Co., 275 NLRB 1358, 120 LRRM 1005 (1985); PYA/Monarch, 275 NLRB 1194, 119 LRRM 1298 (1985); OMSCO, 273 NLRB 872, 118 LRRM 1249 (1984); Airborne Freight Corp. v. NLRB, 728 F2d 357, 115 LRRM 3214 (CA 6, 1984); G&H Prods. v. NLRB, 714 F2d 1397, 114 LRRM 2107 (CA 7, 1983).

For cases where the employer failed to discharge that burden, see NLRB v. Howard Elec. Co., 873 F2d 1287, 131 LRRM 2511 (CA 9, 1989); York Prods. v. NLRB, 881 F2d 542, 132 LRRM 2030 (CA 8, 1989); Woodline Motor Freight, 278 NLRB 1141, 122 LRRM 1355 (1986), *enforcement granted in part and denied in part*, 843 F2d 285, 127 LRRM 3260 (CA 8, 1988); Sanchez v. NLRB, 785 F2d 409, 121 LRRM 3113 (CA 2, 1986), *modifying in part and remanding sub nom.* Goodie Brand Packing Corp., 270 NLRB 451, 116 LRRM 1090 (1984), *supplemented*, 283 NLRB 673, 125 LRRM 1038 (1987); Hunter Douglas Inc. 277 NLRB 1179, 121 LRRM 1064 (1985), *enforcement granted*, 804 F2d 808, 123 LRRM 2912 (CA 3, 1986), *cert. denied*, 481 US 1069, 125 LRRM 2440 (1987); Duroyd Mfg., 276 NLRB 144, 120 LRRM 1095 (1985); NLRB v. Horizon Air Servs., 761 F2d 22, 119 LRRM 2203 (CA 1, 1985); NLRB v. Daniel Int'l Corp., Daniel Constr. Co. Div., 731 F2d 191, 115 LRRM 3574 (CA 4, 1984); Roure Bertrand Dupont, Inc., 271 NLRB 443, 116 LRRM 1394 (1984); Presbyterian/St. Luke's Medical Center v. NLRB, 723 F2d 1468, 115 LRRM 2306 (CA 10, 1983); NLRB v. Townsend & Bottum, 722 F2d 297, 114 LRRM 3548 (CA 6, 1983).

[63]*See, e.g.*, Hunter Douglas, Inc., *supra* note 62. The employer must prove (or persuade) by a preponderance of the evidence that the challenged personnel action would have taken place regardless of employee's protected activity. Hyatt Hotels Corp. dba Hyatt Regency Memphis, *supra* note 61.

challenged personnel action would have taken place regardless of the employee's protected activity and the employer's anti-union animus.[64] If insufficient evidence is offered, or if the evidence is unpersuasive, the employer will not have met its *Wright Line* burden and a violation will be found.[65] Since it is the employer's motivation that is at issue,[66] the employer need not prove the employee actually engaged in conduct on which the discipline is based, but must show that it acted pursuant to a reasonably held good-faith belief regarding the employee's conduct.[67]

The shift of the burdens of production and persuasion to the employer to show the same personnel action would have occurred in the absence of union activity "does not undermine the established concept"[68] that the burden is on the General Counsel to establish an unfair labor practice by a preponderence of the evidence; "the shifting burden merely requires the employer to make out what is actually an affirmative defense."[69] A similar framework for analyzing dual or mixed motive cases involving alleged discrimination under Title VII of the Civil Rights Act of 1964 also has been adopted by the Supreme Court.[70]

The Board also applies *Wright Line* to cases in which there is no evidence of dual or mixed motives, but where the employer's proffered justification for the employment action taken is alleged to be pretexual. But, where pretext findings have been made by an administrative law judge (ALJ), the Board has not required explicit discussion of all the *Wright Line* elements, reasoning that a finding of pretext "necessarily means that the reasons advanced by the employer either did not exist or were

---

[64]Hyatt Hotels Corp. dba Hyatt Regency Memphis, *supra* note 61. Roure Bertrand Dupont, Inc., *supra* note 61; Hicks Oils & Hicksgas, 293 NLRB 84, 132 LRRM 1093 (1989).

[65]F&E Erection Co., *supra* note 57 (proof that alleged discriminatee was less qualified was ambiguous because of subjective hiring practices); R.E.C. Corp., 296 NLRB No. 163, 132 LRRM 1268 (1989) (insufficient evidence of economic need for layoff); Adair Standish Corp., 290 NLRB 317, 130 LRRM 1304 (1988) (testimony unsupported by personnel records and business records make defense unpersuasive).

[66]Phillips Indus., 295 NLRB No. 75, 133 LRRM 1122 (1989) (employer that does not know of misconduct at time of discharge cannot use such conduct to show employee would have been fired for lawful reasons).

[67]GHR Energy Corp., *supra* note 62; Lucky Stores, 269 NLRB 942, 116 LRRM 1463 (1984).

[68]Wright Line, Wright Line Div., *supra* note 53, at 1088 n.11.

[69]*Id.*

[70]Price Waterhouse v. Hopkins, 490 US 228, 49 FEP Cases 954 (1989).

not in fact relied upon."[71] Evidence suggesting that the employer's explanation for its actions is pretextual, moreover, has been used to support the elements of the General Counsel's prima facie case[72] despite the Board's admonition that, "in assessing whether a *prima facie* case has been presented . . . a judge must view the General Counsel's evidence in isolation, apart from a respondent's proffered defense."[73]

Where a violation of section 8(a)(3) is charged, the question of whether the employer in fact changed the employee's tenure or terms or conditions of employment is rarely if ever disputed. What is most often in contention is whether by its actions the employer intended to encourage or discourage union membership. If the employer has expressed itself in connection with the action that resulted in the alleged unfair labor practice, direct proof of intent may be available. However, section 8(c) protects an employer's right of free speech as follows:

> [T]he expressing of any views, argument, or opinion or the dissemination thereof, whether in written, printed, graphic, or visual form, shall not constitute or be evidence of an unfair labor practice under any of the provisions of this Act, if such expression contains no threat of reprisal or force or promise of benefit.

Accordingly, antiunion statements that do not include threats of reprisal, force, or promises of benefit cannot be determinative on this issue,[74] and the focal point of the inquiry remains: What

---

[71] Limestone Apparel Corp., 255 NLRB 722, 107 LRRM 1187, 1188 (1981), *enforced*, 705 F2d 799, 113 LRRM 2517 (CA 6, 1982). *See also* HS Healthcare, *supra* note 56; Raynor Motel Corp. dba Holiday Inn E., 281 NLRB 573, 124 LRRM 1035 (1986); Intermountain Rural Elec. Ass'n v. NLRB, 732 F2d 754, 764, 116 LRRM 2068, 2076 (CA 10, 1984), *cert. denied*, 469 US 932, 117 LRRM 2776 (1984).

[72] *See, e.g.*, Active Transp., *supra* note 58 (pretextual reasons are "indicative of illegal motivation"). When a false reason is advanced "one may infer that there is another reason (an unlawful reason)" for the employer's action (citing Shattuck Denn Mining Corp. v. NLRB, 362 F2d 466, 62 LRRM 2401 (CA 9, 1966)); Holo-Krome Co., 293 NLRB 594, 130 LRRM 1489, *corrected*, 132 LRRM 1182 (1989) (shifting reasons for action indicate animus necessary for prima facie case); HS Healthcare dba Springfield Manor, *supra* note 56 (same).

[73] Bali Blinds Midwest, 292 NLRB No. 14, 131 LRRM 1050 (1989). *See also* Hillside Bus Corp., 262 NLRB 1254, 110 LRRM 1552 (1982). *But see* Holo-Krome Co., *supra* note 72 (*Wright Line*'s "precise and formalized framework" does not prevent consideration of employer's proferred reasons as part of prima facie case).

[74] Indiana Metal Prods. Corp. v. NLRB, 202 F2d 613, 31 LRRM 2490 (CA 7, 1953); Pittsburgh S.S. Co. v. NLRB, 180 F2d 731, 25 LRRM 2428 (CA 6, 1950), *aff'd*, 340 US 498, 27 LRRM 2382 (1951). Such statements may be admissible to show background or union animus, however, despite the apparently literal prohibition of such use by the language of §8(c). *See* Chapter 6, "Interference With Protected Rights," for discussion of §8(c) in relation to independent §8(a)(1) cases.

was the real reason for the discharge?[75]

In determining whether the conduct in question is unlawfully motivated, the Board will rely on circumstantial as well as direct evidence to infer discriminatory motivation on the part of an employer. It will consider circumstantial evidence such as the following: (1) delay in the discharge after knowledge of the offense;[76] (2) departure from established procedures for discharge;[77] (3) failure to warn the employee prior to discharge;[78] (4) failure to tell the employee the reason for the discharge at the time of discharge;[79] (5) changes in position in explaining the reason for the discharge;[80] and (6) timing of the discharge (e.g., discharge immediately after the employer gains knowledge of the employee's union activity).[81] The Board may properly use evidence from a prior unfair labor practice proceeding as evidence of present union animus where other supporting evi-

---

[75]W.T. Grant Co., 210 NLRB 622, 86 LRRM 1365 (1974) (antiunion comments prior to discharge); United Cement Co., 209 NLRB 1137, 86 LRRM 1237 (1974) (comments regarding discharge after discharge); Radiadores Paragon de P. R., 206 NLRB 918, 84 LRRM 1591 (1973), *enforced*, 502 F2d 1160, 87 LRRM 3274 (CA 1, 1974) (default judgment in earlier Board case); Mademoiselle Shoppe, 199 NLRB 983, 82 LRRM 1022 (1972) (comments prior to discharge and other unfair labor practices committed on day of discharge).

[76]Merchants Truck Line v. NLRB, 577 F2d 1011, 99 LRRM 2143 (CA 5, 1978), *enforcing* 232 NLRB 676, 96 LRRM 1318 (1977); National Grange Mut. Ins. Co., 207 NLRB 431, 84 LRRM 1656 (1973); Commonwealth Foods, 203 NLRB 891, 83 LRRM 1214 (1973), *enforcement denied in part and remanded*, 506 F2d 1065, 87 LRRM 2609 (CA 4, 1974); Montgomery Ward & Co., 197 NLRB 519, 80 LRRM 1778 (1972).

[77]Wells Dairy dba Wells Blue Bunny, 287 NLRB 827, 129 LRRM 1248 (1987), *enforced*, 865 F2d 175, 130 LRRM 2269 (CA 8, 1989); Richmond Ref. Co., 212 NLRB 16, 87 LRRM 1255 (1974); D. H. Baldwin Co., 207 NLRB 25, 84 LRRM 1502 (1973), *enforced*, 505 F2d 736, 90 LRRM 2891 (CA 8, 1974); Ostby & Barton Co., 202 NLRB 199, 82 LRRM 1605 (1973). *Accord* Westinghouse Learning Corp., 211 NLRB 19, 86 LRRM 1709 (1974).

[78]Great Atl. & Pac. Tea Co., 210 NLRB 593, 86 LRRM 1444 (1974); Coble Dairy Prods. Coop., 205 NLRB 160, 84 LRRM 1094 (1973); National Food Serv., 196 NLRB 295, 80 LRRM 1017 (1972).

[79]Forest Park Ambulance Serv., 206 NLRB 550, 84 LRRM 1506 (1973); Alamo Express, 200 NLRB 178, 82 LRRM 1148 (1972), *enforced*, 489 F2d 1311, 85 LRRM 2768 (CA 5, 1974).

[80]Coca-Cola Bottling Co., 232 NLRB 794, 97 LRRM 1290 (1977), *enforced in part*, 616 F2d 949, 104 LRRM 2819 (CA 6), *cert. denied*, 449 US 998, 105 LRRM 3168 (1980); J. R. Townsend Lincoln-Mercury, 202 NLRB 71, 82 LRRM 1793 (1973); Holiday Inn, 198 NLRB 410, 80 LRRM 1697 (1972), *enforced*, 488 F2d 498, 84 LRRM 2585 (CA 10, 1973); Goodyear Tire & Rubber Co., 197 NLRB 666, 80 LRRM 1701 (1972).

[81]Clark & Wilkins Indus., 290 NLRB No. 19, 130 LRRM 1362 (1988), *enforced*, 887 F2d 308, 132 LRRM 2758 (CA DC, 1989); Marx-Haas Clothing Co., 211 NLRB 350, 87 LRRM 1054 (1974); Shivvers Corp., 213 NLRB 102, 87 LRRM 1753 (1974); Howard Johnson Co., 209 NLRB 1122, 86 LRRM 1148 (1974); D. M. Rotary Press, 208 NLRB 366, 85 LRRM 1477 (1974), *enforced*, 524 F2d 1342, 91 LRRM 2240 (CA 6, 1975); Uniroyal, Inc., 197 NLRB 1034, 80 LRRM 1694 (1972); Atlantic Marine, 193 NLRB 1003, 78 LRRM 1460 (1971), *enforced*, 512 F2d 1404, 90 LRRM 3138 (CA 5), *cert. denied*, 423 US 995, 90 LRRM 3154 (1975).

dence exists,[82] although the earlier evidence is insufficient standing alone to support a finding of violation.[83]

An essential step in proving the existence of unlawful union animus in most cases is proof that the employer had knowledge of the affected employee's union allegiance or activities when the action was taken.[84] Thus, an employer's discipline of a union adherent does not violate section 8(a)(3) where there is no evidence that the employer was aware of either the union's or the employee's organizational activities.[85]

Under certain circumstances, however, the Board will apply its so-called *small plant doctrine* to establish the requisite employer knowledge.[86] The employer's knowledge of union activities is thus inferred where such activities are conducted at a small plant and are carried on in such a manner or at such times that it may be presumed that the employer must have noticed them.

2. Conduct Inherently Destructive of Section 7 Rights. While section 8(a)(3) violations normally turn "on whether the

---

[82]Tama Meat Packing Corp. v. NLRB, 575 F2d 661, 98 LRRM 2339 (CA 8, 1978), *enforcing as modified* 230 NLRB 116, 96 LRRM 1148 (1977), *cert. denied*, 439 US 1069, 100 LRRM 2268 (1979).

[83]In certain circumstances, the Board will consider antiunion conduct by the employer found in prior Board decisions. J. P. Stevens & Co., 245 NLRB 198, 102 LRRM 1437 (1979), *enforced*, 638 F2d 676, 106 LRRM 2145 (CA 4, 1980); Southwest Janitorial & Maintenance Corp., 209 NLRB 402, 85 LRRM 1590 (1974) (prior cases involving predecessor and successor employer); Dollar Gen. Corp., 204 NLRB 601, 83 LRRM 1713 (1973), *enforced*, 493 F2d 1230, 86 LRRM 2655 (CA 6), *cert. denied*, 419 US 840, 87 LRRM 2398 (1974). *See* G & S Metal Prods. Co., 199 NLRB 705, 81 LRRM 1587 (1972), *enforced*, 489 F2d 441, 85 LRRM 2047 (CA 6, 1973) (prior Board case too remote in time and circumstances to establish element of union animus); Southwest Chevrolet Corp., 194 NLRB 975, 79 LRRM 1156, *enforced*, 82 LRRM 2620 (CA 7, 1972) (unlawful motivation cannot be established by conduct prior to settlement agreement containing nonadmission clause). While the employer's prior unfair labor practice may be relevant, Kenworth Trucks of Philadelphia, 236 NLRB 1299, 99 LRRM 1211 (1978), evidence of past union animus by itself is not sufficient to support a finding of a violation. Sioux Quality Packers v. NLRB, 581 F2d 153, 98 LRRM 3128 (CA 8, 1978), *denying enforcement to* 232 NLRB 1166, 96 LRRM 1372 (1977). A past history of amicable relations with a union does not necessarily disprove evidence of present discriminatory intent and motivation with regard to the discriminatee. Awrey Bakeries, 197 NLRB 705, 80 LRRM 1480 (1972).

[84]*See* Leyendecker Paving, 247 NLRB 28, 103 LRRM 1107 (1980). *See* discussion at notes 200-214 *infra*.

[85]Fry Roofing Co., 237 NLRB 1005, 99 LRRM 1544 (1978), *enforced*, 651 F2d 442, 107 LRRM 2926 (CA 6, 1981). Prior knowledge must be present even when there is proof of union animus. *Cf.* A to Z Portion Meats v. NLRB, 643 F2d 390, 106 LRRM 2844 (CA 6, 1980), *denying enforcement to* 238 NLRB 643, 99 LRRM 1527 (1978).

[86]Coral Gables Convalescent Home, 234 NLRB 1198, 97 LRRM 1435 (1978). *See* Clark & Wilkens Indus., *supra* note 81; Reinauer Fuel Transp. Corp., 251 NLRB 1573, 105 LRRM 1355 (1980); Permanent Label Corp., 248 NLRB 118, 103 LRRM 1513 (1980), *enforced*, 657 F2d 512, 107 LRRM 2985 (CA 3, 1981), *cert. denied*, 455 US 940, 109 LRRM 2778 (1982); Webco Bodies, 237 NLRB 1213, 99 LRRM 1135 (1978), *enforced*, 595 F2d 451, 101 LRRM 2041 (CA 8, 1979). *See* discussion at notes 209-214 *infra*.

discriminatory conduct was motivated by an anti-union purpose,"[87] the Supreme Court in *NLRB v. Erie Resistor Corp.*[88] identified a class of employer conduct in which the requisite unlawful intent "is founded upon the inherently discriminatory or destructive nature of the conduct itself."[89] In such instances, the employer is held

> to intend the very consequences which foreseeably and inescapably flow from his actions . . . [because] his conduct *does* speak for itself—it is discriminatory and it *does* discourage union membership, and whatever the claimed overriding justification may be, it carries with it unavoidable consequences which the employer not only foresaw but must have intended.[90]

Recognizing that employer conduct often presents a complex of motives, some lawful and some unlawful, the Court upheld the Board's authority to perform the admittedly delicate task of balancing one motive against another in finding violations of the Act, even in the face of business exigencies, by "weighing the interest of employees in concerted activity against the interest of the employer in operating his business in a particular manner . . . ."[91] The balance was to be achieved in light of the policy of the Act—the effect upon employee rights was to be weighed against the business ends to be served by the employer's conduct.

In *Erie Resistor* the employer had granted superseniority to striker-replacements and to strikers who returned to work. This action was held to involve "conduct which carried its own indicia of intent and which is barred by the Act unless saved from illegality by an overriding business purpose justifying the invasion of union rights."[92] Turning to the employer's alleged busi-

---

[87]NLRB v. Great Dane Trailers, 388 US 26, 65 LRRM 2465 (1967).

[88]373 US 221, 53 LRRM 2121 (1963).

[89]*Id.* at 223. *See also* NLRB v. Brown, 380 US 278, 58 LRRM 2663 (1965) (employer's right to look out and hire replacements during "whipsaw" strike.)

[90]373 US at 228. (Emphasis in original).

[91]*Id.* at 223. The courts have consistently rejected the argument that conduct otherwise discriminatory is *automatically* excused upon a showing that it was motivated by business exigency. While the Court in *Erie Resistor* upheld the Board's balancing of conflicts in interests, the Court has criticized the Board for assessing and attempting to balance the relative bargaining strength or economic power of the parties. *See* American Ship Bldg. Co. v. NLRB, 380 US 300, 58 LRRM 2672 (1965); NLRB v. Insurance Agents, 361 US 477, 45 LRRM 2704 (1960).

[92]373 US at 231. The Court's analysis of the superseniority plan, emphasized four considerations: (1) The tenure of all strikers was affected, whereas permanent replacement under the doctrine of NLRB v. Mackay Radio & Tel. Co., 304 US 333, 2 LRRM 610 (1938), affects only those strikers who were actually replaced. (2) Superseniority operated to the detriment of participants in the strike, and to the benefit of individual strikers who returned to work. (3) The offer of superseniority was a crippling blow to the strike effort.

ness justification, the Court said it would not disturb "the Board's considered judgment that the Act and its underlying policy require . . . giving more weight to the harm wrought by super-seniority than to the interest of the employer in operating its plant during the strike by utilizing this particular means of attracting replacements."[93] The operative policy at work was the concern expressed in the federal labor laws for the protection of the integrity of the strike weapon, "which in great measure implements and supports the principles of the collective bargaining system."[94]

In *NLRB v. Great Dane Trailers*,[95] the Supreme Court established the basic rules concerning the burden of proving the presence or absence of discriminatory purpose under section 8(a)(3). The Court declared that no proof of antiunion motivation need be advanced and that a violation could be found "if it can reasonably be concluded that the employer's discriminatory conduct was 'inherently destructive' of important employee rights"[96] despite evidence of business motivation. However, where the discriminatory conduct has a "comparatively slight" effect on employee rights, an employer's evi-

---

(4) Future collective bargaining would be made difficult because the bargaining unit was and would for many years remain divided between those who stayed with the union and those who returned to work before the strike ended. *See* Gulton Electro-Voice, 266 NLRB 406, 112 LRRM 1361 (1983), *enforced sub nom*, Electrical Workers (IUE) Local 900 v. NLRB, 727 F2d 1184, 115 LRRM 2760 (CA DC, 1984) (superseniority proper only for union officials with on-the-job contract duties); A.P.A. Transp. Corp., 239 NLRB 1407, 100 LRRM 1165 (1979) (broad superseniority for union stewards); Teamsters Local 20 (Preston Trucking Co.) v. NLRB, 610 F2d 991, 102 LRRM 3080 (CA DC, 1979), *enforcing* 236 NLRB 464, 98 LRRM 1248 (1978) (steward superseniority "for all purposes").

[93]373 US at 232. The Court distinguished and thereby refused to extend its dictum in NLRB v. Mackay Radio & Tel. Co., *supra* note 92, that an employer may operate its plant during a strike and at its conclusion need not discharge those who worked during the strike in order to make way for returning strikers, because the employer's interest in carrying on its business must be deemed to outweigh the damage to concerted activities caused by permanently replacing strikers. The Court's departure in *Erie Resistor* from the logic of *Mackay Radio* is best explained by the "far greater encroachment resulting from super-seniority in addition to permanent replacement," *id.*, for the grant of super-seniority affects all strikers, whether replaced or not, and has a powerful adverse impact on the strike itself.

[94]373 US at 234.

[95]*Supra* note 87.

[96]*Id.* at 34. While an economic strike was in progress, the employer denied strikers vacation benefits, which the union contended had accrued under the expired collective bargaining contract. Shortly thereafter, the employer paid vacation benefits to employees who were working during the strike. The Board found a violation of §§8(a)(1) and 8(a)(3), but the Fifth Circuit denied enforcement. Great Dane Trailers v. NLRB, 363 F2d 130, 62 LRRM 2456 (CA 5, 1966), *denying enforcement to* 150 NLRB 438, 58 LRRM 1097 (1964). The Supreme Court reversed and enforced the Board's order (citing Radio Officers v. NLRB (A.H. Bull S.S. Co.), 347 US 17, 33 LRRM 2417 (1954)). In that case, an employer acceded to a union's demand to remove an employee who had obtained his job without first going through the union. *See* notes 377-396 *infra.*

dence of "legitimate and substantial business justifications for the conduct"[97] will shift the burden of proof to the General Counsel to show antiunion motivation. Consequently, to the extent that business justifications and legitimate employer objectives are a part of the Board's analysis in determining whether discriminatory conduct is "inherently destructive," the employer always has the burden of proof as to these elements, in either "inherently destructive" or "comparatively slight" situations. The nature of the effect of discriminatory conduct on employee rights, as measured in the light of the Act's policies, will determine the weight to be accorded such evidence in Board-conducted unfair labor practice proceedings.[98]

The Supreme Court has expressed no clear standards to define what conduct is "inherently destructive" or "comparatively slight" in its impact, what constitutes "legitimate and substantial business justification," or how any of these matters are to be determined.[99] In *Great Dane* and *NLRB v. Fleetwood*

---

[97]388 US at 34. In *Great Dane* the Court upheld the Board's finding of a violation because the General Counsel had proved the existence of "discriminatory conduct carrying a potential for adverse effect upon employee rights," and the employer offered no evidence of proper motivation. Hence, the Court never decided whether "[t]he act of paying accrued [vacation] benefits to one group of employees while announcing the extinction of the same benefits for another group of employees who are distinguishable only by their participation in protected concerted activity" was inherently destructive or had only a comparatively slight effect on employee rights. *See* NLRB v. Borden, Inc., 600 F2d 313, 101 LRRM 2727 (CA 1, 1979) (*Great Dane* did not decide the question whether such conduct was inherently destructive). *See also* Amoco Oil Co., 285 NLRB 918, 126 LRRM 1265 (1987); Texaco, Inc., 285 NLRB 241, 126 LRRM 1001 (1987); NLRB v. Great Atl. & Pac. Tea Co., 409 F2d 296, 70 LRRM 3246 (CA 5, 1969). *Compare* Service Employees Local 250 v. NLRB (Earringhouse Imports), 600 F2d 930, 101 LRRM 2004 (CA DC, 1979) (*Great Dane* interpreted as holding that termination of benefits was inherently destructive conduct) *with* Wallace Metal Prods., 244 NLRB 41, 102 LRRM 1233 (1979); Westinghouse Elec. Corp., 237 NLRB 1209, 99 LRRM 1184 (1978), *enforced*, 603 F2d 610, 101 LRRM 2870 (CA 7, 1979); Borden, Inc., 235 NLRB 982, 98 LRRM 1098 (1978); Molders Local 155 v. NLRB, 442 F2d 742, 76 LRRM 2133 (CA DC, 1971) (which cases concluded that employers' refusal to pay striking employees accrued vacation pay is inherently destructive of employee §7 rights).

[98]In Earringhouse Imports, 227 NLRB 1107, 94 LRRM 1494 (1977), *enforcement denied sub nom.* Service Employees Local 250 v. NLRB, 600 F2d 930, 101 LRRM 2004 (CA DC, 1979), the Board extended the burden-of-proof rules of *Great Dane* to alleged violations of §8(a)(4). In that case, the employer had terminated a number of its employees who had violated an express order of the employer and had left the plant to attend an NLRB representation hearing. In reversing the Board, the Circuit Court for the District of Columbia refused to extend the *Great Dane* rules to alleged violations of §8(a)(4) and held that the employer was not obliged to come forward with legitimate and substantial business justifications for its actions; instead, the burden of proof remained with the General Counsel to prove a violation of §8(a)(4). *See* note 548 *infra*.

[99]The Court did not state whether the Board was empowered to rule on the sufficiency of the "legitimate and substantial justification" proffered by an employer, thereby leaving open the question whether in comparatively slight impact cases the Board could balance the harm against the alleged justification in order to find a violation of §8(a)(3). *Compare* Portland Williamette Co. v. NLRB, 534 F2d 1331, 92 LRRM 2113 (CA 9, 1976), *denying enforcement to* 212 NLRB 272, 86 LRRM 1677 (1974) *with* NLRB v. Knuth Bros., 584 F2d

Trailers Co.,[100] the Court sustained Board decisions finding violations of section 8(a)(3) where the employer failed to offer any proof of legitimate and substantial business justification for otherwise unlawful discriminatory conduct, and in *Erie Resistor* the Court had reiterated its dictum in *Mackay*[101] that an employer may permanently replace economic strikers in order to continue operations during a strike and need not discharge such replacements at the strike's conclusion unless antiunion motivation could be proved. In *NLRB v. Brown*,[102] the Court held that several employers' use of a lockout and temporary replacements in response to a whipsaw strike against another member of a multi-employer bargaining group had a "comparatively slight" tendency to discourage union membership and was reasonably adopted to achieve legitimate business ends or to deal with business exigencies. Thus, a finding of unlawful discrimination could not be sustained without independent evidence of improper motivation.

In *American Ship Building Co. v. NLRB*,[103] a companion case to *Brown*, the Court stated that "there are some practices which are inherently so prejudicial to union interests and so devoid of significant economic justification . . . that the employer's conduct carries with it an inference of unlawful intention so compelling that it is justifiable to disbelieve the employer's protestations of innocent purpose."[104] Nevertheless, the employer's use of a lockout for the sole purpose of bringing economic pressure to bear in support of its legitimate bargaining position was deemed lawful.[105]

813, 99 LRRM 2784 (CA 7, 1978), *enforcing* 229 NLRB 1204, 95 LRRM 1229 (1977). *See infra* at note 149.

[100]389 US 375, 66 LRRM 2737 (1967). *See* Chapter 19, "The Primary Strike," at note 90 and *infra* this chapter at note 118.

[101]*Supra* note 92.

[102]380 US 278, 58 LRRM 2663 (1965). The Court characterized inherently destructive conduct as that which is demonstrably so destructive of employee rights and so devoid of significant service as a legitimate business end that it cannot be tolerated consistently with the Act.

[103]380 US 300, 58 LRRM 2672 (1965). *See* discussion at notes 248-252 *infra.*

[104]*Id.* at 311.

[105]*Supra* note 103. The Court appeared to refine the limits of inherently destructive conduct in holding that the use of the lockout of the entire bargaining unit does not carry with it any necessary implication that the employer acted to discourage union membership or otherwise to discriminate against union members as such. *See* Radio Officers v. NLRB (A.H. Bull S.S. Co.), 347 US 17, 34 LRRM 2417 (1954); *see also* Georgia Pac., Southern Div., NLRB Gen. Counsel Advice Memo., 5-CA-11747, 104 LRRM 1167 (1980). Thus, a no-distribution rule that could be applied to unprotected as well as protected activity did not necessarily imply that its application was to discourage union membership and, therefore, it was not inherently destructive of employee rights. Texas Instruments v. NLRB, 599 F2d 1067, 102 LRRM 2292 (CA 1, 1979), *denying enforcement to* 236 NLRB 68, 98 LRRM 1299 (1978).

The circuit courts have generally defined "inherently destructive" conduct as that "with far-reaching effects which would hinder future bargaining or conduct which discriminates solely on the basis of participation in strikes or union activity."[106] Prior to the 1980s, the Board more readily found specific employer conduct to be "inherently destructive" of section 7 rights than did many of the courts, and reversals were frequent.[107] For example, in *Portland Williamette Co. v. NLRB*,[108] the Ninth Circuit held that the Board was not warranted in finding that the employer violated section 8(a)(3) by implementing, during an economic strike, a wage proposal giving to employees on the payroll on a specified date during the strike retroactive increases for time worked during a specified period before the strike.[109]

---

[106]Forest Prods. Co., v. NLRB, 888 F2d 72, 132 LRRM 2815, 2818 (CA 10, 1989), *denying enforcement to* 286 NLRB 1336, 127 LRRM 1001 (1987); Boilermakers Local 88 v. NLRB (National Gypsum Co.), 858 F2d 756, 762-64, 129 LRRM 2569 (CA DC, 1988) (employer's hiring of temporary replacements for employees it had locked out was not inherently destructive of employee rights); NLRB v. Sherwin-Williams Co., 714 F2d 1095, 114 LRRM 2506 (CA 11, 1983), *denying enforcement to* 260 NLRB 132, 109 LRRM 1338 (1982) (employer's termination of disability benefits during strike was not inherently destructive of employee rights); Vesuvius Crucible Co. v. NLRB, 668 F2d 162, 169, 108 LRRM 3209 (CA 3, 1981), *denying enforcement to* 252 NLRB 1279, 105 LRRM 1589 (1980) (employer lawfully refused to pay vacation benefits to striking employees); NLRB v. Haberman Constr. Co., 641 F2d 351, 106 LRRM 2998 (CA 5, 1981), *enforcing in part* 236 NLRB 79, 98 LRRM 1221 (1978); Portland Williamette Co. v. NLRB, *supra* note 99. *See also* Amoco Oil Co., *supra* note 97.

[107]Even prior to *Great Dane*, at least two circuit courts of appeals had refused to adopt the Board's view that particular employer conduct was so destructive of employee rights as to require no proof of antiunion motivation even though the employer offered economic and business justification for its conduct. Quality Castings Co. v. NLRB, 325 F2d 36, 54 LRRM 2674 (CA 6, 1963), *denying enforcement to* 139 NLRB 928, 51 LRRM 1422 (1962) (failure to make profit-sharing payments to 64 former employees who had engaged in prolonged strike); Pittsburgh-Des Moines Steel Co. v. NLRB, 284 F2d 74, 47 LRRM 2135 (CA 9, 1960), *denying enforcement to* 124 NLRB 855, 44 LRRM 1518 (1959) (failure to grant Christmas bonus to employees who had engaged in economic strike).

[108]*Supra* note 99.

[109]Of the 162 employees who had originally gone on strike, 107 had returned before the qualifying date, 4 or 5 returned after the qualifying date, a single employee continued to picket, and the rest were not heard from again. The strikers who returned to work after the qualifying date did not receive the retroactive pay; neither did the strike replacements; nor did new employees actively employed on the qualifying date who had not worked the specified period before the strike. Those who had worked during the prestrike period and were on the payroll on the qualifying date received retroactive pay. The Ninth Circuit found, contrary to the Board, that the employer's conduct was not inherently destructive of the employees' right to strike and that, while the conduct had a "comparatively slight" effect on such rights, the employer had a legitimate business purpose for its actions. The court reasoned that the proposal when originally made was not intended to provide a cutoff date for abandonment of the strike, that the employer had a right to insist upon its credibility by not awarding increases to those who did not return to work by that date, and that the conduct could have no continuing adverse consequences like the granting of superseniority. The Board and the court agreed that the employer had neither foreseen nor intended antiunion consequences from its actions. For another example of disagreement between the Board and a circuit court, see Loomis Courier Serv., 235 NLRB 534, 98 LRRM 1083 (1978), *enforcement denied*, 595 F2d 491, 101 LRRM 2450 (CA 9, 1979)

In 1983, however, a Board including several newly appointed members concluded that no violation occurred when a new union was certified as the unit representative during a strike by the incumbent union, and when a new collective bargaining agreement granted a wage bonus to all unit employees who were on the payroll as of the contract ratification date.[110] Even though employees who crossed the old union's picket line received a bonus while former strikers who had not been recalled to work from the preferential hiring list did not, a Board majority found no violation of the Act, observing that "not every detriment which has some nexus to an employee's union activities is thereby automatically rendered an unfair labor practice" or "inherently destructive."[111]

Employer changes in compensation and work force during strikes and lockouts have been a fertile source of cases exploring the outer reaches of "inherently destructive" activity under the *Great Dane* analysis. For example, the Board held that granting preferential job transfer rights to employees who returned to work during a strike (or who individually offered to return at about the same time that the union extended an offer on behalf of all strikers) was unlawful and represented "a real and highly discernible reward to those employees who abandoned the

---

(termination of all branch employees during negotiation of collective bargaining agreement). *Compare* Los Angeles Marine Hardware Co. v. NLRB, 602 F2d 1302, 102 LRRM 2498 (CA 9, 1979), *enforcing* 235 NLRB 720, 98 LRRM 1571 (1978) (termination and refusal to transfer employee when, during contract term, employer transferred operations in part from one division to another, is inherently destructive conduct, and employer's desire to escape financial burden of voluntarily executed contract is insufficient business justification) *with* Ingersoll Rand Co., 247 NLRB 801, 103 LRRM 1224 (1980) (refusal to transfer unit employees while transferring nonunit employees to additional new location is not inherently destructive).

[110]Crown Zellerbach Corp., 266 NLRB 1231, 113 LRRM 1121 (1983).

[111]*Id.*, 113 LRRM at 1124. The changes in membership at the Board may have diminished the disharmony between the Board and the courts on the question of what constitutes inherently destructive conduct. *See* P.W. Supermarkets, 269 NLRB 839, 115 LRRM 1315 (1984), where the Board rejected an ALJ's conclusion that the discharge of two employees following the implementation of a subcontracting decision was "inherently destructive." The Board stated: "[T]he judge's analysis overlooks the *sine qua non* for an 8(a)(3) violation, namely, a causal connection between an employee's protected union activities and an action by the employer detrimental to the employee's tenure or terms and conditions of employment." *Id.* at 840, 115 LRRM at 1317 (footnote omitted). Concerning the ALJ's reliance on *Great Dane*, the Board noted: "Application of the *Great Dane* principle does not, of course, eliminate the requirement of finding unlawful motive or intent in determining that Sec. 8(a)(3) is violated. *Great Dane* simply states that certain employer actions are so manifestly discriminatory against employees engaging in union activities that the unlawful motive will be presumed." *Id.* at 840 n.5, 115 LRRM at 1317 n.5. *Cf.* Challenge-Cook Bros. of Ohio, 282 NLRB 21, 123 LRRM 1237 (1986); Asarco, Mission Unit, 279 NLRB 867, 123 LRRM 1253 (1986).

union's concerted activity."[112] In another case, the Board found inherently destructive the employer's refusal to reinstate two former strikers to welder positions they were qualified to hold even though the employer contended that they were not the best-qualified candidates available.[113] The Board reached this result even after accepting the employer's business justification that it needed highly skilled welders because of a change in the nature of the work performed for its customers.

In *Harter Equipment*,[114] the Board decided an employer's use of temporary replacements during a lockout in support of its legitimate bargaining demands was not inherently destructive of employee rights. Expressly overruling its decision in *Inland Trucking Co.*,[115] the Board held that absent specific proof of antiunion motivation, an employer does not violate sections 8(a)(3) and (1) by hiring temporary replacements in order to engage in business operations during an otherwise lawful lockout. The Board stated that the "substantial" business justification requirement imposed by *Great Dane*[116] means only that the employer's reason be "nonfrivolous." In this regard, the Board emphasized that "there can be no more fundamental employer interest than the continuation of business operations."[117]

The Board's decisions in *Texaco, Inc.*[118] and *Amoco Oil Co.*,[119]

---

[112]American Olean Tile Co., 265 NLRB 1625, 112 LRRM 1080 (1982), *enforcement denied*, 826 F2d 1496, 126 LRRM 2001, (CA 6, 1987); Aqua-Chem, 288 NLRB 1108, 128 LRRM 1237 (1988). For further discussion, *see* Chapter 6, "Interference With Protected Rights," Chapter 19, "The Primary Strike."

[113]Lehigh Metal Fabricators, 267 NLRB 568, 114 LRRM 1064 (1983), *enforced*, 735 F2d 1350, 116 LRRM 3264 (CA 3, 1984). *See also* Grocers Supply Co., 294 NLRB No. 31, 131 LRRM 1386 (1989).

[114]280 NLRB 597, 122 LRRM 1219 (1986), *review denied sub nom.* Operating Eng'rs Local 825 v. NLRB, 829 F2d 458, 126 LRRM 2337 (CA 3, 1987). *See also* Boilermakers Local 88 v. NLRB (National Gypsum Co.), *supra* note 106, *denying enforcement to* 281 NLRB 593, 124 LRRM 1314 (1986). *But cf.* Clemson Bros., 290 NLRB No. 111, 129 LRRM 1150 (1988) (lockout unlawful where employer rehired its own unit employees as temporary hires, and purpose of lockout was to unilaterally implement change in seniority rights that was not encompassed in employer's contract proposal).

[115]179 NLRB 350, 72 LRRM 1486 (1969), *enforced*, 440 F2d 562, 76 LRRM 2929 (CA 7), *cert. denied*, 404 US 858, 78 LRRM 2465 (1971). In overruling *Inland Trucking*, the Board embraced the rationale expressed in the plurality opinion in Ottawa Silica Co., 197 NLRB 449, 80 LRRM 1404 (1972), *enforced*, 482 F2d 945, 84 LRRM 2300 (CA 6, 1973), *cert. denied sub nom.* Teamsters Local 283 v. NLRB, 415 US 916, 85 LRRM 2465 (1974).

[116]NLRB v. Great Dane Trailers, 388 US 26, 65 LRRM 2465 (1967).

[117]Harter Equip., *supra* note 114, at 599.

[118]285 NLRB 241, 126 LRRM 1001 (1987).

[119]285 NLRB 918, 126 LRRM 1265 (1987). *See also* Amoco Oil Co., 287 NLRB 1168, 127 LRRM 1254 (1988); Amoco Oil Co., 286 NLRB 770, 126 LRRM 1268 (1987); Amoco Oil Co., 286 NLRB 441, 126 LRRM 1269 (1987); Amoco Oil Co., 286 NLRB 460, 126 LRRM 1271 (1987); Amoco Oil Co., 286 NLRB 453, 126 LRRM 1273 (1987).

held that whether an employer may lawfully suspend sickness, disability, and other payments to disabled employees during a labor dispute will be determined according to the analysis set forth in *Great Dane*. In *Texaco*, the employer suspended accident and sickness (A&S) payments, medical insurance, and pension credit accrual to certain employees who were disabled when the strike commenced. The Board's original decision[120] held that the employer violated sections 8(a)(3) and (1) by treating the disabled employees as strikers and suspending the disputed benefits. The Board relied on *Emerson Electric Co., E.L. Weigand Div.*,[121] which held that an employer may not presume that disabled employees support a strike. In a supplemental decision, the Board expressly overruled the "*Emerson Electric* theory of violation"[122] and held that cessation of benefits issues would be resolved within the analytical framework of *Great Dane*. That framework is as follows:

> Under this test, the General Counsel bears the prima facie burden of proving at least some adverse effect of the benefit denial on employee rights. The General Counsel can meet this burden by showing that (1) the benefit was accrued and (2) the benefit was withheld on the apparent basis of a strike. We emphasize the need for proof that the disability benefit is accrued, that is, "due and payable on the date on which the employer denied [it]." Absent such proof, there is no basis for finding an adverse effect on employee rights because an employer is not required to finance a strike against itself by paying wages or similar expenses dependent on the continuing performance of services for the employer. . . .[123]

Once the General Counsel makes a prima facie showing, the burden under *Great Dane* shifts to the employer to come forward with proof of a legitimate and substantial business justification for its cessation of benefits. The employer may meet this burden by proving that a collective bargaining representative has clearly and unmistakeably waived its employees' statutory right to be free of such discrimination or coercion. Waiver will not be inferred, but must be explicit. If the employer does not seek to prove waiver, it may still contest the disabled employee's continued entitlement to benefits by demonstrating reliance on a *nondiscriminatory* contract interpretation that is "reasonable and

---

[120]260 NLRB 1192, 109 LRRM 1373 (1982).
[121]246 NLRB 1143, 103 LRRM 1073 (1979), *enforced*, 650 F2d 463, 107 LRRM 2112 (CA 3, 1981), *cert. denied*, 455 US 939, 109 LRRM 2778 (1982).
[122]Texaco, Inc., *supra* note 118, at 245.
[123]*Id.*

. . . arguably correct,"[124] and thus sufficient to constitute a legitimate and substantial business justification for its conduct. Moreover, as under *Great Dane*, even if the employer proves a business justification, the Board may nevertheless find that the employer has committed an unfair labor practice "if the conduct is demonstrated to be inherently destructive of important employee rights or motivated by antiunion intent."[125]

In another *Texaco* decision,[126] the Board invoked these standards and decided that the unilateral termination of A&S benefit payments to employees on medical leave at the beginning of a lawful economic strike was unlawful. First, the Board concluded that the General Counsel established a prima facie case by evidence that the employer had terminated the accrued benefits because of the strike. The Board then held that the employer was unable to establish either a waiver by the union allowing, or a legitimate business reason justifying, the termination of benefits. Accordingly, the Board ruled that the employer violated sections 8(a)(3) and (1) and found it unnecessary to determine whether the termination of benefits was "inherently destructive." But the company did not violate sections 8(a)(1), (3), and (5) when it unilaterally cancelled vacations during the same strike. The Board held that the cancellation was effectively only a postponement rather than a denial of the vacation benefit and, hence, not inherently destructive of employee rights.[127]

On the other hand, in *Amoco Oil Co.*,[128] in which the employer locked out economic strikers, the Board held that the employer did not violate sections 8(a)(3) and (1) by suspending sickness, disability, and occupational injury benefits to eight employees who were disabled prior to the start of the strike. The benefits plan, as described in an employee handbook, provided that

---

[124] *Id.* at 246.

[125] *Id.* (footnotes omitted). *See also* Forest Prods. Co. v. NLRB , *supra* note 106 (employer lawfully refused to distribute matching contributions under Christmas program to permanently replaced strikers); Nuclear Fuel Servs., 290 NLRB 309, 129 LRRM 1089 (1988) (employer lawfully denied striking employees' request for vacation benefits or "vacation pay"); Johns-Manville Sales Corp., 289 NLRB 358, 128 LRRM 1326 (1988) (denial of vacation benefits to strikers was based on reasonable and arguably correct interpretation of contract and was not inherently destructive of employee rights); Jim Walter Resources, 289 NLRB 1441, 129 LRRM 1091 (1988) (employer violated Act by discontinuing insurance premiums for employees disabled prior to strike).

[126] 291 NLRB 508, 129 LRRM 1249 (1988). *See also* Stokely Van Camp v. NLRB, 722 F2d 1324, 114 LRRM 3569 (CA 7, 1983).

[127] *But see* Glover Bottled Gas Corp., 292 NLRB 873, 131 LRRM 1649 (1989) (employer violated Act by denying bereavement and vacation benefits to returning strikers).

[128] 285 NLRB 918, 126 LRRM 1265 (1987).

benefits were not payable when the illness or injury occurred during periods of vacation, suspension, approved leaves of absence, or layoff. The plan further provided that benefits would resume when the employees were "otherwise due to return to work." The Board concluded that the plan established dual eligibility requirements of "being disabled and otherwise scheduled to work."[129] Because of the lawful lockout, no work was available, so the plan afforded a contractual defense under the *Great Dane* criteria adopted in *Texaco*. The Board further found that there was no evidence to support a finding that the cessation of benefits was inherently destructive of important employee rights.[130] *Emerson Electric Co., E.L. Wiegand Div.*,[131] *Conoco*,[132] and *Texaco*[133] were overruled "to the extent that they suggest denial of accrued sick leave benefits necessarily has inherently destructive effects on protected employee rights."[134]

Subsequently, in *Energy Cooperative*,[135] the Board held that the employer did not violate the Act when it withheld A&S benefits from employees during a strike because a strike-settlement agreement constituted a waiver. The settlement agreement provided that in full settlement of any pending or future grievance or unfair labor practice charge related to the denial of benefits during the strike the employer would pay the company portion of health insurance premiums that the employees had assumed during the strike.

Other instances of employer conduct that the Board has found to be inherently destructive of employees' rights include the following: (1) failure to recall any former union-represented employees at the time of resuming operations after an economic

---

[129] *Id.* at 920.

[130] *Id.*

[131] *Supra* note 121.

[132] 265 NLRB 819, 112 LRRM 1001 (1982).

[133] 259 NLRB 1217, 109 LRRM 1104 (1982).

[134] 285 NLRB at 921 n.12. *See also* NLRB v. Sherwin-Williams Co., 714 F2d 1095, 114 LRRM 2506 (CA 11, 1983) (suspension of disability payments after commencement of strike not inherently destructive of §7 rights).

[135] 290 NLRB 635, 129 LRRM 1256 (1988). *See also* Gulf Oil Corp., 291 NLRB 376, 130 LRRM 1096 (1988) (strike-settlement agreement insulated employer from charges alleging that termination of A&S benefits violated Act); Texaco, Inc., 291 NLRB 325, 130 LRRM 1018 (1988) (strike-settlement agreement permitted employer to deny A&S benefits and pension credits); Texaco, Inc., 290 NLRB 1182, 129 LRRM 1253 (1988) (employer did not violate Act when it terminated employees' A&S benefits during strike where strike-settlement agreement clearly and unmistakably waived employees' right to receive benefits during strike); Gulf Oil Co., 290 NLRB 405, 130 LRRM 1103 (1988) (employer's denial of benefits was lawful because of strike settlement agreement).

layoff;[136] (2) discharge of current employees so that they could be replaced by employees referred by the union's hiring hall;[137] (3) refusal to rehire employees because they had previously served as union stewards;[138] (4) refusal to honor strikers' unconditional offers to return to work where one of the objects of the strike was to obtain recognition of their union;[139] (5) conditioning of individuals' employment status on whether they continue to file repetitive grievances;[140] (6) discharge of union stewards who asserted their intent to be active representatives for employees;[141] (7) treating strikers who returned to work as new employees for health insurance purposes and assigning returning strikers to less desirable shifts;[142] (8) requiring employees to change their union affiliation as a condition of continued employment, with a resulting loss of seniority and a reduction in other benefits;[143] (9) providing by contract for superseniority to union officers who do not perform on-the-job duties directly related to contract administrations;[144] and (10) repudiating a labor agreement upon reopening two plants closed for two weeks pursuant to a corporate reorganization.[145] Finally, a union violated sections 8(b)(1)(A) and 8(b)(1)(B) by expelling from membership a part-time supervisor because he testified at a grievance meeting: "Union rules and discipline

---

[136]Rushton & Mercier Woodworking Co., 203 NLRB 123, 83 LRRM 1070 (1973), *enforced*, 502 F2d 1160, 86 LRRM 2151 (CA 1, 1974).

[137]Austin & Wolfe Refrigeration, Air Conditioning & Heating, 202 NLRB 135, 82 LRRM 1521 (1973). The parties apparently sought to implement higher wages without violating a Presidentially decreed wage-price freeze.

[138]Northeast Constructors, 198 NLRB 846, 81 LRRM 1140 (1972).

[139]Barnsider, Inc., 195 NLRB 754, 79 LRRM 1587 (1972).

[140]Hyster Co., 195 NLRB 84, 79 LRRM 1407 (1972), *enforced*, 83 LRRM 2091 (CA 7, 1973).

[141]Pittsburgh Press Co., 234 NLRB 408, 97 LRRM 1371 (1978). *See* Consumers Power Co., 245 NLRB 183, 102 LRRM 1500 (1979) (inherently destructive to discipline steward for administering grievance provisions of labor contract). *But cf.* NLRB v. Wilson Freight Co., 604 F2d 712, 102 LRRM 2269 (CA 1, 1979), *denying enforcement to* 234 NLRB 844, 97 LRRM 1412 (1978), *cert. denied sub nom.* Smith v. Wilson Freight Co., 445 US 962, 103 LRRM 3082 (1980) (contractual clause limiting steward to act through established channels rather than unilaterally); Western Exterminator Co. v. NLRB, 565 F2d 1114, 1117, 97 LRRM 2187 (CA 9, 1977), *enforcing in part*, 223 NLRB 1270, 92 LRRM 1161 (1976) (finding *Great Dane* analysis "inappropriate" in reviewing "an isolated discharge of a single employee").

[142]Moore Business Forms, 224 NLRB 393, 93 LRRM 1437 (1976), *enforced in relevant part*, 574 F2d 835, 98 LRRM 2773 (CA 5, 1978). *See* Providence Medical Center, 243 NLRB 714, 102 LRRM 1099 (1979) (failure to reinstate strikers to substantial equivalent of prestrike jobs); MCC Pac. Valves, 244 NLRB 931, 102 LRRM 1183 (1979). *Cf.* Atlas Metal Parts Co., 252 NLRB 205, 105 LRRM 1582 (1980) (employer unlawfully refused to assign returning strikers to second shift).

[143]Stockton Steel Fabricators, 271 NLRB 524, 117 LRRM 1119 (1984) (union member's expulsion violated §8(b)(2)).

[144]*See* notes 442-458 *infra* and accompanying text.

[145]Esmark, Inc. v. NLRB, 887 F2d 739, 132 LRRM 2710 (CA 7, 1989).

which are designed to discourage or prevent individuals from testifying or being called as witnesses in grievance-arbitration hearings are inherently destructive of the contractual arbitral process and are therefore unlawful."[146]

In many cases, the Board and the courts have avoided the unruly issue of whether conduct was "inherently destructive" by finding that there was insufficient evidence of any legitimate and substantial business justification for the employer's action. That finding leads to the conclusion of illegality whether the action was "inherently destructive" or "comparatively slight" in its effect on employee rights. Thus, in *Laidlaw Corp.*,[147] the Board held that when it bypassed permanently replaced economic strikers who had unconditionally applied for reinstatement to positions vacated by departures of strike replacements, the employer violated section 8(a)(3). The Board described the employer's action as "inherently destructive," but only by way of explaining the legal significance of its failure to prove any legitimate and substantial justification. In enforcing the Board's order, the Seventh Circuit similarly avoided that difficult question which, under *Great Dane*, a showing of adequate business justification would have presented.[148]

---

[146]Oil Workers Local 4-23 (Gulf Oil Co.), 274 NLRB 475, 118 LRRM 1432, 1433 (1985). *Compare* Glaziers Local 558 v. NLRB (PPG Indus.), 787 F2d 1406, 122 LRRM 2008 (CA 10, 1986) (Board erroneously categorized union referral system that resulted in union efforts to replace permit workers with union journeymen, as inherently destructive of employee rights; no violation absent proof union sought to illegally encourage membership).

[147]171 NLRB 1366, 68 LRRM 1252 (1968), *enforced*, 414 F2d 99, 71 LRRM 3054, (CA 7, 1969), *cert. denied*, 397 US 920, 73 LRRM 2537 (1970). *See* Chapter 19, "The Primary Strike." *See also* Arrow Indus., 245 NLRB 1376, 102 LRRM 1525 (1979); NLRB v. Fleetwood Trailers Co., 389 US 375, 66 LRRM 2737 (1967), on which the Board relied in *Laidlaw*. In *Fleetwood*, jobs were not available to economic strikers on the date of their applications for reinstatement. Two months later jobs became available when full production was resumed, but the employer hired new employees instead of qualified strikers, which was held to be a violation of §8(a)(3). In *Fleetwood*, as in *Great Dane*, the Supreme Court did not have to decide whether the conduct involved was "inherently destructive" of employee rights, because the rights of the employees were affected to some extent by the employer's actions and the employer failed to introduce any evidence of a legitimate business objective. *But see* Atlantic Creosoting Co., 242 NLRB 192, 101 LRRM 1144 (1979) (where employer eliminated a position during strike, General Counsel must prove anti-union intent); NLRB v. Wells Fargo Armored Serv. Corp., 597 F2d 7, 101 LRRM 2209 (CA 1, 1979), *denying enforcement to* 237 NLRB 605, 99 LRRM 1069 (1978) (failure to rehire four strikers according to seniority for new positions created after strike, while hiring less senior strikers, held not to be inherently destructive).

[148]See note 147 *supra*. *See also* B.G. Costich & Sons v. NLRB, 613 F2d 450, 103 LRRM 2263 (CA 2, 1980); A.S. Abell Co. v. NLRB, 598 F2d 876, 101 LRRM 2417 (CA 4, 1979); Electro Vector v. NLRB, 539 F2d 35, 93 LRRM 2021 (CA 9, 1976), *cert. denied*, 434 US 821, 96 LRRM 2512 (1977); Johns-Manville Prods. Corp. v. NLRB, 557 F2d 1126, 96 LRRM 2010 (CA 5, 1977); Industrial Workers (AIW) Local 289 v. NLRB (Seeburg Corp.), 476 F2d 868, 82 LRRM 2225 (CA DC, 1973), *enforcing as modified* 192 NLRB 290, 77 LRRM

In a 1977 decision, the Board, in *Knuth Brothers*,[149] avoided a *Great Dane* analysis where the employer refused vacation pay to replaced strikers under an established rule that accrued vacation benefits were payable only to persons on the "active payroll" on a given day. There was no basis for finding a section 8(a)(3) violation, because there was no showing of unlawful motivation and other nonstriking terminated employees were treated in the same manner. However, the denial of benefits to strikers was a consequence of their protected activity, and the practice was therefore violative of section 8(a)(1) as a "clear threat of economic loss to employees for engaging in protected concerted activities."[150] On appeal, the Seventh Circuit affirmed, noting that the *Great Dane* standards applicable in section 8(a)(3) cases should apply to section 8(a)(1) cases, since "employer conduct having the effect of disrupting Section 7 rights should not be permitted without a substantial business justification."[151] The employer's asserted business justification defense was rejected.[152]

1889 (1971); *cf.* Sun Oil Co., 245 NLRB 59, 102 LRRM 1238 (1979); Peyton Packing Co., 129 NLRB 1275, 47 LRRM 1170 (1961) (withholding bonus as punishment for selecting union in election violated §8(a)(1)).

[149]229 NLRB 1204, 95 LRRM 1229 (1977), *enforced*, 584 F2d 813, 99 LRRM 2784 (CA 7, 1978).

[150]*Id.* at 1205.

[151]*Id.*, 584 F2d at 816. *See* NLRB v. Albion Corp., 593 F2d 936, 100 LRRM 2818 (CA 10, 1979); *cf.* NLRB v. Teamsters Local 443 (Connecticut Limousine Serv.), 600 F2d 411, 101 LRRM 2622 (CA 2, 1979) (*Great Dane* analysis in §8(b)(2) case). *But cf.* Service Employees Local 250 v. NLRB (Earringhouse Imports), 600 F2d 930, 101 LRRM 2004 (CA DC, 1979) (*Great Dane* analysis not applicable to §8(a)(4)). The cases relied upon by the Seventh Circuit were: NLRB v. Jemco, Inc., 465 F2d 1142, 1145 n.7, 81 LRRM 2019 (CA 6, 1972), *cert. denied*, 409 US 1109, 82 LRRM 2139 (1973); Tex Tan Welhausen Co. v. NLRB, 419 F2d 1265, 1271, 72 LRRM 2885 (CA 5, 1969), *vacated on other grounds*, 397 US 819, 74 LRRM 2064, *modified on other grounds*, 434 F2d 405, 75 LRRM 2554 (CA 5, 1970), *cert. denied*, 402 US 973, 77 LRRM 2242 (1971); Industrial Workers (AIW) Local 289 v. NLRB (Seeburg Corp.), *supra* note 148. *See also* Loomis Courier Serv. v. NLRB, 595 F2d 491, 101 LRRM 2450 (CA 9, 1979), *denying enforcement to* 235 NLRB 534, 98 LRRM 1083 (1978).

[152]*See* note 99 *supra*. *Cf.* NLRB v. William S. Carroll, Inc., 578 F2d 1, 98 LRRM 2848 (CA 1, 1978), *denying enforcement to* 232 NLRB 1131, 97 LRRM 1037 (1977). For further examples of cases involving "inherently destructive" conduct and strike-related activity, see Lone Star Indus., 279 NLRB 550, 122 LRRM 1162 (1986), *aff'd in part and vacated in part sub nom.* Teamsters Locals 822 & 592 v. NLRB, 813 F2d 472, 125 LRRM 3063 (CA DC, 1987) (failure to recall strikers on basis of seniority was not inherently destructive of employee rights in absence of obligation imposed by past practice or collective bargaining); Foote & Davies, 278 NLRB 72, 121 LRRM 1149 (1986); Garrett R.R. Car & Equip., 275 NLRB 1032, 119 LRRM 1246 (1985), *enforcement denied* 804 F2d 1248, 123 LRRM 3272 (CA 3, 1986); New Galax Mirror Corp., 273 NLRB 1232, 118 LRRM 1519 (1984); Arlington Hotel Co., 273 NLRB 210, 118 LRRM 1506 (1984), *enforced*, 785 F2d 249, 121 LRRM 2926 (CA 8), *cert. denied*, 479 US 914, 123 LRRM 2672 (1986); Harvey Eng'g & Mfg. Corp., 270 NLRB 1290, 116 LRRM 1368 (1984). *See also* NLRB v. Harrison Ready Mix Concrete, 770 F2d 78, 120 LRRM 2077 (CA 6, 1985), *denying enforcement to* 272 NLRB 331, 117 LRRM 1235 (1984); Gaso Pumps, 274 NLRB 532, 119 LRRM 1052 (1985). *But see*

The Sixth Circuit rejected a Board attempt to characterize employer conduct as inherently destructive where a group of 12 laboratory employees voted in a Board election to join a large existing production-and-maintenance unit and, after a contract covering them had been negotiated, the laboratory employees were removed from the "office payroll" and thereby deprived of lunch-time access to an employer-subsidized cafeteria.[153] The court found that the union had waived its right to bargain for continuation of the lunchroom privileges, rendering the employer's conduct entirely outside the ambit of *Great Dane*. As there was no evidence of actual discriminatory motivation, there was no violation.[154] In *NLRB v. Harrison Ready Mix Concrete*,[155] the Sixth Circuit rejected another Board finding that conduct was inherently destructive where the employer reinstated economic strikers with less seniority than that assigned to replacement employees. The court ruled that the Board acted prematurely by characterizing the employer's conduct as a per se violation of the Act without an evaluation of evidence of discriminatory intent, because the case might fit within the rule that an employer need not discharge permanent replacements to create places for returning strikers. The court concluded that there was, in fact, no evidence of discriminatory intent, and denied enforcement of the Board's order.

The Ninth Circuit found that the Board improperly characterized as "inherently destructive," an employer's refusal to allow employees to remove their tools from the plant during a strike, noting that the employer would have been privileged to lock out its employees entirely and that the action taken inflicted no permanent disadvantage on strikers.[156]

Indiana Desk Co., 276 NLRB 1429, 120 LRRM 1309 (1985) (employer held not to have unlawfully failed to reinstate economic strikers); Brady-Standard Motor Co., 273 NLRB 1434, 118 LRRM 1170 (1985) (earnings of replacement employees during strike held not to unlawfully exceed employer's final offer to union). In Trans World Airlines v. Flight Attendants, 489 US 426, 130 LRRM 2657 (1989), a Railway Labor Act case, the Supreme Court ruled that junior "cross overs" who had returned to work before termination of a strike did not have to be laid off in order that senior strikers be reinstated, and upheld job and domicile assignments made during the strike by utilizing the bidding procedure of the contract. The Court declined to extend *Erie Resistor* to this situation.

[153]NLRB v. Henry Vogt Mach. Co., 718 F2d 802, 114 LRRM 2893 (CA 6, 1983).

[154]*Id. See also* NLRB v. Island Typographers, 705 F2d 44, 113 LRRM 2207 (CA 2, 1983) (court rejected Board characterization of layoff of "hot type" craftsmen represented by union, while retaining unrepresented "cold type" employees, as "inherently destructive" where union had ample notice and opportunity to bargain over challenged conduct).

[155]770 F2d 78, 120 LRRM 2077 (CA 6, 1985), *denying enforcement to* 272 NLRB 331, 117 LRRM 1235 (1984).

[156]NLRB v. Kaiser Steel Corp., 700 F2d 575, 112 LRRM 2974 (CA 9, 1983).

The Seventh Circuit rejected the Board's conclusion that inherently destructive conduct included an employer's imposition of a requirement that permanently replaced economic strikers notify the employer every six months of their continued desire for reinstatement as a condition for remaining on a preferential hiring list.[157] The list had originally been established in January 1977. However, the periodic reporting requirement was imposed in March 1979 because, in the two years since the list was established, former strikers had declined reinstatement offers at an increasing rate and had taken an increasingly greater amount of time to consider such offers, leading to excessive delays in filling vacancies. In denying enforcement, the court ruled that the employer had proved a "legitimate and substantial business justification" for imposing the notice requirement. According to the court, the burden imposed by the notice requirement was slight.

The *Milwaukee Spring* cases involved section 8(a)(3) and the question of inherently destructive conduct. In *Milwaukee Spring II*,[158] the Board reconsidered and overruled its *Milwaukee Spring I*[159] decision which held that the employer violated section 8(a)(5) by transferring bargaining unit work to an unorganized plant during the term of a collective bargaining agreement and also violated section 8(a)(3) by laying off the affected employees. The Board labeled as "inherently destructive" the layoffs of employees at the organized plant. In its second opinion, the Board ruled that there was no section 8(a)(5) violation because the employer's conduct did not constitute a modification of any term or condition contained in the agreement. The Board, viewing the section 8(a)(3) violation it had previously found as being entirely derivative of the section 8(a)(5) violation, reversed its prior decision and ruled that there remained no basis for finding that the employer violated section 8(a)(3) by laying off employees after the work transfer. In subsequent cases, the Board has reaffirmed that relocations or subcontracting of bargaining unit work for economic reasons

---

[157]Giddings & Lewis v. NLRB, 710 F2d 1280, 113 LRRM 3361 (CA 7, 1983).

[158]Illinois Coil Spring Co., Milwaukee Spring Div., 268 NLRB 601, 115 LRRM 1065 (1984), *aff'd sub nom.* Auto Workers v. NLRB, 765 F2d 175, 119 LRRM 2801 (CA DC, 1985). *See* further discussion in Chapter 16, "Subjects of Bargaining."

[159]Illinois Coil Spring Co., Milwaukee Spring Div., 265 NLRB 206, 111 LRRM 1486 (1982), *rev'd*, 268 NLRB 601, 115 LRRM 1065 (1984), *aff'd sub nom.* Auto Workers v. NLRB, 765 F2d 175, 119 LRRM 2801 (CA DC, 1985).

do not constitute inherently destructive conduct violative of the Act.[160]

Finally, in *Evening News Ass'n*[161] the Board held, and the Sixth Circuit agreed, that two employers bargaining with the same union may lock out pursuant to a mutual-aid agreement. The Board concluded that such an action had a "bargaining purpose" and hence was not inherently destructive of employee rights.

C. Specific Conduct

1. Discharge or Discipline for Union Activity. Discharge because of an employee's membership in or activities on behalf of a labor organization violates section 8(a)(3).[162] The keystone of the violation is the determination of unlawful motive.[163]

a. Elements of an Unlawful Discharge. The essential elements of a discharge that violates section 8(a)(3) are "a knowledge on the part of the employer that the employee is engaged in union activity and the actual discharge of the employee because of this activity."[164] Generally the fact of discharge will be undisputed,[165] leaving motivation and employer knowledge as the issues most often litigated.[166]

To establish that a discharge violates section 8(a)(3), the General Counsel must prove that the employer knew of the employee's union activity[167] (except in situations where the

---

[160]*See, e.g.*, Suburban Transit Corp., 276 NLRB 15, 120 LRRM 1094 (1985); Griffith-Hope Co., 275 NLRB 487, 119 LRRM 1197 (1985); Inland Steel Container Co., 275 NLRB 929, 119 LRRM 1293 (1985), *review denied sub nom.* Steelworkers Local 2179 v. NLRB, 822 F2d 559, 125 LRRM 3313 (CA 5, 1987).

[161]166 NLRB 219, 65 LRRM 1425 (1967), *enforced sub nom.* Teamsters Local 372 v. NLRB, 404 F2d 1159, 70 LRRM 2061 (CA 6, 1968), *cert. denied*, 395 US 923, 71 LRRM 2294 (1969).

[162]Ogle Protection Serv., 149 NLRB 545, 57 LRRM 1337 (1964), *enforcement granted in part and denied in part*, 375 F2d 497, 64 LRRM 2792 (CA 6), *cert. denied*, 389 US 843, 66 LRRM 2308 (1967).

[163]Hambre Hombre Enters. v. NLRB, 581 F2d 204, 99 LRRM 2541 (CA 9, 1978).

[164]Wheeling-Pittsburgh Steel Corp. v. NLRB, 618 F2d 1009, 104 LRRM 2054 (CA 3, 1980); Sterling Aluminum Co. v. NLRB, 391 F2d 713, 67 LRRM 2686 (CA 8, 1968). In proving unlawful motive, the General Counsel must prove that the employer possessed union animus. See discussion *infra* at notes 215-233.

[165]*But see* discussion of constructive discharge at notes 180-199 *infra* for situations where the issue of discharge is disputed.

[166]The crucial determination is that of motivation. *See* NLRB v. Doug Neal Mgmt. Co., 620 F2d 1133, 104 LRRM 2045 (CA 6, 1980), *denying enforcement to* 226 NLRB 985, 94 LRRM 1254 (1976); NLRB v. Armcor Indus., 535 F2d 239, 92 LRRM 2374 (CA 3, 1976).

[167]Clark & Wilkens Indus., 290 NLRB 106, 130 LRRM 1362 (1988), *enforced*, 887 F2d 308, 132 LRRM 2758 (CA DC, 1989); Metro Center, 267 NLRB 288, 114 LRRM 1215 (1983); Phillip Megdal, Inc., 267 NLRB 82, 113 LRRM 1138 (1983).

"small plant" doctrine applies[168]) and that the employee was discharged or disciplined as a result of the employer's unlawful motivation or "union animus."[169] The General Counsel frequently relies on circumstantial evidence—such as the timing of the employer's action,[170] the pretextual nature of its asserted motivation,[171] or shifting justifications for discharge given by the employer[172]—to support the inference of unlawful motivation.[173] Furthermore, if it is shown that an employer's decision to discharge some members of a group was prompted by protected activity, the discharges of all in the group may be attributed to this same illegal motivation. Such a case is made when it is shown that the employer had actual knowledge of some of the employees' protected activity and a reasonable suspicion that other terminated employees were also union supporters.[174] But, "[a]bsent a showing of anti-union motivation, an employer may discharge an employee for a good reason, a bad reason, or no reason at all without running afoul of the [Act]."[175]

---

[168]*See infra* note 209 and accompanying text.

[169]*See, e.g.*, NLRB v. Brookshire Grocery Co., 837 F2d 1336, 127 LRRM 2776 (CA 5, 1988) (no prima facie case made out where no substantial evidence that discharge was based on union activities and employer had adequate basis for discharge which later proved to be erroneous); NLRB v. Gateway Theatre Corp., 818 F2d 971, 125 LRRM 2466 (CA DC, 1987) (no prima facie case made out where employer statements and actions did not indicate union animus); NLRB v. Chaim Babad dba J.R.R. Realty Co., 785 F2d 46, 121 LRRM 2940 (CA 2), *cert. denied*, 479 US 830, 123 LRRM 2592 (1986); NLRB v. Del Rey Tortilleria, 787 F2d 1118, 122 LRRM 2111 (CA 7, 1986), *enforced*, 823 F2d 1135, 125 LRRM 3140 (CA 7, 1987); NLRB v. Nueva Eng'g, 761 F2d 961, 119 LRRM 2317 (CA 4, 1985); Lemon Drop Inn v. NLRB, 752 F2d 323, 118 LRRM 2290 (CA 8, 1985); NLRB v. Southern Fla. Hotel & Motel Ass'n, 751 F2d 1571, 118 LRRM 2792 (CA 11, 1985).

[170]Northern Wire Corp. v. NLRB, 887 F2d 1313, 132 LRRM 2818 (CA 7, 1989); Southwire Co. v. NLRB, 820 F2d 453, 125 LRRM 2798 (CA DC, 1987); NLRB v. Del Rey Tortilleria, *supra* note 169; Bay State Ambulance & Hosp. Rental, 280 NLRB 1079, 123 LRRM 1055 (1986); Lemon Drop Inn v. NLRB, *supra* note 169; Collectramatic, 267 NLRB 866, 114 LRRM 1226 (1983); Emenee Accessories, 267 NLRB 1344, 114 LRRM 1223 (1983); Phillip Megdal, Inc., *supra* note 167.

[171]NLRB v. Nueva Eng'g, *supra* note 169; Phillip Megdal, Inc., *supra* note 167; Abbey Island Park Manor, 267 NLRB 163, 113 LRRM 1149 (1983); Escambia River Elec. Coop., 265 NLRB 973, 112 LRRM 1335 (1982), *enforced*, 733 F2d 830, 116 LRRM 2630 (CA 11, 1984).

[172]NLRB v. Dorothy Shamrock Coal Co., 833 F2d 1263, 126 LRRM 3313 (CA 7, 1987).

[173]The Second Circuit has suggested that the same circumstantial evidence can be used to prove both knowledge and motivation. Abbey's Transp. Servs. v. NLRB, 837 F2d 575, 127 LRRM 2437 (CA 2, 1988).

[174]ARA Leisure Servs. v. NLRB, 782 F2d 456, 121 LRRM 2598 (CA 4, 1986); Dillingham Marine & Mfg. Co. v. NLRB, 610 F2d 319, 103 LRRM 2430 (CA 5, 1980).

[175]Clothing Workers v. NLRB (AMF, Inc.), 564 F2d 434, 440, 95 LRRM 2821 (CA DC, 1977); *accord* Stephenson v. NLRB, 614 F2d 1210, 103 LRRM 2238 (CA 9, 1980); Syncro Corp. v. NLRB, 597 F2d 922, 101 LRRM 2790 (CA 5, 1979); NLRB v. Knuth Bros., 537 F2d 950, 92 LRRM 3275 (CA 7, 1976); Bayliner Marine Corp., 215 NLRB 12, 87 LRRM 1450 (1974), *petition for review dismissed sub nom.* Brook v. NLRB, 538 F2d 260, 92 LRRM 3420 (CA 9, 1976); S. W. Noggle Co. v. NLRB, 478 F2d 1144, 83 LRRM 2225 (CA 8, 1973); Cannady v. NLRB, 466 F2d 583, 80 LRRM 3425 (CA 10, 1972); NLRB v. Bangor Plastics, 392 F2d 772, 67 LRRM 2987 (CA 6, 1967).

The difficult cases arise when the employer, after the General Counsel has demonstrated that one of the motives was improper, asserts a proper business reason for the discharge. While previously the Board applied an "in part" causation test in dual motivation cases, it has now adopted the two-part *Wright Line* analysis under which the employer will prevail upon proving that the discharge would have occurred even in the absence of protected conduct.[176]

The Board also had adopted the proposition that an employee's discharge is not illegal if, between the time the employer decides to terminate the employee for improper reasons, and the time the termination occurs, a legitimate reason arises for discharging the employee. In *A&T Manufacturing Co.*,[177] the Board held that an employee had been improperly discharged because the decision to discharge the employee arose before any legitimate basis for discharge had occurred. The Sixth Circuit refused to enforce the Board's order because, after the termination decision had been made but before the employee's termination, the employee violated a company rule by failing to report his absence on three occasions. The court stated:

> [T]he Board in effect has established a *per se* rule that once an employer decides to discharge an employee for an illegal reason, it is impossible for that employer to adopt an additional legitimate reason between the time of the determination and the time of its effectuation. This *per se* factual rule comports neither with reality nor with the Board's own precedent.[178]

On remand, the Board agreed that the employer had met its burden of proving by affirmative evidence that it would have discharged the employee notwithstanding the employee's protected activity. Accordingly, the Board held that the discharge of the employee was not violative of section 8(a)(3) regardless of the employer's original reason for deciding to discharge the employee.[179]

b. Constructive Discharge. Obviously, employees cannot claim to be victims of discriminatory discharge unless they have been

---

[176]Wright Line, Wright Line Div., 251 NLRB 1083, 105 LRRM 1169 (1980), *enforced*, 662 F2d 899, 108 LRRM 2513 (CA 1, 1981), *cert. denied*, 455 US 989, 109 LRRM 2779 (1982). *See supra* notes 53-75 and accompanying text.

[177]265 NLRB 1560, 112 LRRM 1312 (1982), *enforced in part and vacated in part*, 738 F2d 148, 116 LRRM 3107 (CA 6, 1984).

[178]*Id.*, 738 F2d at 151-52, 116 LRRM at 3110.

[179]A&T Mfg. Co., 276 NLRB 1183, 120 LRRM 1202 (1985).

discharged. Thus, in most situations, an employee who voluntarily quits cannot contend that the separation was a discriminatory discharge in violation of section 8(a)(3). In many cases, however, the Board and the courts have deemed that employees whose terminations appeared voluntary had been "constructively discharged." In the *Crystal Princeton*[180] case, the Board defined "constructive discharge" as follows:

> There are two elements which must be proven to establish a constructive discharge. First, the burden imposed upon the employee must cause, and be intended to cause, a change in his working conditions so difficult or unpleasant as to force him to resign. Second, it must be shown that those burdens were imposed because of the employee's union activities.[181]

These criteria have been satisfied when the employee has suffered a cut in pay,[182] has been assigned more onerous working conditions,[183] or has been transferred to a less desirable job.[184] Constructive discharge has also been found when an employee received numerous warnings,[185] was denied a pay increase,[186]

---

[180]Crystal Princeton Ref. Co., 222 NLRB 1068, 91 LRRM 1302 (1976).

[181]*Id.* at 1069. *Accord* Cartwright Hardware Co. v. NLRB, 600 F2d 268, 101 LRRM 2652 (CA 10, 1979), *denying enforcement in part to* 229 NLRB 781, 95 LRRM 1262 (1977); J.P. Stevens & Co. v. NLRB, 461 F2d 490, 80 LRRM 2609 (CA 4, 1972) and cases cited therein at 494.

[182]Bilmax dba Ellis Toyota, 266 NLRB 442, 112 LRRM 1380 (1983); NLRB v. Tricor Prods., 636 F2d 266, 105 LRRM 3271 (CA 10, 1980); B.N. Beard Co., 248 NLRB 198, 103 LRRM 1560 (1980); Central Dispatch, 229 NLRB 979, 96 LRRM 1483 (1977). *But see* KRI Constructors, 290 NLRB 802, 131 LRRM 1148 (1988); Caddell-Burns Mfg. Co., 222 NLRB 488, 91 LRRM 1191 (1976).

[183]*Compare* East Bay Properties, 232 NLRB 670, 96 LRRM 1342 (1977) *and* Pre-Cast Mfg. Co., 200 NLRB 135, 82 LRRM 1325 (1972) *with* Monon Trailer, 217 NLRB 257, 89 LRRM 1280 (1975), Gerbes Super Mkt., 217 NLRB 394, 89 LRRM 1160 (1975) *and* NLRB v. J.W. Mortell Co., 440 F2d 455, 76 LRRM 2489 (CA 7, 1971).

[184]Production Plated Plastics, 247 NLRB 595, 103 LRRM 1228 (1980). *See* Production Stamping, 239 NLRB 1183, 100 LRRM 1141 (1979); Razco, Inc., 231 NLRB 660, 97 LRRM 1561 (1977); Dumas Bros. Mfg., 205 NLRB 919, 84 LRRM 1411 (1973), *enforced*, 495 F2d 1371, 87 LRRM 2127 (CA 5, 1974). *See also* Sullivan Transfer Co., 247 NLRB 772, 103 LRRM 1369 (1980) (reduction in work hours constituting constructive discharge); Coating Prods., 251 NLRB 1271, 105 LRRM 1399 (1980), *enforced*, 648 F2d 108, 107 LRRM 2337 (CA 2, 1981); Maywood, Inc., 251 NLRB 979, 105 LRRM 1577 (1980). *But see* Dillingham Marine & Mfg. Co., 239 NLRB 904, 100 LRRM 1109 (1978), *enforced*, 610 F2d 319, 103 LRRM 2430 (CA 5, 1980) (refusal to allow employee to change shifts not constructive discharge); KDEN Broadcasting Co., subsidiary, North Am. Broadcasting Co., 225 NLRB 25, 93 LRRM 1022 (1976) (change in employee hours not constructive discharge); Coliseum Hosp., 202 NLRB 927, 82 LRRM 1802 (1973) (reduction in employee hours not constructive discharge); H.A. Kuhle Co., 205 NLRB 88, 84 LRRM 1147 (1973) (assigning additional duties not constructive discharge).

[185]*Compare* W.T. Grant Co., 195 NLRB 1000, 79 LRRM 1670 (1972) *with* P.E. Van Pelt, Inc., 238 NLRB 794, 99 LRRM 1576 (1978) *and* Central Casket Co., 225 NLRB 362, 92 LRRM 1547 (1976).

[186]*Compare* Mallory Capacitor Co., 169 NLRB 42, 67 LRRM 1122, *enforced*, 400 F2d 956, 69 LRRM 2448 (CA 7, 1968), *cert. denied*, 394 US 918, 70 LRRM 3062 (1969) *with* Tahoe Mgmt. & Leasing Co., 222 NLRB 394, 91 LRRM 1212 (1976) *and* Western Boot & Shoe, 205 NLRB 999, 84 LRRM 1140 (1973).

or was threatened with physical harm.[187] The Board also has found that employers constructively discharge employees on account of union activity by harassing union supporters through assigning unnecessarily arduous work,[188] conducting frequent work inspections,[189] and by unilaterally changing working conditions.[190] Employees who refuse to return to work after a strike to avoid unlawful discipline,[191] who quit in the face of employer harassment for union activity,[192] or who quit as a result of reduction in work hours[193] also have been regarded as constructively discharged.

In *Sure Tan v. NLRB*,[194] the Supreme Court held that an employer had constructively discharged its alien employees by reporting their undocumented status to the INS shortly after a representation election in which the union was certified as the employees' bargaining representative. In finding a constructive discharge, the Supreme Court agreed with the ALJ's conclusion that "but for petitioner's letter to Immigration, the discriminatees would have continued to work indefinitely."[195] The Court specifically noted that, although it was legitimate and even commendable for the employer to report the status of the employees, the reporting of the aliens was in retaliation for their exercise of their section 7 rights and was therefore unlawful.

Constructive discharge may also occur when the employer unlawfully withdraws recognition of the union and imposes unlawful terms and conditions of employment on its employees.[196] In *NLRB v. Campbell Harris Electric Co.*,[197] for example,

---

[187]Mishan & Sons, 242 NLRB 1344, 101 LRRM 1344 (1979); S & K Elec., 226 NLRB 442, 93 LRRM 1303 (1976). *See also* Adscon, Inc. 290 NLRB No. 63, 131 LRRM 1145 (1988) (threat, standing alone, not sufficient to prove constructive discharge).

[188]Einhorn Enters., Star Color Plate Serv. Div., 279 NLRB 576, 122 LRRM 1232 (1986); Scotch & Sirloin Restaurant, 269 NLRB 436, 116 LRRM 1205 (1984).

[189]Great S. Constr., 266 NLRB 364, 112 LRRM 1355 (1983).

[190]Auto Fast Freight, 272 NLRB 561, 117 LRRM 1336 (1984), *enforced*, 793 F2d 1126, 122 LRRM 3058 (CA 9, 1986).

[191]Charge Card Ass'n, 247 NLRB 835, 103 LRRM 1298 (1980).

[192]Galax Apparel Corp., 247 NLRB 159, 103 LRRM 1143 (1980). *See also* Spartan Equip. Co., 297 NLRB No. 3, 132 LRRM 1293 (1989); Vought Corp., 273 NLRB 1290, 118 LRRM 1271 (1984), *enforced*, 788 F2d 1378, 122 LRRM 2168 (CA 8, 1986).

[193]Sullivan Transfer Co., *supra* note 184.

[194]467 US 883, 116 LRRM 2857 (1984).

[195]*Id.* at 895, 116 LRRM at 2862.

[196]*Compare* Crawford Door Sales Co., 226 NLRB 1144, 94 LRRM 1393 (1976) *and* Marquis Elevator Co., 217 NLRB 461, 89 LRRM 1520 (1975) *with* Cartwright Hardware Co. v. NLRB, *supra* note 181 (denying enforcement to Board order on this issue). *See also* Western Pac. Roofing Corp., 244 NLRB 501, 102 LRRM 1220 (1979), and Superior Sprinkler, 227 NLRB 204, 94 LRRM 1253 (1976), for a detailed analysis of the law on this issue.

[197]719 F2d 292, 114 LRRM 2881 (CA 8, 1983).

the Eighth Circuit approved the Board's findings that a unionized electrical contractor that ceased operations and reconstituted itself as a nonunion alter ego had constructively discharged its union employees when it advised them of its intention to operate on an open shop basis, thereby inducing them to decline to work for the nonunion entity.

In *Avecor, Inc.*,[198] the Board ruled that a constructive discharge had not occurred because the employer did not implement changes in operations solely to force complainant to quit. Rather, the evidence showed that the changes in operation were planned long before the union's organizing campaign had commenced and that, although the changes applied equally to other employees, no other employee quit.[199]

c. Employer's Knowledge of Employee's Union Activity. In most cases, in order to prove that a particular discharge was discriminatorily motivated, it must be established that prior to the discharge the employer had knowledge of the discharged employee's union activities.[200] Both the Board and the courts recognize that a finding of knowledge can be based upon inferences drawn from circumstantial evidence; however, such inferences must not be entirely speculative or improbable.[201]

---

[198]296 NLRB No. 94, 133 LRRM 1204 (1989).

[199]*See also* Seville Flexpack Corp., 288 NLRB 518, 130 LRRM 1376 (1989).

[200]Tri-State Truck Serv. v. NLRB, 616 F2d 65, 103 LRRM 2640 (CA 3, 1980). In one limited situation, however, the employee who is discharged need not be the one whose union activity the employer sought to discourage. It is unlawful under §8(a)(3) for an employer to discharge "a nonunion employee to cover up and confer an aura of plausibility upon his alleged 'economic justification' for the simultaneous discharge of an unwanted union activist . . . since such a discharge . . . interferes with, restrains, and coerces all of the employees in the exercise of rights under Section 7 of the Act." Jack August Enters., 232 NLRB 881, 900, 97 LRRM 1560 (1977), *enforced*, 583 F2d 575, 99 LRRM 2582 (CA 1, 1978); *accord* NLRB v. Dorn's Transp. Corp., 405 F2d 706, 70 LRRM 2295 (CA 2, 1969); NLRB v. Ambrose Distrib. Co., 358 F2d 319, 61 LRRM 2575 (CA 9, 1966), *cert. denied*, 385 US 838, 63 LRRM 2235 (1966); Looney Sheet Metal Constr. Co., 160 NLRB 1635, 63 LRRM 1211 (1966); NLRB v. Superex Drugs, 341 F2d 747, 58 LRRM 2455 (CA 6, 1965); NLRB v. Williams Lumber Co., 195 F2d 669, 29 LRRM 2633 (CA 4, 1952); *cf.* Majestic Molded Prods., 330 F2d 603, 606, 55 LRRM 2816 (CA 2, 1964) (mass layoff constitutes §8(a)(3) violation when significant unlawful motive exists "even if some white sheep suffer along with the black"). *See also* Ballou Brick Co. v. NLRB, 798 F2d 339, 123 LRRM 2121 (CA 8, 1986) (mass layoff, knowledge inferred); Dillingham Marine & Mfg. Co. v. NLRB, *supra* note 184 (not necessary to show specific knowledge of union activity of each individual employee).

[201]NLRB v. Fort Vancouver Plywood Co., 604 F2d 596, 102 LRRM 2232 (CA 9, 1979), *cert. denied*, 445 US 915, 103 LRRM 2668 (1980) (knowledge found); Delchamps, Inc. v. NLRB, 585 F2d 91, 99 LRRM 3086 (CA 5, 1978) (no knowledge found); Teamsters Local 633 v. NLRB (Bulk Haulers), 509 F2d 490, 88 LRRM 2072 (CA DC, 1974) (knowledge found); NLRB v. Armitage Sand & Gravel, 495 F2d 759, 86 LRRM 2245 (CA 6, 1974) (no knowledge found); Famet, Inc. v. NLRB, 490 F2d 293, 85 LRRM 2223 (CA 9, 1973) (knowledge found); Von Solbrig Hosp., 465 F2d 173, 80 LRRM 3079 (CA 7, 1972) (same); General Mercantile & Hardware Co. v. NLRB, 461 F2d 952, 80 LRRM 2622 (CA 8, 1972)

Knowledge is often inferred when the discharged employee has engaged in overt union activities, such as soliciting signatures on union authorization cards,[202] wearing union buttons or other insignia,[203] or participating in a strike.[204] Knowledge has also been inferred where the discharged employee was the instigator of the union activity[205] or where the employer learned of the employee's union activities through interrogation[206] or surveillance.[207] If the General Counsel fails to prove that the employer had knowledge of the discharged employee's union activities, no violation will ordinarily be found.[208]

As previously noted, the Board often infers employer knowledge of employee union activities from the small size of the

---

(no knowledge found); Winn-Dixie Stores v. NLRB, 448 F2d 8, 78 LRRM 2375 (CA 4, 1971) (same); Morgan Precision Parts v. NLRB, 444 F2d 1210, 77 LRRM 2870 (CA 5, 1971) (knowledge found); Texas Aluminum Co. v. NLRB, 435 F2d 917, 76 LRRM 2151 (CA 5, 1970) (same).

[202]Lizdale Knitting Mills, 211 NLRB 966, 86 LRRM 1465 (1974), *enforced*, 523 F2d 978, 90 LRRM 3341 (CA 2, 1975); Successful Creations, 202 NLRB 242, 82 LRRM 1505 (1973).

[203]Coca-Cola Bottling Co. Consol., 226 NLRB 894, 93 LRRM 1383 (1976); Wintex Knitting Mills, 216 NLRB 1058, 88 LRRM 1566 (1975); Ramada Inns, 201 NLRB 431, 82 LRRM 1253 (1973).

[204]Hembree v. Georgia Power Co., 637 F2d 423, 106 LRRM 2535 (CA 5, 1981); J.P. Stevens & Co., 247 NLRB 420, 103 LRRM 1187 (1980); Transportation Enters., 240 NLRB 551, 100 LRRM 1330 (1979), *enforced in part*, 630 F2d 421, 105 LRRM 3168 (CA 5, 1980).

[205]Horton Automatics, 289 NLRB 405, 130 LRRM 1463 (1988), *enforced*, 884 F2d 574, 133 LRRM 3112 (CA 5, 1989); Hoffer ta Food Cart Mkt., 286 NLRB 1016, 126 LRRM 1314 (1987); Hunter Douglas, Inc. v. NLRB, 804 F2d 808, 123 LRRM 2912 (CA 3, 1986), *cert. denied*, 481 US 1069, 125 LRRM 2440 (1987); Grand Rapids Die Casting Corp. v. NLRB, 831 F2d 112, 126 LRRM 2747 (CA 6, 1987) (one who actually discharged employee need not have knowledge of employee's union activity); D & D Sewing Co. v. NLRB, 801 F2d 636, 123 LRRM 2464 (CA 3, 1986); Turnbull Cone Baking Co. of Tenn. v. NLRB, 778 F2d 292, 121 LRRM 2025 (CA 6, 1985), *cert. denied*, 476 US 1159, 122 LRRM 2424 (1986); Studio S.J.T., 277 NLRB 1189, 121 LRRM 1070 (1985); Island Film Processing dba Kahala Kai Photo Serv., 274 NLRB 1525, 119 LRRM 1096 (1985), *enforcement denied*, 784 F2d 1446, 121 LRRM 3290 (CA 9, 1986); Jenkins Index Co., 273 NLRB 736, 118 LRRM 1097 (1984); Frey Mechanical Contractors, 270 NLRB 348, 117 LRRM 1061 (1984). *See also* BMD Sportswear Corp., 283 NLRB 142, 124 LRRM 1268 (1987) (discharge of employee who is not known to have engaged in union activity but who has close relationship with known union adherent may give rise to inference of discrimination). For cases where knowledge of union activities was not demonstrated, see Lawyers Coop. Publishing Co., 273 NLRB 129, 118 LRRM 1213 (1984), *rev'd in part and remanded sub nom.* Dash v. NLRB, 793 F2d 1062, 122 LRRM 2931 (CA 9, 1986); International Baking Co., 245 NLRB 220, 102 LRRM 1277 (1979); Nebraska Bulk Transp., 240 NLRB 135, 100 LRRM 1340 (1979); Summer Hill Nursing Home, 222 NLRB 433, 91 LRRM 1316 (1976).

[206]Springfield Dodge, 218 NLRB 1429, 89 LRRM 1736 (1975), *enforced*, 532 F2d 747, 92 LRRM 2112 (CA 3, 1976); Pyro Mining Co., 204 NLRB 607, 83 LRRM 1709 (1973).

[207]Florida Steel Corp., 214 NLRB 264, 88 LRRM 1263 (1974), *enforced in pertinent part*, 551 F2d 306, 94 LRRM 2589 (CA 4, 1977).

[208]Kantor Pepsi-Cola Bottling Co., 248 NLRB 99, 103 LRRM 1388 (1980); Leyendecker Paving, 247 NLRB 28, 103 LRRM 1107 (1980); Proler Int'l Corp., 242 NLRB 676, 101 LRRM 1274 (1979), *enforced in part*, 635 F2d 351, 106 LRRM 2530 (CA 5, 1981); Siltec Corp., 217 NLRB 282, 89 LRRM 1514 (1975); Steel-Tex Mfg. Corp., 206 NLRB 461, 84 LRRM 1384 (1973).

employer's plant or operation.[209] For example, in *United L-N Glass*,[210] the Board applied the "small plant" doctrine and inferred knowledge of union activities by an employer who employed fewer than 50 workers, where the employees socialized together outside of the workplace, and where six managerial employees knew of complainant's union activity. Nonetheless, in *Hadley Manufacturing Corp.*,[211] the NLRB stated that

> the mere fact that [the employer's] plant is of a small size, does not permit a finding that [the employer] had knowledge of the union activities of specific employees, absent supporting evidence that the union activities were carried on in such a manner, or at times that in the normal course of events, [the employer] must have noticed them.[212]

Thus, where the discharged employee engages in no union activity on the employer's premises, regardless of the size of the plant, the Board will usually not infer that the employer possesses knowledge of the discharged employee's union activities.[213] While the courts have accepted the small plant doctrine, they have disagreed on its application.[214]

d. Inferential Proof of Employer's Animus. Employers defending against allegations of discriminatory discharge often assert facially nondiscriminatory reasons for the termination. Such a claim, when supported by evidence, requires the Board to weigh that evidence against conflicting evidence that the alleged justifi-

---

[209]Metro Center, 267 NLRB 288, 114 LRRM 1215 (1983); D & D Sewing Co. v. NLRB, *supra* note 205; Permanent Label Corp., 248 NLRB 118, 103 LRRM 1513 (1980), *enforced*, 657 F2d 512, 107 LRRM 2985 (CA 3, 1981), *cert. denied*, 455 US 940, 109 LRRM 2778 (1982); Nebraska Bulk Transp., *supra* note 205; Wiese Plow Welding Co., 123 NLRB 616, 43 LRRM 1495 (1959).

[210]297 NLRB No. 52, 133 LRRM 1238 (1989).

[211]108 NLRB 1641, 34 LRRM 1246 (1954). *See also* Coral Gables Convalescent Home, 234 NLRB 1198, 97 LRRM 1435 (1978), *enforced*, 85 Lab. Cas. (CCH) ¶11200 (CA 5, 1979); Friendly Mkts., 224 NLRB 967, 92 LRRM 1584 (1976).

[212]108 NLRB at 1659.

[213]Mantac Corp., 231 NLRB 858, 97 LRRM 1016 (1977); Picker Corp., 222 NLRB 296, 91 LRRM 1315 (1976). *But see* B. N. Beard Co., 248 NLRB 198, 103 LRRM 1560 (1980) (small-plant doctrine inappropriate where employee successfully kept union activity secret); K & B Mounting, 248 NLRB 570, 103 LRRM 1541 (1980).

[214]Webco Bodies v. NLRB, 595 F2d 451, 101 LRRM 2041 (CA 8, 1979); Teamsters Local 633 v. NLRB (Bulk Haulers), *supra* note 201; Famet, Inc. v. NLRB, *supra* note 201; Hackett Precision Co. v. NLRB, 459 F2d 463, 79 LRRM 3025 (CA 6, 1972); NLRB v. Sutherland Lumber Co., 452 F2d 67, 78 LRRM 2772 (CA 7, 1971); NLRB v. Meinholdt Mfg., 451 F2d 737, 78 LRRM 2892 (CA 10, 1971); NLRB v. Century Broadcasting Corp., 419 F2d 771, 72 LRRM 2905 (CA 8, 1969); NLRB v. Mid States Sportswear, 412 F2d 537, 71 LRRM 2370 (CA 5, 1969); NLRB v. Pembek Oil Corp., 404 F2d 105, 69 LRRM 2811 (CA 2, 1968); Dubin-Haskell Lining Corp. v. NLRB, 375 F2d 568, 64 LRRM 2757 (CA 4, 1967), *cert. denied*, 393 US 824, 69 LRRM 2434 (1968); NLRB v. Joseph Antell, Inc., 358 F2d 880, 62 LRRM 2014 (CA 1, 1966); NLRB v. Dove Coal Co., 369 F2d 849, 63 LRRM 2561 (CA 4, 1966).

cation was *pretextual* and that the real reason was the employer's union animus.[215] Although the wide application of the *Wright Line* analysis[216] pretermits many inquiries into motivation, there remains a residuum of cases in which the Board must decide whether the employer acted from unlawful motives.[217] In such cases, the Board considers a broad range of circumstantial evidence of employer motivation.

When an employee is discharged shortly after engaging in union activity, the Board often infers that the employer's asserted justifications are pretexts and that the discharge was discriminatorily motivated.[218] The courts agree that timing is an important factor in assessing motivation.[219] Nevertheless, the

---

[215]*E.g.*, Reed-I, Inc., 290 NLRB 1115, 129 LRRM 1229 (1988); Murd Indus., 287 NLRB 864, 129 LRRM 1167 (1987); International Metal Co., 286 NLRB 1106, 130 LRRM 1030 (1987); Southwire Co. v. NLRB, 820 F2d 453, 125 LRRM 2798 (CA DC, 1987) (severity of discipline and prior nonenforcement of work rule indicated discharges of employees were pretextual); NLRB v. Bishopric Prod. Co., 777 F2d 1119, 120 LRRM 3434 (CA 6, 1985). See discussion of burden of proof at notes 55-70 *supra*. *See also* NLRB v. Appletree Chevrolet, 608 F2d 988, 993, 103 LRRM 2066 (CA 4, 1979), *denying enforcement in part to* 237 NLRB 867, 99 LRRM 1505 (1978), where the court reversed the Board because the Board had failed to "find and identify 'an affirmative and persuasive reason' why the employer rejected the good cause and chose a bad one."

[216]*See supra* notes 71-73 and accompanying text.

[217]The distinction between "pretext" cases and "mixed motive" cases is widely accepted, as Justice White demonstrated in his opinion for the Court in NLRB v. Transportation Mgmt. Corp., 462 US 393, 400, n. 5, 113 LRRM 2857 (1983), but the boundary between them is hardly a bright line. Indeed, *Transportation Mgmt.* may, on its facts, be fairly viewed as a case in which the employer's asserted justification for the discharge was rejected as pretextual. When a prototypical "pretext" case is analyzed under *Wright Line*, it will usually be seen that evidence critical to the General Counsel's prima facie case, if credited, will negate the employer's asserted justification. *See, e.g.*,, Taylor & Gaskin, 277 NLRB 563, 120 LRRM 1302 (1985), where the panel noted its disagreement with the ALJ's statement that *Wright Line* did not apply to pretext cases and, in this regard, cited Limestone Apparel Corp., 255 NLRB 722, 107 LRRM 1187 (1981), *enforced*, 705 F2d 799, 113 LRRM 2517 (CA 6, 1982) and Castle Instant Mgmt./Maid, 256 NLRB 130, 107 LRRM 1189 (1981), *enforced*, 685 F2d 440, 110 LRRM 2739 (CA 9, 1982). *See also* Frank Black Mechanical Servs., 271 NLRB 1302 n. 2, 117 LRRM 1183 (1984) ("It is clear . . . that the Board's *Wright Line* analysis applies to all 8(a)(3) and (1) discharge cases regardless of the Board's ultimate conclusion as to motive" [citation omitted]). *Cf.* Davidowitz & Goldberg, 277 NLRB 1046, 121 LRRM 1032, 1035 (1985) ("Respondent's explanation of the discharges, given their pretextual quality, obviously do not overcome the General Counsel's case"). *But see* Raynor Motel Corp. dba Holiday Inn E., 281 NLRB 573, 124 LRRM 1035 (1986), and the cases cited *supra* note 71 where a rigorous application of *Wright Line* was deemed unnecessary in view of specific findings that the employer's proffered reason for taking certain actions was pretextual.

[218]Atlanta Blue Prints & Graphics Co., 244 NLRB 634, 102 LRRM 1242 (1979); Haddon House, 242 NLRB 1057, 101 LRRM 1294 (1979), *modified and enforced sub nom.* Teamsters Local 115 v. NLRB, 640 F2d 392, 106 LRRM 2462 (CA DC), *cert. denied*, 454 US 827, 108 LRRM 2558 (1981); Big "G" Corp., 223 NLRB 1349, 92 LRRM 1127 (1976); Weather-Shield Corp., 222 NLRB 1171, 91 LRRM 1478 (1976); M Restaurants, 221 NLRB 264, 90 LRRM 1494 (1975).

[219]Jim Causley Pontiac v. NLRB, 620 F2d 122, 104 LRRM 2190, 2193 (CA 6, 1980); NLRB v. Warren L. Rose Castings, Inc., 587 F2d 1005, 100 LRRM 2303 (CA 9, 1978); NLRB v. Stark, 525 F2d 422, 90 LRRM 3076 (CA 2, 1975), *cert. denied*, 424 US 967, 91

timing of a discharge is only one factor; while it may make a discharge "suspicious," the discharge may be held lawful if other factors indicate that it was properly motivated.[220] Furthermore, when the discharge occurs long after the employee has engaged in union activity, such passage of time has been relied upon to establish that the discharge was not discriminatorily motivated.[221]

One justification for discharge commonly asserted by employers is dissatisfaction with the employee's work. If, however, the employer gave the employee a recent wage increase, a promotion, or a good evaluation, the Board and the courts have often found the alleged dissatisfaction to be a pretext.[222] When employees are discharged for a single significant incident rather than for a negative evaluation of their overall work performance, the fact that they received increases for satisfactory or meritorious work performance may have little influence on the determination of the employer's motive for the discharge.[223] In single incident cases, however, the Board will consider whether discharge was an appropriate penalty for the infraction.[224]

LRRM 2749 (1976); NLRB v. Ri-Del Tool Mfg. Co., 486 F2d 1406, 84 LRRM 2630 (CA 7, 1973); NLRB v. Armstrong Circuit, 462 F2d 355, 80 LRRM 2897 (CA 6, 1972); NLRB v. Treasure Lake, Inc., 453 F2d 202, 79 LRRM 2085 (CA 3, 1971); NLRB v. Central Power & Light Co., 425 F2d 1318, 74 LRRM 2269 (CA 5, 1970).

[220]Thermo King Corp., 247 NLRB 296, 103 LRRM 1204 (1980); Triana Indus., 245 NLRB 1258, 102 LRRM 1323 (1979); Liberty Mut. Ins. Co. v. NLRB, 592 F2d 595, 100 LRRM 2660 (CA 1, 1979); NLRB v. South Shore Hosp., 571 F2d 677, 97 LRRM 3004 (CA 1, 1978); Penasquitos Village v. NLRB, 565 F2d 1074, 97 LRRM 2244 (CA 9, 1977); General Mercantile & Hardware Co. v. NLRB, 461 F2d 952, 80 LRRM 2622 (CA 8, 1972); Amyx Indus. v. NLRB, 457 F2d 904, 79 LRRM 2930 (CA 8, 1972).

[221]Maine Medical Center, 248 NLRB 707, 104 LRRM 1031 (1980); NLRB v. Florida Medical Center, 576 F2d 666, 98 LRRM 3144 (CA 5, 1978); Rockland-Bamberg Print Works, 231 NLRB 305, 96 LRRM 1237 (1977); NLRB v. Consolidated Diesel Elec. Co., 469 F2d 1016, 81 LRRM 2709 (CA 4, 1972).

[222]*E.g.*, NLRB v. Jack August Enters., 583 F2d 575, 99 LRRM 2582 (CA 1, 1978); Florida Steel Corp. v. NLRB, 529 F2d 1225, 92 LRRM 2040 (CA 5, 1976); NLRB v. Ri-Del Tool Mfg. Co., *supra* note 219; NLRB v. Evans Packing Co., 463 F2d 193, 80 LRRM 2810 (CA 6, 1972); NLRB v. George J. Roberts & Sons, 451 F2d 941, 78 LRRM 2874 (CA 2, 1971); Sweeney & Co. v. NLRB, 437 F2d 1127, 76 LRRM 2321 (CA 5, 1971), *modifying on other grounds* 176 NLRB 208, 71 LRRM 1197 (1969); NLRB v. Coast Delivery Serv., 437 F2d 264, 76 LRRM 2450 (CA 9, 1971); NLRB v. S.E. Nichols-Dover, Inc., 414 F2d 561, 71 LRRM 3149 (CA 3, 1969), *cert. denied*, 400 US 831, 75 LRRM 2379 (1970); NLRB v. Winn-Dixie Greenville, Inc., 379 F2d 958, 65 LRRM 2742 (CA 4), *cert. denied*, 389 US 952, 66 LRRM 2507 (1967); NLRB v. Lively Serv. Co., 290 F2d 205, 48 LRRM 2023 (CA 10, 1961). *But see* Green Giant Co., 223 NLRB 377, 91 LRRM 1468 (1976); NLRB v. Consolidated Diesel Elec. Co., *supra* note 221.

[223]Concrete Technology, 224 NLRB 961, 965, 93 LRRM 1282 (1976); *see also* Berbiglia, Inc. v. NLRB, 602 F2d 839, 101 LRRM 3139 (CA 8, 1979).

[224]*See, e.g.*, Fern Terrace Lodge of Bowling Green, 297 NLRB No. 2, 132 LRRM 1294 (1989); Thore, Inc., Integrated Power Sys. Corp., 296 NLRB No. 110, 133 LRRM 1222 (1989); Fort Wayne Foundry Corp., Machining Div., 296 NLRB No. 18, 132 LRRM 1109 (1989).

A variety of other factors have been relied upon to determine whether an asserted justification is in reality a pretext.[225] Thus "[a] failure to investigate the incidents upon which the employer relied as grounds for discharge may reflect an employer's discriminatory motive."[226] Discharges undertaken without prior warnings as to the seriousness of the conduct are also suspect.[227] Similarly, changes in the employer's reason, assertion of inconsistent or false reasons, or failure to inform the employee of the reason for the discharge may be significant factors.[228] The converse is also true: The presence of specific warnings for specific conduct may suggest that a subsequent discharge based upon similar conduct is not discriminatorily motivated.[229]

The existence of good reasons for a discharge may not always justify the discharge. Discriminatory motive will often be inferred when the employer has long tolerated similar conduct[230] or

---

[225]NLRB v. Gogin, 575 F2d 596, 98 LRRM 2250 (CA 7, 1978); see also KBM Elec., 218 NLRB 1352, 89 LRRM 1728 (1975), for discussion of many of the factors considered by the Board in assessing pretext.

[226]W.W. Grainger, Inc. v. NLRB, 582 F2d 1118, 1121, 99 LRRM 2375 (CA 7, 1978); *accord* Clark Manor Nursing Home, 254 NLRB 455, 106 LRRM 1231 (1981), *enforced in part*, 671 F2d 657, 109 LRRM 3151 (CA 1, 1982); Levingston Shipbuilding Co., 249 NLRB 1, 104 LRRM 1058 (1980); Tendico, Inc., 232 NLRB 735, 97 LRRM 1107 (1977); Marsden Elec. Co., 226 NLRB 1097, 94 LRRM 1176 (1976), *enforced*, 586 F2d 8, 100 LRRM 2314 (CA 6, 1978); NLRB v. Aerovox Corp., 435 F2d 1208, 76 LRRM 2042 (CA 4, 1970).

[227]*E.g.*, Lockwoven Co., 245 NLRB 1362, 102 LRRM 1533 (1979); Akron Gen. Medical Center, 232 NLRB 920, 97 LRRM 1510 (1977); River Manor Health Related Facility, 224 NLRB 227, 93 LRRM 1069 (1976), *enforced*, 562 F2d 38, 95 LRRM 3011 (CA 2, 1977); Chart House, 223 NLRB 100, 92 LRRM 1155 (1976) (absence of prior warnings not sufficient to establish discriminatory motive). The absence of warnings may not be significant if the offense is so serious that immediate discharge is warranted. Edgewood Nursing Center v. NLRB, 581 F2d 363, 99 LRRM 2036 (CA 3, 1978); NLRB v. Warren L. Rose Castings, Inc., *supra* note 219; Sweeney & Co. v. NLRB, *supra* note 222; NLRB v. Midtown Serv. Co., 425 F2d 665, 73 LRRM 2634 (CA 2, 1970); NLRB v. Glenn Berry Mfrs., 422 F2d 748, 73 LRRM 2301 (CA 10, 1970); NLRB v. Kay Elec., 410 F2d 499, 71 LRRM 2106 (CA 8, 1969); NLRB v. Virginia Metalcrafters, 387 F2d 379, 67 LRRM 2139 (CA 4, 1967); NLRB v. Challenge-Cook Bros., 374 F2d 147, 64 LRRM 2481 (CA 6, 1967).

[228]Hercules Bumpers, 248 NLRB 1047, 104 LRRM 1056 (1980); NLRB v. Warren L. Rose Castings, Inc., *supra* note 219; A. J. Krajewski Mfg. Co. v. NLRB, 413 F2d 673, 71 LRRM 2954 (CA 1, 1969); NLRB v. Milco, Inc., 388 F2d 133, 67 LRRM 2202 (CA 2, 1968); NLRB v. Richard W. Kaase Co., 346 F2d 24, 59 LRRM 2290 (CA 6, 1965). *Cf.* NLRB v. Henriksen, Inc., 481 F2d 1156, 83 LRRM 2774 (CA 5, 1973) (failure to give reason for discharge not significant when employee is aware of reason).

[229]Butler-Johnson Corp. v. NLRB, 608 F2d 1303, 102 LRRM 3029 (CA 9, 1979); Teledyne, Inc., 246 NLRB 766, 103 LRRM 1011 (1979); Rockland-Bamberg Print Works, *supra* note 221; Loomis Armored Car Serv., 227 NLRB 256, 94 LRRM 1108 (1976); NLRB v. Midwest Hanger Co., 474 F2d 1155, 82 LRRM 2693 (CA 8, 1973), *cert. denied*, 414 US 823, 84 LRRM 2421 (1973); NLRB v. Speed Queen, 469 F2d 189, 81 LRRM 2742 (CA 8, 1972); NLRB v. Newman-Green, Inc., 401 F2d 1, 69 LRRM 2129 (CA 7, 1968). *Cf.* Florida Steel Corp., 223 NLRB 174, 92 LRRM 1004 (1976) (discriminatory motive found when prior warnings unrelated to conduct upon which discharge was based).

[230]McCauley Assocs., 248 NLRB 346, 103 LRRM 1439 (1980), *enforced in part*, 657 F2d 685, 108 LRRM 2612 (CA 5, 1981); Penn Indus., 233 NLRB 928, 97 LRRM 1299 (1977); Sibilio's Golden Grill, 227 NLRB 1688, 94 LRRM 1439 (1977), *enforced*, 573 F2d 1302, 99

penalized it more leniently.[231] Conversely, evidence that the conduct in question has been dealt with on a consistent basis may rebut charges of pretext[232] even where the employer was shown to be eager to terminate the employee.[233]

2. Lockouts. The subject of lockouts is treated extensively elsewhere.[234] The present discussion is confined to the recurrent and specialized questions that arise from the application of section 8(a)(3) to lockouts. It is clear "that there are circumstances in which employers may lawfully resort to the lockout as an economic weapon."[235] But it is equally clear that an employer violates section 8(a)(3) if the lockout is purposely used to discourage union membership.[236] The purpose, or motive, behind the lockout is therefore the critical factor in determining

---

LRRM 2633 (CA 3, 1978); NLRB v. Broyhill Co., 514 F2d 655, 89 LRRM 2203 (CA 8, 1975); NLRB v. Princeton Inn Co., 424 F2d 264, 73 LRRM 3002 (CA 3, 1970); NLRB v. Beverage-Air Co., 402 F2d 411, 69 LRRM 2369 (CA 4, 1968); NLRB v. Challenge-Cook Bros., *supra* note 227; NLRB v. Elias Bros. Big Boy, 325 F2d 360, 54 LRRM 2733 (CA 6, 1963). The classic case on this point is Edward G. Budd Mfg. Co. v. NLRB, 138 F2d 86, 13 LRRM 512, 564 (CA 3, 1943). *But cf.* NLRB v. Threads, Inc., 308 F2d 1, 2, 51 LRRM 2074 (CA 4, 1962) (no violation where the "prior misconduct . . . was tolerated under circumstances which negate any idea that the employer was searching for some false reasons to discharge the employee on account of his union activities").

[231]NLRB v. Inland Empire Meat Co., 611 F2d 1235, 103 LRRM 2746 (CA 9, 1979); Head Div., AMF, Inc. v. NLRB, 593 F2d 972, 100 LRRM 3035 (CA 10, 1979); Ferland Mgmt. Co., 233 NLRB 467, 97 LRRM 1530 (1977); Tendico, Inc., *supra* note 226; D'Youville Manor Nursing Home v. NLRB, 526 F2d 3, 90 LRRM 3100 (CA 1, 1975); NLRB v. Shepherd Laundries Co., 440 F2d 856, 76 LRRM 3080 (CA 5, 1971); Mikami Bros., 188 NLRB 522, 76 LRRM 1425 (1971); NLRB v. Aerovox Corp., *supra* note 226; Electrical Workers (IUE) v. NLRB (Liberty Coach Co.), 418 F2d 1191, 71 LRRM 2991 (CA DC, 1969); NLRB v. S.E. Nichols-Dover, Inc., *supra* note 222; NLRB v. Lone Star Textiles, 386 F2d 535, 67 LRRM 2221 (CA 5, 1967); Aeronco Mfg. Co. v. NLRB, 385 F2d 724, 66 LRRM 2574 (CA 9, 1967); NLRB v. American Casting Serv., 365 F2d 168, 62 LRRM 2539 (CA 7, 1966); A.P. Green Fire Brick Co. v. NLRB, 326 F2d 910, 55 LRRM 2236 (CA 8, 1964).

[232]Frank Briscoe, Inc., 247 NLRB 13, 103 LRRM 1110 (1980), *enforced*, 637 F2d 946, 106 LRRM 2155 (CA 3, 1981); Firestone Tire & Rubber Co. v. NLRB, 539 F2d 1335, 93 LRRM 2625 (CA 4, 1976); NLRB v. Whitfield Pickle Co., 374 F2d 576, 64 LRRM 2656 (CA 5, 1967). Rockland-Bamberg Print Works, *supra* note 221; Clear Lake Hosp., 223 NLRB 1, 91 LRRM 1450 (1976).

[233]Nacker Packing Co. v. NLRB, 615 F2d 456, 103 LRRM 2634 (CA 7, 1980); Petroleum Transp. Co., 236 NLRB 254, 98 LRRM 1484 (1978).

[234]*See* Chapter 20, "The Lockout."

[235]NLRB v. Teamsters Local 449 (Buffalo Linen Supply Co.), 353 US 87, 92–93, 39 LRRM 2603, 2605 (1957). *See* American Ship Bldg. Co. v. NLRB, 380 US 300, 58 LRRM 2672 (1965).

[236]*Compare* Bali Blinds Midwest, 292 NLRB 243, 131 LRRM 1050 (1989) (nonunion employer violated Act by laying off employees most likely to honor recognitional picket line) *with* National Fabricators, 295 NLRB No. 126, 131 LRRM 1761 (1989) (fear that production and delivery schedules would be interrupted justified partial lockout of employees). *See also* Loomis Courier Serv. v. NLRB, 595 F2d 491, 101 LRRM 2450 (CA 9, 1979), *denying enforcement to* 235 NLRB 534, 98 LRRM 1083 (1978); Shelly & Anderson Furniture Mfg. Co. v. NLRB, 497 F2d 1200, 86 LRRM 2619 (CA 9, 1974); NLRB v. Savoy Laundry, 327 F2d 370, 55 LRRM 2285 (CA 2, 1964); NLRB v. Somerset Shoe Co., 111 F2d 681, 6 LRRM 709 (CA 1, 1940).

whether the lockout violates the Act. For example, in *Allbritton Communications*,[237] the employer desired to lay off mailroom employees but an arbitration award prevented it from doing so. The employer then repudiated the collective bargaining agreement and induced a confrontation that gave the employer the pretext to lock out the mailroom employees.[238] The Board found that the employer had not locked out the employees, but had discharged them in violation of the Act. The Board has also held that an employer's purpose to make unilateral changes in the shift time provision[239] or the seniority provision of its collective bargaining agreement,[240] or to avoid payment of an obligatory cost-of-living increase,[241] constitute improper motives that will invalidate a lockout.

In the development of this branch of the law, the Board and courts once characterized lockouts as either defensive or offensive. The defensive lockout was traditionally used to protect employers' legitimate business interests that might be jeopardized by union activity. For example, in *NLRB v. Teamsters Local 449 (Buffalo Linen Supply Co.)*,[242] the union commenced a whipsaw strike against one employer in a multi-employer bargaining unit. As a defense, the other employers temporarily locked out their employees. The Board found the lockout to be "'defensive and privileged in nature, rather than retaliatory and unlawful.'"[243] The Second Circuit reversed,[244] but the Supreme Court sustained the Board, concluding that the employers' interest in preserving "the integrity of the multi-employer bargaining unit"[245] justified the lockout.

The Board had also held that where union activity would cause inordinate harm, a defensive lockout in the legitimate interest of the employer was lawful. Thus, an employer could shut down a plant in response to "quickie" strikes[246] or lock out employees in response to a threatened sitdown strike.[247]

---

[237]271 NLRB 201, 116 LRRM 1428 (1984), *enforced*, 766 F2d 812, 119 LRRM 3290 (CA 3, 1985), *cert. denied*, 474 US 1081, 121 LRRM 2368 (1986).

[238]*Id.* at 203 n.6 and accompanying text.

[239]Union Terminal Warehouse, 286 NLRB 851, 128 LRRM 1225 (1987).

[240]United Chrome Prods., 288 NLRB 1176, 128 LRRM 1223 (1988).

[241]Clemson Bros., 290 NLRB 944, 129 LRRM 1150 (1988).

[242]*Supra* note 235.

[243]*Id.* at 91 (quoting Buffalo Linen Supply Co., 109 NLRB 447, 448, 34 LRRM 1355, 1356 (1954)).

[244]231 F2d 110, 37 LRRM 2546 (CA 2, 1956).

[245]353 US at 93.

[246]International Shoe Co., 93 NLRB 907, 27 LRRM 1504 (1951).

[247]Link Belt Co., 26 NLRB 227, 6 LRRM 565 (1940). *See also* Betts Cadillac Olds, Inc., 96 NLRB 268, 28 LRRM 1509 (1951) (lockout to preempt strike that would have stranded customers' unassembled cars at repair facility).

The Supreme Court's approval of a broader, "offensive," lockout in *American Ship Building Co. v. NLRB*,[248] however, largely mooted the further refinement of the offensive versus defensive distinction.[249] In *American Ship Building*, the employer, whose business was largely concentrated in the winter months, locked out its employees after an impasse in contract negotiations. The purpose of the lockout was to bring about a favorable contract settlement before the start of the busy season. After a new contract was signed, all employees were recalled to work. The Board concluded that the layoff was not a justified defensive lockout and held that it violated section 8(a)(3).[250] The Supreme Court reversed, holding that after impasse an employer does not commit an unfair labor practice by locking out employees "for the sole purpose of bringing economic pressure to bear in support of his legitimate bargaining position."[251] The Court noted that the union did not have the exclusive right to time the cessation of work; consequently, the employer had not preempted the union's right to strike under section 13. The Court further observed that the employer's action was not designed to frustrate collective bargaining and that evidence of specific discrimination against union members had not been shown. In the absence of unlawful intent, "[t]he purpose and effect of the lockout was only to bring pressure upon the union to modify its demands," and the "arguable possibility that someone . . . [might] feel himself discouraged in his membership" did not establish a violation of section 8(a)(3).[252]

More recently, the Board has rejected any distinction between offensive and defensive economic weapons in determining the legality of an employer lockout and subsequent employment of

---

[248]*Supra* note 235.

[249]In Darling & Co., 171 NLRB 801, 68 LRRM 1133 (1968), *enforced sub nom.* Lane v. NLRB, 418 F2d 1208, 72 LRRM 2439 (CA DC, 1969), the Board recognized that the distinction between offensive and defensive strikes had become largely "obliterated."

[250]142 NLRB 1362, 53 LRRM 1245 (1963), *enforced*, 331 F2d 839, 55 LRRM 2913 (CA DC, 1964).

[251]380 US at 318; *cf.* Movers & Warehousemen Ass'n v. NLRB, 550 F2d 962, 94 LRRM 2795 (CA 4), *cert. denied*, 434 US 826, 96 LRRM 2513 (1977) (lawful to lock out employees after impasse in support of nonmandatory subject of bargaining). For detailed discussion of *American Ship Bldg. Co.*, see Chapter 20, "The Lockout," at notes 58–59.

[252]380 US at 312–13. While such lockouts are deemed not to violate the Act, they may violate a "no strike/no lockout" clause of an unexpired collective bargaining agreement. Acme Mkts. v. Bakery & Confectionery Workers Local 6, 613 F2d 485, 103 LRRM 2394 (CA 3, 1980). *See* Auto Workers Local 592 v. Sundstrand Corp., 650 FSupp 83, 124 LRRM 2262 (ND Ill, 1986) (union withdrawal of notice to terminate agreement allowed automatic renewal; renewed agreement barred lockout).

temporary replacements. Absent specific proof of antiunion motivation, the Board will permit the use of temporary replacements during a lawful lockout where the only purpose of the lockout is to exert economic pressure in support of the employer's otherwise lawful bargaining demands.[253] The Court of Appeals for both the Third and the District of Columbia circuits have sustained the use of temporary replacements during a lockout where there is no inherent destruction of employee rights or where the employer can demonstrate that it has a legitimate and substantial business justification that outweighs the comparatively slight effect on employee rights.[254]

While an employer may lawfully continue to operate during a lockout by employing temporary replacements, there are cases holding it unlawful to hire permanent replacements. The Board, in *Pankratz Forest Industries*,[255] found that, although the employer's lockout was lawful, the employer violated the Act by hiring permanent replacements. The employer "was motivated solely by its desire to avoid its obligations under a valid and existing collective bargaining agreement and to sever completely its relationship with the Union."[256]

Moreover, *permanent* replacement of locked-out workers may be so inherently destructive of employee rights that independent evidence of motive is unnecessary to establish an unfair labor practice.[257]

3. Plant Closings. An employer's decisions concerning the closing or relocation of all or part of its operations "are so peculiarly matters of management prerogative that they would never constitute violations of Section 8(a)(1), whether or not they involved sound business judgment, unless they also violated

---

[253]Harter Equip., 280 NLRB 597, 122 LRRM 1219 (1986), *review denied sub nom.* Operating Eng'rs Local 825 v. NLRB, 829 F2d 458, 126 LRRM 2337 (CA 3, 1987). *See also* Georgia-Pacific Corp., Crossett Div., 281 NLRB 1, 122 LRRM 1353 (1986).

[254]Harter Equip., *supra* note 253; Boilermakers Local 88 v. NLRB (National Gypsum Co.), 829 F2d 458, 126 LRRM 2337 (CA 3, 1987). *See also* C-E Natco/C-E Invalco, 272 NLRB 502, 117 LRRM 1265 (1984), *modified on other grounds*, 282 NLRB 314, 123 LRRM 1332 (1986) (lawful to lock out in support of demand for "performance bond" from union to indemnify employer against vandalism during negotiations).

[255]269 NLRB 33, 115 LRRM 1240 (1984).

[256]*Id.* at 39, 115 LRRM at 1246; *but see* NLRB v. Martin A. Gleason, Inc., 534 F2d 466, 92 LRRM 2446 (CA 2, 1976), where the court approved the employer's hiring of locked-out employees who resigned from the union as replacements, provided the employer did not induce the resignation.

[257]B.N. Beard Co., 248 NLRB 198, 103 LRRM 1560 (1980); Johns-Manville Prods. Corp., 223 NLRB 1317, 92 LRRM 1103 (1976), *enforcement denied*, 557 F2d 1126, 96 LRRM 2010 (CA 5, 1977), *cert. denied*, 436 US 956, 98 LRRM 2617 (1978).

Section 8(a)(3)."[258] Permanent shutting down of a business[259] is to be distinguished from a lockout, and also from a "runaway shop," where the employer "transfer[s] its work to another plant or open[s] a new plant in another locality to replace its closed plant."[260] Depending on how the employer's actions are categorized, different legal principles will govern.

a. Complete Cessation of Business. In the *Darlington* case the Supreme Court ruled that an employer, even though motivated solely by vindictiveness toward a union, may close down its entire business without committing an unfair labor practice. As the Court explained:

> A proposition that a single businessman cannot choose to go out of business if he wants would represent such a startling innovation that it should not be entertained without the clearest manifestation of legislative intent or unequivocal judicial precedent so construing the Labor Act.[261]

Under the *Darlington* rule, a complete closing is not an unfair labor practice because the employer can reap no future benefit from its act. "[The closing] may be motivated more by spite against the union than by business reasons, but it is not the type of discrimination which is prohibited by the Act."[262] The Court reasoned that the employer's personal satisfaction "or the mere possibility that other employers will follow his example are surely too remote to be considered dangers at which the labor statutes were aimed."[263]

In *Contris Packing Co.*,[264] the Board applied the *Darlington* rule to a cessation of business allegedly intended as retaliation against employees for the filing of unfair labor practice charges. The ALJ found that the employer violated section 8(a)(4), but not section 8(a)(3), by closing its business. The ALJ dismissed the

---

[258]Textile Workers v. Darlington Mfg. Co., 380 US 263, 269, 58 LRRM 2657 (1965). *See* note 262 *infra*. While *Darlington* dealt only with closures, "runaway shops" are also subject to examination under §8(a)(3). *See infra* at notes 286-305. For treatment of the bargaining obligation relating to termination of operations at an organized establishment, see Chapter 16, "Subjects of Bargaining," at notes 319–418.

[259]Once the Board determines that a closing is permanent and that no unfair labor practice has been committed, it must dismiss the complaint; it cannot retain jurisdiction to examine the legal implications if the plant in question should subsequently resume operations. Bruce Duncan Co. v. NLRB, 590 F2d 1304, 101 LRRM 2033 (CA 4, 1979).

[260]Textile Workers v. Darlington Mfg. Co., *supra* note 258, at 273. *See also* Lear Siegler, Inc., 295 NLRB No. 83, 131 LRRM 1763 (1989).

[261]380 US at 270.

[262]*Id.* at 272.

[263]*Id.* at 273.

[264]268 NLRB 193, 114 LRRM 1250 (1983).

section 8(a)(3) allegations on the authority of *Darlington*, but held that the discharges of employees consequent from the section 8(a)(4) closing did violate section 8(a)(3). The Board rejected the ALJ's analysis and held that *Darlington* permitted the complete closing of the business regardless of whether section 8(a)(4) or section 8(a)(3) were allegedly violated, and that employee discharges occurring as a result of a plant closing privileged under *Darlington* cannot be found to violate section 8(a)(3).

b. Partial Closings. In *Darlington*, the Supreme Court recognized that "a discriminatory partial closing may have repercussions on what remains of the business,"[265] and specified that different standards apply to the legality of closings which are less than complete. The Court declared the controlling principles as follows:

> [A] partial closing is an unfair labor practice under 8(a)(3) if motivated by a purpose to *chill unionism* in any of the remaining plants of the single employer and if the employer may reasonably have foreseen that such closing will likely have the effect.
>
> . . .
>
> . . . If the persons exercising control over a plant being closed for anti-union reasons (1) have an interest in another business, whether or not affiliated with or engaged in the same line of commercial activity as the closed plant, of sufficient substantiality to give promise of their reaping a benefit from the discouragement of unionization in that business; (2) act to close their plant with the purpose of producing such a result; and (3) occupy a relationship to the other business which makes it realistically foreseeable that its employees will fear that such business will also be closed down if they persist in organizational activities, we think that an unfair labor practice has been made out.[266]

Direct evidence of requisite motive and effect is seldom available. While circumstantial evidence is admissible, it "must produce more than a mere suspicion."[267] Board cases have focused on factors that permit legitimate inferences. The decision in *Bruce Duncan Co.*[268] summarized those factors:

---

[265]380 US at 275.

[266]*Id.* at 275-76 (emphasis added). *See also* Purolator Armored v. NLRB, 764 F2d 1423, 119 LRRM 3228 (CA 11, 1985); Alaska Cummins Servs. dba Groves Truck & Trailer, 281 NLRB 1194, 123 LRRM 1189 (1986); Jasta Mfg. Co., 246 NLRB 48, 102 LRRM 1610 (1979).

[267]Joint Indus. Bd., 238 NLRB 1398, 1401, 99 LRRM 1455 (1978). *See also* De Soto, Inc., 278 NLRB 788, 121 LRRM 1226 (1986).

[268]233 NLRB 1243, 97 LRRM 1027 (1977), *modified on other grounds*, 590 F2d 1304, 101 LRRM 2033 (CA 4, 1979).

Generally, the Board in determining whether or not the proscribed "chilling" motivation and its reasonably foreseeable effect can be inferred considers the presence or absence of several factors including, *inter alia*, contemporaneous union activity at the employer's remaining facilities,[269] geographic proximity of the employer's facilities to the closed operation,[270] the likelihood that employees will learn of the circumstances surrounding the employer's unlawful conduct through employee interchange or contact,[271] and, of course, representations made by the employer's officials and supervisors to other employees.[272]

In *Purolator Armored v. NLRB*,[273] the Eleventh Circuit upheld the Board's finding of discrimination. Relying on the two-pronged *Darlington* test for partial closings, the court found substantial evidence to establish: (1) an employer motive to chill unionism; and (2) the reasonable foreseeability that the employer's actions in terminating its coin-room operation and discharging the coin-room employees one week after they voted for union representation would have a chilling effect. The finding of unlawful motive was based on numerous violations of section 8(a)(1) during the election campaign. The court rejected the employer's argument that its sole reason for closing the coin room was unprofitability, because the employer had known the coin room was losing money but continued to operate it until a week after the election. The discharged employees worked in the same building and had daily contact with the remaining employees, and the court found that proximity sufficient to establish that a chilling effect was reasonably foreseeable.

In *Desoto, Inc.*,[274] however, the Board found the closing of one of the employer's plants to be lawful because (1) the employer did not make any statements indicating discriminatory motivation for closing the plant; (2) it was not established that the closing had a chilling effect on unionization among employees at the other plants of the employer; (3) although wages and fringe

---

[269]*E.g.*, Morrison Cafeterias Consol., 177 NLRB 591, 71 LRRM 1449 (1969), *modified on other grounds*, 431 F2d 254, 74 LRRM 3048 (CA 8, 1970); Sweeney & Co., 176 NLRB 208, 71 LRRM 1197 (1969); Motor Repair, 168 NLRB 1082, 67 LRRM 1051 (1968); A.C. Rochat Co., 163 NLRB 421, 64 LRRM 1321 (1967).

[270]*E.g.*, George Lithograph Co., 204 NLRB 431, 431, 83 LRRM 1402 (1973); Morrison Cafeterias Consol., *supra* note 269.

[271]Motor Repair, *supra* note 269.

[272]Midland-Ross Corp. v. NLRB, 617 F2d 977, 103 LRRM 2908 (CA 3), *cert. denied*, 449 US 871, 105 LRRM 2657 (1980). *E.g.*, George Lithograph Co., *supra* note 270; Motor Repair, *supra* note 269.

[273]764 F2d 1423, 119 LRRM 3228 (CA 11, 1985).

[274]278 NLRB 788, 121 LRRM 1226 (1986). *See also* Spring City Knitting Co., 285 NLRB 426, 126 LRRM 1349 (1987).

benefits at the closed plant were considerably higher than those at the other plants, avoidance of these labor costs was not a motivating factor in closing the plant because direct labor costs were less than 2 percent of the operating budget; and (4) evidence of other circumstances surrounding the plant closure aroused "suspicions" but were insufficient to support an inference of unlawful motivation.

In *Maram v. Universidad Interamericana de Puerto Rico*,[275] the First Circuit, reversing the district court, directed the entry of a section 10(j) injunction to restrain a university from subcontracting its janitorial work in retaliation for its employees' attempt to organize. The court found a prima facie case of unlawful motivation under *Wright Line*, and determined that the regional director had reasonable grounds to disregard the employer's claim that the same action would have been taken without regard to the organizing activities.[276]

Proof of legitimate economic reasons for closing can negate inferences of a chilling purpose.[277] On the other hand, the Board has held proof that a partial closing was accomplished for antiunion reasons will not "*ipso facto* establish" the necessary purpose to chill unionism in the remaining parts of the business; but that proof may "indicate a disposition toward [a chilling purpose] and be sufficient to support a logical inference."[278] In such cases there must be a specific showing of purpose; the Board may not simply rely on evidence that warrants an inference that the effect of closing one plant was to discourage union activity in another. The evidence must support the inference that the plant was closed for the purpose of discouraging union activity in the other plant.[279] "It is . . . clear that the ambiguous act of closing a plant following the election of a union

---

[275]722 F2d 953, 115 LRRM 2118 (CA 1, 1983).

[276]*See also* Teamsters Local 171 v. NLRB (A.G. Boone Co.), 863 F2d 946, 130 LRRM 2033 (CA DC, 1988), *cert. denied*, 490 US 1065, 131 LRRM 2400 (1989).

[277]*E.g.*, Spring City Knitting Co., *supra* note 274; Joint Indus. Bd., *supra* note 267; C & T Mfg. Co., 233 NLRB 1430, 97 LRRM 1140 (1977); Food Fair Stores, 229 NLRB 730, 95 LRRM 1157 (1977); Tectura, Inc., 221 NLRB 1193, 91 LRRM 1079 (1975); South San Francisco Scavenger Co., 215 NLRB 694, 88 LRRM 1113 (1974); Thompson Transp. Co., 165 NLRB 746, 65 LRRM 1370 (1967), *modified on other grounds*, 406 F2d 698, 70 LRRM 2418 (CA 10, 1969).

[278]George Lithograph Co., *supra* note 270, at 431; *accord* Darlington Mfg. Co., 165 NLRB 1074, 1083, 65 LRRM 1391 (1967), 380 US 263, 58 LRRM 2657 (1965), *enforced*, 397 F2d 760, 68 LRRM 2356 (CA 4, 1968), *cert. denied*, 393 US 1023, 70 LRRM 2225 (1969) (proceedings following remand of Textile Workers v. Darlington Mfg. Co., *supra* note 258).

[279]De Soto, Inc., *supra* note 274; Motor Repair, *supra* note 269.

is not, absent an inquiry into the employer's motive, inherently discriminatory."[280] However, in establishing the requisite effect, the General Counsel need not demonstrate that the remaining employees were *actually* "chilled" in their union activities; it need only be shown that a chilling effect was reasonably foreseeable.[281]

The Board's usual remedy for discriminatory closings and transfers of work is to require the employer to restore the operation in question and reinstate all discriminatorily terminated employees.[282] However, in some cases the Board has permitted the employer to avoid restoration of the status quo ante when the employer proved that such restoration would be "unduly burdensome".[283] In other cases the employer could avoid restoration upon proof that restoration would endanger its "continued viability".[284] In *Lear Siegler, Inc.*[285] the Board acknowledged its prior inconsistency and announced that in the future it would apply the "unduly burdensome" test because: (1) it has been accepted by the courts, and (2) the "continued viability" standard is too stringent and could require an employer to reopen a demonstrably unprofitable facility.

4. Transfer of Work: The "Runaway Shop." It is generally accepted that when an employer changes or discontinues its business operations "in order to avoid obligations imposed upon it by the National Labor Relations Act"[286] a violation of section 8(a)(3) has occurred. "The law does not permit an employer to flee the bargaining agent because of hostility to it . . . ."[287]

Although the "runaway shop" appears in different forms, it always involves a transfer of work.[288] The work may be trans-

---

[280]Textile Workers v. Darlington Mfg. Co., 380 US 263, 269 n. 10, 58 LRRM 2657 (1965).

[281]George Lithograph Co., *supra* note 270.

[282]*See, e.g.*, B & P Trucking, 279 NLRB 693, 123 LRRM 1063 (1986). *But see* Textile Workers v. Darlington Mfg. Co., *supra* note 280 (reinstatement of dischargees at other facilities of employer).

[283]*See, e.g.*, Hood Indus., 273 NLRB 1587, 118 LRRM 1211 (1985), *supplementing* 248 NLRB 597, 103 LRRM 1540 (1980); *cf* B & P Trucking, *supra* note 282.

[284]*See, e.g.*, Service Merchandise Co., 278 NLRB 185, 188, 121 LRRM 1179 (1986).

[285]295 NLRB No. 83, 131 LRRM 1763 (1989).

[286]NLRB v. Rapid Bindery, 293 F2d 170, 174, 48 LRRM 2658 (CA 2, 1961); *accord* Schieber Millinery Co., 26 NLRB 937, 7 LRRM 18, *enforced in pertinent part*, 116 F2d 281, 7 LRRM 658 (CA 8, 1940).

[287]Ladies' Garment Workers Local 57 v. NLRB (Garwin Corp.), 374 F2d 295, 299, 64 LRRM 2159 (CA DC), *cert. denied*, 387 US 942, 65 LRRM 2441 (1967).

[288]*See* Frito-Lay, Inc. v. NLRB, 585 F2d 62, 99 LRRM 2658 (CA 3, 1978). Although a "runaway shop" often involves, as an initial step, a closing of all or part of an employer's operations at one location, it is not subject to plant-closure analysis. Because a "runaway

ferred to another plant,[289] to other employees within the same plant,[290] or to an alter-ego corporation.[291] The work may even be subcontracted out to another company.[292]

Most of these section 8(a)(3) cases turn on employer motivation in transferring the work. The justification most commonly asserted is economic necessity.[293] In passing on an employer's asserted justification, "the crucial factor is not whether the business reasons cited . . . were good or bad, but whether they were honestly invoked and were in fact the cause of the change."[294] The "causal nexus between the claimed economic considerations and the move" will be important in determining whether the economic considerations were honestly

---

shop" involves discriminatory employer action for the purpose of obtaining some benefit in the future from the new employees, it is analyzed under the standards generally applicable to §8(a)(3) cases. *Cf.* Textile Workers v. Darlington Mfg. Co., *supra* note 280. Thus, "there must be both discrimination and a resulting discouragement of union membership. . . . [A] finding of violation . . . will normally turn on the employer's motivation." American Ship Bldg. Co. v. NLRB, 380 US 300, 311, 58 LRRM 2672 (1965). In *Lear Siegler, Inc.*, *supra* note 285, the Board expressly declined to apply the *Darlington* analysis in a case involving transfers of work and subcontracting.

[289]*E.g.*, Royal Norton Mfg. Co., 189 NLRB 489, 77 LRRM 1022 (1971); Roman Cleanser Co., 188 NLRB 931, 76 LRRM 1446 (1971) (no discriminatory motive); Les Schwab Tire Centers, 172 NLRB 164, 69 LRRM 1290 (1968).

[290]Howmet Corp., 197 NLRB 471, 80 LRRM 1555 (1972), *enforced*, 495 F2d 1375, 86 LRRM 2572 (CA 7, 1974).

[291]*E.g.*, Woodline Motor Freight, 278 NLRB 1141, 122 LRRM 1355 (1986); *enforced in part*, 843 F2d 285, 127 LRRM 3260 (CA 8, 1988); NLRB v. Big Bear Supermarkets, 640 F2d 924, 103 LRRM 3120 (CA 9), *cert. denied*, 449 US 919, 105 LRRM 2809 (1980); H.S. Brooks Elec., 233 NLRB 889, 97 LRRM 1083 (1977); Remke Cent. Div., 227 NLRB 1969, 95 LRRM 1113 (1977); James K. Sterritt, Inc., 215 NLRB 769, 88 LRRM 1355 (1974), *enforced*, 538 F2d 310, 93 LRRM 2336 (CA 2, 1975). "Runaway shops" can also violate §8(a)(5). *See, e.g.*, Davis v. NLRB, 617 F2d 1264, 103 LRRM 2965 (CA 7, 1980); Triumph Curing Center, 222 NLRB 627, 91 LRRM 1313 (1976), *enforced*, 571 F2d 462, 98 LRRM 2047 (CA 9, 1978).

[292]Caguas Asphalt, 296 NLRB No. 97, 132 LRRM 1195 (1989); Hood Indus., 248 NLRB 597, 103 LRRM 1540 (1980); Brown-Dunkin Co., 125 NLRB 1379, 45 LRRM 1256 (1959), *enforced*, 287 F2d 17, 47 LRRM 2551 (CA 10, 1961).

[293]*E.g.*, Great Chinese Am. Sewing Co. v. NLRB, 578 F2d 251, 99 LRRM 2347 (CA 9, 1978); NLRB v. Townhouse TV & Appliances, 531 F2d 826, 91 LRRM 2636 (CA 7, 1976); Ladies' Garment Workers (McLoughlin Mfg. Co.) v. NLRB 463 F2d 907, 80 LRRM 2716 (CA DC, 1972) (accepting employer's economic reasons); Atlantic Coast News Co., 197 NLRB 392, 80 LRRM 1415 (1972) (same); Roman Cleanser Co., *supra* note 289 (same); NLRB v. Roberts & Sons, 451 F2d 941, 78 LRRM 2874 (CA 2, 1971); Ladies' Garment Workers Local 57 (Garwin Corp.) v. NLRB, *supra* note 287 (rejecting employer's economic reasons); NLRB v. Preston Feed Corp., 309 F2d 346, 51 LRRM 2362 (CA 4, 1962) (initial decision economically justified but immediate decision due to union animus); NLRB v. Rapid Bindery, *supra* note 286 (accepting employer's economic reasons); NLRB v. Adkins Transfer Co., 226 F2d 324, 36 LRRM 2709 (CA 6, 1955) (same); Mount Hope Finishing Co. v. NLRB, 211 F2d 365, 33 LRRM 2742 (CA 4, 1954) (same).

[294]NLRB v. Savoy Laundry, 327 F2d 370, 371, 55 LRRM 2285 (CA 2, 1964). *See also* Armored Transp. of Cal., 282 NLRB 850, 124 LRRM 1180 (1987); Dubuque Packing Co., 287 NLRB 499, 130 LRRM 1151 (1987), *remanded*, 880 F2d 1422, 132 LRRM 2104 (CA DC, 1989); H&H Pretzel Co., 277 NLRB 1327, 121 LRRM 1110 (1985), *enforced*, 831 F2d 650, 126 LRRM 2712 (CA 9, 1987); Handy Andy Assocs., 277 NLRB 208, 120 LRRM 1271 (1985).

invoked.[295] For example, in one case, even though the Board found the employer guilty of violating section 8(a)(5) for refusing to bargain over its decision to subcontract work, the Board dismissed the section 8(a)(3) allegation because the decision was based on cost-saving considerations and there was no evidence of union animus.[296]

"[T]he fact that the employer may have legitimate economic reasons for the transfer or liquidation does not absolve him of his conduct if violation of his employees' statutory rights was also a motivating reason."[297] Thus, in the absence of a legitimate economic justification for the change[298] or when the evidence established union animus as the motivating factor,[299] the change in the employer's operation has been found to be discriminatory. An employer may, however, consider "his relationship with his plant's union as only one part of the broad economic picture he must survey when he is faced with determining the desirability of making changes in his operation."[300]

In earlier cases,[301] the Board found certain changes in operation to be in violation of section 8(a)(3), without regard to direct evidence of the employer's motivation, because the changes

---

[295]Ladies' Garment Workers Local 57 (Garwin Corp.) v. NLRB, *supra* note 287, at 299.

[296]Griffith-Hope Co., 275 NLRB 487, 119 LRRM 1197 (1985).

[297]Ladies' Garment Workers Local 57 (Garwin Corp.), 153 NLRB 664, 677, 59 LRRM 1405 (1965); *accord* C-F Air Freight, 247 NLRB 403, 103 LRRM 1156 (1980); Allied Mills, 218 NLRB 281, 89 LRRM 1891 (1975), *enforced sub nom.* Grain Millers Local 110, 543 F2d 417, 93 LRRM 2842 (CA DC, 1976), *cert. denied*, 431 US 937, 95 LRRM 2509 (1977).

[298]Caguas Asphalt, *supra* note 292; Lear Siegler, Inc., *supra* note 285; Whitewood Oriental Maintenance Co., 292 NLRB 899, 131 LRRM 1629 (1989); A.G. Boone Co., 285 NLRB 1070, 128 LRRM 1041 (1987), *enforced in part sub nom.* Teamsters Local 171 v. NLRB (A.G. Boone Co.), , 863 F2d 946, 130 LRRM 2033 (CA DC, 1988), *cert. denied*, 490 US 1065, 131 LRRM 2400 (1989); Middle Earth Graphics, 283 NLRB 1049, 126 LRRM 1010 (1987), *enforced without opinion*, 872 F2d 1027, 134 LRRM 2431 (CA 6, 1989); Strawsine Mfg. Co., 280 NLRB 553, 123 LRRM 1270 (1986); Carrier Corp. v. NLRB, 768 F2d 778, 119 LRRM 3603 (CA 6, 1985); Lear Siegler, Inc., Safelite Div., 277 NLRB 782, 121 LRRM 1011 (1985); Mashkin Freight Lines, 272 NLRB 427, 117 LRRM 1369 (1984); Universidad Interamericana de P.R., 268 NLRB 1171, 115 LRRM 1330 (1984).

[299]Caguas Asphalt, *supra* note 292; A.G. Boone Co., *supra* note 298; Woodline Motor Freight, *supra* note 291; SMCO, 286 NLRB 1291, 127 LRRM 1003 (1987) (subcontracting); Carrier Corp. v. NLRB, 768 F2d 778, 119 LRRM 3603 (CA 6, 1985); Lear Siegler, Inc., Safelite Div., *supra* note 298; Dextra Indus., 273 NLRB 1660, 118 LRRM 1300 (1985); Ausable Communications, 273 NLRB 1410, 118 LRRM 1295 (1985).

[300]NLRB v. Rapid Bindery, *supra* note 286; *accord* NLRB v. New England Web, 309 F2d 696, 51 LRRM 2426 (CA 1, 1962); Jays Foods v. NLRB, 292 F2d 317, 48 LRRM 2715 (CA 7, 1961); NLRB v. Lassing, 284 F2d 781, 47 LRRM 2277 (CA 6, 1960); NLRB v. Adkins Transfer Co., *supra* note 293.

[301]*See, e.g.*, NLRB v. Industrial Insulation Co., 615 F2d 1289, 103 LRRM 2614 (CA 10, 1980); Brown Co., 243 NLRB 769, 101 LRRM 1608 (1979), *enforcement denied and remanded without opinion*, 663 F2d 1078, 109 LRRM 2663 (CA 9, 1981); Ethyl Corp., 231 NLRB 431, 97 LRRM 1465 (1977); Rushton & Mercier Woodworking Co., 203 NLRB 123, 83 LRRM 1070 (1973), *enforced*, 502 F2d 1160, 86 LRRM 2151 (CA 1), *cert. denied*, 419 US 996, 87 LRRM 2658 (1974).

were inherently destructive of employee interests under *Great Dane*.[302] However, in *Milwaukee Spring II*,[303] the Board concluded that, absent a specific contractual prohibition, an employer's decision to transfer work was not itself inherently destructive of important employee rights where the transfer of work was economically motivated and where there was no evidence of union animus.[304] Thus, in *FMC Corp.*,[305] the Board held that the employer's decision to transfer work to another facility did not violate sections 8(a)(1) and (3) despite unlawful threats of job loss made by lower level supervisors during a time when the employer and union were engaged in concession bargaining. The Board based its finding of no violation upon the credited testimony of the employer's division manager that the decision to transfer the work was predicated solely on business reasons unrelated to the concession bargaining and upon a finding that the supervisor's comments were not authorized by the employer and did not reflect the employer's true reasons for transferring the work.

5. Replacement and Reinstatement of Economic Strikers. The history of the relationship between employers and their economic strikers is the balancing of two basic considerations:[306] first, that employees should not so fear a retaliatory denial of the opportunity to work as to render illusory their right to strike for better wages, hours, and working conditions; second, that an employer should remain free to continue operating its business even in the face of an economic strike.

The Supreme Court foreshadowed much of this history when it decided *NLRB v. Mackay Radio & Telegraph Co.*[307] In *Mackay*, the employer had offered permanent employment to those who had replaced its economic strikers. Five replacements accepted the offer. As a result, at the conclusion of the strike the employer refused to reinstate five strikers, and said only that their applications would be considered for future vacancies. The Board held that the employer had violated what were then sections 8(1) and

---

[302]NLRB v. Great Dane Trailers, 388 US 26, 65 LRRM 2465 (1967).

[303]Illinois Coil Spring Co., Milwaukee Spring Div., 268 NLRB 601, 115 LRRM 1065 (1984), *aff'd sub nom.* Auto Workers v. NLRB, 765 F2d 175, 119 LRRM 2801 (CA DC, 1985).

[304]*See also* Griffith-Hope Co., *supra* note 296; P.W. Supermarkets, 269 NLRB 839, 115 LRRM 1315 (1984).

[305]290 NLRB 483, 131 LRRM 1130 (1988).

[306]*See generally* Chapter 19, "The Primary Strike," at notes 87–109.

[307]304 US 333, 2 LRRM 610 (1938).

8(3) by selecting those most active in union affairs for, at best, delayed reinstatement.

The Supreme Court agreed that the discriminatory selection of the five strikers violated section 8(3). The Court conceded that "the [economic] strikers remained employes [sic] for the purpose of the Act and were protected against the unfair labor practices denounced by it."[308] The Court also declared, deciding an issue that was neither decided by the Board nor presented to the Court, that employers can lawfully "replace . . . striking employees with others in an effort to carry on the business" and that employers need "not . . . discharge those hired to fill the places of strikers, upon the election of the latter to resume their employment, in order to create places for them."[309] The Court reasoned that, while discharging or otherwise discriminating against economic strikers violates the Act, offering and providing permanent employment to those who will replace economic strikers does not amount to discharging or otherwise discriminating against those strikers.[310]

After *Mackay*, the Board and the appellate courts expressly held that discharging economic strikers violates the Act.[311]

For many years following *Mackay* the Board maintained, with the approval of the courts, that employers owed their permanently replaced economic strikers only a duty to consider fairly their applications for reinstatement.[312] "Permanently replaced economic strikers merely have the right not to be penalized for their concerted activity, and are not entitled to preferential status in hiring."[313] It followed that employers were under "no

---

[308]*Id.* at 345.

[309]*Id.* at 345-46.

[310]The Court stated:

"[T]he respondent was not bound to displace men hired to take the strikers' places in order to provide positions for them. It might have refused reinstatement on the grounds of skill or ability but the Board found that it did not do so. It might have resorted to any one of a number of methods of determining which of its striking employees would have to wait because five men had taken permanent positions during the strike but it found that the preparation and use of the list, and the action taken by respondent, was with the purpose to discriminate against those most active in the union. There is evidence to support these findings." *Id.* at 347.

[311]*E.g.*, NLRB v. International Van Lines, 409 US 48, 81 LRRM 2595 (1972); NLRB v. United States Cold Storage Corp., 203 F2d 924, 32 LRRM 2024 (CA 5), *cert. denied*, 346 US 818, 32 LRRM 2750 (1953).

[312]*E.g.*, Bartlett-Collins Co., 110 NLRB 395, 35 LRRM 1006 (1954), *aff'd sub nom.* Flint Glass Workers v. NLRB, 230 F2d 212, 37 LRRM 2409 (CA DC), *cert. denied*, 351 US 988, 38 LRRM 2238 (1956); Brown & Root, Inc., 132 NLRB 486, 48 LRRM 1391 (1961), *enforced*, 311 F2d 447, 52 LRRM 2115 (CA 8, 1963); Atlas Storage Div., 112 NLRB 1175, 36 LRRM 1171 (1955), *enforced*, 233 F2d 233, 38 LRRM 2095 (CA 7, 1956).

[313]Bartlett-Collins Co., *supra* note 312, at 397.

obligation to seek out or prefer the strikers for vacancies which occurred after their application."[314]

In 1967, however, the Supreme Court issued two decisions, both previously noted, which compelled the Board to reconsider its position. In *Great Dane*,[315] the Court declared that even employer conduct that has only a "comparatively slight" impact on the rights of employees violates section 8(a)(3) unless the employer demonstrates "legitimate and substantial business justifications."[316] Later, in *Fleetwood Trailer*,[317] the Court explained that refusing to reinstate economic strikers, if not immediately upon their application for reinstatement, then at least at some later point when vacancies occur, has an adverse impact on the rights of employees. The Court concluded:

> If and when a job for which the striker is qualified becomes available, he is entitled to an offer of reinstatement. The right can be defeated only if the employer can show legitimate and substantial business justifications.[318]

Recognizing the implications of *Fleetwood*, the Board revised its interpretation of *Mackay* and expanded the reinstatement rights of permanently replaced economic strikers. Thus, in *Laidlaw Corp.*,[319] the Board held that

> economic strikers who unconditionally apply for reinstatement at a time when their positions are filled by permanent replacements: (1) remain employees; (2) are entitled to full reinstatement upon the departure of replacements unless they have in the meantime acquired regular and substantially equivalent employment or the employer can sustain his burden of proof that the failure to offer full reinstatement was for legitimate and substantial business reasons.[320]

The "substantially equivalent employment' exception to the general rule was derived from section 2(3) of the Act, which includes in the definition of "employee" a person "who has not

---

[314]Laidlaw Corp., 171 NLRB 1366, 1369, 68 LRRM 1252 (1968) (explaining the holding of *Brown & Root, supra* note 312).

[315]NLRB v. Great Dane Trailers, supra note 302.

[316]*Id.* at 65.

[317]NLRB v. Fleetwood Trailer Co., 389 US 375, 66 LRRM 2737 (1967).

[318]*Id.* at 381. The employer refused to reinstate economic strikers upon the conclusion of their strike because a drop in production had accompanied the strike, and the employer could not yet resume full production. Later, when full production could resume, the employer bypassed strikers and offered such vacancies as occurred to applicants who had never before worked for the employer. This violated §8(a)(3).

[319]171 NLRB 1366, 68 LRRM 1252 (1968), *enforced*, 414 F2d 99, 71 LRRM 3054 (CA 7, 1969), *cert. denied*, 397 US 920, 73 LRRM 2537 (1970).

[320]*Id.* at 1369-70.

obtained any other regular and substantially equivalent employment."

The rights of strike replacements were somewhat enhanced by the Supreme Court decision in *Belknap, Inc. v. Hale.*[321] There the employer had promised strike replacements that they were being hired as permanent employees. However, to end the strike and secure the dismissal of unfair labor practice charges, the employer agreed to dismiss the replacements and reinstate strikers. The dismissed replacements sued the employer in state court for breach of contract. The Supreme Court held that the replacements' state court action was not preempted by the Act because the state had "a substantial interest in protecting its citizens from misrepresentations that have caused them grievous harm."[322]

The basic *Laidlaw* rule remains the law, although the Board has refined its application in several cases.[323] In *Brooks Research & Manufacturing,*[324] the Board refused to place a time limit on the duration of the reinstatement rights of economic strikers, noting that there were various procedures by which the employer could "cope" with the burden of maintaining, indefinitely, a preferential recall list.[325]

---

[321]463 US 491, 113 LRRM 3057 (1983). *See also* Trans World Airlines v. Flight Attendants, 489 US 426, 130 LRRM 2657 (1989) and discussion at Chapter 6, "Interference With Protected Rights," and Chapter 19, "The Primary Strike."

[322]463 US at 500, 113 LRRM at 3065. *Cf.* Chavez v. Food & Commerical Workers, 779 F2d 1353, 121 LRRM 2054 (CA 8, 1985) (court affirms in part jury's finding that union breached duty of fair representation by misrepresenting to strikers that they were "unfair labor practice" strikers and could not be permanently replaced).

[323]*E.g.*, Zapex Corp., 235 NLRB 1236, 98 LRRM 1241 (1978), *enforced*, 621 F2d 328, 104 LRRM 2638 (CA 9, 1980); Bralco Metals, 227 NLRB 973, 94 LRRM 1368 (1977). But striking employees who engage in unprotected activity by picketing in violation of §8(b)(7)(B) are not entitled to reinstatement upon their unconditional application for reinstatement. Claremont Polychem. Corp., 196 NLRB 613, 80 LRRM 1130 (1972); *see also* Castle-Pierce Printing Co., 251 NLRB 1293, 105 LRRM 1567 (1980), *aff'd*, 659 F2d 253, 108 LRRM 2175 (CA DC, 1981); NLRB v. Colonial Haven Nursing Homes, 542 F2d 691, 93 LRRM 2241 (CA 7), *reh'g denied*, 542 F2d 707, 93 LRRM 2596 (CA 7, 1976). For additional discussion of *Laidlaw* developments, see Chapter 19, "The Primary Strike," at notes 95–109.

[324]202 NLRB 634, 82 LRRM 1599 (1973).

[325]For cases dealing with the issue of who is a permanent replacement, *see* Cyr Bottle Gas Co., 204 NLRB 527, 83 LRRM 1505 (1973), *enforced*, 497 F2d 900, 87 LRRM 2253 (CA 6, 1974); Covington Furniture Mfg. Co., 212 NLRB 214, 87 LRRM 1505 (1974), *enforced*, 514 F2d 995, 89 LRRM 3024 (CA 6, 1975); H & F Binch Co., 188 NLRB 720, 76 LRRM 1735 (1971), *enforcement denied in relevant part*, 456 F2d 357, 79 LRRM 2692 (CA 2, 1972). Cases dealing with the issue of which striker has been replaced include Pillows of Cal., 207 NLRB 369, 84 LRRM 1446 (1973), and Pleasant View Rest Home, 194 NLRB 426, 78 LRRM 1683 (1971). Reinstatement to a job for which the striker is not qualified and for which the striker receives no training, followed by the striker's discharge for not meeting production quotas on the job, violates §8(a)(3). Elsing Mfg. Co., 209 NLRB 1089, 86 LRRM 1267 (1974); NLRB v. Penn Corp., 630 F2d 561, 102 LRRM 2753 (CA 8, 1979)

The Board has recognized, however, that reinstatement rights may be limited by a strike-settlement agreement negotiated between the employer and the union.[326] In *General Portland, Inc.*,[327] the Board found an employer did not violate the Act by insisting on a strike settlement which conditioned the reinstatement of economic strikers on the union's agreement to give written notice of any future work stoppage. The Board found no proof of actual antiunion intent, and concluded that the notice requirement was not "inherently destructive" of employees' statutory rights and that the employer had a legitimate and substantial justification for imposing the condition.[328]

Although the union can waive reinstatement rights by agreement, an employer may not abridge those rights by unilateral action. In *Gaso Pumps*,[329] the employer violated section 8(a)(3) by insisting upon to impasse, and implementing, its final proposal that reinstatement rights of economic strikers be limited to six months. But in *La Famosa Foods*,[330] the Board held that an employer did not discharge certain strikers in violation of section 8(a)(3) by sending striking employees a mailgram stating they would be terminated if they did not return to work by a certain date. The employer's later actions, including listing the employees who did not return by the deadline on the voter eligibility list in a representation election, established that no discharges had been effected.

In general, the Board will require that replaced strikers be given a fair and realistic opportunity to claim available vacancies in jobs that they can perform before those vacancies are offered to new employees. Thus, an employer violated section 8(a)(3) by terminating the recall rights of a day-shift employee because she

---

(employer violated §8(a)(3) when it requested permanently replaced economic strikers to execute reinstatement-request form containing requirement that strikers renew their request for reinstatement within six months or be removed from recall list); *see also* American Mach. Corp. v. NLRB, 424 F2d 1321, 73 LRRM 2977 (CA 5, 1970); Pease Co., 251 NLRB 540, 105 LRRM 1314 (1980).

[326]United Aircraft Corp., 192 NLRB 382, 77 LRRM 1785 (1971), *aff'd in part sub nom.* Machinists Lodges 743 & 1746, 534 F2d 422, 90 LRRM 2272 (CA 2, 1975), *cert. denied*, 429 US 825, 93 LRRM 2362 (1976). *See* discussion in Chapter 19, "The Primary Strike," at notes 95–96.

[327]283 NLRB 585, 126 LRRM 1053 (1987).

[328]*See also* Pioneer Holding Co. of Minn., 291 NLRB 1047, 131 LRRM 1514 (1988), where no violation was found when the employer demanded, admittedly to favor employees who crossed a picket line, that economic strikers be recalled on the basis of shifts worked after the strike began and that replacements be given superseniority.

[329]274 NLRB 532, 119 LRRM 1052 (1985).

[330]282 NLRB 316, 125 LRRM 1141 (1986).

rejected a recall to a night-shift job.[331] An offer of reinstatement was not valid where it contemplated reemployment on terms and conditions of employment that the employer unlawfully imposed on employees.[332] Requiring strikers who wanted to return to work to fill out new job applications gave them the impression they had been discharged and, thus, violated the Act.[333] The Board did not find a violation, however, where an employer denied reinstatement to two strikers after it had sent them, in effect, notices to report to work within three working days and neither striker offered acceptable reasons for failing to respond.[334] A violation of section 8(a)(3) also occurred when an employer restricted recall of economic strikers to each individual's prestrike position while hiring new employees for jobs strikers were qualified to perform.[335]

In *NLRB v. American Olean Tile Co.*,[336] however, the Sixth Circuit disagreed with the Board and held that an employer that recalled strikers during an economic strike based on the date of the strikers' offer to return to work was not required to abandon the procedure and recall strikers on the basis of seniority once the strike ended.

In *Aqua-Chem*,[337] the Board announced the rule governing the conflicting rights of reinstated strikers and laid-off permanent replacements during a recall from a post strike layoff.

---

[331] Mike Yurosek & Son, 295 NLRB No. 35, 131 LRRM 1723 (1989).

[332] Richmond Recording Corp. dba PRC Recording Co., 280 NLRB 615, 124 LRRM 1081 (1986), *enforced*, 836 F2d 289, 127 LRRM 2148 (CA 7, 1987).

[333] Champ Corp., 291 NLRB 803, 131 LRRM 1555 (1989); Trident Recycling Corp., 282 NLRB 1255, 125 LRRM 1107 (1987). *But see* Schmidt-Tiago Constr. Co., 286 NLRB 342, 127 LRRM 1246 (1987), where the Board found no violation despite an allegation that the employer had constructively discharged 10 strikers by telling them they would not be reinstated unless they resigned from the union, when none of the strikers had unconditionally offered to return to work and other strikers who returned to work during the strike did not resign from the union.

[334] Axelson, Inc., 285 NLRB 862, 129 LRRM 1344 (1987).

[335] Arlington Hotel Co. v. NLRB, 785 F2d 249, 121 LRRM 2926 (CA 8, 1986), *cert. denied*, 479 US 914, 123 LRRM 2672 (1986). *See also* Medallion Kitchens, 277 NLRB 1606, 121 LRRM 1199 (1986), *enforced as modified*, 811 F2d 456, 124 LRRM 2830 (CA 8, 1987) (employer unlawfully failed to reinstate economic strikers to positions that were "temporary" but "substantially equivalent" to job held by strikers prior to strike); Crown Beer Distribs., 296 NLRB No. 78, 132 LRRM 1149 (1989) (offer not valid when employer offered economic strikers reinstatement as casual employees without seniority rather than as regular employees with seniority rights); Toledo 5 Auto/Truck Plaza, 291 NLRB 319, 131 LRRM 1121 (1988) (offer not valid when striker given only one day to consider offer). *Cf.* Trojan Luggage Co., NLRB Gen. Counsel Advice Memo., Case No. 26-CA-11976, 126 LRRM 1373 (1987) (no violation of §8(a)(3) when employer recalled permanent replacements rather than economic strikers for two-day work assignment that followed poststrike layoff of 30 days, in view of short-term and temporary nature of recall).

[336] 826 F2d 1496, 126 LRRM 2001 (CA 6, 1987).

[337] 288 NLRB 1108, 128 LRRM 1237 (1988).

Generally, the employer may recall the laid-off replacements if they have a reasonable expectancy of recall. Thus, to prove a violation the General Counsel must establish a prima facie case that the layoff truly signified a "departure" of replacements under *Laidlaw*. This requires the General Counsel to show (1) that a strike has occurred, (2) that the strikers have made an unconditional offer to return to work, (3) that a layoff of permanent replacements has occurred, (4) that replacements rather than former strikers were recalled, and (5) that based on objective factors the laid-off permanent replacements had no reasonable expectancy of recall. Once the General Counsel establishes a prima facie case that the layoff signified a departure of replacements which created vacancies to which unreinstated strikers are entitled to be recalled, the burden shifts to the employer to show that, in fact, no such vacancies occurred or that its failure to recall unreinstated strikers was based on legitimate and substantial business justifications.

Applying its test to the facts in *Aqua-Chem*,[338] the Board found that the employer had not met its burden and violated section 8(a)(3) by recalling laid-off replacements before unreinstated strikers. In *Mike Yurosek & Son*,[339] however, the Board found no violation when a seasonal employer reinstated permanent replacements who had been laid off at the end of the preceding season rather than unreinstated strikers who had engaged in an economic strike before the end of the preceding season. Because the replacements had a reasonable expectation of recall to the seasonal jobs, their layoffs did not create vacancies under the *Aqua-Chem* test.

In a clarification of *NLRB v. Fleetwood Trailer Co.*,[340] the Board adopted an ALJ's decision that an employer did not violate the Act when it refused to reinstate economic strikers and thereafter terminated them when the plant closed during the strike for economic considerations neither caused by, nor related to, the strike.[341]

---

[338] *Id.*

[339] *Supra* note 331.

[340] 389 US 375, 66 LRRM 2737 (1967).

[341] Weyerhaeuser Co., 274 NLRB 972, 119 LRRM 1091 (1985). *See also* Washington Materials v. NLRB, 803 F2d 1333, 123 LRRM 2774 (CA 4, 1986) (court rejected Board's finding that employer unlawfully failed to reinstate two economic strikers, where failure to reinstate one was based on strike misconduct and failure to reinstate other was based on "terrible" work performance prior to strike).

The Board has found violations of section 8(a)(3) where employers filled vacant jobs by hiring new employees rather than reinstating strikers qualified to perform the work and the employers could not prove legitimate and substantial business reasons for the failures to reinstate the strikers.[342] Likewise, a violation was found when an employer allowed unreinstated qualified strikers to bid on job vacancies only if nonstrikers and strike replacements failed to bid.[343] In *Trans World Airlines v. Flight Attendants*,[344] a Railway Labor Act case which may have implications under the Act, however, the Supreme Court determined that junior crossovers, that is, strikers who abandoned an economic strike and returned to work before the strike's end, were entitled to the same status as newly hired permanent replacements and need not be displaced from their assignments by more senior strikers at the conclusion of the strike. In *George Banta Co. v. NLRB*,[345] a case unusual because the employer had signed a settlement agreement giving the strikers the rights of unfair labor practice strikers, the Court of Appeals for the District of Columbia Circuit found that an employer who retained crossovers in their prestrike jobs violated section 8(a)(3) by refusing after the strike had concluded to allow the crossovers to be bumped by more senior strikers who had remained on strike until the new contract was signed. According to the court, such conduct stands "'as an ever present reminder of the dangers connected with striking and with union activities in general.'"[346]

When an employer's actions convert an economic strike into an unfair labor practice strike, prolonging the strike, strikers become entitled to immediate reinstatement, and the employer's

---

[342]Southwest Merchandising Corp. 296 NLRB No. 128, 132 LRRM 1333 (1989) (violation found when successor employer hired new employees and failed to hire employees who had been on strike against predecessor and whose unconditional offer to return to work had been rejected by predecessor); Glover Bottle Gas Corp., 292 NLRB 873, 131 LRRM 1649 (1989); Corson & Gruman Co., 284 NLRB 1316, 126 LRRM 1279 (1987); Wright Tool Co., 282 NLRB 1398, 125 LRRM 1172 (1987), *enforced*, 854 F2d 812, 129 LRRM 2157 (CA 6, 1988); Zartic, Inc. v. NLRB, 810 F2d 1080, 124 LRRM 2806 (CA 11, 1987); Rockwood & Co. dba Timber Prods. Co., 281 NLRB 862, 124 LRRM 1154 (1986), *enforced*, 834 F2d 837, 127 LRRM 2070 (CA 9, 1987).

[343]Oregon Steel Mills, 291 NLRB 185, 131 LRRM 1335 (1988).

[344]489 US 426, 130 LRRM 2657 (1989).

[345]686 F2d 10, 110 LRRM 3351 (CA DC, 1982), *cert. denied*, 460 US 1082, 113 LRRM 2112 (1983).

[346]*Id.* at 19, 110 LRRM at 3358 (quoting NLRB v. Erie Resistor Corp., 373 US at 231, 53 LRRM at 2125).

backpay liability commences, upon their unconditional offer to return to work.[347]

6. Discharge or Discipline of Union Officers for Strikes in Breach of Contract. In *Metropolitan Edison Co. v. NLRB*,[348] the Supreme Court agreed with the Board that an employer violates section 8(a)(3) by imposing on union officials sanctions more severe than those imposed on other employees who participated in a contractually prohibited work stoppage. The unanimous Court deferred to the judgment of the Board that such disparate treatment, based solely on the protected activity of holding union office, was "inherently destructive" of employee rights and was not countervailed by legitimate business justifications. The decision approved a line of Board decisions resting on *Precision Castings Co.*[349] Even under the *Precision Castings* rationale, however, an exception is recognized where the union official takes a leadership role in the illegal strike. In that situation the Board holds that the official may justifiably receive a harsher penalty.[350]

Applying this rule in *Eagle Picher Industries*,[351] the Board held that, in the absence of a contractual waiver, a violation of the Act occurs whenever the holding of a union office serves as the sole basis for the decision to discipline or to impose more severe discipline.[352]

The statutory right to be free of such discrimination can be waived by explicit contractual language requiring the official to take affirmative steps to end the prohibited work stoppage.[353] According to the Board, however, a general no-strike/no-lock-

---

[347]*See* Chapter 19, "The Primary Strike," at notes 76–78; National Fresh Fruit & Vegetable Co. v. NLRB, 565 F2d 1331, 97 LRRM 2427 (CA 5, 1978); National Car Rental Sys., 237 NLRB 172, 99 LRRM 1027 (1978), *enforcement denied*, 594 F2d 1203, 100 LRRM 2824 (CA 8, 1979). *See also* Mastro Plastics Corp. v. NLRB, 350 US 270, 37 LRRM 2587 (1956).

[348]460 US 693, 112 LRRM 3265 (1983).

[349]233 NLRB 183, 96 LRRM 1540 (1977). *But see* Indiana & Mich. Elec. Co. v. NLRB, 599 F2d 227, 101 LRRM 2475 (CA 7, 1979), *denying enforcement to* 237 NLRB 226, 99 LRRM 1111 (1978).

[350]Atkinson Co., 251 NLRB 277, 105 LRRM 1108 (1980); Chrysler Corp., 232 NLRB 466, 96 LRRM 1382 (1977); J. P. Wetherby Constr. Corp., 182 NLRB 690, 76 LRRM 1879 (1970).

[351]278 NLRB 696, 121 LRRM 1253 (1986), *enforced*, 831 F2d 295 (CA 6, 1987).

[352]*Id.* at n.13.

[353]*See* Indiana & Mich. Elec. Co. *supra* note 349 (employer who disciplined two union stewards more harshly than other employees engaged in unlawful walkout did not violate §8(a)(3) because contract required union officials to take affirmative action to end strike). *Accord* West Penn Power Co., 274 NLRB 1160, 118 LRRM 1529 (1985).

out clause does not, by itself, impose such affirmative duties on a union official.[354]

7. Discrimination Based on Race or Sex. In *Jubilee Manufacturing Co.*,[355] the Board held that discrimination based on race, color, religion, sex, or national origin, standing alone, is not a violation of the Act, absent "actual evidence, as opposed to speculation, of a nexus between the alleged discriminatory conduct and the interference with, or restraint of, employees in the exercise of those rights protected by the Act."[356]

Discrimination based on race, religion, national origin, or sex has been held to violate the Act, however, when the discriminatory conduct does interfere with, or restrain, the employees in the exercise of their protected rights. In *Black Grievance Committee v. NLRB*,[357] the employer granted one nonmajority employee group privileged status in the presentation and resolution of grievances and refused to accord similar status to another predominantly black nonexclusive employee organization. The court ruled that such conduct violates section 8(a)(1) when there is no business justification and a determining factor in the decision not to accord equal privileges is the racial composition of the organization's leadership and membership. The Board also has found employer discrimination on the basis of race or sex to be a violation of section 8(a)(3), where the employer acquiesces in the maintenance and enforcement of discriminatory seniority lists[358] or hiring-hall arrangements.[359]

Employees are engaged in protected activity, however, when in concert they protest their employer's discriminatory practices. Thus, the Board has held that employers violate section 8(a)(1)

---

[354]John Morrell & Co., 270 NLRB 1, 116 LRRM 1177 (1984), *aff'd*, 770 F2d 1400, 120 LRRM 2342 (CA 6, 1985).

[355]202 NLRB 272, 82 LRRM 1482 (1973), *aff'd sub nom.* Steelworkers v. NLRB, 504 F2d 271, 87 LRRM 3168 (CA DC, 1974). *See* Chapter 6, "Interference With Protected Rights," notes 13–16.

[356]*Id.* The decision rejected a rationale suggeted in Packinghouse Workers v. NLRB, 416 F2d 1126, 70 LRRM 2489 (CA DC), *cert. denied*, 396 US 903, 72 LRRM 2658 (1969), that racial discrimination by an employer inherently impaired §7 rights. In Emporium Capwell Co. v. Western Addition Community Org., 420 US 50, 88 LRRM 2660 (1975), the Supreme Court explicitly left open the question whether the right to be free of racial discrimination has an independent source in the NLRA (citing *Packinghouse Workers)*.

[357]749 F2d 1072, 117 LRRM 3389 (CA 3, 1984), *cert. denied*, 472 US 1008, 119 LRRM 2696 (1985).

[358]Olympic S.S. Co., 233 NLRB 1178, 97 LRRM 1276 (1977).

[359]Pacific Maritime Ass'n, 209 NLRB 519, 85 LRRM 1389 (1974). *But see* J.S. Alberici Constr. Co., 231 NLRB 1030, 96 LRRM 1205 (1977) (no violation for employer to withdraw from referral hall arrangement after union was compelled to end discriminatory operations that violated Title VII).

when they discharge employees for alleging discrimination in filings with federal or state agencies,[360] for attempting to change discriminatory hiring practices,[361] and for attempting to secure racially integrated working conditions.[362] But *Emporium Capwell Co. v. Western Addition Community Organization*[363] stands as an important caveat. The Supreme Court there held that employees lose the protection of the Act when they bypass the exclusive representative and attempt to deal directly with the employer to eliminate racially discriminatory employment practices.

8. Discrimination Based on Terms of Collective Bargaining Agreement. *a. Enforcement of Union-Security Provision.* The enforcement of a lawful union-security agreement is not prohibited discrimination. Faced with a union demand to discharge an employee for alleged failure to comply with a valid union-security provision, an employer must inquire into the circumstances behind the demand if the employer "is aware of facts that would lead him to believe that the discharge may be for an improper purpose."[364] The employer's obligation to investigate the demand depends on the facts known to the employer, the degree of doubt they raise, the burden the inquiry would impose, and the likelihood that an investigation would lead to a prompt resolution of the employer's doubts.[365] Thus, an employer did not violate section 8(a)(3) when it acceded to a union's request for an employee's discharge on a claimed dues delinquency.[366] The employer acted on the basis of a letter from the union business agent and confirmed from a review of the agreement that the request appeared to be in order. Although the union was held liable under section 8(b)(2) for an improper

---

[360]King Soopers, Inc., 222 NLRB 1011, 91 LRRM 1292 (1976), where the collective bargaining agreement contained a no-discrimination clause; Advance Carbon Prods., 198 NLRB 741, 81 LRRM 1418 (1972). *See* Frank Briscoe v. NLRB, 637 F2d 946, 106 LRRM 2155 (CA 3, 1981). *See* Chapter 6, "Interference With Protected Rights," at notes 509–510.

[361]Mason & Hanger-Silas Mason Co., 179 NLRB 434, 72 LRRM 1372 (1969), *enforcement denied on other grounds*, 449 F2d 425, 78 LRRM 2487 (CA 8, 1971), *cert. denied*, 405 US 1066, 79 LRRM 3092 (1972).

[362]Tanner Motor Livery, 148 NLRB 1402, 57 LRRM 1170 (1964), *vacated and remanded*, 349 F2d 1, 59 LRRM 2784 (CA 9, 1965), *original decision aff'd*, 166 NLRB 551, 65 LRRM 1502 (1967), *remanded*, 419 F2d 216, 72 LRRM 2866 (CA 9, 1969).

[363]*Supra* note 356.

[364]Macaulay Foundry Co. v. NLRB, 553 F2d 1198, 1202, 95 LRRM 2581 (CA 9, 1977), *enforcing* 223 NLRB 815, 92 LRRM 1279 (1976) (employer violated §8(a)(3) when it refused to investigate absent employee's claim that his dues could be paid upon his return to work).

[365]*Id.; see also* NLRB v. Zoe Chem. Co., 406 F2d 574, 70 LRRM 2276 (CA 2, 1969), *denying enforcement to* 160 NLRB 1001, 63 LRRM 1052 (1966).

[366]R.H. Macy & Co., 266 NLRB 858, 113 LRRM 1049 (1983).

request, the Board ruled that there could be no section 8(a)(3) violation because the employer had "no reasonable cause" to believe that the union's request was improper.[367] No employee may be discharged under a union-security agreement, however, unless the employee has been put on notice of the obligation alleged to be owed to the union.[368]

b. Compliance With Superseniority Provision. To assure continuity of function and maximum use of a union steward's skill and experience, unions often bargain for and attain superseniority for stewards in a collective bargaining agreement. Collective bargaining provisions granting superseniority to union officers in matters relating to layoff and recall have been upheld where the officer's responsibilities "bear a direct relationship to the effect and efficient representation of unit employees."[369] But under the rule of *Dairylea Cooperative*,[370] contractual provisions that give superseniority to union stewards regarding benefits other than layoff and recall are held to be presumptively unlawful, and the party which asserts the legality of such a provision has the burden of demonstrating substantial and legitimate business justification.[371] Where an employee need not be a union member to be selected steward, the Board has indicated that a superseniority preference may not be improper.[372]

In *Gulton Electro-Voice*,[373] stating that "superseniority is inher-

---

[367] *See* Helmsley-Spear, Inc., 275 NLRB 262, 119 LRRM 1121 (1985). *See also* Electrical Workers (IBEW) Local 1547 (Homer Elec. Ass'n), 280 NLRB 1362, 123 LRRM 1278 (1986).

[368] Teamsters Local 162 v. NLRB (Platt Elec. Supply), 568 F2d 665, 97 LRRM 2917 (CA 9, 1978). However, an employer does not violate the Act merely because the union has failed to adequately inform an employee of dues delinquency. Valley Cabinet & Mfg., 253 NLRB 98, 105 LRRM 1467 (1980). *See generally* Chapter 27, "Union Security."

[369] Allied Indus. Workers Local 148 (Allen Group, Inc.), 236 NLRB 1368, 1370, 98 LRRM 1574 (1978); Electrical Workers (UE) Local 623 (Limpco Mfg.), 230 NLRB 406, 95 LRRM 1343 (1977), *enforced sub nom.* D'Amico v. NLRB, 582 F2d 820, 99 LRRM 2350 (CA 3, 1978); Otis Elevator Co., 231 NLRB 1128, 96 LRRM 1108 (1977); Expedient Servs., 231 NLRB 938, 96 LRRM 1436 (1977). *See* note 374, *infra.*

[370] 219 NLRB 656, 89 LRRM 1737 (1975), *enforced sub nom.* NLRB v. Teamsters Local 338, 531 F2d 1162, 91 LRRM 2929 (CA 2, 1976); *see also* NLRB v. Auto Warehousers, 571 F2d 860, 98 LRRM 2238 (CA 5, 1978), *denying enforcement to* 227 NLRB 628, 94 LRRM 1445 (1976); Laborers Local 380, 275 NLRB 1049, 120 LRRM 1023 (1985); Preston Trucking Co., 236 NLRB 464, 98 LRRM 1248 (1978), *enforced sub nom.* Teamsters Local 20 v. NLRB, 610 F2d 991, 102 LRRM 3080 (CA DC, 1979); Connecticut Limousine Serv., 235 NLRB 1350, 98 LRRM 1299 (1978), *modified and enforced*, 600 F2d 411, 101 LRRM 2622 (CA 2, 1979); W. R. Grace Co., 230 NLRB 259, 95 LRRM 1441 (1977).

[371] *See* notes 442-458 *infra* and accompanying text.

[372] Theatrical Stage Employees Local 780 (McGregor-Werner, Inc.), 227 NLRB 558, 94 LRRM 1230 (1976).

[373] 266 NLRB 406, 112 LRRM 1361 (1983), *enforced sub nom.* Electrical Workers (IUE) Local 900 v. NLRB, 727 F2d 1184, 115 LRRM 2760 (CA DC, 1984). *See also* Arvin Automotive, 285 NLRB 753, 126 LRRM 1105 (1987); NLRB v. Auto Workers Locals 1131 & 1161 (Houdaille Indus.), 777 F2d 1131, 121 LRRM 2080 (CA 6, 1985).

ently discriminatory,"[374] the Board ruled that superseniority is justified only for union officials who perform stewardlike duties such as grievance processing and contract administration. Thus, an employer violated section 8(a)(3) by maintaining a clause granting superseniority to the union's recording secretary and treasurer where their duties did not involve grievance processing or on-the-job contract administration.[375] Applying this restricted standard, the Board has held it unlawful to grant a union steward superseniority with respect to job-bumping rights where the company operated only one shift and the steward did not need to be on any particular job to perform her grievance-handling duties.[376]

III. UNION INDUCEMENT OF EMPLOYER TO DISCRIMINATE

A. Union Inducements as Unfair Labor Practice Prohibited by Section 8(b)(2)

Under section 8(b)(2) it is an unfair labor practice for a union "to cause or attempt to cause" an employer to discriminate in violation of section 8(a)(3). Section 8(a)(3), in turn, prohibits that discrimination based on the exercise of employee rights which has the tendency to encourage or discourage union membership.[377] This statutory standard is qualitatively different

---

[374]*Supra* note 373, at 408. *Gulton* overruled Electrical Workers (UE) Local 623 (Limpco Mfg. Co.), *supra* note 369, and its progeny.

[375]NLRB v. Harvey Hubble, Inc., Ensign Elec. Div., 767 F2d 1100, 119 LRRM 3460, *on reh'g*, 783 F2d 1121, 121 LRRM 2765 (CA 4, 1985), *cert. denied*, 479 US 984, 123 LRRM 3128 (1986). *See* NLRB v. Auto Workers Locals 1131 & 1161 (Kennecott Corp.), *supra* note 373, at 1137, 121 LRRM at 2805. For other applications of the *Gulton* rule, see Auto Workers Local 1384 v. NLRB (Ex-Cell-O Corp.), 756 F2d 482, 118 LRRM 2753 (CA 7, 1985); NLRB v. Niagara Mach. & Tool Works, 746 F2d 143, 117 LRRM 2689 (CA 2, 1984); Electrical Workers (IUE) Local 900 v. NLRB (Gulton Electro-Voice), 727 F2d 1184, 115 LRRM 2760 (CA DC, 1984).

[376]Electrical Workers (IUE) Local 663 (Gulton Electro-Voice), 276 NLRB 1043, 120 LRRM 1150 (1985); *see* Mechanics Local 56 (Revere Copper Prods.), 287 NLRB 935, 127 LRRM 1163 (1987); Frankline, Inc., 287 NLRB 263, 127 LRRM 1132 (1987); United States Steel Corp., 288 NLRB 1074, 130 LRRM 1280 (1988).

[377]*See* Breininger v. Sheet Metal Workers Local 6, 493 US 67, 132 LRRM 3001 (1989); NLRB v. Laborers Local 1140 (Cadet Constr. Co.), 861 F2d 531, 129 LRRM 2973 (CA 8, 1988) (per curiam); NLRB v. Electrical Workers (IBEW) Local 952 (Donald Horton dba Tri-Bar Elec. Co.), 758 F2d 436, 119 LRRM 2254 (CA 9, 1985); Auto Workers Local 1384 v. NLRB (Ex-Cell-O Corp.), *supra* note 375; NLRB v. Niagara Mach. & Tool Works, *supra* note 375; Carpenters Local 2396 (Tri-State Ohbayashi), 287 NLRB 760, 127 LRRM 1307 (1987); Upholsterers Local 406 (Boyertown Casket Co.), 280 NLRB 1227, 123 LRRM 1277 (1986); Graphic Communications Dist. Council No. 2 (Data Documents), 278 NLRB 365, 122 LRRM 1029 (1986); Painters Local 277 (Del E. Webb N.J.), 278 NLRB 169, 121 LRRM 1144 (1986), *enforced*, 860 F2d 1075, 129 LRRM 3144 (CA 3, 1988). For an interesting

from the "restrain or coerce" language of sections 8(a)(1) and 8(b)(1).

The Supreme Court gave early direction to the broad implications of the language of section 8(b)(2) in *Radio Officers v. NLRB (A.H. Bull Steamship Co.)*.[378] It held that union inducement of an employer to discharge a union member for reasons other than failure to pay union dues or fees authorized by the union-shop proviso to section 8(a)(3) violated section 8(b)(2). The Court noted that it had previously held that the terms "discrimination" and "membership in any labor organization" included "discrimination to discourage participation in union activities as well as to discourage adhesion to union membership."[379] The Court stressed that

> [t]he policy of the Act is to insulate employees' job rights from their organizational rights. Thus §§ 8(a)(3) and 8(b)(2) were designed to allow employees to freely exercise their right to join unions, be good, bad, or indifferent members, or abstain from joining any union without imperiling their livelihood.[380]

Thus, aside from dismissals pursuant to valid union-shop agreements, "[n]o other discrimination aimed at encouraging employees to join, retain membership, or stay in good standing in a union is condoned."[381]

Although a wide range of union conduct may "cause" or "attempt to cause" an employer to discriminate, the most typical violations of section 8(b)(2) involve a union that is seeking the discharge of a nonmember[382] or of a member who has incurred

---

discussion of consent decrees under Title VII of the Civil Rights Act of 1964 and hiring halls, see Iron Workers Local 483 (Building Contractors Ass'n of N.J.), 285 NLRB 123, 129 LRRM 1285 (1987), *enforcement granted in part sub nom.* NLRB v. Iron Workers Local 11, 864 F2d 1113, 130 LRRM 2337 (CA 3, 1989).

[378] 347 US 17, 22 LRRM 2417 (1954).

[379] *Id.* at 40 n.39. The Court cited Associated Press v. NLRB, 301 US 103, 1 LRRM 732 (1937).

[380] 347 US at 40.

[381] *Id.* at 41–42.

[382] Plumbers & Pipe Fitters Local 669 v. NLRB (Best-Fire Protection Sys.), 778 F2d 8, 120 LRRM 3541 (CA DC, 1985); NLRB v. Electrical Workers (IBEW) Local 952 (Donald Horton dba Tri-Bar Elec. Co.), 758 F2d 436, 119 LRRM 2254 (CA 9, 1985), *enforcing* 269 NLRB 608, 116 LRRM 1087 (1984); Loft Painting Co., 267 NLRB 74, 113 LRRM 1143 (1983); Food & Commercial Workers Local 454 (Central Soya), 245 NLRB 1295, 102 LRRM 1533 (1979), *enforced*, 625 F2d 1012, 108 LRRM 2280 (CA 5, 1980); Typographical Union No. 18 (Detroit) (Sportgraphics), 244 NLRB 1149, 102 LRRM 1337 (1979); Hickmott Foods, 242 NLRB 1357, 101 LRRM 1342 (1979); Crouse Nuclear Energy Servs., 240 NLRB 390, 100 LRRM 1422 (1979); Electrical Workers (IBEW) Local 112 (Ajax Elec. Co.), 231 NLRB 162, 95 LRRM 1571 (1977); NLRB v. Laborers Local 341 (Hurrell), 564 F2d 834, 97 LRRM 2287 (CA 9, 1977); Plumbers Local 58 (Heyse Sheet Metal), 187 NLRB 152, 76 LRRM 1192 (1970); United Nuclear Corp. v. NLRB, 340 F2d 133, 58 LRRM 2211 (CA 1, 1965); Operating Eng'rs Local 9 (Schmidt Constr.), 147 NLRB 393, 56 LRRM 1225 (1964).

the disfavor of the union's leadership.[383] The discharge of a nonmember directly encourages union membership, while the discharge of the member who has incurred the leader's personal and political disfavor does so indirectly, for it teaches others to be "good" or subservient members and provides an example of union power beyond that which the law permits.[384]

Union retaliation for an employee's criticism of the union also violates section 8(b)(2). In *General Motors Corp.*,[385] the Board held that the union unlawfully caused the employer to change an employee's starting time because that individual opposed a new absenteeism program which was supported by the union. Affirming this finding on appeal, the Sixth Circuit stated that a union violates sections 8(b)(1)(A) and 8(b)(2) by attempting to cause an employer to discriminate in order to "retaliate against that employee for protesting the union's policies, questioning the official conduct of union agents, or incurring the personal hostility of a union official."[386]

---

[383]NLRB v. Laborers Local 644 (Kellerman Bros. Constr. Co.), 810 F2d 665, 124 LRRM 2501 (CA 7, 1987); NLRB v. Laborers Local 576 (Arthur B. Myr Sheet Metal Indus.), 754 F2d 677, 118 LRRM 2742 (CA 6, 1985), *enforcing* 267 NLRB 632, 114 LRRM 1217 (1983); Carpenters Local 2310 (Hazex Constr. Co.), 280 NLRB 425, 123 LRRM 1304 (1986); M.W. Kellogg Constructors, 273 NLRB 1049, 118 LRRM 1616 (1984), *enforcement denied*, 806 F2d 1435, 124 LRRM 2288 (CA 9, 1986); Fischbach/Lord Elec. Co., 270 NLRB 856, 116 LRRM 1229 (1984), *enforced in pertinent part*, 827 F2d 530, 126 LRRM 2292 (CA 9, 1987); Plumbers & Pipe Fitters Local 669 (Best-Fire Protection Sys.), 268 NLRB 1218, 115 LRRM 1308 (1984), *enforced in part*, 778 F2d 8, 120 LRRM 3541 (CA DC, 1985); Plumbers & Pipe Fitters Local 198 v. NLRB (Jacobs/Weise), 747 F2d 326, 117 LRRM 3151 (CA 5, 1984). The General Counsel has determined that labor management participation teams, with employee representatives drawn solely from the union membership, do not violate §8(b)(2). Titanium Metals Corp., NLRB Gen. Counsel Advice Memo., Case Nos. 31-CA-16000 & 31-CB-6773, 125 LRRM 1375 (1987). *See also* Fruin-Colnon Corp. v. NLRB, 571 F2d 1017, 97 LRRM 2845 (CA 8, 1978); Operating Eng'rs Local 106 (Green Island Contracting Co.), 243 NLRB 551, 101 LRRM 1596 (1979); Steelworkers Local 8061 (Arrowhead Eng'g Corp.), 233 NLRB 858, 97 LRRM 1012 (1977); Teamsters Local 282 (Explo, Inc.), 229 NLRB 347, 95 LRRM 1202 (1977); Carpenters Local 2205 (Groves-Granite), 229 NLRB 56, 96 LRRM 1146, *modified*, 232 NLRB 381, 97 LRRM 1164 (1977); Daniel Constr. Co., 227 NLRB 72, 94 LRRM 1547 (1976); Upper Manhattan Medical Group, 225 NLRB 153, 92 LRRM 1585 (1976), *enforced*, 559 F2d 1204, 96 LRRM 2661 (CA 2, 1977) (discharge for nonpayment of dues held pretextual); Rust Eng'g Co. v. NLRB, 445 F2d 172, 77 LRRM 2885 (CA 6, 1971); Lummus Co. v. NLRB, 339 F2d 728, 56 LRRM 2425 (CA DC, 1964).

[384]Radio Officers v. NLRB (A.H. Bull S.S. Co.), *supra* note 378.

[385]272 NLRB 705, 117 LRRM 1391 (1984), *enforced sub nom.* Auto Workers Local 594 v. NLRB, 776 F2d 1310, 120 LRRM 3289 (CA 6, 1985).

[386]*Id.* at 1314, 120 LRRM at 3293. *Accord* Longshoremen (ILA) Local 333 (ITO Corp. of Baltimore), 267 NLRB 1320, 114 LRRM 1207 (1983). *See also* Laborers Local 1140 (Plibrico Sales & Serv. Co.), 295 NLRB No. 87, 131 LRRM 1713 (1989) (employees opposed union decision to close branch office); Heavy & Highway Constr. Workers Local 158 (Contractors' Ass'n of E. Pa. & Worthy Bros. Pipeline Corp.), 280 NLRB 1100, 123 LRRM 1042 (1986), *enforced*, 865 F2d 251 (CA 3, 1988) (union refusal to refer members for employment because of their intraunion activities violates §8(b)(2)); Teamsters Local 79 (Carl Subler Trucking), 269 NLRB 1132, 116 LRRM 1054 (1984), *corrected*, 269 NLRB 1132, 116

Employees may not be discriminated against for opposing union leadership in a union election. The Board has concluded, for example, that a union's efforts to cause an employer to discharge an employee who ran against the incumbent for the position of business representative violated section 8(b)(2).[387] Similarly, the Board has held that unions violated the Act by causing an employer to lay off an employee who assumed the role of chairing a newly formed independent union,[388] and by suspending and requesting that the employer discharge employees because of their support for an outside union attempting to replace the incumbent labor organization.[389] A violation also has been found where a union refused to refer a member for employment because he supported an outside union and testified at a hearing on its representation petition.[390] No violation was found, however, in the layoff of two employees who supported an unsuccessful candidate for union business manager because the evidence did not establish that the union attempted to influence the employer in choosing employees for layoff.[391]

A union's threats to terminate an employee's health and welfare benefits because she filed a decertification petition has been held to violate section 8(b)(2).[392] Nor may a union discriminate against an employee who filed unfair labor practice charges,[393] intraunion charges,[394] or a lawsuit[395] against a union or union officials. And the Board has determined that a union may not attempt to cause the discharge of an employee because of that

---

LRRM 1202 (1984) (retaliation against union steward who opposed course of union during contract negotiations).

[387]Carpenters Local 1016 (Bertram Constr. Co.), 272 NLRB 539, 117 LRRM 1325 (1984). *See also* Carpenters Local 720 (Millwright) (National Maintenance Corp.), 283 NLRB 617, 125 LRRM 1016 (1987) (failure to refer employee because of his support for business agent's political opponent unlawful).

[388]Redway Carriers, 274 NLRB 1359, 119 LRRM 1023 (1985).

[389]Inland Boatmen's Union of the Pac. (Dillingham Tug & Barge Co.), 276 NLRB 1261, 120 LRRM 1215 (1985).

[390]Sheet Metal Workers Local 22 (Paul Miller Sheet Metal), 296 NLRB No. 150, 132 LRRM 1354 (1989).

[391]Eller & Co., 273 NLRB 57, 118 LRRM 1327 (1984). *See also* General Motors Corp., 297 NLRB No. 4, 132 LRRM 1325 (1989); Dillingham Tug & Barge Co., 278 NLRB 83, 121 LRRM 1183 (1986).

[392]Service Employees Local 1-J (Shor Co.), 273 NLRB 929, 118 LRRM 1227 (1984).

[393]Carpenters Local 720 (Millwright) (National Maintenance Corp.), *supra* note 387.

[394]Laborers Local 373 (Arrow Enters.), 282 NLRB 347, 125 LRRM 1200 (1986).

[395]Boilermakers Local 374 (Combustion Eng'g), 284 NLRB 1382, 127 LRRM 1047 (1987).

individual's monitoring of the business agent's administration of a hiring hall.[396]

Section 8(b)(2) applies only to union conduct. The Board and the courts have uniformly held that whether someone acts as an agent under this statute must be determined by common-law principles of agency.[397] As one court noted, "Senator Taft, the life-force behind the bill as enacted, repeatedly remarked on the floor of the Senate that common law rules of agency were to govern the question of who acted for whom for purposes of determining culpability under the Act."[398]

Applying these principles, the Board and the courts have found an agency relationship in a wide variety of circumstances. For example, the Board has held a union liable for the acts of an inactive union official who had not relinquished his office on the ground that his inactivity "could not, by itself, revoke his authority."[399] However, the Seventh Circuit rejected a Board ruling that a union steward and two committeemen acted as agents of the union in seeking the discharge of rival-faction union members.[400] The court noted that the steward and committeemen were elected by their fellow employees, rather than appointed by the union, and were acting as individuals on behalf of themselves and other employees distressed by the rival faction's violent and disruptive conduct.

The Board also has held a union liable for the acts of a newly elected union official who had not yet formally taken office on the ground that the employer could reasonably have believed that the official was acting on behalf of the union.[401] The Board noted that holding an elective union office is "persuasive and substantial evidence that the official is an agent of the union."[402]

---

[396]Carpenters Local 720 (Stone & Webster Eng'g Corp.), 274 NLRB 1506, 118 LRRM 1594 (1985), *remanded*, 798 F2d 781, 123 LRRM 2299 (CA 5, 1986).

[397]*E.g.*, NLRB v. Plasterers & Cement Masons Local 90 (Southern Ill. Builders Ass'n), 606 F2d 189, 102 LRRM 2482 (CA 7, 1979), *enforcing* 236 NLRB 329, 98 LRRM 1263 (1978); Laborers Local 341 v. NLRB (Hurrell), *supra* note 382; NLRB v. Electrical Workers (IBEW) Local 3 (New York Tel. Co.), 467 F2d 1158, 81 LRRM 2483 (CA 2, 1972), *enforcing* 193 NLRB 758, 78 LRRM 1431 (1971).

[398]NLRB v. Longshoremen (ILWU) Local 10 (Pacific Maritime Ass'n), 283 F2d 558, 563, 46 LRRM 3141 (CA 9, 1960).

[399]Electrical Workers (IBEW) Local 453 (National Elec. Contractors Ass'n), 258 NLRB 1427, 108 LRRM 1221, 1222 (1981), *enforced*, 696 F2d 999, 112 LRRM 2896 (CA 8, 1982).

[400]NLRB v. Eldorado Mfg. Corp., 660 F2d 1207, 108 LRRM 2600 (CA 7, 1981).

[401]Penn Yan Express, 274 NLRB 449, 118 LRRM 1448 (1985).

[402]*Id.*, 118 LRRM at 1449; Service Employees Local 9 (Blumenfeld Enters.), 290 NLRB 1, 131 LRRM 1211 (1988).

Union liability also has been found where a trust fund administrator, who was also the union president, suspended and threatened to terminate an employee's health and welfare benefits.[403] In so ruling, the Board also held that, on the facts presented, the trust fund was an agent of the union under section 8(b) of the Act.[404]

In enforcing the Act, the Board and the courts have both invoked the principle that one may imply as well as express the authority necessary to create an agency relationship. For example, in *NLRB v. Plasterers and Cement Masons Local 90 (Southern Illinois Builders Ass'n)*,[405] the Seventh Circuit held that a union could impliedly authorize the wife of a business representative to add the names of union members to a union referral list, and could therefore be liable for the wife's failure to add the name of a particular member. The business representative maintained the referral list in his home, and the representative's wife, who would often answer the referral phone, would often add names to the list. The court explained that the Board may base a finding of an agency relationship on evidence that an individual ". . . was acting with the knowledge and acquiescence of the Union and that he had implied authority to do what he did."[406]

As section 2(13) of the Act appears to mandate, the decisions also have held unions liable for acts within only the *apparent* authority of their agents. Section 2(13) provides: "In determining whether any person [acted] as an 'agent' . . ., the question of whether the specific acts performed were actually authorized or subsequently ratified shall not be controlling." Accordingly, in *NLRB v. Teamsters Local 815 (Montauk Iron & Steel Corp.)*,[407] after concluding that a union had surrounded a shop steward with the indicia of authority to order a work stoppage, the Second Circuit affirmed a Board ruling that the union was liable for the steward's ordering of an otherwise unlawful work stoppage.[408]

---

[403]Service Employees Local 1-J (Shor Co.), 273 NLRB 929, 118 LRRM 1227 (1984).

[404]*Id.*, 118 LRRM at 1230. *See also* Hotel Employees Local 50 (Hafed dba Dick's Restaurant), 287 NLRB 1180, 130 LRRM 1152 (1988) (dispatcher at union office was agent); Communications Workers Local 11509 (Pacific Bell), 283 NLRB 1143, 125 LRRM 1251 (1987) (representative of international union acted as agent of local union).

[405]*Supra* note 397.

[406]*Id.* at 189.

[407]290 F2d 99, 48 LRRM 2065 (CA 2, 1961).

[408]The court explained that

"[w]hen Floyd declared there might be a work stoppage and the men in fact stopped working, inferably as a result of his direction, the latter lay within the area where the union had invested Floyd with at least apparent authority. The Board was amply justified in finding that the evidence belied the contention that Floyd was a mere conduit of employee sentiment." *Id.* at 104.

The court stated that "in this field as elsewhere, a principal may be held responsible for the acts of an agent whom it has placed in such a position that persons dealing with the agent reasonably believe the acts to be authorized. . . ."[409] But even as the court held the union liable for the conduct of the shop steward, it also recognized that the union is not responsible for every act committed by virtue of that position. "If he acts only as an individual rather than within the authority the union has conferred, the union is absolved."[410] Recognizing the *mere conduit* principle, the Board in *Sheet Metal Workers Local 67 (Williams Sheet Metal Co.)*,[411] held that a union did not violate section 8(b)(2) by merely conveying to an employer the attitudes of its members, even though the union's doing so caused the employer to discharge a particular employee.

The courts have upheld findings of union liability for the excesses of their agents on at least two theories. In *NLRB v. Electrical Workers (IBEW) Local 3 (New York Telephone Co.)*,[412] the Second Circuit held that a union was liable for a foreman's enforcing of a secondary boycott even though the foreman had misrepresented his authority to speak for the union by purporting to be a shop steward although he was not one. The court found liability because the foreman's exceeding of his *actual* authority had not affected his *apparent* authority to speak for the union.[413] On the other hand, in *NLRB v. Longshoremen (ILWU) Local 10 (Pacific Maritime Ass'n)*,[414] the Ninth Circuit relied on the entirely different principle that a union is broadly liable for its steward's action. The union refused to allow a member to work, notwithstanding a proper dispatch slip, apparently because the member earlier had sued the union. The Ninth Circuit explained:

> [T]he present situation is not unlike that of an employee who is authorized to cut down designated trees belonging to his employer

---

[409] *Id.* at 103.
[410] *Id.* at 104.
[411] 201 NLRB 1050, 82 LRRM 1617 (1973). *But see* Laborers Local 341 v. NLRB (Hurrell), 564 F2d 834, 97 LRRM 2287 (CA 9, 1977), *enforcing* 223 NLRB 917, 92, LRRM 1112 (1976) (union liable when steward transmitted to employer result of cease-work vote by rank-and-file members.
[412] 467 F2d 1158, 81 LRRM 2483 (CA 2, 1972), *enforcing* 193 NLRB 758, 78 LRRM 1431 (1971).
[413] As the court noted, "[t]he union placed Fedar in a position of authority in which as foreman he also acted as steward. That he may have exceeded his authority in claiming to be steward does not affect his apparent authority when he acted as such." *Id.* at 1160.
[414] 283 F2d 558, 46 LRRM 3141 (CA 9, 1960).

> and who with zeal to increase the employer's profits fells timber belonging to a third party. . . . The Local authorized its stewards to safeguard advantages secured by the union at the bargaining table, yet the stewards exercised their power to achieve advantages to which the union was not entitled. Having created the stewards' power, the Local must take the responsibility if it is wrongly used.[415]

Discrimination under section 8(b)(2) does not always involve a discharge. The discrimination might also take the form of layoff, transfer, demotion, or simply loss of pay.[416]

A violation may occur even though the questioned action, if taken by the employer alone, would not be a violation of section 8(a)(3). If the action was induced by the union for wrongful reasons, a violation of sections 8(a)(3) and (b)(2) will be found.[417] Thus, where an employer may have been within its rights in discharging a particular employee, a violation nevertheless exists if the action was induced by the union for an improper reason. Under the rationale of *Radio Officers*, this result obtains because the other employees will perceive the union's exercise of will and power; accordingly, they may be encouraged to become more active members, or, perhaps, merely to become members. The Board will therefore presume that union activity is encouraged where a union causes a discharge.[418] Likewise, where the employer has in fact delegated to a union the authority to discharge or lay off employees, a wrongful exercise of that authority will result in section 8(b)(2) liability against the union and a section 8(a)(3) violation by the employer.[419]

To violate section 8(b)(2), it is not necessary that a union act with the precise motive of encouraging union membership. A union will be held responsible for the foreseeable consequences of its actions, and if the consequence is encouragement of union

---

[415]*Id.* at 564.

[416]*See, e.g.*, Steelworkers (DuVal Corp.), 226 NLRB 772, 94 LRRM 1239 (1976); Maui Surf Hotel, 235 NLRB 957, 98 LRRM 1001 (1978) *enforcement denied*, Teamsters Local 310 v. NLRB, 587 F2d 1176, 98 LRRM 3186 (CA DC, 1978) (Board majority found that union violated §8(b)(2) when it insisted that employer pressure employees to cease work and forfeit one hour's pay in order to attend union meeting held on employer's premises).

[417]Carpenters Local 2205 (Groves-Granite), 229 NLRB 56, 96 LRRM 1146 (1977).

[418]Operating Eng'rs Local 18 (Ohio Contractors Ass'n), 204 NLRB 681, 83 LRRM 1455 (1973), *enforcement denied*, 496 F2d 1308, 86 LRRM 2672 (CA 6, 1974). The Board applies the *Wright Line* analysis, see notes 53–75, *supra*, to the causation issues presented in these cases. *See* M.W. Kellogg Constructors, 273 NLRB 1049, 118 LRRM 1616 (1984), *enforcement denied and remanded*, 806 F2d 1435, 124 LRRM 2288 (CA 9, 1986).

[419]Fruin-Colnon Corp. v. NLRB, 227 NLRB 59, 94 LRRM 1186 (1976), *enforced*, 571 F2d 1017, 97 LRRM 2845 (CA 8, 1978).

membership or obedience of its members, a violation will be found.[420]

Of course, not all union encouragement is unlawful. A union that is effective may, by that very fact, lawfully encourage union activity or membership. As the Supreme Court has stated:

> [T]he union is a service agency that probably encourages membership whenever it does its job well. But . . . the only encouragement or discouragement of union membership banned by the Act is that which is "accomplished by discrimination."[421]

Unions are allowed a wide range of reasonableness in representing their membership as a whole.[422] Thus, when there is a legitimate business action that results in disparate treatment of employees, a section 8(b)(2) violation will not be found.[423]

When a union or its leadership causes or attempts to cause an employer to take action with respect to an employee for a reason that is arbitrary, invidious, or in bad faith, it breaches its duty of fair representation and section 8(b)(2) is violated.[424] This violation occurs, for example, where a layoff is required and a union leader seeks to protect the job of a relative or friend at the expense of some other member with greater seniority.[425] Similarly, in *U.S. Postal Service*,[426] a union steward's vigorous pursuit of a job for his daughter and failure to fairly represent a unit employee in his efforts to retain that same job were, taken together, held to be a violation of the Act. In *Teamsters Local 42 v. NLRB (J.W. Daly, Inc.)*,[427] the union breached its duty of fair representation by refusing to negotiate a dovetailed seniority list

---

[420]*See, e.g.*, NLRB v. St. Joe Paper Co., 319 F2d 819, 53 LRRM 2633 (CA 2, 1963).

[421]Teamsters Local 357 v. NLRB (Los Angeles-Seattle Motor Express), 365 US 667, 675-76, 47 LRRM 2906 (1961). *See* Chapter 27, "Union Security," at notes 254–258, and *infra* at note 500.

[422]*E.g.*, *see* Ford Motor Co. v. Huffman, 345 US 330, 31 LRRM 2548 (1953), discussed at notes 293–314 in Chapter 26, "The Duty of Fair Representation."

[423]Painters Dist. 2 (Paintsmiths, Inc.), 239 NLRB 1378, 100 LRRM 1152 (1979), *vacated and* remanded, 620 F2d 1326, 104 LRRM 2368 (CA 8, 1980) (court rejected Board's conclusion that union had legitimate reason for appointing job steward from outside employer's work force, thereby causing layoff of employee who was displaced by steward).

[424]Fruin-Colnon Corp. v. NLRB, *supra* note 419; Laborers Local 341 v. NLRB (Patrick J. Hurrell), *supra* note 411; Barton Brands, Ltd. v. NLRB, 529 F2d 793, 91 LRRM 2241 (CA 7), *enforcement denied*, 529 F2d 793, 91 LRRM 2241 (CA 7, 1976); Olympic S.S. Co., 233 NLRB 1178, 97 LRRM 1276 (1977); Teamsters Local 282 (Explo, Inc.), 229 NLRB 347, 95 LRRM 1202 (1977). For a detailed discussion of the duty of fair representation, see Chapter 26, "The Duty of Fair Representation."

[425]Teamsters Local 282 (Explo, Inc.), *supra* note 424; Fruin-Colnon Corp. v. NLRB, *supra* note 419 ("I can't lay my uncle off because he owes money to the bank and I am on his note").

[426]272 NLRB 93, 117 LRRM 1400 (1984).

[427]825 F2d 608, 126 LRRM 2046 (CA 1, 1987).

in a case involving the merger of two units into one facility. Likewise, classifications by union hiring halls based on race or sex have been held prohibited by section 8(b)(2).[428] The rationale of these cases is that a union, when it acts arbitrarily or invidiously, demonstrates that employees must curry its favor to avoid unfavorable treatment at the hand of the employer.

In 1962, in *Miranda Fuel Co.*,[429] the Board held that a breach of the union's duty to properly represent bargaining-unit employees amounted to a violation of sections 8(b)(2) and 8(b)(1)(A), thereby bringing the doctrine of fair representation under NLRB jurisdiction. Accordingly, section 8(b)(1)(A) prohibits a union "when acting in a statutory representative capacity, from taking action against any employee upon considerations or classifications which are irrelevant, invidious or unfair."[430] This obligation is based on the right afforded employees by section 7 "to bargain collectively through representatives of their own choosing" and on duties necessarily implied by the grant of exclusive representation provided to unions by section 9(a).

B. Violations Relating to Seniority Provisions

In addition to the problem posed by a union's attempt to have a disfavored employee divested of seniority, seniority provisions in collective bargaining agreements raise several other problems of discrimination. One type of problem arises when an employer either acquires or merges with another company and there is a reduction in the number of employees because of the consolidated operation. A union does not violate section 8(b)(2) if, prior to the effectuation of the merger, it concludes an agreement calling for the preservation of seniority of the represented employees, with the concomitant result that the unrepresented employees in the other company are placed at the bottom of the consolidated list. Since seniority is defined by contract, the unrepresented employees have no conflicting contractual rights. Moreover, when such an agreement is concluded prior to the consolidation, the union owes no duty to the other employees.[431]

---

[428]*See, e.g.*, Olympic S.S. Co., *supra* note 424.

[429]140 NLRB 181, 51 LRRM 1584 (1962), *enforcement denied*, 326 F2d 172, 54 LRRM 2715 (CA 2, 1963). *See* Chapter 26, "The Duty of Fair Representation," at notes 109–112.

[430]140 NLRB at 185.

[431]Schick v. NLRB, 409 F2d 395, 70 LRRM 3249 (CA 7, 1969); NLRB v. Whiting Milk Corp., 342 F2d 8, 58 LRRM 2471 (CA 1, 1965).

Although a union has a duty to represent fairly all bargaining-unit employees, the interests of some inevitably will have to give way to the interests of others; the Act permits unions a "wide range of reasonableness" in dealing with questions of seniority.[432] In making decisions affecting seniority, however, a union is held to a fair representation standard; thus it may not act arbitrarily, invidiously, or in bad faith. For example, in *Barton Brands, Ltd. v NLRB*,[433] the Seventh Circuit remanded a case to the Board for consideration of whether subordinating the seniority of one group of employees to another amounted to a violation. After a merger of two companies, the union had negotiated a "dovetailing" of the two seniority lists, that is, employees of both companies were to keep their seniority on a merged list. But months after the merger, when layoffs appeared imminent, the larger group of employees, spurred on by one person with internal union ambitions, pressed for a new agreement placing all employees in the other group at the bottom of the list, and the union replaced the "dovetailing" with an "endtailing"[434] agreement. The Board held that, since the union was motivated by the internal political ambitions of one person, section 8(b)(2) was violated.[435] The Seventh Circuit disagreed, holding that the conduct of that one individual was not attributable to the union. The court concluded, however, that the Board's finding of a violation could stand if the Board found that the decision to "endtail" the smaller group was made arbitrarily or to placate the wishes of the majority at the expense of the minority.

On remand, the Board found a violation on the ground that the union had merely sought to placate the desires of the majority.[436]

In *Teamsters Local 42 (J.W. Daly, Inc.)*,[437] two bargaining units of the same employer merged. The union that represented employees in both units violated section 8(b)(2) when, upon merger of the units, it failed to negotiate a "dovetailed" seniority

---

[432]Ford Motor Co. v. Huffman, *supra* note 422, at 338. *See* Chapter 26, "The Duty of Fair Representation," for a detailed treatment of the duty of fair representation.

[433]*Supra* note 424.

[434]"Dovetail," a verb in this usage, alludes to the familiar mortise-and-tenon joint of the cabinet shop. The derived "endtail" is a linguistic monstrosity, but has come into wide use.

[435]213 NLRB 640, 87 LRRM 1231 (1974), *enforcement denied*, 529 F2d 793, 91 LRRM 2241 (CA 7, 1976).

[436]Barton Brands, Ltd., 228 NLRB 889, 95 LRRM 1357 (1977).

[437]281 NLRB 974, 123 LRRM 1278 (1986), *enforced*, 825 F2d 608, 126 LRRM 2046 (CA 1, 1987).

list and instead negotiated a list on which employees of the more recently organized facility were "endtailed". The Board reasoned that the employees at the more recently organized facility were endtailed solely because the employees at the other facility had been union members longer and the union's action thus penalized the endtailed employees because they had exercised their section 7 right to refrain from union activity.[438]

In companion cases, *Teamsters Local 869 (Anheuser-Busch, Inc.)*[439] and *Teamsters Local 896 (Miller Brewing Co.)*,[440] the Board addressed the legality under sections 8(b)(1)(A) and (2) of a bumping-rights provision of a collective bargaining agreement that gave so-called permanent employees, bumped by other employers in the industry who were also signatory to contracts with the same union, a preferential seniority right to work over so-called temporary employees. The provision was developed in the context of multi-employer bargaining and its application continued even after the dissolution of the multi-employer unit. Initially, the Board noted that the provision was not unlawful on its face and that there had been no evidence presented that it actually resulted in any discrimination against an employee on the basis of nonunion status. The Board concluded that the preferential provision was arguably skill-based, designed to furnish the industry with a pool of experienced workers, and susceptible of a nondiscriminatory interpretation. Absent evidence of actual discrimination, the Board found the contract clause to be lawful.[441]

A second area of concern relating to seniority involves agreements calling for "superseniority" for employees who hold union office. In *Dairylea Cooperative*,[442] the Board held that while contractual provisions granting superseniority to union stewards with respect to layoff and recall were lawful, more expansive clauses granting superseniority to stewards for all purposes,

---

[438]*See also* Papcin v. Dichello Distribs., 697 FSupp 73 (D Conn), *aff'd*, 862 F2d 304 (CA 2, 1988) (union did not breach duty of fair representation when two units, each represented by separate local unions, were merged into one facility and employees of one unit were "endtailed" behind others).

[439]296 NLRB No. 132, 132 LRRM 1212 (1989).

[440]296 NLRB No. 133, 132 LRRM 1217 (1989).

[441]*But see* Mine Workers Dist. 23 (Peabody Coal Co.), 293 NLRB 77, 130 LRRM 1393 (1989) (union violated §8(b)(2) by maintaining and enforcing contract provision that did not credit employees with seniority, for recall purposes, with time worked for nonunion companies).

[442]219 NLRB 656, 89 LRRM 1737 (1975), *enforced sub nom.* NLRB v. Teamsters Local 338, 531 F2d 1162, 91 LRRM 2929 (CA 2, 1976).

including job-bidding preference, were a violation of section 8(b)(2).[443] Superseniority clauses are thus to be permitted only to the extent that they are necessary to the collective bargaining process.

Where superseniority for stewards is limited to layoffs, the Board has sustained the provision, finding a legitimate purpose in the retention of an official to process grievances. That purpose was held sufficient to outweigh the obvious tendency of such provisions to encourage union membership, that is, to encourage one to become an "active" union member in order to achieve a steward's position and its superseniority emoluments. Originally the Board limited its approval of superseniority only to stewards, and only with respect to layoffs and recall. Later, however, it approved the extension of superseniority for purposes of layoff and recall to union officials other than stewards.[444] Indeed, this occurred even where the written description of the officer's duties appeared to have little or no relationship to the collective bargaining process; the Board reasoned that it did not desire to "second guess" the union regarding which officers were actually necessary "in effectively representing the unit."[445]

In *Gulton Electro-Voice*,[446] the Board modified and again narrowed the standards under which it will allow a grant of superseniority to union officials in layoff and recall situations. In *Gulton*, the Board found that section 8(b)(2) had been violated by the union's application of a superseniority clause to certain union officials (the union's recording secretary and its financial secretary-treasurer) who were not involved in grievance process

---

[443] A seniority clause giving a union the right to veto the discharge of a union steward is presumptively illegal. Perma-Line Corp. v. Painters Local 230, 639 F2d 890, 106 LRRM 2483 (CA 2, 1981). However, an arbitrator's award upholding a contract provision giving a bonus to a union steward may be affirmed where the bonus is to offset losses the steward might incur by missing his hourly job duties to attend union activities. General Battery Int'l v. Union de Servicios, 678 FSupp. 33, 127 LRRM 2715 (D PR, 1988).

[444] Industrial Workers (AIW) Local 148 (Allen Group, Inc.), 236 NLRB 1368, 98 LRRM 1574 (1978); American Can Co., 235 NLRB 704, 98 LRRM 1012 (1978). Superseniority could also be given to employees who performed several functions that further the collective bargaining interests of the bargaining unit. Electrical Workers (UE) Local 623 (Limpco Mfg.), 230 NLRB 406, 95 LRRM 1343 (1977), *enforced sub nom.* D'Amico v. NLRB, 582 F2d 820, 99 LRRM 2350 (CA 3, 1978). "[C]redible proof that the individual in question was officially assigned duties which helped to implement the collective bargaining agreement in a meaningful way" is required. *Id.*, 582 F2d at 825.

[445] American Can Co., *supra* note 444, at 704–5. The Third Circuit would place the burden on the union to demonstrate the need for superseniority for a union official other than a steward. D'Amico v. NLRB, 582 F2d 820, 99 LRRM 2350 (CA 3, 1978).

[446] 266 NLRB 406, 112 LRRM 1361 (1983), *enforced sub nom.* Electrical Workers (IUE) Local 900 v. NLRB, 727 F2d 1184, 115 LRRM 2760 (CA DC, 1984).

ing or other on-the-job bargaining-agreement administration duties. Applying the *Gulton* rule, the Board and the courts have found section 8(b)(2) violations in cases where unions have maintained and enforced contract provisions that grant superseniority to union officials who are not involved in the administration of the collective bargaining agreement or grievance handling.[447]

Even though the rule in *Dairylea* makes superseniority clauses extending benefits beyond layoff and recall preference presumptively invalid, it does not purport to make them invalid per se. The legality of the parties' inclusion of such a clause in the contract depends upon the existence of an adequate justification at the time of execution.[448] Since the line of cases culminating in *Gulton*, however, the Board has taken a restrictive view of what may constitute adequate justification. In finding a section 8(b)(2) violation in *Complete Auto Transit*,[449] the Board rejected the assertion that greater access to employees by a steward justified the use of superseniority to deny a bid position to a more senior employee. Likewise, the maintenance and enforcement of a contract provision that protected a steward against any bumping was found to violate sections 8(b)(1) and (2) when such protection was not needed to keep the steward on the job in his area of representation.[450] Explicitly overruling a contrary decision,[451] the Board reasoned that a steward may be

---

[447] *See, e.g.*, United States Steel Corp., 288 NLRB 1074, 130 LRRM 1280 (1988) (recording secretary, financial secretary, and treasurer); Goodyear Tire & Rubber Co., 278 NLRB 650, 122 LRRM 1238 (1986) (treasurer, executive board members); NLRB v. Auto Workers Locals 1131 & 1161 (Houdaille Indus.), 777 F2d 1131, 121 LRRM 2080 (CA 6, 1985), *enforcing* 268 NLRB 1468, 115 LRRM 1248 and 271 NLRB 1411, 117 LRRM 1373 (1984) (financial secretary); NLRB v. Harvey Hubble, Inc., Ensign Elec. Div., 767 F2d 1100, 119 LRRM 3460 (CA 4, 1985), *cert. denied*, 479 US 984, 123 LRRM 3128 (1986), *enforcing* 268 NLRB 620, 115 LRRM 1090 (1984) (treasurer and recording secretary); Auto Workers Local 1384 v. NLRB (Ex-Cell-O Corp.), 756 F2d 482, 118 LRRM 2753 (CA 7, 1985), *enforcing* 267 NLRB 1303, 114 LRRM 1198 (1983) (recording secretary and financial secretary-treasurer); NLRB v. Niagara Mach. & Tool Works, 746 F2d 143, 117 LRRM 2689 (CA 2, 1984), *enforcing* 267 NLRB 661, 114 LRRM 1076 (1983) (executive board members); Cooper Indus., Wiss Div., 271 NLRB 810, 117 LRRM 1188 (1984) (executive board members); Ford Motor Co., 269 NLRB 250, 115 LRRM 1229 (1984) (financial secretary and treasurer); Inmont Corp., 268 NLRB 1442, 116 LRRM 1009 (1984) (union trustees and sergeant-at-arms); United States Steel Corp., 268 NLRB 1187, 115 LRRM 1275 (1984) (financial secretary-treasurer, recording secretary, guide, sergeant-at-arms, and trustees). *See also* NLRB v. Wayne Corp., Wayne Transp. Div., 776 F2d 745, 120 LRRM 3321 (CA 7, 1985), *enforcing* 270 NLRB 162, 116 LRRM 1049 (1984) (grant of superseniority to recording secretary unlawful even though officer occasionally handled grievances for absent steward).

[448] NLRB v. Auto Warehousers, 571 F2d 860, 98 LRRM 2238 (CA 5, 1978).

[449] 257 NLRB 630, 107 LRRM 1549 (1981).

[450] Mechanics Local 56 (Revere Copper Prods.), 287 NLRB 935, 127 LRRM 1163 (1987).

[451] Parker-Hannifin Corp., 231 NLRB 884, 96 LRRM 1130 (1977).

afforded superseniority to keep a job, but not necessarily his or her job, in the steward's area of representation.[452] On the other hand, the Board found no violation in a union's enforcement of a provision which allowed employees to leave the bargaining unit to take full-time union jobs and then return to their jobs with the same seniority they had been holding when they left.[453] The Board stressed the fact that union officials were not given any advantage over other employees because a former union official returned to his old job no better off than when he left. As a result, the Board concluded that the provision did not create any incentive to engage in union activity.

In contrast, the Board held unlawful a contractual provision that permitted employees who have been transferred or promoted to nonbargaining-unit positions to return to the unit with full seniority provided they obtained a withdrawal card from the union or maintained their membership in the union.[454] The Board determined that this seniority provision treated employees returning to the unit differently depending on their fulfillment of union obligations and, consequently, the provision encouraged employees to participate in union activities in which they otherwise would not be inclined or required to engage.[455] The disparate effect of the provision was not justified because the provision in no way furthered the effective administration of the collective bargaining agreement.[456] The Board distinguished *Radio & Television Broadcast Engineers Local 1212 (WPIX)*[457] on the ground that the union-leave provision in that case did not encourage union participation but simply removed a condition (the inability to accrue seniority) that would have discouraged employees from taking part in those activities.

The Board also has refused to permit the extension of superseniority of union officials for purposes other than layoff or recall, absent a showing of business necessity for such extension.

---

[452]Mechanics Local 56 (Revere Copper Prods.), *supra* note 450.

[453]Theatrical Stage Employees Local 695 (Twentieth Century Fox), 261 NLRB 590, 110 LRRM 1078 (1982). *See also* Radio & Television Broadcast Eng'rs Local 1212 (WPIX), 288 NLRB 374, 128 LRRM 1219 (1988), *review denied*, 870 F2d 858, 131 LRRM 2075 (CA 2, 1989).

[454]Manitowoc Eng'g Co., 291 NLRB 915, 130 LRRM 1072 (1988).

[455]*Id.*, 130 LRRM at 1075–76.

[456]*Id.* at 1076. The Board expressly overruled its decision in Brown & Williamson Tobacco Co., 227 NLRB 2005, 94 LRRM 1337 (1977), which held that such seniority provisions were lawful.

[457]*Supra* note 453.

In *Laborers Local 380 (Mantz & Oren)*,[458] the Board found presumptively unlawful a clause granting superseniority to union stewards for weekend and holiday work. Because the union failed to show a legitimate business purpose for the extension of superseniority to weekend and holiday work, the clause was held unlawful.

C. Violations Relating to Union-Security Provisions

Although the Board presumes that a union's attempt to cause an employer to discharge an employee is unlawful, this presumption may be rebutted by evidence demonstrating that the union's conduct was based on permissible considerations.[459] Under section 8(b)(2), a union may lawfully cause the discharge of an employee working under a union- or agency-shop agreement pursuant to the union-shop proviso to section 8(a)(3) for failing, in the language of the Act, "to tender the periodic dues and the initiation fees uniformly required as a condition of acquiring or retaining membership."[460]

In *NLRB v. General Motors*[461] the Supreme Court held that the term "membership" as used in the proviso to section 8(a)(3) embodies only a financial obligation limited to the payment of fees and dues. Thus, a union violates section 8(b)(2) of the Act if it causes the discharge of former members for failing to rescind their resignation because section 8(a)(3) does not permit a union to compel active membership.[462] Similarly, a union violates sec-

---

[458]275 NLRB 1049, 120 LRRM 1023 (1985). *See also* Gulton Electro-Voice, 266 NLRB 406, 112 LRRM 1361 (1983), *enforced sub nom.* Electrical Workers (IUE) Local 900 v. NLRB, 727 F2d 1184, 115 LRRM 2760 (CA DC, 1984) (job-specific protection against bumping not warranted); Cronin v. Oscar Mayer Corp., 633 FSupp 159 (ED Pa, 1986) (superseniority not applicable in permanent force reduction).

[459]Teamsters Local 170 (Consolidated Beverages), 282 NLRB 812, 125 LRRM 1007 (1987); Glaziers Local 558 (PPG Indus.), 271 NLRB 583, 116 LRRM 1489 (1984), *enforcement denied*, 787 F2d 1406, 122 LRRM 2008 (CA 10, 1986).

[460]For a detailed consideration of the requirements for and applications of lawful union-security arrangements, *see generally* Chapter 27, "Union Security." *See also* Beck v. Communications Workers, 487 US 735, 128 LRRM 2729 (1988); Electrical Workers (IUE) Local 441 (Phelps Dodge Indus., Phelps Dodge Copper Prods. Co. Div.), 281 NLRB 1008, 123 LRRM 1204 (1986); Pattern Makers League v. NLRB (Rockford-Beloit Pattern Jobbers), 473 US 95, 119 LRRM 2928, 2933 n.16 (1985); Machinists Local Lodge 1414 (Neufeld Porsche-Audi), 270 NLRB 1330, 1333 n.15, 116 LRRM 1257, 1260 n.15 (1984).

[461]373 US 734, 53 LRRM 2313 (1963).

[462]Hershey Foods Corp., 207 NLRB 897, 85 LRRM 1004 (1973), *enforced*, 513 F2d 1083, 89 LRRM 2126 (CA 9, 1975). *Accord* Service Employees Local 680 (Leland Stanford, Jr. Univ.), 232 NLRB 326, 97 LRRM 1186 (1977), *enforced*, 601 F2d 980, 101 LRRM 2212 (CA 9, 1979); Communications Workers Locals 1101 & 1104 (New York Tel. Co.), 211 NLRB 114, 87 LRRM 1253 (1974), *enforced*, 520 F2d 411, 89 LRRM 3028 (CA 2, 1975), *cert. denied*, 423 US 1051, 91 LRRM 2099 (1976).

tion 8(b)(2) by seeking the discharge of employees who resign from the union but continue to pay dues.[463]

Under the union-shop proviso to section 8(a)(3) of the Act, a union-security clause must give employees at least 30 days to become union members. Thus, the maintenance of a union-security clause in a collective bargaining agreement that does not provide the statutory 30-day period violates section 8(b)(2).[464] Likewise, it is unlawful to seek the discharge of employees for failure to pay initiation fees or periodic dues during the statutory grace period.[465]

For union-security purposes, the Board regards supervisors returning to the bargaining unit as "new" employees when the return is to be permanent.[466] However, the line between "supervisor" and "employee" sometimes is not drawn clearly because individuals shuttle back and forth between supervisory and bargaining-unit functions. In such instances, the proper test of status is "whether there is a reasonable expectancy that when an individual becomes a supervisor he may soon return to the unit."[467]

The union-shop proviso of section 8(a)(3) permits an employer and labor organization to negotiate a union-security provision if the organization is the representative of the employees as provided in section 9(a). Thus, a union violates section 8(b)(2) by entering a union-security agreement applicable to a unit of employees in which it does not enjoy majority support.[468] Similarly, the Board has found that a union violated section 8(b)(2) by seeking to apply a union-security clause to employees who had been included in a unit inappropriately.[469]

---

[463]Food & Commercial Workers Local 506 (Alpha Beta Co.), 265 NLRB 1290, 112 LRRM 1127 (1982), *enforced without opinion*, 720 F2d 215, 114 LRRM 3391 (CA DC, 1983).

[464]*See* Typographical Union No. 16 (Chicago) (Klaus Beyer & Continental Composition), 268 NLRB 347, 115 LRRM 1013 (1983).

[465]Teamsters Local 439 (Leandro), 281 NLRB 255, 124 LRRM 1143 (1986), *aff'd without opinion*, 838 F2d 1217 (CA 9, 1988); Machinists Local Lodge 1198, Dist. Lodge 99 (Interstate Food Processing Corp.), 278 NLRB 154, 122 LRRM 1284 (1986).

[466]Electrical Workers (IBEW) Local 329 (Illinois Bell Tel. Co.), 200 NLRB 1050, 82 LRRM 1077 (1972), *enforced*, 499 F2d 56, 86 LRRM 2826 (CA 7), *cert. denied*, 419 US 896, 87 LRRM 2453 (1974).

[467]A.O. Smith Corp., 227 NLRB 854, 857, 94 LRRM 1115 (1977) (where individual accrued dues obligation for short periods spent working in unit between supervisory assignments, Board found neither employer nor union violated Act by denying supervisor right to return to unit because of his expulsion for nonpayment of dues for such periods).

[468]R. Waldo, Inc., 280 NLRB 1237, 124 LRRM 1046 (1986).

[469]St. Luke's Hosp. Center, 221 NLRB 1314, 91 LRRM 1150, *enforced*, 551 F2d 476, 94 LRRM 2083 (CA 2, 1976).

However, the Board has concluded that a union representing one unit does not violate section 8(b)(2) by seeking an arbitrator's determination that its collective bargaining agreement containing a union-security clause should be applied to a separate and distinct unit.[470]

Because section 8(b)(2) permits a union to seek an employer's discipline or discharge of employees only if the employees fail to satisfy their financial obligations to the union, the Board has reasoned that a union may neither selectively invoke dues delinquency in order to procure the discharge of dissidents while overlooking equivalent delinquency by supporters,[471] nor seek payment for a longstanding dues delinquency and ask for the employee's discharge only after the employee has made statements criticizing the union.[472] Likewise, the Board has held a union may not suspend or expel an employee from membership for nonfinancial reasons and then seek the discharge of that employee,[473] or seek the discharge of an employee after refusing tendered[474] dues.

For a union to make a lawful discharge request for dues delinquency, a valid union-security agreement must be in effect at the time of the union's request.[475] Thus, the Board has found a violation when a union requested an employee's discharge after its authority to maintain a union-security clause had been revoked in a deauthorization election, even though the employee's dues obligation arose while the agreement was in effect.[476]

In many cases, the legality of a labor organization's action depends upon the propriety of the claim for dues and fees. The Board has held that the obligation to pay dues under a union-

---

[470]Hotel Employees Local 274 (Hospitality Catering ta Warwick Caterers), 282 NLRB 939, 124 LRRM 1250 (1987), *supplementing* 269 NLRB 482, 115 LRRM 1249 (1984).

[471]Jersey Shore Medical Center-Fitkin Hosp. (Jersey Nurses Economic Sec. Org.), 225 NLRB 1191, 93 LRRM 1133 (1976); Retail, Wholesale & Dep't Store Employees Dist. 1199 (Upper Manhattan Medical Group), 225 NLRB 153, 92 LRRM 1585 (1976), *enforced*, 559 F2d 1204, 96 LRRM 2661 (CA 2, 1977).

[472]Pueblo Int'l, 229 NLRB 770, 95 LRRM 1203 (1977).

[473]Dillingham Tug & Barge Co., 278 NLRB 83, 121 LRRM 1183 (1986).

[474]Upholsterers Local 406 (Boyertown Casket Co.), 280 NLRB 1227, 123 LRRM 1277 (1986).

[475]Hotel Employees Local 19 (Le Baron Hotel), 281 NLRB 524, 124 LRRM 1110 (1986); Graphic Communications Dist. Council No. 2 (Data Documents), 278 NLRB 365, 122 LRRM 1029 (1986); Chestnut Hill Bus Corp., 270 NLRB 212, 117 LRRM 1081 (1984).

[476]Machinists Dist. 15 (Burroughs Corp.), 231 NLRB 602, 96 LRRM 1625 (1977). However, the mere *filing* of a deauthorization petition will not relieve employees of their obligations under an existing union shop agreement. *See* King Elec. Mfg., 229 NLRB 615, 96 LRRM 1370 (1977).

security clause accrues from the date of the execution of the collective bargaining agreement and not from the date to which the agreement was made retroactive.[477] Similarly, discharge for dues delinquency is unlawful where the delinquency is charged for a time period during which the employee was working outside the bargaining unit[478] or was unemployed.[479] However, the Board has ruled it is not a violation for a union to cause the discharge of an employee whose tender of back dues was rejected because, following his suspension from membership, he improperly failed to pay a reinstatement fee properly required under the union's bylaws.[480]

In right-to-work states, a union violates section 8(b)(2) by causing an employer to continue to deduct union dues from the wages of employees who resigned from the union, even when the workers failed to comply with the revocation provisions of dues-checkoff authorizations, where the authorizations made payment of dues a quid pro quo for union membership.[481]

The Board has determined that some initiation fees are unlawfully "excessive"[482] under section 8(b)(5).[483] Thus, seeking an employee's discharge for failure to pay an excessive initiation fee violates sections 8(b)(1)(A) and 8(b)(2).[484]

---

[477]Chestnut Hill Bus Corp., *supra* note 475; Typographical Union No. 53 (Cleveland) (Plain Dealer Publishing Co.), 225 NLRB 1281, 93 LRRM 1151 (1976); Teamsters Local 25 (Tech Weld Corp.), 220 NLRB 76, 90 LRRM 1193 (1975); Namm's, Inc., 102 NLRB 466, 31 LRRM 1328 (1953). *See also* Transit Union Locals 1225 & 1222 (Greyhound Lines), 285 NLRB 1051, 129 LRRM 1077 (1987). In some cases the wording of the dues-checkoff card may be dispositive. *See* Carpenters (Campbell Indus.), 243 NLRB 147, 101 LRRM 1394 (1979); Frito-Lay, Inc., 243 NLRB 137, 101 LRRM 1390 (1979).

[478]Hotel Employees Local 19 (Southbay Partnership dba Sunnyvale Hilton), 275 NLRB 461, 119 LRRM 1158 (1985); Hotel Local 2 (Zim's Restaurants), 240 NLRB 757, 100 LRRM 1324 (1979).

[479]Painters Local 277 (Del. E. Webb N.J.), 278 NLRB 169, 121 LRRM 1144 (1986).

[480]John J. Roche & Co., 231 NLRB 1082, 96 LRRM 1281 (1977), *enforced sub nom.* Larkins v. NLRB, 596 F2d 240, 101 LRRM 2018 (CA 7, 1979).

[481]*See, e.g.*, Food & Commercial Workers Local 425 (Hudson Foods), 282 NLRB 1413, 124 LRRM 1220 (1987); Machinists Local 2045, Dist. 102 (Eagle Signal Indus. Controls), 268 NLRB 635, 115 LRRM 1092 (1984).

[482]Under §8(b)(5), it is unlawful for a labor organization "to require of employees covered by an agreement authorized under subsection (a)(3) . . . the payment, as a condition precedent to becoming a member of such organization, of a fee in an amount which the Board finds excessive or discriminatory under all the circumstances." For discussion of checkoff authorization, *see* Chapter 27 *infra.*

[483]*See, e.g.*, Theatrical Stage Employees Local 841 (National Broadcasting Co), 225 NLRB 994, 94 LRRM 1072 (1976); Television & Radio Broadcasting Studio Employees Local 804 (Triangle Publications), 135 NLRB 632, 49 LRRM 1541 (1962), *enforced*, 315 F2d 398, 52 LRRM 2774 (CA 3, 1963) (Board compared challenged initiation fee with initiation fees prevailing for sister locals in same industry and rejected union's contention that increase was designed to improve union's financial condition.

[484]Theatrical Stage Employees Local 150 (Dynasty Theater dba Garfield Theater), 274 NLRB 30, 118 LRRM 1322 (1985).

Because union security under section 8(a)(3) is limited to payment of fees and dues, the Board has ruled that a union violated section 8(b)(2) when it caused the discharge of an employee for failing or refusing to pay: (1) union fines;[485] (2) improperly imposed "reinstatement fees;"[486] (3) building assessment fees;[487] or (4) loan funds borrowed from the union.[488] The Board has also held that a member's failure to pay previously levied fines or assessments did not justify refusal of tendered dues, and the union's attempt to have the employee denied employment or discharged was accordingly, unlawful.[489]

A union's enforcement of a union- or agency-shop agreement where an employee fails to tender the regular initiation fee or periodic dues is lawful only so long as the union complies with its fiduciary duty of "informing the member of the amount owed, the method used to compute that amount, when such payments are to be made, and that discharge will result from failure to pay."[490] While the Board has not set any particular time limitations on when a union must act to enforce a union-security provision, the failure to give members "reasonable" notice of delinquency and adequate opportunity to make a payment can result in a violation.[491] For example, the Board has found that unions failed to meet their fiduciary obligations by: (1) sending

---

[485]Laborers Local 721 (Scaldini, Inc.), 246 NLRB 691, 102 LRRM 1656 (1979), *enforced*, 649 F2d 33, 107 LRRM 2406 (CA 1, 1981); Pittsburgh Press Co., 241 NLRB 666, 100 LRRM 1542 (1979).

[486]Auto Workers Local 1756 (American Hoechst Corp.), 240 NLRB 281, 100 LRRM 1208 (1979). However, failure of a member to pay a *valid* reinstatement fee entitles the union to cause his discharge.

[487]Teamsters Local 439 (Leandro), 281 NLRB 255, 124 LRRM 1143 (1986), *aff'd without opinion*, 838 F2d 1217 (CA 9, 1988).

[488]Plumbers & Pipe Fitters Local 460 (Graham), 287 NLRB 788, 127 LRRM 1290 (1987). As part of the remedy in this case, the Board required the union to expunge from its constitution a provision stating that all assessments and loans were payable before membership dues.

[489]Painters Local 1627 (Johnson's Plastering Co.), 233 NLRB 820, 97 LRRM 1010 (1977); Longshoremen (ILWU) Local 13 (Pacific Maritime Ass'n), 228 NLRB 1383, 96 LRRM 1450 (1977), *enforced*, 581 F2d 1321, 99 LRRM 2435 (CA 9, 1978), *cert. denied*, 440 US 935, 100 LRRM 2687 (1979).

[490]Distillery Workers Local 38 (Schenley Distillers), 242 NLRB 370, 101 LRRM 1150, 1151 (1979), *enforced*, 642 F2d 185, 107 LRRM 2178 (CA 6), *cert. denied*, 452 US 941, 107 LRRM 2632 (1981). For a detailed discussion of a union's duties in enforcing such requirements, see Chapter 27, "Union Security," Section II-B *infra*. *See also* Helmsley-Spear, Inc., 275 NLRB 262, 119 LRRM 1121 (1985); Teamsters Local 13 (Mobile Pre-Mix Concrete), 268 NLRB 930, 115 LRRM 1137 (1984); R.H. Macy & Co., 266 NLRB 858, 113 LRRM 1049 (1983); Western Publishing Co., 263 NLRB 1110, 111 LRRM 1537 (1982).

[491]*See* Teamsters Local 122 (Busch & Co.), 203 NLRB 1041, 83 LRRM 1235 (1973), *enforced*, 502 F2d 1160, 87 LRRM 3274 (CA 1, 1974). *See also* Valley Cabinet & Mfg., 253 NLRB 98, 105 LRRM 1467 (1980); Food & Commercial Workers Local 1445 (Gallahue's Supermarkets), 247 NLRB 1031, 103 LRRM 1267 (1980), *enforced*, 647 F2d 214, 107 LRRM 2178 (CA 1, 1981); Teamsters Local 572 (Ralph's Grocery), 247 NLRB 934, 103 LRRM 1268 (1980).

conflicting notices as to the amounts owed and failing to specify the precise amount of the reinstatement fee and obligations to perfect membership;[492] (2) holding employees delinquent prematurely after informing the employees that they could wait until the "next" payday after their return to work following sick leave;[493] and (3) seeking to enforce a union-security clause because of a dues delinquency after employees tendered their dues in cash rather than by check, money order, or checkoff authorization as demanded by the union.[494] Moreover, where it has been established that the union failed to give the requisite notice, the Board has not required the establishment of "a causal connection" between that failure and the employee's nonpayment.[495] Likewise, members' inquiries as to their dues obligations do not lessen the union's obligation to provide the members with the necessary information and opportunity to pay.[496] However, the Board has not construed and applied these obligations so rigidly that employees who fail to satisfy their membership obligations due to their own recalcitrance may rely on alleged notice deficiencies.[497]

Finally, the "periodic dues and . . . initiation fees" referred to by section 8(b)(2) must be "uniformly required." Thus, a union operating under an agency-shop agreement violated section 8(b)(2) when it caused the discharge of a nonmember employee who was late in paying service fees since the union's constitution discriminated by affording members a 90-day grace period for dues payments, but permitted nonmembers only 10 days.[498]

D. Violations Relating to Hiring and Referral Halls

Hiring-hall arrangements are another common source of unlawful discrimination under sections 8(a)(3) and 8(b)(2).[499]

---

[492]Helmsley-Spear, Inc., *supra* note 490.

[493]Macaulay Foundry Co., 223 NLRB 815, 92 LRRM 1279 (1976), *enforced*, 553 F2d 1198, 95 LRRM 2581 (CA 9, 1977). *See also* Sheet Metal Workers Local 355 (Zinsco Elec. Prods.), 254 NLRB 773, 106 LRRM 1137 (1981), *enforced in part and remanded*, 716 F2d 1249, 114 LRRM 2569 (CA 9, 1983) (union violated §8(b)(2) by causing discharge of employee who remitted delinquent dues in accord with extension of time granted by union); Telephone Workers (Bell of Pa.), 226 NLRB 427, 93 LRRM 1289 (1976); Simmons Co., 150 NLRB 709, 58 LRRM 1148 (1964).

[494]AMF, Inc., 247 NLRB 231, 103 LRRM 1122 (1980).

[495]Teamsters Local 150 (Delta Lines), 242 NLRB 454, 101 LRRM 1175 (1979).

[496]Teamsters Local 572 (Ralph's Grocery), *supra* note 491.

[497]I.B.I. Sec., 292 NLRB 648, 130 LRRM 1185 (1989).

[498]Hospital & Nursing Home Employees Local 113 (Mounds Park Hosp.), 228 NLRB 1500, 96 LRRM 1422, *enforced*, 567 F2d 831, 97 LRRM 2160 (CA 8, 1977).

[499]For a detailed discussion of hiring halls, see generally Chapter 27, "Union Security."

Teamsters Local 357 v. NLRB (Los Angeles-Seattle Motor Express)[500] is the leading case in which a hiring-hall agreement was drawn into question under these provisions. A trucking association entered into an agreement with the union under which casual employees were dispatched from hiring halls on the basis of seniority in the trucking industry. Seniority began with a minimum of three months' service, "irrespective of whether such employee is or is not a member of the Union."[501] The union procured the discharge of a union member because he had obtained employment without being dispatched by the union. Reversing the Board[502] and the Court of Appeals for the District of Columbia Circuit,[503] which had held that the hiring-hall agreement in question was unlawful and that the member's discharge was in violation of sections 8(a)(3) and 8(b)(2), the Supreme Court held that discrimination could not be inferred from the face of the agreement, for it had specifically prohibited discrimination against casual employees because of union membership or nonmembership.[504]

While a hiring-hall agreement may be nondiscriminatory on its face, its administration may be otherwise.[505] Thus a union may not refuse to refer an employee as a means of imposing union discipline except where necessary to preserve legitimate, objective hiring-hall procedures. For example, refusal to dispatch "travelers" of a sister local,[506] or refusal to refer members

---

[500]365 US 667, 47 LRRM 2906 (1961). *See* Chapter 27, "Union Security," at note 253.

[501]365 US at 668.

[502]121 NLRB 1629, 43 LRRM 1029 (1958).

[503]275 F2d 646, 45 LRRM 2752 (CA DC, 1960).

[504]*See* Chapter 27, "Union Security," at notes 254–257.

[505]*E.g.*, NLRB v. Electrical Workers (IBEW) Local 269 (National Elec. Contractors Ass'n), 357 F2d 51, 61 LRRM 2371 (CA 3, 1966); Cargo Handlers, 159 NLRB 321, 62 LRRM 1228 (1966); NLRB v. Houston Maritime Ass'n, 337 F2d 333, 57 LRRM 2170 (CA 5, 1964); NLRB v. Southern Stevedoring & Contracting Co., 332 F2d 1017, 56 LRRM 2507 (CA 5, 1964).

[506]*See* Plumbers & Pipe Fitters Local 669 v. NLRB (Best-Fire Protection Sys.), 778 F2d 8, 120 LRRM 3541 (CA DC, 1985); Plumbers & Pipe Fitters Local 198 v. NLRB (Jacobs/Weise), 747 F2d 326, 117 LRRM 3151 (CA 5, 1984); Iron Workers Local 111 (Northern States Steel Builders), 274 NLRB 742, 118 LRRM 1484 (1985), *modified*, 792 F2d 241, 122 LRRM 2611 (CA DC, 1986); Fischbach/Lord Elec. Co., 270 NLRB 856, 116 LRRM 1229 (1984); Electrical Workers (IBEW) Local 11 (National Elec. Contractors Ass'n, Los Angeles County Chapter), 270 NLRB 424, 116 LRRM 1141 (1984), *enforced*, 772 F2d 571, 120 LRRM 2647 (CA 9, 1985); Operating Eng'rs Local 181 (Raymond Constr.), 269 NLRB 611, 116 LRRM 1159 (1984) (union did not violate Act by refusing to refer members of sister local). *But cf.* Electrical Workers (IBEW) Local 1547 (National Elec. Contractors Ass'n), 280 NLRB 832, 122 LRRM 1329 (1986) (union acted lawfully, despite claim it discouraged travelers from using referral system and condoned threats against them).

because of their criticism of[507] or opposition to[508] union leadership violates sections 8(b)(1)(A) and 8(b)(2) of the Act. In addition, the Board has found violations of section 8(b)(2) in circumstances where a union: refused to refer a member who held a withdrawal card;[509] refused to consider nonmembers for referral while members were unemployed;[510] afforded preferential treatment to union members in assigning job referrals out of chronological order without explanation;[511] refused to refer members for employment due to their intraunion political activites;[512] refused to refer an individual due to personal animosity between the individual and the business agent;[513] refused to register travelers on its out-of-work book;[514] attempted to cause an employer to discharge employees if they failed to pay union initiation fees and dues;[515] and refused to refer nonmember applicants,[516] union applicants who were not

[507]Carpenters Local 720 (Stone & Webster Eng'g Corp.), 274 NLRB 1506, 118 LRRM 1594 (1985), *enforcement denied*, 798 F2d 781, 123 LRRM 2299 (CA 5, 1986); Operating Eng'rs Local 139 (Associated Gen. Contractors of Am., Wisc. Chapter), 273 NLRB 992, 118 LRRM 1396 (1984), *enforcement granted in part and denied in part*, 796 F2d 985, 123 LRRM 2021 (CA 7, 1986); Iron Workers Local 798 (Associated Gen. Contractors, Mobile Chapter), 272 NLRB 679, 117 LRRM 1337 (1984); Painters Local 277 (Polis Wallcovering Co.), 271 NLRB 58, 116 LRRM 1313 (1984), *enforced*, 760 F2d 258, 118 LRRM 3464 (CA 3, 1985); Laborers Local 383 (Associated Gen. Contractors, Ariz. Bldg. Chapter), 266 NLRB 934, 113 LRRM 1070 (1983).

[508]Carpenters Local 720 (Millwright) (National Maintenance Corp.), 283 NLRB 617, 125 LRRM 1016 (1987); Iron Workers Local 92 (Glenn Mach. Works), 277 NLRB 658, 121 LRRM 1120 (1985). *See also* Toledo World Terminals, 289 NLRB 670, 130 LRRM 1503 (1988).

[509]Teamsters Local 272 (various employers), 280 NLRB 1256, 123 LRRM 1326 (1986).

[510]Laborers Local 644 (Kellerman Bros. Constr. Co.), 278 NLRB 1104, 122 LRRM 1238 (1986), *enforced*, 810 F2d 665, 124 LRRM 2501 (CA 7, 1987).

[511]Iron Workers Local 483 (Building Contractors Ass'n of N.J.), 285 NLRB 123, 129 LRRM 1285 (1987), *enforced in part sub nom.* NLRB v. Iron Workers Local 11, 864 F2d 1113, 130 LRRM 2337 (CA 3, 1989); Electrical Workers (IBEW) Local 211 (National Elec. Contractors Ass'n), 280 NLRB 85, 123 LRRM 1080 (1986), *enforced*, 821 F2d 206, 125 LRRM 2827 (CA 3, 1987).

[512]Carpenters Local 316 (Bay Counties Gen. Contractors Ass'n), 291 NLRB 504, 131 LRRM 1269 (1988); Heavy & Highway Constr. Workers Local 158 (Contractors' Ass'n of E. Pa. & Worthy Bros. Pipeline Corp.), 280 NLRB 1100, 123 LRRM 1042 (1986); NLRB v. Teamsters (Leonard B. Hebert, Jr. & Co.), 778 F2d 207, 121 LRRM 2037 (CA 5, 1985).

[513]NLRB v. Teamsters (Leonard B. Hebert, Jr. & Co.), *supra* note 512.

[514]Plumbers & Pipe Fitters Local 305 (Stone & Webster Eng'g Corp.), *supra* note 507.

[515]Hotel Employees Local 50 (Hafed dba Dick's Restaurant), 287 NLRB 1180, 130 LRRM 1152 (1988).

[516]Wolf Trap Found. for the Performing Arts, 287 NLRB 1040, 127 LRRM 1129 (1988) (sex and nonunion status); NLRB v. Electrical Workers (IBEW) Local 322 (Bechtel Power Corp.), 597 F2d 1326, 101 LRRM 2157 (CA 10, 1979), *enforcing* 223 NLRB 925, 92 LRRM 1220 (1976); Carpenters Local 1089 (E. F. Hargett & Co.), 233 NLRB 275, 96 LRRM 1508 (1977); Operating Eng'rs Local 18 (S. J. Groves & Sons Co.), 227 NLRB 1477, 94 LRRM 1336 (1977); Elevator Constructors Local 16 (Westinghouse Elevator Co.), 229 NLRB 439, 95 LRRM 1191 (1977); Plumbers & Pipe Fitters Local 630, 222 NLRB 524, 91 LRRM 1224 (1976); Carpenters Dist. Council (Denver) (Hensel Phelps Constr. Co.), 222 NLRB 551, 91 LRRM 1178 (1976). *See also* Abraham & Straus, 287 NLRB 951, 130 LRRM 1160 (1989).

members of the union that operated the hiring hall,[517] or applicants who were not employed in a union shop.[518]

Generally, it is unlawful for a union to require that preference in employment be given to employees whose names appear on an "experience" roster, when the qualifying experience necessary for placement on the roster is limited to experience obtained with employers having collective bargaining agreements with the union.[519]

Construction industry unions, however, may lawfully maintain and enforce hiring-hall provisions that give priority in job referrals based on applicants' length of service with employers who are subject to collective bargaining agreements with the union. In *Interstate Electric Co.*,[520] a Board majority rejected the contention that such a provision is implicitly discriminatory because it results in rewarding applicants who are union members and in penalizing applicants with greater experience solely because the latter have worked for nonunion employers or nonsignatory employers to the union's contract. The Board relied on section 8(f)(4), which sanctions an exclusive referral system under which priority in job referral may be "based upon length of service with such employer."[521] The term "such employer" was held to include any employer who had agreed to be bound by the union's contract with a multi-employer association, not just member-employers of the association.[522]

The Ninth Circuit has upheld the Board in finding that a union operating an exclusive hiring hall violated the Act by requiring applicants for Class B hiring-hall status to have Class A workers as sponsors, for all but an insignificant number

---

[517]Sachs Elec. Co., 248 NLRB 669, 104 LRRM 1070 (1980), *enforced in part*, 668 F2d 991, 109 LRRM 2524 (CA 8, 1982).

[518]Typographical Union No. 6 (New York) (Royal Composing Room), 242 NLRB 378, 101 LRRM 1148 (1979), *enforcement denied in pertinent part*, 632 F2d 171, 105 LRRM 2529 (CA 2, 1980).

[519]Typographical Union No. 6 (New York) (Royal Composing Room), *supra* note 518; Theatrical Stage Employees Local 659 (MPO-TV), 197 NLRB 1187, 81 LRRM 1223 (1972), *enforced*, 477 F2d 450, 83 LRRM 2527 (CA DC, 1973), *cert. denied*, 414 US 1157, 85 LRRM 2227 (1974); Directors Guild (Association of Motion Picture Producers), 198 NLRB 707, 81 LRRM 1477 (1972), *enforced*, 494 F2d 692, 85 LRRM 2800 (CA 9, 1974).

[520]227 NLRB 1996, 94 LRRM 1225 (1977).

[521]*See* Chapter 27, "Union Security," at notes 261–281, and Chapter 13, "The Duty to Bargain," at notes 834–850.

[522]*See* Electrical Workers (IBEW) Local 68 (Howard Elec. Co.), 227 NLRB 1904, 94 LRRM 1229 (1977) (overruling National Elec. Contractors Ass'n (Nassau-Suffolk Chapter), 215 NLRB 894, 88 LRRM 1226 (1974), to the extent of any inconsistency with *Interstate Elec. Co.*, *supra* note 520).

of Class A workers were union members.[523] The Board has also held that it is unlawful for a union operating an exclusive job-referral system to refuse to permit nonmember applicants to take the journeymen's examination, thereby limiting their opportunities for job referral.[524] And a union may not require hiring-hall applicants to pay union initiation fees prior to referring them for employment.[525]

The Board has refused to extend its holding in *Dairylea Cooperative*[526] to hiring-hall cases. Thus, in *Pattern Makers (Michigan Pattern Manufacturers Ass'n)*,[527] the Board found unlawful a union practice that placed union executive committee members and former union officers at the top of an out-of-work list used in making referrals to new jobs. The Board distinguished its *Limpco Manufacturing*[528] decision, where it had upheld the applicability of superseniority clauses to union officers for job-retention purposes, from *Pattern Makers*, where the benefit was actual preference for initial hiring, which in turn encompassed eligibility for all contract benefits. The Board also noted that the practice did not appear to bear any direct relation to furthering the effective administration of the contract on the job.

In *Teamsters Local 959 (Ocean Technology)*,[529] however, the Board held that a union that operated an exclusive hiring hall did not violate the Act when it insisted on dispatching its designees as union stewards in preference to other eligible employees. *Pattern Makers* was distinguished on the ground that the hiring preference there had been granted to persons who performed no steward functions at the plant. The Board also distinguished

---

[523]NLRB v. Longshoremen (ILWU) Local 13 (Pacific Maritime Ass'n), 549 F2d 1346, 95 LRRM 2215 (CA 9, 1977), *enforcing* 210 NLRB 952, 86 LRRM 1716 (1974), *cert. denied*, 434 US 922, 96 LRRM 2747 (1977). *But see* NLRB v. Typographical Union No. 6 (New York) (Royal Composing Room), *supra* note 518.

[524]Electrical Workers (IBEW) Local 367 (Billcheck), 230 NLRB 86, 96 LRRM 1182 (1977), *enforced*, 578 F2d 1375, 99 LRRM 2633 (CA 3, 1978), *cert. denied*, 439 US 1070, 100 LRRM 226 (1979).

[525]Oil Workers Local 1-128 (Noble Constr. & Maintenance Co.), 232 NLRB 271, 96 LRRM 1394 (1977).

[526]219 NLRB 656, 89 LRRM 1737 (1975), *enforced sub nom.* NLRB v. Teamsters Local 338, 531 F2d 1162, 91 LRRM 2929 (CA 2, 1976). *See also* discussion at notes 442–458 *supra*.

[527]233 NLRB 430, 96 LRRM 1544 (1977).

[528]Electrical Workers (UE) Local 623 (Limpco Mfg.), 230 NLRB 406, 95 LRRM 1443 (1977), *enforced sub nom.* D'Amico v. NLRB, 582 F2d 820, 99 LRRM 2350 (CA 3, 1978). *See also* Pattern Makers v. NLRB (Michigan Pattern Mfrs. Ass'n), 622 F2d 267, 104 LRRM 2713 (CA 6, 1980).

[529]239 NLRB 1387, 100 LRRM 1160 (1979). *Accord* Carpenters Local 1243 (Arctic Slope, Alaska Gen. Constr. Co.), 240 NLRB 1118, 100 LRRM 1384 (1979).

Dairylea (on which the ALJ had relied), asserting that *Dairylea* does not erect a presumption against steward-preference clauses in hiring-hall agreements.

Violations of section 8(b)(2) also have been found where the union, for irrelevant and invidious reasons, refuses to refer an employee because other employees do not want to work with that individual.[530] Moreover, operation of an exclusive hiring hall without objective criteria and consistency and in disregard of written rules is also violative of section 8(b)(2) of the Act.[531] The Court of Appeals for the District of Columbia Circuit so ruled, affirming the Board's finding of disparate and arbitrary treatment of applicants by a union official and awarding backpay to three applicants who were so treated.[532]

Mere negligence or sloppiness in administration of the hiring hall is not violative of the Act.[533] The Sixth Circuit, denying enforcement of a Board order, held that there was no section 8(b)(2) violation where the union business manager disregarded an existing out-of-work list and made referrals in the order in which members' registration forms were submitted to the union. The court held that the collective bargaining agreement did not clearly and unambiguously require adherence to the list and that the business manager could reasonably have believed that this system was consistent with the contract. The court also held that there was no evidence of hostile motive or arbitrariness although the union could be said to have exercised "poor judgment." Negligence, poor judgment, or ineptitude are insufficient, standing alone, to establish a section 8(b)(2) violation.[534]

---

[530]Theatrical Stage Employees Local 646 (Parker Playhouse), 270 NLRB 1425, 117 LRRM 1080 (1984); Boilermakers Local 433 (Riley Stoker Corp.), 266 NLRB 596, 113 LRRM 1003 (1983).

[531]NLRB v. Teamsters (Leonard B. Hebert, Jr. & Co.), 778 F2d 207, 121 LRRM 2037 (CA 5, 1985).

[532]Boilermakers Local 374 v. NLRB (Combustion Eng'g), 852 F2d 1353, 128 LRRM 3184 (CA DC, 1988).

[533]Plumbers & Pipe Fitters Local 392 v. NLRB (Kaiser Eng'rs), 712 F2d 225, 113 LRRM 3500 (CA 6, 1983).

[534]*See also* Baker v. Laborers Local 264 (Builders Ass'n of Mo.), 822 F2d 781, 125 LRRM 3018 (CA 8, 1987) (a "rush forward" referral system, whereby those union members present in hiring hall who rushed to head of stairs first would receive identification slips necessary for job assignments, was found to be "undignified," but not arbitrary, discriminatory, or conclusive of bad-faith toward its members); Theatrical Stage Employees Local 592 (Saratoga Performing Arts Center), 266 NLRB 703, 113 LRRM 1025 (1983). *Cf.* Carpenters Local 2834 (Fleck), 268 NLRB 150, 114 LRRM 1245 (1983).

IV. DISCRIMINATION BECAUSE OF INVOLVEMENT WITH NLRB PROCEDURES: SECTION 8(a)(4)

Section 8(a)(4) makes it unlawful "to discharge or otherwise to discriminate against an employee because he has filed charges or given testimony under this Act."[535] Thus, activity protected under section 8(a)(4) includes testifying in Board proceedings or filing charges with the Board.[536] But the courts and the Board have given that narrow language a broad interpretation. In *NLRB v. Scrivener*,[537] the Supreme Court held that an employer violated section 8(a)(4) by discharging employees who had given sworn written statements to an NLRB field examiner investigating unfair labor practice charges against the company, even though the discharged employees had neither "filed charges" nor "given testimony" at a hearing.

---

[535]Section 8(a)(4) does not apply to filing charges or testifying under legislation other than the NLRA. *See* B & M Excavating, 155 NLRB 1152, 60 LRRM 1466 (1965), *enforced*, 368 F2d 624, 632 LRRM 2479 (CA 9, 1966). Thus, a discharge in response to an employee's threat to go to "the Labor Department" did not violate that section where the employer did not understand it to be a threat to resort to the NLRB. Inked Ribbon Corp., 241 NLRB 7, 100 LRRM 1480 (1979). But employer discrimination because of non-NLRA activities may constitute interference with concerted activities (under §§7 and 8(a)(1), or discrimination under §8(a)(3)). Salt River Valley Ass'n v. NLRB, 206 F2d 325, 32 LRRM 2598 (CA 9, 1953); Montgomery Ward & Co., 154 NLRB 1197, 60 LRRM 1110 (1965); Spandsco Oil & Royalty Co., 42 NLRB 942, 10 LRRM 208 (1942). *See* Chapter 6, "Interference With Protected Rights," at notes 511–518.

[536]*See, e.g.*, Hyatt Hotels Corp. dba Hyatt Regency Memphis, 296 NLRB No. 36, 132 LRRM 1130 (1989) (discharge motivated by attendance at representation hearing); P.I.E. Nationwide, 295 NLRB No. 43, 131 LRRM 1674 (1989) (discharge motivated by employee ridicule of supervisor's conduct during NLRB proceeding); Scranton Lace Co., 294 NLRB No. 19, 131 LRRM 1602 (1989) (discipline motivated by employee attendance at representation proceeding); Fairprene Indus. Prods. Co., 292 NLRB 797, 131 LRRM 1593, *enforced*, 880 F2d 1318, 133 LRRM 2192 (CA 2, 1989) (discharge motivated by unfair labor practice charge); NLRB v. Louisiana Energy & Dev. Corp., 840 F2d 309, 127 LRRM 3085 (CA 5, 1988) (§8(a)(4) protects supervisors from retaliation by employers for giving testimony in Board proceedings); U.S. Precision Lens, 288 NLRB 505, 128 LRRM 1096 (1988) (employee forced to lose personal paid holiday for testimony at Board hearing); S.E. Nichols, Inc., 284 NLRB 556, 127 LRRM 1298 (1987), *enforced*, 862 F2d 952, 129 LRRM 3098 (CA 2, 1988) *cert. denied*, 490 US 1108, 131 LRRM 2528 (1989) (employer "embarked on a persistent course of discrimination" against employee with respect to wages and working conditions in retaliation for testimony before Board); Ben Susan Restaurant Corp., 288 NLRB 16, 128 LRRM 1175 (1988), *enforced*, 867 F2d 1424, 134 LRRM 2431 (CA 2, 1988); Animal Humane Soc'y of S. Jersey, 287 NLRB 50, 130 LRRM 1108 (1987); P.I.E. Nationwide, 283 NLRB 965, 125 LRRM 1076 (1987) (employer discharged employee for filing charges against former employer); Central Broadcast Co., 280 NLRB 501, 124 LRRM 1076 (1986) (layoffs motivated by employees' testimony at Board representation hearing; employer unlawfully effected change in working conditions immediately after employees testified at hearing); Well-Bred Loaf, 280 NLRB 306, 124 LRRM 1012 (1986) (employee discharged for supplying testimony and affidavit to Board); Ryder/P.I.E. Nationwide, 279 NLRB 207, 122 LRRM 1048 (1986); Isla Verde Hotel Corp. v. NLRB, 702 F2d 268, 112 LRRM 3065 (CA 1, 1982).

[537]405 US 117, 79 LRRM 2587 (1972).

Consistent with the broad interpretation embraced in *Scrivener*, employers have been held to violate section 8(a)(4) by discharging or otherwise retaliating against employees for filing an affidavit with a Board agent investigating an unfair labor practice charge,[538] participating in an investigation,[539] talking to co-workers about future testimony,[540] and refusing to testify voluntarily and otherwise assist the employer in defending unfair labor practice charges.[541] Moreover, discharge of an employee who announces an intention to file unfair labor practice charges has been held to violate the Act.[542] The Board also has found a violation where discharge was based on the employer's suspection that the employee had filed or was about to file a charge with the Board,[543] or because it believed, even erroneously, that the employee had filed a charge.[544] Similarly, by disciplining an employee who was scheduled to testify, but did not, an employer violated the Act.[545] However, the First Circuit

---

[538]NLRB v. King Louie Bowling Corp., 472 F2d 1192, 82 LRRM 2576 (CA 8, 1973); Sinclair Glass Co. v. NLRB, 465 F2d 209, 80 LRRM 3082 (CA 7, 1972), *enforcing* 188 NLRB 362, 76 LRRM 1289 (1971).

[539]NLRB v. Overseas Motor, 721 F2d 570, 114 LRRM 3447 (CA 6, 1983). *But see* Vokas Provisions Co. dba Rich Plan of W. Reserve v. NLRB, 796 F2d 864, 122 LRRM 3136 (CA 6, 1986), *denying enforcement to* 271 NLRB 1010, 117 LRRM 1308 (1984) (Board held not warranted in finding that employer violated §8(a)(4) of Act when it refused to permit six employees to voluntarily attend representation hearing during working hours without subpoenas and when it discharged employees for leaving work contrary to employer's explicit instructions).

[540]Weinreb Mgmt., 292 NLRB 428, 131 LRRM 1051 (1989) (employee scheduled to testify before NLRB discharged for asking co-employee about employer harassment).

[541]NLRB v. Retail Clerks Local 876 (Pennacchini), 570 F2d 586, 97 LRRM 2465 (CA 6), *cert. denied*, 439 US 819, 99 LRRM 2600 (1978); Morrison v. NLRB, 772 F2d 283, 120 LRRM 2471 (CA 6, 1985). *But see* Lawyers Coop. Publishing Co., 273 NLRB 129, 118 LRRM 1213 (1984), *rev'd in part and remanded sub nom.* Dash v. NLRB, 793 F2d 1062, 122 LRRM 2931 (CA 9, 1986) (employer discharge of regional manager for refusal to assist in preparation for unfair labor practice hearing did not violate Act).

[542]Hudson Valley Hotels, 283 NLRB 1146, 125 LRRM 1110 (1987) (employee requested co-workers to write statements in preparation for filing NLRB charges); *see* Grand Rapids Die Casting Corp. v. NLRB, 831 F2d 112, 126 LRRM 2747, *reh'g denied*, 833 F2d 605, 127 LRRM 2215 (CA 6, 1987); Elion Concrete, 287 NLRB 69, 129 LRRM 1371 (1987), *enforcement denied without opinion*, 884 F2d 1389, 132 LRRM 2240 (CA 4, 1989) (violation found where employer refused to rehire employee because of rumor that he had filed charge with NLRB); Midtown Serv. Center, 278 NLRB No. 67, 122 LRRM 1132 (1986); Premier Rubber Co., 272 NLRB 466, 117 LRRM 1406 (1984).

[543]First Nat'l Bank & Trust Co., 209 NLRB 95, 85 LRRM 1324 (1974); *accord* Rock Rd. Trailer Parts & Sales, 204 NLRB 1136, 83 LRRM 1467 (1973). This rule applies even if the employer's suspicion is based on a visit to the Board by the dischargee that did not involve a grievance cognizable under the Act. General Nutrition Center, 221 NLRB 850, 90 LRRM 1736 (1975).

[544]Maple City Stamping Co., 200 NLRB 743, 82 LRRM 1059 (1972); *see* First Nat'l Bank & Trust Co., *supra* note 543; *accord* Summit Nursing & Convalescent Home, 204 NLRB 70, 83 LRRM 1323 (1973).

[545]Fuqua Homes (Ohio), 211 NLRB 399, 87 LRRM 1141 (1974). *Cf.* Nestle Co., 248 NLRB 732, 103 LRRM 1567 (1980), *aff'd*, 659 F2d 252, 108 LRRM 2175 (CA DC, 1981);

distinguished *Scrivener* in a case where an employee had telephoned the Board "to vent his spleen" after an unfair labor practice charge had been dismissed; the court held that the employer had lawfully discharged the employee because the employee's call was not to provide information for a future or pending Board proceeding.[546]

An employer is not required to release employees from their normal work schedules so that they may attend an NLRB hearing as mere spectators, as the Board recently affirmed.[547] In 1977, the Board departed from that general rule, but the Circuit Court for the District of Columbia reversed, holding that section 8(a)(4) was not violated by the discharge of such spectators, for they had not been subpoenaed to attend the hearing, they had offered no substantial reasons for their attendance, and the employer had explicitly refused to excuse them from work.[548]

An employee who deliberately files false charges with the Board and gives false testimony is not protected by section 8(a)(4).[549] On the other hand, the discharge of an employee for testifying untruthfully was a violation of the section where the employee did not willfully testify falsely and where the Board found that the real motivation for the discharge was the employee's union activity.[550] A fortiori, discharging an employee who refuses to give false testimony in a Board proceeding is also a violation.[551]

Section 8(a)(4), like section 8(a)(3), requires the Board to distinguish an employer's pretextual and retaliatory conduct from conduct motivated by legitimate business purposes.[552] To that

---

John Wanamaker, Phila., Inc., 199 NLRB 1266, 82 LRRM 1129 (1972). *See also* Marriott Corp., 290 NLRB 442, 129 LRRM 1124 (1988); A-1 Janitorial Serv. Co., 222 NLRB 664, 91 LRRM 1210 (1976) (testimony concerning another employer).

[546]NLRB v. Wilson Freight Co., 604 F2d 712, 102 LRRM 2269 (CA 1, 1979), *cert. denied*, 445 US 962, 103 LRRM 3082 (1980).

[547]Ohmite Mfg. Co., 290 NLRB 1036, 130 LRRM 1190 (1988). *See* Unique Moving & Storage Co., 240 NLRB 40, 100 LRRM 1226 (1979); Standard Packaging Corp., 140 NLRB 628, 52 LRRM 1088 (1963).

[548]Service Employees Local 250 v. NLRB (Earringhouse Imports), 600 F2d 930, 101 LRRM 2004 (CA DC, 1979), *denying enforcement to* 227 NLRB 1107, 94 LRRM 1494 (1977).

[549]NLRB v. Brake Parts Co., 447 F2d 503, 77 LRRM 2695 (CA 7, 1971), *denying enforcement to* 178 NLRB 247, 74 LRRM 1068 (1969).

[550]Big Three Indus. Gas & Equip. Co., 212 NLRB 800, 87 LRRM 1543 (1974).

[551]J. C. Penney Co., 237 NLRB 643, 99 LRRM 1066 (1978).

[552]*See, e.g.*, Sea-Land Serv., 280 NLRB 720, 123 LRRM 1018 (1986), *enforcement denied*, 837 F2d 1387, 127 LRRM 2757 (CA 5, 1988); M&G Convoy, 287 NLRB 1140, 130 LRRM 1150 (1988); Grand Rapids Die Casting Corp. v. NLRB, *supra* note 542; Hudson Valley Hotels, *supra* note 542 (employer failed to provide specific reasons for discharge); Finlay Bros. Co., 282 NLRB 737, 124 LRRM 1244 (1987) (no violation of §8(a)(4) since employee disobeyed rules and was warned but continued to refuse to obey rules).

end, the Board and the courts apply the Board's *Wright Line* analysis.[553] Thus, the Sixth Circuit has held that the Board was not warranted in finding that the employer violated section 8(a)(4) by discharging an employee where the employer proved that the employee would have been terminated for falsifying time records absent his protected activities of supplying information during a Board investigation.[554] Similarly, the Seventh Circuit has held that the discharge of an employee who testified against the employer at an unfair labor practice hearing was lawful where the employer met its burden of showing that the employee would have been discharged regardless of any improper motivation.[555] In contrast, the Seventh Circuit has upheld the Board's finding of a section 8(a)(4) violation where the reasons given for the employee's termination were determined to be pretextual.[556]

In determining whether an employer has violated section 8(a)(4), as in the comparable inquiry under section 8(a)(3), the Board considers all of the circumstances surrounding the alleged discriminatory action. In both inquiries, the Board relies extensively on inferential proof of motivation. Thus, the time span between the employee's participation in Board proceedings and the disputed employment action may be evidence of unlawful motivation.[557] In addition, evidence of statements to, threats against, and disparate treatment of the employee are also

---

[553]*See* notes 40-73 *supra* and accompanying text.

[554]Airborne Freight Corp. v. NLRB, 728 F2d 357, 115 LRRM 3214 (CA 6, 1984), *denying enforcement to* 263 NLRB 1376, 111 LRRM 1580 (1982). *But see* Baddour, Inc., 281 NLRB 546, 123 LRRM 1200 (1986), *enforced without opinion*, 848 F2d 193, 129 LRRM 2800 (CA 6, 1988), *cert. denied*, 488 US 944, 129 LRRM 2800 (1988); Hudson Valley Hotels, *supra* note 542.

[555]Viracon v. NLRB, 736 F2d 1188, 116 LRRM 3124 (CA 7, 1984). *See also* M&G Convoy, *supra* note 552; Metz Metallurgical Corp., 275 NLRB 1045, 119 LRRM 1239 (1985) (employer did not violate Act since General Counsel failed to establish prima facie case of retaliation); Redway Carriers, 274 NLRB 1359, 119 LRRM 1023 (1985) (same); Esco Elevators, 271 NLRB 1262, 117 LRRM 1158 (1984) (same). *But see* Montag Oil, 271 NLRB 665, 116 LRRM 1452 (1984) (discharge lawful even though prima facie case established).

[556]NLRB v. Bliss & Laughlin Steel Co., 754 F2d 229, 118 LRRM 2676 (CA 7, 1985). *See also* NLRB v. Louisiana Energy & Dev. Corp., *supra* note 536 (Fifth Circuit upheld Board's finding that employer's proffered reasons for discharging employees were pretextual). For other examples of violations of §8(a)(4), see Roadway Express, 274 NLRB 357, 119 LRRM 1056 (1985); Cerock Wire & Cable Group, 274 NLRB 888, 119 LRRM 1060 (1985); North Slope Mechanical, 269 NLRB 869, 116 LRRM 1102 (1984). *enforced*, 760 F2d 276, 119 LRRM 3160 (CA 9, 1985).

[557]Brenal Elec., 284 NLRB 552, 126 LRRM 1360 (1987); Grand Rapids Die Casting Corp. v. NLRB, *supra* note 542; Animal Humane Soc'y of S. Jersey, 287 NLRB 50, 130 LRRM 1108 (1987); Viracon v. NLRB, *supra* note 555.

pertinent.[558] A supervisor's unlawful motivation in taking action that leads to the discharge of, or discrimination against, an employee may be imputed to the employer, even though the officers who actually made the adverse employment decision did not share the employer's antiunion intentions.[559] Of course, there must exist a causal relationship between the unlawful animus and the adverse employment decision in that the supervisor with knowledge of the employee's protected activity influenced or played a significant role in such decision.[560]

Thus, in *Host International*,[561] two restaurant employees at a New York airport were discharged by Host for violating company work rules. The employees filed charges with the Board which were settled by an agreement that did not provide for their reinstatement. Thereafter, the employees obtained similar positions with another food service company at a different New York airport. Two years later, their new employer was acquired by Host, which also acquired operating rights at the terminal facility in which the employees worked. Host refused to hire the two individuals, and later claimed that it had been motivated by their earlier discharge for cause. The Board rejected that claim as pretextual. Based on evidence of inconsistent acts and statements, together with direct evidence of a supervisor's animus toward one of the two employees, the Board held that the refusal to hire was unlawfully based on the charges previously filed with the Board.

Antiunion history and general bias, standing alone, do not provide "causal connection" between the employee's actions and the discharge that is required to support a finding that an

---

[558]P.I.E. Nationwide, 283 NLRB 965, 125 LRRM 1076 (1987) (employer stated that it would not have hired employee if it had known he had filed unfair labor practice charges against his previous employer); Memphis Truck & Trailer, 284 NLRB 900, 126 LRRM 1326 (1987) (president told employee that decision not to employ him would have been reconsidered had he not filed charges). *But see* Williams Motor Transfer, 284 NLRB 1496, 126 LRRM 1030 (1987) (no violation of §8(a)(4) when president told employee that president was "going to be watching" and was "going to be on employee" if he did anything wrong, since statements were made following discussion of employee's purported work deficiencies).

[559]Louisiana Energy & Dev. Corp., 283 NLRB 391, 125 LRRM 1356 (1987), *enforced*, 840 F2d 309, 127 LRRM 3085 (CA 5, 1988); Boston Mut. Life Ins. Co. v. NLRB, 692 F2d 169, 111 LRRM 2983 (CA 1, 1982). *But see* Pioneer Natural Gas Co. v. NLRB, 662 F2d 408, 108 LRRM 3255 (CA 5, 1981).

[560]U.S. Postal Serv., 282 NLRB 686, 125 LRRM 1111 (1987); Garrett Flexible Prods., 270 NLRB 1147, 116 LRRM 1296 (1984); M&G Convoy, *supra* note 552.

[561]290 NLRB 442, 129 LRRM 1124 (1988).

employer has violated section 8(a)(4).[562] Thus, the Board generally lists a variety of factors when it holds that "the real reason" for an employer's action is activity protected by section 8(a)(4) rather than violation of the employment policy which the employer alleges. Common among such factors is that the employer has disciplined or discharged an employee pursuant to a newly announced policy[563] or one that has been in existence but not previously enforced.[564] Additional factors that have supported a finding of violation are an employer's failure to investigate or to take into account an employee's explanation for the conduct at issue,[565] an employer's "inconsistent defenses," and the excessive severity of discharge as a punishment for the conduct in question.[566] Conversely, the employer has been held not to have violated section 8(a)(4) when employees had prior notice of the employment policy relied upon,[567] when employees were treated uniformly,[568] when the employer acted as soon as it learned of the employee's violation of the employment policy,[569] when the employer did not know of the employee's participation in Board proceedings,[570] when there is lack of animus,[571] and when there is discharge or discipline for just cause.[572]

Although Congress excluded "supervisors" from the statutory definition of "employee," the Board has held that supervisors who file charges alleging discrimination based on their union

---

[562]Florida Steel Corp. v. NLRB, 587 F2d 735, 100 LRRM 2451, 2455-56 (CA 5, 1979).

[563]Permanent Label Corp., 248 NLRB 118, 103 LRRM 1513 (1980), *enforced*, 657 F2d 512, 107 LRRM 2985 (CA 3, 1981) (en banc); Pepper Packing Co., 243 NLRB 215, 101 LRRM 1528 (1979); Vornado, Inc., 241 NLRB 64, 100 LRRM 1586 (1979).

[564]Staco, Inc., 244 NLRB 461, 102 LRRM 1223 (1979); Ward Prods. Corp., 243 NLRB 239, 101 LRRM 1578 (1979), *enforced in part*, 653 F2d 958, 108 LRRM 2202 (CA 5, 1981).

[565]Siro Sec. Serv., 247 NLRB 1266, 103 LRRM 1362 (1980).

[566]Mid-State Broadcasting, 248 NLRB 1206, 104 LRRM 1024, *enforced*, 636 F2d 1209, 108 LRRM 2280 (CA 3, 1980).

[567]Joseph Schlitz Brewing Co., 240 NLRB 710, 100 LRRM 1323 (1979).

[568]U.S. Postal Serv., 235 NLRB 307, 100 LRRM 1222 (1978).

[569]McKesson Chem. Co., 246 NLRB 584, 102 LRRM 1629 (1979); Summitville Tile, 245 NLRB 863, 102 LRRM 1552 (1979).

[570]Landgrebe Motor Transp., 295 NLRB No. 118, 131 LRRM 1811 (1989); United Parcel Serv. v. NLRB, 706 F2d 972, 113 LRRM 2174 (CA 3), *vacated*, 464 US 979, 114 LRRM 3168 (1983), *cert. denied*, 469 US 834, 117 LRRM 2552 (1984); U.S. Postal Serv., 266 NLRB 467, 112 LRRM 1429 (1983).

[571]Alamo Cement Co., 270 NLRB 535, 116 LRRM 1104 (1984).

[572]*See* Dahl Fish Co., 279 NLRB 1084, 123 LRRM 1322 (1986), *enforced without opinion*, 813 F2d 1254, 125 LRRM 3063 (CA DC, 1987); Finlay Bros. Co., 282 NLRB 737, 124 LRRM 1244 (1987); Lewis Grocer Co., 282 NLRB 166, 125 LRRM 1143 (1987); U.S. Postal Serv., 283 NLRB 8, 125 LRRM 1014 (1987); Raymond Eng'g, 286 NLRB 1210, 127 LRRM 1334 (1987) (denial of overtime no violation); BASF Wyandotte Corp., 278 NLRB 173, 122 LRRM 1152 (1986); Kawasaki Motors Corp., U.S.A., 268 NLRB 936, 115 LRRM 1127 (1983).

activity are, for purposes of processing the charge, "employee[s]" protected by section 8(a)(4).[573] In *General Services*,[574] the employer was found to have violated that section by refusing to give the employee post-termination pay previously promised, even though the promise of such pay was gratuitous and it was not shown that the discharge itself had been unlawful.

Conditioning continued employment or reinstatement of employees upon their withdrawal of Board charges violates section 8(a)(4).[575] The provision is likewise violated by various retaliatory acts short of discharge, such as imposing closer supervision and unilaterally changing sick leave and lateness policies;[576] subjecting an employee to more onerous working conditions with a reduction in working hours;[577] harassment;[578] surveillance;[579] denying benefits, vacation leave, and other work-related privileges;[580] reducing hours, reducing compensation, or changing work rules;[581] transferring employee to different job or job duties;[582] refusing to give references;[583] and terminating workers' compensation.[584] Similarly, refusing to

---

[573]Hi-Craft Clothing Co., 251 NLRB 1310, 105 LRRM 1356 (1980), *enforcement denied*, 660 F2d 910, 108 LRRM 2657 (CA 3, 1981); General Servs., 229 NLRB 940, 95 LRRM 1174 (1977), *enforcement denied* (CA 5, 1978) (unpublished); Walt Disney World Co., 216 NLRB 836, 89 LRRM 1137 (1975).

[574]*Supra* note 573.

[575]Maspeth Trucking Serv., 240 NLRB 1225, 100 LRRM 1482 (1979), *supplementing* 237 NLRB 1531, 99 LRRM 1574 (1978); Everage Bros. Mkt., 206 NLRB 593, 84 LRRM 1383 (1973); Amsterdam Wrecking Co., 196 NLRB 113, 79 LRRM 1648 (1972).

[576]Pinter Bros., 227 NLRB 921, 94 LRRM 1284 (1977).

[577]Frenchy's K & T, 247 NLRB 1212, 103 LRRM 1397 (1980).

[578]NLRB v. S.E. Nichols, Inc., 862 F2d 952, 129 LRRM 3098 (CA 2, 1988), *cert. denied*, 490 US 1108, 131 LRRM 2528 (1989); Quality C.A.T.V., 278 NLRB 1282, 121 LRRM 1297 (1986), *enforcement denied*, 824 F2d 542, 125 LRRM 3093 (CA 7, 1987); Einhorn Enters., Star Color Plate Serv. Div., 279 NLRB 576, 122 LRRM 1232 (1986); La Reina, 275 NLRB 1494, 120 LRRM 1087 (1985).

[579]La Reina, *supra* note 578.

[580]*See* Independent Stave Co., 278 NLRB 593, 122 LRRM 1104 (1986) (employer violated §8(a)(4) of Act by refusing to award employee deer-hunting rifle won in employer-sponsored contest for employees); U.S. Postal Serv., *supra* note 570; Isla Verde Hotel Corp. v. NLRB, 702 F2d 268, 112 LRRM 3065 (CA 1, 1982); Village IX dba Shenanigans, 264 NLRB 908, 112 LRRM 1096 (1982), *enforced in part*, 723 F2d 1360, 115 LRRM 2297 (CA 7, 1983).

[581]Norris Concrete Materials, 282 NLRB 289, 123 NLRB 1329 (1986); Polymer Prints, 281 NLRB 431, 124 LRRM 1302 (1986), *later proceeding*, 287 NLRB No. 97, 129 LRRM 1087 (1988); Woodline Motor Freight, 278 NLRB 1141, 122 LRRM 1355 (1986), *enforced in part*, 843 F2d 285, 127 LRRM 3260 (CA 8, 1988); NLRB v. Louisiana Energy & Dev. Corp., 283 NLRB 391, 125 LRRM 1356 (1987), *enforced*, 840 F2d 309, 127 LRRM 3085 (CA 5, 1988); Superior Forwarding Co., 282 NLRB 806, 124 LRRM 1156 (1987) (reduced runs of employee truck driver by 38%).

[582]Norris Concrete Materials, *supra* note 581.

[583]La Salle Invest. Co. dba Cafe La Salle, 280 NLRB 379, 122 LRRM 1281 (1986); Metz Metallurgical Corp., 275 NLRB 1045, 119 LRRM 1239 (1985).

[584]Baddour, Inc., 281 NLRB 546, 123 LRRM 1200 (1986), *enforced without opinion*, 848 F2d 193, 129 LRRM 2800 (CA 6), *cert. denied*, 488 US 944, 129 LRRM 2800 (1988).

pay severance pay to an employee who is challenging discharge under the Act violates the section, even though the outcome of the litigation might include the employee's reinstatement with backpay.[585]

In *Bill Johnson's Restaurants v. NLRB*,[586] the Supreme Court considered whether by filing and prosecuting a state court lawsuit against its employees an employer violated section 8(a)(4) and could be enjoined against further prosecution. In that case, an employee filed charges with the Board alleging that the employer had discharged her as a result of her efforts to organize a union. Thereafter, she and co-workers picketed the employer's restaurant and distributed leaflets accusing management of unlawfully discharging the employee, maintaining a filthy restroom, and making unwelcome sexual advances. The employer filed a state court action against the picketers, claiming that they had engaged in mass picketing, harassed customers, and libeled the employer by the statements contained in the leaflets. The discharged employee then filed a second charge with the Board, claiming that the state court suit had been instituted in retaliation for her filing of the original charge. The Board held that the employer's conduct violated section 8(a)(4) and ordered the employer to withdraw its state court complaint and reimburse the employees for all legal expenses.[587] The Ninth Circuit enforced the Board's order.[588]

On review, the Supreme Court vacated the Board's order and remanded. According to the Court, an employer's filing of a *meritorious* state lawsuit against an employee does not constitute a violation of section 8(a)(4), even if retaliatory motivation is demonstrated. Conversely, the prosecution of a state court suit lacking a reasonable basis constitutes a violation of the Act if the suit was filed in retaliation for the filing of charges. The Court concluded that in a section 8(a)(4) case in which an employer demonstrates that its state lawsuit raises genuine issues of state law or material fact, the Board should stay its proceedings until the state court suit has been concluded. If the employer prevails in the lawsuit, then it should also prevail before the Board in the section 8(a)(4) case. However, if judgment is entered against the

---

[585]Manuel San Juan Co., 211 NLRB 812, 87 LRRM 1094 (1974).

[586]461 US 731, 113 LRRM 2647 (1983). See discussion Chapter 6, "Interference With Protected Rights," at notes 382–386.

[587]Bill Johnson's Restaurants, 249 NLRB 155, 104 LRRM 1205 (1980).

[588]660 F2d 1335, 109 LRRM 3027 (CA 9, 1981).

employer in the state lawsuit, the Board could consider that circumstance in determining whether the employer's filing and prosecution of the suit violated section 8(a)(4), the Court added. If a violation is found, the Board may order the employer to reimburse the employees wrongfully sued for their attorneys' fees and other expenses, according to the Court.

On remand, the Board found a violation of section 8(a)(4) with respect to the employer's business interference claims, but found no violation with respect to the libel claim.[589] The state court had granted summary judgment for the employees on the business-interference claims. The Board accepted that judgment as a final adjudication establishing that those claims lacked a reasonable basis in law or fact. However, the parties had entered into a settlement agreement stipulating to the dismissal with prejudice of the libel claim. The Board declined the General Counsel's invitation to enter the "thicket" of determining itself the merits of the state law libel claim, and found instead that the General Counsel had failed to meet the burden of establishing that the libel claim was baseless.

The Board applied *Bill Johnson's Restaurants* in a case involving an employer's state court appeal of an award of unemployment compensation benefits to an employee.[590] Noting that it could not halt the prosecution of the state court suit if the suit has a reasonable basis in fact or law, the Board found that the employer's appeal met this test and thus was not violative of the Act.[591] In *American Pacific Concrete Pipe*,[592] however, the Board held that *Bill Johnson's Restaurants* is limited to claims that are not preempted by the LMRA. In *American Pacific*, the employer and the employee entered into a private settlement agreement in lieu of a Board-ordered judgment and award of backpay. The regional director, who was not a party to the settlement agreement, instituted backpay proceedings against the employer with

---

[589]Bill Johnson's Restaurants, 290 NLRB 29, 129 LRRM 1105 (1988).

[590]Lawyers Coop. Publishing Co., 273 NLRB 129, 118 LRRM 1213 (1984), *rev'd in part and remanded sub nom.* Dash v. NLRB, 793 F2d 1062, 122 LRRM 2931 (CA 9, 1986). *See also* Dahl Fish Co., *supra* note 572; Teamsters Local 705 (Emery Air Freight Corp.), 278 NLRB 1303, 122 LRRM 1050 (1986), *enforced in part*, 820 F2d 448, 125 LRRM 2705 (CA DC, 1987) (filing of well-founded state lawsuit may not be enjoined as unfair labor practice under §8(a)(4), regardless of employer's motive, unless suit lacks reasonable basis in law or fact).

[591]*But see* Key Food Stores Coop., 286 NLRB 1056, 129 LRRM 1172 (1987) (employer violated §8(a)(4) by initiating arbitration proceeding to discharge employee because employee "knowingly filed a false charge" with Board).

[592]292 NLRB 1264, 130 LRRM 1501 (1989).

the knowledge of and agreement by the employee. American Pacific sued the employee in state court for fraud, alleging that the employee failed to honor the private settlement agreement. The Board held that the employer's state action was preempted by the LMRA, that it was brought in retaliation for the employee's participation in the NLRB backpay proceeding, and that, therefore, the employer violated section 8(a)(4).

The Board's General Counsel has also determined that the analytical framework announced in *Bill Johnson's Restaurants* should apply to suits filed in federal court.[593]

V. REMEDIAL ORDERS IN DISCRIMINATION CASES

The Board's power to remedy discrimination in unfair labor practices cases is set forth in section 10(c) of the Act.[594] On finding that an unfair labor practice has been committed, the Board is empowered to issue "an order requiring such person to cease and desist from such unfair labor practice and to take such affirmative action including reinstatement of employees with or without back pay, as will effectuate the policies of this Act." The statute also provides that the Board's order "may further require such person to make reports from time to time showing the extent to which it has complied with the order." Although the 1947 amendments to the Act reiterated that, "where an order directs the reinstatement of an employee, back pay may be required of the employer or the labor organization . . . responsible for the discrimination suffered," the same amendments placed a limitation on the Board's remedial power, to wit: "No order of the Board shall require the reinstatement of any individual as an employee who has been suspended or discharged, or the payment to him of any back pay, if such individual was suspended or discharged for cause."[595] Remedies in discrimina-

---

[593]Carpenters, Ariz. State Dist. Council, NLRB Gen. Counsel Advice Memo., Case No. 28-CB-2183, 115 LRRM 1338 (1984); *see* BASF Wyandotte Corp., *supra* note 572 (employer did not violate §8(a)(4) of Act by action in federal district court seeking order directing union officers to withdraw unfair labor practice charges based on employer's refusal to honor contract entitling union officers to pay for time spent on union business; employer had sought declaratory judgment on genuine legal issue—whether contract violated §302 of Act; withdrawal of charges, but one part of remedy sought; lawsuit not brought in retaliation for filing charges). *See also* BASF Wyandotte Corp. v. Chemical Workers Local 227, 791 F2d 1046, 122 LRRM 2750 (CA 2, 1986).

[594]*See generally* Chapter 32, "NLRB Orders and Remedies."

[595]*See* Chapter 19, "The Primary Strike," at notes 76–78.

tion cases generally take the form of orders for reinstatement of employees who have been discharged and for backpay for loss of wages and other employment benefits. These remedial orders are treated in detail in a later chapter.[596]

VI. JUDICIAL REVIEW IN DISCRIMINATION CASES

Sections 10(e) and (f)[597] of the Act provide that the "findings of the Board with respect to questions of fact if supported by substantial evidence on the record considered as a whole shall be conclusive." That language dates from the Taft-Hartley amendments and replaces a provision of the Wagner Act which made the Board's findings of fact conclusive if supported "by evidence."[598]

In *Universal Camera Corp. v. NLRB*,[599] the Supreme Court explicated the purpose and effect of the changes in sections 10(e) and (f), and articulated the standard of review of NLRB decisions by the circuit courts:

> Whether or not it was ever permissible for courts to determine the substantiality of evidence supporting a Labor Board decision merely on the basis of evidence which in and of itself justified it, without taking into account contradictory evidence or evidence from which conflicting inferences could be drawn, the new legislation definitely precludes such a theory of review and bars its practice. The substantiality of evidence must take into account whatever in the record fairly detracts from its weight. . . .[600]

At one time a question existed as to whether the standard of review in discrimination cases differed from that applicable to other unfair labor practices. The Fifth Circuit had taken the position that an employer's sworn testimony concerning the reason for a discharge was controlling unless the employer's testimony was impeached, or there was substantial contradiction, or circumstances raising grave doubts were inconsistent with its sworn testimony.[601] However, in *NLRB v. Walton Man-*

---

[596]*See* Chapter 32, "NLRB Orders and Remedies," at notes 144–185.

[597]*See* Chapter 33, "Judicial Review and Enforcement," at notes 58–81.

[598]Prior to amendment in 1947, §10(e) read, in pertinent part, as follows: "The findings of the Board as to the facts if supported by evidence shall be conclusive." Section 10(f) contained virtually identical language.

[599]340 US 474, 27 LRRM 2373 (1951).

[600]*Id.* at 487-88.

[601]NLRB v. Walton Mfg. Co., 286 F2d 16, 47 LRRM 2367 (CA 5, 1961); NLRB v. Williamson-Dickie Mfg. Co., 130 F2d 260, 10 LRRM 867 (CA 5, 1942); NLRB v. Tex-O-Kan Flour Mills, 122 F2d 433, 8 LRRM 675 (CA 5, 1941).

ufacturing Co.,[602] the Supreme Court ruled that the Act does not require the substantial-evidence test to be applied more rigorously in reinstatement cases than in other cases. It emphasized that "[t]here is no place in the statutory scheme for one test of the substantiality of evidence in reinstatement cases and another test in other cases."[603] Noting that its decisions in *NLRB v. Pittsburgh Steamship Co.*[604] and *Universal Camera Corp.*[605] had been decided the same day and that both involved reinstatement, the Court reiterated that "[t]hey state a rule for review by Courts of Appeals in all Labor Board cases."[606] The Board is thus free to reject an employer's sworn testimony and to predicate findings of discrimination on the basis of all the evidence, both direct and circumstantial.

The courts continue to hold that substantial evidence in section 8(a)(3) cases is such relevant evidence as a reasonable mind might accept as adequate to support a conclusion, and that it is not appropriate for the appellate courts to substitute their view of the evidence for that of the Board.[607] However, the Seventh Circuit, elaborating on a problem discussed in *Universal Camera*, ruled that analysis of whether the Board's findings of fact are supported by substantial evidence must take into account any contrary findings by the ALJ, with particular attention to findings that turn on the ALJ's firsthand observation of the witness.[608]

Where a party fails to contest a Board finding of fact, a court may determine that the party has abandoned the claim of error and decline to review or disturb that finding.[609] For example, the Third Circuit refused to consider whether an ALJ had erred

---

[602]369 US 404, 49 LRRM 2962 (1962).

[603]*Id.* at 407.

[604]340 US 498, 27 LRRM 2382 (1951).

[605]*Supra* note 599.

[606]369 US at 407. *See* Coleman, *Wright Line; A Variation on the Old Shell Game—"Now You See It, Now You Don't,"* 28 FED. B. NEWS & J. 208 (1981); Remar, *Climbing Mt. Healthy: In Search of the "Wright Line" on Mixed-Motive Discharges Under Section 8(a)(3)*, 4 IND. REL. L. J. 636 (1981).

[607]*See, e.g.*, Whisper Soft Mills v. NLRB, 754 F2d 1381, 117 LRRM 2974 (CA 9, 1984); Belcher Towing Co. v. NLRB, 726 F2d 705, 115 LRRM 3224 (CA 11, 1984); Ajax Paving Indus. v. NLRB, 713 F2d 1214, 113 LRRM 3673 (CA 6, 1983); Champion Parts Rebuilders, Ne. Div. v. NLRB, 717 F2d 845, 114 LRRM 2674 (CA 3, 1983). Even if courts address an issue raised by the Board, the Board sometimes chooses to practice nonacquiescence. *See* Estreicher & Revest, *Nonacquiescence by Federal Administrative Agencies*, 98 YALE L.J. 679 (1989).

[608]NLRB v. Stor-Rite Metal Prods., 856 F2d 957, 129 LRRM 2392 (CA 7, 1988).

[609]NLRB v. Lathers Local 46 (New York & Vicinity) (General Contractors Ass'n of N.Y.), 727 F2d 234, 115 LRRM 2652 (CA 2, 1984).

in refusing to approve a settlement agreement because the employer had failed to raise that issue before the Board.[610] Similarly, the Eleventh Circuit has held that it was without jurisdiction to consider an employer's arguments regarding backpay and reinstatement remedies because those matters were not properly raised before the Board.[611]

Prior differences among the circuits in interpreting the *Wright Line* test[612] were resolved by the Supreme Court in *NLRB v. Transportation Management Corp.*[613] The Court held that once the General Counsel makes a prima facie case, the burden of proof is then properly placed on the employer to prove by a preponderance of the evidence that the employer would have fired the employee for permissible reasons even if the employee had not been involved in the protected union activity.

---

[610]NLRB v. A. Duie Pyle, Inc., 730 F2d 119, 115 LRRM 3428 (CA 3, 1984).

[611]Purolator Armored v. NLRB, 764 F2d 1423, 119 LRRM 3228 (CA 11, 1985). *See also* NLRB v. Schwab Foods dba Mooresville IGA Foodliner, 858 F2d 1285, 129 LRRM 2601 (CA 7, 1988) (employer's failure to file timely motions asking Board to consider changed circumstances was waiver of objections to remedial order); Oldwick Materials v. NLRB, 732 F2d 339, 116 LRRM 2092 (CA 3, 1984) (employer's failure to file exceptions precludes review under §10(e)); St. Francis Fed'n of Nurses & Health Professionals v. NLRB, 729 F2d 844, 115 LRRM 3352 (CA DC, 1984) (union's failure to raise issue before Board precludes court review).

[612]For a further discussion of the *Wright Line* test, *see supra* notes 40-73 and accompanying text.

[613]462 US 393, 113 LRRM 2857 (1983), *rev'g* 674 F2d 130, 109 LRRM 3291 (CA 1, 1982).

CHAPTER 8

EMPLOYER DOMINATION OF AND ASSISTANCE TO LABOR ORGANIZATIONS

I. INTRODUCTION: SECTION 8(a)(2)

It is an unfair labor practice for an employer "to dominate or interfere with the formation or administration of any labor organization or contribute financial or other support to it . . . ."[1] This restriction was included in the Wagner Act as section 8(2) and retained without change as section 8(a)(2) of the Taft-Hartley Act.[2]

Section 8(a)(2)'s prohibition extends only to employer domination or interference with or support to a "labor organization," a term defined in section 2(5) of the Act. Therefore, labor organization status is a threshold issue in every section 8(a)(2) case. An employer does not violate the Act by support of groups

---

[1]Section 8(a)(2). The additional language of the clause reads as follows: "*Provided*, That subject to rules and regulations made and published by the Board pursuant to section 6, an employer shall not be prohibited from permitting employees to confer with him during working hours without loss of time or pay[.]"

[2]The literature dealing with §8(a)(2) includes the following: Kesselring & Brinker, *Contract Difficulties Under §8(a)(2)*, 31 LAB. L.J. 139 (1980); Kesselring & Brinker, *Financial and Material Support Under §8(a)(2)*, 31 LAB. L.J. 3 (1980); Murmann, *The Scanlon Plan Joint Committee and Section 8(a)(2)*, 31 LAB. L.J. 299 (1980); Kesselring & Brinker, *Discriminatory Treatment of Employees Under §8(a)(2)*, 30 LAB. L.J. 611 (1979); Kesselring & Brinker, *Employer Domination Under §8(a)(2)*, 30 LAB. L.J. 340 (1979); Jackson, *An Alternative to Unionization and the Wholly Unorganized Shop: A Legal Basis for Sanctioning Joint Employer-Employee Committees and Increasing Employee Free Choice*, 28 SYRACUSE L. REV. 809 (1977); Getman, *The* Midwest Piping *Doctrine: An Examination of the Need for Reappraisal of Labor Board Dogma*, 31 U. CHI. L. REV. 292 (1964); Crager, *Company Unions Under the National Labor Relations Act*, 40 MICH. L. REV. 831 (1942); Van Dusen, *What Is Employer Domination or Support?*, 13 TEMP. L.Q. 63 (1938); Comment, *Discarding the Doctrine of Supervisory Domination: New Solutions to an Old Conflict of Interest*, 30 HASTINGS L.J. 763 (1979); Note, *The West German Model of Codetermination Under Section 8(a)(2) of the NLRA*, 51 IND. L.J. 795 (1976); Note, *Does Employer Implementation of Employee Production Teams Violate §8(a)(2) of the National Labor Relations Act?*, 49 IND. L.J. 516 (1974); Note, *New Standards for Domination and Support Under Section 8(a)(2)*, 82 YALE L.J. 510 (1973).

that are not labor organizations, such as employee recreation committees and credit unions.[3]

The primary purpose of section 8(2) of the Wagner Act was to eradicate company unionism, a practice whereby employers would establish and control in-house labor organizations in order to prevent organization by autonomous unions.[4] The section thus makes it unlawful for an employer to "dominate" a labor organization.[5] However, section 8(a)(2) is not limited to cases where an employer dominates a labor organization, for it is also an unfair labor practice for an employer to "interfere with" or "contribute financial or other support to" a labor organization. Employer interference with a labor organization is conduct short of domination and often takes the form of participation by low-level supervisors in a labor organization's activities.[6] The prohibition of support requires substantial employer neutrality between contending unions. An employer may not grant recognition to a union when another union has petitioned the Board for an election; but where there is an established lawful bargaining relationship the employer is required to continue bargaining with the incumbent union despite the pendency of a rival union petition.[7] Section 8(a)(2) also prohibits an employer from "contribut[ing] financial or other support" to a labor organization. The provision is cast in broad language which, if given its full literal meaning, would make trivial employer civility unlawful. The Board and the courts therefore draw a line between prohibited employer *support* and permitted employer *cooperation*, an important line that is often difficult to perceive.[8]

Even the well-intentioned employer may render prohibited support or commit other, sometimes technical, 8(a)(2) violations. A violation can arise from action taken in good faith without any intention of violating the Act. The defense of good faith is unavailing in section 8(a)(2) cases. The Supreme Court in *Ladies' Garment Workers (Bernhard-Altmann Texas Corp.) v. NLRB*[9]

---

[3]*E.g.*, Chicago Rawhide Mfg. Co. v. NLRB, 221 F2d 165, 35 LRRM 2665 (CA 7, 1955). The law concerning labor organization status is discussed *infra* at notes 15–41.

[4]*See, e.g.*, Remarks of Senator Wagner, *reprinted in* 1 LEGISLATIVE HISTORY OF THE NATIONAL LABOR RELATIONS ACT, 1935, at 15–16 (1949).

[5]Concerning employer domination of labor organizations, *see* text *infra* at notes 47–78.

[6]Discussed *infra* at notes 79–114.

[7]Concerning recognition of and bargaining with one of two or more rival unions, *see* text *infra* at notes 142–161.

[8]Regarding the distinction between employer support and employer cooperation *see* text *infra* at notes 162–200.

[9]366 US 731, 48 LRRM 2251 (1961). *See infra* at notes 82 and 204.

emphatically rejected an employer's "good-faith" defense by noting that nothing in the statutory language prescribes scienter as an element of an 8(a)(2) violation.[10] The Court observed that to hold otherwise would allow a "permissibly careless" employer and union to completely frustrate employee rights.[11] In *Bernhard-Altmann* the employer violated section 8(a)(2) by extending recognition to a labor organization at a time when the employer and the union held a good-faith, although mistaken, belief that the union represented a majority of the employees. By its participation, the union violated section 8(b)(1)(A). Neither the employer nor the union in *Bernhard-Altmann* was able to use good faith as a defense to the unfair labor practice charges.

In *Majestic Weaving Co.*[12] the Board held invalid negotiations with a minority union and the resulting agreement, even though the parties conditioned the efficacy of the agreement upon the union obtaining majority support. The Board held that such grant of recognition, even when conditioned upon attainment of majority status before execution of an agreement, was similar to formal recognition and thus illegal under *Bernhard-Altmann*.

II. LABOR ORGANIZATION DEFINED

Section 2(5) of the Act defines a labor organization as

> any organization of any kind, or any agency or employee representation committee or plan, in which employees participate and which exists for the purpose, in whole or in part, of dealing with employers concerning grievances, labor disputes, wages, rates of pay, hours of employment, or conditions of work.[13]

Under this broad definition, it is often difficult to determine whether employee committees,[14] or other groups of employees

---

[10]*See* Chapter 6, "Interference With Protected Rights," at notes 18–30, and Chapter 7 "Discrimination in Employment," at notes 40–86, for discussions of scienter in relation to §8(a)(1) and §8(a)(3) conduct, respectively.

[11]366 US at 739.

[12]147 NLRB 859, 56 LRRM 1330 (1964), *enforcement denied on procedural grounds*, 355 F2d 854, 61 LRRM 2132 (CA 2, 1966) (overruling its earlier decision in Julius Resnick, Inc., 86 NLRB 38, 24 LRRM 1581 (1949)); *See also* Wickes Corp., 197 NLRB 860, 80 LRRM 1458 (1972). For a discussion of a union as a party to an employer's §8(a)(2) violation, *see infra* at notes 201–211.

[13]For further discussion of the meaning of employee as used in §2(5), see Chapter 28, "Jurisdiction: Coverage of the Act," notes 212–373.

[14]NLRB v. Fremont Mfg. Co., 558 F2d 889, 95 LRRM 3095 (CA 8, 1977), *enforcing* 224 NLRB 597, 92 LRRM 1508 (1976); Mattiace Indus., 239 NLRB 15, 99 LRRM 1476 (1978); Easy-Heat Wirekraft, 238 NLRB 1695, 99 LRRM 1681 (1978); Kux Mfg. Corp., 233 NLRB 317, 97 LRRM 1052 (1977); Eastern Indus., 217 NLRB 712, 89 LRRM 1134 (1975), *enforced*, 558 F2d 889, 95 LRRM 3095 (CA 3, 1976).

not traditionally viewed as unions,[15] are labor organizations within the meaning of the Act.

Section 2(5) does not require labor organizations to have any formal structure. A group of individuals may comprise a labor organization even though it lacks a constitution or bylaws, elected officials, formal meetings, dues, or other formal structure.[16]

The cases generally focus on two statutory prerequisites: the element of employee participation and the purpose of "dealing with employers concerning grievances, labor disputes, wages, rates of pay, hours of employment, or conditions of work."

A. Requirement of Participation by "Employees"

Section 2(5) states that a labor organization is a group in which "employees participate." The Board and the courts have held that, in the absence of any participation by "employees" as defined in section 2(3) of the Act, no statutory labor organization can exist. Thus, domination of an advisory council of truck drivers who are independent contractors does not violate section 8(a)(2).[17] Similarly, groups composed entirely of individuals excluded from the definition of "employees," such as agricultural laborers,[18] supervisors,[19] managerial employees,[20] and

---

[15]*See, e.g.*, Elliott River Tours, 246 NLRB 935, 103 LRRM 1095 (1979) (association of white-water canoe guides held to be labor organization); Major League Rodeo, 246 NLRB 743, 103 LRRM 1015 (1979) (league of rodeo participants and member clubs held to be labor organization); North Am. Soccer League, 236 NLRB 1317, 98 LRRM 1445 (1978) (association of professional soccer players held to have labor organization status).

[16]*E.g.*, Columbia Transit Corp., 237 NLRB 1196, 99 LRRM 1114 (1978); Arkay Packaging Corp., 221 NLRB 99, 90 LRRM 1728 (1975); Lane Aviation Corp., 211 NLRB 824, 86 LRRM 1518 (1974); Stow Mfg., 103 NLRB 1280, 31 LRRM 1635 (1953), *enforced*, 217 F2d 900, 35 LRRM 2210 (CA 2, 1954), *cert. denied*, 348 US 964, 35 LRRM 2612 (1955).

[17]North Am. Van Lines v. NLRB, 869 F2d 596, 130 LRRM 2837 (CA DC, 1989), *denying enforcement to* 288 NLRB 38, 130 LRRM 1320 (1988).

[18]Di Giorgio Fruit Corp. v. NLRB, 191 F2d 642, 28 LRRM 2195 (CA DC), *cert. denied*, 342 US 869, 29 LRRM 2022 (1951). *But see* Ojai Valley Community Hosp., 254 NLRB 1354, 106 LRRM 1278 (1981) (association composed almost exclusively of public employees is §2(5) labor organization).

[19]*See, e.g.*, Masters, Mates & Pilots v. NLRB (Westchester Marine Shipping Co.), 539 F2d 554, 93 LRRM 2429 (CA 5, 1976); Masters, Mates & Pilots v. NLRB (Marine & Mktg. Int'l Corp.), 486 F2d 1271, 84 LRRM 2439 (CA DC, 1973), *cert. denied*, 416 US 956, 85 LRRM 3018 (1974); Directors Guild (Association of Motion Picture & Television Producers), 198 NLRB 707, 81 LRRM 1477 (1972), *enforced*, 494 F2d 692, 85 LRRM 2800 (CA 9, 1974). However, groups composed entirely of supervisors have been held to be labor organizations under other titles of the Act. *E.g.*, Marine Eng'rs, Dist. 2 v. Amoco Oil Co., 554 F2d 774, 95 LRRM 2241 (CA 6, 1977) (Congress did not intend to exclude organizations comprised entirely of supervisors from coverage of §301 jurisdiction), and cases cited therein.

[20]NLRB v. Yeshiva Univ., 444 US 672, 690, 103 LRRM 2526, 2529–33 (1980).

public employees,[21] are not "labor organizations" within the meaning of section 2(5). However, in cases interpreting section 2(5) in the context of certification proceedings and section 8(b) "labor organization" unfair labor practices, the Board and the courts have found labor organization status even where only a minority of the organization's members are employees as defined by section 2(3) of the Act.[22] For example, in *Masters, Mates & Pilots (Chicago Calumet Stevedoring Co.) v. NLRB*,[23] the Court of Appeals for the District of Columbia Circuit affirmed a Board determination that an 11,000-member union constituted a labor organization for purposes of section 8(b), even though only 170 of its members were "employees" under the Act. The employee-participation requirement has not posed a significant obstacle to finding labor organization status in the context of section 8(a)(2) charges.

B. Requirement of "Dealing With" Employers

Section 2(5) limits labor organization status to an organization "which exists for the purpose, in whole or in part, of *dealing with* employers concerning grievances, labor disputes, wages, rates of pay, hours of employment, or conditions of work."[24] In its early decisions, the Board established that the "dealing with" language broadly included various types of employee committees, such as any employer-employee committees which discussed grievances or working conditions, even though they never engaged in formal collective bargaining.[25]

---

[21]United Truck & Bus Serv. Co., 257 NLRB 343, 107 LRRM 1495 (1981).

[22]*See, e.g.*, Masters, Mates & Pilots v. NLRB (Westchester Marine Shipping Co.), *supra* note 19; (Masters, Mates & Pilots v. NLRB (Marine & Mktg. Int'l Corp.), *supra* note 19; Masters, Mates & Pilots (Chicago Calumet Stevedoring Co.), 146 NLRB 116, 55 LRRM 1265 (1964), *enforced*, 351 F2d 771, 59 LRRM 2566 (CA DC, 1965). "Labor organization" status also has been found where the organization includes supervisory employees, South Nassau Communities Hosp., 274 NLRB 1181, 118 LRRM 1590 (1985) (§§8(a)(1) and 8(a)(3) allegations), although the presence of supervisors may disqualify it from serving as bargaining agent; NLRB v. North Shore Univ. Hosp. 724 F2d 269, 115 LRRM 2001 (CA 2, 1983), *on remand*, 274 NLRB 1289, 118 LRRM 1585 (1985); Highland Hosp., 288 NLRB 750, 128 LRRM 1090 (1988), *enforced*, 861 F2d 56, 129 LRRM 2899 (CA 2, 1988) (association of nurses structured to isolate supervisor/members from collective bargaining process held a labor organization); South Nassau Communities Hosp., *supra* (association of nurses including supervisors held a labor organization in case involving §§8(a)(1) and 8(a)(3) allegations; no §8(a)(5) disqualification issue); Sierra Vista Hosp., 241 NLRB 631, 100 LRRM 1590 (1979).

[23]351 F2d 771, 59 LRRM 2566 (CA DC, 1965).

[24]Emphasis added.

[25]*E.g.*, Standard Coil Prods. Co., 110 NLRB 412, 35 LRRM 1013 (1954), *modified on other grounds and enforced*, 224 F2d 465, 36 LRRM 2463 (CA 1), *cert. denied*, 350 US 902, 37

In 1957, in *Cabot Carbon Co.*,[26] the Board held that an employee-committee system, in which elected employee representatives regularly met with management to discuss matters of mutual interest, was a section 2(5) labor organization because the meeting discussions dealt with grievances and working conditions. That committee system was held to be employer dominated; accordingly, the Board ordered the employer to disestablish it. The Fifth Circuit denied enforcement of the Board's order, holding instead that the employee committee was not a labor organization, and that, therefore, section 8(a)(2) was inapplicable. The circuit held that "dealing with," as used in section 2(5), embraced only activity within the usual meaning of collective bargaining. That court construed the section 9(a) proviso,[27] which as amended by Taft-Hartley allowed employees individually to present their grievances to the employer for adjustment, as being in conflict with the Board's interpretation of "dealing with."

Reversing the Fifth Circuit's decision, the Supreme Court held that the employee-committee system was a labor organization; the Court agreed with the Board that discussions relating to seniority, job classifications, holidays, vacations, and various other conditions of employment constituted "dealing with" for purposes of section 2(5). The Court rejected the employer's argument that the committee's proposals and requests "amounted only to recommendations"[28] and that the final decision remained with the employer. The Court found this to be

---

LRRM 2083 (1955) (employer-employee committee formed to "discuss" working conditions is §2(5) labor organization; Board rejected trial examiner's recommendation to modify its §2(5) decisions to allow for "necessary and proper media of communication"); Stow Mfg., *supra* note 16 (§2(5) labor organization found where company president conducted monthly question-and-answer period at which working conditions were often discussed and which sometimes resulted in changes in working conditions); General Shoe Corp., 90 NLRB 1330, 26 LRRM 1331 (1950), *enforced*, 192 F2d 504, 29 LRRM 2112 (CA 6, 1951), *cert. denied*, 343 US 904, 29 LRRM 2606 (1952); Wrought Iron Range Co., 77 NLRB 487, 22 LRRM 1050 (1948); J. W. Greer Co., 52 NLRB 1341, 13 LRRM 70 (1943); B. Z. B. Knitting Co., 28 NLRB 257, 7 LRRM 129 (1940).

[26]117 NLRB 1633, 40 LRRM 1058 (1957), *enforcement denied*, 256 F2d 281, 42 LRRM 2272 (CA 5, 1958), *rev'd and remanded*, 360 US 203, 44 LRRM 2204 (1959).

[27]The §9(a) proviso states: "[A]ny individual employee or a group of employees shall have the right at any time to present grievances to their employer *and to have such grievances adjusted, without the intervention of the bargaining representative, as long as the adjustment is not inconsistent with the terms of a collective-bargaining contract or agreement then in effect: Provided further, That the bargaining representative has been given opportunity to be present at such adjustment.*" (Italicized portion was added by Taft-Hartley amendment.) *See* Chapter 13, "The Duty to Bargain," at notes 105–112, and Chapter 6, "Interference With Protected Rights," at notes 433–437, for discussion of the proviso to §9(a).

[28]360 US at 214.

"true of all such 'dealings,' whether with an independent or a company administered 'labor organization.' The principal distinction lies in the unfettered power of the former to insist upon its requests."[29] After reviewing the legislative history, the Court found no indication that the broad phrase "dealing with" should be viewed as synonymous with the more limited term "bargaining with." The Court also disagreed with the Fifth Circuit's construction of the section 9(a) proviso. According to the Supreme Court, the proviso merely allows employees personally to present their own grievances to their employer; it does not state that an employer may form or maintain an employee committee for the purpose of dealing with the employer concerning grievances; therefore, the proviso as amended did not limit the traditional section 8(a)(2) proscriptions of employer-dominated or -assisted labor organizations.

Since *Cabot Carbon*, the Board and the courts have generally given a broad interpretation to the "dealing with" requirement.[30] In *Thompson Ramo Wooldridge, Inc.*,[31] an employer argued that an employee committee was not a section 2(5) labor organization, because it merely communicated employee

---

[29]*Id.*

[30]*See, e.g.*, Sahara Datsun v. NLRB, 811 F2d 1317, 124 LRRM 3168 (CA 9, 1987) (employee organization lacking formal structure, history, and financial support constitutes labor organization where purpose encompasses dealing with employers concerning both grievances and working conditions); St. Anthony's Hosp., 292 NLRB 1308, 130 LRRM 1460 (1989), *enforcement denied*, 877 F2d 1291, 131 LRRM 2899 (CA 6, 1989) (nurses association formed to improve labor relations and resolve conflicts constitutes union despite disclaimer to contrary); Camvac Int'l, 288 NLRB 816, 130 LRRM 1447 (1988) (working committee formed to obtain employee input before wage reviews and changes in working conditions was labor organization); UARCO, Inc., 286 NLRB 55, 130 LRRM 1051 (1987) (employee committee that met with employer to discuss terms and conditions of employment is labor organization); Onan Corp., Ona Corp. Div., 285 NLRB 400, 128 LRRM 1013 (1987) (employee action committee is labor organization within meaning of §2(5)); Schwab Foods, 284 NLRB 1055, 125 LRRM 1225 (1987), *enforced*, 858 F2d 1285, 129 LRRM 2601 (CA 7, 1988) ("conference committee" composed of elected employee representatives from employer's four stores is labor organization where committee presented employees' complaints and suggestions that resulted in many employee benefits); Texas Bus Lines, 277 NLRB 626, 120 LRRM 1304 (1985) (employee-elected driver committee that dealt with employer on grievances, policies affecting wages, and other terms and conditions of employment is labor organization under Act); Lawson Co., 267 NLRB 463, 114 LRRM 1173 (1983), *enforced in relevant part*, 753 F2d 471, 118 LRRM 2505 (CA 6, 1985) (employer-sponsored employee committee that discussed list of employee demands with employer is labor organization under Act); Mattiace Indus., 239 NLRB 15, 99 LRRM 1476 (1978); Alta Bates Hosp., 226 NLRB 485, 93 LRRM 1288 (1976); Rensselaer Polytechnic Inst., 219 NLRB 712, 89 LRRM 1879 (1975); Money Oldsmobile Co., 201 NLRB 155, 82 LRRM 1379 (1973); North Am. Rockwell Corp., 191 NLRB 833, 77 LRRM 1634 (1971); Utrad Corp., 185 NLRB 434, 75 LRRM 1069 (1970), *modified on other grounds and enforced*, 454 F2d 520, 79 LRRM 2080 (CA 7, 1971). *But see* NLRB v. Scott & Fetzer Co., 691 F2d 288, 111 LRRM 2673 (CA 6, 1982).

[31]132 NLRB 993, 48 LRRM 1470 (1961), *modified and enforced*, 305 F2d 807, 50 LRRM 2759 (CA 7, 1962).

"views" to management and did not make recommendations; management did not negotiate, but simply made unilateral changes when it saw fit to do so. The Board rejected these arguments, holding that "presentation to management of employee 'views,' without specific recommendations as to what action is needed to accommodate those views," constitutes "dealing with" under section 2(5).[32] In *NLRB v. Ampex Corp.*[33] an employer argued that an employee committee was not a labor organization because it had no formal structure, employees were selected at random to attend meetings, and all employees attended one meeting before any employees were selected to attend a second meeting; furthermore, the employer had a separate grievance procedure, and the matters discussed at committee meetings ranged widely beyond the subjects ordinarily discussed by unions and management. Enforcing the Board's order finding the committee to be a section 2(5) labor organization, the Seventh Circuit opined: "We might well be persuaded that this particular mechanism was not a labor organization in the ordinary sense of the term. The statutory definition, however, is very broad."[34]

The very breadth of the definition has called into question a variety of "participative management" arrangements, bringing the section 8(a)(2) prohibition into conflict with emerging managerial techniques for enhancing employee involvement. In three cases decided in the late 1970s, however, the Board somewhat narrowed its interpretation of what "dealing with" means, perhaps in response to this difficulty. In *Sparks Nugget, Inc.*,[35] a Board panel held that a joint employee-employer grievance committee performed a "purely adjudicatory" function and therefore was not "dealing with" an employer within the meaning of section 2(5). Under rules dictated by the employer, the committee consisted of an employee representative, an employer representative, and a neutral member selected by the

---

[32] *Id.* at 995. *See* Stephens Inst., 241 NLRB 454, 100 LRRM 1603 (1979), where the Board found a university faculty senate to be a labor organization. *But cf.* Northeastern Univ., 218 NLRB 247, 89 LRRM 1862 (1975), where the employer argued unsuccessfully in a representation case that the union's petition was barred because the faculty senate was a labor organization and the faculty handbook was a collective bargaining agreement constituting a contract bar. (*See* Chapter 10, "Representation Proceedings and Elections," for a discussion of the contract-bar doctrine.)

[33] 442 F2d 82, 77 LRRM 2072 (CA 7, 1971), *enforcing* 168 NLRB 742, 67 LRRM 1134 (1967), *cert. denied*, 404 US 939, 78 LRRM 2704 (1971).

[34] *Id.* at 84.

[35] 230 NLRB 275, 95 LRRM 1298 (1977).

two representatives. The committee convened only to hear cases filed by individual employees; it did not initiate grievances, recommend changes in terms and conditions of employment, or advocate employee interests. The Board majority concluded: "[T]he Employees' Council performs a purely adjudicatory function and does not interact with management for any purpose or in any manner other than to render a final decision on the grievance. Therefore it cannot be said that the Employees' Council 'deals with' management. Rather, it appears to perform a function for management, i.e., resolving employee grievances."[36]

In *Mercy-Memorial Hospital*,[37] a three-to-two Board held that a joint employee-employer grievance committee was not "dealing with" the employer, even though the committee discussed individual employee grievances and, on occasion, engaged in dialogue with high-level management officials over various employment conditions. Thus the committee in *Mercy-Memorial* went beyond the strict "purely adjudicatory" grievance committee in *Sparks Nugget*.[38]

In *General Foods Corp.*,[39] a unanimous panel, including the two *Mercy-Memorial* dissenters, held that employee participants in an employer's job enrichment program were not "dealing with" the employer and the program was therefore not a statutory labor organization. The job enrichment program divided the 25–30 affected employees into four teams, which acted by consensus to make job assignments, schedule overtime, and, occasionally, participate in interviewing job applicants. Management officials and a consultant met periodically with the teams to discuss the program and such discussions included at least some reference to section 8(d) subjects,[40] such as wages, vacation schedules, and

---

[36]*Id.* at 276. This dispute occurred in the context of an overall refusal by the employer to continue recognition of a Hotel Employees local. The Board held that the refusal to continue recognition was a §8(a)(5) violation and, accordingly, held that unilateral implementation of the grievance plan was also a §8(a)(5) violation.

[37]231 NLRB 1108, 96 LRRM 1239 (1977). Chairman Fanning and Member Jenkins wrote a strong dissent, stating: "We find no support for *Sparks Nugget* in Board precedent, *Cabot Carbon*, or the Act." *Id.* at 1108 n.2. Moreover, the dissenters expressed the belief that §2(5) status should have been found even assuming that *Sparks Nugget* was correctly decided, because the grievance committee engaged in general discussions with management, unlike the committee in *Sparks Nugget*.

[38]*Cf.* Center for United Labor Action, 219 NLRB 873, 90 LRRM 1004 (1975) (social action group seeking to promote unionism, interests of women, minorities, and consumers did not exist for purpose of dealing with employers and therefore was not §2(5) labor organization).

[39]231 NLRB 1232, 96 LRRM 1204 (1977).

[40]*See generally* Chapter 16, "Subjects of Bargaining."

assignments of overtime. Employee committees also investigated plant safety, reevaluated job procedures, and, on one occasion, drafted a job description. The administrative law judge held that the teams' activities involved "managerial functions [which were] flatly delegated to employees and do not involve any dealing with the employer within the meaning of Section 2(5) however expansively that term is applied . . . . These functions were just other assignments of job duties, albeit duties not normally assigned to rank-and-file personnel."[41]

The Sixth Circuit has displayed similar concern with the distinction between legitimate managerial initiatives and impermissible support for an organization. In *NLRB v. Scott & Fetzer Co.*,[42] the court refused to enforce an order of the Board which found that the employer had unlawfully assisted an employee committee. The court regarded the committee not as a substitute for union representation, but as a device created by management for the purpose of enhancing legitimate communication between employees and management, and observed: "not all management efforts to communicate with employees concerning company personnel policy are forbidden on pain of violating the Act. An overly broad construction of the statute would be as destructive of the objects of the Act as ignoring the provisions entirely."[43] The court followed the precedent of its *Scott & Fetzer* decision in *Airstream, Inc. v. NLRB*,[44] where the court again refused to enforce the Board's order. The court distinguished an intervening decision enforcing an order of the Board in a case under section 8(a)(2)[45] on the ground, among others, that in the intervening case the employer had acted with "an anti-union animus" in setting up the employee committee.

The decision of the Board in *General Foods*, and those of the Sixth Circuit in *Scott & Fetzer* and *Airstream*, may be significant in relation to various worker-participation programs, such as Scanlon plans, quality work circles, codetermination programs,

---

[41]231 NLRB at 1235. *See* S & W Motor Lines, 236 NLRB 938, 98 LRRM 1488 (1978), *enforced in part*, 621 F2d 598, 104 LRRM 2310 (CA 4, 1980); Roytype, 199 NLRB 354, 81 LRRM 1219 (1972).

[42]691 F2d 288, 111 LRRM 2673 (CA 6, 1982), *denying enforcement to* 249 NLRB 396, 104 LRRM 1289 (1980).

[43]*Id.* at 292.

[44]877 F2d 1291, 131 LRRM 2899 (CA 6, 1989), *denying enforcement to* 288 NLRB 220, 130 LRRM 1281 (1988).

[45]Lawson Co. v. NLRB, 753 F2d 471, 118 LRRM 2505 (CA 6, 1985), *enforcing* 267 NLRB 463, 114 LRRM 1173 (1983).

and other plans that are designed to solicit worker involvement in day-to-day job activities and decision making.[46]

III. EMPLOYER DOMINATION

Section 8(a)(2) prohibits employer *domination* of a labor organization. Prohibited domination exists when the organization is directed by the employer, rather than by the employees.[47] The original intent of section 8(a)(2) was principally to eradicate "company unions" created by employers to minimize the threat of employee representation by outside labor organizations. However, Congress did not intend to prohibit employees from freely selecting representation by a "company" or "enterprise" union, that is, an independent union organized solely on a companywide basis.[48]

---

[46] *See generally* NATIONAL CENTER FOR PRODUCTIVITY AND QUALITY OF WORKING LIFE, RECENT INITIATIVES IN LABOR-MANAGEMENT COOPERATION (1976); D. Jenkins, JOB POWER (1973); WORKERS' CONTROL (G. Hunnius, G.D. Garson & J. Case eds., 1973); U.S. DEPARTMENT OF LABOR, U.S. LABOR LAW AND THE FUTURE OF LABOR-MANAGEMENT COOPERATION: FINAL REPORT (1989); WORKER ALIENATION: HEARINGS ON S.3916 BEFORE THE SUBCOMMITTEE ON EMPLOYMENT, MANPOWER, AND POVERTY OF THE SENATE COMMITTEE ON LABOR AND PUBLIC WELFARE, 92d Cong., 2d Sess. (1972); Clarke, *Rethinking the Adversarial Model in Labor Relations: An Argument for the Repeal of Section 8(a)(2)*, 96 YALE L.J. 2021 (1987); Murmann, *The Scanlon Plan Joint Committee and Section 8(a)(2)*, 31 LAB. L.J. 299 (1980); Jackson, *An Alternative to Unionization and the Wholly Unorganized Shop: A Legal Basis for Sanctioning Joint Employer-Employee Committees and Increasing Employee Free Choice*, 28 SYRACUSE L. REV. 809 (1977); Shaw, *Worker Participation—American Style*, 3 EMPLOYEE REL. L.J. 38 (1977); Winpisinger, *An American Unionist Looks at Co-determination*, 2 EMPLOYEE REL. L.J. 133 (1976) (Machinist president is apprehensive about worker participation plans); Sangerman, *Employee Committees: Can They Survive Under the Taft-Hartley Act?*, 24 LAB. L.J. 684 (1973); Walton, *How to Counter Alienation in the Plant*, 50 HARV. BUS. REV. 50 (Nov.–Dec. 1972); Note, *Employee Codetermination: Origins in Germany, Present Practice in Europe, and Applicability to the United States*, 47 HARV. J. ON LEGIS. 946 (1977); Note, *The West German Model of Codetermination Under Section 8(a)(2) of the NLRA*, 51 IND. L.J. 795 (1976), Note, *Does Employer Implementation of Employee Production Teams Violate §8(a)(2) of the National Labor Relations Act?*, 49 IND. L.J. 516 (1974).

Worker committees in unorganized plants have come under §8(a)(2) review almost exclusively. To the extent that such committees are the result of mature, arm's-length collective bargaining at organized plants, §8(a)(2) should not pose a serious obstacle. *See generally* Chapter 16, "Subjects of Bargaining."

[47] *E.g.*, Han-Dee Spring & Mfg. Co., 132 NLRB 1542, 48 LRRM 1566 (1961); Wahlgren Magnetics, 132 NLRB 1613, 48 LRRM 1542 (1961).

[48] "Nothing in the bill prohibits the formation of a company union, if by that term is meant an organization of workers confined by their own volition to the boundaries of a particular plant or employer. What is intended is to make such organization the free choice of the workers, and not a choice dictated by forms of interference which are weighty precisely because of the existence of the employer-employee relationship." H.R. REP. NO. 972, 74th Cong., 1st Sess. 15-16 (1935), *reprinted in* 2 NLRB, LEGISLATIVE HISTORY OF THE NATIONAL LABOR RELATIONS ACT, 1935, at 2971–72 (1949). An international comparative note: Almost all Japanese trade unions are "enterprise" unions, confined to the employees of a single employer. *See generally* Hanami, Japan, 5 INTERNATIONAL ENCYCLOPEDIA FOR LABOUR LAW AND INDUSTRIAL RELATIONS ¶¶188-94 (R. Blanpain ed. 1978).

The Board's first case under the Wagner Act involved Pennsylvania Greyhound Lines, which formed and controlled a company union for the handling of employee grievances, in an effort to avoid dealing with a more militant outside organization.[49] The Board completely disestablished the company union and ordered the employer never to bargain with it again.[50] By the eve of the enactment of the Taft-Hartley amendments in 1947, Board Chairman Herzog was able to observe, in the *Detroit Edison* case,[51] that employer domination of company unions had ceased to be the problem it had been in 1935. The prohibition was nevertheless kept intact in the new Act.

The Board's basic approach to unlawful domination of labor organizations was approved by the Supreme Court in *Newport News Shipbuilding & Drydock Co. v. NLRB*.[52] The Board there ordered disestablishment of an employee committee which gave the employer the power to veto the organization's proposed actions, even though the challenged organization had prevented serious labor disputes and had employee support, and there was no evidence that the employer had actually exercised its power to control it. The Board and the Court found that the employer possessed such "control of the form and structure of an employee organization" as to deprive the employees of the "complete freedom of action guaranteed to them by the Act."[53]

While there is uniform agreement that section 8(a)(2) was designed to facilitate employee free choice and self-organization, the Board and the courts have wrestled with the problem of distinguishing between *cooperation*, which the Act permits, and *domination*, which the Act prohibits.[54] In *Humble Oil & Refining Co. v. NLRB*,[55] the Fifth Circuit noted that the Board is not the

---

[49]Pennsylvania Greyhound Lines, 1 NLRB 1, 1 LRRM 303 (1935), *enforced*, 303 US 261, 2 LRRM 599 (1938).

[50]Disestablishment of company unions is the traditional Board remedy whenever prohibited domination or control is found. *See, e.g.*, Metropolitan Alloys Corp., 233 NLRB 966, 97 LRRM 1220 (1977), *enforced*, 624 F2d 743, 105 LRRM 3419 (CA 6, 1980); Kux Mfg. Corp., 233 NLRB 317, 97 LRRM 1052 (1977). *See infra* at notes 212–227.

[51]74 NLRB 267, 20 LRRM 1160 (1947).

[52]308 US 241, 5 LRRM 665 (1939).

[53]*Id.* at 249. Similarly, in NLRB v. Brown Paper Mill Co., 108 F2d 867, 5 LRRM 782 (CA 5, 1940), the employee association members testified that they were not dominated or coerced by the employer and that they desired representation by the association. Although the Board found no evidence that the employer in fact dominated the association, disestablishment was ordered because the employer had supported its formation.

[54]*See* Hertzka & Knowles v. NLRB, 503 F2d 625, 87 LRRM 2503 (CA 9, 1974), *denying enforcement to* 206 NLRB 191, 84 LRRM 1556 (1973), *cert. denied*, 423 US 875, 90 LRRM 2554 (1975).

[55]113 F2d 85, 6 LRRM 816 (CA 5, 1940).

"guardian or ruler over the employees, but is only empowered to deliver them from restraint at the hands of the employer when it exists."[56] Concerning employees' preference for an inside committee system rather than an outside union, Judge Magruder, in *Coppus Engineering Corp. v. NLRB*,[57] commented that the "choice was theirs," and that the Act was limited to guaranteeing them the "freedom to exercise that choice unimpeded by employer interference or coercion."[58]

In *Spiegel Trucking Co.*[59] the Board found the following factors relevant to the question of domination: (1) the relationship of the employer to the labor organization; (2) the nature of the collective bargaining negotiations between the parties; (3) what control, if any, the employer has over the union's membership; (4) whether the organization has a constitution and bylaws; (5) the nature and place of meetings of the organization; (6) whether employees are compensated for time and attendance at such meetings; and (7) whether supervisory personnel attend such meetings, and if so, their role in the organization.[60]

Generally, the Board considers a labor organization unlawfully dominated if the employer has the *potential power* to control it,[61] but reviewing courts generally have required evidence of *actual control*.[62] This difference in approach was illustrated by the Board's decision in *Northeastern University*[63] and the

---

[56]*Id.* at 88.

[57]240 F2d 564, 39 LRRM 2315 (CA 1, 1957).

[58]*Id.* at 573 (Magruder, C.J., concurring). Judge Magruder added: "[T]he statute does not make it the duty of the employer, nor a function of the Board to 'baby' along the employees in the direction of choosing an outside union as a bargaining representative." *Id.* at 574.

[59]225 NLRB 178, 179, 92 LRRM 1604 (1976) *enforced*, 559 F2d 188, 95 LRRM 3010 (CA DC, 1977); *accord* Wahlgren Magnetics, *supra* note 47.

[60]In *Spiegel*, the Board declined to find unlawful domination, although the employer was the moving force in the formation of the Spiegel Trucking Company Drivers Committee, because of an absence of proof of domination after the formation of the organization.

[61]*See, e.g*, Stephens Inst., 241 NLRB 454, 100 LRRM 1603 (1979); Janesville Prods. Div., 240 NLRB 854, 100 LRRM 1383 (1979), *enforcement granted in part and denied in part*, 610 F2d 819 (CA 7, 1979); Northeastern Univ., 235 NLRB 858, 98 LRRM 1347 (1978), *enforcement denied*, 601 F2d 1208, 101 LRRM 2767 (CA 1, 1979); Duquesne Univ., 198 NLRB 891, 81 LRRM 1091 (1972); Tuscarora Plastics Co., 167 NLRB 1059, 66 LRRM 1229 (1967); Hydraulic Accessories Co., 165 NLRB 864, 65 LRRM 1603 (1967).

[62]As the Ninth Circuit stated in Hertzka & Knowles v. NLRB, *supra* note 54, at 630: "The sum of this is that a section 8(a)(2) finding must rest on a showing that the employees' free choice, either in type of organization or in the assertion of demands, is stifled by the degree of employer involvement at issue." *See* Federal-Mogul Corp. v. NLRB, 394 F2d 915, 918, 68 LRRM 2332 (CA 6, 1968); NLRB v. Prince Macaroni Mfg. Co., 329 F2d 803, 809–12, 55 LRRM 2852 (CA 1, 1964); Coppus Eng'g Corp. v. NLRB, *supra* note 57; Chicago Rawhide Mfg. Co. v. NLRB, 221 F2d 165, 167–68, 35 LRRM 2665 (CA 7, 1955); *but cf.* Newport News Shipbuilding & Drydock Co., *supra* note 52.

[63]*Supra* note 61.

First Circuit's denial of enforcement.[64] The Board found the following evidence of domination: The university allowed meetings on company property and company time, assisted with election procedures, provided printing and secretarial services, and funded some social activities; management representatives attended some meetings of the employee organization, individual members of the organization consulted with management, and the university originally announced that it had "established" the employee organization.[65] In applying its test requiring *actual* domination, the First Circuit commented that "allowing meetings on company property and company time, assisting with election procedures, providing for printing and secretarial services, and funding occasional social activities—does not a domination case make."[66]

The courts have recognized that the potential means for domination are always present to some degree in any employer-employee relationship;[67] however, there is no basis for a finding of a section 8(a)(2) violation without evidence of its realization. "Words and actions which might dominate the employees in their choice of a bargaining agent do not constitute domination proscribed by the Act unless the employees are actually dominated."[68]

Courts have also held that employer cooperation which assists the employees or their bargaining representative in expressing their interests does not violate section 8(a)(2);[69] indeed, such assistance may be needed where the bargaining representative is "a feeble instrument."[70] Several court decisions have insisted that an organization is not *per se* dominated simply because it has no formal membership, no dues, no mass meetings, and no written collective bargaining agreement.[71] In one case, the

---

[64]*Id.*

[65]The Board ordered disestablishment even though there was no outside labor organization seeking to represent the employees, there was no movement among the employees to seek representation by another union, and the admittedly useful services performed by the organization would go undone.

[66]NLRB v. Northeastern Univ., 601 F2d 1208, 1214, 101 LRRM 2767 (CA 1, 1979).

[67]*See, e.g.,* Chicago Rawhide Mfg. Co. v. NLRB, *supra* note 62.

[68]*Id.* at 167.

[69]*See, e.g.,* NLRB v. Northeastern Univ., *supra* note 66.

[70]Coppus Eng'g Corp. v. NLRB, *supra* note 57, at 573 (also quoted in NLRB v. Northeastern Univ., *supra* note 66, at 1213).

[71]*See, e.g,* NLRB v. Northeastern Univ., *supra* note 66; Hertzka & Knowles v. NLRB, *supra* note 54. The courts have held that the Act does not require approval of a purely adversarial model of labor relations. Hertzka & Knowles v. NLRB, *id.* at 631. For criticism of the Board's adversarial approach, *see* Note, *Discarding the Doctrine of Supervisory Domination: New Solutions to an Old Conflict of Interest,* 30 HASTINGS L.J. 763 (1979).

appellate court found insufficient evidence of actual domination where the employer had permitted meetings on company time, had controlled the length of meetings, and had advised an employee representative not to concern himself with a particular safety problem.[72]

The Board and the courts are in general agreement, however, that domination exists where the employer creates an employee committee, selects the employee representatives, requires that committee membership be on a rotating basis, and determines when meetings will be held and also presides over them.[73] The same standards apply equally to labor organizations acting as employers.[74]

The involvement of supervisors in the affairs of labor organizations also can establish unlawful domination. In *Kresge Department Store*[75] the Board held that section 14(a) of the Act, which expressly permits supervisors to join unions and remain members, does not prohibit consideration of supervisor membership in unions as a factor in finding unlawful employer domination. In *Nassau & Suffolk Contractors Ass'n*,[76] the Board found a section 8(a)(2) violation where the employer had acquiesced in the union's placement of supervisors on the union's negotiating committee. Such acquiescence, however, was insufficient to sup-

---

[72]Federal-Mogul Corp. v. NLRB, *supra* note 62; *see also* Hotpoint Co. v. NLRB, 289 F2d 683, 48 LRRM 2101 (CA 7, 1961).

[73]*See, e.g.*, Utrad Corp. v. NLRB, 454 F2d 520, 79 LRRM 2080 (CA 7, 1971), *enforcing* 185 NLRB 434, 75 LRRM 1069 (1970); NLRB v. Ampex Corp., 442 F2d 82, 77 LRRM 2072 (CA 7, 1971), *enforcing* 168 NLRB 742, 67 LRRM 1134 (1967), *cert. denied*, 404 US 939, 78 LRRM 2704 (1971); NLRB v. Reed Rolled Thread Die Co., 432 F2d 70, 75 LRRM 2344 (CA 5, 1970); Camvac Int'l, 288 NLRB 816, 130 LRRM 1447 (1988); Onan Corp., Ona Corp. Div., 285 NLRB 400, 128 LRRM 1013 (1987); Hunter Douglas, Inc., 277 NLRB 1179, 121 LRRM 1064 (1985), *enforced*, 804 F2d 808, 123 LRRM 2912 (CA 3 1986), *cert. denied*, 481 U.S. 1069, 125 LRRM 2440 (1987); Lawson Co., 267 NLRB 463, 114 LRRM 1173 (1983), *enforced*, 753 F2d 471, 118 LRRM 2505 (CA 6, 1985); STR, Inc., 221 NLRB 496, 90 LRRM 1591 (1975); Rensselaer Polytechnic Inst., 219 NLRB 712, 89 LRRM 1879 (1975); Rupp Indus., 217 NLRB 385, 88 LRRM 1603 (1975); Versatube Corp., 203 NLRB 456, 83 LRRM 1118 (1973), *enforced*, 492 F2d 795, 86 LRRM 2128 (CA 6, 1974); American Mfg., 196 NLRB 248, 79 LRRM 1694 (1972). In Kux Mfg. Corp., 233 NLRB 317, 97 LRRM 1052 (1977), the employer paid representatives for time spent in meetings, unilaterally prepared and issued minutes of the meetings, and responded favorably only to those complaints and suggestions brought by representatives which it found beneficial to its own interests. *See also* Liberty Mkts., 236 NLRB 1486, 99 LRRM 1163 (1978); Kurz-Kasch, Inc., 239 NLRB 1044, 100 LRRM 1118 (1978); Rideout Memorial Hosp., 227 NLRB 1338, 94 LRRM 1703 (1977); *but see* NLRB v. Homemaker Shops, 724 F2d 535, 115 LRRM 2321 (CA 6, 1984), *denying enforcement in part to* 261 NLRB 441, 110 LRRM 1082 (1982).

[74]In Teamsters Local 688, 215 NLRB 852, 88 LRRM 1217 (1974), the labor organization-employer violated §8(a)(2) by entering into a collective bargaining agreement with itself as representative of its clerical employees.

[75]77 NLRB 212, 21 LRRM 1345 (1948).

[76]118 NLRB 174, 40 LRRM 1146 (1957).

port a finding of domination, because there was no proof that the employer was in any way responsible for placing the supervisors on the negotiating committee. The issue of supervisory involvement also arises in representation cases where such involvement can be so extensive as to constitute a conflict of interest preventing the labor organization from acting in the employees' interest.[77]

A section 8(a)(2) "domination" violation cannot be based solely on events occurring outside the six-month limitations period imposed by section 10(b) of the Act. But a violation will be found where the prior conduct is sufficiently connected with conduct within the limitations period, as where the employer retains during the period control first gained outside it.[78]

IV. EMPLOYER INTERFERENCE

Another unlawful means of undermining employees' rights to select the bargaining representative of their choice is employer *interference* with the creation or operation of a labor organization. Such activity goes beyond merely interfering with section 7 rights of individual employees;[79] it is aimed instead at the labor organization as an entity.[80] A narrow and often obscure line divides actual or attempted unlawful "interference" or "assistance" from what constitutes unlawful "domination." Board and court decisions often create confusion by using the three terms indiscriminately to describe similar conduct. The difference between domination and interference or assistance is a matter of degree. Domination of a union constitutes an irreversible subjugation of the union to the employer's will; interference or assistance is misconduct sufficiently less severe that the union is deemed capable of functioning as a union once the

---

[77]*E.g.*, Sierra Vista Hosp., 241 NLRB 631, 100 LRRM 1590 (1979); *accord* Rockford Memorial Hosp., 247 NLRB 319, 103 LRRM 1165 (1980); Farber Cancer Inst., 247 NLRB 1, 103 LRRM 1132 (1980); Healdsburg Gen. Hosp., 247 NLRB 212, 103 LRRM 1135 (1980); Exeter Hosp., 248 NLRB 292, 104 LRRM 1052 (1980). *See also* Home Box Office, NLRB Gen. Counsel Advice Memo. No. 31-CA-9104, 103 LRRM 1159 (1979).

[78]*E.g.*, NLRB v. Erie Marine, 465 F2d 104, 80 LRRM 3330 (CA 3, 1972); Consolidated Flavor Corp., 238 NLRB 326, 99 LRRM 1416 (1978); *see* Machinists Local Lodge 1424 v. NLRB (Bryan Mfg. Co.), 362 US 411, 45 LRRM 3212 (1960). *See* Chapter 31, "NLRB Procedures."

[79]*See generally* Chapter 6, "Interference With Protected Rights."

[80]*See, e.g.*, Nassau & Suffolk Contractors Ass'n, *supra* note 76.

interference or assistance is removed.[81] For example, in *Ladies' Garment Workers v. NLRB (Bernhard-Altmann)*,[82] an employer unlawfully assisted a union by recognizing it as the exclusive representative of the employees when it did not have majority status. That was unlawful assistance but not domination; there were no allegations or evidence that the employer was able to control the activities of the union.[83] Even when a showing of majority support for a union can arguably be made, the Board and the courts continue to hold that an employer violates section 8(a)(2) by recognizing and bargaining with that union if the union's majority is tainted by unlawful employer coercion or assistance.[84]

---

[81] For cases discussing the distinction between domination and interference, *see* Liquor Salesmen Local 195 v. NLRB (Brescome Distribs. Corp.), 452 F2d 1312, 78 LRRM 2641 (1971); NLRB v. Dennison Mfg. Co., 419 F2d 1080, 72 LRRM 2972 (CA 1, 1969), *cert. denied*, 397 US 1023, 73 LRRM 2868 (1970); Newman-Green, Inc., 161 NLRB 1062, 63 LRRM 1405 (1966); Lunardi-Central Distrib. Co., 161 NLRB 1443, 63 LRRM 1457 (1966).

[82] 366 US 731, 48 LRRM 2251 (1961).

[83] *See* NLRB v. Pacific Erectors, 718 F2d 1459, 114 LRRM 3230 (CA 9, 1983) (§8(a)(2) violation based on employer's withdrawal of recognition from majority union and concomitant recognition of different union having only minority support); Shortway Suburban Lines, 286 NLRB 323, 126 LRRM 1225 (1987), *enforced*, 862 F2d 309, 129 LRRM 3144 (CA 3, 1988) (successor-employer violated §8(a)(2) by recognizing outside union and applying terms of collective bargaining agreement when outside union did not represent majority of employees); Christopher St. Owners Corp., 286 NLRB 253, 126 LRRM 1158 (1987) (employer violated §8(a)(2) by maintaining and enforcing collective bargaining agreement with outside union that did not represent majority of employees when agreement was executed); Caro Bags, 285 NLRB 656, 128 LRRM 1031 (1987) (employer violated §8(a)(2) by recognizing union that did not represent majority of employees); Roundup Co. dba Fred Meyer, Inc. dba Meyer's Cafe & Konditorei, 282 NLRB 1, 124 LRRM 1005 (1986) (employer violated §8(a)(2) by rendering assistance to and recognizing outside union as representative of newly hired delicatessen employees, where union did not represent uncoerced majority of employees; employees were accretion to unit of employees represented by incumbent union at restaurant); R. Waldo, Inc., 280 NLRB 1237, 124 LRRM 1046 (1986) (employer violated §8(a)(2) by executing renewal collective bargaining agreement with incumbent union when all but one employee had signed authorization cards of another labor organization; employer was aware before it executed renewal contract that incumbent union had lost its majority support); Ryder Sys., 280 NLRB 1024, 124 LRRM 1113 (1986) (employer violated §8(a)(2) by executing collective bargaining agreement with union that did not represent majority of employees); Safeway Stores, 276 NLRB 944, 120 LRRM 1186 (1985) (employer violated §8(a)(2) by recognizing union as bargaining agent at new store where there was no majority support, thus rendering "additional stores" clause of collective bargaining agreement inapplicable); Windsor Place Corp., 276 NLRB 445, 120 LRRM 1101 (1985) (employer violated §8(a)(2) when it recognized union that did not have majority support; one of two unit employees had also signed card designating another union as bargaining agent); Sav-On Drugs, 267 NLRB 639, 114 LRRM 1102 (1983) (Board found that newly opened store was not accretion to existing bargaining unit, and, accordingly, employer violated §8(a)(2) by recognizing union as bargaining agent for employees at that store when it did not have majority support).

[84] Christopher St. Owners Corp., *supra* note 83; Rainey Sec. Agency, 274 NLRB 269, 119 LRRM 1043 (1985) (employer unlawfully recognized union it had assisted in obtaining authorization cards from employees); MGR Equip. Corp., 272 NLRB 353, 117 LRRM 1302 (1984) (employer violated §8(a)(2) by recognizing unlawfully assisted union;

It is also well established that an employer renders unlawful section 8(a)(2) assistance by recognizing and executing a collective bargaining agreement with a union at a time when the employer does not employ a substantial and representative complement of the projected work force in the relevant bargaining unit, or at a time when it is not engaged in normal operations.[85] In *Spiegel Trucking Co.*[86] the Board upheld an administrative law judge's decision that an employer's active role in the formation of an employee group was unlawful interference under section 8(a)(2), but reversed the ALJ's conclusion that such conduct was also unlawful domination. The Board noted that while unlawful interference as the moving force in the formation of the union had indeed occurred, "it did not automatically follow that [the employer] was guilty of unlawful domination" in the absence of proof that the employer controlled the union after its formation.[87] This is an example of employer conduct that falls short of the standard required for a finding of domination but that is nevertheless unlawful under section 8(a)(2) as proscribed interference.

While the distinction between "domination" and "interference" or "assistance" is often obscure, it nevertheless determines the appropriate remedy.[88] The Board imposes the more severe remedy of disestablishment when an employer's conduct constitutes illegal "domination," but uses less severe remedies in cases of "interference" or "assistance."[89]

---

employee was permitted to use working hours and company premises in efforts to form new union); Jet Spray Corp., 271 NLRB 127, 116 LRRM 1379 (1984) (employer violated §8(a)(2) by interfering with and dominating employee association); Farmers Energy Corp., 266 NLRB 722, 113 LRRM 1037 (1983) *enforced*, 730 F2d 1098, 115 LRRM 3469 (CA 7, 1984) (employer improperly initiated idea of bringing independent union into plant, permitted its facilities to be used by employee organizers, paid employees for participating in union activities, determined composition of employee negotiating committee, and threatened plant closure, discharges, and layoffs). *See also* NLRB v. Homemakers Shops, *supra* note 73; National Maritime Union v. NLRB (Monfort of Colo.), 683 F2d 305, 111 LRRM 2286 (CA 9, 1982) (court enforced Board order based on finding that employer unlawfully recognized union it assisted in obtaining authorization cards which were never verified).

[85]Sheraton Great Falls Inn, 242 NLRB 1255, 101 LRRM 1381 (1979); Allied Prods. Corp., 220 NLRB 732, 735, 90 LRRM 1476 (1975).

[86]225 NLRB 178, 92 LRRM 1604 (1976).

[87]*Id.* at 179.

[88]*See, e.g,* Packerland Packing Co. of Tex., 221 NLRB 1119, 91 LRRM 1062 (1975), *enforced in relevant part*, 537 F2d 1343, 93 LRRM 2128 (CA 5, 1976); Graham Ford, Inc., 218 NLRB 980, 89 LRRM 1796 (1975); Harpeth Steel, 208 NLRB 545, 85 LRRM 1174 (1974).

[89]*See* text *infra* at notes 212–241; Jet Spray Corp., *supra* note 84 (dominated union ordered disestablished); Comet Corp., 261 NLRB 1414, 110 LRRM 1276 (1982); Flex Plastics, 262 NLRB 651, 110 LRRM 1365 (1982), *enforced*, 726 F2d 272, 115 LRRM 3036 (CA 6, 1984) (unlawfully assisted union's recognition withdrawn but union not ordered disestablished).

A. Employer Preference Among Contending Unions

Section 8(a)(2) ensures that employees designate a collective bargaining representative of their own independent choice without interference by the employer, who might prefer dealing with an inside or less aggressive labor organization. It is unlawful for an employer to form or urge its employees to form an inside labor organization.[90] Thus, in *NLRB v. Fremont Manufacturing Co.*,[91] the Eighth Circuit upheld a Board decision that an employer had violated section 8(a)(2) by conducting an election to select employees to serve on a newly created "Progress Team" and to present employee grievances to the employer contemporaneously with an outside union's organizational campaign. Similarly, employer conduct that actively benefits a preferred outside labor organization over an incumbent,[92] or prefers one of two rival outside labor organizations,[93] violates the Act, and generally falls within the definition of unlawful "assistance."[94]

---

[90]*E.g.*, UARCO, Inc., 286 NLRB 55, 130 LRRM 1051 (1987); Superior Container, 276 NLRB 521, 120 LRRM 1089 (1985); Flex Plastics, *supra* note 89; Coating Prods., 251 NLRB 1271, 105 LRRM 1399 (1980), *enforced*, 648 F2d 108, 107 LRRM 2337 (CA 2, 1981); Miller Materials Co., 244 NLRB 496, 102 LRRM 1069 (1979); G. Q. Sec. Parachutes, 242 NLRB 508, 101 LRRM 1247 (1979); World Wide Press, 242 NLRB 346, 101 LRRM 1205 (1979); Rideout Memorial Hosp., *supra* note 73; Doces Sixth Ave., 225 NLRB 806, 93 LRRM 1091 (1976); Victor M. Sprys dba Eastern Indus., 217 NLRB 712, 89 LRRM 1134 (1975), *enforced*, 538 F2d 319, 93 LRRM 2336 (CA 3, 1976); Sportspal, Inc., 214 NLRB 917, 88 LRRM 1533 (1974); Tappan Knitting Indus., 201 NLRB 3, 82 LRRM 1447 (1973).

[91]558 F2d 889, 95 LRRM 3095 (CA 8, 1977), *enforcing* 224 NLRB 597, 92 LRRM 1508 (1976).

[92]Independent Ass'n of Steel Fabricators, 231 NLRB 264, 97 LRRM 1391 (1977), *enforcement denied in part*, 582 F2d 135, 98 LRRM 3150 (CA 2, 1978), *cert. denied*, 439 US 1130, 100 LRRM 2334 (1979); Precision Carpet, Inc., 223 NLRB 329, 92 LRRM 1333 (1976); Arkay Packaging Corp., 221 NLRB 99, 90 LRRM 1728 (1975); Freeman G. Gaffney, Inc., 205 NLRB 1012, 84 LRRM 1248 (1973); Carbona Mining Corp., 198 NLRB 293, 80 LRRM 1628 (1972); Penn Bldg. Maintenance Corp., 195 NLRB 183, 79 LRRM 1416 (1972); Columbus Janitor Serv., 191 NLRB 902, 77 LRRM 1737 (1971).

[93]Ralco Sewing Indus., 243 NLRB 438, 101 LRRM 1578 (1979); Ravenswood Elec. Corp., 232 NLRB 609, 97 LRRM 1170 (1977); Hartz Mountain Corp., 228 NLRB 492, 96 LRRM 1589 (1977), *enforced sub nom.* Distributive Workers Dist. 65 v. NLRB, 593 F2d 1155, 99 LRRM 2640 (CA DC, 1978); River Manor Health Related Facility, 224 NLRB 227, 93 LRRM 1069 (1976); Suburban Transit Corp., 203 NLRB 465, 83 LRRM 1588 (1973); Shreveport Packing Corp., 196 NLRB 498, 80 LRRM 1206 (1972); Northrop Corp., 187 NLRB 172, 76 LRRM 1824 (1970).

[94]*See infra* notes 115–141; Park Inn Home for Adults, 293 NLRB No. 130, 132 LRRM 1139 (1989); Systems Mgmt., 292 NLRB 1078, 131 LRRM 1729 (1989); United Artists Communications, 280 NLRB 1056, 122 LRRM 1296 (1986) (employer violated §8(a)(2) by rendering assistance to incumbent union after outside union filed petition; employer unlawfully threatened employees with discharge and promised them benefits to induce them to sign cards); Midwestern Mining & Reclamation, 277 NLRB 221, 121 LRRM 1170 (1985); Olympia Plastics Corp., 266 NLRB 519, 112 LRRM 1416 (1983). *But see* Raley's, Inc. v. NLRB, 703 F2d 410, 112 LRRM 3376 (CA 9, 1983), *vacated and remanded*, 725 F2d 1204, 115 LRRM 2933 (CA 9, 1984) (en banc) (court held that employer's announcement explaining health and welfare benefits to employees in order to induce them to retain incumbent union and reject rival was lawful and protected by §8(c) of Act).

For example, the Sixth Circuit, in *Schlabach Coal Co. v. NLRB*,[95] held that an employer violated section 8(a)(2) when it assisted a preferred outside labor organization, threatened to shut down if the employees supported a rival union, and discharged an employee because he supported the other union. However, an employer may tell its employees that it favors an inside union, or it may even suggest that the employees form such an organization, provided it does not help them plan and organize it.[96] The courts, in general, have enforced the Board's determinations of unlawful interference.[97]

B. Conduct of Supervisors

Participation by an employer's supervisors in a union organizing effort frequently has been held unlawful. In representation cases, the Board has identified certain conduct by supervisors that is deemed so coercive of employee section 7 rights as to "taint" a petitioning labor organization's showing of interest among unit employees, thereby resulting in the Board's dismissal of the representation petition, the setting aside of an election won by the labor organization, or the revoking of the union's certification.[98] In this situation, strict principles of agency are not followed, and an employer violates section 8(a)(2) when its supervisors engage in offending conduct, whether or not such conduct is known, actually authorized, or subsequently ratified by the employer.[99] As the Supreme Court noted in

---

[95]611 F2d 1161, 104 LRRM 2593 (CA 6, 1979).

[96]Missouri Heel Co., 209 NLRB 481, 85 LRRM 1442 (1974); Walker's Midstream Fuel Serv. Co., 208 NLRB 158, 85 LRRM 1065 (1974); Greyhound Airport Servs., 204 NLRB 900, 83 LRRM 1712 (1973). In Hertzka & Knowles v. NLRB, 503 F2d 625, 87 LRRM 2503 (CA 9, 1974), the Ninth Circuit denied enforcement to a Board order which had held that an employer violated §8(a)(2) by allowing employees to meet on company time and premises to set up an inside employee committee. The court noted that the idea for such committee originated with the employees themselves, who had given their approval to the organization in its final form.

[97]NLRB v. Flex Plastics, 726 F2d 272, 115 LRRM 3036 (CA 6, 1984); Coating Prods. v. NLRB, 648 F2d 108, 107 LRRM 2327 (CA 2, 1981). *But see* NLRB v. Homemaker Shops, 724 F2d 535, 115 LRRM 2321 (CA 6, 1984), *denying enforcement to* 261 NLRB 441, 110 LRRM 1082 (1982) (organization found to be effective employee representative; peaceful cooperation held not unlawful).

[98]NLRB v. North Shore Univ. Hosp., 724 F.2d 269, 115 LRRM 2001 (CA 2, 1983), *on remand*, 274 NLRB 1289, 118 LRRM 1585 (1985) (supervisory influence in union as a whole required revocation of certification).

[99]*E.g.*, Plumbers & Pipe Fitters Local 636 v. NLRB (Detroit Ass'n of Plumbing Contractors), 287 F2d 354, 47 LRRM 2457 (CA DC, 1961), *enforcing* 126 NLRB 1381, 45 LRRM 1482 (1960); University of Chicago Library, 205 NLRB 220, 83 LRRM 1678 (1973). *But see* Castaways Mgmt., 285 NLRB 954, 126 LRRM 1231 (1987) (employer's direction to supervisor to perform unlawful act is not in and of itself violation of Act).

Machinists Lodge 35 v. NLRB (Serrick Corp.):[100]

> The employer . . . may be held to have assisted . . . a union even though the acts of the so-called agents were not expressly authorized or might not be attributable to him on strict application of the rules of *respondeat superior*. We are dealing here not with private rights . . . nor with technical concepts pertinent to an employer's legal responsibility to third persons . . . but with a clear legislative policy to free the collective bargaining process from all taint of an employer's compulsion, domination or influence.[101]

In *Stevenson Equipment Co.*[102] the Board explained that supervisory participation in the solicitation of authorization cards could be a basis either for not counting these "tainted" cards in a "showing of interest" card check or for valid objections to an election. Supervisor's solicitation of cards (1) "might well imply to the employee that their employer favors the union"[103] or (2) might coerce employees into signing authorization cards for fear of future retaliation by the supervisors. In the former situation, an employer's vigorous antiunion campaign following the supervisors' pro-union conduct can negate the potential coercion of employees;[104] and in the latter, the employer's termination of the offending supervisor may abate the employees' fears.[105]

Supervisory conduct unlawful under section 8(a)(2) includes supervisors signing authorization cards in the presence of unit employees,[106] soliciting employees to sign authorization cards, whether explicitly or implicitly,[107] requiring other employees to

---

[100]311 US 72, 7 LRRM 282 (1940).

[101]*Id.* at 80.

[102]174 NLRB 865, 70 LRRM 1302 (1969).

[103]*Id.* at 866.

[104]Gary Aircraft, 220 NLRB 187, 90 LRRM 1216 (1975).

[105]Rocky Mountain Bank Note Co., 230 NLRB 922, 95 LRRM 1421 (1977) (employer suspended and discharged offending supervisor before representation election).

[106]Fugazy Continental Corp., 265 NLRB 1301, 112 LRRM 1203 (1982), *enforced*, 725 F2d 1416, 115 LRRM 2571 (CA DC, 1984); Boston Pet Supply, 227 NLRB 1891, 95 LRRM 1096 (1977); Glomac Plastics, 194 NLRB 406, 78 LRRM 1662 (1971); Sopps, Inc., 175 NLRB 296, 70 LRRM 1555 (1969); Boyer Bros., 170 NLRB 1108, 68 LRRM 1494 (1968), *enforced*, 448 F2d 555, 78 LRRM 2225 (CA 3, 1971).

[107]A.M.A. Leasing, 283 NLRB 1017, 125 LRRM 1170 (1987); Ryder Sys., 280 NLRB 1024, 124 LRRM 1113 (1986); Denver Lamb Co., 269 NLRB 508, 116 LRRM 1144 (1984); Hillside Bus Corp., 262 NLRB 1254, 110 LRRM 1552 (1982); Lamar Elec. Membership Corp., 164 NLRB 979, 65 LRRM 1199 (1967); *contra* Red Barn Sys., 224 NLRB 1586, 92 LRRM 1404 (1976); Independent Sprinkler & Fire Protection Co., 220 NLRB 941, 90 LRRM 1564 (1975); Yonkers Hamilton Sanitarium, 214 NLRB 668, 88 LRRM 1357 (1974); Howard Creations, Inc., 212 NLRB 179, 87 LRRM 1466 (1974); Lawrence Rigging, Inc., 202 NLRB 1094, 82 LRRM 1784 (1973); Scottex Corp., 200 NLRB 446, 82 LRRM 1287 (1972); Luby Leasing, Inc., 198 NLRB 951, 81 LRRM 1097 (1972);Prospect Gardens, 177 NLRB 136, 72 LRRM 1173 (1969); Park Inn Hotel, 139 NLRB 669, 51 LRRM 1369 (1962).

sign the union authorization cards,[108] and allowing union organizers unfettered access to employees while standing by and watching in an approving manner.[109] For example, in *Packing House & Industrial Services v. NLRB*,[110] the Eighth Circuit held that an employer violated section 8(a)(2) when its agents passed out union-designation cards at the time job applications were accepted at a facility recently purchased from a predecessor employer.[111] A supervisor's procuring of employee support for an antiunion petition violates section 8(a)(1), but not section 8(a)(2) inasmuch as the conduct does not support or assist any labor organization.[112]

However, not every instance of supervisory participation is unlawful. A low-level supervisor's solicitation of cards does not always warrant a finding of "supervisory taint,"[113] nor will a mere statement of personal preference by a supervisor who favors the union constitute unlawful coercion of employee rights.[114]

V. THE REQUIREMENT OF EMPLOYER NEUTRALITY

Section 8(a)(2) prohibits an employer from contributing "support" to a labor organization. However, in the absence of unlawful interference, the Act does not prohibit an employer from expressing a preference for a particular union over its rival.[115] Nor does the mere filing of a representation petition by an outside, challenging union require or permit an employer to withdraw from bargaining or refrain from executing a contract

---

[108]Ryder Sys., *supra* note 107; Gold Standard Enters., 249 NLRB 356, 104 LRRM 1423 (1980), *enforced*, 679 F2d 673, 110 LRRM 2587 (CA 7, 1982).

[109]Ryder Sys., *supra* note 107; Monfort of Colo., 256 NLRB 612, 107 LRRM 1296 (1981), *enforced sub nom.* National Maritime Union v. NLRB, 683 F2d 305, 111 LRRM 2286 (CA 9, 1982).

[110]590 F2d 688, 100 LRRM 2356 (CA 8, 1978), *enforcing* 231 NLRB 735, 97 LRRM 1215 (1977).

[111]*Id.* at 694; *accord* NLRB v. Mears Coal Co., 437 F2d 502, 76 LRRM 2081 (CA 3, 1970).

[112]*See* Tenneco, Walker Mfg. Co. Div., 288 NLRB 888, 128 LRRM 1104 (1988); Central Wash. Health Servs. Ass'n dba Central Wash. Hosp., 279 NLRB 60, 122 LRRM 1050 (1986), *enforced*, 815 F2d 1493 (CA 9, 1987); Times-Herald, 253 NLRB 524, 528, 105 LRRM 1642 (1980).

[113]Admiral Petroleum Corp., 240 NLRB 894, 100 LRRM 1373 (1979); Willett Motor Coach Co., 227 NLRB 882, 95 LRRM 1082 (1977).

[114]*See* NLRB v. San Antonio Portland Cement Co., 611 F2d 1148, 103 LRRM 2631 (CA 5), *cert. denied*, 449 US 844, 105 LRRM 2657 (1980) (mere presence of supervisor wearing union button at union meeting not coercive).

[115]Alley Constr. Co., 210 NLRB 999, 86 LRRM 1316 (1974); Plymouth Shoe Co., 182 NLRB 1, 73 LRRM 1610 (1970).

with an incumbent union. Rather, an employer will violate section 8(a)(5) by refusing to bargain solely because a petition has been filed by an outside union.

The Board will not find section 8(a)(2) violations in situations involving initial organizing by rival unions when an employer recognizes a labor organization that represents an uncoerced, unassisted majority. However, once an employer is notified of a valid petition for election, the Board requires the employer to refrain from recognizing any of the rival unions.

A. Development of the Requirement: The Rise and Fall of *Midwest Piping*

From 1945 until 1982 the Board, with considerable disapproval from the courts of appeals, interpreted section 8(a)(2) to require an employer to maintain neutrality when two unions were competing for recognition. The requirement had its origin in *Midwest Piping Co.*,[116] in which the Steelworkers and the Steamfitters each petitioned the Board for an election. While both petitions were pending, the employer recognized and entered into a closed-shop contract with the Steamfitters.[117] The Board held that the contract violated section 8(a)(1). The substantive basis of the offense, however, was the violation of section 8(a)(2). The employer's execution of the agreement

> indicated its approval of the Steamfitters, accorded it unwarranted prestige, encouraged membership therein, discouraged membership in the Steelworkers, and thereby rendered unlawful assistance to the Steamfitters, which interfered with, restrained and coerced its employees in the exercise of rights guaranteed in §7 of the Act.[118]

The original *Midwest Piping* decision thus made it an unfair labor practice for an employer to recognize one of two or more competing labor organizations after a representation question had been submitted to the Board by the filing of a petition.

In 1954, the rule was narrowed in *William D. Gibson Co.*[119] The Board held that an incumbent union and an employer acted

---

[116]63 NLRB 1060, 17 LRRM 40 (1945). For a critical analysis of the Board's *Midwest Piping* doctrine, *see* Kesselring & Brinker, *Contract Difficulties Under §8(a)(2)*, 31 LAB. L.J. 139 (1980); Note, *New Standards for Domination and Support Under Section 8(a)(2)*, 82 YALE L.J. 510 (1973).

[117]The closed shop was not illegal under the Wagner Act. *See* Chapter 27, "Union Security," at notes 19–20.

[118]63 NLRB at 1071.

[119]110 NLRB 660, 35 LRRM 1092 (1954); *accord* William Penn Broadcasting Co., 93 NLRB 1104, 27 LRRM 1532 (1951) (company may *bargain* with incumbent while rival election petition is pending).

lawfully in entering into a new contract covering a large unit of production and maintenance employees in the face of a petition by a rival union seeking severance of 30 toolroom employees. But the Board overruled *Gibson* in 1958 in *Shea Chemical Corp.*,[120] and held that section 8(a)(2) was violated when a newly, but lawfully, recognized union and an employer entered into an agreement after a rival union had petitioned for an election. The Board stated its new version of the *Midwest Piping* doctrine as follows:

> [U]pon presentation of a rival or conflicting claim which raises a real question concerning representation an employer may not go so far as to bargain collectively with the incumbent (or any other) union unless and until the question concerning representation has been settled by the board.[121]

But this exception was added:

> The Midwest Piping Doctrine does not apply in situations when, because of contract bar or certification year or other established reason, the rival claim does not raise a real representation question.[122]

Under *Midwest Piping*, "a real question concerning representation" was presented when a competing union filed a petition and the Board determined that there was a showing of interest by taking cognizance of the case.[123]

In *Playskool, Inc.*[124] the Board found a section 8(a)(2) violation, holding that it had "never established any numerical percentage as a condition precedent to establishing the existence of a question concerning representation" and that the "sole requirement . . . is that the claim of the rival union must not be clearly unsupportable and lacking in substance."[125]

---

[120]121 NLRB 1027, 42 LRRM 1486 (1958).

[121]*Id.* at 1028.

[122]*Id.* In an earlier case the same year, the Board had held that an employer could not recognize one of two competing unions once "a real question concerning representation" had arisen. Novak Logging, 119 NLRB 1573, 41 LRRM 1436 (1958).

[123]Swift & Co., 128 NLRB 732, 46 LRRM 1381 (1960).

[124]195 NLRB 560, 79 LRRM 1507 (1972), *enforcement denied*, 477 F2d 66, 82 LRRM 2916 (CA 7, 1973), *supplemented*, 205 NLRB 1009, 84 LRRM 1129 (1973).

[125]*Id.* at 560. In a 1975 case, American Can Co., 218 NLRB 102, 89 LRRM 1585 (1975), *enforced*, 535 F2d 180, 92 LRRM 2251 (CA 2, 1976), where the rival union's claim was not supportable according to the administrative law judge, the Board found that extending recognition to a union which apparently represented an overwhelming majority of the employees in the unit violated §8(a)(2). The Board relied on its holding in Boys Mkts., 156 NLRB 105, 61 LRRM 1001 (1965), *enforced sub nom.* Retail Clerks Local 770 v. NLRB, 370 F2d 205, 64 LRRM 2155 (CA 9, 1966), to the effect that it is sufficient that the rival claim to

The Board never rendered a definitive statement of the amount of support required to raise a real question concerning representation under *Midwest Piping*.[126] In *American Bread Co.*[127] the Board found that a substantial question concerning representation had been raised by a union which possessed only one authorization card in a unit of 92 when it demanded recognition and had only eight authorization cards when the company recognized the rival union.

In *Robert Hall*,[128] however, the Board found a union's claim "insufficient to compel application of the *Midwest Piping* doctrine" and "no more than a naked claim," where the union had 24 authorization cards in a unit of 153 and it had recently withdrawn its petition for a Board election but had continued to assert an interest in the employees in the appropriate unit. Although the Board held that an employer could ignore a "naked claim," whether a claim was "naked" depended on facts ascertained after recognition and during unfair labor practice proceedings.[129]

The presumption of continuing majority status afforded to an incumbent bargaining representative[130] could also prevent an employer from recognizing a rival union, especially if the parties were engaged in litigation concerning the existence of a bargaining agreement between them.[131] But a refusal to negotiate with the incumbent union after a petition was filed by a rival, or by

---

representation is not "clearly unsupportable or specious, or otherwise not a colorable claim," *id.* at 107, and further declared: "An employer faced with conflicting claims of rival unions which give rise to a real question concerning representation may not recognize or enter into a contract with one of these unions until the representation question has been settled under the special procedures of the Act." 218 NLRB at 103. *Accord* U & I, Inc., 227 NLRB 1, 94 LRRM 1064 (1976).

[126]For a general treatment of "question concerning representation," *see* Chapter 10, "Representation Proceedings and Elections," at notes 3–9.

[127]170 NLRB 85, 67 LRRM 1430 (1968), *enforcement denied*, 411 F2d 147, 71 LRRM 2243 (CA 6, 1969).

[128]207 NLRB 692, 84 LRRM 1538 (1973).

[129]*See, e.g.*, Kona Surf Hotel, 201 NLRB 139, 82 LRRM 1279 (1973), *enforcement denied*, 507 F2d 411, 87 LRRM 3075 (CA 9, 1974), where the Board held that the employer unlawfully recognized and executed a contract with one union on the basis of a card check the day after another union had filed a petition. At the time of recognition, there was no way for the employer to know whether or not the petition was adequately supported. *See also* Riviera Manor Nursing Home, 220 NLRB 124, 90 LRRM 1186 (1975), *enforcement denied*, 539 F2d 714, 93 LRRM 2019 (CA 7, 1976).

[130]*See* Chapter 12, "Recognition and Withdrawal of Recognition Without an Election," at notes 313–412.

[131]*See* Greyhound Airport Servs., 204 NLRB 900, 83 LRRM 1712 (1973); Western Commercial Transp., 201 NLRB 17, 82 LRRM 1366 (1973), *enforced*, 487 F2d 332, 84 LRRM 2814 (CA 5, 1973).

dissatisfied employees, was not a refusal to bargain in violation of section 8(a)(5).[132]

The Board also applied the *Midwest Piping* doctrine where an employer granted recognition at a time when rival unions were litigating the scope of the unit in a representation proceeding,[133] or where the unit was in flux.[134]

The *Midwest Piping* doctrine was inapplicable where an employer recognized the rival receiving the most votes in an election while objections were pending, provided the objections were ultimately dismissed.[135] Neither was the doctrine invoked when a local union disaffiliated from its international and demonstrated its continuing uncoerced majority status to the employer and thereafter executed an agreement as an independent union. The Board held that a *Midwest Piping* problem did not exist, even in the face of such claims by the international.[136]

But improper recognition of one of two rival unions was found where recognition was based upon cards signed by employees who, prior to recognition, had signed cards for both unions.[137]

---

[132]Greyhound Airport Servs., *supra* note 131.

[133]Holyoke Food Mart, 191 NLRB 470, 77 LRRM 1772 (1971).

[134]For example, in American Can Co., *supra* note 125, the employer opened a new manufacturing facility and hired many employees from its former plant. At the old plant the employer had recognized two separate bargaining units: a production-and maintenance unit and a smaller unit of lithographic-production employees. At the new facility, prior to start-up of lithographic production, the employer recognized the production-and-maintenance union as the sole representative. But certain lithographic equipment and work was transferred to the new facility, and the employer expected to hire some of the old facility's lithographic workers. The Board held that such expectancy, together with communications from the union representing the lithographic employees, raised a "colorable claim," even though the employer had no obligation to transfer the union's bargaining status to the new facility.

[135]In Gulf & W. Mfg. Co., Taylor Forge Div., 227 NLRB 696, 95 LRRM 1061 (1977), the Board held that the employer acted at its peril when it recognized one of two competing labor organizations under such circumstances, but it did not violate §8(a)(2) of the Act since it had guessed correctly. *Accord* Sundstrand Heat Transfer v. NLRB, 538 F2d 1257, 92 LRRM 3266 (CA 7, 1976).

[136]American Cystoscope Makers, 190 NLRB 590, 77 LRRM 1399 (1971); Pall Corp., 190 NLRB 594, 77 LRRM 1397 (1971); Sinclair Mfg. Co., 178 NLRB 182, 72 LRRM 1035 (1969); Southern Stevedoring, 230 NLRB 609, 96 LRRM 1342 (1977); *See also* Associated Gen. Contractors, Evansville Chapter, 182 NLRB 224, 74 LRRM 1050 (1970); H. L. Washum dba Los Angeles-Yuma Freight, 172 NLRB 328, 68 LRRM 1535 (1968), *reversed on other grounds*, 446 F2d 210, 77 LRRM 3076 (CA 9, 1971); Climax Molybdenum Co., 146 NLRB 508, 55 LRRM 1357 (1964).

[137]NLRB v. Hi-Temp, 503 F2d 583, 87 LRRM 2437 (CA 7, 1974). *See also* Italco Aluminum Corp. v. NLRB, 417 F2d 36, 72 LRRM 2368 (CA 9, 1969); R. L. Sweet Lumber Co., 207 NLRB 529, 85 LRRM 1073 (1973), *enforced*, 515 F2d 785, 89 LRRM 2326 (CA 10, 1975); Allied Super Mkts., 169 NLRB 927, 67 LRRM 1298 (1968). *See generally* Chap-

The Board's *Midwest Piping* doctrine met strong resistance from the circuit courts.[138] Most of the circuits refused to find a violation of section 8(a)(2) when an employer recognized one of two competing unions that had clearly demonstrated its majority support.[139] As expressed by the Seventh Circuit, by extending recognition to a union enjoying majority support, the employer has not rendered "unlawful assistance" or "illegal support," but "has merely obeyed the duty imposed upon him to recognize the agent that his employees have designated."[140] The Fifth Circuit, however, accepted the Board's view.[141]

In two cases decided in July 1982 the Board reevaluated and significantly modified its *Midwest Piping* doctrine. In *RCA del Caribe*[142] a three-to-two Board majority decided that an employer may continue to recognize and bargain with an incumbent union in the face of a valid petition for election by a rival union. The majority reasoned that to prohibit negotiations until the Board ruled on the results of a new election might work an undue hardship on employers, unions, and employees, and that the *Midwest Piping* doctrine did not give proper weight to the Act's concern for stability of collective bargaining relationships. Additionally, the Board observed that in an existing union situation the employer cannot, in any event, maintain strict neutrality

---

ter 14, "Effect of Change in Bargaining Representative During the Term of a Collective Bargaining Agreement," regarding changes in the affiliation or identity of an exclusive representative.

[138]*E.g.*, Wintex Knitting Mill v. NLRB, 610 F2d 430, 104 LRRM 2529 (CA 6, 1979); Buck Knives, Inc. v. NLRB, 549 F2d 1319, 94 LRRM 2813 (CA 9, 1977); NLRB v. Inter-Island Resorts, 507 F2d 411, 87 LRRM 3075 (CA 9, 1974); NLRB v. Suburban Transit Corp., 499 F2d 78, 86 LRRM 2626 (CA 3, 1974); Playskool, Inc. v. NLRB, 477 F2d 66, 82 LRRM 2916 (CA 7, 1973); NLRB v. Peter Paul, Inc., 467 F2d 700, 80 LRRM 3431 (CA 9, 1972); NLRB v. Modine Mfg. Co., 453 F2d 292, 79 LRRM 2109 (CA 8, 1971); Sturgeon Elec. Co. v. NLRB, 419 F2d 51, 72 LRRM 2872 (CA 10, 1969); American Bread Co. v. NLRB, 411 F2d 147, 71 LRRM 2243 (CA 6, 1969); Iowa Beef Packers v. NLRB, 331 F2d 176, 56 LRRM 2071 (CA 8, 1964); NLRB v. John Swift Co., 277 F2d 641, 46 LRRM 2090 (CA 7, 1960); Cleaver-Brooks Mfg. Corp., 264 F2d 637, 43 LRRM 2722 (CA 7, 1959), *cert. denied*, 361 US 817, 44 LRRM 2983 (1959); Pittsburgh Valve Co. v. NLRB, 234 F2d 565, 38 LRRM 2294 (CA 4, 1956); NLRB v. Indianapolis Newspapers, 210 F2d 501, 33 LRRM 2536 (CA 7, 1954).

[139]Buck Knives, Inc. v. NLRB, *supra* note 138; NLRB v. Inter-Island Resorts, *supra* note 138; Playskool, Inc. v. NLRB, *supra* note 138; NLRB v. Peter Paul, Inc., *supra* note 138; Modine Mfg. Co. v. NLRB, *supra* note 138; American Bread Co. v. NLRB, *supra* note 138; Iowa Beef Packers v. NLRB, *supra* note 138; NLRB v. Indianapolis Newspapers, *supra* note 138.

[140]Playskool, Inc. v. NLRB, *supra* note 138, at 70. *Accord* NLRB v. Indianapolis Newspapers, *supra* note 138.

[141]NLRB v. Western Commercial Transp., *supra* note 131; Oil Transp. Co. v. NLRB, 440 F2d 664, 75 LRRM 2609 (CA 5, 1971); NLRB v. Signal Oil & Gas Co., 304 F2d 785, 50 LRRM 2505 (CA 5, 1962).

[142]262 NLRB 963, 110 LRRM 1369 (1982).

and that withdrawal from contract negotiations would signal repudiation of the incumbent and preference for the rival. Finally, the majority recognized that changing economic circumstances might require immediate changes in working conditions.[143]

In *Bruckner Nursing Home*,[144] the Board held that it would no longer find section 8(a)(2) violations in situations involving organizing by rival unions when, before a valid petition for an election is filed, an employer recognizes a labor organization that represents an uncoerced, unassisted majority of employees. The Board noted its continued inability to define a "naked" or "clearly unsupported" rival claim, and its consequent inability to provide a clear standard. The *Midwest Piping* doctrine had, the Board said, frustrated employee free choice by delaying recognition of majority unions while giving minority unions time to gather support or to frustrate their rivals. The Board noted the virtually unanimous rejection of *Midwest Piping* by the circuit courts. However, the Board adhered to its rule that once notified of a valid petition the employer must refrain from recognizing any of the rival unions.[145]

Shortly thereafter, in *Dresser Industries*,[146] the Board held that an employer's obligation to remain neutral does not privilege the suspension of bargaining with an incumbent union solely on the basis of the filing of a decertification petition when the employer does not otherwise have reasonable grounds for doubting the incumbent's majority status. The application of these new principles is discussed more fully below.

B. When a Union Is Incumbent

Although two members appointed soon after *RCA del Caribe* was decided announced reservations as to whether that case was correct,[147] members appointed more recently have expressly

---

[143]The Board noted that an employer could withdraw recognition from the incumbent in good faith based on objective considerations. 262 NLRB at 965 n.13, 110 LRRM at 1371 n.13 (citing United States Gypsum Co., 157 NLRB 652, 61 LRRM 1384 (1966)).

[144]262 NLRB 955, 110 LRRM 1374 (1982).

[145]*Id.* at 957, 110 LRRM at 1376–77.

[146]264 NLRB 1088, 111 LRRM 1436 (1982) (overruling Telautograph Corp., 199 NLRB 892, 81 LRRM 1337 (1972)).

[147]*See* Alexander Muss & Sons, 274 NLRB 1330, 118 LRRM 1629 (1985). In Crown Cork de P.R., 273 NLRB 243, 244 n.6, 118 LRRM 1532, 1533 n.6 (1984), Chairman Dotson and Member Dennis added that "[a]bsent a majority to overrule RCA del Caribe, [they] consider themselves institutionally bound to apply that precedent in this case."

endorsed it.[148] Applying its *RCA del Caribe* decision,[149] the Board has ruled that an employer does not violate section 8(a)(2) either by recognizing and executing a new collective bargaining agreement with an incumbent union despite the filing of a representation petition by another union,[150] or by doing so after the election if the incumbent secured a majority vote, notwithstanding that objections are pending to the incumbent union's conduct during the election.[151]

However, if there are other objective indications of the incumbent union's loss of majority status, execution of a new collective bargaining agreement with the incumbent union will violate the Act.[152] The Board has also held that where an employer properly withdraws recognition from an incumbent union based on a good-faith doubt of the incumbent's continuing majority status, the employer will nevertheless violate section 8(a)(2) by recognizing a rival union which has filed a representation petition supported by a card majority.[153] The Board reasoned that, in light of its holding in *Bruckner Nursing Home,*[154] in an incumbency situation an employer ought not to be privileged to recognize a rival union as long as the incumbent—though it had lost its majority status—still had not abandoned its claim to represent the employer's employees.

An employer whose food store employees were represented by an incumbent union under a master agreement violated the Act when it recognized an outside union as representative of its employees at a newly opened store after the incumbent had obtained cards from a majority of the new employees and was entitled to recognition under the terms of the master agreement.[155]

The filing of a decertification petition alone does not provide a sufficient basis for a refusal to continue to recognize and bargain unless the employer has reasonable grounds for doubting the incumbent union's majority status.[156]

---

[148]Len Martin Corp., 282 NLRB 482, 124 LRRM 1109 (1986) (Members Johansen, Brabson, and Stevens).

[149]*Supra* note 142.

[150]*See, e.g.,* Crown Cork de P.R., *supra* note 147.

[151]Continental Can Co., 282 NLRB 1363, 124 LRRM 1277 (1987).

[152]S.M.S. Automotive Prods., 282 NLRB 36, 125 LRRM 1125 (1986).

[153]Signal Transformer Co., 265 NLRB 272, 111 LRRM 1556 (1982).

[154]*Supra* note 144.

[155]Alpha Beta Co., 294 NLRB No. 13, 131 LRRM 1754 (1989).

[156]St. Agnes Medical Center v. NLRB, 871 F2d 137, 130 LRRM 3022 (CA DC 1989); Bryan Memorial Hosp. v. NLRB, 814 F2d 1259, 124 LRRM 3165 (CA 8), *cert. denied,* 484 US 849, 126 LRRM 2496 (1987); Dresser Indus., *supra* note 146.

C. When No Union Is Incumbent

In an initial organizing situation, the Board, applying *Bruckner Nursing Home*,[157] holds that in the absence of a valid petition for election an employer does not violate section 8(a)(2) by recognizing and bargaining with a union that represents an uncoerced majority of its employees. However, once the employer is informed that a valid petition has been filed, it must refrain from recognizing any of the rival unions.[158] A violation occurs even if the election petition has been blocked for several years by the filing and litigation of unfair labor practice charges.[159]

The Board has held that employer knowledge of the rival union petition is critical and that an employer does not extend unlawful recognition by recognizing a union on the same day that a rival union files a petition, where the employer did not know of the filing of the petition.[160]

Once a union is lawfully recognized, but prior to the conclusion of the first contract, it has the status of an "incumbent" union and the employer does not violate the Act by negotiating a contract in the face of the pendency of a rival union's petition.[161] If an agreement is reached, however, the viability of that agreement is dependent upon the outcome of the decertification election.[162] An employer and a union can agree that the effectiveness of a collective bargaining agreement will depend on the outcome of a decertification election.[163]

VI. SUPPORT VERSUS COOPERATION

In addition to prohibiting employer domination and interference, section 8(a)(2) makes it unlawful for an employer to "contribute financial or other support to a labor organization."

---

[157]*Supra* note 144.

[158]*Id. See also* Caro Bags, 285 NLRB 656, 128 LRRM 1031 (1987); S.M.S. Automotive Prods., *supra* note 152; Haddon House Food Prods., 269 NLRB 338, 115 LRRM 1209 (1984), *enforced*, 764 F2d 182, 119 LRRM 3021 (CA 3, 1985); Film Consortium, 268 NLRB 436 n.4, 115 LRRM 1021 n.4 (1983) (General Counsel has burden of proving lack of majority status); Great S. Constr., 266 NLRB 364, 112 LRRM 1355 (1983).

[159]Caro Bags, *supra* note 158.

[160]Rollins Transp. Sys., 296 NLRB No. 108, 132 LRRM 1185 (1989).

[161]Air La Carte, 284 NLRB 471, 125 LRRM 1161 (1987).

[162]*Id.*

[163]Kelly Broadcasting Co., 273 NLRB 1632, 118 LRRM 1241 (1985). See Chapter 10, "Representation Proceedings and Elections," regarding the effect of such an agreement as a bar to further representation proceedings during its term.

Illegal support or assistance generally takes the form of affirmative acts of tangible benefit to a labor organization that are not sufficiently serious to constitute illegal domination.[164] Because illegal domination under section 8(a)(2) also often involves illegal assistance to a labor organization, the Board and the courts occasionally have created confusion by using the terms indiscriminately. The characterization of certain employer conduct as unlawful assistance or illegal domination is a matter of degree; domination exists when the employer is able to exercise a strong influence over the organization. The distinction between domination and assistance is all-important, for it determines the Board's remedy.[165]

In *Coamo Knitting Mills*,[166] the Board declined to formulate or apply a mechanistic test of unlawful assistance. Noting that the employer had given its support to a union during its successful organizing drive, the Board stated:

> We have held that the use of company time and property does not, *per se*, establish unlawful support and assistance. Rather, each case must be decided on the totality of its facts . . . . We think that the use of company time for these few employees . . . is subject, under the circumstances of this case, to the application of a *de minimis* rule.[167]

The Board and the courts also have recognized a distinction between unlawful support or assistance and lawful cooperation.[168] Lawful cooperation has been described as activity "which does not have the effect of inhibiting self-organization and free collective bargaining."[169] The Board and the courts thus evaluate the totality of an employer's conduct[170] in determining whether the "natural tendency of [that] support would be to inhibit employees in their choice of a bargaining represen-

---

[164]*See supra* at notes 47–78.

[165]*See infra* at notes 212–241.

[166]150 NLRB 579, 58 LRRM 1116 (1964).

[167]*Id.* at 582.

[168]Hertzka & Knowles v. NLRB, 503 F2d 625, 87 LRRM 2503 (CA 9, 1974); Federal-Mogul Corp. v. NLRB, 394 F2d 915, 68 LRRM 2332 (CA 6, 1968); NLRB v. Prince Macaroni Mfg. Co., 329 F2d 803, 55 LRRM 2852 (CA 1, 1964); Chicago Rawhide Mfg. Co. v. NLRB, 221 F2d 165, 35 LRRM 2665 (CA 7, 1955); NLRB v. Wenyss, 212 F2d 465, 34 LRRM 2124 (CA 9, 1954).

[169]Federal-Mogul Corp. v. NLRB, *supra* note 168, at 917.

[170]Distributive Workers Dist. 65 v. NLRB (Hartz Mountain Corp.), 593 F2d 1155, 99 LRRM 2640 (CA DC, 1978), *enforcing* 228 NLRB 492, 96 LRRM 1589 (1977); Duquesne Univ., 198 NLRB 891, 91 LRRM 1091 (1972). *See also* NLRB v. Vernitron Elec. Components, 548 F2d 24, 94 LRRM 2380 (CA 1, 1977), *enforcing* 221 NLRB 464, 90 LRRM 1497 (1975), where the court held that the use of company facilities for a union organizational meeting, "standing alone," was not unlawful support.

tative" and to restrict the employee group in maintaining an arm's-length relationship with the employer.[171] Accordingly, union use of company time and property does not establish a *per se* violation of section 8(a)(2) where the union is lawfully recognized.[172]

Much employer conduct that may be evidence of unlawful domination may also simply be unlawful support, as when an employer furnishes a meeting place on its premises to a union and pays employees for time spent at such meetings[173] or in other union-related activities,[174] or provides supplies and other services of benefit to a union.[175] An employer also engages in unlawful support if it requires job applicants to sign union dues checkoff cards as a condition precedent to their future employment,[176] pays membership fees or other dues to a union on behalf of its employees,[177] or gives direct financial assistance to a

---

[171]*See* Airstream, Inc., 288 NLRB 220, 130 LRRM 1281 (1988); Windsor Place Corp., 276 NLRB 445, 120 LRRM 1101 (1985); (employer violated Act by assisting union in obtaining authorization cards from employees); *see also* NLRB v. Homemaker Shops, 724 F2d 535, 115 LRRM 2321 (CA 6, 1984), *enforcing* 261 NLRB 441, 110 LRRM 1082 (1982); Farmers Energy Corp., 266 NLRB 722, 113 LRRM 1037 (1983), *enforced*, 730 F2d 1098, 115 LRRM 3469 (CA 7, 1984); Monfort of Colo., 256 NLRB 612, 107 LRRM 1296 (1981), *enforced sub nom.* National Maritime Union v. NLRB, 683 F2d 305, 111 LRRM 2286 (CA 9, 1982); Kaiser Found. Hosps., 223 NLRB 322, 322, 91 LRRM 1523 (1976); *accord* NLRB v. Keller Ladders S., 405 F2d 663, 70 LRRM 2001 (CA 5, 1968), *enforcing* 161 NLRB 21, 63 LRRM 1280 (1966).

[172]Baker Mine Servs. dba Coppinger Mach. Serv., 279 NLRB 609, 122 LRRM 1153 (1986) (no evidence demonstrating lack of arm's-length relationship between employer and employee organization; employer's acts helpful to union held "cooperation of ministerial character growing out of amicable labor-management relationship."); BASF Wyandotte Corp., 274 NLRB 978, 119 LRRM 1035 (1985), *enforced*, 798 F2d 849, 123 LRRM 2320 (CA 5, 1986); SMI of Worcester, 271 NLRB 1508, 117 LRRM 1365 (1984).

[173]St. Vincent's Hosp., 244 NLRB 84, 102 LRRM 1196 (1979); World Wide Press, 242 NLRB 346, 101 LRRM 1205 (1979); Tuschak-Jacobson, Inc., 223 NLRB 1298, 92 LRRM 1280 (1976); Rensselaer Polytechnic Inst., 219 NLRB 712, 89 LRRM 1879 (1975); Bee Line Eng'g, 217 NLRB 367, 89 LRRM 1026 (1975); Sportspal, Inc., 214 NLRB 917, 88 LRRM 1533 (1974).

[174]NLRB v. Vernitron Elec. Components, *supra* note 170; Mountaineer Shaft & Tunnel Constr. Co., 234 NLRB 929, 98 LRRM 1148 (1978); Rockville Nursing Center, 193 NLRB 959, 78 LRRM 1519 (1971); *accord* Kurz-Kasch, Inc., 239 NLRB 1044, 100 LRRM 1118 (1978); Kux Mfg. Corp., 233 NLRB 317, 97 LRRM 1052 (1977); Rideout Memorial Hosp., 227 NLRB 1338, 94 LRRM 1703 (1977); C. H. Heist Corp., 186 NLRB 355, 76 LRRM 1062 (1970).

[175]*See* Easy-Heat Wirekraft Div., 238 NLRB 1695, 99 LRRM 1681 (1978) (employer offered to pay union's attorneys' fees); Bee Line Eng'g, *supra* note 173. *See also* Kaiser Found. Hosps., *supra* note 171 (employer provided union with use of company clerical supplies and copying machines for producing its newsletter). *Contra* S & W Motor Lines, 236 NLRB 938, 98 LRRM 1488 (1978) (de minimis assistance); Monon Trailer, 217 NLRB 257, 89 LRRM 1280 (1975) (use of company photocopier held to be de minimis assistance and thus not unlawful).

[176]*E.g.*, Rainey Sec. Agency, 274 NLRB 269, 119 LRRM 1043 (1985); Baggett Indus. Constructors, 219 NLRB 171, 90 LRRM 1175 (1975).

[177]*See* Business Envelope Mfrs., 227 NLRB 280, 94 LRRM 1351 (1976); Stockton Door Co., 218 NLRB 1053, 89 LRRM 1428 (1975). *See also* Dura-Vent Corp., 235 NLRB 1300, 98 LRRM 1225 (1978).

union or its members.[178] Section 302 also prohibits certain payments by an employer to a labor organization.[179] An employer may also provide unlawful assistance to a union by applying a contract only to members of the union, while denying to other bargaining-unit employees contractual wage increases and other benefits.[180]

When an employer urges employees to support a union[181] or directs them to solicit union authorization cards, section 8(a)(2) is violated.[182] For similar reasons, when an employee solicits authorization cards in the presence of supervisors who state that the company wants the union for which the employee is soliciting, unlawful assistance is found because the employees could reasonably believe that the soliciting employee is acting as an agent for the employer.[183] A manager's suggestion that workers form an employee committee, the manager's attendance at the committee meetings, and his discussion of problems and possible solutions, all taken in response to a union organizing campaign, violated section 8(a)(2).[184] Similarly, it was unlawful for an employer to invite union officials to a meeting where applicants completed the hiring process, to pay for a room where organizing activities occurred, and to direct employees to join the union in order to obtain work.[185] Arranging for a union representative to meet employees on the company's property while employees were being paid was unlawful support where the employer had reason to believe that the employees might support another union.[186]

---

[178]Prestige Bedding Co., 212 NLRB 690, 87 LRRM 1299 (1974) (employer offered to pay insurance premiums only for employees who were union members). *See also* United Artists Communications, 280 NLRB 1056, 122 LRRM 1296 (1986) (employer's soliciting its employees to join incumbent union constituted unlawful assistance where there had been no enforcement of collective bargaining agreement, including contract's union-security clause, until rival union began organizing efforts).

[179]*See* Chapter 27, "Union Security," at notes 352–382.

[180]F&C Transfer Co., 277 NLRB 591, 121 LRRM 1086 (1985).

[181]Palmas Del Mar Co., 277 NLRB 71, 120 LRRM 1270 (1985), *enforcement granted*, 797 F2d 39, 123 LRRM 2060 (CA 1, 1986).

[182]Airport Bus Serv., 273 NLRB 561, 118 LRRM 1343 (1984).

[183]Ryder Sys., 280 NLRB 1024, 124 LRRM 1113 (1986).

[184]Hunter Douglas, Inc., 277 NLRB 1179, 121 LRRM 1064 (1985), *enforced*, 804 F2d 808, 123 LRRM 2912 (CA 3, 1986), *cert. denied*, 481 US 1069, 125 LRRM 2440 (1987).

[185]Roundup Co. dba Fred Meyer, Inc. dba Meyer's Cafe & Konditorei, 282 NLRB 1, 124 LRRM 1005 (1986); *see also* North Am. Van Lines, 288 NLRB 38, 130 LRRM 1320 (1988), *enforcement denied*, 869 F2d 596, 130 LRRM 2837 (CA DC, 1989).

[186]Windsor Place Corp., *supra* note 171. The Board noted that such conduct is not per se illegal, but rather must be evaluated against all the surrounding circumstances. *Id.* at 448 (ALJ decision). *See also* Bell Energy Mgmt. Corp., 291 NLRB 168, 130 LRRM 1499 (1988).

In *NLRB v. Vernitron Electrical Components*,[187] an employer assembled its employees on its own premises for organizational meetings with union representatives; it arranged for its supervisors to personally attend those meetings and observe the signing of authorization cards; it recognized the union on that same day; and it shortly thereafter entered into a collective bargaining agreement with the union. The First Circuit upheld the Board's conclusion that such conduct represented unlawful support regardless of whether the employer actually intended to aid the union in an unlawful manner.[188]

Extending voluntary recognition to a union that represents a majority[189] of the employees in an appropriate bargaining unit is lawful. But an employer violates section 8(a)(2) when it recognizes an incumbent union as the representative of its employees at a new facility, in the absence of a lawful accretion, and extends coverage of an existing contract to such employees.[190] It is likewise unlawful to extend union recognition in an inappropriate unit.[191] Similarly, it is unlawful for an employer to recognize a labor organization prior to employment of a representative

---

[187]548 F2d 24, 94 LRRM 2380 (CA 1, 1977).

[188]*Id.* at 27. *See also* Ella Indus., 295 NLRB No. 104, 131 LRRM 1747 (1989) (employer sponsored meeting of one of two rival unions at a restaurant and denied the other union equal access).

[189]*See supra* note 9 and accompanying text.

[190]United States Steel Corp., 280 NLRB 837, 123 LRRM 1309 (1986); Matlack, Inc., 278 NLRB 246, 121 LRRM 1183 (1986); Big E Leasing & Serv. Corp. & RJE Leasing, 275 NLRB 1329, 119 LRRM 1311 (1985) (extension of existing prehire agreement to new employees performing new classification of work violated Act when union did not represent uncoerced majority of employees); Sav-On Drugs, 267 NLRB 639, 114 LRRM 1102 (1983); Save-It Discount Foods, 263 NLRB 689, 111 LRRM 1110 (1982) (extension of collective bargaining agreement to new store where union did not represent uncoerced majority); King Radio Corp., 257 NLRB 521, 107 LRRM 1571 (1981) (extension of union recognition to facility that had been traditionally excluded from bargaining unit when union did not represent uncoerced majority of that facility's employees); Safeway Stores, 256 NLRB 918, 919, 107 LRRM 1338 (1981). *See also* Armco, Inc., Eastern Steel Div., Ashland Works, 279 NLRB 1184, 123 LRRM 1335 (1986), *aff'd in relevant part*, 832 F2d 357, 126 LRRM 2961 (CA 6, 1987), *cert. denied*, 486 US 1042, 130 LRRM 2800 (1988). Accretion was also found unlawful in Harte & Co., 278 NLRB 947, 122 LRRM 1003 (1986), and Metropolitan Teletronics Corp., 279 NLRB 957, 122 LRRM 1107(1986). Meijer, Inc. v. NLRB, 564 F2d 737, 96 LRRM 2738 (CA 6, 1977), *enforcing* 222 NLRB 18, 91 LRRM 1153 (1976); NLRB v. Security-Columbian Banknote Co., 541 F2d 135, 93 LRRM 2049 (CA 3, 1976), *enforcing in relevant part* 215 NLRB 450, 88 LRRM 1043 (1974); NLRB v. General Cinema Corp., 526 F2d 427, 91 LRRM 2193 (CA 5, 1976), *enforcing in relevant part* 214 NLRB 1074, 87 LRRM 1563 (1974); and Arco Elec., 241 NLRB 256, 100 LRRM 1541 (1979).

[191]*E.g.*, Atlas Guard Serv., 229 NLRB 698, 95 LRRM 1207 (1977) (employer recognized union in inappropriate two-state unit). *See also* California Gen. Linen Supply Co., 206 NLRB 203, 84 LRRM 1613 (1973); Northrop Corp., 187 NLRB 172, 76 LRRM 1824 (1970).

work force at a new or existing facility.[192] However, as the Board pointed out in *Hayes Coal Co.*:[193]

> A determination of premature recognition . . . cannot be predicated on whether existing jobs are temporarily unfilled by reason of quit or discharge, or on a possibility that future conditions may warrant an increase in personnel subsequent to the granting of recognition. The correct test is whether, at the time of recognition, the jobs or job classifications designated for the operation involved are filled or substantially filled and the operation is in normal or substantially normal production.[194]

Improper enforcement of union-security and checkoff clauses in a collective bargaining agreement may result in unlawful assistance to a labor organization.[195] Thus, an employer violated section 8(a)(2) when it refused to honor an employee's revocation of dues checkoff authorization where the employee had resigned from union membership.[196] On the other hand, an employer did not act unlawfully when it gave effect to dues checkoff authorizations following the return of the employees to the bargaining unit from nonunit positions without executing new checkoff forms, where there had been a "reasonable expectancy" of a return to the unit.[197] However, it is unlawful for an employer to maintain and give effect to an illegal closed-shop provision in a collective bargaining agreement,[198] or to require union membership prior to the expiration of the

---

[192]*E.g.*, NLRB v. Cen-Vi-Ro Pipe Corp., 457 F2d 775, 79 LRRM 2895 (CA 9, 1972), *enforcing* 180 NLRB 344, 73 LRRM 1089 (1969); Nederlander dba Ned West, Inc., 276 NLRB 32, 120 LRRM 1088 (1985); Sheraton Great Falls Inn, 242 NLRB 1255, 101 LRRM 1381 (1979); Klein's Golden Manor, 214 NLRB 807, 88 LRRM 1418 (1974); Norris Indus., 214 NLRB 629, 88 LRRM 1061 (1974); Helrose Bindery, 204 NLRB 499, 83 LRRM 1388 (1973); Wickes Corp., 197 NLRB 860, 80 LRRM 1458 (1972). *See infra* at note 212.

[193]197 NLRB 1162, 80 LRRM 1501 (1972).

[194]*Id.* at 1163; *accord* Fraser & Johnston Co., 189 NLRB 142, 77 LRRM 1036 (1971), *enforced in part*, 469 F2d 1259, 81 LRRM 2964 (CA 9, 1972); W. L. Rives Co., 136 NLRB 1050, 49 LRRM 1902 (1962), *enforced in part*, 328 F2d 464, 55 LRRM 2428 (CA 5, 1964).

[195]Enforcement of such clauses by an employer often results in the union being a party to the unlawful conduct. *See infra* at notes 203–213. *See generally* Chapter 27, "Union Security."

[196]U.S. Postal Serv., 279 NLRB 40, 121 LRRM 1333 (1986), *enforcement denied*, 827 F2d 548, 126 LRRM 2277 (CA 9, 1987). *Accord* Wickes Cos., Mode O'Day Co. Div., 280 NLRB 253, 122 LRRM 1213 (1986). *See also* Automated Waste Disposal, 288 NLRB 914, 130 LRRM 1287 (1988) (unlawful to deduct dues from paychecks without obtaining valid authorizations).

[197]Cameron Iron Works, 272 NLRB 984, 117 LRRM 1455 (1984).

[198]NLRB v. American Dredging Co., 276 F2d 286, 45 LRRM 2405 (CA 3, 1960), *enforcing as modified* 123 NLRB 139, 43 LRRM 1387 (1959), *cert. denied*, 366 US 908, 48 LRRM 2070 (1961).

30-day grace period provided by section 8(a)(3) of the Act.[199] Likewise, an employer violates section 8(a)(2) when it remits dues to a union in the absence of valid authorization from the affected employee,[200] refuses to honor an otherwise valid revocation of dues checkoff by an employee,[201] or in any way solicits on behalf of the union for authorization of dues checkoff from its employees.[202]

VII. THE UNION AS PARTY TO THE EMPLOYER'S DOMINATION, ASSISTANCE, OR SUPPORT

Employer conduct prohibited by section 8(a)(2) often involves conduct by a labor organization that is prohibited by section 8(b)(1)(A), which makes it unlawful for a labor organization or its agents to "restrain or coerce employees" in the exercise of their rights guaranteed by section 7 of the Act.[203] A joint violation of these provisions occurs when an employer executes a contract with a labor organization representing only a minority of its employees. The union violates section 8(b)(1)(A) by accepting recognition[204] and by entering into such a contract, while the

---

[199]*E.g.*, NLRB v. Western Bldg. Maintenance Co., 402 F2d 775, 69 LRRM 2623 (CA 9, 1968), *enforcing* 162 NLRB 778, 64 LRRM 1120 (1967); NLRB v. Campbell Soup Co., 378 F2d 259, 65 LRRM 2515 (CA 9, 1967), *enforcing* 152 NLRB 1645, 59 LRRM 1369 (1965); Teamsters Health & Welfare Fund, 233 NLRB 814, 97 LRRM 1174 (1977).

[200]*E.g.*, NLRB v. Jo-Jo Mgmt. Corp., 556 F2d 558, 95 LRRM 3011 (CA 2, 1977), *enforcing* 225 NLRB 1133, 93 LRRM 1475 (1976); Fieldstone Ambulance & Medical Sys., 242 NLRB 185, 101 LRRM 1141 (1979); Brown Transp. Corp., 239 NLRB 711, 100 LRRM 1016 (1978); Welsbach Elec. Corp., 236 NLRB 503, 99 LRRM 1271 (1978); American Geriatric Enters., 235 NLRB 1532, 98 LRRM 1220 (1978); Supreme Equip. & Sys. Corp., 235 NLRB 244, 98 LRRM 1600 (1978).

[201]*E.g.*, Trico Prods. Corp., 238 NLRB 1306, 99 LRRM 1473 (1978); Miller Brewing Co., 193 NLRB 528, 78 LRRM 1323 (1971); Nathan's Famous of Yonkers, 186 NLRB 131, 75 LRRM 1321 (1970).

[202]*E.g.*, Tribulani's Detective Agency, 233 NLRB 1121, 97 LRRM 1169 (1977); Atlas Guard Serv., *supra* note 191; Wackenhut Corp., 226 NLRB 1085, 94 LRRM 1328 (1976); Steak & Brew, 213 NLRB 450, 87 LRRM 1664 (1974); Luke Constr. Co., 211 NLRB 602, 87 LRRM 1087 (1974).

[203]*See generally* Chapter 6, "Interference With Protected Rights," at notes 554–626.

[204]Haddon House Food Prods., 269 NLRB 338, 115 LRRM 1209 (1984), *enforced*, 764 F2d 182, 119 LRRM 3021 (CA 3, 1985). *Accord* NLRB v. Cas Walker's Cash Stores, 659 F2d 79, 108 LRRM 3007 (CA 6, 1981), *enforcing* 249 NLRB 316, 104 LRRM 1330 (1980); Wackenhut Corp., 287 NLRB 374, 127 LRRM 1217 (1987); General Instrument Corp., 262 NLRB 1178, 111 LRRM 1017 (1982); Monfort of Colo., 256 NLRB 612, 107 LRRM 1296 (1981), *enforced sub nom.* National Maritime Union v. NLRB, 683 F2d 305, 111 LRRM 2286 (CA 9, 1982). *See also* Port Chester Nursing Home, 269 NLRB 150, 116 LRRM 1403 (1984), where an invalidly merged union violated §§8(b)(1)(A) and 8(b)(2) and the employer violated §§8(a)(1), (2), and (3) by entering into a contract containing union-security and checkoff clauses, even though an arbitrator had upheld the validity of the merger.

employer violates section 8(a)(2) by extending exclusive recognition and conferring the contractual benefits.[205]

A labor organization's "good-faith" mistaken belief that it is a majority representative is not a defense to a section 8(b)(1)(A) violation.[206] And the assisted labor organization also violates section 8(b)(2) if the unlawful contract contains a union-security clause.[207] For example, in *NLRB v. Retail Clerks Local 588 (Raley's, Inc.)*,[208] the Ninth Circuit affirmed the Board's finding that a union violated sections 8(b)(1)(A) and (2) when it demanded and obtained recognition, including application of a contract with a union-security clause, for a unit of employees of an entire store at which another union was recognized in a smaller unit consisting of a portion of the store's employees.[209] The Board has also found violations of section 8(b)(2) when an unlawfully assisted union causes the discharge of an employee

---

[205]*E.g*, Ladies' Garment Workers v. NLRB (Bernhard-Altmann Tex. Corp.), 366 U.S. 731, 48 LRRM 2251 (1961). *See also* NLRB v. Hospital Workers Local 250 (Kaiser Found. Hosps.), 577 F2d 649, 99 LRRM 2431 (CA 9, 1978), *enforcing* 228 NLRB 468, 96 LRRM 1345 (1977); Haddon House Food Prods., *supra* note 204; Carpenters Dist. Council of Miami & Vicinity, 238 NLRB 1683, 99 LRRM 1295 (1978); Supreme Equip. & Sys. Corp., *supra* note 200; Desco Vitro-Glaze, 230 NLRB 379, 96 LRRM 1467 (1977); Atlas Guard Serv., *supra* note 191; Seaview Manor Home for Adults, 222 NLRB 596, 91 LRRM 1198 (1976); Ellery Prods. Mfg. Co., 149 NLRB 1388, 57 LRRM 1478 (1964). The cases cited and discussed *supra* Sections IV and V are also illustrative of union §§8(b)(1)(A) and 8(b)(2) counterparts to employer §8(a)(2) violations. *See e.g.*, National Maritime Union v. NLRB (Monfort of Colo.), 683 F2d 305, 111 LRRM 2286 (CA 9, 1982) (union violated §8(b)(1)(A) by entering into collective bargaining agreement with employer at time when it did not represent uncoerced majority of employees); Caro Bags, 285 NLRB 656, 128 LRRM 1031 (1987) (union violated §§8(b)(1)(A) and 8(b)(2) by executing collective bargaining agreement containing union-security clause when it did not represent majority of employees and when rival union's representation petition was pending); Sav-On Drugs, *supra* note 190 (union violated §§8(b)(1)(A) and 8(b)(2) by accepting recognition and executing collective bargaining agreement containing union-security clause for employees at store where union did not have majority support); Great S. Constr. Co., 266 NLRB 364, 112 LRRM 1355 (1983) (union violated §§8(b)(1)(A) and 8(b)(2) by entering into collective bargaining agreement containing union-security clause with employer at time when rival incumbent union, though it had lost its majority status, had not abandoned its representation claim).

[206]Ladies' Garment Workers v. NLRB (Bernhard-Altmann Tex. Corp.), *supra* note 205.

[207]Bristol Consolidators, 239 NLRB 602, 100 LRRM 1026 (1978); Party Cookies, 237 NLRB 612, 99 LRRM 1468 (1978), *enforced in part*, 681 F2d 820, 111 LRRM 2058 (CA 7, 1982); Desco Vitro-Glaze, *supra* note 205; Southern Ore. Log Scaling & Grading Bureau, 223 NLRB 430, 92 LRRM 1216 (1976). *Contra* Ramey Supermarkets, 238 NLRB 1719, 99 LRRM 1342 (1978). *See generally* Chapter 27 *infra*.

[208]587 F2d 984, 100 LRRM 2299 (CA 9, 1978), *enforcing* 227 NLRB 670, 94 LRRM 1443 (1976).

[209]*See also* Marriott Corp., Bob's Big Boy Family Restaurants Div., 264 NLRB 432, 111 LRRM 1411 (1982); Paper Mfrs. Co., 274 NLRB 491, 119 LRRM 1030 (1985), *enforced*, 786 F2d 163, 121 LRRM 3278 (CA 3, 1986) (violation found where recognition demanded when rival union already certified); Armco, Inc., Eastern Steel Div., Ashland Works, *supra* note 190. *See also* Sav-On-Drugs, *supra* note 190 (execution and enforcement of union-security clause based on unlawful accretion).

who refuses to support the union,[210] when a union obtains recognition in breach of a valid preexisting section 8(f) prehire agreement between the employer and another union,[211] or when a union acquires recognition from an employer at a new facility in the absence of a lawful accretion.[212] A union likewise violates section 8(b)(1)(A) when it accepts recognition whether or not it has knowledge that one of two rival unions has filed a valid petition for election.[213]

VIII. REMEDIES

Before the Taft-Hartley amendments in 1947, the Board determined the appropriate remedy for an employer's violation of section 8(2), based on whether the benefited labor organization was an independent employee group or was an organization affiliated with a national or international federation. In the former situation, the Board ordered the employer to forever withhold recognition from the benefited employee group and ordered complete disestablishment of the organization. In contrast, employer conduct benefiting a labor organization affiliated with a national or international federation was held to be a violation only of section 8(1), and the Board would issue a cease-and-desist order directing the employer to withhold recognition from the organization only until it was certified.[214] The Board based this difference in treatment between affiliated and nonaffiliated organizations on the "belief that a labor organization affiliated with a national or international federation that was outside the ambit of the employer's control could not be permanently and completely subjugated to the will of the

---

[210]*E.g.*, Tuschak-Jacobson, Inc., 223 NLRB 1298, 92 LRRM 1280 (1976).

[211]Fenix & Scission, 207 NLRB 752, 85 LRRM 1380 (1973), *enforced*, 506 F2d 1404, 87 LRRM 3276 (CA 7, 1974). *See generally* Chapter 27, "Union Security," at notes 158–212.

[212]*E.g.*, NLRB v. Hospital Workers Local 250 (Kaiser Found. Hosps.), *supra* note 205; NLRB v. Hershey Foods Corp., 506 F2d 1052, 90 LRRM 2890 (CA 3, 1974), *enforcing* 208 NLRB 452, 85 LRRM 1312 (1974); Teamsters Local 814, 223 NLRB 527, 91 LRRM 1543 (1976); Meijer, Inc., 222 NLRB 18, 91 LRRM 1153 (1976), *enforced*, 564 F2d 737, 96 LRRM 2738 (CA 6, 1977); Laconia Shoe Co., 215 NLRB 573, 88 LRRM 1427 (1974); Teamsters Local 705 (Gasoline Retailers Ass'n of Metro. Chicago), 210 NLRB 210, 86 LRRM 1011 (1974); Fenix & Scission, *supra* note 211. *See supra* at note 192.

[213]Haddon House Food Prods., *supra* note 204, at 340 n.9. *See* text *supra* at notes 158–163.

[214]Carpenter Steel Co., 76 NLRB 670, 21 LRRM 1232 (1948).

employer."[215] The lesser remedy of a cease-and-desist order pending election and certification was deemed sufficient to remedy the effects of employer interference and to restore employee freedom of self-organization.

By amendment of section 10(c),[216] Congress disapproved the distinction between affiliated and nonaffiliated labor organizations, and specifically directed the Board to utilize the same remedies irrespective of the nature of the benefited labor organization. Within several months following the enactment of the Taft-Hartley amendments, the Board, in *Carpenter Steel Co.*,[217] noted the "congressional rejection of [its] prior view that mere affiliation with a national federation" placed a labor organization in a position so different from that of an unaffiliated employee group as to justify the use of different remedies.[218] It observed, however, that there was no evidence that Congress intended to abolish the remedy of disestablishment itself, but rather intended only to prohibit "discrimination in its use."[219] Accordingly, the Board abandoned the distinction between affiliated and unaffiliated labor organizations and announced an enforcement policy under which different remedies would be ordered depending on whether the offensive employer conduct constituted unlawful domination or merely illegal interference or assistance:

> In all cases in which we find that an employer has dominated, or interfered with, or contributed support to a labor organization, or has committed any of these proscribed acts, we will find such conduct a violation of Section 8(a)(2) of the Act . . . regardless of whether the organization involved is affiliated. Where we find that an employer's unfair labor practices have been so extensive as to constitute *domination* of the organization, we shall order its disestablishment, whether or not it be affiliated. The Board believes that disestablishment is still necessary as a remedy . . . in those cases, perhaps few in number, in which the employer's control of *any* labor organization has extended to the point of actual domination. But when the Board finds that an employer's unfair labor practices were limited to interference and support and never reached the point of

[215]*Id.* at 672.

[216]Taft-Hartley added the following proviso language to §10(c): "[I]n determining whether a complaint shall issue alleging a violation of section 8(a)(1) or section 8(a)(2), and in deciding such cases, the same regulations and rules of decision shall apply irrespective of whether or not the labor organization affected is affiliated with a labor organization national or international in scope."

[217]*Supra* note 214.

[218]*Id.* at 672.

[219]*Id.*

domination, we shall only order that recognition be withheld until certification, again without regard to whether or not the organization happens to be affiliated.[220]

As a consequence, the conclusion by the trier of fact as to whether unlawful employer conduct constitutes "domination" or "assistance" under section 8(a)(2) determines the remedy. If disestablishment of a dominated labor organization is ordered, the employer generally will be required to cease all contact with the dominated union[221] and make a public announcement of its intent to cease bargaining with that union.[222] After disestablishment has been ordered, the employees may then form a new union, but the employer cannot take part in its organization.[223] If the employer's support of a labor organization has undermined the majority support of a rival union and is accompanied by other unfair labor practices, the Board may issue a *Gissel* bargaining order requiring the employer to bargain with the disfavored labor organization.[224] For example, in *Kurz-Kasch, Inc.*,[225] the Board granted a *Gissel* bargaining order when the employer formed an "employee committee," dominated that organization in an attempt to forestall an outside union's organizing efforts, and also committed other substantial independent unfair labor practices to the detriment of the outside, disfavored, labor organization. The courts have enforced such orders,[226] but the Second Circuit has cautioned the Board that such a remedy should not become routine.[227]

---

[220]*Id.* at 673 (emphasis in original).

[221]*See e.g.*, American Smelting & Ref. Co. v. NLRB, 126 F2d 680, 10 LRRM 423 (CA 8, 1942); Dade Drydock Corp., 58 NLRB 833, 15 LRRM 67 (1944); Andrew Jergens Co., 43 NLRB 457, 11 LRRM 23 (1942).

[222]NLRB v. Tappan Stove Co., 174 F2d 1007, 24 LRRM 2125 (CA 6, 1949); Kansas City Power & Light Co. v. NLRB, 111 F2d 340, 6 LRRM 938 (CA 8, 1940); Remington Arms Co., 62 NLRB 611, 16 LRRM 199 (1945).

[223]NLRB v. Continental Oil Co., 121 F2d 120, 8 LRRM 907 (CA 10, 1941); Continental Oil Co. v. NLRB, 113 F2d 473, 6 LRRM 1020 (CA 10, 1940).

[224]Camvac Int'l, 288 NLRB 816, 130 LRRM 1447 (1988); Christopher St. Owners Corp., 286 NLRB 253, 126 LRRM 1158 (1987); Carbonex Coal Co., 262 NLRB 1306, 111 LRRM 1147 (1982); Flex Plastics, 262 NLRB 651, 110 LRRM 1365 (1982), *enforced*, 726 F2d 272, 115 LRRM 3036 (CA 6, 1984); Wheelco Co., 260 NLRB 867, 109 LRRM 1229 (1982); Professional Ambulance Serv., 232 NLRB 1141, 97 LRRM 1109 (1977); Federal Alarm, 230 NLRB 518, 96 LRRM 1141 (1977); Surface Indus., 224 NLRB 155, 93 LRRM 1074 (1976). *See also* Hirsch v. Trim Lean Meat Prods., 479 F Supp 1351, 102 LRRM 2950 (D. Del., 1979), where a district court granted a §10(e) temporary injunction compelling bargaining. *See* Chapter 12, "Recognition and Withdrawal of Recognition Without an Election," at notes 155–156.

[225]239 NLRB 1044, 100 LRRM 1118 (1978).

[226]*See, e.g.*, NLRB v. Cas Walker's Cash Stores, 659 F2d 79, 108 LRRM 3007 (CA 6, 1981), *enforcing* 249 NLRB 316, 104 LRRM 1330 (1980).

[227]Coating Prods. v. NLRB, 648 F2d 108, 107 LRRM 2337 (CA 2 1981), *enforcing* 251 NLRB 1271, 105 LRRM 1399 (1980).

Disestablishment frequently has been ordered in cases of dominated company unions or employee committees,[228] even where the complaint has alleged only unlawful employer assistance.[229]

Where the unlawful employer conduct falls short of domination but nevertheless constitutes unlawful assistance, the Board frequently issues a cease-and-desist order that prohibits the employer from recognizing the assisted labor organization and from giving effect to any contract between the employer and the union until the union is properly certified.[230] Although rescission of a collective bargaining agreement entered into by an employer with an unlawfully assisted labor organization is the device commonly used to restore the parties to the status quo ante,[231] the Board also has ordered employers not to alter provisions in a tainted collective bargaining agreement which provide for increased wages, seniority, or other rights over and above the

---

[228]Onan Corp., Ona Corp. Div., 285 NLRB 400, 128 LRRM 1013 (1987); Jet Spray Corp., 271 NLRB 127, 116 LRRM 1379 (1984); Homemaker Shops, 261 NLRB 441, 110 LRRM 1082 (1982), *enforcement denied in part*, 724 F2d 535, 115 LRRM 2321 (CA 6, 1984); Walker Die Casting, 255 NLRB 212, 107 LRRM 1154 (1981), *enforced as modified*, 682 F2d 592, 111 LRRM 2457 (CA 6, 1982), *cert. denied*, 461 US 905, 113 LRRM 2112 (1983); Classic Indus., 254 NLRB 1149, 107 LRRM 1046, *enforced*, 667 F2d 205, 109 LRRM 2057 (CA 1, 1981). The Board is not free to order disestablishment of a group without making a finding that it was "dominated" within the meaning of the Act. Memphis Truck & Trailer, 284 NLRB 900, 126 LRRM 1326 (1987); Fry Foods, 241 NLRB 76, 100 LRRM 1513 (1979), *enforced*, 609 F2d 267, 102 LRRM 2894 (CA 6, 1979); Interstate Eng'g Div., 230 NLRB 1, 96 LRRM 1135 (1977), *enforced*, 583 F2d 1087, 99 LRRM 3245 (CA 9, 1978); International Signal & Control Corp., 226 NLRB 661, 93 LRRM 1384 (1976); STR, Inc., 221 NLRB 496, 90 LRRM 1591 (1975); Lowen Co., 203 NLRB 449, 83 LRRM 1147 (1973); Solmica, 199 NLRB 224, 81 LRRM 1334 (1972); Glover Packing Co., 191 NLRB 547, 77 LRRM 1695 (1971).

[229]NLRB v. Fremont Mfg. Co., 558 F2d 889, 95 LRRM 3095 (CA 8, 1977); Kux Mfg. Corp., 233 NLRB 317, 97 LRRM 1052 (1977). *But see* Kent Corp., 212 NLRB 595, 87 LRRM 1730 (1974), in which the Board refrained from ordering disestablishment where the pleadings did not allege, but the proof at the hearing established, such unlawful employer domination.

[230]*E.g*, NLRB v. Cas Walker's Cash Stores, *supra* note 226; Interstate Material Corp., 290 NLRB 362, 131 LRRM 1101 (1988); Roundup Co. dba Fred Meyer, Inc. dba Meyer's Cafe & Konditorei, 282 NLRB 1, 124 LRRM 1005 (1986); United States Steel Corp., 280 NLRB 837, 123 LRRM 1309 (1986); Safeway Stores, 276 NLRB 944, 120 LRRM 1186 (1985); First Nat'l Maintenance Corp., 254 NLRB 289, 106 LRRM 1211 (1981), *enforced*, 681 F2d 802, 111 LRRM 2058 (CA 2, 1981); Presbyterian Community Hosp., 230 NLRB 599, 95 LRRM 1610 (1977); Diamond Int'l Corp., 229 NLRB 1314, 95 LRRM 1281 (1977); Hartz Mountain Corp., 228 NLRB 492, 96 LRRM 1589 (1977), *enforced sub nom.* Distributive Workers Dist. 65 v. NLRB, 593 F2d 1155, 99 LRRM 2640 (CA DC, 1978); Roberts Elec. Co., 227 NLRB 1312, 95 LRRM 1159 (1977); Press Specialties Mfg. Co., 220 NLRB 361, 90 LRRM 1384 (1975); Colony Knitwear Corp., 217 NLRB 245, 88 LRRM 1552 (1975); Vic's Shop 'n Save, 215 NLRB 28, 88 LRRM 1478 (1974); Traub's Mkt., 205 NLRB 787, 84 LRRM 1078 (1973), *enforcement denied*, 506 F2d 730, 87 LRRM 3275 (CA 3, 1974).

[231]NLRB v. Hunter Outdoor Prods., 440 F2d 876, 76 LRRM 2969 (CA 1, 1971), *enforcing* 176 NLRB 449, 73 LRRM 1632 (1969).

conditions that existed prior to the agreement.[232] More recently, however, the Board has not ordered the employer to maintain the wages and benefits granted in the agreement with the unlawfully assisted unions, but has simply provided that its order "shall not be construed to authorize or require the elimination of wage increases or benefits established under the agreement."[233] A cease-and-desist order, however, is inappropriate if the union's majority status is unaffected by the employer's unlawful support,[234] or in certain instances where more narrowly drawn orders can remedy relatively minor unlawful employer assistance.[235] Nonetheless, as in the case of unlawful employer domination, the Board will utilize a *Gissel* bargaining order as a remedy if the unlawful employer assistance and other employer unfair labor practices have undermined the majority support of a rival, disfavored, labor organization.[236]

Where unlawful assistance taints a representation election, the Board directs that the employer cease and desist from the unlawful assistance and orders a new election "at such time as the regional director decides that the circumstances permit the free choice of a bargaining representative."[237] Where there is

---

[232] Airstream, Inc., 288 NLRB 220, 130 LRRM 1281 (1988); Caro Bags, 285 NLRB 656, 128 LRRM 1031 (1987); R.J.E. Leasing Corp., 262 NLRB 373, 110 LRRM 1313 (1982); King Radio Corp., 257 NLRB 521, 107 LRRM 1571 (1981); Hollander Home Fashion Corp., 255 NLRB 1098, 107 LRRM 1058 (1981); Mego Corp., 254 NLRB 300, 106 LRRM 1196 (1981); Triangle Sheet Metal Works, 237 NLRB 364, 98 LRRM 1585 (1978); Eastern Indus., 217 NLRB 712, 89 LRRM 1134 (1975).

[233] Caro Bags, *supra* note 232; R.J.E. Leasing Corp., *supra* note 232; Special Serv. Delivery, 259 NLRB 993, 994, 109 LRRM 1061 (1982); First Nat'l Maintenance Corp., 254 NLRB 289, 289 n.1, 106 LRRM 1211 (1981) (Board deleted ALJ-recommended order requiring maintenance of wages and benefits). In Mego Corp., *supra* note 232, at 301, 302, 106 LRRM at 1198, which involved an improper accretion under an existing, valid, contract, the Board's order was "without prejudice, however, to any wages or benefits granted" under the agreement. With regard to any insurance provided under a union-sponsored plan the Board ordered the employers to "forthwith provide an equivalent substitute so that no such coverage shall be discontinued or lapse."

[234] St. Joseph's Hosp., 254 NLRB 634, 106 LRRM 1190 (1981); True Temper Corp., 217 NLRB 1120, 89 LRRM 1228 (1975).

[235] *E.g.*, Jeffrey Mfg. Co., 208 NLRB 75, 85 LRRM 1336 (1974) (order merely prohibits employer from dealing with collective bargaining representative who was a supervisor); *see* Schwenk, Inc., 229 NLRB 640, 95 LRRM 1129 (1977); Associated Gen. Contractors of Cal., 220 NLRB 540, 90 LRRM 1719 (1975), *enforcement denied*, 564 F2d 27, 96 LRRM 3331 (CA 9, 1977).

[236] Professional Ambulance Serv., *supra* note 224; Doces Sixth Ave., 225 NLRB 806, 93 LRRM 1091 (1976); General Iron Corp., 224 NLRB 1180, 93 LRRM 1260 (1976). *Contra* Business Envelope Mfrs., 227 NLRB 280, 94 LRRM 1351 (1976). *See* Chapter 12, "Recognition and Withdrawal of Recognition Without an Election," for general treatment of *Gissel* and its progency.

[237] Yaloz Mold & Die Co., 256 NLRB 30, 30 n.4, 107 LRRM 1179 (1981); Raley's, Inc., 256 NLRB 946, 107 LRRM 1363 (1981), *rev'd and remanded in part*, 703 F2d 410, 112 LRRM

unlawful assistance, but no recognition, the employer is simply ordered to cease and desist from the unlawful support.[238] The Board continues to distinguish between narrow and broad cease-and-desist orders. Narrow orders, appropriate in most unlawful assistance cases, require the employer to cease and desist from the specific unlawful acts found, and from infringing on employee rights "in any like or related manner."[239] Broad orders, which prohibit infringement of employee rights "in any manner," are fashioned by the Board where the respondent has shown a proclivity to violate the Act, or where the violations are egregious.[240] In the case of a respondent union, a broad order protects employees beyond those of the particular employer involved in the union's unlawful conduct. In a 1984 case, a broad order was issued against a minority union that had violated sections 8(b)(1)(A) and 8(b)(2) by entering into a contract, with union-security and checkoff clauses, even though the union had not sought to enforce the union-security clause.[241] Because the union had previously committed such a violation, the Board expanded the ALJ's recommended order so as to prohibit the union from "[i]n any manner restraining or coercing employees of Respondent Employer, or any other employer in the exercise of rights guaranteed in Section 7 of the Act."[242]

3376 (CA 9, 1983), *vacated and remanded*, 725 F2d 1204, 115 LRRM 2933 (CA 9) (en banc), *reaff'd on remand*, 272 NLRB 1136, 117 LRRM 1485 (1984).

[238]Crown Cork & Seal Co., 255 NLRB 14, 107 LRRM 1195 (1981), *enforced*, 691 F2d 506, 111 LRRM 2650 (CA 9, 1982); NAB Constr. Corp., 258 NLRB 670, 108 LRRM 1306 (1981).

[239]*See, e.g.*, Interstate Material Corp., 290 NLRB 362, 131 LRRM 1101 (1988); Wickes Cos., Mode O'Day Co. Div., 280 NLRB 253, 122 LRRM 1213 (1988), *modified*, 290 NLRB 1234, 129 LRRM 1276 (1988); Ana Colon, Inc., 266 NLRB 611, 112 LRRM 1434 (1983); Type Rite Ribbon Mfg. Co., 264 NLRB 650, 111 LRRM 1304 (1982); NAB Constr. Corp., *supra* note 238.

[240]American Pac. Concrete Pipe Co., 262 NLRB 1223, 110 LRRM 1540 (1982), *enforced*, 709 F2d 1514, 113 LRRM 2736 (CA 9, 1983). A broad cease-and-desist order was held warranted where, to avoid continuing a bargaining relationship with the representative of its trucking employees, the employer purported to end trucking operations, but then reestablished such operations through an alter ego arrangement. The employer refused to recognize the former bargaining-unit representative and encouraged the employees to support a different union. Such unfair labor practices by the employer were sufficiently egregious "to demonstrate a disregard for its employees' fundamental statutory rights." *Id.* at 1227. *See also* All Kind Quilting, 266 NLRB 1186, 113 LRRM 1129 (1983); Ford Bros., 263 NLRB 92, 111 LRRM 1188 (1982). The breadth of the cease-and-desist order determines whether subsequent violations expose the violator to contempt citations. *See* Hickmott Foods, 242 NLRB 1357, 101 LRRM 1342 (1979).

[241]Port Chester Nursing Home, 269 NLRB 150, 154, 116 LRRM 1403 (1984).

[242]*Id.* at 150. The Board explained that a broad order had been issued in Sanford Home for Adults, 253 NLRB 1132, 106 LRRM 1219, *enforced*, 669 F2d 35, 109 LRRM 3007 (CA2, 1981), for various violations of §§8(b)(1)(A) and 8(b)(2) "including violations similar to those found here." Port Chester Nursing Home, *supra* note 241, at 150. However, in *Sanford Home*, the "extensive and pervasive" violations that prompted the broad order included unlawfully effectuating the discharge of employees. 253 NLRB at 1140.

In addition to its power to disestablish a dominated labor organization, or to compel an employer to stop bargaining with an assisted labor organization, the Board has the discretion to order the employer to reimburse its employees for initiation fees and dues paid to an unlawfully favored labor organization. This remedy is generally used only where an illegal collective bargaining agreement has been used to coerce the employees into paying such dues and fees, as where an employer and a minority union have entered into a collective bargaining agreement providing for union-security and dues checkoff. In *Virginia Electric & Power Co. v. NLRB*[243] the Supreme Court rejected the employer's argument that a reimbursement remedy was penal in nature. The Court stated:

> To hold that the Board is without power here to order reimbursement of the amount so exacted is to hold that an employer is free to fasten firmly upon his employees the cost of maintaining an organization by which he effectively defeats the free exercise of their rights to self-organization and collective bargaining. That this may pervert the purpose of the Act is clear . . . . An order such as this, which deprives an employer of advantages accruing from a particular method of subverting the Act, is a permissible method of effectuating the statutory policy.[244]

The Board routinely requires employers to reimburse their employees for dues and other funds obtained under such circumstances.[245] If the labor organization is named as a respondent and found guilty of section 8(b)(1)(A) violations as a party to an unlawful agreement, the union and the employer may be held jointly and severally liable for the cost of reimbursement to the employees.[246] However, actual coercion of such

---

[243]319 US 533, 12 LRRM 739 (1943).

[244]*Id.* at 540–41.

[245]*E.g.*, Baine Serv. Sys., 248 NLRB 563, 103 LRRM 1518 (1980); Hudson River Aggregates, 246 NLRB 192, 102 LRRM 1524 (1979), *enforced*, 639 F2d 865, 106 LRRM 2313 (CA 2, 1981); Bronxwood Home for Adults, 244 NLRB 905, 102 LRRM 1120 (1979); B. F. G. Gourmet Foods, 236 NLRB 489, 98 LRRM 1344 (1978). In Dyna Corp., 223 NLRB 1200, 92 LRRM 1284 (1976), the Board ordered the employer to reimburse the incumbent disfavored union the amount of its dues, which the employer had withheld pursuant to its contract with that union but which it had transmitted to an outside favored union.

[246]*E.g.*, Caro Bags, *supra* note 232; Armco, Inc., Eastern Steel Div., Ashland Works, 279 NLRB 1184, 123 LRRM 1335 (1986), *enforced in part*, 832 F2d 357, 126 LRRM 2961 (CA 6, 1987); Monfort of Colo., 256 NLRB 612, 107 LRRM 1296 (1981), *enforced sub nom.* National Maritime Union v. NLRB, 683 F2d 305, 111 LRRM 2286 (CA 9, 1982); Save-It Discount Foods, 263 NLRB 689, 111 LRRM 1110 (1982); General Instrument Corp., 262 NLRB 1178, 111 LRRM 1017 (1982); McKesson Drug Co., 257 NLRB 468, 107 LRRM 1509 (1981); Sanford Home for Adults, *supra* note 242. *See also* NAB Constr. Corp., *supra* note 238; Safeway Stores, *supra* note 230 (reimbursement not ordered for employees who

payments must precede the reimbursement remedy, and unless the employer actually coerced the employees to make such payment, the reinstatement remedy is deemed "punitive and beyond the power of the Board."[247] The Board found the requisite coercion where the employer had deducted dues from the wages of employees during the first 45 days of their employment without valid authorization cards.[248] The administrative law judge had recommended that reimbursement was unwarranted because the employees were covered by a contract containing valid dues checkoff and union-security clauses, which would have required the payments.[249] The Board disagreed because the relevant contract clauses did not apply to employees during the first 45 days of their employment. The employees had no obligation to pay dues during that period unless they voluntarily executed authorization cards, and therefore, the deduction of dues was coerced. In another case,[250] the Board ordered repayment of dues withheld by an employer that presented new employees with dues authorization cards immediately upon being hired, even though the contract provided for a 30-day waiting period before employees had to join the union. The Board found that the employer's practice coerced the employees into joining the union.

The coercive deduction of initiation fees, rather than periodic dues, during the 30-day statutory period violates sections 8(a)(2) and 8(b)(1)(A), but reimbursement of the withheld fee amount will not be ordered if the employee worked beyond the 30-day

---

were union members prior to unlawful recognition of union); McKesson Drug Co., *supra* (reimbursement not ordered for employees who voluntarily joined union prior to employer's acts of unlawful assistance); Romar Carrot Co., 228 NLRB 369, 94 LRRM 1734 (1977). In Kaiser Found. Hosp., 228 NLRB 468, 96 LRRM 1345 (1977), *enforced sub nom.* NLRB v. Hospital Workers Local 250, 577 F2d 649, 99 LRRM 2431 (CA 9, 1978), the reimbursement remedy was applied to the union alone where the charge against the employer was dismissed as time-barred.

[247]Carpenters Local 60 v. NLRB, 365 US 651, 47 LRRM 2900 (1961). *See, e.g.*, Haddon House Food Prods. v. NLRB, 764 F2d 182, 119 LRRM 3021 (CA 3, 1985); Cherokee Equity Corp., Cherokee Marine Terminal Div., 287 NLRB 1080, 128 LRRM 1051 (1988); Caro Bags, *supra* note 232; Roundup Co. dba Fred Meyer, Inc. dba Meyer's Cafe & Konditorei, *supra* note 230; United States Steel Corp., *supra* note 230; Armco, Inc., Eastern Steel Div., Ashland Works, *supra* note 246; Safeway Stores, *supra* note 230; SMI of Worcester, 271 NLRB 1508, 117 LRRM 1365 (1984); Harbor Cartage, 269 NLRB 927, 116 LRRM 1016 (1984); Port Chester Nursing Home, *supra* note 241; Hudson River Aggregates, *supra* note 245.

[248]General Instrument Corp., *supra* note 246.

[249]Safeway Stores, *supra* note 230.

[250]Wickes Cos., Mode O'Day Co. Div., 290 NLRB 1234, 129 LRRM 1276 (1988), *supplementing* 280 NLRB 253, 122 LRRM 1213 (1986). The Board disavowed the reimbursement remedy imposed under similar circumstances in General Instrument Corp., *supra* note 246.

period and thereby became liable for the entire initiation fee.[251] By a parity of reasoning, reimbursement of dues will not be ordered, even if they were obtained improperly by an employer from his employees, where the employees were subject to a lawful union-security clause.[252] Neither will the Board order reimbursement if there is no union-security clause[253] or where there is no actual coercion,[254] as where employees joined the union before a union-security clause became effective.[255]

Where an employee has been discharged because of failure to pay dues pursuant to a union-security provision between an employer and an unlawfully recognized union, reinstatement with backpay is the standard remedy.[256] Reimbursement for coerced payment of monies or lost wages includes interest.[257] Additional "make whole" relief and special remedies may also be utilized to remove advantages obtained by a favored union.[258]

---

[251]Wickes Cos., Mode O'Day Co. Div., *supra* note 250.

[252]IBEC Housing Corp., 245 NLRB 1282, 102 LRRM 1420 (1979); American Geriatric Enters., 235 NLRB 1532, 98 LRRM 1220 (1978).

[253]Wintex Knitting Mill, 223 NLRB 1293, 92 LRRM 1113 (1976), *enforcement denied*, 610 F2d 430, 104 LRRM 2529 (CA 6, 1979).

[254]Safeway Stores, 276 NLRB 944, 120 LRRM 1186 (1985) (reimbursement denied to employees who had been members before transferring to new store at which violation occurred); Al Pfister Truck Serv., 236 NLRB 217, 99 LRRM 1024 (1978) (reimbursement inappropriate where employees were longtime union members and were not coerced into joining union).

[255]Unit Train Coal Sales, 234 NLRB 1265, 98 LRRM 1343 (1978); Acme Wire Works, 229 NLRB 333, 96 LRRM 1603 (1977), *enforced*, 582 F2d 153, 98 LRRM 3163 (CA 2, 1978).

[256]*E.g.*, Southern Ore. Log Scaling & Grading Bureau, 223 NLRB 430, 92 LRRM 1216 (1976); Western Exterminator Co., 223 NLRB 1270, 92 LRRM 1161 (1976), *enforced in part*, 565 F2d 1114, 97 LRRM 2187 (CA 9, 1977); Captive Plastics, 209 NLRB 749, 86 LRRM 1235 (1974).

[257]Caro Bags, 285 NLRB 656, 128 LRRM 1031 (1987); United States Steel Corp., 280 NLRB 837, 123 LRRM 1309 (1986); Port Chester Nursing Home, *supra* note 241; Haddon House Food Prods., 269 NLRB 338, 115 LRRM 1209 (1984), *enforced*, 764 F2d 182, 119 LRRM 3021 (CA 3, 1985); Save-It Discount Foods, *supra* note 246; McKesson Drug Co., *supra* note 246; Monfort of Colo., *supra* note 246; Hudson River Aggregates, *supra* note 245. *See generally* Olympic Medical Corp., 250 NLRB 146, 104 LRRM 1325 (1980), *enforced*, 665 F2d 1053, 108 LRRM 3059 (CA 9, 1981).

[258]*See, e.g.*, Colony Knitwear Corp., 217 NLRB 245, 88 LRRM 1552 (1975); Teamsters Local 688, 215 NLRB 852, 88 LRRM 1217 (1974); Kent Corp., 212 NLRB 595, 87 LRRM 1730 (1974); Scottex Corp., 200 NLRB 446, 82 LRRM 1287 (1972). For general treatment of NLRB orders and remedies, *see* Chapter 32, "NLRB Orders and Remedies."

Part III

THE REPRESENTATION PROCESS AND UNION RECOGNITION

CHAPTER 9

RESTRICTIONS ON PREELECTION ACTIVITY: "LABORATORY CONDITIONS"

I. INTRODUCTION

Section 7 of the National Labor Relations Act gives employees "the right to bargain collectively through representatives of their own choosing . . . ." In addition to granting the substantive right, the Act also establishes the procedure through which employees may choose a bargaining representative. As set forth in section 9 of the Act,[1] this procedure is the representation election, which culminates in formal certification of the results by the National Labor Relations Board.

This chapter deals with preelection conduct by employers and unions which improperly interferes with the election process but which is not an unfair labor practice. Preelection conduct which is an unfair labor practice is, a fortiori, conduct which improperly interferes with the election process, but such unfair labor practice conduct is dealt with in other chapters.[2]

A. The Board's Authority Under Section 9

Section 9 vests in the Board "the broad duty of providing election procedures and safeguards . . . ."[3] In particular, the Board has the authority to "police" preelection campaigns in order to assure that the parties do not engage in conduct that prevents the employees from making a free choice in the elec-

---

[1]*See generally* Chapter 10, "Representation Proceedings and Elections."

[2]*See particularly* Chapter 6, "Interference With Protected Rights," dealing with unfair labor practices under §8(a)(1) and Chapter 7, "Discrimination in Employment," dealing with unfair labor practices under §8(a)(3). Unfair labor practices under other sections of the Act may also provide a basis for setting aside an election.

[3]NLRB v. Sanitary Laundry, 441 F2d 1368, 1369, 77 LRRM 2359 (CA 10, 1971).

tion or forces them to act contrary to their desires. Where the results of an election are the product of extraneous and coercive influence and therefore do not represent the free and uninhibited choice of the employees, the Board has the authority to set aside the results and order a new election.[4]

1. Relation to Unfair Labor Practices. Conduct disrupting the free choice of a bargaining representative may also have the effect of interfering with, restraining, or coercing employees in the exercise of their section 7 rights. Thus, certain conduct which is the basis for overturning an election may also be the basis for finding a violation of section 8(a)(1).[5] However, conduct that is not a violation of section 8(a)(1) may nevertheless improperly interfere with the election process and provide a basis for setting aside an election.

2. Development of the *General Shoe* "Laboratory Conditions" Doctrine. In its 1948 *General Shoe Corp.*[6] decision, the Board held that conduct not so egregious as to violate section 8(a)(1) may nevertheless provide a basis for setting aside an election:

> Conduct that creates an atmosphere which renders improbable a free choice will sometimes warrant invalidating an election, even though that conduct may not constitute an unfair labor practice. . . .
>
> . . .
>
> [T]he criteria applied . . . in a representation proceeding . . . need [not] be identical to those employed in testing whether an unfair labor practice was committed. . . .
>
> . . .
>
> In election proceedings, it is the Board's function to provide a laboratory in which an experiment may be conducted, under conditions as nearly ideal as possible, to determine the uninhibited desires of the employees.[7]

Thus, the "laboratory conditions" test enunciated in *General Shoe* holds the parties to a more demanding standard of conduct than the strictures of section 8(a)(1).

It has been argued that the Board's holding in *General Shoe* is not consistent with section 8(c) of the Act, which declares that

---

[4]*See* discussion of remedies at Part III *infra*.

[5]For detailed treatment of unfair labor practices under §8(a)(1), *see* Chapter 6, "Interference With Protected Rights."

[6]77 NLRB 124, 21 LRRM 1337 (1948).

[7]*Id.* at 127. How realistic is this objective? *See* J. GETMAN, S. GOLDBERG, & J. HERMAN, UNION REPRESENTATION ELECTIONS: LAW AND REALITY (1976); Bok, *The Regulation of Campaign Tactics in Representation Elections Under the National Labor Relations Act*, 78 HARV. L. REV. 38, 45–47 (1964).

the finding of an unfair labor practice may not be predicated on a party's communications if such communications contain "no threat of reprisal or force or promise of benefit."[8] The Board has reconciled the two by emphasizing that section 8(c) applies only to unfair labor practice cases and makes no mention of representation proceedings. Thus, under *General Shoe,* communications not containing a threat of reprisal or force or promise of benefit may provide the basis for setting aside an election even though the party making such communications could not have violated section 8.

General Shoe fell into disfavor during the period of the Eisenhower Board, which held that section 8(c) set the applicable standard both in representation and in unfair labor practice proceedings.[9] The result was a relaxation of the regulation of preelection campaigns. Indeed, in some instances, a more demanding standard of conduct was applied in unfair labor practice cases than in representation proceedings.[10]

In 1962, with new members in their seats, the Board returned to *General Shoe* as the standard for judging conduct in a representation proceeding. In *Dal-Tex Optical Co.*[11] the Board stated that "[c]onduct violative of Section 8(a)(1) is, a fortiori, conduct which interferes with the exercise of a free and untrammeled choice in an election." Thus, conduct that constitutes an unfair labor practice will almost always also violate the Board's election rules, although the Board has made exceptions for conduct that could not have affected the election outcome.[12] Other improper conduct which may destroy the "laboratory conditions" for an

---

[8] *See* Chapter 6, "Interference With Protected Rights," at notes 51–64.

[9] *See* National Furniture Co., 119 NLRB 1, 40 LRRM 1442 (1957); Lux Clock Mfg. Co., 113 NLRB 1194, 36 LRRM 1432 (1955); Esquire, Inc., 107 NLRB 1238, 33 LRRM 1367 (1954); American Laundry Mach. Co., 107 NLRB 511, 33 LRRM 1181 (1953).

[10] Wirtz, *The New National Labor Relations Board; Herein of "Employer Persuasion,"* 49 Nw. U.L. REV. 594 (1954).

[11] 137 NLRB 1782, 1786, 50 LRRM 1489 (1962). *See* Chapter 6, "Interference With Protected Rights," at notes 88–92, for discussion of the case and its application.

[12] *See* Clark Equip. Co., 278 NLRB 498, 505, 121 LRRM 1258 (1986), which noted that "the Board has departed from this policy where it is virtually impossible to conclude that the misconduct could have affected the election results" based on the number of violations, their severity, the extent of dissemination, the size of the unit, and other factors. Absent evidence of dissemination of an unlawful threat of plant closure, a single statement by one supervisor to one employee in a unit of 75–80 employees was not alone a sufficient basis to set aside the election. Kokomo Tube Co., 280 NLRB 357, 122 LRRM 1254 (1986). *See also* Keith Austin, Inc., 288 NLRB 646, 129 LRRM 1296 (1988); Hall Indus., 285 NLRB 391, 126 LRRM 1162 (1987). *Cf.* Machinists (Burkart Foam), 286 NLRB 417, 126 LRRM 1223 (1987) (union constitutional provision imposing unlawful restrictions on resignation from membership not likely to affect outcome of election; therefore, in line with *Clark Equip. Co.,* decertification election not set aside).

election, though not an unfair labor practice, may nonetheless be the basis for setting aside an election.[13]

B. Timing of "Laboratory Period"

In contrast to the six-month "statute of limitations" for unfair labor practice charges,[14] in postelection objection proceedings the Board bases its findings only upon conduct that has occurred between an established cutoff date and the election. The establishment of a cutoff date represents an attempt to balance the advantage of "eliminating from postelection consideration conduct too remote to have prevented free choice"[15] with the disadvantage of intentional delays for the purpose of strategic interference. In 1952, in the *A&P* case[16] the Board established the cutoff date as either (1) the execution date of a consent-election agreement, or (2) in contested cases, the issuance of a notice of hearing. Two years later, in *Woolworth,*[17] the Board moved the cutoff date in contested cases closer to the election, namely, to the date of issuance of the direction of election.

In 1961 the Board reconsidered the cutoff date in the light of its experience with the delegation of decisional authority in representation cases to the regional directors.[18] That delegation had decreased the time between the filing of a petition and an election, and considerations of remoteness were no longer as

---

[13]J. GETMAN, S. GOLDBERG, & J. HERMAN, *supra* note 7, analyzed and criticized the assumptions on which the Board's "laboratory conditions" standard is based. Following an empirical inquiry into voting behavior in Board elections, they recommended that the Board should cease regulating speech and, for election purposes, nearly all conduct. Considerable controversy surrounded their findings and recommendations. Some commentators objected to deregulating conduct or speech involving threats of reprisal (*see* Kochan, *Book Review, Legal Nonsense, Empirical Examination and Policy Evaluation,* 29 STAN. L. REV. 1115, 1121 (1977); Goetz & Wike, *Book Review, Union Representation Elections: Law and Reality,* 25 KAN. L. REV. 375, 383 (1977)); others criticized the methodology underlying the Getman study or charged that their data failed to support some of the study's conclusions (*see* Eames, *An Analysis of the Union Voting Study From a Trade-Unionist's Point of View,* 28 STAN. L. REV. 1181, 1182 (1976); Peck, *Book Review, NLRB Election Law, Union Representation Elections: Law and Reality,* 22 WASH. L. REV. 197, 206–8 (1977); Craver, *Book Review, Union Representation Elections, Law and Reality,* 22 VILL. L. REV. 891, 896–97 (1977). The authors have defined their position. *See* Getman, *Ruminations on Organizing in the Private Section,* 53 U. CHI. L. REV. 45 (1986); *Goldberg, Getman, & Brett, The Relationship Between Free Choice and Labor Board Doctrine: Differing Empirical Approaches,* 79 NW. U.L. REV. 721 (1984).

[14]Section 10(b).

[15]Ideal Elec. & Mfg. Co., 134 NLRB 1275, 1277, 49 LRRM 1316 (1961).

[16]Great Atl. & Pac. Tea Co., 101 NLRB 1118, 31 LRRM 1189 (1952).

[17]F. W. Woolworth Co., 109 NLRB 1446, 34 LRRM 1584 (1954).

[18]Ideal Elec. & Mfg. Co., *supra* note 15.

compelling. Thus, in *Ideal Electric,*[19] *Woolworth* was overruled and the date of filing of the petition rather than of the direction of election was established as the cutoff date.[20]

Ideal Electric left unchanged the cutoff date in uncontested elections. The following year, uniformity in cutoff dates was prescribed in *Goodyear Tire.*[21] Thereafter, the filing of the petition marked the commencement of the "laboratory period" in all representation cases.

The *Ideal Electric* rule does not preclude consideration of prepetition conduct that "adds meaning and dimension" to postpetition conduct[22] or prepetition conduct that is "sufficiently serious" to have affected the results of the election.[23] In *NLRB v. Anchorage Times Publishing Co.,*[24] the Ninth Circuit rejected an employer's argument that the "critical period" or "laboratory period" doctrine is a Board-created statute of limitations. Enforcing the Board's bargaining order, the court held that the Board had properly considered the employer's prepeti-

---

[19]*Id.* Objectionable conduct occurring on the day the petition was filed, but before the actual filing, will still be considered as ground for setting aside the election. West Tex. Equip. Co., 142 NLRB 1358, 53 LRRM 1249 (1963).

[20]Clothing & Textile Workers (Lowenstein Corp.) v. NLRB, 736 F2d 1559, 117 LRRM 2453 (CA DC, 1984) (*Ideal Electric* applied to exclude prepetition conduct); NLRB v. Golden Age Beverage Co., 415 F2d 26, 31, 71 LRRM 2924, 2927 (CA 5, 1969) (*Ideal Electric* applied). *See also* Weather Wise Conditioning Corp., 282 NLRB 273, 124 LRRM 1047 (1986) (threat by union agent made before representation petition was filed provided no basis for setting aside election); Knogo Corp., 262 NLRB 1346, 111 LRRM 1104 (1982), *enforced,* 727 F2d 55, 115 LRRM 2756 (CA 2, 1984); Fisher-Haynes Corp. of Ga., 262 NLRB 1274, 110 LRRM 1432 (1982).

[21]Goodyear Tire & Rubber Co., 138 NLRB 453, 51 LRRM 1070 (1962).

[22]Fruehauf Corp., 274 NLRB 403, 119 LRRM 1053 (1985) (prepetition threat considered insofar as it lends meaning and dimension to related conduct during critical period); YKK (U.S.A.), 269 NLRB 82, 115 LRRM 1986 (1984); Shamrock Coal Co., 267 NLRB 625, 114 LRRM 1122 (1983); Evans Bros. Barber & Beauty Salons, 256 NLRB 121, 107 LRRM 1176 (1981); Dresser Indus., 242 NLRB 74, 101 LRRM 1112 (1979). *Cf.* Data Technology Corp., Plastronics Div., 281 NLRB 1005, 123 LRRM 1192 (1986) (prepetition conduct, standing alone, does not provide basis for sustaining objection absent related allegedly objectionable postpetition conduct to which prepetition conduct might give meaning). *See also* White Plains Lincoln Mercury, 288 NLRB 1133, 128 LRRM 1145, 1151 (1988) (related prepetition conduct indicated that postpetition unfair labor practices "were not isolated incidents" and were "sufficiently serious and of widespread impact to have interfered with the conduct of the . . . election"); Royal Packaging Corp., 284 NLRB 317, 125 LRRM 1235 (1987) (election set aside because union prepetition promise to obtain recall of employee likely to have significant impact on election).

[23]Servomation of Columbus, 219 NLRB 504, 506, 89 LRRM 1688, 1690 (1975) (dictum) ("the election will be set aside regardless of the time when the misconduct occurred" where the "fear and coercion . . . persist to the date of the election"); Willis Shaw Frozen Express, 209 NLRB 267, 268, 85 LRRM 1540, 1541 (1974) (dictum) (stabbing and assault prior to filing petition making free election impossible); Weather Seal Corp., 161 NLRB 1226, 1229, 63 LRRM 1428, 1432 (1966) ("unlawfully assisted union on the ballot").

[24]637 F2d 1359, 106 LRRM 2900 (CA 9), *cert. denied,* 454 US 835, 108 LRRM 2558 (1981).

tion unfair labor practices. The Board is not required to adhere to an inflexible *per se* rule to disregard incidents before the filing of an election petition, where such incidents may have had an effect on the election outcome.[25] Indeed, courts have refused to enforce Board orders where application of *Ideal Electric* excluded consideration of egregious prepetition conduct.[26] In *NLRB v. L & J Equipment Co.*,[27] the Third Circuit refused to enforce a bargaining order where the Board applied *Ideal Electric* to exclude egregious prepetition misconduct. In the court's opinion, "the *Ideal Electric* rule should not be applied woodenly," but only "as a rule of thumb and convenience, and not used to exclude important evidence needed to evaluate misconduct."[28]

When a party withdraws a petition, and later files a second petition, the Board will disregard conduct occurring in the hiatus between the petitions if the hiatus constitutes "a significant period during which Board processes [are] not involved."[29] Thus, where an original petition was withdrawn 31 days before the filing of a second petition, the Board refused to consider conduct that occurred during the 31-day intervening period.[30] However, the Board distinguished that case from one where a second petition was filed "immediately on the heels" of the withdrawal of the first petition. In that situation, the Board indicated it would make an exception to the *Ideal Electric* rule, and would consider the alleged misconduct occurring during the pedency of the first petition, because the critical period began on the date of the filing of the first petition.[31]

---

[25]*Id.* at 1365, 106 LRRM at 2904. *See also* NLRB v. L & J Equip. Co., 745 F2d 224, 117 LRRM 2592 (CA 3, 1984), *denying enforcement to* 266 NLRB No. 29, 112 LRRM 1434 (1983) (not printed in bound volume of Board reports) (arson occurring three months prior to filing of petition should be considered in light of incidents occurring after filing of petition).

[26]NLRB v. L & J Equip. Co., *supra* note 25, 237, 117 LRRM at 2601; Catholic Medical Center of Brooklyn & Queens v. NLRB, 589 F2d 1166, 100 LRRM 2225 (CA 2, 1978) *denying enforcement of* 236 NLRB 497, 98 LRRM 1603 (1978) (rejecting as arbitrary and capricious Board's refusal to consider conduct occurring between filing of two petitions); NLRB v. R. Dakin & Co., 477 F2d 492, 494, 82 LRRM 3090, 3091 (CA 9, 1973) (*Ideal Electric* may not be "mechanically" applied to flatly bar "consideration of all pre-petition misconduct"); NLRB v. Typographical Union No. 570 (Lawrence), 376 F2d 643, 652, 653, 65 LRRM 2176, 2182 (CA 10, 1967) (prepetition offer of superseniority to strike replacements "must be given full consideration").

[27]*Supra* note 25.

[28]*Id.* at 237, 117 LRRM at 2601–2.

[29]Carson Int'l, 259 NLRB 1073, 109 LRRM 1066 (1982).

[30]*Id.*

[31]*Id.* (citing Monroe Tube Co., 220 NLRB 302, 305, 90 LRRM 1526 (1975), *enforcement denied on other grounds,* 545 F2d 1320, 94 LRRM 2020 (CA 2, 1976)). *See also* Catholic Medical Center of Brooklyn & Queens, *supra* note 26.

C. Procedural Considerations

The criteria used in judging the lawfulness of employer communications vary with the procedural setting in which the issue arises. If preelection conduct is being ruled upon in a representation case, the criteria for judgment will be compliance with "laboratory conditions." The same conduct in an unfair labor practice proceeding will be judged by the standard of section 8(c), which precludes the Board from finding an unfair labor practice based on a party's communications unless the communications contain threats or promises of benefit.[32]

Where the unfair labor practice and representation cases are consolidated into one action,[33] however, the distinction breaks down. In such circumstances, the administrative law judge presumably has two standards for guidance in judging the same conduct. These standards sometimes become entangled as the case moves from the administrative law judge to the Board, and possibly to the courts.[34]

A petitioner's knowledge, prior to an election, of an employer's improper preelection conduct does not preclude the petitioner from asserting such conduct as grounds for objecting to the conduct of the election. A filing of a request for the Board to proceed to election, notwithstanding the pendency of such unfair labor practice charges based upon the same conduct, does not constitute a waiver of that right.[35] However, where a labor organization files both a petition and unfair labor practice charges, and then withdraws the unfair labor practice charges without prejudice in order to facilitate the representation pro-

---

[32]Dal-Tex Optical Co., 137 NLRB 1782, 50 LRRM 1489 (1962); *see also* Eagle-Picher Indus., 171 NLRB 293 n.1, 68 LRRM 1570 (1968). In Gold Kist, Inc. dba Golden Poultry Co., Agri-International, 271 NLRB 925, 117 LRRM 1127 (1984), the Board held that the employer's timely repudiation of coercive interrogation which was sufficient to avoid liability under section 8(a)(1) was a fortiori sufficient to restore the laboratory conditions necessary for a valid election. *See supra* at notes 7–10 and Chapter 6, "Interference with Protected Rights," at notes 51–72. For added treatment of objection period, *see* Chapter 10, "Representation Proceedings and Elections," at notes 51–78.

[33]Ordinarily both the objection to the election and the unfair labor practice complaint will be consolidated for hearing before the law judge. NLRB FIELD MANUAL 11420.1. *See* discussion of this procedure in Freeport Marble & Tile Co., 153 NLRB 810, 59 LRRM 1561 (1965), *enforced in part,* 367 F2d 371, 63 LRRM 2289 (CA 1, 1966).

[34]*See* Eagle-Picher Indus., *supra* note 32. An illustration of the process of disentangling the standards appears in Sinclair Co., 164 NLRB 261, 65 LRRM 1087 (1967), *enforced,* 397 F2d 157, 68 LRRM 2720 (CA 1, 1968), *aff'd sub nom.* NLRB v. Gissel Packing Co., 395 US 575, 71 LRRM 2481 (1969), where, in the course of recommending a bargaining order, the trial examiner, citing *Dal-Tex Optical, supra* note 32, found employer communications to have violated §8(a)(1) and also to have interfered with the free choice in the election.

[35]Ed Chandler Ford, Inc., 241 NLRB 1201, 101 LRRM 1056 (1979).

ceedings the withdrawal of those charges is treated as an automatic waiver by the petitioning union of the right to use the subject matter of the charges as a basis for objections to the election.[36]

II. GROUNDS FOR SETTING ASIDE ELECTIONS

A. Regulating Preelection Conduct by Adjudication Rather Than Rulemaking

Since its earliest days, the Board has imposed restrictions upon the parties' preelection activities. These have included "rules"[37] prohibiting electioneering activities at the polling place,[38] prohibiting speechmaking to captive audiences within 24 hours preceding the election,[39] and requiring management to provide names and addresses of all employees qualified to vote in the election.[40] These and other rules, made pursuant to the Board's power to conduct elections for certification of a bargaining agent, are mandatory rules for the conduct of elections; their violation furnishes grounds for setting aside the election whether or not the conduct constituted an unfair labor practice.[41]

---

[36]Ellicott Mach. Corp., 54 NLRB 732, 13 LRRM 194 (1944). *See* Redway Carriers, 274 NLRB 1359, 119 LRRM 1023 (1985).

[37]All of these rules were promulgated in adjudicated cases, rather than under the formal rulemaking procedures of the Administrative Procedure Act, 5 USC §553 (1988). *See* Chapter 31, "NLRB Procedures," at notes 236–258, and discussion *infra* at notes 42–43.

[38]Alliance Ware, Inc., 92 NLRB 55, 27 LRRM 1040 (1950); Detroit Creamery Co., 60 NLRB 178, 15 LRRM 221 (1945); Kilgore Mfg. Co., 45 NLRB 468, 11 LRRM 139 (1942); *cf.* Higgins, Inc., 106 NLRB 845, 32 LRRM 1566 (1953); J. I. Case Co., 85 NLRB 576, 24 LRRM 1431 (1949).

[39]Peerless Plywood Co., 107 NLRB 427, 33 LRRM 1151 (1953). In Honeywell, Inc., 162 NLRB 323, 64 LRRM 1007 (1966), the prohibition on speechmaking within 24 hours preceding the election was extended to include informal "question and answer" sessions; however the *Peerless Plywood* rules have been held inapplicable to sound-car broadcasting so long as the broadcasts consisted not of speeches, but merely of appeals interspersed with music. Southland Cork Co., 146 NLRB 906, 55 LRRM 1426 (1964), *enforced in part*, 342 F2d 702, 58 LRRM 2555 (CA 4, 1965). *But see* United States Gypsum Co., 115 NLRB 734, 37 LRRM 1374 (1956). *See* Chapter 6, "Interference With Protected Rights," at notes 159–162.

[40]Excelsior Underwear, 156 NLRB 1236, 61 LRRM 1217 (1966).

[41]*See, e.g.*, Thrifty Auto Parts, 295 NLRB No. 134, 131 LRRM 1801 (1989). In that case, the Board held that it "presumes" that an employer's failure to "substantially comply" with the rule set forth in *Excelsior Underwear, supra* note 40, warrants setting aside an election, stating: "Evidence of bad faith and actual prejudice is unnecessary because the rule is essentially prophylactic, *i.e.*, the potential harm from list omissions is deemed sufficiently great to warrant a strict rule that encourages conscientious efforts to comply." 131 LRRM at 1802.

There are, in theory, two ways in which the Board can promulgate the standards that regulate election campaign activities: (1) through the rulemaking power granted to the Board by section 6 of the National Labor Relations Act, and regulated by the Administrative Procedure Act,[42] or (2) by announcing a principle of general applicability in the context of a particular two-party action. In practice, the Board has regulated preelection activities through the second method only. The myriad rules governing preelection conduct have been formulated by the Board through adjudication in much the same way as the principles of the common law have been formulated by the courts. Rules of conduct announced by the Board in this manner acquire a measure of permanence and may serve to direct the future actions of employers and unions.[43]

B. Employer and Union Conduct

A wide assortment of traditional and imaginative techniques have been employed both to frustrate and to further union organizational efforts. Usually these have been used during election campaigns and have been evaluated by the Board in terms of election interference. In some instances, however, they have been employed at other stages of employer-employee relationships and have been evaluated in the broader context of interference with section 7 rights. The following discussion focuses upon the various techniques in the context of the representation election.[44]

1. Campaign Propaganda and Misrepresentations. During an election campaign, parties may intentionally or unintentionally make statements that are factually inaccurate. Employees may rely upon those inaccurate statements in voting, changing the outcome of the election. The Board for a long

---

[42]USC §551, et seq. (1988). For comment on the Board's rulemaking procedures, see authorities cited in Chapter 31, "NLRB Procedures," at notes 238–240.

[43]*Cf.* NLRB v. Bell Aerospace Co., 416 US 267, 85 LRRM 2945 (1974). The Board has recently shown what may be a new interest in utilizing its rulemaking authority, adopting rules setting appropriate bargaining units in the health care industry. *See* 29 C.F.R. §103.30 (1989). In American Hosp. Ass'n v. NLRB, ___ US ___, 137 LRRM 2001 (1991), the Supreme Court upheld the authority of the Board to promulgate the rule. *See* Morris, *NLRB Rulemaking: Promise and Prospects, reprinted in* BNA Daily Lab. Rep., No. 2, p. D-1, January 3, 1990.

[44]Discussion on unfair labor practices is found in Chapter 6, "Interference With Protected Rights." This chapter considers conduct which, though not constituting an unfair labor practice, may be grounds for setting aside an election.

period was reluctant to undertake the regulation of election propaganda,[45] explicitly stating that "exaggeration, inaccuracies, half-truths, and name calling, though not condoned, will not be grounds for setting aside an election."[46] The Board's view was that "absolute precision of statement and complete honesty are not always attainable in an election campaign, nor are they expected by the employees."[47] Consequently, the Board's preference was to leave misstatements for the opposing parties to correct and for the employees to evaluate.[48] Nevertheless, it sought to balance this preference against "the right of employees to an untrammeled choice, and the right of the parties to wage a free and vigorous campaign with all the normal legitimate tools of electioneering."[49] Over the last 30 years, the manner in which the Board has struck this balance has passed through several stages.

a. Last Minute Misrepresentations Prohibited: The Hollywood Ceramics *Rule.* In *Hollywood Ceramics Co.*[50] the Board formulated a limited prohibition of campaign misrepresentations in the following terms:

> [A]n election should be set aside only where there has been a misrepresentation or other similar campaign trickery, which involves a substantial departure from the truth, at a time which prevents the other party or parties from making an effective reply, so that the misrepresentation, whether deliberate or not, may reasonably be expected to have a significant impact on the election.[51]

The Board applied the *Hollywood Ceramics* rule for 15 years, abandoning it in 1977.[52] That rule required the Board to evaluate the truth or falsity of the parties' assertions. Not every misrepresentation, however, justified setting aside the election. The

---

[45]Cleveland Trencher Co., 130 NLRB 600, 603, 47 LRRM 1371 (1961); Gummed Prods. Co., 112 NLRB 1092, 36 LRRM 1156 (1955); Merck & Co., 104 NLRB 891, 32 LRRM 1160 (1953).

[46]Hollywood Ceramics Co., 140 NLRB 221, 226 n.6, 51 LRRM 1600 (1962). *See infra* note 51.

[47]140 NLRB at 223.

[48]United States Gypsum Co., 130 NLRB 901, 904, 47 LRRM 1436 (1961).

[49]Hollywood Ceramics Co., *supra* note 46, at 224. *Cf.* Linn v. Plant Guard Workers Local 114, 383 US 53, 61 LRRM 2345 (1966).

[50]*Supra* note 46.

[51]*Id.* at 224.

[52]Shopping Kart Food Mkt., 228 NLRB 1311, 94 LRRM 1705 (1977). *Shopping Kart* was, in turn, overruled and *Hollywood Ceramics* briefly revivified in General Knit of Cal., 239 NLRB 619, 99 LRRM 1687 (1978). More recently, in Midland Nat'l Life Ins. Co., 263 NLRB 127, 110 LRRM 1489 (1982), the Board again rejected *Hollywood Ceramics* and embraced *Shopping Kart.*

phrasing of the rule was in the conjunctive so that even a substantial misrepresentation would not upset an election if it concerned an unimportant matter and had only a de minimis effect. Similarly, the misrepresentation might be "so extreme as to put employees on notice of its lack of truth," or the employees themselves might have independent knowledge permitting them to evaluate the statements.[53]

Under *Hollywood Ceramics,* if there was a fair opportunity for rebuttal, even at a late moment, an election would not be set aside.[54] But lack of a fair opportunity for rebuttal was not controlling where the last-minute statement addressed an issue previously raised in the campaign and which the employees had a basis to evaluate.[55]

Under the rule of *Hollywood Ceramics,* whether the speaker or author had special knowledge of the assertions was occasionally controlling. Thus, an employer's statement as to the likelihood of a rise in union dues, based upon hearsay, did not invalidate an election.[56] In the First Circuit's view, the proper test under *Hollywood Ceramics* was not whether the speaker in fact had special knowledge, but whether listeners would believe that he had.[57]

Issues of misrepresentation and campaign trickery took many forms. The use of literature that concealed the true identity of the sponsor was grounds for setting aside an election.[58] Thus, employer issuance of antiunion materials over the signature of popular employees,[59] and union distribution of putative reports from rival union organizers describing employees in insulting terms, were deemed improper.[60] On the other hand, the use of pay stubs by an employer to dramatize the cost of union dues was proper or not depending upon the accuracy of the deduction, the timing, the manner of distribution, and the accompanying

---

[53]140 LRRM at 224.

[54]*Id.* at 223; *see also* General Elec. Co., 162 NLRB 912, 64 LRRM 1104 (1967).

[55]Elmcrest Convalescent Hosp. Mgmt. Corp., 173 NLRB 38, 69 LRRM 1196 (1968). *Cf.* United States Gypsum Co., *supra* note 48, where an election was set aside because the employer's last-minute claims could not be evaluated despite earlier campaign attention to matters raised in those claims.

[56]York Furniture Corp., 170 NLRB 1487, 67 LRRM 1606 (1968).

[57]NLRB v. A. G. Pollard Co., 393 F2d 239, 67 LRRM 2997 (CA 1, 1968). The Board took a similar view in Cranbar Corp., 173 NLRB 1287, 69 LRRM 1581 (1968).

[58]Kelsey-Hayes Co., 126 NLRB 151, 45 LRRM 1290 (1960).

[59]Timken-Detroit Axle Co., 98 NLRB 790, 29 LRRM 1401 (1952), *petition to restrain enforcement dismissed,* 197 F2d 512, 30 LRRM 2328 (CA 6, 1952).

[60]Sylvania Elec. Prods., 119 NLRB 824, 828, 41 LRRM 1188 (1954).

description;[61] portrayal of strikes and violence as the inevitable consequence of unionization could also be grounds for setting aside an election.[62]

The *Hollywood Ceramics* standard was applied to unions as well as to employers.[63] Thus, for example, union misrepresentations concerning profit margins of employers could be the basis for setting aside an election.[64] On the other hand, the Board upheld an election where a union representative stated that the company had "made" approximately one million dollars when, although the company had grossed that amount, its profits were substantially lower.[65]

Incontestable accuracy of expression is unattainable in such matters. Context and nuance always color and define claims about employer profitability, and all the similar claims advanced in organizing campaigns including those comparing the employer's wages and benefits with those of other employers.[66] Thus, *Hollywood Ceramics* opened a potentially wide field of postelection review: the statements and omissions of the prevailing party could be combed by a losing party seeking facially plausible objections. The review required the Board and courts

---

[61]TRW, Inc., 173 NLRB 1425, 70 LRRM 1017 (1968); Crown Laundry & Dry Cleaners, 160 NLRB 746, 63 LRRM 1035 (1966), *enforced* (CA 5, 1967) (unreported), *subsequent contempt proceeding,* 437 F2d 290, 76 LRRM 2336 (CA 5, 1971). Trane Co., 137 NLRB 1506, 50 LRRM 1434 (1962); Mosler Safe Co., 129 NLRB 747, 47 LRRM 1058 (1960).

[62]Louis Gallet, Inc., 247 NLRB 63, 103 LRRM 1125 (1980), *enforced,* 642 F2d 443, 108 LRRM 2279 (CA 3, 1981). Prior to the Board's 1974 decision in Litho Press, 211 NLRB 1014, 86 LRRM 1471 (1974), *enforced,* 512 F2d 73, 89 LRRM 2171 (CA 5, 1975), the film *And Women Must Weep,* depicting strike violence, frequently resulted in findings of objectionable election conduct. In *Litho Press,* the Board overruled precedent and held the film not objectionable regardless of the circumstances of the campaign. *See* Chapter 6, "Interference With Protected Rights," at notes 226–227.

[63]Pointe Enters., 216 NLRB 747, 88 LRRM 1519 (1975); Medical Ancillary Serv., 212 NLRB 582, 86 LRRM 1598 (1974). Indeed, the original *Hollywood Ceramics* case involved union conduct.

[64]Argus Optics v. NLRB, 515 F2d 939, 89 LRRM 2280 (CA 6, 1975); LaCrescent Constant Care Center v. NLRB, 510 F2d 1319, 88 LRRM 2849 (CA 8, 1975). *Accord* Aircraft Radio Corp. v. NLRB, 519 F2d 590, 89 LRRM 3060 (CA 3, 1975).

[65]Henderson Trumbull Supply Corp., 220 NLRB 210, 90 LRRM 1477 (1975). The representative subsequently explained to an employee that he had been referring to total sales before expenses, and this explanation was passed on to other employees.

[66]Russell-Newman Mfg. Co., 158 NLRB 1260, 62 LRRM 1195 (1966) (assertion made just prior to an election that a contract elsewhere "provides for" stated increase without disclosing that increase was spread over three years may be misleading but literally true, absent representation that increases are effective immediately); *but see* S.S. Kresge Co., 173 NLRB 520, 69 LRRM 1382 (1968), *on remand from* Gallenkamp Stores Co., 402 F2d 525, 69 LRRM 2024 (CA 9, 1968), *denying enforcement to* 162 NLRB 498, 64 LRRM 1045 (1966). *See also* Grede Foundries, 153 NLRB 984, 59 LRRM 1552 (1965) (union handbills distributed day before election claimed that "average" take-home pay under one of its contracts was $140 per week when, in fact, only 2 of the 350 employees received that "average").

to evaluate the claims based on the elusive standard of their impact on employees, or suppositions about that impact.[67] The impact of the claims could only be gauged, of course, in the full circumstances in which they were uttered and received.

The Board's approach was criticized because the application of the *Hollywood Ceramics* standards was necessarily fact-specific and, for that reason, often unpredictable.[68] Critics also maintained that the unpredictability was, itself, a further spur to postelection review, and to the review of Board orders in the courts of appeals.[69]

b. Hollywood Ceramics *Overruled: Voters Allowed to Assess Misrepresentations.* In 1977, in its *Shopping Kart* decision,[70] the Board, divided three-to-two, overruled *Hollywood Ceramics,* deciding that it would no longer set aside an election solely because of misleading campaign statements or misrepresentations of fact. The decision was justified on the ground that employees are in a better position than the Board to judge the truth or falsity of campaign statements: "[W]e believe that Board rules in this area must be based on a view of employees as mature individuals who are capable of recognizing campaign propaganda for what it is and discounting it."[71] While indicating that it would not probe the veracity of campaign statements, the Board said that it would continue to intervene in those instances where "a party has engaged in such deceptive campaign practices as improperly involving the Board and its processes," or where forged documents were used, rendering "the voters unable to recognize the propaganda for what it is."[72]

The *Shopping Kart* rule was applied in the following situations: An employer's misrepresentation of wages and fringe benefits paid under the current union contract at other plants did not warrant setting an election aside.[73] Misrepresentations by a

---

[67]*See supra* note 13 for criticism of Board assumptions about voter behavior.

[68]*See generally* Cox, *The Regulation of Campaign Tactics in Representation Elections Under the National Labor Relations Act,* 78 HARV. L. REV. 38 (1964).

[69]*Id.* at 92.

[70]*Supra* note 52. *See* Phalen, *The Demise of* Hollywood Ceramics: *Fact and Fantasy*, 46 U. CIN. L. REV. 450 (1977), and response of Penello, Shopping Kart Food Market, Inc.: *The Cure for the* Hollywood Ceramics *Malaise*, 46 U. CIN. L. REV. 464 (1977).

[71]*Id.* at 1313. The Board claimed reliance upon an empirical study conducted by Professors Getman and Goldberg, *The Behavioral Assumptions Underlying NLRB Regulation of Campaign Misrepresentations: An Empirical Evaluation,* 28 STAN L. REV. 263 (1976). *See* note 13 *supra.*

[72]228 NLRB at 1313.

[73]Thomas E. Gates & Sons, 229 NLRB 705, 95 LRRM 1198 (1977).

union concerning an employer's reasons for engaging in certain business transactions were no basis for granting a new election.[74]

(*1*) General Knit: *A temporary return to* Hollywood Ceramics. In late 1978 the dissenters in *Shopping Kart* gained the third vote needed to overrule it. Again dividing three-to-two, the Board abandoned the policy of nonintervention announced in *Shopping Kart* and reverted to the rule that an election would be set aside where its outcome may have been affected by a substantial and material misrepresentation. Reviving the standards of *Hollywood Ceramics,* the Board wrote in *General Knit of California*:[75]

> In returning to the rule of *Hollywood Ceramics,* we are convinced that the rule better enhances employee free choice and fairness of Board elections than did *Shopping Kart.* The *Hollywood Ceramics* rule further assures the public that the Board will not tolerate substantial and material misrepresentations made in the final hours of an election campaign, and thereby gives stability to any bargaining relationship resulting from the election.[76]

Accordingly, under *General Knit* an election would be set aside when a misrepresentation or similar campaign trickery, deliberate or not, which involved a substantial departure from the truth and occurred at a time that prevented effective rebuttal by the opposition, might reasonably be expected to have had a significant effect on the election.

(*2*) *Return to* Shopping Kart: Hollywood Ceramics *again abandoned.* The resurrection of *Hollywood Ceramics* was short-lived. In August 1982 the Board once again reversed its position; it overruled *General Knit* and *Hollywood Ceramics* and returned to the standards first enunciated in *Shopping Kart.* Again, the Board divided three-to-two, the majority including recently appointed members. In *Midland National Life Insurance Co.*[77] the Board majority indicated their "emphatic" belief that "Shopping Kart is the most appropriate accommodation of all the interests . . . involved, and should be given a fair chance to suc-

---

[74]Cormier Hosiery Mills, 230 NLRB 1052, 95 LRRM 1461 (1977). *But see* Larson Tool & Stamping Co., 296 NLRB No. 112, 132 LRRM 1209 (1989), where the employer sent employees letters which stated that "you could LOSE YOUR JOB TO A PERMANENT REPLACEMENT." The Board held that this was a threat of retaliation sufficiently misleading (in that the "loss" would be qualified by a right to recall) that the election should be set aside.

[75]239 NLRB 619, 99 LRRM 1687 (1978) (overruled by Midland Nat'l Life Ins. Co., 263 NLRB 127, 110 LRRM 1489 (1982)).

[76]239 NLRB at 623.

[77]*Supra* note 75.

ceed."[78] Under *Midland National,* elections will no longer be set aside solely because of misleading campaign statements or misrepresentations of fact: The Board "will no longer probe into the truth or falsity of the parties' campaign statements."[79] However, the Board declared it would intervene in cases where a party "used forged documents which render the voters unable to recognize propaganda for what it is"[80] or where "an official Board document has been altered in such a way as to indicate an endorsement by the Board of a party to the election."[81]

In *Mattera Litho,*[82] the Board concluded that an employer's mischaracterization of portions of the union-filed Labor Organization Annual Report relating to expenditures on behalf of its members was not sufficient grounds for setting an election. With court approval, the Board also refused to set aside an election where "a general atmosphere of confusion" existed among the employees.[83]

Midland National was applied retroactively by the Board with court approval,[84] except where manifest injustice would result.[85]

Decisions from the circuit courts suggest that the *Hollywood Ceramics–Shopping Kart–Midland National* debate may continue. A few courts have expressed reservations about the Board's

---

[78]*Id.* at 132.
[79]*Id.* at 133.
[80]*Id.*
[81]*Id.* at n.25.
[82]267 NLRB 375, 114 LRRM 1023 (1983).
[83]Bridgeport Fittings v. NLRB, 877 F2d 180, 185, 131 LRRM 2732 (CA 2, 1989).
[84]*See, e.g.,* NLRB v. Affiliated Midwest Hosp. dba Riveredge Hosp., 789 F2d 524, 122 LRRM 2224 (CA 7, 1986); NLRB v. Best Prods. Co., 765 F2d 903, 119 LRRM 3265 (CA 9, 1985); Hickman Harbor Serv. Div. v. NLRB, 739 F2d 214, 116 LRRM 3119 (CA 6, 1984); National Posters, Nat'l Litho Div. v. NLRB, 720 F2d 1358, 114 LRRM 3240 (CA 4, 1983); Pierce Corp., 288 NLRB 97, 128 LRRM 1014 (1988).
[85]Mosey Mfg. Co. v. NLRB, 701 F2d 610, 112 LRRM 2822 (CA 7, 1983). Two months after the Board announced its decision in *Shopping Kart,* the union won an election by one vote. Claiming that the union made material misrepresentations during the campaign, the employer filed objections. The Board, citing *Shopping Kart,* found no basis to set aside the election and applied to the Seventh Circuit to enforce its bargaining order. Shortly before the court heard the case, the Board overruled *Shopping Kart* and returned to the material misrepresentation standard of *Hollywood Ceramics.* The court then remanded the case to the Board for further investigation of objections to the election under *Hollywood Ceramics* standards. On remand, the Board found there had been no material misrepresentations, and again applied to the court for enforcement. Before the court handed down its decision, the Board issued its decision in *Midland National.* Under these circumstances, the court held it was unsure that the Board intended *Midland National* to apply to all pending cases, especially where, as here, the Board's indecision over the applicable standard to apply resulted in protracted litigation. The court also expressed uncertainty whether the union, which had won the election five years earlier by one vote, was still preferred by a majority of bargaining-unit employees. Accordingly, the court denied enforcement of the Board's bargaining order, thereby paving the way for a new election.

return to the *Shopping Kart* rule in cases where the misrepresentation was pervasive or the deception so artful that employees would be unable to separate truth from falsity.[86]

2. Misuse of the Board's Election Process. "Misuse of the Board's election process" refers to a particular campaign technique by which one party seeks to create the impression that the Board or government favors a particular outcome in the election. Consistent with its holding in *Midland National Life Insurance Co.,*[87] the Board will set aside an election only where a tactic would mislead a reasonable voter into believing that the Board supported the successful party.[88]

Misrepresentations of Board actions, unlike such "misuse," are subject to the same standard as other misrepresentations.[89] Similarly, misstatement of Board decisional law has been held not to be grounds for setting aside the results of an election.[90] In *National Micronetics,*[91] the Board, overruling its earlier decision in *Glassmaster Plastics,*[92] held that distribution of accurate copies of a Board decision with the LRRM headnotes and portions of the decision highlighted would not be treated as an illegal threat or objectionable conduct.

a. Reproduction of Board Documents. The most frequently encountered form of misuse of the Board's election process is the distribution by a party of a facsimile of a Board document which is altered in such a way as to suggest that the Board endorses a particular choice. In *Allied Electric Products,*[93] the Board specifically ruled that the distribution of marked copies of

---

[86]Van Dorn Plastic Mach. Co. Div. v. NLRB, 736 F2d 343, 116 LRRM 2647 (CA 6, 1984), *cert. denied,* 469 US 1208, 118 LRRM 2576 (1985); NLRB v. New Columbus Nursing Home, 720 F2d 726, 114 LRRM 3304 (CA 1, 1983); *compare* NLRB v. Superior Coatings, 839 F2d 1178, 1182, 127 LRRM 2737 (CA 6, 1988), *enforcing* 277 NLRB No. 104, 121 LRRM 1295 (1985) (employee's misrepresentation of supervisor's statement "not 'pervasive' nor particularly 'artful' so as to require that the election results be set aside").

[87]*Supra* note 75.

[88]*See* SDC Inv., 274 NLRB 556, 118 LRRM 1410, 1412 (1985).

[89]Affiliated Midwest Hosp. dba Riveredge Hosp., 264 NLRB 1094, 111 LRRM 1425 (1982), *enforced,* 789 F2d 524, 122 LRRM 2224 (CA 7, 1986).

[90]John W. Galbreath & Co., 288 NLRB 876, 128 LRRM 1185, 1186 (1988) ("mere fact that a party makes an untrue statement, whether of law or fact, is not grounds for setting aside an election"); Tri Cast, Inc., 274 NLRB 377, 118 LRRM 1380 (1985); Furr's, Inc., 265 NLRB 1300, 112 LRRM 1034 (1982) ("no basis for treating misrepresentations of law differently from other misrepresentations"); Beatrice Foods Co., County Line Cheese Div., 265 NLRB 1519, 112 LRRM 1124 (1982).

[91]277 NLRB 993, 121 LRRM 1035 (1985).

[92]203 NLRB 944, 83 LRRM 1227 (1973).

[93]109 NLRB 1270, 34 LRRM 1538 (1954).

Board election ballots would result in the ordering of a new election:

> The reproduction of a document that purports to be a copy of the Board's official secret ballot, but which is altered for campaign purposes, necessarily, at the very least, must tend to suggest that the material appearing thereon bears the Agency's approval.[94]

Consequently, in *Building Leasing Corp.*,[95] the Board set aside an election where the employer had distributed a copy of the official ballot with a highlighted "NO" box and a statement that "your 'X' in the *NO box will mean you* do not want a union." The Board concluded that the additional comments were indistinguishable from the ballot itself and thus appeared to have the Board's approval.[96]

In 1985, in keeping with the rationale of *Midland National,* the Board relaxed the strict rule of *Allied Electric.* In *SDC Investment,*[97] the Board emphasized that the critical inquiry is whether the party responsible for the alteration is clearly identified on the face of the document itself, in which case the alteration is not objectionable. If the source of the altered Board document does not appear, the inquiry is whether the altered document has a tendency to mislead employees into believing the Board favors or is endorsing the position of one party. In *SDC,* the leaflet distributed by the union contained the Board's sample ballot in English on one side and a handwritten, Spanish-language facsimile of the official Board election ballot on the other, stating (in Spanish) at the bottom: "Remember to vote yes on December 16th," with the Board seal at the top.[98] The Board found the leaflet objectionable because it was likely to lead Spanish-speaking employees to believe the Board was endorsing the union.

In short, the Board, with court approval, has now held that it is permissible for a union or employer to adopt and/or use a Board position statement or document so long as the party is clearly identified as the author of such communication and the employees are not misled as to its origin.[99]

---

[94]*Id.* at 1272.

[95]239 NLRB 13, 99 LRRM 1543 (1978).

[96]*See also* Silco, Inc., 231 NLRB 110, 95 LRRM 1516 (1977); Regency Elecs., 200 NLRB 625, 81 LRRM 1587 (1972), *enforced,* 499 F2d 1129, 84 LRRM 2891 (CA 7, 1973).

[97]*Supra* note 88.

[98]*Id.*, 118 LRRM at 1412.

[99]Bauer Welding & Metal Fabricators v. NLRB, 676 F2d 314, 321, 110 LRRM 2270, 2275 (CA 8, 1982); Crown Cork & Seal Co. v. NLRB, 659 F2d 127, 129–30, 108 LRRM

Reproduction of a complaint which seeks to invoke the support of the government by conveying the impression of actual findings of violations of federal law, as opposed to unproven allegations, is also cause for setting aside an election. In *Mallory Capacitor Co.,*[100] the Board stated:

> [W]e cannot sanction the reproduction of a Board document which is altered for campaign purposes and used under circumstances where it is reasonably calculated to mislead employees into believing that the Board has judged the Employer to have violated federal law whereas, in truth, it has only made allegations which have yet to be proved.[101]

In *Ona Corp.,*[102] a Board panel held that the union interfered with an election by mailing employees copies of a Board complaint against the employer where the union had deleted the paragraphs concerning the time and the place of hearing, the employer's right to answer the complaint, and the effect of failing to answer allegations. That the mailing revealed that a hearing had been set and that the employer denied the allegations of the complaint did not cure the misleading effect of the document. On the other hand, a statement in union campaign literature that issuance of a complaint against the employer shows that "there has to be merit in the case" was deemed permissible.[103]

2224, 2226 (CA 10, 1981), *cert. denied,* 454 US 1150, 109 LRRM 2304 (1982); Hall-Brooke Hosp. v. NLRB, 645 F2d 158, 107 LRRM 2039 (CA 2, 1981); BIW Employees Fed. Credit Union, 287 NLRB 423, 127 LRRM 1098 (1987) (altered ballot with vote "No" attached to memorandum from employer was sufficient identification of employer campaign material); Professional Care Centers of N. Am., 279 NLRB 814, 122 LRRM 1076 (1986) (notice that alterations made to Board document not necessary where union preparing and distributing document clearly identified); Rosewood Mfg. Co., 278 NLRB 722, 121 LRRM 1225 (1986) (handwritten message "Vote No" on Board notice of election "clearly discernible" as employer addition and "sufficiently distinct" from Board notice printed material); Worths Stores Corp., 281 NLRB 1191, 123 LRRM 1215 (1986); R.L. White Co., 262 NLRB 575, 111 LRRM 1078 (1982) (supervisor placing thumb over "yes" box and telling employees to vote "no"); Cambridge Wire Cloth Co., 256 NLRB 1135, 107 LRRM 1393 (1981), *enforced,* 679 F2d 885, 110 LRRM 2167 (CA 4, 1982) (stickers of obvious union origin with words "vote yes" repeatedly placed on plexiglass covering official Board ballot); Monier Roof Tiles, 249 NLRB 703, 104 LRRM 1204 (1980) (Board's neutrality not compromised by reproduction of "Bill of Rights" from its official election notice when hand-printed union statement is attached). *But see* NLRB v. Carroll Contracting & Ready-Mix, 636 F2d 111, 106 LRRM 2491 (CA 5, 1981), *denying enforcement to* 247 NLRB 890, 103 LRRM 1232 (1980) (employer objections sustained by court where union misused sample ballot).

[100]161 NLRB 1510, 63 LRRM 1473 (1966).

[101]*Id.* at 1512.

[102]235 NLRB 595, 98 LRRM 1005 (1978).

[103]George J. London Memorial Hosp., 236 NLRB 797, 98 LRRM 1312 (1978).

b. Misrepresentation of Board Action. Misrepresentation pertaining to the Board and its processes can be a sufficient basis for setting aside an election. Before the decision of *Midland National,* the Board had held, in *Formco, Inc.,*[104] that a union interfered with an election when it distributed a letter which falsely reported that the employer had been guilty of unfair labor practices. The Board reasoned that since only the Board could find the employer "guilty" the union's statement improperly drew the Board into the election.

In 1982, in *Riveredge Hospital,*[105] the Board overruled *Formco* and held that it would treat a misrepresentation of Board action as it treats other election misrepresentations. In so doing, the Board distinguished the physical alteration of a Board document from a misrepresentation of Board action. An allegation by one party that the Board has taken an action against the other party is viewed essentially the same as any other misrepresentation and it is not grounds for setting aside the election if it does not impugn the Board's neutrality.[106]

c. Electioneering at the Polls. In the actual conduct of the election the Board is "especially zealous in preventing instructions"[107] to voters. It has long been held that campaigning too close to the polls may be objectionable.[108] In 1968 the Board adopted the strict *Milchem*[109] rule that, "regardless of the con-

---

[104]233 NLRB 61, 96 LRRM 1392 (1977).

[105]Affiliated Midwest Hosp. dba Riveredge Hosp., 264 NLRB 1094, 111 LRRM 1425 (1982). *See also* NLRB v. Affiliated Midwest Hosp. dba Riveredge Hosp., 789 F2d 524, 122 LRRM 2221 (CA 7, 1986) (subsequent unfair labor practice proceeding; order of Board enforced).

[106]NLRB v. Rhone-Poulenc, Inc. 789 F2d 188, 122 LRRM 2193 (CA 3, 1986) (no substantial misrepresentation found where union stated Board's "bylaws" prohibit reduction in wages and benefits once union wins election and Board agent advised union to file charges against employer); C.J. Krehbiel Co., 279 NLRB 855, 122 LRRM 1105 (1986), *enforced,* 844 F2d 880, 128 LRRM 2203 (CA DC, 1988) (no substantial misrepresentation found where union flyer quoting caption and remedy section of administrative law judge decision embellished with cartoons and slogans readily identifiable as "partisan campaign comments" of union and not endorsement of union by Board); Purolator Prods., 270 NLRB 694, 117 LRRM 1036 (1984) (no substantial misrepresentation found where union handbill contained excerpt from Board publication and misstated status of union's pending charge against employer by implying employer had been found guilty of unfair labor practice). *See also* NLRB v. Omi Ga., 707 F2d 453, 113 LRRM 2919 (CA 11, 1983) (no substantial misrepresentation found where union leaflet asserted employer was "forced" to reinstate several employees with back pay where there had been settlement agreement which contained nonadmission clause); NLRB v. Rolligon Corp., 702 F2d 589, 113 LRRM 2044 (CA 5, 1983) (abuse of Board's subpoena procedure is not adequate basis for setting aside election where employer had opportunity to correct employees' misconceptions); Ethyl Prods. Co., 267 NLRB 219, 114 LRRM 1013 (1983).

[107]Claussen Baking Co., 134 NLRB 111, 112, 49 LRRM 1092 (1961).

[108]*Id.;* Continental Can Co., 80 NLRB 785, 23 LRRM 1126 (1948).

[109]Milchem, Inc., 170 NLRB 362, 67 LRRM 1395, 1395 (1968), emphasizing the importance of ensuring that "[t]he final minutes before an employee casts his vote should be his own, as free from interference as possible."

tent of the remarks exchanged," prolonged conversation by representatives of any party with prospective voters in the polling area "constitutes conduct which, in itself," will invalidate an election.[110]

While "prolonged conversation" by an agent of either party is per se objectionable, the Board usually considers the following factors in determining whether electioneering at or near the polls is objectionable: the extent and nature of the alleged electioneering; whether, when a no-electioneering area was designated, the conduct occurred within the area; the closeness of the election results; and whether the conduct occurred or continued contrary to the instructions of the Board agent.[111] Chance, isolated, or innocuous comments or enquiries do not violate the rule.[112] A lesser standard is applied to third-party electioneering: such conduct will warrant setting aside an election only if the acts disrupt the voting procedure or destroy the atmosphere necessary for the exercise of free choice in the election.[113]

Under the *Milchem* rule, once the polls open, employees waiting outside in line to vote become a part of the polling place and are entitled to safeguards against interference. Electioneering on such lines is improper.[114] The Board has found that an employer interfered with an election when a supervisor, though within a section of the plant that included his area of responsibility, stationed himself, without explanation, 10 to 15 feet from the entrance of the voting area where the employees had to pass in order to vote.[115] But the *Milchem* rule is not mechanically applied. The Board did not set aside an election where, despite

---

[110]*Id.* at 362.

[111]US Ecology v. NLRB, 772 F2d 1478, 120 LRRM 2779 (CA 9, 1985); Pepsi-Cola Bottling Co. of Petersburg, 291 NLRB No. 93, 129 LRRM 1236 (1988); Del Rey Tortilleria, 272 NLRB 1106, 117 LRRM 1449 (1984), *enforced,* 823 F2d 1135, 125 LRRM 3140 (CA 7, 1987); Boston Insulated Wire & Cable Co., 259 NLRB 1118, 1119, 109 LRRM 1081, 1082 (1982), *enforced,* 703 F2d 876, 113 LRRM 2241 (CA 5, 1983).

[112]Clothing & Textile Workers (Angelica Healthcare Servs. Group) v. NLRB, 815 F2d 225, 125 LRRM 2832 (CA 2, 1987) (conversations between union observers and voters near voting booth not objectionable since conversations were short and innocuous); L.C. Cassidy & Son v. NLRB, 745 F2d 1059, 117 LRRM 2518 (CA 7, 1984); NLRB v. Michigan Rubber Prods., 738 F2d 111, 116 LRRM 2876 (CA 6, 1984); Pierce Corp., 288 NLRB 97, 128 LRRM 1014 (1988) (union activist's electioneering conversation with co-worker 30 feet from farthest end of line of voters was basis for setting aside election).

[113]Worley Mills v. NLRB, 685 F2d 362, 366, 110 LRRM 3322, 3325 (CA 10, 1982); EDS-IDAB v. NLRB, 666 F2d 971, 975, 109 LRRM 2653, 2656 (CA 5, 1982); *see also* NLRB v. Carroll Contracting & Ready-Mix, 636 F2d 111, 106 LRRM 2491 (CA 5, 1981).

[114]NLRB v. Carroll Contracting & Ready-Mix, *supra* note 113; Bio-Medical Applications of P.R., 269 NLRB 827, 116 LRRM 1036 (1984). *See also* Pepsi-Cola Bottling Co. of Petersburg, *supra* note 111.

[115]Electric Hose & Rubber Co., 262 NLRB 186, 216, 110 LRRM 1282 (1982).

an agreement that no persons other than voters and observers would come within 150 feet of the polling area, union representatives briefly did so on three occasions; but there was no evidence that any conversations were initiated with voters.[116]

Keeping a list of employees who have voted (aside from the official eligibility list used to check off voters as they receive their ballots) has been found to interfere with the election.[117] An employer may not bar any individuals from entering the voting place and casting a ballot. The Board has held that anyone who presents himself or herself at the polls has the right to cast at least a challenged ballot and to assert, directly to the Board's agent,[118] his or her right to vote. Supervisory participation as an observer has also been found to interfere with an election.[119]

The Board holds its agents to high standards of accuracy and neutrality in the conduct of elections and sets aside elections in which its agents do not meet those high standards.[120] In *Alco Iron & Metal Co.*[121] the Board set aside an election where a Board agent directed the union observer to repeat voting instructions to voters in Spanish. The delegation by a Board agent of such a function to an election participant conveyed the impression that the union, and not the Board, was responsible for conducting the election.

3. Appeals to Racial Prejudice. Racial appeals in a preelection campaign may, but do not necessarily, constitute a valid objection, for the subject may be germane to the issues. Employees are free to allow their prejudices to affect their choice in

---

[116]Connecticut Foundry Co., 254 NLRB 758, 106 LRRM 1207 (1981), *enforcement denied on other grounds*, 688 F2d 871, 880, 110 LRRM 3307, 3314 (CA 2, 1982). The court expressly approved of the Board's decision on this point.

[117]Piggly-Wiggly, 168 NLRB 792, 66 LRRM 1360 (1967), where the making of notations on a list as employees passed by to enter the employer's premises during the balloting caused the election to be set aside. Use of this technique may cause employees to infer that their names are being recorded. A.D. Juilliard & Co., 110 NLRB 2197, 2199, 35 LRRM 1401 (1954). *See also* International Stamping Co., 97 NLRB 921, 29 LRRM 1158 (1951); NLRB Form 722 instructing observers not to keep such lists; and Chapter 10, "Representation Proceedings and Elections," at note 323.

[118]Sabine Towing & Transp. Co., 226 NLRB 422, 93 LRRM 1277 (1976).

[119]Cooper Supply Co., 120 NLRB 1023, 42 LRRM 1094 (1958). *See* Chapter 10, "Representation Proceedings and Elections," at notes 317–318.

[120]Athbro Precision Eng'g Corp., 166 NLRB 966, 65 LRRM 1699 (1967). The Board's interest in protecting the integrity of the election process is also illustrated in its decision to set aside an election where the ballot box was left unsealed and unattended for only two to five minutes, without regard to what might have occurred. Austill Waxed Paper Co., 169 NLRB 1109, 67 LRRM 1366 (1968).

[121]269 NLRB 590, 115 LRRM 1322 (1984) (overruling Regency Hyatt House, 180 NLRB 489, 75 LRRM 1527 (1969) and Deeco Co., 116 NLRB 990, 38 LRRM 1375 (1956) to the extent inconsistent with this decision). *See* US Ecology v. NLRB, *supra* note 111.

union representation matters. But where pure racial prejudice, or fear inspired by racial conflict, is made the dominant theme of a campaign so as to reduce the election to a vote on racial rather than on collective bargaining issues, there will be ground for setting aside the election.[122]

The rules for determining whether an election should be set aside on this ground were first enunciated in *Sewell Manufacturing Co.*[123] The Board there invalidated an election in two Georgia plants where the antiunion campaign was based on appeals to prejudice by excessive publicizing of an AFL-CIO donation of money to the Committee on Racial Equality for the support of desegregation projects in Alabama and Mississippi. The publicity, which included photographs of a white union official dancing with a black woman, was not germane to the election. In setting aside the election, the Board announced its test for application to future cases: When a party injects racial subjects into an election, it must limit comment to truthful statements of the other party's position on racial matters and must not seek to "overstress" or exacerbate racial feelings by irrelevant and inflammatory appeals; the party who brings racial statements into the campaign has the burden of establishing that they were both truthful and germane to the election issues.[124]

This burden was successfully sustained in *Allen Morrison Sign Co.*[125] An employer wrote a truthful letter that the international union seeking to represent the employees had given financial, moral, and official backing to desegregation activities and that one local had been placed in trusteeship when its members voted to purchase bonds to finance segregated white schools in an attempt to combat public school integration. The employer did not have the support of widespread community campaigning in this matter, as was true in some other racial appeal cases, and the letter was not the sole or central theme of the employer's campaign. The Board noted that the letter presented factual argument which the employees could consider in the light of their

---

[122]For a review of the race issue in election campaigns, *see* Pollit, *The National Labor Relations Board and Race Hate Propaganda in Union Organization Drives*, 17 STAN. L. REV. 373 (1965); *see also* Sovern, *The National Labor Relations Act and Racial Discrimination*, 62 COLUM. L. REV. 563 (1962).

[123]138 NLRB 66, 50 LRRM 1532 (1962).

[124]*Id.*

[125]138 NLRB 73, 50 LRRM 1535 (1962); *see also* Archer Laundry Co., 150 NLRB 1427, 58 LRRM 1212 (1965); Aristocrat Linen Supply Co., 150 NLRB 1448, 58 LRRM 1216 (1965).

racial prejudices instead of substituting appeals to racial prejudice for factual argument, as in *Sewell.* The union's loss of the election was certified.

Long before *Sewell,* however, the Board had recognized that racially based harassment and intimidation could impair an election. In *P.D. Gwaltney, Jr. & Co.,*[126] where 80 percent of the employees were black, the employer, the local press, the sheriff, and other public officials in the small Virginia community made known their antiunion sympathies. The threat of Ku Klux Klan reactivation in the event of a union victory was prominently proclaimed; two black union members who had come to the city to speak at a union meeting were frightened away before the meeting began; and the sheriff and the chief of police stationed themselves at the polling place throughout the elections. The Board held that in its "experienced judgment" such circumstances made the freedom of choice guaranteed by the Act impossible.[127]

Similarly in *YKK (U.S.A.),*[128] the Board set aside an election where the union, at meetings with the employees, spoke of the need to stick together against "Japs" and in handbills referred to the "Japs," "Pearl Harbor," and "slant eyes."[129]

On the other hand, the courts and Board have refused to overturn elections where objectionable comments did not rise to the level of a "sustained inflammatory appeal"[130] or were related

---

[126]74 NLRB 371, 20 LRRM 1172 (1947).

[127]*Id.* at 373.

[128]269 NLRB 82, 115 LRRM 1186 (1984).

[129]*Id.* at 84, 115 LRRM at 1188. *See also* Futuramik Indus., 279 NLRB 185, 121 LRRM 1314 (1986) (objectionable conduct for employer to threaten to report employees to Welfare Department and Immigration Service if they selected union).

[130]*See* NLRB v. Utell Int'l, 750 F2d 177, 179, 118 LRRM 2006 (CA 2, 1984) (union statements that employees "may [have] been fired for racist reasons" were "not deliberate inflammatory appeals designed to incite racial hatred"); NLRB v. Krafcor Corp., 712 F2d 1268, 114 LRRM 2054, 2057 (CA 8, 1983) (racial slurs and threats of physical violence against black employee were isolated and such incidents normally occur "between employees who adopt opposing views"); Brightview Care Center, 292 NLRB 352, 130 LRRM 1154, 1155 (1989) (alleged inflammatory remarks that "owners would not give us raises because they were Jews and cheap," and that "maybe Hitler did the right thing," were isolated remarks not rising to level of "sustained inflammatory appeal"); Air Express Int'l Corp., 289 NLRB 608, 130 LRRM 1235, 1236 (1988) (election not set aside despite rumor spread by employees attributing to operations manager statements that the "f . . . Cubans were not going to put the union in there" and that he "was going to terminate all the f . . . Cubans"); Beatrice Grocery Prods., 287 NLRB 302, 127 LRRM 1041 (1987) (objection to election overruled where isolated racial epithet was made at beginning of campaign). *But see* M&M Supermarkets v. NLRB, 818 F2d 1567, 125 LRRM 2918 (CA 11, 1987) (court held Board incorrectly evaluated racial and religious statements); NLRB v. Eurodrive, 724 F2d 556, 115 LRRM 2361 (CA 6, 1984); NLRB v. Triplex Mfg. Co., 701 F2d 703, 112 LRRM 3024 (CA 7, 1983) (Board abused its discretion in refusing to conduct evidentiary hearing on employer's objections even where appeals to racial prejudice were isolated incidents).

to legitimate campaign issues as wages or treatment of employees.[131]

The Board has treated appeals to the racial pride of a particular ethnic minority in a different manner from appeals to racial prejudice. Generally it has found appeals to racial pride to be germane to the issues of the campaign and not designed to inflame racial hatred, but rather to encourage self-respect and concerted efforts for betterment.[132] The Board has explained that

> [c]ampaign material of this type is directed at undoing disadvantages historically imposed . . . upon Negroes because of their race, through an appeal to collective action of the disadvantaged. . . .
>
> . . .
>
> Traditionally, trade unions have sought to unify groups of employees by focusing group attention on common problems, and to further the acceptance of union spokesmen by emphasizing the extent to which the spokesmen have identified themselves with those problems. To hold that this traditional approach may not be utilized because of the ethnic composition of the work force might itself be discriminatory.[133]

In *Bancroft Manufacturing Co.,*[134] the Board, with Fifth Circuit approval, refused to set aside an election because of a union organizer's campaign remarks to employees that "if blacks did not stay together as a group and the union lost the election all the blacks would be fired," and "that seemingly the trend was . . . that the blacks were going to be laid off if they didn't stick together and try to get the plant organized to where they would have some protection . . . ." In a divided opinion, the Board held that in the context of three recent layoffs, in which

---

[131] State Bank of India v. NLRB, 808 F2d 526, 541, 124 LRRM 2001 (CA 7, 1986), *cert. denied,* 483 US 1005, 125 LRRM 3064 (1987) (disputed statement that "[t]he State Bank of India is trying to keep depressed conditions and low wages for its employees because you are of Indian nationality and other minority groups" merely urged employees to vote for the union to prevent discrimination and did not arouse race hatred); NLRB v. Vought Corp., 788 F2d 1378, 122 LRRM 2168 (CA 8, 1986) (black union advocate's remarks on racial discrimination in workplace were legitimate comments relevant to existing racial conditions); Arlington Hotel Co. v. NLRB, 712 F2d 333, 113 LRRM 3381 (CA 8, 1983) (union supporter's comparison of hotel general manager to "Hitler," and union's repeated references to employer's hotel as "slave ship" when read in context were legitimately focused on economic issues); Coca-Cola/Dr. Pepper Bottling Co. of Memphis, 273 NLRB 444, 118 LRRM 1225 (1984) (because mistreatment was legitimate campaign issue, no objectionable conduct where union representative told employees that employer had kept blacks down for long time, that this was their "chance to take care of it," and referred to employer's plant as a "plantation").

[132] Archer Laundry Co., *supra* note 125; Aristocrat Linen Supply Co., *supra* note 125.

[133] Baltimore Luggage Co., 162 NLRB 1230, 1233–34, 64 LRRM 1145, 1146 (1967).

[134] 210 NLRB 1007, 86 LRRM 1376 (1974), *enforced,* 516 F2d 436, 89 LRRM 3105 (CA 5, 1975), *cert. denied,* 424 US 914, 91 LRRM 2410 (1976).

mainly black employees had been laid off, and given that racial polarization would be counterproductive because 57 percent of the eligible voters were white, the statements concerning the impact of future layoffs were not "appeals to racial prejudice on matters unrelated to election issues" but were "germane to the larger issue of the advantages and disadvantages of the union as a means of promoting economic security and job rights."[135]

Not all courts have agreed with the Board's position on appeals to racial pride. The Fourth Circuit, in *NLRB v. Schapiro & Whitehouse*,[136] refused to enforce an order requiring the employer to bargain, since the union in its preelection campaign had made appeals to the racial pride of black employees.

4. Third-Party Interference. There are situations where an employer may be responsible for the conduct of others, or for countermeasures when such conduct occurs. In several cases, outsiders, such as townspeople of the community in which a plant being organized is located, have joined in the campaign against the union. This has presented special problems where the employer did not participate in, condone, or otherwise support the third-party intervention, and in fact, may not have been able to prevent it. Nonetheless, in a representation case the right to a free choice of bargaining representative is not diminished because the campaign against the union is conducted by, or in the name of, townspeople rather than the employer.[137] Likewise, intervention by a state official,[138] by an outside placement service,[139] or by an unknown employee or group of employees may invalidate an election.[140] The Board has traditionally

[135]*Id.* at 1008. *See also* NLRB v. Sumter Plywood Corp., 535 F2d 917, 92 LRRM 3508 (CA 5, 1976), *cert. denied,* 429 US 1092, 94 LRRM 2643 (1977) ("consciousness-raising" calls to racial pride and unity not objectionable).

[136]356 F2d 675, 61 LRRM 2289 (CA 4, 1966).

[137]Universal Mfg. Corp., 156 NLRB 1459, 61 LRRM 1258 (1966); P.D. Gwaltney, Jr. & Co., *supra* note 126. *See also* NLRB v. General Metal Prods. Co., 410 F2d 473, 70 LRRM 3327 (CA 6, 1969), *cert. denied,* 396 US 830, 72 LRRM 2432 (1969); Cagle's, Inc., 234 NLRB 1148, 98 LRRM 1117 (1978), *enforced in part,* 588 F2d 943, 100 LRRM 2590 (CA 5, 1979); Star Kist Samoa, 237 NLRB 238, 98 LRRM 1558 (1978); Claymore Mfg. Co., 146 NLRB 1400, 56 LRRM 1080 (1964); Electra Mfg. Co., 148 NLRB 494, 57 LRRM 1054 (1964); Utica-Herband Tool Div., 145 NLRB 1717, 55 LRRM 1223 (1964); Falmouth Co., 114 NLRB 896, 37 LRRM 1057 (1955).

[138]Richlands Textile, 220 NLRB 83, 90 LRRM 1391 (1975) (state legislator mailed letter to employees threatening plant closure); *see also* Columbia Tanning Corp., 238 NLRB 899, 99 LRRM 1382 (1978) (letter endorsing union mailed by state labor commissioner held to be sufficient grounds for setting election aside).

[139]Montgomery Ward & Co., 228 NLRB 750, 96 LRRM 1383 (1977). *See* note 147 *infra.*

[140]Florida-Tex. Freight, 230 NLRB 952, 95 LRRM 1426 (1977) (Board held that where unknown and unauthorized employees obtained and published secret files of employer, which outlined plan for closing facility if union won election, election should be set aside

accorded less weight to the conduct of third parties, such as employees who do not act under the actual or apparent authority of the union or the employer, than it does to the conduct of the parties.[141]

The reaction of the employer to the third-party campaign may be determinative. Adequate disavowal of objectionable outside campaigning may dissipate the impact of the objectionable features and obviate the need to set the election aside.[142]

In *Falmouth Co.,*[143] a citizens' group actively campaigned to defeat the union, emphasizing and utilizing rumors of plant closure. The employer disclaimed the rumors, but the Board held the disclaimer to be insufficient and ordered a new election despite its failure to find the employer at fault in the preelection campaign. In *Utica-Herband Tool Division,*[144] the employer took positive advantage of objectionable campaigning against unionization, and the Board set aside the election. In *Claymore Manufacturing Co.,*[145] however, an unequivocal disclaimer by the employer was sufficient to forestall remedial action by the Board. At the union's request, the employer issued a letter to

---

because coercive atmosphere was created). *But see* NLRB v. MacDonald's Indus. Prods., 731 F2d 340, 115 LRRM 3547 (CA 6, 1984) (remarks of unidentified person near polling place may have discouraged employee from voting; election valid); Marlowe Mfg. Co., 213 NLRB 278, 87 LRRM 1133 (1974) (leaflet allegedly threatening plant closure distributed by group of unit employees, which employer did not prepare or distribute, was not grounds for setting aside election).

[141]*See* NLRB v. Herbert Halperin Distrib. Corp., 826 F2d 287, 126 LRRM 2152 (CA 4, 1987); Vitek Elecs. v. NLRB, 763 F2d 561, 119 LRRM 2699 (CA 3, 1985); Daylight Grocery v. NLRB, 678 F2d 905, 909, 110 LRRM 2915, 2917–18 (CA 11, 1982) (pro-union threats made by store customer to employees did not create coercive atmosphere which required new election); ATR Wire & Cable Co., 267 NLRB 204, 114 LRRM 1006 (1983), *enforced,* 752 F2d 201, 118 LRRM 2226 (CA 6, 1985); Maremont Corp., World Parts Div., 251 NLRB 1617, 105 LRRM 1535 (1980), *enforcement denied on other grounds,* 666 F2d 1037, 109 LRRM 2861 (CA 6, 1981). *See also* Kitchen Fresh v. NLRB, 716 F2d 351, 355–56, 114 LRRM 2233, 2236–37 (CA 6, 1983). *But see* John M. Horn Lumber Co. v. NLRB, 859 F2d 1242, 129 LRRM 2608 (CA 6, 1988), *denying enforcement to* 282 NLRB 127, 124 LRRM 1183 (1986) (Board erred by not setting aside election based on threats by pro-union employees who were not agents of union); Pepsi-Cola Bottling Co. of Petersburg, 291 NLRB 578, 129 LRRM 1236 (1988) (election set aside based on boistrous gathering and electioneering of pro-union employees at opening of polls).

[142]General Metal Prods. Co., 164 NLRB 64, 65 LRRM 1002 (1967), *enforced,* 410 F2d 473, 70 LRRM 3327 (CA 6, 1969), *cert. denied,* 396 US 830, 72 LRRM 2432 (1969); Electra Mfg. Co., *supra* note 137; Claymore Mfg. Co., *supra* note 137; Utica-Herband Tool Div., *supra* note 137; Falmouth Co., *supra* note 137. *But see* Raytheon Co., 179 NLRB 678, 72 LRRM 1454 (1969), where the Board found no violation when the employer remained silent following a radio news broadcast quoting "informed sources" as predicting the closing of the plant if the union won the election.

[143]*Supra* note 137.

[144]*Supra* note 137.

[145]*Supra* note 137. *See also* Otterbacher Mfg., 279 NLRB 1167, 122 LRRM 1145 (1986) (effective disavowal); Plessey, Inc., 263 NLRB 1392, 111 LRRM 1573 (1982) (same).

employees disavowing rumors created by the community campaign and stating it would continue operations whatever the result of the election.

Where the employer is charged with an unfair labor practice, rather than with objectionable preelection conduct only, considerations of agency status are more significant. An election may be set aside without a showing of fault by a party,[146] but coercive conduct must be attributable to an employer or labor organization before an unfair labor practice can be found.[147]

5. Violence and Threats. The Board will set aside an election where there is an "atmosphere" of violence or threats of violence, since this may impair a free choice by employees. It is "immaterial that fear and disorder may have been created by individual employees or non-employees and that their conduct cannot be attributed either to the employer or to the union. The significant fact is that such conditions existed and that a free election was thereby rendered impossible."[148] But zealous partisanship alone does not justify setting an election aside.[149]

Its test for determining whether the election should be set aside, the Board has said, is "whether the election was held with a general atmosphere among the employees of confusion, violence, and threats of violence, such as might reasonably be expected to generate anxiety and fear of reprisal, and to render impossible a rational uncoerced expression of choice as to bargaining representative."[150] This type of atmosphere destroys

---

[146]Al Long, Inc., 173 NLRB 447, 69 LRRM 1366 (1968). *Cf.* NLRB v. L&J Equip. Co., 745 F2d 224, 117 LRRM 2592 (CA 3, 1984) (members of in-plant organizing committee agents of union).

[147]Dean Indus., 162 NLRB 1078, 64 LRRM 1193 (1967). *E.g.*, where a state legislator mailed letters to employees threatening plant closure, and the employer knew of the mailing and of in-plant circulation of the letter but did not repudiate the letter, the Board held that the employer's conduct constituted ratification; hence there was an unlawful threat of plant closure. Richlands Textile, *supra* note 138. *See also* Star Kist Samoa, *supra* note 137. For unfair labor practice treatment of third-party conduct, see Chapter 6, "Interference With Protected Rights," at notes 348–351.

[148]Al Long, Inc., *supra* note 146, at 448, involving anonymous telephone calls threatening bodily injury, rifle shots by unknown persons, bomb threats, and massed and unruly picketing. *See also* John M. Horn Lumber Co. v. NLRB, *supra* note 141.

[149]American Wholesalers, 218 NLRB 292, 89 LRRM 1352 (1975).

[150]Bauer Welding & Metal Fabricators v. NLRB, 758 F2d 308, 118 LRRM 3193 (CA 8, 1985), *enforcing* 268 NLRB 1416, 116 LRRM 1018 (1984); Poinsett Lumber & Mfg. Co., 116 NLRB 1732, 39 LRRM 1083, (1956). *See* Tony Scott Trucking v. NLRB, 817 F2d 105, 125 LRRM 2910 (CA 6, 1987), *enforcing* 277 NLRB No. 155, 121 LRRM 1295 (1985), *cert. denied*, 484 US 896, 126 LRRM 2696 (1987); Clothing & Textile Workers v. NLRB (Lowenstein Corp.), 736 F2d 1559, 117 LRRM 2453 (CA DC, 1984); NLRB v. ARA Servs., 717 F2d 57, 114 LRRM 2377 (CA 3, 1983); Libbey-Owens Ford Co. v. NLRB, 715 F2d 291,

the "laboratory conditions" in which Board-conducted elections must be conducted.

The Board has held that verbal threats are sufficient to set aside an election only when they have tended to coerce the employees into voting in a particular manner. "For conduct to warrant setting aside an election, not only must that conduct be coercive, but it must be so related to the election as to have had a probable effect on the employees' action at the polls."[151]

In determining the seriousness of threats, the Board evaluates the nature of the threats and the surrounding circumstances—such as whether the threats encompass the entire bargaining unit, whether they were widely disseminated, whether the persons making the threats are capable of carrying them out, whether it is likely the employees acted in fear that the threats would be carried out, and whether the threats were rejuvenated at or near the time of the election.[152]

In *NLRB v. Browning-Ferris Industries of Louisville dba Indiana Home Sanitation,*[153] the court approved the Board's findings that

---

114 LRRM 2226 (CA 7, 1983); NLRB v. Krafcor, *supra* note 130; Certainteed Corp. v. NLRB, 714 F2d 1042, 114 LRRM 2541 (CA 11, 1983); Emerson Elec. Co., Beaird-Poulan Div. v. NLRB, 649 F2d 589, 594, 107 LRRM 2646, 2650 (CA 8, 1981); Sequatchie Valley Coal Corp., 281 NLRB 726, 123 LRRM 1185 (1986); Lovilia Coal Co., 275 NLRB 1358, 120 LRRM 1005 (1985); Westwood Horizons Hotel, 270 NLRB 802, 116 LRRM 1152 (1984); ATR Wire & Cable Co., *supra* note 141. The Board and the courts do not, however, always agree in the application of that test. *See* NLRB v. Newly Weds Foods, 758 F2d 4, 118 LRRM 3213 (CA 1, 1985); Hickman Harbor Serv. Div. v. NLRB, 739 F2d 214, 116 LRRM 3119 (CA 6, 1984), *denying enforcement to* 266 NLRB 476, 112 LRRM 1430 (1983). Where the conduct is attributable to the union, the standard is the same as for employer conduct—does the conduct tend to interfere? *See* NLRB v. Chicago Metallic Corp., 794 F2d 527, 122 LRRM 3163 (CA 9, 1986), *denying enforcement in part to* 275 NLRB 871, 119 LRRM 1288 (1985); NLRB v. Hawaiian Flour Mill, 792 F2d 1459, 122 LRRM 2944 (CA 9, 1986), *enforcing* 274 NLRB 1108, 118 LRRM 1613 (1985); NLRB v. Island Film Processing Co. dba Kahala Kai Photo Serv., 784 F2d 1446, 121 LRRM 3290 (CA 9, 1986), *denying enforcement to* 274 NLRB 1525, 119 LRRM 1096 (1985); Avis Rent-A-Car Sys., 280 NLRB 580, 122 LRRM 1241 (1986); Bristol Textile Co., 277 NLRB 1637, 121 LRRM 1125 (1986); Baja's Place, 268 NLRB 868, 115 LRRM 1122 (1984). *But cf.* Tennessee Plastics, 215 NLRB 315, 88 LRRM 1472 (1974), *enforced,* 525 F2d 670, 91 LRRM 2240 (CA 6, 1975) (employer's objection dismissed where based on union adherents' statement to employee, as she arrived at work on election day, that if she or any other employee did not vote for union, they would get their hair cut off); American Wholesalers, *supra* note 149, 89 LRRM at 1354 (employer's objection dismissed where "statements by pro-union supporters . . . made in a climate of no violence whatever" were considered "overzealous partisanship rather than meaningful threats").

[151]Great Atl. & Pac. Tea Co., 177 NLRB 942, 942–43, 71 LRRM 1554 (1969). Threats of other than physical harm may also be grounds for ordering a new election. In Lyon's Restaurants, subsidiary of Consolidated Foods Co., 234 NLRB 178, 97 LRRM 1116 (1978), the Board set aside an election where employees were threatened with loss of their jobs unless they supported the union. *See also* Aire Flo Corp., 167 NLRB 679, 66 LRRM 1214 (1967); Vicker's, Inc., 152 NLRB 793, 59 LRRM 1196 (1965).

[152]Crown Coach Corp., 284 NLRB 1010, 126 LRRM 1043 (1987), *supplementing* 243 NLRB 984, 101 LRRM 1581 (1979).

[153]803 F2d 345, 123 LRRM 2673 (CA 7, 1986), *enforcing* 275 NLRB No. 199, 120 LRRM 1119 (1985).

isolated threatening remarks by two employees did not indicate a pattern of intimidation or an atmosphere of coercion. In *Bauer Welding & Metal Fabricators v. NLRB,*[154] the court held, in agreement with the Board, that an incident in which four pro-union employees briefly surrounded a fellow employee and threatened him did not warrant setting aside the election. However, in *Electra Food Machinery,*[155] serious written threats, which were widely disseminated, to kill or beat up identified or suspected nonunion adherents and to burn their cars required that the election be set aside. The Board set aside an election after concluding that three months is insufficient time to dissipate the effects of threats of physical harm to an employee in his home and the brutal beating of the employer's president and manager.[156] In *Lovilia Coal Co.,*[157] the election was set aside on the basis of threats by pro-union employees to blow up the employer's mine. In *Westwood Horizons Hotel,*[158] a new election was required after pro-union employees threatened to beat up employees who did not vote for the union. A prior climate of violence and threats is an important determinant[159] in setting aside an election, as is the presence of other factors showing that the threats had a material impact on the election.[160]

In a move toward the position of the courts, the Board, in *Anthony & Karney Scioscia dba Home & Industrial Disposal Service,*[161] explicitly overruled its prior position in *Hickory Springs Manufacturing Co.*[162] and held that preelection threats by a party to engage in violent future conduct may warrant setting an election aside, even if the threatened future conduct is not directly related to the outcome of the election.

---

[154]*Supra* note 150.

[155]279 NLRB 279, 122 LRRM 1046 (1986). The Board's focus is the reasonableness of employee fears as reflected by objective facts: the subjective reactions of employees are irrelevant to whether there was objectionable conduct. *Id.*

[156]Teamsters Local 703 (Kennicott Bros. Co.), 284 NLRB 1125, 126 LRRM 1033 (1987).

[157]*Supra* note 150.

[158]*Supra* note 150.

[159]*See* Connecticut Foundry Co., 254 NLRB 758, 106 LRRM 1207 (1981), *enforcement denied on other grounds,* 688 F2d 871, 110 LRRM 3307 (CA 2, 1982).

[160]Selective misconduct in a small unit and a close vote can persuade the Board and the courts to set aside an election. NLRB v. Chicago Metallic Corp., *supra* note 150. *See also* NLRB v. Production Plated Plastics, 663 F2d 709, 109 LRRM 2328 (CA 6, 1981); NLRB v. Columbus Hi, 652 F2d 614, 108 LRRM 2342 (CA 6, 1981).

[161]266 NLRB 100, 112 LRRM 1257 (1983). *See* Pony Express Courier Corp., 282 NLRB 265, 123 LRRM 1324 (1986).

[162]239 NLRB 641, 99 LRRM 1715 (1978), *enforcement denied,* 645 F2d 506, 107 LRRM 2402 (CA 5, 1981). *Hickory Springs* had overruled Provincial House, 209 NLRB 215, 85 LRRM 1326 (1974) in this regard.

C. Union Conduct

1. In General. Generally, the same standards of preelection conduct apply to both employers and unions. Conduct that will invalidate an election if committed by an employer will usually do so when committed by a union; however, this is not always the case. An employer's promise or grant of benefits violates section 8(a)(1) and constitutes interference if made for the purpose of inducing employees to vote against the union.[163] Union promises, on the other hand, have customarily been considered part of the give-and-take of campaign propaganda and not legally objectionable.[164] The Board has reasoned that the employer has it within its power to implement promises of benefits, whereas the union does not, and the employees will be aware of that distinction:

> Employees are generally able to understand that a Union cannot obtain benefits automatically by winning an election; but must seek to win them through collective bargaining. Union promises . . . are easily recognized by employees to be dependent on contingencies beyond the Union's control and do not carry with them the same degree of finality as if uttered by an employer who has it within his power to implement promises or benefits.[165]

2. Specific Promises and Grants of Benefits. The Board has generally been unwilling to set aside an election because a union *promised* benefits, but it has done so in the uncommon situation in which a union promised a significant benefit that was within its power to confer. In *Alyeska Pipeline Service Co.*,[166] the union promised employees that if they voted for the union they would have a "golden opportunity" to get a membership card and a favorable priority position for job referrals. Because the union,

---

[163]NLRB v. Exchange Parts Co., 375 US 405, 55 LRRM 2098 (1964). *See generally* Chapter 6, "Interference With Protected Rights," at notes 244–249.

[164]Shirlington Supermarket, 106 NLRB 666, 32 LRRM 1519 (1953). *See* El Monte Tool & Die Casting v. NLRB, 633 F2d 160, 105 LRRM 3307 (CA 9, 1980), *enforcing* 244 NLRB 40, 102 LRRM 1139 (1979).

[165]Smith Co., 192 NLRB 1098, 1101, 78 LRRM 1266, 1267 (1971). *See also* Acme Wire Prods. Corp., 224 NLRB 701, 92 LRRM 1482 (1976). *But see* NLRB v. Madisonville Concrete Co., 552 F2d 168, 95 LRRM 2001 (CA 6, 1977), *denying enforcement to* 220 NLRB 668, 90 LRRM 1336 (1976) (union promise to take care of traffic ticket for employee).

[166]261 NLRB 125, 127, 110 LRRM 1011 (1982). *But see* NLRB v. L & J Equip. Co., 745 F2d 224, 117 LRRM 2592 (CA 3, 1984), *denying enforcement on other grounds to* 266 NLRB No. 29, 112 LRRM 1434 (1983) (court accepted Board's determination that union promise to hold victory dinner and dance not objectionable); Adventura Country Club, 253 NLRB 416, 105 LRRM 1587 (1980) (union payment of insurance premiums of members maintained status quo and was not objectionable).

through its referral hall, controlled access to construction jobs for junior employees, the Board set the election aside.

By contrast, the Board has ordered a new election where the union actually *granted* benefits. A gift of life insurance coverage to prospective voters was found to be "akin to an employer's grant of a wage increase in anticipation of a representation election" and therefore required that the election be set aside.[167] Such a gift was deemed different from a waiver of initiation fees because it results in the "enhancement of the employees' economic position" and is not "merely an avoidance of possible future liability."[168] In *Owens-Illinois,*[169] the Board held that the union interfered with the election by giving employees jackets costing $16 between the first and the second voting sessions. In *NLRB v. Labor Services,*[170] the First Circuit refused to enforce the Board's bargaining order, holding that the union had interfered with the election by providing free alcoholic drinks to voters before, during, and after the election. In *Revco v. NLRB,*[171] the Sixth Circuit denied enforcement of a bargaining order where an employee member of the union organizing committee had offered an antiunion employee $100 to vote for the union.

However, where it is not clear that tangible benefits have actually been promised or granted as an inducement to voters, election objections will not be sustained. In *NLRB v. L&J Equipment,*[172] the Third Circuit upheld the Board's finding that the

---

[167]Wagner Elec. Corp., 167 NLRB 532, 66 LRRM 1073 (1967); *but see* Primco Casting Corp., 174 NLRB 244, 70 LRRM 1128 (1969).

[168]Wagner Elec. Corp., *supra* note 167, at 533. *See* Easco Tools, 248 NLRB 700, 103 LRRM 1493 (1980), where the Board set aside an election because of union payments of $5.00 per hour to election observers. The employees' normal rate was $4.25 per hour. Citing its decision in Quick Shops Mkts., 200 NLRB 830, 81 LRRM 1594 (1972), the Board stated that there is no precise test for determining whether payments to union observers are improper. The union's payments resulted in one observer having more than doubled his wages that day. The Board determined that it was doubtful whether the observers could have voted independently, without a sense of obligation to vote for the union. Noting that the observers were sufficient in number to affect the results of the election, the Board concluded that the integrity of the election processes would be better served by directing a new election.

[169]271 NLRB 1235, 117 LRRM 1104 (1984).

[170]721 F2d 13, 114 LRRM 3259 (CA 1, 1983), *denying enforcement to* 265 NLRB 463, 111 LRRM 1650 (1982). On remand, the Board ordered a second election, 274 NLRB 479, 118 LRRM 1407 (1985).

[171]830 F2d 70, 126 LRRM 2535 (CA 6, 1987). The union won the election by one vote. Although the member of the organizing committee may have had no actual authority from the union to offer the $100, the employee to whom the money was offered had been present at a meeting where the two committee members were elected and where the union announced to employees that all questions about the union were to be taken to the organizing committee members. Consequently, the court found that the committee had apparent authority to speak for the union.

[172]*Supra* note 166.

union's promise to hold a dinner dance for all employees in the event of a union victory was not objectionable. The court reasoned that the dinner dance was not a benefit of a monetary nature and there would not be "substantial influence" on the outcome of the election.[173]

3. Waiver of Initiation Fees. Unions have sometimes sought to win preelection support by granting employees a waiver of initiation fees conditioned upon their joining the union before the election, signing an authorization card, or promising to vote in favor of the union. The Board had, alternately, both allowed[174] and prohibited[175] such conditional waivers.

In *NLRB v. Savair Manufacturing Co.*,[176] the Supreme Court rejected the Board's position that a union may offer to waive initiation fees for employees who sign authorization cards before an election. The Court was persuaded that some employees signing a membership or authorization card might feel obligated to carry through on their stated intention to support the union when they vote; thus, unions should not be allowed to "buy endorsements and paint a false portrait of employee support during its election campaign."[177] "[T]he statutory policy of fair elections," declared the Court, "[does not permit endorsements], whether for or against the union, to be bought and sold in this fashion."[178] The Court noted, however, that the union's legitimate interest in overcoming employees' reluctance to pay out money before the union has done anything for them "can be preserved as well by waiver of initiation fees available not only to

---

[173]*Id.* at 232, 117 LRRM at 2597. *See also* NLRB v. Gulf States Canners, 634 F2d 215, 106 LRRM 2270 (CA 5), *enforcing* 242 NLRB 1326, 101 LRRM 1335 (1979), *cert. denied*, 452 US 906, 107 LRRM 2504 (1981) (union purchase of gasoline for employees who attended union meetings not objectionable).

[174]Before 1954, the Board regarded such waivers as "lawful campaign propaganda." DeVilbiss Co., 102 NLRB 1317, 1318, 31 LRRM 1374 (1953).

[175]In Labue Bros., 109 NLRB 1182, 34 LRRM 1528 (1954), the Board held that it would set aside an election where the offer of reduced initiation fees to employees who joined the union was made contingent upon the result of the election. Thereafter, the legality of conditional waivers of initiation fees was in doubt until 1967, when the Board in DIT-MCO, 163 NLRB 1019, 64 LRRM 1476 (1967), *subsequent order to bargain enforced*, 428 F2d 775, 74 LRRM 2664 (CA 8, 1970), returned to its pre–1954 position. The Board said that the offer to waive or reduce initiation fees for those who sign authorization cards before the election is a "legitimate membership-recruiting and campaign device," since there is nothing that coerces these employees into voting in favor of the union.

[176]414 US 270, 84 LRRM 2929 (1973), *aff'g* 470 F2d 305, 82 LRRM 2085 (CA 6, 1972), *rev'g* 194 NLRB 298, 78 LRRM 1605 (1971). Also overruled was the Board's decision on DIT-MCO, *supra* note 175. *See* Chapter 12, "Recognition and Withdrawal of Recognition Without an Election," at notes 281–284.

[177]414 US at 277.

[178]*Id.*

those who have signed up with the union before an election but also to those who join after the election."[179]

Even after *Savair*, a waiver of initiation fees does not interfere with an election absent a showing that the waiver is contingent upon preelection support, the signing of authorization cards, or a commitment to vote only for the union.[180] Consequently, the specific language used by the union in waiving initiation fees is often of critical importance. Where a union offered to waive initiation fees for "charter members" but failed to explain the term to employees, thereby leaving the impression that only those who signed before the election were "charter members," the Board set the election aside.[181] And a union's statement that no initiation fees would be paid by "anyone joining now, during this campaign" was held to be objectionable because it could have been interpreted by employees as being conditioned upon a commitment to support the union.[182]

In *Davlan Engineering*,[183] the Board enlarged the possible sources of such ambiguous statements by holding that employees who solicit authorization cards bind the union by their statements about union fee waivers. Citing *Davlan Engineering*, the Board set aside an election in the case of *University Towers*[184] where it found that while a union official's statements were not of themselves objectionable, they nevertheless were insufficient to neutralize the effects of ambiguous statements of employees who solicited on behalf of the union. An example of an ambiguous statement sufficient to set aside an election was found by the

---

[179]*Id.* at 274 n.4.

[180]NLRB v. First Union Mgmt., 777 F2d 330, 120 LRRM 3437 (CA 6, 1985). However, in McCarty Processors, 286 NLRB 703, 126 LRRM 1211 (1987), the Board set aside a decertification election because the union waived accrued back dues. The waiver was found to have constituted the granting of a financial benefit. Prior to the second election, the union's literature explained that the waiver of dues was an established union policy and there was no obligation to pay dues for any period during which the members were not covered by a contract. 292 NLRB No. 50, 131 LRRM 1714 (1989). *See also* Solon Mfg. Co. v. NLRB, 544 F2d 1109, 93 LRRM 2786 (CA 1, 1976); NLRB v. Sumter Plywood Corp., 535 F2d 917, 92 LRRM 3508 (CA 5, 1976), *cert. denied*, 429 US 1092, 94 LRRM 2643 (1977); Prudential Ins. Co. v. NLRB, 529 F2d 66, 91 LRRM 2422 (CA 6, 1976), *cert. denied*, 425 US 975, 92 LRRM 2502 (1976); Lake Charles Memorial Hosp., 226 NLRB 849, 93 LRRM 1420 (1976). *See also* NLRB v. Whitney Museum of Am. Art, 636 F2d 19, 105 LRRM 3239 (CA 2), *enforcing* 247 NLRB 573, 103 LRRM 1176 (1980).

[181]Inland Shoe Mfg. Co., 211 NLRB 724, 86 LRRM 1498 (1974). *Cf.* Wright Bros. Paper Box Co., 261 NLRB 1162, 110 LRRM 1227 (1982) (waiver available until "new union" formed not unlawful).

[182]Crane Co., 225 NLRB 657, 93 LRRM 1181 (1976).

[183]283 NLRB 903, 125 LRRM 1049 (1987). *Accord* Salem Village I, 288 NLRB 563, 128 LRRM 1069 (1988), *supplementing* 256 NLRB 1015, 107 LRRM 1364 (1981).

[184]285 NLRB 199, 126 LRRM 1127 (1987). *But see* Firestone Steel Prods. Co. Div., 235 NLRB 548, 98 LRRM 1014 (1978).

Board to have occurred where the union made a statement to employees that those who signed cards before the election would not pay any initiation fees, but that those employees could determine whether to impose initiation fees on other employees who signed cards after the election.[185] In another case, the Board set aside an election where the union told employees that there would be a reduced initiation fee of $50 "for organizational purposes for this site" and for "this one time organizational drive."[186] The ambiguity of the time period, the Board stated, must be resolved against the party who used the ambiguous term.

In *Certain-Teed Products Corp. v. NLRB*[187] the Seventh Circuit agreed with the Board that distribution of union literature, which stated that the union "usually does not charge an initiation fee until after giving employees a certain period of time to join the union after a labor board election," was an unconditional waiver of fees for all employees after the election and was therefore permissible under *Savair*. The court also agreed that the use of the word "usually" did not confuse the employees or pressure them into signing cards prior to the election.

The Ninth Circuit, in *NLRB v. L. D. McFarland Co.*,[188] agreed with the Board that the union's offer to waive initiation fees for all "members" and to waive monthly dues until an agreement was signed did not violate *Savair*. The term "members" was held to refer to incoming as well as existing members, and neither waiver of initiation fees nor waiver of dues was held to be improper because both applied regardless of whether the employee joined before or after the election.

Impermissibly ambiguous waivers have been rendered unobjectionable by clarifications or repudiations issued by the unions prior to the election. In *Polyflex M Co.*,[189] the Board denied the employer's motion for reconsideration and reaffirmed its holding that a leaflet which set forth a clearly permissible initiation fee waiver mailed by the union to all unit employees shortly before the election effectively clarified and rendered harmless

---

[185]Claxton Mfg. Co., 258 NLRB 417, 108 LRRM 1171 (1981).

[186]Cataract, 274 NLRB 741, 118 LRRM 1414 (1985). *See also* Equitable Constr. Co., 266 NLRB 668, 113 LRRM 1020 (1983).

[187]562 F2d 500, 96 LRRM 2504 (CA 7, 1977), *enforcing* 225 NLRB 971, 93 LRRM 1192 (1976).

[188]572 F2d 256, 98 LRRM 2037 (CA 9, 1978), *enforcing* 219 NLRB 575, 90 LRRM 1119 (1975), *cert. denied*, 439 US 911, 99 LRRM 2743 (1978).

[189]260 NLRB 1146, 109 LRRM 1290 (1982). *See also* George Lithographics Co., A.G.S. Graphics Div., 262 NLRB 1071, 110 LRRM 1445 (1982).

any arguably ambiguous statements which the union's agent may have made to employees. Further, in *Detroit Receiving Hospital & University Health Center,*[190] the Board found that statements of union officials at meetings with employees that the union's policy and practice for many years has been never to charge initiation fees was sufficient to clarify any ambiguous statements made by a union representative to 3 employees of a 500-member unit.

Conversely, in *Claxton Manufacturing Co.,*[191] the Board held that a union letter to employees containing a guarantee that there would be no initiation fees "as of this day," sent in an attempt to clarify an earlier objectionable statement, was insufficient to clarify or remedy earlier conduct. Similarly, the Sixth Circuit set aside the Board's bargaining order when it found that a fact sheet mailed to bargaining-unit employees just before the election was insufficient to repudiate union representations that violated *Savair.*[192]

In *Aladdin Hotel Corp.*[193] the Board considered a union organizing policy that required prepayment of a reduced initiation fee and one month's dues by a majority of unit employees before the union would file an election petition. If the union lost the election, the amounts prepaid were forfeited to the union to defray the union's campaign expenses; if the union won the election, the dues payments were applied to the first month's dues after a contract was signed, and the reduced initiation fee was open to all employees until the signing of an agreement. In finding this organizational policy lawful, the Board majority reasoned that a union is not obligated to seek to represent employees, and if a majority of employees do not prepay, thus causing the union to abandon its efforts, the employees are denied no rights. If a majority of employees do prepay, those who choose not to do so at the outset are not prejudiced because they can pay the reduced initiation fee after the election. The majority saw no objection that the union's policy might create "an early—though not binding—commitment to favor the Petitioner."[194]

---

[190]277 NLRB 1225, 121 LRRM 1107 (1985).
[191]*Supra* note 185.
[192]*Supra* note 176.
[193]229 NLRB 499, 95 LRRM 1150 (1977).
[194]*Id.* at 500. Members Penello and Walther dissented, observing that the union admitted that one of its reasons for the dues policy was to discourage employees from just "window shopping" for a union. The dissenters viewed this as clear interference with the employees' freedom of choice in direct conflict with *Savair. See also* Jarp Corp., 230 NLRB 660, 95 LRRM 1425 (1977).

4. Other Union Conduct. *a. Interrogation.* In *Springfield Discount,*[195] the Board held that a union's polling of unit employees as to how they would vote does not warrant setting aside an election. The Seventh Circuit agreed, holding there is "no merit in the . . . argument that, because such a poll might have been coercive if conducted by the company, it is likewise coercive when conducted by the union. The employer occupies a far different position with regard to the coercive impact of its actions upon employees than does a Union."[196]

b. Failure to Disclose Information. Is a union under an affirmative duty to disclose any information prior to an election? That question arose in *Florida Mining & Materials Corp. v. NLRB,*[197] where the Fifth Circuit was called upon to resolve, in its words, a "single extremely complex issue." On the day before the election the petitioning local union was placed under temporary trusteeship by its parent international union. Prior to the election, which the union won, the existence of the trusteeship and the reasons therefor were not made known to the public, to the company, or to the employees. The employer filed objections alleging that concealment of the trusteeship invalidated the election results. The Board opposed what, in its view, was the employer's attempt to inject an "affirmative disclosure" requirement into representation campaigns, thus creating an impossible administrative burden in return for only marginal benefits. The circuit court agreed that such a rule had never before been formulated or imposed. It also noted that the union, even though under trusteeship, would still be able to function as a viable union organization and adequately represent the employees.

c. Discrimination on the Basis of Race or Sex. While not involving an objection to union conduct during an election campaign, the

---

[195] 195 NLRB 921, 79 LRRM 1542 (1972), *enforced,* 82 LRRM 2173 (CA 7, 1972).

[196] Louis-Allis Co. v. NLRB, 463 F2d 512, 517, 80 LRRM 2864 (CA 7, 1972). *Accord* Kux Mfg. Co. v. NLRB, 890 F2d 804, 132 LRRM 2935 (CA 6, 1989), *enforcing* 291 NLRB No. 60, 131 LRRM 1718 (1988). *See also* Kusan Mfg. Co. v. NLRB, 749 F2d 362, 117 LRRM 3394 (CA 6, 1984), *enforcing* 267 NLRB 740, 114 LRRM 1075 (1983), *on remand from* 673 F2d 150, 109 LRRM 3087 (CA 6, 1982), *supplementing* 251 NLRB 1629, 105 LRRM 1350 (1980).

[197] 481 F2d 65, 83 LRRM 2793 (CA 5, 1973), *enforcing* 198 NLRB 601, 80 LRRM 1848 (1972), *cert. denied,* 514 US 990, 85 LRRM 2711 (1974). *Accord* Bokum Resources Corp. v. NLRB, 655 F2d 1021, 107 LRRM 3230 (CA 10, 1981). *But see* Pacific Southwest Container, 283 NLRB 79, 124 LRRM 1217 (1987) (election set aside where union listed on ballot had been merged into another union before election date and some eligible voters did not receive notice of change of union identity).

Board and the courts have questioned whether a union which discriminates on the basis of race or sex should be certified. The concern was that by certifying such a union, the Board would beome a partner in illegal discrimination, thereby violating the constitutional guarantees of due process and equal protection.[198]

In *Bekins Moving & Storage Co.,*[199] the Board held, in a split decision, that it would consider an objection to a union's certification, where it was contended that the union engaged in invidious discrimination on the basis of race, alienage, or national origin (but not sex), if such objection were filed within five days of issuance of the tally of ballots. To confer the benefits of certification upon a labor organization which was shown to be engaging in a pattern and practice of invidious discrimination, the majority said, would be to run "afoul of the due process clause of the fifth amendment"; and such action on the Board's part "would clearly be anomalous in view of the federal government's express policy against such discrimination and the many laws which prohibit it."[200]

In *Bell & Howell Co.*[201] the Board again split, but this time denied the employer's postelection motion to disqualify the union from certification because of the union's alleged sex discrimination.

In 1977 the Board, in *Handy Andy,*[202] overruled *Bekins.* The majority held that an employer may no longer, prior to Board certification of the union, raise issues relating to whether the union engages in racial, national origin, or alienage discrimination.[203]

Subsequent to *Handy Andy,* the Board also held that an employer cannot successfully defend against a refusal-to-bargain charge based on a contention that certification was improperly

---

[198]NLRB v. Mansion House Corp., 473 F2d 471, 82 LRRM 2608 (CA 8, 1973). *See* discussion in Chapter 10, "Representation Proceedings and Elections," at notes 440–442, Chapter 12, "Recognition and Withdrawal of Recognition Without an Election," at notes 306–311, and Chapter 26, "Section 8(e): The 'Hot Cargo' Agreement," at notes 124–138.

[199]211 NLRB 138, 86 LRRM 1323 (1974). *See also* Union Carbide Corp., Case No. 13-RC-13269, 86 LRRM 1606 (1974).

[200]211 NLRB at 139.

[201]213 NLRB 407, 87 LRRM 1172 (1974).

[202]228 NLRB 447, 94 LRRM 1354 (1977).

[203]*See also* Skyline Corp. v. NLRB, 613 F2d 1328, 1335–36, 103 LRRM 3003, 3007 (CA 5, 1980); Colonial Manor 1977, 253 NLRB 1183, 106 LRRM 1184 (1981); Electrical Workers (IBEW) Local 1245 v. City of Gridley, 193 Cal. Rptr. 518, 526, 113 LRRM 3729, 3735 (1983) (citing *Handy Andy* with approval).

granted because the certified union discriminated on the basis of sex.[204]

III. REMEDIES

Typically, when the Board sustains a party's objections to an election it will set aside the election and direct a rerun.[205] In addition, it may order the employer to post a *Lufkin Notice* which explains to the employees why the original election was set aside.[206] The Board will normally schedule the rerun election as soon as possible after the original election has been set aside. There are at least two circumstances, however, under which the election may be postponed: (1) where there is a concurrent unfair labor practice case pending against a party, or (2) where a party has been found guilty of unfair labor practices which must be remedied before the rerun.[207]

In *Republic Electronics,*[208] the Board set aside a union-won election where an employee failed to vote because the employer required him to continue performing his job rather than to vote. Although a party to an election is generally estopped from profiting from its own misconduct, the Board recognized a limited exception to this rule. Where a party to an election causes an employee to miss the opportunity to vote, the Board will uphold the wrongdoer's objection if the vote is determinative, there is no evidence of bad faith, and the employee was disenfranchised through no fault of his or her own.[209]

---

[204]Bell & Howell Co., 230 NLRB 420, 95 LRRM 1333 (1977), *enforced,* 598 F2d 136, 100 LRRM 2192 (CA DC), *cert. denied,* 442 US 942, 101 LRRM 2556 (1979).

[205]NLRB CASE HANDLING MANUAL, Pt. 2, Representation Proceedings, ¶11436.

[206]Lufkin Rule Co., 147 NLRB 341, 56 LRRM 1212 (1964). *See also* NLRB CASE HANDLING MANUAL, Pt. 2, Representation Proceedings, ¶11452.1. The language adopted from the *Lufkin* decision is as follows:

"NOTICE TO ALL VOTERS

"The election conducted on __________ was set aside because the National Labor Relations Board found that certain conduct of the (Employer) (Union) interfered with the employees' exercise of a free and reasoned choice. Therefore, a new election will be held in accordance with the terms of this notice of election. All eligible voters should understand that the National Labor Relations Act, as amended, gives them the right to cast their ballots as they see fit, and protects them in the exercise of this right, free from interference by any of the parties."

See Chapter 10, "Representation Proceedings and Elections," at note 434.

[207]NLRB CASE HANDLING MANUAL, Pt. 2, Representation Proceedings, ¶11452.

[208]266 NLRB 852, 113 LRRM 1059 (1983).

[209]*Id.* at 853, 113 LRRM at 1060. *But see* Community Care Sys., 284 NLRB 1147, 126 LRRM 1077 (1987).

In limited circumstances, involving certain types of unfair labor practices, the Board has authority to remedy an employer's election interference by ordering the employer to recognize and bargain with the union in spite of the union's loss of the election. These cases are treated elsewhere.[210]

[210]*See* Chapter 12, "Recognition and Withdrawal of Recognition Without an Election."

Chapter 10

REPRESENTATION PROCEEDINGS AND ELECTIONS

I. Questions Concerning Representation

The process for determining union representation is central to the administration of the National Labor Relations Act.[1] The mandate of the Act is contained in a single sentence:

> Representatives designated or selected for the purposes of collective bargaining by the majority of the employees in a unit appropriate for such purposes, shall be the exclusive representatives of all the employees in such unit for the purposes of collective bargaining in respect to rates of pay, wages, hours of employment or other conditions of employment . . . .[2]

The Act thus provides for union recognition and bargaining when the circumstances of *majority representation* and *appropriate bargaining unit* are present. Although the statute does not require the parties to use the formal processes of the NLRB to determine these questions,[3] it does provide administrative machinery under section 9 to resolve questions concerning representation. A *question concerning representation* (often referred to as a QCR) exists when a labor organization or individual seeks recognition as bargaining agent and the employer declines to recognize it, thus requiring the Board to determine whether the union or individual represents a majority of the employees in an appropriate bargaining unit.

---

[1]*See generally* K.C. McGuiness & J.A. Norris, How to Take a Case Before the NLRB 3–281 (5th ed. 1986).

[2]Section 9(a).

[3]*See* Chapters 12, "Recognition and Withdrawal of Recognition Without an Election," and 13, "The Duty to Bargain."

Employees, labor organizations, or employers may file representation petitions to determine whether a labor organization or individual is entitled to recognition (or to continued recognition) for purposes of collective bargaining. The Board has charged its regional directors[4] with the investigation of these petitions to decide whether "a question of representation affecting commerce exists."[5] When an employer and labor organization agree that the labor organization is in fact the choice of a majority of employees in the bargaining unit,[6] that certain employees constitute an appropriate unit,[7] and that the Act is applicable, the employer may voluntarily recognize the union without any recourse to the Board. But if the Board's processes are invoked by a representation petition, then the Board will decide whether its jurisdictional requirements are met,[8] and if so whether the bargaining unit is appropriate and whether a majority of the employees has selected a representative.

If, pursuant to a petition, the regional director holds a hearing[9] and finds that a question concerning representation exists, an election is directed and the results certified. If two or more petitions involving the same employer are pending, they may be consolidated into one hearing because of common issues. When it appears to the Board, after investigation by the regional director, that an expedited election under section 8(b)(7)(C) is warranted, an election may be held without a prior hearing.[10] An election may also be held without a hearing on the basis of a consent agreement resolving certain issues preliminary to the election.[11]

After the hearing the regional director may transfer the record to the Board for a ruling on the petition. Normally,

---

[4]For a discussion of the 1961 delegation of authority, *see* Chapter 31, "NLRB Procedures," at notes 69–70 and accompanying text.

[5]Section 9(c)(2).

[6]*But see* Bernhard-Altmann Texas Corp., 122 NLRB 1289, 43 LRRM 1283 (1959), *enforced sub nom.* Ladies' Garment Workers v. NLRB, 280 F2d 616, 46 LRRM 2223 (CA DC, 1960), *aff'd,* 366 US 731, 48 LRRM 2251 (1961) (employer and union violated §§8(a)(2) and 8(b)(1)(a) by voluntary recognition when union lacked majority support), discussed in Chapter 8, "Employer Domination and Assistance to Labor Organizations," at notes 9 and 82–83.

[7]*See* Chapter 11, "Appropriate Bargaining Units."

[8]For discussion of the Board's jurisdictional standards, *see* Chapter 28, "Jurisdiction: Coverage of the Act."

[9]*See* Chapter 31, "NLRB Procedures," at notes 64–68 and accompanying text. *See also infra* at notes 218–230.

[10]*See* Chapter 21, "The Primary Strike."

[11]*See* Chapter 31, "NLRB Procedures," at notes 75–77 and accompanying text and *infra* at notes 224–226.

however, the director rules on it initially, and that decision is final subject to discretionary Board review upon timely request.[12] If, pursuant to the director's or the Board's direction, an election is held, ballots may be challenged and objections may be made to the election.[13] The postelection procedure to resolve such issues is similar to the preelection procedure: under the common practice the regional director investigates without a hearing then makes a report and recommendations to the Board, which makes the final determination.[14] The conclusion of the process is marked by certification of the winning union (or individual) as the exclusive bargaining representative, or merely by certification of the results if no union wins.

A. Petitions by Labor Organizations and Employees

1. Showing of Interest. A union (or individual) desiring to be certified as the collective bargaining representative files a petition (in Board parlance an "RC" petition, a reference to the agency's system for numbering case files) describing the bargaining unit alleged to be appropriate. Section 9(c)(1)(A) of the Act provides that the petition must be supported by a "substantial number of employees." The Board by rule defines "substantial" to mean at least 30 percent.[15] The evidence of support, which is usually in the form of signed and dated[16] authorization cards, must accompany the petition or be presented shortly thereafter, generally within 48 hours of its filing.[17] The 30-percent showing is not necessarily required of a union seeking to intervene; its interest may be otherwise shown if it seeks the same unit as the

---

[12]*See* Chapter 31, "NLRB Procedures," at notes 64–68 and accompanying text.

[13]*Id.* at notes 98–110 and accompanying text; *see also* Chapter 9, "Restrictions of Preelection Activity: 'Laboratory Conditions.'"

[14]*But see* NLRB v. Chelsea Clock Co., 411 F2d 189, 71 LRRM 2263 (CA 1, 1969), where the regional director was held to have improperly abdicated to the NLRB his responsibility for deciding disputes arising out of an agreement for a consent election. When the employer filed objections to the election on the grounds that an alleged supervisor engaged in pro-union conduct, the regional director consolidated the representation case for hearing with the unfair labor practice case which had been filed by the same supervisor. *See also* Chapter 31, "NLRB Procedures," at notes 98–110.

[15]NLRB RULES AND REGULATIONS AND STATEMENTS OF PROCEDURE, SERIES 8, §101.18 (as last amended, Jan. 8, 1976) (1976) (hereinafter referred to as Rules and Regs. and Statements of Procedure); Esso Standard Oil Co., 124 NLRB 1383, 45 LRRM 1020 (1959).

[16]A showing of interest is deemed inadequate where none of the cards is dated, Werman & Sons, 114 NLRB 629, 37 LRRM 1021 (1955), although exceptions to this rule may exist; *see* Windemuller Elec., 180 NLRB 686, 686 n.1, 73 LRRM 1111 (1970) (validity of petition merely "questionable" where cards undated).

[17]K.C. MCGUINESS & J.A. NORRIS, *supra* note 1, at 63–64.

petitioner.[18] A cross-petitioning union seeking a substantially different unit from that claimed to be appropriate by the initial petitioner must comply with the 30-percent showing.[19]

Investigation of the cards includes checking them against a current payroll list of employees furnished by the employer to the regional director's agent. The agent's responsibility is to determine whether the cards are current and sufficient in number. The employer is not permitted to inspect the cards,[20] and at the hearing no litigation is permitted concerning fraud, forgery, or coercion in obtaining cards. The adequacy of petitioner's showing in general is by prehearing administrative determination of the Board, "not subject to direct or collateral attack at hearings."[21]

The Act also authorizes procedures for decertification and deauthorization petitions.[22] A decertification petition (an "RD" petition)[23] seeks certification that an incumbent union no longer has the support of the unit; a deauthorization petition (a

---

[18]NLRB, 1958 ANNUAL REPORT 14 (1959). *See* NLRB FIELD MANUAL, issued by the General Counsel of the NLRB, Aug. 1, 1968 (hereinafter referred to as NLRB Field Manual), 11022.3c and d: "A [*full* intervenor] union which seeks to intervene on the basis of a showing of designation by at least 10 percent of the employees . . . may 'block' any consent election in such unit; and it may participate fully in any hearing thereon. *Cf.* Corn Prods. Ref. Co., 87 NLRB 187, 25 LRRM 1085 (1949). . . . A [*participating* intervenor] union which seeks to intervene on a timely showing of less than 10 percent (it may be only one of two designations) in any unit may not 'block' a consent election in such unit. However, it should be accorded a place on the ballot under the terms agreed upon by the other parties. If a hearing is held it may participate fully. Union Carbide & Carbon Corp., 89 NLRB 460, 25 LRRM 1585 (1950)."

[19]NLRB Field Manual 11022.3b.

[20]The Board has successfully resisted employer efforts to gain disclosure of authorization cards under the Freedom of Information Act. 5 U.S.C. §552 (1988). *See, e.g.*, NLRB v. Martins Ferry Hosp. Ass'n, 649 F2d 445, 107 LRRM 2569 (CA 6), *cert. denied*, 454 US 1083, 108 LRRM 3104 (1981); Howard Johnson Co. v. NLRB, 618 F2d 1, 103 LRRM 2888 (CA 6, 1980); Pacific Molasses Co. v. NLRB, 577 F2d 1172, 99 LRRM 2048 (CA 5, 1978); Committee on Masonic Homes v. NLRB, 556 F2d 214, 95 LRRM 2457 (CA 3, 1977). However, it has been held that subpoenaed authorization cards must be disclosed to the attorneys of an employer and a union under criminal indictment on charges of conspiracy and obstruction of administrative proceedings. Irving v. DiLapi, 600 F2d 1027, 101 LRRM 2903 (CA 2), *cert. denied*, 444 US 866, 102 LRRM 2240 (1979). At least one court has reached a different result with respect to Board Form 4069 used by Board agents to report facts concerning a union's showing of interest in support of a representation proceeding. Pacific Molasses Co. v. NLRB, *supra*.

[21]O.D. Jennings & Co., 68 NLRB 516, 518, 18 LRRM 1133 (1946). *See also* Wright Memorial Hosp. v. NLRB, 771 F2d 400, 120 LRRM 2193 (CA 8, 1985); Union Mfg. Co., 123 NLRB 1633, 44 LRRM 1188 (1959) (decertification proceedings). Adequacy of showing of interest may be contested by submission of affidavits to the regional director. Globe Iron Foundry, 112 NLRB 1200, 36 LRRM 1170 (1955).

[22]Section 9(c)(1)(A)(ii).

[23]Rules and Regs. §102.61; Statements of Procedure §101.18. The unit for purposes of an RD election is coextensive with the contract unit. Arlan's Dep't Store, 131 NLRB 565, 567 n.7, 48 LRRM 1115 (1961).

"UD"petition)[24] seeks rescission of the union's authority to make an existing union-shop agreement with the employer. Such petitions may be filed by an employee or group of employees or an individual or labor organization acting in their behalf, and the petitioner must demonstrate that at least 30 percent of the employees in the unit support the petition.

No showing of interest is required for an expedited election under section 8(b)(7)(C) of the Act.[25]

2. Employer Denial of Recognition. Section 9(c)(1)(A) contemplates an allegation that an employer "declines to recognize" the union representative through which the employees wish to engage in collective bargaining. However, the failure of the union to demand recognition before filing the petition is not a basis for its dismissal[26] provided the employer refuses to recognize the union at the hearing. Indeed, after a union has gained recognition from an employer without certification, it may nonetheless seek and obtain an election by petition in order to reap the statutory benefits conferred especially by the 1947 Taft-Hartley amendments upon unions that are certified by the NLRB as representatives.[27]

3. Joint Petitions. Joint petitions may be filed by two or more labor organizations that desire to act as a joint representative.[28] The employees' authorizations may be made in the individual name of any of the joint petitioners, and the cards may even be silent as to the question of joint representation.[29] If the unions are successful in the election, certification will issue in the joint names of the unions, and the employer may insist that they bargain jointly.[30]

---

[24]Section 9(e)(1) Rules and Regs. Subpart E; Statements of Procedure Subpart E. *See* Chapter 27, "Union Security," at notes 149–157 and accompanying text.

[25]*See* Chapter 21, "Picketing for Organization and Recognition," at notes 258–262 and accompanying text.

[26]"M" Sys., 115 NLRB 1316, 38 LRRM 1055 (1956).

[27]General Box Co., 82 NLRB 678, 23 LRRM 1589 (1949).

[28]*See* Mid-South Packers, 120 NLRB 495, 41 LRRM 1526 (1958). In the absence of petitioners' intention to represent the employees jointly and to bargain jointly with the employer, the Board will not allow a joint petition. *See, e.g.*, Suburban Newspaper Publications, 230 NLRB 1215, 95 LRRM 1482 (1977), where the Board declared the election a nullity and dismissed the joint petition after the posthearing investigation revealed that the unions had assured employees that the joint representation election was only a formality and that each union would continue to represent its traditional constituency.

[29]Stickless Corp., 115 NLRB 979, 37 LRRM 1466 (1956).

[30]Jackson Manor Nursing Home, 194 NLRB 892, 79 LRRM 1166 (1972); Swift & Co., 115 NLRB 752, 37 LRRM 1392 (1956).

B. Petitions by Employers[31]

1. History Under the Wagner Act. Although the original statute declared that "whenever a question affecting commerce arises concerning the representation of employees, the Board may investigate such controversy,"[32] it provided no mechanism for bringing the controversy to the Board's attention. Drawing upon the experience of other governmental agencies, the Board adopted a procedure authorizing any person or labor organization desiring investigation of a controversy concerning representation to file a petition.[33] There was no provision for employer petitions.[34]

This policy met with widespread opposition, especially as it affected an employer caught in the middle of a jurisdictional dispute.[35] The American Bar Association's Committee on Labor Employment and Social Security called for amendment of the Act.[36]

The American Federation of Labor also advocated amendment of the Act. It had charged that the Board, in acting upon union petitions, had exercised its discretion in favor of the CIO and against the AFL. In 1939, to remedy this situation, it supported a bill[37] to amend section 9(c) to require the Board to investigate union petitions; the bill would also have amended section 9(c) to provide for employer petitions. The bill was not enacted into law. The Board opposed the bill, criticizing the proposal for employer petitions:

> The reasons for not permitting employers an unlimited right of petition are first, that normally the employer has no legitimate interest in the question whether or when his employees wish to choose representatives or whom they wish to choose; and second,

---

[31]For general discussion of this subject, *see* Lewis, *Employer Petitions—New York and Federal—A Comparison,* NYU FIFTH ANNUAL CONFERENCE ON LABOR 249 (1952).

[32]Section 9(c), deleted in 1947.

[33]NLRB RULES AND REGS., SERIES 1, art. III, §1 (1935).

[34]Nevertheless, it was not unusual for the regional director, at the instance of the employer, to induce the union to file a petition. BOWMAN, PUBLIC CONTROL OF LABOR RELATIONS 298 (1942); ROSENFARB, THE NATIONAL LABOR POLICY 303 (1940).

[35]For example, one editorial advised: "Many of those connected with the NLRB admit in private that the employer is often at the mercy of two conflicting unions, neither of which will concede that the other has the right to bargain for the workers, though neither, until it is certain it has a majority, will ask for an election." N.Y. Times, Nov. 30, 1937, at 22.

[36]25 A.B.A. J. 119, 124 (1936).

[37]S. 1000, 76th Cong., 1st Sess. (1939). For its legislative history, *see* H. MILLIS & E. BROWN, FROM THE WAGNER ACT TO TAFT-HARTLEY 347–53 (1950).

> that if an employer is given the right to demand an election at will he can, by choosing a strategic time, effectively hinder or block self-organization among his employees. The right of employees to choose their representatives when and as they wish is normally no more the affair of the employer than the right of the stockholders to choose directors is the affair of the employees.[38]

However, in response to strong public pressure, the Board in 1939 amended its rules to grant employers a limited right to petition if the petition alleged that two or more unions were making conflicting claims of representative status.[39] This right was not altered under the statute or the rules until the Taft-Hartley amendments.

2. History Under the Taft-Hartley Act. The most frequently voiced objection to employer petitions in the debate on the 1947 amendments was that they could be used to force a premature test and thereby obtain a vote rejecting the union. A further objection was based upon another amendment which would disenfranchise permanently replaced economic strikers. President Truman's veto message stressed that employer petitions could be used to obtain elections during strikes and thereby capitalize on the strikers' disenfranchisement.[40]

To meet those objections, the measure as enacted conditioned the employer's right to petition for an election upon a prior claim for recognition by a union. Accordingly, section 9(c)(1) reads as follows:

> Whenever a petition shall have been filed . . . by an employer, alleging that one or more individuals or labor organizations have presented to him a claim to be recognized as the representative defined in Section 9(a); the Board shall investigate such petition. . . .

This amendment was designed to grant an employer the right to petition in two situations previously unavailable to it. The first involves a claim for recognition by one union only; previously an employer's right to petition was contingent upon claims for recognition by two or more unions. The second concerns an employer desire to question the current majority standing of

---

[38] *Report of NLRB Before Sen. Comm. on Education and Labor, Hearings on National Labor Relations Act and Proposed Amendments,* 76th Cong., 1st Sess., Part 3, pp. 467, 540–43 (1939).

[39] NLRB RULES AND REGS., SERIES 2, art. III, §§1–3 (1939).

[40] H.R. 334, 93 CONG. REC. 7486 (1947). For similar criticism, see 93 CONG. REC. 4032, 6527 (1947) (remarks of Senators Murray and Pepper).

an incumbent union; before 1947 the Board would not entertain an employer petition (an "RM" petition) in such a situation.[41]

a. Unrecognized Unions. Section 9(c)(1)(B) specifies that an employer petition must contain an allegation that a union (or individual) has "presented to [the employer] a claim to be recognized as the representative defined in section 9(a)." The Board considers that absent such a claim it would be without jurisdiction to proceed with its investigation.[42] The phrase "representative defined in section 9(a)" means a labor organization (or individual) chosen by a majority of employees in a unit appropriate for collective bargaining to be the exclusive representative of all employees therein for such purposes. Mere campaigning by a union and knowledge of such campaigning by the employer are not the equivalent of a claim by the union that it represents a majority of the employees, nor do they constitute a request for exclusive bargaining rights under the Act.[43] It is not necessary, however, that a claim of majority representation be made in the exact terms of section 9(a). It is sufficient if the union submits or requests a proposed contract,[44] other than a prehire agreement authorized by section 8(f).[45]

When an employer receives the requisite claim of representative status, the employer is permitted to file a petition, but is not required by the Act to do so. In *Linden Lumber Co. v. NLRB*[46] the Court held that an employer which has not committed independent unfair labor practices does not violate section 8(a)(5) of the Act by refusing to recognize authorization cards as evidence

[41]*E.g.*, Cincinnati Times-Star Co., 66 NLRB 414, 17 LRRM 340 (1946); Toledo Steel Prods. Co., 65 NLRB 56, 17 LRRM 211 (1945); Colonial Life Ins. Co. of Am., 65 NLRB 58, 17 LRRM 195 (1945); Landis Mach. Co., 65 NLRB 60, 17 LRRM 210 (1945).

[42]Herman Loewenstein, Inc., 75 NLRB 377, 21 LRRM 1032 (1947).

[43]Baldwin Co., 81 NLRB 927, 23 LRRM 1438 (1949); Electro Metallurgical Co., 72 NLRB 1396, 19 LRRM 1291 (1947).

[44]Johnson Bros. Furniture Co., 97 NLRB 246, 29 LRRM 1089 (1951); Kimel Shoe Co., 97 NLRB 127, 29 LRRM 1069 (1951). *See* Chapter 21, "Picketing for Organization and Recognition," at notes 52–76 and accompanying text for a discussion of the nature of evidence used to show recognitional objectives.

[45]By its nature, a union's request for a §8(f) agreement does not assert a claim of majority status. Thus, such a request did not satisfy the statutory requisite of a demand to be recognized "as the representative," and an employer petition was dismissed. Albuquerque Insulation Contractor, 256 NLRB 61, 107 LRRM 1254 (1981).

[46]419 US 301, 87 LRRM 3236 (1974). *See* Chapter 12, "Recognition and Withdrawal of Recognition Without an Election," at notes 48–76 and 228–237. The decision resolved a question that the Court had expressly reserved in NLRB v. Gissel Packing Co., 395 US 575, 595, 601 n.18, 71 LRRM 2481 (1969).

of a union's majority status, even though the employer fails to petition the Board for an election.

b. Incumbent Unions. Section 9(c)(1)(B) is not restricted to situations where an unrecognized union claims recognition. A request by an incumbent union for renewal of its contract constitutes a "claim to be recognized" within the meaning of this section.[47] Therefore, an employer who questions a union's continuing support by a majority of the employees may file a petition for an election.

Under former Board policy it was not necessary that the employer have a reasonable basis for doubting majority status, nor was withdrawal of recognition required.[48] The reasonable, or good-faith, basis for the doubt was an issue only in the event of subsequent unfair labor practice charges alleging a refusal to bargain.[49] In *United States Gypsum Co.*[50] the Board changed that rule, thenceforth dismissing an employer petition where no "reasonable basis" was shown for questioning the status of an incumbent union. It formulated an "objective evidence" test, premising the rule in part upon its reading of the legislative history of section 9(c)(1)(B). It asserted that the provision was designed to give relief to employers who had "reasonable grounds for believing" that the claiming union was not really the choice of the majority, for "[t]here is no indication that Congress . . . contemplated the creation of a device by which an employer acting without good-faith doubt of the union's status . . . could disrupt collective bargaining and frustrate the policy of the Act favoring stable relations."[51] The Board therefore held that,

> in petitioning the Board for an election to question the continued majority of a previously certified incumbent union, an employer, in addition to showing the union's claim for continued recognition, must demonstrate by objective considerations that it has some reasonable grounds for believing that the union has lost its majority status since its certification.[52]

---

[47]Philadelphia Elec. Co., 95 NLRB 71, 28 LRRM 1296 (1951); Whitney's, 81 NLRB 75, 23 LRRM 1297 (1949).

[48]J.P. O'Neil Lumber Co., 94 NLRB 1299, 28 LRRM 1190 (1951); J.C. Penney Co., 86 NLRB 920, 25 LRRM 1039 (1949); Continental S. Corp., 83 NLRB 668, 24 LRRM 1127 (1949).

[49]Celanese Corp. of Am., 95 NLRB 664, 28 LRRM 1362 (1951).

[50]157 NLRB 652, 61 LRRM 1384 (1966).

[51]*Id.* at 656.

[52]*Id.* For a detailed discussion of this history, see Talent, *United States Gypsum Co.—More of the Same,* 17 LAB. L.J. 559 (1966).

In considering the sufficiency of the "objective considerations," it is not the fact of the union's majority status that is in question, but whether the employer has reasonable cause to believe that the union has lost its majority status.[53] Objective considerations which constitute reasonable grounds for believing that the union has lost its majority status have been found in a variety of situations.[54] Examples include admissions by union officials that the union has lost majority support[55] and written and oral statements by union employees repudiating the union.[56] Some circuit courts, rejecting the contrary view of the Board, have held that such statements may be obtained by an employer-conducted poll of employees.[57] A combination of factors, such as a decline in dues checkoff authorizations, the union's inactivity in failing to monitor contract provisions or to process grievances, or to recommend employees for promotion or to safety committees, and significant turnover in the work force may serve as a basis for reasonable doubt of the union's continued majority.[58]

The Board has also decided that an employer's demonstration of the "objective considerations" is to be submitted confidentially to the regional director for administrative determination as to the *prima facie* showing. As an administrative determination, that issue would thus not be litigable at any stage of the representation proceeding.[59]

---

[53]NLRB Field Manual 11042.5. *Cf.* Chapter 12, "Recognition and Withdrawal of Recognition Without an Election," at notes 313–412, for discussion of withdrawal of recognition without an election.

[54]In the absence of a collective bargaining agreement, *see, e.g.,* NLRB v. Buckley Broadcasting Corp. of Cal. dba Station KKHI, 891 F2d 230, 133 LRRM 2175 (CA 9, 1989), an employer with objective grounds to support a good-faith belief that the incumbent union no longer enjoys majority support may also simply withdraw recognition and cease dealing with the union, *see* NLRB v. Curtin Matheson Scientific, 494 US 775, 133 LRRM 3049 (1990). Accordingly, most decisions dealing with such objective considerations arise in unfair labor practice proceedings contesting withdrawals of recognition. *See* Chapter 12, "Recognition and Withdrawal of Recognition Without an Election," at notes 313–412, and Chapter 13, "The Duty to Bargain," at notes 819–833.

[55]Machinists Lodge 1746 v. NLRB (United Aircraft Corp.), 416 F2d 809, 71 LRRM 2336 (CA DC, 1969), *cert. denied,* 396 US 1058, 73 LRRM 2278 (1970).

[56]NLRB v. Gallaro Bros., 419 F2d 97, 73 LRRM 2043 (CA 2, 1969); Riverside Produce Co., 242 NLRB 615, 101 LRRM 1371 (1979).

[57]Thomas Indus. v. NLRB, 687 F2d 863, 111 LRRM 2233 (CA 6, 1982). *See* Struksnes Constr. Co., 165 NLRB 1062, 65 LRRM 1385 (1967) for general guidelines adopted by Board for conducting such polls. NLRB v. A.W. Thompson, 651 F2d 1141, 107 LRRM 3245 (CA 5, 1981) (notice of intention to poll must be given to union).

[58]Ingress-Plastene, Inc. v. NLRB, 430 F2d 542, 74 LRRM 2658 (CA 7, 1970); *see also* NLRB v. Massachusetts Mach. & Stamping, 578 F2d 15, 98 LRRM 2939 (CA 1, 1978).

[59]United States Gypsum Co., 161 NLRB 601, 63 LRRM 1308 (1966).

Where an employer is signatory to a section 8(f) agreement, the Board observed that the employer may utilize section 9(c)(1)(B) to compel the union to "fish or cut bait" with respect to its status as a section 9(a) representative.[60] If the union claims majority status (or at least does not disclaim such status), an election will be directed. If, on the other hand, either the union disclaims or has achieved exclusive representative status through voluntary recognition, the petition will be dismissed. If the union disclaims or loses an election, the employer may then disavow the section 8(f) agreement without violating section 8(a)(5).[61]

The Board has often found that no question concerning representation exists where an employer's petition requests a unit that is narrower than the unit sought by a labor organization. In *Sonic Knitting Industries*,[62] this rule was applied to dismiss an employer's petition for an election in a single-plant unit where the union historically had represented employees in a multiplant unit.

3. Disclaimer of Interest. Section 9(c)(1)(B) was designed to permit an employer to file an election petition when a union claims to be an exclusive representative for purposes of collective bargaining. The possibility that a union, having made such a claim, might withdraw it was apparently unforeseen by the drafters.

The issue was first presented in *Ny-Lint Tool & Manufacturing Co.*[63] A union which had represented the employees for several years without benefit of Board certification submitted a new contract proposal covering the same employees. The employer expressed doubt that the union continued to represent a majority of the employees, refused to negotiate a new contract, and filed a petition. The union disavowed any claim to majority representation and asked that the employer's petition be dismissed. The Board did so, on the ground that a question concerning representation no longer existed and it was without

---

[60]*Id.*; Albuquerque Insulation Contractor, *supra* note 45. *See supra* note 45.

[61]John Deklewa & Sons, 282 NLRB 1375, 124 LRRM 1185 (1987), *enforced sub nom.* Iron Workers Local 3 v. NLRB, 843 F2d 770, 128 LRRM 2020 (CA 3), *cert. denied,* 488 US 889, 129 LRRM 2528 (1988).

[62]228 NLRB 1319, 95 LRRM 1076 (1977).

[63]77 NLRB 642, 22 LRRM 1061 (1948). Both majority and dissenting opinions observed that the situation of an incumbent contractual representative presented the same issue and called for the same construction of the statute as that of an unrecognized union.

jurisdiction to proceed. The Board continues to adhere to this policy, dismissing employer petitions whenever the union disclaims interest.[64]

Similarly, a disclaimer of interest by the union may result in a dismissal of certain other petitions. For example, in *Federal Shipbuilding & Drydock Co.*[65] the Board held that a union may disclaim interest even after the Board has directed an election, but before the date of the election, on a decertification petition. In *Hartz Mountain Corp.*,[66] the Board allowed the winning union to disclaim after the losing rival union filed a meritorious charge that the employer had unlawfully assisted the winner.

The failure of a union to appear at the hearing,[67] or the failure of a union to intervene,[68] will not constitute a disclaimer of interest. And a union's filing of a refusal-to-bargain charge is not deemed inconsistent with a disclaimer of interest.[69] In addition, a union may, in certain instances, disclaim interest but engage in picketing.[70] It was argued in *Hubach & Parkinson Motors*[71] that the continued picketing impeached the union's disclaimer and that the union was continuing to assert its claim to be the statutory representative of the employees. The Board disagreed, stating that in order "to defeat an employer's petition or a petition for decertification, a union's disclaimer of status as exclusive bargaining representative must be clear and unequivocal,"[72] although the determination of the sufficiency of a disclaimer may involve considering not only the words used but

---

[64]*E.g.*, Josephine Furniture Co., 172 NLRB 404, 68 LRRM 1311 (1968); Coeur d'Alene Grocers Ass'n, 88 NLRB 44, 25 LRRM 1301 (1950); Murray B. Marsh Co., 79 NLRB 76, 22 LRRM 1377 (1948); Brockton Wholesale Grocery Co., 78 NLRB 663, 22 LRRM 1264 (1948); Louella Balierino, 77 NLRB 738, 22 LRRM 1076 (1948).

[65]77 NLRB 463, 22 LRRM 1034 (1948).

[66]260 NLRB 323, 109 LRRM 1204 (1982). *See also* Hartz Mountain Corp. v. Dotson, 727 F2d 1308, 115 LRRM 3137 (CA DC, 1984) (district court lacked jurisdiction to review order of Board allowing postelection disclaimer by winning union and directing second election).

[67]Felton Oil Co., 78 NLRB 1033, 22 LRRM 1332 (1948).

[68]Penn Paper & Stock Co., 88 NLRB 17, 25 LRRM 1279 (1950).

[69]Franz Food Prods., 137 NLRB 340, 50 LRRM 1143 (1962).

[70]Hubach & Parkinson Motors, 88 NLRB 1202, 25 LRRM 1466 (1950). To the same effect, see Martino's Complete Home Furnishings, 145 NLRB 604, 55 LRRM 1003 (1963); General Paint Corp., 95 NLRB 539, 28 LRRM 1345 (1951). *See also* Tribune Publishing Co., 147 NLRB 841, 56 LRRM 1273 (1964); Hamilton's Ltd., 93 NLRB 1076, 27 LRRM 1538 (1951); Palace Knitwear Co., 93 NLRB 872, 27 LRRM 1481 (1951); Bur-Bee Co., 90 NLRB 9, 26 LRRM 1153 (1950). *But see* Ladies' Garment Workers Local 155 (Boulevard Knitwear Corp.), 167 NLRB 763, 66 LRRM 1157 (1967) (regarding picketing in violation of §8(b)(7) after disclaimer).

[71]*Supra* note 70.

[72]*Id.* at 1204. For treatment of organizational and recognitional picketing, see Chapter 21, "Picketing for Organization and Recognition."

also other conduct of the union. The Board concluded, however, that despite the resumption of picketing, the union's disclaimer had been clear and unequivocal.[73]

Not all disclaimers of interest by unions result in the dismissal of the employer's petition. Where the disclaimer is not "clear and unequivocal,"[74] or where the union's picket signs may be interpreted as expressing a continued claim to majority representation, the Board will refuse, notwithstanding the disclaimer, to dismiss the employer's petition.[75]

II. TIMELINESS OF PETITIONS

A. One-Year Rule

1. The Statutory Bar. Representation elections may not be conducted more often than once a year in any given bargaining unit or subdivision of a unit. This limitation was imposed in 1947 by the addition of section 9(c)(3). Accordingly, when a representation petition is filed within 60 days preceding the anniversary date of the earlier election, it will be processed but the election itself will be scheduled for a date after the expiration of the one-year period. A petition filed more than 60 days before the anniversary date will be dismissed as untimely.[76] The prohibition applies only to conclusive elections; the Board is not precluded from directing a rerun or runoff election within the year, or from directing a second election within the year where the first election was set aside on the basis of valid objections timely filed.[77] A deauthorization election to revoke a union's authority

---

[73]*Id. See also* John's Valley Foods, 237 NLRB 425, 99 LRRM 1414 (1978), where the Board found insufficient evidence that a union's current informational picketing had a recognitional objective. The regional director had improperly relied on an unsupported presumption that an earlier recognitional objective continued despite a substantial hiatus in picketing which followed an injunctive order. Nor had he sufficiently considered the union's avowed informational objective and the absence of union conduct inconsistent with its disclaimer. Accordingly, the Board dismissed the employer's petition for an election.

[74]*E.g.,* Johnson Bros. Furniture Co., 97 NLRB 246, 29 LRRM 1089 (1951); Coca-Cola Bottling Co., 80 NLRB 1063, 23 LRRM 1160 (1948). *See also* Ogden Enters., 248 NLRB 290, 103 LRRM 1395 (1980), where the Board directed an election on an employer's petition even though the union picketing the employer had disclaimed an interest in representing the employees, since its "activity prior to the disclaimer" was "tantamount" to a demand for recognition and its picketing thereafter furthered that objective; McClintock Mkt., 244 NLRB 555, 102 LRRM 1141 (1979) (there had been no hiatus in picketing, no leaflets advising public of purpose of picketing, and union's disclaimer of interest had followed its demand for a contract by only a few days).

[75]Kimel Shoe Co., 97 NLRB 127, 29 LRRM 1069 (1951).

[76]Randolph Metal Works, 147 NLRB 973, 56 LRRM 1348 (1964).

[77]NAPA N.Y. Warehouse, 76 NLRB 840, 21 LRRM 1251 (1948).

to execute a union-security contract is not barred by any form of election other than another deauthorization election within the 1-year period.[78]

Elections conducted by responsible private or state agencies which afford employees an opportunity to express their true desires and which respect the fundamentals of due process will bar NLRB elections in the same unit within the 1-year period.[79]

Where no union is certified, the year begins to run from the date of the election (i.e., date of balloting).[80] The Board maintains this position even where there are postelection objections or challenges that are not resolved for several months.[81]

The 1-year rule applies only to new elections in the same bargaining unit or in a subdivision of that unit. An election in a given unit will not preclude the holding of an election in a broader, more inclusive unit within the year.[82] Nor will a prior election in a larger unit preclude an election within a year in a smaller unit of employees who were barred from voting in the first election.[83] The bar applies, however, if the smaller unit is within the broader unit in which the prior election was held.[84]

---

[78]Monsanto Chem. Co., 147 NLRB 49, 56 LRRM 1136 (1964).

[79]West Indian Co., 129 NLRB 1203, 47 LRRM 1146 (1961); Olin Mathieson Chem. Corp., 115 NLRB 1501, 38 LRRM 1099 (1956); T-H Prods. Co., 113 NLRB 1246, 36 LRRM 1471 (1955); Interboro Chevrolet Co., 111 NLRB 783, 35 LRRM 1567 (1955). For the development of this policy, *compare* National Container Corp., 87 NLRB 1065, 25 LRRM 1234 (1949) *with* Punch Press Repair Corp., 89 NLRB 614, 26 LRRM 1012 (1950). A Board majority failed to give effect to such an election in applying §8(b)(7) in Bartenders Local 58 (Fowler Hotel), 138 NLRB 1315, 51 LRRM 1180 (1962). In NLRB v. Western Meat Packers, 350 F2d 804, 60 LRRM 2101 (CA 10, 1965), the Board was chided for refusing to honor such an election. *Compare* Monroe Coop. Oil Co., 86 NLRB 95, 24 LRRM 1591 (1949) *with* National Waste Material Corp., 93 NLRB 477, 27 LRRM 1413 (1951).

[80]Palmer Mfg. Co., 103 NLRB 336, 31 LRRM 1520 (1953); Mallinckrodt Chem. Works, 84 NLRB 291, 24 LRRM 1253 (1949). When balloting is conducted over a period of several weeks or months, the year begins at the end of the balloting period. Alaska Salmon Indus., 90 NLRB 168, 26 LRRM 1199 (1950).

[81]Bendix Corp., 179 NLRB 140, 72 LRRM 1264 (1969). In Tri-ExTower Corp., 230 NLRB 1006, 96 LRRM 1490 (1977), *enforced,* 595 F2d 1, 105 LRRM 2896 (CA 9, 1979), an election was held in July 1975, but the union's objections to the election were not resolved until June 1976, when the Board overruled the objections and certified the election results. In the meantime, the union petitioned for another election in the same unit which was held in August 1976, and won by the union. Since that election occurred more than one year after the first election, the Board rejected the employer's contention that the 1-year rule was violated.

[82]Robertson Bros. Dep't Store, 95 NLRB 271, 28 LRRM 1335 (1951).

[83]Philadelphia Co., 84 NLRB 115, 24 LRRM 1251 (1949). *See also* Ideal Roller & Mfg. Co. v. Douds, 111 F Supp 156, 32 LRRM 2030 (SDNY, 1953).

[84]Krambo Food Stores, No. 13-RC-57 (NLRB Feb. 14, 1958); Allied Chem. & Dye Corp., No. 5-RC-1745, 1748 (NLRB Aug. 19, 1955) (not reported in Board volumes). Note that the prohibition on the holding of a representation election within a year of a previous election is not a defense to an employer's refusal to bargain with a union on the basis of authorization cards. Conren, Inc., 156 NLRB 592, 61 LRRM 1090 (1966), *enforced,* 368 F2d 173, 63 LRRM 2273 (CA 7, 1966), *cert. denied,* 386 US 974, 64 LRRM 2640

2. The Certification Year. To foster collective bargaining and stabilize industrial relations, the Board has long required that in the absence of unusual circumstances a certified union's majority status must be honored for 1 year; and a petition filed during the 1-year period will ordinarily be barred. In *Brooks v. NLRB*[85] the Court approved the Board's requirement that an employer must recognize a union for the entire "certification year" even if it has evidence of the union's loss of majority, except in "unusual circumstances." Unusual circumstances, according to the Court, include (1) a schism within the certified union or its defunctness and (2) radical fluctuation in the size of the bargaining unit within a short period of time.[86]

The presumption of the union's continuing majority status during the first year of certification is almost conclusive. Even where the employer has objective evidence that the union has lost its majority status during the first year of certification, the duty to bargain must ordinarily be honored for the entire year.[87]

In *Mar-Jac Poultry Co.*[88] the Board modified the policy which the Supreme Court had approved in *Brooks* by extending the presumption of majority status beyond 1 year when the employer's misconduct denies the union a year's fair opportunity to bargain. In *Mar-Jac*, the employer had refused to bargain with the certified union, but later executed a settlement containing a promise to bargain. The Board granted the union

---

(1967). *See* Chapter 12, "Recognition and Withdrawal of Recognition Without an Election."

[85]348 US 96, 35 LRRM 2158 (1954), and cases cited therein; *see also* Nick Trutanich & John Vilicich, 133 NLRB 238, 46 LRRM 1529 (1961); Rocky Mountain Phosphates, 138 NLRB 292, 51 LRRM 1019 (1962). For discussion of schism and defunctness, *see* text at notes 175–181 *infra*. *See also* Chapter 12, "Recognition and Withdrawal of Recognition Without an Election," at notes 313–332.

[86]*See* Children's Habilitation Centers, 289 NLRB No. 109, 129 LRRM 1084 (1988), *enforced*, 887 F2d 130, 132 LRRM 2780 (CA 7, 1989) (duty to recognize union not affected by departure of 4 of 5 employees and reduction of unit size from 5 to 3 during 2 weeks following certification).

[87]Airport-Shuttle Cincinnati, 257 NLRB 955, 108 LRRM 1044 (1981), *enforced*, 703 F2d 220, 112 LRRM 3169 (CA 6, 1983) (union's "total inactivity," coupled with "disaffection" petition signed by 70% of unit employees did not extinguish rights of union during year after certification). *See* NLRB v. Pepsi-Cola Bottling Co., 613 F2d 267, 103 LRRM 2233 (CA 10, 1980). There was a change of ownership during the first year of certification. The successor employer hired 80% of the former employees, operated the business in substantially the same manner as the predecessor, and served the same customers. Even though the company may have been correct in its belief that the union no longer represented a majority of the employees, that good-faith belief was deemed irrelevant in light of the almost conclusive presumption of continuing majority status.

[88]136 NLRB 785, 49 LRRM 1854 (1962) (overruling Daily Press, 112 NLRB 1434, 36 LRRM 1228 (1955), and similar inconsistent cases). *See also* Chicago Health & Tennis Clubs, 251 NLRB 140, 105 LRRM 1009 (1980); J.P. Stevens & Co. 239 NLRB 738, 100 LRRM 1052 (1978).

an additional period of an entire year, dating from the settlement agreement, for actual bargaining. It announced that it would do the same in future cases where similar factors were present. A corollary of this policy is the denial, as untimely, of petitions filed in the extended period. Thus, in *Lamar Hotel*[89] the Board dismissed a decertification petition and gave the union an additional 6 months from the resumption of negotiations because the union had been deprived of its right to an unimpeded opportunity to bargain during 6 months of the certification year.

3. Voluntary Recognition Bar. Voluntary recognition agreements, written or oral, may also constitute a bar to an election.[90] The sufficiency of a recognition agreement depends upon the existence of a union majority at the time of recognition;[91] majority support may be shown by a card check by an impartial third party.[92] Under the Board's *Keller Plastics* rule, once a valid recognition agreement is consummated, the parties have a "reasonable time" in which to negotiate a collective bargaining agreement.[93]

The rule that a recognition agreement is an election bar for a reasonable period of time applies only to the initial organization of the employer's employees. Such an agreement does not bar a decertification election where an alleged successor employer has recognized an incumbent union as the representative of its employees, and where, at the time the decertification petition is filed, the successor employer has not accepted the collective

---

[89]137 NLRB 1271, 50 LRRM 1366 (1962); *see also* Interstate Brick Co., 167 NLRB 831, 66 LRRM 1160 (1967); Mid-City Foundry Co., 167 NLRB 795, 66 LRRM 1154 (1967); Cincinnati Gasket, Packing & Mfg. Co., 163 NLRB 763, 64 LRRM 1455 (1967).

[90]Dale's Super Valu, 181 NLRB 698 (1970); Keller Plastics E., 157 NLRB 583, 61 LRRM 1396 (1966). In Mojave Elec. Coop., 210 NLRB 88, 86 LRRM 1085 (1974), the Board noted that while collective bargaining agreements must be in writing in order to bar representation petitions, a recognition agreement need not be. It held, however, that oral recognition would not bar the petition of an outside union because the employer knew, at the time it orally recognized the incumbent union, that the outside union had substantial support among unit employees.

[91]Keller Plastics E., *supra* note 90. *Cf.* Ladies' Garment Workers (Bernhard-Altmann) v. NLRB, 366 US 731, 48 LRRM 2251 (1961), discussed at notes 9 and 82–83 in Chapter 8, "Employer Domination and Assistance to Labor Organizations."

[92]American Ship Bldg. Co., No. 8-RC-8037, 77 LRRM 1313 (1971) (not reported in Board volumes). The Board found that the incumbent union had made a clear and positive demonstration of employee support which satisfied the employer of its majority status. Additionally, the employer had extended recognition to the incumbent union at a time when no other organizational activity was occurring.

[93]Keller Plastics E., *supra* note 90. *But see* Down River Forest Prods., 205 NLRB 14, 83 LRRM 1504 (1973) (recognition agreement not a bar when 5 months elapsed without consummation of contract, and unit changed from two divisions to a single division with substantial reduction in number of employees.)

bargaining agreement of the predecessor or executed a new agreement with the union.[94] In addition, a voluntary recognition agreement will not be a bar to an election petition where the employer recognizes one union at a time when another union is seeking to organize its employees.[95]

A valid recognition agreement constitutes a bar only if the unit involved meets the requisite standard of appropriateness.[96] The unit need not be precisely described, however. In *Central General Hospital*,[97] the Board held that the parties' recognition agreement covering "medical records employees" was not intended to establish a separate unit of those employees, which would have been inappropriate; rather, it found that the parties had merely intended the recognition agreement to add those employees to an existing unit. The resultant unit was considered "sufficiently appropriate" to render the recognition agreement a bar, since the Board permits parties "the broadest permissible latitude to mutually define the context in which collective bargaining should take place."[98]

B. Pendency of Unfair Labor Practice Charges

Generally, unless the charging party requests the Board to proceed, the Board will decline to direct an election while unfair labor practice charges which affect the unit are pending. The rationale is that the charges, if true, would destroy the "laboratory conditions"[99] necessary to permit employees to cast their ballots freely and without restraint or coercion. This practice is not governed by statute, apart from the exceptional expedited election under section 8(b)(7)(C), or by rules or regulations; rather, it lies within the Board's discretion as part of its responsi-

---

[94]Southern Moldings, 219 NLRB 119, 89 LRRM 1623 (1975). *See* Chapter 15, "Effect of Change in the Employment Unit," for general treatment of successorship.

[95]Rollins Transp. Sys., 296 NLRB No. 108, 132 LRRM 1185 (1989). In that case, the Board declined to "transplant" the rationale of Bruckner Nursing Home, 262 NLRB 955, 110 LRRM 1374 (1982) and, thus, refused to allow the employer to bar an election by granting lawful recognition to one of two competing unions. *See also* Bridgeport Jai Alai, 227 NLRB 1519, 94 LRRM 1435 (1977).

[96]The Board has stated that nothing in the statute requires that the unit for bargaining be the "only" appropriate unit, or the ultimate unit or the most appropriate unit; it need only be appropriate to ensure the employees in each case the fullest freedom in exercising the rights guaranteed by the Act. Morand Bros. Beverage Co., 91 NLRB 409, 26 LRRM 1501 (1950). *See* Chapter 11, "Appropriate Bargaining Units."

[97]223 NLRB 110, 91 LRRM 1433 (1976).

[98]*Id.* at 112.

[99]*See generally* Chapter 9, "Restrictions of Preelection Activity: 'Laboratory Conditions.'"

bility to decide whether an election will effectuate the policies of the Act.[100] This *blocking charge* rule has been held not to violate due process[101] and not to constitute an abuse of discretion by the Board.[102]

The blocking charge rule may be applied even where the charging party requests the Board to proceed, if the issues raised in the charge require resolution in an unfair labor practice proceeding before the holding of an election can be deemed appropriate.[103] Normally, however, when a *request to proceed* is filed the pendency of an unfair labor practice charge will not block an election. In *NLRB v. Tri-City Linen Supply*,[104] the Ninth Circuit held that the Board did not abuse its discretion by scheduling an election during the pendency of unfair labor practice charges against the employer where a request to proceed had been filed by the union; the court also held that the investigation of the charges by a Board agent the day before the election did not adversely affect the voters or the Board's laboratory conditions.[105]

Various exceptions have developed as a result of the Board's common practice of directing elections forthwith as a means of effectuating the policies of the Act. Factors on which the Board has relied to proceed with a representation case, despite the pendency of unfair labor practice charges, include the following: (1) the length of time the proceeding has been pending, (2) the fact that employees in the unit have been without an election during that period, (3) the dismissal of earlier charges that were grounded upon the same basic pattern of conduct as

---

[100]American Metal Prods. Co., 139 NLRB 601, 51 LRRM 1338 (1962). NLRB Field Manual 11730 sets forth the "Blocking Charge Rule" in detail.

[101]Hausley v. NLRB, 81 LRRM 2254 (ED Tenn., 1972).

[102]Gem Int'l v. Hendrix, 80 LRRM 3302 (WD Mo., 1972). *But see* Chapter 33, "Judicial Review and Enforcement," at notes 142–146. The "blocking charge" practice has not been without judicial criticism. *See, e.g.*, NLRB v. Gebhard-Vogel Tanning Co., 389 F2d 71, 67 LRRM 2364 (CA 7, 1968); NLRB v. Minute Maid Corp., 283 F2d 705, 47 LRRM 2072 (CA 5, 1960).

[103]E. & R. Webb, 194 NLRB 1135, 79 LRRM 1163 (1972). The election would have been barred by the agreement between the employer and incumbent union unless the employer's recognition of the incumbent was itself unlawful and violative of §§8(a)(2) and 8(b)(1)(A) and (2) of the Act. The Board reasoned that to make such a determination in the representation case would be contrary to established Board policy that unfair labor practice allegations are not properly litigable in a representation proceeding. *See also* Mistletoe Express Serv. of Tex., 268 NLRB 1245, 115 LRRM 1153 (1984). *But see* Conair Corp. v. NLRB, 721 F2d 1355, 114 LRRM 3169 (CA DC, 1983), *cert. denied sub. nom.* Ladies' Garment Workers Local 222 v. NLRB, 467 US 1241, 116 LRRM 2632 (1984).

[104]579 F2d 51, 98 LRRM 2155 (CA 9, 1978), *enforcing* 226 NLRB 669, 93 LRRM 1431 (1976).

[105]*See also* Bishop v. NLRB, 502 F2d 1024, 87 LRRM 2524 (CA 5, 1974).

the pending charges, (4) "eleventh hour" filing of the charges, (5) the existence of a strike, or (6) a past practice by the charging party of using the filing of charges as a tactic to delay representation proceedings.[106]

The Board has also directed an immediate election on a union's petition notwithstanding the employer's pending section 8(e) charge against the union.[107] The charge was based on an allegedly unlawful hot-cargo contract between the union and an employer association. The Board noted that in contrast to section 8(a) and (b) cases, a section 8(e) charge deals only with the terms of an agreement between an employer and a labor organization. Such an agreement, even if prohibited, would not necessarily restrain or coerce employees or in any other way prevent the holding of a fair election or influence the employees' choice of a bargaining representative.

The Board has also directed an immediate election, despite pending charges, in order to hold the election within 12 months of the beginning of an economic strike so as not to disenfranchise economic strikers.[108]

A petition dismissed because of a pending unfair labor practice charge is subject to reinstatement when the charge is resolved.[109] In *City Markets*,[110] decertification petitions were dismissed in view of the incumbent union's filing of a refusal-to-bargain charge. While the charge was being processed, the union and the employer agreed on a contract and the charge was withdrawn. The Board held that the contract did not bar reinstatement of the decertification petitions and that the dismissal of the petitions did not operate as a determination that the petitions themselves were defective. The original filing date of the petitions controlled for contract-bar purposes.

---

[106]NLRB v. Typographical Union No. 570 (Lawrence), 376 F2d 643, 65 LRRM 2176 (CA 10, 1967); Surprenant Mfg. Co., 144 NLRB 507, 54 LRRM 1097 (1963); West-Gate Sun Harbor Co., 93 NLRB 830, 27 LRRM 1474 (1951); Columbia Pictures Corp., 81 NLRB 1313, 23 LRRM 1504 (1949); Bercut Richards Packing Co., 70 NLRB 84, 18 LRRM 1336 (1946).

[107]Holt Bros., 146 NLRB 383, 55 LRRM 1310 (1964). *See* note 146 *infra.*

[108]Section 9(c)(3) of the Act provides: "Employees engaged in an economic strike who are not entitled to reinstatement shall be eligible to vote . . . in any election conducted within twelve months after the commencement of the strike." *See* American Metal Prods. Co., *supra* note 100. *See* notes 104–105 and accompanying text in Chapter 19, "The Primary Strike."

[109]Passavant Health Center, 278 NLRB 483, 121 LRRM 1230 (1986); Island Spring, 278 NLRB 913, 121 LRRM 1280 (1986).

[110]273 NLRB 469, 118 LRRM 1279 (1984).

C. Unlawful Employer Assistance

Even though no charge is pending, an election petition may be dismissed because of employer domination of, or assistance to, the petitioning union. As noted above, whether the requisite showing of interest has been made is ordinarily an issue for administrative determination rather than for resolution in an adversary proceeding. However, allegations that authorization cards have been obtained with the help of supervisors, accompanied by supporting evidence, will be heard on collateral request to the regional director. If the cards are tainted by reason of supervisory participation, the showing of interest may be found to be impaired and the petition will be dismissed.[111] The dismissal of a petition on these grounds does not affect subsequent proceedings on a new petition, provided a new showing of interest is obtained without the assistance of supervisors.[112]

D. Fluctuating Work Force

A petition for an election in a fluctuating work force will be dismissed, without prejudice to the filing of a petition at a more appropriate time, if it appears that a representative employment complement has not yet been established or if other substantial changes are occurring in the employing entity.[113] However, the Board will not dismiss a petition, despite the employer's anticipated expansion, if the present number of employees represents a substantial percentage of the anticipated employee complement and if they are performing nearly all of the projected job classifications. A substantial and representative segment of the ultimate projected complement of employees has been held

---

[111]Union Mfg. Co., 123 NLRB 1633, 44 LRRM 1188 (1959); Georgia Craft Co., 120 NLRB 806, 42 LRRM 1066 (1958). *See also* Southeastern Newspapers, 129 NLRB 311, 46 LRRM 1541 (1960); Modern Hard Chrome Serv. Co., 124 NLRB 1235, 44 LRRM 1624 (1959); Desilu Prods., 106 NLRB 179, 32 LRRM 1418 (1953); American Dist. Tel. Co., 89 NLRB 1635, 26 LRRM 1135 (1950); Alaska Salmon Indus., 78 NLRB 185, 22 LRRM 1190 (1948). *See* Chapter 8, "Employer Domination and Assistance to Labor Organizations," for general treatment of employer assistance to labor organizations.

[112]Toledo Stamping & Mfg. Co., 56 NLRB 1291, 14 LRRM 192 (1944).

[113]K-P Hydraulics Co., 219 NLRB 138, 89 LRRM 1601 (1975); Some Indus., 204 NLRB 1142, 83 LRRM 1481 (1973); Noranda Aluminum, 186 NLRB 217, 75 LRRM 1328 (1970); Cramet, Inc., 112 NLRB 975, 36 LRRM 1138 (1955).

sufficient to order an election.[114] Moreover, mere speculation[115] as to the uncertainty of future operations will not render a petition untimely.[116]

In seasonal industries, the Board usually directs that the election be held at or about the approximate seasonal peak. If the peak has already passed, the Board will generally fix the election date at or about the next seasonal peak.[117]

No election will be conducted where an employer ceases its operations and the employees have no reasonable expectation of employment in the near future. In *Tracinda Investment Corp.*[118] the Board dismissed a petition for a unit of stagehands where the employer had closed the stage show at a resort facility for economic reasons. The Board held, however, that should the employer open a new show in the near future, the regional director would be authorized to reinstate the petition without prejudice.

E. Contract-Bar Doctrine

In an effort to stabilize the employer-union relationship, the Board has established the *contract-bar* doctrine whereby a current and valid contract will ordinarily prevent the holding of an election. Although now recognized by implication in section 8(b)(7), the doctrine is discretionary, and not statutorily mandated. The formulation, application, and modification of

---

[114]Y & S Candies, 233 NLRB 1311, 97 LRRM 1035 (1977); Cincinnati S.I. Co., 225 NLRB 1196, 93 LRRM 1197 (1976); Hearth Craft, 222 NLRB 1304, 91 LRRM 1387 (1976); World S. Corp., 215 NLRB 287, 87 LRRM 1633 (1974); Some Indus., *supra* note 113; Bell Aerospace Co., 190 NLRB 509, 77 LRRM 1278 (1971).

[115]Canterbury of P.R., 225 NLRB 309, 92 LRRM 1486 (1976); Meramec Mining Co., 134 NLRB 1675, 49 LRRM 1386 (1961); Douglas Motors Corp., 128 NLRB 307, 46 LRRM 1292 (1960); Gordon B. Irvine, 124 NLRB 217, 44 LRRM 1336 (1959); General Eng'g, 123 NLRB 586, 43 LRRM 1486 (1959); General Elec. Co., 106 NLRB 364, 32 LRRM 1465 (1953).

[116]Bekaert Steel Wire Corp., 189 NLRB 561, 76 LRRM 1698 (1971); in Gerlach Meat Co., 192 NLRB 559, 77 LRRM 1832 (1971), the employer's work force at the time of the hearing consisted of 35% of the employee complement working in 50% of the job classifications projected for the nine months following the hearing. The regional director was found to have erroneously applied a projection for a date almost 2 years subsequent to the hearing. The Board applied the earlier projection date and directed an election. *See also* Witteman Steel Mills, 253 NLRB 320, 105 LRRM 1561 (1980). *But see* Risdon Mfg. Co., 195 NLRB 579, 79 LRRM 1442 (1972) (posthearing motion to reopen record appropriate where employer had decided to make substantial corporate changes, which involved moving unit employees from their existing location, thus affecting appropriateness of unit).

[117]Cleveland Cliffs Iron Co., 117 NLRB 668, 39 LRRM 1319 (1957); Bordo Prods. Co., 117 NLRB 313, 39 LRRM 1220 (1957); Dick Kelchner Excavating Co., 236 NLRB 1414, 98 LRRM 1442 (1978).

[118]235 NLRB 1167, 98 LRRM 1089 (1978). *But see* Allegheny Pepsi-Cola Bottling Co., 222 NLRB 1298, 91 LRRM 1369 (1976).

the Board's contract-bar rules are committed to the Board's judgment and are not subject to ordinary judicial review.[119]

1. Requisites of the Contract. In order to bar an otherwise timely petition, a contract must be reduced to writing and executed by the parties.[120] It must also be clearly identifiable as a controlling document[121] and must contain substantial terms and conditions of employment.[122] Ratification by the union membership is not a necessity for upholding a contract as a bar unless the contract itself requires ratification.[123] Ordinarily, the question of whether an agreement constitutes a bar is determined in a representation proceeding based on the face of the document and not upon extrinsic evidence.[124] However, in implementing

---

[119]Carpenters Local 1545 v. Vincent, 286 F2d 127, 47 LRRM 2304 (CA 2, 1960). *But see* NLRB v. Wyman-Gordon Co., 394 US 759, 70 LRRM 3345 (1969); Leedom v. Electrical Workers (IBEW) Local 108, 278 F2d 237, 45 LRRM 3005 (CA DC, 1960). *See* Chapter 33, "Judicial Review and Enforcement."

[120]The agreement need not be formally executed to constitute a bar. Gaylord Broadcasting, Television Station WVTC, 250 NLRB 198, 104 LRRM 1360 (1980) (parties' initials constituted sufficient signatures for contract-bar purposes); Georgia Purchasing, 230 NLRB 1174, 1175, 95 LRRM 1469 (1977) (exchange of telegrams between employer and union, when read in conjunction with prior agreement which it incorporated by reference, charted "with adequate precision a continuing contractual relationship between the parties"); Diversified Servs., 225 NLRB 1092, 93 LRRM 1068 (1976) (employer's signed cover letter accompanying unsigned proposal, coupled with union's execution of proposal prior to filing of petition, created contract bar). *See also* Bendix Corp., 210 NLRB 1026, 86 LRRM 1547 (1974) (informal letter of agreement signed by parties on date that petition was filed). *Cf.* Lane Constr. Corp., 222 NLRB 1224, 91 LRRM 1337 (1976). Where the history of collective bargaining reveals that persons or entities other than the certified bargaining agent and the employer have become parties to the contract, all such parties, such as the national union, must sign the contract. Crothall Hosp. Servs., 270 NLRB 1420, 117 LRRM 1072 (1984); *but see* Pharmaseal Laboratories, 199 NLRB 324, 81 LRRM 1215 (1972) (contract signed by only one of two jointly certified local unions constituted a bar).

[121]In Delto Co., 202 NLRB 921, 82 LRRM 1725 (1973), the Board was confronted with two substantially identical collective bargaining agreements between the same parties. One contained an automatic renewal clause, whereas the other did not. An outside union filed a petition which would have been timely if the disputed renewal clause was invalid. The incumbent union relied upon the contract containing the renewal clause, while the employer argued for the contract which lacked the renewal clause. Unable to determine which contract was controlling, the Board decided there was no contract bar.

[122]*See* J.P. Sand & Gravel Co., 222 NLRB 83, 91 LRRM 1187 (1976) (contract provided neither employees nor employer with "guidance in governing their day-to-day relations" and did not impart "sufficient stability to the bargaining relationship" to justify a bar).

[123]Appalachian Shale Prods. Co., 121 NLRB 1160, 42 LRRM 1506 (1958) (overruling numerous earlier cases and eliminating exceptions). In Merico, Inc., 207 NLRB 101, 84 LRRM 1395 (1973), the agreement stated that "the Union Committee is unanimous for acceptance and each member is hereby pledged to recommend this agreement for ratification by the membership." The Board held that such language required ratification as a condition precedent to the agreement's validity, and accordingly did not find a contract bar.

The Board has also ruled that where a number of locals of an incumbent union negotiate a master contract which is "subject to ratification by the Local Unions," the agreement may operate as a bar if a majority of locals vote in favor of it prior to filing of a petition. Swift & Co., 213 NLRB 49, 87 LRRM 1041 (1974).

[124]Jet-Pak Corp., 231 NLRB 552, 96 LRRM 1112 (1977); Loree Footwear Corp., 197 NLRB 360, 80 LRRM 1339 (1972); Pine Transp., 197 NLRB 256, 80 LRRM 1334 (1972);

its discretionary contract-bar rules the Board has developed an exception to this general principle: A bar will not be found where it appears that the alleged contract is not "'one imparting sufficient stability to the bargaining relationship to justify . . . withholding a present determination of representation.'"[125] An agreement authorized by section 8(f) does not bar an election.[126]

2. Duration of the Contract. A contract must also have a definite duration if it is to serve as a bar to an election; it will then preclude petitions by either the employer or a certified incumbent union for the entire term of the agreement.[127] Petitions by rival unions, however, are barred only for a reasonable part of the term of an agreement if the agreement is of unreasonably long duration. An uncertified incumbent union may file a petition during the term of an agreement where it seeks the benefits of certification—the *General Box* doctrine.[128]

In the 1958 *Pacific Coast* case the Board abandoned, as "administratively burdensome,"[129] a rule that made the reasonable duration of a barring contract vary by industry. Two years was determined to be a reasonable period applicable to all indus-

---

Paragon Prods. Corp., 134 NLRB 662, 49 LRRM 1160 (1961). *But see infra* note 133 and accompanying text.

[125]Frank Hager, Inc., 230 NLRB 476, 476, 96 LRRM 1117 (1977) (quoting Raymonds, Inc., 161 NLRB 838, 840, 63 LRRM 1363 (1966)). In order to bar a petition, a contract must embrace an appropriate unit. Moveable Partitions, 175 NLRB 915, 71 LRRM 1095 (1969); Appalachian Shale Prods. Co., *supra* note 123. *Cf.* Stur-Dee Health Prods., 248 NLRB 1100, 104 LRRM 1012 (1980), where the Board held that an agreement providing for interest arbitration is sufficiently complete, even prior to the arbitration award, on the ground that "the agreement . . . contains substantial terms and conditions of employment as well as a definite and readily ascertainable method for determining economic terms." *Id.* at 1101.

[126]John Deklewa & Sons, 282 NLRB 1375, 124 LRRM 1185 (1987), *enforced sub nom.* Iron Workers Local 3 v. NLRB, 843 F2d 770, 128 LRRM 2020 (CA 3), *cert. denied,* 488 US 889, 129 LRRM 2528 (1988). But if the union wins the election, it becomes the §9(c) representative and the prior §8(f) agreement enjoys the status of a bar. *See supra* note 61.

[127]Cind-R-Lite Co., 239 NLRB 1255, 100 LRRM 1138 (1979); Kroger Co., 173 NLRB 397, 69 LRRM 1333 (1968); Pacific Coast Ass'n of Pulp & Paper Mfrs., 121 NLRB 990, 42 LRRM 1477 (1958). *See* Absorbent Cotton Co., 137 NLRB 908, 50 LRRM 1258 (1962); Montgomery Ward & Co., 137 NLRB 346, 50 LRRM 1137 (1962).

[128]General Box Co., 82 NLRB 678, 23 LRRM 1589 (1949).

[129]Pacific Coast Ass'n of Pulp & Paper Mfrs., *supra* note 127, at 992. The Board's position had evolved after experience with a variety of tests. Originally, a one-year contract was thought to be reasonable in conjunction with the test of "custom in the industry." Presumptions of reasonableness would vary in accordance with industry custom. That rule, with its many problems of proof, was difficult to administer. For a discussion of this earlier development and application, see Cushman's Sons, 88 NLRB 121, 25 LRRM 1296 (1950); Puritan Ice Co., 74 NLRB 1311, 20 LRRM 1268 (1947); Reed Roller Bit Co., 72 NLRB 927, 19 LRRM 1227 (1947).

tries. Then in 1962, in *General Cable Corp.*,[130] the Board discarded that rule in favor of a uniform 3-year rule which is still in effect. Thus, contracts of a definite duration for terms up to 3 years bar election petitions for the entire period, and contracts for longer fixed terms operate as a bar to rival petitions for the first 3 years.

If, during the term of a contract, the parties agree to an amendment, or execute a new contract which contains a terminal date later than that of the existing contract, the amendment or new contract will be considered "premature"; a prematurely extended contract will not bar an election if the petition is otherwise timely.[131] This *premature extension* doctrine does not apply (1) to contracts executed during the insulated period preceding the terminal date (or first 3 years) of the old contract, (2) after the terminal date (or first 3 years) of the old contract, or (3) at a time when the existing contract would not have barred an election because of other contract-bar rules.[132]

The duration dates contained in a contract are not always determinative, for the Board will look behind "inartful drafting" to establish actual contract duration in the light of bargaining history.[133]

3. Unlawful Clauses. The Board has frequently considered whether an election should be barred by an existing contract which contains provisions that are, or might be, unlawful. As with many other issues concerning contract-bar application, it has attempted to strike a balance between the interests of industrial stability and the right of employees to select bargaining representatives.

a. Union Security. In the 1958 *Keystone* case,[134] the Board ruled that contracts containing union-security and checkoff provisions

---

[130]139 NLRB 1123, 51 LRRM 1444 (1962).

[131]*See* discussion *infra* at notes 184–200 for rules concerning timeliness of petitions.

[132]Shen-Valley Meat Packers, 261 NLRB 958, 110 LRRM 1121 (1982) (5-year agreement was bar where parties renegotiated terms after 3 years); Deluxe Metal Furniture Co., 121 NLRB 995, 42 LRRM 1470 (1958). *But see* Crompton Co., 260 NLRB 417, 109 LRRM 1161 (1982) (new agreement for fixed duration less than 90 days not a bar).

[133]Youngstown Osteopathic Hosp. Ass'n, 216 NLRB 766, 88 LRRM 1591 (1975). However, parties to a contract may be estopped from asserting that the effective dates of the agreement are other than as shown on the cover of printed copies if a petitioning union is thereby precluded from making a clear determination as to the proper time for filing its petition. Marriott Corp., Bob's Big Boy Family Restaurants, Div., 259 NLRB 153, 108 LRRM 1296 (1981), *enforcement denied*, 693 F2d 904, 111 LRRM 3132 (CA 9, 1984).

[134]Keystone Coat, Apron & Towel Supply Co., 121 NLRB 880, 42 LRRM 1456 (1958). *See generally* Chapter 27, "Union Security," for treatment of checkoff and union-security agreements.

would not bar elections unless on their face they conformed to the express terms of the Act. The effect of this rule of interpretation in *Keystone* was to "require a presumption of illegality"[135] with respect to any contract containing a union-security clause that did not expressly reflect the precise language of the statute. In 1961, in the *News Syndicate* case,[136] the Supreme Court cast serious doubt upon the exercise of administrative discretion based on the attachment of presumptions of illegality to provisions in collective bargaining agreements. Accordingly, in *Paragon Products Corp.*,[137] the Board, adverting to the "unsettling" of bargaining relationships engendered by the *Keystone* rules, reformulated its position as follows:

> [O]nly those contracts containing a union-security provision which is clearly unlawful on its face, or which has been found to be unlawful in an unfair labor practice proceeding, [will fail to] bar a representation petition. A clearly unlawful union-security provision for this purpose is one which by its express terms clearly and unequivocally goes beyond the limited form of union-security permitted by Section 8(a)(3) of the Act, and is therefore incapable of a lawful interpretation.[138]

Provisions unlawful under this rule would include: a clause by which the employer agrees to give union members preference in hiring, layoff, or other terms of employment; a clause specifically denying new employees, or incumbent nonunion employees, the statutory 30-day grace period; or a clause requiring the payment to the union of money other than "periodic dues and initiation fees uniformly required.[139]

In further clarification, the Board held that absent express contractual saving features, the "mere existence of a clearly unlawful union security provision in a contract will render it no bar"[140] regardless of whether it was intended to be enforced. However, two means of curing the defect were recognized: (1) inclusion of an express contractual provision clearly deferring the effectiveness of the unlawful clause or (2) elimination of

---

[135]Paragon Prods. Corp., *supra* note 124, at 664.
[136]NLRB v. News Syndicate Co., 365 US 695, 47 LRRM 2916 (1961).
[137]*Supra* note 124.
[138]*Id.*
[139]Section 8(a)(3).
[140]134 NLRB at 667. For applications of the *Paragon Products* principle, see Sentry Investigation Corp., 198 NLRB 1074, 81 LRRM 1046 (1972); Liquid Transport, No. 7-RC-10741, 78 LRRM 1248 (1971) (not reported in Board volumes).

the unlawful clause by properly executed rescission or amendment.[141] The Supreme Court accorded these so-called "deferral clauses" this saving virtue in two 1961 cases.[142]

b. Checkoff. The Board has similarly relaxed the rule governing checkoff clauses, since *Keystone* was applicable to such clauses in the same manner as to other union-security provisions.[143] Currently, a checkoff clause does not affect the standing of a contract as a bar to an election unless it is unlawful on its face, or has been held unlawful in an unfair labor practice proceeding or in a court proceeding brought by the Attorney General.[144]

c. Racial Discrimination. A contract that discriminates between groups of employees by reason of race will not operate as a bar to an election.[145] Such discrimination is inherent in agreements that sanction groupings of employees along racial lines, and the Board has concluded that to permit its rules to be used to shield such contracts from election petitions would in effect extend governmental sanction to such discrimination.

d. "Hot Cargo." Although a clause may violate section 8(e), the Board distinguishes between "hot-cargo" and unlawful union-security provisions, holding that the hot-cargo clause does not act as a restraint upon the employees' choice of a bargaining representative. Therefore, the presence of a clause that violates section 8(e) does not remove the contract as a bar.[146]

4. Expanding Units. The contract-bar doctrine formulated in *General Extrusion*[147] establishes guidelines for determining whether an election should be directed in an expanding unit in the face of a valid contract. Decided in 1958 along with many of

---

[141]134 NLRB at 667. For a specific application, see American Broadcasting Co., 134 NLRB 1458, 49 LRRM 1365 (1961); Columbia Broadcasting Sys., 134 NLRB 1466, 49 LRRM 1366 (1961).

[142]NLRB v. News Syndicate Co., *supra* note 136; Typographical Union Local 38 v. NLRB (Haverhill Gazette), 365 US 705, 47 LRRM 2920 (1961).

[143]The first modification was a response to certain Department of Justice interpretations. William Wolf Bakery, Inc., 122 NLRB 630, 43 LRRM 1447 (1958). Further relaxation came in Boston Gas Co., 129 NLRB 369, 46 LRRM 1546 (1960) *and* 130 NLRB 1230, 47 LRRM 1429 (1961).

[144]Gary Steel Supply Co., 144 NLRB 470, 54 LRRM 1082 (1963).

[145]Pioneer Bus Co., 140 NLRB 54, 51 LRRM 1546 (1962). *See* Chapter 26, "The Duty of Fair Representation," at note 138.

[146]Food Haulers, 136 NLRB 394, 49 LRRM 1774 (1962) (overruling Calorator Mfg. Corp., 129 NLRB 704, 47 LRRM 1109 (1960); American Feed Co., 129 NLRB 321, 46 LRRM 1541 (1960); Pilgrim Furniture Co., 128 NLRB 910, 46 LRRM 1427 (1960)). The same policy obtains when the §8(e) question takes the form of a blocking charge of unfair labor practice. Holt Bros., 146 NLRB 383, 55 LRRM 1310 (1964). For general treatment of "hot-cargo" clauses, see Chapter 24, "Section 8(e): The 'Hot-Cargo' Agreement."

[147]121 NLRB 1165, 42 LRRM 1508 (1958).

the landmark contract-bar cases,[148] *General Extrusion* laid down a series of rules relating to prehire agreements, relocation and consolidation, and good-faith purchasers.

a. Prehire Agreements. A contract executed before any employees have been hired, or prior to a "substantial increase" in personnel, does not bar an election. When a question of a substantial increase in personnel exists, an agreement will bar an election only if (1) "at least 30 percent of the complement employed at the time of the hearing had been employed at the time the contract was executed"[149] *and*[150] (2) "50 percent of the job classifications in existence at the time of the hearing were in existence at the time the contract was executed."[151]

When a successor employer lawfully negotiates an agreement with the incumbent union, the agreement is a bar. Unlike an employer in a premature contract situation, who is under an obligation *not* to bargain until a representative complement of employees has been hired, a successor employer is under an immediate and continuing obligation to bargain.[152]

b. Relocation and Consolidation. In *General Extrusion* the Board distinguished between a "relocation of operations" and a "consolidation of two or more operations."[153] It stated that a contract would not be a bar if changes had occurred in the "*nature* as

---

[148]*See* Deluxe Metal Furniture Co., *supra* note 132; Appalachian Shale Prods. Co., 121 NLRB 1160, 42 LRRM 1506 (1958); Hershey Chocolate Corp., 121 NLRB 901, 42 LRRM 1460 (1958); Keystone Coat, Apron & Towel Supply Co., *supra* note 134; Pacific Coast Ass'n of Pulp & Paper Mfrs., 121 NLRB 990, 42 LRRM 1447 (1958).

[149]General Extrusion Co., *supra* note 147, at 1167. But the actual date of signing may not in all instances be determinative. *See* H.L. Klion, 148 NLRB 656, 660, 57 LRRM 1073 (1964).

[150]Although the conjunctive "and" is used in General Extrusion Co., *supra* note 147, it was reemphasized in West Penn Hat & Cap Corp., 165 NLRB 543, 543 n.1, 65 LRRM 1417 (1967). *See also* United Serv. Co., 227 NLRB 1469, 94 LRRM 1250 (1977).

[151]121 NLRB at 1167. A contract executed with a minority union pursuant to §8(f), although a legal contract, cannot function as a bar to a representation petition. John Deklewa & Sons, 282 NLRB 1375, 124 LRRM 1185 (1987), *enforced sub nom.* Iron Workers Local 3 v. NLRB, 843 F2d 770, 128 LRRM 2020 (CA 3), *cert. denied,* 488 US 889, 129 LRRM 2528 (1988). However, if the union attained majority status prior to the execution of the agreement, the ordinary rules of contract bar will apply. Mishara Constr. Co., 171 NLRB 471, 68 LRRM 1120 (1968); Island Constr. Co., 135 NLRB 13, 49 LRRM 1417 (1962). *See* Chapter 13, "The Duty to Bargain," at notes 834–850, and Chapter 27, "Union Security," at notes 158–191.

[152]General Elec. Co., 173 NLRB 511, 69 LRRM 1395 (1968); Western Freight Ass'n, 172 NLRB 303, 68 LRRM 1364 (1958). There is more than a little conflict in the rationale of these cases. That difficulty has been reduced by the evolving requirement of a substantial and representative complement as a precondition to any duty to bargain by a putative successor employer. *See* NLRB v. Fall River Dyeing & Finishing Corp., 482 US 27, 125 LRRM 2441 (1987).

[153]Kroger Co., 155 NLRB 546, 548, 60 LRRM 1351 (1965). The Board in *General Extrusion* did not actually use the term "consolidation," but in *Kroger* the distinction was so characterized.

distinguished from the *size* of the operations between the execution of the contract and the filing of the petition, involving (1) a merger of two or more operations resulting in the creation of an entirely new operation with major personnel changes,"[154] *or* "(2) resumption of operations at either the same or a new location, after an indefinite period of closing, with new employees."[155] The Board distinguishes these patterns from a "mere relocation" involving a considerable transfer of employees to another plant without a change in the character of the jobs and the functions of the employees. In the latter situation, the contract will not be removed as a bar.

Following a merger of two or more corporate entities covered by separate contracts with different unions, a resulting integration of operations may be found to be a new operation. In these circumstances the existing bargaining agreements may be deemed abrogated, and previously existing separate bargaining units may no longer be considered appropriate.[156]

---

[154]121 NLRB at 1167 (emphasis added). In *Kroger,* the contract bar was not upheld because of a merger of two or more operations. Plants *A* and *B* were closed and their operations transferred to plant *C*. Of the 69 employees at *C*, 42 were from *A* and 27 from *B*. The Board held that this created an entirely new operation with major personnel changes on the ground that plant *C* could not be regarded simply as a relocation of *B* to the exclusion of *A*. *Accord* General Elec. Co., 170 NLRB 1272, 67 LRRM 1561 (1968), where facilities *A* and *B* merged into *C* and the Board found *C* to be an "amalgam of the two separate facilities" rather than a "relocation." Determinative factors were (1) the uncertainty of the proportion of employees transferring, (2) consolidation of different product lines, and (3) changes in supervisory personnel. *See also* Mego Corp., 223 NLRB 279, 92 LRRM 1080 (1976). *Contra* Arrow Co., 147 NLRB 829, 56 LRRM 1303 (1964), where the Board found a "relocation" and upheld the bar where plants *A* and *B* closed and operations were transferred to *C*. Of 78 employees at *C*, 45 were from *A* and 5 tentatively from *B*. The basis of the holding was that "when the relocation . . . is complete," a "considerable portion" of the employees at *A* and *B* "will have been transferred" to *C*. On this basis, the decision is difficult to square with *General Extrusion* on timeliness and with *Kroger* and *General Electric* on the conclusion reached. Also puzzling was the Board's use of the term "consolidation" along with "relocation." The other ground for decision was that intervenor at *C* was the incumbent at both *A* and *B*. *See also* Bowman Dairy Co., 123 NLRB 707, 43 LRRM 1519 (1959), where a contract bar was upheld. *Bowman* was distinguished in *Kroger* on the ground that it simply involved plant *A* merging into an existing plant *B*, without there being a newly constructed plant *C*, as in *Kroger*.

[155]121 NLRB at 1167. For this precise fact situation, see Slater Sys. Md., 134 NLRB 865, 49 LRRM 1294 (1961). *See also* Sheets & Mackey, 92 NLRB 179, 27 LRRM 1087 (1950).

[156]Martin Marietta Chems., 270 NLRB, 821, 116 LRRM 1150 (1984); Massachusetts Elec. Co., 248 NLRB 155, 103 LRRM 1404 (1980); Hooker Electrochem. Co., 116 NLRB 1393, 38 LRRM 1482 (1965); Pacific Isle Mining Co., 118 NLRB 740, 40 LRRM 1253 (1957); Industrial Stamping & Mfg. Co., 111 NLRB 1038, 35 LRRM 1648 (1955); L.B. Spear & Co., 106 NLRB 687, 32 LRRM 1535 (1953); Greyhound Garage, 95 NLRB 902, 28 LRRM 1388 (1951). *See also* Hudson Berlind Corp., 203 NLRB 421, 83 LRRM 1090 (1973), *enforced,* 494 F2d 1200, 86 LRRM 2008 (CA 2), *cert. denied,* 419 US 897, 87 LRRM 2453 (1974); General Elec. Co., *supra* note 154 (where this issue was raised in an accretion context); National Carloading Corp., 167 NLRB 801, 66 LRRM 1166 (1967); Panda Terminals, 161 NLRB 1215, 63 LRRM 1419 (1966).

On the other hand, if, after merger, the previously independent companies continue as separate operating divisions of the newly created corporate entity (absent evidence of substantial integration and the factors of common operation discussed above), the preexisting bargaining units, together with their collective bargaining relationships, will remain in existence.[157]

c. Purchasers. Under another *General Extrusion* rule, assumption of an operation by a good-faith purchaser who had not bound itself to assume the contract of a predecessor would remove the contract as a bar. This was a reaffirmance of an earlier rule.[158] The Board later held that, absent unusual circumstances, a successor employer was bound as a matter of law by the contract of the predecessor,[159] but the Supreme Court rejected that ruling, declaring that a successor does not automatically assume the predecessor's contract.[160] Thus, the *General Extrusion* rule continues to apply to a purchase situation where the contract is not assumed.

5. Accretions. An employer's acquisition or construction of an additional operation or facility after the execution of the contract frequently gives rise to a claim of accretion. One or both of the contracting parties may seek to have the additional facility "accreted." If the additional facility is found to be an accretion to the existing operation, the preexisting contract may be extended to cover employees in the new operation and thus bar an election there. The question of accretion can arise in myriad factual and procedural contexts,[161] but in most instances the Board follows

---

[157]Consolidated Edison Co., 132 NLRB 1518, 48 LRRM 1539, *supplemented,* 134 NLRB 1137, 49 LRRM 1341 (1961); Illinois Malleable Iron Co., 120 NLRB 451, 41 LRRM 1510 (1958); United Illuminating Co., No. 1-RC-6586 (1962) (not reported in Board volumes).

[158]Jolly Giant Lumber Co., 114 NLRB 413, 36 LRRM 1585 (1955).

[159]Burns Int'l Sec. Serv., 182 NLRB 348, 74 LRRM 1098 (1970), *enforcement denied in pertinent part,* 441 F2d 911, 77 LRRM 2081 (CA 2, 1971), *aff'd,* 406 US 272, 80 LRRM 2225 (1972).

[160]*Id. Accord* Howard Johnson Co. v. Hotel Employees, Detroit Executive Bd., 417 US 249, 86 LRRM 2449 (1974). *See* NLRB v. Fall River Dyeing & Finishing Corp., *supra* note 152. *See* Chapter 15, "Effect of Change in the Employing Unit: Successorship," at notes 62–69.

[161]Procedurally, accretion may become an issue in situations in addition to the "contract-bar" disputes, including: (1) unit-clarification proceedings, *infra,* and (2) as a defense to an unfair labor practice charge. Masters-Lake Success, 124 NLRB 580, 44 LRRM 1437 (1959), *enforced as modified,* 287 F2d 35, 47 LRRM 2607 (CA 2, 1967). *See also* Great Atl. & Pac. Tea Co., 140 NLRB 1011, 52 LRRM 1155 (1963) (exhaustive discussion of accretion doctrine by trial examiner). Factually, accretion can involve a prototype situation such as the opening of a new store by a retail chain, Sunset House, 167 NLRB 870, 66 LRRM 1243 (1967), *enforced,* 415 F2d 545, 72 LRRM 2283 (CA 9, 1969); or a subdivision of store units, Parkview Drugs, 138 NLRB 194, 50 LRRM 1564 (1962); or categories of employees, Horn & Hardart Co., 173 NLRB 1077, 69 LRRM 1522 (1968). It can also involve extremely complex fact situations, as where two unions each seek to accrete the facility at which the other has a contract. Panda Terminals, *supra* note 156.

established guidelines in deciding whether an election will be conducted in the added operation or facility.

The guidelines take into account a variety of factors such as: (1) the degree of interchange among employees;[162] (2) geographical proximity;[163] (3) integration of operations; (4) integration of machinery and product lines;[164] (5) centralized administrative control;[165] (6) similarity of working conditions, skills, and functions;[166] (7) common control over labor relations;[167] (8) collective bargaining history; and (9) the number of employees at the facility proposed for accretion as compared with the existing operation.[168] These factors determine the basic issue of whether the new[169] facility is sufficiently integrated into the existing operation to justify the application of the contract as a bar.[170] The board has consistently indicated a somewhat restrictive attitude toward accretions in deference to the important statutory policy of employee free choice.[171] Thus, a new

---

[162]Dura Corp., 153 NLRB 592, 59 LRRM 1519 (1965), *enforced*, 375 F2d 707, 64 LRRM 2828 (CA 6, 1967); Buy Low Supermarket, 131 NLRB 23, 47 LRRM 1586 (1961).

[163]Meijer, Inc. v. NLRB, 564 F2d 737, 96 LRRM 2738 (CA 6, 1977), *enforcing* 222 NLRB 18, 91 LRRM 1153 (1976); Sunset House, *supra* note 161; Pay Less Drug Stores, 127 NLRB 160, 45 LRRM 1520 (1960).

[164]Beacon Photo Serv., 163 NLRB 706, 64 LRRM 1439 (1967).

[165]Masters-Lake Success, *supra* note 161.

[166]Public Serv. Co., 190 NLRB 350, 77 LRRM 1129 (1971).

[167]Buy Low Supermarket, *supra* note 162.

[168]Panda Terminals, *supra* note 156 (no accretion where new operation had four times as many employees as old one). *See also* Renaissance Center Partnership, 239 NLRB 1247, 100 LRRM 1121 (1979), in which a union was certified as the bargaining representative for security officers and guards employed by the employer for certain facilities. The employer began providing security for a hotel and consolidated its existing security force with that already serving the hotel. The union sought to clarify the existing certified unit to include the hotel's security force, and the employer objected. The Board found that the hotel's security force was not an accretion to the certified bargaining unit and that the certified unit was no longer appropriate, and directed an election among all the employees. The Board relied on the fact that the employees the union sought to add to the certified unit exceeded the number already within that unit. *See also* United Hosps., 249 NLRB 562, 104 LRRM 1163 (1980) (hospital's unrepresented admitting-department employees and those of another facility with which it was merging did not constitute accretion to a service and maintenance unit covered by a multi-employer contract, since these employees were traditionally excluded from the multi-employer unit).

[169]However, the Board's accretion guidelines may also apply to a consolidation of existing facilities. Public Serv. Co., *supra* note 166.

[170]*E.g.*, Bryan Infants Wear, 235 NLRB 1305, 98 LRRM 1140 (1978). *But see* Safeway Stores, 256 NLRB 918, 107 LRRM 1338 (1981) (guidelines not controlling where employer manipulated acquisition process to favor particular union).

[171]Super Valu Stores, 283 NLRB 134, 124 LRRM 1294 (1987); Rainey Sec. Agency, 274 NLRB 269, 119 LRRM 1043 (1985); Safeway Stores, 276 NLRB 944, 120 LRRM 1186 (1985); Towne Ford Sales, 270 NLRB 311, 116 LRRM 1066 (1984), *enforced*, 759 F2d 1477, 119 LRRM 2488 (CA 9, 1985). *See also* NLRB v. Stevens Ford, 773 F2d 468, 120 LRRM 2589 (CA 2, 1985), *denying enforcement to* 272 NLRB 907, 117 LRRM 1404 (1984); Martin Marietta Chems., *supra* note 156. In Lear Siegler, Safelite Div., 277 NLRB 782, 121 LRRM 1011 (1985), the Board found a runaway shop to be an accretion to the branch unit it sought to replace. The runaway shop was opened before the first branch closed, performed identical work, and served two-thirds of the first branch's customers.

facility would likely be treated as an independent operation and not an accretion where (1) new employees are hired specifically for the new facility, (2) the facility is separately managed, (3) there is no interchange of employees between the new and previous operations, and (4) either the facilities are geographically distant or the operation of the new facility is autonomous despite close geographical proximity.[172]

A conflict occasionally arises where the contracting parties have negotiated an "accretion clause" that clearly covers any new operation the employer may subsequently own or operate. The Board is then confronted with the alternatives of (1) treating this issue as one of contract interpretation or (2) determining for itself, in accordance with its own guidelines, whether an accretion exists. The Board has refused to find the contract a bar to a petition without its own independent determination that the new facilities represented an accretion to the contract unit.[173] The Board has also held that where the union seeking to apply an accretion clause in a collective agreement fails to present the employer with proof that it has acquired majority status at the new facility, the employer is not obligated to extend recognition.[174]

6. Schism, Defunctness, and Disclaimer. The Board has long held that a mere change in designation or affiliation of the contractual representative of the employees does not remove an otherwise valid and subsisting contract as a bar. However, the Board does disregard the contract when the contracting union has become defunct. It also holds the contract to be no longer a bar if a schism arises and destroys the identity of the contractual bargaining representative.

---

[172]Renaissance Center Partnership, *supra* note 168; W.C. DuComb Co, 239 NLRB 964, 100 LRRM 1061 (1978); Pay Less Drug Stores, *supra* note 163. *See also* Denver Publishing Co., 238 NLRB 207, 99 LRRM 1222 (1978); Illinois Bell Tel. Co., 222 NLRB 485, 91 LRRM 1274 (1976).

[173]Pullman Indus., 159 NLRB 580, 62 LRRM 1273 (1966). *See also* W.C. DuComb Co., *supra* note 172; Anheuser-Busch, 170 NLRB 46, 67 LRRM 1376 (1968); Beacon Photo Serv., *supra* note 164. *But compare* Horn & Hardart Co., *supra* note 161 *and* Westinghouse Elec. Corp., 162 NLRB 768, 64 LRRM 1082 (1967) *with* Raley's, Inc., 143 NLRB 256, 53 LRRM 1347 (1963), involving interpretations of contracts regarding preexisting facilities or employee categories. Accommodation of Board action to the arbitration process is treated in detail in Chapter 18, "Accommodation of Board Action to the Arbitration Process." See particularly discussion of representation cases therein at notes 322–338.

[174]Geo. V. Hamilton, Inc., 289 NLRB 1335, 129 LRRM 1067 (1988) (overruling in this respect Public Serv. Co., *supra* note 166). *See* Central Soya Co., 281 NLRB 1308, 124 LRRM 1026 (1986), *aff'd*, 867 F2d 1245, 130 LRRM 2915 (CA 10, 1988) (accretion found where slight majority of employees at new facility were transferred from similar existing facility).

a. Schism. Generally speaking, a schism occurs when a substantial number of the employees in the unit express dissatisfaction with their representation. The crosscurrent must be so compelling that (1) there is a basic intraunion conflict over fundamental policy questions and (2) employees take action which creates such confusion in the bargaining relationship that stability can be restored only by an election. To be described as a "schism" for this purpose, the conflict must pervade the local as well as the national or international level and be so disruptive as to warrant the conclusion that industrial stability would be served by affording the employees an opportunity to select a new bargaining representative. Thus far, however, the only kinds of policy splits which the Board has considered schismatic have involved issues relating to communism or corruption.[175]

b. Defunctness. A contract by an employer with a union that has become defunct will not operate as a bar.[176] Generally, the Board holds a union to be defunct if it has ceased to exist as an effective labor organization and is no longer able or willing to fulfill its responsibilities in administering the contract. The Board looks to whether the union has been processing grievances, holding meetings of the members, collecting dues, and electing officers, but the inquiry concentrates on present willingness and ability to represent, and not on mere inactivity.[177] The absence of anyone remaining in the union to discharge the representative's responsibilities would show that the union is defunct. However, procedural steps taken to disaffiliate and sever all connection with the national or international union ordinarily are not sufficient to establish defunctness.[178]

Moreover, the Board has recognized that unions may be tempted to use the claim of schism or defunctness as a means to

---

[175]Hershey Chocolate Corp., 121 NLRB 901, 42 LRRM 1460 (1958); Great Atl. & Pac. Tea Co., 120 NLRB 656, 42 LRRM 1022 (1958); Lawrence Leather Co., 108 NLRB 546, 34 LRRM 1022 (1954). *See also* Swift & Co., 145 NLRB 756, 55 LRRM 1033 (1963); Clayton & Lambert Mfg. Co., 128 NLRB 209, 46 LRRM 1275 (1960). *Cf.* American Seating Co., 106 NLRB 250, 32 LRRM 1439 (1953); Prudential Ins. Co., 106 NLRB 237, 32 LRRM 1448 (1953).

[176]Francis L. Bennett, 139 NLRB 1422, 51 LRRM 1518 (1962).

[177]*Cf.* Kent Corp., 272 NLRB 735, 117 LRRM 1333 (1984) (union not defunct where newly appointed officer declared readiness to represent bargaining-unit employees).

[178]Aircraft Turbine Serv., 173 NLRB 709, 69 LRRM 1406 (1968); Swift & Co., *supra* note 175; Polar Ware Co., 139 NLRB 1006, 51 LRRM 1452 (1962); Hebron Brick Co., 135 NLRB 245, 49 LRRM 1463 (1962); Pepsi-Cola Bottling Co., 132 NLRB 1441, 48 LRRM 1514 (1961); W.H. Nicholson & Co., 119 NLRB 1412, 41 LRRM 1319 (1958); A.O. Smith Corp., 107 NLRB 1415, 33 LRRM 1393 (1954).

circumvent the contract-bar doctrine. Accordingly, the Board considers the element of good faith. Where it appeared that the real purpose of the claim was to rid the local members of a disfavored contract, the Board has held the contract to be a bar to effectuate the policies of the Act.[179] The Board has also rejected arguments that an "old" union was defunct, where it has found that the "new" union was in fact the "alter ego" or "successor" to the old union.[180]

c. Disclaimer. When a viable incumbent union disclaims interest in continuing to represent the employees covered by a contract, the situation is different from schism or defunctness; the union has experienced no internal change and is capable of administering the contract. The disclaimer might result from genuine employee rejection of the union, but it might also be a means to permit escape from an unfavorable contract by having another union replace the incumbent and attempt to negotiate a more favorable contract.[181] In either event, the stability of the bargaining relationship engendered by the existing contract is impaired. It has been difficult for the Board, in these disclaimer cases, to reconcile the competing interests of free employee choice of a representative and stability in the bargaining relationship. In the same year, it held in one case that a disclaimer does not remove a contract as a bar[182] but in another case held that it may have such an effect, absent evidence of collusion between the incumbent and intervening unions.[183]

---

[179]*Schism*: Allied Container Corp., 98 NLRB 580, 29 LRRM 1388 (1952); Saginaw Furniture Shops, 97 NLRB 1488, 29 LRRM 1281 (1952).

Defunctness: News-Press Publishing Co., 145 NLRB 803, 55 LRRM 1045 (1964); Hebron Brick Co., *supra* note 178.

[180]Charles Beck Mach. Corp., 107 NLRB 874, 33 LRRM 1248 (1954). *See also* Harbor Carriers v. NLRB, 306 F2d 89, 50 LRRM 2863 (CA 2, 1962), *cert. denied*, 372 US 917, 52 LRRM 2471 (1963); NLRB v. Weyerhaeuser Co., 276 F2d 865, 45 LRRM 3088 (CA 7, 1960); Carpinteria Lemon Ass'n v. NLRB, 240 F2d 554, 39 LRRM 2185 (CA 9, 1957), *enforcing* 112 NLRB 121, 35 LRRM 1724 (1955). *Cf.* Visitainer Corp., 237 NLRB 257, 98 LRRM 1553 (1978); Fluhrer Bakeries, 232 NLRB 212, 96 LRRM 1491 (1977); Arthur C. Harvey Co., 110 NLRB 338, 34 LRRM 1650 (1954). *But cf.* Cleveland Decals, 99 NLRB 745, 30 LRRM 1129 (1952).

[181]The new union is not bound by the existing contract. American Sunroof Corp., 243 NLRB 1128, 102 LRRM 1086 (1979); American Seating Co., *supra* note 175.

[182]East Mfg. Corp., 242 NLRB 5, 101 LRRM 1079 (1979). *See also* Estate of Bella Moses, 247 NLRB 144, 103 LRRM 1081 (1980).

[183]American Sunroof Corp., *supra* note 181. The Board relied on the following considerations in finding that the disclaimer removed the contract as a bar: (1) the disclaimer was made in response to a deauthorization petition filed by an employee, (2) the disclaimer was made one and one-half months before a representation petition was filed by the other union, (3) the incumbent union took no actions inconsistent with its disclaimer, and (4) there was no evidence of collusion between the two unions.

7. Expiration of the Contract Bar: Timeliness. As the period of the contract bar approaches its expiration date,[184] three distinct procedural stages arise. In an attempt to reduce uncertainty, the Board has developed rules of timeliness as to each stage.[185]

a. The Open Period. In order to provide employees with an opportunity for a free choice of bargaining representative at reasonable and predictable intervals, the Board has established an *open period* during which petitions may be filed. This open period begins 90 days prior to the terminal date, i.e., the expiration date of the contract or, if the contract exceeds 3 years, the last day of the third year, and ends 60 days prior to that date.[186] A slightly different period is prescribed for health care institutions.[187]

b. The Insulated Period. A petition is not timely if it is filed during the 60-day period preceding the terminal date. This is the *insulated period* and immediately follows the open period. It is during this period that the parties will be permitted to negoti-

---

[184]For most collective bargaining contracts, the period of the contract—3 years—will be coextensive with the period of the contract bar. *See* General Cable Corp., 139 NLRB 1123, 51 LRRM 1444 (1962).

[185]*See* Deluxe Metal Furniture Co., 121 NLRB 995, 42 LRRM 1470 (1958), which superseded an earlier doctrine of recognizing a petition as timely filed if filed within 10 days following claim for recognition; General Elec. X-Ray Corp., 67 NLRB 997, 18 LRRM 1047 (1946). *See* notes 190–192 *infra* and accompanying text.

[186]Leonard Wholesale Meats Co., 136 NLRB 1000, 49 LRRM 1901 (1962). A petition filed before the commencement of an "open" period, however, may be entertained as to seasonal operations. *See, e.g.*, Cooperativa Azucarera Los Canos, 122 NLRB 817, 43 LRRM 1193 (1958). The Board has also held that, even though a petition is prematurely filed, it will not be dismissed if a hearing is directed, despite the prematurity of the petition, and that the Board's decision issues on or after the commencement of the open period. Royal Crown Cola Co., 150 NLRB 1624, 58 LRRM 1306 (1965). *See also* W.A. Foote Memorial Hosp., 230 NLRB 540, 96 LRRM 1099 (1977).

Because of a presidential wage-price freeze, in 1972 the Board granted a special exception to the open-period rule in several cases. Otherwise timely petitions were dismissed as untimely because the freeze had prevented intelligent bargaining during the insulated period; the Board therefore granted the bargaining parties new, uninterrupted periods of time in which to negotiate a contract. Litton Business Sys., 199 NLRB 354, 81 LRRM 1219 (1972); Dennis Chem. Co., 196 NLRB 226, 79 LRRM 1659 (1972); Hill & Sanders-Wheaton, 195 NLRB 1137, 79 LRRM 1617 (1972); West India Mfg. & Serv. Co., 195 NLRB 1135, 79 LRRM 1619 (1972).

[187]The open period in the health care industry is 120 to 90 days prior to an agreement's terminal date or the first 3 years of the agreement, whichever is sooner, thereby making the insulated period 90 days. The Board adopted these modifications for the health care industry in order to accommodate its contract-bar rules to amended §8(d)(4) of the Act, requiring 90 days' notice to the other party of the proposed termination or modification of a health care collective bargaining agreement. Trinity Lutheran Hosp., 218 NLRB 199, 89 LRRM 1238 (1975). *See* Chapter 13, "The Duty to Bargain," at notes 893–909.

ate "free from the 'threat of overhanging rivalry and uncertainty.'"[188]

In the borderline case, petitions filed on the sixtieth day preceding and including the terminal date will normally be considered untimely as falling within the insulated period, and the Board has specifically held that where a contract provides that it is in effect "until" or "to" a specific date, the date following the word "until" or "to" will not be counted in the 60-day computation.[189]

c. *After the Terminal Date.* If an employer and a union do not enter into a contract during the 60-day insulated period, the Board will entertain a petition filed after the terminal date, subject to new tests of timeliness.[190] Previously, under the Board's *General Electric X-Ray* doctrine,[191] a union's bare claim to representation prevented another union's subsequent contract from being a bar if the claiming union filed a petition within 10 days following the claim. The Board discarded this rule in *Deluxe Metal*[192] because it found that it had become a means of disrupting the stability of labor relations rather than a means of protecting the employees' free choice of representative.

In *Deluxe Metal*, the Board established the following rules:

(1) A contract executed after the expiration of a prior contract will not bar an election if a petition is filed with the Board (a) before the execution date of a contract to be effective immediately or retroactively, or (b) before the effective date of a contract to be effective at some time after its execution.[193]

(2) In the borderline case, a petition filed on the day the contract is executed is not timely unless the employer has "been

---

[188]Deluxe Metal Furniture Co., *supra* note 185, at 1001; General Dynamics Corp., 158 NLRB 956, 62 LRRM 1132 (1966). In the health care industry, the insulated period is 90 days. *See supra* note 187. In *General Dynamics,* a petition filed during the insulated period was dismissed even though it was not processed until after the terminal date. *But see* Vanity Fair Mills, 256 NLRB 1104, 107 LRRM 1331 (1981) (petition filed during insulated period was processed where petitioner delayed filing based on erroneous advice given by NLRB regional office).

[189]Hemisphere Steel Prods., 131 NLRB 56, 47 LRRM 1595 (1961).

[190]For purposes of timeliness at this stage, there would be no difference between petitions filed with respect to "old" contracts and petitions filed with respect to "first" contracts.

[191]General Elec. X-Ray Corp., *supra* note 185.

[192]Deluxe Metal Furniture Co., *supra* note 185.

[193]In Weather Vane Outerwear Corp., 233 NLRB 414, 96 LRRM 1621 (1977), the Board reaffirmed the rule established in General Dyestuff Corp., 100 NLRB 72, 30 LRRM 1230 (1952), that when one petition is timely filed and a second petition is filed during the pendency of the unresolved representation question raised by the earlier one, the contract-bar doctrine will not apply to the later petition.

informed at the time of the execution that a petition has been filed."[194]

(3) A petition filed the day before the contract's execution will always be timely.[195]

While the Board seeks to avoid having its contract-bar rules circumvented by premature extensions of contract expiration dates, it has declined to penalize the parties by attaching more stringent rules than would otherwise have been applicable to an initial contract of like duration. Thus, it noted:

> The primary purpose of the premature-extension rule is to protect petitioners in general from being faced with prematurely executed contracts at a time when the Petitioner would normally be permitted to file a petition. However, the Board's rule is not an absolute ban on premature extensions, but only subjects such extensions to the condition that if a petition is filed during the open period calculated from the expiration date of the old contract, the premature extension will not be a bar.[196]

As indicated above, petitions filed during the insulated period of the old contract remain untimely.[197] Similarly, the *premature extension* doctrine does not apply to a contract executed at a time when the existing contract would have failed as a bar because of other contract-bar rules, for example, a contract containing a union-security provision clearly unlawful on its face.[198]

Notice to modify the contract, or actual modification short of termination, will not remove the contract as a bar to an election, regardless of the scope of any such clause.[199] This has not always been the case, however. Returning to its earlier *Western Electric* rule,[200] the Board in *Deluxe Metal*[201] overturned intervening decisions which had held that the reopening destroyed the bar.

F. Clarification of Units

Either party to a bargaining relationship may obtain a clarification of the bargaining unit from the Board, regardless of

---

[194]Deluxe Metal Furniture Co., *supra* note 185, at 999. As to what constitutes being "informed" in timely fashion, see Portland Associated Morticians, 163 NLRB 614, 64 LRRM 1402 (1967); Rappahannock Sportswear Co., 163 NLRB 703, 64 LRRM 1417 (1967).

[195]The cutoff date in applying these rules is midnight, even though the contract eventually executed after midnight is the result of continuous bargaining. Deluxe Metal Furniture Co., *supra* note 185.

[196]H.L. Klion, Inc., 148 NLRB 656, 660, 57 LRRM 1073 (1964).

[197]Deluxe Metal Furniture Co., *supra* note 185.

[198]St. Louis Cordage Mills, 168 NLRB 981, 67 LRRM 1017 (1967).

[199]*Id.*

[200]Western Elec. Co., 94 NLRB 54, 28 LRRM 1002 (1951). *See also* Greenville Finishing Co., 71 NLRB 436, 19 LRRM 1023 (1946).

[201]Deluxe Metal Furniture Co., *supra* note 185.

whether the unit was established by formal NLRB representation procedures.[202] In the absence of a question concerning representation, a labor organization or an employer may file a petition for clarification of an existing bargaining unit or a petition for amendment of certification.[203] In 1964, the Board held in the *Locomotive Firemen* case[204] that such a petition may be considered and decided even though the Board has never passed on the appropriateness of the bargaining unit and no certification exists. In that case, the Board treated an employer's representation petition as a motion for clarification in view of (1) the parties' long bargaining history, (2) the recognition of the union as majority representative of the employees, and (3) a finding that the existing bargaining unit was not repugnant to the Act.

Locomotive Firemen has been construed as holding only that, on proper motion, the Board will undertake to clarify an uncertified unit, not that any petition for an election may be treated as one for clarification. And the Board will not certify or recertify a union as an incident to clarifying a unit[205] unless an election is conducted. Whether certified or not, a definite unit must exist or the Board will dismiss the motion for clarification.[206] Because there must be no question concerning representation,[207] clarification procedures cannot be used as an alternative to a petition for election when the object is to add a classification of employees

---

[202]Rules and Regs. §102.60(b): "A petition for clarification of an existing bargaining unit or a petition for amendment of certification, in the absence of a question concerning representation, may be filed by a labor organization or by an employer. Where applicable the same procedures set forth in section 102.60(a) above [pertinent to conventional petitions] shall be followed." *See also* Chapter 18, "Accommodation of Board Action to the Arbitration Process," at notes 322–338.

[203]Rules and Regs. §102.61(d), outlines the contents of a petition for clarification. Unlike election petitions, unit-clarification petitions are not limited to the 90-to-60-day open period. *But see* Arthur C. Logan Memorial Hosp., 231 NLRB 778, 96 LRRM 1063 (1977).

[204]Locomotive Firemen & Enginemen, 145 NLRB 1521, 55 LRRM 1177 (1964). The Board overruled Bell Tel. Co., 118 NLRB 371, 40 LRRM 1179 (1957).

[205]Crown Zellerbach Corp., 147 NLRB 1223, 56 LRRM 1438 (1964).

[206]FWD Corp., 131 NLRB 404, 48 LRRM 1055 (1961).

[207]Rules and Regs. §102.60(b); Renaissance Center Partnership, 239 NLRB 1247, 100 LRRM 1121 (1979). In Southern Cal. Water Co., 241 NLRB 771, 100 LRRM 1583 (1979), an employer's enterprise had substantially changed by the addition of a unit of employees already represented by another certified labor organization operating under a collective bargaining agreement then in force. The Board held that a question of representation existed and dismissed the employer's petition to clarify the original unit.

The Board has also refused to allow the unit-clarification procedure to be used as a device to resolve jurisdictional disputes. Printing Pressmen Local 663 (Norway), 258 NLRB 438, 108 LRRM 1159 (1981); Graphic Communications Local 289, 246 NLRB 981, 103 LRRM 1025 (1979). *See* Chapter 25, "Jurisdictional Disputes and 'Featherbedding.'"

which had been deliberately omitted from the unit.[208] However, a petition for unit clarification will be entertained if there has been a proper accretion to the unit.[209] In *Western Cartridge Co.*,[210] the Board found a proper accretion because the employees in question were interchangeable with the existing unit, had a community of interest in employment conditions, performed the same duties, and worked under common supervision.

The Board has dismissed petitions for clarification or amendment where professionals were entitled to an election,[211] where a union sought to amend and transfer certifications,[212] where a union sought to substitute the name of another local for its own,[213] and where a union was attempting to effectuate a change in work assignments.[214] The clarification requested must not have been precluded by a previous Board determination,[215] (although to be preclusive, a previous determination must have resolved the exact question upon which clarification is sought).[216]

---

[208]Wallace-Murray Corp., 192 NLRB 1090, 78 LRRM 1046 (1971). *See also* NLRB v. Mississippi Power & Light Co., 769 F2d 276, 120 LRRM 2302 (CA 5, 1985); Washington Post Co., 256 NLRB 1243, 107 LRRM 1441 (1981); Machinists (I.A.M. Representative Ass'n), 242 NLRB 44, 101 LRRM 1098 (1979); Lufkin Foundry & Mach. Co., 174 NLRB 556, 70 LRRM 1262 (1969); Dayton Power & Light Co., 137 NLRB 337, 50 LRRM 1147 (1962). In Desert Palace, 209 NLRB 950, 85 LRRM 1594 (1974), the Board dismissed a clarification petition seeking the accretion of plainclothes investigators to a unit of security officers. It rejected as irrelevant the fact that the exclusion of the plainclothes investigators at the time of the certification may have resulted from Board precedent which had since changed. The Board reasoned that the investigators had never had an opportunity to express themselves as to union representation. *But see* Austin Cablevision, 279 NLRB 535, 122 LRRM 1084 (1986) (petition processed).

[209]Boston Gas Co., 235 NLRB 1354, 98 LRRM 1146 (1978); Western Cartridge Co., 134 NLRB 67, 49 LRRM 1098 (1961). *See* discussion of accretions at notes 161–174 *supra*.

[210]*Supra* note 209.

[211]Lockheed Aircraft Corp., 155 NLRB 702, 60 LRRM 1390 (1965).

[212]Monon Stone Co., 137 NLRB 761, 50 LRRM 1248 (1962).

[213]Gulf Oil Corp., 135 NLRB 184, 49 LRRM 1465 (1962).

[214]Cincinnati Gas & Elec. Co., 235 NLRB 424, 97 LRRM 1523 (1978); T.I.M.E.-D.C., 225 NLRB 1175, 93 LRRM 1270 (1976); Borg-Warner Corp., 150 NLRB 912, 58 LRRM 1168 (1965).

[215]Security Guard Serv., 154 NLRB 33, 59 LRRM 1684 (1965). *But see* Fairleigh Dickinson Univ., 227 NLRB 239, 94 LRRM 1044 (1976), where the Board clarified a unit of university professors by adding department chairpersons to the faculty unit found appropriate by the Board in a prior representation proceeding. In the earlier proceeding, the employees in question had been found to be supervisors and were excluded from voting. The Board ruled that the duties of the department chairpersons had been changed by the parties' collective bargaining agreement, so they were no longer supervisors. *But cf.* NLRB v. Yeshiva Univ., 444 US 672, 103 LRRM 2526 (1980), discussed at notes 231–255 in Chapter 11, "Appropriate Bargaining Units," and at notes 250–268 in Chapter 28, "Jurisdiction: Coverage of the Act"; College of Osteopathic Medicine & Surgery, 265 NLRB 295, 111 LRRM 1523 (1982), discussed in Chapter 28, "Jurisdiction: Coverage of the Act," at note 251. *See also* note 442 *infra*.

[216]West Virginia Pulp & Paper Co., 140 NLRB 1160, 52 LRRM 1196 (1963); Boston Gas Co., 136 NLRB 219, 49 LRRM 1742 (1962).

Ultimately, the normal enforcement mechanism for a unit-clarification decision, like other decisions in representation cases,[217] will be a refusal-to-bargain unfair labor practice proceeding. Thus, in *Libbey-Owens-Ford v. NLRB*,[218] following protracted litigation, the Third Circuit enforced a Board order finding the employer in violation of section 8(a)(5) when it refused to add a single-plant unit to an existing multiplant unit pursuant to the Board's prior unit-clarification order.

III. ELECTION PROCEDURES

A. Preelection Matters

A cardinal policy of the Act is to protect the exercise by employees of full freedom to express their desires on union representation. A union (or individual) becomes the sole representative for purposes of collective bargaining if "designated or selected for the purposes of collective bargaining by the majority of the employees in a unit appropriate for such purposes."[219] For a union (or individual) to become a *certified* representative, however, there must be an "election by secret ballot" conducted by the NLRB after the filing of a proper petition and a determination that a question of representation exists.[220]

Pursuant to section 3(b) of the Act, the Board has delegated to the regional directors its powers to conduct elections under section 9.[221] The regional director under whose supervision the election is conducted is responsible for its proper conduct.[222] Following long-established policy, the regional director, under ordinary circumstances, is allowed to exercise discretion concerning the conduct of elections.[223] The regional director may,

---

[217]*See* Chapter 32, "NLRB Orders and Remedies," at notes 17–22.

[218]495 F2d 1195, 85 LRRM 2668 (CA 3, 1974), *enforcing* 202 NLRB 29, 82 LRRM 1417 (1973), *cert. denied,* 419 US 998, 87 LRRM 2658 (1974).

[219]Section 9(a). *See* Chapter 12, "Recognition and Withdrawal of Recognition Without an Election," for treatment of the process of obtaining recognition without an election.

[220]Section 9(c)(1). Until the Taft-Hartley amendments, the Board had (though it did not use) "wide discretion" in determining how to insure free employee choice. NLRB v. A.J. Tower Co., 329 US 324, 19 LRRM 2128 (1946); Southern S.S. Co. v. NLRB, 316 US 31, 10 LRRM 544 (1942). *See* Chapter 3, "The Taft-Hartley Changes," and Chapter 12, "Recognition and Withdrawal of Recognition Without an Election."

[221]Statements of Procedure §101.21(a). *See supra* at notes 9–14.

[222]Rules and Regs. §102.69; NLRB Field Manual 11300.

[223]V. La Rosa & Sons, 121 NLRB 671, 42 LRRM 1418 (1958); Independent Rice Mill, 111 NLRB 536, 35 LRRM 1509 (1955).

however, transfer parts of the case to the Board for determination. The director acts through an assigned Board agent, a field attorney, or a field examiner, any of whom may hold informal preelection conferences with interested parties in an attempt to settle the details of the election.[224]

1. Types of Elections. If the parties can voluntarily resolve the details of the election, either of two types of consent election agreements may be used:[225] (1) Agreement for Consent Election[226] (a "pure consent" agreement), providing for determination by the regional director of any dispute arising from the subsequent proceedings; and (2) Stipulation for Certification on Consent Election (a "stip" agreement), providing for a determination by the Board of any subsequent dispute.[227] In either case the parties enter into a written agreement setting forth the details of the election (e.g., time and place), which must be approved by the regional director. The regional director rules on all requests or motions made after the execution of the agreement and conducts the election. The regional director's rulings (unless arbitrary or capricious) are final in connection with a "pure consent" election but are reviewable by the Board under a "stip" agreement. Before approval by the regional director, or before a hearing in a case where there is no agreement, any petitioning or intervening party may withdraw.

In the absence of either form of consent election agreement, the regional director will proceed to a hearing. If the evidence at the hearing establishes the existence of a question concerning representation (QCR) and the appropriateness of the unit sought by the petitioner, the regional director will issue a Decision and Direction of Election. In cases that are transferred to the Board, the Board may, upon a finding that a QCR exists, issue a Direction of Election.[228]

After approval, or hearing: (1) a petitioning union may withdraw prior to the election if no inconsistent action is taken (such as recognition picketing), subject to 6 months' prejudice regarding the filing of a new petition; (2) an intervening union may withdraw until administrative functions have begun (i.e., the

[224]Statements of Procedure §101.19(a)(1): NLRB Field Manual 11300.
[225]Section 9(c)(4).
[226]Rules and Regs. §102.62(a).
[227]*Id.* §102.62(b).
[228]*Id.* §§102.63, 102.64, 102.67.

printing of ballots or notices);[229] and (3) a petitioning employer may withdraw only if unusual and compelling reasons exist or no union party opposes the withdrawal.[230]

The usual preliminaries are modified for expedited elections conducted under section 8(b)(7)(C): no showing of substantial interest is required if the petition is filed within 30 days of the commencement of picketing for organizational or recognitional objectives. Regional offices conduct these elections, but the usual investigatory and hearing prerequisites are omitted.[231]

2. Details of the Election. *a. Date.* An election may not be held within 10 days following the date the regional director schedules for receipt of the required list of eligible voters and their addresses.[232] Unless a waiver of review of the direction of election is filed, the regional director normally will not schedule an election until a date more than 20 days but less than 30 days from the date of the direction of election. This is to allow the Board to rule on any request for review.[233] If an election is directed by the Board, the election may be held at any time within 30 days of the date of the direction of election.[234] The exact day on which the election is held will usually be one when it is likely that the greatest number of eligible employees will be present and able to vote.[235]

b. Time.[236] The election may be held on company time with the employer's permission; otherwise it is held on the employees' own time. The actual time or times for voting will be set so as to

---

[229]NLRB Field Manual 11098.1. *See* Thiokol Chem. Corp., 114 NLRB 21, 36 LRRM 1508 (1955); Sears, Roebuck & Co., 107 NLRB 716, 33 LRRM 1233 (1954); Waumbec Dyeing & Finishing Co., 101 NLRB 1069, 31 LRRM 1185 (1952); American Meter Co., 89 NLRB 401, 25 LRRM 1584 (1950).

[230]NLRB Field Manual 11114.2; Alloy Mfg. Co., 107 NLRB 1201, 33 LRRM 1352 (1954).

[231]Section 8(b)(7)(C). *See* Chapter 21, "Picketing for Organization and Recognition," for treatment of organizational and recognitional picketing and expedited elections under §8(b)(7)(C). *See also* Rules and Regs. §102.67(b), on the decision and direction of election by the regional director, and paragraph (j) on such orders by the Board; Woodco Corp., 129 NLRB 1188, 47 LRRM 1143 (1961), for a discussion of appropriate unit considerations in expedited elections.

[232]NLRB Field Manual 11302.1. *See* notes 239–251 *infra*.

[233]Statements of Procedure §101.21(d); NLRB Field Manual 11302.1.

[234]NLRB Field Manual 11302.1; K.C. MCGUINESS & J.A. NORRIS, HOW TO TAKE A CASE BEFORE THE NLRB 184 (5th ed. 1986).

[235]*E.g.*, a day in the middle of the workweek or a payday. NLRB Field Manual 11302.1. However, the Ninth Circuit held that the Board did not abuse its discretion when it declined to schedule the election for payday and designated a different day when 26 employees were absent. Beck Corp. v. NLRB, 590 F2d 290, 100 LRRM 2719 (CA 9, 1978), *enforcing* 231 NLRB 907, 96 LRRM 1627 (1977).

[236]For specific rules relating to time and procedural aspects of the election, see NLRB Field Manual 11300–11342.

give all eligible employees adequate opportunity to vote, with minimum interference with the workday.

In a multishift, multiplant, or multi-employer situation, the polls may be kept open long enough to give each employee sufficient opportunity to vote, then moved or reopened later so that another shift, plant, or unit may vote.

When appropriate, such as where long distances are involved or where voters are widely scattered, voting may be conducted by mail, and the time for voting will be lengthened accordingly.[237]

c. Place. The polls are to be situated for easy accessibility and convenience to the voters.[238] For this reason the election is usually held on company property, if the employer agrees.

3. Voter List and Eligibility. *a. The* Excelsior *List.* After the direction of the election or approval of the consent election agreement, the employer will be required to prepare a list of eligible voters and their addresses, and file it with the regional director. This requirement was announced in *Excelsior Underwear,*[239] where the Board held that the failure of an employer to provide a list of names and addresses of employees eligible to vote would provide grounds, upon proper objection, for setting aside an election. The list must be filed with the regional director within 7 days of the direction of election or approval of a consent election agreement. The regional director then makes the list available to all parties.[240]

Disclosure of the list is intended both to facilitate communication in order to insure a free and reasoned choice by the employees and to avoid the necessity of a challenge when an employee previously unknown to the union, but whose name is on the eligibility list, appears to vote. The names and addresses should be listed systematically (e.g., alphabetically, or by clock or card

---

[237]NLRB Field Manual 11336. *See* notes 328–331 *infra* and accompanying text.

[238]Manchester Knitted Fashions, 108 NLRB 1366, 34 LRRM 1214 (1954); NLRB Field Manual 11302.2.

[239]156 NLRB 1236, 61 LRRM 1217 (1966). The Board determined that the early release of voters' names and addresses is necessary to a fair election. The Supreme Court directed enforcement of the Board's subpoena for an *Excelsior* list, but without concurrence of a majority in support of the reasons for enforcement. NLRB v. Wyman-Gordon Co., 394 US 759, 70 LRRM 3345 (1969). The subpoena was enforced notwithstanding that a majority of the justices, although for differing reasons, were of the opinion that the *Excelsior* requirement should have been promulgated pursuant to the formal rulemaking procedures specified in the Administrative Procedure Act. 5 U.S.C. §553 (1976).

[240]NLRB Field Manual 11312.1; Blaise Parking Serv., Case No. 15-CA-3646, 65 LRRM 1707 (1967) (not reported in Board volumes).

number, either as a whole or by department or unit). This list will also serve as the basis for composing the voting list.[241] The list should be checked and approved promptly by the parties in order to allow maximum time for resolving eligibility questions prior to the election, and the list should be kept up to date while the election procedures are pending.[242] If the list is not received, or if it contains names but not addresses, the director will proceed to hold the election unless requested in writing not to do so by the petitioner or an intervenor with sufficient showing of interest.[243] The *Excelsior* requirement is not dependent on the union's need for the information—the Board has rejected the argument that the list need not be furnished because the union already possesses all the information.[244]

Deviations from *Excelsior* requirements, either failure to properly list eligible voters or failure to meet time requirements, constitute grounds for setting aside an election. However, the Board has accepted deviations in some cases, finding that the requirements were satisfied by substantial compliance.[245]

In *Pole-Lite Industries,*[246] the Board outlined the major factors that it takes into account when considering a union objection to an election based on untimely submission of the *Excelsior* list: (1) the number of days by which the list was overdue, (2) the number of days for which the union has had the list prior to the election, (3) the number of employees eligible to vote in the election, and (4) whether the employer acted in good faith in providing the union with the required information. Since *Pole-Lite,* the Board has set aside an election where, because of delays by both the Board and the postal service, the union did not

---

[241]NLRB Field Manual 11312.3. *See* discussion *infra* at note 321.

[242]Statements of Procedure §101.19(a)(1); NLRB Field Manual 11312.4.

[243]NLRB Field Manual 11312.6. An intervenor with less than 30% cannot block the election but may file objections, and the Board may set the election aside for failure to supply the list.

[244]Gray Drug Stores, 197 NLRB 924, 80 LRRM 1449 (1972). The Board refused to admit evidence of the union's lack of need, reasoning that the list would be beneficial to the union in correcting and updating its information, and that furnishing the list would tend to reduce challenges because it would enable the union to know prior to the election the employer's position on voter eligibility.

[245]In one case a petitioning union objected to the time limits, claiming that 7 days from the direction of an election was too long to wait, in view of the fact that the proceeding in issue was the third election to be conducted following the filing of its petition. The Board found this reason unpersuasive and denied the motion to reconsider the union's objection to that policy. Sabine Towing & Transp. Co., 226 NLRB 422, 93 LRRM 1277 (1976). In the same case, the Board set aside the election because alleged off-duty employees whose names did not appear on the list were prevented by the employer from asserting their right to vote to the Board agent conducting the election.

[246]299 NLRB 196, 95 LRRM 1080 (1977).

receive the list until eight days before the election.[247] In another case,[248] rejecting the employer's contention that it was justified in delivering the *Excelsior* list 15 days late because it had filed a motion to set aside the consent agreement, the Board ordered a new election. It pointed out that the employer could have submitted the list while its motion was under consideration, and its failure to do so had denied the union up to 40 percent of its election campaigning time.

Substantial compliance as to the names on the list appears to satisfy *Excelsior* requirements. The Board excused an employer's 7-percent error factor in submitting incorrect addresses and omitting names, finding that an error of that magnitude did not amount to "insubstantial compliance" with the rule.[249] Similarly, a 13-percent error factor in the addresses of eligible voters was held to constitute neither gross negligence nor an absence of good faith warranting a new election.[250] However, a list that omitted 10 percent of the eligible voters and had incorrect addresses for 18 percent was found not to constitute substantial compliance and, therefore, provided grounds for setting aside the election.[251] In the latter case, the Board stated that omissions are more serious than inaccurate addresses and indicated that the election would have been set aside on the basis of the omissions alone.

---

[247]McGraw Edison Co., 234 NLRB 630, 97 LRRM 1262 (1978). For a contrary decision before *Pole-Lite, see* Peerless Eagle Coal Co., 220 NLRB 357, 90 LRRM 1229 (1975).

[248]Rockwell Int'l, 235 NLRB 1159, 98 LRRM 1077 (1978). *See also* C & G Mkts., 272 NLRB 294, 117 LRRM 1261 (1984) (Board neglected to mail list to petitioner: election set aside); Arpro Co. m/v Arctic Producer, 265 NLRB 313, 112 LRRM 1022 (1982) (list submitted 2 days before election: election set aside).

[249]Kentfield Medical Hosp., 219 NLRB 174, 89 LRRM 1697 (1975). *See also* Lemaster Steel Erectors, 271 NLRB 1391, 117 LRRM 1160 (1984) (refusal to disclose temporary addresses allowed where disclosure of permanent addresses gave union adequate access); Houston Distrib. Co., 261 NLRB 145, 110 LRRM 1029 (1982) (omission of 42 names excused where employer had provided names and addresses directly to union two months earlier during negotiations; *but see* Dutch Boy, Glow Lite Div., 262 NLRB 4, 110 LRRM 1249 (1982), *enforced sub nom.* Artra Group v. NLRB, 730 F2d 586, 115 LRRM 3242 (CA 10, 1984) (40% omission warranted overturning election); Ponce Television Corp., 192 NLRB 115, 77 LRRM 1622 (1971) (22% error factor not substantial compliance); Sonfarrel, Inc., 188 NLRB 969, 76 LRRM 1497 (1971) (omission of 5 names out of unit of 52 held to warrant new election).

[250]Days Inns, 216 NLRB 384, 88 LRRM 1224 (1975). The Board has also held that providing a list of only surnames and first and middle initials and failing to volunteer subsequently updated addresses did not violate the Act because there was no showing that it was a "product of intent to frustrate communication or impede Board processes." St. Francis Hosp., 249 NLRB 180, 104 LRRM 1213 (1980).

[251]Chromalloy Am. Corp., 245 NLRB 934, 102 LRRM 1405 (1979). In Centre Eng'g, 253 NLRB 419, 105 LRRM 1637 (1980), an employer did not comply with the *Excelsior* requirements when its list was not alphabetized, nor arranged according to department or plant location, and contained Zip codes for only 25 of the 424 addresses.

b. Eligibility. Generally, all employees in the unit found appropriate who were employed during the payroll period immediately preceding the date of the direction of election or approval of the consent agreement, are eligible to vote provided they are still employed at the time of the election.[252] Laid-off employees who have a "reasonable expectation of re-employment" in the foreseeable future are also eligible to vote.[253] Probationary employees are eligible to vote if their duties and working conditions are substantially the same as those of regular employees and they have reasonable expectation of permanent employment.[254] Employees on sick leave or leave of absence are eligible to vote if they are to be automatically restored to their duties when ready to resume work.[255] Employees who have quit or been discharged for cause before the election are generally ineligible,[256] but employees who have been discriminatorily dis-

---

[252]Columbia Pictures Corp., 61 NLRB 1030, 16 LRRM 128 (1945); Vultee Aircraft, 24 NLRB 1184, 6 LRRM 459 (1940). *But see* Carl B. King Drilling Co., 164 NLRB 419, 65 LRRM 1096 (1967); Great Lakes Pipe Line Co., 64 NLRB 1296, 17 LRRM 169 (1945); Remington Rand Corp., 50 NLRB 819, 12 LRRM 219 (1943). An employee must be actively employed on the eligibility date; an employee who was hired 2 days before the eligibility date and took his physical on that date, but who did not actually begin work until a later date is not eligible to vote. B.L.K. Steel, Inc., 245 NLRB 1347, 102 LRRM 1532 (1980). *Accord* Airport-Shuttle Cincinnati, 257 NLRB 955, 108 LRRM 1044 (1981), *enforced,* 703 F2d 220, 112 LRRM 3169 (CA 6, 1983) (participation in training, orientation, or other matters preliminary to actual work will not make one eligible to vote).

[253]Kustom Elec. v. NLRB, 590 F2d 817, 100 LRRM 2097 (CA 10, 1978), *enforcing* 230 NLRB 1037, 96 LRRM 1454 (1977); NLRB v. Jesse Jones Sausage Co., 309 F2d 664, 51 LRRM 2501 (CA 4, 1962); Marley Co., 131 NLRB 866, 48 LRRM 1168 (1961). *But see* Thomas Engine Corp., 196 NLRB 706, 80 LRRM 1755 (1972) (employees laid off and told to find other work because employer could not estimate duration of layoff were ineligible to vote, even though they were called back to work shortly after the election). *See also* Red Arrow Freight Lines, 278 NLRB 965, 121 LRRM 1257 (1986); S & G Concrete Co., 274 NLRB 895, 118 LRRM 1420 (1985); Precision Tumbling Co., 252 NLRB 1014, 105 LRRM 1365 (1980).

[254]Vogue Art Ware & China Co., 129 NLRB 1253, 47 LRRM 1169 (1961); V.I.P. Radio, 128 NLRB 113, 46 LRRM 1278 (1960); Sheffield Corp., 123 NLRB 1454, 44 LRRM 1155 (1959); Beattie Mfg. Co., 77 NLRB 361, 22 LRRM 1015 (1948). *See* Data Technology Corp., Plastronics Div., 281 NLRB 1005, 123 LRRM 1192 (1986) (laid-off probationary employees eligible).

[255]NLRB v. Atkinson Dredging Co., 329 F2d 158, 55 LRRM 2598 (CA 4, 1964), *cert. denied,* 377 US 965, 56 LRRM 2416 (1964). Where the leave is for a definite duration, the Board considers it more likely that the employee will return. Sid Eland, Inc., 261 NLRB 11, 109 LRRM 1369 (1982) (open-ended leave with no notice of when employee will return, as opposed to maternity leave, will defeat voter eligibility). *Cf.* Dane County Dairy, 274 NLRB 291, 118 LRRM 1473 (1985), *enforced,* 795 F2d 1313, 122 LRRM 3051 (CA 7, 1986) (employee on maternity leave who did not report on her scheduled date of return was ineligible to vote). There is a rebuttable presumption that employees on sick leave remain employed until they recover. NLRB v. Newly Weds Foods, 758 F2d 4, 118 LRRM 3213 (CA 1, 1985), *enforcing* 270 NLRB 357, 116 LRRM 1179 (1984).

[256]Rish Equip. Co., 150 NLRB 1185, 58 LRRM 1274 (1965), *enforced,* 359 F2d 391, 61 LRRM 2719 (CA 4, 1966); Gemex Corp., 117 NLRB 656, 39 LRRM 1312 (1957); Dura Steel Prods. Co., 111 NLRB 590, 35 LRRM 1522 (1955); United States Rubber Co., 86 NLRB 338, 24 LRRM 1621 (1949).

charged[257] are entitled to vote. Employees whom the employer plans to terminate after the election are eligible voters if still employed on the date of election.[258]

Employees who have given notice of intent to quit[259] or retire,[260] but are still on the payroll at the time of the election are entitled to vote. But in one case the Board held that an employee who had given notice of his resignation before the election and who did not work on election day was ineligible to vote even though he was on the payroll, because "'it is well settled that, in order to be eligible to vote, an individual must be employed *and working* on the established eligibility date, unless absent for one of the reasons set out in the Direction of Election.'"[261] The Board's policy in this regard is not to "fractionalize" workdays, and it has held that an employee who worked a full shift but was discharged prior to voting was an eligible voter;[262] although the Seventh Circuit denied enforcement of a bargaining order based on that vote,[263] the Board continues to adhere to this policy.[264] The Board has held that an employee who quit in the middle of a payroll eligibility period, but was rehired and worked on the day of the election, was eligible to vote on the ground that "payroll eligibility is in fact conferred by some work during the payroll eligibility *period*."[265] On the other hand, an employee who had been previously retired, and who was placed

---

[257]Tampa Sand & Material Co., 137 NLRB 1549, 50 LRRM 1438 (1962); Sioux City Brewing Co., 85 NLRB 1164, 24 LRRM 1534 (1949); *see also* B.E. & K., Inc., 252 NLRB 256, 105 LRRM 1495 (1980), *enforced in part,* 672 F2d 906, 111 LRRM 2650 (CA 4, 1981); Pacific Tile & Porcelain Co., 137 NLRB 1358, 50 LRRM 1394 (1962) (voting permitted even though pending grievance or arbitration procedure over discharged employee had not been made subject of unfair labor practice charge).

[258]Ethyl Prods. Co., 267 NLRB 219, 114 LRRM 1013 (1983).

[259]NLRB v. General Tube Co., 331 F2d 751, 56 LRRM 2161 (CA 6, 1964); Ely & Walker, 151 NLRB 636, 58 LRRM 1513 (1965); Reidbord Bros. Co., 99 NLRB 127, 30 LRRM 1047 (1952).

[260]Radio Free Eur./Radio Liberty, 262 NLRB 549, 110 LRRM 1330 (1982). *See also* Amoco Oil Corp., 289 NLRB 280, 131 LRRM 1088 (1988) (retiring employee on final vacation leave at end of employment eligible).

[261]Roy N. Lotspeich Publishing Co., 204 NLRB 517, 517, 83 LRRM 1380 (1973) (emphasis in original) (quoting Ra-Rich Mfg. Corp., 120 NLRB 1444, 1447, 42 LRRM 1182 (1958)).

[262]Choc-Ola Bottlers, 192 NLRB 1247, 78 LRRM 1049 (1971).

[263]Choc-Ola Bottlers v. NLRB, 478 F2d 461, 83 LRRM 2204 (CA 7, 1973).

[264]*E.g.,* Firestone Tire & Rubber Co., 206 NLRB 614, 84 LRRM 1582 (1973), *enforced,* 503 F2d 759 (CA 10, 1974) (employee absent from work for several months, who returned to work on election day but did no unit work before voting, was eligible to vote even though he was assigned to probationary supervisory position after election).

[265]Leather by Grant, 206 NLRB 961, 961 n.1 84 LRRM 1448 (1973) (emphasis in original).

on leave-of-absence status prior to the election but returned to work six days after the election, was held ineligible.[266]

Seasonal, casual, or temporary employees are generally not eligible to vote unless they have a reasonable expectation of reemployment and a substantial interest in working conditions at the employer's place of business.[267] With respect to temporary employees, the Board has held that those "who are employed on the eligibility date, and whose tenure of employment remains uncertain, are eligible to vote."[268] The Board has applied two standards to determine the eligibility of temporary employees: a reasonable expectation of further employment test[269] and a date certain test.[270] After reviewing the cases, the First Circuit has held that the date certain test is "the better and more prevalent standard."[271] Under that standard, "an employee may be fully aware that his or her employment will be short lived, but, as long as no definite termination date is known and the employee was employed on the eligibility and election dates, he or she will be eligible to vote."[272]

Regular part-time, as distinguished from casual, employees are permitted to vote.[273] Likewise, temporarily transferred employees may vote.[274] Dual-function employees who spend part of their time doing bargaining-unit work may have sufficient interest in conditions of employment in the unit to be eligible to vote, even though they do not spend a majority of

---

[266]Universal Paper Goods Co. v. NLRB, 638 F2d 1159, 102 LRRM 2218 (CA 9, 1979), *enforcing* 238 NLRB 1088, 99 LRRM 1579 (1978).

[267]Sentinel Printing & Publishing Co., 137 NLRB 1610, 50 LRRM 1469 (1962); S. Martinelli & Co., 99 NLRB 43, 30 LRRM 1031 (1952). *But see* Evergreen Legal Servs., 246 NLRB 964, 103 LRRM 1028 (1979) (employees employed under Comprehensive Employment and Training Act (CETA) who share community of interest with employer's regular employees are not ineligible as temporary employees). *See also* Mt. Graham Hosp., 250 NLRB 433, 104 LRRM 1375 (1980); Montgomery County Opportunity Bd., 249 NLRB 880, 104 LRRM 1238 (1980).

[268]Personal Prods. Corp., 114 NLRB 959, 960, 37 LRRM 1079 (1955).

[269]*See, e.g.*, Trustees of Stevens Inst. of Technology, 222 NLRB 16, 91 LRRM 1087 (1976); Georgia-Pacific Corp., 201 NLRB 831, 82 LRRM 1355 (1973).

[270]M.J. Pirolli & Sons, 194 NLRB 241, 78 LRRM 1631 (1971), *enforced without published opinion*, 80 LRRM 3170 (CA 1), *cert. denied*, 409 US 1008, 81 LRRM 2672 (1972); Lloyd A. Fry Roofing Co., 121 NLRB 1433, 43 LRRM 1013 (1958).

[271]NLRB v. New England Lithographic Co., 589 F2d 29, 33, 100 LRRM 2001 (CA 1, 1978).

[272]*Id.* at 34.

[273]Motz Poultry Co., 244 NLRB 573, 102 LRRM 1198 (1979); Tol-Pac, Inc., 128 NLRB 1439, 46 LRRM 1485 (1960); Providence Pub. Mkt. Co., 79 NLRB 1482, 23 LRRM 1011 (1948).

[274]Huntley-Van Buren Co., 122 NLRB 957, 43 LRRM 1228 (1959) (production employee assigned as night watchman).

their time on unit work.[275] To determine the eligibility of day laborers, the Board balances the factors of length, regularity, and currency of employment.[276]

Employees engaged in an economic strike who are "not entitled to reinstatement" (i.e., who have been permanently replaced) are eligible under Board regulations to vote in any election held within 12 months of the commencement of the strike.[277] Conversely, the Board has held that replaced economic strikers who were on a recall list were not eligible to vote in a decertification election held more than 12 months after the strike began.[278] Unreplaced strikers retain their right to vote absent some affirmative act (such as the acceptance of permanent employment elsewhere, elimination of their jobs, discharge, or denial of reinstatement for conduct rendering them unsuitable for reemployment) indicating that their employment has ended.[279] The Board has applied the same principles in determining the eligibility of replaced sympathy strikers, holding that they have the same status as the economic strikers they are supporting.[280]

The Board has rejected an employer's argument that a pending strike caused such a substantial reduction in available work that none of the strikers could reasonably expect to be recalled in the foreseeable future and hence were ineligible to vote. The elimination of jobs as the result of a strike was not deemed justification for disenfranchisement of strikers within the 12-month period prescribed in section 9(c)(3).[281]

---

[275]NLRB v. Joclin Mfg. Co., 314 F2d 627, 52 LRRM 2415 (CA 2, 1963); Berea Publishing Co., 140 NLRB 516, 52 LRRM 1051 (1963).

[276]The most common cutoff point is to allow irregular employees, who otherwise have a community of interest with unit employees, to vote if they have worked 15 days in the calendar quarter immediately preceding the direction of election. *See, e.g.,* Capitol Insulation Co., 233 NLRB 902, 96 LRRM 1592 (1977) (citing Scoa, Inc., 140 NLRB 1379, 52 LRRM 1244 (1963)). *See also* Avon Prods., 250 NLRB 1479, 105 LRRM 1128 (1980) (parties' agreement that "reserve employees" who had worked 4 or more hours in 9 of 13 weeks preceding direction of election would be eligible was not inconsistent with the Act).

[277]Section 9(c)(3). The Board's regulation has been upheld by the Ninth Circuit. Bio-Science Labs. v. NLRB, 542 F2d 505, 93 LRRM 2154 (CA 9, 1976). *See* Chapter 19, "The Primary Strike," at note 104.

[278]Wahl Clipper Corp., 195 NLRB 634, 79 LRRM 1433 (1972).

[279]W. Wilton Wood, Inc., 127 NLRB 1675, 46 LRRM 1240 (1960). *Cf.* Laidlaw Corp., 171 NLRB 1366, 68 LRRM 1252 (1968), *enforced,* 414 F2d 99, 71 LRRM 3054 (CA 7, 1969), *cert. denied,* 397 US 920, 73 LRRM 2537 (1970). *See* Chapter 19, "The Primary Strike," at note 105.

[280]Levitz Furniture Co., 248 NLRB 15, 103 LRRM 1320 (1980).

[281]Globe Molded Plastics Co., 200 NLRB 377, 81 LRRM 1433 (1972).

An eligible striker does not lose eligibility simply by working elsewhere during a strike, even if at a higher rate of pay.[282] Statements by a striker to his new employer that he had no intention of returning to his unit job were held insufficient to prove affirmatively that the striker had abandoned all interest in returning.[283]

Replacements employed on a permanent basis prior to the voting eligibility cutoff date are also eligible to vote.[284] However, the Fifth Circuit enforced a Board decision holding that permanent replacements who had been hired before the eligibility date and worked on the day of the election, but did not actually report for work until one month after the eligibility cutoff date, were not entitled to vote.[285] Employees who *are* entitled to reinstatement (unfair labor practice strikers) are entitled to vote regardless of the 12-month statutory limitation.[286] Replacements for such strikers are not.[287] However, the Board has held that employees discharged prior to the representation election for striking to protest the termination of a fellow employee were not eligible to vote where no unfair labor practice charge had been filed with respect to the discharges.[288] Because unfair labor practices cannot be adjudicated in representation proceedings, the Board presumed that the discharges were lawful.

Under a principle first enunciated in *Norris-Thermador Corp.*,[289] the Board will respect a written agreement between the parties expressly settling specific questions of eligibility, unless it

---

[282]Woodview Calabasas Hosp., 257 NLRB 497, 107 LRRM 1575 (1981), *enforced*, 702 F2d 184, 112 LRRM 3290 (CA 9, 1983).

[283]Q-T Tool Co., 199 NLRB 500, 81 LRRM 1520 (1972). *Accord* Foote & Davies, 262 NLRB 238, 110 LRRM 1270 (1982). *But see* Lake Dev. Mgmt. Co., 259 NLRB 791, 109 LRRM 1027 (1981) (striker who accepted other job and testified, after election, to lack of interest in returning was ineligible).

[284]Pacific Tile & Porcelain Co., 137 NLRB 1358, 50 LRRM 1394 (1962). If the strike occurs after the direction of election, permanent replacements of economic strikers attain eligibility if they remain employees on election day. Tampa Sand & Material Co., 129 NLRB 1273, 47 LRRM 1166 (1961) (strike began after direction of election and ended before election). But if the strike is called before the direction of election, replacements enjoy no exception to the general rule specifying eligibility both at the time of direction of election and on election day. Greenspan Engraving Corp., 137 NLRB 1308, 50 LRRM 1380 (1962).

[285]NLRB v. Dalton Sheet Metal Co., 472 F2d 257, 82 LRRM 2468 (CA 5, 1973). The court distinguished Tampa Sand & Material Co., *supra* note 284, where replacements employed after the eligibility deadline but before the election were permitted to vote, on the ground that in *Tampa Sand* the union had attempted to control eligibility by its timing of the strike after the eligibility cutoff date had passed.

[286]Kellburn Mfg. Co., 45 NLRB 322, 11 LRRM 142 (1942).

[287]Larand Leisurelies, 222 NLRB 838, 91 LRRM 1305 (1976).

[288]Spray Sales & Sierra Rollers, 225 NLRB 1089, 93 LRRM 1025 (1976).

[289]119 NLRB 1301, 41 LRRM 1283 (1958).

is contrary to the Act or Board policy. For example, the Board has upheld an agreement that enfranchised an employee who did not begin work until after the eligibility period and who would have been ineligible but for the agreement.[290] The Board said that the customary basis for determining eligibility to vote is neither a requirement of the Act nor a policy of the Board, but rather a rule of administrative convenience that may be waived. The Board has also upheld an employer's challenge to the ballot of an employee whom the parties had agreed to exclude from the list because he had worked on a casual basis and had recently been discharged.[291] *Norris-Thermador* agreements will not, however, preclude a challenge based on a statutory exclusion, e.g., inclusion of a supervisor under the Act.[292] The Board has extended the *Norris-Thermador* rule to include an unequivocal oral agreement and sustained a challenge to a voter where there was clear evidence that the parties had orally agreed to the voter's ineligibility.[293]

4. Notice of Election. When a petition is filed, the parties receive a Board poster outlining their rights. The Board urges but does not require that this notice be posted. Prior to the date of election, however, the election must be adequately publicized by the posting of official notices to inform eligible voters of the election details.[294] A standard Board form,[295] which reproduces a sample ballot and outlines such details as location of polls, time of voting, and eligibility rules, is used. The notices are posted by the employer in its place of business in conspicuous places, such as on bulletin boards and timecard racks whenever possible. Notices may also be posted in other places, or

---

[290]Trilco City Lumber Co., 226 NLRB 289, 93 LRRM 1360 (1976).

[291]Pilgrim Foods, 234 NLRB 136, 97 LRRM 1187 (1978), *modified*, 591 F2d 110, 100 LRRM 2494 (CA 1, 1978). After the election, the Board determined that the employee had been unlawfully discharged but upheld the challenge based on the agreement because the question of the employee's eligibility involved a determination of his community of interest with other employees rather than the application of a statutory exclusion.

[292]Esten Dyeing & Finishing Co., 219 NLRB 286, 89 LRRM 1621 (1975). Likewise, the parties cannot by agreement confer eligibility upon a person who is not an employee of the employer. Inacomp Am., 281 NLRB 271, 123 LRRM 1096 (1986). In addition, the Board has refused to give effect to a *Norris-Thermador* agreement excluding certain classifications of employees who belong within the bargaining unit because "the parties are not free to agree that certain classes of employees, although admittedly in the bargaining unit, may not vote." Illinois Valley Community Hosp., 249 NLRB 410, 104 LRRM 1154 (1980).

[293]Banner Bedding, 214 NLRB 1013, 87 LRRM 1417 (1974). *But see* Esten Dyeing & Finishing Co., *supra* note 292 (existence and terms of oral agreement must be fully accepted by both parties).

[294]NLRB Field Manual 11314.

[295]NLRB Form 707.

the publicizing of the election may be achieved by the "use of other means considered appropriate and effective."[296]

The Board has never specified a required time prior to the election for the posting of election notices, leaving such details to the discretion of the regional director; but it has set aside elections because of late postings,[297] though the appellate courts have disagreed in at least two such cases.[298]

The Board has an affirmative duty to present election notices to employees in languages they will understand.[299] The Board will provide notices in such languages if requested by a party. The Board has set aside an election on the ground that bilingual notices requested by the employer were not provided until a few days before the election.[300]

---

[296]Statements of Procedure §101.19(a)(1); NLRB Field Manual 11314.3.

[297]*E.g.*, in Congoleum Indus., 227 NLRB 108, 93 LRRM 1503 (1976), a Board panel set aside an election where notices were not posted until 2 days before the election, even though 97% of the eligible employees voted. The Board said that there was no excuse offered by the employer for the last-minute posting, and for the Board to ignore the employer's inaction would encourage other employers to do the same. The Board additionally pointed out that the notices contain important information with respect to employees' rights under the Act. Similarly, in Singer Co., 238 NLRB 264, 99 LRRM 1462 (1978), the Board set aside an election because the employer had not posted the official Board notices in the eight stores in which the election was conducted in time to allow the employees to read and adequately study them. *But see* Printhouse Co., 246 NLRB 741, 102 LRRM 1663 (1979), where the Board did not set an election aside even though the employer posted the notice only 1 day in advance of the election. Similarly, in Kane Indus., 246 NLRB 738, 102 LRRM 1664 (1979), notice was held to be sufficient even though a plantwide layoff prevented voters from reading the posted notice until the day of the election. In Contractors Redi-Mix, 250 NLRB 121, 104 LRRM 1339 (1980), the Board did not set aside an election, which the union had won, where the notice had not been posted until the day before the election, since the employer was found to have contributed to the delay by failing to post the notice until the third day after receiving it. In Flo-Tronic Metal Mfg., 251 NLRB 1546, 105 LRRM 1144 (1980), the Board set aside an election where, as a result of a mistake by the Board's regional office, the notice of election was in English only but the unit consisted primarily of Spanish-speaking employees.

[298]In Cerlo Mfg. Corp. v. NLRB, 585 F2d 847, 99 LRRM 3054 (CA 7, 1978), the Seventh Circuit denied enforcement of the Board's bargaining order on the ground that the Board had erred in setting aside a representation election which the union had lost. The Board had set the election aside because no official notice of the election had been published. The court found that the regional director had failed to supply the employer with an official notice, and the employer had instead posted a copy of the stipulation for certification, an official Board document. In NLRB v. Kilgore Corp., 510 F2d 1165, 88 LRRM 2833 (CA 6, 1975), the Sixth Circuit refused to enforce a Board order based on an election that had been set aside because the employer had posted the notices only in inconspicuous places shortly before the election. The court relied on the fact that the employees had actually been notified of the procedures, almost 100% of them had voted, the employer had offered to postpone the election, and there was no evidence of bad faith.

[299]Tanforan Park Food Purveyors Council v. NLRB, 656 F2d 1358, 108 LRRM 2630 (CA 9, 1981). *See also* Unibilt Indus., 278 NLRB 825, 121 LRRM 1240 (1986).

[300]Thermalloy Corp., 233 NLRB 428, 96 LRRM 1505 (1977). *See also* Rattan Art Gallery, 260 NLRB 255, 109 LRRM 1149 (1982) (objection sustained: translation of notice into Filipino dialect was defective and incomplete). *But see* Wicks Forest Indus., 227 NLRB 299, 94 LRRM 1029 (1976) (objection to absence of Spanish-language notice overruled: no showing that eligible employees with Hispanic surnames could not read or understand English).

5. Review of Direction of Election. The order of a regional director, setting forth findings and conclusions, and ordering or directing an election, is final.[301] However, within 10 days of service of the direction, any party may file a request for review with the Board. Such request must be a self-contained document enabling the Board to rule on the basis of its contents without recourse to the record.[302] The Board will grant a request for review only where one or more of the following "compelling reasons" exist: (1) a substantial question of law or policy is raised, and there is an absence of or departure from officially reported Board precedent; (2) the regional director's decision on a substantial factual issue is both clearly erroneous on the record and prejudicial; (3) the conduct of the hearing resulted in prejudicial error; or (4) compelling reasons exist for reconsideration of an important Board rule or policy.[303] Within 7 days of the deadline for filing a request for review, any party may file a statement in opposition to the request.[304] If the request for review is granted, the parties may file briefs within 7 days of the order granting review, and the Board will consider the entire record in light of the grounds relied on for review.[305]

A case may be transferred to the Board for decision if it appears to the regional director that the proceeding raises questions that should be decided by the Board. If the case is so transferred, the parties may file with the Board the briefs previously filed (or due to be filed) with the regional director.[306] Immediately upon issuance of an order transferring the case or granting the request for review, the regional director may transmit the record to the Board.[307]

Further briefs or reply briefs are permitted only by special leave of the Board. The Board decides the issues referred to it (or reviews the regional director's decision), either on the record or after oral argument or following submission of briefs or further hearing. The Board then directs an election, dismisses the petition, affirms or reverses the regional director's order, or

---

[301]Rules and Regs. §102.67(b). *See* §3(b) of the Act and Chapter 4, "The Landrum-Griffin Changes," at note 50.

[302]Rules and Regs. §102.67(d).

[303]*Id.*, §102.67(c).

[304]*Id.*, §102.67(e).

[305]*Id.*, §102.67(g).

[306]*Id.*, §§102.67(h), 102.67(i).

[307]*Id.*, §102.68.

disposes of the matter in such other way as it deems appropriate.[308]

Normally, Board orders in election and certification proceedings under section 9(c) are not directly reviewable by the courts.[309] The Supreme Court in *Leedom v. Kyne*[310] held that a party might, however, by proceeding against the Board members in a district court, attack an order of election and unit determination made "in excess of [the Board's] delegated powers and contrary to a specific prohibition in the Act."[311] But the Court later emphasized that the *Leedom* exception is a narrow one.[312] Such Board orders are more conventionally reviewable by an indirect procedure: in a refusal-to-bargain unfair labor practice proceeding in which the correctness of the certification of a representative may be put in issue.[313]

B. The Election Proper

1. Observers. Any party may be represented at the voting by observers of its own selection. In directed elections, this privilege is extended by the Board; in consent elections, the consent agreement or stipulation form supplied by the Board provides for the observers, making their use a matter of right.[314] Each party appoints an equal number of observers, the number to be determined by the Board agent based on the circumstances of the election (such as number of voters and voting places). Parties may waive, expressly or by default, the opportunity to be represented by observers.[315]

The use of observers is also subject to such limitations as the regional director may prescribe, for they are to be "appropriate"

---

[308]Id., §102.67(j).

[309]Custom Recovery v. NLRB, 597 F2d 1041, 101 LRRM 2784 (CA 5, 1979).

[310]358 US 184, 43 LRRM 2222 (1958), *aff'g* 249 F2d 490, 40 LRRM 2600 (CA DC, 1957), *aff'g* 148 F Supp 597, 39 LRRM 2197 (D DC, 1956).

[311]*Id.* at 188. The Board had included both professional and nonprofessional employees in the same unit without a vote of the professional employees, in contravention of §9(b)(1) of the Act.

[312]Boire v. Greyhound Corp., 376 US 473, 55 LRRM 2694 (1964). *See also* Goldberg, *District Court Review of NLRB Representation Proceedings,* 42 IND. L.J. 455, 487, 489 (1967); Railway & S.S. Clerks v. Association for the Benefit of Non-Contract Employees, 380 US 650, 59 LRRM 2051 (1965). *See* Chapter 33, "Judicial Review and Enforcement," at notes 118–149.

[313]*See* §9(d) of the Act and Administrative Procedure Act, 5 U.S.C. §554 cl. 6 (1988). For a general discussion of judicial review, see Chapter 33, "Judicial Review and Enforcement."

[314]Breman Steel Co., 115 NLRB 247, 37 LRRM 1273 (1956).

[315]Rules and Regs. §102.69(a); NLRB Field Manual 11310.

representatives.[316] Board policy requires that observers be nonsupervisory employees[317] and not be "persons closely identified" with the employer.[318] An employee who is eligible to vote may act as an election observer and still vote.[319] Neither nonparticipating unions nor "no-union" groups are permitted to select observers.[320]

A *preelection conference* of the parties and the Board agent is usually held. At this conference, the voter eligibility list[321] is checked, the authorized observers are identified, and other election details are handled.

Observers are given their instructions[322] by the Board agent prior to the election. They check procedures at the balloting and the counting of ballots, aid in identifying voters, and generally assist the Board agent. Their most important function is that of challenging voters. For this purpose, they may keep a list of voters whose ballots they intend to challenge but not a list to establish who votes.[323]

2. Balloting. *a. The Ballot.* Ballots are furnished by the Board in all cases. According to established Board practice, no one but the Board agent and the voter may handle a ballot.[324] The color of the ballot for a particular group or unit will not be disclosed to the parties prior to the voting. If the regional director concludes that the voters will not be misled, a union may be permitted to use a shortened name, regardless of whether the matter was raised in the hearing. The phrasing of the question on the ballot

---

[316]Rules and Regs. §102.69(a); Statements of Procedure §101.19(a)(2).

[317]NLRB Field Manual 11310; Worth Food Mkt. Stores, 103 NLRB 259, 31 LRRM 1527 (1953). *But cf.* Soerens Motor Co., 106 NLRB 1388, 33 LRRM 1021 (1953) (presence of union secretary who was former employee of employer permitted, since (1) discharge was subject of unfair labor practice charges at time of election and (2) presence did not exert undue influence on voters). *See also* Diamond Int'l Corp. v. NLRB, 646 F2d 1, 107 LRRM 2165 (CA 1, 1981), *enforcing* 252 NLRB 95, 105 LRRM 1350 (1980) (union official permitted as observer).

[318]Watkins Brick Co., 107 NLRB 500, 33 LRRM 1176 (1953) (employer's vice-president, treasurer, and office manager); International Stamping Co., 97 NLRB 921, 29 LRRM 1158 (1951) (son and sister-in-law of employer's president); Peabody Eng'g Co., 95 NLRB 952, 28 LRRM 1391 (1959) (employer's attorney). *But see* Mountain States Tel. & Tel. Co., 207 NLRB 552, 84 LRRM 1483 (1973) (Board approved election where employer's observer was former supervisor who temporarily occupied nonsupervisory position).

[319]Kroder-Reubel Co., 72 NLRB 240, 19 LRRM 1155 (1947).

[320]NLRB Field Manual 11310. *See* Chapter 9, "Restrictions of Preelection Activity: 'Laboratory Conditions,'", at notes 139–162.

[321]*See* notes 239–251 *supra* and accompanying text.

[322]NLRB Form 722.

[323]Milwaukee Cheese Co., 112 NLRB 1383, 36 LRRM 1225 (1955) (use of duplicate of official voting list to check off employees voting held improper); Bear Creek Orchards, 90 NLRB 286, 26 LRRM 1204 (1950).

[324]NLRB Field Manual 11306.

is determined by the direction of election.[325] The ballot gives the employee a choice whether or not to be represented by the petitioner. In a craft-severance election, however, the only question is: By whom does the employee wish to be represented?[326]

b. Voting. The actual polling is always conducted and supervised by Board agents.[327] Voting is by secret ballot and takes place in voting booths, because of the necessity that the employees be furnished a place where they can vote in absolute secrecy. As each voter is identified, the name is checked against the eligibility list and the Board agent hands the voter a ballot. The voter marks only his or her choice on the ballot (any other mark may affect the validity of the ballot) and puts it directly into the ballot box provided by the Board.

c. Mail Ballots. When an election involves long distances or widely scattered voters,[328] the regional director may conduct the voting by mail, in whole or in part. Specific provision for voting by mail in the direction of election is not required.[329] Prospective voters are mailed a notice of the election and a voting "kit" containing a ballot and return envelope. The parties are given notice at least 24 hours prior to dispatching the mail ballots. The returned envelopes are treated as voters for the purpose of identification and challenge, and the mail ballots are commingled with any regular ballots before counting.[330] The ballots must generally be returned by the time set for receipt of ballots, but the Board made an exception to this rule in a case where a late ballot was mailed three days before due, on the basis of a finding that it was mailed at a time when the employee could reasonably have anticipated timely receipt.[331]

d. Defective Ballots. Unmarked[332] or improperly marked[333] ballots are void, as are write-in ballots.[334] A ballot is invalid if

---

[325]*Id.*

[326]*See* discussion of craft severance in Chapter 11, "Appropriate Bargaining Units," notes 78–101.

[327]Statements of Procedure §101.19(a)(2).

[328]NLRB Field Manual 11336.

[329]Simplot Fertilizer Co., 107 NLRB 1211, 33 LRRM 1357 (1954).

[330]NLRB Field Manual 11336.2, 11336.3, 11336.5.

[331]Queen City Paving Co., 243 NLRB 71, 101 LRRM 1472 (1979).

[332]NLRB v. Vulcan Furniture Mfg. Corp., 214 F2d 369, 34 LRRM 2449 (CA 5, 1954), *cert. denied,* 348 US 873, 35 LRRM 2058 (1954); Q-F Wholesalers, 87 NLRB 1085, 25 LRRM 1254 (1949).

[333]Semi-Steel Casting Co. v. NLRB, 160 F2d 388, 19 LRRM 2458 (CA 8, 1947), *cert. denied,* 332 US 758, 20 LRRM 2673 (1947).

[334]Woodmark Indus., 80 NLRB 1105, 23 LRRM 1209 (1948).

identification of the voter is possible,[335] or if the voter shows his or her marked ballot to other voters.[336] However, a defaced ballot is valid if the voter's intent is clearly indicated and the ballot has none of the above infirmities.[337] In *Hydro Conduit Corp.*,[338] the Board abandoned the policy that a ballot that contains no markings on its face, but indicates clear voter intent on the reverse side, is void.

The Board has also announced that it will not void a ballot as a result of random markings if they are in addition to an "X" marked only in either the "Yes" or "No" blocks.[339] Overruling its rationale in *San Joaquin Compress & Warehouse Co.*[340] that such markings may indicate a desire by the voter to cancel an initial vote and enter a "no-choice" vote, the Board held that it will regard a mark in only one box, despite some irregularities, as a presumptively clear indication of the intent of the voter.

The Board has set aside elections where a multilingual ballot was found to contain inadequate and confusing translations[341] and where an interpreter was late in arriving for the balloting.[342] However, where the errors on a multilingual ballot are insignificant and the ballot is not "unreasonably difficult" for the voters to read, the Board will uphold the election.[343]

3. Challenges. The Board agent or any party (through its authorized observers) has the privilege of challenging for good cause the eligibility of any person to apply for a ballot and vote in the election. The ballots of such challenged persons are segre-

---

[335]George K. Garrett Co., 120 NLRB 484, 41 LRRM 1519 (1958); Eagle Iron Works, 117 NLRB 1053, 39 LRRM 1379 (1957); Burlington Mills Corp., 56 NLRB 365, 14 LRRM 148 (1944). *See also* NLRB v. A.G. Parrott Co., 630 F2d 212, 105 LRRM 2035 (CA 4, 1980), involving multiple ballot errors.

[336]General Photo Prods., 242 NLRB 1371, 101 LRRM 1352 (1979). *But cf.* Sewell Plastics, 241 NLRB 887, 100 LRRM 1589 (1979), where the Board refused to set aside an election in which two observers had seen how some ballots were marked as they were being deposited in the ballot box.

[337]Abtex Beverage Corp., 237 NLRB 1271, 99 LRRM 1107 (1978); Belmont Smelting & Ref. Works, 115 NLRB 1481, 38 LRRM 1104 (1956); American Cable & Radio Corp., 107 NLRB 1090, 333 LRRM 1324 (1954); General Motors Corp., 107 NLRB 1096, 33 LRRM 1318 (1954).

[338]260 NLRB 1352, 109 LRRM 1320 (1982) (overruling Columbus Nursing Home, 188 NLRB 825, 76 LRRM 1417 (1971)).

[339]Kaufman's Bakery, 264 NLRB 225, 111 LRRM 1261 (1982). *See also* Horton Automatics, 286 NLRB 1413, 127 LRRM 1017 (1987) ("no" marked across both boxes, ballot valid).

[340]251 NLRB 23, 105 LRRM 1007 (1980), where the Board held random marks in addition to an "X" in the "No" box voided a ballot.

[341]Kraft, Inc., 273 NLRB 1484, 118 LRRM 1242 (1985).

[342]Gory Associated Indus., 275 NLRB 1303, 119 LRRM 1277 (1985).

[343]Bridgeport Fittings, 288 NLRB 124, 127 LRRM 1289 (1988), *enforced*, 877 F2d 180, 131 LRRM 2732 (CA 2, 1989).

gated and impounded,[344] thus allowing the Board temporarily to reserve ruling on questions of voter eligibility; but the process preserves the challenged votes in the event they are found relevant. The Board agent must challenge any voter whose name is not on the official eligibility list and any voter who the agent knows or has reason to believe is ineligible. The reason for the challenge should be stated at the time the challenge is made.[345] Anyone in a job classification specifically excluded by the direction of election will be denied a ballot unless plausible reasons for voting are presented, despite the exclusion, or there is some question as to whether he or she is actually within the excluded group.[346]

In *NLRB v. A.J. Tower Co.*,[347] the Supreme Court approved the requirement that challenges to the eligibility of voters be made "prior to the actual casting of ballots," thereby giving all uncontested votes absolute finality. The Court compared this rule with the rule in political elections that once a ballot has been cast without challenge and its identity lost, its validity can no longer be challenged. It follows from this rule that the Board will not permit challenges in the guise of "objections" after the election.[348] Each voter's ballot must be challenged individually when the voter appears at the polls; a party's statement at the opening of the polls that it challenges each and every voter is not a sufficient challenge.[349]

Board agents may make challenges requested by a party. In one case, for example, an election was set aside because a Board

---

[344]Rules and Regs. §102.69(a); Statements of Procedure §101.19(a)(2).

[345]NLRB Field Manual 11338.

[346]*Id.*, 113385.5. In NLRB v. W.R. Grace & Co., 571 F2d 279, 98 LRRM 2001 (CA 5, 1978), the Fifth Circuit upheld a Board decision rejecting an employer's contention that the election should have been set aside because the Board agent failed to investigate the employee status of an individual who was temporarily filling a supervisory position and did not offer him an opportunity to cast a challenged ballot, which could have affected the outcome of the election.

[347]329 US 324, 19 LRRM 2128 (1946); NLRB Field Manual 11360.

[348]Norris, Inc., 63 NLRB 502, 17 LRRM 4 (1945), *enforced*, 162 F2d 50, 20 LRRM 2304 (CA 5, 1947).

[349]Whittaker Co., 94 NLRB 1151, 28 LRRM 1150 (1951); Cities Serv. Oil Co., 87 NLRB 324, 25 LRRM 1112 (1949). *See also* Westinghouse Elec. Corp., 118 NLRB 1625, 40 LRRM 1440 (1957). The Eighth Circuit, however, has held that the Board should have set aside an election because an elderly, illiterate employee, who might have been confused by a challenge to his ballot, voted for the union contrary to his intent. In so deciding this "unusual case," the court refused to apply the general rule that considerations of ballot secrecy and election finality preclude consideration of evidence as to how an employee voted or intended to vote. Alpers Jobbing Co. v. NLRB, 547 F2d 402, 94 LRRM 2145 (CA 8, 1976).

agent failed to challenge a ballot on the union's behalf;[350] the objection was sustained because there was no union observer present during the voting, and the agent was aware of a preelection agreement between the parties that the employee would vote subject to challenge. The District of Columbia Circuit has announced the following guidelines to be applied when it is necessary for a Board agent to state challenges: (1) The Board agent must be completely impartial and show no favoritism in any manner in stating the challenge; (2) the Board agent must not state challenges except when necessitated by an unexpected occurrence; and (3) if an allegation is made that the Board agent was not completely impartial, the burden rests on the alleging party to prove partiality.[351]

A challenged vote is cast as follows: The voter is given a ballot and an envelope which identifies the voter, the reason for challenge, and the challenger. The voter then marks the ballot, puts it into an unmarked envelope which is sealed and placed inside the marked envelope, and casts the sealed envelope in the ballot box. At the time of the count, the challenged ballots are segregated. If the number of challenged ballots is sufficient to affect the outcome of the election, the validity of the challenges must be determined. The regional director or Board need rule only on what is necessary to decide the election. If the number of challenged ballots is insufficient to affect the outcome, the challenges will not be resolved. If a ballot is ruled valid, the challenge is waived unless objection is made within three days.[352] Generally the Board will not open a challenged ballot until the individual has been determined to be eligible. The Board has held that the premature opening of challenged ballots constitutes grounds for vacating an election, because it might create an appearance that the Board had prejudged the eligibility questions.[353] The Board's normal procedure is to hold the ballots of challenged voters in abeyance until a determination of their

---

[350]Laubenstein & Portz, 226 NLRB 804, 93 LRRM 1367 (1976). *But see* Fern Laboratories, 232 NLRB 379, 97 LRRM 1315 (1977). (Board agent had no duty to make party's challenge, noted in preelection agreement, when that party had observer present who could have exercised challenge but failed to do so).

[351]NLRB v. Schwartz Bros., 475 F2d 926, 82 LRRM 2376 (CA DC, 1973).

[352]Rules and Regs. §102.69(h).

[353]D & N Delivery Corp., 201 NLRB 27, 82 LRRM 1208 (1973).

voting eligibility has been made, even if the determination must await the outcome of unfair labor practice charges.[354]

C. Standards for the Conduct of Elections

The procedures for the conduct of elections are designed to insure, insofar as possible, that the outcome reflects a free and fair choice of the voters; "[i]t has long been established that '[t]he Board is responsible for assuring properly conducted elections. . . .'"[355] The Board's goal is to conduct elections "in a laboratory under conditions as nearly ideal as possible to determine the uninhibited desires of employees" and to provide "an atmosphere conducive to the sober and informed exercise of the franchise, free not only from interference, restraint, or coercion violative of the Act, but also from other elements which prevent or impede a reasonable choice."[356] However, the Board has also cautioned against the application of "unrealistic standards," noting that conduct which might be determinative in a small unit election might be isolated and thus insignificant in a larger unit.[357]

In order to test whether an election was conducted consistently with the required safeguards, parties to an election may file objections to *conduct of the election.* Such objections should be distinguished from objections to *conduct affecting the results of the*

---

[354]El Fenix Corp., 234 NLRB 1212, 98 LRRM 1020 (1978).

[355]Kerona Plastics Extrusion Co., 196 NLRB 1120, 1120, 80 LRRM 1231 (1972) (quoting New York Tel. Co., 109 NLRB 788, 790, 34 LRRM 1441 (1954)).

[356]Sewell Mfg. Co., 138 NLRB 66, 70, 50 LRRM 1532 (1962), *supplemented,* 140 NLRB 220, 51 LRRM 1611 (1962). *See generally* Chapter 9, "Restrictions of Preelection Activity: 'Laboratory Conditions.'"

[357]Newport News Shipbuilding & Dry Dock Co., 239 NLRB 82, 99 LRRM 1518 (1978). The Board overruled numerous objections from the employer and an incumbent union, holding that there were no substantial and material issues warranting a hearing. The Fourth Circuit denied enforcement of a §8(a)(5) order against the employer for refusal to bargain following the Board's certification. Newport News Shipbuilding & Dry Dock Co. v. NLRB, 594 F2d 8, 100 LRRM 2798 (CA 4, 1979). The court observed that the use of paper ballots presented special risks of vote fraud, and concluded that a hearing was necessary for the limited purpose of ascertaining whether there was a reasonable likelihood that the election was corrupted by chain voting. Because of the presence of blank ballots found in trash receptacles outside the polling area, coupled with objections suggesting that a substantial number of blank ballots had been left in voting booths, and other objections that the Board was not able to account adequately for all ballots, a hearing was ordered. Upon remand and after hearing, the Board found that logistical difficulties made it not "reasonably likely" that chain voting had occurred, and it again certified the union. Newport News Shipbuilding & Dry Dock Co., 243 NLRB 99, 102 LRRM 1051 (1979). The Circuit Court enforced a bargaining order based on that certification. Newport News Shipbuilding & Dry Dock Co. v. NLRB, 602 F2d 73, 102 LRRM 2531 (CA 4, 1979).

election. The latter involve alleged misconduct by a party during the campaign leading up to an election and frequently involve behavior that constitutes an independent violation of section 8 of the Act.[358] Objections to the conduct of an election, in contrast, may involve behavior by the Board agent, union representative, employer representatives, observers, or voters, and are as likely to involve inadvertent departures from requisite standards as deliberate attempts to influence voters. In general, the Board's standards for conduct of an election involve questions regarding the opportunity to vote, conduct in and around the polling area, protection of the ballot box, and conduct of Board agents that might be construed as, or tend to imply, partiality by the Board.

1. The Opportunity to Vote. Because a certification as exclusive representative is based on the majority of those who vote, the Board has set aside elections where eligible voters have been deprived of an opportunity to vote, either by departures from the scheduled time of the election or by being prevented from reaching the polls.[359]

For example, the Board has set aside elections where there had been departures from the scheduled voting period involving either delayed opening or early closing of the polls. Where a Board agent had arrived 40 minutes late, the election was set aside because the votes of those "possibly excluded" from voting may have affected the outcome, and "the ensuing votes may have been affected by the conduct of the Board agent."[360] In another case involving a 40-minute delay in the opening of the polls, the Board set aside the election even though the number of eligible voters who did not vote could not have affected the outcome; the Board agreed with the regional director's finding that "the votes cast may have been affected by the conduct of the Board agent."[361] In a later case, however, the Board declined to set aside an election where the Board agent was an hour and a half late in opening the polls; the Board stated that "[i]n order to find such conduct objectionable, we require also that the late arrival of the Board agent caused, or may have caused, eligible

---

[358]*See* Chapters 6, "Interference With Protected Rights," and 9, "Restrictions of Pre-election Activity: 'Laboratory Conditions.'"

[359]In addition, as discussed *supra* at notes 294–300, the Board may set aside elections where there has been inadequate posting of notices.

[360]B & B Better Baked Foods, 208 NLRB 493, 493, 85 LRRM 1092 (1974).

[361]Nyack Hosp., 238 NLRB 257, 260, 99 LRRM 1362 (1978).

voters to be disenfranchised."[362] Elections have also been set aside for early closing of the polls where the number of eligible voters who did not vote was sufficient to affect the outcome.[363]

Where every reasonable opportunity should be provided to allow employees to vote, closing the polls at the scheduled time, even if employees are thereby prevented from voting, is generally not considered objectionable conduct.[364] However, if an employee is permitted to cast a ballot after the polls are scheduled to be closed, the Board will usually allow the ballot to be counted,[365] although the Fourth Circuit refused to enforce a bargaining order in a case where a Board agent had permitted at least 30 employees to vote after the polls were closed and had improperly excluded at least one voter.[366]

The Board has also set aside an election where an employer refused to permit possibly eligible voters to cast a ballot.[367] Elections will normally not be set aside where voters are prevented from voting for personal reasons or by circumstances outside the control of the parties.[368] However, the Board has set aside an election where an employee was prevented from voting by the need to correct an emergency situation which was found to be within the control of the employer.[369]

---

[362]Jim Kraut Chevrolet, 240 NLRB 460, 460, 100 LRRM 1227 (1979). *See also* Jobbers Meat Packing Co., 252 NLRB 41, 105 LRRM 1184 (1980).

[363]Kerona Plastics Extrusion Co., 196 NLRB 1120, 80 LRRM 1231 (1972) (polls were closed 20 minutes early in first of two voting sessions); Repcal Brass Mfg. Co., 109 NLRB 4, 34 LRRM 1277 (1954) (polls were closed 1½ to 2 minutes early and number of employees who had not voted was sufficient to affect outcome). *See also* Dominguez Valley Hosp., 251 NLRB 842, 105 LRRM 1122 (1980).

[364]Bancroft Mfg. Co., 210 NLRB 1007, 86 LRRM 1376 (1974), *enforced*, 516 F2d 436, 89 LRRM 3105 (CA 5, 1975), *cert. denied*, 424 US 914, 91 LRRM 2410 (1976). *But see* Hanford Sentinel, Inc., 163 NLRB 1004, 64 LRRM 1482 (1967) (Board set aside election for failure to extend voting time because of "special circumstances," including, *inter alia*, brief duration of voting period, Board agent's awareness that two employees had presented themselves to vote previously, and fact that they sought to vote "only minutes" after polls were closed and prior to opening of ballot box).

[365]Howard Johnson Co., 221 NLRB 542, 90 LRRM 1575 (1975).

[366]NLRB v. Bata Shoe Co., 377 F2d 821, 65 LRRM 2318 (CA 4), *cert. denied*, 389 US 917, 66 LRRM 2370 (1967). The court held that the Board had abused its discretion by not setting aside the election in light of the extreme closeness of the vote (1,082-to-1,036) and the high probability that the Board agent's conduct had deterred other employees from voting.

[367]Neuhoff Bros. Packers, 154 NLRB 438, 59 LRRM 1761 (1965), *enforced*, 362 F2d 611, 62 LRRM 2380 (CA 5, 1966).

[368]Southland Corp., 232 NLRB 631, 96 LRRM 1279 (1977); Yerges Van Liners, 162 NLRB 1259, 64 LRRM 1173 (1967); Versail Mfg., 212 NLRB 592, 86 LRRM 1603 (1974). *See also* Lemco Constr., 283 NLRB 459, 124 LRRM 1329 (1987) (properly conducted election not set aside even though only one of eight eligibles appeared and voted).

[369]Cal Gas Redding, 241 NLRB 290, 100 LRRM 1486 (1979). It was the employer who filed the objections. Noting that it would not normally set aside an election on the basis of the conduct of the objecting party, the Board did so here because of the special circumstance that the employer had no reason to anticipate the emergency situation.

2. Conduct in and Around the Polling Areas. The Board has held that "the final minutes before an employee casts his vote should be his own, as free from interference as possible."[370] Accordingly, the Board prohibits prolonged conversations between parties and voters waiting to vote.[371] This practice also applies to prolonged conversations between observers and voters[372] and even applies to other conversations, regardless of whether they involve electioneering.[373] The same principle was extended to conduct in which an employer representative shook hands with employees waiting to vote.[374] In another case, union partisans wearing T-shirts displaying the words "Vote UAW" paraded back and forth in view of the voters—conduct which the Fifth Circuit, in disagreement with the Board, held to be illegal electioneering.[375] The Board set aside an election where employer officials were present near the voting area.[376] The Board has held, however, that the wearing of union insignia by the union's election observers does not constitute interference with an election,[377] even in circumstances where the employer's observers were required to remove their badges identifying them as section supervisors.[378] Protracted consumption of alcohol at the election site may be a basis for invalidating an election.[379]

3. The Integrity of the Ballots and the Ballot Box. The Board has always been concerned with the integrity of the ballots

---

[370]Milchem, Inc., 170 NLRB 362, 362, 67 LRRM 1395 (1968).

[371]*Id. See also* Midwest Stock Exch. v. NLRB, 620 F2d 629, 104 LRRM 2243 (CA 7), *cert. denied*, 449 US 873, 105 LRRM 2657 (1980); Star Expansion Indus. Corp., 170 NLRB 364, 67 LRRM 1400 (1968).

[372]General Dynamics Corp., 181 NLRB 874, 73 LRRM 1535 (1970). *Cf.* Princeton Refinery, 244 NLRB 1, 101 LRRM 1603 (1979), where conversations between an observer and a voter, which did not involve electioneering, were found not to have interfered with an election because they were not prolonged or sustained. Similarly, when the union's observer invited employees to come in and vote, this was not deemed interference. Amalgamated Indus. Union Local 76B, 246 NLRB 727, 102 LRRM 1666 (1979).

[373]Modern Hard Chrome Serv. Co., 187 NLRB 82, 75 LRRM 1498 (1970).

[374]Volt Technical Corp., 176 NLRB 832, 71 LRRM 1608 (1969).

[375]NLRB v. Decibel Prods., 657 F2d 727, 108 LRRM 2598 (1981), *denying enforcement to and remanding* 248 NLRB 1337, 104 LRRM 1055 (1980). *But see* Clothing & Textile Workers (Angelica Healthcare Servs. Group) v. NLRB, 815 F2d 225, 125 LRRM 2832 (CA 2, 1987), *enforcing* 280 NLRB 864, 123 LRRM 1252 (1986) (repeated pro-union chanting by employee group near polling place insufficient to invalidate election).

[376]Performance Measurements Co., 148 NLRB 1657, 57 LRRM 1218, *supplemented*, 149 NLRB 1451, 58 LRRM 1037 (1964). *But cf.* Components, Inc., 197 NLRB 163, 80 LRRM 1834 (1972); Serv-Air, Inc., 183 NLRB 263, 74 LRRM 1284 (1970).

[377]Colfor, Inc., 243 NLRB 465, 101 LRRM 1495 (1979).

[378]Firestone Textiles Co., 244 NLRB 168, 102 LRRM 1197 (1979) (employer's observers were not statutory supervisors).

[379]Labor Servs., 274 NLRB 479, 118 LRRM 1407 (1985).

and the ballot box, and avers that it "has gone to great lengths to establish and maintain the highest standards possible to avoid any taint of the balloting process; and where a situation . . . casts a doubt or cloud over the integrity of the ballot box itself, the practice has been, without hesitation, to set aside the election."[380] In determining whether there is a cloud on the integrity of the ballot box, all relevant facts are examined.[381] Thus the Board has set aside an election where the ballot box was left unattended for between two and five minutes,[382] though it declined to set aside an election where the Board agent had left the ballot box and the unmarked ballots in the possession of the parties' observers.[383] Similarly, where an envelope containing blank ballots had been outside the Board agent's possession for a short period and there was no evidence of anyone else in the vicinity, the Board upheld the election, noting that "[i]t is not every conceivable possibility of irregularity which requires setting an election aside but only reasonable possibilities."[384]

4. Conduct of Board Agents. The Board has usually sought to maintain the integrity and neutrality of its procedures by insisting on high standards of conduct from Board agents, holding that

> [t]he commission of an act by a Board Agent conducting an election which tends to destroy confidence in the Board's election process, or which could reasonably be interpreted as impugning the election standards we seek to maintain, is a sufficient basis for setting aside that election.[385]

---

[380]Austill Waxed Paper Co., 169 NLRB 1109, 1109, 67 LRRM 1366 (1968). *See also* Henry St. Settlement, 277 NLRB 901, 120 LRRM 1333 (1985) (discrepancy between election tally and number of votes cast).

[381]Polymers, Inc., 174 NLRB 282, 70 LRRM 1148 (1969), *enforced*, 414 F2d 999, 71 LRRM 3107 (CA 2, 1969), *cert. denied*, 396 US 1010, 73 LRRM 2121 1970).

[382]Austill Waxed Paper Co., *supra* note 380. *But see* Bell Foundry Co. v. NLRB, 827 F2d 1340, 126 LRRM 2705 (CA 9, 1987), *enforcing* 278 NLRB 282, 122 LRRM 1127 (1986) (election upheld even though Board agent left sealed ballot box unattended for 5 minutes). In Ashland Chem. Co. Div., 295 NLRB No. 117, 131 LRRM 1722 (1989), the Board determined that the integrity of the ballot box was not impugned when the Board agent slit the ballot box open prior to the arrival of the employer's election observer.

[383]Benavent & Fournier, 208 NLRB 636, 85 LRRM 1143 (1974).

[384]Trico Prods. Corp., 238 NLRB 380, 381, 99 LRRM 1265 (1978). *But see* Paprikas Fono, 273 NLRB 1326, 118 LRRM 1150 (1984) (irregularity in handling challenged ballots).

[385]Athbro Precision Eng'g Corp., 166 NLRB 966, 966, 65 LRRM 1699 (1967), *vacated sub nom.* Electrical Workers (IUE) v. NLRB, 67 LRRM 2361 (CA DC, 1968), *acq. sub nom.* Athbro Precision Eng'g Corp., 171 NLRB 21, 68 LRRM 1001 (1968), *enforced*, 423 F2d 573, 73 LRRM 2355 (CA 1, 1970). *Athbro* has a curious litigation history. The Board originally set aside an election on the basis of the Board agent's misconduct. The union then obtained an injunction in federal district court forcing the Board to issue a certification, and the Board acquiesced in that decision. The employer, who had not appealed the

For example, in one case the Board set aside an election where an employee, who had already voted, observed the Board agent having a drink with a union representative between sessions of an election.[386]

Not all ambiguous or arguably partial conduct requires the Board or the courts to set aside an election. Elections were not set aside where, at the beginning of a voting period, a Board agent announced that the polls were opened and the employees could, if they desired, "'now vote for your union representative'";[387] where, after the counting of the ballots, the Board agent told two new Board lawyers who had accompanied her to the election that they were lucky, because "'[y]ou've got yourself a winner'";[388] and where the Board agent told the employer's observer that he thought the union would win the election and that would do the people a lot of good.[389]

Occasionally, the courts have held the Board to a more exacting standard than the Board had embraced. The Fifth Circuit refused to enforce a bargaining order based on an election where a Board agent, while traveling from one polling place to another, had stopped at a motel room of a union representative and was thus observed by a company supervisor.[390] The Sixth Circuit held that the Board erred in refusing to set aside an election won by the union where a Board agent, while conducting an investigation of unfair labor practice charges,[391] had allowed himself to be introduced to employees at a union organization meeting. The court held that the agent, whether inadvertently or not, had allowed himself to be used in a manner that seriously affected the neutrality of the Board's procedures. On the other hand, the Ninth Circuit upheld the Board's rejection of an employer's contention that a Board agent's investigation of

---

district court decision, attempted to have the First Circuit set aside a bargaining order based on that certification, which the court refused because both the Board and the employer had failed to appeal from the district court's judgment. The court did, however, agree with the Board's position with respect to the importance of the fairness and integrity of election procedures, stating: "We cannot think that the Board any less than a court, is uninterested in maintaining, as well as fairness, the appearance of fairness. The Board's public image provides the basis for its existence. The running of an election is a small price to pay for the preservation of public respect." *Id.*, 423 F2d at 575.

[386] Athbro Precision Eng'g Corp., *supra* note 385.

[387] Wabash Transformer Corp., 205 NLRB 148, 148, 83 LRRM 145 (1973), *aff'd*, 509 F2d 647, 88 LRRM 2545 (CA 8), *cert. denied*, 423 US 827, 90 LRRM 2553 (1975).

[388] Wald Sound, Inc., 203 NLRB 366, 367, 83 LRRM 1125 (1973).

[389] NLRB v. Dobbs Houses, 435 F2d 704, 76 LRRM 2120 (CA 5, 1970).

[390] Delta Drilling Co. v. NLRB, 406 F2d 109, 70 LRRM 2272 (CA 5, 1969).

[391] Provincial House v. NLRB, 568 F2d 8, 97 LRRM 2307 (CA 6, 1977).

unfair labor practice charges filed by the union on the day before the election had destroyed the requisite laboratory conditions.[392] The court found no evidence that the agent's actions indicated favoritism or partiality. Likewise, the First Circuit held that no substantial or material fact issues warranted a hearing based on an employee's sworn allegation that the Board agent conducting the election had attempted to influence him to vote for the union.[393] Although the court stated that the Board had erred in applying only an "impact" standard to that allegation, it sustained the Board on the ground that there was no evidence that any employee's vote had been influenced by the alleged conduct.

The issuance of instructions to parties during the voting process is an important responsibility of the Board agent for which the Board holds its agents to strict standards. The Board agent's responsibility for explaining voting procedures may not be delegated to an election observer.[394] Similarly, where a Board agent misled an employer's observer into thinking that a formal challenge to a particular voter's eligibility was unnecessary and that he could not use any kind of employee list to make challenges, the election was set aside.[395]

D. Resolution of Challenges and Objections to the Election

1. Challenges. Prior to the count of the votes the parties may wish to dispose of some challenged ballots by withdrawing challenges. Although the Board agent may encourage such action, it should not be urged on reluctant parties.[396] If the number of challenges remaining is sufficient to affect the results of the election,[397] the regional director investigates the challenges.[398] This investigation is deemed nonadversary. The regional director's investigator is responsible for obtaining all available rele-

---

[392]NLRB v. Tri-City Linen Supply, 579 F2d 51, 98 LRRM 2155 (CA 9, 1978), *enforcing* 226 NLRB 669, 93 LRRM 1431 (1976). *See also* NLRB v. Osborn Transp., 589 F2d 1275, 100 LRRM 2787 (CA 5, 1979).

[393]NLRB v. Fenway Cambridge Motor Hotel, 601 F2d 33, 101 LRRM 2858 (CA 1, 1979).

[394]Alco Iron & Metal Co., 269 NLRB 590, 115 LRRM 1322 (1984) (agent improperly allowed Spanish-speaking partisan observer to explain vote procedure to Spanish-speaking voters).

[395]Harry Lunstead Designs, 270 NLRB 1163, 116 LRRM 1289 (1984).

[396]NLRB Field Manual 11340.3.

[397]Statements of Procedure §101.19(a)(4); NLRB Field Manual 11360.

[398]Rules and Regs. §102.69(c); United States Rubber Co. v. NLRB, 373 F2d 602, 64 LRRM 2393 (CA 5, 1967).

vant facts so that full consideration may be given to all matters elicited by the investigation, whether or not urged by, or known to, the parties.[399]

2. Objections to the Election. In 1986, reacting to strong judicial criticism,[400] the Board promulgated new regulations designed to bring uniformity to its rules governing the filing of objections.[401] The rule imposed two important changes: (1) the time period in which to file objections was extended from 5 to 7 days; and (2) the objections must actually be received by the Board within the 7-day period.[402] The rules have been strictly enforced since their issuance, and the Board has held that election objections postmarked prior to the due date but not received by the Board until after the due date were not timely filed.[403] The Board has also made clear that the time period will not be extended even where a holiday falls during the first 6 days of the period for filing objections, rather than on the seventh day.[404] The Board will consider objections timely filed if they are deposited in any Board office whether it be designated as a regional office, subregional office, or a resident office, and are received by an agent with an official Board stamp, or deposited with an authorized agent of the regional director and marked as received within the designated period.[405]

Upon receipt of timely objections, the regional director must conduct an investigation unless the party filing the objections is unable to furnish sufficient evidence to support a *prima facie* case.[406] The Board will sustain a dismissal of objections if the

---

[399]NLRB Field Manual 11362; J. Weingarten, Inc., 172 NLRB 2020, 69 LRRM 1118 (1968). In 1981 the Board amended §102.69(d) of its Rules and Regulations to make it clear that the regional director should hold a hearing when objections raise "substantial and material factual issues."

[400]*E.g.*, NLRB v. Washington Star Co., 732 F2d 974, 977, 116 LRRM 2131 (CA DC, 1984) (court criticized Board for rejecting documents as untimely filed without "articulat[ing] its reasons for a strict rule that requires filings to be in hand on the due date and announc[ing] that it will apply this rule uniformly with specific stated exceptions. . . .").

[401]NLRB Rules and Regs. §§102.69 (a) and (b).

[402]*Id.*

[403]Drum Lithographers, 287 NLRB 22, 127 LRRM 1227 (1987) (overruling Rio de Oro Uranium Mines, 119 NLRB 153, 41 LRRM 1057 (1957)); *see also* North Star Steel Co., 289 NLRB 1188, 129 LRRM 1024 (1988); W.B. Brown & Sons, 288 NLRB 746, 128 LRRM 1189 (1988); Everett Prods., 287 NLRB 309, 127 LRRM 1230 (1987); Berk, Inc., 287 NLRB 425, 127 LRRM 1231 (1987).

[404]Drum Lithographers, *supra* note 403.

[405]Sacramento Union, 258 NLRB 1074, 108 LRRM 1193 (1980). The Eleventh Circuit has approved this rule in Piggly Wiggly, Tuscaloosa Div. v. NLRB, 705 F2d 1537, 113 LRRM 2810 (CA 11, 1983). The court also held that objections were timely filed even though they were filed with the resident office after the regional office had closed on the fifth and final day for filing.

[406]NLRB Field Manual 11392.5.

objecting party does not furnish supporting evidence in a timely manner;[407] however, this may be a matter of some discretion, for the Board has found that a regional director's failure to extend the time limit to be an abuse of discretion.[408] The Fourth Circuit reversed a Board decision which rejected objections supported by specific allegations of fact and directed an investigation, holding that the regional director should have conducted an investigation as required by Board rules where the information submitted suggested that laboratory conditions could have been destroyed.[409]

The Board requires that the objections include a statement of reasons.[410] But Board policy also permits a regional director to set aside an election based on conduct discovered during the investigation of objections to the election, even though the particular conduct relied on was not the subject of a specific objection.[411] The Board's rationale for this approach is that it is consistent with the trend of modern pleading practice, which tends to lessen if not eliminate technical niceties. The Sixth Circuit has agreed, rejecting an employer's argument that the election was improperly overturned because the union objections did not specify the ground upon which the election was thereafter set aside.[412] The court held the objection sufficient even though it did not refer to an antiunion speech by the employer's general manager, upon which the union had relied in successfully challenging the election, since it did not appear that the company was prejudiced or taken by surprise.

---

[407]Kano Trucking Serv., 295 NLRB No. 58, 131 LRRM 1710 (1989). *But see* Excalibur Extrusions, 296 NLRB No. 159, 132 LRRM 1267 (1989) (Board remanded case to regional director to determine whether Board agent had granted oral extension of time to file evidence, and it stressed need for strict and uniform application of procedural rules). *See also* Classic Courts, 246 NLRB 603, 102 LRRM 1631 (1979).

[408]Midland Nat'l Life Ins. Co., 244 NLRB 3, 102 LRRM 1156 (1979), *enforced*, 621 F2d 901, 104 LRRM 2293 (CA 8, 1980); Vintage Homes, 240 NLRB 609, 100 LRRM 1303 (1979).

[409]Electronic Components Corp. v. NLRB, 546 F2d 1088, 93 LRRM 2280 (CA 4, 1976).

[410]Rules and Regs. §102.69(a).

[411]Clark Manor Nursing Home Corp., 254 NLRB 455, 106 LRRM 1231 (1981), *enforced in part and rev'd in part on other grounds*, 671 F2d 657, 109 LRRM 3151 (CA 1, 1982); Seneca Foods Corp., 244 NLRB 558, 102 LRRM 1085 (1979); Midland Nat'l Life Ins. Co., *supra* note 408; Siskin Steel & Supply Co., 240 NLRB 177, 100 LRRM 1263 (1979); Dayton Tire & Rubber Co., 234 NLRB 504, 97 LRRM 1308 (1978); American Safety Equip. Corp., 234 NLRB 501, 97 LRRM 1305 (1978), *enforcement denied*, 643 F2d 693, 106 LRRM 2836 (CA 10, 1981). *See also* Moody Nursing Home, 251 NLRB 147, 105 LRRM 1126 (1980).

[412]NLRB v. Leslie Metal Arts Co., 530 F2d 720, 92 LRRM 2428 (CA 6, 1976). *But see* San Francisco Sausage Co., 291 NLRB 384, 130 LRRM 1140 (1988); Burns Int'l Sec. Servs., 256 NLRB 959, 107 LRRM 1425 (1981) (evidence raised in "supplementary" objections too remote).

The time span of conduct subject to investigation generally begins with the filing of the petition.[413] This restriction, however, has been held not to apply in certain circumstances; for example, the Board has set aside elections based on prepetition misconduct occurring in connection with a union's effort to develop a showing of interest.[414]

3. Resolution of Challenges and Objections. If the election was held under a direction of election and it appears to the regional director that substantial and material factual issues exist which can be resolved only after a hearing, a hearing must be held on such issues; otherwise the holding of a hearing is within the regional director's discretion.[415] Whether or not a hearing is held, as to a directed election the regional director may (1) issue a report on the objections and/or challenges, specifically recommend a disposition, and forward the report to the Board; or (2) issue a supplemental decision appropriately disposing of the objections and challenges. If the regional director issues a report to the Board, the parties have a right to file exceptions with the Board within 10 days. If the regional director issues a supplemental decision, the parties may seek Board review. As in the case of orders directing elections, review is limited to four categories, namely: (1) departure from reported Board precedent involving a substantial question of law or policy, (2) clear and prejudicial error on the record regarding a substantial issue of fact, (3) prejudicial error in the conduct of the hearing, and (4) compelling reasons to reconsider an important Board rule or policy.[416]

In a "pure consent" election the foregoing procedure is not applicable because the regional director's decision is virtually final on all issues, without even a discretionary appeal. In rare situations, however, the Board may consider a motion to set aside the regional director's decision as being arbitrary or capricious.[417]

---

[413]Jerome J. Jacomet, 222 NLRB 899, 91 LRRM 1370 (1976); Ideal Elec. & Mfg. Co., 134 NLRB 1275, 49 LRRM 1316 (1961). *See* Chapter 9, "Restrictions of Preelection Activity: 'Laboratory Conditions,'" at notes 14–31.

[414]Consolidated Foods Co., 234 NLRB 178, 97 LRRM 1116 (1978); Gibson's Discount Center, 214 NLRB 221, 87 LRRM 1291 (1974).

[415]Rules and Regs. §102.69(c); Home Town Foods v. NLRB, 379 F2d 241, 65 LRRM 2681 (CA 5, 1967) (holding that if there are substantial and material issues of fact, employer must be given opportunity for a hearing to establish its charges).

[416]Rules and Regs. §§102.67(c), 102.69(c); but where objections raise substantial and material issues, a hearing should be held. §102. *See* Chapter 31, "NLRB Procedures," at note 105.

[417]*Id.*, §102.62(a).

In a "stipulated" election the Board, rather than the regional director, makes final determinations of challenges and objections. The regional director prepares a report on the investigation, serves it on the parties, and forwards it to the Board. But if the regional director orders a hearing, the report may be omitted.[418] When the regional director forwards a report to the Board, the parties have a right to file exceptions within 10 days. Such exceptions may be accompanied by briefs and may be opposed by an answering brief from any other party within 17 days of the regional director's report. If no exceptions are filed, the Board may decide the case on the record or otherwise dispose of it.[419] If the election was held pursuant to a stipulation agreement, and the exceptions filed to the Board's decision do not appear to raise substantial and material issues, the Board may decide the case forthwith. But if the exceptions do appear to raise such issues, the Board may order a further hearing and a report, in which case the parties would again have the right to file (within 10 days) exceptions to the report, which the Board will then consider on their merits.[420]

If the objections to the election are overruled, a certification will be issued, provided there are no problems pending due to unresolved challenges. If the objections are found to have merit, the election will be set aside and a new election conducted.[421] A decision of the Board sustaining objections, setting aside an election, and ordering a new vote is not directly reviewable in the courts.[422]

E. Runoff and Rerun Elections

A prerequisite to the holding of a *runoff election* is that none of the three or more choices that appeared on the ballot in the original election has received a majority of the valid votes cast. For example, in an election involving 18 eligible voters, union *A* receives seven votes, "neither" receives six votes, and union *B* receives five votes—this would be considered an inconclusive election; the regional director would then conduct a runoff

---

[418]*Id.*, §102.69(c).
[419]*Id.*
[420]*Id.*, §102.69(e).
[421]Statements of Procedure §101.19(a)(4).
[422]Bonwit Teller, Inc. v. NLRB, 197 F2d 640, 30 LRRM 2305 (CA 2, 1952). *See generally* Chapter 33, "Judicial Review and Enforcement."

election between the choices on the ballot that received the highest and the next highest number of votes, i.e., union *A* and "neither."[423] There can be no runoff of an election in which there are only two choices.[424] The runoff election is held as soon as possible after the original election, but not while objections are pending or still timely.[425] A timely objection to a runoff election will be considered only insofar as it relates to circumstances occurring subsequent to the original election.[426] Those eligible to vote are those who were eligible at the time of the original election.[427] However, the Board did make one exception to its general eligibility rule: Where there was a long lapse of time between the elections, with substantial employee turnover,[428] a current eligibility date was used in order to provide a more representative vote.

A runoff election may not be appropriate where voters in the original election are faced with answering two questions by a single vote. In one such *Globe election* case,[429] a single vote was taken among powerhouse employees to ascertain whether they preferred a separate unit and, if so, which union, if any, they desired to represent them. The election was conclusive concerning the preference of the employees for a separate unit, but no union on the ballot received a majority. The Board rejected the employer's contention that a second election should be deemed a runoff election with the ballot limited to the two choices in the original election that received the highest vote. Instead, the Board deemed its investigation concerning representation incomplete, and ordered a second election, since one union had not sought to represent the separate unit in the original election.

A *rerun election* is an exception to the runoff procedure (which is premised on the emergence of the top two nonmajority choices). On occasion, two of the nonmajority choices may receive the same number of votes, while the third choice may receive a higher vote but still less than a majority. In that event,

---

[423]NLRB Field Manual 11350.1.

[424]This would include a craft severance election where there were only two choices on the ballot. *Id.*

[425]*Id.*, 11350.3.

[426]*Id.*

[427]Thus the list can only change "downward." *Id.* 11350.5.

[428]Interlake S.S. Co., 178 NLRB 128, 72 LRRM 1008 (1969).

[429]B. P. Alaska, Inc., 234 NLRB 125, 98 LRRM 1060 (1978); *see* Sohio Petroleum Corp. v. NLRB, 625 F2d 223, 104 LRRM 2804 (CA 9, 1980). *See also* discussion of *Globe* election doctrine in Chapter 11, "Appropriate Bargaining Units," at notes 29–33.

the election is considered a *nullity* and is rerun.[430] A runoff may result from a rerun,[431] but a second nullity will cause a dismissal of the petition.[432] For rerun purposes, the payroll period determining eligibility is a "recent" one set by the regional director or the Board.[433]

Rerun elections will also be conducted pursuant to an order setting aside the original election because of violations of "laboratory conditions." When the first election has been set aside because of employer or union interference, the notice of election may include a paragraph explaining why the election is being rerun.[434]

A further exception to the runoff procedure occurs when all eligible votes have been cast, two or more choices have received an equal number of votes, the other choice has received no votes, and there are no challenges; for example, of 16 valid votes, union *A* receives none, union *B* receives eight, and "neither" receives eight.[435] In that situation, the election will not be rerun and there will be no certification of representative; the regional director will merely certify the results of the election.

F. Certification and Revocation

When there are no timely filed objections and the voting is determinative, the regional director issues a certification of the results of the election and, where appropriate, a certification of representative. This certification has the same force and effect as if issued directly by the Board, and the proceeding is thereby closed.[436] If no union receives more than half the votes, the results of the election will be certified, showing that the union or unions are not the choice of the majority of the employees.

A union that receives a majority of the valid votes cast will be certified as the representative of the employees in the unit for purposes of collective bargaining. Thus, a union cannot be cer-

---

[430]NLRB Field Manual 11350.1.

[431]*Id.*, 11456.

[432]*Id.*, 11350.1.

[433]*Id.*, 11452.

[434]*Id.*, 11452.1, incorporating the device adopted by the Board in Lufkin Rule Co., 147 NLRB 341, 56 LRRM 1212 (1964) (notice to employees in second election included statement that first election was set aside because of employer interference and that the Act gives employees right to cast ballots as they see fit and protects them in exercise of that right).

[435]*Id.*, 11350.2.

[436]Rules and Regs. §102.69(b).

tified on the basis of a tie vote.[437] The Board may refuse certification if the legality of any stage in the representation proceeding is properly called into question,[438] or if the labor organization would be precluded from representing the employees because of supervisory domination or control, or as a result of a conflict of interest.[439]

The Board has consistently held that certifications are subject to reconsideration and that it may police its certifications by amendment, clarification, or even revocation.[440] In *Hughes Tool Co.*,[441] for example, the Board rescinded a certification where the certified unions had executed racially discriminatory contracts and had administered them in a manner that tended to perpetuate racial discrimination in employment. A certification may also be revoked where the certified union has exhibited a pattern of coercion or violence.[442]

The Board has extended comity to a certification issued pursuant to an election conducted by a responsible state agency, where the state agency's election procedures conformed to due process and effectuated the policies of the Act.[443] However, the Third Circuit Court of Appeals denied enforcement to a bargaining order based on the extension of comity, on the basis of its finding that the state-certified unit was inappropriate under the Act.[444]

---

[437]John W. Thomas Co., 111 NLRB 226, 36 LRRM 1444 (1955).

[438]Worthington Pump & Mach. Corp., 99 NLRB 189, 30 LRRM 1052 (1952).

[439]*See* Sierra Vista Hosp., 241 NLRB 631, 100 LRRM 1590 (1979).

[440]*See* K.C. MCGUINESS & J.A. NORRIS, HOW TO TAKE A CASE BEFORE THE NLRB 231–281; Rules and Regs. §§102.60(b), 102.61(d), 102.61(e).

[441]147 NLRB 1573, 56 LRRM 1289 (1964). *See* Chapter 26, "The Duty of Fair Representation," at note 113.

[442]Union Nacional de Trabajadores, 219 NLRB 862, 90 LRRM 1023 (1975), *enforced*, 540 F2d 1, 92 LRRM 3425 (1976), *cert. denied*, 429 US 1039, 94 LRRM 2201 (1977). *See also* College of Osteopathic Medicine & Surgery, 265 NLRB 295, 111 LRRM 1523 (1982), where union's certification of faculty unit was revoked after Board reclassified all faculty members as managerial employees, leaving no covered employees in unit.

[443]Doctors Osteopathic Hosp., 242 NLRB 447, 101 LRRM 1192 (1979), *enforced*, 624 F2d 1089, 106 LRRM 2546 (CA 3, 1980); Allegheny Gen. Hosp., 230 NLRB 954, 96 LRRM 1022 (1977).

[444]Memorial Hosp. of Roxborough v. NLRB, 545 F2d 351, 93 LRRM 2571 (CA 3, 1976), *denying enforcement to* 220 NLRB 402, 90 LRRM 1369 (1975).

CHAPTER 11

APPROPRIATE BARGAINING UNITS

I. BACKGROUND

A bargaining unit is a grouping of two or more employees aggregated for the assertion of organizational rights or for collective bargaining. The bargaining unit provides the formal arena of the entire collective bargaining process. Section 9(a) of the National Labor Relations Act provides that

> [r]epresentatives designated or selected for the purposes of collective bargaining by the majority of the employees in *a unit appropriate for such purposes*, shall be the exclusive representatives of all the employees in such units . . . .[1]

The size and composition of the bargaining unit is often a subject of dispute between union and employer and between contending unions, since this decision can determine whether the union is entitled to representative status. A union which may enjoy majority support within a small unit may not be able to establish its majority in a larger unit. Similarly, the size and composition of the bargaining unit may determine which of two contending unions gains representative status.

When the parties to a representation proceeding disagree,[2] the Board determines whether the unit of employees in which the petitioner seeks an election is an "appropriate unit" for collective bargaining. In resolving the unit issue, "the Board's primary concern is to group together only employees who have substantial mutual interests in wages, hours, and other condi-

---

[1]Emphasis added.

[2]NLRB v. J.J. Collins Sons, 332 F2d 523, 56 LRRM 2375 (CA 7, 1964). For discussion of consent election agreements, see Chapter 10, "Representation Proceedings and Elections," at notes 11 and 225–227, and Chapter 31, "NLRB Procedures," at notes 62–63.

tions of employment."[3] Stated in another fashion, the Board determines whether the employees share a *community of interests*. The Board need not determine "the *only* appropriate unit, or the *ultimate* unit, or the *most* appropriate unit: the Act requires only that the unit be 'appropriate.'"[4]

The Board has found the "appropriate bargaining unit" concept elastic and, except for its recent efforts involving the health care industry,[5] has not employed the discretion conferred by the Act to establish rules defining units for broad categories of cases. Instead, it makes bargaining-unit determinations by use of a number of tests, including (1) extent and type of union organization of the employees; (2) bargaining history in the industry, as well as with respect to the parties before the Board; (3) similarity of duties, skills, interests, and working conditions of the employees; (4) organizational structure of the company; and (5) the desires of the employees.

Because of the wide differences in forms of employee organizations, the complexities of modern industry, and other variables, it was virtually impossible for Congress to include in the Wagner Act detailed criteria to guide the Board in making unit determinations. Instead, by use of the discretionary term "appropriate" and the inclusion of the broad standard, "in order to assure to employees the fullest freedom in exercising the rights guaranteed by this Act,"[6] Congress delegated to the Board wide latitude to determine appropriate bargaining units.[7] When the National Labor Relations Act was amended in 1947, Congress reenacted the same broad delegation for general unit determination;[8] but imposed some specific limitations, as follows:

---

[3]NLRB, 1950 ANNUAL REPORT 39 (1951).

[4]Morand Bros. Beverage Co., 91 NLRB 409, 418, 26 LRRM 1501 (1950), *enforced*, 190 F2d 576, 28 LRRM 2364 (CA 7, 1951) (emphasis in original); *accord* Florida Steel Corp., 222 NLRB 546, 91 LRRM 1189 (1976); Capital Bakers, 168 NLRB 904, 66 LRRM 1385 (1967); Federal Elec. Corp., 157 NLRB 1130, 61 LRRM 1500 (1966); F.W. Woolworth Co., 144 NLRB 307, 54 LRRM 1043 (1963). Thus, if a petitioning union seeks a unit that is found to be appropriate, the employer's alternative proposals will not be considered. P.J. Dick Contracting, 290 NLRB 150, 129 LRRM 1144 (1988).

[5]*See infra* notes 194–203.

[6]Section 9(b).

[7]In NLRB v. Hearst Publications, 322 US 111, 134, 14 LRRM 614 (1944), a case under the Wagner Act, the Supreme Court noted the Board's broad discretion in unit determination as follows:

> Wide variations in the forms of employee self-organization and the complexities of modern industrial organization make difficult the use of inflexible rules as the test of an appropriate unit. Congress was informed of the need for flexibility in shaping the unit to the particular case and accordingly gave the Board wide discretion in the matter.

[8]Section 9(b).

(1) Professional employees may not be included in a unit with other employees unless a majority of the professionals vote for inclusion in that unit.[9]

(2) The Board may not decide that any craft unit is inappropriate on the ground that prior Board determinations established a different unit.[10]

(3) Guards may not be included in a unit with other employees, and any organization representing guards may not be affiliated with any organization that admits other employees to membership.[11]

(4) The extent of union organization shall not be controlling in determining whether a unit is appropriate.[12]

Outside the area of these restrictions, the Board still has extremely broad discretion in determining appropriate bargaining units under the statutory polestar of "assur[ing] employees the fullest freedom in exercising the rights guaranteed by this Act."[13]

---

[9]Section 9(b)(1).

[10]Section 9(b)(2).

[11]Section 9(b)(3).

[12]Section 9(c)(5).

[13]Section 9(b). NLRB v. Mercy Hosps. of Sacramento, 589 F2d 968, 98 LRRM 2800 (CA 9, 1978); Stephens Produce Co. v. NLRB, 515 F2d 1373, 89 LRRM 2311 (CA 8, 1975) (Board unit determination should not be set aside unless "arbitrary" or "capricious").

For discussion of the Board's overall approach to unit determinations, see Kaminsky, *Overview of the Law, and the Basic Manufacturing Unit*, in APPROPRIATE UNITS FOR COLLECTIVE BARGAINING 1 (P. Nash & G. Blake eds. 1979). For an economics-oriented analysis of bargaining units, see Leslie, *Labor Bargaining Units*, 70 VA. L. REV. 353 (1984).

The statutory provisions and procedures for determination of bargaining units under the NLRB may be contrasted with those of the Railway Labor Act, 45 USC §§151–188 (1974), under which the National Mediation Board (NMB) has the duty of deciding in what *craft* or *class* the election and bargaining shall take place. Railway Labor Act §2 (Ninth), 45 USC §152 (Ninth) (1976). The NMB does not have as wide a discretion to structure bargaining units, although its determinations of craft or class are not subject to judicial review. Railway & S.S. Clerks v. Association for the Benefit of Non-Contract Employees (United Airlines), 380 US 650, 59 LRRM 2051 (1965); Switchmen v. National Mediation Bd., 320 US 297, 13 LRRM 616 (1943); *see* A.R. Weber, THE STRUCTURE OF COLLECTIVE BARGAINING 228 (1961); Comment, *Procedure and Judicial Review Under Section 2, Ninth of the Railway Labor Act*, 32 J. AIR L. & COM. 249 (1966); *see generally* Eischen, *Representation Disputes and Their Resolution in the Railroad and Airline Industries*, in THE RAILWAY LABOR ACT AT FIFTY: COLLECTIVE BARGAINING IN THE RAILROAD AND AIRLINE INDUSTRIES 23–70 (C.M. Rehmus ed. 1977). Judicial review of NLRB unit determinations is discussed in Chapter 33, "Judicial Review and Enforcement." For a comparison of procedures under the RLA and the NLRA, see Morris, *Procedural Reform in Labor Law—A Preliminary Paper*, 35 J. AIR L. & COM. 537 (1969).

II. GENERAL FACTORS IN UNIT DETERMINATIONS

A. Community of Interest Among Employees

Community of interest is the fundamental factor in bargaining-unit determination involving not only previously unrepresented employees but also attempts to sever a group of already represented employees from a larger bargaining unit.[14] In *Kalamazoo Paper Box Corp.*,[15] a unit-severance case, the Board enumerated the factors in determining whether community of interest sets a group of employees apart from other employees:

> [A] difference in method of wages or compensation; different hours of work; different employment benefits; separate supervision; the degree of dissimilar qualifications, training and skills; differences in job functions and amount of working time spent away from the employment or plant situs . . . ; the infrequency or lack of contact with other employees; lack of integration with the work functions of other employees or interchange with them; and the history of bargaining.[16]

Community of interest controls the appropriateness of all bargaining units: multi-employer as well as single-employer, plant-wide as well as multiplant, and craft as well as departmental.

The Act itself suggests the possible appropriateness of aggregating employees by "employer unit, craft unit, plant unit, or subdivision thereof."[17] And the Board has asserted the presumptive appropriateness of the single-location unit.[18] On the other hand, the specific amendments of 1947 attach special significance to the community of skills among professionals and

---

[14]The Board's emphasis on community of interest has received wide judicial approval. *E.g.*, NLRB v. Action Automotive, 469 U.S. 490, 118 LRRM 2577 (1985). In bargaining-unit severance cases, the group of employees seeking a separate bargaining unit must not only show that they share a community of interest among themselves, they must also meet several other Board criteria for severance, as discussed at notes 78–108 *infra*.

[15]136 NLRB 134, 48 LRRM 1715 (1962). *Cf.* Olincraft, Inc., 179 NLRB 414, 72 LRRM 1337 (1969) (refusing to sever truck drivers from production and maintenance unit because of similarity of employee duties and interests).

[16]136 NLRB at 137, 49 LRRM at 1716. While the *Kalamazoo* case dealt specifically with severance of truck drivers from a production unit, the principles announced in that case have been given general application in cases involving unit severance and in cases involving previously unrepresented employees. *See* NLRB v. Campbell Sons' Corp., 407 F2d 969, 70 LRRM 2886 (CA 4, 1969). For application of the principle to unit clarification, see Kennecott Copper Corp., 176 NLRB 96, 71 LRRM 1188 (1969).

[17]Section 9(b).

[18]Frisch's Big Boy Ill-Mar, 147 NLRB 551, 56 LRRM 1246 (1964). For an argument challenging the Board's position, see Siegel, *Problems and Procedures in the NLRB Election Process*, in LABOR LAW DEVELOPMENTS 1968 (Fourteenth Annual Institute on Labor Law, Southwestern Legal Foundation) 29, 43 (1969).

craftsmen, and to the security needs of the employer regarding plant guards.[19]

Thus, the Board's basic function in determining the appropriateness of a potential bargaining unit is to decide whether or not the employees in a proposed unit share a sufficient "community of interest" and to group together for purposes of collective bargaining employees who share a common interest in wages, hours, and other conditions of employment. Community of interest is not susceptible to precise definition or to mechanical application. As illustrated by the cases discussed throughout this chapter, the ultimate determination much more often depends on detailed factual analysis on a case-by-case basis than on the application of rules of law.

B. Extent of Union Organization

The scope of the union's organizing campaign, that is, the groups of employees on which the union has focused its organizing efforts, may play a significant role in the Board's decision as to what constitutes an appropriate unit. This factor is now treated separately in the Act[20] and is referred to as *extent of organization*.

Prior to 1947, the Board found extent of organization to be an especially significant factor in determining appropriateness of a unit on the theory that it is often desirable to render collective bargaining a reasonably early possibility for the employees involved, lest prolonged delay expose these organized employees to the temptation of striking to obtain recognition.[21] The weight given this factor by the Board aroused considerable criticism.[22]

Critics of the Board's approach persuaded Congress in 1947 to enact section 9(c)(5), which provides that

> [i]n determining whether a unit is appropriate . . . the extent to which the employees have organized shall not be controlling.

Thus, a unit based solely or essentially on extent of organization is inappropriate.[23] However, the Board may give weight to the

---

[19]*See* notes 9–11 *supra* and accompanying text.

[20]Section 9(c)(5).

[21]NLRB, 1947 ANNUAL REPORT 21 (1948).

[22]See dissent by Member Reynolds in Garden State Hosiery Co., 74 NLRB 318, 20 LRRM 1149 (1947), claiming that the Board's application of the doctrine permitted "gerrymandering" by the petitioning union so as to establish a unit in which it could win an election.

[23]John A. Sundwall & Co., 149 NLRB 1022, 57 LRRM 1435 (1964); Quality Food Mkts., 126 NLRB 349, 45 LRRM 1316 (1960).

extent of organization in finding a unit appropriate, provided there are other substantial factors on which to base the unit determination.[24] Accordingly,

> [i]t is not the Board's policy to compel labor organizations to represent the most comprehensive grouping; nor is it the Board's function to compel all employees to be represented or unrepresented at the same time or to require that a labor organization represent employees it does not wish to represent unless an appropriate unit does not otherwise exist.[25]

So long as the Board gives less than controlling weight to the extent of organization, its unit determination does not contravene the statute.[26] It may even treat extent of organization as a determinative factor which tilts the balance in favor of a particular unit and still comply with the statutory command that extent of organization not be a controlling factor.[27] Problems may arise, however, where the Board rules on extent of organization but fails to indicate precisely the weight which it is given.[28]

C. Desires of the Employees—The *Globe* Doctrine

The effectiveness of collective bargaining depends in large part on the cohesiveness of the employees in the unit.[29] Where

---

[24]Beck Corp. v. NLRB, 590 F2d 290, 100 LRRM 2719 (CA 9, 1978); NLRB v. Morganton Full Fashioned Hosiery Co., 241 F2d 913, 39 LRRM 2493 (CA 4, 1957); NLRB v. Smythe, 212 F2d 664, 34 LRRM 2108 (CA 5, 1954); Mosler Safe Co., 188 NLRB 650, 651, 76 LRRM 1524 (1971); Overnite Transp. Co., 141 NLRB 384, 52 LRRM 1361 (1963), *enforced as modified*, 327 F2d 36, 55 LRRM 2126 (CA 4, 1963); Waldensian Hosiery Mills, 83 NLRB 742, 24 LRRM 1129 (1949).

[25]Ballentine Packing Co., 132 NLRB 923, 925, 48 LRRM 1451 (1961).

[26]NLRB v. Metropolitan Life Ins. Co., 380 US 438, 58 LRRM 2721 (1965); NLRB v. Salant & Salant, 171 F2d 292, 23 LRRM 2265 (CA 6, 1948) (per curiam); Dixie Belle Mills, Inc., 139 NLRB 629, 631 n.7, 51 LRRM 1344 (1962).

[27]NLRB v. Southern Metal Serv., 606 F2d 512, 102 LRRM 2907 (CA 5, 1979), *enforcing* 236 NLRB 827, 98 LRRM 1490 (1978). *See also* Allied Stores of N.Y., 150 NLRB 799, 807, 58 LRRM 1081 (1965), where the Board stated that the petitioner's motive in seeking a particular unit is immaterial as long as the Board does not give controlling weight to extent of organization.

[28]*See* Metropolitan Life Ins. Co. v. NLRB, 330 F2d 62, 55 LRRM 2930 (CA 6, 1964), *vacated and remanded*, 380 US 525, 59 LRRM 2063 (1965). On statewide units, see Central Power & Light Co., 195 NLRB 743, 79 LRRM 1489 (1972); Retail Clerks Local 1325 v. NLRB (Adams Drug Co.), 414 F2d 1194, 71 LRRM 2721 (CA DC, 1969).

[29]The idea of the cohesiveness of the employees has been especially important in craft and departmental severance questions, and the *Globe* doctrine has special impact in these areas. *See infra* at notes 78–107. For determining whether separate multiplant units should be merged into a single-employer unit, see Libbey-Owens-Ford Glass Co., 169 NLRB 126, 67 LRRM 1096 (1968); *cf.* Rinker Materials Corp., 294 NLRB No. 58, 131 LRRM 1382 (1989). On the necessity of a self-determination election to determine a petition for addition of classifications in existence at the time of certification, see National Cash Register Co., 170 NLRB 1022, 67 LRRM 1541 (1968), *enforcement denied*, 415 F2d 1012, 72 LRRM 2051 (CA 5, 1969). Before such a self-determination election is held, the

there are two or more equally appropriate units, the desires of the employees oftentimes become the critical factor. When such a situation arises, the Board's *Globe* doctrine[30] comes into play, and an election is held to determine the employees' desires on the unit issue. The doctrine is derived from *Globe Machine & Stamping Co.*[31] In a typical *Globe* situation, craft employees

> are afforded the opportunity to indicate that they prefer to be established as a separate bargaining unit, apart from a broader industrial unit in which they would otherwise be included, by voting for the craft union that seeks to represent them separately, as against the industrial union that desires to represent them as part of the broader unit. But in such an election, a majority of the employees in the craft group will sometimes vote for the "no-union" choice, or for an industrial union which fails to win a majority in the balance of the industrial unit for which it desires to bargain.[32]

The *Globe* procedure requires two or more ballots in the same election (or holding two or more elections simultaneously among the different groups). To illustrate: The employees in the smaller group—ordinarily but not necessarily a craft group—vote separately to indicate whether they desire representation by (1) the union seeking to represent them in the smaller (craft) unit or (2) the union seeking to represent all of the employees in a broader (e.g., production and maintenance) unit. If a majority of the smaller group selects its own representation, its choice of unions will be certified for the smaller unit. Representation of the remaining employees in the broader "industrial" unit will be by majority vote in a unit which excludes the smaller group. If the smaller group does not choose separate representation, and if the "industrial" union polls a majority among both groups combined, its certification will cover both groups of employees in a single unit.

A *Globe*-type election may also be ordered where only one union is seeking representation and the Board finds either (1) a larger all-inclusive unit or (2) a smaller unit of a group within the

---

Board must determine what units would be appropriate. Pacific Southwest Airlines v. NLRB, 587 F2d 1032, 100 LRRM 2566 (CA 9, 1978), *denying enforcement to* 227 NLRB 1578, 94 LRRM 1704 (1977).

[30]3 NLRB 294, 1-A LRRM 122 (1937). The doctrine was upheld in NLRB v. Underwood Mach. Co., 179 F2d 118, 25 LRRM 2195 (CA 1, 1959). The *Globe* procedure received Supreme Court approval in Pittsburgh Plate Glass Co. v. NLRB, 313 US 146, 8 LRRM 425 (1941).

[31]*Supra* note 30.

[32]NLRB, 1949 ANNUAL REPORT 33 n.26 (1950); *see also* Western Condensing Co., 85 NLRB 981, 24 LRRM 1506 (1949).

larger unit to be appropriate. That was the situation in *Underwood Machinery Co.*,[33] where the Board found that the decisive factor was the wishes of the smaller group of employees. Accordingly, it ordered separate elections among the two employee groups and awaited the results of the elections before determining the appropriate unit or units. It declared that if the union secured a majority of the votes cast by the larger (production) group only, it would find that the larger (production) group, excluding the smaller group (erection and maintenance department), constituted the appropriate unit; but if, in addition, a majority of the smaller group also selected the union, the smaller group would be included in the same bargaining unit.

D. Bargaining History

The Board is reluctant to disturb longstanding bargaining units, whether established by agreement or by certification, when bargaining in those units has been successful. Bargaining history is therefore an important factor in unit determination.[34]

Nevertheless, although bargaining history is customarily accorded great weight, it is not given such weight where the history runs counter to well-established Board policy,[35] where the history resulted from a consent election,[36] where the history was "checkered," brief, ambiguous, or ineffective,[37] where there have been changes in the bargaining unit, or the scope of the

---

[33]59 NLRB 42, 15 LRRM 109 (1944). *See also* NLRB v. Lorimar Prods., 771 F2d 1294, 120 LRRM 2425 (CA 9, 1985), *denying enforcement to* 270 NLRB 18, 116 LRRM 1359 (1984); Hamilton Test Sys., N.Y. v. NLRB, 743 F2d 136, 117 LRRM 2248 (CA 2, 1984), *denying enforcement to* 268 NLRB No. 175, 115 LRRM 1278 (1984).

[34]Tool Craftsmen v. Leedom, 276 F2d 514, 45 LRRM 2826 (CA DC), *cert. denied*, 364 US 815, 46 LRRM 3080 (1960); Buffalo Broadcasting Co., 242 NLRB 1105, 101 LRRM 1306 (1979); Gulf Oil Corp., 4 NLRB 133, 1-A LRRM 270 (1937). *But cf.* NLRB v. Porter County Farm Bureau Coop. Ass'n, 314 F2d 133, 52 LRRM 2485 (CA 7, 1963), *denying enforcement to* 133 NLRB 1019, 48 LRRM 1760 (1961) (bargaining history, not predicated on Board certification, is not controlling as to what constitutes appropriate bargaining unit). See also Puerto Rico Marine Mgmt., 242 NLRB 181, 101 LRRM 1134 (1979), where bargaining history was determinative because it was the only evidence adduced regarding the unit issue.

[35]Manufacturing Woodworkers Ass'n of Greater N.Y., 194 NLRB 1122, 79 LRRM 1214 (1972); Land Title Guar. & Trust Co., 194 NLRB 148, 78 LRRM 1500 (1971).

[36]A.L. Mechling Barge Lines, 192 NLRB 1118, 78 LRRM 1119 (1971); Mid-West Abrasive Co., 145 NLRB 1665, 55 LRRM 1209 (1964); Macy's San Francisco, 120 NLRB 69, 41 LRRM 1433 (1958).

[37]Coplay Cement Co., 288 NLRB 66, 128 LRRM 1038 (1988); Duke Power Co., 191 NLRB 308, 77 LRRM 1417 (1971); Western Elec. Co., 98 NLRB 1018, 29 LRRM 1463 (1952).

employer's operations,[38] or where the unit does not conform reasonably well to other standards of appropriateness.[39]

E. Employer's Organizational Structure

Generally, an employer strongly desires to have the collective bargaining unit coincide with its organizational or administrative structure. Similarity of working conditions among employees, lines of supervision, and degree of functional integration[40] in the employer's operations are important factors in unit determinations, and these factors are given considerable weight in the Board's unit determinations.[41] Changes in an employer's organizational structure may so affect workplace conditions as to require the alteration of established bargaining units.[42]

III. TYPES OF UNITS

A. Unit Classifications Required by the Act

Section 9(b) of the Act places certain statutory limitations on the Board with respect to its unit determinations for two specific classes of employees: professional employees and guards.

1. Professionals. Prior to passage of the Taft-Hartley Act, the Board treated professional employees as it treated other employees. Persuaded that professionals are different from other employees and that their legitimate interests could be submerged if they were grouped with other employees, Con-

[38]Big Y Foods v. NLRB, 651 F2d 40, 107 LRRM 2971 (CA 1, 1981), *enforcing* 251 NLRB 869, 105 LRRM 1323 (1980); Western Commercial Transp., 288 NLRB 214, 127 LRRM 1313 (1988); Batesville Casket Co., 283 NLRB 795, 125 LRRM 1052 (1987) (distinguishing Rock-Tenn Co., 274 NLRB 772, 118 LRRM 1377 (1985)); Pacific Northwest Bell Tel. Co., 253 NLRB 795, 106 LRRM 1006 (1980); Plymouth Shoe Co., 185 NLRB 732, 75 LRRM 1169 (1970); General Elec. Co., 185 NLRB 13, 74 LRRM 1710 (1970).

[39]NLRB v. Hudson River Aggregates, 639 F2d 865, 106 LRRM 2313 (CA 2, 1981), *enforcing* 246 NLRB 192, 102 LRRM 1524 (1979); Crown Zellerbach Corp., 246 NLRB 202, 102 LRRM 1434 (1979).

[40]Kaiser Aluminum & Chem. Corp., 177 NLRB 682, 71 LRRM 1422 (1969); Minnesota Mining & Mfg. Co., 129 NLRB 789, 47 LRRM 1061 (1960). *See* J. Ray McDermott & Co., 240 NLRB 864, 100 LRRM 1401 (1979).

[41]Metro Distribs. dba Kansas City Coors, 27 NLRB 1388, 117 LRRM 1148 (1984); Birdsall, Inc., 268 NLRB 186, 114 LRRM 1257 (1982); Central Greyhound Lines, 88 NLRB 13, 25 LRRM 1273 (1950); Douglas Aircraft Co., 49 NLRB 819, 12 LRRM 212 (1943).

[42]Frito-Lay, Inc., 177 NLRB 820, 71 LRRM 1442 (1969); Mahoning Mining Co., 61 NLRB 792, 16 LRRM 110 (1945).

gress provided in section 9(b)(1) that a unit including both professionals and other employees is inappropriate "unless a majority of such professional employees vote for inclusion in such unit."[43]

Professional employees are entitled to a separate election even though they may have on a prior occasion voted in favor of inclusion in a larger unit with nonprofessionals.[44] The right to a separate election cannot be limited "to a single opportunity in the course of their employment for a particular employer."[45]

A separate election must be afforded even when the number of nonprofessionals seems insignificant. In *Leedom v. Kyne,*[46] the Supreme Court held that the failure of the Board to afford 233 professionals an opportunity to vote on whether they wished to be included in a unit with nine nonprofessionals violated the plain command of the statute.

The Board has interpreted section 9(b)(1) as being applicable "only in situations where a representation election is sought in a unit including professional employees among others."[47] Applying this rule, the Board dismissed a petition to decertify a professional segment of a larger unit.[48] The Board found such a petition appropriate, however, where the existing unit was

---

[43]Section 2(12), also added by Taft-Hartley, defines "professional" employee as

> (a) any employee engaged in work (i) predominantly intellectual and varied in character as opposed to routine mental, manual, mechanical, or physical work; (ii) involving the consistent exercise of discretion and judgment in its performance; (iii) of such a character that the output produced or the result accomplished cannot be standardized in relation to a given period of time; (iv) requiring knowledge of an advanced type in a field of science or learning customarily acquired by a prolonged course of specialized intellectual instruction and study in an institution of higher learning or a hospital, as distinguished from a general academic education or from an apprenticeship or from training in the performance of routine mental, manual, or physical processes; or (b) any employee, who (i) has completed the courses of specialized intellectual instruction and study described in clause (iv) of paragraph (a), and (ii) is performing related work under the supervision of a professional person to qualify himself to become a professional employee as defined in paragraph (a).

Compare Ryan Aeronautical Co., 132 NLRB 1160, 48 LRRM 1502 (1961) *with* Starrett Bros. & Eken, 77 NLRB 275, 22 LRRM 1003 (1948).

Depending on their job duties, however, professionals may be exempted from the NLRA's coverage as supervisors or managerial employees. NLRB v. Yeshiva Univ., 444 US 672, 103 LRRM 2526 (1980). *See infra* at notes 231–246. See also discussion of managerial employees in Chapter 28, "Jurisdiction: Coverage of the Act," at notes 246–268.

[44]Westinghouse Elec. Corp., 116 NLRB 1545, 39 LRRM 1039 (1956); *see also* Sunrise, 282 NLRB 252, 123 LRRM 1301 (1986).

[45]116 NLRB at 1547.

[46]358 U.S. 184, 43 LRRM 2222 (1958). See the discussion of this case in Chapter 33, "Judicial Review and Enforcement," at notes 124–129.

[47]Westinghouse Elec. Corp., 115 NLRB 530, 542, 37 LRRM 1341 (1956).

[48]*Id.* The proper method to achieve separation is thus through a representation proceeding, not through decertification.

established by agreement and the professionals had never been given an opportunity to vote.[49] Where a union enters into a contract covering a professional and nonprofessional unit without first having an election, there is no violation of the law.[50] Moreover, such a contract can bar a subsequent petition.[51] The Board holds that such a unit is appropriate on an historical basis and that an election is mandatory only when the Board establishes the unit.

On a case-by-case basis, the Board has applied the statutory definition of a "professional" to the particular jobs in dispute to determine whether or not "professional" indicia are present.[52] Under section 2(12), the controlling factor is generally the work required of the job, rather than the individual employee's qualifications.[53] However, section 2(12) also allows for examination of an individual's personal qualifications.[54]

Although cast in general terms, section 2(12) contains concrete criteria which must be met before the Board will find professional status. For example, in *Express-News Corp.*,[55] the Board concluded that "journalists" (reporters, staff writers, columnists, copy editors, editorial writers, and a cartoonist) were not professionals within the meaning of the Act, because they did not have a "prolonged course of specialized intellectual instruction and study in an institution of higher learning . . . as distinguished from a general academic education" as required by section 2(12)(a)(iv). According to the Board, most "journalists" had a general college education but lacked specialized education in the field of journalism or communications.[56]

---

[49]Utah Power & Light, 258 NLRB 1059, 108 LRRM 1145 (1981).

[50]Retail Clerks Local 324, 144 NLRB 1247, 54 LRRM 1226 (1963), where the Board stated: "We find nothing in Section 9(b)(1) or in its legislative history to suggest that Congress intended . . . to invalidate as inappropriate a historically established contract unit simply because of a joinder of professional and nonprofessional employees." *Id.* at 1252.

[51]Corporation de Servicios Legales de P.R., 289 NLRB 612, 128 LRRM 1270 (1988).

[52]For a comprehensive listing of such cases by specific professions, see Annotation, 40 A.L.R. FED. 25 (1978).

[53]*See, e.g.*, Ohio State Legal Servs. Ass'n, 239 NLRB 594, 100 LRRM 1001 (1978); Willett Motor Coach Co., 227 NLRB 882, 95 LRRM 1082 (1977); Aeronca, Inc., 221 NLRB 326, 90 LRRM 1709 (1975); Chesapeake & Potomac Tel. Co., 192 NLRB 483, 77 LRRM 1807 (1971).

[54]*See, e.g.*, Catholic Bishop of Chicago, 235 NLRB 776, 98 LRRM 1037 (1978), in which the Board found teachers and social workers to be professionals based on the individuals' educational background and experience. The Supreme Court later decided that the Board lacked jurisdiction over such religious schools, Catholic Bishop of Chicago v. NLRB, 440 US 490, 100 LRRM 2913 (1979).

[55]223 NLRB 627, 628, 91 LRRM 1489 (1976).

[56]See also Binghamton Press Co., 226 NLRB 808, 93 LRRM 1355 (1976), where the Board followed the strict construction approach of *Express-News*.

2. Guards. Section 9(b)(3), which was added by the Taft-Hartley Act, prevents the Board from including in a unit which includes any nonguard employees "any individual employed as a guard to enforce against employees and other persons rules to protect property of the employer or to protect the safety of persons on the employer's premises." That provision also prevents the Board from certifying any labor organization as the representative of a guard unit "if such organization admits to membership, or is affiliated directly or indirectly with an organization which admits to membership, employees other than guards."[57] Congress enacted section 9(b)(3) "to insure to an employer that during strikes or labor unrest among his other employees he would have a core of plant-protection employees who would enforce the employer's rules for the protection of his property and persons thereon without being confronted with a division of loyalty between the employer and dissatisfied fellow union members."[58]

In situations where employees perform the duties of guards in addition to other duties, the Board will find guard status only if the guard function is an essential part of the employees' duties.[59] Thus, for example, the Board has held that firefighters are guards where "an essential part of their duties and responsibilities is the enforcement of the employer's other plant protection rules and regulations."[60] Likewise, plainclothesmen who

---

[57]The Board has said that "mutual sympathy, common purpose, and assistance between a guard union and a nonguard union is not, without more, indicative of indirect affiliation within the meaning of Section 9(b)." Bonded Armored Carrier, 195 NLRB 346, 346, 79 LRRM 1317 (1972); *see* International Harvester Co., 145 NLRB 1747, 55 LRRM 1227 (1964) (certification revoked where union representing guards used nonguard union as its negotiator, allowed nonguard union to participate in internal union affairs, and received substantial financial aid from nonguard union). That a union representing nonguard employees also represents members of a local police force in public sector bargaining does not bring it within the ban of section 9(b)(3). Ojai Valley Community Hosp., 254 NLRB 1354, 106 LRRM 1278 (1981).

[58]McDonnell Aircraft Corp., 109 NLRB 967, 969, 34 LRRM 1489 (1954) (Senator Taft "stated that Section 9(b)(3) of the Act was inserted because the conferees were impressed with the reasoning of the Court of Appeals for the Sixth Circuit in N.L.R.B. v. Jones and Laughlin Steel Corp., 154 F.2d 932, 17 LRRM 982 [(CA 6, 1946)], deciding that guards could not be represented by the same union as represented the production and maintenance employees at their plant because otherwise they would be confronted with conflicting loyalties during periods of industrial unrest and strikes." *Id.* at 969 n.3).

[59]For a detailed summary of decisions concerning guard status, see Annotation, 45 A.L.R. FED. 428 (1979).

[60]Chance Vought Aircraft, 110 NLRB 1342, 1346, 35 LRRM 1338 (1954); *see also* McDonnell Aircraft Co. v. NLRB, 827 F2d 324, 126 LRRM 2140 (CA 8, 1987), *denying enforcement to* 279 NLRB 357, 122 LRRM 1083 (1986) (fire prevention/suppression specialists); Baker Protective Servs., Wells Fargo Alarm Servs. Div., 289 NLRB 562, 128 LRRM 1217 (1988) (service technicians); A.W. Schlesinger Geriatric Center, 267 NLRB

investigate traffic accidents and, on occasion, theft are considered guards, even though they lack the authority to restrain or arrest other employees.[61] On the other hand, persons who are called "guards" and "watchmen" but who lack responsibility for the enforcement of the employer's rules are not subject to the statutory exclusion from bargaining units.[62] Thus, servicemen of alarm systems are not guards within the meaning of section 9(b)(3) because they do not enforce the employer's rules against employees, search for intruders, or restrain persons from entering the employer's premises.[63] On two occasions, the Board has held that employees engaged in traffic control were part of the production process and were not guards within the meaning of the Act.[64]

The Board, with court approval, also applies section 9(b)(3) to guard-services employees who act as guards for other employers.[65] In applying this rule, the Board has extended guard status to armored-car company employees whose job consists of transporting other employers' money and valuables.[66]

1363, 114 LRRM 1221 (1983) (maintenance employees); Purolater Courier Corp., 266 NLRB 384, 112 LRRM 1322 (1983), *enforced* 732 F2d 43, 116 LRRM 2386 (CA 2, 1984) (couriers); Wright Memorial Hosp., 255 NLRB 1319, 107 LRRM 1121 (1981), *enforced*, 771 F2d 400, 120 LRRM 2193 (CA 8, 1985) (ambulance drivers); United Technologies Corp., 245 NLRB 932, 102 LRRM 1328 (1979).

[61]Burns Sec. Sys., 188 NLRB 222, 76 LRRM 1267 (1971) (plainclothesmen included in unit with uniformed guards who perform full range of police functions). *See also* Desert Palace, 209 NLRB 950, 85 LRRM 1594 (1974) (union unsuccessfully sought unit clarification to include plainclothes investigators in unit of uniformed guards).

[62]Shattuck School, 189 NLRB 886, 77 LRRM 1164 (1971); Container Research Corp., 188 NLRB 586, 76 LRRM 1369 (1971). *See also* Lion Country Safari, 246 NLRB 156, 102 LRRM 1419 (1979) (nursery attendants not guards because primary function is animal care; reporting rule infractions only incidental). But see Wackenhut Corp., 196 NLRB 278, 79 LRRM 1673 (1972), where the Board excluded as "guards" employees who possessed and exercised responsibility to observe and report infractions of the employer's rules, despite the fact that they lacked power to compel compliance with such rules.

[63]Wells Fargo Alarm Servs. v. NLRB, 533 F2d 121, 92 LRRM 2009 (CA 3, 1976), *enforcing* 218 NLRB 68, 89 LRRM 1368 (1975).

[64]Deluxe Gen., 241 NLRB 229, 100 LRRM 1478 (1979) (movie company whistlemen and flagmen who regulate flow of traffic during filming); City of Boston Cab Ass'n, 177 NLRB 64, 71 LRRM 1370 (1969) (taxicab "starters" who monitor flow of taxicabs at airport and report drivers who violate taxicabs rules).

[65]*E.g.*, Brink's, Inc., 226 NLRB 1182, 94 LRRM 1022 (1976). The Board initially held that §9(b)(3) applied only to an employer's own plant-protection employees. Brink's, Inc., 77 NLRB 1182, 22 LRRM 1133 (1948). However, in Armored Motor Serv. Co., 106 NLRB 1139, 32 LRRM 1628 (1953), the Board overruled the earlier *Brink's* decision, expressly adopting the Third Circuit's reasoning in NLRB v. American Dist. Tel. Co., 205 F2d 86, 32 LRRM 2210 (CA 3, 1953).

[66]*E.g.*, Brink's, Inc., 226 NLRB 1182, 94 LRRM 1022 (1976) (couriers who deliver nonnegotiable instruments and bank correspondence in vans held "guards" under the Act; couriers included in unit with armored-car guards); Teamsters Local 639 (Dunbar Armored Express), 211 NLRB 687, 86 LRRM 1396 (1974); Armored Motor Serv. Co., *supra* note 65.

Guards who have been temporarily assigned out of a guard unit are analogous to employees on temporary layoff and, as such, are eligible to vote in a guard-unit election.[67] Similarly, a unit of guards is appropriate even though one of the unit members works part-time for the employer in a nonguard capacity.[68] [*See* **Editor's Note** below.]

As with professional employees, an employer and a union may voluntarily establish a unit that includes guards with other employees, since only units established by the Board fall within the statutory prohibition.[69] But the prohibition extends to any use of the Board's processes to achieve certification, including intervention in a representation proceeding or appearance on the ballot in a Board election.[70] Nor may a union representing guards and other employees picket for recognition without violating section 8(b)(7)(C) of the Act, even though it had previously appeared on the ballot in a Board election.[71] The Board will order a severence election where guards petition to sever themselves from a unit that includes nonguards, even though the larger unit had a history of successful collective bargaining.[72] Moreover, the Board will conduct a decertification election for guards, even though they do not comprise a separate bargaining unit, but rather are part of a longstanding unit of guards and nonguards.[73]

Section 9(b)(3) also precludes the representation of guards by a union affiliated with a union that represents nonguards.[74] The mere presence of an official of the nonguard union at collective

---

[67]United States Steel Corp., 188 NLRB 309, 76 LRRM 1266 (1971).

[68]NLRB v. J.W. Mays, Inc., 675 F2d 442, 110 LRRM 2218 (CA 2, 1982). [**Editor's Note:** A union is not disqualified from representing guards of a statutory employer because it also represents nonguard employees of municipalities and is affiliated with a union that represents nonguard public employees. Children's Hosp. of Mich., 299 NLRB No. 63, 135 LRRM 1033 (1990). *See also* University of Tulsa, 304 NLRB No. 101, 138 LRRM 1118 (1991).]

[69]NLRB v. J.J. Collins Sons, 332 F2d 523, 56 LRRM 2375 (CA 7, 1964). But the employer may freely withdraw recognition when the contract expires. Wells Fargo Armored Servs. Corp., 270 NLRB 787, 116 LRRM 1129 (1984), *enforced sub nom.* Teamsters Local 807 v. NLRB, 755 F2d 5, 118 LRRM 2613 (CA 2, 1985), *cert. denied*, 474 US 901, 120 LRRM 2728 (1985).

[70]Brink's, Inc., 272 NLRB 868, 117 LRRM 1385 (1984) (overruling Bally's Park Place, 257 NLRB 777, 107 LRRM 1580 (1981)); *see also* University of Chicago, 272 NLRB 873, 117 LRRM 1377 (1984).

[71]Teamsters Local 710 (University of Chicago), 274 NLRB 956, 118 LRRM 1514 (1985); Teamsters Local 851 (Purolator Courier Corp.), 268 NLRB 452, 115 LRRM 1041 (1983), *enforced*, 732 F2d 43, 116 LRRM 2386 (CA 2, 1984).

[72]Los Angeles Bonaventure Hotel, 235 NLRB 96, 97 LRRM 1453 (1978). See discussion of bargaining history as factor in unit determinations at notes 34–39 *supra*.

[73]Fisher-New Center Co., 170 NLRB 909, 67 LRRM 1502 (1968).

[74]Brink's, Inc., 274 NLRB 970, 118 LRRM 1409 (1985).

bargaining negotiations between the guard union and the employer does not in itself establish impermissible affiliation.[75] But full-time business agents of a union representing general employees cannot represent guards, even on their free time, even though it was permissible that some officers of a newly certified guard unit also served as stewards of another, nonguard, union.[76] The Board has also found unlawful affiliation where a newly formed guard union took advice and assistance from a nonguard union, which had initially sought to represent the same unit of employees.[77]

B. Unit Classifications in General

1. Craft Units. Since passage of the Wagner Act in 1935, the Board has continuously been faced with the issue: Under what circumstances will separate-unit status be granted to the various crafts? In the late 1930s, the CIO was conducting massive organizing campaigns usually seeking plant or industrial units. The AFL, however, was organizing along craft lines, and it was often confronted with established plant or industrial units that included craft employees. Consequently, the AFL often argued that the Board should allow for craft-severance elections, enabling employees in a specific craft to obtain a separate bargaining unit.

The Board's 1939 *American Can*[78] decision was the first in a 25-year series of major craft-severance decisions. In *American Can* the Board held that it was "not authorized by the Act to split [an] appropriate unit thus established by collective bargaining . . . . To permit such small groups to break up an appropriate unit . . . would make stability and responsibility in collective bargaining impossible."[79] The effect of this approach was to foreclose craft representation once the craft group was included in a broader industrial unit.

---

[75]Wells Fargo Guard Servs., 269 NLRB 236, 115 LRRM 1224 (1984).

[76]Armored Transp. of Cal., 269 NLRB 683, 115 LRRM 1309 (1984). However, that some officers of a newly certified guard union were also stewards of another union did not justify an employer's refusal to bargain. Brink's Inc., 283 NLRB 711, 125 LRRM 1271 (1987). *See also* NLRB v. J.W. Mays, Inc., *supra* note 68.

[77]Stewart-Warner Corp., Alemite & Instrument Divs., 273 NLRB 1736, 118 LRRM 1292 (1985).

[78]American Can Co., 13 NLRB 1252, 4 LRRM 392 (1939).

[79]*Id.* at 1256. For a discussion of the craft-severance problem, see Case Note, 8 B.C. INDUS. & COM. L. REV. 988 (1967). For definition of a craft, see note 85 *infra*.

The *American Can* doctrine was not rigidly applied,[80] however, and in its 1944 decision in *General Electric Co.*,[81] the Board modified the doctrine, declaring that severance would be permitted if the group (1) constituted a true craft, (2) had maintained its identity while bargaining in the more comprehensive unit, and (3) had protested its inclusion in the broader unit, or the broader unit had been established without its knowledge and there had been no previous consideration of the merits of a separate unit.[82]

To diminish the restrictive effect of the *American Can* doctrine,[83] Congress included in the Taft-Hartley Act a proviso, section 9(b)(2), to the effect that

> the Board shall . . . not decide that any craft unit is inappropriate . . . on the ground that a different unit has been established by a prior Board determination, unless a majority of the employees in the proposed craft unit votes against separate representation.

Enactment of the proviso did not immediately alter Board policy in craft-unit determinations. The Board retained its policy of severely limiting craft severance, though it reduced its emphasis on collective bargaining history. Starting in 1948, the Board issued a series of decisions known collectively as the *National Tube* doctrine,[84] under which the Board emphasized the integration of general production and craft operations in the industries involved and imposed a restrictive definition of what constitutes a true craft.[85] Under the *National Tube* doctrine, the

---

[80]International Minerals & Chem. Corp., 71 NLRB 878, 19 LRRM 1059 (1946); Remington Rand, Inc., 62 NLRB 1419, 16 LRRM 274 (1945), General Elec. Co., 58 NLRB 57, 15 LRRM 33 (1944); Aluminum Co. of Am., 42 NLRB 772, 10 LRRM 202 (1942); Bendix Aviation Corp., 39 NLRB 81, 10 LRRM 4 (1942).

[81]*Supra* note 80, as discussed in Case Note, *supra* note 79, at 989–90.

[82]General Elec. Co., *supra* note 80.

[83]S. REP. No. 105, 80th Cong., 1st Sess. 13 (1947), charged: "Since the decision in the *American Can* case (13 NLRB 1252), where the Board refused to permit craft units to be carved out from a broader bargaining unit already established, the Board, except under unusual circumstances, has virtually compelled skilled artisans to remain parts of a comprehensive plant unit."

[84]Permanente Metals Co., 89 NLRB 804, 26 LRRM 1039 (1950) (basic aluminum industry); Weyerhaeuser Timber Co., 87 NLRB 1076, 25 LRRM 1173 (1949) (lumber industry); Corn Prods. Ref. Co., 80 NLRB 362, 23 LRRM 1090 (1948) (wet milling industry); National Tube Co., 76 NLRB 1199, 21 LRRM 1292 (1948) (basic steel industry).

[85]For a group to be defined as a craft, the Board said, its members must possess skills requiring a substantial period of training, the group seeking severance must be homogeneous, and its members must have little or no interchange with the employees working at unskilled or semiskilled jobs. Allis-Chalmers Mfg. Co., 77 NLRB 719, 22 LRRM 1085 (1948); Caterpillar Tractor Co., 77 NLRB 457, 22 LRRM 1033 (1948); American Mfg. Co., 76 NLRB 647, 21 LRRM 1232 (1948); Lockheed Aircraft Corp., 57 NLRB 41, 14 LRRM 216 (1944).

Board denied craft severance and initial establishment of craft units in four industries,[86] on the rationale that the industries were so highly integrated that to allow severance, even of a true craft, would upset stable labor relations in these industries contrary to the purpose of the Act.

In 1954, in *American Potash & Chemical Corp.*,[87] the Board took an important step toward lessening the restrictions on craft severance. The Board reexamined the legislative history of the 1947 proviso and concluded that "the right of separate representation should not be denied the members of a craft group merely because they are employed in an industry which involves highly integrated production processes and in which the prevailing pattern of bargaining is industrial in character."[88] Henceforth, "a craft group will be appropriate for severance purposes in cases where a true craft group is sought and where, in addition, the union seeking to represent it is one which traditionally represents that craft."[89] Although *American Potash* abandoned *National Tube*, the Board announced it would continue to deny craft severance in those industries to which the *National Tube* doctrine already had been applied.

The Board's 1966 decisions in *Mallinckrodt Chemical Works*[90] and two related cases[91] concluded the series. In *Mallinckrodt* the Board sharply criticized the *American Potash* decision for "confining consideration solely to the interests favoring severance"[92] and for "arbitrarily [freezing] the so-called *National Tube* industries."[93] Instead, the Board declared that henceforth craft severance would be based on all the relevant factors, including, but not limited to the following:

> 1. Whether or not the proposed unit consists of a distinct and homogeneous group of skilled journeymen craftsmen performing the functions of their craft on a nonrepetitive basis, or of employees constituting a functionally distinct department, working in trades or occupations for which a tradition of separate representation exists.

---

[86]The four industries were basic steel, basic aluminum, lumbering, and wet milling. *See supra* note 84.

[87]107 NLRB 1418, 33 LRRM 1380 (1954).

[88]*Id.* at 1421.

[89]*Id.* at 1422. The Board defined a true craft unit as consisting of "a distinct and homogeneous group of skilled journeymen craftsmen, working as such, together with their apprentices and/or helpers. To be a 'journeyman craftsman' an individual must have a kind and degree of skill which is normally acquired only by undergoing a substantial period of apprenticeship or comparable training." *Id.* at 1423.

[90]162 NLRB 387, 64 LRRM 1011 (1966).

[91]Holmberg, Inc., 162 NLRB 407, 64 LRRM 1025 (1966). E.I. du Pont de Nemours & Co., 162 NLRB 413, 64 LRRM 1021 (1966).

[92]Mallinckrodt Chem. Works, *supra* note 90, at 396, 64 LRRM at 1016.

[93]*Id.*

2. The history of collective bargaining of the employees sought and at the plant involved, and at other plants of the employer, with emphasis on whether the existing patterns of bargaining are productive of stability in labor relations, and whether such stability will be unduly disrupted by the destruction of the existing patterns of representation.

3. The extent to which the employees in the proposed unit have established and maintained their separate identity during the period of inclusion in a broader unit, and the extent of their participation or lack of participation in the establishment and maintenance of the existing pattern of representation and the prior opportunities, if any, afforded them to obtain separate representation.

4. The history and pattern of collective bargaining in the industry involved.

5. The degree of integration of the employer's production processes, including the extent to which the continued normal operation of the production processes is dependent upon the performance of the assigned functions of the employees in the proposed unit.

6. The qualifications of the union seeking to "carve out" a separate unit, including that union's experience in representing employees like those involved in the severance action.[94]

In *Mallinckrodt* the union had sought a unit composed of all instrument mechanics, apprentices, and helpers. There were 12 such employees out of a total of 280 production and maintenance employees, all 12 of whom were represented in the existing bargaining unit. Units of electricians and powerhouse employees were already separately represented. In dismissing the petition, the Board based its decision primarily on the facts that (1) the work of the instrument mechanics was intimately related to the production process, (2) they had been represented as part of a production and maintenance unit for the preceding 25 years, and (3) the petitioner had not traditionally represented the craft of instrument mechanic.

Mallinckrodt remains the standard against which the Board measures craft-severance petitions. The cases[95] and the com-

---

[94] *Id.* Although *Mallinckrodt* dealt with craft severance, the Board, in a companion case to *Mallinckrodt*, held that the same factors would be applied to cases involving the appropriateness of establishing craft units at unorganized employers. E.I. du Pont de Nemours & Co., *supra* note 91.

[95] *See, e.g.*, La-Z-Boy Chair Co., 235 NLRB 77, 97 LRRM 1490 (1978) (discussed *infra* at note 98); Boise Cascade Corp., 238 NLRB 1022, 99 LRRM 1411 (1978) (instrument men); International Found., 234 NLRB 277, 97 LRRM 1144 (1978) (printing and composing employees); Bendix Corp., 227 NLRB 1534, 94 LRRM 1596 (1976) (metal platers); Beaunit Corp., 224 NLRB 1502, 92 LRRM 1458 (1976) (electrical mechanics and instrument mechanics); Firestone Tire & Rubber Co., 223 NLRB 904, 91 LRRM 1561 (1976) (attempt to sever multicraft group from general production and maintenance unit);

mentators[96] have indicated that the *Mallinckrodt* standard usually results in a denial of craft severance. For example, in *Dow Chemical Co.*,[97] the Board denied petitions for severance of five separate groups of craftsmen (electrical workers, pipe fitters, painters, sheet metal workers, and carpenters) on the grounds that they shared substantially common working conditions and benefits with production employees, that their work was highly integrated with the employer's entire production process, and that the bargaining history favored a single overall unit.

Likewise, in *La-Z-Boy Chair Co.*,[98] a petition to sever tool and die employees from a unit of production and maintenance employees was rejected by a divided Board. In applying the *Mallinckrodt* standard, the majority gave controlling weight to the successful 20-year bargaining history, the high degree of functional integration, the degree of participation by tool and die employees in contract negotiations, the overlapping of supervision, the common seniority system, and the lack of evidence that the petitioner was specially qualified to represent tool and die employees or that the incumbent union had failed to represent them adequately.

Craft severance has been granted only sparingly under *Mallinckrodt*.[99] For example, in *Mason & Hanger-Silas Mason Co.*,[100] the Board granted severance to a unit of approximately 44 tool and die makers, machinists, apprentices, helpers and welders who were part of a production and maintenance unit. In ruling

---

Union Carbide Corp., 205 NLRB 794, 84 LRRM 1065 (1973) (machinists and instrument makers); E.I. du Pont de Nemours & Co., 205 NLRB 552, 84 LRRM 1036 (1973) (engineers); Dow Chem. Co., 202 NLRB 17, 82 LRRM 1594 (1973) (discussed *infra* at note 97); ASG Indus., 190 NLRB 557, 77 LRRM 1245 (1971) (electricians and powerhouse employees); Lear-Siegler, Inc., 170 NLRB 766, 67 LRRM 1522 (1968) (union petitioned for nine separate craft units); Timber Prods. Co., 164 NLRB 1060, 65 LRRM 1189 (1967) (maintenance electricians); North Am. Aviation, 162 NLRB 1267, 64 LRRM 1146 (1967) (welders). For cases in which craft severance has been granted, see Golden Gateway Center, 195 NLRB 492, 79 LRRM 1437 (1972) (maintenance painters); Mason & Hanger-Silas Mason Co., 180 NLRB 467, 73 LRRM 1010 (1969) (discussed *infra* at note 100); Buddy L Corp., 167 NLRB 808, 66 LRRM 1150 (1968) (toolroom employees).

[96]Fanning, *The Taft-Hartley Act—Twenty Years Later*, in N.Y.U. TWENTIETH ANNUAL CONFERENCE ON LABOR 209 (1968); DuRoss, *Craft Severance and National Labor Policy—The Aftermath of* Mallinckrodt, 30 U. PITT. L. REV. 577 (1969). See Miller & Robbins, *Accretions and Craft Severance*, in APPROPRIATE UNITS FOR COLLECTIVE BARGAINING, *supra* note 12 at 98–104, and Abodeely, *NLRB Craft Severance Policies: Preeminence of the Bargaining History Factor After* Mallinckrodt, 11 B.C. INDUS. & COM. L. REV. 411 (1970), where the Board is criticized for relying too heavily on bargaining history in its post-*Mallinckrodt* decisions.

[97]*Supra* note 95.

[98]*Supra* note 95.

[99]*See* cases cited in *supra* note 95.

[100]*Supra* note 95.

that severance was appropriate, the Board emphasized that the employer's 6,000 employees were represented by 10 different unions and the bargaining history in the production and maintenance unit was limited to a single 3-year agreement, which had been preceded by a long period of separate representation. The Board concluded that granting severance would not disrupt labor relations in the plant.

The Board's reluctance to disrupt an established stable bargaining relationship will generally prevail over a claim that a separate craft unit is entitled to different representation. Where there is no established bargaining history, however, a separate craft unit will be approved if appropriate under generally applicable unit determination criteria.[101]

2. Departmental Units. Board policy regarding departmental units has been greatly influenced by Board policy regarding craft severance.[102] In the aftermath of *Mallinckrodt*,[103] the Board has approached departmental unit issues, whether involving unit severance or unorganized employers, by examining all of the facts on a case-by-case basis without applying strict tests. Departmental unit decisions emphasize several factors, including (1) differences in skills, (2) difference in training, (3) degree of common supervision, (4) interchange with other employees, and (5) differences in types of performance ratings.[104] For example, in *Stephens Produce Co.*,[105] the Board concluded that meat department employees constituted a separate and distinct unit from bakery and dairy employees, based on evidence of differences in skills, jobs, training, compensation, benefits, working conditions, degree of supervision, the interchange and contact with other employees, the nature of the unit sought by the petitioner, predominant industry practices, and

---

[101] *E.g., compare* Dodge City of Wauwatosa, 282 NLRB 459, 124 LRRM 1038 (1986) *with* Brown & Root, 258 NLRB 1002, 108 LRRM 1188 (1981).

[102] *See* notes 78–100 *supra* and accompanying text.

[103] *Supra* note 90. *Mallinckrodt* overruled *American Potash, supra* note 87, under which departmental units would be held appropriate only if strong evidence was presented establishing that (1) the departmental group was functionally distinct and separate and (2) the petitioner has traditionally devoted itself to serving the special interests of employees in similar departments.

[104] *See, e.g.*, Anaheim Operating dba Sheraton-Anaheim Hotel, 252 NLRB 959, 105 LRRM 1333 (1980); Stephens Produce Co., 214 NLRB 131, 88 LRRM 1363 (1974), *enforced*, 515 F2d 1373, 89 LRRM 2311 (CA 8, 1975) (discussed *infra* text at note 105); Witt-Armstrong Equip. Co., 214 NLRB 721, 87 LRRM 1574 (1974); Juilliard School, 208 NLRB 153, 85 LRRM 1129 (1974); Cone Mills Corp., 187 NLRB 759, 76 LRRM 1179 (1971). Employee desires may, however, be determinative. Lianco Container Co., 177 NLRB 907, 71 LRRM 1483 (1969).

[105] *Supra* note 104.

prior bargaining history.[106] As part of this trend toward flexibility, separate departmental units have frequently been held appropriate in cases involving retail stores.[107] More recently, the Board has abandoned what it described as a "rigid rule" that only employerwide units are appropriate in the hotel/motel industry.[108]

3. Plant and Employer Units. In determining whether to direct an election in a unit encompassing more than one plant, store, or office, or to limit the unit to a single facility or less than an employerwide grouping, the Board considers a number of factors including (1) prior bargaining history; (2) centralization of management, particularly regarding labor relations; (3) extent of employee interchange; (4) degree of interdependence or autonomy of facilities; (5) differences or similarities in skills and functions of employees; and (6) geographical location of facilities in relation to each other.[109]

The Board has also embraced a slowly evolving pattern of presumptions in favor of single-plant units in various industries. In early decisions the Board relied on the statutory reference to "plant unit[s]" in section 9(b), finding a presumption in favor of plant units over types of units not expressly mentioned in sec-

---

[106]The Board, however, has refused to separate meat department employees from a grocery's other employees where such factors did not exist. Save Mart of Modesto, 293 NLRB 1190, 131 LRRM 1791 (1989); Hall's Super Mkts., 281 NLRB 1116, 123 LRRM 1158 (1986); Yaohan of Cal., 252 NLRB 309, 105 LRRM 1293 (1980); Great Day, 248 NLRB 527, 103 LRRM 1451 (1980); Ashcraft Mkt., 246 NLRB 471, 102 LRRM 1592 (1979); NLRB v. Foodland, 744 F2d 735, 117 LRRM 2482 (CA 10, 1984), *enforcing* 261 NLRB 995, 110 LRRM 1158 (1982) (meat department excluded from storewide unit); *see accord* Great Scot of Fla., 256 NLRB 885, 107 LRRM 1317 (1981). *See also* Weber's Food Serv., 244 NLRB 594, 102 LRRM 1148 (1979) (meat department employees not included in overall storewide unit; bakery and "deli" employees also excluded since closely identified with meat department employees).

[107]*See, e.g.*, Wickes Furniture, 231 NLRB 154, 95 LRRM 1545 (1977) (selling employees); J.C. Penney Co., 196 NLRB 708, 80 LRRM 1071 (1972) (automotive service department employees); Arnold Constable Corp., 150 NLRB 788, 58 LRRM 1086 (1965) (selling, office, and restaurant employees). *But see* Beco Stores, 197 NLRB 1105, 80 LRRM 1493 (1972) (separate unit for nonselling employees held inappropriate on overall review of facts). But a separate unit of warehouse employees is less likely to be approved in the retail industry than in a wholesale operation. *Compare* Roberds, Inc., 272 NLRB 1318, 117 LRRM 1465 (1984) *and* Salem Furniture Co., 272 NLRB 1321, 117 LRRM 1467 (1984) *with* NLRB v. Great W. Produce, 839 F2d 555, 127 LRRM 2662 (CA 9, 1988).

[108]Omni Int'l Hotel of Detroit, 283 NLRB 475, 124 LRRM 1370 (1987); *see also* Dinah's Hotel Corp., 295 NLRB No. 127, 131 LRRM 1797 (1989); Western Lodging Corp. dba Stanford Park Hotel, 287 NLRB 1291, 127 LRRM 1208 (1988); Pratt/North Plaza Assocs. dba Maxim's de Paris Suite Hotel, 285 NLRB 377, 126 LRRM 1083 (1987); Hilton Hotels Corp., 287 NLRB 359, 127 LRRM 1141 (1987).

[109]Trustees of Columbia Univ., 222 NLRB 309, 91 LRRM 1276 (1976).

tion 9(b).[110] In a 1958 decision involving manufacturing operations, the Board stated that "a single plant unit is generally appropriate for collective bargaining purposes, unless such plant unit has been so effectively merged with another as to destroy its identity."[111] This presumption with regard to manufacturing units has been frequently repeated and continues to apply today.[112]

The Board also applies this presumption in favor of single "plant" units to the retail industry. Before 1962 the Board's policy preferred multistore units: "absent unusual circumstances, the appropriate bargaining unit should embrace employees of all stores located within an employer's administrative division or geographic area."[113] However, in its 1962 decision in *Sav-On Drugs*,[114] the Board abandoned the administrative-division/geographic-area policy, stating:

> Reviewing our experience under that policy we believe that too frequently it has operated to impede the exercise by employees in retail chain operations of their rights to self-organization guaranteed in Section 7 of the Act. In our opinion that policy has overemphasized the administrative grouping of merchandising outlets at the expense of factors such as geographic separation of the several outlets and the local managerial autonomy of the separate outlets; and it has ignored completely as a factor the extent to which the claiming labor organization had sought to organize the employees of the retail chain. We have decided to modify this policy and to apply to retail chain operations the same unit policy which we apply to multiplant enterprises in general. Therefore, whether a proposed

---

[110]Beaumont Forging Co., 110 NLRB 2200, 35 LRRM 1410 (1954) (plant unit presumptively favored over two departmental units); Hy-Grade Food Prods. Co., 85 NLRB 841, 848, 24 LRRM 1491 (1949) (Member Murdock, concurring opinion). Section 9(b) expressly mentions the "employer unit, craft unit, plant unit, or subdivision thereof."

[111]Temco Aircraft Corp., 121 NLRB 1085, 1088, 42 LRRM 1538 (1958).

[112]*E.g.*, Airco, Inc., 273 NLRB 348, 118 LRRM 1052 (1984); Penn Color, 249 NLRB 1117, 104 LRRM 1229 (1980); J. Ray McDermott & Co., 240 NLRB 864, 100 LRRM 1401 (1979); Hamburg Knitting Mills, 239 NLRB 1231, 100 LRRM 1237 (1979); Kendall Co., 184 NLRB 847, 74 LRRM 1623 (1970); Kent Plastics Corp., 183 NLRB 612, 74 LRRM 1312 (1970); Leslie Metal Arts Co., 167 NLRB 693, 66 LRRM 1134 (1967); National Cash Register Co., 166 NLRB 173, 65 LRRM 1441 (1967); Marks Oxygen Co., 147 NLRB 228, 56 LRRM 1187 (1964); Dixie Belle Mills, Inc., 139 NLRB 629, 51 LRRM 1344 (1962). *Cf.* Pickering & Co., 248 NLRB 772, 103 LRRM 1489 (1980) (presumptive appropriateness of single-employer manufacturing unit was rebutted). For judicial approval of the Board's presumption favoring a single-plant unit, see, e.g., NLRB v. New Enter. Stone & Lime Co., 413 F2d 117, 71 LRRM 2802 (CA 3, 1969).

[113]Robert Hall Clothes, Inc., 118 NLRB 1096, 1098, 40 LRRM 1322 (1957); *accord, e.g.*, Father & Son Shoe Stores, 117 NLRB 1479, 40 LRRM 1032 (1957); Sparkle Mkts. Co., 113 NLRB 790, 36 LRRM 1388 (1955); Safeway Stores, 96 NLRB 998, 28 LRRM 1622 (1951).

[114]138 NLRB 1032, 51 LRRM 1152 (1962).

unit which is confined to one of two or more retail establishments making up an employer's retail chain is appropriate will be determined in the light of all the circumstances of the case.[115]

Six years following *Sav-On Drugs*, the Board noted that it had "consistently found [single store] units appropriate unless countervailing factors were present";[116] it therefore concluded that "a single store in a retail chain, like single locations in multilocation enterprises in other industries, is *presumptively* an appropriate unit for bargaining."[117] The Board has continued to apply the presumption in retail store cases.[118]

In the insurance industry the early cases likewise favored multilocation units. In its 1944 decision in *Metropolitan Life*[119] the Board adopted a statewide unit presumption under which "in the absence of unusual circumstances, the practice of setting up units of insurance agents smaller than state-wide in scope should be avoided."[120] In its 1961 *Quaker City Life Insurance*

---

[115]*Id.* at 1033.

[116]Haag Drug Co., 169 NLRB 877, 877, 67 LRRM 1289 (1968) (*see* cases cited at 877 n.3; Board analyzes mixed reaction of circuit courts to post–*Sav-On* decisions, *id.* at 879).

[117]*Id.* (emphasis in original).

[118]*E.g.*, Albertson's, 270 NLRB 132, 116 LRRM 1061, *reconsideration denied*, 273 NLRB 286, 118 LRRM 1090 (1984); Big Y Foods, 238 NLRB 860, 99 LRRM 1366 (1978); Bud's Food Store, 236 NLRB 1203, 98 LRRM 1386 (1978); Buehler's Food Mkts., 232 NLRB 785, 96 LRRM 1322 (1977); Wickes Furniture Corp., 231 NLRB 154, 95 LRRM 1545 (1977); Pneumo Corp., 228 NLRB 1443, 95 LRRM 1018 (1977); *see* Sears, Roebuck & Co., 253 NLRB 211, 105 LRRM 1512 (1980) (decertification election ordered for single-store unit notwithstanding history of multistore bargaining). The single-store presumption does not apply, however, when the petitioning union seeks a broader unit. Stop N' Go, 279 NLRB 344, 122 LRRM 1183 (1986); *see also* NLRB v. Carson Cable TV, 795 F2d 879, 123 LRRM 2225 (CA 9, 1986), *enforcing* 275 NLRB No. 201, 120 LRRM 1119 (1985).

For examples of cases where the presumption applies but has been rebutted, see Charrette Drafting Supplies Corp., 275 NLRB 1294, 119 LRRM 1301 (1985) (centralized control, employee interchange, broad community of interest); Westman Interiors, 273 NLRB 610, 118 LRRM 1130 (1984) (common supervision, similar wages and benefits, frequent interchange); Ohio Valley Supermarkets, 269 NLRB 353, 115 LRRM 1238 (1984) (centralized management of labor relations, geographical proximity); ITT Continental Baking Co., 231 NLRB 326, 96 LRRM 1002 (1977) (store managers lacked authority over employee relations; close geographic proximity of stores); Petrie Stores Corp., 212 NLRB 130, 86 LRRM 1509 (1974) (high degree of employee transfer; store managers lacked authority over employee relations; close geographic proximity of stores). For circuit court reaction to the single-store unit presumption, see NLRB v. Chicago Health & Tennis Clubs, 567 F2d 331, 96 LRRM 3249 (CA 7, 1977) (in consolidated cases, court reviewed history of single-store unit presumption and approved of single-store unit in one case and disapproved of single-store unit in another. *See* Schnitzler & Giovannetti, *Retail Stores*, in APPROPRIATE UNITS FOR COLLECTIVE BARGAINING 120–27 (P. Nash & G. Blake eds. 1979).

[119]Metropolitan Life Ins. Co. (New York), 56 NLRB 1635, 14 LRRM 187 (1944).

[120]*Id.* at 1640. The Board had previously approved of "provisional units" that were less-than-statewide, relying heavily on the extent of union organization and the belief that the "provisional units" would grow into statewide units. *See* cases discussed *id.* and in Washington Nat'l Ins. Co., 64 NLRB 929, 930 n.1, 17 LRRM 154 (1945).

Co.[121] decision the Board changed its policy, stating: "the [statewide-unit] rule was adopted *solely* in anticipation of broader organization on a companywide or statewide basis . . . [which] has not materialized, and the result of the rule has been to arrest the organizational development of insurance agents to an extent certainly never contemplated by the Act . . . . Accordingly, . . . we shall apply our normal unit principles to the cases as they arise." However, the decisions under the *Quaker City* case-by-case approach lacked coherency[122] and produced conflicting circuit court decisions, with the First Circuit concluding that the Board was giving controlling weight to the extent of organization in violation of section 9(c)(5).[123] The Supreme Court, addressed this confusion in its 1965 *NLRB v. Metropolitan Life Insurance Co. (Woonsocket, R.I.)*[124] decision, and remanded the case to the Board. Because the Board had failed to articulate its reasons for finding that debit insurance agents at a district office constituted an appropriate unit the Court could not determine whether controlling weight had been given to the extent of organization. On remand, the Board reviewed its policy and the structure of the insurance industry and concluded: "[T]he district office is the insurance industry's analogue of the single manufacturing plant, or the single store of a retail chain. Accordingly, if petitioned for, we will ordinarily find a single district office to be an appropriate bargaining unit for insurance agents . . . ."[125] The Board has continued to apply this presumption in favor of single district office units,[126] although in specific cases it has favored

---

[121]134 NLRB 960, 962, 49 LRRM 1281 (1961), *aff'd*, 319 F2d 690, 53 LRRM 2519 (CA 4, 1963).

[122]*Compare* Metropolitan Life Ins. Co. (Cleveland), 141 NLRB 1074, 52 LRRM 1451 (1963), *enforced*, 330 F2d 62, 55 LRRM 2930 (CA 6, 1964), *vacated and remanded per curiam*, 380 US 525, 59 LRRM 2063 (1965) (unit of six city offices and three suburban offices held appropriate) *with* Metropolitan Life Ins. Co. (Chicago), 144 NLRB 149, 54 LRRM 1005 (1963) (unit of city offices, excluding suburban offices, held appropriate).

[123]*Compare* NLRB v. Metropolitan Life Ins. Co. (Woonsocket, R.I.), 327 F2d 906, 55 LRRM 2444 (CA 1, 1964), *vacated and remanded*, 380 US 438, 58 LRRM 2721 (1965) *with* Metropolitan Life Ins. Co. (Cleveland) v. NLRB, 330 F2d 62, 55 LRRM 2930 (CA 6, 1964), *vacated and remanded per curiam*, 380 US 525, 59 LRRM 2063 (1965) *and* Metropolitan Life Ins. Co. (Wilmington, Del.) v. NLRB, 328 F2d 820, 55 LRRM 2448 (CA 3, 1964), *vacated and remanded per curiam*, 380 US 523, 59 LRRM 2063 (1965).

[124]*Supra* note 123.

[125]Metropolitan Life Ins. Co., 156 NLRB 1408, 1414–15, 61 LRRM 1249 (1966).

[126]*E.g.*, Empire Mut. Ins. Co., 195 NLRB 284, 79 LRRM 1348 (1972); Equitable Life Ins. Co., 163 NLRB 154, 64 LRRM 1300 (1967), *enforced*, 395 F2d 750, 68 LRRM 2251 (CA 6), *cert. denied*, 393 US 849, 69 LRRM 2435 (1968).

regional units over district office units.[127]

The Board has thus shown a general policy towards finding single-plant units presumptively appropriate.[128] As will be observed in the next section, this presumption has also been applied to the health care industry, notwithstanding the congressional admonition against unit fragmentation in that industry.[129] The general policy, however, is not without exceptions, for the Board has favored systemwide units over single-location units in the public utility,[130] and oceanic transport industries.[131] The building and construction industry has posed special problems of unit determination because of the fluctuating nature of the work force and the constant changes in job sites.[132]

---

[127]Farmers Ins. Group, 187 NLRB 844, 76 LRRM 1133 (1971); Allstate Ins. Co., 171 NLRB 142, 68 LRRM 1039 (1968).

[128]The single-facility presumption has been applied in a number of service industries. The Board has applied it to banks, with mixed success in the courts. *See* Wyandotte Sav. Bank v. NLRB, 669 F2d 386, 109 LRRM 2859 (CA 6, 1982), *denying enforcement to* 250 NLRB 362, 104 LRRM 1404 (1980); Alaska State Bank v. NLRB, 653 F2d 1285, 108 LRRM 2048 (CA 9, 1981). Among the other services to which the presumption has been applied are transportation industries, Beckett Aviation Corp.-Cleveland, 254 NLRB 88, 106 LRRM 1105 (1981); restaurants, Eschenbach-Boysa Mgmt. Co., 268 NLRB 550, 115 LRRM 1046 (1984); beauty salons, Emporium-Capwell Div., 273 NLRB 621, 118 LRRM 1348 (1984); and entertainment, United Artists Communications, 280 NLRB 1056, 122 LRRM 1296 (1986). The presumption has been applied, but rebutted specific settings, in connection with property management, Seligman & Assocs. v. NLRB, 639 F2d 307, 106 LRRM 2413 (CA 6), *cert. denied*, 454 US 838, 108 LRRM 2559 (1981); and pest control, Orkin Exterminating Co., 258 NLRB 773, 108 LRRM 1170 (1981).

[129]*See* discussion at notes 204–206 *infra*.

[130]*See* New England Tel. & Tel. Co., 242 NLRB 940, 101 LRRM 1263 (1979); New England Tel. & Tel. Co., 242 NLRB 793, 101 LRRM 1239 (1979); National Telecommunications, 215 NLRB 184, 87 LRRM 1696 (1974); National Tel. Co., 215 NLRB 176, 87 LRRM 1688 (1974); Atlantic Gas & Light Co., 158 NLRB 311, 62 LRRM 1026 (1966); Southwestern Bell Tel., 108 NLRB 1106, 34 LRRM 1146 (1954); New England Tel. & Tel. Co., 90 NLRB 639, 26 LRRM 1259 (1950). In Tidewater Tel. Co., 181 NLRB 867, 867, 73 LRRM 1512 (1970), the Board noted:

> While the Board has generally considered that the optimum unit in public utilities is systemwide, it has not required that it be multi-department at all times and in all circumstances, particularly where, as here, no labor organization seeks to represent the employees on a more comprehensive basis. In such circumstances, a more limited unit, such as one coextensive with a smaller administrative subdivision, may also be appropriate.

Accord New England Tel. & Tel. Co., 280 NLRB 162, 122 LRRM 1202 (1986); Concord Tel. Co., 248 NLRB 253, 103 LRRM 1363 (1979); Michigan Wis. Pipe Line Co., 164 NLRB 359, 65 LRRM 1065 (1967).

[131]*See* Inter-Ocean S.S. Co., 107 NLRB 330, 33 LRRM 1132 (1953); Ocean Tow, 99 NLRB 480, 30 LRRM 1086 (1952). In Moore-McCormack Lines, 139 NLRB 796, 51 LRRM 1361 (1962), the Board acknowledged persumption in favor of fleetwide units, but held in favor of a smaller unit due to unusual facts.

[132]*E.g.*, Electric Mach. Enters., 269 NLRB 499, 115 LRRM 1273 (1984). In John Deklewa & Sons, 282 NLRB 1375, 124 LRRM 1185 (1987), *enforced sub nom.* Iron Workers Local 3 v. NLRB, 843 F2d 770, 128 LRRM 2020 (CA 3), *cert. denied*, 488 US 889, 129 LRRM 2528 (1988), the Board indicated that it would normally find appropriate a list of the employees covered by the most recent §8(f) agreement, if any, and it has followed this approach in some subsequent cases. P.J. Dick Contracting, 290 NLRB 150, 129 LRRM 1144 (1988); William N. Taylor, Inc., 288 NLRB 1049, 129 LRRM 1219 (1988). More recent

C. Specialized Units

1. Units in Health Care Institutions. *a. Background: The 1974 Amendment to the Act.* In 1974 the Act was amended to extend coverage to nonprofit hospitals,[133] which previously had been excluded from the statutory definition of "employer."[134] This legislation included a number of special provisions applicable to all "health care institutions,"[135] including those previously subject to the Act.[136]

Bargaining-unit determination issues in the health care industry received significant attention from Congress during consideration of the 1974 amendments.[137] During the congressional hearings leading to passage of the amendments, concern was expressed that unit fragmentation in health care institutions would increase labor disputes and adversely affect patient care.[138] Committee members responded to this concern by specifically directing in both the Senate and House committee reports that "[d]ue consideration should be given by the Board to preventing proliferation of bargaining units in the health care

---

decisions, however, suggest that the unit described in the §8(f) agreement is far from controlling, and that unit determinations in the construction industry will be based on criteria similar to those used generally. *See* Ralph Rogers & Co. v. NLRB, 870 F2d 379, 130 LRRM 2979 (CA 7, 1989), *enforcing* 287 NLRB No. 114, 129 LRRM 1085 (1988); A.C. Pavement Striping Co., 296 NLRB No. 38, 132 LRRM 1113 (1989); Dezcon, Inc., 295 NLRB No. 19, 131 LRRM 1675 (1989).

[133]Pub. L. No. 93-360, 88 Stat. 395 (1974).

[134]Section 2(2).

[135]Section 2(14). *See also* Chapter 19, "The Primary Strike," at notes 52–57, and Chapter 13, "The Duty to Bargain," at notes 893–909.

[136]S. REP. NO. 93-766, 93d Cong., 2d Sess. 3 (1974).

[137]For bibliographic materials, see the following: Corbett, *Problems and Predictions From the Management Perspective*, in LABOR RELATIONS LAW PROBLEMS IN HOSPITALS AND THE HEALTH CARE INDUSTRY 246 (A. Knapp ed. 1977) [hereinafter cited as LABOR RELATIONS LAW PROBLEMS]; D'Alba, *Health Care Decisions of the National Labor Relations Board Since the 1974 Amendments to the National Labor Relations Act*, in LABOR RELATIONS LAW PROBLEMS, *supra*, at 15; Emanuel, *Hospital Bargaining Unit Decisions*, in LABOR RELATIONS LAW PROBLEMS, *supra*, at 187; Fanning, *Health Care Labor Relations: Problems and Predictions*, in LABOR RELATIONS LAW PROBLEMS, *supra*, at 237; King, *Legislative Review: Is Congressional Intent Being Realized—Or Are Significant Changes Needed?*, in LABOR RELATIONS LAW PROBLEMS, *supra*, at 147; Pepe, *An Overview of the Changes and Their Significance*, in LABOR RELATIONS LAW PROBLEMS, *supra*, at 3; Kilgour, *The Health-Care Bargaining Unit Controversy: Community of Interest Versus Disparity of Interest*, 40 LAB. L.J. 81 (1989); Sharo, *Appropriate Bargaining Units in the Health Care Industry*, 5 LAB. LAW. 787 (1989); Bumpass, *Appropriate Bargaining Units in Health Care Institutions: An Analysis of Congressional Intent and Its Implementation by the National Labor Relations Board*, 20 B.C.L. REV. 867 (1979); Farkas, *National Labor Relations Act: The Health Care Amendments*, 29 LAB. L.J. 259 (1978); Miller, *National Labor Relations Act—History and Interpretation of the Health Care Amendments*, 60 MARQ. L. REV. 921 (1977).

[138]*See* SUBCOMM. ON LABOR OF THE SENATE COMM. ON LABOR AND PUBLIC WELFARE, 93d Cong., 2d Sess., LEGISLATIVE HISTORY OF NONPROFIT HOSPITALS UNDER THE NATIONAL LABOR RELATIONS ACT (1974).

industry."[139] The reports cited with approval two preamendment health care industry decisions in which the Board had found inappropriate a unit of maintenance department employees in a nursing home[140] and a unit of X-ray technicians in a hospital.[141] The committee reports also approved the "trend toward broader units" reflected in another preamendment case, where a separate unit of technical employees had been found inappropriate.[142] However, the committees criticized one element of that decision—the Board's approval of a separate unit of licensed practical nurses—because it was inconsistent with the trend toward broader units.

The congressional debates which preceded enactment of the amendments gave further attention to the problem of bargaining-unit definitions in health care institutions. The cosponsors of the legislation decried unit proliferation, claiming that it would lead to jurisdictional disputes, work stoppages, wage whipsawing, and a higher cost for medical care. Legislators adjured the Board to examine the public interest and use great caution in deciding health care unit cases.[143]

Congress, nevertheless, did not amend section 9(b)'s sweeping grant of discretion to the Board. Rather, it acknowledged the Board's expertise in unit determinations, as evidenced by Senator Williams's statement at the time the Senate conference report was being considered: "While the [conference] committee clearly intends that the Board give due consideration to its admonition to avoid an undue proliferation of units in the health care industry, it did not intend to preclude the Board acting in the public interest from exercising its specialized expertise and expert knowledge in determining appropriate bargaining units."[144]

In the exercise of that "specialized experience and expert knowledge," the Board began the regulation of the newly covered facilities by applying its familiar test of community of

---

[139]S. REP. NO. 93-766, 93d Cong., 2d Sess. 5 (1974), and H.R. REP. NO. 93-1051, 93d Cong., 2d Sess. 7 (1974).

[140]*Id.* (citing Four Seasons Nursing Center of Joliet, 208 NLRB 403, 85 LRRM 1093 (1974)).

[141]*Id.* (citing Woodland Park Hosp., 205 NLRB 888, 84 LRRM 1075 (1973)).

[142]*Id.* (citing Extendicare of W. Va. dba St. Luke's Hosp., 203 NLRB 1232, 83 LRRM 1242 (1973)).

[143]120 CONG. REC. 12,944–45, 13,559, 22,949 (1974) (comments of Sen. Taft and Rep. Ashbrook).

[144]120 CONG. REC. 22,575 (1974).

interests. Given the intricacies of modern hospitals, that test threatened to produce numerous bargaining units in most hospitals. In the face of mounting criticism, much of it from the Courts of Appeal, the Board experimented briefly with a requirement of vastly broader units. More recently, by notice-and-comment rulemaking, the Board has reverted to an adaptation of the original approach, declaring that eight specified units will ordinarily be appropriate. These developments are reviewed below.

b. Application of Community of Interest Standard and the Eight-Unit Result. The Board's case-by-case application of the community of interest standard to health care units following the 1974 amendments eventually yielded eight basic units[145] which were found appropriate if sought by a labor organization: (1) physicians, (2) registered nurses (RNs), (3) other professional employees, (4) technical employees, (5) business office clerical employees, (6) service and maintenance employees, (7) either maintenance department employees or stationary engineers, and (8) guards. The appellate courts often took a more literal view of the unit nonproliferation instructions contained in the legislative history, denigrating to that extent the authority of the unamended section 9(b). That approach led to the reversal of many Board decisions. These court decisions, as well as the Board decisions establishing the basic unit structure, are the topic of this section.

(1) Physicians, excluding interns and residents. In *Ohio Valley Hospital Ass'n*[146] the Board decided that separate units of employed physicians are appropriate, and that physicians should be excluded from units of other professional employees. This was based on a conclusion that physicians share a distinct community of interests and that "[w]ithin the hospital hierarchy, physicians are the pivotal employees and all other patient care employees are subject to their professional direction."[147] In *Cedars-Sinai Medical Center*[148] the Board decided that hospital interns and

[145]Other units emerged from time to time due to special circumstances. For example, a unit of chauffeur-drivers was approved in Michael Reese Hosp. & Medical Center, 242 NLRB 322, 101 LRRM 1157 (1979), largely because it was an unrepresented residual group that otherwise would have been denied representation.

[146]230 NLRB 604, 95 LRRM 1430 (1977).

[147]*Id.* at 605. See note 240 *infra* for discussion of managerial status for hospital staff physicians.

[148]223 NLRB 251, 91 LRRM 1398 (1976).

residents should be excluded from any unit because they are primarily students and not "employees" as defined in the Act.[149]

(2) Registered nurses. The Board's decision to separate registered nurses from other professionals was announced in *Mercy Hospitals of Sacramento*,[150] a decision based primarily on the rationale that registered nurses had an "impressive history of exclusive representation and collective bargaining."[151] Later, the Board abandoned national bargaining history as a major underpinning of its RN unit policy, holding instead that a separate RN unit was justified on traditional community of interest grounds and that one relevant factor in evaluating community of interests is *area* practice and patterns of bargaining.[152] Despite the shift of rationale, the Board retained the bright-line rule allowing a separate unit.[153]

---

[149]Section 2(3). This position was reiterated in Kansas City Gen. Hosp., 225 NLRB 108, 93 LRRM 1362 (1976), and in numerous cases involving the status of interns and residents. *See, e.g.*, Samaritan Health Servs., 238 NLRB 629, 99 LRRM 1551 (1978); St. Clare's Hosp. & Health Center, 229 NLRB 1000, 95 LRRM 1180 (1977); University of Chicago Hosp. & Clinics, 223 NLRB 1032, 92 LRRM 1039 (1976). The Board later obtained a federal court injunction to prevent a state labor relations board from taking jurisdiction over interns and residents, arguing that federal law preempts the regulation of labor relations involving interns and residents, even though they are not employees under the Act. NLRB v. Committee of Interns & Residents, 556 F2d 810, 96 LRRM 2342 (CA 2, 1977), *cert. denied*, 435 US 904, 97 LRRM 2809 (1978). Litigation seeking to overturn the Board's *Cedars-Sinai* decision was ultimately unsuccessful. Physicians Nat'l House Staff Ass'n v. Murphy, 100 LRRM 3055 (CA DC, 1979), *reh'g en banc sub nom.* Physicians Nat'l House Staff Ass'n v. Fanning, 642 F2d 492, 104 LRRM 2940 (CA DC, 1980), *cert. denied*, 450 US 917, 106 LRRM 2513 (1981). Legislation intended to overrule *Cedars-Sinai* was defeated in 1979. H.R. Res. 2222, 96th Cong., 1st Sess. (1979).

[150]217 NLRB 765, 89 LRRM 1097 (1975), *rev'd and remanded*, 589 F2d 968, 98 LRRM 2800 (CA 9, 1978), *cert. denied sub nom.* Hospital & Institutional Workers Local 250 v. NLRB, 440 US 910, 100 LRRM 2687, *decision on remand*, 244 NLRB 229, 102 LRRM 1016 (1979). *Accord* Texas Inst. for Rehabilitation & Research, 228 NLRB 578, 94 LRRM 1513, 1514 (1977); Sutter Community Hosps. of Sacramento, 227 NLRB 181, 94 LRRM 1450 (1976); Morristown-Hamblen Hosp. Ass'n, 226 NLRB 76, 93 LRRM 1166 (1976); Valley Hosp., 220 NLRB 1339, 90 LRRM 1411, *modified*, 221 NLRB 1239, 91 LRRM 1061 (1975); Kaiser Found. Hosps., 219 NLRB 325, 89 LRRM 1763 (1975); Gnaden Huetten Memorial Hosp., 219 NLRB 235, 89 LRRM 1761 (1975); Presbyterian Medical Center, 218 NLRB 1266, 89 LRRM 1752 (1975); Bishop Randall Hosp., 217 NLRB 1129, 89 LRRM 1249 (1975).

[151]217 NLRB at 767.

[152]Allegheny Gen. Hosp. (II), 239 NLRB 872, 100 LRRM 1030 (1978), *enforcement denied*, 608 F2d 965, 102 LRRM 2784 (CA 3, 1979).

[153]The Board was sharply rebuked for this "per se" rule in NLRB v. St. Francis Hosp. of Lynwood, 601 F2d 404, 101 LRRM 2943 (CA 9, 1979), *denying enforcement to* 232 NLRB 32, 97 LRRM 1297 (1977). Citing Congress' "directive" against undue proliferation, the court announced that proper standard was not whether RNs have a separate community of interests, but whether a "disparity of interests" separated RNs from other professional employees. *Id.* at 419. For other examples of judicial criticism of the Board's treatment of RN units *see* NLRB v. Frederick Memorial Hosp., 691 F2d 191, 111 LRRM 2680 (CA 4, 1982); NLRB v. HMO Int'l Cal. Medical Group Health Plan, 678 F2d 806, 110 LRRM 2745 (CA 9, 1982); Presbyterian/St. Luke's Medical Center v. NLRB, 653 F2d 450, 107 LRRM 2753 (CA 10, 1981), *cert dismissed sub nom.* St. Luke's Fed'n of Nurses & Health

In 1980, the Board disavowed any irrebutable presumption that a separate RN unit is appropriate and acknowledged that a separate RN unit might be inappropriate where unusual facts exist. A separate unit would be approved, however, whenever the customary hospital fact pattern of RN community of interests is present.[154]

The Board has included in an RN unit "on-call" RNs[155] as well as graduate nurses (graduates of an accredited nursing school who have not passed the RN licensing examination).[156] Nurse practitioners (RNs with additional education and responsibilities) were also included,[157] but physician extenders (specialized RNs with advanced training) have been separated from RNs and placed in a unit of other professional employees.[158]

(3) Other professionals. A separate unit of all professional employees except registered nurses was first approved in *Mercy Hospitals of Sacramento.*[159] There the Board reasoned that although a diversity of health care functions exists among various professional groups, their skills, interests, and working conditions are in many respects no more diverse than those of employees in a production and maintenance unit in the indus-

---

Professionals v. Presbyterian/St. Luke's Medical Center, 459 US 1025 (1982), *on remand*, 289 NLRB 249, 129 LRRM 1263 (1988).

[154]Newton-Wellesley Hosp., 250 NLRB 409, 104 LRRM 1384 (1980). *See also* Mount Airy Found. dba Mount Airy Psychiatric Center, 253 NLRB 1003, 106 LRRM 1071 (1981) (unit of registered nurses at 80-bed psychiatric hospital held inappropriate where there were nonnurse professional "team leaders" and other professionals who shared a community of interests with the nurses). The Board applied its RN unit policy only when a petitioning union sought a separate unit. *See, e.g.*, Walker County Medical Center, 260 NLRB 862, 109 LRRM 1287 (1982), *enforced*, 722 F2d 1535, 115 LRRM 2553 (CA 11, 1984); Ralph K. Davies Medical Center, 256 NLRB 1113, 107 LRRM 1372 (1981); Long Island College Hosp., 256 NLRB 202, 107 LRRM 1205 (1981); Milwaukee Children's Hosp. Ass'n, 255 NLRB 1009, 107 LRRM 1024 (1981); Frederick Memorial Hosp., 254 NLRB 36, 106 LRRM 1102 (1981), *enforcement denied*, 691 F2d 191, 111 LRRM 2680 (CA 4, 1982); Addison-Gilbert Hosp., 253 NLRB 1010, 106 LRRM 1059 (1981). When a petitioning union sought a combined unit of all professionals, and no intervenor sought a separate RN unit, the combined unit was allowed, Valley Hosp., 221 NLRB 1239, 91 LRRM 1061 (1975), even when an employer contended that the RN unit should be separate. Family Doctor Medical Group, 226 NLRB 118, 93 LRRM 1193 (1976).

[155]*See* cases cited in note 150 *supra*.

[156]Lydia E. Hall Hosp., 227 NLRB 573, 94 LRRM 1105 (1976). Decisions regarding RN-LPN (Licensed Practical Nurse) units were in apparent conflict, with one such petition having been granted and another denied. *Compare* Maple Shade Nursing Home, 228 NLRB 1457, 96 LRRM 1411 (1977) (petitioned-for RN-LPN unit held appropriate) *with* Presbyterian Medical Center, 218 NLRB 1266, 89 LRRM 1752 (1975) (petitioned-for RN-LPN unit held inappropriate). Both decisions recognized that any RN-LPN unit would require majority approval by RNs, since LPNs are nonprofessionals.

[157]Rockridge Medical Care Center, 221 NLRB 560, 90 LRRM 1721 (1975).

[158]Kaiser Found. Health Plan of Colo. & Permanente Servs. of Colo., 230 NLRB 438, 95 LRRM 1376 (1977).

[159]*Supra* note 150.

trial sphere, or in an overall service and maintenance unit in the health care industry. The Board has followed this view in numerous cases,[160] in the absence of special circumstances inherent in the nature of the particular health care institution.[161]

(4) Technical employees. A unit confined to technical employees was approved as part of the Board's basic unit structure in *Barnert Memorial Hospital Ass'n.*[162] The Board explained that while a "separate community of interest is frequently evidenced by the fact that such employees are certified, registered or licensed," this will not be required in every case.[163] The Board later added that technical employees will be excluded from a service and maintenance unit when the petitioning union seeks to exclude them.[164] The Board has frequently reaffirmed this determination,[165] which has been enforced by the Sixth, Seventh, and Eighth circuits.[166]

Pursuant to the Board's technical unit policy, licensed practical nurses or vocational nurses (LPNs or LVNs) were not allowed to be represented in a separate unit and were ordinarily,

---

[160]Allegheny Gen. Hosp. (II), *supra* note 152. Ohio Valley Hosp. Ass'n, 230 NLRB 604, 95 LRRM 1430 (1977); San Jose Hosp. & Health Center, 228 NLRB 21, 96 LRRM 1391 (1977); Sutter Community Hosps. of Sacramento, *supra* note 150; Methodist Hosp. of Sacramento, 223 NLRB 1509, 92 LRRM 1198 (1976); Beth Israel Hosp. & Geriatrics Center, 219 NLRB 520, 89 LRRM 1685 (1975); Dominican Santa Cruz Hosp., 218 NLRB 1211, 89 LRRM 1504 (1975). The professional status of laboratory technologists is still an open question, however. *Compare* St. Barnabas Hosp., 283 NLRB 472, 124 LRRM 1388 (1987) *with* Norton Community Hosp., 291 NLRB 1174, 130 LRRM 1218 (1988). On the propriety of excluding social workers from a professional unit, see Foundation for Comprehensive Health Servs., 251 NLRB 161, 105 LRRM 1056 (1980), *enforcement denied*, 654 F2d 731, 108 LRRM 2344 (CA 9, 1981), *on remand*, 261 NLRB 124, 109 LRRM 1377 (1982).

[161]*See* Jack L. Williams, DDS, 219 NLRB 1045, 90 LRRM 1188 (1975) (separate unit for dentists employed by dental clinic).

[162]217 NLRB 775, 89 LRRM 1083 (1975).

[163]*Id.* at 776.

[164]Newington Children's Hosp., 217 NLRB 793, 89 LRRM 1108 (1975). *But see* Appalachian Regional Hosps., 233 NLRB 542, 96 LRRM 1528 (1977) (technical employees combined with maintenance and service employees on request of petitioner); National G.S. dba Memorial Medical, 230 NLRB 976, 95 LRRM 1478 (1977) (same).

[165]Middlesex Gen. Hosp., 239 NLRB 837, 100 LRRM 1024 (1978); Allegheny Gen. Hosp. (II), *supra* note 152; Pontiac Osteopathic Hosp., 227 NLRB 1706, 94 LRRM 1417 (1977); Children's Hosp. of Pittsburgh, 222 NLRB 588, 91 LRRM 1440 (1976); St. Luke's Episcopal Hosp., 222 NLRB 674, 91 LRRM 1359 (1976); Taylor Hosp., 218 NLRB 1188, 89 LRRM 1506 (1975); Trinity Memorial Hosp. of Cudahy, 219 NLRB 215, 90 LRRM 1099 (1975); Sweetwater Hosp. Ass'n, 219 NLRB 803, 90 LRRM 1055 (1975); Heights Medical Center, 221 NLRB 563, 90 LRRM 1675 (1975). *See* A.W. Schlesinger Geriatric Center, 260 NLRB 452, 109 LRRM 1171 (1982) (technical employees and LVNs excluded from service and maintenance unit).

[166]NLRB v. Res-Care, 705 F2d 1461, 113 LRRM 2336 (CA 7, 1983); NLRB v. Sweetwater Hosp. Ass'n, 604 F2d 454, 102 LRRM 2246 (CA 6, 1979); Watonwan Memorial Hosp., 263 NLRB No. 99, 111 LRRM 1191 (1982), *enforced*, 711 F2d 848, 113 LRRM 3481 (CA 8, 1983).

but not uniformly, included with the other technical classifications.[167]

(5) Business office clericals. A separate unit of "business office clerical" employees was approved in *Mercy Hospitals of Sacramento.*[168]

The Board has continued to find appropriate a separate unit of business office clerical employees,[169] and to exclude such employees from a service and maintenance unit when requested by the petitioning union.[170]

However, the Board has found patient-admitting clerks and patient-records clerks not to be business office clericals because of their substantial patient contact; it has, rather, included them

---

[167]St. Catharine's Hosp., 217 NLRB 787, 89 LRRM 1070 (1975). *But see* Pine Manor, 238 NLRB 1654, 99 LRRM 1323 (1978) (LPNs granted self-determination election to choose between separate unit or inclusion in service and maintenance unit); Pontiac Osteopathic Hosp., *supra* note 165 (LPNs excluded from technical unit because they had prior bargaining history in separate unit); Maple Shade Nursing Home, 228 NLRB 1457, 96 LRRM 1411 (1977), *enforced*, 577 F2d 727, 98 LRRM 2438 (CA 3, 1978) (LPNs included with registered nurses); Children's Hosp. of Pittsburgh, *supra* note 165 (LPNs excluded from technical unit because they did not perform technical work); Bay Medical Center, 218 NLRB 620, 89 LRRM 1310 (1975), *enforced*, 558 F2d 1174, 100 LRRM 2213 (CA 6, 1978), *related case*, Bay Medical Center, 239 NLRB 731, 100 LRRM 1012 (1978) (same result in similar but more complicated factual setting).

[168]217 NLRB 765, 89 LRRM 1097 (1975), *rev'd and remanded*, 589 F2d 968, 98 LRRM 2800 (CA 9, 1978), *cert. denied sub nom.* Hospital & Institutional Workers Local 250 v. NLRB, 440 US 910, 100 LRRM 2867, *decision on remand*, 244 NLRB 229, 102 LRRM 1016 (1979). The Board drew a distinction between "business office clerical employees, who perform mainly business-type functions, and other types of clerical employees whose work is more closely related to the function performed by personnel in the service and maintenance unit and who have, in the past, been traditionally excluded by the Board from bargaining units of business office clerical employees." *Id.* at 770. *See* Sisters of St. Joseph of Peace, 217 NLRB 797, 89 LRRM 1082 (1975); St. Catharine's Hosp., *supra* note 167.

[169]The Board later defined business office clericals as "those clerical employees who, because they perform business office functions, have minimal contact with unit employees or patients, work in geographical areas of the hospital, or perform functions, separate and apart from service and maintenance employees, and thus do not share a community of interest with the service and maintenance unit employees." St. Luke's Episcopal Hosp., *supra* note 165, at 676.

[170]Allegheny Gen. Hosp. (II), *supra* note 152; Sutter Community Hosps. of Sacramento, 227 NLRB 181, 94 LRRM 1450 (1976); Family Doctor Medical Group, 226 NLRB 118, 93 LRRM 1193 (1976); Seton Medical Center, 221 NLRB 120, 90 LRRM 1436 (1975); Oakwood Hosp. Corp., 219 NLRB 620, 90 LRRM 1026 (1975); William W. Backus Hosp., 220 NLRB 414, 90 LRRM 1696 (1975). However, in one case the Board included business office clericals in a service and maintenance unit although the employer contended that there should be two separate units, but that decision was based on "special circumstances." Appalachian Regional Hosps., *supra* note 164. The business office clerical definition was applied to medical-records-department employees with conflicting results, *compare* Central Gen. Hosp., 223 NLRB 110, 91 LRRM 1433 (1976) *with* St. Luke's Episcopal Hosp., *supra* note 165. Again with conflicting results, the definition was applied in cases involving admitting clerks, *compare* Southwest La. Hosp. Ass'n dba Lake Charles Memorial Hosp., 226 NLRB 849, 93 LRRM 1420 (1976) *with* St. Luke's Episcopal Hosp., *supra.*

in a service and maintenance unit along with other nonprofessional employees.[171]

(6) Service and maintenance employees. In *Newington Children's Hospital,*[172] the Board reiterated that "a service and maintenance unit in a service industry is the analogue to the plant-wide production and maintenance unit in the industrial sector, and as such is the classic appropriate unit" for the health service industry.[173]

In late 1975, the Board heard oral argument in a series of cases dealing with separate maintenance units including *Jewish Hospital Ass'n of Cincinnati.*[174] However, in *St. Vincent's Hospital,*[175] the Board found a unit of four boiler operators to be appropriate. Subsequent decisions were inconsistent, with maintenance units found inappropriate in most cases[176] but appropriate in some.[177]

The Board's inconsistency, and its reliance on traditional unit factors when maintenance units were found appropriate, led to judicial criticism and a number of reversals.[178] Despite judicial

---

[171]Southwest La. Hosp. Ass'n dba Lake Charles Memorial Hosp., *supra* note 170; Appalachian Regional Hosps., *supra* note 164; National G.S. dba Memorial Medical, *supra* note 164.

[172]Newington Children's Hosp., *supra* note 164, at 794. *See also* Allegheny Gen. Hosp. (II), *supra* note 152.

[173]In Mount Airy Found. dba Mount Airy Psychiatric Center, 217 NLRB 802, 89 LRRM 1067 (1975), the Board refused to bifurcate a service and maintenance unit into separate units of "direct" and "indirect" patient care employees. Other attempts to split such units were also rejected. *See* Bay Medical Center, 218 NLRB 620, 89 LRRM 1310 (1975), *enforced*, 588 F2d 1174, 100 LRRM 2213 (CA 6, 1978) (housekeeping unit); Mad River Community Hosp., 219 NLRB 25, 89 LRRM 1499 (1975) (unit of laboratory and X-ray departments).

[174]223 NLRB 614, 617, 91 LRRM 1499 (1976).

[175]223 NLRB 638, 91 LRRM 1513 (1976), *enforcement denied*, 567 F2d 588, 97 LRRM 2119 (CA 3, 1977).

[176]Peter Bent Brigham Hosp., 231 NLRB 929, 96 LRRM 1546 (1977); Northeastern Hosp., 230 NLRB 1042, 95 LRRM 1464 (1977); Baptist Memorial Hosp., 224 NLRB 199, 92 LRRM 1223 (1976); St. Joseph Hosp., 224 NLRB 270, 92 LRRM 1209 (1976); Greater Bakersfield Memorial Hosp., 226 NLRB 971, 93 LRRM 1386 (1976); Anaheim Memorial Hosp., 227 NLRB 161, 94 LRRM 1058 (1976); Riverside Methodist Hosp., 223 NLRB 1084, 92 LRRM 1033 (1976); Jewish Hosp. Ass'n of Cincinnati, *supra* note 174; Shriner's Hosps. for Crippled Children, 217 NLRB 806, 89 LRRM 1076 (1975) (separate unit of stationary engineers rejected).

[177]Allegheny Gen. Hosp. (II), 239 NLRB 872, 100 LRRM 1030 (1978), *enforcement denied*, 608 F2d 965, 102 LRRM 2784 (CA 3, 1979); McLean Hosp., 234 NLRB 424, 97 LRRM 1322 (1978); Hebrew Rehabilitation Center, 230 NLRB 255, 95 LRRM 1279 (1977); St. Francis Hosp.-Medical Center, 223 NLRB 1451, 92 LRRM 1172 (1976); West Suburban Hosp., 224 NLRB 1349, 92 LRRM 1369 (1976); Eskaton Am. River Healthcare Center, 225 NLRB 755, 92 LRRM 1569 (1976). In Mercy Center for Health Care Servs., 227 NLRB 1814, 94 LRRM 1534 (1977), the Board found a maintenance department unit inappropriate, but approved a separate unit of stationary engineers.

[178]*See, e.g.*, Memorial Hosp. of Roxborough v. NLRB, 545 F2d 351, 93 LRRM 2571 (CA 3, 1976), *denying enforcement to* 220 NLRB 402, 90 LRRM 1369 (1975). In Long Island College Hosp. v. NLRB, 566 F2d 833, 843–44, 96 LRRM 3119 (CA 2, 1977), *denying*

criticism,[179] the Board routinely approved separate maintenance units when sought by a petitioning union.[180]

(7) Guards. Some hospitals employ "guards" as defined in section 9(b)(3) of the Act.[181] That section, which precludes the Board from including guards and nonguards in the same unit, is fully applicable to health care institutions. The Board has held that mixed units of guards and nonguards established prior to the amendments may be separated in a unit-clarification proceeding.[182]

c. Adoption of the "Disparity of Interest" Standard in St. Francis (II). In 1984, in *St. Francis Hospital (II)*,[183] the Board responded to the appellate courts' criticisms[184] of its bargaining-unit deter-

---

enforcement to 228 NLRB 83, 94 LRRM 1438 (1977), *cert. denied*, 435 US 996, 98 LRRM 2069 (1978), the Second Circuit described the Board's maintenance unit decisions as being in "disarray," and commented that "no one really knows how the Board would decide any case in this area of the law." In St. Vincent's Hosp. v. NLRB, *supra* note 175, relying on the congressional admonition, the Third Circuit refused to enforce the Board's order approving a unit of four boiler operators. The Seventh Circuit did likewise in NLRB v. West Suburban Hosp., 570 F2d 213, 97 LRRM 2929 (CA 7, 1978). The court criticized the Board for giving "mere lip service" to Congress' "directive" against proliferation of units. *Id.* at 216.

[179]The Board's persistence in its view was sharply criticized by the Third Circuit. Allegheny Gen. Hosp. (II) v. NLRB, 608 F2d 965, 970, 102 LRRM 2784 (CA 3, 1979). The Seventh and Second circuits also rejected the Board's unit approach in *Allegheny (II)*, and refused enforcement of decisions in which the Board approved a separate maintenance unit. Mary Thompson Hosp. v. NLRB, 621 F2d 858, 103 LRRM 2739 (CA 7, 1980); NLRB v. Mercy Hosp. Ass'n, 606 F2d 22, 102 LRRM 2259 (CA 2, 1979), *cert. denied*, 445 US 971, 103 LRRM 3082 (1980).

[180]In its 1982 St. Francis Hospital (I), 265 NLRB 1025, 112 LRRM 1153 (1982), decision, the Board reiterated that separate maintenance units would, on a case by case basis, be found appropriate if the community of interest of maintenance workers was sufficiently distinguished from other employees at the facility. The Board reasoned that maintenance employees possessed greater skills and required greater experience and on-the-job training than service employees, and that the job function, direction, and supervision of service employees was completely different from that of maintenance employees. The Board minimized the maintenance employees' consistent frequent contacts with service workers because the contacts were incidental and did not constitute job integration. *See also* Garden City Hosp., 244 NLRB 778, 102 LRRM 1146 (1979); Carney Hosp., 243 NLRB 826, 101 LRRM 1581 (1979); Fresno Community Hosp., 241 NLRB 521, 100 LRRM 1528 (1979); Long Island College Hosp., 239 NLRB 1135, 100 LRRM 1085 (1978).

[181]*See supra* at notes 57–77.

[182]Peninsula Hosp. Center & Peninsula Gen. Nursing Home Corp., 219 NLRB 139, 90 LRRM 1034 (1975). See Chapter 10, "Representation Proceedings and Elections," at notes 202–218 for treatment of unit-clarification procedures.

[183]271 NLRB 948, 116 LRRM 1465 (1984), *remanded sub nom.* Electrical Workers (IBEW) Local 474 v. NLRB, 814 F2d 697, 124 LRRM 2993 (CA DC, 1987) (overturning its earlier decision which found maintenance unit appropriate as one of seven "traditional" units and then applied and adopted two-tiered analysis whereby it was first determined if unit sought was appropriate under traditional community of interest standards, 265 NLRB 1025, 112 LRRM 1153 (1982)). *See supra* note 180.

[184]*See, e.g.*, Southwest Community Health Servs. v. NLRB, 726 F2d 611, 115 LRRM 2529 (CA 10, 1984); NLRB v. Res-Care, 705 F2d 1461, 113 LRRM 2336 (CA 7, 1983); Trustees of Masonic Hall & Asylum Fund v. NLRB, 699 F2d 626, 112 LRRM 2908 (CA 2, 1983); NLRB v. HMO Int'l/Cal. Medical Group Health Plan, 678 F2d 806, 110 LRRM

minations in the health care industry. Reconsidering an earlier decision which had allowed a unit largely confined to skilled maintenance employees, the Board purported to abandon the community of interest standard and to adopt, in its place, a "disparity of interests" standard. Under the new standard, discrete groups of employees would be allowed representation separate from other professional or nonprofessional employees only when it could be determined that their interests were sharply disparate from those of other such employees.[185] The Board announced that the new standard would be applied flexibly and disavowed any rigid presumption that there could be only two appropriate units. A concurring opinion suggested that as many as four units might be appropriate in large and diverse comprehensive hospitals: professional employees, service and maintenance employees, technical employees, and business office clerical employees.[186]

The Court of Appeals for the District of Columbia Circuit granted review, vacated the Board's decision, and remanded,[187] rejecting the conclusion that Congress' admonitions and adjurations required the Board to abandon its traditional community of interest standard. The Board might be free to adopt a more restricted standard in the health care industry, but it was not required to do so.[188] On remand, the Board reaffirmed its use of the disparity of interests standard.[189]

Applying *St. Francis (II)*, the Board: (1) refused, in general, to approve petitions for exclusive RN units, usually finding that the smallest appropriate unit in which the RNs could be represented was an all-professional unit;[190] (2) applied a "disparity of interest" analysis and approved a petition for a separate technical unit;[191] (3) ceased the routine exclusion of business office cler-

---

2745 (CA 9, 1982); NLRB v. Frederick Memorial Hosp., 691 F2d 191, 111 LRRM 2680 (CA 4, 1982).

[185]*Supra* note 183.

[186]*Id.* at 955 (Member Dennis concurring).

[187]Electrical Workers (IBEW) Local 474 v. NLRB, 814 F2d 697, 124 LRRM 2993 (CA DC, 1987).

[188]*Id.*

[189]St. Francis Hosp., 286 NLRB 1305, 126 LRRM 1361 (1987).

[190]North Arundel Hosp. Ass'n, 279 NLRB 311, 122 LRRM 1001 (1986); Keokuk Area Hosp., 278 NLRB 242, 121 LRRM 1168 (1986); Middletown Hosp. Ass'n, 282 NLRB 541, 124 LRRM 1260 (1986), *supplemented*, 291 NLRB No. 79, 129 LRRM 1261 (1988); Manor Healthcare Corp., 285 NLRB 224, 125 LRRM 1333 (1987). *See also* Southern Md. Hosp., 274 NLRB 1470, 118 LRRM 1599 (1985).

[191]Southern Md. Hosp., *supra* note 190, at 1474. The Board relied on wage disparities, qualifications and training differences, and the absence of interchange between the technical employees and the service and maintenance employees. *But see* St. Luke's

ical employees from service and maintenance or technical units when requested by the petitioning party;[192] and (4) refused to approve a petition for a separate maintenence unit, finding that the maintenance employees' interests were not sufficiently disparate from those of all the hospital's nonprofessional employees to warrant separate representation.[193]

d. The Board Engages in Rulemaking and the Supreme Court Approves: The Return to the Eight-Unit Standard. The Board's struggle with unit determination in the health care industry, and the conflict with the courts of appeals which this struggle engendered led the Board to undertake rulemaking to resolve the unit issues. In 1989 the Board enacted a rule that defines bargaining units for acute care facilities (excluding psychiatric hospitals and nursing homes).[194] Absent extraordinary circumstances, eight units are appropriate under the Final Rule: registered nurses, physicians, other professionals, technical employees, skilled maintenance employees, business office clericals, service and other nonprofessional employees, and guards.

In *American Hospital Ass'n v. NLRB*,[195] the Supreme Court upheld the Board's authority to establish general rules for bargaining-unit determinations through administrative rulemaking, rather than through adjudication, and affirmed the substance of the Board's eight-unit rule for acute care health care facilities. The litigation arose when an association of employers in the health care industry challenged the rule as invalid on its face. The district court enjoined enforcement of the rule on the ground that the Board's presumption in favor of eight valid units impermissibly offended the congressional admonition against proliferation.[196] The Seventh Circuit found no merit in that proposition and reversed.[197] The Supreme Court affirmed.

Memorial Hosp., 274 NLRB 1431, 118 LRRM 1545 (1985). The Board refused to approve a petition for a unit of all LPNs and graduate practical nurses, holding that a history of separate bargaining cannot overcome a lack of disparity of interest and that such employees should be included in a larger all-technical or all-nonprofessional unit.

[192]In Baker Hosp., 279 NLRB 308, 122 LRRM 1015 (1986), the Board refused to approve a petition for a combined unit of technical employees and service and maintenance employees because the unit would have excluded business office clericals who shared significant common interests with the included groups.

[193]Community Hosp. at Glen Cove, 278 NLRB 80, 121 LRRM 1126 (1986) (maintenance employees' skills and knowledge comparable to or exceeded levels of other nonprofessional employees with whom they had frequent contact and shared common employment terms).

[194]52 Fed. Reg. 3920–27 (Apr. 21, 1989). *See* Miller, *The NLRB and Rule Making: Determining Bargaining Units in the Health Care Industry*, 42 LAB. L.J. 711 (1990).

[195]___ U.S. ___, 137 LRRM 2001 (1991).

[196]American Hosp. Ass'n v. NLRB, 718 F Supp 704, 132 LRRM 2033 (ND Ill, 1989).

[197]American Hosp. Ass'n v. NLRB, 899 F2d 651, 133 LRRM 3073 (CA 7, 1990).

Reviewing three major contentions advanced in the lower courts, the Court reached these conclusions:

First, the mandate of section 9(b) of the Act that "the Board shall decide on each case . . . the unit appropriate for . . . collective bargaining" did not preclude rulemaking on the subject of bargaining-unit composition. The Court explained that the statutory provision "cannot fairly or logically be read to command the Board to exercise standardless discretion in each case."[198] The Court also observed that the rule established no more than a general rule, and that

> [a]s with its prior rules, the Board must still apply the rule "in each case." For example, the Board must decide in each case, among a host of other issues, whether a given facility is properly classified as an acute care hospital and whether particular employees are properly placed in particular units.[199]

Second, the "admonition" contained in the reports of congressional committees, which urged the Board to avoid large numbers of bargaining units in health care facilities, did not have the force of law. According to the Court, the statement was "best understood as a form of notice to the Board that if it did not give appropriate consideration to the problem of proliferation in this industry, Congress might respond with a legislative remedy."[200] The admonition was, in any event, only an adjuration to give "due consideration" to the special problems that would follow from the "proliferation" of bargaining units in acute care hospitals, and the Board had given extensive consideration to those problems.

Third, the decision of the Board to treat the eight units as presumptively appropriate was not arbitrary or capricious. The Court deemed that the adjudicatory, case-by-case, application of the rule, including its exception for "unusual circumstances," would allow the Board to take account of "critical differences among the more than 4,000 acute care hospitals in the United

---

[198]137 LRRM at 2004.

[199]*Id.* The Court's decision of this aspect of the case was hardly surprising. In NLRB v. Wyman-Gordon Co., 394 US 759, 70 LRRM 3345 (1969), the Court criticized the Board for having promulgated it *Excelsior Underwear* rule (which requires preelection disclosure of employee names and addresses) through an adjudicatory proceeding in which the Board announced a rule of prospective application, rather than through formal rulemaking consonant with the Administrative Procedure Act. Excelsior Underwear, 156 NLRB 1236, 61 LRRM 1217 (1966). For a fuller discussion of *Wyman-Gordon* and rulemaking at the Board, *see* Chapter 31, "NLRB Procedures," Section V.

[200]137 LRRM at 2006.

States, including differences in size, location, operations, and work force organization."[201]

After emphasizing the discretion of the Board concerning the substantive issues addressed by the rule,[202] the Court concluded with this summary of its decision:

> In this opinion, we have deliberately avoided any extended comment on the wisdom of the rule, the propriety of the specific unit determinations, or the importance of avoiding work stoppages in acute care hospitals. We have pretermitted such discussion not because these matters are unimportant but because they primarily concern the Board's exercise of its authority rather than the limited scope of our review of the legal arguments presented . . . .[203]

e. Related Issues. (1) Single-facility vs. multifacility units. In the health care industry, the appropriateness of single-facility units has become increasingly important because of the growth of chains of hospitals, nursing homes, and other types of health care institutions. The Board has applied its general presumption in favor of single-facility units to health care institutions, stating that "there is no legislative or practical imperative for excepting health care industry operations from the general presumption in favor of single-facility units."[204] The Board will thus find single-facility units appropriate, absent a history of multifacility bargaining or strong proof of functional integration of facilities, that is, centralized control of labor relations, common benefits and working conditions, interchange of employees, and geographic proximity.[205] For example, in one case the Board found

[201]*Id.*

[202]"[W]e would not be troubled even if there were inconsistencies between the current rule and prior NLRB pronouncements." *Id.* at 2006–7.

[203]*Id.* at 2007. The extensive jurisprudence of bargaining units in this industry in the period preceding the Board's rulemaking procedure is summarized in detail in the Second Edition of this work, at 436–55.

[204]Samaritan Health Servs., 238 NLRB 629, 632, 99 LRRM 1551 (1978). *Accord* National G.S. dba Memorial Medical, 230 NLRB 976, 978 n.5, 95 LRRM 1478 (1977) (noting that legislative concern about undue proliferation of units referred to unit composition, not unit scope).

[205]*Compare* Samaritan Health Servs., *supra* note 204 (single hospital unit appropriate), National G.S. dba Memorial Medical, *supra* note 204 (single nursing home unit appropriate) *and* Saint Anthony Center, 220 NLRB 1009, 90 LRRM 1405 (1975) (same) *with* Saddleback Community Hosp., 223 NLRB 247, 92 LRRM 1147 (1976) (separate units for hospital and medical center inappropriate where facilities are only 400 feet apart and where there is significant employee interaction and interchange), Kaiser Found. Health Plan of Or., 225 NLRB 409, 92 LRRM 1412 (1976) (single clinic unit inappropriate where employer operates nine facilities in same metropolitan area and there is regular interchange of employees) *and* Mercy Hosps. of Sacramento, 217 NLRB 765, 89 LRRM 1097 (1975), *rev'd and remanded*, 589 F2d 968, 98 LRRM 2800 (CA 9, 1978), *cert. denied sub nom.* Hospital & Institutional Workers Local 250 v. NLRB, 440 US 910, 100 LRRM 2687, *decision on remand*, 244 NLRB 229, 102 LRRM 1016 (1979) (single hospital-complex unit

appropriate a single-facility nursing home unit even though "most of the [e]mployer's policies were centrally controlled and basically uniformly applied to the [89] various individual facilities."[206] The Board emphasized that the administrator of the single facility maintained a significant degree of control over hiring and firing of employees, oriented new employees, scheduled vacations, and was held accountable for the overall adequacy of the services rendered to the nursing home occupants.

(2) Prior bargaining history in the institution. Where there has been prior bargaining history in the institution, the Board generally has refused to disrupt an existing unit structure, even though it may conflict with the basic hospital unit structure.[207] However, in one case the Board declined to perpetuate "a relatively small splinter group as a bargaining unit."[208]

(3) Stipulated units. In *Otis Hospital, Inc.*[209] the Board decided to "give effect to all stipulations designating unit compositions that do not contravene the provisions or purposes of the Act or well-settled Board policies," even though a stipulation is not in conformity with the Board's basic unit structure. This policy has been followed in subsequent cases.[210]

(4) Decertification elections. The appropriate unit for a decertification election is the existing contractual unit, regardless of whether the unit was formed as a result of an NLRB certification or voluntary recognition.[211] This policy is also applied to the

---

inappropriate where other hospital is functionally integrated and only 13 miles away). *See also* West Jersey Health Club, 293 NLRB No. 88, 131 LRRM 1111 (1989) (presumption rebutted under conventional unit analysis); Manor Healthcare Corp., *supra* note 190 (evidence of undue proliferation); Montefiore Hosp. & Medical Center, 261 NLRB 569, 110 LRRM 1048 (1982) (highly centralized management).

[206]National G.S. dba Memorial Medical, *supra* note 204, at 977.

[207]Bay Medical Center, 218 NLRB 620, 89 LRRM 1310 (1975), *enforced*, 588 F2d 1174, 100 LRRM 2213 (CA 6, 1978); Kansas City College of Osteopathic Medicine, 220 NLRB 181, 90 LRRM 1189 (1975); St. Joseph Hosp. & Medical Center, 219 NLRB 892, 90 LRRM 1088 (1975); Kaiser Found. Hosps., 219 NLRB 168, 89 LRRM 1667 (1975). *But cf.* Valley Hosp., 220 NLRB 1339, 90 LRRM 1411, *modified*, 221 NLRB 1239, 91 LRRM 1061 (1975) (Board rejected employer's argument that employees covered by existing agreements must be part of overall nonprofessional unit; however, the Board cautioned that it would not indiscriminately "place [its] imprimatur on such preexisting units." *Id.* at 1343).

[208]North Memorial Medical Center, 224 NLRB 218, 92 LRRM 1212 (1976).

[209]219 NLRB 164, 89 LRRM 1545, 1545 (1975).

[210]*See, e.g.*, Southwest Community Hosp., 219 NLRB 351, 90 LRRM 1116 (1975). *But see* Mercy Hosps. of Sacramento, *supra* note 205 (Board set aside stipulation establishing service and maintenance unit and all-clerical unit, because it conflicted with Board's policy of approving separate unit for business office clericals and including other clericals in service and maintenance unit).

[211]*See, e.g.*, Campbell Soup Co., 111 NLRB 234, 35 LRRM 1453 (1955). *See* Chapter 10, "Representation Proceedings and Elections," at notes 22–23.

health care industry, even though the existing contractual unit may not be consistent with the basic hospital unit structure.[212]

(5) Supervisory determinations. In *Doctor's Hospital of Modesto,*[213] decided prior to the 1974 health care amendments, the Board announced its standard for determining which professional employees at a proprietary health care institution are supervisors. It held that charge nurses who gave directions to other employees in the exercise of professional judgment, where such directions were purely incidental to the treatment of patients, were not supervisors within the meaning of section 2(11). In contrast, head nurses who could make effective recommendations affecting the job and pay status of the employees working under them were found to be supervisors.

This approach was approved in the committee reports accompanying the amendments. The committees stated:

> [T]he Board has carefully avoided applying the definition of "supervisor" to a health care professional who gives direction to other employees in the exercise of professional judgment, which direction is incidental to the professional's treatment of patients, and thus is not the exercise of supervisory authority in the interest of the employer. The Committee expects the Board to continue evaluating the facts of each case in this manner when making its determinations.[214]

After the amendments, the Board indicated it would continue to follow the policy announced in *Doctor's Hospital of Modesto,* as well as traditional standards, for determining supervisory status.[215] Under this standard, an employee who possesses any of the attributes enumerated in section 2(11) will be found to be a supervisor.[216]

---

[212]Foote Memorial Hosp., 230 NLRB 540, 96 LRRM 1099 (1977).

[213]183 NLRB 950, 76 LRRM 1784 (1970), *enforced,* 489 F2d 772, 85 LRRM 2228 (CA 9, 1973).

[214]S. REP. NO. 93-766, 93d Cong., 2d Sess. 6 (1974), and H.R. REP. NO. 93-1051, 93d Cong., 2d Sess. 7 (1974).

[215]Extendico-Professional Care, 272 NLRB 599, 117 LRRM 1330 (1984), *enforced,* 767 F2d 926, 120 LRRM 2631 (CA 7, 1985); Northwood Manor, 260 NLRB 854, 109 LRRM 1226 (1982); St. Mary's Home, 258 NLRB 1024, 108 LRRM 1329 (1981), *enforcement granted in part and denied in part,* 690 F2d 1062, 111 LRRM 2580 (CA 4, 1982); American Geri-Care, 258 NLRB 1116, 108 LRRM 1295 (1981), *enforced,* 697 F2d 56, 112 LRRM 2529 (CA 2, 1982), *cert. denied,* 461 US 906, 113 LRRM 2112 (1983); Milwaukee Children's Hosp. Ass'n, 255 NLRB 1009, 107 LRRM 1024 (1981); French Hosp. Medical Center, 254 NLRB 711, 106 LRRM 1149 (1981); Mount Airy Found. dba Mount Airy Psychiatric Center, 253 NLRB 1003, 106 LRRM 1071 (1981); Trustees of Noble Hosp., 218 NLRB 1441, 89 LRRM 1806 (1975); Wing Memorial Hosp. Ass'n, 217 NLRB 1015, 89 LRRM 1183 (1975); Doctors Hosp., 217 NLRB 611, 89 LRRM 1525 (1975).

[216]*See, e.g.,* Vic's Shop 'n Save, 215 NLRB 28, 88 LRRM 1478 (1974); Illinois Steel Fabricators, 197 NLRB 296, 80 LRRM 1582 (1972). *See generally* Chapter 28, "Jurisdiction: Coverage of the Act," at notes 213–245.

The Board has generally found that shift and departmental supervisors are statutory supervisors.[217] However, "head nurses" and "nursing coordinators" have been deemed to be statutory supervisors only when sufficient evidence has indicated that these nurses have the authority to effectively recommend wage increases, hire and fire employees, settle grievances, and assign work.[218] "Head nurses" and "nursing coordinators" who lack this authority have been found to be employees rather than supervisors.[219] The same standards have been applied in determining supervisory status of in-service and assistant in-service education directors.[220]

In cases decided after *Doctor's Hospital of Modesto*, the Board has been reluctant to find that "charge nurses" or "team leader nurses" are statutory supervisors,[221] even when they appear to satisfy some of the attributes enumerated in section 2(11). For example, in *McAlester General Hospital*[222] the Board refused to find that charge nurses were supervisors even though their performance evaluations of other employees were the determinant of pay increases. The Board indicated that in health care cases it would consider supervision over nonunit employees only if the alleged supervisor spends more than 50 percent of his or her time engaged in this supervisory function. Thus, a charge

---

[217]Newton-Wellesley Hosp., 250 NLRB 409, 104 LRRM 1384 (1980); Women Care, 246 NLRB 753, 103 LRRM 1109 (1979); Trustees of Noble Hosp., *supra* note 215; Wing Memorial Hosp. Ass'n, *supra* note 215; Doctor's Hosp., *supra* note 215.

[218]Ohio Masonic Home, 295 NLRB No. 45, 131 LRRM 1520 (1989); A. Barton Hepburn Hosp., 238 NLRB 95, 99 LRRM 1230 (1978); Associated Hosps. of the E. Bay, 237 NLRB 1473, 99 LRRM 1069 (1978); Gnaden Huetten Memorial Hosp., 219 NLRB 235, 89 LRRM 1761 (1975).

[219]Misericordia Hosp. Medical Center, 246 NLRB 351, 102 LRRM 1562 (1979); Texas Inst. for Rehabilitation & Research, 228 NLRB 578, 94 LRRM 1513 (1977); Sutter Community Hosps. of Sacramento, 227 NLRB 181, 94 LRRM 1450 (1976); Brattleboro Memorial Hosp., 226 NLRB 1036, 94 LRRM 1129 (1976); St. Rose de Lima Hosp., 223 NLRB 1511, 92 LRRM 1181 (1976); Trustees of Noble Hosp., *supra* note 215; Wing Memorial Hosp. Ass'n, *supra* note 215; Doctors Hosp., *supra* note 215.

[220]*See, e.g.*, Woonsocket Health Center, 245 NLRB 652, 102 LRRM 1494 (1979); A. Barton Hepburn Hosp., *supra* note 218.

[221]Springfield Jewish Nursing Home for the Aged, 292 NLRB 1269, 130 LRRM 1431 (1989); Turtle Creek Convalescent Centers, 235 NLRB 400, 98 LRRM 1407 (1978); Shadecrest Health Care Center, 228 NLRB 1081, 94 LRRM 1670 (1977); Sutter Community Hosps. of Sacramento, *supra* note 219; St. Rose de Lima Hosp., *supra* note 219; Pinecrest Convalescent Home, 222 NLRB 13, 91 LRRM 1082 (1976); Western Medical Enters. dba Driftwood Convalescent Hosp., 217 NLRB 1026, 89 LRRM 1493 (1975); Doctors Hosp., *supra* note 215. *But see* Gnaden Huetten Memorial Hosp., *supra* note 218 (charge nurses who spend only 20% of their time performing staff nurse duties were found to be statutory supervisors).

[222]233 NLRB 589, 96 LRRM 1524 (1977).

nurse's supervision of LVNs and other technical employees generally will not be determinative of supervisory status.

The Board has also applied the *Doctor's Hospital of Modesto* standard to LVNs and LPNs—who are considered nonprofessional employees—and has generally held that these employees are not supervisors.[223] In doing so, the Board has emphasized that participating in the interviewing of employees and making effective recommendations in the hiring and firing of employees are critical to a finding that the employee is a statutory supervisor.[224]

On this issue, the Board's decisions have fared well in the courts. The Board has wide discretion in determining which employees are supervisors, and, inasmuch as the Board's conclusion rests on findings of fact, the court must defer to it "if the evidence is supported by substantial evidence in the record."[225]

2. Units in Colleges and Universities. *a. Background.* In 1951, in *Trustees of Columbia University*,[226] the Board declined to assert jurisdiction over private nonprofit colleges and universities. Its 1970 decision in *Cornell University*[227] reversed this longstanding policy. In arriving at the decision to assert jurisdiction over private institutions of higher learning, the Board reexamined the legislative history of the Act with respect to nonprofit institutions and noted the rapid growth of higher education since 1951. Shortly thereafter, by formal rulemaking,[228] the Board established a minimum gross annual revenue figure of

---

[223]Beverly Manor Convalescent Centers v. NLRB, 661 F2d 1095, 108 LRRM 2746 (CA 6, 1981), *on remand*, 264 NLRB 966, 111 LRRM 1336 (1982), *enforcement denied*, 727 F2d 591, 115 LRRM 2898 (CA 6, 1984); Phelps Community Medical Center, 295 NLRB No. 55, 131 LRRM 1522 (1989); St. Mary's Home, *supra* note 215; Eskaton Sunrise Community, 279 NLRB 68, 121 LRRM 1348 (1986). *See* Pine Manor Nursing Home, 230 NLRB 320, 95 LRRM 1356 (1977), *enforced*, 578 F2d 575, 99 LRRM 2156 (CA 5, 1978); Greenpark Care Center, 231 NLRB 753, 96 LRRM 1066 (1977); Pinecrest Convalescent Home, *supra* note 221.

[224]*See, e.g.*, Greenpark Care Center, *supra* note 223.

[225]NLRB v. St. Francis Hosp. of Lynwood, 601 F2d 404, 101 LRRM 2943 (CA 9, 1979) (assistant head nurses found not to be supervisors); Methodist Home v. NLRB, 596 F2d 1173, 101 LRRM 2139 (CA 4, 1979), *enforced*, 672 F2d 911, 108 LRRM 3152 (CA 4, 1981) (charge nurses found not to be supervisors). *Cf.* Universal Camera Corp. v. NLRB, 340 US 474, 27 LRRM 2373 (1951). *See* Chapter 32, "NLRB Orders and Remedies," at notes 67–83.

[226]97 NLRB 424, 29 LRRM 1098 (1951).

[227]183 NLRB 329, 74 LRRM 1269 (1970).

[228]NLRB RULES AND REGULATIONS AND STATEMENTS OF PROCEDURE, SERIES 8 (as last amended, Jan. 8, 1976); Section 103.1 (GPO, 1976). For discussion of rulemaking by the Board, see Chapter 31, "NLRB Procedures," at notes 236–258.

$1 million for assertion of Board jurisdiction over private nonprofit educational institutions.[229]

The Board has divided college and university bargaining units into two basic groupings: (1) professional units usually centered around full-time faculty members, and (2) nonprofessional units. The Board and the courts have attempted to compose these professional units by adapting the principles of industrial labor relations to the sharply different conditions of work in academia. This section discusses these decisions concerning professional units. The nonprofessional units are readily governed by criteria applicable to service and manufacturing industries,[230] and are not treated separately.

b. Basic Structure of Professional Units. (1) The unit of all full-time faculty members. Prior to the Supreme Court's 1980 decision in *NLRB v. Yeshiva University*,[231] the basic professional unit at colleges and universities had centered around the full-time faculty, including the various levels of full-time professors and instructors. The Board's approach was to build a basic professional unit around the full-time faculty, but including other assorted professional employees according to the skills and functions which they exercise and the desires of the petitioning labor organization. For example, in an early professional unit case, *C. W. Post Center of Long Island University*,[232] the union sought a unit of all professionals engaged in teaching, including full-time professors and instructors, part-time professors and lecturers,

---

[229]The line between public and private has not always been easy to determine. *See* Howard Univ., 224 NLRB 385, 92 LRRM 1249 (1976) (Board reverses its earlier decision in Howard Univ., 211 NLRB 247, 86 LRRM 1389 (1974), and exercises jurisdiction over Howard University despite its close relationship with federal government); Temple Univ., 194 NLRB 1160, 79 LRRM 1196 (1972) (high degree of state control makes Temple University a "state related university"; the Board declines to assert its jurisdiction); *cf.* Cornell Univ., *supra* note 227 (jurisdiction extended to Cornell University, including New York State School of Industrial and Labor Relations, "contract" college funded by state of New York). *See* Chapter 28, "Jurisdiction: Coverage of the Act," at notes 189–203, for a discussion of the Act's coverage of quasi-public employers.

The Supreme Court's decision in NLRB v. Catholic Bishop of Chicago, 440 US 490, 100 LRRM 2913 (1979), raises questions concerning the Act's coverage of church-operated and church-affiliated colleges and univerities. *See* Chapter 28, "Jurisdiction: Coverage of the Act," at notes 19–39, for a discussion of that case and subsequent Board decisions asserting jurisdiction over church-affiliated schools.

[230]*See, e.g.*, Harvard College (I), 229 NLRB 586, 587, 95 LRRM 1390 (1977) ("[t]raditional principles for determining appropriate bargaining units [are] applic[able] to universities operating several facilities"); Tuskegee Inst., 209 NLRB 773, 86 LRRM 1082 (1974) (Board applies traditional community-of-interest factors in deciding composition of service and maintenance unit). *But see* Harvard College (II), 269 NLRB 821, 115 LRRM 1290 (1984) (*Harvard I* overruled).

[231]444 US 672, 103 LRRM 2526 (1980).

[232]189 NLRB 904, 77 LRRM 1001 (1971).

librarians, laboratory personnel, a research associate, guidance counselors, admission counselors, and academic counselors. The employer argued initially that jurisdiction should not be applied to a university's professional employees, and later took the position that a separate unit should be established for full-time faculty. The Board found appropriate a unit of full-time professors and instructors, part-time professors and lecturers, professional librarians, and guidance counselors. The Board has continued this case-by-case structuring of faculty bargaining units, although it has also established certain rules and patterns, discussed below.

(2) Faculty as managerial and supervisory employees—NLRB v. Yeshiva University. *Yeshiva*[233] has had a major impact on decisions dealing with the composition of professional units at colleges and universities. Rejecting a long line of Board decisions,[234] a five-to-four Court refused to enforce a bargaining order because the bargaining unit, comprised of various full-time faculty members, included managerial employees excluded from the coverage of the Act.[235] The decision thus makes managerial status a threshold issue in representation cases involving faculty members.

In *Yeshiva* the Board held appropriate a unit of faculty members, including assistant deans, department chairpersons, senior professors, associate professors, assistant professors and instructors, at 10 of the university's 13 colleges.[236] The Board rejected the employer's argument that the university faculty were managerial employees. After the petitioner was certified the Second Circuit refused to enforce the bargaining order, holding that the faculty exercised managerial authority and thus were excluded from coverage of the Act.[237]

The Supreme Court's decision is premised entirely on the high degree of authority and participation in decision making which was exercised by the Yeshiva faculty. The Court summarized those factors as follows:

> The controlling consideration in this case is that the faculty of Yeshiva University exercise authority which in any other context

---

[233]NLRB v. Yeshiva Univ., *supra* note 231.

[234]*See, e.g.*, Northeastern Univ., 218 NLRB 247, 89 LRRM 1862 (1975); University of Miami, 213 NLRB 634, 87 LRRM 1634 (1974).

[235]*See* Chapter 28, "Jurisdiction: Coverage of the Act," at note 220 and notes 250–251.

[236]Yeshiva Univ., 221 NLRB 1053, 91 LRRM 1017 (1975).

[237]NLRB v. Yeshiva Univ., 582 F2d 686, 98 LRRM 3245 (CA 2, 1978).

> unquestionably would be managerial. Their authority in academic matters is absolute. They decide what courses will be offered, when they will be scheduled, and to whom they will be taught. They debate and determine teaching methods, grading policies, and matriculation standards. They effectively decide which students will be admitted, retained, and graduated. On occasion their views have determined the size of the student body, the tuition to be charged, and the location of a school. When one considers the function of a university, it is difficult to imagine decisions more managerial than these. To the extent the industrial analogy applies, the faculty determines within each school the product to be produced, the terms upon which it will be offered, and the customers who will be served.[238]

The Board argued that faculty members were called upon to exercise "independent professional judgment," which is different from managerial decision making. The Court rejected the Board's distinction as inconsistent with the goal of "ensur[ing] that employees who exercise discretionary authority on behalf of the employer will not divide their loyalty between employee and union."[239]

The majority opinion concluded with a footnote, indicating the limited reach of the Court's holding:

> We recognize that this is a starting point only, and that other factors not present here may enter into the analysis in other contexts. It is plain, for example, that professors may not be excluded merely because they determine the content of their own courses, evaluate their own students, and supervise their own research. There thus may be institutions of higher learning unlike Yeshiva where the faculty are entirely or predominantly nonmanagerial. There also may be faculty members at Yeshiva and like universities who properly could be included in a bargaining unit. It may be that a rational line could be drawn between tenured and untenured faculty members, depending upon how a faculty is structured and operates. But we express no opinion on these questions, for it is clear that the unit approved by the Board was far too broad.[240]

---

[238]NLRB v. Yeshiva Univ., *supra* note 231, at 686.

[239]*Id.* at 687–88. The Court described "[t]he problem of divided loyalty [as] particularly acute for a university like Yeshiva, which depends on the professional judgment of its faculty to formulate and apply crucial policies constrained only by necessarily general institutional goals." *Id.* at 689.

[240]*Id.* at 690 n.31. In Ithaca College, 261 NLRB 577, 110 LRRM 1059 (1982); Thiel College, 261 NLRB 580, 110 LRRM 1041 (1982); and Duquesne Univ. of the Holy Ghost, 261 NLRB 587, 110 LRRM 1046 (1982), the Board dismissed representation petitions, holding that the full-time faculty members at those institutions were managerial employees because they exercised extensive control over policy in a manner similar to the *Yeshiva* faculty. In Bradford College, 261 NLRB 565, 110 LRRM 1055 (1982), however, it ordered an election, finding that the college president, not the faculty, ran the school. In Montefiore Hosp. & Medical Center, 261 NLRB 569, 110 LRRM 1048 (1982), the Board

The Ninth Circuit distinguished *Yeshiva* in a case involving the faculty at an art institute.[241] The court rejected the employer's argument that the faculty were managerial employees, stating: "In *Yeshiva* the Court . . . relied heavily on the policy making role of the faculty. . . . The instructors at the [art institute] hardly share such a role. They have no input into policy decisions, and do not engage in management level decision making. They simply are employees."[242]

The Supreme Court did not address the issue of *supervisory status* of the Yeshiva faculty. The Board, in cases decided prior to the Court's *Yeshiva* decision, had refused to find that an entire faculty consisted of supervisors.[243] Instead, it found that certain faculty and administrative positions were supervisory, but only on a case-by-case basis after careful scrutiny of the particular positions.[244] In some early cases, the Board applied its "50 percent rule," under which professionals are excluded as supervisors if more than 50 percent of their time is spent supervising personnel.[245] This rule was abandoned, however, in *Detroit College of Business*;[246] now, a chairperson, coordinator, or other faculty member will be deemed a supervisor where the basic

declined to extend the *Yeshiva* conception of managerial status to the health care field, finding that the medical center's highly centralized structure justified ordering an election among staff doctors and dentists, including doctors with faculty appointments to the Albert Einstein College of Medicine. *See supra* at notes 146–147; *see also* Joint Diseases, North Gen. Hosp., 288 NLRB 291, 130 LRRM 1220 (1988), *review denied*, 875 F2d 350, 131 LRRM 2528 (CA DC, 1989).

[241]Stephens Inst. v. NLRB, 620 F2d 720, 104 LRRM 2524 (CA 9, 1980), *cert. denied*, 449 US 953, 105 LRRM 2968 (1980).

[242]*Id.* at 727. In Ithaca College v. NLRB, 623 F2d 224, 104 LRRM 2493, *cert. denied*, 449 US 975, 105 LRRM 2969 (1980), the Second Circuit criticized the Board for refusing to reopen the record in a faculty unit case in light of the Second Circuit's decision in *Yeshiva*. The case was heard after the Supreme Court's affirmance of the Second Circuit's *Yeshiva* decision. The court denied enforcement of the Board's bargaining order and declined to remand for further hearings because the Board's prior refusal to address the issue of faculty status "exposed the College to needless expense and unwarranted prejudicial publicity." *Id.* at 230.

[243]*E.g.*, Northeastern Univ., *supra* note 234; University of Miami, *supra* note 234.

As to a related issue, in New York Univ. (I), 205 NLRB 4, 83 LRRM 1549 (1973), the Board held that faculty members in general are not independent contractors, stating: "Instruction is performed on the Employer's premises with its equipment; faculty may become tenured; and they receive sabbatical leave, a fixed annual salary, and Employer contributions to a retirement fund. The faculty are not subject to the entrepreneurial risks and profits normally associated with independent contractors." *Id.* at 5–6. *See* Chapter 28, "Jurisdiction: Coverage of the Act," at notes 292–348, for discussion of independent contractor status.

[244]See discussion *infra* in this chapter under separate subhearings for department chairpersons, principal investigators, administrative officials, program directors, and librarians.

[245]*E.g.*, New York Univ. (II), 221 NLRB 1148, 91 LRRM 1165 (1975).

[246]296 NLRB No. 40, 132 LRRM 1081 (1989).

duties of the position involve significant supervisory authority over other faculty members, regardless of the percentage of time spent on such activities.

In the aftermath of *Yeshiva*, the Board evaluates the decision-making authority and input of an institution's faculty in general, and the various levels of faculty positions in particular, in order to determine which faculty members, if any, are nonmanagerial.[247] The Board thus constructs a basic professional unit around the nonmanagerial faculty, where such faculty exists.

The Board has determined the supervisory and/or managerial status of faculty members by examining their duties and responsibilities in governing academic and administrative matters including faculty hiring, tenure, sabbaticals, termination, and promotion,[248] participation on academic boards or evaluation committees,[249] as well as the role of a board of trustees in setting policy,[250] curriculum determination,[251] and student admissions.[252] The Board has recognized that managerial status may be based upon faculty participation in policymaking of either academic or administrative matters or professional activities outside of the classroom.[253] In general, the Board will find faculty members to be managerial where they have direct authority over academic affairs and significant influence upon the hiring, promotion, and tenure of faculty members, notwithstanding the fact that a president or the board of trustees may have ultimate authority over such matters.[254]

---

[247]See cases cited in note 240 *supra* and also College of Osteopathic Medicine & Surgery, 265 NLRB 295, 111 LRRM 1523 (1982), discussed in Chapter 10, "Representation Proceedings and Elections," at note 442, and in Chapter 28, "Jurisdiction: Coverage of the Act," at note 251.

[248]*See* Lewis Univ., 265 NLRB 1239, 112 LRRM 1206 (1982), *enforcement denied*, 765 F2d 616, 119 LRRM 2993 (CA 7, 1985).

[249]*See* Puerto Rico Junior College, 265 NLRB 72, 111 LRRM 1499 (1982).

[250]*See* Loretto Heights College, 264 NLRB 1107, 111 LRRM 1680 (1982), *enforced*, 742 F2d 1245, 117 LRRM 2225 (CA 10, 1984).

[251]*See* Florida Memorial College, 263 NLRB 1248, 111 LRRM 1547 (1982).

[252]*See* New York Medical College, 263 NLRB 903, 111 LRRM 1128 (1982).

[253]*See* University of Dubuque, 289 NLRB 349, 128 LRRM 1259 (1988); Livingstone College, 286 NLRB 1308, 126 LRRM 1332 (1987); Lewis Univ., *supra* note 248.

[254]Trustees of Boston Univ., 281 NLRB 798, 123 LRRM 1144 (1986), *petition for review denied sub nom.* Boston Univ. Chapter, AAUP v. NLRB, 835 F2d 399, 127 LRRM 2193 (CA 1, 1987); American Int'l College, 282 NLRB 189, 123 LRRM 1284 (1986); University of New Haven, 267 NLRB 939, 114 LRRM 1140 (1983); Duquesne Univ. of the Holy Ghost, *supra* note 240; College of Osteopathic Medicine & Surgery, *supra* note 247.

The Board has found faculty members not to be managerial employees in the absence of such authority.[255]

(3) Other specific inclusions and exclusions. (a) Department chairpersons. Prior to the Supreme Court's *Yeshiva* decision, department chairpersons had been excluded from faculty units in some cases on the ground that they were "supervisors" within the meaning of section 2(11) and, in other cases, included in such units on the ground that they were not "supervisors." The decisions often turned on whether the department chairpersons had the power to "make effective recommendations as to hiring, firing, or change of status" or whether such power has been "effectively diffused among the department faculty pursuant to the principle of collegiality."[256] In cases where the Board found that department chairpersons were merely a conduit for faculty recommendations regarding personnel matters, they were included in the faculty unit.[257] Alternatively, where department chairpersons had the power to make effective recommendations in personnel matters, the Board excluded them from faculty units as supervisors.[258]

---

[255]*See* Kendall School of Design, 279 NLRB 281, 122 LRRM 1177 (1986), *modified*, 866 F2d 157, 130 LRRM 2374 (CA 6, 1989) (faculty could not make independent decisions regarding curriculum; administration tightly controlled committee membership, agendas, and final products; no systematic mechanism for ascertaining faculty views); Marymount College of Va., 280 NLRB 486, 122 LRRM 1299 (1986) (program coordinators and librarians lack significant managerial or supervisory authority); Cooper Union for the Advancement of Science & Art, 273 NLRB 1768, 118 LRRM 1333 (1985), *enforced*, 783 F2d 29, 121 LRRM 2561 (CA 2), *cert. denied*, 479 US 815, 123 LRRM 2591 (1986) (participation in goverance and academic committees did not render faculty members managerial employees because they constituted minority on committees, a dean chaired each administrative committee and set its agenda; dean could unilaterally disband committee (and had done so); and faculty had no effective control over which academic degrees school would offer); Universidad Cent. de Bayamon, 273 NLRB 1110, 118 LRRM 1592 (1984), *enforced*, 778 F2d 906, 120 LRRM 3457 (CA 1, 1985), *enforcement denied en banc*, 793 F2d 383, 122 LRRM 2582 (CA 1, 1986) (faculty members were not managerial employees because they had no role in faculty personnel decisions and no control over curriculum, admissions, tuition, or financial affairs); Puerto Rico Junior College, *supra* note 249, at 75 (faculty members were elected or appointed to administrative body; their policy-making role was limited because they constituted at most only 50% of any policy-making committee).

[256]Northeastern Univ., 218 NLRB 247, 251–52, 89 LRRM 1862 (1975).

[257]Stephens College, 240 NLRB 166, 100 LRRM 1268 (1979); Yeshiva Univ., 221 NLRB 1053, 91 LRRM 1017 (1975), *enforcement denied on other grounds*, 582 F.2d 686, 98 LRRM 3245 (CA 2, 1978), *aff'd on other grounds*, 444 US 672, 103 LRRM 2526 (1980); Fordham Univ. (II), 214 NLRB 971, 87 LRRM 1643 (1974); Rosary Hill College, 202 NLRB 1137, 82 LRRM 1768 (1973); Fordham Univ. (I), 193 NLRB 134, 78 LRRM 1177 (1971); University of Detroit, 193 NLRB 566, 78 LRRM 1273 (1971); *see* Trustees of Boston Univ. v. NLRB, 575 F2d 301, 98 LRRM 2070 (CA 1, 1978), *enforcing* 228 NLRB 1008, 96 LRRM 1408 (1977).

[258]University of Vt., 223 NLRB 423, 91 LRRM 1570 (1976); New York Univ. (II), *supra* note 245; Rensselaer Polytechnic Inst., 218 NLRB 1435, 89 LRRM 1844 (1975); Syracuse

In its decisions after *Yeshiva*, the Board has more readily discerned the elements of supervisory authority in the normal duties of department heads. For example, in *Trustees of Boston University*,[259] a 1977 decision antedating *Yeshiva*, the Board included department heads in a unit with other faculty and professional employees on the grounds, among others, that the heads consulted widely with the faculty before making recommendations concerning tenure and promotion, and that ultimate authority lay in the board of trustees. On remand following the decision of *Yeshiva*, the Board reached the opposite conclusion and excluded the heads from the unit on the ground that they not only effectively review the performance of faculty members, they also hire, supervise, and fire nonunit clericals and other university employees.[260] In deference to the Board's discretion in factual determinations, the First Circuit accepted the Board's determination in both instances.[261]

(b) "Principal investigators." Principal investigators are faculty members who prepare grant proposals and administer the projects once the funds have been awarded by government or private granting agencies.[262] In *New York University (II)*[263] the Board included principal investigators in the bargaining unit, because "principal investigators do not 'supervise' employees of the University, they 'supervise' faculty only seasonally, and the work is not performed at the direction of the University."[264] However, principal investigators were excluded from units in four cases where they had supervisory authority over research associates who were included in the bargaining unit.[265]

(c) Administrative officials. Ordinarily, administrative officials—including deans, assistant and associate deans, admissions

---

Univ., 204 NLRB 641, 83 LRRM 1373 (1973); C.W. Post Center of Long Island Univ., 189 NLRB 904, 77 LRRM 1001 (1971); Long Island Univ., 189 NLRB 909, 77 LRRM 1006 (1971).

[259]*Supra* note 257.

[260]Trustees of Boston Univ., 281 NLRB 798, 123 LRRM 1144 (1986), *aff'd sub nom.* Boston Univ. Chapter, AAUP v. NLRB, 835 F2d 399, 127 LRRM 2193 (CA 1, 1987). *But see* Florida Memorial College, 263 NLRB 1248, 111 LRRM 1547 (1982) (department heads included in unit where supervision of nonunit employees minimal).

[261]*See supra* notes 259, 260.

[262]Faculty often drift in and out of principal investigator status on a year-to-year basis depending upon whether they are currently working on a grant. The process of "popping in and out" of the bargaining unit, in units excluding principal investigators, has been termed in at least one Board decision as the creation of a "popcorn unit." Northeastern Univ., *supra* note 256, at 253.

[263]*Supra* note 245.

[264]*Id.* at 1155. *See also* New York Univ. (I), 205 NLRB 4, 83 LRRM 1549 (1973); Fordham Univ. (I), *supra* note 257.

[265]University of Vt., *supra* note 258; Yeshiva Univ., *supra* note 257; Rensselaer Polytechnic Inst., *supra* note 258; Northeastern Univ., *supra* note 256.

directors, and registrars—are excluded from a faculty bargaining unit as supervisory employees.[266] In some cases, however, including *Yeshiva*, the Board has included in the faculty bargaining unit assistant or associate deans whose primary duty is to teach.[267] Moreover, a separate unit of nonacademic administrative officials is appropriate when that group merely implements decisions established by higher authority.[268]

(d) Program directors. Whether individuals holding the title of "program director" are included or excluded from a faculty unit depends upon the particular functions and duties they perform. In some instances, "program directors" have been excluded from a faculty unit because they hold supervisory status.[269] In other cases, program directors have been included in faculty bargaining units.[270] The Supreme Court's *Yeshiva* decision suggests that program directors whose jobs involve substantial decision-making authority and participation, as opposed to a predominantly ministerial function, will be excluded as managerial employees.[271]

(e) Coaches. Athletic coaches whose academic credentials are comparable to other faculty members, and whose duties include teaching, are held to be professionals and are included in faculty units.[272] However, coaching positions that do not require advanced degrees or teaching are deemed nonprofessional and are excluded from faculty bargaining units.[273]

(f) Visiting faculty. The Board has excluded visiting faculty members from faculty bargaining units because they usually have no expectation of permanent employment by the institution at which they are teaching as visitors.[274]

---

[266]In most cases administrative officials such as deans are excluded by stipulation. *See, e.g.*, Syracuse Univ., *supra* note 258; University of Detroit, *supra* note 257.

[267]Yeshiva Univ., *supra* note 257; University of Miami, 213 NLRB 634, 87 LRRM 1634 (1974).

[268]Pratt Inst., 256 NLRB 1166, 107 LRRM 1404 (1981).

[269]*See, e.g.*, Loretto Heights College, 205 NLRB 1134, 84 LRRM 1163 (1973) (full-time and part-time program directors excluded as supervisors).

[270]*See, e.g.*, University of Miami, *supra* note 267; Adelphi Univ., 195 NLRB 639, 79 LRRM 1545 (1972).

[271]See discussion at notes 233–242 *supra*.

[272]Rensselaer Polytechnic Inst., *supra* note 258; Manhattan College, 195 NLRB 66, 79 LRRM 1253 (1972) (teaching duties related to extracurricular activities, not classroom teaching for college credit).

[273]University of Miami, *supra* note 267.

[274]Goddard College, 216 NLRB 457, 88 LRRM 1228 (1975) (visiting faculty excluded even though they had full-time teaching loads and were entitled to full participation in governance, including voting privileges); *see* Trustees of Boston Univ., 228 NLRB 1008, 96 LRRM 1408 (1977), *enforced*, 575 F2d 301, 98 LRRM 2070 (CA 1, 1978).

(g) Members of religious orders. In early decisions after *Cornell University*[275] the Board excluded members of religious orders from faculty units where the order controlled or strongly influenced the operation of the institution and the members of the order returned a large part of their salaries to the order pursuant to spiritual vows or contractual obligations.[276] Under such circumstances, the faculty members of the order were deemed "in a sense part of the employer since the Order owns and administers the College."[277] However, faculty members of orders were included in faculty bargaining units where the institution was operated by a different religious order,[278] and where the institution was not church operated but merely church affiliated and the faculty members' obligations to their order were significantly independent of their obligations to the institution.[279]

These decisions by the Board preceded the Supreme Court's 1979 decision in *Catholic Bishop of Chicago v. NLRB*,[280] where the Court held that the Act impliedly excluded lay teachers and, a fortiori, clergy teachers at church-operated schools. That decision effectively limited Board jurisdiction in this area to faculty at colleges and universities that are church affiliated, excluding those that are church operated.

The distinction between church-affiliated and church-operated educational institutions has been problematic. Applying *Catholic Bishop* in *Universidad Central de Bayamon*[281] the Board concluded that the university, which had been established origi-

---

[275] 183 NLRB 329, 74 LRRM 1269 (1970).

[276] Seton Hill College, 201 NLRB 1026, 82 LRRM 1434 (1973); *see* Niagara Univ. (I), 226 NLRB 918, 94 LRRM 1082 (1976), *enforcement denied*, 558 F2d 1116, 95 LRRM 3354 (CA 2, 1977); St. Francis College, 224 NLRB 907, 92 LRRM 1551 (1976), *enforcement denied*, 562 F2d 246, 96 LRRM 2134 (CA 3, 1977).

[277] Seton Hill College, *supra* note 276, at 1027.

[278] Niagara Univ. (II), 227 NLRB 313, 94 LRRM 1001 (1976). In Niagara Univ. (I), *supra* note 276, an election was conducted and a bargaining order issued for a unit excluding 18 faculty who were members of religious orders. In Niagara Univ. (II), *supra*, the Board, in a unit-clarification proceeding, included in the faculty unit three nuns and a priest who were not members of the religious order that operated the university. The Second Circuit subsequently denied enforcement to *Niagara Univ. (I)*, holding that all faculty members of religious orders should have been included in the faculty unit. Niagara Univ. v. NLRB, 558 F2d 1116, 95 LRRM 3354 (CA 2, 1977). *See also* NLRB v. St. Francis College, 562 F2d 246, 96 LRRM 2134 (CA 3, 1977).

[279] D'Younville College, 225 NLRB 792, 92 LRRM 1578 (1976) (by stipulation of parties; regional director held that *Seton Hill, supra* note 276, required exclusion from unit despite parties' agreement to the contrary); Fordham Univ. (II), 214 NLRB 971, 87 LRRM 1643 (1974) (by stipulation of parties).

[280] 440 US 490, 100 LRRM 2913 (1979). See Chapter 28, "Jurisdiction: Coverage of the Act," at notes 19–25, for a discussion of *NLRB v. Catholic Bishop of Chicago*.

[281] 273 NLRB 1110, 118 LRRM 1592 (1984).

nally with the approval of the Dominican Order of the Roman Catholic Church, was not a religious institution exempt from the coverage of the Act. The Board emphasized that neither the Dominican Order nor the Roman Catholic Church owned, financed, or controlled the university and that the university's academic mission was secular. The Board did find, however, that one of the university's programs, which had as its primary objective training priests for the ministry, was exempt from the Act's coverage.

The First Circuit initially enforced the Board's order requiring the university to bargain but reheard the case en banc, and divided equally thereby denying enforcement.[282] The issue which divided the full court was whether an educational institution could be "church-controlled," as defined by *Catholic Bishop*, if its primary mission was to provide secular education. The full court agreed that was the university's primary mission and that its religious mission was secondary. However, three judges deemed the university "church-controlled," and thus beyond the Board's jurisdiction, despite the secular nature of its primary mission. The opinion of these judges emphasized the university's founding by the Dominican Order, its history as a branch of the Catholic University of Ponce, and its integration into an educational system maintained by the Dominicans. They further emphasized that the university administration was comprised of officials in the Dominican Order and these religious officials actively controlled the hiring, firing, promotion, and tenure of nonreligious faculty members.

The opposing opinion viewed the university as "church-affiliated," emphasizing that the university's primary purpose was to deliver secular education and that faculty members were hired without regard to religion and according to the same standards generally applied at most secular institutions. This opinion concluded that the unique "church-teacher" relationship which led to the holding of *Catholic Bishop* was not present. Thereafter, the Board embraced a broader reading of *Catholic Bishop* which appears to exempt a broad range of religiously oriented colleges.[283]

---

[282]Universidad Cent. de Bayamon v. NLRB, 778 F2d 906, 120 LRRM 3457 (CA 1, 1985), *on reh'g*, 793 F2d 383, 122 LRRM 2582 (CA 1, 1986).

[283]Trustees of St. Joseph's College, 282 NLRB 65, 123 LRRM 1281 (1986) (declining jurisdiction over college supported by Sisters of Mercy). *Cf.* Livingstone College, 286 NLRB 1308, 126 LRRM 1332 (1987) (asserting jurisdiction over church-affiliated college).

(h) Part-time faculty. After the Board asserted jurisdiction over private higher educational institutions, it initially decided, consistent with its policy in the industrial sector, to include part-time faculty members in a unit of full-time faculty.[284] However, in 1973, in *New York University (I)*,[285] the Board abandoned that policy and decided to exclude all part-time faculty members from the faculty unit. The Board relied upon the "substantial" differences usually found between full-time and part-time faculty, including: (1) differences in compensation, (2) the lack of participation by part-time faculty in university governance, (3) the unavailability of tenure for part-time faculty, and (4) differences in working conditions.[286] The *New York University* precedent has been followed in subsequent decisions.[287]

In *University of San Francisco*,[288] the Board approved a unit comprised exclusively of part-time faculty members. The Board concluded that a disclaimer of tenure rights in the faculty members' one-year contracts was not sufficiently indicative of temporary status.

(i) Librarians. Librarians are normally includable in a faculty bargaining unit since they "possess a sufficient community of interest to be included in the unit, as a closely allied professional group whose ultimate function, aiding and furthering the educational and scholarly goals of the University, converges with that of the faculty, though pursued through different means and in a different manner."[289]

---

[284]C.W. Post Center of Long Island Univ., 189 NLRB 904, 77 LRRM 1001 (1971). *See also* University of New Haven, 190 NLRB 478, 77 LRRM 1273 (1971); Fordham Univ. (I), 193 NLRB 134, 78 LRRM 1177 (1971). In University of Detroit, 193 NLRB 566, 78 LRRM 1273 (1971), the Board adopted a four-to-one rule, under which part-time faculty would be included in a faculty unit only if they taught at least 25% of a full-time teaching load. *See* Catholic Univ., 201 NLRB 929, 82 LRRM 1385 (1973) (formula modified slightly for part-time law faculty); Florida S. College, 196 NLRB 888, 80 LRRM 1160 (1972); Tusculum College, 199 NLRB 28, 81 LRRM 1345 (1972).

[285]205 NLRB 4, 83 LRRM 1549 (1973).

[286]*Id.* at 6.

[287]NLRB v. Wentworth Inst. & Wentworth College of Technology, 515 F2d 550, 89 LRRM 2033 (CA 1, 1975); Bradford College, 261 NLRB 565, 110 LRRM 1055 (1982); Point Park College, 209 NLRB 1064, 85 LRRM 1542 (1974); University of San Francisco, 207 NLRB 12, 84 LRRM 1403 (1973). *But see* Kendall School of Design v. NLRB, 866 F2d 157, 130 LRRM 2374 (CA 6, 1989), *enforcing as modified*, 283 NLRB No. 44, 125 LRRM 1077 (1987). (part-time faculty included in unit with full-time where compensation, status, and working conditions were alike); Kendall College v. NLRB, 570 F2d 216, 97 LRRM 2878 (CA 7, 1978) (semble).

[288]265 NLRB 1221, 112 LRRM 1113 (1982). *See also* NLRB v. New School for Social Research, Parsons School of Design Div., 793 F2d 503, 122 LRRM 2845 (CA 2, 1986), *denying enforcement on other grounds to* 275 NLRB 173, 119 LRRM 1021 (1985) (court approved Board's finding that unit of part-time instructors was appropriate).

[289]New York Univ. (I), *supra* note 285, at 8; *accord* Fordham Univ. (II), *supra* note 279; C.W. Post Center of Long Island Univ., *supra* note 284. *But cf.* Northeastern Univ., 218

This unit concept, however, was not applicable where the library was a distinct entity within the university community. In *Teachers College, Columbia University*,[290] the Board there found a separate unit of professional librarians appropriate because the librarians were not faculty members, did not share faculty prerogatives, salary scales, or fringe benefits, and had little contact or interchange with faculty members.

(j) Research associates and assistants. Research associates and research assistants are normally included in a faculty unit, since such persons usually have educational qualifications comparable to those of the faculty, have similar benefits and working conditions as faculty, and engage in some form of teaching.[291]

(k) Graduate students. Graduate students working on advanced degrees often perform teaching functions and receive financial assistance for performing such duties. Generally, however, they are directed by faculty members and do not have significant input in governance. The Board has found graduate assistants to be primarily students and lacking a community of interest with the faculty; accordingly, graduate students are normally excluded from the faculty unit.[292]

(l) Counselors. Counselors who hold advanced degrees and perform activities such as career counseling have been included in faculty units as professional employees; but absent such duties they are excluded.[293]

NLRB 247, 89 LRRM 1862 (1975) (all but two professional librarians excluded as supervisors because they exercised supervisory authority over other professional librarians or spent more than 50% of their time supervising nonprofessional library staff). See Chapter 28, "Jurisdiction: Coverage of the Act," at notes 240–241, for a discussion of the "50 percent rule." *See also* Marymount College of Va., 280 NLRB 486, 122 LRRM 1299 (1986); Brooklyn Psychosocial Rehabilitation Inst., 264 NLRB 114, 111 LRRM 1275 (1982), *enforced*, 742 F2d 1438, 116 LRRM 2552 (CA 2), *cert. denied*, 467 US 1226, 116 LRRM 2552 (1984).

[290]226 NLRB 1236, 93 LRRM 1481 (1976); *accord* Claremont Univ. Center, 198 NLRB 811, 81 LRRM 1317 (1972) (separate unit for librarians found appropriate, librarians given option to vote for inclusion with unit of nonprofessional library staff).

[291]University of Vt., 223 NLRB 423, 91 LRRM 1570 (1976); Northeastern Univ., *supra* note 289; C.W. Post Center of Long Island Univ., *supra* note 284. *But cf.* New York Univ. (I), *supra* note 285 *and* Fordham Univ. (I), *supra* note 284, where research personnel were held not to be university employees. *See also* Bradford College, *supra* note 287.

[292]*E.g.*, Leland Stanford Junior Univ., 214 NLRB 621, 87 LRRM 1519 (1974) (graduate students who received stipends and grants to perform research for advanced degrees held not to be employees within meaning of §2(3) of the Act); Adelphi Univ., 195 NLRB 639, 79 LRRM 1545 (1972).

[293]Mount Vernon College, 228 NLRB 1237, 95 LRRM 1349 (1977) (college's academic advisor-career counselor excluded from faculty unit as nonprofessional employee); Northeastern Univ., *supra* note 289 (career counselors included in faculty unit; academic counselors excluded); C.W. Post Center of Long Island Univ., *supra* note 284 (guidance counselors included in faculty unit; admissions and academic counselors excluded); *see*

(4) Scope of the units. (a) Multicampus units. Universities with more than one campus raise issues concerning single-campus *versus* multiple-campus units. In general, the scope of the unit is determined under generally applicable criteria, and either a campus- or collegewide unit is presumptively appropriate.[294] The Board has approved an institutionwide, multicampus faculty bargaining unit where there was (1) integration and centralization of administrative functions between campuses; (2) some campus interchange between faculty members; (3) a university senate which included representatives from all campuses; (4) similarity of wages, hours, and working conditions for faculty members at all campuses; and (5) a petitioner that was seeking a universitywide unit.[295] But the Board found appropriate two separate units for two of a university's three campuses where separate units had been sought by the petitioner and the employer did not object to separate units.[296]

(b) Separate units for professional and graduate school faculty. The Board has generally excluded the law school faculty from overall faculty units or has ordered self-determination elections, depending upon the units sought by the petitioning unions. In *Fordham University (I)*[297] one union sought a faculty unit excluding law school faculty while another union sought a unit solely for the law school faculty. Stating that "it is clear that [a universitywide unit of professional employees] may be appropriate here,"[298] the Board nevertheless held that a separate law school faculty unit was appropriate because the law school faculty's "community of interest is not irrevocably submerged in the broader community of interest which they share with other

---

Goddard College, *supra* note 274 (counselors held to be professional employees; however, counselors who worked in psychological services office were excluded from faculty unit along with various other professionals).

[294]University of Hartford, 295 NLRB No. 79, 131 LRRM 1641 (1989); Livingstone College, 290 NLRB 304, 129 LRRM 1079 (1988).

[295]Fairleigh Dickinson Univ., 205 NLRB 673, 84 LRRM 1033 (1973); *cf.* Tulane Univ., 195 NLRB 329, 79 LRRM 1366 (1972) (Board rejects petitioner's request for main campus nonprofessional unit; unit must include university's three other facilities located within a 40-mile radius of the main campus); Cornell Univ., *supra* note 275 (statewide unit of nonprofessional employees held to be only appropriate unit, even though university operated facility in New York City some 280 miles away from rural upstate New York campus and union sought separate unit for New York City facility).

[296]C.W. Post Center of Long Island Univ., *supra* note 284; Long Island Univ., 189 NLRB 909, 77 LRRM 1006 (1971).

[297]*Supra* note 284 (followed in University of San Francisco, *supra* note 287, and Catholic Univ., *supra* note 284).

[298]Fordham Univ. (I), *supra* note 284, at 136.

faculty members,"[299] and no union sought to include the law school faculty in a broader unit. Subsequently, in *Syracuse University*,[300] the Board ordered a self-determination election for law school faculty where one union sought a universitywide unit and another union sought a separate unit for the law school faculty. The Board gave the law school faculty a self-determination election and added the unusual choice to vote for no representation regardless of the vote among other faculty members.[301]

Generally, the Board has included or excluded other professional school faculty from overall faculty units depending on the scope of the units sought by the unions. For example, medical school faculty have been excluded in cases in which unions sought overall faculty units that excluded medical school faculty.[302] In one case the Board required that a dentistry school be included in an overall faculty unit where the school was located near a major campus, the dentistry faculty participated in university programs and governance, and no union sought a separate unit for the dentistry school.[303] In another case, an overall unit, excluding the dentistry school as well as the law and medical schools, was held appropriate where the dentistry school was located away from the campus, even though no union sought to represent dentistry school faculty.[304] The Board has also excluded graduate school faculty from overall faculty bargaining units when the graduate school faculty did not share a substantial community of interest with other faculty.[305]

---

[299] *Id.* at 137. *Fordham Univ. (I)* was followed under similar circumstances in University of Miami, 213 NLRB 634, 87 LRRM 1634 (1974).

[300] 204 NLRB 641, 83 LRRM 1373 (1973). *Accord* New York Univ. (I), *supra* note 285 (*Syracuse Univ.* followed).

[301] 204 NLRB at 643 (followed in New York Univ. (I), *supra* note 285). This separate choice of no representation is not usually given to employees in self-determination elections. See discussion of *Globe* doctrine at notes 30–33 *supra*.

[302] Trustees of Boston Univ. v. NLRB, 575 F2d 301, 98 LRRM 2070 (CA 1, 1978), *enforcing* 228 NLRB 1008, 96 LRRM 1408 (1977) (law and graduate dentistry faculty excluded for same reason); University of Vt., *supra* note 291; University of Miami, *supra* note 299 (school of marine and atmospheric science excluded on same basis).

[303] Fairleigh Dickinson Univ., *supra* note 295.

[304] Trustees of Boston Univ. v. NLRB, *supra* note 302.

[305] Goddard College, 216 NLRB 457, 88 LRRM 1228 (1975) (graduate faculty and their programs located far away from campus and operated apart from campus governance structure; union sought inclusion in overall unit); University of Miami, *supra* note 299 (school of marine and atmospheric sciences located away from main campus and had substantially different educational mission; union sought overall unit excluding, inter alia, marine and atmospheric sciences school).

3. Units in the U.S. Postal Service. *a. Background.* In 1970 Congress enacted the Postal Reorganization Act (PRA)[306] establishing the U.S. Postal Service as an independent establishment of the executive branch of the federal government.[307] Chapter 12 of the PRA,[308] effective in 1971, brought the Postal Service and its employees under the jurisdiction of the Board, and to the extent not inconsistent with the PRA, under the coverage of the National Labor Relations Act. The intent of Congress, as reflected in Chapter 12, was that labor relations in the Postal Service should be similar to those in the private sector.[309]

Prior to the effective date of the PRA, collective bargaining between the Post Office Department and labor unions representing postal employees was governed by Executive Order,[310] pursuant to which the Postal Office Department determined in 1962 that appropriate bargaining units should be national in scope and coincide with seven traditional "craft" lines.[311] At that time the seven craft groups were (1) letter carriers, (2) mailhandlers, (3) clerks, (4) special delivery messengers, (5) rural letter carriers, (6) motor vehicle employees, and (7) maintenance employees.[312] In elections held in 1962 and 1963, a majority of the employees voting in the seven national craft units selected seven national craft unions, which the Department of Labor certified as national exclusive representatives for postal employees in those units. Thereafter, the Post Office Department and the seven craft unions entered into successive collective bargaining agreements.[313]

To facilitate the transition from the national craft unit bargaining pattern established in 1962 by the Department of Labor to the Board-governed method newly enacted by the PRA, section 10(a) of the PRA provided:

> As soon as practicable after the enactment of this Act, the Postmaster General and the labor organizations which as of the effective date of

---

[306]Pub. L. No. 91-375, 84 Stat. 719 (1970) (codified in Title 39 USC).
[307]*See* Chapter 5, "The Post–Landrum-Griffin Period," at notes 1–4.
[308]39 USC §1209(a).
[309]*See generally* Granof & Moe, *Grievance Arbitration in the U.S. Postal Service; The Postal Service View*, 29 ARB. J. 1 (1974).
[310]Exec. Order No. 10,988, 3 CFR §130 (1962); Exec. Order No. 11,491, 3 CFR §451 (1970).
[311]Kennedy, *The Postal Reorganization Act of 1970: Heading Off Future Postal Strikes?*, 59 GEO. L.J. 305 (1970).
[312]*Id.*
[313]*See generally* Postal & Fed. Employees v. Klassen, 514 F2d 189, 89 LRRM 2558 (CA DC), *cert. denied*, 423 US 1037, 90 LRRM 3258 (1975).

> this section hold national exclusive recognition rights granted by the Post Office Department, shall negotiate an agreement or agreements covering wages, hours, and working conditions of the employees represented by such labor organizations.[314]

Pursuant to that statutory mandate, the Postmaster General and the national craft unions have entered into successive national agreements under which the national craft unions have been recognized as the exclusive bargaining agents for postal workers.[315]

b. The Basic Unit. The congressional mandate to the Board in the comprehensive PRA legislation is to determine "in each case the unit appropriate for collective bargaining in the Postal Service."[316] While an explicit standard for determining unit appropriateness is not set forth in the PRA, the legislative history reveals that Congress expected the Board to apply its private sector criteria. The conference report stated:

> It is the intent of the conference committee that these provisions of the conference substitute leave to the National Labor Relations Board the judgment as to what will be the appropriate units for collective bargaining in the Postal Service on the basis of the same criteria applied by the Board in determining appropriate bargaining units in the private sector. The conference substitute deems it desirable to leave the determination of appropriate bargaining units entirely in the judgment of the NLRB rather than to predetermine such matters in any way.[317]

In 1974 the Board rendered its landmark decision concerning postal employee bargaining units.[318] The Board had consoli-

---

[314] 39 USCA §1201. Section 10(a) withstood constitutional challenge. Unions other than the national craft unions protested that §10(a) denied their members equal protection of law by entrenching the national craft unions as exclusive bargaining representatives. The courts held that the congressional grant of exclusive bargaining rights during a "transitional period" to labor organizations which had been successful in previous elections administered by the Department of Labor was a reasonable scheme to incorporate the status quo in labor representation among postal employees. Additionally, it was determined that the "transitional period" provided for in the PRA was not intended by Congress to be limited to a period of two years, but was to extend until the Board had established bargaining units and provided for the election of representatives, or until accomplishment of such other actions as might be taken by the Board defining the rights and obligations of the Postmaster General, the labor organizations representing postal employees, and their members. National Postal Union v. Blount, 341 F Supp 370, 79 LRRM 2861 (DDC, 1972); Postal & Fed. Employees v. Klassen, 369 F Supp 747, 85 LRRM 2609 (DDC, 1974), *aff'd*, 514 F2d 189, 89 LRRM 2558 (CA DC, 1975).

[315] Postal & Fed. Employees v. Klassen, *supra* note 313.

[316] 39 USC §1202.

[317] CONF. REP. NO. 91-1363, 91st Cong., 2d Sess. 81-82 (1970), *reprinted in* 1970 U.S. CODE CONG. & ADMIN. NEWS 3715.

[318] U.S. Postal Serv., 208 NLRB 948, 85 LRRM 1212 (1974).

dated for hearing six petitions filed by various unions to represent units as large as 70,000 employees (part, not all, of the New York region) and as small as 90 motor vehicle employees working at different Baltimore, Maryland, facilities. In dismissing all six petitions, the Board stated that "any less-than-nationwide unit which does not at least encompass all employees within a district or sectional center is too fragmented for meaningful collective bargaining."[319] The Board reasoned as follows:

> The Employer's size, collective-bargaining history, number of employees, geographic dispersion, and centralized operational organization impose certain practical limitations on the numerical proliferation of bargaining units. It is obvious that meaningful collective bargaining could not realistically occur at each of the Employer's 32,000 individual facilities. On the other hand, we are aware that certain broad horizontal or vertical divisions of employees into homogenous units with the requisite community of interests might well promote meaningful, or at least feasible, collective bargaining.[320]

Additional bargaining units have been delineated by the Board, however, in several cases involving Postal Service employees engaged in duties ancillary to regular mail processing and delivery operations. Employees of the Postal Service's two area supply centers, located in New Jersey and Kansas, were combined with employees of the Postal Service's 14 Mail Bag Depositories to form an appropriate bargaining unit.[321] In the same decision, the Board found appropriate a separate unit for employees at the Mail Equipment Shops in Washington, D.C.[322]

In a subsequent decision the Board found employees at the Postal Service's six postal data centers to constitute an appropriate bargaining unit.[323] In so finding, the Board relied upon the fact that the employees at all of the data centers enjoyed similar working conditions, terms of employment, fringe benefits, and

---

[319]*Id.* at 954.

[320]*Id.* at 953. The Board reserved for future consideration the question of whether a unit encompassing all employees within a region, metropolitan center, metropolitan area, district, or sectional center would in fact constitute an appropriate unit.

[321]U.S. Postal Serv., 200 NLRB 1143, 82 LRRM 1049 (1972). Area Supply Centers provide all types of supplies and equipment to postmasters throughout the country and to certain large mailing customers. Employees at Mail Bag Depositories receive, examine, and store mail bags and eventually ship them to locations where there is a shortage. Mail Equipment Shops manufacture mail bags and various types of clocks and keys.

[322]The Board emphasized that while Area Supply Center and Mail Bag Depository employees were operationally integrated and had common supervision, Mail Equipment Shop employees shared no such community of interest, inasmuch as Mail Equipment Shops were a separate entity as to both function and operation.

[323]U.S. Postal Serv., 210 NLRB 477, 86 LRRM 1097 (1974).

overall supervision, and that the centers represented "a highly-integrated data processing operation whose employees share a community of interest."[324]

c. The U.S. Postal Service's Challenge to the Basic Units. Between 1962 and 1970 four successive national agreements were negotiated jointly between the Postal Service and the seven unions representing the nationwide "craft" units which the Post Office Department had determined were appropriate. In 1971, four of the craft unions merged into the American Postal Workers Union (APWU) and, together with the three remaining craft unions, jointly negotiated a collective bargaining agreement. Thereafter, the bargaining fragmented. In 1978, the National Rural Letter Carriers Association (NRLCA) negotiated a separate agreement with the Postal Service. In 1981, the unions split into two groups for bargaining. The APWU and the National Association of Letter Carriers (NALC) desired to jointly negotiate one contract, and the National Post Office Mail Handlers, Watchmen, Messengers and Group Leaders Division of the Laborer's International Union of North America (Mail Handlers), and NRLCA announced that they intended to jointly negotiate a separate agreement.

In response to this bargaining configuration and amid charges that the two largest unions, APWU and NALC, were conducting raiding campaigns to win members from the other unions, the Postal Service filed an RM petition which sought an election in a single nationwide bargaining unit comprised of all Postal Service employees.[325]

The Service contended that the existing units were inappropriate because they did not constitute traditional crafts and because the technological changes in the structure of the Service and the unions' raiding activities made separate units inappropriate. Concluding that no question concerning representation was raised, the Board dismissed the petition without a hearing. The Board noted that none of the unions wished to represent the employees in a single unit, and it reasoned that it would not order an election in a larger unit merely because existing units might be inappropriate.

---

[324]*Id.* at 478. *See also* U.S. Postal Serv., 232 NLRB 556, 97 LRRM 1062 (1977) (unit of Research and Development Department employees held appropriate).

[325]U.S. Postal Serv., 256 NLRB 502, 107 LRRM 1249 (1981), *enforced sub nom.* NLRB v. Northwest Publishing Co., 727 F2d 1112, 116 LRRM 2191 (CA 7, 1984).

The Board refused to accept the Service's contention that the PRA provided an independent basis for processing the petition:

> Congress intended that the collective bargaining in the Postal Service be treated like any other . . . under the NLRA (except for specifically stated exceptions such as prohibiting strikes by postal workers and imposing binding arbitration in the event parties reach an impasse in collective bargaining).[326]

D. Multi-Employer Bargaining Units

This section examines the multi-employer bargaining unit: how it is formed, how the parties may enter it, and how they may withdraw from it. Once the unit is formed, the multi-employer group becomes the employer for purposes of bargaining and assumes the obligation under sections 8(a)(5) and 8(d) to bargain collectively with the representative of all the employees in the unit.[327] The bargaining obligations of the "multi-employer" are substantially the same as for any employer. The major differences are noted in this section.[328]

1. The Role of Multi-Employer Units in the Bargaining Process. The institution of multi-employer bargaining, that is, bargaining between a union or unions and groups of employers, has existed in this country for over 85 years.[329] Employers first grouped together in the 1880s, forming associations of large corporations, not for the purpose of collective bargaining, but in order to achieve a coordinated counterforce to the Knights of Labor.[330] Since the establishment of the principle of collective bargaining, however, multi-employer bargaining has come to be seen as a device employed by small employers to offset the bargaining strength of powerful unions.[331] Unions nevertheless recognize a number of important advantages in multi-employer

---

[326] *Id.* at 505.

[327] *E.g.*, NLRB v. Strong, 393 US 357, 70 LRRM 2100 (1969).

[328] See Chapter 13, "The Duty to Bargain," for a discussion of the requirements of good-faith bargaining generally, and Chapter 20, "The Lockout," for a discussion of the body of law relating to lockouts affecting multi-employer units.

[329] *See* F. PIERSON, MULTI-EMPLOYER BARGAINING: NATURE AND SCOPE 35 (1949); Sommers, *Pressures on an Association in Collective Bargaining*, 6 INDUS. & LAB. REL. REV. 557 (1953).

[330] *See* S. PERLMAN, A HISTORY OF TRADE UNIONISM IN THE UNITED STATES 94, 194, 252 (1950); Note, 66 HARV. L. REV. 886 (1953).

[331] J. BACHMAN, MULTI-EMPLOYER BARGAINING 14 (1951); J. FREIDEN, THE TAFT-HARTLEY ACT AND MULTI-EMPLOYER BARGAINING 4–5 (1949). *See* NLRB v. Truck Drivers Local 449 (Buffalo Linen Supply Co.), 353 US 87, 94–95, 39 LRRM 2603, 2606 (1957).

bargaining. The standardization of wage rates and working conditions within an industry is a fundamental union objective.[332] Decertification petitions, which require a 30-percent showing of interest, become increasingly less practical as the size of the unit expands.[333] Economies of scale accrue when a union must negotiate only one contract covering several employers. Finally, both weak and powerful unions can join together, thereby avoiding an employer's "divide and conquer" strategy.

Large corporations may not feel union pressures strongly enough to justify their entering an association for collective bargaining,[334] although some industries, such as basic steel and refractories, have engaged in industrywide—hence, multi-employer—bargaining for years. Such bargaining is also prevalent in industries like longshore and construction, where workers frequently change employers and hiring halls[335] are common.[336] Employers recognize that an employers' association can eliminate wage competition,[337] help to prevent whipsaw strikes,[338] and achieve certain economies of scale.

The Wagner Act did not explicitly authorize the Board to find multi-employer units appropriate, although such bargaining was not uncommon in 1935. However, in a 1938 decision, the Board, with Supreme Court approval, construed the Act to allow for multi-employer units.[339] The Board noted that section 9(b) provided for "employer" units, that section 2(2) defined

---

[332]*See* Apex Hosiery Co. v. Leader, 310 US 469, 503, 6 LRRM 647, 657 (1940); GENERAL SUBCOMM. ON LABOR OF THE HOUSE COMM. ON LABOR AND EDUCATION, 88th Cong., 2d SESS., MULTI-EMPLOYER ASSOCIATION BARGAINING AND ITS IMPACT ON THE COLLECTIVE BARGAINING PROCESS (Comm. Print 1965) (Testimony of James A. Suffridge, President, Retail Clerks Int'l Ass'n).

[333]Employees of a single employer in a multi-employer unit cannot obtain a decertification election; the petition must be filed on behalf of all employees in the unit. *See, e.g.*, American Consolidating Co., 226 NLRB 923, 93 LRRM 1446 (1976); Alston Coal Co., 13 NLRB 683, 4 LRRM 337 (1939). *See generally* Chapter 10, "Representation Proceedings and Elections," at notes 22–23.

[334]*See* Bachman, *supra* note 331, at 60–61.

[335]*See generally* Chapter 27, "Union Security," at notes 252–349.

[336]*See* NLRB v. Truck Drivers Local 449 (Buffalo Linen Supply Co.), *supra* note 331, at 94; Rains, *Legal Aspects and Problems of Multi-Employer Bargaining*, 34 B.U.L. REV. 159 (1954). See *infra* notes 359–360, for a discussion of multi-employer bargaining in the construction industry.

[337]Bachman, *supra* note 331, at 16–18. *See also* Chapter 30, "Accommodations to Other Federal Enactments," at notes 22–99, for a discussion of the antitrust laws and variations of multi-employer bargaining.

[338]*See* Chapter 20, "The Lockout."

[339]Shipowners' Ass'n of the Pac. Coast, 7 NLRB 1002, 1024–25, 2 LRRM 377 (1938), *review denied sub nom.* AFL v. NLRB, 103 F2d 933, 4 LRRM 78 (CA DC, 1939), *aff'd*, 308 US 401, 5 LRRM 670 (1940); Waterfront Employers Ass'n, 71 NLRB 80, 110, 18 LRRM 1465, 1469 (1946).

"employer" to include any "person" acting in an employer's interest, and that section 2(1) defined "person" to include "associations." Therefore, the Act contemplated that an employer unit could consist of an association acting in the employer's interest, that is, a multi-employer unit.

In the course of the Taft-Hartley debates, many proposals to limit multi-employer bargaining were introduced usually in the interest of curbing perceived excesses of union power. The Hartley bill, passed by the House of Representatives, placed severe restrictions upon multi-employer bargaining.[340] However, none of these proposals survived in the final version of the Taft-Hartley Act.

The Taft-Hartley amendments of 1947 substituted for "any person acting in the interest of an employer" the phrase "any person acting as an agent of the employer." The Board implicitly read this amendment as detracting nothing from its authority to conduct elections in multi-employer units.[341] In *NLRB v. Truck Drivers Local 449* (*Buffalo Linen Supply Co.*),[342] the Supreme Court reviewed the failure of legislative efforts to curb such bargaining and concluded that Congress intended the Board to "continue its established administrative practice of certifying multi-employer units."[343]

The procedures referred to as "multi-employer bargaining" include industrywide and multi-association bargaining as well as bargaining between a union and several companies associated on the side of the employer. The Board applies the same principles to all these subtypes.[344]

---

[340]Section 9(f)(1) of H.R. 3020, with certain provisos, declared unions representing employees of one employer ineligible to be certified as the representative of the employees of a competing employer of more than 100 workers at a facility less than 50 miles distant. LEGISLATIVE HISTORY OF THE LABOR MANAGEMENT RELATIONS ACT, 1947, 187–88 (1948). *See, e.g.*, Wolman, *Industry-Wide Bargaining*, 1 LAB. L.J. 167 (1949).

[341]Associated Shoe Indus. of Southeastern Mass., 81 NLRB 224, 23 LRRM 1320 (1949). Dissenting Members Houston and Murdock interpreted the legislative history as expanding the Board's authority to find multi-employer units appropriate. *Id.* at 235 n.28.

[342]*Supra* note 331.

[343]*Id.* at 95–96.

[344]*See* Chester County Beer Distribs. Ass'n, 133 NLRB 771, 48 LRRM 1712 (1961); Morgan Linen Serv., 131 NLRB 420, 48 LRRM 1054 (1961); Mutual Rough Hat Co., 82 NLRB 440, 24 LRRM 1641 (1949). Multi-employer unit issues are not to be confused with "joint employer" issues presented in such cases as Greyhound Corp. v. Boire, 205 F Supp 686, 50 LRRM 2485 (SD Fla., 1962), *aff'd*, 309 F2d 397, 51 LRRM 2509 (CA 5, 1962), *rev'd*, 376 US 473, 55 LRRM 2694 (1964). See Chapter 28, "Jurisdiction: Coverage of the Act," at notes 148–169, for a discussion of the joint-employer issue; see also Chapter 13, "The Duty to Bargain," at notes 960–1004, for a discussion of the "double-breasted" issue.

Multi-employer bargaining should also be distinguished from "coordinated" and "coalition" bargaining. Unions have developed a "coordinated" bargaining strategy in response to the diversification of many major corporations through mergers and acquisi-

2. Establishment of the Multi-Employer Unit: Its Consensual Nature. Unlike other bargaining units, the multi-employer unit is *consensual*. A multi-employer association need not have a formal organizational structure; nor must the members delegate to the association the authority to execute a final and binding contract; nor must the resulting contract be signed by all members of the group. The essential criterion for the establishment of a multi-employer unit is the unequivocal manifestation by each member of the group that all be bound in collective bargaining by group, rather than by individual, action.[345] The formation of the unit must be entirely voluntary, the assent of the union having representative status also being required. The Board will not approve the creation of such a unit over the objection of any party, union, or employer.[346]

An employer's objective intent must be manifest either by express delegation to the association's bargaining arm or by participation in the group bargaining process.[347] In the absence

---

tions, and to coordinated or centralized bargaining by management within and among large corporations. Having organized the numerous plants of conglomerates and corporate giants in separate collective bargaining units, unions have often felt overpowered in a framework of separate negotiations, for the employer could deal first with the weaker unions and then impose the pattern settlement on the stronger unions, who could not strike successfully because production could be shifted to other plants of the same company. Through coordinated bargaining, by negotiating a series of separate contracts containing common or similar terms, unions have sought the benefits of multi-employer bargaining, but without merging into a single bargaining unit. Coordinated bargaining thus represents an intermediate position between single-employer bargaining and multi-employer bargaining. For a discussion of coordinated bargaining and a related form, "coalition" bargaining, see Chapter 13, "The Duty to Bargain," at notes 910–935.

[345]Kroger Co., 148 NLRB 569, 57 LRRM 1021 (1964); York Transfer & Storage Co., 107 NLRB 139, 33 LRRM 1078 (1953). *Kroger* also illustrates that a multi-employer unit does not require the execution of a single, master agreement. It is sufficient if members of the group have bargained as a group over a period of time (17 years in that case) and, as a result of joint negotiations, have executed separate, but substantially similar, contracts with the union representing their employees. *See also* Crane Sheet Metal, 248 NLRB 75, 103 LRRM 1365 (1980), *enforcement denied*, 675 F2d 256, 110 LRRM 2235 (CA 10, 1982); Bel-Window, 240 NLRB 1315, 100 LRRM 1464 (1979); A.B. Hirschfeld, Inc., 140 NLRB 212, 51 LRRM 1607 (1962); Rayonier, Inc., 52 NLRB 1269, 13 LRRM 91 (1943). An employer's membership in a multi-employer unit is assumed by a corporation that purchases the employer's stock. RKB Int'l Corp., 240 NLRB 1082, 100 LRRM 1426 (1979).

[346]Artcraft Displays, 262 NLRB 1233, 110 LRRM 1462, *clarified*, 263 NLRB 804, 111 LRRM 1074 (1982); United Fryer & Stillman, 139 NLRB 704, 51 LRRM 1385 (1962). Early in the Wagner Act period, the Board created a multi-employer unit over the objections of the employers. Shipowners' Ass'n of the Pac. Coast, *supra* note 339. In Alston Coal Co., *supra* note 333, the Board first required unanimous employer consent. The union's consent may be implied from its failure to object. Authorized Air Conditioning Co. v. NLRB, 606 F2d 899, 102 LRRM 2647 (CA 9, 1979). Forcing an employer, by threatening to strike, to bargain through a multi-employer association violates §§8(b)(1)(A) and 8(b)(4)(A). Mine Workers Local 1854 (Amax Coal Co.), 99 LRRM 1670 (1978). *See also* note 368 *infra* and Chapter 6, "Interference With Protected Rights," at note 627.

[347]Greenhoot, Inc., 205 NLRB 250, 83 LRRM 1656 (1973); Rock Springs Retail Merchants Ass'n, 188 NLRB 261, 76 LRRM 1254 (1971); Van Eerden Co., 154 NLRB 496,

of both participation and delegation of authority, the Board will not accept, over the objection of any party, a mere showing of a custom of past adoption of terms of a multi-employer agreement.[348]

The history of collective bargaining—not only in the particular industry but with respect to particular units—is always an important consideration in determining the appropriateness of a unit. In the multi-employer context, bargaining history assumes unique significance. The absence of any history of multi-employer bargaining in a proposed multi-employer unit is usually determinative against such a unit.[349] However, there have been instances of approval of new multi-employer units in industries where such units are characteristic.[350] On the other hand, a multi-employer bargaining history of brief duration not predicated upon a Board certification does not ensure that only a multi-employer unit is appropriate.[351] Thus, when an employer with a history of individual bargaining joins a multi-employer association and adopts its contract, a rival petition for a single-employer unit will prevail if timely filed before the insulated period of the last individual contract, whether or not the multi-employer contract would otherwise bar a petition.[352] Bargaining history is considered qualifying even when successive

---

59 LRRM 1770 (1965); Kroger Co., *supra* note 345. In *Rock Springs*, for example, the Board ruled inappropriate a unit of employees of 31 members of an association, but directed an election in a unit composed of the five employer-members who had previously negotiated or signed contracts with the union and had indicated their intent to be bound by joint action.

[348]NLRB v. E-Z Davies Chevrolet, 395 F2d 191, 68 LRRM 2228 (CA 9, 1968); Typographical Union No. 6 (New York) (Royal Composing Room), 242 NLRB 378, 101 LRRM 1148 (1979), *enforcement granted in part*, 632 F2d 171, 105 LRRM 2529 (CA 2, 1980); A.B. Hirschfeld, Inc., *supra* note 345; Colonial Cedar Co., 119 NLRB 1613, 41 LRRM 1353 (1958); West End Brewing Co., 107 NLRB 1542, 33 LRRM 1432 (1954); Pacific Metals Co., 91 NLRB 696, 26 LRRM 1558 (1950); Associated Shoe Indus. of Southeastern Mass., *supra* note 341.

[349]Arden Farms, 117 NLRB 318, 39 LRRM 1216 (1957); Rainbo Bread Co., 92 NLRB 181, 27 LRRM 1067 (1950). *But see* Taylor Motors, Inc., 241 NLRB 711, 100 LRRM 1558 (1979).

[350]*E.g.*, Calumet Contractors Ass'n, 121 NLRB 80, 42 LRRM 1279 (1958); Western Ass'n of Eng'rs, Architects & Surveyors, 101 NLRB 64, 31 LRRM 1010 (1952). A new unit without multi-employer bargaining history is appropriate if no party seeks a single-employer unit. Broward County Launderers & Cleaners Ass'n, 125 NLRB 256, 45 LRRM 1113 (1959). *See also* Checker Cab Co., 141 NLRB 583, 52 LRRM 1357 (1963) *and* 153 NLRB 651, 59 LRRM 1503 (1965), *enforced*, 367 F2d 692, 63 LRRM 2243 (CA 6, 1966), *cert. denied*, 385 US 1008, 64 LRRM 2108 (1967).

[351]Miron Bldg. Prods. Co., 116 NLRB 1406, 39 LRRM 1002 (1956).

[352]Etna Equip. Co., 236 NLRB 1578, 98 LRRM 1591 (1978). The first multi-employer contract is not a bar where the employees have not ratified their inclusion in the larger unit. U.S. Pillow Corp., 136 NLRB 584, 50 LRRM 1216 (1962). See Chapter 10, "Representation Proceedings and Elections," at notes 119–201, for discussion of the contract-bar doctrine.

agreements contain clauses held to violate the Act.[353] Individual bargaining on a limited basis, under a mutually recognized privilege to do so concomitant with group bargaining on subjects of general concern, does not negate a desire to be bound on a multi-employer basis.[354] But if either the union or an employer manifests an unequivocal intent to pursue an individual course of action, or if resulting individually bargained agreements substantially vary conditions established on a multi-employer basis, even a substantial history of multi-employer bargaining will not suffice to establish such a unit in the face of the determination to bargain individually.[355] A substantial history of multi-employer bargaining was also deemed insufficient to maintain the multi-employer unit after the dissolution of the local union representing the employees and its merger with another local left no successor union with a claim to represent all employees in the multi-employer unit.[356]

The freedom of choice extended an employer under the foregoing rules is subject to a limitation which results from the freedom of association accorded employees by the Act. The Board has held that an employer "could not unilaterally and without the express or implied consent of its employees bind them to representation in a multi-employer unit" by signing a multi-employer collective bargaining agreement which granted recognition to a particular union.[357] When the employer seeks to enter the multi-employer bargaining unit, the relevant majority is that of the employees of the particular employer. However, once the multi-employer bargaining unit is established, the relevant majority is the entire unit. Thus, even if a majority of the employees of a single employer within the multi-employer unit no longer wish to be represented by the union, "that fact would

---

[353]Tom's Monarch Laundry & Dry Cleaning Co., 168 NLRB 217, 66 LRRM 1277 (1967).

[354]Kroger Co., *supra* note 345. The resulting multi-employer agreement may be executed in a series of individual-member agreements embodying the terms of joint bargaining (and also side agreements reached by individual bargaining). Detroit News, 119 NLRB 345, 41 LRRM 1085 (1957); Balaban & Katz, 87 NLRB 1071, 25 LRRM 1197 (1949).

[355]Burns Int'l Sec. Servs., 257 NLRB 387, 107 LRRM 1501 (1981); Donaldson Sales, Inc., 141 NLRB 1303, 1305, 52 LRRM 1500 (1963).

[356]McKesson Wine & Spirits Co., 232 NLRB 208, 96 LRRM 1465 (1977).

[357]Mohawk Business Mach. Corp., 116 NLRB 248, 249, 38 LRRM 1239, 1240 (1956); *accord* Dancker & Sellew, 140 NLRB 1824, 52 LRRM 1120 (1963), *enforced sub nom.* NLRB v. Teamsters Local 210, 330 F2d 46, 55 LRRM 2902 (CA 2, 1964); Pepsi-Cola Bottling Co. of Kansas City, 55 NLRB 1138, 14 LRRM 75 (1944). *Cf.* Douds v. Anheuser-Busch, Inc., 99 F Supp 474, 28 LRRM 2277 (DNJ, 1951); Lamson Bros., 59 NLRB 1561, 15 LRRM 209 (1945).

not relieve [the employer] of its obligation to bargain with the Union as to the appropriate multi-employer unit, nor justify an untimely withdrawal from such unit."[358]

The Board's new approach to section 8(f) agreements in the construction industry announced in *John Deklewa & Sons*[359] has incidentally affected the establishment of multi-employer units in that industry. A section 8(f) agreement, even if negotiated or adopted in the context of multi-employer bargaining, results only in an enforceable agreement covering a unit of the signatory employer's own employees.[360]

3. Dissolution of the Unit. *a. Total Dissolution.* By 1958, it was well established that even in the face of a long history of multi-employer bargaining, an employer could unilaterally withdraw from its association and thus reduce the size of the unit.[361] Conversely, it was equally well established that a union could not unilaterally terminate a multi-employer bargaining relationship and could not negotiate with individual members of the association without first bargaining to impasse under the existing framework; even after such an impasse, the Board emphasized, separate negotiations did not signal the end of the multi-employer relationship.[362]

In 1958 the Board first indicated that unions, as well as employers, had the right to withdraw from a multi-employer bargaining relationship. In *Retail Associates*[363] the Board conditioned either party's withdrawal upon adequate written notice given either prior to the contractually established date for modi-

---

[358]Sheridan Creations, 148 NLRB 1503, 57 LRRM 1176, 1178 (1964), *enforced*, 357 F2d 245, 61 LRRM 2586 (CA 2, 1966), *cert. denied*, 385 US 1005, 64 LRRM 2108 (1967). Similarly, a decertification petition must be filed for the multi-employer unt; a petition filed on a single-employer basis will be dismissed. American Consolidating Co., 226 NLRB 923, 93 LRRM 1446 (1976).

[359]282 NLRB 1375, 124 LRRM 1185 (1987), *enforced sub nom.* Iron Workers Local 3 v. NLRB, 843 F2d 770, 128 LRRM 2020 (CA 3, 1988), *cert. denied*, 488 US 889, 129 LRRM 2528 (1988). For a fuller discussion of *Deklewa* and §8(f) agreements see Chapter 13, "The Duty to Bargain."

[360]In Stack Elec., 290 NLRB 575, 129 LRRM 1293 (1988), which overruled Vincent Elec. Co., 281 NLRB 903, 123 LRRM 1233 (1986), the Board applied the one-man unit rule and, accordingly, refused to find a violation of §8(a)(5). *See also* Joseph Stern & Sons, 297 NLRB No. 1, 133 LRRM 1082 (1989); Bufco Corp., 291 NLRB 1132, 130 LRRM 1116 (1988), *enforced*, 899 F2d 608, 134 LRRM 2044 (CA 7, 1990). Even before *Deklewa*, one Court had rejected a union's claim of majority status in a multi-employer unit based on a §8(f) agreement. Building & Constr. Trades Council (Baton Rouge) v. E.C. Schafer Constr. Co., 657 F2d 806, 108 LRRM 2634 (CA 5, 1981).

[361]McAnary & Welter, 115 NLRB 1029, 37 LRRM 1483 (1956); Johnson Optical Co., 87 NLRB 539, 25 LRRM 1135 (1949).

[362]Stouffer Corp., 101 NLRB 1331, 31 LRRM 1200 (1952); Morand Bros. Beverage Co., 91 NLRB 409, 26 LRRM 1501 (1950), *enforced*, 190 F2d 576, 28 LRRM 2364 (CA 7, 1951).

[363]120 NLRB 388, 41 LRRM 1502, *supplemented*, NLRB No. 8-RM-185, 42 LRRM 1119 (1958).

fication of the collective agreement or prior to the agreed-upon date for the commencement of multi-employer negotiations. Once actual bargaining had begun, either party could withdraw only by mutual consent[364] or under "unusual circumstances."[365] The *Retail Associates* rules require that notice of withdrawal be both timely and unequivocal. To be unequivocal, "the decision to withdraw must contemplate a sincere abandonment, with relative permanency, of the multi-employer unit and the embracement of a different course of bargaining on an individual employer basis."[366] Should timeliness of the notice of withdrawal turn upon the date agreed upon for the start of negotiations, the date in question relates to the actual negotiations, not to the service of a notice or demand for conference.[367] After either party gives such timely and unequivocal notice, the other party may not exert economic pressure to preserve the multi-employer relationship.[368]

---

[364]The essence of multi-employer bargaining is a tripartite relationship between the union, the multi-employer bargaining association, and the individual employer-members of the association. An employer who wishes to perfect an untimely withdrawal must secure the consent of both the union and the multi-employer association of which it has been a member. A union violates §8(b)(3) by executing an independent contract with a former association member where the association has not consented to the withdrawal, or by asserting that the unit employees are covered by a multi-employer agreement despite the union's earlier participation in individual bargaining. Service Employees Local 32B-32J (Allied Maintenance Corp.), 258 NLRB 430, 108 LRRM 1157 (1981). Conversely, an employer violates §8(a)(5) by an untimely withdrawal from the unit without the association's and the union's consent. Teamsters Local 378 (Capital Chevrolet Co.), 243 NLRB 1086, 102 LRRM 1007 (1979), *vacated and remanded*, 672 F2d 741, 110 LRRM 2213 (CA 9, 1982). Consent to an employer's withdrawal was not inferred from a union's four and one-half month delay in requesting the employer to execute the association contract. Reliable Roofing Co., 246 NLRB 716, 103 LRRM 1006 (1979).

[365]Retail Assoc., *supra* note 363, at 395. *See also* Evening News Ass'n, 154 NLRB 1494, 60 LRRM 1149 (1965), *enforced sub nom.* Detroit Newspaper Publishers Ass'n v. NLRB, 372 F2d 569, 64 LRRM 2403 (CA 6, 1966); Wilborn, *A New Look at NLRB Policy on Multiemployer Bargaining*, 60 N.C.L. REV. 455 (1982); Comment, *Employer Withdrawal From Multi-Employer Bargaining Units: A Proposal for Self-Regulation*, 130 U. PA. L. REV. 689 (1982); Comment, *Withdrawal From Multi-Employer Bargaining—Reconsidering* Retail Associates, 115 U. PA. L. REV. 464 (1967).

[366]Retail Assocs., *supra* note 363, at 394.

[367]Carmichael Floor Covering Co., 155 NLRB 674, 60 LRRM 1364 (1965); Quality Limestone Prods., 153 NLRB 1009, 59 LRRM 1589 (1965); Building Serv. Employees Local 139 (Daelvte Serv. Co.), 126 NLRB 63, 45 LRRM 1275 (1960).

[368]Section 8(b)(4)(A) prohibits a union from exerting pressure to force an employer "to join any labor or employer organization." Longshoremen (ILWU) (General Ore, Inc.), 126 NLRB 172, 45 LRRM 1296 (1960). *See* Chapter 6, "Interference with Protected Rights," at note 627, note 346, *supra* this chapter and related text. Section 8(b)(1)(B) prohibits a union from coercing an employer in the selection of a representative for purposes of collective bargaining. *See* Chapter 6, at notes 627–651. Hotel Employees, Local 2 (Zim's Restaurant), 240 NLRB 757, 100 LRRM 1324 (1979). Section 8(b)(3) prohibits a union from unilaterally attempting to enlarge a bargaining unit. Amax Coal Co. v. NLRB, 614 F2d 872, 103 LRRM 2482 (CA 3, 1980); Electrical Workers (IUE) Local 323 (Active Enters.), 242 NLRB 305, 101 LRRM 1179 (1979). *See* Chapter 16, "Subjects of

b. Withdrawal After Impasse: The Bonanno Linen *Rule.* Following *Retail Associates*, the Board generally limited application of the term "unusual circumstances" to cases where the withdrawing employer has faced dire economic circumstances such that "the very existence of an employer as a viable business entity has ceased or is about to cease."[369] However, the Board has, in some cases, found "unusual circumstances" and allowed an employer to withdraw where the bargaining power of the association had been dissipated by a series of consensual withdrawals and the execution of separate agreements by the majority of the association's members.[370]

Bargaining," at notes 477–478. Section 8(a)(3) prohibits an employer from locking out employees to force their union's adherence to a multi-employer unit. Great Atl. & Pac. Tea Co., 145 NLRB 361, 54 LRRM 1384 (1964), *enforced in pertinent part*, 340 F2d 690, 58 LRRM 2232 (CA 2, 1965). The employer's right to lock out to protect the integrity of the multi-employer bargaining unit from whipsaw strikes, *e.g.*, NLRB v. Truck Drivers Local 449 (Buffalo Linen Supply Co.), 353 US 87, 39 LRRM 2603 (1957), is discussed in Chapter 20, "The Lockout."

[369]Hi-Way Billboards, 206 NLRB 22, 23, 84 LRRM 1161, 1162 (1973), *enforcement denied*, 500 F2d 181, 87 LRRM 2203 (CA 5, 1974). The Board held that an employer may withdraw from a multi-employer bargaining association after negotiations have begun: (1) where the employer is subject to extreme economic difficulties resulting in an arrangement under the bankruptcy laws, U.S. Lingerie Corp., 170 NLRB 750, 67 LRRM 1482 (1968); (2) where the employer is faced with the imminent prospect of such adverse economic conditions as would require it to close its plant, Spun-Jee Corp., 171 NLRB 557, 68 LRRM 1121 (1968); and (3) where the employer is faced with the prospect of being forced out of business for lack of qualified employees and the union refuses to assist the employer by providing employees, Atlas Elec. Serv. Co., 176 NLRB 827, 71 LRRM 1625 (1969). The Board refused to find "unusual circumstances": (1) where an employer asserted a good-faith doubt of the union's majority status among his own employees, Sheridan Creations, 148 NLRB 1503, 57 LRRM 1176 (1964), *enforced*, 357 F2d 245, 61 LRRM 2586 (CA 2, 1966), *cert. denied*, 385 US 1005, 64 LRRM 288 (1967); (2) where all the employer's unit employees were discharged, John J. Corbett Press, Inc., 163 NLRB 154, 64 LRRM 2108 (1967), *enforced*, 401 F2d 673, 69 LRRM 2480 (CA 2, 1968); (3) where the union executed separate agreements with individual employer-members of the association, We Painters, Inc., 176 NLRB 964, 72 LRRM 1089 (1969); (4) where the employer had been suspended from the association for failure to pay its dues, Senco, Inc., 177 NLRB 882, 71 LRRM 1532 (1969); (5) where the employer was subjected to a strike, State Elec. Serv., 198 NLRB 592, 80 LRRM 1763 (1972), *enforced*, 477 F2d 749, 82 LRRM 3154 (CA 5), *cert. denied*, 414 US 911, 84 LRRM 2458 (1973); and (6) where the employer suffered a sharp decline in its business, Serv-All Co., 199 NLRB 1131, 81 LRRM 1495 (1972), *enforcement denied on other grounds*, 491 F2d 1273, 85 LRRM 2677 (CA 10, 1974). Dire economic circumstances will not justify withdrawal from the unit after an agreement is reached. Arco Elec. Co. v. NLRB, 618 F2d 698, 103 LRRM 3114 (CA 10, 1980); Co-Ed Garment Co., 231 NLRB 848, 97 LRRM 1502 (1977).

[370]Typographic Serv. Co., 238 NLRB 1565, 99 LRRM 1649 (1978); Connell Typesetting Co., 212 NLRB 918, 87 LRRM 1001 (1974). *But see* Tobey Fine Papers Div., 245 NLRB 1393, 102 LRRM 1343 (1979), *enforced*, 659 F2d 841, 107 LRRM 2221 (CA 8, 1981); Graham Paper Co., 245 NLRB 1388, 102 LRRM 1345 (1979); Butler Paper Co., 245 NLRB 1398, 102 LRRM 1347 (1979). The Board failed to find "unusual circumstances" that would allow an employer to withdraw from a multi-employer unit where the union had negotiated a series of interim agreements with more than two-thirds of the employer-members of the association. Callier's Custom Kitchens, 243 NLRB 1114, 102 LRRM 1008 (1979), *enforced*, 630 F2d 595, 105 LRRM 2510 (CA 8, 1980).

The Board and the courts of appeals have disagreed as to two situations. First, where a minority of the employers in an association argued that the majority had ignored their interests in negotiations, the Board found no "unusual circumstances."[371] While recognizing that mere dissatisfaction with the results of the group bargaining does not justify an untimely withdrawal, the Eighth Circuit concluded that where the multi-employer association fails to fairly represent the interests of a class of employer members, their withdrawal is justified.[372] Second, and more important, the Board consistently held that a bargaining impasse does not constitute "unusual circumstances" justifying an employer's withdrawal from a multi-employer unit once negotiations have begun. In *Hi-Way Billboards*[373] the Board explained that impasse is an expected part of negotiations, as to which both parties may utilize economic weapons to restart negotiations. The Board reasoned that multi-employer negotiations could be destroyed if members of the unit could withdraw upon reaching impasse, since a member could avoid its bargaining obligations by intentionally creating an impasse whenever an impending agreement seemed unfavorable. Five courts of appeals rejected the Board's position,[374] for they equated a union's right to strike selectively (to obtain interim agreements with individual employer members of the multi-employer unit after reaching impasse) with an employer's unilateral right to withdraw from the bargaining unit. The courts reasoned that

---

[371]Siebler Heating & Air Conditioning, 219 NLRB 1124, 90 LRRM 1239 (1975).

[372]NLRB v. Siebler Heating & Air Conditioning, 563 F2d 366, 96 LRRM 2613 (CA 8, 1977), *cert. denied*, 437 US 911, 98 LRRM 2705 (1978). *See also* NLRB v. Unelko Corp., 478 F2d 1404, 83 LRRM 2447 (CA 7, 1973).

[373]*Supra* note 369. *Accord* Florida Fine Sprinklers, 237 NLRB 1034, 99 LRRM 1078 (1978); Charles D. Bonanno Linen Serv., 229 NLRB 629, 95 LRRM 1128 (1977), *reconsidered*, 243 NLRB 1093, 102 LRRM 1001 (1979), *enforced*, 630 F2d 25, 105 LRRM 2477 (CA 1, 1980), *aff'd*, 454 US 404, 109 LRRM 2257 (1982) (*see infra* at note 376); Goodsell & Vocke, 223 NLRB 60, 92 LRRM 1187 (1976), *enforced*, 559 F2d 1141, 96 LRRM 2370 (CA 9, 1977); Bill Cook Buick, Inc., 224 NLRB 1094, 92 LRRM 1582 (1976); Associated Shower Door Co., 205 NLRB 677, 84 LRRM 1108 (1973), *enforced on other grounds*, 512 F2d 230, 88 LRRM 3024 (CA 9, 1975), *cert. denied*, 423 US 893, 90 LRRM 2614 (1975).

[374]H & D v. NLRB, 633 F2d 139, 105 LRRM 3070 (CA 9, 1980); NLRB v. Independent Ass'n of Steel Fabricators, 582 F2d 135, 98 LRRM 3150 (CA 2, 1978), *cert. denied*, 439 US 1130, 100 LRRM 2334 (1979); NLRB v. Beck Engraving Co., 522 F2d 475, 90 LRRM 2089 (CA 3, 1975); NLRB v. Associated Shower Door Co., 512 F2d 230, 88 LRRM 3024 (CA 9, 1975), *cert. denied*, 423 US 893, 90 LRRM 2614 (1975); NLRB v. Hi-Way Billboards, *supra* note 373; Fairmont Foods Co. v. NLRB, 471 F2d 1170, 82 LRRM 2017 (CA 8, 1972). *Contra* NLRB v. Charles D. Bonanno Linen Serv., 630 F2d 25, 105 LRRM 2477 (CA 1, 1980), *aff'd*, 454 US 404, 109 LRRM 2257 (1982). *See generally Effect of Negotiating Impasse on an Employer's Right to Withdraw From a Multi-Employer Bargaining Association*, 17 B.C. INDUS. & COM. L. REV. 525 (1976).

the union's right to strike created an imbalance of power between the union and employer members of the unit, including a potential for whipsaw strikes, sufficient to justify granting the employer an "equivalent" right of unilateral withdrawal.

In *Charles D. Bonanno Linen Service*,[375] the Board reconsidered its prior decisions. Restating its *Hi-Way Billboards* rationale, it clarified its understanding of the function of interim agreements. A true interim agreement establishes terms and conditions of employment for one or more employer-members pending the outcome of renewed group bargaining. It does not diminish or subvert the association's bargaining authority because any succeeding contract with the association will supersede the interim agreement. Under these circumstances, the Board reasoned, all employer-members of the association remain interested in the terms of the ultimate agreement. In contrast, the multi-employer unit would be fragmented by a pseudo-interim agreement which did not conform to the union's pre-impasse proposals and was offered with variations to employer-members of the group. In this latter circumstance, employer-members with favorable interim agreements might seek to prolong the impasse in order to gain a competitive advantage. The Board concluded that true interim agreements will operate to further the integrity of the bargaining unit by preserving the members' mutual interest in a final association-wide contract; thus, the union's right to negotiate interim agreements after impasse should not excuse an employer's untimely withdrawal from the multi-employer unit.

The First Circuit enforced *Bonanno*.[376] It reasoned that the balance of economic power arguably created by the union's right to negotiate an interim agreement should have little bearing on whether impasse justifies withdrawal; the union's right to negotiate interim agreements had never been contingent upon reaching impasse. The Supreme Court granted certiorari and affirmed.[377] The Court accepted the conclusion urged by the Board, "that interim agreements, on balance, tend to deter

---

[375]*Supra* note 373; *see* Seattle Auto Glass, 246 NLRB 94, 102 LRRM 1376 (1979), *enforced*, 669 F2d 1332, 109 LRRM 3350 (CA 9, 1982); Birkenwald Distrib. Co., 243 NLRB 1151, 102 LRRM 1005 (1979); Maine Mach. Works, 243 NLRB 1098, 102 LRRM 1006 (1979), *enforced*, 635 F2d 522, 106 LRRM 2656 (CA 5, 1981).

[376]NLRB v. Bonanno Linen Serv., *supra* note 374. See discussion of the Supreme Court's opinion in Chapter 13, "The Duty to Bargain," at notes 736–740.

[377]*Id.*

rather than promote unit fragmentation since they preserve a continuing mutual interest by all employer members in a final association-wide contract."[378]

Withdrawal from the multi-employer unit may be total or partial. A total withdrawal dissolves the entire multi-employer unit. Partial withdrawal takes different forms. An individual employer may timely withdraw as far as his own employees are concerned. Comparably, the union may elect to withdraw only as to the employees of some employers.[379] In either situation, the multi-employer unit continues as to the remaining employer-members; the union must bargain with the departing employers on an individual employer basis. And after lawfully withdrawing from a multi-employer unit, the employer must negotiate with the union, for the union's majority status is presumed to continue despite the changed structure of the unit.[380]

Partial withdrawal may also involve the severance of certain crafts from the multi-employer unit. Upon a timely petition by the incumbent or an outside union, in a unit appropriate for severance, the Board will conduct an election among all employees in specified crafts or job classifications employed by all the employers in the unit, in effect creating a second multi-employer unit.[381] However, the Board will not conduct an election to sever

---

[378]*Id.* at 415. Subsequent decisions have been governed by the *Bonanno Linen* decision. *See* Universal Enters., 291 NLRB 670, 131 LRRM 1031 (1988) (international union's rejection of negotiated agreement and resultant fragmentation of unit justified withdrawal, but employer required to honor interim agreement reached prior to withdrawal); Corson & Gruman Co., 284 NLRB 1316, 126 LRRM 1279 (1987); Marbro Co., 284 NLRB 1303, 1316, 126 LRRM 1282 (1987) (union's execution of final contract with one member of multi-employer unit fragments unit, permitting withdrawal of other employers). *See also* H & D. v. NLRB, 670 F2d 120, 109 LRRM 3296 (CA 9, 1982) (resignation of majority of employer's employees from union does not justify withdrawal); NLRB v. L.B. Priester & Sons, 669 F2d 355, 109 LRRM 3208 (CA 5, 1982) (unsubstantiated and belated claim of financial hardship does not justify withdrawal).

[379]*See, e.g.*, Pacific Coast Ass'n of Pulp & Paper Mfrs., 163 NLRB 892, 64 LRRM 1420 (1967).

[380]Holiday Hotel & Casino, 228 NLRB 926, 94 LRRM 1702 (1977), *enforced*, 604 F2d 605, 102 LRRM 2484 (CA 9, 1979); Tahoe Nugget, 227 NLRB 357, 94 LRRM 1343 (1976), *enforced*, 584 F2d 293, 99 LRRM 2509 (CA 9, 1978), *cert. denied*, 442 US 921, 101 LRRM 2428 (1979); Nevada Lodge, 227 NLRB 368, 94 LRRM 1345 (1976), *enforced sub nom.* NLRB v. Tahoe Nugget, 584 F2d 2983, 99 LRRM 2509 (CA 9, 1978); Barney's Club, 227 NLRB 414, 94 LRRM 1444 (1976). The presumption was rebutted where the employer reclassified its employees to change the composition of the unit and thereby reduced the union's support in the newly defined unit. NLRB v. Sac Constr. Co., 603 F2d 1155, 102 LRRM 2513 (CA 5, 1979). *See generally* Chapter 12, "Recognition and Withdrawal of Recognition Without an Election," at notes 313–412, and Chapter 13, "The Duty to Bargain," at notes 819–833.

[381]Allen, Lane & Scott, 137 NLRB 223, 50 LRRM 1140 (1962); Printing Indus. of Del., 131 NLRB 1100, 48 LRRM 1196 (1961); Employing Printers of Peoria, 130 NLRB 1511, 47 LRRM 1537 (1961). *See supra* notes 74–100 for treatment of craft severance in general.

specific classifications at only one of the employers in the unit[382] or where there is substantial interchange among employees in the various classifications.[383] With mutual consent, the parties may also sever classifications to create a second multi-employer unit.

4. Scope of the Multi-Employer Unit. Until 1952, the Board took the position that the appropriateness of a multi-employer unit was controlling as to all categories of employees of the employers in the unit.[384] Thus, once multi-employer bargaining was established with respect to some employees, all subsequent organization involving participating employers had to proceed on a multi-employer basis.

The Board's concern that this requirement would impede organization led to its abandonment in *Joseph E. Seagram & Sons.*[385] Although the *Seagram* rule was enunciated in a case involving a multiplant unit of a single employer, it soon found application in multi-employer cases as well. Under the new policy, the Board has approved single-employer units of office clericals[386] and of salesmen,[387] for example, although the employer had been bargaining as to other employees in a multi-employer unit. The essential criterion for the creation of a single-employer unit is that the employee classifications sought have an "internal homogeneity and cohesiveness" permitting them to stand alone.[388]

If the unrepresented employees do not form a cohesive group, but comprise groups of miscellaneous employees having in common only the fact that they lack representation, the Board has found a unit consisting of such employees appropriate simply as a "residual" unit. But a residual unit is deemed appropriate only if it includes all unrepresented employees in the multi-

---

[382]Jahn-Tyler Printing & Publishing Co., 112 NLRB 167, 35 LRRM 1730 (1955); Washington Hardware Co., 95 NLRB 1001, 28 LRRM 1406 (1951); Coca-Cola Bottling Works Co., 91 NLRB 351, 26 LRRM 1488 (1950); Pioneer, Inc., 86 NLRB 1316, 25 LRRM 1068 (1949); Coeur d'Alene Mines Corp., 77 NLRB 570, 22 LRRM 1069 (1948).

[383]Teamsters Local 705 (Roper Corp.), 244 NLRB 522, 102 LRRM 1081 (1979); Packaging Corp. of Am., 146 NLRB 1620, 56 LRRM 1104 (1964).

[384]Kenosha Auto Transp. Corp., 98 NLRB 482, 29 LRRM 1370 (1952); Columbia Pictures Corp., 84 NLRB 746, 24 LRRM 1291 (1949).

[385]101 NLRB 101, 31 LRRM 1022 (1952).

[386]Hyatt House Motel, 174 NLRB 1009, 70 LRRM 1378 (1969); Continental Baking Co., 109 NLRB 33, 34 LRRM 1298 (1954); Sovereign Prods., 107 NLRB 359, 33 LRRM 1171 (1953); Miller & Miller Motor Freight Lines, 101 NLRB 581, 31 LRRM 1118 (1952).

[387]NLRB v. E-Z Davies Chevrolet, 395 F2d 191, 68 LRRM 2228 (CA 9, 1968); Lownsbury Chevrolet Co., 101 NLRB 1752, 31 LRRM 1261 (1952).

[388]Los Angeles Statler Hilton Hotel, 129 NLRB 1349, 1351, 47 LRRM 1194 (1961) (single-employer unit denied).

employer group.[389] Where multi-employer bargaining has been confined to certain craft and special interest groups, a residual multi-employer unit cannot be considered the only appropriate unit, on the basis of bargaining history, when such a unit would in effect embrace the main force of employees.[390] Should an employee classification be employed by one or more but by fewer than all the employer-members, such classification may be represented in a unit smaller than the all-employer unit.[391]

Once a multi-employer unit is established, the employers' consent to the inclusion of other categories of employees in the unit is unnecessary. Thus, the Board placed unrepresented timekeepers in an existing multi-employer unit despite an express resolution by association members denying the association the authority to represent them with respect to such employees. The Board held that the Act's requirement that bargaining be conducted in an appropriate unit must supersede the employers' choice to exclude timekeepers from the multi-employer unit, where the timekeepers shared a community of interests with the other employees who were part of the multi-employer unit.[392]

5. Multilevel Bargaining Units. While multi employer bargaining units are generally thought to be conducive to industrial peace and are thus favored by national policy, unions and employers recognize that associationwide solutions are not practical for all subjects of bargaining. Thus, within the framework of multi-employer bargaining, the parties may agree to bargain individually or in smaller groups on specific issues. Bargaining in the trucking industry, for example, evolved into a master agreement dealing primarily with economic and other national issues and numerous geographic supplements covering essen-

---

[389]*Id.* Daily Press, 110 NLRB 573, 35 LRRM 1048 (1954).

[390]Pacific Drive-In Theatres Corp., 167 NLRB 661, 66 LRRM 1119 (1967).

[391]Holiday Hotel, 134 NLRB 113, 49 LRRM 1095 (1961); Desaulniers & Co., 115 NLRB 1025, 37 LRRM 1481 (1956).

[392]Steamship Trade Ass'n of Baltimore, 155 NLRB 232, 60 LRRM 1257 (1965). *See also* I.T.O. Corp. of Baltimore v. NLRB, 818 F2d 1108, 125 LRRM 2477 (CA 4, 1987), *enforcing sub nom.* Steamship Trade Ass'n of Baltimore, 279 NLRB 338, 122 LRRM 1087 (1986); NLRB v. American Printers & Lithographers, 820 F2d 878, 125 LRRM 2593 (CA 7, 1987), *enforcing* 275 NLRB 1490, 120 LRRM 1054 (1985) (court approved Board's view that it may add to multi-employer unit employees of one member employer without adding similarly classified employees of other member employers. The court also found no departure from the Board's general rule that a bargaining history of including "fringe" classifications is controlling; here the employees did not lack homogeneity or cohesiveness with the main unit).

tially regional matters such as seniority and local grievance procedures.[393]

Multilevel bargaining may also occur in a less developed form where one or more members of an association specifically reserve the right to bargain separately on matters peculiar to their respective plants. However, the union must consent to this limited delegation of bargaining authority to the association.[394] Such an agreement is the equivalent of a waiver during negotiations and is effective for the duration of the bargaining. If the union revokes its acquiescence during the renegotiation of the contract, the employer is obligated to negotiate the issue on a multi-employer basis.[395] Where an employer party to a multi-employer association implements local rules changes, it must bargain with the affected union on request.[396]

When a union that is party to a national or multi-employer agreement organizes a previously unrepresented facility of a covered employer, the new facility will be included in the multi-employer unit only with the parties' implicit or explicit consent. If the new facility is included by consent, the employer may refuse to bargain with the union as to matters covered by the master agreement, but must bargain on local issues.[397]

Another form of multilevel bargaining occurs when parties to a multi-employer agreement cannot agree upon a successor contract and they submit the unresolved issues to a panel composed of representatives of parent union and employer bodies. The Board has held that an employer does not violate the Act by referring to the panel disputed issues, including the continued application of the panel system in the next contract.[398]

---

[393]*See, e.g.*, Davey v. Fitzsimmons, 413 F Supp 670, 92 LRRM 2130 (DDC, 1976).

[394]Rice Lake Creamery Co., 131 NLRB 1270, 48 LRRM 1251 (1961), *enforced sub nom.* Teamsters Local 662 v. NLRB, 302 F2d 908, 50 LRRM 2243 (CA DC), *cert. denied*, 371 US 827, 51 LRRM 2222 (1962); Kroger Co., 141 NLRB 564, 52 LRRM 1352 (1963), *aff'd sub nom.* Retail Clerks Local 1550 v. NLRB, 330 F2d 210, 55 LRRM 2212 (CA DC), *cert. denied*, 379 US 828, 57 LRRM 2239 (1964).

[395]Pacific Coast Ass'n of Pulp & Paper Mfrs., 133 NLRB 690, 48 LRRM 1696 (1961), *enforced*, 304 F2d 760, 50 LRRM 2626 (CA 9, 1962).

[396]NLRB v. Miller Brewing Co., 408 F2d 12, 70 LRRM 2907 (CA 9, 1969).

[397]Eltra Corp., 205 NLRB 1035, 84 LRRM 1234 (1973); Radio Corp. of Am., 135 NLRB 980, 49 LRRM 1606 (1962).

[398]*See* Mechanical Contractors Ass'n of Newburgh, 202 NLRB 1, 82 LRRM 1438 (1973). The Board has distinguished this procedure from interest arbitration. *See* Chapter 16, "Subjects of Bargaining," at notes 496–497.

Chapter 12

RECOGNITION AND WITHDRAWAL OF RECOGNITION WITHOUT AN ELECTION

I. Introduction

An employer may be required to recognize and bargain with a union that has not been certified by the National Labor Relations Board. This duty to recognize the representative "designated or selected for the purposes of collective bargaining by the majority of the employees in a unit appropriate for such purposes"[1] may exist independently of NLRB election procedures. An employer may also extend recognition voluntarily to a union without a Board election. In such cases, however, the employer must act with due care in ascertaining the majority status of the union, for section 8(a)(2) of the Act forbids the recognition of a union that does not in fact represent a majority of the employees in the unit.[2] In addition, in the limited circumstances discussed in this chapter, the Board may remedy an employer's unfair labor practices by ordering the employer to bargain with a union even though an election has not been held.

Prior to 1947, section 9(c) of the Wagner Act authorized the Board to certify unions by using secret-ballot elections or "any other suitable method," to ascertain that the union enjoyed

---

[1]Section 9(a).

[2]Ladies' Garment Workers (Bernhard-Altmann Tex. Corp.) v. NLRB, 366 US 731, 48 LRRM 2251 (1961). This chapter does not treat the "sweetheart" contract and its kindred, recognition deemed unlawful under §8(a)(2); *see* Chapter 8, "Employer Domination and Assistance to Labor Organizations," at notes 9, 83, and 203–207. Refusal of an employer to recognize a previously established bargaining agent is also treated elsewhere; *see* Chapter 13, "The Duty to Bargain."

majority support.[3] A *card check* was the most frequently invoked "other suitable method." That is the procedure by which signatures on union authorization cards are compared with the signatures of employees on the employer's payroll documents to determine whether a majority have selected the union.[4]

The Board's use of card checks has evolved in several stages. Until 1939, the Board relied extensively upon authorization cards as sufficient evidence of majority status to establish a violation of the former section 8(5) duty to bargain and to sustain a certification. In 1939, the Board abandoned the "other suitable method" approach and began relying almost exclusively upon elections in representation cases as the basis of issuing certifications. In the 1947 Taft-Hartley amendments, Congress made the election process the *only* basis for certification.[5] In the 1950s, a new Board policy governing the effect of a union's participation in an election resulted in a near-total eclipse of the card check device.[6] In the mid-1960s, reverting to its earlier decision in *Joy Silk Mills, Inc.*,[7] the Board changed its policy again and revived the card check as a legitimate means for establishing an employer's duty to bargain. Although the *Joy Silk* doctrine was accepted by the courts initially,[8] some courts of appeals disap-

---

[3]Section 9(c) of the Wagner Act stated:

> Whenever a question affecting commerce arises concerning the representation of employees, the Board may investigate such controversy and certify to the parties, in writing, the name or names of the representatives that have been designated or selected. In any such investigation, the Board shall provide for an appropriate hearing upon due notice, either in conjunction with a proceeding under section 10 or otherwise, and may take a secret ballot of employees, or utilize any other suitable method to ascertain *such* representatives.

For a discussion of the early Board history, see H. MILLIS & E. BROWN, FROM THE WAGNER ACT TO TAFT-HARTLEY 133–34 (1950); *Hearings on S.256 Before the Subcomm. of Labor of the Senate Comm. on Labor and Public Welfare*, 89th Cong., 1st Sess. 19, 20 (1965) (memorandum from Secretary of Labor Willard Wirtz to Senator Jacob Javits); NLRB, 1937 ANNUAL REPORT 108 (1937)

[4]Other devices, such as petitions or polls, have also been used to establish majority authorization. In San Clemente Publishing Corp., 167 NLRB 6, 65 LRRM 1726 (1967), a bargaining order was based on an unofficial poll of employees, which had been agreed upon by the union and the employer, conducted by a third person.

[5]The amendment deleted from §9 the provision allowing "any other suitable method."

[6]*See* note 23 *infra* and accompanying text.

[7]85 NLRB 1263, 24 LRRM 1548 (1949), *modified and enforced*, 185 F2d 732, 27 LRRM 2012 (CA DC, 1950), *cert. denied*, 341 US 914, 27 LRRM 2633 (1951). *See* notes 17–20 *infra* and accompanying text.

[8]NLRB v. Taitel & Son, 261 F2d 1, 43 LRRM 2025 (CA 7, 1958), *cert. denied*, 359 US 944, 43 LRRM 2741 (1959); NLRB v. Wheeling Pipe Line, 229 F2d 391, 37 LRRM 2403 (CA 8, 1956); NLRB v. Pyne Molding Corp., 226 F2d 818, 37 LRRM 2007 (CA 2, 1955); NLRB v. Armco Drainage & Metal Prods., 220 F2d 573, 35 LRRM 2536 (CA 6 1955); NLRB v. Hamilton Co., 220 F2d 492, 35 LRRM 2658 (CA 10, 1955); NLRB v. Trimfit of Cal., 211 F2d 206, 33 LRRM 2705 (CA 9, 1954); NLRB v. Epstein, 203 F2d 482, 31 LRRM 2619 (CA 3, 1953); NLRB v. Ken Rose Motors, Inc., 193 F2d 769, 29 LRRM 2343 (CA 1, 1952); NLRB v. Inter-City Advertising Co., 190 F2d 420, 28 LRRM 2321 (CA 4, 1951).

proved of its resurrected application by the Board.[9] In 1969, in *NLRB v. Gissel Packing Co.*,[10] the Supreme Court settled major questions that had split the circuits by holding that the Board has authority to issue a remedial bargaining order where the union has demonstrated its majority status through authorization cards.

This chapter first describes the practice under the Wagner Act and traces the development and modification of the *Joy Silk* doctrine. Next, the standards that replaced *Joy Silk*, as fashioned first by the Board, ratified by the Supreme Court in *Gissel*, and thereafter elaborated in the case law, are discussed.[11] That is followed by discussion of the Supreme Court's decision in *Linden Lumber Division v. NLRB*[12] that an employer who commits no unfair labor practices need not petition for an election after rejecting an offer of authorization cards. The chapter concludes with an examination of the employer's affirmative defenses to the bargaining obligation and of the conditions under which an employer may withdraw recognition from a union.

II. HISTORY

A. The Practice Under the Wagner Act

Under the original Wagner Act, a union was not required to win an NLRB election to be certified as the exclusive bargaining representative of a unit of employees. Section 9(c) of that Act

---

[9]The Board's standards were rejected by the courts of appeals in NLRB v. S.S. Logan Packing Co., 386 F2d 562, 66 LRRM 2596 (CA 4, 1967); NLRB v. S.E. Nichols-Dover Co., 380 F2d 438, 65 LRRM 2655 (CA 2, 1967); Engineers & Fabricators v. NLRB, 376 F2d 482, 64 LRRM 2849 (CA 5, 1967). They were approved in NLRB v. Dan Howard Mfg. Co., 390 F2d 304, 67 LRRM 2278 (CA 7, 1968); NLRB v. Swan Super Cleaners, 384 F2d 609, 66 LRRM 2385 (CA 6, 1967); Furr's, Inc. v. NLRB, 381 F2d 562, 64 LRRM 2422 (CA 10, 1967); NLRB v. Southbridge Sheet Metal Works, 380 F2d 851, 65 LRRM 2916 (CA 1, 1967).

[10]395 US 575, 71 LRRM 2481 (1969). *See infra* at notes 48–76.

[11]The literature discussing these standards includes: Cooper, *Authorization Cards and Union Representation Election Outcome: An Empirical Assessment of the Assumption Underlying the Supreme Court* Gissel *Decision*, 79 NW. U.L. REV. 87 (1984); Beeson, *Recognition Without Election*, in LABOR LAW DEVELOPMENTS—1970 (Sixteenth Annual Institute on Labor Law, Southwestern Legal Foundation) 89 (1970); Lewis, Gissel Packing: *Was the Supreme Court Right?*, 56 A.B.A. J. 877 (1970); Sheinkman, *Recognition of Unions Through Authorization Cards*, 3 GA. L. REV. 319 (1969); Browne, *Obligation to Bargain on Basis of Card Majority*, 3 GA. L. REV. 334 (1969); Gordon, *Union Authorization Cards and the Duty to Bargain*, in LABOR RELATIONS YEARBOOK—1968, 128 (1969), 19 LAB. L.J. 201 (1968); Lesnick, *Establishment of Bargaining Rights Without an NLRB Election. See also* Note, NLRB v. Gissel Packing Co.: *Bargaining Orders and Employee Free Choice*, 45 N.Y.U. L. REV. 318 (1970).

[12]419 US 301, 87 LRRM 3236 (1974).

provided that the Board should "take a secret ballot election or utilize any other suitable method" to determine whether a unit of employees wanted the union to be its certified bargaining agent.[13] Although authorization cards were typically regarded as a "suitable method" of ascertaining employee desires, the Board's willingness to rely on authorization cards in the certification process waned. In 1939, in *Cudahy Packing Co.*,[14] the Board declared that "in the interest of investing . . . certifications with more certainty and prestige by basing them on free and secret elections conducted under the Board's auspices," it would no longer base them on other methods.[15] When an employer was confronted with a majority of authorization cards signed by its employees, the Board's new policy was to order an election unless it could be shown that the employer lacked a good-faith doubt of the union's majority status. This showing was often, but not always, made by evidence of the commission of unfair labor practices while representation matters were pending. These standards met with general judicial approval.[16]

B. The *Joy Silk* Period

Following the Board's decision in *Joy Silk* an employer was ordered to recognize and bargain with a union if the General Counsel established four elements:[17] (1) the union represented a majority of the employees in an appropriate unit, (2) the union had requested recognition, (3) the employer had denied the request for recognition while lacking a good-faith doubt as to the union's majority status, and (4) the employer had taken action calculated to dissipate the union's majority status.

As the Court of Appeals for the District of Columbia Circuit declared in *Joy Silk*:

> An employer may refuse recognition to a union when motivated by a good-faith doubt as to that union's majority status. . . . When,

---

[13]*See supra* note 3.

[14]13 NLRB 526, 4 LRRM 321 (1939).

[15]*Id.* at 531–32. In Joe Hearin Lumber, 66 NLRB 1276, 1283, 17 LRRM 399 (1946), the Board stated that it did "not feel . . . that a card check reflects employees' true desires with the same degree of certainty" as a secret-ballot election.

[16]Medo Photo Supply Corp. v. NLRB, 321 US 678, 14 LRRM 581 (1944); NLRB v. P. Lorillard Co., 314 US 512, 9 LRRM 410 (1942); Lebanon Steel Foundry v. NLRB, 130 F2d 404, 10 LRRM 760 (CA DC), *cert. denied*, 317 US 659, 11 LRRM 839 (1942).

[17]Aaron Bros. Co., 158 NLRB 1077, 62 LRRM 1160 (1966). *See also* Jem Mfg., 156 NLRB 643, 61 LRRM 1074 (1966); John P. Serpa, Inc., 155 NLRB 99, 60 LRRM 1235 (1965), *order set aside sub nom.* Retail Clerks Local 1179 v. NLRB, 376 F2d 186, 64 LRRM 2764 (CA 9, 1967).

however, such refusal is due to a desire to gain time and to take action to dissipate the union's majority, the refusal is no longer justifiable and constitutes a violation of the duty to bargain set forth in Section 8(a)(5) of the Act.[18]

Thus, under the *Joy Silk* doctrine, unless an employer's good-faith doubt related to the union's majority status, there was no legal justification for insistence upon an election.[19] Although an employer might have doubted in good faith that the unit proposed by the union was appropriate, if it was later found to be so, the employer had a duty to bargain notwithstanding its preference for a different unit. An employer whose refusal to bargain stemmed solely from disagreement as to the appropriate unit acted "at its peril and in violation of the Act."[20]

Although this "good-faith doubt" test was retained in name for 20 years, two factors affecting its application, and the frequency with which it was applied, changed during that period. The first was the overruling of a 1951 Board decision that a union that participated in an election and lost could nonetheless obtain the unfair labor practice remedy of a bargaining order if the employer had unlawfully refused to recognize the union based on its preelection card majority.[21] In 1954, in *Aiello Dairy Farms Co.*,[22] the Board abandoned that position and held that if a union participated in an election after its request for recognition had been denied, it waived a bargaining-order remedy under section 10 in favor of an election remedy under section 9. The union would thus be confined to the election process to prove majority status. The Board adhered to this "waiver" doctrine for 10 years, and the incidence of *Joy Silk* cases drastically declined.

---

[18]Joy Silk Mills, Inc. v. NLRB, 185 F2d 732, 741, 27 LRRM 2012 (CA DC, 1950), *modifying and enforcing* 85 NLRB 1263, 24 LRRM 1548 (1949), *cert. denied*, 341 US 914, 27 LRRM 2633 (1951). The Supreme Court recognized the *Joy Silk* doctrine in Mine Workers v. Arkansas Oak Flooring Co., 351 US 62, 37 LRRM 2828 (1956). *See also* Franks Bros. v. NLRB, 321 US 702, 14 LRRM 591 (1944).

[19]NLRB v. Ralph Printing & Lithographing Co., 379 F2d 687, 65 LRRM 2800 (CA 8, 1967), *cert. denied*, 401 US 925, 76 LRRM 2500 (1971).

[20]Tom Thumb Stores, Inc., 123 NLRB 833, 835, 44 LRRM 1005 (1959); Benson Wholesale Co., 164 NLRB 536, 65 LRRM 1278 (1967) (good-faith belief that another unit is appropriate, if erroneous, is irrelevant); *see also* NLRB v. Morris Novelty Co., 378 F2d 1000, 65 LRRM 2577 (CA 8, 1967); Oklahoma Sheraton Corp., 156 NLRB 681, 61 LRRM 1115 (1966); Southland Paint Co., 156 NLRB 22, 60 LRRM 1546 (1965); Clermont's, Inc., 154 NLRB 1397, 60 LRRM 1141 (1965).

[21]Davidson Co., 94 NLRB 142, 28 LRRM 1026 (1951).

[22]110 NLRB 1365, 35 LRRM 1235 (1954).

In 1964, in *Bernel Foam*,[23] the Board expressly overruled *Aiello* and reverted to its prior policy. The Board reasoned that

> the so-called "choice" which the union is forced to make under Aiello between going to an election or filing an 8(a)(5) charge is at best a Hobson's choice. Although an election is a relatively swift and inexpensive way for the union to put the force of law behind its majority status, the procedure is highly uncertain entailing the real possibility that because of conduct by the employer no fair election will be held.
>
> . . .
>
> Since this difficult and rather dubious "choice" is created by the employer's unlawful conduct, there is no warrant for imposing upon the union which represents the employees an irrevocable option as to the method it will pursue . . . while permitting the offending party to enjoy at the expense of public policy the fruits of such unlawful conduct.[24]

The resulting *Bernel Foam* rule allowed the issuance of a bargaining order based on employer preelection misconduct, however, only when the election was set aside on the basis of meritorious objections.[25]

Aaron Brothers[26] had made clear that it was the General Counsel's burden to establish the existence of the employer's lack of good-faith doubt as to the union's majority. The Board had added that "[w]hether an employer is acting in good faith or bad faith in questioning the union's majority is a determination which must be made in light of all the relevant facts of the case, including any unlawful conduct of the employer, the sequence of events, and the time lapse between the refusal and the

---

[23]Bernel Foam Prods. Co., 146 NLRB 1277, 56 LRRM 1039 (1964). The doctrine was approved in NLRB v. Southbridge Sheet Metal Works, *supra* note 9.

[24]146 NLRB at 1280, 56 LRRM at 1041. This doctrine was approved by the Supreme Court in NLRB v. Gissel Packing Co., *supra* note 10. See text accompanying notes 48–76, *infra*, relating to the *General Steel* case. *See also* Colson Corp. (Boilermakers) v. NLRB, 347 F2d 128, 59 LRRM 2512 (CA 8), *cert. denied*, 382 US 904, 60 LRRM 2353 (1965); Electrical Workers (IUE) v. NLRB (S.N.C. Mfg. Co.), 352 F2d 361, 59 LRRM 2232 (CA DC), *cert. denied*, 382 US 902, 60 LRRM 2353 (1965). *Cf.* NLRB v. Flomatic Corp., 347 F2d 74, 59 LRRM 2535 (CA 2, 1965).

[25]Irving Air Chute Co., 149 NLRB 627, 57 LRRM 1330 (1964), *enforced*, 350 F2d 176, 59 LRRM 3052 (CA 2, 1965). In Green Bay Aviation, 165 NLRB 1026, 65 LRRM 1499 (1967), the Board refused to issue a postelection bargaining order where the employer's unfair labor practices occurred prior to the filing of the petition for an election. The election may be set aside on the basis of objections filed by the employer following a union victory, as well as by the union. Photobell Co., 158 NLRB 738, 62 LRRM 1091 (1966).

[26]*Supra* note 17 and accompanying text. "Absent an affirmative showing of bad faith, an employer, presented with a majority card showing and a bargaining request, will not be held to have violated his bargaining obligation under the law simply because he refuses to rely upon cards, rather than an election, as the method for determining the union's majority." *Id.* at 1078.

unlawful conduct."[27] The Board expressly eschewed a mechanical position, that employers were "automatically precluded" from having a good-faith doubt simply because unfair labor practices had been committed, in favor of an analysis of all the facts and circumstances of the particular case.[28] Thus, the Board considered such factors as (1) the employer's past experience in dealing with union activities;[29] (2) the employer's willingness to proceed with an expedited election;[30] (3) the timing,[31] nature, and effect of unlawful conduct;[32] and (4) the employer's disavowal of unlawful supervisory conduct[33] in making its determination regarding the employer's good-faith doubt. And just as employer unfair labor practices were not always fatal to an assertion of good-faith doubt, the bad faith necessary to support a bargaining order was occasionally demonstrated by employer conduct which did not amount to an independent unfair labor practice.[34] Thus, employers were ordered to bargain in the absence of a secret-ballot election where they repudiated the results of a previously agreed-upon card check.[35]

---

[27]*Id.* at 1079; Converters Gravure Serv., 164 NLRB 397, 65 LRRM 1098 (1967). In NLRB v. River Togs, 382 F2d 198, 65 LRRM 2987 (CA 2, 1967), the Second Circuit denied enforcement of a bargaining order, pointing out that where the evidence shows a good-faith doubt, the antiunion activities of an employer—including his unfair labor practices—are "as consistent with a desire to prevent the acquisition of a majority status as with a purpose to destroy an existing majority" (quoting Lesnick, *supra* note 11, at 855). But see Furr's, Inc. v. NLRB, *supra* note 9, enforcing a bargaining order and sustaining a finding of bad faith. The court in *Furr's* accepted a violation of §8(a)(1) as strong evidence of the lack of good-faith doubt.

[28]*See, e.g.*, Cameo Lingerie, 148 NLRB 535, 538, 57 LRRM 1044 (1964); A. L. Gilbert Co., 110 NLRB 2067, 35 LRRM 1314 (1954). *See also* River Togs, *supra* note 27. In Hammond & Irving, 154 NLRB 1071, 1073, 60 LRRM 1073, 1074 (1965) (footnote omitted), the Board noted that

> not every act of misconduct necessarily vitiates the respondent's good faith. For, there are some situations in which the violations of the Act are not truly inconsistent with a good-faith doubt that the union represents a majority of the employees. Whether the conduct involved reflects on the good faith of the employer requires an evaluation of the facts of each case.

[29]Walmac Co., 106 NLRB 1355, 33 LRRM 1019 (1953).

[30]Marr Knitting, 90 NLRB 479, 26 LRRM 1237 (1950).

[31]Sunset Lumber Prods., 113 NLRB 1172, 36 LRRM 1426 (1955).

[32]Beaver Mach. & Tool Co., 97 NLRB 33, 29 LRRM 1051 (1951).

[33]KTRH Broadcasting Co., 113 NLRB 125, 36 LRRM 1260 (1955).

[34]Aaron Bros. Co., *supra* note 17 (citing Snow & Sons, 134 NLRB 709, 49 LRRM 1228 (1961), *enforced*, 308 F2d 687, 51 LRRM 2199 (CA 9, 1962)); Dixon Ford Shoe Co., 150 NLRB 861, 58 LRRM 1160 (1965); Kellogg Mills, 147 NLRB 342, 56 LRRM 1223 (1964), *enforced*, 347 F2d 219, 59 LRRM 2340 (CA 9, 1965); Greyhound Terminal, 137 NLRB 87, 50 LRRM 1088 (1962), *enforced*, 314 F2d 43, 52 LRRM 2335 (CA 5, 1963). *See* Christensen & Christensen, Gissel Packing *and "Good Faith Doubt": The Gestalt of Required Recognition of Unions Under the NLRB*, 37 U. CHI. L. REV. 411 (1970). *Cf.* Wilder Mfg. Co., 185 NLRB 175, 75 LRRM 1023 (1970).

[35]Snow & Sons, *supra* note 34. *Accord* Kellogg Mills, *supra* note 34; Dixon Ford Shoe Co., *supra* note 34; Greyhound Terminal, *supra* note 34. However, bad faith was not to be inferred simply from the rejection of a proposal to submit the cards to an impartial determination. Strydel, Inc., 156 NLRB 1185, 61 LRRM 1230 (1966).

The two most significant tests for lack of good faith were whether the employer "deliberately engaged in unfair labor practices in order to dissipate the Union's majority and make the holding of a fair election impossible,"[36] and whether the employer, in effect, had actual independent knowledge of the union's majority.[37] Since *serious* employer unfair labor practices were interpreted as indicating a desire to gain time to undermine the union or a rejection of the principle of collective bargaining,[38] evidence of such practices was the most frequent method of establishing the lack of a good-faith doubt.[39] Applied in such a manner, the *Joy Silk* doctrine was endorsed by every circuit court of appeals.[40]

In the years following *Joy Silk*, increasing emphasis was placed on an employer's unfair labor practices as establishing the absence of good faith when the employer refused recognition based on a card majority. The General Counsel argued that the unfair labor practices dissipated the union's majority status, as the employer had intended. Thus, the employer's unlawful conduct was said to betoken awareness of the union's majority status, thereby negating the possibility of a good-faith belief that the cards were inadequate indicators of the union's majority. Moving away from examination of the totality of an employer's conduct, the Board stated that the "test for determining good-faith doubt of a union's majority is whether the employer has engaged in substantial unfair labor practices calculated to dissipate union support."[41] While conceding that a secret-ballot election would normally be the most reliable means of ascertaining the employees' desire for representation, the Board reasoned that if "an employer engages in unfair labor practices which make impossible the holdings of a free election, the Board has no alternative but to look to signed authorization cards as the only available proof of the choice employees would have made absent

---

[36]Southeastern Rubber Mfg. Co., 106 NLRB 989, 32 LRRM 1590, 1590 (1953).

[37]Snow & Sons, *supra* note 34.

[38]Commission of unfair labor practices which were either too insubstantial to warrant an inference of bad faith or were not inconsistent with a good-faith doubt of majority status would not support a bargaining order. Hercules Packing Corp., 163 NLRB 264, 64 LRRM 1331, *aff'd*, 386 F2d 790, 66 LRRM 2751 (CA 2, 1967); Hammond & Irving, *supra* note 28.

[39]Joy Silk Mills, Inc., 85 NLRB 1263, 24 LRRM 1548 (1949), *modified and enforced*, 185 F2d 732, 27 LRRM 2012 (CA DC, 1950), *cert. denied*, 341 US 914, 27 LRRM 2633 (1951); Benson Wholesale Co., *supra* note 20; Taitel & Son, 119 NLRB 910, 41 LRRM 1230 (1957).

[40]*See* cases cited in *supra* note 8.

[41]National Cash Register Co., 167 NLRB 1047, 66 LRRM 1206, 1206 (1967).

the employer's unfair labor practices."[42] In *Aaron Brothers*,[43] the Board observed that the *Joy Silk* rule used the "most reliable means available"[44] to afford employees free choice in the selection of a bargaining representative. The Board reasoned that "[w]here an employer has engaged in unfair labor practices, the results of a Board-conducted election are a less reliable indication of the true desires of employees than authorization cards, whereas, in a situation free of such unlawful interference, the converse is true."[45]

Under *Aaron Brothers*, the employer's right to insist upon an election was enhanced where no unfair labor practices had been committed. The Board held that an employer would "not be subject to an 8(a)(5) violation simply because he is unable to substantiate a reasonable basis for his doubt."[46] Accordingly, an employer who committed no unfair labor practices could insist on an election even where his doubt is "founded on no more than a distrust of cards."[47]

C. The *Gissel* Decision

In its landmark decision in *NLRB v. Gissel Packing Co.*,[48] the Supreme Court approved the Board's approach, which it described by saying that "an employer's good-faith doubt [of a union's majority] is largely irrelevant, and the key to the issuance of a bargaining order is the commission of serious unfair labor practices that interfere with the election process and tend to

---

[42]Bryant Chucking Grinder Co., 160 NLRB 1526, 63 LRRM 1185, 1187 (1966), *enforced*, 389 F2d 565, 67 LRRM 2017 (CA 2, 1967), *cert. denied*, 392 US 908, 68 LRRM 2408 (1968). In Aaron Bros., 158 NLRB 1077, 62 LRRM 1160 (1966), the Board defined the policy as follows:

> While an employer's right to a Board election is not absolute, it has long been established Board policy that an employer may refuse to bargain and insist upon such an election as proof of a union's majority . . . . An election by secret ballot is normally a more satisfactory means of determining employees' wishes, although authorization cards signed by a majority may also evidence their desires. Absent an affirmative showing of bad faith, an employer, presented with a majority card showing and a bargaining request, will not be held to have violated his bargaining obligation under the law simply because he refuses to rely upon cards, rather than an election, as the method for determining the union's majority.

Id. at 1078, 62 LRRM at 1161 (footnotes omitted).

[43]*Supra* note 42.

[44]*Id.*, 62 LRRM at 1161 n.10.

[45]*Id.*

[46]H & W Constr. Co., 161 NLRB 852, 857, 63 LRRM 1346 (1966).

[47]*Id.*

[48]395 US 575, 71 LRRM 2481 (1969).

preclude the holding of a fair election."[49] The Court's description of the Board's approach was based on statements of counsel for the Board during oral argument which indicated "that [the Board] had virtually abandoned the Joy Silk doctrine altogether."[50] That description accurately summarized the course of Board decisions which, long before *Gissel,* had equated substantial employer unfair labor practices with a lack of good-faith doubt of majority status.

In *Gissel,* the Court consolidated four cases for decision, *Gissel, Heck's,* and *General Steel*[51] from the Fourth Circuit and *Sinclair*[52] from the First Circuit. In each of the Fourth Circuit cases, the union obtained authorization cards from a majority of the employees in an appropriate bargaining unit and demanded recognition. In each instance, the employer refused to extend voluntary recognition on the ground that authorization cards were inherently unreliable indicators of employee desires. Each employer then waged an antiunion campaign during which it committed numerous unfair labor practices. In *Gissel* and *Heck's* the Board ordered the employers to bargain even though an election had not been held. In *General Steel* the Board set aside the election, which the union had lost, and the employer was ordered to bargain on the basis of preelection unfair labor practices. In each case the Board ruled that the union had valid authorization cards from a majority of the employees in an appropriate unit and, therefore, the employer's refusal to bargain "was motivated not by a 'good faith' doubt of the unions' majority status, but by a desire to gain time to dissipate that status."[53] The Fourth Circuit refused to enforce the Board's orders to bargain but affirmed the other unfair labor practice findings.[54]

---

[49]*Id.* at 594, 71 LRRM at 2488. In Schrementi Bros., 179 NLRB 853, 72 LRRM 1481 (1969), decided after the Supreme Court's decision in *Gissel,* the Board noted that the employer's good-faith doubt in refusing to recognize a union is now "largely irrelevant." For a discussion of the open question of how irrelevant is "largely irrelevant," see Christensen & Christensen, *supra* note 34.

[50]395 US at 594, 71 LRRM at 2488.

[51]NLRB v. Gissel Packing Co., 398 F2d 336, 68 LRRM 2636 (CA 4, 1968); NLRB v. Heck's, 398 F2d 337, 68 LRRM 2638 (CA 4, 1968); NLRB v. General Steel Prods., 398 F2d 339, 68 LRRM 2639 (CA 4, 1968).

[52]NLRB v. Sinclair Co., 397 F2d 157, 68 LRRM 2720 (CA 1, 1968), *enforcing,* 164 NLRB 261, 65 LRRM 1087 (1967).

[53]NLRB v. Gissel Packing Co., *supra* note 48, at 583, 71 LRRM at 2483.

[54]NLRB v. General Steel Prods., *supra* note 51.

The facts in *Sinclair* were similar to those in the Fourth Circuit cases, except that an additional issue was raised as to whether specific statements made by the employer—found by the Board to be unfair labor practices—fell outside the protection of the First Amendment of the Constitution and section 8(c) of the Act.[55] The First Circuit upheld both the Board's findings of unfair labor practices and its order requiring the employer to recognize and bargain with the union.[56]

The Supreme Court framed the questions as follows:

> [1] [W]hether the duty to bargain can arise without a Board election under the Act; [2] whether union authorization cards, if obtained from a majority of employees without misrepresentation or coercion, are reliable enough to provide a valid, alternate route to majority status; [3] whether a bargaining order is an appropriate and authorized remedy where an employer rejects a card majority while at the same time committing unfair labor practices that tend to undermine the union's majority and make a fair election an unlikely possibility.[57]

The Court answered each question in the affirmative.

First, the Court noted that the establishment of a bargaining obligation by means other than a Board election was an accepted principle under both the Wagner Act and the Taft-Hartley Act.[58] It emphasized that Congress had rejected a House bill[59] in 1947 which would have conditioned a section 8(a)(5) violation upon either a Board election or current recognition of a union.[60] The Court saw nothing in section 9(c)(1)(B), by which the 1947 amendments gave employers the right to petition for elections, to suggest that Congress intended to relieve an employer of his bargaining obligation "where, without good faith, he engaged in unfair labor practices disruptive of the Board's election machinery."[61] The Court noted that, although

---

[55]*See* Chapter 6, "Interference With Protected Rights," at notes 58–67, for a discussion of the Supreme Court's treatment of this issue. *See also* Margulies, NLRB v. Gissel Packing Co.: *A Standard Without a Following (The Need for Reappraisal of Employer Free Speech Rights in the Organizing Campaign)*, 22 WILLAMETTE L. REV. 459 (1986).

[56]*Supra* note 52.

[57]395 US at 579, 71 LRRM at 2482. A fourth question related to free speech and §8(c) of the Act. *See supra* note 55.

[58]*Supra* note 48, 71 LRRM at 2489 (citing Mine Workers v. Arkansas Oak Flooring Co., 351 US 62, 37 LRRM 2828 (1956); Franks Bros. v. NLRB, 321 US 702, 14 LRRM 591 (1944); NLRB v. Bradford Dyeing Ass'n, 310 US 318, 339–40, 6 LRRM 684 (1940)).

[59]Section 8(1)(5) of H.R. 3020, 80th Cong., 1st Sess. (1947).

[60]*See supra* note 3.

[61]395 US at 600, 71 LRRM at 2490.

a union had to win a secret-ballot election in order to obtain the benefits of a Board *certification*, an employer's *duty to bargain* might arise even in the absence of such an election.

On the second question, the Court decided that authorization cards could be reliable evidence of a union's majority status where, due to employer unfair labor practices, "a fair election probably could not have been held, or where an election that was held was in fact set aside."[62] The Court agreed with the Board that "cards, though admittedly inferior to the election process, can adequately reflect employee sentiment when that process has been impeded . . . ."[63]

In each of the four cases before the Court, the union had used a "single-purpose" card, that is, a card that clearly designated the union as the employees' bargaining representative and that did not state that it might also be used to obtain an election. The only case that raised an issue as to the validity of these "single purpose" cards, or the manner in which they were obtained, was *General Steel*. In that case, in reliance on and in approval of the Board's *Cumberland Shoe*[64] doctrine, the Court upheld the validity of such cards and specifically approved the Board's findings as to the manner in which they had been solicited by the union:

> [I]f the card itself is unambiguous (*i.e.*, states on its face that the signer authorizes the union to represent the employee for collective bargaining purposes and not to seek an election), it will be counted unless it is proved that the employee was told that the card was to be used *solely* for the purpose of obtaining an election.[65]

---

[62]*Id.* at 601 n.18, 71 LRRM at 2491–92, n.18.

[63]*Id.* at 603, 71 LRRM at 2491. The Court rejected the employers' general arguments that the cards were inherently unreliable because of group pressure, that cards did not allow employees to express an informed choice, and that misrepresentation and coercion are too often present in card solicitation. However, the Court expressly refused to decide whether a union could rely on authorization cards as a "freely interchangeable substitute for elections where there has been no election interference." *Id.* at 601 n.18, 71 LRRM at 2491 n.18.

[64]144 NLRB 1268, 54 LRRM 1233 (1963), *enforced*, 351 F2d 917, 60 LRRM 2305 (CA 6, 1965). *See* discussion *infra* at notes 268–272.

[65]395 US at 584, 71 LRRM at 2484 (emphasis in original).

Resolving a conflict among the circuits,[66] the Court concluded that

> employees should be bound by the clear language of what they sign unless that language is deliberately and clearly canceled by a union adherent with words calculated to direct the signer to disregard and forget the language above his signature.[67]

The Court thus approved the solicitation of such cards, even when accompanied by a statement that the card would probably first be used to obtain an election. The Court noted that elections are held in the vast majority of cases and Board rules require signatures from at least 30 percent of the employees before the Board will entertain a union's petition for an election.[68]

The Court recognized that probing an employee's subjective motivation in signing a card would be inherently unreliable, noting that "employees are more likely than not, many months after a card drive and in response to questions by company counsel, to give testimony damaging to the union . . . ."[69] Thus, single-purpose cards should be invalidated only if the employee was actually told that the sole purpose of the card was to obtain a Board election. The Court expressly declined to comment on the validity of "ambiguous, dual-purpose cards."[70]

Finally, the Court in *Gissel* delineated three categories of unfair labor practices, based on the relative severity of the vio-

---

[66]The Court reviewed the differing views of the circuits as follows:

> [E]ven where the cards are unambiguous on their face, both the Second Circuit and the Fifth Circuit have joined the Fourth Circuit below in rejecting the Board's rule that the cards will be counted unless the solicitor's statements amounted under the circumstances to an assurance that the cards would be used only for an election. And even those circuits which have adopted the Board's approach have criticized the Board for tending too often to apply the Cumberland rule too mechanically, declining occasionally to uphold the Board's application of its own rule in a given case. Among those who reject the Cumberland rule, the Fifth Circuit agrees with the Second Circuit that a card will be vitiated if an employee was left with the impression that he would be able to resolve any lingering doubts and make a final decision in an election, and further requires that the Board probe the subjective intent of each signer, an inquiry expressly avoided by Cumberland. Where the cards are ambiguous on their face, the Fifth Circuit, joined by the Eighth Circuit departs still further from the Board rule. And there is a conflict among those courts which otherwise follow the Board as to single-purpose cards.

Id. at 604–5, 71 LRRM at 2492 (citations omitted).

[67]*Id.* at 606, 71 LRRM at 2493.

[68]*See* Chapter 10, "Representation Proceedings and Elections."

[69]395 US at 608, 71 LRRM at 2493.

[70]*Id.* at 609, 71 LRRM at 2493. *See* notes 85–86 *infra* and accompanying text.

lations, which it would consider in deciding whether a bargaining order would be an appropriate remedy in card-based majority cases. In the first category, where the employer has committed "outrageous" and "pervasive" unfair labor practices which rendered the holding of an untainted election *impossible*, a bargaining order would be an appropriate remedy "without need of inquiry into majority status on the basis of cards or otherwise."[71] In the second category, cases "marked by less pervasive practices which nonetheless still have the tendency to undermine majority strength and impede the election processes,"[72] a bargaining order could likewise be an appropriate remedy. This was the appropriate category, the Court said, for the cases before it. The Court also identified a third category of cases in which the unfair labor practices are so minor that, "because of their minimal impact on the election machinery, [they] will not sustain a bargaining order."[73]

Noting the wide agreement that a bargaining order was inappropriate in the third category, the Court stated that "[t]he only effect of our holding here is to approve the Board's use of the bargaining order" in cases falling into the second category.[74] In this second category, the Court wrote, a bargaining order may issue if the Board finds that the possibility of "erasing the effects" of past unfair labor practices and insuring a fair election by "traditional means" is "slight" and that the interests of the employees who had signed cards would be better protected by a bargaining order.[75] Despite the Court's dictum that bargaining orders could issue in cases in the first category, even absent proof of the union's majority status, it was not until 1981 that the Board asserted the authority to issue bargaining orders in such cases.[76]

---

[71]*Id.* at 613, 71 LRRM at 2495.

[72]*Id.* at 614, 71 LRRM at 2495. In Gottfried v. Mayco Plastics, 615 F2d 1360, 103 LRRM 3104, 3105 (CA 6, 1980), the Sixth Circuit affirmed the district court's bargaining order, 472 F Supp 1161, 101 LRRM 2815 (ED Mich, 1979), pending final disposition of unfair labor practice charges before the NLRB, where the parties had stipulated that reasonable cause existed to believe that the employer's actions were in violation of the LMRA and that a bargaining order was a "just and proper relief and 10(j) is a proper remedy to preserve the status quo."

[73]395 US at 614–15, 71 LRRM at 2496.

[74]*Id.* at 614–15, 71 LRRM at 2495.

[75]*Id.* at 614–15, 71 LRRM at 2496.

[76]*See* notes 211–226 *infra* and accompanying text.

III. ELEMENTS OF A BARGAINING OBLIGATION IN THE ABSENCE OF AN ELECTION

A. Majority Representation

The initial inquiry in these cases is whether a majority of the employees in an appropriate unit have signed authorization cards as of the date of the employer's alleged refusal to bargain.[77] The refusal may occur either when the employer receives the demand[78] or when the employer sends a reply.[79] In *Conren, Inc.*[80] a union was not precluded from insisting on recognition based on a card majority during the 1-year period following an election even though a second election could not be held.

1. Form of Designation. The card may be a regular union membership card,[81] an application for membership,[82] a dues checkoff authorization,[83] or simply a card that explicitly designates the union as the signer's bargaining representative.[84] The status of dual-purpose cards is not entirely clear. Although the Board traditionally honored such cards,[85] many appellate

---

[77] *See* Jasta Mfg. Co., 246 NLRB 48, 102 LRRM 1610 (1979), *enforced*, 634 F2d 623, 108 LRRM 2103 (CA 4, 1980) (card of employee whose name appeared on *Excelsior* (Excelsior Underwear, 156 NLRB 1236, 61 LRRM 1217 (1966) list counted as being that of unit employee); Dadco Fashions, 243 NLRB 1193, 102 LRRM 1027 (1979), *enforced*, 632 F2d 493, 106 LRRM 2022 (CA 5, 1980) (card of employee whose name was not on payroll records during pertinent period was not counted).

[78] Allegheny Pepsi-Cola Bottling Co. v. NLRB, 312 F2d 529, 52 LRRM 2019 (CA 3, 1962), *enforcing* 134 NLRB 388, 49 LRRM 1169 (1961).

[79] NLRB v. Burton Dixie Corp., 210 F2d 199, 33 LRRM 2483 (CA 10, 1954), *enforcing* 103 NLRB 880, 31 LRRM 1589 (1953).

[80] 156 NLRB 592, 61 LRRM 1090 (1966), *enforced*, 368 F2d 173, 63 LRRM 2273 (CA 7, 1966), *cert. denied*, 386 US 974, 64 LRRM 2640 (1967). The Board held that neither the legislative history of the 12-month rule in §9(c)(3), "nor its plain terms, manifest any congressional purpose to preclude a union from obtaining recognition either without an election or within a year after an election which it did not win, if it in fact acquires majority status in an appropriate unit." *Id.* at 599.

[81] NLRB v. Federbush Co., 121 F2d 954, 8 LRRM 531 (CA 2, 1941).

[82] NLRB v. Valley Broadcasting Co., 189 F2d 582, 28 LRRM 2148 (CA 6, 1951); NLRB v. Dahlstrom Metallic Door Co., 112 F2d 756, 6 LRRM 746 (CA 2, 1940).

[83] Lebanon Steel Foundry v. NLRB, 130 F2d 404, 10 LRRM 760 (CA DC), *cert. denied*, 317 US 659, 11 LRRM 839 (1942).

[84] NLRB v. Stow Mfg. Co., 217 F2d 900, 35 LRRM 2210 (CA 2, 1954), *cert. denied*, 348 US 964, 35 LRRM 2612 (1955).

[85] *E.g.*, World-Wide Press, 242 NLRB 346, 101 LRRM 1205 (1979). However, in a case decided after the Supreme Court's decision in *Gissel*, the Board rejected as ambiguous certain dual-purpose cards where the top half of the card stated that its purpose was to obtain an election and the bottom half contained a reference to the signer being invited to join the union "should the union be elected" to represent him. John S. Barnes Corp., 180 NLRB 911, 73 LRRM 1215 (1970), *enforced*, 77 LRRM 2372 (CA DC), *cert. denied*, 404 US 854, 78 LRRM 2465 (1971). For a general discussion of the types and purposes of union authorization cards, see S.I. SCHLOSSBERG & J.A. SCOTT, ORGANIZING AND THE LAW 58–61 (4th ed. 1991).

courts disagreed with the Board's practice.[86] In 1989, the Board refused to grant a bargaining order in favor of a union whose majority status was asserted on the basis of cards that included both an unambiguous grant of representation rights on its front, and a statement on its reverse side that "The purpose of signing this Authorization card is to have the [NLRB] conduct a Secret Ballot Election . . . at your place of work."[87] The Board ruled that the card was ambiguous, then looked to the conduct of its solicitors to determine whether the ambiguity had been so removed that signatory employees would understand that signing the cards could lead to representation without an election. Finding that the ambiguity had not been removed during solicitation, the Board withheld the bargaining order.

2. Name of Union. It is sufficient if union designation is indicated in general terms, without identifying either a particular local or even the international union. Cards bearing the simple designation "AFL-CIO" have been held valid.[88]

3. Status of the Solicitor. Any person other than a representative of management may normally solicit an employee's signature on an authorization card. Cards that have been solicited directly by a supervisor will usually be held invalid.[89] The Board has held, however, that the mere "passing along" of a card or other incidental involvement by a supervisor does not constitute invalidating solicitation.[90]

4. Time of Execution. In order to be counted in determining a union's majority status, cards must have been signed during

---

[86]*See* NLRB v. Lenz Co., 396 F2d 905, 68 LRRM 2577 (CA 6, 1968), *denying enforcement in pertinent part to* 153 NLRB 1399, 59 LRRM 1638 (1965); Dayco Corp. v. NLRB, 382 F2d 577, 65 LRRM 3092 (CA 6, 1967); NLRB v. S.E. Nichols-Dover Co., 380 F2d 438, 65 LRRM 2655 (CA 2, 1967); NLRB v. Peterson Bros., 342 F2d 221, 58 LRRM 2570 (CA 5, 1965).

[87]Nissan Research & Dev., 296 NLRB No. 80, 132 LRRM 1169, 1169 (1989).

[88]NLRB v. Southbridge Sheet Metal Works, 380 F2d 851, 65 LRRM 2916 (CA 1, 1967); Air Traffic Controllers, 261 NLRB 922, 110 LRRM 1129 (1982). *See also* World-Wide Press, *supra* note 85 (cards valid although name and number of local union were not filled in). But if an employee executes similar cards for rival unions, neither card will be counted. Human Dev. Ass'n, 293 NLRB 1228, 132 LRRM 1068 (1989); International Metal Prods. Co., 104 NLRB 1076, 32 LRRM 1194 (1953). However, cards signed for two unions *will* be deemed valid where the employees understood that they authorized joint representation. Bolsa Drainage, 242 NLRB 728, 101 LRRM 1372 (1979).

[89]Neuman Nursing Home, 270 NLRB 663, 116 LRRM 1447 (1984); Leas & McVitty, 155 NLRB 389, 60 LRRM 1333 (1965); Insular Chem. Corp., 128 NLRB 93, 46 LRRM 1268 (1960); Flint River Mills, 107 NLRB 472, 33 LRRM 1177 (1953).

[90]Engineers & Fabricators v. NLRB, 376 F2d 482, 64 LRRM 2849 (CA 5, 1967). *See also* Tall Pines Inn, 268 NLRB 1392, 116 LRRM 1389 (1984) (supervisor attended union meeting and signed card after majority of employees had signed cards).

the union's current organizing campaign.[91] In a protracted campaign, however, cards signed more than a year prior to the union's demand for recognition may be considered "stale" and thus not count toward the union's majority.[92]

5. Authentication. The General Counsel bears the burden of proving a card's authenticity.[93] The employees may be called as witnesses to identify their signatures. Other competent evidence, such as the testimony of a witness to the card's execution, may also be used for this purpose.[94]

B. Demand for Recognition in an Appropriate Unit

A union must request, or "demand," recognition before an employer can be required to recognize the union. The union need not explicitly state that it enjoys majority status,[95] but its

---

[91]Grand Union Co., 112 NLRB 589, 43 LRRM 1165 (1958), *enforced*, 279 F2d 83, 46 LRRM 2492 (CA 2, 1960). In Greenfield Components Corp. v. NLRB, 317 F2d 85, 53 LRRM 2145 (CA 1, 1963), the Board counted cards signed nine months before the demand was made, there having been no hiatus in the union's organizational effort. And a period exceeding 2 years was not too long where there was a delay in proceeding upon a petition for election. Northern Trust Co., 69 NLRB 652, 18 LRRM 1252 (1946). Undated cards have been counted where they were received by the NLRB's regional office prior to the union's demand for recognition, Curlee Clothing Co., 240 NLRB 355, 100 LRRM 1423 (1979), *enforced*, 607 F2d 1213, 102 LRRM 2675 (CA 8, 1979), and where there was credible evidence as to when they were signed. World-Wide Press, *supra* note 85. *But see* Burger King, 258 NLRB 1293, 108 LRRM 1318 (1981), *enforced sub nom.* NLRB v. Greyhound Food Mgmt., 709 F2d 1506, 113 LRRM 3816 (CA 6, 1983) (undated card not counted in absence of any reliable evidence of date of execution).

[92]Sertafilm, Atlas Microfilming Div., 267 NLRB 682, 114 LRRM 1120 (1983), *enforced*, 753 F2d 313, 118 LRRM 2628 (CA 3, 1985); Blade-Tribune Publishing Co., 161 NLRB 1512, 63 LRRM 1484 (1966); Grand Union Co., *supra* note 91. *See* Mandel Mgmt. Co., 245 NLRB 273, 102 LRRM 1449 (1979) (cards of former employees held invalid when shown that they were not signed on dates indicated on cards). *But see* NLRB v. Fort Vancouver Plywood Co., 604 F2d 596, 102 LRRM 2232 (CA 9, 1979), *cert. denied*, 445 US 915, 103 LRRM 2668 (1980) (cards backdated to point prior to employees' discharges were held valid); Axton Candy & Tobacco Co., 241 NLRB 1034, 101 LRRM 1043 (1979), *enforcement granted in part and denied in part*, 645 F2d 555, 107 LRRM 2863 (CA 6, 1981) (misdated cards counted toward union's majority absent evidence they were purposely misdated and did not show union support).

[93]Ona Corp., 261 NLRB 1378, 110 LRRM 1271 (1982), *enforcement granted in part and denied in part*, 729 F2d 713, 115 LRRM 3665 (CA 11, 1984); Dixie Cup, 157 NLRB 167, 61 LRRM 1329 (1966). However, the General Counsel is under no obligation to prove that the employees read the cards before signing. World-Wide Press, *supra* note 85; Southern Cotton Oil Crude Mill, 144 NLRB 959, 54 LRRM 1161 (1963); Franke's, Inc., 142 NLRB 551, 53 LRRM 1086 (1963).

[94]Colson Corp. v. NLRB, 347 F2d 128, 59 LRRM 2512 (CA 8), *cert. denied*, 382 US 904, 60 LRRM 2353 (1965); NLRB v. Economy Food Center, 333 F2d 468, 56 LRRM 2263 (CA 7, 1964); Crest Indus. Corp., 276 NLRB 490, 120 LRRM 1101 (1985). *But see* Stop N' Go, 279 NLRB 344, 122 LRRM 1183 (1986) (cards not authenticated, union agent neither saw them executed nor received them directly from signatories).

[95]Lincoln Mfg. Co., 160 NLRB 1866, 63 LRRM 1245 (1966), *enforced*, 382 F2d 411, 65 LRRM 2913 (CA 7), *cert. denied*, 389 US 972, 66 LRRM 2663 (1967).

request must be made when the union in fact possesses signed authorizations from a majority of the employees in an appropriate unit.[96] If the Board deems an initial demand to be a continuing one, however, the union's initial deficiency in cards may be overcome by the subsequent solicitation of additional cards.[97] The union's request may also be insufficient if, under all the circumstances, it is too ambiguous to apprise the employer of the contemplated unit.[98]

A request or demand is not required, however, when the bargaining order is designed to remedy unfair labor practices other than a refusal to bargain.[99] The Board's theory in such cases is that the employer, whether or not guilty of a refusal to bargain, has impaired the election process by committing unfair labor practices, thereby reducing the union from majority to minority status.[100] This rule applies even if the union has petitioned the Board for an election.[101]

A valid demand for recognition or bargaining need not be made in any particular form so long as it clearly indicates a desire to negotiate and bargain on behalf of employees in an appropri-

---

[96]Decision, Inc., 166 NLRB 464, 65 LRRM 1660 (1967). For treatment of bargaining units generally, *see* Chapter 11, "Appropriate Bargaining Units."

[97]Ed's Foodland of Springfield, 159 NLRB 1256, 62 LRRM 1465 (1966). *See also* Fall River Dyeing & Finishing Corp. v. NLRB, 482 US 27, 125 LRRM 2441 (1987), where the Supreme Court approved the Board's finding of a continuing demand for recognition in a successorship setting. *But see* Filler Prods. v. NLRB, 376 F2d 369, 65 LRRM 2029 (CA 4, 1967), denying enforcement of a bargaining order based on authorization cards where the employer had refused to read the letter containing the request and claim of majority status.

[98]National Can Co. v. NLRB, 374 F2d 796, 64 LRRM 2607 (CA 7, 1967), *denying enforcement to* 159 NLRB 647, 62 LRRM 1403 (1966); Bryant Chucking Grinder Co., 160 NLRB 1526, 63 LRRM 1185 (1966), *enforced,* 389 F2d 565, 67 LRRM 2017 (CA 2, 1967), *cert. denied,* 392 US 908, 68 LRRM 2408 (1968). *See* Marion Center Supply, 277 NLRB 262, 120 LRRM 1299 (1985) (vague demand offset by employer's notice of union's election petition specifying unit).

[99]Quality Aluminum Prods., 278 NLRB 338, 121 LRRM 1187 (1986), *enforced,* 813 F2d 795, 125 LRRM 2838 (CA 6, 1987); Naum Bros., 240 NLRB 311, 100 LRRM 1219 (1979), *enforced,* 637 F2d 589, 106 LRRM 2939 (CA 6, 1980). *See generally* NLRB v. Gissel Packing Co., 395 US 575, 71 LRRM 2481 (1969). *See also* discussion *infra* at notes 194–210.

[100]Steelworkers v. NLRB (Northwest Eng'g Co.), 376 F2d 770, 64 LRRM 2650 (CA DC, 1967), *enforcing* 148 NLRB 1136, 57 LRRM 1116 (1964) *and* 158 NLRB 624, 62 LRRM 1089 (1966), *cert. denied,* 389 US 932, 66 LRRM 2444 (1967); American Sanitary Prods. Co. v. NLRB, 382 F2d 53, 65 LRRM 3122 (CA 10, 1967); Quality Aluminum Prods., *supra* note 99; Bryant Chucking Grinder Co., *supra* note 98. *But see* NLRB v. Li'l Gen. Stores, 422 F2d 571, 73 LRRM 2522, 2525 (CA 5, 1970). The Fifth Circuit refused to enforce a bargaining order where there were unfair labor practices described as "extensive if not bordering on the flagrant," because the union had neither claimed a majority nor demanded recognition and there was no finding that the employer was aware of the union's majority when the petition for an election was filed.

[101]Mink-Dayton, Inc., 166 NLRB 604, 65 LRRM 1642 (1967), *enforced,* 416 F2d 327, 72 LRRM 2232 (CA 6, 1969), *cert. denied,* 400 US 829, 75 LRRM 2378 (1970); Tonkin Corp. of Cal., 165 NLRB 607, 65 LRRM 1521 (1967). *Cf.* Filler Prods. v. NLRB, *supra* note 97.

ate unit.[102] A union's request could therefore be addressed to almost any upper level representative of management.[103] A management representative's actual lack of authority to discuss the matter does not relieve the employer of its duty to recognize the union.[104] And where the refusal of recognition is unlawful, the employer is not assisted by the reply that the matter "is in the hands of an attorney."[105] The demand need not be stated in formal or precise terms. For example, in *Laclede Cab Co.*[106] the Board held that a union did not request recognition when its agent, asserting that he represented a discharged employee, requested that the latter be reinstated.[107] However, later that same day the union agent asked a supervisor to set a time to negotiate a collective bargaining agreement in a unit covering all employees at the facility; the Board held that the latter request constituted a valid demand for recognition and bargaining.[108]

Additionally, an employer's refusal to accept a union's letter demanding recognition will not invalidate the demand if the employer has notice of the contents of the letter.[109] In such a case the employer was held to have "reasonably suspected" a letter to be a demand for recognition, for the employer had previously committed extensive violations of section 8(a)(1) and the letter clearly came from the union.[110]

C. Employer Unfair Labor Practices

In *Gissel*, the Supreme Court approved what it characterized as the Board's "current practice.":[111]

---

[102]NLRB v. Cofer, 637 F2d 1309, 106 LRRM 2471 (CA 9, 1981), *enforcing* 233 NLRB 527, 96 LRRM 1613 (1977); Soil Eng'g & Exploration Co., 269 NLRB 55, 116 LRRM 1343 (1984).

[103]NLRB v. Tri-City Linen Supply, 579 F2d 51, 98 LRRM 2155 (CA 9, 1978); S.E. Nichols-Dover Co., 156 NLRB 1201, 61 LRRM 1234 (1966), *enforcement denied on other grounds*, 380 F2d 438, 65 LRRM 2655 (CA 2, 1967).

[104]S.E. Nichols-Dover Co., *supra* note 103, at 1201, 1212.

[105]*Id.* Furthermore, if the union's initial request is adequate, it need not be repeated to the employer's attorney. *Id.*

[106]236 NLRB 206, 98 LRRM 1426 (1978).

[107]*Id.*

[108]*Id.*

[109]Wayne Trophy Corp., 236 NLRB 299, 99 LRRM 1438 (1978), *enforced*, 595 F2d 1213, 103 LRRM 2604 (CA 3, 1979).

[110]*Id. But see* R & H Diesel & Trailer Serv., 238 NLRB 1432, 99 LRRM 1374 (1978) (where employer marked letter from union "moved, left no address" and returned it unopened, Board did not infer that employer knew letter contained demand for recognition).

[111]NLRB v. Gissel Packing Co., *supra* note 99, at 591, 71 LRRM at 2487.

> When confronted by a recognition demand based on possession of cards allegedly signed by a majority of his employees, an employer need not grant recognition immediately, but may, unless he has knowledge independently of the cards that the union has a majority, decline the union's request and insist on an election, either by requesting the union to file an election petition or by filing such a petition himself under §9(c)(1)(B). If, however, the employer commits independent and substantial unfair labor practices disruptive of election conditions, the Board may withhold the election or set it aside, and issue instead a bargaining order as a remedy for the various violations. A bargaining order will not issue, of course, if the union obtained the cards through misrepresentation or coercion or if the employer's unfair labor practices are unrelated generally to the representation campaign.[112]

Thus, the propriety of a bargaining order depends in part on the nature and extent of the employer's misconduct. The Court indicated that where the misconduct was egregious, the bargaining order might issue regardless of the union's majority status. In 1981, in *United Dairy Farmers Cooperative Ass'n*,[113] the Board issued an order to bargain where there was no proof of the union's majority after the Third Circuit, directing the Board to reconsider the matter, remanded an earlier order which had withheld that remedy.[114] The Board issued another such order in *Conair Corp.*,[115] but the Court of Appeals for the District of Columbia Circuit, disagreeing with the Third Circuit, refused enforcement.[116] The court wrote: "Without a clear direction from Congress, we are not prepared to recognize administrative authority, or arrogate power to ourselves, to remedy one possible injustice by taking the substantial chance of imposing another."[117] Shortly later the Board embraced that reasoning, concluded that such orders are unwarranted, and ceased issuing them.[118]

---

[112]*Id.*

[113]257 NLRB 772, 107 LRRM 1577 (1981).

[114]242 NLRB 1026, 101 LRRM 1278 (1979), *aff'd and remanded for reconsideration of bargaining-order remedy*, 633 F2d 1054, 105 LRRM 3034 (CA 3, 1979).

[115]261 NLRB 1189, 110 LRRM 1161 (1982).

[116]Conair Corp. v. NLRB, 721 F2d 1355, 114 LRRM 3169 (CA DC, 1983), *cert. denied sub nom.* Ladies' Garment Workers Local 222 v. NLRB, 467 US 1241, 116 LRRM 2632 (1984).

[117]*Id.* at 1383, 114 LRRM at 3189.

[118]Gourmet Foods, 270 NLRB 578, 116 LRRM 1105 (1984) (overruling United Dairy Farmers, *supra* note 113 and Conair, *supra* note 115). *See* NLRB v. Pace Oldsmobile, 739 F2d 108, 116 NLRB 3137 (CA 2, 1984), *denying enforcement to* 265 NLRB 1527, 112 LRRM 1186 (1982) (court expressed approval of *Gourmet Foods*). *See also* Abbey's Transp. Servs., 284 NLRB 698, 125 LRRM 1242 (1987), *enforced*, 837 F2d 575, 127 LRRM 2437 (CA 2, 1988).

Whether or not a bargaining order in the absence of majority status is ever appropriate in "'exceptional' cases marked by 'outrageous' and 'pervasive' unfair labor practices,"[119] the *Gissel* decision approved the bargaining order in the second category of "less extraordinary cases marked by less pervasive practices which nonetheless still have the tendency to undermine majority strength and impede the election processes" when "at one point the union had a majority."[120]

1. Conduct Warranting a *Gissel* Bargaining Order. *a. No Per Se Rules.* The Board has rejected any mechanical application of *Gissel* standards governing the issuance of bargaining orders. When the Board considers whether employer unfair labor practices warrant a *Gissel* bargaining order, its task is

> somehow to quantify the impact upon employees which follows from unlawful conduct by their employer. In such an inquiry, there can be few per se rules. [The Board] must be alert in each case to the . . . infinitely various circumstances which will influence employee perceptions of such prohibited conduct.[121]

In general, bargaining orders have issued where the union has at some point attained majority status and the employer has committed unfair labor practices which, in the Board's view, rendered the holding of a fair election unlikely.[122] The application

---

[119] NLRB v. Gissel Pkg. Co., *supra* note 99, at 613, 71 LRRM at 2495.

[120] *Id.* at 614, 71 LRRM 2495–96.

[121] General Stencils, Inc., 195 NLRB 1109, 1112, 79 LRRM 1608, 1611 (1972) (Chairman Miller, dissenting; footnote omitted), *enforcement denied*, 472 F2d 170, 82 LRRM 2081 (CA 2, 1972).

[122] *See, e.g.*, Faith Garment Co. Div., 246 NLRB 299, 102 LRRM 1515 (1979), *enforced*, 630 F2d 630, 105 LRRM 2568 (CA 8, 1980); Rexart Color & Chem. Co., 246 NLRB 240, 102 LRRM 1512 (1979); Kermit Super Valu, 245 NLRB 1077, 102 LRRM 1512 (1979). Early cases in which the Board charted this course include: Marie Phillips, Inc., 178 NLRB 340, 72 LRRM 1103 (1969), *enforced sub nom.* Ladies' Garment Workers Local 153 v. NLRB, 443 F2d 667, 75 LRRM 2539 (CA DC, 1970), *cert. denied*, 403 US 905, 77 LRRM 2404 (1971); Garland Knitting Mills, 178 NLRB 396, 72 LRRM 1112 (1969); Schrementi Bros., 179 NLRB 853, 72 LRRM 1481 (1969). In Central Soya of Canton, 180 NLRB 546, 73 LRRM 1069 (1970), the Board stressed that relatively minor unfair labor practices were not sufficient to indicate that a coercion-free rerun election could not be held; for that reason a bargaining order was not issued. In Gibson Prods. Co., 185 NLRB 362, 75 LRRM 1055, 1057 (1970), the Board held that *Gissel* "contemplated that the propriety of the bargaining order would be judged as of the time of the commission of the unfair labor practices and not in the light of subsequent events"; *see also* American Cable Sys., 179 NLRB 846, 72 LRRM 1524 (1969), where the Board ordered the employer to bargain because of unfair labor practices which were committed in 1965 and which "undermined the Union's majority and caused an election to be a less reliable guide . . . than the signed authorization cards . . . ." The Fifth Circuit refused to enforce the order and remanded because of the Board's failure to consider events in the intervening years which could have made a free election possible. NLRB v. American Cable Sys., 427 F2d 446, 73 LRRM 2913 (CA 5), *cert. denied*, 400 US 957, 75 LRRM 2810 (1970).

of these broad principles to specific situations is examined below.

b. "Hallmark" Violations: Invasive Employer Conduct. Some employer unfair labor practices are so likely to impair employee free choice that they will usually justify a bargaining order against the employer who commits them. These violations are likely to take the form of actions rather than threats. As the Second Circuit explained

> Certain violations have been regularly regarded by the Board and the courts as highly coercive. These are the so-called "hallmark" violations and their presence will support the issuance of a bargaining order unless some significant mitigating circumstance exists. They include such employer misbehavior as the closing of a plant or threats of plant closure or loss of employment, the grant of benefits to employees, or the reassignment, demotion or discharge of union adherents in violation of §8(a)(3) of the Act.[123]

Although the Board has never fully catalogued these violations, it has consistently recognized that some employer violations are more invasive of employee free choice than others. The Board has explained, for example, that

> The discharge of employees because of union activity is one of the most flagrant means by which an employer can hope to dissuade employees from selecting a bargaining representative because no event can have more crippling consequences to the exercise of Section 7 rights than the loss of work.[124]

By similar reasoning, a bargaining order has been deemed appropriate where the employer (1) closed one store in order to discourage union activity at several of its other stores that were also being organized;[125] (2) partially closed a plant;[126] (3) partially closed a plant and subcontracted other unit work;[127] (4) laid off all unit employees and transferred the work to another location;[128] (5) subcontracted all of the work of the bargaining unit;[129] and (6) unlawfully disciplined, dis-

---

[123]NLRB v. Jamaica Towing Co., 632 F2d 208, 212, 105 LRRM 2959, 2962 (CA 2, 1980), *denying enforcement in pertinent part to* 247 NLRB 353, 103 LRRM 1161 (1980) (footnotes omitted). *See also* General Stencils, Inc., *supra* note 121 (dissent of Chairman Miller).

[124]Apple Tree Chevrolet, 237 NLRB 867, 99 LRRM 1505, 1507 (1978), *enforcement denied in pertinent part and remanded*, 608 F2d 988, 103 LRRM 2066 (CA 4, 1979), *on remand*, 251 NLRB 666, 105 LRRM 1220 (1980), *enforcement denied*, 671 F2d 838, 109 LRRM 2946 (CA 4, 1982).

[125]Serv-U-Stores, 225 NLRB 37, 93 LRRM 1033 (1976).

[126]Great Chinese Am. Sewing Co. v. NLRB, 578 F2d 251, 99 LRRM 2347 (CA 9, 1978). *See also* Elliot River Tours, Inc., 246 NLRB 935, 103 LRRM 1095, 1096 (1979) (closing of school found to be a violation of §8(a)(5)).

[127]Great Chinese Am. Sewing Co. v. NLRB, *supra* note 126.

[128]Case, Inc., 237 NLRB 798, 99 LRRM 1159 (1978), *enforcement denied in pertinent part sub nom.* NLRB v. Gibraltar Indus., 653 F2d 1091, 107 LRRM 3307 (CA 6, 1981).

[129]Townhouse TV & Appliances, 213 NLRB 716, 88 LRRM 1295 (1974), *enforcement granted in part*, 531 F2d 826, 91 LRRM 2636 (CA 7, 1976).

charged,[130] or locked out employees,[131] or refused to reinstate strikers who made unconditional offers to return to work.[132] In some cases, the Board has granted these bargaining orders on the explicit ground that the employer's unfair labor practices constituted "hallmark" violations.[133] The courts have made clear, however, that even the presence of such hallmark violations will not support a bargaining order if there are unusual or extenuating circumstances.[134]

Bargaining orders have also been deemed appropriate where, in the face of union activity, work rules have been enforced more stringently,[135] or new, more onerous, work rules have been introduced,[136] and where the employer transferred or reduced the work hours of union adherents,[137] or denied a vacation

---

[130]NLRB v. Gordon, 792 F2d 29, 122 LRRM 2489 (CA 2), *cert. denied*, 479 US 931, 123 LRRM 2904 (1986), *enforcing* 273 NLRB 420, 118 LRRM 1084 (1984); Lotts Elec. Co., 293 NLRB 297, 131 LRRM 1657 (1989); Gupta Permold Corp., 289 NLRB 1234, 131 LRRM 1018 (1988); Honeycomb Plastics, 288 NLRB 413, 130 LRRM 1511 (1988); Montgomery Ward Co., 288 NLRB 126, 130 LRRM 1369 (1988); Ambulette Trans. Serv. Corp., 287 NLRB 224, 127 LRRM 1044 (1987). *See also* NLRB v. Digital Paging Sys., 659 F2d 725, 108 LRRM 3141 (CA 6, 1981), *enforcing* 249 NLRB 127, 104 LRRM 1033 (1980); Pay 'n Save Corp. v. NLRB, 641 F2d 697, 106 LRRM 3040 (CA 9, 1981), *enforcing* 247 NLRB 1346, 103 LRRM 1334 (1980); NLRB v. Bighorn Beverage Co., 614 F2d 1238, 103 LRRM 3008 (CA 9, 1980); Medline Indus. v. NLRB, 593 F2d 788, 100 LRRM 3202 (CA 7, 1979), *enforcing in part* 233 NLRB 627, 97 LRRM 1562 (1977); Bandag, Inc. v. NLRB, 583 F2d 765, 99 LRRM 3226 (CA 5, 1978); Hambre Hombre Enters. v. NLRB, 581 F2d 204, 99 LRRM 2541 (CA 9, 1978); NLRB v. Woodline, Inc., 577 F2d 463, 98 LRRM 2869 (CA 8, 1978); Multi-Medical Convalescent & Nursing Center v. NLRB, 550 F2d 974, 95 LRRM 2021 (CA 4, 1977), *cert. denied*, 434 US 835, 96 LRRM 2514 (1977); NLRB v. Montgomery Ward & Co., 554 F2d 996, 95 LRRM 2433 (CA 10, 1977); NLRB v. Pacific Southwest Airlines, 550 F2d 1148, 94 LRRM 2772 (CA 9, 1977); NLRB v. Townhouse TV & Appliances, 531 F2d 826, 91 LRRM 2636 (CA 7, 1976); NLRB v. Federated Publications (State Journal), 544 F2d 908, 93 LRRM 2877 (CA 6, 1976); NLRB v. Tahoe Vangas, 517 F2d 747, 89 LRRM 2508 (CA 9, 1975); Ethan Allen, 247 NLRB 552, 103 LRRM 1251 (1980).

[131]Crockett-Bradley, Inc., 212 NLRB 435, 87 LRRM 1597 (1974), *enforced*, 523 F2d 449, 90 LRRM 3116 (CA 5, 1975).

[132]Massachusetts Coastal Seafoods, 293 NLRB 496, 132 LRRM 1035 (1989); Hargis Mine Supply, 225 NLRB 660, 93 LRRM 1370 (1976).

[133]*E.g.*, Larid Printing, 264 NLRB 369, 111 LRRM 1631 (1982); Marion Rohr Corp., 261 NLRB 971, 110 LRRM 1149 (1982), *enforcement denied in pertinent part*, 714 F2d 228, 114 LRRM 2126 (CA 2, 1983).

[134]NLRB v. Windsor Indus., 730 F2d 860, 115 LRRM 3649 (CA 2, 1984); NLRB v. Marion Rohr Corp., *supra* note 133. *See also* Impact Indus. v. NLRB, 847 F2d 379, 128 LRRM 2455 (CA 7, 1988), *denying enforcement to* 285 NLRB 5, 128 LRRM 1122 (1987) (bargaining order refused enforcement because of lapse of 7 years, turnover in employee complement, and changed management of employer). *See generally*, Bethel & Melfi, *Judicial Enforcement of NLRB Bargaining Orders: What Influences Courts?*, 22 U.C. DAVIS L. REV. 139 (1988).

[135]Schwab Foods, 223 NLRB 394, 92 LRRM 1285 (1976), *enforced*, 549 F2d 805, 95 LRRM 2108 (CA 7, 1977).

[136]*Id.*

[137]C & W Super Mkts. v. NLRB, 581 F2d 618, 98 LRRM 3311 (CA 7, 1978); Lotts Elec. Co., *supra* note 130; Hinky Dinky Super Mkts., 247 NLRB 1176, 103 LRRM 1314 (1980), *aff'd*, 636 F2d 231, 106 LRRM 2112 (CA 8, 1980); Frederick's Foodland, 247 NLRB 284, 103 LRRM 1219 (1980), *enforcement denied in pertinent part*, 655 F2d 88, 107 LRRM 3216

request because of an employee's union activities.[138]

c. Other Specific Employer Unfair Labor Practices. (1) Threats. For a bargaining order to be an appropriate remedy, an employer need not actually take adverse action against employees. A threat of harm, even if not carried out, can be sufficiently invasive of employee free choice to render a fair election unlikely. Thus, bargaining orders have issued based on employer threats (1) to close the plant or take other such serious reprisals because of union activities;[139] (2) to impose more onerous working conditions;[140] (3) to withhold paychecks until employees' authorization cards are retrieved;[141] (4) to eliminate unit work,[142] the employees' pension and profit-sharing plan,[143] or other fringe benefits;[144] (5) to institute a time clock procedure;[145] (6) to require employees to work harder if the plant becomes unionized;[146] and to report undocumented alien employees to immigration officials.[147] The Board has also granted the bargaining order to remedy employer threats of bodily harm to employ-

---

(CA 6, 1981); Maxi Mart, Inc., 246 NLRB 1151, 103 LRRM 1105 (1979); Kroger Co., 228 NLRB 149, 94 LRRM 1586 (1977).

[138]Pope Maintenance Corp., 228 NLRB 326, 96 LRRM 1186 (1977), *enforced*, 573 F2d 898, 98 LRRM 2644 (CA 5, 1978).

[139]Midland-Ross Corp. v. NLRB, 617 F2d 977, 103 LRRM 2908 (CA 3, 1980), *cert. denied*, 449 US 871, 105 LRRM 2657 (1980); Frito-Lay, Inc. v. NLRB, 585 F2d 62, 99 LRRM 2658 (CA 3, 1978); NLRB v. Matouk Indus., 582 F2d 125, 99 LRRM 2136 (CA 1, 1978); C & W Super Mkts. v. NLRB, *supra* note 137; Great Chinese Am. Sewing Co. v. NLRB, *supra* note 126; NLRB v. Prineville Stud Co., 578 F2d 1292, 98 LRRM 3322 (CA 9, 1978); NLRB v. Pope Maintenance Corp., 573 F2d 898, 98 LRRM 2644 (CA 5, 1978); NLRB v. Solboro Knitting Mills, 572 F2d 936, 97 LRRM 3047 (CA 2), *cert. denied*, 439 US 864, 99 LRRM 2601 (1978); Drug Package Co. v. NLRB, 570 F2d 1340, 97 LRRM 2851 (CA 8, 1978); Salvation Army, Williams Memorial Residence, 293 NLRB 944, 131 LRRM 1289 (1989); Camvac Int'l, 288 NLRB 816, 130 LRRM 1447 (1988); Jacques Syl Knitwear, 247 NLRB 1525, 103 LRRM 1358 (1980), *enforced without opinion*, 672 F2d 904, 108 LRRM 2816 (CA 3, 1981), *cert. denied*, 455 US 946, 109 LRRM 2778 (1982); Wright Plastic Prods., 247 NLRB 635, 103 LRRM 1206 (1980); Ste-Mel Signs, Inc., 246 NLRB 1110, 103 LRRM 1120 (1979); Philadelphia Ambulance Serv., 238 NLRB 1070, 99 LRRM 1320 (1978); Albertson Mfg. Co., 236 NLRB 663, 98 LRRM 1402 (1978); Chatfield-Anderson Co., 236 NLRB 50, 98 LRRM 1190 (1978), *enforcement denied in pertinent part*, 606 F2d 266, 102 LRRM 2576 (CA 9, 1979); Unimedia Corp., 235 NLRB 1561, 98 LRRM 1176 (1978).

[140]Donovan v. NLRB, 520 F2d 1316, 89 LRRM 3127 (CA 2, 1975), *cert. denied*, 423 US 1053, 91 LRRM 2099 (1976); MPC Restaurant Corp. v. NLRB, 481 F2d 75, 83 LRRM 2769 (CA 2, 1973).

[141]Great Chinese Am. Sewing Co. v. NLRB, *supra* note 126.

[142]NLRB v. Eagle Material Handling, 558 F2d 160, 95 LRRM 2934 (CA 3, 1977); Ideal Elevator Corp., 295 NLRB No. 39, 132 LRRM 1078 (1989); Camvac Int'l, *supra* note 139.

[143]Chatfield-Anderson Co., *supra* note 139.

[144]Drug Package Co. v. NLRB, *supra* note 139.

[145]L'Eggs Prods., 236 NLRB 354, 99 LRRM 1304 (1978).

[146]Drug Package Co. v. NLRB, *supra* note 139.

[147]Air Prods. & Chems., 263 NLRB 341, 111 LRRM 1024 (1982), *enforced*, 717 F2d 141, 114 LRRM 2397 (CA 4, 1983).

ees,[148] or statements that violent and costly strikes would be the consequence of unionization.[149]

(2) Promise or grant of benefits. An employer may also impair employee free choice by granting or promising benefits to discourage union support. Thus, the Board has imposed a bargaining order where an employer promised or granted such benefits or solicited grievances and promised to remedy them in order to discourage union activity or membership.[150] For example, employers who granted large pay increases,[151] or Christmas bonuses,[152] to induce employee rejection of the union were ordered to bargain with the union.

(3) Unlawful efforts to undermine or discourage union support. Bargaining orders have also been issued where the employer (1) stated that selection of a union would be futile or that it would not bargain with a union;[153] (2) stated that money that could have gone to employees was spent on legal fees to fight the union;[154] (3) assisted a rival union or encouraged employees to

---

[148]Studio S.J.T., 277 NLRB 1189, 121 LRRM 1070 (1985); Ohio New & Rebuilt Parts, 267 NLRB 420, 114 LRRM 1053 (1983), *enforced*, 760 F2d 1443, 119 LRRM 2473 (CA 6), *cert. denied*, 474 US 1020, 120 LRRM 3456 (1985).

[149]NLRB v. Daybreak Lodge Nursing & Convalescent Home, 585 F2d 79, 99 LRRM 2985 (CA 3, 1978).

[150]Bandag, Inc. v. NLRB, *supra* note 130; Great Chinese Am. Sewing Co. v. NLRB, 578 F2d 251, 99 LRRM 2347 (CA 9, 1978); C & W Super Mkts. v. NLRB, *supra* note 137; Ideal Elevator Corp., *supra* note 142; Camvac Int'l, *supra* note 139; Madison Indus., 290 NLRB 1226, 129 LRRM 1323 (1988); Lapeer Foundry & Mach., 289 NLRB 952, 129 LRRM 1001 (1988); Studio S.J.T., *supra* note 148; Ohio New & Rebuilt Parts, *supra* note 148; Grandee Beer Distribs., 247 NLRB 1280, 103 LRRM 1338 (1980); Alumbaugh Coal Corp., 247 NLRB 895, 103 LRRM 1210 (1980); Apple Tree Chevrolet, 237 NLRB 867, 99 LRRM 1505 (1978), *enforcement denied in pertinent part and remanded*, 608 F2d 988, 103 LRRM 2066 (CA 4, 1979), *on remand*, 251 NLRB 666, 105 LRRM 1220 (1980), *enforcement denied*, 671 F2d 838, 109 LRRM 2946 (CA 4, 1982); Central Cartage, 236 NLRB 1232, 98 LRRM 1554 (1978).

[151]Tipton Elec. Co. v. NLRB, 621 F2d 890, 104 LRRM 2073, 2080 (CA 8, 1980) (employer granting increases after election, when objections were still pending, destroyed laboratory conditions). Raley's, Inc., 236 NLRB 971, 98 LRRM 1381 (1978), *enforced*, 608 F2d 1374, 105 LRRM 2304 (CA 9, 1979), *cert. denied*, 449 US 871, 105 LRRM 2657 (1980). *See* J.J. Newberry Co., 249 NLRB 991, 104 LRRM 1244, 1247 (1980) (grant of substantial wage increase to all employees was "sufficient to render it unlikely that a fair election could be held"), *enforcement denied in pertinent part*, 645 F2d 148, 107 LRRM 2018 (CA 2, 1981).

[152]Machine Tool & Gear, 237 NLRB 1109, 99 LRRM 1153 (1978), *enforced without opinion*, 633 F2d 216, 106 LRRM 2968, *opinion reported at* 652 F2d 596, 126 LRRM 2335 (CA 6, 1980), *cert. denied*, 450 US 1040, 106 LRRM 2997 (1981).

[153]J.P. Stevens & Co., 247 NLRB 420, 103 LRRM 1187 (1980); Professional Ambulance Serv., 232 NLRB 1141, 97 LRRM 1109 (1977); Curtin Matheson Scientific, 228 NLRB 996, 94 LRRM 1742 (1977), *enforced*, 602 F2d 759, 102 LRRM 2946 (CA 6, 1979); Sparkle Mills, Inc., 227 NLRB 1981, 94 LRRM 1448 (1977); Red Barn Sys., 224 NLRB 1586, 92 LRRM 1404 (1976), *enforced*, 574 F2d 315, 98 LRRM 2935 (CA 6, 1976).

[154]Pilot Freight Carriers, 223 NLRB 286, 92 LRRM 1246 (1976).

form a company union;[155] (5) suggested that an employee committee be formed;[156] (6) told strikers that they might be able to arrange to return to work on more favorable terms if they met with the company without a union representative;[157] (7) offered to permit strikers to form their own union;[158] (8) solicited employees' grievances and asked employees to persuade other employees to abandon the union;[159] and (9) solicited employees to repudiate signed authorization cards.[160]

(4) Interrogation. Bargaining orders are also appropriate where the employer engages in severely coercive interrogation, polling, or surveillance[161] of employees. For example, in *Horizon Air Services,*[162] a bargaining order was issued where, among other offenses, the employer interrogated several employees in a small bargaining unit and maintained a "hit list" of union supporters.

(5) Other offenses. Bargaining orders have been issued in a variety of other situations. Such orders have been deemed

---

[155]Professional Ambulance Serv., *supra* note 153.

[156]NLRB v. Rollins Telecasting, 494 F2d 80, 86 LRRM 2735 (CA 2), *cert. denied,* 419 US 964, 87 LRRM 2508 (1974); NLRB v. Hendel Mfg. Co., 483 F2d 350, 83 LRRM 2657 (CA 2, 1973); C & W Mining Co., 248 NLRB 270, 103 LRRM 1563 (1980).

[157]Merkel & Sons, 232 NLRB 140, 97 LRRM 1081 (1977). *See* Jamaica Towing, 247 NLRB 353, 103 LRRM 1161 (1980), *enforcement denied in pertinent part,* 632 F2d 208, 105 LRRM 2959 (CA 2, 1980) (employer told employees that their demands would be met by dealing with management and that union representation would be of no advantage to them).

[158]Merkel & Sons, *supra* note 157.

[159]Farah Supermarkets, 228 NLRB 984, 95 LRRM 1201 (1977).

[160]NLRB v. Matouk Indus., 582 F2d 125, 99 LRRM 2136 (CA 1, 1978); NLRB v. Pope Maintenance Corp., 573 F2d 898, 98 LRRM 2644 (CA 5, 1978); Arkansas Lighthouse for the Blind, 284 NLRB 1214, 126 LRRM 1060 (1987), *enforcement denied on other grounds,* 851 F2d 180, 128 LRRM 2819 (CA 8, 1988).

[161]Bandag, Inc. v. NLRB, 583 F2d 765, 99 LRRM 3226 (CA 5, 1978); Great Chinese Am. Sewing Co. v. NLRB, *supra* note 150; NLRB v. Prineville Stud Co., 578 F2d 1292, 98 LRRM 3322 (CA 9, 1978); NLRB v. Pope Maintenance Corp., *supra* note 160; NLRB v. Solboro Knitting Mills, 572 F2d 936, 97 LRRM 3047 (CA 2), *cert. denied,* 439 US 864, 99 LRRM 2601 (1978); Multi-Medical Convalescent & Nursing Center v. NLRB, 550 F2d 974, 95 LRRM 2021 (CA 4), *cert. denied,* 434 US 835, 96 LRRM 2514 (1977); Ann Lee Sportswear, Inc. v. NLRB, 543 F2d 739, 93 LRRM 2653 (CA 10, 1976); Hicks Oils & Hicksgas, 293 NLRB 84, 132 LRRM 1093 (1989); Studio S.J.T., *supra* note 148; Ohio New & Rebuilt Parts, *supra* note 148; Enterprise Prods. Co., 265 NLRB 544, 112 LRRM 1412 (1982), *enforced,* 744 F2d 93, 118 LRRM 2967 (CA 5, 1984); Tartan Marine Co., 247 NLRB 646, 103 LRRM 1247 (1980); Boatel Alaska, 236 NLRB 1458, 99 LRRM 1005 (1978); Plastic Film Prods. Corp., 238 NLRB 135, 99 LRRM 1216 (1978); Daybreak Lodge Nursing & Convalescent Home, 230 NLRB 800, 96 LRRM 1345 (1977), *enforced in pertinent part,* 585 F2d 79, 99 LRRM 2985 (CA 3, 1978); Broadmoor Lumber Co., 227 NLRB 1123, 95 LRRM 1117 (1977), *enforced,* 578 F2d 238, 98 LRRM 3134 (CA 9, 1978); Woodline, Inc., 231 NLRB 863, 97 LRRM 1288 (1977), *enforced,* 577 F2d 463, 98 LRRM 2869 (CA 8, 1978).

[162]272 NLRB 243, 117 LRRM 1312 (1984), *enforced,* 761 F2d 22, 119 LRRM 2203 (CA 1, 1985).

appropriate where an employer promulgated an invalid no-solicitation rule[163] or applied a lawful rule in a discriminatory manner.[164] For example, in *Medline Industries*,[165] the Board issued a bargaining order based in part on an employer's prohibition of conversations about the union and solicitation during nonworking time.

Bargaining orders have been imposed on employers who used racial slurs,[166] fired shots to intimidate employees,[167] or caused the arrest of a relative of two union adherents.[168] This result also obtained where the employer substituted a pay increase for a free lunch program which it discontinued[169] and where the employer induced employees to withdraw unfair labor practice charges against it.[170]

2. Conduct Not Warranting a *Gissel* Bargaining Order. The decision whether to issue a *Gissel* bargaining order is committed in the first instance to the discretion of the Board, which is usually exercised at the request of the General Counsel and in light of the decision of the ALJ. The decision requires the Board to evaluate not only the unlawful conduct of the employer, but also the probable impact of that conduct on the employees over time. Among other considerations, *Gissel* requires the Board to deny the bargaining order if, in the circumstances of the particular case, the application of traditional remedies would open the way for a fair election. Any such judgment introduces subjective variability. Because of that, and because the Board's remedial orders are so highly responsive to the facts of each case, they defy easy classification. Thus, in several cases the Board has refused to issue bargaining orders notwithstanding findings that the employer committed extensive and pervasive violations of sections 8(a)(1) and (3) of the Act.[171] The Board has also

---

[163] NLRB v. Tischler, 615 F2d 509, 103 LRRM 3033 (CA 9, 1980); Bandag, Inc. v. NLRB, *supra* note 161; NLRB v. Montogmery Ward & Co., 554 F2d 996, 95 LRRM 2433 (CA 10, 1977); Southern Moldings, 255 NLRB 839, 107 LRRM 1203 (1981), *enforced en banc*, 728 F2d 805, 115 LRRM 3325 (CA 6, 1984).

[164] Production Plating Co., 233 NLRB 116, 96 LRRM 1470 (1977), *enforced*, 614 F2d 1117, 104 NLRB 2661 (CA 6, 1980).

[165] 233 NLRB 627, 97 LRRM 1562 (1977), *enforcement of bargaining order denied for insufficient proof of majority status*, 593 F2d 788, 100 LRRM 3202 (CA 7, 1979).

[166] Romal Iron Works Corp., 285 NLRB 1178, 129 LRRM 1335 (1987).

[167] Hargis Mine Supply, 225 NLRB 660, 93 LRRM 1370 (1976).

[168] Albertson Mfg. Co., 236 NLRB 663, 98 LRRM 1402 (1978).

[169] Elmwood Nursing Home, 238 NLRB 346, 99 LRRM 1202 (1978).

[170] Medline Indus., *supra* note 165.

[171] Cato Show Printing Co., 219 NLRB 739, 90 LRRM 1139 (1975); Rensselaer Polytechnic Inst., 219 NLRB 712, 89 LRRM 1879 (1975); Grismac Corp., 205 NLRB 1108, 84

declined to issue bargaining orders in some cases where the employer committed hallmark violations such as discriminatorily discharging employees,[172] or refusing to reinstate economic strikers.[173] Bargaining orders are also sometimes denied where the employer's unlawful conduct, though serious, affects only a small number of employees in a large bargaining unit.[174]

The Board has declined to issue bargaining orders in some cases (1) where the employer solicited and remedied grievances,[175] created the impression of, and engaged in, surveillance of employees' union activities,[176] made threats of reprisal or granted or promised to grant benefits in response to union activity;[177] (2) where the employer interrogated employees or suggested that unionization would be futile;[178] (3) where wage and benefit increases were postponed or withheld;[179] and (4) where the employer circumvented the union and sought to engage in individual bargaining with employees.[180]

LRRM 1256 (1973), *enforced*, 86 LRRM 2152 (CA 7, 1974); Fuqua Homes Mo., 201 NLRB 130, 82 LRRM 1142 (1973); Georgetown Dress Corp., 201 NLRB 102, 82 LRRM 1318 (1973). *See* Schultes I.G.A. Foodliner, 241 NLRB 855, 101 LRRM 1048, 1050 (1979) (bargaining order inappropriate where employer unfair labor practices were not "outrageous and pervasive").

[172]Beckett Aviation Corp., 218 NLRB 238, 89 LRRM 1341 (1975); Munro Enters., 210 NLRB 403, 86 LRRM 1620 (1974) (a single, unlawful discharge so long before recognition demand as to leave a minimal impact).

[173]Mead Corp., 211 NLRB 657, 86 LRRM 1501 (1974).

[174]Americraft Mfg. Co., 242 NLRB 1312, 101 LRRM 1378 (1979); Dependable Lists, 239 NLRB 1304, 100 LRRM 1148 (1979); May Dep't Stores Co., 211 NLRB 150, 86 LRRM 1423 (1974), *enforced*, 514 F2d 894, 90 LRRM 2844 (CA DC, 1975).

[175]Lasco Indus., 217 NLRB 527, 89 LRRM 1058 (1975); White Pine, 213 NLRB 566, 87 LRRM 1386 (1974); Franklin Park Mall, Inc., 212 NLRB 21, 87 LRRM 1255 (1974); Central Diagnostic Laboratory, 206 NLRB 754, 84 LRRM 1636 (1973); Georgetown Dress Corp., *supra* note 171; Flight Safety, 197 NLRB 223, 80 LRRM 1298 (1972).

[176]Sands Indus., 218 NLRB 461, 89 LRRM 1730 (1975); Fuqua Homes Mo., *supra* note 171; J.J. Newberry Co., 202 NLRB 420, 82 LRRM 1584 (1973); Gold Circle Dep't Stores Div., 207 NLRB 1005, 85 LRRM 1033 (1973).

[177]Chef's Pantry, 247 NLRB 77, 103 LRRM 1126 (1980); Bruce Duncan Co., 233 NLRB 1243, 97 LRRM 1027 (1977); Sturgis-Newport Business Forms, 227 NLRB 1426, 94 LRRM 1611 (1977), *enforced*, 563 F2d 1252, 96 LRRM 3383 (CA 5, 1977); South Station Liquor Store, 223 NLRB 1115, 92 LRRM 1083 (1976); Walgreen Co., 221 NLRB 1096, 91 LRRM 1177 (1975); Lasco Indus., *supra* note 175; Treadway Inn, 217 NLRB 51, 89 LRRM 1005 (1975); Franklin Park Mall, Inc., *supra* note 175; Litho Press of San Antonio, 211 NLRB 1014, 86 LRRM 1471 (1974), *enforced*, 512 F2d 73, 89 LRRM 2171 (CA 5, 1975); Rockland Chrysler Plymouth, 209 NLRB 1045, 86 LRRM 1233 (1974); Gold Circle Dep't Stores Div., *supra* note 176; J.J. Newberry Co., *supra* note 176; Ring Metals Co., 198 NLRB 1020, 81 LRRM 1001 (1972), *enforced*, 87 LRRM 2128 (CA DC, 1973); Claremont Polychemical Corp., 196 NLRB 613, 80 LRRM 1130 (1972); Restaurant Assocs. Indus., 194 NLRB 1066, 79 LRRM 1145 (1972).

[178]Hennessy Serv. Corp., 204 NLRB 266, 83 LRRM 1573 (1973).

[179]Ring Metals Co., *supra* note 177; Consolidated Fibers, 197 NLRB 843, 80 LRRM 1817 (1972).

[180]Rensselaer Polytechnic Inst., *supra* note 171.

Moreover, bargaining orders were withheld where the employer: encouraged employees to revoke authorization cards;[181] coerced employees into signing cards for a rival union;[182] offered encouragement or assistance in the formation of a company union;[183] and entered into an unlawful security agreement with a rival union.[184] The same result obtained where the employer prohibited organizational activity[185] and unlawfully assisted an antiunion campaign.[186]

Board bargaining orders may be voided if they fail to comply with standards for enforcement developed by the courts of appeals. Thus, Board bargaining orders have gone unenforced where the Board failed to explain the nexus between the employer's unfair labor practices and the unlikelihood of holding a fair election.[187] This result has also followed where the reviewing court found no evidence to establish that the employer's unfair labor practices undermined the union's majority[188] or were sufficiently egregious to preclude the holding of a fair election.[189] And courts of appeals have refused to enforce bargaining orders on finding that the Board either

---

[181]L.O.F. Glass, Inc., 216 NLRB 845, 88 LRRM 1654 (1975); Tennessee Shell Co., 212 NLRB 193, 86 LRRM 1704 (1974), *petition for review denied*, 515 F2d 1018, 90 LRRM 2844 (CA DC, 1972); Dakota Sand & Gravel Co., 211 NLRB 1026, 86 LRRM 1555 (1974); Consolidated Fibers, *supra* note 179.

[182]Colony Knitwear Corp., 217 NLRB 245, 88 LRRM 1552 (1975).

[183]Rensselaer Polytechnic Inst., *supra* note 171; Litho Press of San Antonio, *supra* note 177; May Dep't Stores Co., *supra* note 174.

[184]Colony Knitwear, *supra* note 182.

[185]Cato Show Printing Co., *supra* note 171; Litho Press of San Antonio, *supra* note 177; Grismac Corp., *supra* note 171; Montgomery Ward & Co., 198 NLRB 52, 80 LRRM 1814 (1972).

[186]Rensselaer Polytechnic Inst., *supra* note 171.

[187]*E.g.*, NLRB v. Gruber's Super Mkt., 501 F2d 697, 87 LRRM 2037 (CA 7, 1974); NLRB v. Gibson Prods. Co., 494 F2d 762, 86 LRRM 2636 (CA 5, 1974); Peerless, Inc. v. NLRB, 484 F2d 1108, 83 LRRM 3000 (CA 7, 1973); NLRB v. General Stencils, Inc., 438 F2d 894, 76 LRRM 2288 (CA 2, 1971).

[188]NLRB v. Apple Tree Chevrolet, 608 F2d 988, 103 LRRM 2066 (CA 4, 1979), *on remand*, 251 NLRB 666, 105 LRRM 1220 (1980), *enforcement denied*, 671 F2d 838, 109 LRRM 2946 (CA 4, 1982); Rapid Mfg. Co. v. NLRB, 612 F2d 144, 103 LRRM 2162, 2166 (CA 3, 1979); Harper & Row Publishers v. NLRB, 476 F2d 430, 83 LRRM 2199 (CA 8, 1973); Arbie Mineral Feed Co. v. NLRB, 438 F2d 940, 76 LRRM 2613 (CA 8, 1971).

[189]Donn Prods. v. NLRB, 613 F2d 162, 103 LRRM 2338, 2342 (CA 6, 1980); Rapid Mfg. Co. v. NLRB, *supra* note 188; NLRB v. Apple Tree Chevrolet, *supra* note 188; NLRB v. Chatfield-Anderson Co., 606 F2d 266, 102 LRRM 2576 (CA 9, 1979); NLRB v. Pilgrim Foods, 591 F2d 110, 100 LRRM 2494 (CA 1, 1978); Shulman's, Inc. v. NLRB, 519 F2d 498, 89 LRRM 2729 (CA 4, 1975); NLRB v. East Side Shopper, 498 F2d 1334, 86 LRRM 2817 (CA 6, 1974); NLRB v. Leslie Metal Arts Co., 472 F2d 584, 82 LRRM 2002 (CA 6, 1972); Dawson Metal Prods. v. NLRB, 450 F2d 47, 78 LRRM 2674 (CA 8, 1971). See also NLRB v. Western Drug, 600 F2d 1324, 101 LRRM 3023 (CA 9, 1979), where the court, denying enforcement, criticized what it characterized as the Board's mechanical application of the *Gissel* criteria and disregard of employee turnover.

failed to adequately account for prior inconsistent decisions[190] or acted arbitrarily and capriciously by determining that certain authorization cards were secured by misrepresentation while others obtained in similar circumstances were not (where the latter gave the union a majority).[191]

There has been disagreement between the Board and some circuit courts concerning the effect of delays in the implementation of the remedy or of intervening changes in the employee complement in the bargaining unit. The Board, for its part, has steadfastly refused to withhold the remedial bargaining order, where warranted, simply because there has been turnover of employees in the bargaining unit or passage of time.[192] Courts which have been critical of the Board's practice, most notably the Second Circuit, have held that the remedial order, based as it is on a conclusion that a fair election is unlikely, must take account of potentially ameliorating events following the employer unfair labor practices.[193] However, the Court of Appeals for the District of Columbia Circuit and other courts have enforced remedial bargaining orders based on pervasive unfair labor practices without requiring detailed inquiry by the Board regarding turnover.[194]

---

[190]Midwest Stock Exch. v. NLRB, 620 F2d 629, 104 LRRM 2243, 2247 (CA 7, 1980); Peerless, Inc. v. NLRB, *supra* note 187; NLRB v. General Stencils, Inc., *supra* note 187.

[191]Fort Smith Outerwear v. NLRB, 499 F2d 223, 86 LRRM 2753 (CA 8, 1974).

[192]Massachusetts Coastal Seafoods, 293 NLRB No. 47, 132 LRRM 1035 (1989); Salvation Army, Williams Memorial Residence, 293 NLRB 944, 131 LRRM 1289 (1989); 299 Lincoln St., Inc., 292 NLRB 172, 130 LRRM 1065 (1988).

[193]NLRB v. Koenig Iron Works, 856 F2d 1, 129 LRRM 2229 (CA 2, 1988); NLRB v. Knogo Corp., 727 F2d 55, 115 LRRM 2756 (CA 2, 1984); NLRB v. Windsor Indus., 730 F2d 860, 115 LRRM 3649 (CA 2, 1984). *But see* NLRB v. Einhorn Enters., Star Color Plate Serv. Div., 843 F2d 1507, 127 LRRM 3161 (CA 2, 1988) (bargaining order enforced despite delay caused by Board and high employee turnover); NLRB v. Gordon, 792 F2d 29, 122 LRRM 2489 (CA 2), *cert. denied*, 479 US 931, 123 LRRM 2904 (1986), *enforcing* 273 NLRB 420, 118 LRRM 1084 (1984) (bargaining order enforced where turnover caused by unlawful discharge of bargaining-unit employees). *See also* Impact Indus. v. NLRB, 847 F2d 379, 128 LRRM 2455 (CA 7, 1988), *denying enforcement to* 285 NLRB 5, 128 LRRM 1122 (1987) (bargaining order refused enforcement because of lapse of 7 years, turnover in employee complement, and changed management of employer); NLRB v. Gruber's Super Mkt., *supra* note 187; NLRB v. Ship Shape Maintenance Co., 474 F2d 434, 81 LRRM 2865 (CA DC, 1972); Peerless, Inc. v. NLRB, *supra* note 187. *See generally* Bethel & Melfi, *Judicial Enforcement of NLRB Bargaining Orders: What Influences Courts?*, 22 U.C. DAVIS L. REV. 139 (1988).

[194]Amazing Stores v. NLRB, 887 F2d 328, 132 LRRM 2753 (CA DC, 1989), *enforcing* 289 NLRB 163, 131 LRRM 1066 (1988) (to require fuller inquiry would reward employer by alerting new employees to employer's union antipathy and by further delaying proceedings). *See* NLRB v. Buckley Broadcasting Corp. dba Station KKHI, 891 F2d 230, 133 LRRM 2175 (CA 9, 1989), *enforcing* 284 NLRB 1339, 125 LRRM 1281 (1987), *cert. denied*, _____ US _____, 134 LRRM 2432 (1990); Indiana Cal-Pro v. NLRB, 863 F2d 1292, 130 LRRM 2222 (CA 6, 1988), *enforcing* 287 NLRB 796, 129 LRRM 1128 (1987); Koons Ford v. NLRB, 833 F2d 310, 126 LRRM 3032 (CA 4, 1987), *enforcing* 282 NLRB 506, 124 LRRM

D. The Bargaining Order as an Extraordinary Remedy

Seriously coercive unfair labor practices may warrant issuance of a bargaining order even though the employer does not independently violate section 8(a)(5).[195] In *Steel-Fab, Inc.*[196] the Board held that "it is unnecessary to predicate the bargaining order on any 8(a)(5) violation."[197] It stated that by issuing a bargaining order to remedy an employer's 8(a)(1) violations that have dissipated a union's majority and prevented the holding of a fair election, the Board was "removing . . . a semantic difficulty which . . . has clouded the central issue over the years."[198] Under *Steel-Fab*, however, bargaining orders not predicated upon section 8(a)(5) violations imposed the duty to bargain from the date of decision only. That left unremedied unilateral changes in working conditions made by an employer after the union had obtained a card majority but before the date of the Board's order to bargain.[199] This limitation of the remedy under *Steel-Fab* was short-lived. In *Trading Port*,[200] the Board concluded, that "while there may be certain truths to the approaches each takes to the issuance of and legal basis for a bargaining order, we are now of the opinion that the correct approach lies somewhere in between" the conflicting principles of *Gissel* and *Steel-Fab*.[201] In *Trading Port*, the Board concluded that its *Steel-Fab* holding

> led to the unwanted result that an employer, by committing serious unfair labor practices, could delay the holding of an election indefinitely (since a fair one could no longer be held), and insure himself a substantial period of time until the Board issued a remedial bargaining order, during which period he would not have to deal with a union. Since the events which "triggered" the bargaining duty occurred much earlier, i.e., at the time of the unfair labor practices,

---

1167 (1986); Piggly Wiggly v. NLRB, 705 F2d 1537, 113 LRRM 2810 (CA 11, 1983), *enforcing* 258 NLRB 1081, 108 LRRM 1323 (1981).

[195] NLRB v. Delight Bakery, 353 F2d 344, 60 LRRM 2501 (CA 6, 1965); Piasecki Aircraft Corp. v. NLRB, 280 F2d 575, 46 LRRM 2469 (CA 3, 1960), *cert. denied*, 364 US 933, 47 LRRM 2365 (1961); Kinter Bros., 167 NLRB 57, 66 LRRM 1004 (1967); Crystal Tire Co., 165 NLRB 563, 65 LRRM 1459 (1967); Better Val-U Stores of Mansfield, 161 NLRB 762, 63 LRRM 1326 (1966); John Hammonds, 160 NLRB 927, 63 LRRM 1057 (1966); Bishop & Malco, 159 NLRB 1159, 62 LRRM 1498 (1965).

[196] 212 NLRB 363, 86 LRRM 1474 (1974).

[197] *Id.*, 86 LRRM at 1476.

[198] *Id.* at 365, 86 LRRM at 1478.

[199] This was the subject of Member Jenkins's concurring and dissenting opinion. *Id.* at 371.

[200] 219 NLRB 298, 89 LRRM 1565 (1975).

[201] *Id.* at 301, 89 LRRM at 1569.

> and since the employees had earlier expressed their desire for union representation, the Board's prospective bargaining order fell short of reinstating the situation as it would have been had [the employer] obeyed the law and allowed a fair election to proceed.[202]

Stressing that its "main concern in granting bargaining orders has been, and is, to correct and give redress for an employer's misconduct and to protect the employees from the effects thereof,"[203] the Board held that "an employer's obligation under a bargaining order remedy should commence as of the time the employer has embarked on a clear course of unlawful conduct or has engaged in sufficient unfair labor practices to undermine the union's majority status."[204] Read together, *Steel-Fab* and *Trading Port* establish that a section 8(a)(5) violation need not be present to support a bargaining order, and that a bargaining order predicated on other than section 8(a)(5) conduct will be retroactive to the date that the employer "embarked on a clear course of unlawful conduct . . . sufficient . . . to undermine the union's majority status."[205]

The date to which a bargaining order will be retroactive may vary. If the employer has committed unfair labor practices sufficient to warrant a bargaining order, and the union has not demanded recognition, the duty to bargain will extend back to the point at which the union attained majority status.[206] If the bargaining order is intended to remedy only a section 8(a)(5) violation, the Board has held that the order should be retroactive to the date of the union's demand for recognition.[207] If the employer first engages in unfair labor practices *after* the union has either attained majority status or demanded recognition, the bargaining order will extend back no further than the point at which the employer "embarked on a clear course of unlawful

---

[202]*Id.*

[203]*Id.*

[204]*Id.*

[205]*Id. See* NLRB v. Gordon, *supra* note 193 (bargaining order appropriate remedy for discharge of all employees in bargaining unit).

[206]Permanent Label Corp., 248 NLRB 118, 103 LRRM 1513 (1980) (order effective as of date union attained majority status); Dresser Indus., 248 NLRB 33, 103 LRRM 1473 (1980); J. P. Stevens & Co., 244 NLRB 407, 102 LRRM 1039 (1979); International Mfg. Co., 238 NLRB 1361, 99 LRRM 1328 (1978); Machine Tool & Gear, 237 NLRB 1109, 99 LRRM 1153 (1978); Woodland Supermarket, 237 NLRB 1481, 99 LRRM 1113 (1978); Seven-Up Bottling Co., 235 NLRB 297, 98 LRRM 1515 (1978). *See also* Lockwoven Co., 245 NLRB 1362, 102 LRRM 1533 (1979).

[207]Albertson Mfg. Co., 236 NLRB 663, 98 LRRM 1402 (1978); *see* Robin Am. Corp., 245 NLRB 822, 102 LRRM 1563 (1979).

conduct."[208] Where the achievement of majority status, the demand for recognition, and the commencement of the employer's unfair labor practices all occurred more than six months *prior* to the filing of the charges, the bargaining obligation is deemed retroactive to the first day of the six-month limitation period set forth in section 10(b) of the Act.[209]

In a related proceeding, the Second Circuit held that in *Gissel* cases a Board regional director may, under section 10(j) of the Act, obtain preliminary injunctive relief to require an employer to bargain pending a final determination by the Board concerning the union's status as bargaining representative.[210]

In *Gissel* the Supreme Court indicated in dicta that where "outrageous" and "pervasive" unfair labor practices made a fair election impossible, a bargaining order might be appropriate "without need of inquiry into majority status on the basis of cards or otherwise."[211] However, until 1981 the Board declined to issue bargaining orders absent evidence that the union at one time enjoyed majority status.[212] In *United Dairy Farmers Cooperative Ass'n,*[213] the Board considered such a remedy but, dividing

---

[208]Jasta Mfg. Co., 246 NLRB 48, 102 LRRM 1610 (1979), *enforced,* 634 F2d 623, 108 LRRM 2103 (CA 4, 1980); Bighorn Beverage, 236 NLRB 736, 98 LRRM 1396 (1978); Chatfield-Anderson Co., 236 NLRB 50, 98 LRRM 1190 (1978), *enforcement denied in pertinent part,* 606 F2d 266, 102 LRRM 2576 (CA 9, 1979); Idak Convalescent Center, 238 NLRB 410, 99 LRRM 1542 (1978); L'Eggs Prods., 236 NLRB 354, 99 LRRM 1304 (1978); Michigan Prods., 236 NLRB 1143, 98 LRRM 1515 (1978).

[209]Chromalloy Mining & Minerals, 238 NLRB 688, 99 LRRM 1642 (1978).

[210]Seeler v. Trading Port, 517 F2d 33, 89 LRRM 2513 (CA 2, 1975). *See also* Asseo v. Pan Am. Grain Co., 805 F2d 23, 123 LRRM 2996 (CA 1, 1986); Levine v. C & W Mining Co., 610 F2d 432, 102 LRRM 3093 (CA 6, 1979). District courts, both in the Second Circuit and elsewhere, had previously refused to grant such relief in situations involving a union's initial organizing attempts. Boire v. Pilot Freight Carriers, 86 LRRM 2976 (MD Fla, 1974), *aff'd,* 515 F2d 1185, 89 LRRM 2908 (CA 5, 1975); Fuchs v. Steel-Fab, Inc., 356 F Supp 385, 83 LRRM 2635 (D Mass, 1973); Kaynard v. Lawrence Rigging, Inc., 80 LRRM 2600 (EDNY, 1972). *See* Note, *The Propriety of Section 10(j) Bargaining Orders in* Gissel *Situations,* 82 MICH. L. REV. 112 (1983).

[211]NLRB v. Gissel Packing Co., 395 US 575, 613, 71 LRRM 2481, 2495 (1969).

[212]*See* Sambo's Restaurant, 247 NLRB 777, 103 LRRM 1181 (1980), *enforced,* 641 F2d 794, 107 LRRM 2332 (CA 9, 1981); Haddon House Food Prods., 242 NLRB 1057, 101 LRRM 1294 (1979), *aff'd sub nom.* Teamsters Local 115 v. NLRB, 640 F2d 392, 106 LRRM 2462 (CA DC), *cert. denied,* 454 US 837, 108 LRRM 2559 (1981); GTE Automatic Elec., 196 NLRB 902, 80 LRRM 1155 (1972); Loray Corp., 184 NLRB 557, 74 LRRM 1513 (1970); Electrical Workers (IUE) (Scott's, Inc.), 159 NLRB 1795, 62 LRRM 1543 (1966), *enforced as modified,* 383 F2d 230, 66 LRRM 2081 (CA DC, 1967), *cert. denied,* 390 US 904, 67 LRRM 2308 (1968); J.P. Stevens & Co., 157 NLRB 869, 61 LRRM 1437 (1966), *enforced as modified,* 380 F2d 292, 65 LRRM 2829 (CA 2), *cert. denied,* 389 US 1005, 66 LRRM 2728 (1967); H.W. Elson Bottling, 155 NLRB 714, 60 LRRM 1381 (1965), *enforced as modified,* 379 F2d 223, 65 LRRM 2673 (CA 6, 1967).

[213]242 NLRB 1026, 101 LRRM 1278 (1979), *aff'd and remanded for reconsideration of bargaining-order issue,* 633 F2d 1054, 105 LRRM 3034 (CA 3, 1979), *on remand,* 257 NLRB 772, 107 LRRM 1577 (1981).

three ways, declined to impose it. Two members asserted that the Board has the authority to issue a bargaining order, regardless of any evidence that the union had attained majority status.[214] Two other members stated that although "the Board's remedial authority . . . may well encompass the authority to issue a bargaining order in the absence of a prior showing of majority support,"[215] they would decline to issue a bargaining order where the union had at no time obtained a showing of majority support. These members noted that the employer's unfair labor practices were indeed "outrageous" and "pervasive," but they decided that a bargaining order would not "effectuate the policies of the Act" where there had been no showing of majority status at any point.[216] The fifth member of the Board wrote that, notwithstanding the dicta in *Gissel*, the Board lacked authority to issue a bargaining order where the union had never commanded majority support.[217]

On review of *United Dairy Farmers*, the Third Circuit concluded not only that the Board has authority to issue bargaining orders despite the union's lack of majority in "'exceptional' cases marked by 'outrageous' and pervasive unfair labor practices," but also that the failure to recognize such authority "would undermine the underlying goal of the Act to further the majority preference of all employees."[218] The court noted that "[u]nions which would have attained a majority in a free and uncoerced election if the employer had not committed unfair labor practices would be deprived of recognition merely because of the employer's illegal conduct."[219] The court expressed con-

---

[214]*Id.* at 1032 (concurring and dissenting opinion of Chairman Fanning and Member Jenkins). *See* Shillman, *Nonmajority Bargaining Orders: The Only Effective Remedy for Pervasive Employer Unfair Labor Practices During Union Organizing Campaigns*, 20 U. MICH. J.L. REF. 617 (1987).

[215]*Id.* at 1027 (opinion of Members Murphy and Truesdale).

[216]*Id.* at 1028. They conceded that other remedies might not be sufficient to eradicate totally the effects of the unfair labor practices, but they would "tend to restore an atmosphere in which employees are given a meaningful opportunity to exercise their Section 7 rights in an election." *Id.*

[217]*Id.* at 1038 (concurring and dissenting opinion of Member Penello).

[218]United Dairy Farmers Coop. Ass'n v. NLRB, 633 F2d 1054, 1068, 105 LRRM 3034 (CA 3, 1979).

[219]*Id.* The court noted that "virtually every court that has discussed the issue has stated that a bargaining order may be issued in the absence of a card majority." *Id. See* NLRB v. Armcor Indus., 535 F2d 239, 92 LRRM 2374 (CA 3, 1976) and Judge Rosenn's comments therein at 244. *See also* NLRB v. Garry Mfg. Co., 630 F2d 934, 105 LRRM 2113 (CA 3), *cert. denied*, 449 US 871 (1980); Electrical Prods. Div. v. NLRB, 617 F2d 977, 103 LRRM 2908 (CA 3, 1980); Rapid Mfg. Co. v. NLRB, 612 F2d 144, 103 LRRM 2162 (CA 3, 1979); NLRB v. Daybreak Lodge Nursing & Convalescent Home, 585 F2d 79, 99 LRRM 2985 (CA 3, 1978); Struthers-Dunn, Inc. v. NLRB, 574 F2d 796, 98 LRRM 2385 (CA 3, 1978); NLRB

cern that "the absence of such authority might create incentives for employers to engage in illegal prophylactic action with the purpose of preventing the attainment of a card majority."[220] The court remanded the case so that the Board could make the prerequisite findings as to whether the employer's unfair labor practices embodied the critical elements that would warrant issuance of a bargaining order. On remand, the Board issued a bargaining order.

In *Conair Corp.*,[221] the Board issued a bargaining order where the employer had committed "outrageous" and "pervasive" unfair labor practices and where the union had never achieved majority status. The Board concluded that the lingering effects of the employer's "massive and unrelenting" violations[222] foreclosed any possibility of a fair election, for such conduct could not be dissipated by either traditional or milder extraordinary remedies. In a companion case in which the union never achieved majority status, the Board withheld the bargaining order, explaining that the employer's unfair labor practices had not been as pervasive as those in *Conair*, and had occurred at only one of several facilities.[223]

On review of *Conair*, the Court of Appeals for the District of Columbia Circuit refused enforcement of the bargaining order.[224] The court concluded that the Act does not authorize the Board to impose a bargaining agent not chosen by the

---

v. Eagle Material Handling, 558 F2d 160, 95 LRRM 2934 (CA 3, 1977); Hedstrom Co. v. NLRB, 558 F2d 1137, 95 LRRM 3069 (CA 3, 1977); NLRB v. Montgomery Ward & Co., 554 F2d 996, 1002, 95 LRRM 2433 (CA 10, 1977); J.P. Stevens Co. v. NLRB, 441 F2d 514, 76 LRRM 2817 (CA 5, 1971), *cert. denied*, 404 US 830, 78 LRRM 2464 (1971); NLRB v. S.S. Logan Packing Co., 386 F2d 562, 66 LRRM 2596 (CA 4, 1967); *but cf.* NLRB v. Roney Plaza Apartments, 597 F2d 1046, 101 LRRM 2794 (CA 5, 1979).

[220] 633 F2d at 1068.

[221] 261 NLRB 1189, 110 LRRM 1161 (1982), *enforcement denied in pertinent part*, 721 F2d 1355, 114 LRRM 3169 (CA DC, 1983), *cert. denied sub nom.* Ladies' Garment Workers Local 222 v. NLRB, 467 US 1241, 116 LRRM 2632 (1984).

[222] The employer's conduct consisted of holding a series of meetings at which employees were threatened with plant closure, discharge, and loss of benefits if they supported the union. The employer also promised certain new benefits, solicited grievances which it implied would be remedied, interrogated employees, and created an impression of surveillance. After two employees struck to protest those unfair labor practices, the employer threatened to discharge, then discharged, all the strikers. It also repeated many of the former threats and engaged in new unfair labor practices, including the granting of increased benefits to nonstrikers. Following the strike it discriminated among the strikers in its reinstatement policy; and shortly before the election it committed further unfair labor practices, including threatening to move the plant to Hong Kong if the union won the election. *Id.*

[223] United Supermarkets, 261 NLRB 1291, 110 LRRM 1173 (1982), *aff'd*, 699 F2d 1161 (CA 5, 1983).

[224] Conair Corp. v. NLRB, 721 F2d 1355, 114 LRRM 3169 (CA DC, 1983), *cert. denied sub nom.* Ladies' Garment Workers Local 222 v. NLRB, 467 US 1241, 116 LRRM 2632 (1984).

employees themselves and wrote: "Without a clear direction from Congress, we are not prepared to recognize administrative authority, or arrogate power to ourselves, to remedy one possible injustice by taking the substantial chance of imposing another."[225] Shortly later, in *Gourmet Foods*,[226] the Board embraced the reasoning of the District of Columbia Circuit, concluded that such orders are unwarranted, and ceased issuing them.

IV. BARGAINING OBLIGATION ESTABLISHED BY EMPLOYER CARD CHECKS, POLLS, AND OTHER INDEPENDENT MEANS

In *Gissel*, the Supreme Court expressly reserved decision as to the following questions:

> [W]hether, absent election interference by an employer's unfair labor practices, he may obtain an election only if he petitions for one himself; whether, if he does not, he must bargain with a card majority if the union chooses not to seek an election; and whether, in the latter situation, he is bound by the Board's ultimate determination of the card results regardless of his earlier good-faith doubts, or whether he can still insist on a Union-sought election if he makes an affirmative showing of his positive reasons for believing there is a representation dispute.[227]

The Court answered those questions in *Linden Lumber Div. v. NLRB*.[228]

In *Linden Lumber*, the union demanded recognition based on a card majority. The employer refused, and, at its suggestion, the union petitioned the Board for an election. But the union withdrew the petition when the employer, claiming that supervisors had improperly assisted the union's organizing campaign, refused to enter into a consent-election agreement or be bound by the results of an election. The union again demanded recognition and the employer again refused. The union then struck for recognition and filed an unfair labor practice charge alleging

---

[225] *Id.* at 1383, 114 LRRM at 3189.

[226] 270 NLRB 578, 116 LRRM 1105 (1984) (overruling United Dairy Farmers Coop. Ass'n, 242 NLRB 1026, 101 LRRM 1278 (1979) *and* Conair Corp., *supra* note 221). *See* NLRB v. Pace Oldsmobile, 739 F2d 108, 116 LRRM 3137 (CA 2, 1984), *denying enforcement to* 265 NLRB 1527, 112 LRRM 1186 (1982) (court expressed approval of *Gourmet Foods*). *See also* Abbey's Transp. Servs., 284 NLRB 698, 125 LRRM 1242 (1987), *enforced*, 837 F2d 575, 127 LRRM 2437 (CA 2, 1988).

[227] *Supra* note 211, at 601 n.18, 71 LRRM 2481, 2491 n.18.

[228] 419 US 301, 87 LRRM 3236 (1974).

unlawful refusal to bargain. There was no allegation of any other unfair labor practice.

The Board held that the employer "should not be found guilty of a violation of Section 8(a)(5) solely upon the basis of [its] refusal to accept evidence of majority status other than the results of a Board election"[229] and that the employer should not be required to petition the Board for an election if it has not committed any unfair labor practices. The Court of Appeals for the District of Columbia Circuit reversed, however, stating that while recognitional strikes, "ambiguous utterances of the employer," and signed cards do not necessarily constitute "convincing evidence of majority support" which would compel issuance of a bargaining order, they do give rise to "a sufficient probability of majority support as to require an employer asserting a doubt of majority status to resolve the possibility through a petition for an election . . . ."[230]

The Supreme Court adopted the Board's position. Writing for the majority, Justice Douglas observed that, in the Board's view, a union faced with an "unwilling employer" had two options: "It can file for an election; or it can press unfair labor practices against the employer under *Gissel*."[231] Noting that the election process is typically much less time-consuming and thus more desirable, the Court stated that "[t]he question remains—should the burden be on the union to ask for an election or should it be the responsibility of the employer?"[232]

A majority of the Court concluded that it could "not say that the Board's decision that the union should go forward and ask for an election on the employer's refusal to recognize the authorization cards was arbitrary and capricious or an abuse of discretion."[233] The Court commented that there was no suggestion that Congress, in enacting section 9(c)(1)(B), "wanted to place the burden of getting a secret election on the employer."[234] Justices Stewart, White, Marshall, and Powell dissented.[235]

Under the rule of *Linden Lumber*, an employer who has neither committed unfair labor practices nor agreed to be bound by the

---

[229]Linden Lumber Div., 190 NLRB 718, 721, 77 LRRM 1305 (1971).

[230]Teamsters Local 413 (Linden Lumber Div.) v. NLRB, 487 F2d 1099, 1111, 84 LRRM 2177, 2186 (CA DC, 1973).

[231]*Supra* note 228, at 306.

[232]*Id.* at 307.

[233]*Id.* at 309–10.

[234]*Id.* at 307.

[235]*Id.* at 310.

results of some other method of ascertaining majority status cannot be required to bargain with a union absent an election.[236] Noting that the question was not presented on the record before it, the Court declined comment on what result would obtain "if the employer breaches its agreement to permit majority status to be determined by means other than a Board election."[237]

The Board has consistently held, however, that where an employer responds to a union's demand for recognition by unilaterally attempting to determine majority status by, for example, interrogating or otherwise polling employees, it may not lawfully disavow the results.[238] The union's demand for recognition must precede the employer's inquiry into the union's majority status. The Board reasons that it is only *after* the union demands recognition that the employer must select the means by which it will verify a union's claim of majority status.[239] Thus, interrogations occurring before the demand for recognition, which were not completed and which therefore failed to establish a union majority, did not waive the employer's right to a Board election to ascertain the employees' sentiments regarding the union.[240] On the other hand, the employer may withdraw from an agreed verification procedure with impunity if the withdrawal comes before the procedure has operated to verify the union's status.[241]

The Board's decision in *Struksnes Construction Co.*[242] sets the standards for a lawful employer inquiry into a union's claim of

---

[236]*See, e.g.*, NLRB v. Creative Food Design t/a Broker, 852 F2d 1295, 128 LRRM 3089 (CA DC, 1988); Service Employees Local 250 v. NLRB (Earringhouse Imports), 600 F2d 930, 101 LRRM 2004 (CA DC, 1979); Without Reservation, 280 NLRB 1408, 123 LRRM 1323 (1986).

[237]419 US at 310 n.10.

[238]Sullivan Elec. Co., 199 NLRB 809, 81 LRRM 1313 (1972), *enforced*, 479 F2d 1270, 83 LRRM 2513 (CA 6, 1973). *Accord* NLRB v. Gogin, 575 F2d 596, 98 LRRM 2250 (CA 7, 1978); Jerr-Dan Corp., 237 NLRB 302, 98 LRRM 1569 (1978), *enforced*, 601 F2d 575, 103 LRRM 2603 (CA 3, 1979); Idaho Pac. Steel Warehouse Co., 227 NLRB 326, 94 LRRM 1135 (1976); E.S. Merriman & Sons, 219 NLRB 972, 90 LRRM 1161 (1975) (interrogation); Rockwell Int'l Corp., 220 NLRB 1262, 90 LRRM 1481 (1975) (third-party card check); Taylor-Roe Mfg. Corp., 205 NLRB 262, 84 LRRM 1017 (1973), *enforced*, 493 F2d 1398, 86 LRRM 2152 (CA 2, 1974) ("handcount" poll); Nation-Wide Plastics Co., 197 NLRB 996, 81 LRRM 1036 (1972) (secret-ballot poll); Summersville Indus. Equip. Co., 197 NLRB 731, 80 LRRM 1664 (1972).

[239]Tennessee Shell Co., 212 NLRB 193, 86 LRRM 1704 (1974), *petition for review denied*, 515 F2d 1018, 90 LRRM 2844 (CA DC, 1975).

[240]*Id.* The Eighth Circuit has refused to enforce a bargaining order predicated upon the results of a card check where the list used to establish the union's majority included employees who were not part of the appropriate unit. Harding Glass Indus. v. NLRB, 533 F2d 1065, 92 LRRM 2147 (CA 8, 1976).

[241]Georgetown Hotel v. NLRB, 835 F2d 1467, 127 LRRM 2129 (CA DC, 1987), *denying enforcement to* 281 NLRB 357, 123 LRRM 1149 (1986).

[242]165 NLRB 1062, 65 LRRM 1385 (1967). *See* Chapter 6, "Interference With Protected Rights," at notes 286–299.

majority support. In *Struksnes* the Board held that polling employees is a violation of section 8(a)(1) unless "1) the purpose of the poll is to determine the truth of a union's claim of majority, 2) this purpose is communicated to the employees, 3) assurances against reprisal are given, 4) the employees are polled by secret ballot, and 5) the employer has not engaged in unfair labor practices or otherwise created a coercive atmosphere."[243]

Although the need for the "safe harbor" of the *Struksnes* standards might be diminished in light of the calm forecast in *Linden Lumber*, those standards continue to apply.[244] Moreover, a poll that fails to satisfy *Struksnes* standards may became the basis for an order to bargain if it establishes a union majority. In *Bushnell's Kitchens*,[245] the Board reasoned that since the employees had openly indicated their union sentiments and invited the employer to verify them, the employer did not coerce them by acceding to their request. Since the employer's poll merely verified what the employees had already told him, the Board found no interference.[246]

Other informal means of inquiring into a union's majority may also result in imposition of a bargaining order. Thus, an employer was deemed to have recognized a union when, after examining signed authorization cards, he stated, "You got them all."[247] The same result was reached where a union representative brought a majority of the unit's nonsupervisory employees, all wearing union buttons, into the employer's office, thereby convincing him of the union's majority.[248] The

[243]165 NLRB at 1063. The Board further held that §8(a)(1) is violated when the poll is taken after the filing of an election petition.

[244]American Nat'l Ins. Co., 281 NLRB 713, 124 LRRM 1116 (1986); Liberty Nursing Homes, 245 NLRB 1194, 102 LRRM 1517 (1979); B & L Plumbing, 243 NLRB 1016, 101 LRRM 1616 (1979); Baptist Memorial Hosp., 229 NLRB 45, 95 LRRM 1043 (1977); B. C. Hawk Chevrolet, Inc., 226 NLRB 527, 93 LRRM 1304 (1976), *enforced*, 582 F2d 491, 99 LRRM 3173 (CA 9, 1978); Burns Int'l Sec. Servs., 225 NLRB 271, 92 LRRM 1439 (1976), *enforcement denied*, 567 F2d 945, 97 LRRM 2350 (CA 10, 1977).

[245]222 NLRB 110, 91 LRRM 1113 (1976). *See* Chapter 6, "Interference With Protected Rights," at note 293.

[246]Jerome J. Jacomet, 222 NLRB 899, 91 LRRM 1370 (1976). *See* Chapter 6, "Interference With Protected Rights," at note 293. *Cf.* Mid-Continent Refrigerated Serv. Co., 228 NLRB 917, 94 LRRM 1733 (1977).

[247]Jerr-Dan Corp., *supra* note 238. *See also* Brown & Connolly, 237 NLRB 271, 98 LRRM 1572 (1978), *enforced*, 593 F2d 1373, 100 LRRM 3072 (CA 1, 1979).

[248]Brown & Connolly, *supra* note 247. *See also* Lyon & Ryan Ford, 246 NLRB 1, 102 LRRM 1448 (1979), *enforced*, 647 F2d 745, 107 LRRM 2345 (CA 7), *cert. denied*, 454 US 894, 108 LRRM 2656 (1981).

employer was not allowed to withdraw that expression of "recognition" one week later. The Board has consistently held that once recognition is voluntarily granted, it may not be withdrawn until a reasonable time for bargaining to take place has elapsed.[249] The Board has also sharply restricted the use of polls to test the continuing majority status of an incumbent union by requiring that the employer have an objectively based, good-faith doubt of the union's majority *before* conducting any such poll.[250]

V. DEFENSES TO THE REMEDIAL BARGAINING ORDER

A. Union Lack of Majority Status

Since the decision of *Gourmet Foods*,[251] it has been the Board's view that a remedial bargaining order is completely precluded by the absence of proof of majority support for the union. Thus, an employer who can rebut or discredit the evidence offered to establish such majority status, or who can prove that the union did not at any time enjoy majority support, can avoid the entry of a remedial bargaining order. The standards for establishing majority status by authorization cards or other means are dealt with extensively elsewhere.[252] This section treats a few matters that have particular application to *Gissel* bargaining orders.

In *Grismac Corp.*,[253] for example, the employer avoided the bargaining order remedy by showing that the union lacked majority status. The union obtained signed cards from 43 of the unit's 83 employees. Two of the cards, however, were executed by employees who had been lawfully terminated prior to the union's demand for recognition. Thus, despite the employer's extensive unfair labor practices, the Board refused to issue a

---

[249]Jerr-Dan Corp., *supra* note 238; Brown & Connolly, *supra* note 247. *See also* Phelps Cement Prods., 257 NLRB 19, 107 LRRM 1474 (1981).

[250]Montgomery Ward & Co., 210 NLRB 717, 86 LRRM 1273 (1974). *See* Texas Petrochemicals Corp., 296 NLRB No. 136, 132 LRRM 1279 (1989).

[251]270 NLRB 578, 116 LRRM 1105 (1984). *See supra* notes 224–226.

[252]*See supra* notes 77–94. *See generally* Chapter 10, "Representation Proceedings and Elections."

[253]205 NLRB 1108, 84 LRRM 1256 (1973), *enforced*, 86 LRRM 2152 (CA 7, 1974). *See also* United Supermarkets, 261 NLRB 1291, 110 LRRM 1173 (1982), *aff'd*, 699 F2d 1161 (CA 5, 1983).

bargaining order because the 41 valid cards did not constitute a majority of the unit.[254]

In *Business Envelope Manufacturers*[255] the Board considered conflicting presumptions of majority status and withheld the bargaining-order remedy. An incumbent union enjoyed the presumption of continuing majority status at a time when a rival union had a card majority. Notwithstanding the employer's "egregious and coercive conduct" in violation of sections 8(a)(1) and (2), the Board refused to order the employer to bargain with the rival union.[256] It concluded that the conflicting presumptions of majority status canceled each other; therefore a second election should be held.[257]

The union's majority status need not be evidenced by signed cards alone. In *Pinter Brothers*[258] the Board issued a bargaining order even though the union had never possessed a card majority; majority status was established by adding signed cards of nonvoters to union votes in an election that had been set aside. In *Benjamin Coal Co.,*[259] the Board accepted as sufficient evidence of majority an earlier union victory in an election that was set aside by agreement of the parties.

In *Struthers-Dunn, Inc.*[260] the Board rejected the employer's argument that since the union lost its majority status through employee-card revocations prior to the commission of any unfair labor practices, a bargaining order could not issue. The revocations were deemed ineffective because the union had not been informed of them before it demanded recognition. The Third Circuit denied enforcement, finding that the revocations were effective and were not made in response to conduct by the employer that "in some way undermined union majority

---

[254]Grismac Corp., *supra* note 253. *See also* Honolulu Sporting Goods Co., 239 NLRB 1277, 100 LRRM 1172 (1979). Other cases in which the Board has refused to issue bargaining orders absent a showing that the union had ever achieved majority status include: Triana Indus., 245 NLRB 1258, 102 LRRM 1323 (1979); Woonsocket Health Centre, 245 NLRB 652, 102 LRRM 1494 (1979); Daniel Constr. Co., 244 NLRB 704, 102 LRRM 1399 (1979); Haddon House Foods Prods., 242 NLRB 1057, 101 LRRM 1294 (1979); Miami Springs Properties, 245 NLRB 278, 102 LRRM 1556 (1979).

[255]227 NLRB 280, 94 LRRM 1351 (1976).

[256]*Id.*

[257]*Id.*

[258]227 NLRB 921, 94 LRRM 1284 (1977).

[259]294 NLRB No. 44, 133 LRRM 1058 (1989).

[260]228 NLRB 49, 95 LRRM 1204 (1977), *enforcement denied,* 574 F2d 796, 98 LRRM 2385 (CA 3), *on remand,* 237 NLRB 892, 99 LRRM 1048 (1978).

strength."[261] On remand, the Board ordered a new election without requiring a fresh showing of interest because the first election had been set aside for valid objections.[262]

1. Timing of the Demand for Recognition. The union need not enjoy majority status on the date when it first demands recognition. The Board's view that a demand for recognition ordinarily continues once made validates cards which are executed after the union's demand. In *Brown Group*,[263] the union demanded recognition by letter dated February 12. Although the union did not enjoy majority status at the time, its letter stated that the demand should be considered "continuing"; and the union did achieve majority status three days later. In issuing a *Gissel* bargaining order in response to various unfair labor practices which the employer had committed in the interim, the Board concluded that the employer had unlawfully refused to bargain as of February 15. Similarly, when a union demanded recognition on September 20 but did not attain majority status until October 1, the Board's *Gissel* bargaining order was based on the employer's refusal to bargain as of the latter date.[264] The "continuing demand" theory was also invoked in a case where the Board concluded that it would have been futile for the union to make another demand after receiving more cards, the employer having previously ignored the union's written demand for recognition.[265]

Although the "continuing demand" theory has met some judicial resistance,[266] its application to a successor employer was approved by the Supreme Court in *Fall River Dyeing & Finishing Corp. v. NLRB*.[267]

2. Invalid Authorization. *a. In General.* The most frequently asserted claim of invalid authorization relies on evidence that those who solicited the cards misrepresented their purpose, or the consequence of signing them. Such claims of misrepresenta-

---

[261]*Id.*

[262]*Id.*

[263]223 NLRB 1409, 92 LRRM 1297 (1976), *enforced sub nom.* Hedstrom Co. v. NLRB, 558 F2d 1137, 95 LRRM 3069 (CA 3, 1977).

[264]Schwab Foods, 223 NLRB 394, 92 LRRM 1285 (1976), *enforced*, 549 F2d 805, 95 LRRM 2108 (CA 7, 1977).

[265]Area Disposal, 200 NLRB 350, 82 LRRM 1173 (1972). *See also* J.P. Stevens & Co., 157 NLRB 869, 61 LRRM 1437 (1966), *enforced as modified*, 380 F2d 292, 65 LRRM 2829 (CA 2), *cert. denied*, 389 US 1005, 66 LRRM 2728 (1967).

[266]*See* Hedstrom Co. v. NLRB, 558 F2d 1137, 95 LRRM 3069 (CA 3, 1977).

[267]482 US 27, 125 LRRM 2441 (1987). *See also* Montgomery Ward Co., 288 NLRB 126, 130 LRRM 1369 (1988) (demand deemed continuing). *See* Chapter 15, "Effect of Change in the Employing Unit: Successorship."

tion are dealt with below insofar as they are particularly pertinent here,[268] and at greater length above.[269] Invalid authorization is also asserted at times on the ground that the authorization cards were revoked prior to the union's demand for recognition.[270] The Board will not accept this argument if the revocations are the product of the employer's unfair labor practices.[271] Of course, cards bearing forged signatures are invalid absent adequate evidence of assent by the putative signatory.[272]

b. Nature of the Card. A critical inquiry focuses on whether the authorization cards are ambiguous, even if they are multipurpose. Thus, in *Area Disposal,*[273] the Board counted unambiguous cards where employees had been told that the "principal purpose" of the cards was to obtain an election. In *Colonial Lincoln Mercury Sales,*[274] the Board counted unambiguous authorizations signed by employees who allegedly believed they were only for the purpose of obtaining a union meeting. In *Unarco Industries,*[275] unambiguous cards were counted where employees had been told that the union needed "'so many more cards before they could go ahead and get an election.'"

c. Misrepresentations. An employer must show evidence of clearly material misrepresentations in order to invalidate unambiguous authorization cards. Evidence that card signers were told the cards would be used to petition for an election, to show interest in the union, and to get a representative to come to talk to employees about the union has been held insufficient to

---

[268]*See infra* notes 273–280.

[269]*See supra* notes 77–87.

[270]Reilly Tar & Chem. Corp. v. NLRB, 352 F2d 913, 60 LRRM 2437 (CA 7, 1965); TMT Trailer Ferry, 152 NLRB 1495, 59 LRRM 1353 (1965). *See also* Struthers-Dunn, Inc., *supra* note 260 (cards revoked prior to commission of any unfair labor practices not counted toward majority necessary to support bargaining order).

[271]Gupta Permold Corp., 289 NLRB 1234, 131 LRRM 1018 (1988); Quality Mkts., 160 NLRB 44, 62 LRRM 1582 (1966); Abrasive Salvage Co., 127 NLRB 381, 46 LRRM 1033 (1960).

[272]Imco Container Co., 148 NLRB 312, 56 LRRM 1497 (1964). *See* W.B. Johnson Properties, 241 NLRB 358, 100 LRRM 1547 (1979) (card signed by solicitor on behalf of employee held invalid where employee did not give permission). *But see* J.P. Stevens, *supra* note 265 (card signed by solicitor counted as that of employee who told solicitor, "If you want it signed, sign it yourself," where employee subsequently gave solicitor his telephone and post office box numbers).

[273]*Supra* note 265. *But see* Superior Container, 276 NLRB 521, 120 LRRM 1089 (1985) (English-language card not valid where signer, who spoke little English, was solicited in English).

[274]197 NLRB 54, 80 LRRM 1842 (1972), *enforced,* 485 F2d 455, 84 LRRM 2528 (CA 5, 1973).

[275]197 NLRB 489, 80 LRRM 1621, 1623 (1972).

invalidate such cards.[276] If, however, an employer can show that the employees were told that the sole purpose of the cards was to obtain an election, even clear and unambiguous cards will be deemed invalid for determining the union's majority status.[277] Thus, in *Bookland, Inc.*,[278] the Board invalidated a card where the employee was told that it was solicited solely to enable the union to keep in touch with the employees and it did not mean that the employee wanted a union. In reliance upon this misrepresentation, the employee signed the card without reading it.

Cards signed by employees of a predecessor company have been deemed valid designations of the union as the bargaining representative of the successor employer's employees.[279] Similarly, the merger of other unions with the union that solicited the cards neither voids the cards nor undermines the union's majority status, especially where the employer's unfair labor practices prevented the card signers from becoming union members eligible to vote in the merger election.[280]

d. Coercion and Related Interference. In *NLRB v. Savair Manufacturing Co.*,[281] the Supreme Court held that a union's offer to waive initiation fees for those employees who signed authorization cards prior to an election constituted election interference and grounds for setting aside the election. The Court stated that this practice "allows the union to buy endorsements and paint a false portrait of employee support during its election cam-

---

[276]Peerless, Inc. v. NLRB, 484 F2d 1108, 83 LRRM 3000 (CA 7, 1973); NLRB v. WKRG-TV, 470 F2d 1302, 82 LRRM 2146 (CA 5, 1973); Sahara Datsun, 278 NLRB 1044, 121 LRRM 1329 (1986), *enforced*, 811 F2d 1317, 124 LRRM 3168 (CA 9, 1987); Bookland, Inc., 221 NLRB 35, 90 LRRM 1492 (1975). For cases in which the Board has rejected the claim that solicitors represented that cards were to be used solely to procure an election, see, e.g., Pedro's Restaurant, 246 NLRB 567, 102 LRRM 1600 (1979); Motor Inn of Perrysburg, 243 NLRB 280, 101 LRRM 1526 (1979); Janesville Prods. Div., Amtel, Inc., 240 NLRB 854, 100 LRRM 1383 (1979). *See also* Happach v. NLRB, 353 F2d 629, 60 LRRM 2489 (CA 7, 1965); Winn-Dixie Stores, 166 NLRB 227, 65 LRRM 1637 (1967); American Cable Sys., 161 NLRB 332, 63 LRRM 1296 (1966), *enforced in part and remanded in part*, 414 F2d 661, 71 LRRM 2979 (CA 5), *on remand*, 179 NLRB 846, 72 LRRM 1524 (1969), *remanded*, 427 F2d 446, 73 LRRM 2913 (CA 5), *cert. denied*, 400 US 957, 75 LRRM 2810 (1970); Aero Corp., 149 NLRB 1283, 57 LRRM 1483 (1964), *enforced*, 363 F2d 702, 62 LRRM 2361 (CA DC), *cert. denied*, 385 US 973, 63 LRRM 2527 (1966).

[277]Fort Smith Outerwear v. NLRB, 499 F2d 223, 86 LRRM 2753 (CA 8, 1974); W & W Tool & Die Mfg. Co., 225 NLRB 1000, 93 LRRM 1006 (1976); Walgreen Co., 221 NLRB 1096, 91 LRRM 1177 (1975).

[278]*Supra* note 276.

[279]Unit Train Coal Sales, 234 NLRB 1265, 98 LRRM 1343 (1978), *enforcement denied*, 636 F2d 1121, 105 LRRM 3455 (CA 6, 1980). *See also* W. B. Johnson Properties, *supra* note 272.

[280]Goodfriend W. Corp., 232 NLRB 527, 97 LRRM 1074 (1977). *See also* Pedro's Restaurant, *supra* note 276.

[281]414 US 270, 84 LRRM 2929 (1973). For detailed discussion of *Savair*, see Chapter 9, "Restrictions on Preelection Activity: 'Laboratory Conditions,'" at notes 176–182.

paign."[282] Although the Court was primarily concerned with the coercive effect of artificially inflated union support on uncommitted employees in the preelection period, it also expressed concern about and disapproval of the use of authorization cards thus obtained as proof of majority status to support a *Gissel* bargaining order. The Board has since invalidated cards solicited in violation of the *Savair* restriction.[283] But authorization cards obtained in response to a waiver of initiation fees that are not contingent upon support for the union and which are available to all eligible voters before and after the election are valid.[284]

e. Supervisory Interference. Supervisory involvement in a union's organizational campaign is not necessarily impermissible and is not a per se basis for overturning a union's card majority. However, extensive or serious supervisory interference is prohibited; thus, cards solicited directly by supervisors from rank-and-file employees will normally be invalidated. The Board and the reviewing courts seem to have taken a pragmatic approach, whereby the totality of the supervisor's conduct is evaluated in each case.[285]

Limited supervisory involvement may be deemed insufficient to impair employee free choice.[286] For example, cards were not invalidated where a supervisor merely signed a card himself, on his own behalf, attended union meetings, and brought a coworker's signed card to a union representative.[287] The same result has obtained where a supervisor's union activity was limited to answering employees' questions, making authorization cards available to employees, and delivering signed cards to the union.[288]

---

[282]414 US at 277.

[283]Paul Distrib. Co., 264 NLRB 1378, 112 LRRM 1094 (1982).

[284]NLRB v. Gunton Co., 596 F2d 175, 101 LRRM 2181 (CA 6, 1979); NLRB v. Wabash Transformer Corp., 509 F2d 647, 88 LRRM 2545 (CA 8, 1975), *cert. denied,* 423 US 827, 90 LRRM 2553 (1975); NLRB v. Dunkirk Motor Inn, 524 F2d 663, 90 LRRM 2961 (CA 2, 1975); NLRB v. Con-Pac, Inc., 509 F2d 270, 88 LRRM 2977 (CA 5, 1974); Evans Rotork, Inc., 242 NLRB 1317, 101 LRRM 1333 (1979); Endless Mold, 210 NLRB 159, 86 LRRM 1033 (1974).

[285]*See, e.g.,* Circo Resorts, 244 NLRB 880, 102 LRRM 1262 (1979), *enforced,* 646 F2d 403, 107 LRRM 2608 (CA 9, 1981); D. V. Copying & Printing, 240 NLRB 1276, 100 LRRM 1531 (1979); El Rancho Mkt., 235 NLRB 468, 98 LRRM 1153 (1978), *enforced,* 603 F2d 223, 104 LRRM 2612 (CA 9, 1979).

[286]Kona 60 Minute Photo, 277 NLRB 867, 120 LRRM 1313 (1985); Tall Pines Inn, 268 NLRB 1392, 116 LRRM 1389 (1984).

[287]Jasta Mfg. Co., 246 NLRB 48, 102 LRRM 1610 (1979); Boston Pet Supply, 227 NLRB 1891, 95 LRRM 1096 (1977).

[288]Kroger Co., 228 NLRB 149, 94 LRRM 1586 (1977).

An example of supervisory conduct where the impact was sufficient to invalidate cards occurred in *Glomac Plastics*.[289] Two supervisors solicited between 25 and 30 of the 44 cards signed in a unit of 52 employees, distributed union literature to employees, attended union meetings, and obtained employees' names and addresses for the union.[290] The Board declined to order the employer to bargain with the union. Similarly, supervisory interference was held to taint the union's card majority where the plant manager contacted the union to initiate the organizational drive, and his wife, a plant supervisor, helped arrange the initial union meeting and solicited authorization cards.[291]

B. Change of Circumstances

The Board has held that "the validity of a bargaining order depends on an evaluation of the situation as of the time the unfair labor practices were committed."[292] Some courts have required that in order to warrant the issuance of a *Gissel* bargaining order, the Board must find that a fair election cannot be held *at the time it issues the order*.[293] In making this determination, the courts have considered such circumstances as the lapse of time between the violations and the order,[294] a significant change in employee complement,[295] subsequent picket-line misconduct by

---

[289]194 NLRB 406, 78 LRRM 1662 (1971).

[290]*Id.*

[291]Central Casket Co., 225 NLRB 362, 92 LRRM 1547 (1976).

[292]Highland Plastics, 256 NLRB 146, 147, 107 LRRM 1271 (1981). *See also* NLRB v. Wilhow Corp. dba Town & Country Supermarkets, 666 F2d 1294, 109 LRRM 2116 (CA 10, 1981).

[293]*E.g.*, NLRB v. Koenig Iron Works, 856 F2d 1, 129 LRRM 2229 (CA 2, 1988); NLRB v. Knogo Corp., 727 F2d 55, 115 LRRM 2756 (CA 2, 1984); NLRB v. Windsor Indus., 730 F2d 860, 115 LRRM 3649 (CA 2, 1984). *See also* Impact Indus. v. NLRB, 847 F2d 379, 128 LRRM 2455 (CA 7, 1988), *denying enforcement to* 285 NLRB 5, 128 LRRM 1122 (1987) (bargaining order refused enforcement because of lapse of 7 years, turnover in employee complement, and changed management of employer); NLRB v. Ship Shape Maintenance Co., 474 F2d 434, 81 LRRM 2865 (CA DC, 1972); NLRB v. Armcor Indus., 535 F2d 239, 92 LRRM 2374 (CA 3, 1976). The Third Circuit has required the Board to specifically state its reasons for issuing a bargaining order in a given case. This requirement may be met, however, by the Board's adoption of the ALJ's statement of reasons supporting recommendation of a bargaining order. Kenworth Trucks v. NLRB, 580 F2d 55, 99 LRRM 2157 (CA 3, 1978). *See* discussion *supra* at notes 192–194.

[294]NLRB v. J. Coty Messenger Serv., 763 F2d 92, 119 LRRM 2779 (CA 2, 1985); NLRB v. East Side Shopper, 498 F2d 1334, 86 LRRM 2817 (CA 6, 1974); NLRB v. Gibson Prods. Co., 494 F2d 762, 86 LRRM 2636 (CA 5, 1974).

[295]NLRB v. Gruber's Super Mkt., 501 F2d 697, 87 LRRM 2037 (CA 7, 1974); NLRB v. Ship Shape Maintenance Co., *supra* note 293; NLRB v. Coca Cola Bottling Co. of San Mateo, 472 F2d 140, 82 LRRM 2088 (CA 9, 1972).

unfair labor practice strikers,[296] and a change in ownership and management.[297]

Some courts of appeals have also required that the Board detail its rationale for determining that a fair second election cannot be conducted—a requirement with which the Board has strongly disagreed. The Third Circuit has denied enforcement of bargaining orders and remanded cases to the Board for "'a detailed analysis' of the lingering effect of the unfair labor practices and the likelihood of a fair rerun election."[298] In one such case, *Armcor Industries,*[299] the Board stated that although it "respectfully recognizes the . . . court['s judgment] as binding upon us for the purposes of deciding this case," the validity of a bargaining order "in the present case and in all similar cases should properly rest upon [the Board's] analysis of the seriousness and pervasiveness of the unlawful conduct at the time that conduct was first presented for . . . scrutiny."[300] The Board then reissued the bargaining order, enforcement of which was again denied by the Third Circuit.[301]

Other courts of appeals, however, have supported the Board's position.[302] In *NLRB v. Pacific Southwest Airlines*[303] the employer argued that the bargaining order was not an appropriate remedy because 5 years had elapsed since the unfair labor practice charges were first presented to the Board. Rejecting this argument, the Ninth Circuit said that the passage of time itself did

---

[296]Evison J. Dent, 210 NLRB 547, 86 LRRM 1357 (1974).

[297]General Steel Prods. v. NLRB, 445 F2d 1350, 77 LRRM 2801 (CA 4, 1971).

[298]Hedstrom Co. v. NLRB, 558 F2d 1137, 95 LRRM 3069, 3080 (CA 3, 1977).

[299]227 NLRB 1543, 95 LRRM 1523 (1977), *enforcement denied by equally divided court*, 588 F2d 821, 103 LRRM 2604 (CA 3, 1978).

[300]*Id.* at 1545. *See also* Hitchiner Mfg. Co., 243 NLRB 927, 102 LRRM 1091 (1979), *enforced*, 634 F2d 1110, 105 LRRM 3265 (CA 8, 1980). *See also* Northfield Cheese Co., 242 NLRB 1117, 101 LRRM 1539 (1979), *enforced without opinion*, 620 F2d 289, 106 LRRM 2546 (CA 3), *cert. denied*, 449 US 829 (1980) (bargaining order granted despite parties having entered into collective bargaining agreement after unfair labor practice hearing, because employer's actions indicated it was still trying to oust union).

[301]*Supra* note 299.

[302]Amazing Stores v. NLRB, 887 F2d 328, 132 LRRM 2753 (CA DC, 1989), *enforcing* 289 NLRB 163, 131 LRRM 1066 (1988) (to require fuller inquiry would reward employer by alerting new employees to employer's union antipathy and by further delaying proceedings). *See* NLRB v. Buckley Broadcasting Corp. dba Station KKHI, 891 F2d 230, 133 LRRM 2175 (CA 9, 1989), *enforcing* 284 NLRB 1339, 125 LRRM 1281 (1987), *cert. denied*, ___ US ___, 134 LRRM 2432 (1990); Indiana Cal-Pro v. NLRB, 863 F2d 1292, 130 LRRM 2222 (CA 6, 1988), *enforcing* 287 NLRB 796, 129 LRRM 1128 (1987); Koons Ford v. NLRB, 833 F2d 310, 126 LRRM 3032 (CA 4, 1987), *enforcing* 282 NLRB 506, 124 LRRM 1167 (1986); Piggly Wiggly v. NLRB, 705 F2d 1537, 113 LRRM 2810 (CA 11, 1983), *enforcing* 258 NLRB 1081, 108 LRRM 1323 (1981). *See* discussion *supra* at notes 192–194.

[303]550 F2d 1148, 94 LRRM 2772 (CA 9, 1977).

not necessarily compel a new election and "the appropriate time for determination of a bargaining order relates back to the time when the case arose before the Board."[304]

The Board has indicated its expectation that the Supreme Court must resolve the conflict among the circuits on this issue.[305]

C. Union Discrimination or Misconduct

In 1973, *NLRB v. Mansion House Corp.*,[306] the Eighth Circuit refused for constitutional reasons to enforce a *Gissel* remedy because of possible racial discrimination in union membership practices, holding that Board machinery should not be available to a union that either practiced racial discrimination or was unwilling to reform a past practice of racial discrimination. Thereafter, in *Bekins Moving & Storage Co.*,[307] the Board held that it would entertain as an objection to a union's certification a timely filed claim that the union engaged in invidious discrimination on the basis of race, alienage, or national origin,[308] but not sex.[309] Although *Bekins* was not an unfair labor practice case, the Board's reasoning was deemed applicable to *Gissel* bargaining orders. Later, in a 1977 decision, *Handy Andy, Inc.*,[310] the Board abandoned *Bekins* and announced that it would no longer consider issues relating to union discrimination based on race, national origin, or alienage prior to certification. Thus, the Board considers a section 8(b) unfair labor practice proceeding to be "the appropriate vehicle for resolving such issues and for devising the appropriate remedies for unlawful discrimination, including revocation of certification."[311] As to the effect of

---

[304]*Id.* at 1153. *But see* NLRB v. Western Drug, 600 F2d 1324, 101 LRRM 3023, 3024 (CA 9, 1979) (court stated that the "Board's perfunctory conclusion that a bargaining order [should issue] denied the present employees their freedom of choice without warrant").

[305]Chandler Motors, 236 NLRB 1565, 98 LRRM 1528 (1978).

[306]473 F2d 471, 82 LRRM 2608 (CA 8, 1973). *See generally* Chapter 9, "Restrictions on Preelection Activity: 'Laboratory Conditions,'" at notes 198–204, and Chapter 26, "The Duty of Fair Representation," at notes 132–138.

[307]211 NLRB 138, 86 LRRM 1323 (1974).

[308]*Id.*

[309]Bell & Howell, 213 NLRB 407, 87 LRRM 1172 (1974).

[310]228 NLRB 447, 94 LRRM 1354 (1977).

[311]*Id.* at 448. *But see* NLRB v. Heavy Lift Serv., 607F2d 1121, 102 LRRM 3061, 3063 (CA 5, 1979), *enforcing* 234 NLRB 1078, 98 LRRM 1177 (1978) (court indicated it will not enforce bargaining order "'when the employer has proffered specific evidence sufficient to demonstrate a pattern of racially discriminatory behavior by the union which would support a finding of a definite propensity for racially unfair representation,'" (quoting NLRB v. Sumter Plywood Corp., 535 F2d 917, 92 LRRM 3508, 3519 (CA 5, 1976)) (unless the Board has considered the question after hearing). *See* Meltzer, *The National Labor Relations Act and Racial Discrimination: The More Remedies the Better?*, 42 U. CHI. L. REV. 1 (1974).

union misconduct, disorderly conduct including threats of violence against strikebreakers during a long strike, did not warrant the withholding of an otherwise appropriate *Gissel* bargaining order in *Donovan v. NLRB*.[312] The Second Circuit there held that the Board is obliged to balance the respective wrongdoings of the employer and the union. If the employer is the more offending party, the Board should issue a bargaining order.

VI. WITHDRAWAL OF RECOGNITION

An employer may withdraw recognition from an incumbent union at any time when such withdrawal is not precluded by law,[313] if it can affirmatively establish either (1) that the union no longer enjoyed majority status when recognition was withdrawn, or (2) that the withdrawal was predicated on a reasonably grounded doubt as to the union's continued majority status, which doubt was asserted in good faith, based upon objective considerations, and raised in a context free of employer unfair labor practices.[314] Furthermore, the employer must be aware of the objective facts upon which its doubt is based at the time it withdraws recognition.[315] And finally, because the Act protects the right of employees freely to support or reject the incumbent, the Board will consider the impact of the employer's unfair labor practices on the union's alleged loss of majority status.[316]

---

[312]520 F2d 1316, 89 LRRM 3127 (CA 2, 1975), *cert. denied*, 423 US 1053, 91 LRRM 2099 (1976).

[313]*See* discussion *infra* at notes 317–326.

[314]NLRB v. Curtin Matheson Scientific, 494 US 775, 133 LRRM 3049 (1990), *reversing and remanding* 859 F2d 362, 129 LRRM 2801 (CA 5, 1988), *denying enforcement to* 287 NLRB 350, 127 LRRM 1114 (1987); Buckley Broadcasting Corp. dba Station KKHI, 284 NLRB 1339, 125 LRRM 1281 (1987), *enforced*, 891 F2d 230, 133 LRRM 2175 (CA 9, 1989), *cert. denied*, ____ US ____, 134 LRRM 2432 (1990); NLRB v. Windham Memorial Hosp., 577 F2d 805, 99 LRRM 2242 (CA 2, 1978); Retired Persons Pharmacy v. NLRB, 519 F2d 486, 89 LRRM 2879 (CA 2, 1975); NLRB v. Dayton Motels, 474 F2d 328, 82 LRRM 2651 (CA 6, 1973). Upon rebuttal by the employer of the presumption of continuing majority status after expiration of the certification year, the burden shifts to the General Counsel to prove that the union represented a majority of unit employees on the day the employer withdrew recognition. Dalewood Rehabilitation Hosp. v. NLRB, 566 F2d 77, 97 LRRM 2632 (CA 9, 1977), *denying enforcement to* 224 NLRB 1618, 92 LRRM 1372 (1976); Orion Corp. v. NLRB, 515 F2d 81, 89 LRRM 2135 (CA 7, 1975).

[315]Orion Corp. v. NLRB, *supra* note 314; Dayton Motels, 212 NLRB 553, 87 LRRM 1341 (1974), *enforced*, 525 F2d 476, 90 LRRM 3084 (CA 6, 1975). *See* Lammert Indus. Div., 229 NLRB 895, 96 LRRM 1557 (1977), *enforced*, 578 F2d 1223, 98 LRRM 2992 (CA 7, 1978) (good-faith doubt not supported by employee resignations from union that occurred after employer withdrew recognition).

[316]NLRB v. Anvil Prods., 496 F2d 94, 86 LRRM 2822 (CA 5, 1974), *supplemental decision on remand*, 216 NLRB 158, 88 LRRM 1223 (1975); National Cash Register Co. v. NLRB, 494 F2d 189, 85 LRRM 2657 (CA 8, 1974); Anderson Cabinets, 241 NLRB 513, 100 LRRM 1606 (1979), *enforced*, 611 F2d 1225, 103 LRRM 2103 (CA 8, 1979); Warehouse Mkt., 216 NLRB 216, 88 LRRM 1145 (1975).

Withdrawal of recognition will ordinarily be precluded by law if the union has recently been certified or recognized, or if a collective bargaining agreement is in effect. Under the rule of *Brooks v. NLRB*,[317] a union enjoys an irrebuttable presumption of continuing majority status for 1 year after it is certified by the Board. During the period of the presumption, an employer may not withdraw recognition even if the union has, in fact, lost the support of a majority of the employees in the bargaining unit. As the Court explained in *Brooks*, the rule is intended, among other things, to deter employer subversion of the bargaining process and to insulate the union from "exigent pressure to produce hothouse results."[318]

Where an employer extends voluntary recognition to a union, a comparable presumption of majority status arises and continues for a reasonable period of time.[319] Thus, in *Brennan's Cadillac*,[320] after the employer had voluntarily recognized the union, the parties met on eight occasions, over a three-month period, to negotiate an initial agreement. The union then struck. Shortly thereafter, three of the five employees in the bargaining unit wrote to the employer stating that they were withdrawing from the union and returning to work, whereupon the employer withdrew recognition. The Board held that whether a "reasonable time" has passed "turns on what transpired during [negotiations] . . . and what was accomplished therein."[321] It concluded that the bargaining relationship had been given "a fair chance to succeed," and the employer's subsequent withdrawal of recognition was lawful.[322]

Under a settlement agreement in which the employer agrees to bargain with the union, the 1-year period commences as of the effective date of the agreement.[323] Where, however, the consid-

---

[317]348 US 96, 35 LRRM 2158 (1954). *See* Chapter 10, "Representation Proceedings and Elections," at notes 85–89. *See also* Chapter 13, "The Duty to Bargain," at notes 819–833, for detailed treatment of the effect of the presumption, or its rebuttal, in the duty to bargain.

[318]348 US at 100.

[319]NLRB v. Sierra Dev. Co., 604 F2d 606, 102 LRRM 2160 (CA 9, 1979); NLRB v. Cayuga Crushed Stone, 474 F2d 1380, 82 LRRM 2951 (CA 2, 1973); Pioneer Inn Assocs. v. NLRB, 578 F2d 835, 99 LRRM 2354 (CA 9, 1978); Capitol Temptrol Corp., 243 NLRB 575, 102 LRRM 1106 (1979); Winco Petroleum Co., 241 NLRB 1118, 101 LRRM 1100 (1979).

[320]231 NLRB 225, 96 LRRM 1004 (1977).

[321]*Id.* at 226.

[322]*Id.*

[323]Straus Communications, 246 NLRB 846, 102 LRRM 1679 (1979), *enforced*, 625 F2d 458, 104 LRRM 3061 (CA 2, 1980); Pride Ref., 224 NLRB 1353, 92 LRRM 1553 (1976), *enforcement denied*, 555 F2d 453, 95 LRRM 2958 (CA 5, 1977).

eration for a non-Board settlement of a refusal-to-bargain charge does not include an agreement to bargain with the union, an employer may lawfully withdraw recognition in less than 1 year.[324]

The irrebuttable presumption of continuing majority status also attaches for the duration of a collective bargaining agreement.[325] When an employer withdraws from a multi-employer unit, "the presumption of majority status flowing from the contract in the multi-employer unit survives [the employer's] . . . withdrawal from that unit and carries over to the newly created single employer unit."[326]

In *NLRB v. Curtin Matheson Scientific*,[327] the Supreme Court accepted and applied this matrix of rules and presumptions. In that case, the employer withdrew recognition after a lockout and a strike both of which occurred during negotiations for a renewal collective bargaining agreement. During the strike, five of the strikers abandoned the strike and worked behind the picket line and the employer hired permanent replacements for other strikers so that, on the day when recognition was withdrawn "the bargaining unit consisted of 19 strikers, 25 permanent replacements, and the 5 employees who had crossed the picket line at the strike's inception."[328] The employer contended that its good-faith doubt of the union's majority was justified because the replacements and nonstriking employees, who should be presumed to oppose the union, outnumbered the strikers. The Board rejected that argument and held that the employer violated section 8(a)(5) by withdrawing recognition.[329] The Fifth Circuit refused to enforce, holding that the Board had erred in rejecting the employer's position.[330]

The Supreme Court agreed with the Board that there was no necessary presumption that either the strike replacements or the

---

[324]NLRB v. Vantran Elec. Corp., 580 F2d 921, 99 LRRM 2207 (CA 7, 1978); Crestwood Auto Supply Co., 240 NLRB 826, 100 LRRM 1480 (1979).

[325]NLRB v. Marine Optical, 671 F2d 11, 109 LRRM 2593 (CA 1, 1982). *See* NLRB v. Burns Int'l Sec. Servs., 406 US 272, 290 n.12, 80 LRRM 2225 (1972); Osteopathic Hosp. Founders Ass'n v. NLRB, 618 F2d 633, 638, 103 LRRM 2814 (CA 10, 1980).

[326]Nevada Club, 229 NLRB 1186, 1186, 96 LRRM 1466 (1977), *enforced in pertinent part sub nom.* NLRB v. Silver Spur Casino, 623 F2d 571, 104 LRRM 3068 (CA 9, 1980), *cert. denied*, 451 US 906, 106 LRRM 3077 (1981). *See also* NLRB v. Sierra Dev. Co., *supra* note 319. *But cf.* Western Distrib. Co. v. NLRB, 608 F2d 397, 102 LRRM 2510 (CA 10, 1979) (no presumption of continuing majority status found in merger-successorship setting).

[327]*Supra* note 314.

[328]*Id.*, 133 LRRM at 3051.

[329]*Id.*

[330]*Id.*

nonstriking employees no longer desired representation by the union. Accordingly, the Court held that it was allowable for the Board to require the employer to support its claim by some specific evidence showing that those employees did not desire such representation. Justice Marshall wrote for the Court, explaining that the conflict of interest between strikers and replacements did not demand a presumption that the replacements opposed the union. Especially if the union were relatively weak and could not compel the employer to discharge the replacement in favor of the strikers, Justice Marshall observed,

> [The replacing employees] may still want that union's representation after the strike, . . . despite the union's lack of bargaining strength during the strike, because of the union's role in processing grievances, monitoring the employer's actions, and performing other non-strike roles. Because the circumstances of each strike and the leverage of each union will vary greatly, it was not irrational for the Board to reject the antiunion presumption and adopt a case-by-case approach in determining replacements' union sentiments.[331]

Dissenting, Justice Scalia contended that the conflict between the unreinstated strikers and the replacements over the right to fill scarce jobs would ordinarily be so great, and the tendency of the union to support the strikers so manifest, that the Board should be required to presume that the replacements did not desire to be represented by the union.[332]

A. Employee Activity or Inactivity as a Justifying Consideration

As *Curtin Matheson* confirms, an employee may desire continued representation by a union even while engaging in a wide range of actions that disclose conflict with or opposition to the union's goals or tactics. An employee already represented by a union is rarely asked precisely the question that is squarely posed by an authorization card or by the ballot in a Board election: "Do I wish to be represented by this union?" Moreover, the questions that more commonly do confront such an employee ("Do I wish to abandon this strike? To resign from membership in the union?") are usually imperfect surrogates for the specific question whether continued representation is desired. Thus, an

---

[331] *Id.*, 133 LRRM at 3055.
[332] *Id.*, 133 LRRM at 3059 (dissenting opinion).

employer did not justify its withdrawal of recognition by producing union business records showing that only a minority of the employees in the bargaining unit were union members.[333] Likewise, an employer's showing of a decline in dues checkoff authorizations[334] (even in a right-to-work state),[335] a decline in employee membership in and support of the union, and even a majority vote to withdraw a union-shop authorization,[336] have all been held inadequate objective bases upon which to justify withdrawal of union recognition.

For similar reasons, general employee dissatisfaction with the union often has been held to be an inadequate basis upon which to justify withdrawal of recognition.[337] This was the result where the claim of dissatisfaction was based on oral complaints by employees,[338] even when made prior to the withdrawal of recognition.[339] Numerous employee statements to supervisors that the employees had no interest in the union have been deemed insufficient basis,[340] as have supervisory reports of employee dissatisfaction with the union.[341] In like manner, an employer

---

[333]Sparks Nugget, 230 NLRB 275, 95 LRRM 1298 (1977). *See also* Premium Foods v. NLRB, 709 F2d 623, 113 LRRM 3261 (CA 9, 1983) (numerous requests to union for withdrawal cards); Restaurant Employers Bargaining Ass'n, 213 NLRB 651, 87 LRRM 1194 (1974).

[334]NLRB v. Koenig Iron Works, 681 F2d 130, 110 LRRM 2995 (CA 2, 1982); NLRB v. North Am. Mfg. Co., 563 F2d 894, 96 LRRM 2635 (CA 8, 1977); NLRB v. Washington Manor, 519 F2d 750, 89 LRRM 3044 (CA 6, 1975); Imperial House Condominium, 279 NLRB 1225, 122 LRRM 1289 (1986); Grand Lodge of Ohio, 233 NLRB 143, 96 LRRM 1457 (1977); Dalewood Rehabilitation Hosp. v. NLRB, *supra* note 314; United Supermarkets, 214 NLRB 958, 87 LRRM 1434 (1974), *petition for review denied*, 90 LRRM 3344 (CA 5, 1975).

[335]Pilgrim Indus., 286 NLRB 244, 127 LRRM 1327 (1987); Imperial House Condominium, 279 NLRB 1225, 122 LRRM 1289 (1986), *enforced*, 831 F2d 999, 126 LRRM 2988 (CA 11, 1987); North Am. Mfg. Co., 224 NLRB 1252, 93 LRRM 1191 (1976). *See* Wald Transfer & Storage Co., 218 NLRB 592, 89 LRRM 1346 (1975).

[336]Orion Corp. v. NLRB, 515 F2d 81, 89 LRRM 2135 (CA 7, 1975).

[337]Retired Persons Pharmacy v. NLRB, 519 F2d 486, 89 LRRM 2879 (CA 2, 1975); Felsenthal Plastics, 224 NLRB 1312, 92 LRRM 1591 (1976). *See also* Achilles Constr. Co., 283 NLRB 87, 124 LRRM 1393 (1987); Lammert Indus. Div., 229 NLRB 895, 96 LRRM 1557 (1977); Autoprod, Inc., 223 NLRB 773, 92 LRRM 1076 (1976).

[338]Burns Int'l Sec. Servs., 225 NLRB 271, 92 LRRM 1439 (1976), *enforcement denied*, 567 F2d 945, 97 LRRM 2350 (CA 10, 1977).

[339]NLRB v. North Am. Mfg. Co., *supra* note 334. *See* Grand Lodge of Ohio, *supra* note 334.

[340]Sierra Dev. Co., 231 NLRB 22, 95 LRRM 1597 (1977); Physicians & Surgeons Community Hosp., 231 NLRB 512, 96 LRRM 1344 (1977).

[341]Bryan Memorial Hosp. v. NLRB, 814 F2d 1259, 124 LRRM 3165 (CA 8), *cert. denied*, 484 US 849, 126 LRRM 2496 (1987), *enforcing* 279 NLRB 222, 123 LRRM 1135 (1986); Dalewood Rehabilitation Hosp. v. NLRB, 566 F2d 77, 97 LRRM 2632 (CA 9, 1977), *denying enforcement to* 224 NLRB 1618, 92 LRRM 1372 (1976); C & J Transpo dba Northeast Truck Center, 296 NLRB No. 93, 132 LRRM 1253 (1989); Mingtree Restaurant dba Forbidden City Restaurant, 265 NLRB 409, 111 LRRM 1630 (1982) (employer relied on affidavits of supervisors).

poll of 300 unit employees which resulted in the receipt of 50 letters critical of the union was deemed an inadequate basis upon which to withdraw recognition.[342]

The same result has obtained where there was a lack of attendance at union meetings;[343] where there was a lack of support for a strike;[344] and where unit employees, prior to expiration of the current collective bargaining agreement, signed authorization cards of a rival union.[345] The Board has also held that the employer may not justify its withdrawal of recognition on the basis of antiunion sentiments of employees hired as strike replacements.[346]

Despite the Board's refusal to treat employees' generalized dissatisfaction with a union as the equivalent of their repudiation of its representation, specific complaints that a majority do not want union representation have been held to be a sufficient basis for an employer to withdraw recognition when the circumstances of such expressions supported the inference of repudiation.[347] Such employee sentiment has been manifested by antiunion views expressed by many unit employees,[348] by personal and specific statements from most or all unit employees that they did not want the union,[349] and by expressions of

---

[342]Burns Int'l Sec. Servs., *supra* note 338.

[343]NLRB v. A.W. Thompson, Inc., 651 F2d 1141, 107 LRRM 3245, *amended*, 651 F2d 1141, 108 LRRM 2336 (CA 5, 1981); NLRB v. North Am. Mfg. Co., *supra* note 334; Grand Lodge of Ohio, *supra* note 334; Cut & Curl, 227 NLRB 1869, 94 LRRM 1332 (1977).

[344]NLRB v. Curtin Matheson Scientific, 494 US 775, 133 LRRM 3049 (1990), *reversing and remanding* 859 F2d 362, 129 LRRM 2801 (CA 5, 1988), *denying enforcement to* 287 NLRB 350, 127 LRRM 1114 (1987); NLRB v. Buckley Broadcasting Corp. dba Station KKHI, 891 F2d 230, 133 LRRM 2175 (CA 9, 1989), *cert. denied,* ______ US ______, 134 LRRM 2432 (1990), *enforcing* 284 NLRB 1339, 125 LRRM 1281 (1987); NLRB v. Wallkill Valley Gen. Hosp., 866 F2d 632, 131 LRRM 2442 (CA 3, 1989), *enforcing* 288 NLRB 103, 127 LRRM 1318 (1988); NLRB v. Windham Memorial Hosp., 577 F2d 805, 99 LRRM 2242 (CA 2, 1978); Strange & Lindsey Beverages, 219 NLRB 1200, 90 LRRM 1236 (1975). *See* Mar-Len Cabinets, 243 NLRB 523, 101 LRRM 1613 (1979), *enforced*, 659 F2d 995, 108 LRRM 2838 (CA 9, 1981) (employees resigned from union during strike to avoid possible union fines for crossing picket line but did not thereby manifest intent to repudiate union as bargaining representative).

[345]Triplett Corp., 234 NLRB 985, 97 LRRM 1406 (1978), *enforcement denied,* 619 F2d 586, 105 LRRM 2369 (CA 6, 1980). *See also* Premium Foods v. NLRB, *supra* note 333 (numerous employee requests for withdrawal cards).

[346]Hajoca Corp., 291 NLRB No. 16, 129 LRRM 1296 (1988), *enforced*, 872 F2d 1169, 131 LRRM 2447 (CA 3, 1989); Dold Foods, 289 NLRB 1323, 129 LRRM 1174 (1988).

[347]Hartz Mountain Corp., 295 NLRB No. 48, 132 LRRM 1160 (1989); Airport Aviation Servs., 292 NLRB 823, 131 LRRM 1013 (1989); Southern Wipers, 192 NLRB 816, 78 LRRM 1070 (1971). *See* Dalewood Rehabilitation Hosp. v. NLRB, *supra* note 341.

[348]Hotel Employees Local 19 v. NLRB (Burger Pits), 785 F2d 796, 121 LRRM 3305 (CA 9, 1986), *aff'g* 273 NLRB 1001, 118 LRRM 1123 (1984) (majority of employees signed petition stating union representation not desired); Houston Shopping News Co., 233 NLRB 105, 96 LRRM 1632 (1977).

[349]Faye Nursing Home, 215 NLRB 658, 88 LRRM 1404 (1974).

several unit employees that they no longer wanted to be represented by the union.[350] The same result obtained where the dissatisfaction with the union which had been communicated to the employer was substantiated by a subsequent employer poll that revealed a majority of unit employees no longer wished union representation[351] and where the employer received a petition repudiating the union signed by 60 percent of the unit employees.[352] An employer was also held justified in withdrawing union recognition based on oral criticism of the union by unit employees made over the six-month period that preceded the withdrawal of recognition.[353] And where there was evidence that a majority of the unit employees were not members of and did not support the union, withdrawal of recognition was lawful.[354]

The Board and the circuit courts have occasionally disagreed as to whether particular facts justified withdrawal of recognition. A sharp decrease in dues checkoff authorizations, combined with a union-shop authorization vote, was held sufficient for withdrawal of recognition from a union.[355] Similarly, a valid basis for withdrawal was found where only one fourth of all unit employees had executed checkoff authorizations[356] and the union was inactive.[357]

Employers were also held to have acted lawfully in withdrawing union recognition where only a minority of employees chose to accept employment at a new plant site;[358] where a substantial number of strikers crossed the picket line and requested

---

[350]Houston Shopping News Co., *supra* note 348.

[351]White Castle Sys., 224 NLRB 1089, 92 LRRM 1591 (1976).

[352]Carolina Am. Textiles, 219 NLRB 457, 90 LRRM 1074 (1975). *See* Hotel Employees Local 19 v. NLRB (Burger Pits), *supra* note 348; NLRB v. Alvin J. Bart & Co., 598 F2d 1267, 101 LRRM 2457 (CA 2, 1979).

[353]Burns Int'l Sec. Servs. v. NLRB, 567 F2d 945, 97 LRRM 2350 (CA 10, 1977), *denying enforcement to* 225 NLRB 271, 92 LRRM 1439 (1976); Wilshire Foam Prods., 282 NLRB 1137, 125 LRRM 1212 (1987).

[354]Bil-Mar Foods, 286 NLRB 786, 126 LRRM 1275 (1987); Houston Shopping News Co., *supra* note 348.

[355]Dalewood Rehabilitation Hosp. v. NLRB, *supra* note 341. *Cf.* Peoples Gas Sys., 214 NLRB 944, 87 LRRM 1430 (1975), *reversed and remanded sub nom.* Teamsters Local 769 v. NLRB, 532 F2d 1385, 92 LRRM 2077 (CA DC, 1976), *reh'g*, 238 NLRB 1008, 99 LRRM 1423 (1978), *enforced in part*, 629 F2d 35, 104 LRRM 2224 (CA DC, 1980) (court found Board's bargaining order unreasonable remedy where evidence indicated employees no longer wished union representation).

[356]Star Mfg. Co. v. NLRB, 536 F2d 1192, 92 LRRM 3179 (CA 7, 1976), *enforcing in part* 220 NLRB 582, 90 LRRM 1360 (1975).

[357]*Id.* Among other things, the union failed to appoint a steward or file valid grievances.

[358]NLRB v. Massachusetts Mach. & Stamping, 578 F2d 15, 98 LRRM 2939 (CA 1, 1978), *denying enforcement in part to* 231 NLRB 801, 96 LRRM 1187 (1977).

reinstatement;[359] and where a substantial number of permanent replacements, who either were not interested in the union or were victims of picket-line violence, were hired.[360]

B. Activity or Inactivity by the Union

For reasons like those set out above concerning employee dissatisfactions, the apparent dormancy of the union will not, alone, justify a withdrawal of recognition. The controlling question is whether the employees continue to desire representation by the union despite its inactivity. Thus, withdrawals of recognition have been condemned when based on a union's general inactivity,[361] lack of formal organization,[362] or failure to process grievances.[363] This result was also reached where an employer relied on the infrequency of visits to the plant by union representatives[364] and the absence of bargaining for three months prior to the withdrawal of recognition.[365] Additionally, the Board found that lack of communication with the union for a 10-month period during negotiations was not a sufficient basis for withdrawal of recognition where the employer knew the union was busy negotiating contracts with other employers.[366]

Similarly, there was an inadequate basis for withdrawal of recognition where: (1) union affiliation changed, or the international union imposed a trusteeship,[367] (2) the union failed to file required reports with the Department of Labor,[368] (3) the union

---

[359]NLRB v. Randle-Eastern Ambulance Serv., 584 F2d 720, 99 LRRM 3377 (CA 5, 1978).

[360]*Id.*

[361]NLRB v. Flex Plastics, 726 F2d 272, 115 LRRM 3036 (CA 6, 1984); Pennex Aluminum Corp., 288 NLRB 439, 128 LRRM 1157 (1988); Triplett Corp., *supra* note 345.

[362]NLRB v. North Am. Mfg. Co., 563 F2d 894, 96 LRRM 2635 (CA 8, 1977). *See* Grand Lodge of Ohio, 233 NLRB 143, 96 LRRM 1457 (1977).

[363]Airport-Shuttle Cincinnati v. NLRB, 703 F2d 220, 112 LRRM 3169 (CA 6, 1983); Nevada Club, 229 NLRB 1186, 96 LRRM 1466 (1977), *enforced in pertinent part sub nom.* NLRB v. Silver Spur Casino, 623 F2d 571, 104 LRRM 3068 (CA 9, 1980), *cert. denied*, 451 US 906, 106 LRRM 3077 (1981); Burns Int'l Sec. Servs. v. NLRB, *supra* note 353.

[364]Cut & Curl, 227 NLRB 1869, 94 LRRM 1332 (1977).

[365]United Supermarkets, 214 NLRB 958, 87 LRRM 1434 (1974), *petition for review denied*, 90 LRRM 3344 (CA 5, 1975).

[366]NLRB v. Leatherwood Drilling Co., 513 F2d 270, 89 LRRM 2460 (CA 5), *cert. denied sub nom.* Brahaney Drilling Co. v. NLRB, 423 US 1016, 90 LRRM 3176 (1975), *enforcing* 209 NLRB 618, 86 LRRM 1187 (1974) *and* Brahaney Drilling Co., 209 NLRB 624, 86 LRRM 1188 (1974). *See also* Airport-Shuttle Cincinnati v. NLRB, *supra* note 363.

[367]NLRB v. Financial Inst. Employees Local 1182 (Seattle-First Nat'l Bank), 475 US 192, 121 LRRM 2741 (1986) (change in union affiliation); Triplett Corp., 234 NLRB 985, 97 LRRM 1406 (1978), *enforcement denied*, 619 F2d 586, 105 LRRM 2369 (CA 6, 1980); Nevada Club, *supra* note 363.

[368]Burns Int'l Sec. Servs. v. NLRB, *supra* note 353.

waived claims against the employer for payments that had not been made to the union's welfare funds,[369] and (4) the union engaged in race and sex discrimination.[370]

In withdrawing recognition from a union, employers may not lawfully rely on a union's attempts to organize employees prior to the withdrawal of recognition,[371] a union's reportedly unsuccessful recent organizing campaigns,[372] or a union's dilatory tactics which delayed an election that it ultimately lost.[373]

Despite the general rule that inactivity of the union will not, alone, justify a good-faith belief that the union has lost majority status, such inactivity has contributed to a successful employer defense in some cases.[374] These have included cases in which the union (1) failed to hold meetings for some time;[375] (2) failed to communicate with the employer for six months;[376] generally failed to handle grievances,[377] as by processing only one substantial grievance in 20 years;[378] or by failing to prosecute beyond the first step the two grievances that were filed within a 3-year period,[379] together with failure to file grievances challenging the employer's nonadherence to the contract.[380]

An employer also successfully withdrew recognition where the union's bargaining committee contained no union-member shop stewards or employees.[381] This same result obtained where the union officers comprising the negotiating committee resigned and the employer was not notified of the election of new officers.[382] Employers have also successfully withdrawn recognition in response to "unusual conduct" by union repre-

---

[369]Cut & Curl, *supra* note 364.

[370]R. C. Cobb, Inc., 231 NLRB 99, 95 LRRM 1576 (1977).

[371]Westinghouse Elec. Corp., 238 NLRB 763, 99 LRRM 1400 (1978).

[372]Nevada Club, *supra* note 363.

[373]Lammert Indus. Div., 229 NLRB 895, 96 LRRM 1557 (1977); Felsenthal Plastics, 224 NLRB 1312, 92 LRRM 1591 (1976); Autoprod, Inc., 223 NLRB 773, 92 LRRM 1076 (1976).

[374]Southern Wipers, 192 NLRB 816, 78 LRRM 1070 (1971).

[375]White Castle Sys., 224 NLRB 1089, 92 LRRM 1591 (1976).

[376]Southern Wipers, *supra* note 374.

[377]Burns Int'l Sec. Servs. v. NLRB, 567 F2d 945, 97 LRRM 2350 (CA 10, 1977), *denying enforcement to* 225 NLRB 271, 92 LRRM 1439 (1976).

[378]White Castle Sys., *supra* note 375.

[379]Star Mfg. Co. v. NLRB, 536 F2d 1192, 92 LRRM 3179 (CA 7, 1976), *enforcing in part* 220 NLRB 582, 90 LRRM 1360 (1975).

[380]*Id.*

[381]White Castle Sys., *supra* note 375.

[382]Burns Int'l Sec. Servs. v. NLRB, *supra* note 377.

sentatives during negotiations,[383] and where, during negotiations, union representatives made statements implying the union's lack of majority support.[384] And, in the context of other facts indicating loss of majority support, employers have lawfully withdrawn recognition based upon a union's failure to file required reports with the Department of Labor,[385] to produce a membership list as contractually required,[386] and to appoint a shop steward during a period of more than 1 year.[387] This was also the case where a union representative informed the employer that "50 to 25 to 20%" of the striking employees would not return to work.[388]

C. Filing of Decertification Petition

In 1972, in *Telautograph Corp.*,[389] the Board held that an employer did not violate section 8(a)(5) by refusing to negotiate a new agreement with an incumbent union after the filing of a valid petition for a decertification election, and where the employer had committed no unfair labor practices. The holding rested on an extension of the rule of *Shea Chemical Corp.*,[390] that an employer could not lawfully negotiate with an incumbent during the pendency of a real question concerning representation raised by the filing of a rival union's valid petition for an election.[391] In 1982, the Board first overruled *Shea Chemical*,[392] and then, in *Dresser Indus.*,[393] overruled *Telautograph*. In *Dresser* the Board held that the filing of a decertification petition will

---

[383]Peoples Gas Sys., 214 NLRB 944, 87 LRRM 1430 (1975), *reversed and remanded sub nom.* Teamsters Local 769 v. NLRB, 532 F2d 1385, 92 LRRM 2077 (CA DC, 1976), *reh'g*, 238 NLRB 1008, 99 LRRM 1423 (1978), *enforced in part*, 629 F2d 35, 104 LRRM 2224 (CA DC, 1980) (union's "unusual conduct" was change in its bargaining position, including reversing its announced intention to strike by recommending, 3 days later, that membership accept employer's offer).

[384]White Castle Sys., *supra* note 375.

[385]Burns Int'l Sec. Servs. v. NLRB, *supra* note 377.

[386]Star Mfg. Co. v. NLRB, *supra* note 379.

[387]*Id.*

[388]NLRB v. Randle-Eastern Ambulance Serv., 584 F2d 720, 99 LRRM 3377 (CA 5, 1978).

[389]199 NLRB 892, 81 LRRM 1337 (1972).

[390]121 NLRB 1027, 42 LRRM 1486 (1958).

[391]Such negotiations were deemed assistance to the incumbent union prohibited by §8(a)(2). *Id.*

[392]*See* RCA del Caribe, 262 NLRB 963, 110 LRRM 1369 (1982); Chapter 8, "Employer Domination and Assistance to Labor Organizations," at notes 138–146.

[393]264 NLRB 1088, 111 LRRM 1436 (1982). *See also* Bryan Memorial Hosp. v. NLRB, 814 F2d 1259, 124 LRRM 3165 (CA 8), *cert. denied*, 484 US 849, 126 LRRM 2496 (1987), *enforcing* 279 NLRB 222, 123 LRRM 1135 (1986).

not, alone, justify an employer's withdrawal from bargaining with an incumbent union, nor preclude the execution of an agreement reached with it. However, the Board did not preclude the withdrawal of recognition where circumstances, including the petition, justify the conclusion that the union has lost majority support as bargaining representative:

> The rule . . . in no way erodes the principle that an employer is privileged to withdraw from bargaining if, on the basis of objective evidence, it has a good-faith doubt as to the union's continued majority status. Thus . . . if an employer is presented with a valid decertification petition supported by a majority of the unit employees, it may be privileged to withdraw from bargaining.[394]

The rule requires in this setting, as in all others, that the employer not have interfered with, restrained, or coerced the employees in the petition or election process.[395] Neither may the employer invoke the rule if its own refusal to bargain, dilatory tactics, or other misconduct engendered employee dissatisfaction which led to the filing of the petition.[396]

D. Bargaining-Unit Factors

Ordinarily, the Board applies the rebuttable presumption that new employees support the union in the same proportion as employees who are already in the unit or employees whom they replace.[397] This general rule is subject to the *Curtin Matheson*[398]

---

[394]264 NLRB 1438 at n.7. *See also* Cadillac Mfg. Corp., 232 NLRB 586, 96 LRRM 1281 (1977) (letter requesting decertification sent to the Board by five of six unit employees and rival union obtained authorization cards from every unit employee and demanded recognition); Essex Int'l, 222 NLRB 121, 91 LRRM 1413 (1976) (timely petition filed by union members and supported by adequate showing of interest in context free of employer unfair labor practices). *But see* Lammert Indus. Div., 229 NLRB 895, 96 LRRM 1557 (1977) (recognition unlawfully withdrawn despite almost unanimously supported decertification petition because employer unaware of petition at time of withdrawal).

[395]United Supermarkets v. NLRB, 862 F2d 549, 130 LRRM 2212 (CA 5, 1989), *enforcing* 287 NLRB 119, 127 LRRM 1210 (1987); American Linen Supply Co., 297 NLRB No. 18, 132 LRRM 1313 (1989); Cargill, Inc., 294 NLRB No. 74, 131 LRRM 1621 (1989); Hercules Automotive, 285 NLRB 944, 127 LRRM 1060 (1987); Lomasney Combustion, 273 NLRB 1241, 118 LRRM 1501 (1984).

[396]Xidex Corp., 297 NLRB No. 9, 132 LRRM 1331 (1989); United Technologies Corp., 296 NLRB No. 79, 132 LRRM 1240 (1989).

[397]Dalewood Rehabilitation Hosp., 224 NLRB 1618, 92 LRRM 1372 (1976), *enforcement denied*, 566 F2d 77, 97 LRRM 2632 (CA 9, 1977); Laystrom Mfg. Co., 151 NLRB 1482, 58 LRRM 1624 (1965), *enforcement denied*, 359 F2d 799, 62 LRRM 2033 (CA 7, 1966); John S. Swift Co., 133 NLRB 185, 48 LRRM 1601 (1961), *enforced*, 302 F2d 342, 50 LRRM 2017 (CA 7, 1962). *Cf.* Pennco, Inc., 242 NLRB 467, 101 LRRM 1195 (1979), *enforced*, 684 F2d 340, 111 LRRM 2821 (CA 6), *cert. denied*, 459 US 994, 111 LRRM 2823 (1982) (presumption applied in bargaining unit where some, but not all, turnover was caused by employment of strike replacements).

[398]NLRB v. Curtin Matheson Scientific, 494 US 775, 133 LRRM 3049 (1990), *reversing and remanding* 859 F2d 362, 129 LRRM 2801 (CA 5, 1988), *denying enforcement to* 287 NLRB 350, 127 LRRM 1114 (1987). *See supra* notes 327–332.

exception for employees hired as permanent replacements for strikers, as to whom neither support for nor opposition to the union is presumed. Thus, employers have unlawfully withdrawn recognition when they relied on high turnover in a unit[399] or on the fact that the size of the unit had tripled.[400] This was the result even where turnover was 1,700 percent annually and 50 percent between pay periods, because such high turnover was found to be commonplace in the industry.[401] Furthermore, an employer's doubt as to a union's majority status at a facility that had been included in a multiplant unit was held an inadequate basis on which to withdraw recognition.[402]

E. Miscellaneous Factors

In *NLRB v. Financial Institution Employees Local 1182 (Seattle-First National Bank)*,[403] the Supreme Court held that withdrawal of recognition was not warranted where a previously independent incumbent union had become affiliated with an international union in a process that denied union nonmembers in the bargaining unit the opportunity to vote on the question of affiliation. In so holding, the Court rejected a rule, newly adopted by the Board,[404] that would have required participation by nonmembers as a condition for any valid affiliation, without regard to whether the change of affiliation significantly altered the identity or continuity of the organization. Emphasizing the pol-

---

[399]NLRB v. Washington Manor, 519 F2d 750, 89 LRRM 3044 (CA 6, 1975); NLRB v. Leatherwood Drilling Co., 513 F2d 270, 89 LRRM 2460 (CA 5), *cert. denied sub nom.* Brahaney Drilling Co. v. NLRB, 423 US 1016, 90 LRRM 3176 (1975), *enforcing* 209 NLRB 618, 86 LRRM 1187 (1974), *and* Brahaney Drilling Co., 209 NLRB 624, 86 LRRM 1188 (1974); Pennex Aluminum Corp., 288 NLRB 439, 128 LRRM 1157 (1988); Dalewood Rehabilitation Hosp., *supra* note 397; Wald Transfer & Storage Co., 218 NLRB 592, 89 LRRM 1346 (1975).

[400]Sierra Dev. Co., 231 NLRB 22, 95 LRRM 1597 (1977), *enforced*, 604 F2d 606, 102 LRRM 2160 (CA 9, 1979).

[401]NLRB v. Hondo Drilling Co., 525 F2d 864, 91 LRRM 2133 (CA 5), *cert. denied*, 429 US 818, 93 LRRM 2362 (1976). *See also* Burns Int'l Sec. Servs. v. NLRB, 567 F2d 945, 97 LRRM 2350 (CA 10, 1977), *denying enforcement to* 225 NLRB 271, 92 LRRM 1439 (1976); Sierra Dev., Co., *supra* note 400; Physicians & Surgeons Community Hosp., 231 NLRB 512, 96 LRRM 1344 (1977). *But see* Corallo v. Merrick Cent. Carburetor, 733 F2d 248, 251–52, 116 LRRM 2237, 2239–40 (CA 2, 1984) (significant change in operations resulting in complete employee turnover was sufficient basis to withdraw recognition); Abbott-Northwestern Hosp., 274 NLRB 1063, 118 LRRM 1521 (1985) (withdrawal of recognition lawful after employer merger).

[402]Westinghouse Elec. Corp., 238 NLRB 763, 99 LRRM 1400 (1978).

[403]475 US 192, 121 LRRM 2741 (1986).

[404]Seattle-First Nat'l Bank, 265 NLRB 426, 111 LRRM 1637 (1982), *review granted and remanded sub nom.* Financial Inst. Employees Local 1182 v. NLRB, 752 F2d 356, 116 LRRM 3409 (CA 9, 1984), *reh'g denied en banc*, 750 F2d 757, 118 LRRM 2208 (CA 9, 1985).

icy value of continuity and stability in collective bargaining relationships and the need for strong reasons for disturbing those relationships, the Court struck down the Board's new rule.

Withdrawal of recognition has been held unlawful where employers sought to justify it on a variety of other factors. Thus, it was unlawful for an employer to withdraw recognition because it had failed to obtain any evidence of the union's majority status when recognition had been extended voluntarily outside the section 10(b) period,[405] or (2) where the union lacked Board certification,[406] or (3) because of the closeness in time of the original election.[407] It has also been held that the employer could not lawfully rely on supervisory taint of which it was unaware at the time recognition was withdrawn.[408] Neither the employer's financial problems[409] nor bankruptcy proceedings[410] will justify withdrawal of recognition. A union's picket-line misconduct that violated section 8(b)(1)(A) did not justify withdrawal.[411] Finally, one employer met defeat on the argument that its presence in a right-to-work state justified its decision to withdraw recognition.[412]

---

[405]Sierra Dev. Co., *supra* note 400.

[406]*Id.*

[407]NLRB v. Washington Manor, *supra* note 399; Wald Transfer & Storage Co., *supra* note 399.

[408]NLRB v. Dayton Motels, 525 F2d 476, 90 LRRM 3084 (CA 6, 1975), *enforcing* 212 NLRB 553, 87 LRRM 1341 (1974).

[409]Edward Cooper Painting, Inc., 273 NLRB 1870, 118 LRRM 1289 (1985), *enforced,* 804 F2d 934, 123 LRRM 2905 (CA 6, 1986).

[410]Airport Bus Serv., 273 NLRB 561, 118 LRRM 1343 (1984). *See* NLRB v. Bildisco & Bildisco, 465 US 513, 115 LRRM 2805 (1984).

[411]Proxy Communications of Manhattan, 290 NLRB 540, 129 LRRM 1175 (1988), *enforced,* 873 F2d 552, 131 LRRM 2072 (CA 2, 1989).

[412]Nevada Club, 229 NLRB 1186, 1186, 96 LRRM 1466 (1977), *enforced in pertinent part sub nom.* NLRB v. Silver Spur Casino, 623 F2d 571, 104 LRRM 3068 (CA 9, 1980), *cert. denied,* 451 US 906, 106 LRRM 3077 (1981).

Part IV

THE COLLECTIVE BARGAINING PROCESS

CHAPTER 13

THE DUTY TO BARGAIN

I. INTRODUCTION

A. Historical Background

The reciprocal duty of an employer and the representative of its employees to bargain "in good faith" is among the most unruly of the obligations imposed by the National Labor Relations Act.[1] What constitutes "good faith," in the performance of the employer's duty to bargain under section 8(a)(5), or of the union's under section 8(b)(3), is not readily ascertainable, although hundreds of cases and exhaustive commentaries have undertaken the task.[2] The duty to bargain in good faith is an

[1]Section 8(d) of the National Labor Relations Act provides: "For the purposes of this section, to bargain collectively is the performance of the mutual obligation of the employer and the representative of the employees to meet at reasonable times and confer in good faith with respect to wages, hours, and other terms and conditions of employment, or the negotiation of an agreement, or any question arising thereunder, and the execution of a written contract incorporating any agreement reached if requested by either party, but such obligation does not compel either party to agree to a proposal or require the making of a concession . . . ." Under §8(a)(5), it is an unfair labor practice for an employer "to refuse to bargain collectively with the representatives of his employees, subject to the provisions of section 9(a)." Under §8(b)(3), it is an unfair labor practice for a labor organization "to refuse to bargain collectively with an employer, provided it is the representative of his employees subject to the provisions of section 9(a)." See Chapter 16, "Subjects of Bargaining," at notes 1–17, for a discussion of the historical development of the statutory language.

[2]As one commentator has observed: "If one were to select the single area of our national labor law which has posed the greatest difficulties for the National Labor Relations Board, that area could be encompassed within the phrase "the duty to bargain in good faith." Cooper, *Boulwarism and the Duty to Bargain in Good Faith*, 20 RUTGERS L. REV. 653 (1966). For other commentaries, see the following partial listing: Abrams, *Negotiating in Anticipation of Arbitration: Some Guideposts for the Initiated*, 29 CASE W. RES. L. REV. 428 (1979); Modjeska, *Guess Who's Coming to the Bargaining Table*, 39 OHIO ST. L.J. 415 (1978); Morris, *The Role of the NLRB and the Courts in the Collective Bargaining Process: A Fresh Look at Conventional Wisdom and Unconventional Remedies*, 30 VAND. L. REV. 661 (1977); *Labor Law: Unionization and Collective Bargaining* 399–495 (1976); Brooks, *Stability Versus Employee Free Choice*, 61 CORNELL L. REV. 344 (1976); Nelson & Howard, *The Duty to Bargain During*

evolving concept, rooted in statute. The Board has characterized the test of good faith as a fluctuating one, "dependent in part upon how a reasonable man might be expected to react to the bargaining attitude displayed by those across the table."[3] Such a "test," however, should not be confused with the definitional standards that the Board and the courts have developed to describe the concept.[4]

1. Origin of Concept of Collective Bargaining. Originally, most of the case law and much of the legislation in the field of labor relations were concerned with the prevention of open hostility resulting from disputes, rather than the prevention of the friction between employers and employees that was the direct cause of the disputes.[5] The United States Commission Report on the Chicago Strike of 1894,[6] the Erdman Act of 1898,[7] and the Supreme Court's 1908 decision in *Adair v. United States*,[8] three of the earliest executive, legislative, and judicial

---

the Term of an Existing Agreement, 27 LAB. L.J. 573 (1976); Pulle, *The Private Collective Bargaining Process; A Human Dignity Approach*, 5 SAN FERN. V. L. REV. 1 (1976); Kleiman, *Collective Bargaining in Perspective*, 13 DUQ. L. REV. 481 (1975); Feller, *A General Theory of the Collective Bargaining Agreement*, 61 CALIF. L. REV. 663 (1973); Gould, *Black Power in the Unions; The Impact Upon Collective Bargaining Relationships*, 79 YALE L.J. 46 (1969); Summers, *Collective Agreements and the Law of Contracts*, 78 YALE L.J. 525 (1969); Gross, Cullen & Hanslowe, *Good Faith in Labor Negotiations: Tests and Remedies*, 53 CORNELL L. REV. 1009 (1968); Duvin, *The Duty to Bargain: Law in Search of Policy*, 64 COLUM. L. REV. 248, 266 (1964); Fleming, *The Obligation to Bargain in Good Faith*, 16 SW. L.J. 43 (1962); Feinsinger, *The National Labor Relations Act and Collective Bargaining*, 57 MICH. L. REV. 807, 812 (1959); Cox, *The Duty to Bargain in Good Faith*, 71 HARV. L. REV. 1401 (1958); Humphrey, *The Duty to Bargain*, 16 OHIO ST. L.J. 403, 418 (1955); Taplitz, *Refusal to Bargain*, NYU SEVENTH ANNUAL CONFERENCE ON LABOR 171 (1954); Cox, *Government Regulation of the Negotiation and Terms of Collective Bargaining Agreement*, 101 U. PA. L. REV. 1137 (1953); Cox & Dunlop, *The Duty to Bargain Collectively During the Term of an Existing Agreement*, 63 HARV. L. REV. 1097 (1950); Sherman, *Employer's Obligation to Produce Data for Collective Bargaining*, 35 MINN. L. REV. 24, 32 (1950); Note, *Automation and Collective Bargaining*, 84 HARV. L. REV. 1822 (1971); Note, *Coordinated-Coalition Bargaining: Theory, Legality, Practice and Economic Effects*, 55 MINN. L. REV. 599 (1971); Comment, *Coordinated Bargaining: The Unions' Attempt to Answer a Need*, 3 U.S.F. L. REV. 353 (1969); Comment, *The Status of Multi-employer Bargaining Under the National Labor Relations Act*, 67 DUKE L.J. 558 (1967); Note, *Boulwarism and Good Faith Collective Bargaining*, 63 MICH. L. REV. 1473 (1965); Note, *Employer's Duty to Supply Economic Data for Collective Bargaining*, 57 COLUM. L. REV. 112 (1957); Note, *Slowdowns and Work Stoppages Not Evidence of Union's Failure to Bargain in Good Faith*, 69 HARV. L. REV. 1337 (1956); Note, *Harassment by Unions as a Refusal to Bargain Under Section 8(b)(3) of the National Labor Relations Act*, 64 YALE L.J. 766 (1955); Note, *Labor Law—Collective Bargaining—Duty of an Employer to Bargain*, 36 MINN. L. REV. 109 (1951); Note, *Employer's Duty to Bargain Under the National Labor Relations Act*, 22 NOTRE DAME LAW. 95 (1946).

[3]Times Publishing Co., 72 NLRB 676, 682–83, 19 LRRM 1199 (1947).

[4]See notes 34–50 *infra* and accompanying text.

[5]*See generally* Chapter 1, "Historical Background of the Wagner Act."

[6]*See* Chapter 1, "Historical Background of the Wagner Act," at notes 44–47.

[7]Ch. 370, 30 Stat. 424 (1898) (repealed 1926). *See* Chapter 1, "Historical Background of the Wagner Act," at notes 48–52.

[8]208 US 161 (1908). *See* Chapter 1, "Historical Background of the Wagner Act," at notes 50–53 and 62.

forays into the labor relations area, were concerned primarily with the conciliation and arbitration of disputes. The Clayton Act[9] and the Norris-LaGuardia Act[10] also dealt largely with control of concerted activity and employment disputes rather than with the prevention of disputes.

When it became apparent in 1917, however, that governmental intervention would be necessary to prevent labor disputes from interfering with war production, the establishment of the War Labor Board gave recognition to the right of workers to organize in trade unions and to bargain collectively through their chosen representatives.[11] This granting of governmental protection to collective bargaining was a step toward federal regulation to encourage settlement of conditions of employment at the bargaining table. The War Labor Board put this principle into effect in the *Western Cold Storage*[12] case by requiring that the parties "take up the differences that still exist in an earnest endeavor to reach an agreement on all points at issue."

The old National Labor Board, set up under the National Industrial Recovery Act,[13] followed the War Labor Board in announcing that it would adhere to the "incontestably sound principle that the employer is obligated by the statute to negotiate in good faith with his employees' representatives; to match their proposals, if unacceptable, with counterproposals; and to make every reasonable effort to reach an agreement."[14] Compromise was an essential part of the statutory obligation under the National Recovery Act, and the National Labor Board decided that this statutory concept conferred a duty on employers to bargain, which was more than a bare requirement to meet and confer. The National Labor Board thus contemplated that both parties would approach negotiations with an open mind and make reasonable efforts to reach a common ground of agreement.[15]

---

[9]Ch. 323, 38 Stat. 730 (1914) (current version at 15 USC §12 et seq.) (1976). *See* Chapter 1, "Historical Background of the Wagner Act," at notes 54–61.

[10]Ch. 90, 47 Stat. 70 (1932), 29 USC §101 et seq. (1976). *See* Chapter 1, "Historical Background of the Wagner Act," at notes 72–79.

[11]National War Labor Board, Principles and Rules of Procedure 4 (1919).

[12]No. 80 (War Lab. Bd. 1919).

[13]The National Industrial Recovery Act was declared unconstitutional under the Commerce Clause, and also as an illegal delegation of legislative power, in Schechter Poultry Corp. v. United States, 295 US 495 (1935). *See* Chapter 2, "The Wagner Act Period," at notes 2–6.

[14]Houde Eng'g Corp., 1 NLRB (old series) 35 (1935).

[15]National Lock Co., 1 NLRB (old series) 15 (1934); Hall Baking Co., 1 NLRB (old series) 83 (1934); Dresner & Son, 1 NLRB (old series) 26 (1934); Budd Mfg. Co., 1 NLRB (old series) 58 (1933).

2. The Wagner Act. Section 8(5) of the original National Labor Relations Act required that an employer "bargain collectively with the representatives of his employees." Section 9(a) stated that such bargaining should be "in respect to rates of pay, wages, hours of employment, or other conditions of employment." These two brief statements constituted the entire expression of the duty to bargain collectively imposed by the Wagner Act.

Section 8(5) had been deleted from the bill in the hearings on S.2926, but was restored in S.1958 at the urging of Lloyd K. Garrison, chairman of the old National Labor Board. While the legislators agreed that section 8(5) did not compel anyone to make a contract,[16] the opinions among congressmen varied with regard to what section 8(5) did require. For example, Senator Walsh stated that "[a]ll the bill proposed to do is escort representatives to the bargaining door, not control what goes on behind the door."[17] But Senator Wagner saw a stronger requirement: "The bill requires the parties to match unacceptable proposals and to make every effort to reach agreement."[18]

In its first effort to clarify the Act, in its *Jones & Laughlin*[19] holding, the Supreme Court stressed that the Act encourages free opportunity for negotiation to bring about adjustments and agreements. Soon after, in *Pennsylvania Greyhound Lines*,[20] the Court emphasized the importance of union recognition in securing collective bargaining and declared that the legislative intent expressed in the NLRA was an extension of Railway Labor Act[21] principles. Finally, in the 1938 *Consolidated Edison* case,[22] the Court stated that the manifest objective of the Act in providing for collective bargaining was "the making of contracts with labor organizations."[23]

3. The Taft-Hartley Amendments: The Statutory Language. The basic shortcomings relative to bargaining which Congress

---

[16]79 CONG. REC. 7571 (1935). For history of the Wagner Act, see Chapters 1, "Historical Background of the Wagner Act," and 2, "The Wagner Act Period."

[17]79 CONG. REC. 7660 (1935). *See* Chapter 16, "Subjects of Bargaining," at note 20.

[18]*Hearings on H.R. 6288*, 74th Cong., 1st Sess. 16 (1935). Senator Wagner's concept proved to be the more accurate as a prediction of how the law would actually develop.

[19]NLRB v. Jones & Laughlin Steel Corp., 301 US 1, 1 LRRM 703 (1937). For discussion of the constitutional issue in the case, see Chapter 28, "Jurisdiction: Coverage of the Act," at notes 1–11.

[20]NLRB v. Pennsylvania Greyhound Lines, 303 US 261, 2 LRRM 599 (1938).

[21]44 Stat. 577 (1926), 45 USC §§161–63 (1964).

[22]Consolidated Edison Co. v. NLRB, 305 US 197, 3 LRRM 645 (1938).

[23]*Id.* at 236.

sought to remedy in the Taft-Hartley amendments were the lack of a statutory obligation (reciprocal to that of employers) that unions must bargain, and the lack of an objective standard by which the courts and the Board could determine whether a party had unlawfully refused to bargain. The House of Representatives detected in some Board decisions a tendency to judge the reasonableness of employers' proposals or counterproposals and concessions.[24] Some court decisions also tended to examine the terms of the proposals rather than the nature of the bargaining.[25] The House proposed a lengthy and detailed objective test for determining what constituted good faith in collective bargaining.[26]

While the proposed Senate bill, which was subsequently passed almost intact, did not prescribe a purely objective test, it had substantially that effect since it precluded the Board from determining the merits of the parties' positions.[27] The Senate's use of the word "concession" as to requirements that might not be made of the employer, rather than the word "counterproposal," was intended to meet the objection of the then-chairman of the National Labor Relations Board that eliminating any duty to make counterproposals would remove one of the readiest indicia of good or bad faith.[28] The requirements provided by Congress in section 8(d) of the Taft-Hartley amendments, that the parties "confer in good faith," were almost identical to the requirements that had been propounded by the Supreme Court in *NLRB v. Jones & Laughlin Steel Corp.*[29]

---

[24]*See, e.g.*, J. I. Case Co., 71 NLRB 1145, 19 LRRM 1100 (1946) (refusal to consider closed shop); Burgie Vinegar Co., 71 NLRB 829, 19 LRRM 1055 (1946) (demand that union agree to reimburse employer for any damages from strike); Jasper Blackburn Prods. Corp., 21 NLRB 1240, 6 LRRM 169 (1940) (requiring union to make itself legally responsible for contract violations); Dallas Cartage Co., 14 NLRB 411, 4 LRRM 445 (1939) (insistence on collective bargaining rather than arbitration provisions); Globe Cotton Mills, 6 NLRB 461, 2 LRRM 172 (1938), *enforced in part*, 103 F2d 91, 4 LRRM 621 (CA 5, 1939) (refusal to make counterproposals held refusal to bargain); S. L. Allen & Co., 1 NLRB 714, 1 LRRM 29 (1936) (refusal to make concessions with respect to any clause in proposed agreement held to violate duty to bargain). *See* Kuelthau, *The NLRB and the Duty to Make Concessions in Bargaining*, 18 LAB. L.J. 201, 202 (1967). The history of the Taft-Hartley Act is treated in Chapter 3, "The Taft-Hartley Changes."

[25]"The fair dealing . . . must be exhibited by the parties . . . in their specific treatment of the particular subjects or items for negotiation." NLRB v. Pilling & Son Co., 119 F2d 32, 37, 8 LRRM 557 (CA 3, 1941). *See also* H.J. Heinz Co. v. NLRB, 311 US 514, 7 LRRM 291 (1941); Texas Foundries v. NLRB, 211 F2d 791, 33 LRRM 2883 (CA 5, 1954).

[26]H.R. REP. NO. 245, 80th Cong., 1st Sess. 21 (1947).

[27]*See* HOUSE COMM. OF CONF. REP. NO. 510, 80th Cong., 1st Sess. 34, *reprinted in* 1947 U.S. CODE CONG. & ADMIN. NEWS 1135, 1140.

[28]S. REP. NO. 105, 80th Cong., 1st Sess. 24 (1947).

[29]*Supra* note 19. *See* Chapter 28, "Jurisdiction: Coverage of the Act," at notes 1–9.

Both the House and the Senate agreed that section 8(b)(3)[30] simply promoted equality and responsibility in bargaining by making the duty to bargain mutual.[31] Such mutuality of obligation in the duty to bargain had already been considered by a few courts.[32] The provision was added to the statute as part of the Taft-Hartley amendments.

B. Elements of the Bargaining Obligation

1. The Duty to Meet, Confer, and Negotiate. While the Act does not prescribe any particular frequency with which the parties are required to negotiate, it does expressly require them "to meet at reasonable times and confer in good faith with respect to . . . the negotiation of an agreement . . . ."[33] Where an employer had repeatedly declared that it would sign no written agreement, the Fourth Circuit, in *NLRB v. Highland Park Manufacturing Co.*,[34] declared that

> [t]he Act, it is true, does not require that the parties agree; but it does require that they negotiate in good faith *with the view of reaching an agreement if possible*; and mere discussion with the representatives of employees, with a fixed resolve on the part of the employer not to enter into any agreement with them, even as to matters as to which there is no disagreement, does not satisfy its provisions.[35]

While various decisions, such as *NLRB v. George P. Pilling & Son Co.*,[36] *NLRB v. Montgomery Ward & Co.*,[37] *NLRB v. Reed & Prince Manufacturing Co.*,[38] and *NLRB v. Boss Manufacturing Co.*,[39] have elaborated on the *Highland Park* definition, the basic require-

---

[30] *See supra* note 1.

[31] H.R. REP. NO. 245, 80th Cong., 1st Sess. 19 (1947).

[32] Globe Cotton Mills v. NLRB, 103 F2d 91, 4 LRRM 621 (CA 5, 1939); NLRB v. Sands Mfg. Co., 96 F2d 721, 2 LRRM 712 (CA 6, 1938), *aff'd*, 306 US 332, 4 LRRM 530 (1939).

[33] Section 8(d).

[34] 110 F2d 632, 6 LRRM 786 (CA 4, 1940).

[35] *Id.* at 637 (emphasis added).

[36] *Supra* note 25 (requiring that good faith be exhibited in parties' approach and attitude to negotiations as well as in their specific treatment of particular subjects, plus common willingness to discuss their claims and demands freely and fully and, when opposed, to justify them by reason).

[37] 133 F2d 676, 12 LRRM 508 (CA 9, 1943) (requiring active participation indicating present intent to find basis for agreement).

[38] 118 F2d 874, 8 LRRM 478 (CA 1, 1941), *cert. denied*, 313 US 595, 8 LRRM 458 (1941) (allowing Board to find refusal to bargain from fact that employer displayed completely closed mind without any spirit of cooperation and complete absence of required good faith).

[39] 118 F2d 187, 8 LRRM 729 (CA 7, 1941) (requiring open and fair mind plus endeavor to overcome existing obstacles and difficulties).

ment set forth therein remains the same: the parties must negotiate with the view of trying to reach an agreement.[40]

2. The Obligation to Deal in Good Faith. The Wagner Act had no explicit requirement that the employer bargain in good faith, only that it bargain. The Board, however, almost immediately included the additional requirement that such bargaining be done in good faith,[41] with a "*bona fide* intent to reach an agreement."[42]

When first called upon to enforce Board orders, the federal courts did not adopt the good-faith requirement as such. But they did require an employer to engage in sincere negotiations with an intent to settle differences and arrive at an arrangement.[43] Some cases continued to follow that view of the bargaining obligation even after Taft-Hartley had specifically added the good-faith requirement.[44] Under the original Wagner Act, the Supreme Court in *NLRB v. Sands Manufacturing Co.*[45] upheld a test which did not specify good faith but did consider the "sincerity" of the employer's effort.[46] Two years later, in *National Licorice Co. v. NLRB*,[47] the Court adopted "good faith" as the standard for an employer's conduct.

Bad-faith bargaining typically must be inferred from a party's conduct at or away from the bargaining table, since an intent to frustrate agreement is rarely articulated. The distinction between lawful "hard" bargaining and unlawful "bad-faith" or "surface" bargaining is a difficult one to draw and depends on the facts of each case.[48] Section 8(d) of the Act does not "compel

---

[40]NLRB v. Southwestern Porcelain Steel Corp., 317 F2d 527, 53 LRRM 2307 (CA 10, 1963); NLRB v. Herman Sausage Co., 275 F2d 229, 45 LRRM 2829 (CA 5, 1960); Majure v. NLRB, 198 F2d 735, 30 LRRM 2441 (CA 5, 1952); California Girl, 129 NLRB 209, 46 LRRM 1533 (1960).

[41]NLRB, 1937 ANNUAL REPORT 82, 82–85 (1937); Atlas Mills, 3 NLRB 10, 1 LRRM 60 (1937).

[42]3 NLRB at 21.

[43]NLRB v. Biles-Coleman Lumber Co., 98 F2d 18, 2 LRRM 757 (CA 9, 1938). *See also* Globe Cotton Mills v. NLRB, *supra* note 32; Jeffery-DeWitt Insulator Co. v. NLRB, 91 F2d 134, 1 LRRM 634 (CA 4, 1937), *cert. denied*, 302 US 731, 2 LRRM 623 (1937).

[44]*E.g.*, NLRB v. Shannon, 208 F2d 545, 33 LRRM 2270 (CA 9, 1953).

[45]306 US 332, 4 LRRM 530 (1939), *aff'g* 96 F2d 721, 2 LRRM 712 (CA 6, 1938).

[46]"The sincerity of the employer's effort is to be tested by the length of time involved in the negotiations, their frequency, and the persistence with which the employer offers opportunity for agreement." 96 F2d at 725.

[47]309 US 350, 6 LRRM 674 (1940). *See also* H.J. Heinz Co. v. NLRB, 311 US 514, 7 LRRM 291 (1941).

[48]Soule Glass & Glazing Co. v. NLRB, 652 F2d 1055, 107 LRRM 2781 (CA 1, 1981), *denying enforcement in part to* 246 NLRB 792, 102 LRRM 1693 (1979); Virginia Holding Corp. dba Hotel Roanoke, 293 NLRB 182, 132 LRRM 1229 (1989) (Board reviewed totality of employer's conduct at and away from bargaining table); Overnite Transp. Co.,

either party to agree to a proposal or require the making of a concession . . . ."[49] But the Board does consider the justification for proposals and a willingness to make concessions in evaluating whether "the totality of the circumstances" shows good-faith bargaining.[50]

3. The Subjects of Bargaining. While section 8(5) of the original Wagner Act established the employer's duty to "bargain collectively" with the employees' representative "subject to the provisions of Section 9(a)," nowhere in the original Act were the subjects of collective bargaining enumerated or defined. Section 9(a) did, however, provide that the representatives designated or selected by the employees in an appropriate unit would be the exclusive representatives "for the purposes of collective bargaining in respect to rates of pay, wages, hours of employment, or other conditions of employment . . . ." This provision was later used by the courts to determine the scope of the bargaining obligation.[51]

Three categories of bargaining subjects have evolved since 1935: mandatory, permissive, and illegal.[52] Because of the absence of a precise statutory definition of the subjects over which parties were required to bargain under the Act, the Board very early assumed the role of defining compulsory bargaining subjects.[53]

---

296 NLRB No. 77, 132 LRRM 1176, 1179 (1989) (unlawful statements prior to bargaining "established the context in which [the parties] commenced negotiations"); Eltec Corp., 286 NLRB 890, 127 LRRM 1021 (1987).

[49]Barry-Wehmiller Co., 271 NLRB 471, 472, 116 LRRM 1496 (1984); *see also* American Commercial Lines, 291 NLRB 1066, 131 LRRM 1561 (1988).

[50]American Commercial Lines, *supra* note 49. *See also* K-B Resources dba Commercial Candy Vending Mach., 294 NLRB No. 82, 131 LRRM 1477 (1989); Cook Bros. Enters. dba Challenge-Cook Bros., 288 NLRB 387, 128 LRRM 1074 (1988); Houston County Elec. Coop., 285 NLRB 1213, 129 LRRM 1337 (1987); Schwab Foods dba Mooresville IGA Foodliner, 284 NLRB 1055, 125 LRRM 1225 (1987), *enforced*, 858 F2d 1285, 129 LRRM 2601 (CA 7, 1988); Hyatt Regency New Orleans, 281 NLRB 279, 124 LRRM 1142 (1986).

[51]*See generally* Chapter 16, "Subjects of Bargaining."

[52]Chapter 16, "Subjects of Bargaining," provides a general historical perspective on all three categories. *See generally* Rabin, Fibreboard *and the Termination of Bargaining Unit Work: The Search for Standards in Defining the Scope of the Duty to Bargain*, 71 COLUM. L. REV. 803 (1971); Schwarz, *Plant Relocation or Partial Termination—The Duty to Decision-Bargain*, 39 FORDHAM L. REV. 81 (1970); Sheinkman, *Plant Removal Under the National Labor Relations Act: Can Bargaining Be Avoided and Should Bargaining Be Avoided*, NYU SIXTEENTH ANNUAL CONFERENCE ON LABOR 81 (1963); Case Comment, *Duty to Bargain About Termination of Operations:* Brockway Motor Trucks, Inc. v. NLRB, 92 HARV. L. REV. 768 (1979); Note, *Application of the Mandatory-Permissive Dichotomy to the Duty to Bargain and Unilateral Action: A Review and Reevaluation*, 15 WM. & MARY L. REV. 918 (1974); Comment, *Union Dues Checkoff as a Subject in Labor Management Negotiations: Good Faith Bargaining and NLRB Remedies*, 39 FORDHAM L. REV. 299 (1970).

[53]In 1940 the Board held that "[p]aid holidays, vacations, and bonuses constitute an integral part of the earnings and working conditions of the employees and . . . are

Interpretation of the statutory language requiring parties to "confer in good faith with respect to wages, hours, or other terms and conditions of employment" led to a distinction between *mandatory* and *permissive* subjects of bargaining. In *NLRB v. Borg-Warner Corp., Wooster Division*,[54] the Supreme Court in 1958 affirmed and adopted this distinction. It observed that the duty to bargain created by sections 8(a)(5) and 8(d) is "limited to those subjects" enumerated in those sections, "and within that area neither party is legally obligated to yield."[55] Distinguishing permissive bargaining subjects, the Court noted that "as to [such] other matters, however, each party is free to bargain or not to bargain and to agree or not to agree."[56]

Examples of *permissive* subjects of bargaining include collective bargaining provisions covering supervisors[57] or agricultural labor,[58] performance bonds,[59] legal-liability clauses,[60] and internal union affairs.[61]

---

matters which are generally the subject of collective bargaining . . . . [I]nsistence upon treating such matters as gratuities[,] to be granted and withdrawn at will, constitutes a refusal to bargain . . . ." Singer Mfg. Co., 24 NLRB 444, 470, 6 LRRM 405 (1940), *enforced*, 119 F2d 131, 8 LRRM 740 (CA 7), *cert. denied*, 313 US 595, 8 LRRM 458 (1941).

Following the *Singer* case, the Board held that other integral aspects of the employment relationship were "rates of pay, wages, hours of employment or other conditions of employment" within the meaning of section 9(a), and were therefore mandatory bargaining subjects. *See* Chapter 16, "Subjects of Bargaining," at notes 5–16. *See also* Cox & Dunlop, *Regulation of Collective Bargaining by the National Labor Relations Board*, 63 HARV. L. REV. 389, 397–401 (1950).

[54]356 US 342, 42 LRRM 2034 (1958). *See generally* Chapter 16, "Subjects of Bargaining," at notes 24–29.

[55]356 US at 349.

[56]*Id.*, citing NLRB v. American Nat'l Ins. Co., 343 US 395, 30 LRRM 2147 (1952). For an earlier and somewhat analogous categorization, see Cox & Dunlop, *supra* note 53.

[57]NLRB v. Retail Clerks (Safeway Co.), 203 F2d 165, 31 LRRM 2606 (CA 9, 1953), adjudging union in contempt for insisting on bargaining for supervisory employees in violation of a consent decree, *enforcing* 96 NLRB 581, 28 LRRM 1554 (1951), *cert. denied*, 348 US 839, 34 LRRM 2898 (1954); Plumbers & Pipe Fitters, Southern Cal. Pipe Trades Dist. Council 16 (Aero Plumbing Co.), 167 NLRB 1004, 66 LRRM 1233 (1967), *enforced*, 449 F2d 668, 78 LRRM 2260 (CA 9, 1971).

[58]Mine Workers Dist. 50 (Central Soya Co.), 142 NLRB 930, 939, 53 LRRM 1178 (1963).

[59]NLRB v. Reeves & Sons, 47 LRRM 2480 (CA 10, 1961), *adjudicating contempt for violating* 273 F2d 710, 45 LRRM 2295 (CA 10, 1959), *cert. denied*, 366 US 914, 48 LRRM 2071 (1961); Newberry Equip. Co., 135 NLRB 747, 49 LRRM 1571 (1962); Teamsters Local 294 (Conway's Express), 87 NLRB 972, 978–79, 25 LRRM 1202, 1210 (1949), *enforced sub nom.* Rabouin v. NLRB, 195 F2d 906, 29 LRRM 2617 (CA 2, 1952); Amory Garment Co., 80 NLRB 182, 23 LRRM 1081 (1948), *enforced*, 24 LRRM 2274 (CA 5, 1949); Cookeville Shirt Co. & P.M. French, 79 NLRB 667, 22 LRRM 1438 (1948). *See also* Painters Local 164 v. NLRB (Cheatham Painting Co.), 293 F2d 133, 48 LRRM 2060 (CA DC), *cert. denied*, 368 US 824, 48 LRRM 3110 (1961) (union insistence on employer performance bond).

[60]Radiator Specialty Co., 143 NLRB 350, 53 LRRM 1319 (1963), *enforced in part*, 336 F2d 495, 57 LRRM 2097 (CA 4, 1964). *See also* North Carolina Furniture, 121 NLRB 41, 42 LRRM 1271 (1958).

[61]NLRB v. Corsicana Cotton Mills, 178 F2d 344, 24 LRRM 2494 (CA 5, 1949) (per curiam).

Although the law permits, but does not compel, bargaining about permissive subjects, there is another category, *illegal* subjects, about which the parties are forbidden to bargain. Among these subjects are closed-shop provisions,[62] hiring-hall provisions that give preference to union members,[63] "hot cargo" clauses that violate section 8(e),[64] contract provisions inconsistent with a union's duty to fair representation,[65] and contract clauses that discriminate among employees on invidious bases, such as race, religion, sex, or national origin.[66]

II. PER SE VIOLATIONS

In determining whether an unlawful refusal to bargain has occurred, the Board and the courts usually probe the conduct of the parties for evidence of the presence or absence of subjective "good faith." However, certain types of conduct have been viewed as independent or per se refusals to bargain, without regard to any considerations of good or bad faith.[67] As the following cases demonstrate, such conduct generally involves an absence of bargaining, frequently selective as to subjects; thus it is the *failure to negotiate*, rather than the absence of good faith, which lies at the heart of any violation involving this type of conduct.

A. Unilateral Changes[68]

Unilateral changes by an employer during the course of a collective bargaining relationship concerning matters that are

---

[62]Penello v. Mine Workers, 88 F Supp 935, 25 LRRM 2368 (DDC, 1950). *See* Chapter 22, "Secondary Strikes and Picketing."

[63]NLRB v. National Maritime Union (Texas Co.), 175 F2d 686, 24 LRRM 2268 (CA 2, 1949), *cert. denied*, 338 US 954, 25 LRRM 2395 (1950). *See* Chapter 22, "Secondary Strikes and Picketing."

[64]Lithographers Local 17 (Graphic Arts Employers Ass'n), 130 NLRB 985, 47 LRRM 1374 (1961), *aff'd*, 309 F2d 31, 51 LRRM 2093 (CA 9, 1962), *cert. denied*, 372 US 943, 52 LRRM 2673 (1963). *see* Chapter 24, "Section 8(e): The 'Hot-Cargo' Agreement."

[65]Longshoremen (ILA) Local 1367 (Galveston Maritime Ass'n), 148 NLRB 897, 57 LRRM 1083 (1964), *enforced*, 368 F2d 1010, 63 LRRM 2559 (CA 5, 1966), *cert. denied*, 389 US 837, 66 LRRM 2307 (1967). *See* Chapter 26, "The Duty of Fair Representation."

[66]*E.g.*, Metal Workers (Hughes Tool Co.), 147 NLRB 1573, 56 LRRM 1289 (1964). *See* Chapter 26, "The Duty of Fair Representation."

[67]During the period prior to passage of Taft-Hartley, this same category of cases existed, but the distinction did not become pronounced until the passage of the Taft-Hartley amendments added a good-faith requirement separate from the general duty-to-bargain requirement.

[68]This section treats unilateral changes as per se refusals to bargain. See discussion at notes 353–369 *infra*, for treatment of unilateral changes as *evidence* of bad-faith bargaining. *See also* McGuckin, *Clipping the Fringes: An Employer's Duty to Bargain Prior to Unilaterally Changing Employee Benefits*, 10 U.S.F. L. REV. 175 (1975).

mandatory subjects of bargaining are normally regarded as per se refusals to bargain.[69] These actions, committed without negotiation and achieved through bypassing the union, may sometimes support an inference of lack of good faith.[70] While such conduct has been analyzed by the Board and the circuit courts both in per se terms[71] and in terms based on a good-faith standard,[72] the Supreme Court did not give express recognition to the per se determination in this context until the 1962 case of *NLRB v. Katz*.[73] In *Katz* the employer's unilateral changes in conditions of employment (changes in sick-leave and merit-wage policies, and general wage increase) were characterized by the Court as follows:

> A refusal to negotiate *in fact* as to any subject which is within §8(d), and about which the union seeks to negotiate, violates §8(a)(5) though the employer has every desire to reach agreement with the union upon an over-all collective agreement and earnestly and in all good faith bargains to that end.[74]

Thus, a violation was found despite the absence of bad faith; indeed, where there was even a possibility of subjective good faith.

The Court in *Katz* referred to its earlier decision in *NLRB v. Crompton-Highland Mills*,[75] where a wage increase greater than that offered to the union was granted immediately after an impasse had developed. While that opinion was not framed in per se language, the absence of any other indicia of bad faith

[69]NLRB v. Katz, 369 US 736, 50 LRRM 2177 (1962); NLRB v. American Mfg. Co., 351 F2d 74, 60 LRRM 2122 (CA 5, 1965) (granting wage increase under pressure of Interstate Commerce Commission); NLRB v. Zelrich Co., 344 F2d 1011, 59 LRRM 2225 (CA 5, 1965) (unilateral wage increase); McLean v. NLRB, 333 F2d 84, 56 LRRM 2475 (CA 6, 1964) (granting health insurance); NLRB v. Citizens Hotel Co., 326 F2d 501, 55 LRRM 2135 (CA 5, 1964) (discontinuing Christmas bonus); NLRB v. Central Ill. Pub. Serv. Co., 324 F2d 916, 54 LRRM 2586 (CA 7, 1963) (discontinuing employee discount); Hyatt Hotels Corp., 296 NLRB No. 36, 132 LRRM 1130 (1989); Peelle Co., 289 NLRB 113, 130 LRRM 1365 (1988); GTE Automatic Elec., 240 NLRB 297, 100 LRRM 1204 (1979). Exceptions have been made concerning impasse, necessity, and waiver; *see infra* at notes 741–833. *But cf.* Rust Craft Broadcasting, 225 NLRB 327, 92 LRRM 1576 (1976), where the Board considered the unilateral installation of time clocks to be solely within the employer's managerial discretion "which it was free to exercise" and therefore not a proper subject of bargaining.

[70]*See infra* at notes 353–369.

[71]NLRB v. Katz, *supra* note 69, at 738.

[72]*See, e.g.*, NLRB v. Reeves & Sons, 273 F2d 710, 713, 45 LRRM 2295 (CA 10, 1959), *enforcing* 121 NLRB 543, 42 LRRM 1555 (1958), *cert. denied*, 366 US 914, 48 LRRM 2071 (1961); NLRB v. Century Cement Mfg. Co., 208 F2d 84, 33 LRRM 2061 (CA 2, 1953).

[73]*Supra* note 69.

[74]*Id.* at 743 (emphasis in original).

[75]337 US 217, 24 LRRM 2088 (1949).

placed the decision in a per se context, and a number of later cases rested upon this approach,[76] some expanding it,[77] others distinguishing it.[78]

In *Katz* the Court did note, however, that certain circumstances might justify unilateral employer action;[79] and exceptions dealing with impasse,[80] necessity,[81] and waiver[82] have been developed.[83]

The obligation to refrain from unilaterally changing terms and conditions of employment continues after contract expiration and until a good-faith bargaining results in an impasse.[84]

---

[76]Electri-Flex Co. v. NLRB, 570 F2d 1327, 97 LRRM 2888 (CA 7), *cert. denied*, 439 US 911, 99 LRRM 2743 (1978) (institution of written warning system, 60-day probationary period, and call-in rule); Korn Indus. v. NLRB, 389 F2d 117, 67 LRRM 2148 (CA 4, 1967); NLRB v. Almeida Bus Lines, 333 F2d 729, 56 LRRM 2548 (CA 1, 1964).

[77]NLRB v. Erie Resistor Corp., 373 US 221, 53 LRRM 2121 (1963) (superseniority to strike replacements); NLRB v. Tom Joyce Floors, Inc., 353 F2d 768, 60 LRRM 2434 (CA 9, 1965) (increased wages to strike replacements); Taft Broadcasting Co., 185 NLRB 202, 75 LRRM 1076 (1970), *aff'd*, 441 F2d 1382, 77 LRRM 2257 (CA 8, 1971) (unilateral elimination of arbitration procedure).

[78]NLRB v. Southern Coach & Body Co., 336 F2d 214, 57 LRRM 2102 (CA 5, 1964) (employer may continue "automatic" increases to which it is already committed since these are not a "change" in working conditions); NLRB v. Tex-Tan, 318 F2d 472, 53 LRRM 2298 (CA 5, 1963) (employer may make changes, but only to extent of previous offers to union, after impasse is reached); NLRB v. Superior Fireproof Door & Sash Co., 289 F2d 713, 47 LRRM 2816 (CA 2, 1961) (employer may make isolated individual wage adjustments); Armstrong Cork Co. v. NLRB, 211 F2d 843, 33 LRRM 2789 (CA 5, 1954); NLRB v. Dealers Engine Rebuilders, 199 F2d 249, 31 LRRM 2007 (CA 8, 1952); NLRB v. Landis Tool Co., 193 F2d 279, 29 LRRM 2255 (CA 3, 1952) (employer may make wage increase which union has rejected, but only after notice to and consultation with union); NLRB v. Bradley Washfountain Co., 192 F2d 144, 29 LRRM 2064 (CA 7, 1951).

[79]NLRB v. Katz, *supra* note 69, at 747–48.

[80]NLRB v. Tex-Tan, *supra* note 78. *See* NLRB v. U.S. Sonics Corp., 312 F2d 610, 52 LRRM 2360 (CA 1, 1963). *See also* discussion of impasse *infra* at notes 694–740.

[81]*See* Duvin, *The Duty to Bargain: Law in Search of Policy*, 64 COLUM. L. REV. 248, 278 n.210 (1964). *See also* Peerless Publications, 283 NLRB 334, 124 LRRM 1331 (1987), *supplementing* 231 NLRB 244, 95 LRRM 1611 (1977) (publisher's code of employee conduct was not mandatory subject of bargaining where narrowly tailored to protect core purpose of enterprise).

[82]Where a union is put on notice of an intended change and does not seek to bargain about it, the employer may act unilaterally. United States Lingerie Corp., 170 NLRB 750, 67 LRRM 1482 (1968). See discussion of waiver *infra* at notes 796–805.

[83]Work rules generally are within the scope of mandatory bargaining. *See, e.g.*, McCotter Motors Co., 291 NLRB 764, 131 LRRM 1370 (1988); G.J. Aigner Co., 257 NLRB 669, 107 LRRM 1586 (1981). But the Board has sometimes found exceptions to the rule, for instance, where an existing rule was more rigidly enforced. U.S. Postal Serv., 275 NLRB 360, 119 LRRM 1057 (1985). *But see* Hyatt Hotels Corp., *supra* note 69 (more stringent enforcement of time sheets rule was violation) or where a change was not material or substantial, LaMousse, 259 NLRB 37, 108 LRRM 1356 (1981), *enforced without opinion*, 703 F2d 576, 112 LRRM 3168 (CA 9, 1983).

[84]*See* Schmidt-Tiago Constr. Co., 286 NLRB 342, 127 LRRM 1246 (1987) (pension contributions); White Oak Coal Co., 295 NLRB No. 64, 131 LRRM 1802 (1985) (holiday pay, birthday pay, pension benefits). In Laborers Health & Welfare Trust Fund for N. Cal. v. Advanced Lightweight Concrete Co., 484 US 539, 127 LRRM 2657 (1988), the Supreme Court held that an employer's postcontract cessation of contributions to a pension fund

This rule requires continuation of the grievance procedure established pursuant to an expired contract.[85]

A unilateral change is unlawful even where the employer has a good-faith, albeit mistaken, belief that the parties are at an impasse[86] or that the union has not been negotiating in good faith.[87] A legal impasse cannot be reached if the employer has engaged in surface bargaining.[88] However, if the implemented change involves a nonmandatory subject of bargaining, there is no violation.[89] An employer may lawfully make some changes, at least, in the terms and conditions of employment for replacement workers during a strike[90] or lockout.[91] The Board has found that the cancellation of accident and sickness benefit payments to employees on medical leave at the inception of the strike was unlawful.[92] On the other hand, the cancellation of scheduled vacations during a strike was privileged.[93]

An isolated departure from an established company policy does not constitute a unilateral change if the policy itself does not change.[94] However, the addition of an HMO option to existing medical coverage was a unilateral change even though the basic insurance plan remained unchanged.[95]

A successor employer's failure to continue a benefit of which it was unaware was held to violate its bargaining obligation because

---

was subject to the Board's primary jurisdiction, and not regulable under collection provisions of the Employee Retirement Income Security Act, as amended.

[85]White Oak Coal Co., *supra* note 84.

[86]Columbia Portland Cement Co., 294 NLRB 410, 133 LRRM 1009 (1989); Saunders House, 265 NLRB 1632, 112 LRRM 1405 (1982), *enforcement denied*, 719 F2d 683, 114 LRRM 2977 (CA 3, 1983) *and* 115 LRRM 3712 (CA 3), *cert. denied sub nom.* Hospital & Health Care Employees Dist. 1199C v. Saunders House, 466 US 958, 116 LRRM 2096 (1984).

[87]Stone Boat Yard v. NLRB, 715 F2d 441, 114 LRRM 2407 (CA 9, 1983), *cert. denied*, 466 US 937, 115 LRRM 3640 (1984).

[88]Benjamin F. Winninger & Son, 286 NLRB 1177, 128 LRRM 1159 (1987).

[89]Allied Chem. & Alkali Workers Local 1 v. Pittsburgh Plate Glass Co., 404 US 157, 78 LRRM 2974 (1971). *Compare* Johnson-Bateman Co., 295 NLRB No. 26, 131 LRRM 1393 (1989) (employee drug-testing mandatory subject) *with* Star Tribune Div., 295 NLRB No. 63, 131 LRRM 1404 (1989) (applicant drug-testing nonmandatory subject).

[90]Marbro Co., 284 NLRB 1303, 126 LRRM 1282 (1987) (unilateral reduction of benefits no violation).

[91]Lincoln, subsidiary of Pentair, NLRB Gen. Counsel Advice Memo., Case No. 14-CA-18744, 125 LRRM 1374 (1987).

[92]Texaco, Inc., 291 NLRB 508, 129 LRRM 1249 (1988).

[93]*Id.*

[94]Champion Parts Rebuilders, Northeast Div. v. NLRB, 717 F2d 845, 114 LRRM 2674 (CA 3, 1983).

[95]Martin Marietta Energy Sys., 283 NLRB 173, 124 LRRM 1395 (1987), *enforced*, 842 F2d 332, 131 LRRM 3072 (CA 6, 1988).

such failure breached a general commitment by the successor to maintain the previous employer's compensation package.[96]

The *Katz* analysis, which is confined to unilateral changes in working conditions made by employers, is not readily applicable to unions because of their relative inability to effect unilateral changes.[97] Whether a union may actually compel a company to accede to its demands is usually a matter of economic power, and the possession and exercise of such power is "not at all inconsistent with the duty to bargain in good faith."[98] However, the Ninth Circuit has viewed a union's unilateral imposition of production quotas, enforced by fines upon member-employees, as a refusal to bargain on a mandatory subject and thus a violation of section 8(b)(3).[99] This represented the first application to a union of the *Katz-Fibreboard*[100] approach. The case has been distinguished on the ground that the union there was modifying a term contained in an existing collective bargaining agreement without meeting the requirements of section 8(d).[101]

An attempt to modify or terminate a collective bargaining agreement by means of a strike, without serving the requisite statutory notice upon federal and state mediation agencies as

---

[96]NLRB v. Pepsi-Cola Distrib. Co. of Knoxville, Tenn., 646 F2d 1173, 107 LRRM 2252 (CA 6, 1981), *enforcing* 241 NLRB 869, 100 LRRM 1626 (1979), *cert. denied*, 456 US 936, 109 LRRM 3368 (1982). *See also* Kallmann dba Love's Barbeque Restaurant No. 62 v. NLRB, 640 F2d 1094, 107 LRRM 2011 (CA 9, 1981); Shortway Suburban Lines, 286 NLRB 323, 126 LRRM 1225 (1987), *enforced*, 862 F2d 309, 129 LRRM 3144 (CA 3, 1988).

[97]In NLRB v. Insurance Agents (Prudential Ins. Co.), 361 US 477, 45 LRRM 2704 (1960), the Supreme Court expressly left open the question of whether a union's unilateral imposition of new terms and conditions is subject to the same treatment under section 8(b)(3) as an employer's unilateral action. In Musicians Local 802, 164 NLRB 23, 65 LRRM 1048 (1967), *aff'd*, 395 F2d 287, 68 LRRM 2317 (CA 2, 1968), the Board distinguished the *Katz* case and declined to find a per se refusal to bargain where the union had amended its bylaws during negotiations to specify a higher wage scale and to establish a new welfare fund. Union members were placed under threat of union discipline for failing to observe the scales. Distinguishing *Katz*, the Second Circuit pointed out that the union could not unilaterally effect changes, and could only demand that the employer make them, 395 F2d at 290. *See also* Letter Carriers, 240 NLRB 519, 100 LRRM 1315 (1979). *But see* NLRB v. System Council T-6, 599 F2d 5, 101 LRRM 2413 (CA 1, 1979) (union violated §8(b)(3) when it unilaterally promulgated rule prohibiting union members from accepting temporary supervisory assignments, contrary to established employer practice).

[98]NLRB v. Insurance Agents (Prudential Ins. Co.), *supra* note 97, at 490–91. *See infra* notes 658–661 for further discussion of *Insurance Agents* and union conduct in collective bargaining.

[99]Associated Home Builders, 352 F2d 745, 60 LRRM 2345 (CA 9, 1965). *But see* Scofield v. NLRB, 393 F2d 49, 67 LRRM 2673 (CA 7, 1968), *aff'd*, 394 US 423, 70 LRRM 3105 (1969), where a union's enforcement of production quotas was held not to be violative of §8(b)(1). *See* Chapter 6, "Interference With Protected Rights," at notes 569–571.

[100]NLRB v. Katz, 369 US 736, 50 LRRM 2177 (1962); Fibreboard Paper Prods. Corp. v. NLRB, 379 US 203, 57 LRRM 2609 (1964). *See* Chapter 16, "Subjects of Bargaining," at notes 324–332.

[101]Musicians Local 802, *supra* note 97.

required by section 8(d), is deemed an attempt to secure a unilateral change in a bargaining relationship and therefore a violation of the union's bargaining obligation.[102] And in *Chemical Workers Local 29 (Morton-Norwich Products)*[103] the Board held that by demanding the right to tape-record grievance meetings, after a 10-year history of handwritten note-taking, the union was attempting to change the implied terms of the collective bargaining agreement and in effect terminate the processing of employee grievances provided for in the collective bargaining agreement.[104]

B. Bargaining Directly With Employees

The collective bargaining obligation requires "recognition that the statutory representative is the one with whom [the employer] must deal in conducting bargaining negotiations, and that it can no longer bargain directly or indirectly with the employees."[105] Just as a unilateral promulgation of a change in a mandatory subject of bargaining is a per se violation of section 8(a)(5) because the employer has bypassed the bargaining agent, a like change effected by the employer dealing directly with the employees rather than with the bargaining agent is also a violation.[106] Some cases, however, treat such bypassing as merely evidence of lack of good faith in the duty to bargain.[107]

The Board has found direct-dealing violations in conduct such as promising benefits to employees if they would change the union's bargaining agent,[108] direct dealing in violation of a

---

[102]Mine Workers (McCoy Coal Co.), 165 NLRB 592, 65 LRRM 1450 (1967); Sheet Metal Workers Local 141 (American Sign Co.), 153 NLRB 537, 59 LRRM 1512 (1965).

[103]228 NLRB 1101, 94 LRRM 1696 (1977).

[104]*Id.* at 1101. *See also* Emery Worldwide, 295 NLRB No. 137, 132 LRRM 1019 (1989) (union which unlawfully coerced employer to accept higher-priced insurance plan than that originally negotiated violated §8(b)(3) and was ordered to reimburse employer for all expenses incurred); Communications Workers (Chesapeake & Potomac Tel. Co.), 280 NLRB 78, 124 LRRM 1009 (1986), *enforced*, 818 F2d 29, 125 LRRM 2352 (CA 4, 1987) (union violated §8(b)(3) by refusing to comply with provision of agreement requiring preparation, use, and sharing of costs of transcripts in nonexpedited arbitration proceedings); Plumbers & Pipe Fitters Local 420 (Paragon Mechanical), 254 NLRB 445, 106 LRRM 1183 (1981) (union attempt to coerce employer to abandon national agreement in favor of local agreement).

[105]General Elec. Co., 150 NLRB 192, 194, 57 LRRM 1491 (1964), *enforced*, 418 F2d 736, 72 LRRM 2530 (CA 2, 1969), *cert. denied*, 397 US 965, 73 LRRM 2600 (1970).

[106]Medo Photo Supply Corp. v. NLRB, 321 US 678, 14 LRRM 581 (1944); R & L Carthage & Sons, 292 NLRB No. 59, 131 LRRM 1695 (1989); Wings & Wheels, 139 NLRB 578, 51 LRRM 1341 (1962), *enforced*, 324 F2d 495, 54 LRRM 2455 (CA 3, 1963).

[107]*E.g.*, General Elec. Co., *supra* note 105.

[108]Hancock Fabrics, 294 NLRB No. 4, 131 LRRM 1306 (1989); Armour Oil Co., 253 NLRB 1104, 106 LRRM 1127 (1981).

contract,[109] or conducting attitude surveys while refusing to bargain.[110] Conversely, the Board has refused to find such violations in an employer's accurate, direct communication to its employees of the terms of its collective bargaining proposals[111] or in a forthright discussion of possible improvements in quality and production and request for employees comments and suggestions.[112]

C. Refusal to Execute Written Contract

Section 8(d) requires "the execution of a written contract incorporating any agreement reached." The refusal to sign a written memorandum of the agreement made has been uniformly regarded as a per se refusal to bargain.[113] Even prior to the enactment of section 8(d) as part of Taft-Hartley, the Supreme Court in 1941, in *H.J. Heinz v. NLRB*,[114] viewed such failure as an independent refusal to bargain. While that decision did not specifically announce the rule that refusal to execute is a per se violation, the Court's analysis supplies the precedent for the rule. The same per se approach has been applied under section 8(b)(3) in cases of union refusals to execute an agreed-

---

[109]*See* Standard Fitting Co. v. NLRB, 845 F2d 1311, 128 LRRM 2613 (CA 5, 1988); Pano, 295 NLRB No. 90, 131 LRRM 1717 (1989).

[110]American Commercial Barge Lines Co., 296 NLRB No. 124, 132 LRRM 1257 (1989); Marriott Corp., Bob's Big Boy Family Restaurant Div., 264 NLRB 432, 111 LRRM 1411 (1982). *See also* Care Ambulance, 255 NLRB 417, 107 LRRM 1043 (1981), *enforced,* 692 F2d 762, 111 LRRM 2650 (CA 9, 1982).

[111]Machinists Dist. Lodge 190, Local 1414 v. NLRB (Putnam Buick), 827 F2d 557, 126 LRRM 2247 (CA 9, 1987), *enforcing* 280 NLRB 868, 122 LRRM 1344 (1986); NLRB v. United Technologies Corp., Pratt & Whitney Aircraft Div., 789 F2d 121, 122 LRRM 2250 (CA 2, 1986); Huck Mfg. Co. v. NLRB, 693 F2d 1176, 112 LRRM 2245 (CA 5, 1982); Lear Siegler, 283 NLRB 929, 126 LRRM 1073 (1987), *enforced in part,* 890 F2d 1573, 133 LRRM 2479 (CA 10, 1989).

[112]Emhart Indus., Hartford Div., 297 NLRB No. 29, 133 LRRM 1066 (1987).

[113]NLRB v. Big Run Coal & Clay Co., 385 F2d 788, 66 LRRM 2640 (CA 6, 1967), *enforcing* 152 NLRB 1144, 59 LRRM 1287 (1965); Lozano Enters. v. NLRB, 327 F2d 814, 55 LRRM 2510 (CA 9, 1964) (employer signed contract, but refused to return it to union); NLRB v. Wate, Inc., 310 F2d 700, 51 LRRM 2701 (CA 6, 1962); SKS Die Casting & Machining, 294 NLRB No. 25, 132 LRRM 1357 (1989); Hydrologics, Inc., 293 NLRB 1060, 131 LRRM 1350 (1989) (refusal to execute supplemental wage agreement after conclusion of reopener negotiations); Midvalley Steel Fabricators, 243 NLRB 516, 101 LRRM 1503 (1979), *order enforced as modified,* 621 F2d 49, 104 LRRM 2062 (CA 2, 1980); Crimptex, Inc., 211 NLRB 855, 87 LRRM 1093 (1974). This requirement is also applicable to individual employer members of multi-employer bargaining units. NLRB v. Strong, 393 US 357, 70 LRRM 2100 (1969); NLRB v. Sheridan Creations, 357 F2d 245, 61 LRRM 2586 (CA 2, 1966). Nonmembers of employer associations who, during the course of association bargaining, have agreed to be bound by the terms of the multi-employer agreement are also subject to this requirement. Buffalo Bituminous v. NLRB, 564 F2d 267, 96 LRRM 2884 (CA 8, 1977), *enforcing* 227 NLRB 99, 94 LRRM 1398 (1977). *See* discussion of multi-employer bargaining units in Chapter 11, "Appropriate Bargaining Units," at notes 327–398.

[114]311 US 514, 7 LRRM 291 (1941).

upon contract.[115] An employer may not insist upon union membership ratification as a condition to executing the contract, unless that condition has been agreed to by both parties.[116] Of course, refusal to sign is lawful if there has been a failure to gain requisite approval of a principal,[117] or a misunderstanding as to terms,[118] or failure to agree on all material terms.[119]

D. Refusal to Meet at Reasonable Times

Section 8(d) also requires the parties "to meet at reasonable times" but does not define the term "reasonable." That language commands not only that the parties "meet," but that they do so as appropriate and without unreasonable delays.[120] Where an employer insists upon bargaining by mail or insists that the union submit all its proposals in writing despite union requests for personal meetings, an unlawful refusal to bargain results.[121]

---

[115]In NLRB v. Longshoremen (ILA), South Atl. & Gulf Coast Dist. (Lykes Bros. S.S. Co.), 443 F2d 218, 77 LRRM 2366 (CA 5, 1971), *enforcing* 181 NLRB 590, 76 LRRM 1700 (1970), the court found it unnecessary to determine whether the union's violation of §8(b)(3) was its refusal to reduce the final agreement to writing, or its insistence upon the nonmandatory subject of expansion of its bargaining authority beyond its own jurisdiction and its own bargaining unit. Enforcing the Board's §8(b)(3) order, the court held that, in the context presented, "the two characterizations are no more than two sides of the same coin." *Id.* at 220. *See also* Hospital & Health Care Employees Dist. 1199C, (Episcopal Hosp.), 241 NLRB 270, 101 LRRM 1030 (1979); Operating Eng'rs Local 12 (Tri-County Ass'n), 168 NLRB 173, 66 LRRM 1270 (1967); Standard Oil Co., 137 NLRB 690, 50 LRRM 1238 (1962), *aff'd*, 322 F2d 40, 54 LRRM 2076 (CA 6, 1963).

[116]Sierra Publishing Co., 296 NLRB No. 65, 132 LRRM 1189 (1989).

[117]Hiney Printing Co., 262 NLRB 157, 110 LRRM 1255 (1982), *enforced*, 733 F2d 1170, 116 LRRM 2404 (CA 6, 1984). *But see* Cablevision Indus., 283 NLRB 22, 126 LRRM 1102 (1987) (employer violated §8(a)(5) when it refused to execute contract, claiming that its final offer, which union membership had ratified, had not been approved by its sole stockholder and CEO).

[118]Aztec Bus Lines, 289 NLRB 1021, 131 LRRM 1214 (1988); Mercedes Benz of N. Am., 258 NLRB 803, 108 LRRM 1134 (1981). *But see* Lenox Hill-Hosp., 296 NLRB No. 41, 132 LRRM 1351 (1989).

[119]McClean County Roofing, 290 NLRB 685, 131 LRRM 1126 (1988); Luther Manor Nursing Home, 270 NLRB 949 n.1, 116 LRRM 1277 (1984), *aff'd sub nom.* Food & Commercial Workers Local 304A v. NLRB, 772 F2d 421, 120 LRRM 2288 (CA 8, 1985); Laredo Packing Co., 254 NLRB 1, 106 LRRM 1350 (1981). *But see* Cutter Laboratories, 265 NLRB 577, 112 LRRM 1026 (1982).

[120]Carbonex Coal Co., 248 NLRB 779, 104 LRRM 1009 (1980), *enforced*, 679 F2d 200, 110 LRRM 2566 (CA 10, 1982) (2½ month hiatus before scheduled hearing held unlawful); Rhodes St. Clair Buick, 242 NLRB 1320, 101 LRRM 1448 (1979) (hiatus of 2 months after union certification held unlawful); Preterm, Inc., 240 NLRB 654, 100 LRRM 1344 (1979). *See* Dunau, *The Duty to Bargain: Law in Search of Policy*, 64 COLUM. L. REV. 248, 264–70 (1964). *See also* discussion of dilatory tactics *infra* at notes 297–317.

[121]NLRB v. United States Cold Storage Corp., 203 F2d 924, 32 LRRM 2024 (CA 5, 1953); NLRB v. P. Lorillard Co., 117 F2d 921, 7 LRRM 475 (CA 6, 1941), *rev'd per curiam on other grounds*, 314 US 512, 9 LRRM 410 (1942); Alle Arecibo Corp., 264 NLRB 1267, 111 LRRM 1322 (1982); Chemetron Corp., Cardox Div., 258 NLRB 1202, 108 LRRM 1202 (1981), *enforcement denied and remanded*, 699 F2d 148, 112 LRRM 2743 (CA 3, 1983), *supplemented*, 268 NLRB 335, 114 LRRM 1273 (1983). *See also* NLRB v. Yutana Barge

A party's busy schedule is not a defense to a continued failure to meet or schedule meetings.[122]

E. Refusal to Confer

Section 8(d) also requires the parties to "confer in good faith with respect to wages, hours, and other terms and conditions of employment." Although the subjective condition of "good faith" is set forth in the Act, the further requirement that the parties "confer" provides the primary basis for the per se determinations indicated in the *Katz* case. A refusal to bargain about a mandatory subject or an insistence to the point of impasse about a permissive subject may constitute a per se violation, not only because of the nature of those positions, but also because each of those activities amounts to a failure to confer in good faith.[123] On the other hand, there may be a conceptual overlap between a failure to "meet at reasonable times" and the "failure to confer"—for both may be viewed as mechanics of bargaining.[124]

F. Insisting on Nonmandatory Subjects of Bargaining

In 1958 the Supreme Court affirmed and adopted the distinction between mandatory and permissive subjects of bargaining contained in *NLRB v. Borg-Warner Corp., Wooster Div.*[125] The proposals at issue in *Borg-Warner* were a "recognition" clause and a "ballot" clause, both of which had been insisted upon by the employer during collective bargaining. The recognition clause disregarded the Board's certification of the local union and parent international as bargaining agent and would have given contractual recognition only to the local union. The ballot clause provided for a secret-ballot vote of all bargaining-unit employees—union as well as nonunion—on the employer's pen-

---

Lines, 315 F2d 524, 52 LRRM 2750 (CA 9, 1963) (refusal to bargain with respect to part of bargaining unit); NLRB v. American Aggregate Co., 305 F2d 559, 50 LRRM 2580 (CA 5, 1962) (ignoring requests for bargaining); Duro Fittings Co., 121 NLRB 377, 42 LRRM 1368 (1958) (refusal to sit across table and bargain in person).

[122]Fern Terrace Lodge of Bowling Green, 297 NLRB No. 2, 132 LRRM 1294 (1989) (unavailability of attorney-negotiator).

[123]NLRB v. Katz, 369 US 736, 50 LRRM 2177 (1962).

[124]For a critical analysis of the application of per se rules to this aspect of bargaining, see Duvin, *The Duty to Bargain: Law in Search of Policy, supra* note 120, at 271.

[125]356 US 342, 42 LRRM 2034 (1958).

ultimate and last offers in negotiations; only after exhausting this procedure would the union be free to strike. The employer maintained that both clauses were prerequisites to its reaching an agreement.

The Board found that the employer had not bargained in bad faith, but the insistence upon inclusion of both clauses in any agreement signed by the employer was held to be per se violative of section 8(a)(5).[126] Agreeing with the Board's analysis, the Supreme Court declared:

> [G]ood faith does not license the employer to refuse to enter into agreements on the ground that they do not include some proposal which is not a mandatory subject of bargaining. . . . [S]uch conduct is, in substance, a refusal to bargain about the subjects that are within the scope of mandatory bargaining. This does not mean that bargaining is to be confined to the statutory subjects. Each of the two controversial clauses is lawful in itself. Each would be enforceable if agreed to by the unions. But it does not follow that, because the company may propose these clauses, it may lawfully insist upon them as a condition to any agreement.[127]

Borg-Warner thus teaches that regardless of a party's good faith in bargaining it commits an unfair labor practice by insisting to impasse upon incorporation in the collective bargaining contract of permissive subject matter, that is, subject matter outside the scope of "wages, hours, and other terms and conditions of employment."[128]

Permissive subjects of bargaining are treated in detail elsewhere.[129] Some examples of such subjects, employer insistence upon which have resulted in findings of per se violations of section 8(a)(5), include (1) clauses requiring the union to post a performance bond,[130] (2) "ballot" clauses requiring a strike vote on the employer's last offer,[131] (3) legal-liability clauses (subject-

---

[126]113 NLRB 1288, 36 LRRM 1439 (1955), *enforced*, 236 F2d 898, 38 LRRM 2660 (CA 6, 1956), *aff'd*, 356 US 342, 42 LRRM 2034 (1958).

[127]356 US at 349.

[128]*See generally* Chapter 16, "Subjects of Bargaining"; Goetz, *The Duty to Bargain About Changes in Operations*, 1964 DUKE L.J. 1; Fleming, *The Changing Duty to Bargain*, 14 LAB. L.J. 297 (1963); *see also* Comment, *Subjects Included Within Management's Duty to Bargain Collectively*, 26 LA. L. REV. 630 (1966); Comment, *Employer's Duty to Bargain About Subcontracting and Other "Management" Decisions*, 64 COLUM. L. REV. 294 (1964).

[129]*See generally* Chapter 16, "Subjects of Bargaining."

[130]NLRB v. American Compress Warehouse, 350 F2d 365, 59 LRRM 2739 (CA 5, 1965), *cert. denied*, 382 US 982, 61 LRRM 2147 (1966); Union Mfg. Co., 76 NLRB 322, 21 LRRM 1187 (1948), *enforced*, 179 F2d 511, 25 LRRM 2302 (CA 5, 1950); Jasper Blackburn Prods. Corp., 21 NLRB 1240, 6 LRRM 169 (1940).

[131]NLRB v. Borg-Warner Corp., Wooster Div., *supra* note 125.

ing unions to legal liability for violation of a no-strike clause, including liability for all injury or damage resulting from such violation),[132] (4) interference with internal union affairs,[133] and (5) exclusion from a bargaining unit of certain categories of employees included under the certification.[134] Further, a party unlawfully refuses to bargain by insisting to impasse that employees waive the right to seek redress from the NLRB for strike discipline imposed by the employer.[135] Similarly, insistence upon the presence of a stenographer at negotiations,[136] the payment of construction industry advancement funds,[137] multi-unit negotiations,[138] or the inclusion of an "ecclesiastical clause,"[139] a loyalty clause,[140] or an interest-arbitration clause, constitutes refusal to bargain.[141] A change in the bargaining unit is a permissive subject and cannot be insisted upon to impasse,[142] although there has not always been agreement as to what constitutes a proposed change in the bargaining unit.[143]

---

[132]Radiator Specialty Co., 143 NLRB 350, 53 LRRM 1319 (1963). *See also* North Carolina Furniture, 121 NLRB 41, 42 LRRM 1271 (1958).

[133]NLRB v. Superior Fireproof Door & Sash Co., 289 F2d 713, 47 LRRM 2816 (CA 2, 1961); NLRB v. Darlington Veneer Co., 236 F2d 85, 38 LRRM 2574 (CA 4, 1956). *Cf.* Bethlehem Steel, 133 NLRB 1400, 49 LRRM 1018 (1961) (dictum indicating it would be unlawful for employer to insist upon clause requiring individual signatures on grievances).

[134]Preterm, Inc., *supra* note 120.

[135]Reichhold Chems., 288 NLRB 69, 127 LRRM 1265 (1988), *supplementing* 277 NLRB 639, 120 LRRM 1339 (1985).

[136]Nassau Ins. Co., 280 NLRB 878, 124 LRRM 1075 (1986).

[137]American Thoro-Clean, 283 NLRB 1107, 125 LRRM 1115 (1987).

[138]Boise Cascade Corp., 283 NLRB 462, 124 LRRM 1391 (1987), *enforced*, 860 F2d 471, 129 LRRM 2744 (CA DC, 1988); Swatts v. Steelworkers, 120 LRRM 2542 (SD Ind, 1985), *aff'd*, 808 F2d 1221, 124 LRRM 2165 (CA 7, 1986).

[139]NLRB v. Salvation Army of Mass. Dorchester Day Care Center, 763 F2d 1, 119 LRRM 2587 (CA 1, 1985), *enforcing* 271 NLRB 195, 116 LRRM 1410 (1984) (employer demanded clause by which union recognized religious mission of employer).

[140]Meda-Care Ambulance, 285 NLRB 471, 128 LRRM 1276 (1987) (clause requiring employees and union to use best efforts to promote employer's interests).

[141]Electrical Workers (IBEW) Local 135 (LaCrosse Elec. Contractors Ass'n), 271 NLRB 250, 116 LRRM 1329 (1984).

[142]Boise Cascade Corp. v. NLRB, 860 F2d 471, 129 LRRM 2744 (CADC, 1988); Standard Register Co., 288 NLRB 1409, 128 LRRM 1268 (1988); Idaho Statesman, 281 NLRB 272, 124 LRRM 1141 (1986), *enforced*, 836 F2d 1396, 127 LRRM 2429 (CA DC, 1988); Grey Line Scenic Tours dba California Nev. Golden Tours, 283 NLRB 58, 125 LRRM 1015 (1987); Bozzutto's, 277 NLRB 977, 120 LRRM 1337 (1985).

[143]Newspaper Printing Corp. v. NLRB, 692 F2d 615, 111 LRRM 2824 (CA 6, 1982), *denying enforcement to* 250 NLRB 1144, 104 LRRM 1495 (1980) (employer's proposed change in unit description/work assignment clause held by court to be mandatory subject, contrary to Board's conclusion that it was permissive subject). *Compare* Newspaper Printing Corp. v. NLRB, 625 F2d 956, 104 LRRM 2432 (CA 10, 1980), *cert. denied*, 450 US 911, 106 LRRM 2512 (1981), where the court enforced the Board's finding that the employer violated its bargaining obligation by insisting upon a clause allowing it to designate what work was within the bargaining unit at any particular time. *See also* Idaho Statesman, *supra* note 142.

A union's insistence upon permissive subjects to the point of impasse likewise constitutes a per se refusal to bargain.[144] Examples include unions' demands to (1) combine or alter existing bargaining units,[145] (2) include additional employees,[146] (3) include supervisors in a contract,[147] (4) include agricultural labor,[148] (5) provide bonds for the payment of employees' wages and benefits,[149] (6) display the union label,[150] (7) support industry promotion funds,[151] and (8) agree to interest-arbitration clauses.[152]

---

[144]NLRB v. Hod Carriers (Laborers) Local 1082 (E.L. Boggs Plastering Co.), 384 F2d 55, 66 LRRM 2333 (CA 9, 1967), *cert. denied,* 390 US 920, 67 LRRM 2385 (1968); Bricklayers Local 3 (Associated Gen. Contractors, Eastern Wash.), 162 NLRB 476, 64 LRRM 1085 (1966), *enforced,* 405 F2d 469, 69 LRRM 2944 (CA 9, 1968); Painters Dist. Council 36 (Commercial Drywall Constructors), 155 NLRB 1013, 60 LRRM 1431 (1965). *See also* Plumbers & Pipe Fitters, Southern Cal. Pipe Trades Dist. Council 16 (Aero Plumbing Co.), 167 NLRB 1004, 66 LRRM 1233 (1967), *enforced,* 449 F2d 668, 78 LRRM 2260 (CA 9, 1971), where a number of nonmandatory subjects were insisted upon. Union insistence upon hot-cargo agreements may also, in certain circumstances, be violative. Bricklayers Local 2 (Chris. Paschen Co.), 152 NLRB 1582, 59 LRRM 1320 (1965), *enforced,* 381 F2d 381, 65 LRRM 3103 (CA 6, 1967); Sheet Metal Workers Local 26 (Reno Employers Council), 168 NLRB 893, 67 LRRM 1130 (1967). For general treatment of permissive subjects of bargaining, *see* Chapter 16, "Subjects of Bargaining."

[145]NLRB v. Longshoremen (ILA), South Atl. & Gulf Coast Dist. (Lykes Bros. S.S. Co.), 443 F2d 218, 77 LRRM 2366 (CA 5, 1971), *enforcing* 181 NLRB 590, 76 LRRM 1700 (1970); Douds v. Longshoremen (ILA), 241 F2d 278, 39 LRRM 2388 (CA 2, 1957); Electrical Workers (IBEW) Local 323 (Active Enters.), 242 NLRB 305, 101 LRRM 1179 (1979); Longshoremen (ILA), 118 NLRB 1481, 40 LRRM 1408 (1957), *set aside on other grounds,* 277 F2d 681, 45 LRRM 2551 (CA DC, 1960).

[146]Electrical Workers (IBEW) Local 1049 (Lewis Tree Serv.), 244 NLRB 124, 102 LRRM 1166 (1979); Steere Broadcasting Corp., 158 NLRB 487, 62 LRRM 1083 (1966); Typographical Union (Haverhill Gazette Co.), 123 NLRB 806, 823, 43 LRRM 1538 (1959), *rev'd in pertinent part,* 278 F2d 6, 46 LRRM 2132 (CA 1, 1960), *aff'd in part and rev'd in part,* 365 US 705, 47 LRRM 2920 (1961), *without considering this issue. See* AFL-CIO Joint Negotiating Comm. (Phelps Dodge Corp.), 184 NLRB 976, 74 LRRM 1705 (1970), *rev'd,* 459 F2d 374, 79 LRRM 2939 (CA 3, 1972), *cert. denied,* 409 US 1059, 81 LRRM 2893 (1972) (unions violated §8(b)(3) when they demanded and struck to obtain companywide bargaining instead of bargaining within established bargaining units).

[147]NLRB v. Retail Clerks (Safeway Co.), 203 F2d 165, 31 LRRM 2606 (CA 9, 1953), *cert. denied,* 348 US 839, 34 LRRM 2898 (1954) (union in contempt for insisting on bargaining for supervisory employees in violation of consent decree); Plumbers & Pipe Fitters, Southern Cal. Pipe Trades Dist. Council 16 (Aero Plumbing Co.), *supra* note 144.

[148]Mine Workers, Dist. 50 (Central Soya Co.), 142 NLRB 930, 53 LRRM 1178 (1963).

[149]Excello Dry Wall Co., 145 NLRB 663, 55 LRRM 1015 (1963). *See also* NLRB v. American Compress Warehouse, *supra* note 130. *Cf.* Bricklayers Local 3 (Associated Gen. Contractors, Eastern Wash.), *supra* note 144 (union may not insist on penalty clause calling for reimbursement to union for dues and initiation fees lost as result of improper subcontracting).

[150]Kit Mfg. Co., 150 NLRB 662, 671, 58 LRRM 1140 (1964), *enforced per curiam,* 365 F2d 829, 62 LRRM 2856 (CA 9, 1966).

[151]NLRB v. Sheet Metal Workers Local 38 (Elmsford Sheet Metal Works), 575 F2d 394, 98 LRRM 2147 (CA 2, 1978), *enforcing* 231 NLRB 699, 96 LRRM 1190 (1977); Detroit Resilient Floor Decorators Local 2265 (Mill Floor Covering), 136 NLRB 769, 49 LRRM 1842 (1962), *enforced,* 317 F2d 269, 53 LRRM 2311 (CA 6, 1963).

[152]NLRB v. Sheet Metal Workers Local 38 (Elmsford Sheet Metal Works), *supra* note 151.

III. THE GOOD-FAITH REQUIREMENT

The Board and the courts recognized at an early date that simply compelling the parties to meet was insufficient to promote the purposes of the Act.[153] Early attempts by employers to satisfy the bargaining obligation by merely going through the motions without actually seeking to adjust differences were condemned.[154] The concept of "good faith" was brought into the law of collective bargaining as a solution to the problem of bargaining without substance.[155] In 1947 Congress explicitly incorporated the "good faith" requirement into section 8(d).

A. Totality of Conduct Assessed: *General Electric* and the Proper Roles of the Parties

The duty to bargain in good faith is an "obligation . . . to participate actively in the deliberations so as to indicate a present *intention* to find a basis for agreement . . . ."[156] This implies both "an open mind and a sincere desire to reach an agreement"[157] as well as "a sincere effort . . . to reach a common ground."[158] The presence or absence of intent "must be discerned from the record."[159] Except in cases where the conduct fails to meet the minimum obligation imposed by law or constitutes an outright

---

[153]NLRB, 1936 ANNUAL REPORT 85. "Collective bargaining is something more than the mere meeting of an employer with the representative of his employees; the essential thing is rather the serious intent to adjust differences and to reach an acceptable common ground."

[154]NLRB v. Montgomery Ward & Co., 133 F2d 676, 12 LRRM 508 (CA 9, 1943); Benson Produce Co., 71 NLRB 888, 19 LRRM 1060 (1946).

[155]Cox, *The Duty to Bargain in Good Faith*, 71 HARV. L. REV. 1401, 1413 (1958). See discussion of the meaning of the good-faith bargaining requirement, *supra*, at notes 33–50. Assessing the impact of that requirement, one commentator observed: "Whether imposing a statutory duty to bargain in good faith could ever amount to more than a pious exhortation has been the subject of much controversy. . . . Over the years, however, there has been increasing evidence the statute has had a practical effect, including voluntary compliance by management. Thus, one survey revealed that successful bargaining relationships were eventually established in 75% of the cases sampled that went through to a final Board order, and in 90% of the cases that were voluntarily adjusted after the issuance of a complaint." St. Antoine, *The Role of Law*, U.S. INDUSTRIAL RELATIONS 1950–1980: A CRITICAL ASSESSMENT 159, 172–73 (J. Stieber, R. McKersie & D. Mills eds. 1981). *See* P. Ross, THE GOVERNMENT AS A SOURCE OF UNION POWER 180–230 (1965); McCulloch, *The Development of Administrative Remedies*, 14 LAB. L.J. 339 (1963). *See, e.g.*, NLRB v. Montgomery Ward & Co., *supra* note 154.

[156]NLRB v. Montgomery Ward & Co., *supra* note 154, at 686, 12 LRRM at 517.

[157]*Id. See* NLRB v. Truitt Mfg. Co., 351 US 149, 38 LRRM 2042 (1956).

[158]NLRB v. Montgomery Ward & Co., *supra* note 154, at 686. *See* NLRB v. Herman Sausage Co., 275 F2d 229, 45 LRRM 2829 (CA 5, 1960).

[159]General Elec. Co., 150 NLRB 192, 194, 57 LRRM 1491 (1964), *enforced*, 418 F2d 736, 72 LRRM 2530 (CA 2, 1969), *cert. denied*, 397 US 965, 73 LRRM 2600 (1970).

refusal to bargain,[160] relevant facts of a case must be studied to determine whether the employer or the union is bargaining in good or bad faith. The "totality of conduct" is the standard by which the "quality" of negotiations is tested.[161] Thus, even though some specific actions, viewed alone, might not support a charge of bad-faith bargaining, a party's overall course of conduct in negotiations may reveal a violation of the Act.[162]

Because the Board considers the entire course of conduct in bargaining, isolated misconduct will not be viewed as a failure to bargain in good faith. Thus, an employer's withdrawal of tentative agreements, standing alone, does not constitute bad faith in contravention of the bargaining obligation.[163] In *Roman Iron Works*,[164] for example, the employer violated section 8(a)(5) by its unilateral wage increase during negotiations. The employer also engaged in hard bargaining including a reduction of the

---

[160]Intent will not even be in issue if the outward conduct amounts to refusal to bargain. *See* NLRB v. Katz, 369 US 736, 50 LRRM 2177 (1962). *But cf.* NLRB v. Cascade Employers Ass'n, 296 F2d 42, 49 LRRM 2049 (CA 9, 1961), where the court held that the Board had erroneously applied the per se rule rather than looking to the "totality of circumstances" surrounding the bargaining. *See* discussion *supra* at notes 67–152.

[161]B. F. Diamond Constr. Co., 163 NLRB 161, 64 LRRM 1333 (1967), *enforced per curiam*, 410 F2d 462, 71 LRRM 2112 (CA 5), *cert. denied*, 396 US 835, 72 LRRM 2432 (1969); Stevenson Brick & Block Co., 160 NLRB 198, 62 LRRM 1605 (1966), *enforcement denied in pertinent part*, 393 F2d 234, 68 LRRM 2086 (CA 4, 1968); General Elec. Co., *supra* note 159; McCulloch Corp., 132 NLRB 201, 48 LRRM 1344 (1961). In Rhodes-Holland Chevrolet Co., 146 NLRB 1304, 1304–5, 56 LRRM 1058 (1964), the Board stated: "In finding that Respondent violated its obligation to bargain in good faith, we, like the Trial Examiner, have not relied solely on the position taken by Respondent on substantive contract terms, a factor which, standing alone, . . . might not have provided sufficient basis for the violation found, but have considered that factor as simply one item in the totality of circumstances reflecting Respondent's bargaining frame of mind." The "totality of conduct" doctrine, generally, stems from NLRB v. Virginia Elec. & Power Co., 314 US 469, 9 LRRM 405 (1941).

[162]*See, e.g.*, NLRB v. Cable Vision, 660 F2d 1, 108 LRRM 2357 (CA 1, 1981); Continental Ins. Co. v. NLRB, 495 F2d 44, 86 LRRM 2003 (CA 2, 1974), *enforcing* 204 NLRB 1013, 83 LRRM 1406 (1973) (employer's delaying tactics in negotiations, unreasonable bargaining demands, efforts to bypass and undermine union, and unilateral changes in mandatory subjects of bargaining); United Technologies Corp., Hamilton Standard Div., 296 NLRB No. 79, 132 LRRM 1240 (1989); Lustrelon, Inc., 289 NLRB 378, 130 LRRM 1398 (1988), *enforced*, 869 F2d 590, 131 LRRM 2128 (CA 3, 1989). *See also* Pillowtex Corp., 241 NLRB 40, 100 LRRM 1546 (1979); Milgo Indus., 229 NLRB 25, 96 LRRM 1347 (1977); Byrd's Terrazzo & Tile Co., 227 NLRB 866, 94 LRRM 1412 (1977); Underwriters Adjusting Co., 214 NLRB 388, 87 LRRM 1372 (1974); Ramona's Mexican Food Prods., 203 NLRB 663, 83 LRRM 1705 (1973), *enforced per curiam*, 531 F2d 390, 92 LRRM 2611 (CA 9, 1975); John Zink Co., 196 NLRB 942, 80 LRRM 1232 (1972), *modified*, 83 LRRM 3045 (CA 10, 1973). *But see* NLRB v. Advanced Business Forms Corp., 474 F2d 457, 82 LRRM 2161 (CA 2, 1973) (court refused to find bad-faith bargaining from totality of conduct); Hartz Mountain Corp., 295 NLRB No. 48, 132 LRRM 1160 (1989) (no surface bargaining).

[163]Williams, 279 NLRB 82, 121 LRRM 1313 (1986).

[164]275 NLRB 449, 119 LRRM 1144 (1985). *See also* Auto Workers Local 1712 v. NLRB (Sun Elec. Corp.), 732 F2d 573, 116 LRRM 2178 (CA 7, 1984); American Commercial Lines, 291 NLRB 1066, 131 LRRM 1561 (1988).

wage offer during bargaining, denial of a union request for employee addresses, insistence on a right to subcontract, and a demand for significant cost reductions. However, the Board found that the employer met frequently with the union, made complete contract proposals, and made several significant concessions. Under all of these circumstances, the Board found that the employer did not engage in bad-faith bargaining.[165]

In reviewing the totality of the employer's conduct, the Board also takes into consideration an employer's antiunion behavior away from the bargaining table.[166] However, the Board has held that such conduct away from the table does not establish bad faith where there exists no other evidence that the employer failed to bargain in good faith.[167]

Application of these principles has been both difficult and controversial. Much of the trouble arises from the uneasy coexistence of two conflicting approaches to regulation, first by objective, per se, rules typified by *Katz* and second by subjective and amorphous "rules" that have evolved from efforts to judge "the totality" of conduct. The conflict was placed on prominent display in *General Electric Co.*,[168] the celebrated "Boulwarism" case.[169]

---

[165]Roman Iron Works, *supra* note 164. *See also* Allbritton Communications Co. v. NLRB, 766 F2d 812, 119 LRRM 3290 (CA 3, 1985) *enforcing* 271 NLRB 201, 116 LRRM 1428 (1984), *cert. denied*, 474 US 1081, 121 LRRM 2368 (1986); Financial Inst. Employees Local 1182 v. NLRB, 738 F2d 1038, 117 LRRM 2139 (CA 9, 1984), *enforcing sub nom.* Seattle-First Nat'l Bank, 267 NLRB 897, 114 LRRM 1072 (1983), *aff'd*, 475 US 192, 121 LRRM 2741 (1986); WPIX, Inc., 293 NLRB 10, 131 LRRM 1780 (1989); Gulf States Mfrs., 287 NLRB 26, 127 LRRM 1182 (1987); United Technologies Corp., 274 NLRB 1069, 118 LRRM 1556 (1985), *enforced sub nom.* NLRB v. United Technologies Corp., Pratt & Whitney Aircraft Div., 789 F2d 121, 122 LRRM 2250 (CA 2, 1986). *But see* Coast Engraving Co., 282 NLRB 1236, 125 LRRM 1215 (1987) (reasons for finding bad-faith bargaining included employer's unilateral changes in conditions prior to impasse).

[166]NLRB v. Billion Motors, 700 F2d 454, 112 LRRM 2873 (CA 8, 1983); United Technologies Corp., Hamilton Standard Div., *supra* note 162; White-Evans Serv. Co., 285 NLRB 81, 127 LRRM 1070 (1987); Meda-Care Ambulance, 285 NLRB 471, 128 LRRM 1276 (1987); Port Plastics, 279 NLRB 362, 123 LRRM 1320 (1986); Hedaya Bros., 277 NLRB 942, 121 LRRM 1073 (1985).

[167]Allbritton Communications Co. v. NLRB, 766 F2d 812, 119 LRRM 3290 (CA 3, 1985), *cert. denied*, 474 US 1081, 121 LRRM 2368 (1986); River City Mechanical, 289 NLRB 1503, 131 LRRM 1026 (1988); Peelle Co., 289 NLRB 113, 130 LRRM 1365 (1988); Reichhold Chems., 288 NLRB 69, 127 LRRM 1265 (1988); Frontier Dodge, 272 NLRB 722, 117 LRRM 1411 (1984), *supplemented*, 277 NLRB 1242, 121 LRRM 1294 (1985).

[168]*Supra* note 159.

[169]The term "Boulwarism" was used in the trial examiner's report, but not in the Board's opinion, to denote General Electric's bargaining practices. *See, e.g.*, 150 NLRB at 207. "Boulwarism" was named for Lemuel R. Boulware, a vice-president of General Electric, who formulated the concept following a bitter and costly strike at General Electric in 1946. Briefly, the tactic was designed to convince its employees that the company was responsive to their needs and that the union was not needed to force the company to grant that which it would voluntarily provide. This was accomplished

On the basis of its own research, General Electric formulated a single offer that anticipated the union's demands. Some 6 weeks of meetings (18 sessions) and a massive publicity campaign involving virtually all media of communication preceded the company's presentation of the offer to the union on August 30, 1960. The company characterized its offer as fair and firm—one which would give no reason for the union to strike—but it would be open and subject to change if new information showed that the original offer was not "right."[170] However, by September 9, the company had made but four changes in the offer. A contract on the company's terms eventually was signed on November 10, 1960, after the union abandoned an ineffectual strike.

The company was charged with violating sections 8(a)(1), (3), and (5).[171] The Board found a failure to bargain in good faith in the company's (1) failure to furnish information requested by the union,[172] (2) attempt to bargain with local unions and thereby undermine the international's position,[173] (3) presentation of its insurance proposal on a take-it-or-leave-it basis,[174] and (4) overall attitude or approach as evidenced by the totality of its conduct.[175] In a split decision, the Second Circuit agreed with these rulings and enforced the Board's order in its entirety.

General Electric describes and focuses upon the complex nature of the duty to "bargain collectively" created by sections 8(a)(5) and 8(b)(3).[176] The duty imposed by the Act contemplates a *bilateral* procedure through which the employer and the bargaining representative *jointly* attempt to set wages and

---

through a massive communications program to employees, a continual research program to discover what was "best" for its employees, and the formulation of a "firm and fair" offer to the union based upon the facts it had gathered. For a full explanation of the history of the 1960 negotiations and the concept of Boulwarism, see Cooper, *Boulwarism and the Duty to Bargain in Good Faith*, 20 RUTGERS L. REV. 653 (1966). *See also* H.R. Northrup, BOULWARISM (1964); Gross, Cullen & Hanslowe, *Good Faith in Labor Negotiations: Tests and Remedies*, 53 CORNELL L. REV. 1009 (1968); Note, *"Boulwareism": Legality and Effect*, 76 HARV. L. REV. 807 (1963).

[170]150 NLRB at 270.

[171]Similar charges had been filed by the union in 1954 and 1958, but were dismissed. Northrup, *supra* note 169, at 60.

[172]150 NLRB at 193. *See also* discussion *infra* at notes 409–657.

[173]150 NLRB at 262–66.

[174]150 NLRB at 269. Although the trial examiner treated this as a separate violation, the Board considered General Electric's position on the insurance proposal to be indicative of the employer's overall bad faith. *Id.* at 196.

[175]150 NLRB at 193.

[176]The original declaration of policy in the Wagner Act, reenacted in §1 of the Taft-Hartley Act, declared that it is "the policy of the United States to eliminate the causes of certain substantial obstructions to the free flow of commerce and to mitigate and eliminate these obstructions when they have occurred *by encouraging the practice and procedure of collective bargaining*. . . ." (emphasis added).

working conditions for the employees.[177] The objective that Congress hoped to achieve by this process was described by the Supreme Court in *H.K. Porter Co.*:[178]

> The object of this Act was . . . to ensure that employers and their employees could work together to establish mutually satisfactory conditions. The basic theme of the Act was that through collective bargaining the passions, arguments, and struggles of prior years would be channeled into constructive, open discussions leading, it was hoped, to mutual agreement.[179]

Under the statutory scheme, when there is an absence of collective bargaining, good faith may be an irrelevant consideration.[180] The term *per se violation* has generally been used to describe the bypassing of the bargaining process; and *lack of good faith* has often been used to describe refusing to bargain or sham bargaining. But lack of good faith may also refer to a subjective state of mind evidenced by various types of overt conduct, as described in this chapter. *General Electric* illustrates many of the subtle requirements of this elusive "duty to bargain."

The majority of the reviewing court in *General Electric* reviewed in detail the long history of the negotiations. It approved the Board's findings as to specific refusals to bargain: the unilateral promulgation of an accident insurance plan and the employer's refusal to "indicate the cost of union proposals, or how much [GE] was willing to expend . . . ."[181] Relying on *Truitt*[182] and other decisions requiring disclosure of bargaining information, the court stated:

> [I]f the purpose of collective bargaining is to promote the "rational exchange of facts and arguments" that will measurably increase the chance for amicable agreement, then sham discussions in which unsubstantiated reasons are substituted for genuine arguments should be anathema.[183]

Concerning the employer's conduct in dealing separately with several Electrical Workers (IUE) locals, the court sustained the

---

[177]The current chapter defines the requirements of that procedure. The subjects about which the parties must bargain, that is, "the wages, hours, and other terms and conditions of employment" of §8(d), are treated in Chapter 16, "Subjects of Bargaining."

[178]397 US 99, 73 LRRM 2561 (1970).

[179]*Id.* at 103.

[180]NLRB v. Katz, *supra* note 160.

[181]418 F2d at 750.

[182]NLRB v. Truitt Mfg. Co., 351 US 149, 38 LRRM 2042 (1956). *See* discussion at notes 413–427 *infra*.

[183]418 F2d at 750, 72 LRRM at 2541 (citing Cox, *The Duty to Bargain in Good Faith*, 71 HARV. L. REV. 1401 (1958)).

Board's conclusion that in each instance when the employer "went behind the back of the national negotiators and offered separate peace settlements to locals"[184] it committed an unfair labor practice.

The court also agreed that the employer was guilty of a refusal to bargain based on the "totality of circumstances."[185] It took note of the take-it-or-leave-it basis of the insurance proposal, that GE "occasionally took untenable and unreasonable positions and then defended them, with no apparent purposes other than to avoid yielding to the Union,"[186] and other conduct which was deemed inconsistent with a genuine desire to reach a mutual accommodation. The court observed that the employer's aim "was to deal with the union through the employees, rather than the employees through the union"[187]—the antithesis of collective bargaining.

Underlying the decisions of both the Board and the court of appeals was the view that the employer had locked itself in.[188] GE had put certain benefits into effect for employees not in the bargaining units, and—invoking its longstanding policy of maintaining uniformity among all its employees—had taken the public position that there was "nothing more to come." Thus, "having created a view of the bargaining process that admitted no compromise," the court concluded that GE "was trapped by its own creation."[189] The court also emphasized what it had not held:

> We do not today hold that an employer may not communicate with his employees during negotiations. Nor are we deciding that the "best offer first" bargaining technique is forbidden. Moreover, we do not require an employer to engage in "auction bargaining," or, as the dissent seems to suggest, compel him to make concessions, "minor" or otherwise.[190]

Disagreeing with the majority's reasoning in this regard, Judge Friendly concurred and dissented, warning that the holding constituted a "serious indentation of §8(c) and (d), if not,

---

[184] 418 F2d at 755.
[185] *Id.* at 756.
[186] *Id.* at 758.
[187] *Id.* at 759.
[188] *See* Jaffe, *Major Developments of the Year Under the National Labor Relations Act*, NYU EIGHTEENTH ANNUAL CONFERENCE ON LABOR 61, 67 (1966).
[189] 418 F2d at 760.
[190] *Id.* at 762.

indeed, of the First Amendment . . . the familiar instance of a hard case producing bad law."[191]

Since 1969, when the Second Circuit decided *General Electric*, the Board and the courts have further considered some of the elements examined in *General Electric*. They have not always agreed on what constitutes the requisite showing of bad faith in bargaining.[192]

In *Finch Baking Co. v. NLRB*[193] the Second Circuit ruled that the employer breached its duty to bargain in good faith by informing employees of the terms of its "firm, fair" offer *prior* to the time such offer was made to the union and by thereafter notifying the employees that, unless the union accepted the offer prior to the expiration of the existing contract, the offer would be made directly to the employees in the hope that they would accept it and continue on the job. The offer finally was made to the union just hours before the expiration of the old contract.[194]

The Eighth Circuit, however, in *United States Gypsum Co. v. NLRB*,[195] set aside the Board's order even though (1) the employer's initial and final contract proposals were essentially identical and reflected an intransigent attitude toward bargaining, (2) the employer made its final offer before bargaining could narrow the differences between the parties, and (3) the employer circulated among the employees letters denigrating the union. The court held that the employer had the right to

---

[191]*Id.* at 774.

[192]*General Electric* was distinguished in Rangaire Corp., 157 NLRB 682, 61 LRRM 1429 (1966). *See also* Stark Ceramics, 155 NLRB 1258, 60 LRRM 1487 (1965), *enforced*, 375 F2d 202, 64 LRRM 2781 (CA 6, 1967); Memorial Consultants, 153 NLRB 1, 59 LRRM 1375 (1965); *cf.* Procter & Gamble Mfg. Co., 160 NLRB 334, 62 LRRM 1617 (1966) (noncoercive communication campaign did not demonstrate bad faith, especially since record established employer's good faith in seeking to reach common ground for agreement, as evidenced by its extensive negotiations, proposals, counterproposals, and concessions).

[193]479 F2d 732, 83 LRRM 2361 (CA 2, 1973), *enforcing* 199 NLRB 414, 81 LRRM 1616 (1972), *cert. denied*, 414 US 1032, 84 LRRM 2683 (1973).

[194]Noting that such a technique seriously impaired the union's ability to function as a bargaining representative, the court further found that (1) the timing of the offer to the union prevented any meaningful evaluation or discussion, (2) the company became so enamored with its "firm, fair" offer technique that it ignored its basic duty to allow adequate time or opportunity for discussion, and (3) the employees were assured specific increases regardless of union acceptance or rejection before the increases had even been presented to the union. The company's technique was thus not an "offer" but a "decision" completely removing the element of bargaining. According to the court, "the fountain was poisoned before it ever began to flow." *Id.* at 736.

[195]484 F2d 108, 84 LRRM 2129 (CA 8, 1973), *denying enforcement to* 200 NLRB 1098, 82 LRRM 1064 (1972).

refuse to make concessions during bargaining as long as it agreed to meet and discuss its proposals with the union.

In *Arnold Graphic Industries v. NLRB*[196] the Sixth Circuit set aside that portion of a Board order holding that the employer had engaged in "take-it-or-leave-it" bargaining, agreeing with the ALJ that the employer had bargained further, had modified its demands, and had otherwise evidenced its good faith by taking the union's wage offer to its board of directors. Later, however, the Sixth Circuit enforced a Board holding that an employer "as a practical matter" had made a "take-it-or-leave-it" economic offer on 20 bargaining subjects by insisting that the entire proposal would lapse automatically 5 days later unless accepted by the union, and by refusing the union additional time to study the proposal.[197]

On the other hand, the Board has also held that an employer's take-it-or-leave-it position during negotiations does not constitute bad faith where the *union* refuses to compromise on any of its demands or to pursue negotiations diligently to help resolve bargaining differences.[198]

Nor in the Board's view does an employer violate the Act merely by communicating with employees during bargaining while at the same time taking a hard-line bargaining posture. Accordingly, no violation was found where an employer told an assembled group of employees that it would refuse to accede to the union's demands.[199] Observing that the *General Electric* case only proscribes "a massive campaign of employee persuasion designed to undercut the bargaining representative and win support for the company's 'take-it-or-leave-it' bargain [sic] methods," the Board concluded that the employer's conduct amounted to little more than publicly taking a position on a bargaining issue and then notifying employees of that position.[200] The opinion observed that employees today are sufficiently sophisticated to appreciate such an approach.

---

[196]505 F2d 257, 87 LRRM 2753 (CA 6, 1974), *denying enforcement in part to* 206 NLRB 327, 84 LRRM 1343 (1973).

[197]Federal Mogul Corp., 212 NLRB 950, 87 LRRM 1105 (1974), *enforced*, 524 F2d 37, 91 LRRM 2207 (CA 6, 1975).

[198]Romo Paper Prods. Corp., 208 NLRB 644, 85 LRRM 1165 (1974).

[199]Oneita Knitting Mills, 205 NLRB 500, 83 LRRM 1670 (1973).

[200]*Id.* at 500.

B. Indicia of Good or Bad Faith

1. Surface Bargaining. When examination of the "totality" of a party's conduct during bargaining discloses that the forms of negotiation have been employed to conceal a purpose to frustrate or avoid mutual agreement, the party is said to have engaged in "surface bargaining."[201] Any single factor, standing alone, is usually insufficient to support such a conclusion, but its "persuasiveness grows as the number of issues increases."[202]

Although an employer may be willing to meet at length and confer with the union, the Board will find a refusal to bargain in good faith if it concludes the employer is merely going through the "motions" of bargaining.[203] Surface bargaining has been

---

[201]"[T]he question of whether an employer is acting in good or bad faith at the time of the refusal is . . . one which . . . must be determined in the light of all relevant facts in the case, including any unlawful conduct of the employer, the sequence of events, and the time lapse between the refusal and the unlawful conduct." Joy Silk Mills, Inc. v. NLRB, 185 F2d 732, 27 LRRM 2012, 2019 (CA DC, 1950), *cert. denied*, 341 US 914, 27 LRRM 2633 (1951). *See* Shieber, *Surface Bargaining: The Problem and a Proposed Solution*, 5 U. TOL. L. REV. 656 (1974). *See also* WPIX, Inc., 293 NLRB 10, 131 LRRM 1780 (1989) (good-faith bargaining where employer was willing to meet and confer with union, exchange proposals and modify its positions in order to reach agreement); K-B Resources dba Commercial Candy Vending Mach., 294 NLRB No. 82, 131 LRRM 1477 (1989) (no surface bargaining where employer modified, redrafted, and withdrew proposals in major areas in response to union's concerns, and where employer's conduct away from bargaining table did not support finding of bad-faith bargaining). *But see* Lapham-Hickey Steel Corp., 294 NLRB No. 27, 131 LRRM 1448 (1989) (bad-faith bargaining where employer declared impasse and unilaterally implemented new terms and conditions of employment after only two bargaining sessions, where employer had reasons to believe that its final offer would be rejected by employees); Virginia Holding Corp. dba Hotel Roanoke, 293 NLRB 182, 132 LRRM 1229 (1989) (bad-faith bargaining where employer committed acts of unlawful interference and introduced new contract proposals at last stage of negotiations); Modern Mfg. Co., 292 NLRB 10, 130 LRRM 1269 (1988) (bad-faith bargaining where employer repeatedly demonstrated it had no intention of reaching agreement with union).

[202]Cox, *supra* note 183, at 1421.

[203]*See* Greensboro News Co., 222 NLRB 893, 91 LRRM 1308 (1976), *enforced per curiam*, 549 F2d 308, 94 LRRM 2752 (CA 4, 1977) (union's insistence on interest-arbitration provision, coupled with advancement in last negotiating session of new proposal for agreement of 12 years' duration with wage rates in excess of those sought by it in previous sessions, held evidence of surface bargaining in violation of §8(b)(3); Texas Coca Cola Bottling Co., 146 NLRB 420, 55 LRRM 1326 (1964), *enforced per curiam*, 365 F2d 321, 62 LRRM 2487 (CA 5, 1966) (employer's refusal to accept union's proposed management-rights clause even though it had suggested same clause to union, refusal to agree to arbitration clause after securing union's agreement to no-strike clause, failure to submit counterproposal on dues checkoff, rejection of agreement on workweek, inter alia, led to conclusion that employer was merely going through motions of negotiation without sincere desire to reach agreement); My Store, 147 NLRB 145, 56 LRRM 1176 (1964), *enforced*, 345 F2d 494, 58 LRRM 2775 (CA 7), *cert. denied*, 382 US 927, 60 LRRM 2424 (1965) (furnishing erroneous wage information to union and failing to correct it after discovering error, questioning of union's majority by raising issue covered by consent election, failure to submit counterproposal until 4 months after certification, and making minor agreements to give "appearances of bargaining" considered as "evidence of

found where an employer rejected a union's proposal, tendered its own, and did not try to reconcile the differences.[204] Likewise, the offering of a proposal that cannot be accepted, coupled with an inflexible attitude on major issues and no proposal of reasonable alternatives, has been condemned as violative of the good-faith obligation.[205] However, regressive contract proposals are not unlawful, absent other indicia of bad faith,[206] even in the

---

Respondent's bad faith"); Tower Hosiery Mills, 81 NLRB 658, 23 LRRM 1397 (1949), *enforced*, 180 F2d 701, 25 LRRM 2509 (CA 4), *cert. denied*, 340 US 811, 26 LRRM 2611 (1950) (employer's insistence on union bond payable in event of breach of no-strike clause, and substitution of a more burdensome requirement after 7 months of negotiation without modifying its requirement for open shop, showed "lack of a sincere purpose to reach an agreement"). *See also* Tex Tan Welhausen Co. v. NLRB, 419 F2d 1265, 72 LRRM 2885 (CA 5, 1969); Walter Pape, Inc., 205 NLRB 719, 84 LRRM 1055 (1973); West Coast Casket Co., 192 NLRB 624, 78 LRRM 1026 (1971), *enforced in part*, 469 F2d 871, 81 LRRM 2857 (CA 9, 1972); Collins & Aikman Corp., 165 NLRB 678, 65 LRRM 1484 (1967), *enforced in part*, 395 F2d 277, 68 LRRM 2320 (CA 4, 1968); Southern Transp., 145 NLRB 615, 55 LRRM 1023 (1963), *enforced*, 343 F2d 558, 58 LRRM 2822 (CA 8, 1965); Atlanta Broadcasting Co., 90 NLRB 808, 26 LRRM 1287 (1950), *enforced*, 193 F2d 641, 29 LRRM 2327 (CA 5, 1952).

[204]Neon Sign Corp., 229 NLRB 861, 95 LRRM 1161 (1977), *enforcement denied*, 602 F2d 1203, 102 LRRM 2485 (CA 5, 1979) (failure of employer to move from its initial economic proposals in face of some union movement in this area, its failure to accept union's noneconomic proposals, and its inquiry concerning union's position on crossing picket lines viewed as evidence of surface bargaining); A. H. Belo Corp., 170 NLRB 1558, 69 LRRM 1239 (1968), *modified*, 411 F2d 959, 71 LRRM 2437 (CA 5, 1969).

[205]NLRB v. Wright Motors, 603 F2d 604, 102 LRRM 2021 (CA 7, 1979); Brownsboro Hills Nursing Home, 244 NLRB 269, 102 LRRM 1118 (1979); K-Mart Corp., 242 NLRB 855, 101 LRRM 1406 (1979), *enforced*, 626 F2d 704, 105 LRRM 2431 (CA 9, 1980); Clear Pine Mouldings, 238 NLRB 69, 99 LRRM 1221 (1978), *aff'd*, 632 F2d 721, 105 LRRM 2132 (CA 9, 1980), *cert. denied*, 451 US 984, 107 LRRM 2384 (1981); Case, Inc., 237 NLRB 798, 99 LRRM 1159 (1978), *enforced in part*, 653 F2d 1091, 107 LRRM 3307 (CA 6, 1981); Neon Sign Corp., *supra* note 204; San Isabel Elec. Servs., 225 NLRB 1073, 93 LRRM 1055 (1976); Yearbook House, 223 NLRB 1456, 92 LRRM 1191 (1976); Morena & Sons, 163 NLRB 1071, 65 LRRM 1054 (1967); Roy E. Hanson, Jr., Mfg., 137 NLRB 251, 50 LRRM 1134 (1962).

[206]I. Bahcall Indus., I. Bahcall Steel & Pipe Div., 287 NLRB 1257, 128 LRRM 1159 (1988), *review denied sub nom.* Teamsters Local 75 v. NLRB, 866 F2d 1537, 130 LRRM 2581 (CA DC, 1989); Cook Bros. Enters. dba Challenge-Cook Bros., 288 NLRB 387, 128 LRRM 1074 (1988); Hamady Bros. Food Mkts., 275 NLRB 1335, 120 LRRM 1019, 1022 (1985) (employer's insistence upon position which reduced benefits is not by itself evidence of bad faith); Rescar, 274 NLRB 1, 118 LRRM 1371, 1372 (1985) ("[T]he withdrawal and substitution of alleged regressive economic terms occurred in the context of changes both in the economy of the industry and the relative strengths of the participants. It is not unlawful for a party to take advantage of a shift in strength in order to seek more favorable contract terms"); ACL Corp., 271 NLRB 1600, 1603, 117 LRRM 1224, 1228 (1984) (employer's insistence on 1-year extension of current contract did not by itself evidence bad-faith or surface bargaining but rather established that employer engaged in hard bargaining). *Cf.* Excelsior Pet Prods., 276 NLRB 759, 120 LRRM 1117 (1985) (Board affirmed ALJ's finding of bad-faith bargaining by employer engaged in negotiations for new contact who had no intention of reaching agreement, notwithstanding sincere belief that executing new contract would affect survival of its business) *and* Leeds Cablevision, 277 NLRB 103, 120 LRRM 1225 (1985), *aff'd*, 835 F2d 1438, 128 LRRM 2792 (CA 11, 1987). For earlier cases finding bad-faith bargaining, see Quality Engineered Prods. Co., 267 NLRB 593, 114 LRRM 1100 (1983); Rockingham Mach. Lunex Co., 255 NLRB 89, 107 LRRM 1222 (1981), *enforced*, 665 F2d 303, 108 LRRM 3228 (CA 8, 1981), *cert. denied*, 457 US 1107, 110 LRRM 2608 (1982); K&S Circuits, 255 NLRB 1270, 107 LRRM 1230 (1981).

context of a strike or picketing activities.[207]

In *Irvington Motors*,[208] the employer was held to have violated the Act by engaging in surface bargaining where its offer merely reiterated existing practices and its first written counterproposal was not submitted until 3½ months after it had been requested.[209] An employer's (1) predetermined and inflexible position toward union security and merit increases,[210] (2) dilatory tactics and an apparent intent to reach an impasse,[211] (3) arbitrary scheduling of the day and time of a bargaining meeting,[212] (4) failure to designate an agent with sufficient authority,[213] (5) withdrawal of provisions already agreed upon,[214] and (6) injecting significant new proposals at an advanced stage in negotiations,[215] have each been held to be an element which, when coupled with other factors, proves an intent to engage in surface bargaining rather than reach a mutually satisfactory basis for agreement.

But the mere tendering by an employer of a counterproposal which is "predictably unacceptable" is not, standing alone, sufficient to justify a finding of lack of good faith, provided the proposal does not foreclose future discussion.[216] In *NLRB v. Tomco Communications*,[217] the Ninth Circuit disagreed with Board findings that the employer had engaged in bad-faith bargaining: The employer had insisted to impasse on a detailed

---

[207]Cook Bros. Enters. dba Challenge-Cook Bros., *supra* note 206; Hendrick Mfg. Co., 287 NLRB 310, 127 LRRM 1097 (1987); Eltec Corp., 286 NLRB 890, 127 LRRM 1021 (1987), *enforced*, 870 F2d 1112, 130 LRRM 3080 (CA 6), *cert. denied*, 493 US 891, 132 LRRM 2624 (1989).

[208]147 NLRB 565, 56 LRRM 1257 (1964), *enforced per curiam*, 343 F2d 759, 58 LRRM 2816 (CA 3, 1965).

[209]*See also* MacMillan Ring-Free Oil Co., 160 NLRB 877, 63 LRRM 1073 (1966), *enforcement denied on other grounds*, 394 F2d 26, 68 LRRM 2004 (CA 9, 1968).

[210]Duro Fittings Co., 121 NLRB 377, 42 LRRM 1368 (1958).

[211]Hilton Mobile Homes, 155 NLRB 873, 60 LRRM 1411 (1965), *modified*, 387 F2d 7, 67 LRRM 2140 (CA 8, 1967) (by implication); Wheeling Pac. Co., 151 NLRB 1192, 58 LRRM 1580 (1965). For the effect of an impasse on the bargaining obligation, see *infra* at notes 694–740.

[212]Moore Drop Forging Co., 144 NLRB 165, 54 LRRM 1024 (1963).

[213]Billups W. Petroleum Co., 169 NLRB 964, 67 LRRM 1323 (1968), *enforced per curiam*, 416 F2d 1333, 72 LRRM 2687 (CA 5, 1969); Bonham Cotton Mills, 121 NLRB 1235, 42 LRRM 1542 (1958), *enforced per curiam*, 289 F2d 903, 48 LRRM 2086 (CA 5, 1961).

[214]Valley Oil Co., 210 NLRB 370, 86 LRRM 1351 (1974).

[215]Yearbook House, *supra* note 205; Greensboro News Co., *supra* note 203.

[216]Neon Sign Corp. v. NLRB, 602 F2d 1203, 102 LRRM 2485 (CA 5, 1979), *denying enforcement to* 229 NLRB 861, 95 LRRM 1161 (1977); NLRB v. Crockett-Bradley Inc., 598 F2d 971, 101 LRRM 3040 (CA 5, 1979); NLRB v. Tomco Communications, 567 F2d 871, 97 LRRM 2660 (CA 9, 1978), *denying enforcement to* 220 NLRB 636, 90 LRRM 1321 (1975).

[217]*Supra* note 216.

management-rights clause, a broad zipper clause, a waiver-of-past-practices provision, and a no-strike provision that covered strikes over matters not covered by the employer's proposed grievance-arbitration provision; the employer's final economic offer consisted of a tendered increase of 10 cents an hour to seven of the nine bargaining-unit employees and a wage review for the remaining two employees. The Board had concluded that the employer engaged in surface bargaining, and condemned the employer's final proposals as "terms which no self respecting union could be expected to accept," amounting to a demand that the union "abdicate virtually every right it would normally possess to represent effectively the employees involved during the contract term."[218] The Ninth Circuit concluded, however, that the case only involved "hard bargaining between two parties who were possessed of disparate economic power: a relative weak union and a relative strong company," and that the employer's use of its economic-power advantage was not inconsistent with its statutory duty to negotiate in good faith. Rejecting the Board's "self respecting union" test for good-faith negotiations, the court said that such a standard "comes perilously close to determining what the employer should give by looking at what the employees want."[219]

The Second Circuit noted in *NLRB v. Fitzgerald Mills Corp.*[220] that "[i]n the realities of the bargaining process, neither party expects its first proposal to be accepted."[221] And the fact that

---

[218]*Id.*, 220 NLRB at 637.

[219]567 F2d at 883. *Accord* Gulf States Mfrs. v. NLRB, 579 F2d 1298, 99 LRRM 2547 (CA 5, 1978), *aff'd in part and remanded in part, en banc*, 598 F2d 896, 101 LRRM 2805 (CA 5, 1979); *but cf.* NLRB v. Mar-len Cabinets, 659 F2d 995, 108 LRRM 2838 (CA 9, 1981).

[220]133 NLRB 877, 48 LRRM 1745 (1961), *enforced*, 313 F2d 260, 52 LRRM 2174 (CA 2), *cert. denied*, 375 US 834, 54 LRRM 2312 (1963).

[221]*Id.*, 313 F2d at 265. "Consideration of the negotiations themselves, rather than the proposed contracts within whose framework they were conducted, is a better guide to whether there was good faith bargaining." *Id.* at 266. This view also prevails under the Railway Labor Act. *See* Atlantic Coast Line R.R. v. Railroad Trainmen, 262 F Supp 177, 64 LRRM 2177, 2182 (DDC, 1967), *rev'd on other grounds*, 383 F2d 225, 66 LRRM 2115 (CA DC, 1967). In Kohler Co., 128 NLRB 1062, 46 LRRM 1389 (1960), *enforced in part, modified and remanded in part*, 300 F2d 699, 49 LRRM 2485 (CADC, 1962), the union had charged that the company had engaged in "surface bargaining" during prestrike negotiations by making few concessions and remaining firm on its original offer. In rejecting this charge, the Board pointed to the company's request to get to the "meat" of the contract, its regular attendance at bargaining sessions, and its exploration of alternatives and the reasonableness of arguments in support of its bargaining positions. *Id.* at 1069. The Board did find that Kohler's poststrike conduct in unilaterally increasing the wages of nonstrikers after having previously attached conditions to its offer of the same increase to the union, coupled with surveillance and discharge of strikers, constituted a §8(a)(5) violation. *Id.* at 1078. *See also* Star Expansion Indus. Corp., 164 NLRB 563, 65 LRRM 1127 (1967), *aff'd*, 409 F2d 150, 70 LRRM 2529 (CADC, 1969).

extensive negotiations fail to produce a contract does not justify an inference that the company is engaged in "surface bargaining," since the Act does not compel the parties to reach an agreement. In one case the parties had exchanged contract proposals, had met and discussed them, and the union negotiator had written the company a letter stating he felt that the parties were not too far apart on the issues; the Board found no bad faith even though no agreement had been reached.[222] An employer's adherence to a "package" proposal during contract negotiations has been allowed in view of the employer's willingness to concede other points.[223] In addition, bargaining without concealing existing "mutual hostility,"[224] or negotiating in a "cool atmosphere,"[225] will not "dilute a finding of good faith where the totality of the party's conduct conforms to the dictates of the statute."[226] Indeed, even where an employer's conduct might have been viewed as surface bargaining, the Board has been reluctant to so hold if the union has been equally intransigent.[227]

2. Concessions, Proposals, and Demands. *a. Concessions.* "Although . . . state of mind may occasionally be revealed by declarations, ordinarily the proof must come by inference from external conduct."[228] Thus, even though section 8(d) does not require the making of a concession, the courts' and the Board's definitions of good faith[229] suggest that willingness to compromise is an important if not an essential ingredient.[230] The grant-

---

[222]Lakeland Cement Co., 130 NLRB 1365, 47 LRRM 1499 (1961). the employer committed independent §8(a)(1) violations by assisting employees in the processing of withdrawal petitions and interrogating an employee with regard to his union sympathies.

[223]Midwestern Instruments, 133 NLRB 1132, 48 LRRM 1793 (1961). But offering a union a contract on a take-it-or-leave-it basis consistently has been held to be a repudiation of collective bargaining. *See, e.g.*, NLRB v. Insurance Agents' (Prudential Ins. Co.), 361 US 477, 45 LRRM 2704 (1960); NLRB v. Truitt Mfg. Co., 351 US 149, 38 LRRM 2042 (1956). See also discussion of the *General Electric* case *supra* at notes 156–191.

[224]McCulloch Corp., 132 NLRB 201, 48 LRRM 1344 (1961); *but see* Brownsboro Hills Nursing Home, *supra* note 205.

[225]NLRB v. Almeida Bus Lines, 333 F2d 729, 731, 56 LRRM 2548 (CA 1, 1964), *setting aside* 142 NLRB 445, 53 LRRM 1055 (1963).

[226]*Id.* at 731.

[227]Unoco Apparel, 208 NLRB 601, 85 LRRM 1169 (1974), *enforced*, 508 F2d 1368, 88 LRRM 2956 (CA 5, 1975).

[228]Cox, *The Duty to Bargain in Good Faith*, 71 HARV. L. REV. 1401, 1418 (1958).

[229]*See, e.g.*, NLRB v. Highland Park Mfg. Co., 110 F2d 632, 6 LRRM 786 (CA 4, 1940), and Part I *supra* for general definitions of good faith.

[230]Cox, *supra* note 228, at 1414. For this reason, Professor Cox concluded "that the conventional definition of good faith bargaining as a sincere effort to reach an agreement goes beyond the statute." *Id.* at 1416. *See also* Specialty Container Corp., 171 NLRB 24, 68 LRRM 1018 (1968). However, an employer's refusal to grant a particular demand or to counterpropose on an issue does not necessarily constitute bad-faith bargaining. *See*

ing or withholding of concessions may be of vital importance in defending against charges of refusal to bargain in good faith. The historic language in *Reed & Prince*[231] bears this out:

> [W]hile the Board cannot force an employer to make a "concession" on any specific issue or to adopt any particular position, the employer is obliged to make *some* reasonable effort in *some* direction to compose his differences with the union, if §8(a)(5) is to be read as imposing any substantial obligation at all.[232]

In *Herman Sausage Co.*[233] the Board found, as evidence of the employer's bad faith, its unwillingness "to accept or consider any contract other than its proposed contract," which, though similar to a contract previously executed by the same union, "constituted such a radical departure from the previous contract in eliminating approximately 26 existing benefits . . . as to be predictably unacceptable to the Union."[234]

Kankakee-Iroquois County Employers Ass'n (KICEA) v. NLRB, 825 F2d 1091, 125 LRRM 2820 (CA 7, 1987), *denying review of* 274 NLRB 1176, 118 LRRM 1497 (1985) (union did not bargain in bad faith when it refused to recede from its position, advanced and maintained in good faith, that employers association must accept contract containing same provisions as union's contract with another association). Schaeff Namco, 280 NLRB 1317, 123 LRRM 1058 (1986); SCA Servs. of Ga., 275 NLRB 830, 119 LRRM 1247 (1985); Kansas Van & Storage Co., 273 NLRB 855, 118 LRRM 1162 (1984) *See also* Sanderson Farms, 271 NLRB 1477, 117 LRRM 1196 (1984) (employer did not bargain in bad faith where, under totality of circumstances, employer was not obligated to make concession regarding management-rights clause it wished preserved from prior contract); Frontier Dodge, 272 NLRB 722, 117 LRRM 1411 (1984), *supplemented*, 277 NLRB 1242, 121 LRRM 1291 (1985) (employer did not bargain in bad faith where it made several concessions and indicated its willingness to consider union's proposals). *Accord* National Steel Corp., Weirton Steel Div. v. NLRB, 689 F2d 504, 111 LRRM 2297 (CA 4, 1982), *denying enforcement of* 259 NLRB 666, 109 LRRM 1004 (1981); NLRB v. Bancroft Mfg. Co., 635 F2d 492, 106 LRRM 2603 (CA 5), *cert. denied*, 452 US 917, 107 LRRM 2632 (1981); National Council of Young Israel dba Shalom Nursing Home, 276 1123, 120 LRRM 1237 (1985) (no bad-faith bargaining by employer where employer met with union representatives, although parties failed to reach agreement on issue of economic strikers' reinstatement); Emboss-ing Printers, 268 NLRB 710, 115 LRRM 1110 (1984), *enforced*, 742 F2d 1456, 118 LRRM 2967 (CA 6, 1984) (no violation of §8(a)(5) despite evidence that employer would not agree to union-security and dues checkoff); Keller Mfg. Co., 272 NLRB 763, 117 LRRM 1425 (1984) (no violation where employer refused to offer any form of union-security proposal; employer's position was consistent with previous position taken during negotiation with previous representative of employees). *But see* Goren Printing Co., 284 NLRB 30, 126 LRRM 1157 (1987), *aff'd*, 843 F2d 1385 (CA 1, 1988) (employer bargained in bad faith where employer failed to make promised counterproposal and did not meet with union at all).

[231] Reed & Prince Mfg. Co., 96 NLRB 850, 28 LRRM 1608 (1951), *enforced*, 205 F2d 131, 32 LRRM 2225 (CA 1), *cert. denied*, 346 US 887, 33 LRRM 2133 (1953).

[232] *Id.*, 205 F2d at 134–35.

[233] 122 NLRB 168, 43 LRRM 1090 (1958), *enforced*, 275 F2d 229, 45 LRRM 2829 (CA 5, 1960).

[234] *Id.* at 170. *See also* K-Mart Corp., 242 NLRB 855, 101 LRRM 1406 (1979), *enforced*, 626 F2d 704, 105 LRRM 2431 (CA 9, 1980); Pillowtex Corp., 241 NLRB 40, 100 LRRM 1546 (1979); Preterm, Inc., 240 NLRB 654, 100 LRRM 1344 (1979).

Alluding to the futility of future negotiations unless the union accepts certain management proposals,[235] insisting that economic items not be discussed until all other terms are agreed upon,[236] failing to offer "concessions of value,"[237] and creating the impression that there can be no wage increase in order to assure that negotiations would founder[238] have each been considered factors[239] pointing to bad-faith bargaining.[240] But as the Board stated in *Partee Flooring Mill*,[241] "[t]he significant fact is not whether [the employer] was [in a position] to grant such concessions, but rather whether it had bargained in good faith on the subject."[242]

---

[235]Howmet Corp., 197 NLRB 471, 80 LRRM 1555 (1972) (a party cannot condition its making of counterproposals upon "more realistic" offers by other side); Lewin-Mathes Co., 126 NLRB 936, 45 LRRM 1416 (1960), *enforcement denied*, 285 F2d 329, 47 LRRM 2288 (CA 7, 1960)

[236]South Shore Hosp., 245 NLRB 848, 102 LRRM 1565 (1979), *enforced*, 630 F2d 40, 105 LRRM 2640 (CA 1, 1980), *cert. denied*, 450 US 965, 106 LRRM 2560 (1981); K-Mart Corp., *supra* note 234; Federal Mogul Corp., 212 NLRB 950, 87 LRRM 1105 (1974), *enforced*, 524 F2d 37, 91 LRRM 2207 (CA 6, 1975); Rhodes-Holland Chevrolet Co., 146 NLRB 1304, 56 LRRM 1058 (1964). *See also* Vanderbilt Prods., 129 NLRB 1323, 47 LRRM 1182 (1961), *enforced per curiam*, 297 F2d 833, 49 LRRM 2286 (CA 2, 1961).

[237]NLRB v. Columbia Tribune Publishing Co., 495 F2d 1384, 86 LRRM 2078 (CA 8, 1974), *enforcing and remanding* 201 NLRB 538, 82 LRRM 1553 (1973); Collins & Aikman Corp., 165 NLRB 678, 65 LRRM 1484 (1967), *enforced in part*, 395 F2d 277, 68 LRRM 2320 (CA 4, 1968). *See also* East Tex. Steel Castings Co., 154 NLRB 1080, 60 LRRM 1097 (1965).

[238]Cincinnati Cordage & Paper Co., 141 NLRB 72, 52 LRRM 1277 (1963). "For the Company to refuse at this time [at the parties' last meeting and after a strike vote had been taken] to divulge that it would consider a more modest demand than had been theretofore advanced, and for it to state to the Union a position which the plant manager later admitted on the witness stand was a falsity—namely, that it could not grant *any* increase because of competition—establishes that it was not bargaining in good faith." *Id.* at 77.

[239]In Marden Mfg. Co., 106 NLRB 1335, 33 LRRM 1025 (1953), *enforced*, 217 F2d 567, 35 LRRM 2217 (CA 5, 1954), *cert. denied*, 348 US 981, 35 LRRM 2709 (1955), the Board expressly declined to "adopt a possible implication . . . in . . . the Intermediate Report that the . . . failure to make concessions to the Union with respect to wages or financial benefits was *per se* a refusal to bargain . . . rather than only 'a material factor' in assessing good faith." *Id.* at 1338.

[240]Other factors considered include an employer's insistence on a broad management-prerogatives clause while refusing to negotiate about a wage increase and declining to consent to arbitration. "M" Sys., 129 NLRB 527, 47 LRRM 1017 (1960) (employer also violated §8(a)(5) by instituting wage incentive plan and granting individual pay raises without consulting union while steadfastly refusing to enter any agreement containing wage increase of any size). *See also* Farmers Coop. Gin Ass'n, 161 NLRB 887, 63 LRRM 1400 (1966) (employer agreed to payroll deductions not involving union while refusing a request for checkoff provision). In NLRB v. Fitzgerald Mills Corp., *supra* note 220, the employer in contract-renewal negotiations submitted a counterproposal that was, in effect, the expiring contract. Thereafter "the Union receded from its original position and made a great many progressively lesser requests but . . . the Respondent at all times maintained an uncompromising attitude, rejecting the Union's request without explanation or discussion . . . . While an employer is not obligated to make any concession, it is required to make a reasonable effort to reach an agreement." *Id.* at 880. *See also* Alba-Waldensian, 167 NLRB 695, 66 LRRM 1445 (1967), *aff'd per curiam*, 404 F2d 1370, 69 LRRM 2882 (CA 4, 1968).

[241]107 NLRB 1177, 33 LRRM 1342 (1954).

[242]*Id.* at 1178. *But see* NLRB v. Minute Maid Corp., 283 F2d 705, 47 LRRM 2072 (CA 5, 1960), *denying enforcement to* 124 NLRB 355, 44 LRRM 1376 (1959).

Granting numerous concessions may be an indication of good-faith bargaining. Although some decisions purport to look beyond the number of concessions granted or withheld,[243] others indicate that consideration is given to the quantity as well as the quality of concessions. In one case, for instance, the Fifth Circuit took note of "thirty-eight instances where [the employer] adjusted its proposals in striving to induce the Union to agree" and made "numerous concessions on substantive issues."[244] By the same token, quantitative considerations have also influenced findings of lack of good faith.[245]

Agreement on a number of major bargaining subjects may be used as evidence to overcome a refusal-to-bargain charge based on a single issue.[246] In *John S. Swift Co.*[247] a union representing only a portion of the employees at one plant sought to institute its own health and welfare plan; whereas the employer insisted upon retaining its existing companywide plan embracing several plants. In finding that the employer had bargained in good faith with respect to the health and welfare plan, the Board noted the employer's continued willingness to discuss the issue and the fact that agreement had been reached "on virtually every major bargaining item excepting health and welfare."[248]

In the *Cummer-Graham*[249] case, where the employer would not agree to an arbitration clause but was adamant in insisting upon inclusion of a no-strike clause, the Board found a refusal to

---

[243]*See, e.g.*, Vickers, Inc., 153 NLRB 561, 59 LRRM 1516 (1965).

[244]NLRB v. General Tire & Rubber Co., 326 F2d 832, 833, 55 LRRM 2150 (CA 5, 1964), *denying enforcement to* 135 NLRB 269, 49 LRRM 1469 (1962). In Star Expansion Indus. Corp., 164 NLRB 563, 65 LRRM 1127 (1967), *review denied*, 409 F2d 150, 70 LRRM 2529 (CA DC, 1969), "the company agreed to some 12 or more proposals made by the union. In subsequent negotiations, it made other concessions and offered proposals of its own on wage increases and other matters." In Dierks Forests, Inc., 148 NLRB 923, 57 LRRM 1086 (1964), "the Union [initially] presented its proposed contract, consisting of 25 articles, with a total of 61 subsections." *Id.* at 927. The employer submitted counterproposals on every issue except a no-discrimination clause, checkoff, and insurance. By the end of the negotiations, 54 of the subsections had been agreed upon. *Id.* at 928.

[245]Abingdon Nursing Center, 197 NLRB 781, 80 LRRM 1470 (1972); Florida Mach. & Foundry Co., 190 NLRB 563, 77 LRRM 1272 (1971), *enforced*, 441 F2d 1005, 78 LRRM 2895 (CADC, 1971), *cert. denied*, 409 US 846, 81 LRRM 2390 (1972).

[246]*See, e.g.*, McCourt v. California Sports, 600 F2d 1193 (CA 6, 1979); Procter & Gamble Mfg. Co., 160 NLRB 334, 62 LRRM 1617 (1966).

[247]124 NLRB 394, 44 LRRM 1388 (1959), *enforced in part and denied in part*, 277 F2d 641, 46 LRRM 2090 (CA 7, 1960).

[248]*Id.* at 395. However, the employer was found to have violated §8(a)(5) by failing to furnish data on wages and the cost of its health and welfare plan; the finding was upheld on appeal.

[249]Cummer-Graham Co., 122 NLRB 1044, 43 LRRM 1253 (1959), *enforcement denied*, 279 F2d 757, 46 LRRM 2374 (CA 5, 1960).

bargain in good faith, but the Fifth Circuit denied enforcement, stating that it did "not think that the Supreme Court held, or intended to hold, in *Lincoln Mills*, that a no-strike clause and an arbitration clause were so much one that a persistent demand for the one without acquiescing in the other is a refusal to bargain in good faith."[250]

As these cases demonstrate, no rule of thumb is available to measure the significance of specific concessions. Reference must usually be made to the "totality" of negotiations in order to find good or bad faith. Where a review of the record as a whole has shown neither dilatory tactics nor an attempt to stall efforts[251] to reach an agreement,[252] *hard bargaining* rather than unlawful bargaining has been inferred from an unyielding position by an employer on security,[253] wage offers,[254] checkoff,[255] management rights,[256] and arbitration and no-strike clauses discussed above. The failure of management to retreat from a rigid position has also been justified, at least partially, by the failure of the union to recede from its position or to grant concessions "for which it could reasonably expect a *quid pro quo* from the [employer]."[257]

---

[250]*Id.*, 279 F2d at 759–60. Textile Workers v. Lincoln Mills, 353 US 448, 40 LRRM 2113 (1957). *See* Chapter 17, "Relation of Board Action to Enforcement of Agreements Under Section 301," at notes 30–38.

[251]NLRB v. Wonder State Mfg. Co., 344 F2d 210, 59 LRRM 2065 (CA 8, 1965).

[252]"The fact that respondent did not accede to the Union's proposal but endeavored to secure a contract which it regarded would be compatible with its financial condition, does not of itself establish lack of good faith. The Act does not compel either party to agree to a proposal or require the making of a concession." *Id.* at 217.

[253]McCulloch Corp., 132 NLRB 201, 48 LRRM 1344 (1961). *But see* NLRB v. Newton-New Haven Co., 101 LRRM 2917 (Special Master, 1979) *aff'd as modified*, 101 LRRM 2922 (CA 2, 1979) (civil contempt for violating bargaining order); Brownsboro Hills Nursing Home, 244 NLRB 269, 102 LRRM 1118 (1979); K-Mart Corp., *supra* note 234; ENDO Laboratories, 239 NLRB 1074, 100 LRRM 1110 (1978).

[254]Neon Sign Corp. v. NLRB, 602 F2d 1203, 102 LRRM 2485 (CA 5, 1979); Webster Outdoor Advertising Co., 170 NLRB 1395, 67 LRRM 1589 (1968); Midwestern Instruments, 133 NLRB 1132, 48 LRRM 1793 (1961). *But see* Orion Tool, Die & Mach. Co., 195 NLRB 1080, 79 LRRM 1636 (1972) (hard-bargaining argument rejected—no effort by company to establish that it could not afford benefits-proposal it had rejected). *See also* American Express Reservations, 209 NLRB 1105, 86 LRRM 1362 (1974); Longhorn Mach. Works, 205 NLRB 685, 84 LRRM 1307 (1973).

[255]NLRB v. General Tire & Rubber Co., 326 F2d 832, 55 LRRM 2150 (CA 5, 1964); Cone Mills Corp., 169 NLRB 449, 67 LRRM 1241 (1968), *modified on other grounds*, 413 F2d 445, 71 LRRM 2916 (CA 4, 1969); McLane Co., 166 NLRB 1036, 65 LRRM 1729 (1967), *aff'd per curiam*, 405 F2d 483, 70 LRRM 2095 (CA 5, 1968); Raybestos-Manhattan, General Asbestos & Rubber Div., 168 NLRB 396, 67 LRRM 1012 (1967). *But see* Farmers Coop. Gin Ass'n, *supra* note 240. *See* H.K. Porter, 397 US 99, 73 LRRM 2561 (1960), and discussion of checkoff, *infra*, at notes 278–284.

[256]Procter & Gamble Mfg. Co., 160 NLRB 334, 62 LRRM 1617 (1966).

[257]Broadway Hosp., 244 NLRB 341, 102 LRRM 1259 (1979); Memorial Consultants, 153 NLRB 1, 15, 59 LRRM 1375 (1965). *See* NLRB v. Stevenson Brick & Block Co., 393 F2d 234, 68 LRRM 2086 (CA 4, 1968).

b. Proposals and Demands. The Board will consider the advancement of proposals by a party as a factor in determining overall good faith.[258] The fact that a proposal is "predictably unacceptable" will not justify an inference of bad faith if the proposal does not foreclose future negotiations,[259] unless it is so harsh or patently unreasonable as to frustrate agreement.[260] Moreover, the fact that a proposal merely embodies existing practices or advances less desirable working conditions is not, in itself, supportive of a finding of bad faith. Such fact may, nonetheless, be a consideration in evaluating the totality of bargain-

---

[258]Hondo Drilling Co., 213 NLRB 229, 87 LRRM 1760 (1974), *aff'd*, 525 F2d 864, 91 LRRM 2133 (CA 5, 1976), *cert. denied*, 429 US 818, 93 LRRM 2362 (1976); WCUE Radio, 209 NLRB 181, 86 LRRM 1191 (1974); Reisman Bros., 165 NLRB 390, 65 LRRM 1409 (1967), *aff'd per curiam*, 401 F2d 770, 69 LRRM 2521 (CA 2, 1968); Channel Master Corp., 162 NLRB 632, 64 LRRM 1102 (1967); Anderson's, 161 NLRB 1470, 63 LRRM 1456 (1966); Procter & Gamble Mfg. Co., *supra* note 256.

[259]NLRB v. Crockett-Bradley, 598 F2d 971, 975–77, 101 LRRM 3040 (CA 5, 1979); Gulf States Mfrs. v. NLRB, 579 F2d 1298, 99 LRRM 2547 (CA 5, 1978), *reh'g en banc granted*, 598 F2d 896, 101 LRRM 2805 (CA 5, 1979), *enforcing in part, denying and remanding in part* 230 NLRB 558, 96 LRRM 1032 (1977); NLRB v. Big Three Indus., 497 F2d 43, 86 LRRM 3031 (CA 5, 1974); NLRB v. Fitzgerald Mills Corp., 133 NLRB 877, 48 LRRM 1745 (1961), *enforced*, 313 F2d 260, 52 LRRM 2174 (CA 2), *cert. denied*, 375 US 834, 54 LRRM 2312 (1963); Preterm, Inc., 240 NLRB 654, 100 LRRM 1344 (1979). *See* Rangaire Corp., 157 NLRB 682, 61 LRRM 1429 (1966). The Ninth Circuit has stated: "We may also assume arguendo that in certain exceptional cases the extreme or bizarre character of a party's proposals may give rise to a persuasive inference that they were made only as a delaying tactic or that they should be viewed as a facade concealing an intention to avoid reaching any agreement . . . . We believe, however, that such a principle, if accepted at all, must be narrowly restricted. Otherwise, the policy supporting section 8(d)'s provision that the duty to bargain in good faith does not 'require the making of a concession' would be undermined if not more." NLRB v. MacMillan Ring-Free Oil Co., 394 F2d 26, 29, 68 LRRM 2004 (CA 9 1968), *cert. denied*, 393 US 914, 69 LRRM 2481 (1968). *See also* Taylor Instrument Co., 169 NLRB 162, 67 LRRM 1145 (1968).

[260]NLRB v. Wright Motors, 603 F2d 604, 102 LRRM 2021 (CA 7, 1979); Southside Elec. Coop., 247 NLRB 705, 103 LRRM 1393 (1980) (employer proposed 3-year contract with no wage increases or changes in existing benefits coupled with elimination of existing pension plan). *See* Skrl Die Casting, 245 NLRB 1041, 102 LRRM 1530 (1979), *enforced in part*, 651 F2d 1218, 108 LRRM 2549 (CA 6, 1981); United Contractors, 244 NLRB 72, 102 LRRM 1012 (1979), *enforced*, 631 F2d 735, 108 LRRM 3152 (CA 7, 1980); Northfield Cheese Co., 242 NLRB 1117, 101 LRRM 1539 (1979), *enforced*, 620 F2d 289, 106 LRRM 2546 (CA 3), *cert. denied*, 449 US 829 (1980); K-Mart Corp., 242 NLRB 855, 101 LRRM 1406 (1979), *enforced*, 626 F2d 704, 105 LRRM 2431 (CA 9, 1980); Architectural Fiberglass, 165 NLRB 238, 65 LRRM 1331 (1967). *See also* NLRB v. Tower Hosiery Mills, 180 F2d 701, 25 LRRM 2509 (CA 4), *cert. denied*, 340 US 811, 26 LRRM 2611 (1950) (conditioning agreement on union acceptance of proposal requiring payment of fines and liquidated damages in event of strike); Hospitality Motor Inn, 249 NLRB 1036, 104 LRRM 1276 (1980), *enforced*, 667 F2d 562, 109 LRRM 2945 (CA 6), *cert. denied*, 459 US 969, 111 LRRM 2744 (1982) (the Board, while adopting the ALJ's finding of bad-faith bargaining, specifically disavowed his "no self-respecting union could agree" rationale for reaching this result.) *Cf.* Arkansas La. Gas Co., 154 NLRB 878, 60 LRRM 1055 (1965) (company-proposed changes in no-strike, management-rights, arbitration-and-grievance, and insurance-and-pension provisions not so onerous or unreasonable as to bespeak bad faith); United States Gypsum Co., 94 NLRB 112, 28 LRRM 1015 (1951), *amended*, 97 NLRB 889, 29 LRRM 1171 (1951), *enforced in part and denied in part*, 206 F2d 410, 32 LRRM 2553 (CA 5, 1953), *cert. denied*, 347 US 912, 33 LRRM 2456 (1954).

ing conduct.[261] On the other hand, the withdrawal of an employer's solitary proposal which itself embodies only existing conditions[262] and the rejection or withdrawal of proposals that had previously been tentatively accepted have been considered elements of bad faith.[263]

In its 1988 *Reichhold Chemicals (II)*[264] decision, the Board set forth the circumstances in which it will examine the substance of a party's bargaining proposals in determining whether there has been bad-faith bargaining. Clarifying what it termed "an imprecise description of the process the Board undertakes" in evaluating a refusal-to-bargain claim, the Board announced that it has not "precluded itself from reading the language of con-

---

[261]Existing or less favorable terms embodied in an employer's proposal (more stringent requirements to qualify for holiday pay); no violation found. McCulloch Corp., *supra* note 253. *See also* Continental Bus Sys., 128 NLRB 384, 46 LRRM 1308 (1960), *enforced*, 294 F2d 264, 48 LRRM 2579 (CADC, 1961) (employer proposed renewal of old contract); *cf.* Marathon-Clark Coop. v. NLRB, 315 F2d 269, 52 LRRM 2723 (CA 7, 1963) (across-the-board reduction in benefits). *But see* the following cases where violations were found: Southside Elec. Coop., *supra* note 260; Satilla Rural Elec. Membership Corp., 137 NLRB 387, 50 LRRM 1159 (1962), *enforced*, 322 F2d 251, 53 LRRM 2841 (CA 5, 1963) (withdrawal of proposal of conditions already in effect and failure to make counterproposal); *cf.* Houston Sheet Metal Contractors Ass'n, 147 NLRB 774, 56 LRRM 1281 (1964) (company's last offer substantially below previous contract and its own earlier offers); Irvington Motors, 147 NLRB 565, 56 LRRM 1257 (1964), *enforced per curiam*, 343 F2d 759, 58 LRRM 2816 (CA 3, 1965) (proposal to continue existing practices conditioned upon union acceptance of new wage plan offered by company); Schnell Tool & Die Corp., 144 NLRB 385, 54 LRRM 1064 (1963), *enforced in part*, 359 F2d 39, 62 LRRM 2091 (CA 6, 1966). *See also* Weinacker Bros., 153 NLRB 459, 59 LRRM 1542 (1965).

[262]*See* Berry Kofron Dental Laboratory, 160 NLRB 493, 62 LRRM 1643 (1966).

[263]NLRB v. Industrial Wire Prod. Corp., 455 F2d 673, 79 LRRM 2593 (CA 9, 1972), *enforcing* 177 NLRB 328, 74 LRRM 1128 (1969); San Antonio Mach. & Supply Corp. v. NLRB, 363 F2d 633, 62 LRRM 2674 (CA 5, 1966); NLRB v. Shannon, 208 F2d 545, 33 LRRM 2270 (CA 9, 1953); Skrl Die Casting, *supra* note 260 (employer withdrew agency-shop proposal and substituted maintenance-of-membership clause); Brownsboro Hills Nursing Home, *supra* note 253; Carpenters Local 1780, 244 NLRB 277, 102 LRRM 1150 (1979); Satilla Rural Elec. Membership Corp., *supra* note 261. *See also* NLRB v. Holmes Tuttle Broadway Ford, 465 F2d 717, 81 LRRM 2036 (CA 9, 1972), *enforcing* 186 NLRB 73, 75 LRRM 1298 (1970) (employer rejected union's unconditional acceptance of terms previously suggested by employer); Wichita Eagle & Beacon Publishing Co., 222 NLRB 742, 91 LRRM 1227 (1976) (employer is not required to make concessions on items already agreed to, absent showing of clear illegality in language previously agreed to); Borden, Inc., Dairy & Serv. Div., 196 NLRB 1170, 80 LRRM 1240 (1972). *But see* Typographical Union Local 190 (Omaha) v. NLRB (World Publishing Co.), 545 F2d 1138, 93 LRRM 3063 (CA 8, 1976) (no inference of bad faith should be drawn from modification of final offer to reflect substantially changed conditions which occurred during strike); Warehousemen & Mail Order Employees Local 743 v. NLRB (Aetna Plywood & Veneer Co.), 302 F2d 865, 49 LRRM 2466 (CADC, 1962); Wallace Metal Prods., 244 NLRB 41, 102 LRRM 1233 (1979) (employer lawfully withdrew contract proposals previously agreed to after they had been rejected by union); Loggins Meat Co., 206 NLRB 303, 84 LRRM 1270 (1973) (lawful to withdraw two proposals after acceptance by union); Food Serv. Corp., 202 NLRB 790, 82 LRRM 1746 (1973); Taylor Chevrolet Corp., 199 NLRB 1064, 81 LRRM 1405 (1972); Sunderland's, Inc., 194 NLRB 118, 78 LRRM 1553 (1971).

[264]288 NLRB 69, 127 LRRM 1265 (1988), *supplementing* 277 NLRB 639, 120 LRRM 1339 (1985) (*Reichhold I*).

tract proposals and examining insistence on extreme proposals in certain situations."[265]

The Board generally does not find bad-faith bargaining solely because of the content of very aggressive contract demands made by the employer. Thus, the Board found no bad faith where the employer's demands included a broad management-rights clause, no union participation in grievances, and little weight to seniority in promotion and layoff decisions, but where the employer had yielded on the union's no-strike position. In finding no violations, the Board emphasized the frequency of meetings and the employer's willingness to discuss proposals and counterproposals.[266]

In several decisions applying *Reichhold II*, the Board has found bad-faith bargaining where the employer's proposals and conduct indicated an intent to frustrate bargaining.[267]

---

[265]*Id.*, 127 LRRM at 1266. In *Reichhold I, supra* note 264, the Board had announced that it "will not attempt to evaluate the reasonableness of a party's bargaining proposals," as distinguished from its bargaining tactics. *Id.*, 120 LRRM at 1341. In reconsidering the evidence under the standard announced in *Reichhold II*, the Board concluded that the employer violated §8(a)(5) by insisting to impasse on a no-strike clause which would have waived the right of unit employees to seek redress from the NLRB for strike discipline imposed by the employer. The Board nonetheless concluded that the employer had not engaged in overall bad-faith bargaining, and that the strike subsequently called by the union was not an unfair labor practice strike. 127 LRRM at 1268.

[266]Boaz Carpet Yarns, 280 NLRB 40, 122 LRRM 1139 (1986). *See* American Thread Co., 274 NLRB 1112, 118 LRRM 1499 (1985) (overruling Markle Mfg. Co., 239 NLRB 1353, 100 LRRM 1230 (1979), to the extent that it held that an employer's insistence on deletion of a dues checkoff provision was a violation of §8(a)(5)). *See also* K-B Resources dba Commercial Candy Vending Mach., 294 NLRB No. 82, 131 LRRM 1477 (1989) (no bad-faith bargaining in employer's insistence on broad management-rights clause and in holding firm on initial wage proposal). *Cf.* Port Plastics, 279 NLRB 362, 123 LRRM 1320 (1986), where bad-faith bargaining was found in (1) the employer's stated intent to give no ground to the union; (2) its demand for absolute authority over hours, job classifications, and subcontracting; (3) no agreement to allow union participation in grievances; (4) demand for a 12-month wage and benefit freeze; and (5) an uncompromising attitude during bargaining. Moreover, the Board ruled that management insistence that a collective bargaining agreement be unilaterally terminable at will is per se bad-faith bargaining. *See also* Massillon Hosp. Ass'n dba Massillon Community Hosp., 282 NLRB 675, 124 LRRM 1125 (1987). *But see* Walter A. Zlogar, Inc., 278 LRRM 1089, 121 LRRM 1347 (1986) (not bad-faith bargaining to demand flexible wage rate where base rate was negotiable).

[267]Cleveland Sales Co., Clesco Mfg. Div., 292 NLRB No. 126, 130 LRRM 1312 (1989) (employer insisted on 1-year agreement while telling employees that they would be better off without union and conducting poll of employees on their interest in union); Josten Concrete Prods. Co., 295 NLRB No. 114, 131 LRRM 1758 (1989) (wage offer calculated to frustrate bargaining). In Modern Mfg. Co., 292 NLRB 10, 130 LRRM 1269 (1988), the Board explicitly refused to analyze the proposals to determine whether they were sufficiently generous; Board based its decision on the employer's refusal to bargain on noneconomic matters unless the union capitulated on economic matters, while characterizing every matter as economic. The employer also insisted on retaining discretion and control over every important economic term of employment. The Board found that this conduct prevented the union from exploiting the employer's position on noneconomic matters and therefore substantially reduced the possibility of reaching a contract.

The timing of demands or proposals may also be a factor in ascertaining good faith. The interjection of numerous new proposals for the first time after several months of bargaining,[268] or the submission of new issues after the parties have reached agreement[269] in order to frustrate or stall contract execution, have been found to be indications of bad faith.[270]

In one decision, the Board found that an employer had engaged in bad-faith bargaining when it conditioned a final wage offer on successfully obtaining concessions from a third party. The employer's bargaining tactics rendered the union unable to negotiate and demonstrated that the offer was tendered without the intent to arrive at an agreement.[271]

Specialized legal principles have evolved in response to specific types of proposals and demands:

(1) Contract duration. Proposals for contracts of excessively long or short duration may indicate bad faith when judged in the light of attending circumstances.[272] A proposal for a 5-year contract has been considered by the Board as evidence of bad faith.[273] Proposals for contracts to be effective for very short periods, when obviously keyed to the expiration of the certification year,[274] have been similarly viewed. Such holdings appear grounded on the proposition that

---

[268]MRA Assocs., 245 NLRB 676, 102 LRRM 1338 (1979); Southside Elec. Coop., 243 NLRB 390, 101 LRRM 1605 (1979); Hi-Grade Materials Co., 239 NLRB 947, 100 LRRM 1113 (1978); B.F. Diamond Constr. Co., 163 NLRB 161, 64 LRRM 1333 (1967), *enforced*, 410 F2d 462, 71 LRRM 2112 (CA 5), *cert. denied*, 396 US 835, 72 LRRM 2432 (1969); Altex Mfg. Co., 134 NLRB 614, 49 LRRM 1212 (1961), *enforced*, 307 F2d 872, 51 LRRM 2139 (CA 4, 1962).

[269]Midvalley Steel Fabricators, 243 NLRB 516, 101 LRRM 1503 (1979), *modified and enforced*, 621 F2d 49, 104 LRRM 2062 (CA 2, 1980); Cabinet Mfg. Corp., 144 NLRB 842, 54 LRRM 1144 (1963).

[270]*See* Shovel Supply Co., 162 NLRB 460, 64 LRRM 1080 (1966); New England Die Casting Co., 116 NLRB 1, 38 LRRM 1175 (1956), *enforced per curiam*, 242 F2d 759, 39 LRRM 2616 (CA 2, 1957).

[271]Krausman, Perlberg, & Perlberg dba Park Inn Home for Adults, 293 NLRB 1082, 132 LRRM 1139 (1989).

[272]*See* Holmes Tuttle Broadway Ford, 186 NLRB 73, 75 LRRM 1298 (1970), *enforced*, 465 F2d 717, 81 LRRM 2036 (CA 9, 1972); Borg-Warner Corp., 128 NLRB 1035, 46 LRRM 1459 (1960).

[273]Wonder State Mfg. Co., 147 NLRB 179, 56 LRRM 1181 (1964), *enforcement denied in pertinent part*, 344 F2d 210, 59 LRRM 2065 (CA 8, 1965); Mooney Aircraft, 132 NLRB 1194, 48 LRRM 1499 (1961), *enforced per curiam*, 310 F2d 565, 51 LRRM 2615 (CA 5, 1962); Vanderbilt Prods., 129 NLRB 1323, 47 LRRM 1182 (1961), *enforced*, 297 F2d 833, 49 LRRM 2286 (CA 2, 1961).

[274]NLRB v. Strauss & Son, 536 F2d 60, 92 LRRM 3581 (CA 5, 1976); NLRB v. Hall Distrib., 341 F2d 359, 58 LRRM 2378 (CA 10, 1965), *enforcing* 144 NLRB 1285, 54 LRRM 1231 (1963); NLRB v. Henry Heide, Inc., 219 F2d 46, 35 LRRM 2378 (CA 2), *cert. denied*, 349 US 952, 36 LRRM 2203 (1955); Solo Cup Co., 142 NLRB 1290, 53 LRRM 1253 (1963), *enforced*, 332 F2d 447, 56 LRRM 2383 (CA 4, 1964).

> [w]hile the expiration date of the contract, like its substantive provisions, is a bargainable matter, a contract terminable at the will of a party, or a contract for less than a year to expire at the end of the certification year, is normally not one that will give force and effect to the Board's certification.[275]

(2) Checkoff. The Board and the courts have long recognized that the bargaining obligation extends to a proposed checkoff clause[276] and refusals to accede to and failure to offer counterproposals to union demands for checkoff or other forms of union security have been treated as evidence of breach of the duty to bargain in good faith. Nevertheless, the Board did not condemn an employer's adamant stand against such a clause where it had shown willingness to discuss the issue even though such discussions proved fruitless.[277] On the other hand, if the adamant stand is merely a "device to frustrate agreement,"[278] or

---

[275]Insulating Fabricators, 144 NLRB 1325, 1329–30, 54 LRRM 1246 (1963), *enforced per curiam*, 338 F2d 1002, 57 LRRM 2606 (CA 4, 1964). Similar reasoning has been applied where the employer insisted on a 1-year contract. *See, e.g.*, NLRB v. My Store, 345 F2d 494, 58 LRRM 2775 (CA 7), *cert. denied*, 382 US 927, 60 LRRM 2424 (1965). *But see* Grace & Hornbrook Mfg. Co., 225 NLRB 15, 92 LRRM 1637 (1976), where the Board held that the employer's proposal that the contract expire on the same date as the union's certification, in 2½ weeks, was permissible because the employer's good-faith doubt as to the union's majority status was based on objective considerations. (The Board found that (1) some employees had orally expressed their dissatisfaction with union, (2) a majority of employees had subsequently signed a petition asking for new election, and (3) the parties had been engaged in negotiations for 10 months, during which time there had been an unsuccessful 12-week strike.) *Cf.* Star Expansion Indus. Corp., 164 NLRB 563, 65 LRRM 1127 (1967), *aff'd*, 409 F2d 150, 70 LRRM 2529 (CA DC, 1969), where the Board found no bad faith in an employer's insistence on a contract expiration date coinciding with the termination of the certification year, since the contracting union had recently supplanted the incumbent union in a close election and the employer had reasonable cause to believe the contracting union was no longer supported by the majority of employees.

[276]Reed & Prince Mfg. Co., 96 NLRB 850, 28 LRRM 1608 (1951), *enforced*, 205 F2d 131, 32 LRRM 2225 (CA 1), *cert. denied*, 346 US 887, 33 LRRM 2133 (1953); United States Gypsum Co., *supra* note 260. *See* Chapter 16, "Subjects of Bargaining," at note 227.

[277]Star Expansion Indus. Corp., *supra* note 275; McLane Co., 166 NLRB 1036, 65 LRRM 1729 (1967), *aff'd per curiam*, 405 F2d 483, 70 LRRM 2095 (CA 5, 1968); Raybestos-Manhattan, General Asbestos & Rubber Div., 168 NLRB 396, 67 LRRM 1012 (1967). *See also* Capitol Aviation v. NLRB, 355 F2d 875, 877, 61 LRRM 2307 (CA 7, 1966) (citing McCulloch Corp., 132 NLRB 201, 211, 48 LRRM 1344 (1961)).

[278]H.K. Porter Co., 153 NLRB 1370, 1372, 59 LRRM 1462 (1965), *enforced*, 363 F2d 272, 62 LRRM 2204 (CADC, 1966), *cert. denied*, 385 US 851, 63 LRRM 2236 (1966) (*see* notes 281–284 *infra* for further history of this case). *See also* Queen Mary Restaurants Corp. v. NLRB, 560 F2d 403, 96 LRRM 2456 (CA 9, 1977) (court and Board rejected employer's "moral principle" excuse for refusal to agree to union-security and hiring-hall proposals, where both employer and its parent corporation had previously agreed to similar language with another union); Roanoke Iron & Bridge Works, 160 NLRB 175, 62 LRRM 1464 (1966), *enforced*, 390 F2d 846, 67 LRRM 2450 (CADC, 1967), *cert. denied*, 391 US 904, 68 LRRM 2097 (1968); Stevenson Brick & Block Co., 160 NLRB 198, 62 LRRM 1605 (1966), *enforcement denied in pertinent part*, 393 F2d 234, 68 LRRM 2086 (CA 4, 1968); Flowers Baking Co., 161 NLRB 1429, 63 LRRM 1462 (1966). *But cf.* American Oil Co., 164 NLRB 36, 65 LRRM 1007 (1967) (employer's intransigent position not based on desire to frustrate agreement).

if it is taken despite a practice of deducting nonunion items from employees' paychecks,[279] the Board has considered such conduct indicative of bad faith.[280]

In *H.K. Porter*[281] the employer withheld a dues checkoff solely to avoid giving aid and comfort to the union, for in his view the collection of union dues was the "union's business."[282] The employer contended that this was merely "hard bargaining."[283] The Board found, and was sustained by the District of Columbia Circuit, that the refusal to bargain about checkoff was not done in good faith, but was done solely to frustrate the making of any collective bargaining agreement, and hence was in violation of section 8(a)(5).[284]

(3) Management rights. The landmark case on provisions dealing with management rights is the Supreme Court's decision in

---

[279]Farmers Coop. Gin Ass'n, 161 NLRB 887, 63 LRRM 1400 (1966); H.K. Porter Co., *supra* note 278.

[280]Textron, Inc., Caroline Farms Div., 163 NLRB 854, 64 LRRM 1465 (1967), *rev'd* 401 F2d 205, 69 LRRM 2257 (CA 4, 1968). *See also* Alba-Waldensian, 167 NLRB 695, 66 LRRM 1145 (1967), *aff'd*, 404 F2d 1370, 69 LRRM 2882 (CA 4, 1968); General Tire & Rubber Co., 135 NLRB 269, 49 LRRM 1469 (1962), *enforcement denied*, 326 F2d 832, 55 LRRM 2150 (CA 5, 1964).

[281]*Supra* note 278. On subsequent motion to clarify the District of Columbia Circuit's decree, the case was remanded to the Board for consideration of whether checkoff should be granted to the union as a remedy for bad-faith bargaining. The circuit court stated that §8(d) defines the limit of the duty but does not circumscribe the remedy for the breach of that duty; it is within the Board's broad remedial powers to order the employer to grant a checkoff in return for reasonable union concessions or, in a proper case, for no concessions at all. Steelworkers (H. K. Porter Co.) v. NLRB, 389 F2d 295, 66 LRRM 2761 (CADC, 1967). On remand, the Board directed the employer to grant the checkoff provision. 172 NLRB 966, 68 LRRM 1337 (1968). The Supreme Court reversed as to remedy, holding that the Board had no authority to compel agreement as to any substantive provision in a collective bargaining contract. 397 US 99, 73 LRRM 2561 (1970). See Chapter 32, "NLRB Orders and Remedies," at notes 248–250, for further discussion of the remedial aspect of the case.

[282]153 NLRB at 1372.

[283]*Id.*

[284]The District of Columbia Circuit has also enforced a Board finding of bad faith where the sole issue was the company's refusal to grant a checkoff. The company had rejected seven alternative dues collection proposals, on the principle that no cooperation would be given in union dues collection. The Board viewed the company's history of refusing to grant checkoff in the past as a stratagem to weaken and destroy the union. The Court found support for this view in the company's disavowal of any business reason for refusal to grant checkoff. The court (citing NLRB v. Katz, 369 US 736, 50 LRRM 2177 (1962), stated that a party may not assume an intrasigent position in bad faith on a mandatory subject "even though its purpose to frustrate an agreement on that issue coincides with a willingness to reach some overall agreement." Steelworkers v. NLRB (Roanoke Iron & Bridge Works), 390 F2d 846, 849, 67 LRRM 2450 (CA DC, 1968). The District of Columbia Circuit's *Roanoke* decision goes beyond its earlier *H.K. Porter* decision, *supra* note 278, where the Board had found that the employer's refusal was intended to frustrate *any* agreement. Though purporting to base its finding on subjective good faith, the reliance on *Katz* suggested a per se approach reminiscent of General Elec. Co., 150 NLRB 192, 194, 57 LRRM 1491 (1964), *enforced*, 418 F2d 736, 72 LRRM 2530 (CA 2, 1969), *cert. denied*, 397 US 965, 73 LRRM 2600 (1970). *See also* text accompanying *supra* note 105.

NLRB v. American National Insurance Co.[285] In that case the union had submitted a proposed agreement which, in effect, called for unlimited arbitration. In response, the company proposed a management-functions clause in which all matters pertaining to promotions, discipline, and work scheduling were to be within management's exclusive control and not subject to arbitration.[286] The parties deadlocked on the clause but continued bargaining and reached agreement on other matters. Nonetheless, the Board found that insistence upon the management-functions clause constituted a per se violation of section 8(a)(5), without regard to considerations of good faith. The Fifth Circuit denied enforcement of the Board's holding on the management-functions clause,[287] and the Supreme Court affirmed, holding that bargaining for such a clause was neither a per se violation nor evidence of bad faith.

The Court reasoned that good-faith bargaining is a "two way street," and that the parties' inability to reach an agreement was due not only to the employer's unyielding position, but also to the steadfast position of the union in opposing the management-functions clause. The broader significance of the decision lies in its affirmation of collective bargaining as a method of resolving industrial disputes, while minimizing the role of the Board in policing the content of the bargaining proposals.[288]

The Board subsequently has found evidence of bad faith in an employer's insistence on a management-prerogative clause so broad as to undermine the union's ability to represent the employees adequately.[289] Other related indicators that an employer is not bargaining in good faith include insistence

---

[285]343 US 395, 30 LRRM 2147 (1952). *See also* Chapter 16, "Subjects of Bargaining," at notes 21–22.

[286]The clause provided: "The right to select, hire, to promote, demote, discharge, discipline, for cause, to maintain discipline and efficiency of employees, and to determine schedules of work is the sole prerogative of the Company and . . . such matters shall never be the subject of arbitration." 343 US at 397 n.2.

[287]187 F2d 307, 27 LRRM 2405 (CA 5, 1951), *aff'd*, 343 US 395, 30 LRRM 2147 (1952).

[288]"In its general aspect, the decision appears to be an admonition to the Board to moderate its close scrutiny of the play and byplay of collective bargaining negotiations in the application of the 'good faith' standard." From address of Professor Russell A. Smith, Labor Relations Law Section of American Bar Ass'n, Aug. 24, 1953, *reprinted in part*, 32 LRRM 68, 73 (1953).

[289]Carbonex Coal Co., 248 NLRB 779, 104 LRRM 1009 (1980), *enforced*, 679 F2d 200, 110 LRRM 2566 (CA 10, 1982) (proposed management-rights clause would have required union "to waive practically all its rights"); "M" Sys., 129 NLRB 527, 47 LRRM 1017 (1960) (employer's proposal preserved job preference, allowed termination of seniority upon discharge for just cause based on management determination, reserved final determination of grievances to management). *But cf.* Preterm, Inc., 240 NLRB 654, 100 LRRM 1344 (1979).

that the union waive most of its rights under the Act,[290] or a demand for a unilateral control of wages, hours, or terms of employment.[291]

Despite the Board's position regarding demands for broad management-rights provisions, insistence upon a management-rights clause reserving the power to assign work and to protect replacements after a strike has begun was upheld by the Seventh Circuit in *NLRB v. Lewin-Mathes Co.*[292] The court criticized the Board's finding of bad faith as passing judgment "on the reasonableness of the proposals . . . ."[293] In *Texas Industries,*[294] the Board dismissed a complaint which was based in part on a management-rights clause that reserved, inter alia, the final decision in the grievance procedure as a management prerogative, where the employer had willingly negotiated and explained his proposal. Similarly, no evidence of bad faith was found where the employer had insisted upon reserving the right to grant individual merit increases[295] or to subcontract.[296]

3. Dilatory Tactics: Refusing to Confer at Reasonable Times and Intervals. The duty to bargain in good faith imposes on the parties the obligation to confer at reasonable times and at reasonable intervals. Obviously, refusal to meet at all with the union would fail to satisfy the positive duty imposed on the employer.[297] Less flagrant conduct, however, such as procrastination in executing an agreement,[298] or delay in schedul-

---

[290]East Tex. Steel Castings Co., 154 NLRB 1080, 60 LRRM 1097 (1965) (employer's proposal reserved, inter alia, right to allocate work, transfer work from unit, reduce work force, and establish and change plant rules).

[291]Dixie Corp., 105 NLRB 390, 32 LRRM 1259 (1953); Heider Mfg. Co., 91 NLRB 1185, 26 LRRM 1641 (1950). *But see* Woodworkers Local 3-10 v. NLRB (Long Lake Lumber Co.), 458 F2d 852, 79 LRRM 2259 (CADC, 1972).

[292]285 F2d 329, 47 LRRM 2288 (CA 7, 1960).

[293]*Id.* at 332.

[294]140 NLRB 527, 52 LRRM 1054 (1963).

[295]Atlantic Research Corp., 144 NLRB 285, 54 LRRM 1049 (1963). *But see* Smyth Mfg. Co., Beacon Indus., 247 NLRB 1139, 103 LRRM 1432 (1980).

[296]Star Expansion Indus. Corp., 164 NLRB 563, 65 LRRM 1127 (1967), *aff'd,* 409 F2d 150, 70 LRRM 2529 (CADC, 1969); Peerless Distrib. Co., 144 NLRB 1510, 54 LRRM 1285 (1963).

[297]NLRB v. Little Rock Downtowner, 341 F2d 1020, 58 LRRM 2510 (CA 8, 1965). Although an outright refusal to negotiate was only of 5 days' duration, the Tenth Circuit agreed with the Board that it nonetheless violated §8(a)(5) since it occurred at a critical time—just prior to the expiration of the contract and in the face of a threatened strike. NLRB v. Albion Corp. dba Brooks, Inc., 593 F2d 936, 100 LRRM 2818 (CA 10, 1979).

[298]NLRB v. Ogle Protection Serv., 375 F2d 497, 64 LRRM 2792 (CA 6, 1967), *cert. denied,* 389 US 843, 66 LRRM 2308 (1967); NLRB v. Vander Wal, 316 F2d 631, 52 LRRM 2761 (CA 9, 1963); Wate, Inc., 132 NLRB 1338, 48 LRRM 1535 (1961), *enforced,* 310 F2d 700, 51 LRRM 2701 (CA 6, 1962). This duty extends to unions as well. *See, e.g.,* Ice Cream Drivers Local 717 (Ice Cream Council), 145 NLRB 865, 55 LRRM 1059 (1964); Auto Workers Local 453 (Maremont Automotive Prods.), 134 NLRB 1337, 49 LRRM 1357 (1961).

ing of meetings,[299] has also been found to evidence lack of good faith. Willful avoidance of meetings[300] or resorting to delaying and evasive tactics[301] have likewise been considered evidence of bad faith. Specifically, the Board has held that an employer violates section 8(a)(5) by refusing to accept certified mail from the union requesting the start of negotiations, by persistently not agreeing to meet at suggested times, by canceling scheduled meetings without proposing any additional sessions, and by failing to make meaningful counterproposals.[302] In *United Tech-*

---

[299]Henry M. Hald High School Ass'n, 213 NLRB 463, 87 LRRM 1753 (1974), *enforced*, 559 F2d 1204, 95 LRRM 3011 (CA 2, 1977) (no merit to employer's contention that bargaining sessions ought to be postponed pending court decision on government aid to parochial schools); Federal Pac. Elec. Co., 203 NLRB 571, 83 LRRM 1201 (1973), *enforced in pertinent part sub nom.* Electrical Workers (IBEW) Local 2338 v. NLRB, 499 F2d 542, 86 LRRM 2814 (CADC, 1974) (among other factors, Board noted that employee had been solicited at same time to circulate decertification petition). *See also* NLRB v. Southwestern Porcelain Steel Corp., 317 F2d 527, 53 LRRM 2307 (CA 10, 1963) (employer's efforts to delay scheduling of bargaining sessions was one factor in overall pattern of conduct indicating lack of good faith); Frank E. Nash Fence Co., 242 NLRB 233, 101 LRRM 1153 (1979) (2-month delay in setting initial meeting outside §10(b) period but still critical background evidence in finding §8(a)(5) violation); Insulating Fabricators, 144 NLRB 1325, 54 LRRM 1246 (1963), *enforced*, 338 F2d 1002, 57 LRRM 2606 (CA 4, 1964); "M" Sys., *supra* note 289.

[300]Exchange Parts Co., 139 NLRB 710, 51 LRRM 1366 (1962), *enforced*, 339 F2d 829, 58 LRRM 2097, *petition for reh'g denied*, 341 F2d 584, 58 LRRM 2456 (CA 5, 1965).

[301]Dilatory or evasive tactics are considered by the Board in assessing the totality of an employer's conduct to determine good or bad faith. Crane Co., 244 NLRB 103, 102 LRRM 1351 (1979); Rhodes St. Clair Buick, 242 NLRB 1320, 101 LRRM 1448 (1979). These tactics, standing alone, would not be per se violations of §8(a)(5). *See, e.g.*, Fry Roofing Co. v. NLRB, 216 F2d 273, 35 LRRM 2009 (CA 9, 1954), *amended per curiam*, 220 F2d 432, 35 LRRM 2662 (CA 9, 1955); National Amusements, 155 NLRB 1200, 60 LRRM 1485 (1965); Insulating Fabricators, *supra* note 299; Exchange Parts Co., *supra* note 300, 51 LRRM at 1368 (failure to meet at reasonable times "occurring as it did in the context of a history of unfair labor practices committed by Respondents" constituted §8(a)(5) violation); Bewley Mills, 111 NLRB 830, 35 LRRM 1578 (1955) (authority of negotiator considered factor, but not sole factor, in reaching conclusion that employer did not bargain in good faith). In Architectural Fiberglass, 165 NLRB 238, 65 LRRM 1331 (1967), the employer's insistence on using a tape recorder throughout the bargaining sessions was held to be evidence of bad faith. *See also* Borg Compressed Steel Corp., 165 NLRB 394, 65 LRRM 1474 (1967) (employer representative's claimed inability to locate company president did not justify delays in scheduling bargaining session). *Cf.* Inter-Polymer Indus., 196 NLRB 729, 80 LRRM 1509 (1972), *petition for review denied*, 480 F2d 631, 83 LRRM 2735 (CA 9, 1973) (despite condemning host of delaying and evasive tactics by employer, Board did not regard as indicia of bad faith representative's attempt to limit size of union's negotiating committee; use of stenographic reporter to record sessions; canceling several scheduled meetings; and imposing 4-hour limit on bargaining sessions). *See* Chapter 16, "Subjects of Bargaining," at notes 427–440.

[302]NLRB v. Platte Valley Plumbing & Heating, 748 F2d 444, 117 LRRM 3050 (CA 8, 1984); Fern Terrace Lodge of Bowling Green, 297 NLRB No. 2, 132 LRRM 1294 (1989); Midway Foodmart, 293 NLRB 152, 131 LRRM 1125 (1989); Vainio dba Professional Eye Care, 289 NLRB 738, 131 LRRM 1230 (1988); *but see* E.I. Du Pont de Nemours & Co., 294 NLRB 563, 131 LRRM 1749 (1989) (no violation for employer to insist that negotiations take place on company time and property); Nagio Restaurant dba Captain's Table, 289 NLRB 22, 128 LRRM 1183 (1988); Goren Printing Co., 284 NLRB 30, 126 LRRM 1157

nologies,[303] the Board found bad faith when the employer had engaged in a pattern of delaying tactics, including a failure to make an economic proposal, after almost 1 year of bargaining with the union. The Board has also found bad faith where the employer fragmented collective bargaining by refusing to discuss economic issues for 6 months,[304] by refusing to execute an agreed-upon contract in order to extract more concessions,[305] and by repeatedly withdrawing proposals the union had affirmed and stating that it would not comply with proposals already agreed to.[306] Bad faith also has been found where the employer refused to provide the union an adequate notice and opportunity to bargain concerning layoffs.[307]

The duty to bargain is a bilateral one, however, so that where both parties have been equally dilatory,[308] or where the union has broken off negotiations and made no further request for bargaining,[309] or has failed to request the employer to bar-

---

(1987); Storall Mfg. Co., 275 NLRB 220, 119 LRRM 1132 (1985), *enforced,* 786 F2d 1169, 122 LRRM 2832 (CA 8, 1986); Leeds Cablevision, 277 NLRB 103, 120 LRRM 1225 (1985), *aff'd,* 835 F2d 1438, 128 LRRM 2792 (CA 11, 1987); Queen Anne Record Sales dba Tower Books, 273 NLRB 671, 118 LRRM 1113 (1984), *enforced,* 772 F2d 913, 121 LRRM 2048 (CA 9, 1985); Washington Steel Brass & Iron Foundry, 268 NLRB 338, 114 LRRM 1276 (1983); Schnelli Enters. dba Cellar Restaurant, 262 NLRB 796, 110 LRRM 1362 (1982); Taurus Waste Disposal, 263 NLRB 309, 111 LRRM 1031 (1982). *But see* Hyatt Hotels Corp., 296 NLRB No. 37, 132 LRRM 1158 (1989) (refusal to meet lawful where no evidence meeting would be fruitful); Potter's Medical Center, 289 NLRB 201, 131 LRRM 1321 (1988) (previously arranged schedule of employer's counsel does not alleviate employer from meeting with union).

[303]United Technologies Corp., Hamilton Standard Div., 296 NLRB No. 79, 132 LRRM 1240 (1989).

[304]John Wanamaker, Philadelphia, 279 NLRB 1034, 123 LRRM 1271 (1986) (employer also refused to execute agreement until union withdrew unfair labor practice charges).

[305]Josten Concrete Prods., 295 NLRB No. 114, 131 LRRM 1758 (1989); Fashion Furniture Mfg., 279 NLRB 705, 122 LRRM 1229 (1986).

[306]Southwestern Portland Cement Co., 289 NLRB 1264, 131 LRRM 1063 (1988); Hilton Inn N., 279 NLRB 45, 123 LRRM 1136 (1986), *enforced and review denied,* 817 F2d 391, 125 LRRM 2351 (CA 6, 1987). *But see* Bickerstaff Clay Prods. v. NLRB, 871 F2d 980, 131 LRRM 2378 (CA 11, 1989), *denying enforcement to* 286 NLRB 295, 127 LRRM 1118 (1987), *cert. denied sub nom.* Laborers Local 246 v. Bickerstaff Clay Prods. Co., 493 US 924, 132 LRRM 2624 (1989) (no violation for employer to refuse to execute its proposals when union accepted them after employer properly withdrew its recognition of union).

[307]USA McDonald Corp. dba Norco Prods., 288 NLRB 1416, 129 LRRM 1183 (1988).

[308]Dunn Packing Co., 143 NLRB 1149, 53 LRRM 1471 (1963). *But cf.* McLean v. NLRB, 333 F2d 84, 88, 56 LRRM 2475 (CA 6, 1964), *enforcing* 142 NLRB 235, 53 LRRM 1021 (1963) (where court agreed with Board's view that union's failure to negotiate during 8-month period was no defense to employer's subsequent refusal to meet and negotiate since "it seems to us that it constituted more of a violation of duty owing to its members than to McLean").

[309]NLRB v. Lambert, 250 F2d 801, 41 LRRM 2345 (CA 5, 1958) (dismissing contempt proceedings against employer for alleged refusal to bargain in compliance with previous court order.)

gain,[310] the Board has refused to find bad faith on the part of the dilatory employer.

Delay in supplying requested information necessary for negotiations or for administration of the contract may also be considered bad faith.[311] Failure to supply wage information promptly,[312] or delay in furnishing the union a current list of employees, wage rates, and job classifications[313] or a copy of the pension plan,[314] has been treated as evidence of bad faith.

No hard-and-fast rule has evolved with regard to the number, frequency, and duration of meetings between the parties. In *Insulating Fabricators,*[315] the Board seemed to suggest that the test, consistent with other aspects of good-faith conduct, is whether the party's conduct reflects a subjective willingness to reach an agreement. It has been noted that "neither the Board nor the courts have evolved, or indeed can evolve, any particular formula by which to test whether any given frequency of meetings or amount of time spent in negotiations, satisfies the statutory requirement 'to meet at reasonable times' . . . ."[316] Nonetheless, frequency of meetings is relied upon for evidence of an employer's intent.[317]

---

[310]Lori-Ann, Inc., 137 NLRB 1099, 50 LRRM 1340 (1962).

[311]Crane Co., *supra* note 301; Fitzgerald Mills Corp., 133 NLRB 877, 48 LRRM 1745 (1961), *enforced,* 313 F2d 260, 52 LRRM 2174 (CA 2), *cert. denied,* 375 US 834, 54 LRRM 2312 (1963).

[312]Rhodes-Holland Chevrolet Co., 146 NLRB 1304, 56 LRRM 1058 (1964); Fitzgerald Mills Corp., *supra* note 311; Butcher Boy Refrigerator Door Co., 127 NLRB 1360, 46 LRRM 1192 (1960), *enforced,* 290 F2d 22, 48 LRRM 2058 (CA 7, 1961).

[313]International Powder Metallurgy Co., 134 NLRB 1605, 49 LRRM 1388 (1961); Gateway Luggage Mfg. Co., 122 NLRB 1584, 43 LRRM 1342 (1959).

[314]Rangaire Corp., 157 NLRB 682, 61 LRRM 1429 (1966).

[315]*Supra* note 299.

[316]Radiator Specialty Co., 143 NLRB 350, 368, 53 LRRM 1319 (1963) (trial examiner's report), *enforced in part,* 336 F2d 495, 57 LRRM 2097 (CA 4, 1964).

[317]*See, e.g.,* Rhodes St. Clair Buick, *supra* note 301 (violation found where employer postponed first meeting for 2 months following certification and request to bargain, agreed to meet only six times within 6-month period following certification, and limited length of meetings to (1½ hours); Exchange Parts Co., 139 NLRB 710, 51 LRRM 1366 (1962), *enforced,* 339 F2d 829, 58 LRRM 2097 (CA 5, 1965) (meeting average of 8 hours a month over 8-month period was insufficient). *But cf.* Honaker, 147 NLRB 1184, 56 LRRM 1371 (1964) (meeting on 11 occasions over 5-month period, with meetings averaging 3½–4 hours each, was not failure to meet); Radiator Specialty Co., *supra* note 316, at 369 ("[T]he parties met . . . 37 times during a 10-month period. Some of these meetings . . . were at close intervals and a few meetings were lengthy. However, the great bulk of the meetings were of short duration, lasting about 2 hours, and the lags between many were considerable." Nevertheless, Board's finding of bad faith was rejected on ground that evidence did not show bad faith); Texas Indus., 140 NLRB 527, 52 LRRM 1054 (1963) (meeting 11 times during 4-month period was frequent enough to satisfy Act); McCulloch Corp., 132 NLRB 201, 48 LRRM 1344 (1961) (employer, having met 79 times in 11 months and not having caused substantial delay, was not guilty of refusing to meet).

4. Representative With Inadequate Authority to Bargain. The employer is under a duty to vest its negotiators with sufficient authority to carry on meaningful bargaining.[318] Thus, nonavailability of the employer's negotiator[319] or its labor counsel[320] has been held to manifest bad faith,[321] as has the failure to provide a bargaining representative sufficiently knowledgeable about the company's operations and pay practices to permit fruitful, informed discussion of working conditions and employee pay.[322] Further, an employer violates section 8(a)(5) when it sends representatives to the bargaining table who have no authority to enter into a contract or to advance binding contract proposals.[323] The refusal to execute an agreement made by a representative having apparent authority is unlawful where the employer has not expressly reserved the right to ratify or reject it.[324] But the Board found no bad-faith

---

[318]NLRB v. Fitzgerald Mills Corp., *supra* note 311; Valley Imported Cars, 203 NLRB 873, 83 LRRM 1477 (1973); Han-Dee Spring & Mfg. Co., 132 NLRB 1542, 48 LRRM 1566 (1961). In NLRB v. Alterman Transp. Lines, 587 F2d 212, 100 LRRM 2269 (CA 5, 1979), the Fifth Circuit found the employer in contempt of an earlier bargaining order, where its president sought to reject substantially all of the terms agreed to by its negotiator over a nearly 2-year period under the guise of a reserved right of ratification.

[319]General Motors Acceptance Corp. v. NLRB, 476 F2d 850, 82 LRRM 3093 (CA 1, 1973), *enforcing* 196 NLRB 137, 79 LRRM 1662 (1972); Solo Cup Co., 142 NLRB 1290, 53 LRRM 1253 (1963), *enforced*, 332 F2d 447, 56 LRRM 2383 (CA 4, 1964) (company's vice-president and company's counsel); Allis Chalmers Mfg. Co., 106 NLRB 939, 32 LRRM 1585 (1953), *rev'd on other grounds*, 213 F2d 374, 34 LRRM 2202 (CA 7, 1954) (scheduling of negotiating sessions only at times when they would not interfere with company routine). *But cf.* Radiator Specialty Co., *supra* note 316 (enforcement denied as to failure to bargain based on unavailability of negotiator).

[320]*See, e.g.*, NLRB v. Milgo Indus., 567 F2d 540, 97 LRRM 2079 (CA 2, 1977) (court upheld Board determination that employer impermissibly delayed negotiations by making its attorney-negotiator available only 17 times in 15 months, even though union negotiators also were responsible for substantial portion of delay); Franklin Equip., 194 NLRB 643, 79 LRRM 1112 (1971) ("busy lawyer" defense rejected); Insulating Fabricators, 144 NLRB 1325, 54 LRRM 1246 (1963), *enforced*, 338 F2d 1002, 57 LRRM 2606 (CA 4, 1964) (company's labor lawyer resided in Boston, approximately 800 miles from client's plant). *See also* Skyland Hosiery Mills, 108 NLRB 1600, 34 LRRM 1254 (1954).

[321]B.F. Diamond Constr. Co., 163 NLRB 161, 64 LRRM 1333 (1967), *enforced*, 410 F2d 462, 71 LRRM 2112 (CA 5), *cert. denied*, 396 US 835, 72 LRRM 2432 (1969); "M" Sys., 129 NLRB 527, 47 LRRM 1017 (1960).

[322]Coronet Casuals, 207 NLRB 304, 84 LRRM 1441 (1973).

[323]Cablevision Indus., 283 NLRB 22, 126 LRRM 1102 (1987); S-B Mfg. Co., 270 NLRB 485, 116 LRRM 1334 (1984); Bedford Farmers Coop., 259 NLRB 1226, 109 LRRM 1113 (1982); *see also* Vainio dba Professional Eye Care, 289 NLRB 1376, 131 LRRM 1185 (1988) (family-owned and-operated business violated §8(a)(5) by sending negotiator who had no knowledge of present terms and conditions of employment and lacked authority); Penntech Papers, 263 NLRB 264, 111 LRRM 1622 (1982), *enforced*, 706 F2d 18, 113 LRRM 2219 (CA 1), *cert. denied*, 464 US 892, 114 LRRM 2648 (1983).

[324]Metco Prods. Div. v. NLRB, 884 F2d 156, 132 LRRM 2777 (CA 4, 1989), *enforcing* 289 NLRB 76, 130 LRRM 1351 (1988); Roslyn Gardens Tenants Corp., 294 NLRB No. 40, 132 LRRM 1087 (1989); Plattdeutsche Park Restaurant, 296 NLRB No. 26, 132 LRRM 1109 (1989); Property Resources Corp., 285 NLRB 1105, 127 LRRM 1187 (1987), *enforced*, 863 F2d 964, 130 LRRM 2266 (CADC, 1988); Medical Towers, 285 NLRB 1011, 127

bargaining where an employer repudiated a tentative agreement that had not yet been ratified by the union where the employer's negotiator mistakenly assumed authority to agree.[325]

5. Imposing Conditions. The duty to bargain extends to good-faith consideration of all proper subjects for collective bargaining. Attempts to place conditions upon either bargaining or the execution of a contract are scrutinized closely by the Board to determine whether the proposed condition is so onerous or unreasonable as to indicate bad faith.[326] For example, in *Fitzgerald Mills Corp.*,[327] components of the employer's bad-faith bargaining were its demand for a union waiver of grievances which were pending under the old contract and its conditioning further bargaining upon a waiver of strikers' reinstatement rights. The Board found the latter to be tantamount to requiring abandonment of the union's pending unfair labor practice charges against the employer, a condition that the Board has frequently condemned.[328]

Conditioning further negotiations on cessation of a strike also violates the Act, since the obligation to bargain continues during a strike.[329] As the Fifth Circuit noted in *NLRB v. Safway Steel*

LRRM 1080 (1987), *enforced*, 862 F2d 309, 129 LRRM 3144 (CA 3, 1988); Ben Franklin Nat'l Bank, 278 NLRB 986, 122 LRRM 1283 (1986).

[325]Roslyn Gardens Tenants Corp., *supra* note 324 (employer's negotiators never expressed to union fact that their authority was limited); Williams, 265 NLRB 506, 111 LRRM 1684 (1982).

[326]*See, e.g.*, Chemung Contracting Corp., 291 NLRB 773, 129 LRRM 1305 (1988); SAS Ambulance Serv. dba Florida Ambulance Serv., 258 NLRB 459, 108 LRRM 1242 (1981); Dining & Kitchen Admin. dba DAKA, 257 NLRB 325, 107 LRRM 1514 (1981), *enforcement denied sub nom.* International House v. NLRB, 676 F2d 906, 110 LRRM 2206 (CA 2, 1982). In American Flagpole Equip. Co., Case No. 29-CA-1052 (no exceptions filed), 68 LRRM 1384 (1968), an employer's reopening of negotiations was conditioned upon the union's execution of contracts with the employer's competitors. The fact that the purpose of the condition was to avoid economic disadvantage was held to be no defense to a refusal-to-bargain charge. *See also* Kroger Co., 164 NLRB 362, 65 LRRM 1089 (1967), *enforced in part and denied in part*, 401 F2d 682, 69 LRRM 2425 (CA 6, 1968); S & M Mfg. Co., 165 NLRB 663, 65 LRRM 1350 (1967) (submission of contract proposal to union conditioned upon its acceptance on same day held unlawful); Lebanon Oak Flooring Co., 167 NLRB 753, 66 LRRM 1172 (1967).

[327]*Supra* note 311.

[328]*See, e.g.*, Lion Oil Co. v. NLRB, 245 F2d 376, 40 LRRM 2193 (CA 8, 1957); Patrick & Co., 248 NLRB 390, 103 LRRM 1457 (1980), *enforced*, 644 F2d 889, 108 LRRM 2175 (CA 9, 1981); Palm Beach Post-Times, 151 NLRB 1030, 58 LRRM 1561 (1965), *enforced sub nom.* NLRB v. Perry Publications, 375 F2d 118, 65 LRRM 2064 (CA 5), *cert. denied*, 389 US 842, 66 LRRM 2307 (1967); Kit Mfg. Co., 142 NLRB 957, 53 LRRM 1178 (1963), *enforced in part*, 335 F2d 166, 56 LRRM 2988 (CA 9, 1964), *cert. denied*, 380 US 910, 58 LRRM 2496 (1965); Taormina Co., 94 NLRB 884, 28 LRRM 1118 (1951), *enforced*, 207 F2d 251, 32 LRRM 2684 (CA 5, 1953).

[329]General Elec. Co., 163 NLRB 198, 64 LRRM 1312 (1967), *enforced in part and denied in part*, 400 F2d 713, 69 LRRM 2081 (CA 5, 1968), *cert. denied*, 394 US 904, 70 LRRM 2828 (1969); Rice Lake Creamery, 131 NLRB 1270, 48 LRRM 1251 (1961), *enforced sub nom.*

Scaffolds Co.,[330] "the use of economic pressure by a union does not relieve the company of the duty to bargain."

Requiring agreement on certain subjects of bargaining as a prerequisite to further negotiation has been viewed as evidence of bad faith. Thus, employers have exhibited bad faith by requiring the union to accept "open shop" and "freedom to discharge" provisions before the company would engage in economic discussion,[331] by refusing to negotiate unless the union signed a 120-day moratorium that required, in effect, that the union cease representing the employees for a period of 4 months,[332] and by requiring that the union post an indemnity bond as a condition to the signing of a contract.[333] Attempting to dictate the composition of the union's negotiating committee,[334] and refusing to bargain with the union unless a former employee on the union committee was removed,[335] have been similarly treated. Requiring agreement on nonmandatory subjects of bargaining as a condition to further negotiation thus falls in the same category as insisting to impasse on such subjects, which under the *Borg-Warner* doctrine[336] constitutes a refusal to bargain. Moreover, a party cannot insist that bargaining take place through the mail-exchange of proposals.[337]

An employer unlawfully conditioned payment of a Christmas bonus and profit-sharing benefit upon contract ratification and

General Drivers Local 662 v. NLRB, 302 F2d 908, 50 LRRM 2243 (CADC), *cert. denied*, 371 US 827, 51 LRRM 2222 (1962).

[330]383 F2d 273, 66 LRRM 2136, 2141 (CA 5, 1967), *enforcing in part* 153 NLRB 417, 59 LRRM 1486 (1965), *cert. denied*, 390 US 955, 67 LRRM 2632 (1968). *See also* NLRB v. Rutter-Rex Mfg. Co., 245 F2d 594, 40 LRRM 2213 (CA 5, 1957).

[331]Vanderbilt Prods., 129 NLRB 1323, 47 LRRM 1182 (1961), *enforced*, 297 F2d 833, 49 LRRM 2286 (CA 2, 1961). In NLRB v. Strong Roofing & Insulating Co., 386 F2d 929, 65 LRRM 3012 (CA 9, 1967), *cert. denied*, 390 U.S. 920, 67 LRRM 2385 (1968), the Ninth Circuit held that the Board was entitled to consider an employer's refusal to sign a contract, which occurred more than 6 months before the charge was filed, as background evidence of similar refusals occurring within the §10(b) period.

[332]Crusader-Lancer Corp., 144 NLRB 1309, 54 LRRM 1254 (1963). In Architectural Fiberglass, 165 NLRB 238, 65 LRRM 1331 (1967), an employer's proposal requiring both parties to waive their right to bargain during the term of the agreement, as well as the right to information pertaining to wages, hours, and other terms of employment, whether mentioned in the collective bargaining agreement or not, was viewed as a requirement that the union abandon its statutory obligation to bargain collectively as the representative of the employees; hence, it was a violation of §8(a)(5).

[333]Davison, 136 NLRB 742, 49 LRRM 1831 (1962), *enforced*, 318 F2d 550, 53 LRRM 2462 (CA 4, 1963).

[334]Cabinet Mfg. Corp., 140 NLRB 576, 52 LRRM 1064 (1963).

[335]Fetzer Television, 131 NLRB 821, 48 LRRM 1165 (1961), *enforced per curiam*, 299 F2d 845, 49 LRRM 2766 (CA 6, 1962). *See also* Sears, Roebuck & Co., 139 NLRB 471, 51 LRRM 1327 (1962) (refusal to meet with international union representative participating in local negotiations violated §8(a)(5)).

[336]*See supra* notes 54–61 and accompanying text.

[337]Fountain Lodge, 269 NLRB 674, 116 LRRM 1006 (1984). *See also* Signatory Labor Comm., Colorado Contractors Ass'n, 261 NLRB 1459, 110 LRRM 1224 (1982).

unlawfully conditioned further movement in negotiations upon setting a date for contract ratification.[338] Another employer unlawfully insisted that a union retroactively agree to the employer's unilateral midterm modifications of the expiring contract.[339] Other unlawful conditions have included: insisting on the presence of a court reporter,[340] insisting on the inclusion of a loyalty clause in the contract,[341] insisting that a unit of employees be excluded from contract coverage,[342] insisting that a former "disgruntled" employee be excluded from the union's bargaining team,[343] insisting that claims against the employer for delinquent health and welfare fund contributions be dropped,[344] insisting on employee ratification as a condition of the employer's agreement,[345] refusing to sign the contract without withdrawal of the union's unfair labor practice charges,[346] conditioning future meetings on the union's withdrawal of its demands,[347] and refusing to negotiate economic proposals without agreement on noneconomic issues.[348] On the other hand, a refusal to meet with a physically abusive negotiator was not unlawful.[349]

6. Unilateral Changes. Unilateral action by an employer affecting its employees' wages, hours, or working conditions during bargaining is often a strong indication that it is not bargaining in good faith.[350] During contract negotiations an

---

[338]Freedom WLNE-TV, 278 NLRB 1293, 122 LRRM 1214 (1986).

[339]R.E.C. Corp., 296 NLRB No. 163, 132 LRRM 1268 (1989).

[340]NLRB v. Bartlett-Collins Co., 639 F2d 652, 106 LRRM 2272 (CA 10), *cert. denied*, 452 US 961, 107 LRRM 2768 (1981); United Gilsonite Laboratories, 291 NLRB 924, 131 LRRM 1034 (1988), *enforced and review denied*, 884 F2d 1384, 132 LRRM 2240 (CA 3, 1989). *See also* NLRB v. Pennsylvania Tel. Guild (Bell Tel. Co. of Pa.), 799 F2d 84, 123 LRRM 2214 (CA 3, 1986).

[341]Meda-Care Ambulance, 285 NLRB 471, 128 LRRM 1276 (1987).

[342]Gibbs & Cox, 280 NLRB 953, 123 LRRM 1034 (1986).

[343]Colfor, Inc., 282 NLRB 1173, 124 LRRM 1204 (1987), *enforced*, 838 F2d 164, 127 LRRM 2447 (CA 6, 1988).

[344]Plattdeutsche Park Restaurant, *supra* note 324.

[345]Zayre Dep't Stores, 289 NLRB 1183, 131 LRRM 1238 (1988).

[346]Lustrelon Inc., 289 NLRB 378, 130 LRRM 1398 (1988); John Wanamaker, Philadelphia, 279 NLRB 1034, 123 LRRM 1271 (1986).

[347]Lustrelon, Inc., *supra* note 346.

[348]*Id.*; Eastern Me. Medical Center v. NLRB, 658 F2d 1, 108 LRRM 2234 (CA 1, 1981), *enforcing* 253 NLRB 224, 105 LRRM 1665 (1980). *But see* K-B Resources dba Commercial Candy Vending Mach., 294 NLRB No. 82, 131 LRRM 1477 (1989).

[349]Auto Workers v. NLRB, (FitzSimons Mfg. Co.), 670 F2d 663, 109 LRRM 2810 (CA 6, 1982), *enforcing* 251 NLRB 375, 105 LRRM 1083 (1980).

[350]*See, e.g.*, NLRB v. Parents & Friends of the Specialized Living Center, 879 F2d 1442, 131 LRRM 3119 (CA 7, 1989), *enforcing* 286 NLRB 511, 130 LRRM 1009 (1987) (employer engaged in bad-faith bargaining by making changes in employees' work schedules without prior bargaining; "compelling economic circumstances" exception to duty to bargain not applicable after union is certified); NLRB v. Westinghouse Broadcasting & Cable

employer may not implement proposed changes or those tentatively agreed to by the parties, even if an opportunity to bargain is first given the union, absent a valid preexisting impasse or consent of the union.[351] Even if impasse is reached, however, a unilateral implementation of terms not reasonably contemplated in a pre-impasse offer violates section 8(a)(5) and indicates that the employer failed to bargain in good faith.[352]

A violation of section 8(a)(5) will also be found where an employer insists on bargaining to impasse, then unilaterally implements proposals it had made during negotiations that alter the scope of the bargaining unit, as such proposals are not mandatory subjects of bargaining.[353] The Second Circuit has

---

(WBZ-TV), 849 F2d 15, 128 LRRM 2665 (CA 1, 1988), *enforcing* 285 NLRB 205, 128 LRRM 1166 (1987); R.E.C. Corp., *supra* note 339 (employer may not unilaterally cease contributing to pension and welfare funds or paying wage rates specified in collective bargaining agreement); Colorado-Ute Elec. Ass'n, 295 NLRB No. 67, 131 LRRM 1457 (1989) (employer violated §8(a)(5) by granting merit raises to employees without bargaining over timing and amount of raises, despite bargaining to impasse over proposal to implement merit increase program); WPIX, Inc., 293 NLRB 10, 131 LRRM 1780 (1989); Virginia Holding Corp. dba Hotel Roanoke, 293 NLRB 182, 132 LRRM 1229 (1989); United Technologies Corp., Hamilton Standard Div., 296 NLRB No. 79, 132 LRRM 1240 (1989); Roslyn Gardens Tenants Corp., 294 NLRB No. 40, 132 LRRM 1087 (1989); Krausman, Perlberg, & Perlberg dba Park Inn Home for Adults, 293 NLRB 295, 132 LRRM 1139 (1989); Storer Communications, 294 NLRB No. 78, 133 LRRM 1118 (1989); Microdot Valley Mould Div., 288 NLRB 1015, 128 LRRM 1134 (1988); O'Neill, Ltd., 288 NLRB 1354, 129 LRRM 1315 (1988); L.W. LeFort Co., 290 NLRB 344, 130 LRRM 1180 (1988); Bennett Packaging Co. of Ky., 285 NLRB 602, 129 LRRM 1245 (1987); Nuclear Fuel Servs., 286 NLRB 705, 129 LRRM 1166 (1987). *See also* Hoover Enters., 293 NLRB 654, 131 LRRM 1057 (1989) (§§8(a)(1) and 8(a)(5) violations found where employer improperly withdrew recognition of voluntarily recognized union, then implemented unilateral changes in terms and conditions of employment). *But see* Attwood & Morrill Co., 289 NLRB 794, 129 LRRM 1210 (1988); Murphy Oil USA, 286 NLRB 1039, 127 LRRM 1111 (1987); Nielsen Lithographing Co., 279 NLRB 877, 123 LRRM 1217 (1986), *review granted and set aside*, 854 F2d 1063, 129 LRRM 2367, *amended*, 129 LRRM 2732 (CA 7, 1988); Great Lakes Coal Co., 268 NLRB 1207, 116 LRRM 1310 (1984), *supplemented*, 280 NLRB No. 70, 123 LRRM 1224 (1986); Robbins Door & Sash Co., 260 NLRB 659, 109 LRRM 1181 (1982). *See also* NLRB v. M.A. Harrison Mfg. Co., 682 F2d 580, 111 LRRM 2449 (CA 6, 1982), *enforcing* 253 NLRB 675, 106 LRRM 1021 (1980) *and* 256 NLRB 427, 107 LRRM 1263 (1981); Isla Verde Hotel Corp. v. NLRB, 702 F2d 268, 112 LRRM 3065 (CA 1, 1982); Procter & Gamble Mfg. Co. v. NLRB, 658 F2d 968, 108 LRRM 2177 (CA 4, 1981), *enforcing* 248 NLRB 953, 104 LRRM 1207 (1980), *cert. denied*, 459 US 879, 111 LRRM 2528 (1982); Joe Carroll Orchestras & Entertainment Agency, 254 NLRB 1158, 106 LRRM 1304 (1981).

[351]Accurate Die Casting Co., 292 NLRB 982, 131 LRRM 1706 (1989) (unlawful to alter terms and conditions of employment even though contract expired and strike replacements hired); Connecticut Color, 288 NLRB 699, 128 LRRM 1211 (1988); Milwaukee Terminal Servs., 282 NLRB 637, 124 LRRM 1120 (1987); Marriott Corp., Marriott In-Flite Servs. Div., 258 NLRB 755, 108 LRRM 1287 (1981), *enforced*, 729 F2d 1441, 113 LRRM 3528 (CA 2), *cert. denied*, 464 US 829, 114 LRRM 2568 (1983).

[352]Cuyamaca Meats v. San Diego & Imperial Counties Butchers' & Food Employers' Pension Trust Fund, 827 F2d 491, 126 NLRB 2193 (CA 9, 1987), *cert. denied*, 485 US 1008 (1988); Pano, 295 NLRB No. 90, 131 LRRM 1717 (1989); Laminated Prods., 294 NLRB No. 69, 131 LRRM 1603 (1989).

[353]Boise Cascade Corp. v. NLRB, 860 F2d 471, 129 LRRM 2744 (CADC, 1988), *enforcing* 283 NLRB 462, 124 LRRM 1391 (1987).

noted that a "wage increase [during bargaining] is by far the most important 'unilateral act.'"[354] That court considered such an action a deliberate attempt by the employer to deal directly with its employees and to convince them that benefits come solely from the employer. The court also noted that if the increase is contemporaneous with a strike, the "timing is particularly convincing support for the conclusion that prior negotiations were not conducted in good faith."[355] Wage increases granted to employees in excess of any previous offer to the union are normally violative of section 8(a)(5),[356] as are unilateral increases in wage-related fringe benefits, such as holiday pay,[357] expense allowances,[358] and incentive programs.[359] Reduction or discontinuance of a wage benefit, such as a Christmas bonus, may also be indicative of a refusal to bargain.[360]

---

[354]NLRB v. Fitzgerald Mills Corp., 313 F2d 260, 267, 52 LRRM 2174 (CA 2, 1963). *See supra* note 327. *See also* Trinity Valley Iron & Steel, 127 NLRB 417, 46 LRRM 1030 (1960), *enforced*, 290 F2d 47, 48 LRRM 2110 (CA 5, 1961) (granting wage increases to nonstrikers during economic strike).

[355]313 F2d at 268.

[356]Aztec Ceramics Co., 138 NLRB 1178, 51 LRRM 1226 (1962), *enforced in part and denied in part*, 320 F2d 757, 53 LRRM 2489 (CADC, 1963); Crater Lake Mach. Co., 131 LRRM 1106, 48 LRRM 1211 (1962); Yale Upholstering Co., 127 NLRB 440, 46 LRRM 1031 (1960); Dinion Coil Co., 110 NLRB 196, 34 LRRM 1623 (1954). *Cf.* Phil-Modes, Inc., 162 NLRB 1435, 64 LRRM 1303 (1967), *enforced in part and denied in part*, 406 F2d 556, 70 LRRM 2247 (CA 5, 1969) (employer's unilateral wage increase constituted illegal change in working conditions despite fact that increases conformed with past practice, but evidence was insufficient to establish discriminatory motive in employer's change of method of wage computation). *See also* Blue Cab Co., 156 NLRB 489, 61 LRRM 1085 (1965), *enforced*, 373 F2d 661, 64 LRRM 2317 (CADC), *cert. denied*, 389 US 837, 66 LRRM 2306 (1967).

[357]Mooney Aircraft, 138 NLRB 1331, 51 LRRM 1230 (1962).

[358]Cutter Boats, 127 NLRB 1576, 46 LRRM 1246 (1960).

[359]Phil-Modes, Inc., *supra* note 356; "M" Sys., 129 NLRB 527, 47 LRRM 1017 (1960) (merit increases may not lawfully be unilaterally instituted).

[360]Keystone Consol. Indus., Keystone Steel & Wire Div., 237 NLRB 763, 99 LRRM 1036 (1978), *enforced as modified*, 606 F2d 171, 102 LRRM 2664 (CA 7, 1979) (replacement of administrator/processor of claims under employer's self-insured major medical plan). *Compare* Nello Pistoresi & Son, 203 NLRB 905, 83 LRRM 1212 (1974), *enforcement denied in relevant part*, 500 F2d 399, 86 LRRM 2736 (CA 9, 1974) (discontinuation of Christmas bonus paid to employees previous 2 years), *with* Benchmark Indus., 270 NLRB 22, 116 LRRM 1032 (1984), *aff'd sub nom.* Clothing & Textile Workers v. NLRB, 760 F2d 267, 119 LRRM 3160 (CA 5, 1985) (unilateral termination of 3-year practice of gift ham at Christmas not violation: *Nello Pistoresi* overruled). *See* Radio Television Technical School v. NLRB, 488 F2d 457, 84 LRRM 2794 (CA 3, 1973), *enforcing* 199 NLRB 570, 81 LRRM 1296 (1972); Century Elec. Motor Co. v. NLRB, 447 F2d 10, 78 LRRM 2042 (CA 8, 1971), *enforcing in part* 180 NLRB 1051, 73 LRRM 1307 (1970); NLRB v. McCann Steel Co., 448 F2d 277, 78 LRRM 2237 (CA 6, 1971), *enforcing in part* 184 NLRB 779, 76 LRRM 1556 (1970) (employer reduced Christmas bonus 1 day after union election victory); NLRB v. Zelrich Co., 344 F2d 1011, 59 LRRM 2225 (CA 5, 1965); NLRB v. Exchange Parts, 339 F2d 829, 58 LRRM 2097, *petition for reh'g denied*, 341 F2d 584, 58 LRRM 2456 (CA 5, 1965) (violation regardless of whether decision to make reduction was made before or after union certification); Clear Pine Mouldings, 238 NLRB 69, 99 LRRM 1221 (1978), *aff'd*, 632 F2d 721, 105 LRRM 2132 (CA 9, 1980), *cert. denied*, 451 US 984, 107 LRRM 2384

There are, however, certain situations in which an employer may lawfully make unilateral changes: (1) after the lapse of the certification year, if there are reasonable grounds to believe the certified union has lost majority support.[361] But, justification for such change may require not only that the belief be reasonable, but that it be accurate.[362] (2) An employer may grant a rejected wage increase after a bona fide impasse has been reached,[363] unless the impasse was caused by the employer's lack of good faith.[364] However, a unilateral change as to subject matter which was not included in the negotiations is not permissible even after impasse.[365] (3) In certain circumstances an increase may be granted even before impasse is reached.[366] For example, the

---

(1981) (discontinuance of contributions to health and welfare fund after expiration of contract); Gas Mach. Co., 221 NLRB 862, 90 LRRM 1730 (1975) (withholding of Christmas "gifts" employer had given to employee in each of previous 7 years); Scam Instrument Corp., 163 NLRB 284, 64 LRRM 1327 (1967), *enforced*, 394 F2d 884, 68 LRRM 2280 (CA 7, 1968) (imposing policy rider which reduced benefits to employees who received sums under other insurance policies); Mooney Aircraft, *supra* note 357 (ceasing to allow employees to make up pay lost in periods of absence). *Cf.* Federal-Mogul Corp., 209 NLRB 343, 85 LRRM 1353 (1974) (held employer violated §8(a)(5) by unilaterally imposing collective bargaining agreement covering preexisting unit on emloyees who had voted for inclusion in that unit, resulting in loss of benefits to new unit employees). *But see* NLRB v. Abex Corp., 543 F2d 719, 93 LRRM 2669 (CA 9, 1976), *denying enforcement to* 215 NLRB 665, 88 LRRM 1157 (1974) (in which Board followed, but court distinguished, its decision in *Federal-Mogul*). *See also* Smith Co. of Cal., 200 NLRB 772, 82 LRRM 1269 (1972); Marland One-Way Clutch Co., 192 NLRB 601, 78 LRRM 1127 (1971), *enforced in part and denied in part*, 520 F2d 856, 89 LRRM 2721 (CA 7, 1975); Michigan Power Co., 192 NLRB 830, 78 LRRM 1091 (1971).

[361] McCulloch Corp., 132 NLRB 201, 48 LRRM 1344 (1961); American Laundry Mach. Co., 107 NLRB 1574, 33 LRRM 1457 (1954).

[362] NLRB v. Superior Fireproof Door & Sash Co., 289 F2d 713, 47 LRRM 2816 (CA 2, 1961); Master Slack Corp., 230 NLRB 1054, 96 LRRM 1309 (1977), *enforced*, 618 F2d 6, 105 LRRM 2308 (CA 6, 1980) (violation found for unilateral implementation of procedure to recall unit employees to reopened plant closed for more than 1 year). *See* Chapter 12, "Recognition and Withdrawal of Recognition Without an Election," for detailed treatment of the requirements for withdrawal of recognition.

[363] Massey-Ferguson, Inc. v. NLRB, 78 LRRM 2289 (CA 7, 1971), *enforcing* 184 NLRB 640, 74 LRRM 1565 (1970); Continental Nut Co., 195 NLRB 841, 79 LRRM 1575 (1972); American Laundry Mach. Co., *supra* note 361. *But see* KCW Furniture Co., 247 NLRB 541, 103 LRRM 1194 (1980).

[364] NLRB v. Reed & Prince Mfg. Co., 205 F2d 131, 32 LRRM 2225 (CA 1), *cert. denied*, 346 US 887, 33 LRRM 2133 (1953); Iron Workers Local 103 (Associated Gen. Contractors of Am.), 195 NLRB 980, 79 LRRM 1598 (1972), *enforced*, 81 LRRM 2705 (CA 7, 1972).

[365] Caravelle Boat Co., 227 NLRB 1355, 95 LRRM 1003 (1977); Intracoastal Terminal, 125 NLRB 359, 45 LRRM 1104 (1959), *enforced as modified in other respects*, 286 F2d 954, 47 LRRM 2629 (CA 5, 1961). *But cf.* Laclede Gas Co., 173 NLRB 243, 69 LRRM 1316 (1968), *remanded*, 421 F2d 610, 73 LRRM 2364 (CA 8, 1970), discussed in Chapter 20, "The Lockout," at notes 165–166.

[366] Wichita Eagle & Beacon Publishing Co., 222 NLRB 742, 91 LRRM 1227 (1976) (unilateral reduction in eligibility waiting period under hospitalization policy for both unit and nonunit employees lawful where union had insisted that unit members receive same improvements in benefits as nonunit employees); AAA Motor Lines, 215 NLRB 793, 88 LRRM 1253 (1974) (union's dilatory bargaining tactics made unilateral changes permissible); Fort Smith Chair Co., 143 NLRB 514, 53 LRRM 1313 (1963), *aff'd*, 336 F2d

continuation of traditional payments or implementation of increases already promised to employees is not unlawful;[367] nor is an employer proscribed from unilaterally taking action to avoid loss of fringe benefits upon the expiration of a collective bargaining agreement.[368] (4) An employer may also put wage increases into effect for nonunit employees without incurring an obligation to make the same increase to unit employees, absent receipt of any quid pro quo from the union.[369]

7. Bypassing the Representative; Individual Contracts of Employment. As early as 1944 the Supreme Court, in *J.I. Case v. NLRB*,[370] upheld the Board's decision that an employer violates its duty to bargain by refusing to negotiate portions of a collective agreement on grounds that the unit employees were already covered by lawful individual contracts of employment. The Court's landmark opinion established that the collective bargaining contract superseded the individual employment contracts. The Court wrote:

> Individual contracts, no matter what the circumstances that justify their execution or what their terms, may not be availed of to defeat or delay . . . collective bargaining . . . ; nor may they be used to forestall bargaining or to limit or condition the terms of the collective agreement . . . . Whenever private contracts conflict with [the Board's] functions, they obviously must yield or the Act would be reduced to a futility.[371]

738, 55 LRRM 2990 (CADC), *cert. denied*, 379 US 838, 57 LRRM 2239 (1964) (employer ceased bargaining and granted increases when union went on strike in violation of §8(d)(3) time limits); Betty Brooks Co., 99 NLRB 1237, 30 LRRM 1210 (1952) (union had rejected offer which new profit and loss statement showed employer capable of paying).

[367]McCulloch Corp., *supra* note 361 (contributions to profit-sharing plan); Cutter Boats, *supra* note 358 (providing free home insurance arranged before certification, but not immediately conferred due to insurance-brokerage difficulties). Isolated wage changes for a few employees during negotiations do not necessarily establish bad faith, White v. NLRB, 255 F2d 564, 42 LRRM 2001 (CA 5, 1958), but are often vulnerable to such findings. Sharkey's Tire & Rubber Co., 222 NLRB 261, 91 LRRM 1183 (1976), *enforced by consent judgment*, 542 F2d 1163, 94 LRRM 2125 (CA 1, 1976) (unilateral grant of wage increases to two employees); Insulating Fabricators, 144 NLRB 1325, 54 LRRM 1246 (1963), *enforced*, 338 F2d 1002, 57 LRRM 2606 (CA 4, 1964) (individual merit increases for most of bargaining unit); "M" Sys., *supra* note 359 (individual wage adjustments in accordance with unilaterally established incentive plan).

[368]AAA Motor Lines, *supra* note 366. *But see* Mountaineer Excavating Co., 241 NLRB 414, 100 LRRM 1505 (1979), *enforced*, 618 F2d 102, 105 LRRM 2895 (CA 4), *cert. denied*, 449 US 835, 105 LRRM 2969 (1980) (lack of any advance notice to union evidence of bad faith).

[369]McCulloch Corp., *supra* note 361.

[370]321 US 332, 14 LRRM 501 (1944). *See also* Moisi & Son Trucking, 197 NLRB 198, 80 LRRM 1325 (1972) (employer seeking individual contracts after having recognized union).

[371]321 US at 337.

The Court then acknowledged that individual bargaining might yield benefits for individual employees greater than those available under the collective bargaining agreement:

> [I]t is urged that some employees may lose by the collective agreement, that an individual workman may sometimes have, or be capable of getting, better terms than those obtainable by the group . . . . [W]e find the mere possibility that such agreements might be made no ground for holding generally that individual contracts may survive or surmount collective ones. The practice and philosophy of collective bargaining looks with suspicion on such individual advantages.[372]

Regarding the proper function of the individual contract of employment where the circumstances favor such contracts and where the bargaining agent consents, the Court said:

> Of course, where there is great variation in circumstances of employment or capacity of employees, it is possible for the collective bargain to prescribe only minimum rates or maximum hours or expressly to leave certain areas open to individual bargaining. But except as so provided, advantages to individuals may prove as disruptive to industrial peace as disadvantages.[373]

In the *Insurance Agents*[374] case the Supreme Court stated that "the duty of management to bargain in good faith is essentially a corollary of its duty to recognize the union." This obligation is said to require "at a minimum recognition that the statutory representative is the one with whom [the employer] must deal in conducting bargaining negotiations, and that it can no longer bargain directly or indirectly with the employees."[375] The stat-

---

[372]*Id.* at 338.

[373]*Id.* For example, individual contracts are sanctioned and fostered by collective agreements in many branches of the entertainment industry, notably including professional sports.

[374]NLRB v. Insurance Agents' (Prudential Ins. Co.), 361 US 477, 484–85, 45 LRRM 2704 (1960). *See* notes 659–661 *infra* and accompanying text.

[375]General Elec. Co., 150 NLRB 192, 57 LRRM 1491, 1499 (1964), *enforced*, 418 F2d 736, 72 LRRM 2530 (CA 2, 1969), *cert. denied*, 397 US 965, 73 LRRM 2600 (1970). *See* notes 168–191 *supra* and accompanying text; Medo Photo Supply Corp. v. NLRB, 321 US 678, 14 LRRM 581 (1944). *See also* NLRB v. Rude Carrier Corp., 93 LRRM 2297 (CA 4, 1976), *enforcing in part* 215 NLRB 883, 88 LRRM 1556 (1974); NLRB v. Goodyear Aerospace Corp., 497 F2d 747, 86 LRRM 2763 (CA 6, 1974), *enforcing in part* 204 NLRB 831, 83 LRRM 1461 (1973); Kaiser-Permanente Medical Care Program, 248 NLRB 147, 103 LRRM 1374 (1980); General Athletics Prods. Co., 227 NLRB 1565, 95 LRRM 1130 (1977); Safeway Trails, 233 NLRB 1078, 96 LRRM 1614 (1977), *enforced*, 641 F2d 930, 102 LRRM 2328 (CADC, 1979), *cert. denied*, 444 US 1072, 103 LRRM 2668 (1980); Hearst Corp., 230 NLRB 216, 95 LRRM 1274 (1977), *enforced*, 590 F2d 554, 100 LRRM 2320 (CA 4, 1979) (violation of §8(a)(5) found in employer's economic inducement to 13 employees to retire because of lack of available work); Obie Pac., 196 NLRB 458, 80 LRRM 1169 (1972) (employer violated §8(a)(5) by soliciting employee sentiment for use against union during negotiations); Plastics Transp., 193 NLRB 54, 78 LRRM 1185 (1971); Cal-Pacific

utory obligation thus imposed is to deal with the employees through the union rather than to deal with the union through the employees. Thus, attempts to bypass the representative may be considered evidence of bad faith.

The employer's bargaining obligation is premised upon the majority status of the union. Individual dealings with employees at a time when the union claims, but does not actually represent, a majority may not be used as evidence of bad faith.[376] But a belief that the union has lost its majority is not a ground for refusing to bargain where the majority issue is "raised by the employer in a context of illegal antiunion activities, or other conduct by the employer aimed at causing disaffection from the union" or designed to gain "time in which to undermine the union."[377]

The "injury suffered by the union,"[378] where unilateral changes in wages or other employment conditions are made without notice or consultation with the union, is "not that flowing from a breach of contract [but] 'to the union's status as a bargaining representative.'"[379] Flagrant attempts to deal directly with the employees so as to undermine a certified bargaining agent, such as offering the employees a wage increase if they will disavow the union,[380] making speeches or statements to employees demonstrating union animus,[381] or soliciting strikers to return to work[382] will be vulnerable to Board censure.[383]

Poultry, 163 NLRB 716, 64 LRRM 1462 (1967); Channel Master Corp., 162 NLRB 632, 64 LRRM 1102 (1967); Wings & Wheels, 139 NLRB 578, 51 LRRM 1341 (1962), *enforced*, 324 F2d 495, 54 LRRM 2455 (CA 3, 1963). In a real sense, bypassing the representative means failing to bargain collectively—a per se refusal to bargain; however, the cases also treat "bypassing" as evidence of lack of good faith in the duty to bargain.

[376]Insular Chem. Co., 128 NLRB 93, 46 LRRM 1268 (1960).

[377]C&C Plywood Corp., 163 NLRB 1022, 64 LRRM 1488, 1489 (1967) (quoting Celanese Corp. of Am., 95 NLRB 664, 673, 28 LRRM 1362 (1951)). *See* note 378, *infra*, for subsequent history of *C&C Plywood. See also* Chapter 17, "Relation of Board Action to Enforcement of Agreements Under Section 301," at notes 283–295.

[378]163 NLRB at 1024. *See* NLRB v. C&C Plywood, 385 US 421, 64 LRRM 2065 (1967).

[379]163 NLRB at 1074 (quoting Laystrom Mfg. Co., 151 NLRB 1482, 58 LRRM 1624 (1965)).

[380]Flowers Baking Co., 161 NLRB 1429, 63 LRRM 1462 (1966); Houston Sheet Metal Contractors Ass'n, 147 NLRB 774, 56 LRRM 1281 (1964); Cincinnati Cordage & Paper Co., 141 NLRB 72, 52 LRRM 1277 (1963); Walsh-Lumpkin Wholesale Drug Co., 129 NLRB 294, 46 LRRM 1535 (1960), *enforced*, 291 F2d 751, 46 LRRM 1535 (CA 8, 1960).

[381]K-D Mfg. Co., 169 NLRB 57, 67 LRRM 1140 (1968), *enforced*, 419 F2d 467, 73 LRRM 2013 (CA 5, 1969); Colony Furniture Co., 144 NLRB 1582, 54 LRRM 1308 (1963).

[382]Chanticleer, Inc., 161 NLRB 241, 63 LRRM 1237 (1966); Crater Lake Mach. Co., 131 NLRB 1106, 48 LRRM 1211 (1961); National Furniture Mfg. Co., 130 NLRB 712, 47 LRRM 1414 (1961); Federal Dairy Co., 130 NLRB 1158, 47 LRRM 1465 (1961), *enforced*, 297 F2d 487, 49 LRRM 2214 (CA 1, 1962).

[383]Hajoca Corp. v. NLRB, 872 F2d 1169, 131 LRRM 2447 (CA 3, 1989), *enforcing* 291

Likewise, granting general wage increases during negotiations without first consulting the union has been deemed a reflection of the employer's coercive "efforts to curtail the statutory rights of the union . . . ."[384] Where the employer's activity has only a negligible effect on the authority of the bargaining agent, however, there is no violation. For example, where an employer made a direct announcement to employees inviting them to bid for a job vacancy the Board found no violation, though the matter was a subject of active discussion between the employer and the union.[385]

Failure by an employer to notify the majority representative and bargain with it concerning the adjustment of employee grievances and the imposition of employee discipline is a violation of section 8(a)(5) of the Act. The representative's right not to be bypassed in such circumstances is explicitly protected by the proviso to section 9(a) of the Act, which declares:

> *Provided,* That any individual employee or a group of employees shall have the right at any time to present grievances to their employer and to have such grievances adjusted, without the inter-

---

NLRB 104, 129 LRRM 1296 (1988); EPE v. NLRB, 845 F2d 483, 128 LRRM 2246 (CA 4, 1988), *enforcing in part* 284 NLRB 191, 125 LRRM 1166 (1987). *See* NLRB v. Babad dba J.R.R. Realty Co., 785 F2d 46, 121 LRRM 2940 (CA 2, 1986), *enforcing* 273 NLRB 1523, 118 LRRM 1230 (1985), *cert. denied,* 479 US 830, 123 LRRM 2592 (1986); NLRB v. Billion Oldsmobile-Toyota, 700 F2d 454, 112 LRRM 2873 (CA 8, 1983); Ad-Art, Inc., 290 NLRB 590, 131 LRRM 1319 (1988); Charles Parker Co. and Union Mfg. Co., 285 NLRB 56, 126 LRRM 1123 (1987); Otis Elevator Co. (Otis Elevator III), 283 NLRB 223, 124 LRRM 1334 (1987); Earl C. Smith, Inc., 278 NLRB 664, 121 LRRM 1255 (1986); TLI, Inc., 271 NLRB 798, 117 LRRM 1169 (1984), *enforced sub nom.* Teamsters Local 326 v. NLRB, 772 F2d 894, 120 LRRM 2631 (CA 3, 1985); Hiney Printing Co., 262 NLRB 157, 110 LRRM 1255 (1982), *enforced,* 733 F2d 1170, 116 LRRM 2404 (CA 6, 1984); Taft Broadcasting Co., WBRC-TV, 264 NLRB 185, 111 LRRM 1340 (1982), *petition dismissed,* 712 F2d 1418, 113 LRRM 3816 (CA 11, 1983); Marriott Corp., Bob's Big Boy Family Restaurants Div., 264 NLRB 432, 111 LRRM 1411 (1982).

[384]Flambeau Plastics, 151 NLRB 591, 611, 58 LRRM 1470 (1965). *See also* Crestline Co., 133 NLRB 256, 48 LRRM 1623 (1961). In addition, dealing individually with employees concerning employee placement at a new plant location has been viewed by the Board as being in derogation of the union's bargaining rights. Cooper Thermometer Co., 160 NLRB 1902, 63 LRRM 1219 (1966), *enforcement denied on other grounds,* 376 F2d 684, 65 LRRM 2113 (CA 2, 1967).

[385]Union Elec. Co., 196 NLRB 830, 80 LRRM 1110 (1972). *See also* Leland Stanford Univ. & Stanford Univ. Hosp., 240 NLRB 1138, 100 LRRM 1391 (1979) (employer who distributed opinion survey among unionized employees did not violate Act; Board based its decision in large measure on issuance of memorandum to employees shortly after circulation of survey disclaiming any intention to deal directly with employees); Dow Chem. Co., 215 NLRB 910, 88 LRRM 1625 (1975), *review granted, case remanded and order vacated sub nom.* Steelworkers v. NLRB, 536 F2d 550, 92 LRRM 2545 (CA 3, 1976) ("Speak Out" program for employee submission of anonymous, job-related complaints and questions to management held by Board not to bypass grievance and arbitration procedure; court disagreed); Ingraham Indus., 178 NLRB 558, 72 LRRM 1245 (1969) (employer had refused to permit union representatives to attend sessions conducted by management to explain profit-sharing plan adopted pursuant to collective bargaining agreement).

> vention of the bargaining representative, as long as the adjustment is not inconsistent with the terms of a collective-bargaining contract or agreement then in effect: *Provided further,* That the bargaining representative has been given opportunity to be present at such adjustment.[386]

Thus, in *Texaco, Inc.,*[387] a 1967 case, where the employer had information that an employee had been seen leaving its premises with company property, the Board held that a union representative had the section 9(a) right to attend the employee interview concerned with the investigation of these facts, where the probability of punishment emerging from that interview was great.

A violation occurs where an employer bypasses the union while the collective bargaining agreement is still in effect. In *Walkill Valley General Hospital,*[388] the court enforced the Board's decision that the employer violated section 8(a)(5) by conducting an "employee benefit" survey shortly before it began contract negotiations. The Board has also held that an employer violates the duty to bargain by unilaterally issuing a handbook encouraging employees who feel they have legitimate grievances to report them directly to management, where no provision was made to include the union in the procedure.[389] However, in *United Technologies Corp.,*[390] the employer did not engage in unlawful direct dealing by publicizing to the employees its offer to the union and stating its position on the offer. Similarly, in *Lear Siegler, Inc.,*[391] there was no violation where the employer's

---

[386]The Supreme Court explained the limited intent of the proviso in Emporium Capwell Co. v. Western Addition Community Org., 420 US 50, 88 LRRM 2660 (1975): "The intendment of the *proviso* is to permit employees to present grievances and to authorize the employer to entertain them without opening itself to liability for dealing directly with employees in derogation of the duty to bargain only with the exclusive bargaining representative, a violation of §8(a)(5) . . . . The Act nowhere protects this 'right' by making it an unfair labor practice for an employer to refuse to entertain such a presentation. . . ." Id. at 61 n.12. *See* Chapter 6, "Interference With Protected Rights," at notes 428–432.

[387]168 NLRB 361, 66 LRRM 1296 (1967), *enforcement denied,* 408 F2d 142, 70 LRRM 3045 (CA 5, 1970). *See also* Jacobe-Pearson Ford, 172 NLRB 594, 68 LRRM 1305 (1968); Chevron Oil Co., 168 NLRB 574, 66 LRRM 1353 (1967). While the majority representative derives its right not to be bypassed in matters involving employee discipline from §9(a), a closely related doctrine was announced by the Supreme Court in NLRB v. Weingarten, Inc., 420 US 251, 88 LRRM 2689 (1975).

[388]NLRB v. Wallkill Valley Gen. Hosp., 866 F2d 632, 131 LRRM 2442 (CA 3, 1989), *enforcing* 288 NLRB 103, 127 LRRM 1318 (1988).

[389]Heck's, Inc., 293 NLRB No. 132, 131 LRRM 1281 (1989).

[390]United Technologies, Pratt & Whitney Aircraft Div., 274 NLRB 609, 118 LRRM 1445 (1985), *enforced,* 789 F2d 121, 122 LRRM 2250 (CA 2, 1986). *See also* Radio Broadcasting Co., 277 NLRB 1112, 121 LRRM 1052 (1985), *review denied sub nom.* Teamsters Local 115 v. NLRB, 802 F2d 448, 124 LRRM 2360 (CA 3, 1986).

[391]283 NLRB 929, 126 LRRM 1073 (1987), *enforced in part,* 890 F2d 1573, 133 LRRM 2479 (CA 10, 1989).

speech to the employees, outlining the employer's contract proposals, included a statement that the employees would be permanently replaced if they struck.

8. Commission of Unfair Labor Practices. The commission of unfair labor practices during negotiations may reflect adversely upon the good faith of the guilty party.[392] Where an employer threatened to close the plant, promoted withdrawal from the union, reduced working hours, and engaged in discriminatory layoffs during bargaining, the Board found section 8(a)(5) violations.[393] Engaging in other unfair labor practices during the certification year may also be indicative of a course of conduct inconsistent with good faith.[394]

An employer's doubt as to a union's continued majority status may not excuse its refusal to continue negotiations if the refusal is made in the context of other unlawful employer conduct.[395] If it cannot be shown with certainty how many of the employees would have withdrawn from the union in the absence of illegal conduct by the employer, a violation may be found, even though other factors might have contributed to the employees' change in attitude. This rule is premised on the propositions that doubts are to be resolved against the party whose conduct created the situation and that the union's continued majority status is to be presumed.[396] Moreover, a good-faith doubt is not one based upon employee expressions that have been encouraged, prompted, or solicited by the employer.[397] Thus, assisting employees in the preparation of decertification petitions has

---

[392]Virginia Holding Corp. dba Hotel Roanoke, 293 NLRB 182, 132 LRRM 1229 (1989) (employer bargained in bad faith where it committed numerous acts of unlawful interference during negotiations, including unilaterally implementing terms and conditions of employment and threatening not to enter into any contract with union); Josten Concrete Prods. Co., 295 NLRB No. 114, 131 LRRM 1758 (1989); John Wanamaker, Philadelphia, 279 NLRB 1034, 123 LRRM 1271 (1986); Bedford Farmers Coop., 259 NLRB 1226, 109 LRRM 1113 (1982). *See also* Schwab Foods dba Mooresville IGA Foodliner, 284 NLRB 1055, 125 LRRM 1225 (1987), *enforced*, 858 F2d 1285, 129 LRRM 2601 (CA 7, 1988).

[393]Imperial Mach. Corp., 121 NLRB 621, 42 LRRM 1406 (1958).

[394]Evergreen Rambler, 160 NLRB 864, 63 LRRM 1062 (1966); Coachman's Inn, 147 NLRB 278, 56 LRRM 1206 (1964), *enforced*, 357 F2d 134, 61 LRRM 2445 (CA 8, 1966); Berger Polishing, 147 NLRB 21, 56 LRRM 1140 (1964); Carter Mach. & Tool Co., 133 NLRB 247, 48 LRRM 1625 (1961); Borg-Warner Corp., 128 NLRB 1035, 46 LRRM 1459 (1960).

[395]C&C Plywood, *supra* note 377. *See generally* Chapter 12, "Recognition and Withdrawal of Recognition Without an Election."

[396]Movie Star, 145 NLRB 319, 54 LRRM 1387 (1963), *enforced in part and denied in part*, 361 F2d 346, 62 LRRM 2234 (CA 5, 1966).

[397]Rohlik, Inc., 145 NLRB 1236, 1243, 55 LRRM 1130 (1964).

been deemed evidence of bad faith, since the foreseeable result of such assistance is to obstruct the bargaining process.[398]

The extent to which prior unfair labor practices may be relied upon as evidence of a present violation has undergone some revision by the Board. The old rule, stated in a 1951 case, *Larrance Tank Corp.*,[399] was that the Board would not consider conduct antedating a settlement agreement as evidence of a postsettlement unfair labor practice unless the party charged had (1) failed to comply with the terms of the agreement or (2) engaged in independent unfair labor practices since the settlement.[400] The old rule was modified in the 1965 *Hod Carriers* decision.[401] The Board reexamined *Larrance* and held that presettlement conduct was admissible as "background evidence" to establish the motive or object of a party in its postsettlement activities. The settlement agreement itself, however, may not be used to establish union animus.[402]

Even prior to the *Larrance* modification, evidence of conduct preceding a prior finding of an unfair labor practice, as opposed to a settlement, was admitted as a factor to be considered in determining whether subsequent bargaining was in good faith.[403] In *Associated Machine*,[404] the Board concluded that the employer's unlawful wage reductions "poisoned" the bargaining climate and precluded good-faith negotiations.[405]

---

[398]Wahoo Packing Co., 161 NLRB 174, 63 LRRM 1290 (1966); W.R. Hall Distrib., 144 NLRB 1285, 54 LRRM 1231 (1963), *enforced*, 341 F2d 359, 58 LRRM 2378 (CA 10, 1965). For treatment of decertification petitions generally, see Chapter 10, "Representation Proceedings and Elections," at notes 22–23, and Chapter 31, "NLRB Procedures," at note 35.

[399]94 NLRB 352, 28 LRRM 1045 (1951).

[400]In *Larrance* the trial examiner had found that the employer had not bargained in good faith after the settlement agreement and that the employer's "conduct after [the date of settlement] was of the 'same type' as its prior conduct." *Id.* at 353. This evaluation of the employer's postsettlement conduct was thus colored by the presettlement conduct, which the Board considered to be inconsistent with Board policy.

[401]Hod Carriers (Laborers), Northern Cal. Dist. Council (Joseph's Landscaping Serv.), 154 NLRB 1384, 60 LRRM 1156 (1965), *enforced*, 389 F2d 721, 67 LRRM 2502 (CA 9, 1968).

[402]Metal Assemblies, 156 NLRB 194, 61 LRRM 1023 (1965). *Cf.* Bangor Plastics, 156 NLRB 1165, 61 LRRM 1210 (1966), *enforcement denied*, 392 F2d 772, 67 LRRM 2987 (CA 6, 1967).

[403]H.K. Porter Co., 153 NLRB 1370, 59 LRRM 1462 (1965), *enforced*, 363 F2d 272, 62 LRRM 2204 (CA DC), *cert. denied*, 385 US 851, 63 LRRM 2236 (1966). For discussion of settlements generally, see Chapter 31, "NLRB Procedures," at notes 137–151.

[404]271 NLRB 367, 116 LRRM 1460 (1984), *aff'd*, 782 F2d 1051, 128 LRRM 2792 (CA 9, 1986).

[405]*See also* Albion Corp. dba Brooks Towers v. NLRB, 682 F2d 874, 110 LRRM 2952 (CA 10, 1982), *enforcing* 251 NLRB 757, 105 LRRM 1521 (1980); Hedaya Bros., 277 NLRB

The Ninth Circuit's decision in *NLRB v. MacMillan Ring-Free Oil Co.*[406] limited the Board's use of "background evidence" in establishing section 8(a)(5) violations where the section 10(b) period[407] is a factor. In *MacMillan* the Board found a refusal to bargain within the section 10(b) period based on negotiating attitudes unchanged from the period preceding the 6-month cutoff date. The court rejected the finding that an unfair labor practice had been committed within the 6-month period. Regarding the sufficiency of evidence antedating the cutoff date, the court declared that "while . . . filing of a charge may be used to 'shed light' upon events taking place within the six-month period, the evidence of a violation drawn from within that period must be reasonably substantial in its own right" though not necessarily sufficient within itself to sustain an unfair labor practice finding.[408] Since there was no substantial evidence of violation within the section 10(b) period, a finding of unlawful bargaining was not warranted.

IV. THE DUTY TO FURNISH INFORMATION

A. The Role of Information in the Collective Bargaining Relationship—An Overview

The collective bargaining process requires that the bargaining *antagonists*—or *partners*, depending on whether one emphasizes the adversary or cooperative nature of the process—have adequate information about the immediate subjects at issue in bargaining or contract administration. The underlying rationale is that, without the exchange of essential information, the collective bargaining process cannot function properly. Indeed, an employer's refusal to supply information may convert an economic strike to an unfair labor practice strike.[409] Several key

---

942, 121 LRRM 1073 (1985); Maietta Contracting, 265 NLRB 1279, 112 LRRM 1195 (1982), *enforced*, 729 F2d 1448, 115 LRRM 3536 (CA 3, 1984); Marriott Corp., Marriott In-Flite Servs. Div., 258 NLRB 755, 108 LRRM 1287 (1981), *enforced*, 729 F2d 1441, 113 LRRM 3528 (CA 2), *cert. denied*, 464 US 829, 114 LRRM 2568 (1983); Rockingham Mach-Lunex Co., 255 NLRB 89, 107 LRRM 1222 (1981), *enforced*, 665 F2d 303, 108 LRRM 3228 (CA 8, 1981), *cert. denied*, 457 US 1107, 110 LRRM 2608 (1982).

[406]394 F2d 26, 68 LRRM 2004 (CA 9), *cert. denied*, 393 US 914, 69 LRRM 2481 (1968).

[407]*See* Chapter 31, "NLRB Procedures," at notes 126–128.

[408]394 F2d at 33.

[409]NLRB v. Jarm Enters. dba Blu-Fountain Manor, 785 F2d 195, 121 LRRM 3105 (CA 7, 1986).

decisions have underscored the importance of the exchange of essential information in collective bargaining. The brief overview which follows introduces those decisions and provides the background for the discussions which follow on the nature of the duty to furnish information,[410] the occasions when the duty arises,[411] and the specific kinds of information which must be furnished.[412]

1. Bargaining Over New Terms and Conditions. The Supreme Court, in *NLRB v. Truitt Manufacturing Co.*,[413] held that employers have an obligation to furnish relevant information to union representatives during contract negotiations. The Court reasoned as follows:

> Good-faith bargaining necessarily requires that claims made by either bargainer should be honest claims. . . . If . . . an argument is important enough to present in the give and take of bargaining, it is important enough to require some sort of proof of its accuracy.[414]

Disclosure of relevant information is integral to the bargaining process. It encourages mutual respect between the negotiators and makes the American collective bargaining system, which so heavily relies on cooperation and open exchange, a viable approach to fashioning "a generalized code" establishing "a system of industrial self-government."[415] As the Fourth Circuit noted, unions cannot be expected to represent unit employees in an effective manner where they do not possess information that "is necessary to the proper discharge of the duties of the bargaining agent."[416]

Historically, the Board and the courts have taken the position that an employer which claims it is financially unable to meet the union's demands is obligated to corroborate such claims on

---

[410]*See infra* at notes 450–569.

[411]*See infra* at notes 570–597.

[412]*See infra* at notes 598–657.

[413]351 US 149, 38 LRRM 2042 (1956). See Morris, *The Role of the NLRB and the Courts in the Collective Bargaining Process: A Fresh Look at Conventional Wisdom and Unconventional Remedies*, 30 VAND. L. REV. 661, 663–67 (1977); Fanning, *The Obligation to Furnish Information During the Contract Term*, 9 GA. L. REV. 375 (1975); Bartosic & Hartley, *The Employer's Duty to Supply Information to the Union—A Study of the Interplay of Administrative and Judicial Rationalization*, 58 CORNELL L. REV. 23 (1972); Note, *A Union's Duty to Furnish Information to an Employer for Purposes of Collective Bargaining*, 4 U. DAYTON L. REV. 257 (1979); Note, *Psychological Aptitude Tests and the Duty to Supply Information*, 91 HARV. L. REV. 869 (1978).

[414]351 US at 153, 38 LRRM at 2043.

[415]Steelworkers v. Warrior & Gulf Navigation Co., 363 US 574, 578, 580, 46 LRRM 2416, 2418 (1960).

[416]NLRB v. Whitin Mach. Works, 217 F2d 593, 594, 35 LRRM 2215 (CA 4, 1954), *cert. denied*, 349 US 905, 35 LRRM 2730 (1955).

request. There are no "magic" words to be used in order for the Board to find that a claim of financial hardship has been made. It is sufficient if the employer's words and conduct specifically link its bargaining position to economic hardship.[417] An employer's claims, in support of its bargaining position, that it must remain "competitive" with other employers, may be considered as tantamount to a claim of inability to pay. If so, the employer must furnish supporting data.[418] A refusal to honor a legitimate request for information can foreclose further meaningful bargaining, can convert an economic strike to an unfair labor practice strike,[419] and can preclude a good-faith bargaining impasse.[420]

An employer that had at all times simply expressed an unwillingness to pay rather than an *inability* to pay was not required to make disclosure.[421] That an employer does not want to continue paying the same level of wages does not mean it cannot afford to do so.[422] By contrast, an employer's reliance upon increasing costs and decreasing orders was held to constitute a plea of inability to pay, requiring the production of tax returns, audit reports, and financial statements.[423] Similarly, an employer's statement that a wage freeze was necessary "'to stay in business and recoup some bad losses . . . '" obligated it to provide information requested by the union.[424]

---

[417]NLRB v. Truitt Mfg. Co., *supra* note 413; Sioux City Stockyards Div., 293 NLRB 1, 130 LRRM 1427 (1989); Accurate Die Casting Co., 292 NLRB 284, 131 LRRM 1659 (1989).

[418]Harvstone Mfg. Corp., 272 NLRB 939, 943–44, 117 LRRM 1447 (1984), *enforced in part*, 785 F2d 570, 121 LRRM 3371 (CA 7), *cert. denied sub nom.* Electrical Workers (IBEW) Local 134 v. Harvstone Mfg. Co., 479 US 821, 123 LRRM 2591 (1986).

[419]Fountainhead Dev. Corp., 270 NLRB 199, 206, 116 LRRM 1219 (1984), *enforcement granted sub nom.* NLRB v. Jarm Enters. dba Blu-Fountain Manor, 785 F2d 195, 121 LRRM 3105 (CA 7, 1986). In such a case there is no need to adduce specific proof of a causal connection between the employer's action and the strike. *Id.* at 206 & n.14. Although, as the court of appeals observed, commission of an unfair labor practice does not automatically transform a strike into an unfair labor practice strike. *Accord* C-Line Express, 292 NLRB No. 63, 130 LRRM 1359 (1989) (economic strike not converted to unfair labor practice strike where strikers did not know of unlawful refusal to supply information).

[420]Sioux City Stockyards Div., *supra* note 417; Pertec Computer Corp., 284 NLRB 810, 126 LRRM 1134 (1987); Harvstone Mfg. Corp., *supra* note 418; *accord* Cowin & Co., 277 NLRB 802, 121 LRRM 1029 (1985).

[421]Richmond Recording Corp. dba PRC Recording Co., 280 NLRB 615, 124 LRRM 1081 (1986); Advertisers Mfg. Co., 275 NLRB 100, 119 LRRM 1123 (1985). *Cf.* Accurate Die Casting, *supra* note 417 (employer falsely claimed bargaining position was not based on poor financial condition).

[422]Gilberton Coal Co., 291 NLRB 344, 131 LRRM 1329 (1988), *enforced*, 888 F2d 1381, 134 LRRM 2568 (CA 3, 1989).

[423]S-B Mfg. Co., 270 NLRB 485, 116 LRRM 1334 (1984); *accord* American Model & Pattern, 277 NLRB 176, 120 LRRM 1267 (1985), *enforced*, 816 F2d 678 (CA 6, 1987) (claims of "bad financial position" and need to "remain competitive" triggered obligation to produce records).

[424]Coast Engraving Co., 282 NLRB 1236, 1236 n.1, 125 LRRM 1215 (1987).

Refusing to enforce a Board order, the Second Circuit held that an employer did not violate section 8(a)(5) of the Act by establishing certain qualifications for the union's auditor who was to examine the employer's financial records to verify the employer's claim of inability to pay wage increases.[425] The Sixth Circuit has held that an employer required to produce its financial records is entitled to assurances from the union that it would protect their confidentiality.[426] The Board's decision in *Oakland Press Co.*,[427] that unions have a like duty to furnish information to employers, follows naturally from the *Truitt* rationale.

2. Representation Under an Existing Collective Agreement. The second Supreme Court decision dealing with the duty to furnish information was *NLRB v. Acme Industrial Co.*[428] The Court held that the employer's duty to furnish information, like its duty to bargain, "extends beyond the period of contract negotiations and applies to labor-management relations during the term of an agreement."[429] Thus the Supreme Court required disclosure of certain information pertaining to a grievance filed by the union.

Acme Industrial emphasized the importance of information relevant to the union in its effort to police and administer the collective bargaining agreement. It endorsed the "discovery-type standard" applied by the Board.[430] For example, the Board

---

[425]NLRB v. St. Joseph's Hosp., 755 F2d 260, 118 LRRM 2765, 2769 (CA 2), *cert. denied sub nom.* New York State Nurses Ass'n v. St. Joseph's Hosp., 474 US 827, 120 LRRM 2632 (1985) (hospital's concern over qualifications was legitimate and substantial because of prospect of labor strike if unqualified accountant should produce report that wage increase was reasonable); *but see* Tama Meat Packing, 291 NLRB 657, 130 LRRM 1242 (1988) (employer may not insist on audit according to AICPA standards).

[426]E.W. Buschman Co., 277 NLRB 189, 120 LRRM 1253 (1985), *enforcement denied*, 820 F2d 206, 125 LRRM 2642 (CA 6, 1987); *cf.* Pony Express Courier Corp., 297 NLRB No. 19, 132 LRRM 1321 (1989) (production not required where union business manager was also management consultant for customers).

[427]Printing & Graphic Communications Local 13 (Detroit) (Oakland Press Co.), 233 NLRB 994, 97 LRRM 1047 (1977), *aff'd*, 598 F2d 267, 101 LRRM 2036 (CADC, 1979). *See infra* at notes 439–443.

[428]385 US 432, 64 LRRM 2069 (1967).

[429]*Id.* at 436.

[430]*Id.* at 437. *See infra* at notes 442 and 483–486. That standard is still applied. *Cf.* Detroit Edison Co. v. NLRB, 440 US 301, 100 LRRM 2728 (1979); Holyoke Water Power Co., 273 NLRB 1369, 118 LRRM 1179 (1985), *enforced*, 778 F2d 49, 120 LRRM 3487 (CA 1, 1985), *cert. denied*, 477 US 905, 122 LRRM 2656 (1986) (access to fan room must be given to conduct noise-level studies); Salt River Valley Water Users Ass'n, 272 NLRB 296, 117 LRRM 1295 (1984), *enforced*, 769 F2d 639, 120 LRRM 2265 (CA 9, 1985); W-L Molding Co., 272 NLRB 1239, 118 LRRM 1140 (1984). *See also* Bentley-Jost Elec. Corp., 283 NLRB 564, 125 LRRM 1112 (1987) (where union had evidence tending to show that employer and nonunion company were "alter egos," union needed information concerning relationship between signatory employer and other company so that it could administer and enforce existing contract); Oil, Chem. & Atomic Workers Local 6-418 v. NLRB (Min-

also has found a violation where the employer refused to supply information concerning the implementation of changes which had an effect on the wages, seniority, and promotion rights of employees.[431]

A common demand for information during the term of a contract concerns information pertaining to grievances. The union's access to adequate information concerning grievances enables the union to make a considered judgment about the strength of its claim, to eliminate unmeritorious claims at an early stage in the grievance process, and to prepare for arbitration.[432] Indeed, it is common for collective bargaining agreements to have provisions requiring disclosure of relevant information during the contract term.[433] An employer's duty to provide information relative to a grievance does not cease when the union files a demand for arbitration.[434]

3. Refusal to Furnish Information as an Unfair Labor Practice. Is a refusal to supply requested and relevant information a per se violation of the duty to bargain, merely evidence of lack of good faith, or not a violation of the statute at all? The Supreme Court's majority opinion in *Truitt*[435] addressed this query but failed to supply a complete answer. Concerning a union's demand for information during bargaining, the Court stated:

> We do not hold . . . that in every case in which economic inability is raised as an argument against increased wages it automatically follows that the employees are entitled to substantiating evidence . . . . The inquiry must also be whether or not under the circumstances . . . the statutory obligation to bargain in good faith has been met.[436]

And according to Justice Frankfurter's concurring opinion,[437] the Board had applied the wrong standard in ruling that the

---

nesota Mining & Mfg. Co.), 711 F2d 348, 113 LRRM 3163 (CADC, 1983) (notwithstanding that unions' request for information was not tied to specific problems at plants, employers had duty to supply certain health and safety information so that unions could effectively enforce and administer health and safety provisions of contracts or intelligently seek their modification).

[431]Boise Cascade Corp., Paper Group, 279 NLRB 422, 123 LRRM 1253 (1986).

[432]NLRB v. Electrical Workers (IBEW) Local 309 (Pfizer), 763 F2d 887, 119 LRRM 2947 (CA 7, 1985); General Motors Corp. v. NLRB, 700 F2d 1083, 112 LRRM 2976 (CA 6, 1983), *enforcing* 257 NLRB 1068, 108 LRRM 1030 (1981).

[433]*E.g.*, United Aircraft Corp., 204 NLRB 879, 83 LRRM 1411 (1973).

[434]Chesapeake & Potomac Tel. Co. v. NLRB, 687 F2d 633, 111 LRRM 2165 (CA 2, 1982).

[435]NLRB v. Truitt Mfg. Co., 351 US 149, 38 LRRM 2042 (1956).

[436]*Id.* at 153.

[437]Justice Frankfurter also dissented, insofar as he would have remanded the case to the Board.

employer's failure to supply information constituted a per se refusal to bargain. The view that *Truitt,* properly interpreted, means that refusal to supply information is only evidence of bad faith, not a per se violation, has been followed in a number of circuit court decisions, though some courts have continued to apply a per se standard.[438]

4. The Union's Duty to Supply Information. The duty to furnish information is not an obligation imposed on employers alone; a similar duty is owed by unions. This principle was established in the *Oakland Press* case.[439] Oakland Press printed a daily newspaper. The press room employees at the plant were represented by a local union which had agreed in the collective bargaining contract to an arrangement whereby it would attempt to supply the company with extra employees to handle overload work at straight-time rates. In practice, however, the union gave the assignments to regular employees, whom the company had to pay at overtime rates. The employer questioned whether the union was making a good-faith effort to find extra employees before giving overtime work to regular employees. In conjunction with negotiations for a new labor contract, the employer requested certain information from the union regarding its referral system, which the union refused to disclose; thereupon the employer filed a charge alleging a violation of section 8(b)(3).

The Board held that "'a union's duty to furnish information relevant to the bargaining process is parallel to that of an employer.'"[440] Reasoning that it was essential for the employer, in structuring its economic demands, to know how the referral system operated, as well as the actual availability of extra workers for overload work, the Board concluded that the information sought was relevant to the bargaining process and that therefore the union violated its statutory bargaining obligation by failing

---

[438]*See* Woodworkers Locals 6-7 & 6-22 v. NLRB (Pine Indus. Relations Comm.), 263 F2d 483, 43 LRRM 2462 (CADC, 1959); J.I. Case Co. v. NLRB, 253 F2d 149, 41 LRRM 2679 (CA 7, 1958), *enforcing as amended* 118 NLRB 520, 40 LRRM 1208 (1957). *But see* Curtiss-Wright Corp. v. NLRB, 347 F2d 61, 59 LRRM 2433 (CA 3, 1965), *enforcing* 145 NLRB 152, 54 LRRM 1320 (1963), where the court stated that once it is established that information is relevant, it is a per se refusal to bargain for the employer to fail to produce the information on request.

[439]Printing & Graphic Communications Local 13 (Detroit) (Oakland Press Co.), *supra* note 427.

[440]*Id.* at 996, 97 LRRM at 1049 (quoting dictum in Tool & Die Makers Lodge 78 (Square D Co.), 224 NLRB 111, 92 LRRM 1202 (1976)).

to respond to the employer's inquiries. The District of Columbia Circuit affirmed, holding that just as an employer is required to disclose information during bargaining, a union "is likewise obliged to furnish the employer with relevant information."[441] The court reiterated that the standard for determining relevancy is a liberal one, "much akin to that applied in discovery proceedings,"[442] and the information requested by Oakland Press fell well within this standard.

In decisions since *Oakland Press,* the Board has required unions to turn over relevant information to employers.[443] For example, a union representative, who was also a fringe-benefit-fund trustee, had a bargaining obligation not to obstruct an employer's access to information in control of the fund.[444] However, the Board overruled that decision in 1984[445] on the basis of an intervening Supreme Court decision[446] holding that fund trustees are not agents of their respective parties. The Board now holds that, absent evidence that the union is in de facto control of the fund, it has no obligation to seek, for the employer, information that is in possession of the fund.[447] If, however, the union possesses the information sought, it may have an obligation to provide it if the information is not readily available to the employer from another source.[448] The Board has also held that although the parties had agreed to discuss agency fees, that is a nonmandatory subject of bargaining and thus the union is under no obligation to provide information concerning the union's operating expenses.[449]

---

[441]598 F2d at 271.

[442]*Id.* See notes 484–485 *infra* and accompanying text.

[443]*See infra* at notes 655–657; *see also* NLRB v. Electrical Workers (IBEW) Local 497 (Apple City Elec.), 795 F2d 836, 122 LRRM 3259 (CA 9, 1986), *enforcing* 275 NLRB 1290, 120 LRRM 1045 (1985) (union must furnish names and addresses of all individuals who use hiring hall); Laborers (Heavy Contractors Ass'n), 285 NLRB 688, 128 LRRM 1023 (1987) (union unlawfully denied multi-employer association's request for data on hiring hall); Plasterers Local 346 (Brawner Plastering), 273 NLRB 1143, 118 LRRM 1246 (1984).

[444]Retail, Wholesale & Dep't Store Union Dist. 1199-E (Sinai Hosp. of Baltimore), 248 NLRB 631, 103 LRRM 1459 (1980), *enforced without opinion,* 673 F2d 1314, 108 LRRM 3252 (CA 4, 1981) (overruled by Food & Commercial Workers Local 1439 (Layman's Mkt.), 268 NLRB 780, 115 LRRM 1089 (1984)).

[445]*Id. See also* Hotel Employees Local 355 (Di Lido Hotel), 272 NLRB 265, 117 LRRM 1263 (1984).

[446]Amax Coal Co. Div. v. NLRB, 453 US 322, 107 LRRM 2769 (1981); *see also* Jordan v. Sundt, 6 EB Cases 1382 (WD Wash, 1985).

[447]American Commercial Lines, 291 NLRB 1066, 131 LRRM 1561 (1988).

[448]Food & Commercial Workers Local 1439 (Layman's Mkt.), *supra* note 444.

[449]Service Employees Local 535 (North Bay Dev. Disabilities Servs. dba North Bay Regional Center), 287 NLRB 1223, 127 LRRM 1184 (1988).

B. Nature of the Duty to Furnish Information

The Board has long held that intertwined with the duty to bargain in good faith is a duty on the part of the employer to supply the union, upon request, with sufficient information to enable it to understand and intelligently discuss the issues raised in bargaining.[450] Although the duty is reciprocal, most of the required information must flow from the employer to the union; hence most of the case law concerns employer recalcitrance in supplying information requested by unions, either in the bargaining process or in the administration of the collective agreement.

The employer's duty to furnish information is imposed because without such information the union would be unable to perform its statutory duties as bargaining agent.[451] Thus, information must be furnished to the union for purposes of representing employees in negotiations for a future contract and also for policing the administration of an existing contract.[452] The employer's refusal to supply information is as much a violation of the duty to bargain as if it had failed to meet and confer with the union in good faith.[453]

The duty to furnish information is a statutory obligation which exists independent of any agreement between the parties;[454] however, the union's right to disclosure of relevant and necessary data can be waived by the union in a collective bargaining agreement.[455] But even where the union has made such a waiver in the agreement, the employer must still furnish information at an appropriate time when it is relevant to the negotia-

---

[450]S.L. Allen & Co., 1 NLRB 714, 1 LRRM 29, 29–30 (1936) ("Interchange of ideas, [communication of facts peculiarly within the knowledge of either party are] of the essence of the bargaining process"). *See also* Industrial Welding Co., 175 NLRB 477, 71 LRRM 1076 (1969); Oregon Coast Operators Ass'n, 113 NLRB 1338, 36 LRRM 1448 (1955), *aff'd*, 246 F2d 280, 40 LRRM 2312 (CA 9, 1957); Southern Saddlery Co., 90 NLRB 1205, 26 LRRM 1322 (1950).

[451]Aluminum Ore Co. v. NLRB, 131 F2d 485, 11 LRRM 693 (CA 7, 1942).

[452]J.I. Case Co. v. NLRB, 253 F2d 149, 41 LRRM 2679 (CA 7, 1958); Kroger Co., 226 NLRB 512, 93 LRRM 1315 (1976); Weber Veneer & Plywood Co., 161 NLRB 1054, 63 LRRM 1395 (1966); Curtiss-Wright Corp., 145 NLRB 152, 54 LRRM 1320 (1963), *enforced*, 347 F2d 61, 59 LRRM 2433 (CA 3, 1965); B.F. Goodrich Co., 89 NLRB 1151, 26 LRRM 1090 (1950); General Controls, 88 NLRB 1341, 25 LRRM 1475 (1950).

[453]Curtiss-Wright Corp., *supra* note 452. *See* Levingston Shipbuilding Co., 244 NLRB 119, 102 LRRM 1127 (1979), *enforced*, 617 F2d 294, 106 LRRM 2546 (CA 5, 1980).

[454]American Standard, 203 NLRB 1132, 83 LRRM 1245 (1973).

[455]*See* United Aircraft Corp., 204 NLRB 879, 83 LRRM 1411 (1973), *aff'd*, 525 F2d 237, 90 LRRM 2922 (CA 2, 1975).

tion of a new agreement.[456] Thus in *American Standard,*[457] a 1973 case, the Board held that where a contract is silent on the obligation to furnish information, a request for information bearing on a possible grievance is based on a statutory, rather than a contractual, right, and the Board will therefore not defer the dispute to arbitration under its *Collyer* doctrine.[458] Later in the same year, however, in *United Aircraft Corp.,*[459] where the labor contract contained a provision requiring the production of pertinent information at Step 1 of the grievance procedure, the Board held that the contract language implied a waiver of the right to have information at an earlier stage of the proceedings, and charges concerning earlier requests were therefore "clearly matters of contract interpretation" best resolved by arbitration.[460]

United Aircraft may have been overruled sub silentio. In *International Harvester Co.,*[461] without citing *United Aircraft,* the Board held that a provision in a collective bargaining agreement, which vested the arbitrator of a grievance with authority to order disclosure of information, did not require deferral of unfair labor practice charges alleging wrongful refusal to turn over information that would assist the union in determining whether to initiate the grievance process.

In later decisions the Board has refused to defer to arbitration in cases where the information sought relates directly to the subject matter of other pending grievances.[462] Even where an employer claimed that the underlying subject matter was arbitrable, the Board refused to defer to arbitration.[463] An employer's reliance on an arbitration award as a defense to a section 8(a)(5) complaint for refusing to produce informa-

---

[456]McDonnell Douglas Corp., 224 NLRB 881, 93 LRRM 1280 (1976).

[457]*Supra* note 454.

[458]*Id.* at 1132. *See* Collyer Insulated Wire, 192 NLRB 837, 77 LRRM 1931 (1971), treated extensively in Chapter 18, "Accommodation of Board Action to the Arbitration Process."

[459]*Supra* note 455.

[460]*Id.* at 880.

[461]241 NLRB 600, 100 LRRM 1588 (1979).

[462]U.S. Postal Serv., 280 NLRB 685, 122 LRRM 1337 (1986), *enforced,* 841 F2d 141, 127 LRRM 2807 (CA 6, 1988); E.W. Buschman Co., 277 NLRB 189, 120 LRRM 1253 (1985), *enforcement denied,* 820 F2d 206, 125 LRRM 2642 (CA 6, 1987); U.S. Postal Serv., 276 NLRB 1282, 120 LRRM 1277 (1985); United Technologies Corp., 274 NLRB 504, 118 LRRM 1464 (1985). For earlier cases on the deferral question, *see* General Dynamics Corp., Quincy Shipbuilding Div., 268 NLRB 1432, 115 LRRM 1199 (1984); Loral Elec. Sys., 253 NLRB 851, 106 LRRM 1061 (1980); Collyer Insulated Wire, *supra* note 458.

[463]United Technologies Corp., *supra* note 462.

tion[464] has been examined in light of the *Spielberg*[465] doctrine. Deferral has been deemed inappropriate where the arbitrator failed to consider the statutory right to information[466] or rendered an award that was repugnant to the Act.[467]

1. Request or Demand. An employer's duty to supply the bargaining representative with information does not arise until the union makes a request or a demand that the information be furnished.[468] While the request must be made in good faith,[469] this requirement is met if at least one reason for the demand can be justified.[470]

---

[464]*E.g.*, NLRB v. Designcraft Jewel Indus., 675 F2d 493, 109 LRRM 3341 (CA 2, 1982), *enforcing* 254 NLRB 791, 107 LRRM 1034 (1981); Kroger Co., *supra* note 452.

[465]Spielberg Mfg. Co., 112 NLRB 1080, 36 LRRM 1152 (1955).

[466]NLRB v. Designcraft Jewel Indus., *supra* note 464.

[467]Sherwood Diversified Servs., Federated Answering Serv. Div., 228 NLRB 341, 128 LRRM 1162 (1988); General Motors Corp. v. NLRB, 700 F2d 1083, 112 LRRM 2976 (CA 6, 1983). *But see* NLRB v. United Parcel Serv., 677 F2d 421, 113 LRRM 2035 (CA 6, 1982) (Board did not depart from standards in *Spielberg* by hearing employee's grievance even though it had already been the subject of arbitration proceeding).

[468]NLRB v. Boston Herald-Traveler Corp., 210 F2d 134, 33 LRRM 2435 (CA 1, 1954), *enforcing* 102 NLRB 627, 31 LRRM 1337 (1953); Westinghouse Elec. Supply Co. v. NLRB, 196 F2d 1012, 30 LRRM 2169 (CA 3, 1952). *But see* Boston Herald-Traveler Corp., 110 NLRB 2097, 35 LRRM 1309 (1954), *aff'd*, 223 F2d 58, 36 LRRM 2220 (CA 1, 1955).

[469]Cases are legion in which the Board has upheld an employer refusal to turn over information because the union request or demand was unreasonable. *See, e.g.*, NLRB v. Abbott Publishing Co., 331 F2d 209, 55 LRRM 2994 (CA 7, 1964) (employer refusal to turn over its financial records for union audit did not violate Act, despite poverty-plea response to union's demand for wage increase, where employer offered to supply and discuss weekly profit-and-loss statements, and agreed to allow company bookkeepers who were union members to discuss financial status of company with union negotiators); General Elec. Co., 163 NLRB 198, 64 LRRM 1312 (1967), *enforced*, 400 F2d 713, 69 LRRM 2081 (CA 5, 1968), *cert. denied*, 394 US 904, 70 LRRM 2828 (1969) (employer's refusal to furnish information relating to laid-off employees was not violation of §8(a)(5) because request was made during pendency of unfair labor practice charges complaining of layoff); McCulloch Corp., 132 NLRB 201, 48 LRRM 1344 (1961) (employer did not breach duty when it turned over 29-company wage-range study to union, with list of participating companies and job classifications, but withheld specific wage rates paid by each of the companies because of confidentiality agreement); Albany Garage, 126 NLRB 417, 45 LRRM 1329 (1960) (employer satisfied duty to turn over information where financial statements it supplied union had been accepted by banks doing business with employer, by Bureau of Internal Revenue Service, and by employer's stockholders, and union had accepted same type of information in preceding years); California Portland Cement Co., 101 NLRB 1436, 31 LRRM 1220 (1952) (employer did not violate Act where information requested was posted on plant bulletin board). *Compare* the preceding cases *with* B. F. Diamond Constr. Co., 163 NLRB 161, 64 LRRM 1333 (1967), *enforced*, 410 F2d 462, 71 LRRM 2112 (CA 5), *cert. denied*, 396 US 835, 72 LRRM 2432 (1969) (employer presented with general demand for wage information cannot refuse to turn over such data solely on ground that information is available from employees.)

[470]Utica Observer-Dispatch v. NLRB, 229 F2d 575, 37 LRRM 2441 (CA 2, 1956) (union could not obtain information solely for purpose of collecting dues, but desire for wage information for bargaining purpose as well justified demand); Potter's Medical Center, 289 NLRB 201, 131 LRRM 1321 (1988). *But see* NLRB v. Hawkins Constr. Co., 857 F2d 1224, 129 LRRM 2486 (CA 8, 1988), *denying enforcement to* 285 NLRB 1313, 126 LRRM 1251 (1987) (disclosure not required where union demand was not in good faith,

The specificity required in formulating the demand depends upon the presumptive relevance of the information requested. Where the information relates to unit employees and the presumption of relevance is not rebutted, less precision is required than if it relates to nonunion employees.[471] The request need not be in writing and the union is not required to repeat its request.[472] However, where the request was directed to an inappropriate employer official and not raised again, the Board found no violation in the employer's failure to provide the requested information.[473] Similarly, the Board found no violation where the union failed to attend meetings to which the employer had brought the requested information.[474]

However, where the employer had demonstrated hostility to the union steward and responded to a request for information in an untimely and inadequate manner, the Board found a violation, even though there may have been some ambiguity in the request. In these circumstances, the employer should have sought clarification from the union.[475]

A request for information that goes beyond the members of the bargaining unit will place some additional burdens upon the requesting party. Thus, the Board has required a showing of specificity as to scope as well as relevancy where information was sought relating to employees outside the bargaining unit.[476] However, a closely held company may be required to provide financial data concerning its nonunion operation where the employer is claiming inability to pay.[477] Furthermore, the employer will be obligated to provide information as to its relationship with nonunion firms where the union has a reasonable objective basis to believe that a "double-breasted" operation

---

but to retaliate against employer for filing of suit against union); Snively Groves, Inc., 109 NLRB 1394, 34 LRRM 1568 (1954) (inconsistent and confusing requests by union relieved employer of obligation to furnish information).

[471]Fairfield Publishing Co., 275 NLRB 7, 118 LRRM 1636 (1985), *enforced without opinion*, 782 F2d 1052 (CA 9, 1986); Bauer Welding & Metal Fabricators, 256 NLRB 39, 107 LRRM 1163 (1981), *enforcement denied on other grounds*, 676 F2d 314, 110 LRRM 2270 (CA 8, 1982).

[472]Bundy Corp., 292 NLRB 671, 131 LRRM 1645 (1989); Harvstone Mfg. Corp., 272 NLRB 939, 117 LRRM 1447 (1984), *enforced in part*, 785 F2d 570, 121 LRRM 3371 (CA 7), *cert. denied*, 479 US 821, 123 LRRM 2591 (1986).

[473]Redway Carriers, 274 NLRB 1359, 119 LRRM 1023 (1985).

[474]Michigan Transp. Co., 273 NLRB 1418, 118 LRRM 1287 (1985).

[475]NLRB v. Designcraft Jewel Indus., *supra* note 464; U.S. Postal Serv., 280 NLRB 685, 122 LRRM 1337 (1986); LaGuardia Hosp., 260 NLRB 1455, 109 LRRM 1371 (1982).

[476]Island Creek Coal Co., 292 NLRB 480, 130 LRRM 1292 (1989); Fairfield Publishing Co., *supra* note 471.

[477]Sioux City Stockyards Div., 293 NLRB 1, 130 LRRM 1427 (1989); American Model & Pattern, 277 NLRB 176, 120 LRRM 1267 (1985), *enforced*, 816 F2d 678 (CA 6, 1987).

exists[478] or that the employer subcontracts to a shop that is the employer's alter ego.[479]

2. Relevance or Necessity. The information demanded must be relevant to the relationship between the employer and the union in the latter's capacity as representative of the employees.[480] When the request is in general rather than specific terms, the employer has the right to determine the initial relevance of the requested information.[481] However, the Board and the courts have adopted a liberal definition of relevancy, requiring only that the information be directly related to the union's function as bargaining representative[482] and that it appear "reasonably necessary" for the performance of this function.[483] Data appropriate for disclosure "should not necessarily be limited to that which would be pertinent to a particular existing controversy."[484] As the Supreme Court pointed out in *Acme Industrial,* this is basically a "discovery-type standard."[485]

In general, requested information "must be disclosed unless it plainly appears irrelevant" in accordance with the prevailing rule in discovery procedures under "modern codes."[486] "There the information must be disclosed unless it plainly appears irrelevant."[487] According to the Board, wage and related informa-

---

[478]Pence Constr. Co., 281 NLRB 322, 124 LRRM 1063 (1986); Proctor Mechanical Corp., 279 NLRB 201, 123 LRRM 1152 (1986); Corson & Gruman Co., 278 NLRB 329, 121 LRRM 1325 (1986), *enforced,* 811 F2d 1504, 124 LRRM 2560 (CA 4, 1987).

[479]Blue Diamond Co., 295 NLRB No. 111, 131 LRRM 1752 (1989); Maben Energy Corp., 295 NLRB No. 23, 131 LRRM 1782 (1989); C.E.K. Indus. Mechanical Contractors, 295 NLRB No. 70, 131 LRRM 1737 (1989); George Koch Sons, 295 NLRB No. 73, 132 LRRM 1106 (1989); Weinreb Mgmt., 292 NLRB 428, 131 LRRM 1051 (1989); Stephen Oderwald, Inc., 284 NLRB 277, 126 LRRM 1359 (1987).

[480]NLRB v. Item Co., 220 F2d 956, 35 LRRM 2709 (CA 5), *cert. denied,* 350 US 836, 36 LRRM 2716 (1955); NLRB v. Jacobs Mfg. Co., 196 F2d 680, 30 LRRM 2098 (CA 2, 1952); Transport of N.J., 233 NLRB 694, 97 LRRM 1204 (1977); Ellsworth Sheet Metal, 224 NLRB 1506, 92 LRRM 1590 (1976); Webster Outdoor Advertising, 170 NLRB 1395, 67 LRRM 1589 (1968); Midwestern Instruments, 133 NLRB 1132, 48 LRRM 1793 (1961).

[481]Food Serv. Co., 202 NLRB 790, 82 LRRM 1746 (1973) (union request for general access to employer's records).

[482]Otis Elevator Co., 170 NLRB 395, 67 LRRM 1475 (1968); J.I. Case Co. v. NLRB, 253 F2d 149, 41 LRRM 2679 (CA 7, 1958).

[483]NLRB v. Item Co., *supra* note 480.

[484]NLRB v. Whitin Mach. Works, 217 F2d 593, 593, 35 LRRM 2215 (CA 4, 1954).

[485]NLRB v. Acme Indus. Co., 385 US 432, 437, 64 LRRM 2069 (1967).

[486]NLRB v. Yawman & Erbe Mfg. Co., 187 F2d 947, 949, 27 LRRM 2524 (CA 2, 1951). The court went on to say that "[a]ny less lenient rule in labor disputes would greatly hamper the bargaining process, for it is virtually impossible to tell in advance whether the requested data will be relevant . . . ." *Id.*

[487]Teleprompter Corp. v. NLRB, 570 F2d 4, 8, 97 LRRM 2455 (CA 1, 1977), *enforcing* 227 NLRB 705, 95 LRRM 1058 (1977) (quoting NLRB Chairman Farmer in the *Whitin* case, *supra* note 484; Boston Herald Traveler v. NLRB, 223 F2d 58, 36 LRRM 2220 (CA 1, 1955)). In *Teleprompter,* the First Circuit added a caveat: "The unqualified discovery-type rule . . . does not seem to us tailored to [the plea-of-poverty situation]. The union is

tion should be made available "without regard to its immediate relationship" to the negotiation or administration of the agreement, or to its "precise relevancy" to particular bargaining issues.[488] Subsequent execution of a contract by a union without the information does not render the information irrelevant, since the union may simply have decided that the advantages of a contract in hand would outweigh those that it might enjoy with all the information available to it.[489]

One consideration in determining relevancy and necessity is the union's need for the information. Where a request is rendered moot by subsequent events, the employer has no statutory obligation to furnish information.[490] Such requests have no "current relevancy."[491]

Difficult questions concerning relevance and necessity often arise when a union demands information concerning nonunit employees. In such circumstances, the bargaining representative must demonstrate the probable or potential relevance of the information to its representation of unit employees.[492] In analyzing such amorphous criteria as "relevance" and "necessity," the Board examines the employer's obligation to supply information on a case-by-case basis, reasoning that "the rule is not *per se,* and in each case the Board must determine whether the requested information is relevant, and if relevant, whether it is sufficiently important or needed to invoke a statutory obligation of the other party to produce it."[493] Information concerning terms and conditions of employment of employees represented by a union is presumptively relevant and neces-

---

entitled only to what is reasonably necessary properly to represent its members in light of the employer's triggering claim of financial inability." 570 F2d at 11.

[488]Whitin Mach. Works, 108 NLRB 1537, 34 LRRM 1251 (1954), *enforced,* 217 F2d 593, 35 LRRM 2215 (CA 4, 1954). *See* NLRB v. Boston Herald-Traveler Corp., 209 F2d 134, 33 LRRM 2435 (CA 1, 1954), where the relevance of wage data was presumed. *See also* NLRB v. Fitzgerald Mills Corp., 313 F2d 260, 52 LRRM 2174 (CA 2, 1963), *cert. denied,* 375 US 834, 54 LRRM 2312 (1963).

[489]NLRB v. Fitzgerald Mills Corp., *supra* note 488; NLRB v. Yawman & Erbe Mfg. Co., *supra* note 486.

[490]Glazers Wholesale Drug Co., 211 NLRB 1063, 87 LRRM 1249 (1974), *enforced,* 523 F2d 1053, 90 LRRM 3138 (CA 5, 1975), *cert. denied,* 425 US 913, 91 LRRM 2916 (1976).

[491]C-B Buick, Inc. v. NLRB, 506 F2d 1086, 87 LRRM 2878 (CA 3, 1974), *denying enforcement in part to* 206 NLRB 6, 84 LRRM 1173 (1973).

[492]Newspaper Guild Local 95 (San Diego) v. NLRB, 548 F2d 863, 94 LRRM 2923 (CA 9, 1977); Adams Insulation Co., 219 NLRB 211, 89 LRRM 1699 (1975).

[493]White-Westinghouse Corp., Columbus Prods. Co. Div., 259 NLRB 220, 108 LRRM 1313 (1981).

sary.[494] When the relevance of requested information is not obvious, and when its disclosure implicates employee privacy, an employer is entitled to a statement of its relevance before it is produced.[495] Even though the drug-testing of applicants is not necessarily a mandatory subject of bargaining, information about the identity of such persons who underwent testing was deemed relevant where the union leaders suspected that the testing procedures were discriminatorily administered.[496] Similarly, the results of the employer's survey of employees' attitudes toward the workplace and their benefits were ruled to be relevant.[497] Even where information is in this "presumptively relevant" category, however, there can be questions as to the breadth of information that must be supplied.[498]

Information concerning employees and employers outside the bargaining unit requires a special showing of relevancy.[499] Such relevancy can be shown by presenting "objective facts, or other circumstances which establish the relevance of requested information."[500] The Board and the courts do not require "an

---

[494]Island Creek Coal Co., *supra* note 476; Laminates Unlimited, 292 NLRB 595, 130 LRRM 1352 (1989) (information regarding probationary employees relevant since they were entitled to certain rights under labor contract); Coalite, 278 NLRB 293, 122 LRRM 1030 (1986); Bohemia, 272 NLRB 1128, 117 LRRM 1433 (1984). *See generally* NLRB v. Truitt Mfg. Co., 351 US 149, 38 LRRM 2042 (1956); E.I. du Pont de Nemours & Co., 276 NLRB 335, 120 LRRM 1108 (1985) (certain information as to proposed job restructuring was presumptively relevant); American Marine Decking Sys., 277 NLRB 433, 120 LRRM 1301 (1985), *enforced without opinion*, 804 F2d 145, 123 LRRM 3336 (CA 1, 1986) (identifying employee and fringe-benefit information presumptively relevant).

[495]Szabo v. U.S. Marine Corp., 819 F2d 714, 125 LRRM 2572 (CA 7, 1987); Shrader's Inc., 293 NLRB No. 76, 131 LRRM 1072 (1989).

[496]Star Tribune Div., 295 NLRB No. 63, 131 LRRM 1404 (1989).

[497]NLRB v. United Technologies Corp., Pratt & Whitney Aircraft Div., 789 F2d 121, 122 LRRM 2250 (CA 2, 1986).

[498]Equitable Gas Co. v. NLRB, 637 F2d 980, 106 LRRM 2201 (CA 3, 1981), *denying enforcement to* 245 NLRB 260, 102 LRRM 1470 (1979); NLRB v. Gilbraltar Indus., 653 F2d 1091, 107 LRRM 3307 (CA 6, 1981), *enforcing in part* 237 NLRB 798, 99 LRRM 1159 (1978), *later proceeding*, 265 NLRB 102, 111 LRRM 1446 (1982); Atlas Metal Parts Co. v. NLRB, 660 F2d 304, 108 LRRM 2474 (CA 7, 1981), *denying enforcement in part to* 252 NLRB 205, 105 LRRM 1582 (1980).

[499]*See, e.g.*, Accurate Die Casting Co., 292 NLRB 982, 131 LRRM 1706 (1989) (information on retirees' health insurance lacked relevance); E.I. du Pont de Nemours & Co., 268 NLRB 1031, 115 LRRM 1156 (1984); Leland Stanford Junior Univ., 262 NLRB 136, 110 LRRM 1275 (1982), *enforced*, 713 F2d 473, 114 LRRM 2444 (CA 9, 1983); Amphlett Printing Co., 258 NLRB 86, 108 LRRM 1073 (1981); Times-Herald, 258 NLRB 1041, 108 LRRM 1147 (1981); Leonard B. Hebert, Jr. & Co., 259 NLRB 881, 109 LRRM 1041 (1981), *enforced*, 696 F2d 1120, 112 LRRM 2672 (CA 5), *cert. denied*, 464 US 817, 114 LRRM 2567 (1983). See also the discussion and cases cited in Part IV.B.I, *supra*.

[500]Blue Diamond Co., 295 NLRB No. 111, 131 LRRM 1752 (1989) (objective belief that several companies constitute single employer demonstrates relevancy); Ironton Publications, 294 NLRB No. 73, 131 LRRM 1426 (1989) (details of profit-sharing plan adopted for nonunit employees relevant while negotiations for new agreement were being conducted); Boyd-Mulford Constr. Co., 277 NLRB 1631, 121 LRRM 1271 (1986).

initial, burdensome showing" by a union regarding requests for information that is not presumptively relevant. Rather, a "good faith showing of some relevance" will accord the union "liberal discovery."[501] On the other hand, the courts have rejected certain union demands: for information concerning employees not transferred into the bargaining unit,[502] for information regarding the purchase of new equipment,[503] and for personnel data on nonunion employees being trained as replacements in the event of a strike.[504]

Various other demands for information concerning nonunit employees have been both sustained[505] and rejected.[506] In some cases the Board has held that a union has a right to wage information for nonunit personnel,[507] information regarding unit supervisors,[508] managers' and supervisors' salary rates and job descriptions,[509] the salaries of "confidential secretaries,"[510] as well as information about employees in another division not represented by the union.[511] An employer was required to provide the names, addresses, and wages of temporary employees who performed bargaining-unit work since the information was relevant to the union's policing of the labor contract.[512] Simi-

---

[501]New York Times Co., 270 NLRB 1267, 117 LRRM 1117, 1118 (1984). *See* Barnard Eng'g Co., 282 NLRB 617, 124 LRRM 1107 (1987) (union did not forfeit its right to information because it failed to state basis of its belief that employer and another company were related); Boyers Constr. Co., 267 NLRB 227, 229, 114 LRRM 1008 (1983) (initial showing need not demonstrate that information triggering request for information concerning alleged "dual shop" is "accurate nonhearsay or even ultimately reliable"). *See also* Hawkins Constr. Co., 285 NLRB 1313, 126 LRRM 1251 (1987), *enforcement denied*, 857 F2d 1224, 129 LRRM 2486 (CA 8, 1988) (presumption that union's request for information is in good faith until contrary is shown); O&G Indus., 269 NLRB 986, 987, 116 LRRM 1046 (1984) (presumption that union is acting in good faith).

[502]NLRB v. Western Elec., 559 F2d 1131, 95 LRRM 3230 (CA 8, 1977).

[503]Seafarers (SAG) Local 777 v. NLRB (Yellow Cab Co.), 603 F2d 862, 99 LRRM 2903 (CADC, 1978) (purchase of new cabs and assignment to nonunion drivers).

[504]Newspaper Guild Local 95 (San Diego) v. NLRB, *supra* note 492.

[505]*See* NLRB. v. Goodyear Aerospace Corp., 388 F2d 673, 67 LRRM 2447 (CA 6, 1968); Curtiss-Wright Corp. v. NLRB, 347 F2d 61, 59 LRRM 2433 (CA 3, 1965); California Portland Cement Co., 103 NLRB 1375, 31 LRRM 1630 (1953).

[506]NLRB v. Leland-Gifford Co., 200 F2d 620, 31 LRRM 2196 (CA 1, 1952); Fetzer Television v. NLRB, 317 F2d 420, 53 LRRM 2224 (CA 6, 1963).

[507]Brazos Elec. Power Coop., 241 NLRB 1016, 101 LRRM 1003 (1979), *aff'd*, 615 F2d 1100, 104 LRRM 2123 (CA 5, 1980).

[508]Globe Stores, 227 NLRB 1251, 94 LRRM 1336 (1977); Northwest Publications, 211 NLRB 464, 86 LRRM 1345 (1974).

[509]International Harvester Co., 241 NLRB 600, 100 LRRM 1588 (1979).

[510]Greensboro News Co., 244 NLRB 689, 102 LRRM 1164 (1979).

[511]Temple-Eastex, Inc., 228 NLRB 203, 96 LRRM 1424 (1977), *rev'd*, 579 F2d 932, 99 LRRM 2467 (CA 5, 1978). *But see* Binswanger Glass Co., 245 NLRB 253, 102 LRRM 1541 (1979). *See* discussion *infra* at notes 617–620.

[512]United Graphics, 281 NLRB 463, 123 LRRM 1097 (1986). *See also* Hawkins Constr. Co., *supra* note 501 (Board found employer obligated to supply list of projects, subcontractors, subcontracting agreements, and wage and benefit data on employees on

larly, a union is entitled to information regarding the subcontracting of work even though the employer insists it is complying with the contract requirements.[513] Furthermore, a union is entitled to the names of its officials who apply for supervisory positions where the union's interest in the information is relevant to its duty to provide loyal representation to the unit employees and is not outweighed by the employer's interest in preserving confidentiality of the information and its right to select its supervisors.[514]

3. Availability. Once the union makes a good-faith demand for relevant information, the employer must make a diligent effort to provide the information in a reasonably prompt manner and useful form.[515] Even though an employer has not expressly refused to furnish the information, lack of a diligent effort to obtain or to provide the information "reasonably" promptly may be equated with a flat refusal.[516] A long and unexplained delay in furnishing even partial information (9 months) has supported a conclusion that later bargaining was not in good faith, even though the company had expressly agreed to provide the information.[517] Although the Board finds a delay of several months to be inconsistent with good faith,[518] a short delay may be reasonable if justified.[519] However, the

---

projects since it was relevant and there was no evidence that sole motive for request was to retaliate for employer's filing of lawsuit against unions).

[513]Island Creek Coal Co., 292 NLRB 480, 130 LRRM 1292 (1989); Pertec Computer Corp., 284 NLRB 810, 126 LRRM 1134 (1987).

[514]NLRB v. U.S. Postal Serv., 841 F2d 141, 127 LRRM 2807 (CA 6, 1988), *enforcing* 280 NLRB 685, 122 LRRM 1337 (1986).

[515]General Elec. Co., 290 NLRB 1138, 131 LRRM 1230 (1988); Quaker Oats Co., NLRB Gen. Counsel Advice Memo., Case No. 4-CA-13849, 114 LRRM 1277 (1983) (insurance company's physician's rate schedule).

[516]NLRB v. John S. Swift Co., 277 F2d 641, 46 LRRM 2090 (CA 7, 1960) (the court stated that "Company's inaction spoke louder than its words").

[517]NLRB v. Fitzgerald Mills Corp., 313 F2d 260, 52 LRRM 2174 (CA 2, 1963), *cert. denied*, 375 US 834, 54 LRRM 2312 (1963) (the court also noted that withdrawal by union of earlier unfair labor practice charge based on same refusal of information did not indicate compliance or that union was satisfied, only that union believed employer had begun to comply with its request). *See also* NLRB v. My Store, 345 F2d 494, 58 LRRM 2775 (CA 7), *cert. denied*, 382 US 927, 60 LRRM 2424 (1965) (employer supplied incorrect information, then failed to correct mistake "for months"); NLRB v. Feed & Supply Center, 294 F2d 650, 48 LRRM 2993 (CA 9, 1961) (6-month delay); International Powder Metallurgy Co., 134 NLRB 1605, 49 LRRM 1388 (1961) (11-month delay); Peyton Packing Co., 129 NLRB 1358, 47 LRRM 1211 (1961) (3-month delay is too long, even when data are incomplete and persons necessary to compile information are absent from work).

[518]Colonial Press, 204 NLRB 852, 83 LRRM 1648 (1973), *enforced*, 564 F2d 101, 97 LRRM 2111 (CA 8, 1977); Arkansas Rice Growers Coop. Ass'n, 165 NLRB 577, 65 LRRM 1567 (1967), *aff'd*, 400 F2d 565, 69 LRRM 2119 (CA 8, 1968).

[519]United Engines, 222 NLRB 50, 91 LRRM 1208 (1976) (employer did not violate Act when it provided most of information requested within a month of request and 2 weeks before bargaining was scheduled to start); Partee Flooring Mill, 107 NLRB 1177, 33 LRRM 1342 (1954) (15-day delay not unreasonable).

Board has held that a 10½-month delay in production was justifiable where there was no evidence that the employer could produce the information faster or that the union was prejudiced by the delay.[520] In contrast, the Board has held that an employer violated section 8(a)(5) by failing for approximately 6 months to provide readily available information.[521] The availability of the information from another source does not alter a party's duty to provide relevant information that it has readily available.[522] Similarly, even where access to information could jeopardize an employer's trade secrets, a union, which executed a trade secret agreement with the employer, was granted access.[523]

4. Manner and Form. The Board requires that information must be furnished "in a manner not so burdensome or time consuming as to impede the process of bargaining," although not necessarily in the form requested by the union.[524]

An employer fulfills its obligation by making reasonable efforts to accommodate the union's request for information and

---

[520]Union Carbide Corp., Nuclear Div., 275 NLRB 197, 119 LRRM 1077 (1985). Further, the requested information was not centrally located and the employer could document an ongoing effort to obtain the information. *See also* Dallas & Mavis Forwarding Co., 291 NLRB 980, 131 LRRM 1272 (1988) (7-month delay lawful).

[521]Tennessee Steel Processor, 287 NLRB 1132, 127 LRRM 1140 (1988). *See also* Bundy Corp., 292 NLRB 671, 131 LRRM 1645 (1989) (2½-month delay unreasonable where union required information in order to prepare for negotiations).

[522]ASARCO, Tennessee Mines Div. v. NLRB, 805 F2d 194, 123 LRRM 2985 (CA 6, 1986); Holyoke Water Power Co., 273 NLRB 1369, 118 LRRM 1179 (1985), *enforced*, 778 F2d 49, 120 LRRM 3487 (CA 1, 1985), *later proceeding*, 793 F2d 18 (CA 1), *cert. denied*, 477 US 905, 122 LRRM 2656 (1986); Colgate-Palmolive Co., 261 NLRB 90, 109 LRRM 1352 (1982), *enforced sub nom.* Oil, Chem. & Atomic Workers Local 6-418 v. NLRB (Minnesota Mining & Mfg. Co.), 711 F2d 348, 113 LRRM 3163 (CADC, 1983).

[523]Hercules, Inc. v. NLRB, 833 F2d 426, 126 LRRM 3187 (CA 2, 1987). *But compare* USAir v. National Mediation Bd., 711 F Supp 285, 132 LRRM 2395 (ED Va, 1989), *aff'd*, 894 F2d 403, 133 LRRM 2072 (CA 4, 1989) (Under Railway Labor Act (RLA), 45 U.S.C. §151 et seq., the union's interest in procuring the employees' home addresses must be balanced against the employees' privacy interests. Thus, when the employer sends a letter to the home of each employee asking whether that employee wishes to authorize the release of his or her home address to the union, the RLA mandates that the union is entitled to the addresses of only those employees who have responded affirmatively to the letter).

[524]Cincinnati Steel Castings Co., 86 NLRB 592, 593, 24 LRRM 1657 (1949) (oral information sufficient). *See* Old Line Life Ins. Co., 96 NLRB 499 (1951), *aff'd*, 200 F2d 52, 31 LRRM 2118 (CA 7, 1952) (where information was being supplied regularly on monthly basis, employer's offer to verify accuracy of union's current list fulfilled statutory obligation); B.F. Goodrich Co., 89 NLRB 1151, 26 LRRM 1090 (1950) (wage data identified by employee department number rather than by name not sufficient); *See also* NLRB v. Southwestern Elec. Coop., 794 F2d 276, 122 LRRM 2747 (CA 7, 1986), *enforcing* 274 NLRB 922, 118 LRRM 1453 (1985); NLRB v. Tex-Tan, Inc., 318 F2d 472, 53 LRRM 2298 (CA 5, 1963) (data requested were considered too voluminous to compile, thus request was overly burdensome).

providing the information, albeit in an alternate form.[525] The employer may violate its obligation if the information is incomplete or contains unwarranted inaccuracies.[526]

If the employer claims that compiling the data will be unduly burdensome, it must assert that claim at the time of the request for the information so that an arrangement can be made to lessen the burden.[527] The employer may not simply present the information in any form which it considers adequate but which is, nonetheless, unsuitable for informed consideration.[528] However, if the employer presents information on its financial position in a form generally accepted in business, it will usually be considered adequate.[529] An employer may also attach conditions to the furnishing of such financial information that are reasonably related to its own business interest.[530] Thus, an employer's refusal to allow a union to photocopy a one-page document was justified where the document could easily be read and understood.[531] Where the employer allows the union free

---

[525]Oil, Chem. & Atomic Workers Local 6-418 v. NLRB (Minnesota Mining & Mfg. Co.), 711 F2d 348, 113 LRRM 3163 (CADC, 1983) (furnishing data in form that does not identify individuals acceptable); Airport Aviation Servs., 292 NLRB No. 87, 131 LRRM 1013 (1989); H.M.S. Mach. Works, 284 NLRB 1482, 127 LRRM 1056 (1987) (employer required to furnish union with information on cash Christmas bonuses from memory since no formal records kept and information was not factually complex).

[526]Airport Aviation Servs., *supra* note 525.

[527]J.I. Case Co. v. NLRB, 253 F2d 149, 41 LRRM 2679 (CA 7, 1958).

[528]*Id.* at 150 (employer violated Act when it orally presented complicated information at single bargaining session rather than producing copies of records in question, where union had offered to pay copying charges); NLRB v. Otis Elevator Co., 208 F2d 176, 33 LRRM 2129 (CA 2, 1953) (contract provision specifying that certain information will be furnished to union does not preclude union from obtaining other information to which it is entitled); General Elec. Co., 186 NLRB 14, 75 LRRM 1265 (1970) (employer violated §8(a)(5) when it offered union videotape presentation instead of allowing it to conduct in-plant time study of job in question).

[529]Albany Garage, 126 NLRB 417, 45 LRRM 1329 (1960) (a leading case outlining type of documents that would constitute adequate, voluntary disclosure). *But cf.* Metlox Mfg. Co. v. NLRB, 378 F2d 728, 65 LRRM 2637 (CA 9, 1967), *cert. denied,* 389 US 1037, 67 LRRM 2231 (1968).

[530]Fruit & Vegetable Packers Local 760 v. NLRB (Yakima Frozen Foods), 316 F2d 389, 52 LRRM 2537 (CADC, 1963).

[531]Roadway Express, 275 NLRB 1107, 120 LRRM 1024 (1985). *But see* Communications Workers Local 1051 v. NLRB (AT&T), 644 F2d 923, 106 LRRM 2960, 2963 (CA 1, 1981), *enforcing* 250 NLRB 47, 104 LRRM 1381 (1980) ("We are satisfied that there is substantial evidence to support the Board's decision that the Company rule impeded the grievance process in these four cases. The evidence establishes that the 'no-photocopy' rule made it expensive and time consuming, if not impossible, for the union to obtain the reliable copies it required to discharge its duties as bargaining representative. The rule plainly disadvantaged the union in evaluating and prosecuting grievances and was likely to discourage resort to the grievance process at all in some cases." *Compare* NLRB v. Pennsylvania Tel. Guild (Bell Tel. Co. of Pa.), 799 F2d 84, 90, 123 LRRM 2214 (CA 3, 1986) (right to photocopy grievance-related materials does not extend to allowing right to tape-recorded transcript of negotiations themselves).

access to its records and fully cooperates with the union in answering questions, it need not furnish information in a more organized form than that in which it keeps its own records.[532]

Although a union may be required in certain circumstances to pay the reasonable costs of providing copies in accordance with a request for information, the Board has held that the parties should bargain in good faith over which party shall bear such costs.[533] An employer violated the duty to bargain when it conditioned the grant of the information on the union's paying all "copying and administrative expenses" in advance. The employer did not specify the copying cost per page, the approximate number of copies, or the administrative hourly expense, and the union had no objective basis on which to decide whether it wished to incur these charges.[534]

5. Employer Defenses. A union's interest in arguably relevant information does not always predominate over other legitimate interests, as the Supreme Court ruled in *Detroit Edison Co. v. NLRB*,[535] rejecting any "absolute rule"[536] relating to disclosure of information:

> A union's bare assertion that it needs information to process a grievance does not automatically oblige the employer to supply all the information in the manner requested. The duty to supply information under § 8(a)(5) turns upon "the circumstances of the particular case" . . . and much the same may be said for the type of disclosure that will satisfy that duty.[537]

Employers are limited, however, as to the defenses which they may successfully invoke against a charge of refusal to bargain arising from failure to provide relevant information. Defenses based on the circumstances of specific cases—for example, defenses relating to relevancy, form, or availability—have been previously noted; and like defenses will be noted in relation to the timing of the union's request[538] and to the nature of the

---

[532]NLRB v. Tex-Tan, Inc., *supra* note 524. *See also* Fafnir Bearing Co. v. NLRB, 362 F2d 716, 62 LRRM 2415 (CA 2, 1966) (even after employer makes time studies and releases results to union, union may demand access to plans and records to make its own studies to substantiate company information). *But see* NLRB v. Otis Elevator Co., *supra* note 528.

[533]Food Employers Council, 197 NLRB 651, 80 LRRM 1440 (1972).

[534]Queen Anne Record Sales dba Tower Books, 273 NLRB 671, 118 LRRM 1113 (1984), *enforced*, 772 F2d 913, 121 LRRM 2048 (CA 9, 1985).

[535]440 US 301, 100 LRRM 2728 (1979). *See infra* at notes 543 and 561.

[536]440 US at 318.

[537]*Id.* at 314 (quoting NLRB v. Truitt Mfg. Co., 351 US 149, 153, 38 LRRM 2042 (1956)).

[538]*See infra* at notes 570–597.

information requested.[539] This section concerns certain limited exceptions which might be termed "affirmative defenses."

In *NLRB v. Movie Star*[540] an employer was excused from the duty to provide information where its failure to do so was attributable to a breakdown in negotiations not caused by the employer's lack of good faith. However, employer contentions that information is confidential or privileged have been rejected,[541] as have similar contentions that the divulgence of such information violates employees' right of privacy,[542] although the latter position was upheld in relation to the results of psychological testing.[543] A few cases have pardoned an employer's refusal to furnish information on the ground that the union had waived its right to information by "clearly and unmistakably" bargaining the right away.[544] Even fewer have inferred a waiver from the union's bargaining conduct.[545] Most cases involving waiver stress that, since the duty to furnish information arises under the Act, the union's right to such information can be waived only in express terms and such a waiver cannot arise by implication.[546] Thus, forfeiture of the right must be by "clear and unmistakable" language and not merely by omission from the contract.[547] Thus, claims that a union waived its statutory right to information through past practice,[548] pre-

---

[539]*See infra* at notes 598–657.

[540]361 F2d 346, 62 LRRM 2234 (CA 5, 1966).

[541]Aluminum Ore Co. v. NLRB, 131 F2d 485, 11 LRRM 693 (CA 7, 1942); Kroger Co., 163 NLRB 441, 64 LRRM 1364 (1967), *enforcement denied*, 399 F2d 455, 68 LRRM 2731 (CA 6, 1968); Boston Herald-Traveler Corp., 102 NLRB 627, 31 LRRM 1337 (1953), *enforced*, 210 F2d 134, 33 LRRM 2435 (CA 1, 1954).

[542]Utica Observer-Dispatch v. NLRB, 229 F2d 575, 37 LRRM 2441 (CA 2, 1956) (employer's notification to employees that it would furnish information if they did not object, and withholding of information concerning those who did object, is refusal to bargain); Northwestern Photo Engraving Co., 140 NLRB 24, 51 LRRM 1550 (1962). *But see* Webster Outdoor Advertising Co., 170 NLRB 1395, 67 LRRM 1589 (1968) (employer refused to supply wage data for replacements of economic strikers; replacements had been subject to harassment and threats, and employer requested assurance from union that data would not be used to facilitate further harassment).

[543]Detroit Edison Co. v. NLRB, *supra* note 535, and discussion at note 561, *infra*.

[544]Hearst Corp., International News Serv. Div., 113 NLRB 1067, 36 LRRM 1454 (1955); Hughes Tool Co., 100 NLRB 208, 30 LRRM 1265 (1952).

[545]*E.g.*, Square D Co. v. NLRB, 332 F2d 360, 56 LRRM 2147 (CA 9, 1964); Berkline Corp., 123 NLRB 685, 43 LRRM 1513 (1959).

[546]NLRB v. Perkins Mach. Co., 326 F2d 488, 55 LRRM 2204 (CA 1, 1964); Skyway Luggage Co., 117 NLRB 681, 39 LRRM 1310 (1957).

[547]Timken Roller Bearing Co. v. NLRB, 325 F2d 746, 54 LRRM 2785 (CA 6, 1963), *cert. denied*, 376 US 971, 55 LRRM 2878 (1964); California Portland Cement Co., 103 NLRB 1375, 31 LRRM 1630 (1953).

[548]General Motors Corp. v. NLRB, 700 F2d 1083, 112 LRRM 2976 (CA 6, 1983); American Broadcasting Co., 290 NLRB 86, 131 LRRM 1252 (1988).

vious grievance settlements,[549] or acceptances of prior arbitration awards[550] normally will not be sustained. Inclusion of a grievance procedure in the contract is not a waiver of the right to information,[551] but prior settlement agreements may be.[552] An employer may not refuse to provide information by arguing that the union lost its majority status, if at the time of the request it neither refused to bargain with nor withdrew recognition of the union.[553] A general contract "zipper" provision to the effect that the agreement has settled all issues and all collective bargaining obligations for its term does not normally waive rights to information.[554]

The Board has upheld specific and substantial claims that confidentiality or employee privacy justify denial of a union's request for information.[555] However, the Board has rejected such a claim which was not timely raised, or was brought up only as an afterthought.[556] General claims of privilege will be rejected[557] and the party asserting confidentiality has the burden of proof.[558] Information contained in personnel files is not

---

[549]PPG Indus., 255 NLRB 296, 106 LRRM 1334 (1981), *enforcement denied*, 692 F2d 753, 111 LRRM 2698 (CA 4, 1982).

[550]General Motors Corp. v. NLRB, *supra* note 548.

[551]Stephen Oderwald, Inc., 284 NLRB 277, 126 LRRM 1359 (1987); Clinchfield Coal Co., 275 NLRB 1384, 120 LRRM 1003 (1985).

[552]Southwestern Bell Tel. Co. v. NLRB, 667 F2d 470, 109 LRRM 2602 (CA 5, 1982), *denying enforcement to* 251 NLRB 612, 105 LRRM 1246 (1980) (settlement agreement provided for access to material in employees' personnel files, but prohibited its removal from company premises and allowed photocopying only if employee executed a release).

[553]Weathercraft Co. of Topeka, 282 NLRB 1127, 125 LRRM 1064 (1987). *But see* Curtin Matheson Scientific v. NLRB, 859 F2d 362, 129 LRRM 2801 (CA 5, 1988), *denying enforcement to* 287 NLRB 350, 127 LRRM 1114 (1987), *reversed on other grounds*, 494 US 775, 133 LRRM 3049 (1990) (employer lawfully refused to furnish union with requested information on same day employer lawfully withdrew recognition from union based on good-faith doubt of union's majority status); Airport Aviation Servs., 292 NLRB 823, 131 LRRM 1013 (1989).

[554]J.I. Case Co. v. NLRB, 253 F2d 149, 41 LRRM 2679 (CA 7, 1958). *See* further discussion of waiver in Part VII, *infra*.

[555]Minnesota Mining & Mfg. Co., 261 NLRB 27, 109 LRRM 1345 (1982); Borden Chem. Div., 261 NLRB 64, 109 LRRM 1358 (1982), *enforced*, Oil, Chem. & Atomic Workers Local 6-418 v. NLRB (Minnesota Mining & Mfg. Co.), 711 F2d 348, 113 LRRM 3163 (CADC, 1983).

[556]Gas Spring Co., 296 NLRB No. 14, 132 LRRM 1054 (1989).

[557]New England Newspapers dba Transcript Newspapers, 286 NLRB 124, 128 LRRM 1168 (1987), *enforced*, 856 F2d 409, 129 LRRM 2305 (CA 1, 1988) (agreement of sale is not generally confidential and employer must specifically denote confidential sections); O&G Indus., 269 NLRB 986, 116 LRRM 1046 (1984) (contract with outside party); Washington Star Co., 273 NLRB 391, 118 LRRM 1542 (1984) (contract for sale of facility must be produced but with sale prices deleted).

[558]U.S. Postal Serv. (Main Post Office), 289 NLRB 942, 129 LRRM 1169 (1988), *enforced*, 888 F2d 1568, 133 LRRM 2152 (CA 11, 1989); Island Creek Coal Co., 289 NLRB 851, 129 LRRM 1244 (1988), *enforced sub nom.* Mine Workers Dist. 31 v. NLRB, 879 F2d 939, 131 LRRM 3134 (CA DC, 1989); Pertec Computer Corp., 284 NLRB 810, 126 LRRM 1134 (1987); Washington Gas Light Co., 273 NLRB 116, 118 LRRM 1001 (1984).

per se confidential and the employer must show that harm will result from the disclosure.[559] With respect to information claimed to be confidential for business reasons (e.g., trade secrets), the parties must bargain in good faith to reach an accommodation of interests. Such a claim will not support an employer's categorical refusal to supply information.[560] If the parties cannot resolve the matter through bargaining, the Board will balance the parties' competing interests pursuant to *Detroit Edison v. NLRB*.[561]

Although employee medical information is confidential, the possibility that the furnishing of nonmedical records may include some references to medical problems will not invalidate an information request to the extent that it includes information as to which an adequate defense has not been raised.[562]

An employer may be required to provide aggregate medical data and individual medical records from which identifying data have been excised.[563] In one case, the Board ruled that the employer was not obligated to provide the union with the names of employees identified as having lung disease. The Board rea-

---

[559]Midwest Communications, WCCO Radio Div. v. NLRB, 844 F2d 511, 128 LRRM 2069 (CA 8), *enforcing* 282 NLRB 1199, 125 LRRM 1046 (1987), *cert. denied*, 488 US 824 (1988) (preference for confidentiality on part of some employers does not nullify union's right to information normally relevant but it does underscore need to guarantee against inappropriate disclosure); Salt River Valley Water Users' Ass'n v. NLRB, 769 F2d 639, 120 LRRM 2265 (CA 9, 1985); New Jersey Bell Tel. Co., 289 NLRB 318, 131 LRRM 1315 (1988) (employer-initiated privacy plan ineffective to prevent disclosure where at least some employees authorized disclosure). *But cf.* New Jersey Tel. Co. v. NLRB, 720 F2d 789, 114 LRRM 3337 (CA 3, 1983), where the court refused to enforce a Board order finding unlawful an employer's refusal to release employees' absence and tardiness records to the union, without employee authorization for same. The court ruled that N.J. Bell could require employee consent in accordance with the terms of its Employee Privacy Protection Plan, which applied to anyone seeking information about company employees. The court noted that the union itself had prevented the receipt of the information by directing employees not to authorize its release.

[560]*See* Oil, Chem. & Atomic Workers Local 6-418 v. NLRB (Minnesota Mining & Mfg. Co.), 711 F2d 348, 113 LRRM 3163, 3173–74 (CADC, 1983); E.W. Buschman Co., 277 NLRB 189, 120 LRRM 1253 (1985), *enforcement denied*, 820 F2d 206, 125 LRRM 2642 (CA 6, 1987).

[561]440 US 301, 100 LRRM 2728 (1979), *on remand*, 595 F2d 365, 101 LRRM 2835 (CA 6, 1979). *See* Oil, Chem. & Atomic Workers Local 6-418 v. NLRB (Minnesota Mining & Mfg. Co.), *supra* note 560, 113 LRRM at 3174; *see also* NLRB v. Burkart Foam, 848 F2d 825, 128 LRRM 2772 (CA 7, 1988), *enforcing* 283 NLRB 351, 124 LRRM 1394 (1987) (employer not justified in refusing to provide union with list of strike replacements, strikers who returned to work during strike, and list of strikers not recalled after strike. Employer's defense of fear of retaliation against employees rejected because of lack of reasonable good-faith belief on part of employer that union retaliation would occur. Also, employer failed to seek assurance from union that information would not be used for improper purposes).

[562]Washington Gas Light Co., *supra* note 558, 118 LRRM at 1002.

[563]Oil, Chem. & Atomic Workers Local 6-418 v. NLRB (Minnesota Mining & Mfg. Co.), *supra* note 560, 113 LRRM at 3166–67.

soned that there was "a legitimate aura of confidentiality" surrounding the identity of the employees, the union did not need that information to proceed with its objective of notifying employees of their rights, and the employer had sought to accommodate the union by soliciting the consent of individual employees to disclose their identities to the union.[564]

The union's need for information contained in portions of patients' medical charts has been held to outweigh the patients' concern with an invasion of their privacy where the information would be used in connection with processing grievances.[565] Further, the Board reasoned that since the names of the patients involved were not essential to the resolution of the grievances, the parties were to "act in good faith" to ensure the accuracy of the relevant materials so that the patients' identities need be revealed only to nurses who were in a confidential relationship with such patients and then only if this were in fact necessary.[566]

The Federal Privacy Act of 1974 generally restricts the dissemination of information pertaining to individuals that is in the possession of federal government agencies and certain of their contractors.[567] Although the Privacy Act generally prohibits the release of information about an individual without that individual's express authorization, the statute provides an exception where the information is not individually identifiable and the user will agree to keep the information confidential. Thus, where the union falls within the exception, the employer cannot rely on the Privacy Act to excuse its refusal to fulfill its duty to furnish information.[568]

Information prepared in anticipation of litigation may be confidential.[569]

C. When the Duty Exists

In the 1954 case of *NLRB v. Whitin Machine Works*[570] the Fourth Circuit concluded that it was "well settled that it is an unfair labor practice within the meaning of section 8(a)(5) of the

---

[564]Johns-Manville Sales Corp., 252 NLRB 368, 105 LRRM 1379, 1380 (1980).

[565]Howard Univ., 290 NLRB 1006, 129 LRRM 1136 (1988); LaGuardia Hosp., 260 NLRB 1455, 109 LRRM 1371 (1982).

[566]LaGuardia Hosp., *supra* note 565.

[567]Goodyear Atomic Corp., 266 NLRB 890, 113 LRRM 1057 (1983), *enforced*, 738 F2d 155, 116 LRRM 3023 (CA 6, 1984).

[568]*Id.*

[569]General Dynamics Corp., Quincy Shipbuilding Div., 268 NLRB 1432, 115 LRRM 1199 (1984) (study bearing on union's subcontracting grievances).

[570]217 F2d 593, 35 LRRM 2215 (CA 4, 1954), *cert. denied*, 349 US 905, 35 LRRM 2730 (1955).

Act for an employer to refuse to furnish a bargaining union [such information as] is necessary to the proper discharge of the duties of the bargaining agent."[571] As previously noted, this duty to furnish to the union relevant information was given explicit approval by the Supreme Court in the *Truitt* case.[572] But *when* does the duty exist?

The duty arises as soon as the union is elected bargaining representative. An employer acts at its peril if it refuses to provide requested information following a Board election, even though the request is made prior to certification and while objections are pending.[573]

The duty "does not terminate with the signing of the collective bargaining contract" but "continues through the life of the agreements so far as it is necessary to enable the parties to administer the contract and resolve grievances or disputes."[574] During the term of the contract, a union must be able to apprise the employees of the benefits to which they are entitled under the contract and of its readiness to enforce compliance with the agreement for their protection.[575] Since collective bargaining is a continuing process, the union has not only the duty to negotiate collective bargaining agreements, but also the statutory obligation to police and administer existing agreements;[576] thus, its right to information within the sphere of its function as bargaining representative continues after an agreement is signed.[577]

---

[571]*Id.* at 594. *See also* Sinclair Ref. Co. v. NLRB, 306 F2d 569, 50 LRRM 2830 (CA 5, 1962); NLRB v. Yawman & Erbe Mfg. Co., 187 F2d 947, 27 LRRM 2524 (CA 2, 1951) (employer conceded that duty to provide information was incidental to its duty to bargain in good faith); Aluminum Ore Co. v. NLRB, 131 F2d 485, 487, 11 LRRM 693 (CA 7, 1942) (the court stated: "[W]e do not believe that it was the intent of Congress in this legislation that, in the collective bargaining prescribed, the union, as representative of the employees, should be deprived of the pertinent facts . . .").

[572]NLRB v. Truitt Mfg. Co., 351 US 149, 38 LRRM 2042 (1956).

[573]Sundstrand Heat Transfer v. NLRB, 538 F2d 1257, 92 LRRM 3266 (CA 7, 1976). *See also* Pony Express Courier Corp., 286 NLRB 1286, 128 LRRM 1109 (1987); East Coast Equip. Corp., 229 NLRB 825, 95 LRRM 1166 (1977), *enforced sub nom.* NLRB v. Steco Sales, 577 F2d 727, 98 LRRM 2438 (CA 3, 1978) (employer who contended that certified unit was not appropriate violated Act when it denied union's request for information).

[574]Sinclair Ref. Co. v. NLRB, *supra* note 571, at 570. *See also* Western Mass. Elec. Co. v. NLRB, 589 F2d 42, 100 LRRM 2315 (CA 1, 1978); Budde Publications, 242 NLRB 243, 101 LRRM 1140 (1979).

[575]*See* Prudential Ins. Co. v. NLRB, 412 F2d 77, 71 LRRM 2254 (CA 2, 1969), *cert. denied*, 396 US 928, 72 LRRM 2695 (1969).

[576]J.I. Case Co. v. NLRB, 253 F2d 149, 41 LRRM 2679 (CA 7, 1958); Southwestern Bell Tel. Co., 173 NLRB 172, 69 LRRM 1251 (1968) (subcontracting cost information ordered disclosed for use in processing grievances relating to subcontracting); Twin City Lines, 170 NLRB 625, 67 LRRM 1553 (1968), *enforced*, 425 F2d 164, 74 LRRM 2024 (CA 8, 1970).

[577]NLRB v. John S. Swift Co., 277 F2d 641, 46 LRRM 2090 (CA 7, 1960); Sheet Metal Contractors, 246 NLRB 886, 103 LRRM 1018 (1979). *See also* Hoerner-Waldorf Paper

Often the information sought by the union will be used to determine if an employer has modified or breached the terms of the collective agreement.[578] The union requires such information for the performance of its statutory duties and responsibilities, particularly when employer actions affect employees' rights under the contract.[579] The inquiry must always be whether or not, under the circumstances of the individual case, the employer has satisfied its statutory obligation.[580]

A question that has arisen in this regard is whether the right to information useful in processing grievances is limited by the scope of a particular grievance and by the grievance machinery, or whether a broader right exists under the Act.[581] In *Acme Industrial Co.*[582] the Supreme Court upheld the Board's determination that a section 8(a)(5) violation had occurred when the employer refused to furnish information which would have

---

Prods. Co., 163 NLRB 772, 64 LRRM 1469 (1967), *aff'd*, 422 F2d 1258, 73 LRRM 2670 (CA 9), *cert. denied*, 400 US 839, 75 LRRM 2379 (1970). *See also* NLRB v. Davol, Inc., 597 F2d 782, 101 LRRM 2242 (CA 1, 1979), where the First Circuit enforced a Board order requiring an employer to disclose certain subcontracting information, even though the contract granted the employer an unlimited right to contract-out work, and the union may have been attempting to capture work it had never previously performed. (*Cf.* National Woodwork Mfrs. Ass'n v. NLRB, 386 US 612, 64 LRRM 2801 (1967); Chapter 24, "Section 8(e): The 'Hot-Cargo' Agreement," at notes 100–171). The court reasoned that the information could be relevant to future contract negotiations. *But see* Safeway Stores, 240 NLRB 836, 100 LRRM 1328 (1979), where the Board refused to require the employer to furnish information regarding female supervisors on the ground that the union's role did not extend to policing promotions from out of the unit to management.

[578]Michigan Drywall Corp., 232 NLRB 120, 96 LRRM 1305 (1977), *enforced*, 616 F2d 966, 104 LRRM 2718 (CA 6, 1980). *See also* American Oil Co., 238 NLRB 294, 99 LRRM 1253 (1978), *enforced*, 602 F2d 184, 101 LRRM 2981 (CA 8, 1979); Florida Steel Corp., 235 NLRB 941, 100 LRRM 1187 (1978), *enforced as modified*, 601 F2d 125, 101 LRRM 2671 (CA 4, 1979).

[579]NLRB v. Acme Indus. Co., 385 US 432, 64 LRRM 2069 (1967).

[580]NLRB v. Truitt Mfg. Co., *supra* note 572.

[581]*See* Sinclair Ref. Co. v. NLRB, *supra* note 571, where the Fifth Circuit stated that when a determination of the relevancy of requested information requires "determination of the critical substantive issue of the grievance itself," the Board may not adjudicate the grievance dispute "under the guise of determining relevance" any more than a court could determine the merits of the grievance under the guise of determining its arbitrability. *Id.*, 50 LRRM at 2835. The court went on to hold that since the employer sought earnestly to submit the dispute over relevance of the data to the grievance process, the Board was foreclosed from considering the intrinsic merits of the complaint. *Compare* Sinclair Ref., *supra*, *with* Timken Roller Bearing Co. v. NLRB, 325 F2d 746, 54 LRRM 2785 (CA 6, 1963), where the Sixth Circuit, in upholding the union's right to similar information, relied essentially on the value of the information in the general administration of the contract. *See* Curtiss-Wright Corp. v. NLRB, 347 F2d 61, 59 LRRM 2433 (CA 3, 1965), where the Third Circuit attempted to reconcile the differences between the *Sinclair* and *Timken* cases. *See also* American Oil Co., *supra* note 578; Puerto Rico Tel. Co. v. NLRB, 359 F2d 983, 62 LRRM 2069 (CA 1, 1966). Information requested by the union in both cases might have assisted in disposition of grievances, hence was deemed relevant. *See* Chapter 18, "Accommodation of Board Action to the Arbitration Process," at notes 200–208.

[582]NLRB v. Acme Indus. Co., *supra* note 579.

allowed the union to determine at the outset whether there had been a breach of the collective bargaining agreement. The circuit court had refused to enforce the order on the ground that an arbitration clause foreclosed the Board from exercising its statutory power.[583] In reversing and remanding, the Supreme Court concluded that the Board was not making a binding construction of the labor contract: "It was only acting upon the probability that the desired information was relevant, and that it would be of use to the union in carrying out its statutory duties and responsibilities."[584] The duty to bargain in good faith thus obliges the employer to furnish information enabling the union to make an informed decision about processing grievances.

The employer must also furnish information to the union in order to assist it in properly preparing for arbitration, provided the information is relevant to the grievance scheduled for arbitration.[585] With the information thus supplied, the union can make "an intelligent appraisal of the merits of the member's complaint."[586] It may decide not to take the grievance to arbitration in the first place. In the arbitral processes, however, neither party should be required "to play the game of blind man's bluff."[587] But in the *Square D*[588] case, where the employer was seeking information from the union for use in arbitration, the Board held that there was no statutory obligation on the part of either the employer or the union to turn over to the other "evidence of an undisclosed nature that the possessor of the information believes relevant and conclusive with respect to its rights in an arbitration proceeding."[589]

---

[583]Acme Indus. Co. v. NLRB, 351 F2d 258, 60 LRRM 2220 (CA 7, 1965), *rev'd*, 385 US 432, 64 LRRM 2069 (1967).

[584]*Id.*, 385 US at 437.

[585]Montgomery Ward & Co., 234 NLRB 588, 98 LRRM 1022 (1978); Kroger Co., 226 NLRB 512, 93 LRRM 1315 (1976).

[586]P.R. Mallory & Co., 171 NLRB 457, 68 LRRM 1097, *enforced*, 411 F2d 948, 71 LRRM 2412 (CA 7, 1969).

[587]Fafnir Bearing Co., 146 NLRB 1582, 56 LRRM 1108 (1964), *enforced*, 362 F2d 716, 62 LRRM 2415 (CA 2, 1966). Unions have been allowed to conduct time studies in the employer's plant in connection with the investigation and processing of grievances. General Elec. Co. v. NLRB, 414 F2d 918, 71 LRRM 2562 (CA 4, 1969), *cert. denied*, 396 US 1005 (1970).

[588]Machinists Dist. 10 (Square D Co.), 224 NLRB 111, 92 LRRM 1202 (1976) (employer sought copy of purported company document to which union representative had referred during grievance procedure, but would not identify, boasting that it would prove union's case in arbitration).

[589]*Id.* at 112. *Compare* Transport of N.J., 233 NLRB 694, 97 LRRM 1204 (1977) (employer lawfully withheld witness statements taken during investigation) *with* Square D Elec. Co., 266 NLRB 795, 113 LRRM 1045 (1983) (evidence other than witness statements). *See also* Whirlpool Corp., 281 NLRB 17, 124 LRRM 1138 (1986) (undercover agent not made available until arbitration hearing).

Information requests in the context of plant relocations present special problems. When there is no duty to bargain over a decision to transfer and consolidate operations, an employer does not violate the Act by refusing to furnish information pertinent to that *decision*.[590] However, the relocation of a plant will not relieve an employer of the duty to furnish information relevant to bargaining over the *effects of* that decision.[591] An employer violated the Act when it refused to furnish details and sales contracts concerning the purchase and sale of a facility where the information was necessary for the union to determine which entity was responsible for unfunded pension liability.[592] Similarly, an employer was required to provide the sales contract to the employees' representative in order for the representative to properly ascertain the employees' rights against the buyer and seller of the business entity concerning lifetime employment under the expired collective bargaining agreement.[593]

An appeals court held that a company did not have to supply any information concerning the union's processing of grievances where a bankruptcy court had enjoined the grievances from being processed.[594] And an employer did not violate the Act when it refused a request for financial information made after a contractual wage reopener period had expired. Since the information was requested in connection with a wage proposal that was then moot, the requested information was no longer relevant to the union's bargaining duties.[595] Also, there was no violation in the refusal of an employer to provide information which was requested after expiration of the prehire agree-

---

[590]Dubuque Packing Co., 287 NLRB 499, 130 LRRM 1151 (1987), *remanded sub nom.* Food & Commercial Workers Local 150-A v. NLRB, 880 F2d 349, 132 LRRM 2104 (CADC, 1989); Litton Sys. Microwave Cooking Prods. Div., v. NLRB, 868 F2d 854, 130 LRRM 2773 (CA 6, 1989), *denying enforcement to* 283 NLRB 973, 125 LRRM 1081 (1987); Otis Elevator, subsidiary of United Technologies (Otis Elevator II), 269 NLRB 891, 115 LRRM 1281 (1984), *rev'g* 255 NLRB 235, 106 LRRM 1343 (1981) (Otis Elevator I). [**Editor's Note**: On remand, the Board overruled prior cases and announced new criteria governing bargaining on issues of work relocation. *See* Chapter 16, "Subjects of Bargaining," at note 58.]

[591]Challenge-Cook Bros. of Ohio, 282 NLRB 21, 123 LRRM 1237 (1986), *enforced*, 843 F2d 230, 127 LRRM 3181 (CA 6, 1988).

[592]Super Valu Stores, 279 NLRB 22, 123 LRRM 1136 (1986).

[593]NLRB v. New England Newspapers dba Transcript Newspapers, 856 F2d 409, 129 LRRM 2305 (CA 1, 1988).

[594]NLRB v. Superior Forwarding, 762 F2d 695, 119 LRRM 2619 (CA 8, 1985).

[595]Schaeff Namco, 280 NLRB 1317, 123 LRRM 1058 (1986). *See also* Houston Chapter, Associated Gen. Contractors, NLRB Gen. Counsel Advice Memo., Case No. 23-CA-10049, 128 LRRM 1047 (1988) (employer not obligated to supply any financial information to union to support its claim of inability to pay during negotiations for new prehire contract under §8(f)).

ment.[596] In order for the duty to attach, the union, not an individual employee, must request the information.[597]

D. Information That Must Be Furnished

1. Financial Information. Financial information is relevant to negotiations in which an employer asserts financial inability to meet a union wage demand. As previously noted, the Supreme Court declared in *NLRB v. Truitt Manufacturing Co.*[598] that "[g]ood-faith bargaining necessarily requires that claims made by either party should be honest claims" and that if an inability-to-pay argument "is important enough to present in the give and take of bargaining, it is important enough to require some sort of proof of its accuracy."[599] The Court relied on a series of Board cases holding that if an employer "does no more than take refuge in the assertion" of poor financial condition, refusing either to prove its statement or permit independent verification, "[t]his is not collective bargaining."[600] Even before the *Truitt* decision, the Second Circuit, in *NLRB v. Jacobs Manufacturing Co.*,[601] had attempted to clarify the degree of substantiation required, stating that compliance with the statute does not necessitate that an employer produce proof that its business decision as to what it can afford to do is correct, but only that it produce whatever relevant information it has "to indicate whether it can or cannot afford"[602] to meet union demands.

596E.L. Wagner Co., 294 NLRB No. 38, 131 LRRM 1368 (1989).

597Ohio Medical Prods., NLRB Gen. Counsel Advice Memo., Case No. 30-CA-7635, 113 LRRM 1087 (1983); Spector Red Ball, NLRB Gen. Counsel Advice Memo., Case No. 33-CA-5846, 110 LRRM 1368 (1982).

598351 US 149, 38 LRRM 2042 (1956).

599*Id.* at 152. For a critical analysis of the Supreme Court's "honest claims" rules and its reliance on good-faith terminology in the *Truitt* opinion, see Duvin, *The Duty to Bargain: Law in Search of Policy*, 64 COLUM. L. REV. 248, 282 (1964).

600*Supra* note 598, at 153. *See* McLean-Arkansas Lumber Co., 109 NLRB 1022, 34 LRRM 1496 (1954); Southern Saddlery Co., 90 NLRB 1205, 26 LRRM 1322 (1950); Pioneer Pearl Button Co., 1 NLRB 837, 1 LRRM 26 (1936).

601196 F2d 680, 30 LRRM 2098 (CA 2, 1952). *See also* NLRB v. Southland Cork Co., 342 F2d 702, 58 LRRM 2555 (CA 4, 1965).

602196 F2d at 684. *See also* William J. Burns Int'l Detective Agency, 137 NLRB 1235, 50 LRRM 1367 (1962); Tennessee Chair Co., 126 NLRB 1357, 45 LRRM 1472 (1960); B.L. Montague Co., 116 NLRB 554, 38 LRRM 1289 (1956) (employer must show contracts on which it claims to have lost money). The *Truitt* case has not been limited to claims of inability to pay related to wage demands, since other economic benefits may be as important as wages. Stanley Bldg. Specialties, 166 NLRB 984, 65 LRRM 1684 (1967), *enforced*, 401 F2d 434, 69 LRRM 2196 (CA DC, 1968), *cert. denied*, 395 US 946, 71 LRRM 2426 (1969).

Since the validity of a claim is not at issue until it is actually made, an employer is not obligated to demonstrate that it is unable to raise wages unless it first claims such an inability.[603] The Board, however, with judicial support, has broadened the category of claims that trigger the requirement of substantiation. In *Cincinnati Cordage & Paper Co.*,[604] the Board held that an employer's resistance to a union's wage demand on the ground that it could not remain competitive with comparable employers in the industry constituted a poverty plea. Notwithstanding the contention that the employer was not literally pleading "inability to pay," as in *Truitt*, the Board found *Truitt* applicable "because the employer expressed the view that the wage increases would lead to impoverishment. . . ."[605] Accordingly, the refusal to furnish data showing that it could not stay competitive was held to be unlawful. Similarly, in *Taylor Foundry Co.*[606] the Board equated the employer's contention, that it could not increase its labor costs without losing its profit margin and competitive position, to a plea of inability to pay.

In *NLRB v. Western Wirebound Box Co.*,[607] *Truitt* was extended even further. There the employer resisted wage increases because of price competition but declined a request for supporting data, insisting that it was not claiming an inability to pay, simply that price competition dictated its position. Enforcing an order to supply the data, the Ninth Circuit asserted that *Truitt* is "not confined to cases where the employer's claim is that he is unable to pay the wages demanded by the union."[608] Bargaining, the court reasoned, "is hampered and rendered ineffectual when an employer mechanically repeats his claim but makes no effort to produce substantiating data."[609]

---

[603]Pine Indus. Relations Comm., 118 NLRB 1055, 40 LRRM 1315 (1957), *enforced sub nom.* Woodworkers Locals 6-7 & 6-22, 263 F2d 483, 43 LRRM 2462 (CADC, 1959). *See also* Printing Pressmen Local 51 (New York) v. NLRB (Milbin Printing), 538 F2d 496, 92 LRRM 3207 (CA 2, 1976).

[604]141 NLRB 72, 52 LRRM 1277 (1963). For a forerunner of this decision, see U.S. Steel Corp., Tennessee Coal & Iron Div., 122 NLRB 1519, 43 LRRM 1325 (1959).

[605]141 NLRB at 77.

[606]141 NLRB 765, 52 LRRM 1407 (1963), *enforced*, 338 F2d 1003, 57 LRRM 2560 (CA 5, 1964). *See also* Goodyear Aerospace Corp., 204 NLRB 831, 83 LRRM 1461 (1973), *enforcement denied*, 497 F2d 747, 86 LRRM 2763 (CA 6, 1974); Stockton Dist. Kidney Bean Growers, 165 NLRB 223, 65 LRRM 1300 (1967) (employer denial of access to books after saying it was in "no mood" to increase costs is tantamount to pleading inability to pay).

[607]356 F2d 88, 61 LRRM 2218 (CA 9, 1966), *enforcing* 145 NLRB 1539, 55 LRRM 1193 (1964).

[608]*Id.* at 90.

[609]*Id.* at 91. *See also* NLRB v. Celotex Corp., 364 F2d 552, 62 LRRM 2475 (CA 5, 1966) (the opinion is cast in terms of whether information was "plainly irrelevant").

The Board has also held that a multiplant employer who deals with separate locals at each plant location and pleads inability to meet the union's wage demands must furnish specific information concerning profitability at each plant if so requested by the union.[610] The employer does not satisfy its section 8(a)(5) obligations by merely furnishing information concerning its lack of overall corporate profitability.[611] However, a union is not entitled to financial information for the purpose of harassing the employer, with the possible result of jeopardizing its financial position further.[612]

2. Other Information. The Board has consistently upheld the right of a union to obtain information that it needs to bargain intelligently and "to service and police the contract."[613] Since wage information is often critical to the union in fulfilling both obligations, and since employers commonly regard such information as confidential in nature, many cases have involved employer refusals to provide wage information.[614] "[A] union's right to such information cannot be seriously challenged"[615]—a

---

[610]Teleprompter Corp. v. NLRB, 570 F2d 4, 97 LRRM 2455 (CA 1, 1977).

[611]*Id. But see* Fruit & Vegetable Packers Local 760 v. NLRB (Yakima Frozen Foods), 316 F2d 389, 52 LRRM 2537 (CADC, 1963) (employer may attach reasonable conditions to furnishing of financial information in its own business interest); Braswell Motor Freight Lines, 141 NLRB 1154, 52 LRRM 1467 (1963), *enforced sub nom.* Teamsters Local 745 v. NLRB, 370 F2d 226, 63 LRRM 2288 (CADC, 1966) (employer need not furnish financial information on entire corporate chain controlled by owners of unit in question).

[612]NLRB v. Abbott Publishing Co., 331 F2d 209, 55 LRRM 2994 (CA 7, 1964). *But see* Metlox Mfg. Co., 153 NLRB 1388, 59 LRRM 1657 (1965), *enforced*, 378 F2d 728, 65 LRRM 2637 (CA 9, 1967), *cert. denied*, 389 US 1037, 67 LRRM 2231 (1968), holding that an employer's claimed inability to meet a union's pay demands gave the union a right to look at the salaries being paid management officials. When the employer asserted that it could not grant the union's request for wage increases or other economic benefits because of its financial plight, the union suggested that the trouble might be due to a deliberate bleeding of the assets by officers and/or controlling stockholders. The employer offered to permit an examination of its books by a certified public accountant (CPA) at the expense of the union. The CPA, however, could advise the union only as to whether the employer's profit-and-loss statements were true. The court agreed with the NLRB that the profit-and-loss statements did not disclose sufficient information for the union to make a fair estimate of the employer's financial inability to pay. An order requiring redress of wrongs suffered by employees who struck over the denial of information was enforced by the court.

[613]Viewlex, Inc., 204 NLRB 1080, 1080, 83 LRRM 1634 (1973). *See also* Conrock Co., 263 NLRB 1293, 111 LRRM 1271 (1982), *enforced*, 635 F2d 1371, 118 LRRM 2968 (CA 9, 1984); Hiney Printing Co., 262 NLRB 157, 110 LRRM 1255 (1982), *enforced*, 733 F2d 1170, 116 LRRM 2404 (CA 6, 1984).

[614]Korn Indus. v. NLRB, 389 F2d 117, 67 LRRM 2148 (CA 4, 1967), *clarified*, 67 LRRM 2976 (CA 4, 1968); NLRB v. John S. Swift Co., 277 F2d 641, 46 LRRM 2090 (CA 7, 1960); NLRB v. Boston Herald-Traveler Corp., 210 F2d 134, 33 LRRM 2435 (CA 1, 1954); NLRB v. Yawman & Erbe Mfg. Co., 187 F2d 947, 27 LRRM 2524 (CA 2, 1951); West Side Transfer, 162 NLRB 699, 64 LRRM 1098 (1967).

[615]Woodworkers Locals 6-7 & 6-22 v. NLRB (Pine Indus. Relations Comm.), 263 F2d 483, 484, 43 LRRM 2462 (CADC, 1959).

conclusion which was given impetus in *NLRB v. F. W. Woolworth Co.*,[616] in which the Supreme Court reversed, without argument or opinion, the Ninth Circuit's refusal to enforce a Board order requiring production of wage information. This right to information on wages, based on the requirement of section 8(d) that collective bargaining take place with respect to "wages, hours, and other terms and conditions of employment," extends to wages paid particular employees, groups of employees, and methods of computing compensation.[617] The outer limits of a union's right to wage information are difficult to determine because of the presumption of relevance applied to such information. Even disclosure of information regarding compensation of employees outside the bargaining unit has been required with increasing liberality,[618] as has information on wage rates paid at other plants maintained by the employer.[619] In certain instances, an employer may even be required to divulge information on wage rates paid by its competitors.[620]

Items of information related to "hours, and other terms and conditions of employment" have been ordered disclosed on the same basis as wage information. Insurance and pension plan information must be furnished, including the employer's insurance plan cost information and employee benefits there-

---

[616]352 US 938, 39 LRRM 2151 (1956), *rev'g* 235 F2d 319, 38 LRRM 2362 (CA 9, 1956).

[617]Puerto Rico Tel. Co. v. NLRB, 359 F2d 983, 62 LRRM 2069 (CA 1, 1966); Curtiss-Wright Corp. v. NLRB, 347 F2d 61, 59 LRRM 2433 (CA 3, 1965); Anaconda Am. Brass Co., 148 NLRB 474, 57 LRRM 1001 (1964).

[618]*See* discussion *supra* at notes 499–514. *See also* Goodyear Aerospace Corp. v. NLRB, 388 F2d 673, 67 LRRM 2447 (CA 6, 1968); Curtiss-Wright Corp. v. NLRB, *supra* note 617; Skyland Hosiery Mills, 108 NLRB 1600, 34 LRRM 1254 (1954); California Portland Cement Co., 103 NLRB 1375, 31 LRRM 1630 (1953). *But see* Fetzer Television v. NLRB, 317 F2d 420, 53 LRRM 2224 (CA 6, 1963); NLRB v. Leland-Gifford Co., 200 F2d 620, 31 LRRM 2196 (CA 1, 1952).

[619]Hollywood Brands, 142 NLRB 304, 53 LRRM 1012 (1963), *enforced*, 324 F2d 956, 54 LRRM 2780 (CA 5, 1963), *cert. denied*, 377 US 923, 56 LRRM 2095 (1964).

[620]General Elec. Co. v. NLRB, 466 F2d 1177, 81 LRRM 2303 (CA 6, 1972), *enforcing* 192 NLRB 68, 77 LRRM 1561 (1971). Here the Sixth Circuit enforced a series of Board orders requiring the company to provide the union with correlated wage data the company had obtained from area wage surveys taken at four of its plant locations. The company agreed generally to furnish the union with the results of the surveys, but refused to correlate the wage data with the names of the employers supplying it, arguing that it had obtained the data under assurances of confidentiality, and that employers would no longer supply it with data if it had to provide the correlated information to the union. The court held that the information requested was relevant because without it the union could not meaningfully analyze and discuss the results of the company's surveys. *But cf.* Westinghouse Elec. Supply Co. v. NLRB, 196 F2d 1012, 30 LRRM 2169 (CA 3, 1952) (employer not required to turn over wage-survey chart where union had merely requested proof of company's contention that its salary structure compared favorably with its competitors).

under.[621] Because the union might desire to forgo such insurance in favor of increased take-home pay, information about the cost of an insurance plan is considered "necessary to effective negotiation."[622] The Board and the courts also have uniformly required disclosure of the details of a profit-sharing plan,[623] information on employee job classifications and how they are determined,[624] information about employee status and job changes,[625] time-study material, and information used in setting wage rates or incentives.[626]

---

[621]NLRB v. Borden, Inc., Borden Chem. Div., 600 F2d 313, 101 LRRM 2727 (CA 1, 1979) (employer required to furnish union insurance cost figures on per employee, per hour basis); NLRB v. Feed & Supply Center, 294 F2d 650, 48 LRRM 2993 (CA 9, 1961); NLRB v. John S. Swift Co., *supra* note 614 (health and welfare plan); Ironton Publications, 294 NLRB No. 73, 131 LRRM 1426 (1989) (subsidiary required to provide information on parent's profit-sharing plan that it adopted); O. Voorhees Painting Co., 275 NLRB 779, 119 LRRM 1228 (1985); Accurate Web, 266 NLRB 487, 112 LRRM 1337 (1983), *enforced*, 818 F2d 273, 125 LRRM 2358 (CA 2, 1987); Bakery, Inc., 259 NLRB 766, 109 LRRM 1025 (1981); Crane Co., 244 NLRB 103, 102 LRRM 1351 (1979) (pension coverage information); Industrial Welding Co., 175 NLRB 477, 71 LRRM 1076 (1969); Skyland Hosiery Mills, *supra* note 618 (insurance coverage and portions of premiums paid by employers and employees). *See also* NLRB v. United Technologies Corp., Pratt & Whitney Aircraft Div., 789 F2d 121, 122 LRRM 2250 (CA 2, 1986) (attitude surveys).

[622]Sylvania Elec. Prods. v. NLRB, 358 F2d 591, 61 LRRM 2657 (CA 1), *cert. denied*, 385 US 852, 63 LRRM 2236 (1966); Cone Mills Corp., 169 NLRB 449, 67 LRRM 1241 (1968), *enforced in part and denied in part*, 413 F2d 445, 71 LRRM 2916 (CA 4, 1969). In Sylvania Elec. Prods. v. NLRB, 291 F2d 128, 48 LRRM 2313 (CA 1), *cert. denied*, 368 US 926, 49 LRRM 2173 (1961), the First Circuit held that the employer's cost in a noncontributory group insurance program was neither wages nor conditions of employment and that refusal to furnish cost information did not constitute a refusal to bargain, since no issue of costs arose during negotiations that would bear on the company's willingness to consider any proposal the union might make with respect to changes in the plan. The Board disagreed with the court's distinction between "costs" and "benefits" in Electric Furnace Co., 137 NLRB 1077, 50 LRRM 1322 (1962), *enforcement denied*, 327 F2d 373, 55 LRRM 2398 (CA 6, 1964), and General Elec. Co., 150 NLRB 192, 57 LRRM 1491 (1964), *enforced*, 418 F2d 736, 72 LRRM 2530 (CA 2, 1969), *cert. denied*, 397 US 965, 73 LRRM 2600 (1970). In 1965 the Board again found Sylvania had bargained in bad faith in failing to supply the requested information, 154 NLRB 1756, 60 LRRM 1178 (1965), but this time the First Circuit enforced the Board's order, 358 F2d 591, 61 LRRM 2657 (CA 1, 1966). Although holding to its 1961 opinion, the court ruled that, since the company had proposed changes in the plan, the union had a right to cost information so that it could weigh the company offer against an equivalent increase in take-home pay.

[623]NLRB v. Toffenetti Restaurant Co., 311 F2d 219, 51 LRRM 2601 (CA 2, 1962).

[624]Lock Joint Pipe Co., 141 NLRB 943, 52 LRRM 1410 (1963); American Sugar Ref. Co., 130 NLRB 634, 47 LRRM 1361 (1961); Stanislaus Implement & Hardware Co., 101 NLRB 394, 31 LRRM 1079 (1952).

[625]NLRB v. John S. Swift Co., *supra* note 614; NLRB v. New Britain Mach. Co., 210 F2d 61, 33 LRRM 2461 (CA 2, 1954); Keller Indus., 170 NLRB 1715, 69 LRRM 1078 (1968). *But see* Pacific Tel. & Tel. Co., 246 NLRB 327, 102 LRRM 1543 (1980), where the employer was not required to disclose transfer information.

[626]In Fafnir Bearing Co., 146 NLRB 1582, 56 LRRM 1108 (1964), *enforced*, 362 F2d 716, 62 LRRM 2415 (CA 2, 1966), the employer violated the Act by failing to permit the union to enter the company's production facilities for the purpose of conducting time studies. *See also* Timken Roller Bearing Co. v. NLRB, 325 F2d 746, 54 LRRM 2785 (CA 6, 1963); Emeryville Research Center, 174 NLRB 114, 70 LRRM 1099 (1969), *enforcement denied*, 441

Other types of information that the Board has ordered an employer to disclose include seniority lists and data,[627] employees' ages,[628] equipment types and specifications,[629] names and addresses of customers,[630] information about vending machines and cafeteria catering services,[631] names and addresses of unit employees,[632] names and addresses of successful and unsuccessful job applicants,[633] information relating to benefits received by retirees under the employer's pension and insurance

---

F2d 880, 77 LRRM 2043 (CA 9, 1971); Johns-Manville Prods., 171 NLRB 451, 69 LRRM 1068 (1968); Wilson Athletic Goods Mfg. Co., 169 NLRB 621, 67 LRRM 1193 (1968). *But see* General Aniline & Film Corp., 124 NLRB 1217, 44 LRRM 1617 (1959) (such information must have been used in wage rates, not just for employer cost-determination purpose, in order that employer be required to furnish it).

[627]NLRB v. Gulf Atl. Warehouse Co., 291 F2d 475, 48 LRRM 2376 (CA 5, 1961); Staff Builders Servs., 289 NLRB 373, 130 LRRM 1178 (1988), *enforced*, 879 F2d 1484, 131 LRRM 3067 (CA 7, 1989); Phoenix Co., 274 NLRB 995, 118 LRRM 1456 (1985); Van Dorn Plastic Mach. Co., 265 NLRB 864, 112 LRRM 1408 (1982), *modified on other grounds*, 736 F2d 343, 116 LRRM 2647 (CA 6, 1984), *cert. denied*, 469 US 1208, 118 LRRM 2576 (1985); Crane Co., *supra* note 621; Post Publishing Co., 102 NLRB 648, 31 LRRM 1336 (1953). See Oliver Corp., 162 NLRB 813, 64 LRRM 1092 (1967), where a union's request for information about the length of employment and the reasons for the discharge of employees during their probationary period was held relevant to future contract negotiations. An employee was discharged during his probationary period and the employer refused to tell the union the reason for the termination. The union then asked the employer for data on all employees discharged during their probationary period over a 2-year span. The employer denied that the information was relevant or necessary to prepare for bargaining. The Board held that withholding these data would significantly impair the union's ability to engage in meaningful bargaining concerning the terms and conditions of employment of probationary employees. In Standard Oil Co. of Cal. v. NLRB, 399 F2d 639, 69 LRRM 2014 (CA 9, 1968), the employer was required to supply the union with a mailing list of names and home addresses of all employees in the bargaining unit after the employer had mailed literature to the employees in support of its bargaining position. In Prudential Ins. Co. v. NLRB, 412 F2d 77, 71 LRRM 2254 (CA 2, 1969), the employer was required to supply names and addresses of employees in a nationwide bargaining unit, which the union contended it needed to communicate regarding contract benefits and policing the agreement.

[628]Reed & Prince Mfg. Co., 96 NLRB 850, 28 LRRM 1608 (1951), *enforced*, 205 F2d 131, 32 LRRM 2225 (CA 1, 1953).

[629]Oregon Coast Operators Ass'n, 113 NLRB 1338, 36 LRRM 1448 (1955), *enforced*, 246 F2d 280, 40 LRRM 2312 (CA 9, 1957).

[630]Custom Excavating, 228 NLRB 285, 94 LRRM 1415 (1977), *enforced*, 575 F2d 102, 98 LRRM 2259 (CA 7, 1978) (the Board found that risk of harm to customer relations resulting from union contact was outweighed by union's need to ascertain employer's compliance with terms of collective bargaining agreement and with applicable laws).

[631]*See, e.g.*, B.F. Goodrich Co., 221 NLRB 288, 90 LRRM 1595 (1975) (company violated §8(a)(5) by refusing to furnish information concerning financial arrangements with cafeteria-catering service where company had duty to bargain over subcontracting of its in-plant cafeteria service. *Cf.* Ford Motor Co. v. NLRB, 441 US 488, 101 LRRM 2222 (1979); Chapter 16, "Subjects of Bargaining," at notes 40–46 and 155–160. *But see* NLRB v. Package Mach. Co., 457 F2d 936, 79 LRRM 2948 (CA 1, 1972), *denying enforcement to* 191 NLRB 268, 77 LRRM 1456 (1971).

[632]Summer Home for the Aged, 226 NLRB 976, 93 LRRM 1489 (1976), *enforcement granted in part, denied in part and remanded*, 599 F2d 762, 101 LRRM 2494 (CA 6, 1979); Autoprod, Inc., 223 NLRB 773, 92 LRRM 1076 (1976); Viewlex, Inc., *supra* note 613.

[633]Southwestern Bell Tel., 247 NLRB 171, 103 LRRM 1127 (1980).

plans,[634] information relating to employee grievances,[635] and information pertaining to possible loss of work through a proposed leasing arrangement[636] or a layoff.[637]

The Board also has determined that unions are entitled to certain information in the event of a strike. Specifically, the employer must provide the names and addresses of strike replacements and update the list;[638] it must supply wage information for nonstrikers and replacements,[639] including bonuses,[640] as well as information regarding striker reinstatement and placement on a preferential hiring list.[641] The Board also has indicated that an employer must furnish to the union the names of striking employees who, according to the employer, have forfeited reinstatement rights by misconduct during the strike.[642] Employers also have been required to furnish strike-related subcontracting information, including actual copies of contracts,[643] as well as information showing the total number of subcontracting man-hours involved.[644] However, the Board has held that an employer did not violate the Act by refusing to provide the union with a list of employees who crossed a picket line to work during a strike, where the sole

---

[634]Union Carbide Corp., 197 NLRB 717, 80 LRRM 1429 (1972), *supplementing* 187 NLRB 113, 75 LRRM 1548 (1970).

[635]ACF Indus., 231 NLRB 83, 96 LRRM 1291 (1977), *enforced*, 592 F2d 122, 100 LRRM 2710 (CA 8, 1979). There the Board held that an employer which obtained an analysis of an employee's handwriting in order to substantiate its decision to discharge the employee for falsifying sickness and accident claims had violated the Act by refusing to furnish the analysis to the union that was processing the employee's grievance. The union's right to the information was not defeated merely because it might have acquired similar information by independent investigation. *See* discussion *supra* at notes 585–589.

[636]Yellow Cab Co., 229 NLRB 1369, 95 LRRM 1249 (1977), *enforced in part and denied in part*, 603 F2d 862, 99 LRRM 2903 (CADC, 1978), *petition for reh'g denied*, 101 LRRM 2628 (CADC, 1979).

[637]NLRB v. Production Molded Plastics, 604 F2d 451, 102 LRRM 2040 (CA 6, 1979); Florida Steel Corp. v. NLRB, 601 F2d 125, 101 LRRM 2671 (CA 4, 1979).

[638]Georgetown Assocs., 235 NLRB 485, 98 LRRM 1162 (1978).

[639]Soule Glass & Glazing Co., 246 NLRB 792, 102 LRRM 1693 (1979), *enforcement granted in part and denied in part*, 652 F2d 1055, 107 LRRM 2781 (CA 1, 1981).

[640]Rubatex Corp., 235 NLRB 833, 97 LRRM 1534 (1978), *enforced*, 601 F2d 147, 101 LRRM 2660 (CA 4, 1979). *But see* Crane Co., *supra* note 621, where an employer was not required to disclose whether it intended to continue payment of benefits during a strike.

[641]Southern Fla. Hotel & Motel Ass'n, 245 NLRB 561, 102 LRRM 1578 (1979); Florida Steel Corp., 242 NLRB 1333, 101 LRRM 1370 (1979); Ohio Power Co., 216 NLRB 987, 88 LRRM 1646 (1975), *enforced*, 531 F2d 1381, 92 LRRM 3049 (CA 6, 1979). *See also* Markle Mfg. Co., 239 NLRB 1142, 100 LRRM 1125 (1979).

[642]*Cf.* Food Serv. Co., 202 NLRB 790, 82 LRRM 1746 (1973).

[643]Wallace Metal Prods., 244 NLRB 41, 102 LRRM 1233 (1979).

[644]ACF Indus., Amcar Div. v. NLRB, 596 F2d 1344, 100 LRRM 3074 (CA 8, 1979). *See also* Markle Mfg. Co., *supra* note 642.

reason for the request was to enable the union to discipline members who worked.[645]

The Board has held that employers must disclose certain equal employment opportunity data. Thus, in *Westinghouse Electric Corp.*,[646] the Board ruled that the employer must furnish the following information on unit employees (but not on nonunit employees): (1) statistical data on minority-group and female employees, and (2) charges and complaints filed by employees against the employer under federal and state fair employment practice laws. Such information with respect to unit employees was "presumptively relevant"; whereas, with respect to nonunit employees, the union "must ordinarily demonstrate more precisely the relevance of the data requested."[647] But the Board failed to find an employer's affirmative action plans presumptively relevant and held that copies did not have to be produced for the union unless it demonstrated relevance.[648] In *East Dayton Tool & Die Co.*[649] the employer was required to furnish data as to race and sex of job applicants, but not "subjective" reasons for not hiring more minorities and women. In both cases the Board relied upon nondiscrimination clauses contained in the collective bargaining contract.[650]

A union was entitled to a roster of association members who had once been signatories to the master agreement, but not to the names of the members who had never been bound by the master agreement.[651] When an employer claimed that the state effectively controlled its labor policies, the union was entitled to access to the employer's state contracts and other information.[652] Likewise, an employer was obligated to provide an expurgated payroll record where the state labor code did not specifically prevent disclosure of such information to an employee's authorized collective bargaining representative.[653]

---

[645]Nordstrom, Inc., 229 NLRB 601, 96 LRRM 1092 (1977).

[646]239 NLRB 106, 99 LRRM 1482 (1978), *modified and enforced sub nom.* Electrical Workers (IUE) v. NLRB, 648 F2d 18, 105 LRRM 3337 (CADC, 1980) *and* 107 LRRM 2734 (CADC, 1981). *Accord* New York Post Corp., 283 NLRB 430, 124 LRRM 1377 (1987).

[647]239 NLRB at 110.

[648]Bendix Corp., 242 NRLB 1005, 101 LRRM 1459 (1979); Kentile Floors, 242 NLRB 755, 101 LRRM 1236 (1979).

[649]239 NLRB 141, 99 LRRM 1490 (1978).

[650]*Id.* at 150.

[651]Southern Nev. Home Builders Ass'n, 274 NLRB 350, 118 LRRM 1368 (1985).

[652]Community Living, 285 NLRB 312, 128 LRRM 1167 (1987).

[653]A-Plus Roofing, 295 NLRB No. 101, 132 LRRM 1112 (1989).

Although decisions involving employer requests for information controlled by unions are not plentiful, the decided cases disclose that employers may obtain hiring hall and manning information,[654] information pertinent to union pension and welfare plans,[655] collective bargaining agreements with other employers,[656] and a list of employees on a union out-of-work list.[657]

V. ECONOMIC PRESSURE DURING BARGAINING[658]

The Supreme Court's 1960 decision in *NLRB v. Insurance Agents (Prudential Ins. Co.)*[659] affirmed the principle that economic power goes hand in hand with "reasoned discussion" in determining the outcome of collective bargaining negotiations. The Court held that the Board cannot find a lack of good-faith bargaining by a party solely because tactics designed to exert economic pressure were employed during bargaining. To exert such pressure during the period of bargaining, union members refused to solicit new business, held half-day walkouts, and refused to perform a variety of ordinary duties. The Board found such action to be a per se violation of section 8(b)(3) despite the union's desire to reach an agreement, but the District of Columbia Circuit denied enforcement.[660] The Supreme

---

[654]Printing & Graphic Communications Local 13 (Detroit) (Oakland Press Co.), 233 NLRB 994, 97 LRRM 1047 (1977), *aff'd*, 598 F2d 267, 101 LRRM 2036 (CADC, 1979).

[655]Hospital & Health Care Employees Dist. 1199E (Sinai Hosp. of Balt.), 248 NLRB 631, 103 LRRM 1459 (1980); Teamsters Local 959 (Frontier Transp. Co.), 244 NLRB 19, 102 LRRM 1117 (1979).

[656]Hotel Employees Local 355 (Doral Beach Hotel), 245 NLRB 774, 102 LRRM 1410 (1979).

[657]Asbestos Workers Local 80 (West Virginia Master Insulators Ass'n), 248 NLRB 143, 103 LRRM 1370 (1980).

[658]*See generally* Carroll, *Economic Pressure in Collective Bargaining; Lockout and Permanent Replacements in the Fifth Circuit*, 10 ST. MARY'S L.J. 179 (1978); Bernhardt, *Lockouts: An Analysis of Board and Court Decisions Since* Brown *and* American Ships, 57 CORNELL L. REV. 211 (1972); Pollock, *Bargaining Lockout Prior to an Impasse in Negotiations Is Not a Violation of Sections 8(a)(1) or 8(1)(3)*, 44 NOTRE DAME LAW. 270 (1968); Note, *The Offensive Bargaining Lockout*, 52 VA. L. REV. 464 (1966); Comment, *Use of Lockout to Strengthen Bargaining Position Legal After Impasse Has Been Reached*, 30 ALB. L. REV. 173 (1966).

[659]361 US 477, 45 LRRM 2704 (1960).

[660]Insurance Agents v. NLRB (Prudential Ins. Co.), 260 F2d 736, 43 LRRM 2003 (CADC, 1958). This same issue had reached the District of Columbia Circuit on two prior occasions in the mid-1950s. Mine Workers (Boone County Coal Corp.) v. NLRB, 257 F2d 211, 42 LRRM 2264 (CADC, 1958); Textile Workers Local 1172 (Personal Prods.) v. NLRB, 227 F2d 409, 36 LRRM 2778 (CADC, 1955). Refusing enforcement in both instances, the court found no violation of §8(b)(3) despite harassing tactics, and took the view that Congress had not limited the use of such economic pressure in support of lawful demands.

Court, affirming, recognized that such economic activity may be unprotected by the Act, but held that the use of such pressure is not in and of itself inconsistent with the duty to bargain in good faith. The Court rendered a classic description of the American collective bargaining process:

> [C]ollective bargaining, under a system where the Government does not attempt to control the results of negotiations, cannot be equated with an academic collective search for truth . . . . The parties—even granting the modification of views that may come from a realization of economic interdependence—still proceed from contrary, and to an extent antagonistic viewpoints and concepts of self-interest. The system has not reached the ideal of the philosophic notion that perfect understanding among people would lead to perfect agreement among them on values. The presence of economic weapons in reserve, and their actual exercise on occasion by the parties is part and parcel of the system . . . . [T]he truth of the matter is . . . the two factors—necessity for good-faith bargaining between parties, and the availability of economic pressure devices to each to make the other party incline to agree on one's terms—exist side by side.[661]

Overt[662] economic activity by employers during bargaining has primarily involved the use of a lockout.[663] Prior to 1965 this tactic was permitted only in limited defensive situations.[664] In 1957, for example, the Supreme Court upheld the right of members of a multi-employer bargaining unit to lock out employees in an effort to counter a union's use of a "whipsaw" strike against one of the members of the employer group.[665] In 1965, however, the Court in *American Ship Building Co. v. NLRB*[666] decided that an offensive lockout by an employer did not violate sections 8(a)(1) or 8(a)(3). The Court held that a single employer, after a bargaining impasse has been reached, may temporarily shut down its plant "for the sole purpose of

---

[661]361 US at 488–89, 45 LRRM at 2708–9.

[662]The most common form of employer economic pressure is, of course, a passive response—merely refusing to give in to threatened or actual strike pressure, thus forcing or prolonging the economic consequences of impasse or strike upon the employees.

[663]For detailed treatment of lockouts, see Chapter 20, "The Lockout."

[664]*See, e.g.*, Betts Cadillac Olds, 96 NLRB 268, 28 LRRM 1509 (1951); International Shoe Co., 93 NLRB 907, 27 LRRM 1504 (1951); Duluth Bottling Ass'n, 48 NLRB 1335, 12 LRRM 151 (1943); Link-Belt Co., 26 NLRB 227, 6 LRRM 565 (1940). *See* Comment, 37 N.Y.U. L. REV. 1152 (1962).

[665]NLRB v. Teamsters Local 449 (Buffalo Linen Supply Co.), 353 US 87, 39 LRRM 2603 (1957). *See also* Herold, *Multiemployer Bargaining and the Whipsaw Strike: The Use of a Lockout as an Economic Weapon*, 21 BROOKLYN BARRISTER 54 (1969); Comment, 48 VA. L. REV. 1313 (1962).

[666]380 US 300, 58 LRRM 2672 (1965). *See* Chapter 20, "The Lockout," at notes 27 and 58–89.

bringing economic pressure to bear in support of [its] legitimate bargaining position."[667] Since *American Ship Building*, the Board and the courts have adopted a tolerant view of lockouts, so long as they are not motivated by union animus.[668]

Because of the unilateral changes involved in a lockout, a question arises as to whether an impasse in bargaining must be reached as a prerequisite to a lockout conducted by a single employer. In *Darling & Co.*[669] the Board upheld a pre-impasse lockout, and was affirmed by the Court of Appeals for the District of Columbia Circuit,[670] on the basis of several factual considerations, including (1) the absence of an antiunion motive, (2) the large number of negotiating sessions occurring both before and after the lockout (there was no allegation of bad-faith bargaining), (3) the relative strength of the union, (4) the many concessions that the employer had made during negotiations, (5) the possibility of the union calling a strike at a time of its own choosing, (6) the highly seasonal nature of the employer's business, and (7) the unusual harm that would have resulted from a strike. In later decisions, the Board has allowed pre-impasse lockouts when no union animus exists and the employer is acting in support of its bargaining position.[671]

One circuit court of appeals upheld an employer's lockout of its employees upon the expiration of a collective bargaining

---

[667]380 US at 318.

[668]*See, e.g.*, Teamsters Local 372 (Detroit Newspaper Publishers Ass'n) v. NLRB, 404 F2d 1159, 70 LRRM 2061 (CA 6, 1968), *aff'g* 166 NLRB 219, 65 LRRM 1425 (1967), where an employer's lockout to support the bargaining position of another struck employer was permitted on the ground that any concessions on important issues granted by the struck employer could have impact on the nonstruck employer's ability to maintain its own bargaining position. *See also* NLRB v. Martin A. Gleason, Inc., 534 F2d 466, 91 LRRM 2682 (CA 2, 1976) (employer that lawfully locks out its employees during "whipsaw" strike may state in response to employee inquiries that they could not return to their jobs as members of union engaging in whipsaw strike, so long as this was not accompanied by any solicitation or encouragement to resign from union); Publishers Ass'n of New York City v. NLRB, 364 F2d 293, 62 LRRM 2722 (CA 2, 1966) (even where union withdraws from multi-employer unit, lockout can be utilized); Body & Tank Corp. v. NLRB, 344 F2d 330, 59 LRRM 2123 (CA 2, 1965); Acme Mkts., 156 NLRB 1452, 61 LRRM 1281 (1966) (allowing lockout in stores not in unit); Weyerhaeuser Co., 155 NLRB 921, 60 LRRM 1425 (1965) (employers do not have to be recognized as multi-employer unit). For a more detailed treatment of the subject of lockouts, see Chapter 20, "The Lockout."

[669]171 NLRB 801, 68 LRRM 1133 (1968). *See also* Comment, 44 Notre Dame Law. 270 (1968).

[670]Lane v. NLRB, 418 F2d 1208, 72 LRRM 2439 (CADC, 1969).

[671]Harter Equip. Co., 280 NLRB 597, 122 LRRM 1219 (1986), *aff'd sub nom.* Operating Eng'rs Local 825 v. NLRB, 829 F2d 458, 126 LRRM 2337 (CA 3, 1987). *See also* Evening News Ass'n, 166 NLRB 219, 221, 65 LRRM 1425 (1967), *aff'd*, 404 F2d 1159, 70 LRRM 2061 (CA 6, 1968), where the Board stated that *American Ship Bldg., supra* note 666, "obliterated, as a matter of law, the line previously drawn by the Board between offensive and defensive lockouts." *See* Chapter 20, "The Lockout."

agreement and of the 60-day notice period under section 8(d)(1) but within the 30-day notice period provided by section 8(d)(3).[672] Since the union had initiated the section 8(d)(1) notice, it was the union's responsibility to provide timely notice to the mediation services. The employer fulfilled its statutory obligations by bargaining in good faith and was free to resort to economic pressure in support of its position once the contract had expired.

A substantial amount of litigation arose in the 1970s over whether an employer who uses an offensive lockout as an economic weapon during bargaining may utilize replacements for locked-out employees.

In *NLRB v. Brown,*[673] decided the same day as *American Ship Building,*[674] the Court held that members of a multi-employer bargaining unit which locked out their employees in response to a "whipsaw" strike could lawfully operate with temporary replacements. The Court, however, left open the questions of whether an employer who uses the lockout as an offensive bargaining weapon may utilize temporary replacements. In 1986, in *Harter Equipment Co.,*[675] the Board held that temporary replacements may be so utilized without violation of section 8(a)(3).

Previously, in its *Inland Trucking Co.*[676] decision, the Board found that the employer violated the Act by hiring and using temporary replacements during a lockout. In so holding, the Board adopted, without comment, the trial examiner's findings that the employer's actions had had some adverse impact on employee rights and that the employer failed to meet its burden of proving that the lockout and use of temporaries served a sufficiently legitimate objective. Later, in its *Ottawa Silica Co.*[677]

---

[672]Hooker Chems. & Plastics Corp. v. NLRB, 573 F2d 965, 97 LRRM 3194 (CA 7, 1978); NLRB v. Painting & Decorating Contractors, Peoria Chapter, 500 F2d 54, 86 LRRM 2914 (CA 7, 1974). *See also* Adamson, *The Lockout Loophole*, 24 EMORY L.J. 495 (1975). For a fuller discussion of notice requirements under §8(d), see *infra* at notes 874–909.

[673]380 US 278, 58 LRRM 2663 (1965). As in American Ship Bldg. Co. v. NLRB, *supra* note 666, the Court noted the absence of union animus in the employer's actions. *See also* Musa, *Lockouts and Replacements in Bargaining—Management on the Offensive*, 9 LOY. L.A.L. REV. 67 (1975); Forkosch, *Bargaining and Economic Pressure—The New Trilogy*, 16 LAB. L.J. 323 (1965); Note, *The Offensive Bargaining Lockout*, 52 VA. L. REV. 464 (1966). See discussion in Chapter 6, "Interference With Protected Rights," at notes 18–30, on motive as an element of a §8(a)(1) violation.

[674]*Supra* note 666.

[675]*Supra* note 671.

[676]179 NLRB 350, 72 LRRM 1486 (1969), *enforced*, 440 F2d 562, 76 LRRM 2929 (CA 7), *cert. denied*, 404 US 858, 78 LRRM 2465 (1971).

[677]197 NLRB 449, 80 LRRM 1404 (1972).

decision, the Board limited *Inland Trucking* and found no violation in the offensive use of a lockout coupled with the hiring of temporary replacements where there was no union animus and strong business reasons supported the action.[678] In *Harter,* a majority of the Board expressly adopted the firm rule of the *Ottawa Silica* plurality opinion and held, regardless of business justification, that "absent specific proof of antiunion motivation, an employer does not violate Sections 8(a)(3) and (1) by hiring temporary replacements in order to engage in business operations during an otherwise lawful lockout."[679] The ruling has been reaffirmed in subsequent cases.[680]

A lockout over a *nonmandatory* subject of bargaining violates the Act, and the Board has held that "a lockout unlawful at its inception retains its initial taint of illegality until it is terminated and the affected employees are made whole."[681] Thus, an employer association violated sections 8(a)(3) and (5) when it locked out the employees during contract negotiations, where one object of the lockout was to compel the union to submit the employer's offer to ratification by a mail ballot. The retraction of this demand on the second day of the lockout did not remove the taint of illegality.[682]

In *Johns-Manville Products Corp.*[683] the Board held that an employer violated the Act by unilaterally hiring *permanent* replacements for locked-out employees "without consulting or notifying the Union of such intention," since such action "completely destroyed the bargaining unit." The Fifth Circuit, however, refused to enforce the Board's order.[684] The court found that a continuing pattern of in-plant sabotage and production disruptions by employees during the negotiations for a new

---

[678]Two members would have embraced a firm rule allowing such replacements. Chairman Miller concurred, based on the business justification for their use in the particular case.

[679]*Supra* note 671, 122 LRRM at 1220.

[680]Marquette Co., Gulf & W. Natural Resources Group, 285 NLRB 774, 126 LRRM 1121 (1987); B-Bar-B, 281 NLRB 250, 123 LRRM 1104 (1986).

[681]Movers & Warehousemen's Ass'n, 224 NLRB 356, 357, 92 LRRM 1236 (1976), *enforced*, 550 F2d 962, 94 LRRM 2795 (CA 4), *cert. denied*, 434 US 826, 96 LRRM 2513 (1977).

[682]*Id.* at 358.

[683]223 NLRB 1317, 92 LRRM 1103 (1976). *See also* Walker, *Sabotage by Unidentified Employees Held Tantamount to In-Plant Strike Allowing Permanent Replacement of Locked-Out Employees*, 52 TUL. L. REV. 878 (1978).

[684]Johns-Manville Prods. Corp. v. NLRB, 557 F2d 1126, 96 LRRM 2010 (CA 5, 1977), *cert. denied sub nom.* Oil, Chem. & Atomic Workers v. NLRB, 436 US 956, 98 LRRM 2617 (1978). *See* Chapter 20, "The Lockout," at notes 139–145.

agreement amounted to an "in-plant strike," thereby making permanent replacements permissible.

In *National Fabricators,*[685] the employer violated sections 8(a)(1) and (3) when it selected for temporary lockout those employees whom it felt would likely honor a picket line should there be a strike. The employer attempted to justify its decision based on business necessity, namely the fear that the employees it was selecting would not be available for work should there be a strike. The Board found this overtly discriminatory. Similarly, an employer violated sections (8)(a)(1) and (3) when it locked out its employees and conditioned their reinstatement on their agreement to waive contractually established benefits.[686]

In a variation of the hiring of temporary replacements in a lockout, an employer was found in violation of sections (8)(a)(1) and (3) when it hired its own bargaining-unit employees as temporary replacements. The Board found that the employer was not seeking to use legitimate economic pressure but rather was attempting to subvert the bargaining process in an attempt to unilaterally implement changes not included in the final contract offer.[687]

An employer that insisted to impasse on, and implemented, its proposal to limit the duration of economic strikers' reinstatement rights to 6 months violated sections 8(a)(1), (3), and (5) of the Act.[688] However, an employer who ceased paying employee's health insurance premiums because they were not in "active service" following the commencement of a strike[689] and an employer who paid replacements at a rate higher than the striking employees, but whose actual wages were not higher than those offered the union, did not violate the Act.[690] In *Texaco, Inc.,*[691] the Board adopted a new principle for deciding when a suspension of benefits for disabled employees at the beginning of a strike violates the Act. The Board held that the legality of

[685]295 NLRB No. 126, 131 LRRM 1761 (1989).

[686]Clemson Bros., 290 NLRB 944, 129 LRRM 1150 (1988).

[687]United Chrome Prods., 288 NLRB 1176, 128 LRRM 1223 (1988).

[688]Gaso Pumps, 274 NLRB 532, 119 LRRM 1052 (1985).

[689]Sherwin-Williams Co., 269 NLRB 678, 115 LRRM 1314 (1984). *See also* Forest Prods. Co. v. NLRB, 888 F2d 72, 132 LRRM 2815 (CA 10, 1989) (not an unfair labor practice for employer to cease matching Christmas savings program contributions for permanently replaced economic strikers).

[690]Brady-Stannard Motor Co., 273 NLRB 1434, 118 LRRM 1170 (1985), *review denied sub nom.* Auto Workers Local 259 v. NLRB, 776 F2d 23, 120 LRRM 3102 (CA 2, 1985).

[691]285 NLRB 241, 126 LRRM 1001 (1987).

such an act depends on whether the employer had a legitimate and substantial business justification. This could be supplied by an explicit waiver by the union or by the employer's reliance on a nondiscriminatory contract interpretation that is reasonable and arguably correct.[692]

The Board held that denial of accrued holiday pay to strikers was not violative of the Act because the preexisting employee handbook required that employees be on active duty the working day before and after the holiday in order to earn holiday pay. However, the announcement to strikers that they would be eligible upon return to work for medical insurance only if they satisfied a requalification period and where similar requalification requirements were imposed for disability and life insurance, a violation was found because there was no contractual basis with the carriers for such an imposition, and, with respect to the life insurance requalification period, the employer could have sought a waiver but failed to do so.[693]

VI. BARGAINING IMPASSES[694]

A. Elements of Impasse

The duty to bargain does not require a party "to engage in fruitless marathon discussions at the expense of frank statement and support of his position."[695] Where there are irreconcilable differences in the parties' positions after exhaustive good-faith negotiations, the law recognizes the existence of an impasse.[696] Some difficulty exists in establishing the "inherently vague and fluid . . . standard" applicable to an impasse reached by hard

---

[692]*See also* Gulf Oil Co., 290 NLRB 1158, 130 LRRM 1103 (1988) (no violations found where sickness and accident benefits were withheld from employees during strike since strike settlement agreement clearly and unmistakably waived employees' rights to receive such benefits during strike); *but see* Conoco, Inc., 287 NLRB 619, 130 LRRM 1081 (1987) (violation of §§8(a)(1) and (3) found when employer discontinued disability benefits at beginning of strike where employer had no reasonable belief that it had such right under disability plan).

[693]Advertiser's Mfg. Co., 294 NLRB No. 51, 132 LRRM 1024 (1989).

[694]Stewart & Engeman, *Impasse, Collective Bargaining and Action*, 39 U. CIN. L. REV. 233 (1970).

[695]NLRB v. American Nat'l Ins. Co., 343 US 395, 404, 30 LRRM 2147 (1952).

[696]Usually the more meetings, the better the chance of a finding that an impasse has arisen. Fetzer Television v. NLRB, 317 F2d 420, 53 LRRM 2224 (CA 6, 1963). On the doctrine of impasse generally, see Schatzki, *The Employer's Unilateral Act—A Per Se Violation—Sometimes*, 44 TEX. L. REV. 470, 495 (1966); Comment, *Impasse in Collective Bargaining*, 44 TEX. L. REV. 769 (1966).

and steadfast bargaining, as distinguished from one resulting from an unlawful refusal to bargain.[697] It may be that in collective bargaining "part of the difficulty arises from the fact that the law recognizes the possibility of the parties reaching an impasse."[698]

The existence or nonexistence of an impasse is normally put in issue when, after negotiations have been carried on for a period of time, the positions of the parties become fairly fixed and talks reach the point of stalemate. When this occurs, the employer is free to make unilateral changes in working conditions (i.e., wages, hours, etc.) consistent with its offers that the union has rejected.[699] By the very nature of the bargaining process, it is not always apparent when an impasse has been reached. Prior to making unilateral changes,[700] however, an impasse must exist.

In *Taft Broadcasting Co.*[701] the Board stated that impasse occurs "after good-faith negotiations have exhausted the prospects of concluding an agreement,"[702] and enumerated some of the considerations in making such a determination:

> Whether a bargaining impasse exists is a matter of judgment. The bargaining history, the good faith of the parties in negotiations, the length of the negotiations, the importance of the issue or issues as to which there is disagreement, the contemporaneous understanding of the parties as to the state of negotiations are all relevant factors to be considered in deciding whether an impasse in bargaining existed.[703]

---

[697]NLRB v. Borg-Warner Corp., Wooster Div., 356 US 342, 352, 42 LRRM 2034 (1958) (Justice Harlan concurring in part and dissenting in part). *See also* National Fresh Fruit & Vegetable Co. v. NLRB, 565 F2d 1331, 97 LRRM 2427 (CA 5, 1978).

[698]Speech of Board Member Joseph A. Jenkins, 40 LRRM 98, 105–6 (1957).

[699]NLRB v. Katz, 369 US 736, 50 LRRM 2177 (1962); NLRB v. Almeida Bus Lines, 333 F2d 729, 56 LRRM 2548 (CA 1, 1964); Taft Broadcasting Co., 163 NLRB 475, 64 LRRM 1386 (1967), *aff'd sub nom.* Television & Radio Artists v. NLRB, 395 F2d 622, 67 LRRM 3032 (CADC, 1968); Eddie's Chop House, 165 NLRB 861, 65 LRRM 1408 (1967); American Laundry Mach. Co., 107 NLRB 1574, 33 LRRM 1457 (1954). *See also* notes 722–726 *infra* and accompanying text.

[700]NLRB v. U.S. Sonics Corp., 312 F2d 610, 52 LRRM 2360 (CA 1, 1963); Cheney Cal. Lumber Co. v. NLRB, 319 F2d 375, 53 LRRM 2598 (CA 9, 1963) (a belief that talks or negotiations are deadlocked or stalemated is sufficient). *See also* NLRB v. Cambria Clay Prods. Co., 215 F2d 48, 34 LRRM 2471 (CA 6, 1954) (presence of federal mediator may indicate impasse if agreement still cannot be reached after mediator is called in; since Federal Mediation and Conciliation Service has duty to use its best efforts to bring parties to agreement, a mediator's refusal to call more meetings may indicate there is no chance of agreement).

[701]163 NLRB 475, 64 LRRM 1386 (1967).

[702]*Id.* at 478.

[703]*Id.* There can be no impasse until there appears to be no realistic possibility that a continuation of bargaining at the time would be fruitful. I. Bahcall Indus., I. Bahcall Steel & Pipe Div., 287 NLRB 1257, 128 LRRM 1159 (1988); Richmond Recording Corp. dba PRC Recording Co., 280 NLRB 615, 124 LRRM 1081 (1986), *enforced,* 836 F2d 289, 127

The Board may also consider additional factors,[704] for the existence of an impasse is very much a question of fact.[705] These may include:

1. Whether there has been a strike or the union has consulted the employees about one. However, a strike does not necessarily create an impasse and may even break a preexisting one.[706]
2. Fluidity of position.[707]
3. Continuation of bargaining.[708]

LRRM 2148 (CA 7, 1987); Oak Rubber Co., 277 NLRB 1322, 121 LRRM 1114 (1985); Sann dba Briarcliff Pavilion for Specialized Care, 260 NLRB 1374, 109 LRRM 1383 (1982), *enforced*, 725 F2d 669, 115 LRRM 2712 (CA 3, 1983); Marriott Corp., Marriott In-Flite Servs. Div., 258 NLRB 755, 108 LRRM 1287 (1981), *enforced*, 729 F2d 1441, 113 LRRM 3528 (CA 2), *cert. denied*, 464 US 829, 114 LRRM 2568 (1983); Morco dba Towne Plaza Hotel, 258 NLRB 69, 108 LRRM 1126 (1981); J.D. Lunsford Plumbing, Heating & Air Conditioning, 254 NLRB 1360, 107 LRRM 1033 (1981), *aff'd*, 684 F2d 1033, 110 LRRM 3367 (CADC, 1982).

[704]Carpenter Sprinkler Corp. v. NLRB, 605 F2d 60, 102 LRRM 2199 (CA 2, 1979); Harding Glass Indus., 248 NLRB 902, 104 LRRM 1073 (1980), *enforced*, 672 F2d 1330, 109 LRRM 3044 (CA 10, 1982); Talbert Mfg., 250 NLRB 174, 104 LRRM 1543 (1980), *enforced*, 676 F2d 698, 109 LRRM 2662 (CA 7, 1982). *See* Comment, *supra* note 696.

[705]*See, e.g.*, Dust-Tex Serv., 214 NLRB 398, 88 LRRM 1292 (1974), *enforced*, 521 F2d 1404, 90 LRRM 3074 (CA 8, 1975) (no impasse where employer determined to change wage structure immediately upon expiration of contract regardless of status of negotiations); Servis Equip. Co., 198 NLRB 266, 80 LRRM 1704 (1972) (no impasse on wages when parties met only twice and union was not given enough advance notice of employer's action to respond); Supak & Sons Mfg. Corp., 192 NLRB 1228, 78 LRRM 1289 (1971), *enforced*, 470 F2d 998, 82 LRRM 2560 (CA 4, 1973) (no impasse on wages when employer did not make its counteroffer until last regular bargaining session).

[706]Huck Mfg. Co. v. NLRB, 693 F2d 1176, 112 LRRM 2245 (CA 5, 1982); Marriott Corp., Marriott In-Flite Servs. Div., *supra* note 703. *Cf.* Presto Casting Co., 262 NLRB 346, 111 LRRM 1111 (1982), *enforced in part*, 708 F2d 495, 113 LRRM 3013 (CA 9), *cert. denied*, 464 US 994, 114 LRRM 3392 (1983) (impasse found at time of strike where it was designed to break "deadlock").

[707]J. Josephson, Inc., 287 NLRB 1188, 127 LRRM 1344 (1988) (constant discussion and movement precluded impasse); Arrow Automotive Indus., 284 NLRB 487, 125 LRRM 1188 (1987), *enforcement denied*, 853 F2d 223, 128 LRRM 3137 (CA 4, 1988); Richmond Recording Corp. dba PRC Recording Co., *supra* note 703 (impasse broken when employer asked union for formal counteroffer); Presto Casting Co., *supra* note 706 (impasse found where both sides held to their "final offers" after only two meetings); Saunders House, 265 NLRB 1632, 112 LRRM 1405 (1982), *enforcement denied*, 719 F2d 683, 114 LRRM 2977 (CA 3, 1983) *and* 115 LRRM 3712 (CA 3), *cert. denied sub nom.* Hospital & Health Care Employees Dist. 1199C v. Saunders House, 466 US 958, 116 LRRM 2096 (1984) (mere shift from position off record to same position on record is not sufficient to preclude finding of impasse); Morco dba Towne Plaza Hotel, *supra* note 703 (no-impasse finding predicated in part upon recent union concession).

[708]Huck Mfg. Co. v. NLRB, *supra* note 706 (no impasse: "Of importance is the fact that the parties continued to meet and negotiate"); Shangri-La Rest Home dba Shangri-La Health Care Center, 288 NLRB 334, 130 LRRM 1204 (1988) (impasse not reached because another bargaining session scheduled); Colfor, Inc., 282 NLRB 1173, 124 LRRM 1204 (1987), *enforced*, 838 F2d 164, 127 LRRM 2447 (CA 6, 1988) (temporary impasse broken when parties agreed to another meeting); Richmond Recording Corp. dba PRC Recording Co., *supra* note 703 (impasse broken by continuation of bargaining). Continued bargaining, however, is not always inconsistent with impasse. J.D. Lunsford Plumbing, Heating & Air Conditioning, *supra* note 703.

4. Statements or understandings of the parties concerning impasse.[709]

5. Union animus evidenced by prior or concurrent acts.[710]

6. The nature and importance of issues and the extent of difference or opposition.[711]

7. Bargaining history.[712]

8. Demonstrated willingness to consider the issue further.[713]

---

[709]Huck Mfg. Co. v. NLRB, *supra* note 706; Seattle-First Nat'l Bank v. NLRB, 638 F2d 1221, 106 LRRM 2621 (CA 9, 1981), *denying enforcement to* 241 NLRB 753, 100 LRRM 1624 (1979), *supplemented*, 267 NLRB 897, 114 LRRM 1072 (1983) (employer's letter clearly expressed position as to impasse as did union's position that proposals were too onerous to accept); Presto Casting Co., *supra* note 706 (impasse found where negotiators considered themselves at impasse and union representative's notes of union negotiator's statement to employees in union meeting recited: "we are deadlocked"); J.D. Lunsford Plumbing, Heating & Air Conditioning, *supra* note 703 (employer letter reciting impasse and intent to implement went unchallenged and no new proposals by either party were submitted during remainder of meeting). *Cf.* Richmond Recording Corp. dba PRC Recording Co., *supra* note 703 (use of word "impasse" or "deadlock" is not determinative of legal conclusion whether impasse is reached).

[710]Huck Mfg. Co. v. NLRB, *supra* note 706 (concurrent and preelection §8(a)(1) violations); D.C. Liquor Wholesalers Ass'n, 292 NLRB 1237, 130 LRRM 1256 (1989) (employer conduct in aggregate evinced intent to bargain in bad faith and break union); Virginia Holding Corp. dba Hotel Roanoke, 293 NLRB 182, 132 LRRM 1229 (1989); Globe Business Furniture, 290 NLRB 841, 130 LRRM 1492 (1988), *enforced*, 889 F2d 1087 (CA 6, 1989) (lockout prior to impasse unlawful); Marriott Corp., Marriott In-Flite Servs. Div., *supra* note 703 (direct dealing with employees).

[711]Excavation-Construction v. NLRB, 660 F2d 1015, 108 LRRM 2561 (CA 4, 1981), *denying enforcement to* 248 NLRB 649, 104 LRRM 1088 (1980); NLRB v. Gibraltar Indus., 653 F2d 1091, 107 LRRM 3307 (CA 6, 1981); Sierra Publishing Co., 291 NLRB 552, 131 LRRM 1377 (1988), *enforced*, 888 F2d 1394 (CA 9, 1989) (even if parties reached impasse on union security, deadlock was not reached in entire negotiations and duty to bargain on other critical issues continued); Water Ass'n, 290 NLRB 838, 129 LRRM 1064 (1988) (employer unlawfully insisted to impasse on audiotaping grievance meeting); Standard Register Co., 288 NLRB 1409, 128 LRRM 1268 (1988) (employer unlawfully insisted to impasse on proposal altering scope of unit); I. Bahcall Indus., I. Bahcall Steel & Pipe Div., *supra* note 703 (impasse reached as economic relief was of immediate and overriding importance to employer); Boise Cascade Corp., 283 NLRB 462, 124 LRRM 1391 (1987), *enforced*, 860 F2d 471, 129 LRRM 2744 (CADC, 1988) (employer may not insist on proposal that consolidated bargaining units as scope of bargaining unit is not mandatory subject of bargaining; however, lawful impasse reached over economic issues); Forester Beverage Corp., 265 NLRB 285, 111 LRRM 1554 (1982) (impasse found where parties had reached agreement on all issues except union demand that replacements be released to make room for returning strikers); R.A. Hatch Co., 263 NLRB 1221, 111 LRRM 1569 (1982) (union insistence that employer execute short form binding employer to yet-to-be concluded contract of multi-employer association from which employer had recently withdrawn); Presto Casting Co., *supra* note 706 (first contract disagreement over long-standing merit system); J.D. Lunsford Plumbing, Heating & Air Conditioning, *supra* note 703 (impasse was found where, had union not insisted on standard contract, it would have been required to grant concessions to significant number of other employers under "most favored nations" clause).

[712]Sierra Publishing Co., *supra* note 711; I. Bahcall Indus., I. Bahcall Steel & Pipe Div., *supra* note 703; *cf.* Seattle-First Nat'l Bank v. NLRB, *supra* note 709; J.D. Lunsford Plumbing, Heating & Air Conditioning, *supra* note 703.

[713]Marriott Corp., Marriott In-Flite Servs., *supra* note 703 (union negotiator "made it quite clear . . . that the union would consider the Respondent's . . . final proposal" and respond later); Morco dba Towne Plaza Hotel, *supra* note 703 (although considerable

9. Duration of hiatus between bargaining meetings.[714]
10. Number and duration of bargaining sessions.[715]
11. Other actions inconsistent with impasse.[716]

Impasse on one, or several, issues does not suspend the obligation to bargain on remaining, unsettled issues.[717] Nor does the

---

hiatus, no impasse because employer did not "test the finality" of union's position and failed to return telephone calls).

[714]Southern Newspapers dba The Baytown Sun, 255 NLRB 154, 107 LRRM 1058 (1981). Impasse occurred in: NLRB v. Gibraltar Indus., *supra* note 711 (two meetings and three written communications during 2 months of bargaining); Excavation-Construction v. NLRB, *supra* note 711; R.A. Hatch Co., *supra* note 711 (one meeting with union representing one unit and two meetings with another union representing separate unit were sufficient); Presto Casting Co., *supra* note 706 (two meetings); J.D. Lunsford Plumbing, Heating & Air Conditioning, *supra* note 703 (three meetings during less than 1 month in face of union intransigence). No impasse was found in: Huck Mfg. Co. v. NLRB, *supra* note 706 (six meetings, but bargaining occurred during only four); Electric Mach. Co. v. NLRB, 653 F2d 958, 108 LRRM 2202 (CA 5, 1981), *enforcing in part* 243 NLRB 239, 101 LRRM 1428 (1979) (bargaining spanned only 8 days and two meetings); Marriott Corp., Marriott In-Flite Servs. Div., *supra* note 703 (premium pay and free meal benefits instituted after 37 meetings, but neither party had made wage offer and there were still 26 open items, many of which had not been seriously discussed).

[715]Sierra Publishing Co., *supra* note 711; Marriott Corp., Marriott In-Flite Servs. Div., *supra* note 703.

[716]Microdot, Valley Mould Div., 288 NLRB 1015, 128 LRRM 1134 (1988) (no bona fide impasse when employer made "final offer" that included proposals requiring further study, gave union only 3 days to respond, and stated it would accept no counteroffers); Powell Elec. Mfg. Co., 287 NLRB 969, 127 LRRM 1239 (1987) (solicitation of mediator's assistance in arranging further negotiations indicates parties had not yet exhausted bargaining over core economic issues); Pertec Computer Corp., 284 NLRB 810, 126 LRRM 1134 (1987) (genuine impasse could not be reached when employer failed to supply relevant information necessary to bargaining); Massillon Hosp. Ass'n dba Massillon Community Hosp., 282 NLRB 675, 124 LRRM 1125 (1987) (no legally cognizable impasse if caused by employer's bad-faith insistence that union accept contract terminable at will); Southern Newspapers dba The Baytown Sun, *supra* note 714 (post-impasse change instituted in order to avoid premium pay violated Act because pre-impasse proposal sought to eliminate shift). *See also* Forester Beverage Corp., *supra* note 711. *Cf.* Stone Boat Yard, 264 NLRB 981, 111 LRRM 1427 (1982), *enforced*, 715 F2d 441, 114 LRRM 2407 (CA 9, 1983), *cert. denied*, 466 US 937, 115 LRRM 3640 (1984) (notice to union, in response to its request for bargaining, that employer intended "to offer substantial changes in their contract," followed by union's refusal to meet for more than 2 months, was not sufficiently specific to privilege unilateral implementation of new insurance plan following contract expiration; employer must "provide union with written copy of its proposed contract changes prior to unilaterally implementing them").

[717]Patrick & Co., 248 NLRB 390, 103 LRRM 1457 (1980), *enforced*, 644 F2d 889, 108 LRRM 2175 (CA 9, 1981); Providence Medical Center, 243 NLRB 714, 102 LRRM 1099 (1979); Chambers Mfg. Corp., 124 NLRB 721, 44 LRRM 1477 (1959), *enforced*, 278 F2d 715, 46 LRRM 2316 (CA 5, 1960); Pool Mfg. Co., 70 NLRB 540, 18 LRRM 1364 (1946), *remanded*, 24 LRRM 2147 (CA 5, 1949), *vacated*, 339 US 577, 26 LRRM 2127 (1950). There is a distinction, however, between generally refusing to bargain merely because of an impasse on one issue, as in *Chambers*, and the situation where the impasse on a single but critical issue precludes an agreement. *See, e.g.*, Television & Radio Artists v. NLRB, 395 F2d 622 n.13, 67 LRRM 3032 (CADC, 1968), *aff'g sub nom.* Taft Broadcasting Co., 163 NLRB 475, 64 LRRM 1386 (1967); Teamsters Local 745 v. NLRB (Empire Terminal Warehouse Co.), 355 F2d 842, 61 LRRM 2065 (CADC, 1966); NLRB v. Intracoastal Terminal, 286 F2d 954, 47 LRRM 2629 (CA 5, 1961). In the latter situation, the employer may make "unilateral changes that are reasonably comprehended within his preimpasse proposals." Taft Broadcasting Co., *supra*, at 478. *See also* Sierra Publishing Co., *supra* note 711.

existence of a general impasse insulate a party from the duty to bargain, since an impasse normally only suspends the duty to bargain,[718] and changed circumstances may end the suspension.[719]

B. Effect on the Bargaining Obligation

When an impasse is reached, the duty to bargain is not terminated but only suspended.[720] During this suspension the employer may not take action disparaging to the collective bargaining process or amounting to a withdrawal of recognition of the union's representative status.[721]

When an impasse is reached, the employer may make unilateral changes in working conditions, but such changes must "not [be] substantially different or greater than any [offers] which the employer . . . proposed during the negotiations."[722] Thus, an employer violates section 8(a)(5) by granting wage increases that exceed those previously offered at the bargaining table, even if negotiations were at impasse when the increases were granted.[723] Moreover, an overall bargaining impasse will not justify a unilateral change concerning a subject over which there had been no bargaining.[724] In *Manor Mining & Contracting Corp.*[725] the employer violated section 8(a)(5), notwithstanding an overall bargaining impasse, by unilaterally granting a wage increase. The Board emphasized that: (1) although the certification year had passed, the union had not lost its majority; (2) the bargaining impasse had not occurred over the wage increase, which the employer had never offered to the union; and (3) the

---

[718]See notes 727–729 *infra* and accompanying text.

[719]*See* notes 730–733 *infra* and accompanying text.

[720]NLRB v. Tex-Tan, Inc., 318 F2d 472, 53 LRRM 2298 (CA 5, 1963); Philip Carey Mfg. Co., 140 NLRB 1103, 52 LRRM 1184 (1963); Boeing Airplane Co., 80 NLRB 447, 23 LRRM 1107 (1948), *rev'd on other grounds*, 174 F2d 988, 24 LRRM 2101 (CADC, 1949).

[721]Central Metallic Casket Co., 91 NLRB 572, 26 LRRM 1520 (1950). An employer may not insist, to impasse, on altering the existing contractual unit description. Newspaper Printing Corp. v. NLRB, 625 F2d 956, 104 LRRM 2432 (CA 10, 1980), *cert. denied*, 450 US 911, 106 LRRM 2512 (1981); Newport News Shipbuilding Co. v. NLRB, 602 F2d 73, 101 LRRM 2998 (CA 4, 1979). *See* NLRB v. Borg-Warner Corp., Wooster Div., 356 US 342, 42 LRRM 2034 (1958), and Chapter 16, "Subjects of Bargaining," at notes 24–29.

[722]Atlas Tack Corp., 226 NLRB 222, 227, 93 LRRM 1236 (1976), *enforced*, 559 F2d 1201, 96 LRRM 2660 (CA 1, 1977).

[723]NLRB v. Crompton-Highland Mills, 337 US 217, 24 LRRM 2088 (1949); Falcon Tank Corp., 194 NLRB 333, 78 LRRM 1587 (1971).

[724]NLRB v. Intracoastal Terminal, *supra* note 717.

[725]197 NLRB 1057, 80 LRRM 1535 (1972), *enforced*, 478 F2d 1399, 83 LRRM 2409 (CA 3, 1973).

business needs of the employer did not excuse the bypassing of the union.[726]

If a party's bad-faith bargaining or unfair labor practice precludes agreement, the resulting impasse is not a valid one, and any changes the party unilaterally makes will be illegal.[727] In *National Fresh Fruit & Vegetable Co.*[728] the employer advanced a nonmandatory subject of bargaining (the removal from the certified bargaining unit of some job classifications) during negotiations prior to impasse. The union's final position rejected the employer's entire package, which included the nonmandatory proposal. The Board held that the fact that this was one of the "unresolved points" before the parties was enough to taint the impasse, even though the overall impasse was largely due to the failure to agree on mandatory subjects. The Fifth Circuit refused to enforce the Board's decision, ruling that the nonmandatory proposal was "a bargaining tactic" taken by the employer in response to the union's increased demands, and that the advancement of the subject by the employer did not "rise to the level of an impermissible insistence."[729] Since the court found that the employer was still flexible on the subject, it did not preclude or taint the impasse.

As noted, existence of an impasse does not permanently relieve a party of its duty to bargain. In fact, a legal impasse may end suddenly; almost any changed condition or circumstance that renews the possibility of fruitful discussion will terminate the suspension of the duty to bargain.[730] A strike begun after an impasse has been reached changes the bargaining atmosphere and indicates that bargaining must be resumed,[731] as do changes

---

[726]*See also* American Gypsum Co., 285 NLRB 100, 128 LRRM 1105 (1987) (during bona fide impasse, employer unlawfully implemented proposal inconsistent with final offer); Southwest Forest Indus., 278 NLRB 228, 121 LRRM 1158 (1986), *enforced*, 841 F2d 270, 127 LRRM 2913 (CA 9, 1988) (same); Atlas Tack Corp., *supra* note 722 (employer violated Act by, inter alia, unilaterally instituting new system of rest periods which had not been discussed during negotiations).

[727]NLRB v. Herman Sausage Co., 275 F2d 229, 45 LRRM 2829 (CA 5, 1960) (employer bad faith in bargaining). *See also* United Contractors, 244 NLRB 72, 102 LRRM 1012 (1979), *enforced*, 631 F2d 735, 108 LRRM 3152 (CA 7, 1980) (no impasse in presence of bad-faith bargaining); Neon Sign Corp., 229 NLRB 861, 95 LRRM 1161 (1977), *enforcement denied*, 602 F2d 1203, 102 LRRM 2485 (CA 5, 1979) (surface bargaining by employer); Palomar Corp. & Gateway Serv. Co., 192 NLRB 592, 78 LRRM 1030 (1971) (employer refusal to provide necessary bargaining information to union).

[728]227 NLRB 2014, 95 LRRM 1011 (1977).

[729]National Fresh Fruit & Vegetable Co. v. NLRB, 565 F2d 1331, 97 LRRM 2427, 2429 (CA 5, 1978).

[730]Gulf States Mfg. v. NLRB, 704 F2d 1390, 113 LRRM 2789 (CA 5, 1983).

[731]NLRB v. United States Cold Storage Corp., 203 F2d 924, 32 LRRM 2024 (CA 5,

in the business outlook of the general industry or of the employer's specific firm,[732] or a substantial change in the bargaining position of either party.[733]

Impasse does not justify withdrawal of recognition.[734] Even after the certification year has passed, if changed circumstances end the impasse, the employer must bargain, unless it has reasonable grounds for believing that the union has lost its majority.[735]

In *Bonanno Linen Service v. NLRB*,[736] the Supreme Court agreed with the Board that impasse in multi-employer negotiations is not an unusual circumstance that will justify a member's unilateral withdrawal from the multi-employer bargaining unit. The decision resolved an issue on which the Board[737] and the appellate courts[738] had been sharply divided. The *Bonanno* case involved a linen supply association of 10 employers that negotiated as a multi-employer unit with the Teamsters Union. After 10 bargaining sessions, the negotiators reached agreement on a

---

1953). The occurrence of a strike does not necessarily mean that negotiations prior to the strike have reached an impasse. Neon Sign Corp. v. NLRB, 602 F2d 1203, 102 LRRM 2485 (CA 5, 1979); J.H. Bonck Co., 170 NLRB 1471, 69 LRRM 1172 (1968), *enforced*, 424 F2d 634, 74 LRRM 2103 (CA 5, 1970).

[732]Kit Mfg. Co., 138 NLRB 1290, 51 LRRM 1224 (1962), *enforced*, 319 F2d 857, 53 LRRM 3010 (CA 9, 1963) (general industry increase in production and sales, union obtaining wider membership and certification in entire industry, and employer's financial condition improved).

[733]NLRB v. Sharon Hats, Inc., 289 F2d 628, 48 LRRM 2098 (CA 5, 1961), *enforcing* 127 NLRB 947, 46 LRRM 1128 (1960) (dropping part of benefit-clause requests).

[734]Prentice-Hall, 290 NLRB 646, 129 LRRM 1052 (1988) (employer's doubt of union's majority status in context of bad-faith bargaining was rendered a "nullity" even if doubt was based in part on petition signed by apparent majority of employees); Plymouth Locomotive Works, 261 NLRB 595, 110 LRRM 1155 (1982); Flex Plastics, 262 NLRB 651, 110 LRRM 1365 (1982), *enforced*, 726 F2d 272, 115 LRRM 3036 (CA 6, 1984).

[735]Celanese Corp. of Am., 95 NLRB 664, 28 LRRM 1362 (1951). *See* discussion *infra* at notes 819–833.

[736]Charles D. Bonanno Linen Serv., 229 NLRB 629, 95 LRRM 1128 (1977), *aff'd by the full Board on reh'g*, 243 NLRB 1093, 102 LRRM 1001 (1979), *enforced*, 630 F2d 25, 105 LRRM 2477 (CA 1, 1980), *aff'd*, 454 US 404, 109 LRRM 2257 (1982). *See* Hi-Way Billboards, 206 NLRB 22, 84 LRRM 1161 (1973), *enforcement denied*, 500 F2d 181, 87 LRRM 2203 (CA 5, 1974). The Board held that a genuine impasse between a union and a multi-employer bargaining association does not constitute such an "unusual circumstance" justifying an employer's unilateral withdrawal from the multi-employer unit. *See also* Harding Glass Indus., 248 NLRB 902, 104 LRRM 1073 (1980); Florida Fire Sprinklers, 237 NLRB 1034, 99 LRRM 1078 (1978).

[737]Along with *Bonanno, supra* note 736, the Board handed down five other decisions affirming the rule that unilateral withdrawal from a multi-employer unit is not permitted merely because impasse occurs. *See, e.g.*, Birkenwald Distrib. Co., 243 NLRB 1151, 102 LRRM 1005 (1979), *enforcement denied sub nom.* Seattle Auto Glass v. NLRB, 669 F2d 1332, 109 LRRM 3350 (CA 9, 1982).

[738]Four circuit courts of appeals disagreed with the Board, holding that an impasse in bargaining justified an employer's unilateral withdrawal from a multi-employer unit. NLRB v. Steel Fabricators, 582 F2d 135, 98 LRRM 3150 (CA 2, 1978), *cert. denied*, Iron Workers Local 455 v. NLRB, 439 US 1130, 100 LRRM 2334 (1979); NLRB v. Beck Engraving Co., 522 F2d 475, 90 LRRM 2089 (CA 3, 1975); Hi-Way Billboards, *supra* note 736; Fairmont Foods Co. v. NLRB, 471 F2d 1170, 82 LRRM 2017 (CA 8, 1972).

proposed contract, but it was rejected by the union membership. An impasse over compensation remained unresolved for 7 weeks, whereupon the union initiated a selective strike against one member of the association, Bonanno. Most of the association members responded with a lockout of their drivers, and the stalemate continued for several months. Bonanno hired permanent replacements for all of his striking drivers and notified the association and the union that he was withdrawing from the association. Soon after, the lockout was ended, negotiations were resumed without Bonanno's participation, and a settlement was reached.

When Bonanno refused to sign the contract, the union, which had not consented to Bonanno's withdrawal from the bargaining unit, filed unfair labor practice charges. The Board found a violation of section 8(a)(5) and ordered Bonanno to sign and implement the contract retroactively. The Board reiterated the view it had expressed in *Hi-Way Billboards*[739]—namely, that an impasse is not sufficiently destructive of multi-employer bargaining to justify a unilateral withdrawal. The Supreme Court affirmed, for "although [the Board's rule] may deny an employer a particular economic weapon, [it] does so in the interest of the proper and pre-eminent goal, maintaining the stability of the multi-employer unit."[740]

VII. DEFENSES AND EXCEPTIONS: WAIVER, SUSPENSION, AND TERMINATION OF BARGAINING RIGHTS

A. Waiver of Bargaining Rights

NLRB v. Jacobs Manufacturing Co.[741] stands for the general proposition that, unless discharged or waived, the duty to bargain continues during the term of the collective bargaining

---

[739]*Supra* note 736.

[740]109 LRRM at 2263. *See* Chapter 11, "Appropriate Bargaining Units," at notes 371–378.

[741]196 F2d 680, 30 LRRM 2098 (CA 2, 1952), *enforcing* 94 NLRB 1214, 28 LRRM 1162 (1951). Under the Wagner Act an employer was under a duty, upon request, to bargain with the union as to terms and conditions of employment whether or not the subject had been discussed and previously embodied in a collective bargaining agreement. *See* NLRB v. Sands Mfg. Co., 306 US 332, 4 LRRM 530 (1939). The addition of §8(d) modified this obligation by expressly stating that parties to the agreement are not required "to discuss or agree to any modification of the terms and conditions . . . if such modification is to become effective before such terms and conditions can be reopened under the provisions of the contract." *Id.* In *Jacobs, supra,* at 684, the Second Circuit agreed with the Board that §8(d) does not relieve the employer of the duty to bargain "as to subjects which were neither discussed nor embodied in any of the terms and conditions of the contract." *See also* NLRB v. Niles-Bement-Pond Co., 199 F2d 713, 31 LRRM 2057 (CA 2, 1952); Proctor Mfg. Corp., 131 NLRB 1166, 48 LRRM 1222 (1961). See discussion of the duty to bargain during the term of an existing agreement at notes 936–959 *infra.*

agreement. Frequently the waiver issue arises in connection with unilateral employer action allegedly violative of section 8(a)(5); for example, in cases involving removal of work from the bargaining unit, where the defenses might be that the subject matter is not a mandatory subject of collective bargaining and that the union has waived whatever right it may have had to bargain.[742]

A waiver may result from either action or inaction by a party. A party may agree to contractual language specifically waiving its right to bargain about a particular matter,[743] or it may relinquish its right during negotiations for the collective agreement.[744] Established past practices of the parties may be persuasive evidence of a waiver.[745] In addition, the failure to protest unilateral action[746] or the failure to request bargaining despite knowledge of a contemplated unilateral change[747] may constitute a waiver. Nonetheless, consistent with the traditional common law view of waiver, the Board and the courts have confined the waiver doctrine narrowly and have been reluctant to infer a waiver.[748] The Supreme Court has stated that a waiver of bargaining rights will only be found in clear and unmistakable conduct.[749]

1. Waiver by Express Agreement. A party may contractually waive its right to bargain about a subject.[750] Where such a waiver is claimed, the test applied has been whether the waiver is in "clear and unmistakable" language.[751] In this regard, a waiver is

---

[742]ACF Indus. v. NLRB, 592 F2d 422, 100 LRRM 2710 (CA 8, 1979); U.S. Lingerie Corp., 170 NLRB 750, 67 LRRM 1482 (1968); American Oil Co., 151 NLRB 421, 58 LRRM 1412 (1965); New York Mirror, 151 NLRB 834, 58 LRRM 1465 (1965).

[743]*See, e.g.*, Ador Corp., 150 NLRB 1658, 58 LRRM 1280 (1965).

[744]*See, e.g.*, Speidel Corp., 120 NLRB 733, 42 LRRM 1039 (1958).

[745]*Id.* at 741; New York Mirror, *supra* note 742; American Oil Co., *supra* note 742.

[746]Justesen's Food Stores, 160 NLRB 687, 63 LRRM 1027 (1966); Motoresearch Co., 138 NLRB 1490, 51 LRRM 1240 (1962).

[747]NLRB v. Spun-Jee Corp., 385 F2d 379, 66 LRRM 2485, *amended*, 67 LRRM 2308 (CA 2, 1967), *decision on remand*, 171 NLRB 557, 68 LRRM 1121 (1968); U.S. Lingerie Corp., *supra* note 742; Montgomery Ward & Co., 137 NLRB 418, 50 LRRM 1162 (1962). *See also* Fruehauf Trailer Co., 162 NLRB 195, 64 LRRM 1037 (1966).

[748]*See, e.g.*, New York Mirror, *supra* note 742, and cases cited therein.

[749]Metropolitan Edison Co. v. NLRB, 460 US 693, 708 n.12, 112 LRRM 3265 (1983); Rockwell Int'l Corp., 260 NLRB 1346, 109 LRRM 1366 (1982). *See* Suffolk Child Dev. Center, 277 NLRB 1345, 121 LRRM 1103 (1985) (where union's failure to protest prior changes, and management-rights and zipper clauses, was not a waiver). *See also* Nordpal Corp. dba Twin City Garage Door Co., 297 NLRB No. 13, 133 LRRM 1234 (1989). Texaco, Inc., 291 NLRB 613, 129 LRRM 1273 (1988); Energy Coop., 290 NLRB 635, 129 LRRM 1256 (1988).

[750]Ador Corp., *supra* note 743; Druwhit Metal Prods. Co., 153 NLRB 346, 59 LRRM 1359 (1965) (containing clause identical to that in *Ador*).

[751]In Norris Indus., 231 NLRB 50, 96 LRRM 1078 (1977), the employer made a contract proposal to terminate the medical group insurance of employees on medical

normally construed as applicable only to the specific item mentioned.[752] Conversely, a specific waiver will not embrace a more general grouping. For example, a waiver as to particular compensation for an individual employee does not necessarily constitute a waiver with respect to unilateral changes for groups of employees.[753]

In determining whether a contractual waiver exists, the Board considers the bargaining history of the contract language and the parties' interpretation of the language.[754] Where an employer relies on contract language as a purported waiver to establish unilaterally its right to change terms and conditions of employment not contained in the contract, the Board requires evidence that the matter in issue was "fully discussed and consciously explored during negotiations and the union must have consciously yielded or clearly and unmistakably waived its interest in the matter."[755]

---

leaves of absence. This was incorporated in a "letter of understanding" signed at the same time as the contract. Although the union may have misunderstood the scope of the proposal, the Board held that the clear language in the letter which the union signed constituted a waiver, even though the matter was not thoroughly discussed in the negotiations. On the other hand, in Elizabethtown Water Co., 234 NLRB 318, 97 LRRM 1210 (1978), the parties to a collective bargaining agreement had not discussed changes to the employee retirement plan during the negotiations, since the plan agreement expired 1 year later. The fact that the new collective bargaining agreement (which incorporated the plan by reference) was to "remain in full force and effect" beyond the anniversary date of the plan did not act as a waiver of the union's right to request changes in the plan when the plan agreement expired during the term of the collective agreement. *See also* Plumbers & Pipe Fitters Local 669 (A-1 Fire Protection) v. NLRB, 600 F2d 918, 101 LRRM 2014 (CADC, 1979); Office & Professional Employees Local 425 v. NLRB, 419 F2d 314, 70 LRRM 3047 (CADC, 1969); Leeds & Northrup Co. v. NLRB, 391 F2d 874, 67 LRRM 2793 (CA 3, 1968); NLRB v. Perkins Mach. Co., 326 F2d 488, 55 LRRM 2204 (CA 1, 1964); Timken Roller Bearing Co. v. NLRB, 325 F2d 746, 54 LRRM 2785 (CA 6, 1963), *cert. denied*, 376 US 971, 55 LRRM 2878 (1964); Consumers Power Co., 245 NLRB 183, 102 LRRM 1500 (1979); Bunker Hill Co., 208 NLRB 27, 85 LRRM 1264 (1973), *modified*, 210 NLRB 343, 86 LRRM 1157 (1974); Conval-Ohio, Inc., 202 NLRB 85, 82 LRRM 1701 (1973).

[752]New York Mirror, *supra* note 742.

[753]C&C Plywood Corp., 148 NLRB 414, 57 LRRM 1015 (1964), *enforcement denied*, 351 F2d 224, 60 LRRM 2137 (CA 9, 1965), *rev'd and remanded*, 385 US 421, 64 LRRM 2065 (1967).

[754]Auto Workers Local 449 v. NLRB (Keystone Consol. Indus., National Metalcrafters Div.), 802 F2d 969, 123 LRRM 2677 (CA 7, 1986); Pertec Computer Corp., 284 NLRB 810, 126 LRRM 1134 (1987) (contract language requiring employer to "discuss" prospective relocation of part of operation held not a waiver of union's right to bargain over relocation and subcontracting of work); Reynolds Elec. & Eng'g Co., NLRB Gen. Counsel Advice Memo., Case No. 31-CA-16234, 125 LRRM 1368 (1987); European Parts Exch., 270 NLRB 1244, 116 LRRM 1279 (1984).

[755]Rockwell Int'l Corp., *supra* note 749, at 1347. *See also* Mead Corp. v. NLRB, 697 F2d 1013, 112 LRRM 2797 (CA 11, 1983) (inclusion of same wage rate provisions in contract held not a waiver of union's right to bargain over wage rates of new or changed jobs during contract term); Southern Cal. Edison Co., 284 NLRB 1205, 126 LRRM 1324 (1987), *enforced*, 852 F2d 572 (CA 9, 1988); Brown Co., 278 NLRB 783, 121 LRRM 1250 (1986),

a. "Zipper" Clauses. Prior to 1974, the Board strictly applied the rule that only "clear and unmistakable" language in the contract expressly waiving the right to negotiate over a particular subject would suffice to relieve a party of the duty to bargain. This was especially the case with broad "zipper" clauses which stated that the contract was the complete agreement between the parties on all subjects. Such clauses, standing alone, did not constitute a sufficiently clear and unmistakable waiver as to a specific bargaining item.[756]

The Board's 1974 decision in *Radioear Corp.*[757] retreated somewhat from such a rigid interpretation. The contract in question contained a broad zipper clause. During the term of the agreement, the union sought to bargain with the employer over the employer's unilateral withdrawal of a "turkey money" bonus, which was not mentioned in the contract. Two members of the Board[758] voted with the majority on the ground that the union had waived the right to bargain over the bonuses, in light of the negotiating history and other surrounding circumstances. The

---

enforced and remanded, 833 F2d 1015, 128 LRRM 2223 (CA 9, 1987), *cert. denied*, 485 US 1039, 128 LRRM 2224 (1988). *Cf.* Johnson-Bateman Co., 295 NLRB No. 26, 131 LRRM 1393 (1989); GTE Automatic Elec., 261 NLRB 1491, 110 LRRM 1193 (1982), *supplementing* 240 NLRB 297, 100 LRRM 1204 (1979) (general waiver clause was "shield" against bargaining over union's demand that improvement in nonunit employee benefit be extended to unit employees). In General Tire & Rubber Co., 274 NLRB 591, 118 LRRM 1400 (1985), *enforced*, 795 F2d 585, 122 LRRM 3152 (CA 6, 1986), in the absence of any bargaining history or past practice, a clause in a collective bargaining agreement which provided that certain benefits "shall be provided for 90 days following the termination" of the agreement was not a "clear and unmistakable waiver" of the union's right to bargain over the discontinuance of those benefits after the 90-day period. Conversely, bargaining rights were waived where a union "specifically agreed," in contemplation of a proposed merger of two employee groups, that it would not represent a group of previously unrepresented employees after it was combined with a smaller group of represented employees. *See also* Abbott-Northwestern Hosp., 274 NLRB 1063, 118 LRRM 1521 (1985); *cf.* Armco, Eastern Steel Div., Ashland Works, 279 NLRB 1184, 123 LRRM 1335 (1986), *enforced*, 832 F2d 357, 126 LRRM 2961 (CA 6, 1987), *cert. denied*, 486 US 1042, 130 LRRM 2800 (1988). In Southwestern Steel & Supply v. NLRB, 806 F2d 1111, 123 LRRM 3290 (CADC, 1986), an agreement between the employer and the trust funds, which allowed the employer to terminate contributions, was held not a waiver of the union's bargaining rights over the discontinuance of contributions at contract expiration. *See also* KBMS, 278 NLRB 826, 122 LRRM 1287 (1986) (language in trust agreement tying contributions to labor agreement held not a waiver of right to bargain over discontinuance of benefits at contract expiration).

[756] *See, e.g.*, Bunker Hill Co., *supra* note 751; Conval-Ohio, Inc., *supra* note 751; New York Mirror, *supra* note 742; Beacon Journal Publishing Co., 164 NLRB 734, 65 LRRM 1126 (1967), *modified*, 401 F2d 366, 69 LRRM 2232 (CA 6, 1968); Eaton, Yale & Towne, Unit Drop Forge Div., 171 NLRB 600, 68 LRRM 1129 (1968), *enforced*, 412 F2d 108, 71 LRRM 2519 (CA 7, 1969).

[757] 214 NLRB 362, 87 LRRM 1330 (1974), *supplementing* 199 NLRB 1161, 81 LRRM 1402 (1972).

[758] Chairman Miller and Member Penello.

two members emphasized that the union had unsuccessfully sought—had consciously explored and yielded—a maintenance-of-benefits clause during the negotiations.[759]

The Board has, by and large, adhered to this broader position taken in *Radioear Corp.*[760] The circuit courts, however, are split on the issue, with some circuits following the more flexible approach,[761] while others continue to apply other analyses.[762]

b. "Management-Rights" Clauses. When a "management-rights" clause is the source of an asserted waiver, it is normally scrutinized by the Board to ascertain whether it affords specific justification for unilateral action. Thus, in *Ador Corp.*[763] the discontinuance of a line of products and the consequent layoff of employees without notice to the union was held to be justified by a management-rights clause that gave to the employer the right to take the precise action unilaterally. The Board reasoned that in agreeing to such a clause the parties had, in effect, bargained about the manner in which such decisions were to be made during the term of the collective bargaining agreement, and had agreed that the company could take such unilateral action.[764] Similarly, where a management-rights clause afforded the

---

[759]*See* Columbus & Southern Ohio Elec. Co., 270 NLRB 686, 116 LRRM 1148 (1984), *enforced sub nom.* Electrical Workers (IBEW) Local 1466 v. NLRB, 795 F2d 150, 122 LRRM 2948 (CADC, 1986) (where bargaining history showed union's awareness of its broad application, zipper clause was a waiver of right to bargain over elimination of "turkey bonuses" not mentioned in contract).

[760]Temple-Eastex, Inc., 228 NLRB 203, 96 LRRM 1424 (1977), *rev'd on other grounds*, 579 F2d 932, 99 LRRM 2467 (CA 5, 1978); A-1 Fire Protection, 233 NLRB 38, 96 LRRM 1440 (1977), *remanded in part sub nom.* Plumbers & Pipe Fitters Local 669 v. NLRB, 600 F2d 918, 101 LRRM 2014 (CADC, 1979). A few cases suggest that the Board's analysis may have narrowed. *See* Johnson-Bateman Co., *supra* note 755; Rockwell Int'l Corp., *supra* note 749; Pepsi-Cola Distrib. Co., 241 NLRB 869, 100 LRRM 1626 (1979), *enforced*, 646 F2d 1173, 107 LRRM 2252 (CA 6, 1981), *cert. denied*, 456 US 936, 109 LRRM 3368 (1982); Arizona Pub. Serv. Co., 247 NLRB 321, 103 LRRM 1154 (1980). *See also* GTE Automatic Elec., 261 NLRB 1491, 110 LRRM 1193 (1982), *supplementing* 240 NLRB 297, 100 LRRM 1204 (1979).

[761]NLRB v. Auto Crane Co., 536 F2d 310, 92 LRRM 2363 (CA 10, 1976); NLRB v. Southern Materials Co., 447 F2d 15, 77 LRRM 2814 (CA 4, 1971).

[762]Plumbers & Pipe Fitters Local 669 (A-1 Fire Protection) v. NLRB, *supra* note 751. *See also* ACF Indus. v. NLRB, *supra* note 742, at 429 ("The failure to mention a right in a bargaining agreement does not constitute a waiver of it even though there is a clause stating that the contract represents the entire agreement between the parties"). For further discussion of zipper clauses *see supra* at note 751.

[763]*Supra* note 743.

[764]*Id. See also* Druwhit Metal Prods. Co., *supra* note 750; International Shoe Co., 151 NLRB 693, 58 LRRM 1483 (1965); *but see* General Motors Corp., 149 NLRB 396, 57 LRRM 1277 (1964), *remanded sub nom.* Auto Workers v. NLRB, 60 LRRM 2283 (CADC, 1965), *on remand*, 158 NLRB 229, 62 LRRM 1009 (1966), *rev'd*, 381 F2d 265, 64 LRRM 2489 (CADC), *cert. denied*, 389 US 857, 66 LRRM 2307 (1967) (District of Columbia Circuit took more restrictive view of waiver language than did Board and reversed Board's dismissal of complaint).

employer the sole right to determine employee qualifications, the Board held that the union had waived its right to bargain over the subject of physical examinations during the term of the collective agreement.[765]

On the other hand, the Board refused to find a specific waiver of the right to bargain on a retirement plan despite a management-rights clause reserving exclusive control over the retirement of employees as a management prerogative.[766] Normally, a mere catchall phrase in a management-rights clause to the effect that the "Company retains the responsibility and authority of managing the Company's business,"[767] or that "all management rights not given up in the contract are expressly reserved to it,"[768] or reciting that the exclusive functions and rights of management include the right to establish, continue, or modify policies, practices, or procedures will fall short of being a "clear and unmistakable" relinquishment.[769]

In a 1989 decision, the Board determined in *Johnson-Bateman Co.*[770] that neither the management-rights clause which was "couched in the most general of terms and makes no reference to any particular subject areas, much less a specific reference to drug/alcohol testing"[771] nor the zipper clause constituted an express, clear, unequivocal, and unmistakable waiver by the union of its statutory rights to bargain about implementation of the drug/alcohol testing requirements.

c. Board Jurisdiction to Construe Collective Bargaining Agreements. In *NLRB v. C & C Plywood*[772] the Supreme Court held that the

---

[765]Leroy Mach. Co., 147 NLRB 1431, 56 LRRM 1369 (1964).

[766]Tide Water Associated Oil Co., 85 NLRB 1096, 24 LRRM 1518 (1949).

[767]Leeds & Northrup v. NLRB, 391 F2d 874, 877, 67 LRRM 2793, 2795 (CA 3, 1968), *enforcing* 162 NLRB 987, 64 LRRM 1110 (1967). *See also* Tenneco Chems., 249 NLRB 1176, 104 LRRM 1347 (1980).

[768]Proctor Mfg. Corp., 131 NLRB 1166, 48 LRRM 1222, 1223 (1961).

[769]Litton Sys., Microwave Cooking Prods. Div., 283 NLRB 973, 125 LRRM 1081 (1987), *enforcement denied*, 868 F2d 854, 130 LRRM 2773 (CA 6, 1989) (management-rights clause was not waiver of union's right to bargain over work relocation); Kansas Nat'l Educ. Ass'n, 275 NLRB 638, 119 LRRM 1213 (1985) (language reserving to management "right to carry out the ordinary and customary functions of management" was not waiver of union's right to bargain over employee transfers).

[770]*Supra* note 755.

[771]*Id.*, 131 LRRM at 1399.

[772]385 US 421, 64 LRRM 2065 (1967). *See generally* Chapter 17, "Relation of Board Action to Enforcement of Agreements Under Section 301," for discussion of Board action in relation to enforcement of collective agreements, and Chapter 18, "Accommodation of Board Action to the Arbitration Process," for treatment of the accommodation between Board action and the arbitration process.

Board had jurisdiction to interpret collective bargaining agreements to the extent necessary to determine whether the union had waived its right to bargain about a specific mandatory subject. The Court explained that the Board had not "construed a labor agreement to determine the extent of contractual rights which were given the union by the employer," but only whether the union had waived its right to bargain.[773]

While the Board has jurisdiction to construe a labor agreement for such purposes, it has nonetheless demonstrated, under the *Collyer* doctrine,[774] a willingness to defer the question of contractual waiver to an arbitrator. In *Radioear Corp.*,[775] the Board deferred to an arbitrator the question of whether the zipper clause in the collective bargaining agreement allowed the employer unilaterally to discontinue a bonus.[776] The arbitrator determined that the contract did not guarantee the continuation of the bonuses, but stated that he was without authority to decide whether the zipper clause, under the circumstances, constituted a waiver of the duty to bargain over discontinuation of the bonuses.[777] The Board held that it was within the arbitrator's power to decide the waiver issue since it was a "matter particularly suited to resolution in the forum of arbitration."[778]

2. Waiver by Bargaining History. Where a mandatory subject of bargaining has been discussed in contract negotiations but has not been specifically provided for in the resulting contract, a waiver will be found only where the union has "consciously yielded" its position.[779] This normally requires that the matter

---

[773]385 US at 428, 64 LRRM at 2067–68. *See also* NLRB v. Huttig Sash & Door Co., 377 F2d 964, 65 LRRM 2431 (CA 8, 1967); Gravenslund Operating Co., 168 NLRB 513, 66 LRRM 1323 (1967) (discussing effect of availability of grievance and arbitration machinery in contract and desirable procedural priorities).

[774]Collyer Insulated Wire, 192 NLRB 837, 77 LRRM 1931 (1971). For a full discussion of the *Collyer* doctrine, see Chapter 18, "Accommodation of Board Action to the Arbitration Process."

[775]*Supra* note 757.

[776]In refusing to apply automatically a "rigid rule" as to clear and unequivocal waiver, the Board stated that it was "unwilling to ignore what has taken place at the bargaining table and decide the parties' dispute on the basis of a simplistic formula . . . ." *Id.*, 199 NLRB at 1161.

[777]*Id.*, 214 NLRB at 363.

[778]*Id.*

[779]New York Mirror, 151 NLRB 834, 58 LRRM 1465 (1965); Proctor Mfg. Corp., *supra* note 768; Press Co., 121 NLRB 976, 42 LRRM 1493 (1958). *See* Chapter 17, "Relation of Board Action to Enforcement of Agreements Under Section 301."

be "fully discussed" and "consciously explored."[780] Thus, in *TTP Corp.*,[781] the Board held that the absence of any provisions in a labor agreement regarding a unilaterally adopted pension plan did not constitute a waiver of the union's right to bargain over the termination of the plan, notwithstanding that (1) the unilaterally adopted plan contained express provisions reserving to the employer the right unilaterally to terminate the plan, (2) the union was fully aware of the termination provisions of the pension plan, and (3) during three successive contract negotiations the union had at no time voiced any objection to the termination provisions of the plan.[782]

In *Texaco, Inc.*[783] the Board found that an employer's "practice" of discontinuing accident and sickness benefits during three previous strikes was ambiguous and did not establish an "agreed-on procedure." Thus, the "practice" fell "far short of persuasively demonstrating a clear and unmistakable waiver by the union."[784]

The payment of bonuses has been a frequent source of controversy because the collective bargaining agreement is often silent on this topic. The effect accorded an unsuccessful attempt by the union to incorporate this benefit into the agreement, either directly or by way of a "maintenance of benefits" clause, may turn on close factual circumstances. Where the demand is withdrawn from negotiations without "full discussion" there is a likelihood that no waiver will result.[785] This is especially true where the employer gives assurances that it has no intention of discontinuing the bonus.[786] However, where the employer specifically explains the reasons for its rejection and the union

---

[780]Bunker Hill Co., 208 NLRB 27, 85 LRRM 1264 (1973), *modified*, 210 NLRB 343, 86 LRRM 1157 (1974); Press Co., *supra* note 779. Mere silence or inaction is not "conscious exploration." Litton Precision Prods., 156 NLRB 555, 61 LRRM 1096 (1966); J.C. Penney Co., 161 NLRB 69, 63 LRRM 1309 (1966). *But cf.* Berkline Corp., 123 NLRB 685, 43 LRRM 1513 (1959). In the absence of bargaining over an issue, waiver will not be presumed unless there is "'clear and unequivocal' evidence pointing to a 'conscious relinquishment.'" Henry Vogt Mach. Co., 251 NLRB 363, 105 LRRM 1088, 1089 (1980), *enforcement denied*, 718 F2d 802, 114 LRRM 2893 (CA 6, 1983).

[781]190 NLRB 240, 77 LRRM 1097 (1971).

[782]Chairman Miller dissented. In his view, the majority decision held that silence had the effect of amending the pension plan to eliminate the provisions permitting the employer unilaterally to terminate it.

[783]291 NLRB 508, 129 LRRM 1249 (1988).

[784]*Id.*, 129 LRRM at 1251.

[785]Beacon Journal Publishing Co., 164 NLRB 734, 65 LRRM 1126 (1967), *modified*, 401 F2d 366, 69 LRRM 2232 (CA 6, 1968) (union's unsuccessful attempt to incorporate Christmas bonus provision in the agreement was not persuasive evidence of waiver).

[786]General Tel. Co., 144 NLRB 311, 54 LRRM 1055 (1963), *enforced as modified*, 337 F2d 452, 57 LRRM 2211 (CA 5, 1964).

remains silent, the absence of any contractual provision may be deemed a conscious acquiescence by the union in the position that the employer took during negotiations.[787]

A waiver does not usually turn on the presence or absence of a single factor.[788] Even clear contractual language is not always determinative. In *Kennecott Copper Corp.*,[789] for example, the employer unilaterally subcontracted work, relying upon a broad and inclusive management-rights clause which the trial examiner held reserved to the employer "the right to take precisely the action it took."[790] Although the Board dismissed the complaint, it did so because of the "particular circumstances" of the case, including the facts that the employees in the appropriate unit had suffered "no significant detriment"[791] and the employer had agreed to bargain when the union protested. This rationale of lack of significant detriment to bargaining-unit employees, relied upon in *Kennecott*, was followed in a series of Board decisions which upheld subcontracting without prior notification to the union.[792] Even so, a union's failure to obtain a contractual restriction on subcontracting has sometimes been viewed as persuasive.[793] While the Board has seemed reluctant to decide these cases in terms of a waiver doctrine,[794] the reasoning and the result appear to be the same.

Cases in which union acquiescence in the employer's past practice constitutes a maintenance of the status quo (e.g., an employer's continued unilateral subcontracting during the term of the agreement) should be distinguished from cases where a

---

[787]Radioear Corp., 214 NLRB 362, 87 LRRM 1330 (1974), *supplementing* 199 NLRB 1161, 81 LRRM 1402 (1972); Speidel Corp., 120 NLRB 733, 42 LRRM 1039 (1958) (union dropped demand for "maintenance of privileges" clause and remained silent in face of employer's explanation that such provision would make unilateral practice contractually binding and, as such, objectionable). *See* Tucker Steel Corp., 134 NLRB 323, 49 LRRM 1164 (1961) (employer predicted unilateral termination of bonuses if union's vacation demands were met; union's silence and absence of contractual provision created "estoppel"). *But see* Pine Manor Nursing Home, 230 NLRB 320, 95 LRRM 1356 (1977), *enforced*, 578 F2d 575, 99 LRRM 2156 (CA 5, 1978) (no waiver when union withdrew its proposal merely as a tactic to encourage movement at bargaining table).

[788]For an examination of some of the relevant factors, see Radioear Corp., *supra* note 787 and accompanying text.

[789]148 NLRB 1653, 57 LRRM 1217 (1964).

[790]*Id.* at 1656.

[791]*Id.* at 1654.

[792]Westinghouse Elec. Corp. (Mansfield Plant), 150 NLRB 1574, 58 LRRM 1257 (1965); American Oil Co., 151 NLRB 421, 58 LRRM 1412 (1965); Allied Chem. Corp., 151 NLRB 718, 58 LRRM 1480 (1965), *aff'd*, 358 F2d 234, 61 LRRM 2632 (CA 4, 1966); Shell Oil Co., 149 NLRB 283, 57 LRRM 1271 (1964); Shell Chem. Co., 149 NLRB 298, 57 LRRM 1275 (1964).

[793]*See, e.g.*, American Oil Co., *supra* note 792.

[794]Westinghouse Elec. Corp. (Mansfield Plant), *supra* note 792.

change in the status quo is made without consulting the union. In *Leeds & Northrup*[795] the employer had unilaterally instituted a supplementary compensation plan, renewing it annually. In defending its right to alter unilaterally the formula by which benefits were computed, the employer asserted an implied waiver, relying upon the Board's subcontracting decisions. This defense was rejected by the Board and the Third Circuit on the ground that the status quo had been represented by the formula that the employer unilaterally altered; whereas, in the subcontracting cases, the employers had simply continued the norm of subcontracting and thus had not altered the status quo.

3. Waiver by Inaction. The duty to bargain arises upon request; but where an opportunity exists to bargain and no request is made, a waiver may result.[796] For example, if a union has been notified that the employer plans removal of its operations but makes no attempt to bring issues relating to plant removal to the bargaining table, it waives its rights in the matter.[797] The union need not be given formal notice of the intended unilateral change if the union does in fact know of the plans and a formal announcement would be futile,[798] but the Board is generally reluctant to give broad effect to a waiver by inaction.[799] Timely notice must include information that allows

---

[795]Leeds & Northrup Co. v. NLRB, 391 F2d 874, 67 LRRM 2793 (CA 3, 1968), *enforcing* 162 NLRB 987, 64 LRRM 1110 (1967).

[796]*See, e.g.*, Clarkwood Corp., 233 NLRB 1172, 97 LRRM 1034 (1977); Medicenter, Mid-South Hosp., 221 NLRB 670, 90 LRRM 1576 (1975); Coppus Eng'g Corp., 195 NLRB 595, 79 LRRM 1449 (1972); Triplex Oil Ref., 194 NLRB 500, 78 LRRM 1711 (1971). *See also* notes 742 and 747 *supra*. A "union cannot charge an employer with refusal to negotiate when it has made no attempt to bring the employer to the bargaining table." NLRB v. Alva Allen Indus., 369 F2d 310, 63 LRRM 2515, 2521 (CA 8, 1966) (citing NLRB v. Columbian Enameling & Stamping Co., 306 US 292, 4 LRRM 524 (1939)).

[797]U.S. Lingerie Corp., 170 NLRB 750, 67 LRRM 1482 (1968). *See also* W.W. Grainger, Inc. v. NLRB, 860 F2d 244, 129 LRRM 2718 (CA 7, 1988) (waiver by failing to assert bargaining rights after being given ample opportunity to bargain over change of contractor); American Geri-Care, 278 NLRB 676, 122 LRRM 1240 (1986) (no evidence union requested bargaining over wages); Rochester Inst. of Technology, 264 NLRB 1020, n.2, 111 LRRM 1361 (1982), *enforcement denied on other grounds*, 724 F2d 9, 115 LRRM 2208 (CA 2, 1983); Love's Barbeque Restaurant, 245 NLRB 78, 102 LRRM 1546 (1979), *enforced in part*, 640 F2d 1094, 107 LRRM 2011 (CA 9, 1981) (subcontracting).

[798]*See supra* note 797; American Bus Lines, 164 NLRB 1055, 65 LRRM 1265 (1967). *Cf.* McLoughlin Mfg. Corp., 164 NLRB 140, 65 LRRM 1025 (1967), *enforced as modified*, 463 F2d 907, 80 LRRM 2716 (CADC, 1972); Southern Cal. Stationers, 162 NLRB 1517, 64 LRRM 1227 (1967); Dove Flocking & Screening Co., 145 NLRB 682, 55 LRRM 1013 (1963). While the union need not receive formal notice, it must receive sufficient notice of the change to give it the opportunity to make a meaningful response. *See e.g.*, Metromedia, Inc. v. NLRB, 586 F2d 1182, 99 LRRM 2743 (CA 8, 1978); Electri-Flex Co. v. NLRB, 570 F2d 1327, 97 LRRM 2888 (CA 7, 1978), *cert. denied*, 439 US 911, 99 LRRM 2743 (1978).

[799]*See* Peerless Publications, 231 NLRB 244, 95 LRRM 1611 (1977), *remanded*, 636 F2d 550, 105 LRRM 2001 (CADC, 1980), *and modified*, 283 NLRB 334, 124 LRRM 1331 (1987), and cases cited therein, 231 NLRB at 258.

the union to make an informed decision as to what action it wishes to take on the matter.[800] Thus, a union waived its right to bargain over a unilateral job transfer where the union had 1 month's advance notice and failed to respond until 1 month after the action was taken.[801] However, where a union receives notice contemporaneous with the action itself,[802] or where a demand to bargain would be futile,[803] there is no waiver by inaction.

The interrelationship of waiver and futility was aptly illustrated in *U.S. Lingerie Corp.*,[804] where the union rejected a demand for cooperation to relieve the employer's economic condition. Despite the clear warning to the union that plant removal would otherwise be necessitated, the union remained intransigent. The subsequent failure of the employer to advise the union formally of its decision to remove and to bargain with it was therefore excused on the ground of futility, and the union's failure to request bargaining over the removal was held to be a waiver. In *Johns-Manville Sales Corp.*,[805] however, the

---

[800]Coalite, Inc., 278 NLRB 293, 122 LRRM 1030 (1986). *See also* USA McDonald Corp. dba Norco Prods., 288 NLRB 1416, 129 LRRM 1183 (1988) (insufficient notice of layoffs); Litton Sys., Microwave Cooking Prods. Div., 283 NLRB 973, 125 LRRM 1081 (1987), *enforcement denied*, 868 F2d 854, 130 LRRM 2773 (CA 6, 1989) (union's failure to challenge layoffs resulting from gradual work reduction did not waive union's right to bargain over relocation of work).

[801]Kansas Nat'l Educ. Ass'n, 275 NLRB 638, 119 LRRM 1213 (1985). *Cf.* Greenleaf Motor Express, 285 NLRB 844, 126 LRRM 1320 (1987), *enforced*, 872 F2d 1027, 134 LRRM 2431 (CA 6), *cert. denied*, 493 US 954 (1989) (no waiver of right to bargain over representation of new drivers where union did not receive timely notice of employer's failure to recognize new drivers).

[802]NLRB v. American Distrib. Co., 715 F2d 446, 115 LRRM 2046 (CA 9, 1983), *cert. denied*, 466 US 958, 116 LRRM 2096 (1984). *See* NLRB v. Henry Vogt Mach. Co., 718 F2d 802, 114 LRRM 2893 (CA 6, 1983); Gulf States Mfg. v. NLRB, 704 F2d 1390, 113 LRRM 2789 (CA 5, 1983) (union did not waive its right to bargain over layoffs when it was notified of them only 5 minutes before they occurred); NLRB v. National Car Rental Sys., 672 F2d 1182, 109 LRRM 2832 (CA 3, 1982), *enforcing as modified* 252 NLRB 159, 105 LRRM 1263 (1980) (notice to union not timely); GHR Energy Corp., 294 NLRB No. 76, 133 LRRM 1069 (1989) (union advised of revised conditions under which polygraph testing would be conducted but was given no time to consider plan for testing which was to begin that same night); Gulf & W. Mfg., 286 NLRB 1122, 127 LRRM 1018 (1987) (fait accompli); Michigan Ladder Co., 286 NLRB 21, 127 LRRM 1092 (1987) (no waiver where decision to subcontract unit work was fait accompli); Owens-Corning Fiberglas Corp., 282 NLRB 609, 124 LRRM 1105 (1987) (union did not waive bargaining rights over changes to employee discount purchase plan where changes were not discussed during negotiations and were presented by employer as fait accompli); Kay Fries, Inc., 265 NLRB 1077, 112 LRRM 1377 (1982), *enforced without opinion*, 722 F2d 732, 115 LRRM 2904 (CA 3, 1983) (union faced with fait accompli); Johnson dba Print-Quic, 262 NLRB 857, 111 LRRM 1055 (1982).

[803]Intersystems Design & Technology Corp., 278 NLRB 759, 121 LRRM 1229 (1986). *See also* Emsing's Supermarket, 284 NLRB 302, 125 LRRM 1178 (1987), *enforced*, 872 F2d 1279, 131 LRRM 2296 (CA 7, 1989) (no waiver where employer mentioned discontinuance of benefit payments during negotiations, but matter was never discussed by parties).

[804]*Supra* note 797.

[805]282 NLRB 182, 123 LRRM 1315 (1986).

Board refused to find a waiver of the right to bargain over a change in layoff by seniority where the union indicated it desired to canvass employees' desires in the matter but the new policy was then implemented before further discussion between the parties.

B. Suspension During Illegal or Unprotected Activity

Although the duty to bargain is a continuing one, certain aspects of a party's duty may be temporarily suspended when the other party is engaged in unlawful activity. For example, it was held that an employer was not obligated to continue negotiations during periods in which the union endorsed illegal strike conduct including violence and vandalism[806] and encouraged mass demonstrations at the homes of nonstriking employees.[807] Employers also have been deemed justified in suspending negotiations when the union engaged in a strike in violation of a contractual no-strike pledge.[808] However, the obligation to bargain is suspended only so long as the period of the breach or unlawful action continues.[809]

---

[806]Lyman Steel Co., 249 NLRB 296, 104 LRRM 1323 (1980). The union must have been responsible for or have condoned such conduct, however.

[807]Kohler Co., 128 NLRB 1062, 46 LRRM 1389 (1960), *enforced in part and remanded in part*, 300 F2d 699, 49 LRRM 2485 (CADC, 1962), *supplemented by* 148 NLRB 1434, 57 LRRM 1148 (1964), *enforced*, 345 F2d 748, 58 LRRM 2847 (CADC, 1965). *See also* Johns-Manville Prods. Corp. v. NLRB, 557 F2d 1126, 96 LRRM 2010 (CA 5, 1977), *cert. denied sub nom.* Oil, Chem. & Atomic Workers v. NLRB, 436 US 956, 98 LRRM 2617 (1978), where the court refused to enforce a Board decision finding, inter alia, that the employer had refused to bargain with the union. After numerous acts of in-plant vandalism and sabotage by employees, the employer locked out the employees and hired permanent replacements. The court found that the employees' conduct amounted to an "in-plant strike" and that the employer could therefore hire permanent replacements without bargaining with the union. *See* notes 683–684 *supra* and accompanying text for a fuller discussion of the case.

[808]Arundel Corp., 210 NLRB 525, 86 LRRM 1180 (1974). The Board held that an employer did not violate the Act and was under no obligation to bargain with the union while the union was engaging in an unprotected strike in violation of an oral agreement between the parties. *See also* International Shoe Corp., 152 NLRB 699, 59 LRRM 1176 (1965), *enforced*, 357 F2d 330, 61 LRRM 2559 (CA 1, 1966); Marathon Elec. Mfg. Corp., 106 NLRB 1171, 1180, 32 LRRM 1645 (1953); United Elastic Corp., 84 NLRB 768, 24 LRRM 1294 (1949). Older cases held that a union-led slowdown justified a suspension of bargaining. *See, e.g.*, Phelps Dodge Copper Prods. Corp., 101 NLRB 360, 31 LRRM 1072 (1952). Those decisions antedate NLRB v. Insurance Agents (Prudential Ins. Co.), 361 US 477, 45 LRRM 2704 (1960), which held that such actions are not, per se, refusals to bargain. *See* Carroll Contracting & Ready-Mix, 247 NLRB 890, 103 LRRM 1232 (1980), *enforcement denied*, 636 F2d 111, 106 LRRM 2491 (CA 5, 1981) (slowdown did not justify employer refusal to bargain).

[809]Arundel Corp., *supra* note 808; United Elastic Corp., *supra* note 808; Dorsey Trailers, Inc., 80 NLRB 478, 23 LRRM 1112 (1948). *See* Carroll Contracting & Ready Mix, *supra* note 808 (dictum).

A party's obligation to bargain with a particular negotiator may be suspended if that negotiator's behavior makes good-faith negotiations impossible.[810] Further, if the union commits an unfair labor practice or asks the employer to commit one directly related to the employer's alleged refusal to bargain,[811] or if the union has been improperly certified,[812] the employer may not be required to bargain. Unlawful insistence to impasse on a permissive subject also suspends the bargaining duty.[813]

The illegal or unprotected conduct, however, must be substantial, generally unprovoked, and closely related to the bargaining in question in order to support suspension of the bargaining duty.[814] In one case where a "handfull" of strikers engaged in mass picketing, threats, assaults, and some damaging of property during a strike that had been caused by the employer's disciplinary suspension of a union activist, the employer's own extensive illegal conduct warranted issuance of a bargaining order against the employer.[815] Defamatory statements made by a union during an election campaign are not enough to relieve the employer of its duty to bargain.[816] And claims that a union[817] or an employer[818] have engaged in illegal

---

[810]Auto Workers v. NLRB (FitzSimons Mfg. Co.), 670 F2d 663, 109 LRRM 2810 (CA 6, 1982); Sahara Datsun, 278 NLRB 1044, 121 LRRM 1329 (1986), *enforced*, 811 F2d 1317, 124 LRRM 3168 (CA 9, 1987).

[811]Kaiser Found. Hosps., Kaiser Found. Health Plan of Or., 258 NLRB 29, 108 LRRM 1093, *supplemented*, 259 NLRB 393, 108 LRRM 1363 (1981).

[812]Brink's, Inc., 276 NLRB 1, 120 LRRM 1069 (1985) (employer's contention that union admitted nonguards warrants hearing). *See also* North Shore Univ. Hosp., 274 NLRB 1289, 119 LRRM 1585 (1985), *supplementing* 259 NLRB 852, 109 LRRM 1047 (1981); Sub-Zero Freezer Co., 271 NLRB 47, 116 LRRM 1281 (1984).

[813]Nassau Ins. Co., 280 NLRB 878, 124 LRRM 1075 (1986).

[814]*See* Santa Rosa Blueprint Serv., 288 NLRB 762, 130 LRRM 1403 (1988); Edward Z. Holmes Detective Bureau, 256 NLRB 824, 107 LRRM 1305 (1981) (union's "appalling level of bigotry" in referring to employees insufficient).

[815]Donovan v. NLRB, 520 F2d 1316, 89 LRRM 3127 (CA 2, 1975), *cert. denied*, 423 US 1053, 91 LRRM 2099 (1976), *enforcing* 206 NLRB 688, 85 LRRM 1227 (1973). *Cf.* Laura Modes Co., 144 NLRB 1592, 54 LRRM 1299 (1963). *See also* Evening News Publishing Co., 196 NLRB 530, 80 LRRM 1230 (1972), where the Board held that the employer could not unilaterally order its employees to cease their accepted practice of inflating their expense accounts; questions of morality and violations of tax laws, which would be raised by a continuation of the practice, did not relieve the employer of the duty to bargain on the changes. *See also* Marin Arsham Sewing Co., 244 NLRB 918, 102 LRRM 1119 (1979).

[816]Paramount Gen. Hosp., 223 NLRB 1017, 92 LRRM 1171 (1976), *aff'd*, 554 F2d 1202, 95 LRRM 2626 (CADC, 1977).

[817]Colonial Manor 1977, 253 NLRB 1183, 106 LRRM 1184 (1981); Bell & Howell Co., 230 NLRB 420, 95 LRRM 1333 (1977), *supplementing* 220 NLRB 881, 90 LRRM 1448 (1975), *aff'd*, 598 F2d 136, 100 LRRM 2192 (CADC, 1979), *cert. denied*, 442 US 942, 101 LRRM 2556 (1979). *See also* Handy Andy, Inc., 228 NLRB 447, 94 LRRM 1354 (1977).

[818]Graphic Arts Local 280 (James H. Barry Co.), 235 NLRB 1084, 98 LRRM 1188 (1978), *aff'd*, 596 F2d 904, 101 LRRM 2664 (CA 9, 1979).

age, sex, or race discrimination will not support a suspension of the duty to bargain.

C. Union Loss of Majority

The Act requires the employer to recognize and bargain with the representative of the majority of its employees in an appropriate bargaining unit; thus, under the literal language of the statute the employer would not be required to bargain with a union that loses its majority status. However, there are several recognized exceptions to the literal requirement of majority status. These have been developed by both statutory provision and case law for the purpose of stabilizing industrial relations.[819] This complex body of regulation is dealt with in detail in Chapters 10, "Representation Proceedings and Elections," and 12, "Recognition and Withdrawal of Recognition Without an Election." Here we summarize matters of particular importance in regard to the duty to bargain in good faith.

A certified union must be recognized for a full year following certification, absent "unusual circumstances," even when it has lost its majority.[820] Majority status is irrebuttably presumed to continue during the term of a collective bargaining contract. A rebuttable presumption of majority status also applies, and with it the duty to bargain, in the absence of a collective bargaining agreement.[821] This latter presumption applies "to situations where the refusal to bargain is with a Board certified union or with an incumbent union which has theretofore achieved a bargaining status evidenced by a collective-bargaining agreement, or, at least, by prior recognition."[822] The presumption establishes a prima facie requirement that the employer is obligated to bargain with the incumbent union. As the Board outlined in *Terrell Machine Co.*:[823]

---

[819]See discussion of the *1-year rule* and the *contract-bar doctrine* in Chapter 10, "Representation Proceedings and Elections," at notes 76–98 and 119–201.

[820]*See, e.g.*, Mar-Jac Poultry Co., 136 NLRB 785, 49 LRRM 1854 (1962).

[821]*See generally* Chapter 12, "Recognition and Withdrawal of Recognition Without an Election," at notes 313–360. Special rules apply to relationships in the construction industry under §8(f). *See* note 836 *infra*.

[822]Ramada Inns, 171 NLRB 1060, 1062, 68 LRRM 1209, 1211 (1968). The presumption must be based on a clear unit description in prior collective bargaining agreements or past practice as to the relevant unambiguous unit. NLRB v. West Sand & Gravel Co., 612 F2d 1326, 103 LRRM 2255 (CA 1, 1979). *See also* Glenlynn, Inc., 204 NLRB 299, 83 LRRM 1356 (1973).

[823]173 NLRB 1480, 1480–81, 70 LRRM 1049 (1969), *enforced*, 427 F2d 1088, 73 LRRM 2381 (CA 4, 1970). *See also* Guerdon Indus., 218 NLRB 658, 89 LRRM 1389 (1975); Bartenders Ass'n of Pocatello, 213 NLRB 651, 87 LRRM 1194 (1974); Glenlynn, Inc., *supra* note 822; Celanese Corp. of Am., 95 NLRB 664, 28 LRRM 1362 (1951).

The *prima facie* case may be rebutted if the employer affirmatively establishes either (1) that at the time of the refusal the union in fact no longer enjoyed majority representative status, or (2) that the employer's refusal was predicated on a good-faith and reasonably grounded doubt of the union's continued majority status. As to the second of these, i.e., "good faith doubt," two prerequisites for sustaining the defense are that the asserted doubt may be based on objective considerations and it must not have been advanced for the purpose of gaining time in which to undermine the union.[824]

Employee turnover alone is not sufficient to support a good-faith doubt,[825] nor is the filing of a decertification petition[826] or a petition by a rival union.[827] This rule is applicable to contract-bar cases in section 9 (representation) proceedings and to the employer's obligation to bargain.[828]

Although there is no presumption that replacements for economic strikers support the union in the same ratio as do the strikers, neither is there a presumption that they do not support the union. In order to establish a good-faith doubt of majority status, the employer must show "some further evidence of union non-support."[829]

An employer may not lawfully withdraw recognition from a union if the employer's unlawful conduct improperly undermines the union's majority status.[830] The Ninth Circuit has agreed, holding that an employer could not use a decertification

---

[824]173 NLRB at 1480–81. *See also* Eastern Wash. Distrib. Co., 216 NLRB 1149, 1152–53, 88 LRRM 1453 (1975); Bartenders Ass'n of Pocatello, *supra* note 823.

[825]H&H Pretzel Co., 277 NLRB 1327, 121 LRRM 1110 (1985), *enforced*, 831 F2d 650, 126 LRRM 2712 (CA 6, 1987).

[826]Dresser Indus., 264 NLRB 1088, 111 LRRM 1436 (1982) (overruling Teleautograph, 199 NLRB 892, 81 LRRM 1337 (1972), which had allowed suspension of bargaining upon the filing of a valid decertification petition). *See also* NLRB v. Wallkill Valley Gen. Hosp., 866 F2d 632, 131 LRRM 2442 (CA 3, 1989); Hancock Fabrics dba Fabric Warehouse, 294 NLRB No. 4, 131 LRRM 1306 (1989), *enforced without opinion*, 902 F2d 28, 134 LRRM 2064 (CA 4, 1990); Hercules Automotive, 285 NLRB 944, 127 LRRM 1060 (1987).

[827]RCA del Caribe, 262 NLRB 963, 110 LRRM 1369 (1982). *See also* Hercules Automotive, *supra* note 826.

[828]*See* United States Gypsum Co., 157 NLRB 652, 61 LRRM 1384 (1966). *See also* note 819 *supra*.

[829]NLRB v. Curtin Matheson Scientific, 494 US 775, 133 LRRM 3049 (1990). *See* Hajoca Corp., 291 NLRB 104, 129 LRRM 1296 (1988), *enforced*, 872 F2d 1169, 131 LRRM 2447 (CA 3, 1989); Buckley Broadcasting Corp. of Cal. dba Station KKHI, 284 NLRB 1339, 125 LRRM 1281 (1987).

[830]Bay Area-Los Angeles Express, 275 NLRB 1063, 119 LRRM 1255 (1985); Choctawhatchee Elec. Coop., 274 NLRB 595, 118 LRRM 1431 (1985); Mark Twain Marine Indus., 254 NLRB 1095, 107 LRRM 1008 (1981); Jax Mold & Mach., 255 NLRB 942, 107 LRRM 1197 (1981), *aff'd without opinion*, 683 F2d 418, 111 LRRM 2137 (CA 11, 1982). *But see* Landmark Int'l Trucks v. NLRB, 775 F2d 148, 120 LRRM 2865 (CA 6, 1985); Viking Connectors Co., 297 NLRB No. 15, 133 LRRM 1235 (1989); Eastern States Optical Co., 275 NLRB 371, 119 LRRM 1107 (1985) (no unlawful assistance from employer in decertification).

petition as a defense to a refusal-to-bargain charge where the employer's fair labor practices undermined the union's status.[831]

A change in the employer's condition which does not have significant impact on the bargaining unit will not support an employer's doubt of the union's majority status, and a subsequent refusal to bargain will violate the Act. Thus, absent special circumstances, a union is presumed to retain majority status when a successor employer takes over a going business for which the union is the bargaining representative.[832] Likewise, withdrawal from a multi-employer bargaining unit does not negate the presumption of continued union majority status.[833]

VIII. THE CONSTRUCTION INDUSTRY: SECTION 8(f)

A. History of Bargaining in the Industry and Application of Section 8(f)

The Labor-Management Reporting and Disclosure Act of 1959[834] added section 8(f) to the National Labor Relations Act. Designed to meet certain problems in the building and construction industry, the section acts as a savings clause allowing union-security agreements under circumstances which would otherwise constitute unfair labor practices.[835] Thus, an employer engaged primarily in the building and construction industry may enter into a prehire agreement requiring union mem-

---

[831]NLRB v. Carilli dba Antonio's Restaurant, 648 F2d 1206, 107 LRRM 2961 (CA 9, 1981), *enforcing* 246 NLRB 833, 103 LRRM 1013 (1979).

[832]*See* NLRB v. Burns Int'l Detective Agency, 406 US 272, 80 LRRM 2225 (1972); Pick-Mt. Laurel Corp. v. NLRB, 625 F2d 476, 104 LRRM 2703 (CA 3, 1980); NLRB v. Pepsi-Cola Bottling Co., 613 F2d 267, 103 LRRM 2233 (CA 10, 1980); NLRB v. Fabsteel Co., 587 F2d 689, 100 LRRM 2349 (CA 5), *cert. denied*, 442 US 943, 101 LRRM 2556 (1979); NLRB v. Middleboro Fire Apparatus, 590 F2d 4, 100 LRRM 2182 (CA 1, 1978); M & H Mach. Co., 243 NLRB 817, 102 LRRM 1038 (1979); Barrington Plaza & Tragniew, 185 NLRB 962, 75 LRRM 1226 (1970), *enforcement denied*, 470 F2d 669, 81 LRRM 2336 (CA 9, 1972). *Cf.* Western Distrib. Co. v. NLRB, 608 F2d 397, 102 LRRM 2510 (CA 10, 1979). For general treatment of the effect of change in the employing unit, see Chapter 15, "Effect of Change in the Employing Unit: Successorship."

[833]NLRB v. Silver Spur Casino, 623 F2d 571, 104 LRRM 3068 (CA 9, 1980), *cert. denied*, 451 US 906, 106 LRRM 3077 (1981); NLRB v. Roger's I.G.A., 605 F2d 1164, 103 LRRM 3126 (CA 10, 1979); NLRB v. Sierra Dev. Co., 604 F2d 606, 102 LRRM 2160 (CA 9, 1979); NLRB v. Carda Hotels, 604 F2d 605, 102 LRRM 2484 (CA 9, 1979); NLRB v. Tahoe Nugget, 584 F2d 293, 99 LRRM 2509 (CA 9, 1978), *cert. denied*, 444 US 887, 101 LRRM 2428 (1979); Sahara-Tahoe Corp. v. NLRB, 581 F2d 767, 99 LRRM 2837 (CA 9, 1978), *cert. denied*, 442 US 917, 101 LRRM 2428 (1979).

[834]*See* Chapter 4, "The Landrum-Griffin Changes."

[835]*See generally* King & La Vaute, *Current Trends in Construction Industry Labor Relations, The Double Breasted Contractor and the Prehire Contract*, 29 SYRACUSE L. REV. 901 (1978).

bership as a condition of employment, where not prohibited by state law, notwithstanding the undetermined majority status of the union.[836] Under conventional doctrine such an employer would be guilty of an unfair labor practice by extending recognition to a minority union,[837] and any agreement executed under such circumstances would be invalid even though bargained for under the erroneous but good-faith belief that the employer was dealing with a majority union. A limited though significant departure from the traditional bargaining obligation therefore exists in the building and construction industry. Two important statutory qualifications diminish the potential impact of this section, however. First, section 8(f) does not validate prehire agreements where the union has been established, maintained, or assisted by any action of the employer otherwise violative of section 8(a)(2). Second, a valid prehire agreement is no bar to an election petition subsequently filed to determine the majority representative.[838]

In the 1970s the Board consistently held that a "prehire agreement is merely a preliminary step that contemplates further action for the development of a full bargaining relationship."[839] In one case the Board held that an employer that had signed a prehire agreement with a union did not violate section 8(a)(5) when it unilaterally repudiated the agreement during its term, because the union never obtained majority status;[840] since the union's majority could be tested under section 8(f) at any time during the agreement, the union was not entitled to a presumption of majority status.[841]

---

[836]Administrative Ruling SR-813, 46 LRRM 1515 (1960). The General Counsel refused to issue a complaint where a construction industry employer had complained that the minority union had coerced it into signing a contract. Although a poll of the employees showed that the majority did not wish to be represented by the union, the Act specifically allows union-security agreements within the industry.

[837]Ladies' Garment Workers (Bernhard-Altmann Tex. Corp.) v. NLRB, 366 US 731, 48 LRRM 2251 (1961). *See* Chapter 8, "Employer Domination and Assistance to Labor Organizations," at notes 9–12.

[838]Bear Creek Constr. Co., 135 NLRB 1285, 49 LRRM 1674 (1962). *See* Chapter 10, "Representation Proceedings and Elections," at notes 149–151.

[839]Ruttman Constr. Co., 191 NLRB 701, 702, 77 LRRM 1497 (1971).

[840]R.J. Smith Constr. Co., 191 NLRB 693, 695 n.5, 77 LRRM 1493 (1971), *rev'd and remanded sub nom.* Operating Eng'rs Local 150, 480 F2d 1186, 83 LRRM 2706 (CADC, 1973). *See also* Plott, *Pre-Hire Contracts in the Construction Industry*, 15 B.C. INDUS. & COM. L. REV. 862 (1974).

[841]R.J. Smith Constr. Co., *supra* note 840, at 694. A rebuttable presumption would be appropriate, however, if the prehire agreement contains a union-security clause, which was absent in this case. *Id.* at 695 n.5. Board cases also held that once a union achieved majority support in a "core" work force, it gained an irrebuttable presumption of majority status for the term of the agreement, and an irrebuttable presumption upon its expiration. *See* McWhorter dba McWhorter Trucking, 273 NLRB 369, 118 LRRM 1544 (1984); Hageman Underground Constr., 253 NLRB 60, 105 LRRM 1385 (1980).

In *NLRB v. Iron Workers Local 103 (Higdon Contracting Co.)*[842] the Supreme Court agreed with the Board's interpretation of section 8(f), albeit in a very narrow setting. The employer signed a prehire agreement with a union and thereafter formed a separate corporation to utilize nonunion labor on certain construction jobs (a "double breasted"[843] operation). The union set up picket lines to compel the employer to apply the prehire agreement to its nonunion corporation. The employer responded by filing a section 8(b)(7)(C)[844] charge against the union for picketing without a representation petition having been filed. The Board held that the union violated section 8(b)(7)(C) since it never represented a majority of the employees of the nonunion corporation or of the employer itself.[845] Although the prehire agreement did not violate the Act, absent union majority status the employer was at liberty to repudiate the agreement at any time. Thus, the prehire agreement did not insulate the union from the provisions of section 8(b)(7)(C). The District of Columbia Circuit reversed, holding that the employer's sole remedy, if it wished to annul a prehire agreement, was to request a representation election.[846]

The Supreme Court, however, reversed the circuit court and affirmed the Board.[847] The Court held that the purpose of section 8(f) was to permit the *making* of prehire agreements with a minority union in the construction industry, not to enforce them:

> §8(f) itself does not purport to authorize picketing to enforce prehire agreements where the union has not achieved majority support. Neither does it expand the duty of an employer under §8(a)(5), which is to bargain with a *majority* representative, to require the employer to bargain with a union with which he has executed a prehire agreement but which has failed to win majority support in the covered unit.[848]

So construed, section 8(f) allows a voluntary prehire agreement between an employer and a minority union, but does not mandate good-faith bargaining between the parties.[849] Follow-

[842] 434 US 335, 97 LRRM 2333 (1978). *See* Chapter 27, "Union Security," at notes 170–174.

[843] *See infra* at notes 960–1004.

[844] *See generally* Chapter 21, "Picketing for Organization and Recognition."

[845] Iron Workers Local 103 (Higdon Contracting Co.), 216 NLRB 45, 88 LRRM 1067 (1975).

[846] Iron Workers Local 103 (Higdon Contracting Co.) v. NLRB, 535 F2d 87, 91 LRRM 2986 (CADC, 1976).

[847] NLRB v. Iron Workers Local 103 (Higdon Contracting Co.), *supra* note 842.

[848] *Id.* at 346 (emphasis in original).

[849] R.J. Smith Constr. Co., *supra* note 840.

ing the Supreme Court's decision in *Higdon,* the courts divided on the enforceability of prehire agreements in the absence of majority status.[850]

In *Jim McNeff, Inc. v. Todd,*[851] a suit brought by fringe-benefit-fund trustees, the Supreme Court resolved the issue of enforceability of prehire agreements under section 301 where the union has not attained majority status. The Court noted that it had previously approved the Board's conclusion that prehire agreements are "voluntary" and "voidable" until a union has reached majority status.[852] But the Court perceived "a critical distinction" between an employer's obligation to recognize a union as majority representative under section 8(b)(7)(C) and an employer's duty to satisfy "lawful contractual obligations."[853] The Court held that such prehire agreements were enforceable under section 301 until and unless repudiated by the employer.[854]

Recognizing that a party has an "undoubted right" to repudiate, the Court left open the question of what specific act or acts would suffice to accomplish the repudiation.[855] Cases decided since have not consistently delineated the specific acts necessary before repudiation of a prehire agreement will be judicially recognized.[856]

---

[850]A number of courts have held that prehire agreements are judicially enforceable and that nonmajority status is no defense. *See* Washington Area Carpenters Welfare Fund v. Overhead Door Co. of Metro. Wash., 681 F2d 1, 110 LRRM 2752 (CADC, 1982); Todd v. Jim McNeff, Inc., 667 F2d 800, 109 LRRM 2802 (CA 9, 1982); Western-Washington Laborers-Employers Health & Sec. Trust Fund v. McDowell, 109 LRRM 3104 (CA 9, 1982); Carpenters, New Mexico Dist. Council v. Mayhew Co., 664 F2d 215, 107 LRRM 2930 (CA 10, 1981); W.C. James, Inc. v. Oil, Chem. & Atomic Workers, 646 F2d 1292, 107 LRRM 2226 (CA 8, 1981); Health & Welfare Plan v. Associated Wrecking Co., 638 F2d 1128, 106 LRRM 2257 (CA 8, 1980). *See also* Iron Workers Local 387 v. Southern Stress Wire Corp., 509 F Supp 1097, 108 LRRM 2982 (ND Ga, 1981); Florida Marble Polishers Health & Welfare Trust Fund v. Megahee, 102 LRRM 2740 (ND Fla, 1979).

However, some courts have reached the opposite result. *See* Building & Constr. Trades Council of Baton Rouge v. E.C. Schafer Constr. Co., 657 F2d 806, 108 LRRM 2634 (CA 5, 1981); NLRB v. Haberman Constr. Co., 641 F2d 351, 106 LRRM 2998 (CA 5, 1981) (en banc) (dictum). *See also* Paddack v. Clark, 107 LRRM 2325 (D Or, 1980).

[851]461 US 260, 113 LRRM 2113 (1983).

[852]*Id.*, 113 LRRM at 2116.

[853]*Id.* at 2115. The Court explained that in NLRB v. Iron Workers Local 103 (Higdon Contracting Co.), *supra* note 842, the issue was whether a union with a prehire contract could picket under §8(b)(7)(C) as "representative of [the employer's] employees." 113 LRRM at 2115.

[854]113 LRRM at 2116.

[855]*Id.* at 2117 and 2117 n.11.

[856]Repudiation by conduct has been recognized. Carpenters Local 2247 v. Endicott Enters., 806 F2d 918, 124 LRRM 2265 (CA 9, 1986), *cert. denied*, 484 US 850, 126 LRRM 2496 *and* 484 US 913, 126 LRRM 2776 (1987) (employer conduct sufficiently "bald" to give union notice); Contractors, Laborers, Teamsters & Eng'rs Health & Welfare Plan v.

B. The *Deklewa* Decision: Binding Section 8(f) Agreements and the Duty to Bargain

A major shift in the Board's approach to section 8(f) was announced in *John Deklewa & Sons.*[857] The Board in *Deklewa* overruled *R.J. Smith,*[858] abandoned the "conversation" doctrine, and modified its rules defining the scope of bargaining units in section 8(f) cases. The Board announced that these principles were to be applied in section 8(f) cases:

1. Section 8(f) agreements permitted under the Act would be enforceable through the mechanism of sections 8(a)(5) and 8(b)(3) and could not be unilaterally repudiated during their term.
2. Agreements under section 8(f) would not bar a petition filed pursuant to section 9(c) or (e) of the Act.
3. In processing a petition filed under section 9(c) or 9(e), the appropriate unit would "normally" be a single-employer unit.
4. Upon the expiration of the agreement the union would enjoy no "presumption of majority status, and either party may repudiate the 8(f) bargaining relationship."[859]

The Board also determined that the principles newly enunciated would be applied retroactively.[860]

Harkins Constr. & Equip. Co., 733 F2d 1321, 1326, 116 LRRM 2425, 2429 (CA 8, 1984) (acts putting union and employees on notice are sufficient); Operating Eng'rs Pension Trust v. Beck Eng'g & Surveying Co., 746 F2d 557, 117 LRRM 3041, 3047 (CA 9, 1984) (single-employee situation); *cf.* Washington Area Carpenters' Welfare Fund v. Overhead Door Co. of Metro. Wash., 681 F2d 1, 9, 110 LRRM 2752, 2758 (CADC, 1982), *cert. denied,* 461 US 926, 113 LRRM 2448 (1983). But mere noncompliance does not equal repudiation. Iron Workers Local 103 v. Higdon Constr. Co., 739 F2d 280, 116 LRRM 3265 (CA 7, 1984); Todd v. Jim McNeff, Inc., 667 F2d 800, 109 LRRM 2802 (CA 9, 1982), *aff'd,* 461 US 260, 113 LRRM 2113 (1983). Formal notice in writing has been deemed effective. John S. Griffith Constr. Co. v. Carpenters, 119 LRRM 2247 (CD Cal, 1984), *rev'd,* 785 F2d 706, 121 LRRM 3385 (CA 9, 1986); *cf.* Building & Constr. Trades Council of San Mateo County v. Alberici/Denver, 119 LRRM 2240, 2246 (ND Cal, 1985); Painters Dist. Council No. 3 Pension Fund v. Johnson dba De Be Painting Co., 566 F Supp 592, 597 (WD Mo, 1983); Ion Constr. v. Painters Dist. Council No. 16, 593 F Supp 233, 239, 121 LRRM 3099 (ND Cal, 1984), *aff'd,* 803 F2d 1050, 125 LRRM 3110 (CA 9, 1986). *See also* Mesa Verde Constr. Co. v. Laborers, Northern Cal. Dist. Council, 598 F Supp 1092, 1100, 121 LRRM 3490 (ND Cal, 1984), *aff'd,* 820 F2d 1006, 125 LRRM 2849, *reh'g en banc granted, prior opinion withdrawn,* 832 F2d 1164, 128 LRRM 2780 (CA 9, 1987), *remanded en banc,* 861 F2d 1124, 129 LRRM 3073 (CA 9, 1988) (repudiation when no employees employed in bargaining unit).

[857] 282 NLRB 1375, 124 LRRM 1185 (1987), *enforced sub nom.* Iron Workers Local 3 v. NLRB, 843 F2d 770, 128 LRRM 2020 (CA 3), *cert. denied,* 488 US 889, 129 LRRM 2528 (1988).

[858] R.J. Smith Constr. Co., *supra* note 840.

[859] 282 NLRB at 1378, 124 LRRM at 1187.

[860] *Id.* at 1389, 124 LRRM at 1198.

Deklewa made it clear that voluntary prehire agreements could not be unilaterally repudiated by either party. The Board has consistently enforced this mandate, but subject to the one-man unit rule.[861] An agreement entered into under section 8(f) may become unenforceable only when a union, the employees, or an employer file a petition pursuant to section 9(c) or 9(e). Should the union win the election, it would enjoy the "full panoply of Section 9 rights."[862] Should the union lose, the contract would be unenforceable and the parties would violate the Act if another section 8(f) agreement were entered into within the succeeding 12 months.[863]

The *Deklewa* opinion made clear that a construction industry employer and union could enter into a section 9(a) relationship through voluntary recognition where such recognition was "based on a clear showing of majority support among the unit employees . . . ."[864] The Board later ruled that to establish voluntary recognition in the construction industry, there must be "evidence that the union unequivocally demanded recognition as the employees' 9(a) representative and that the employer unequivocally accepted it as such."[865]

Deklewa makes clear that a construction union has no presumption of majority status upon the expiration of the agreement. The opinion went on to state that "any coercive union efforts, including strikes and picketings" to compel renewal of the relationship would violate the Act.[866] That this was not meant to prohibit all picketing for section 8(f) agreement was clarified in later cases. In *Laborers Local 1184 (Cates Constructors)*,[867] the Board recognized that its statement in *Deklewa* concerning strikes or picketing was inaccurate. In clarifying the matter, the Board held that the employer must be free only from unlawful coercion, for example, unlimited picketing. A con-

---

[861] *See, e.g.*, Nordpal Corp. dba Twin City Garage Door Co., 297 NLRB No. 13, 133 LRRM 1234 (1989); Bufco Corp., 291 NLRB 1015, 130 LRRM 1116 (1988), *aff'd*, 899 F2d 608, 134 LRRM 2044 (CA 7, 1990); W.E. Colglazier, Inc., 289 NLRB 1219, 130 LRRM 1241 (1988). In Stack Elec., 290 NLRB 575, 129 LRRM 1293 (1988), the Board held that the employer could disavow the agreement where there was only one employee in the bargaining unit.

[862] John Deklewa & Sons, *supra* note 857, at 1385, 124 LRRM at 1195.

[863] *Id.*

[864] *Id.* at 1387 n.53, 124 LRRM at 1196 n.53.

[865] J & R Tile, 291 NLRB 1034, 130 LRRM 1005, 1007 (1988). *See also* Precision Striping, 284 NLRB 1110, 1112 n.6, 126 LRRM 1117 (1987) (employer poll may establish §9(a) relationship).

[866] John Deklewa & Sons, *supra* note 857, at 1386, 124 LRRM at 1195.

[867] 296 NLRB No. 165, 132 LRRM 1273 (1989).

struction union was free to picket an employer for a section 8(f) contract so long as it comported with the time limitations of section 8(b)(7)(C).[868] It would seem to follow that normal bargaining tactics are available to the parties negotiating a section 8(f) agreement.

As noted, the *Deklewa* opinion provided that its principles would be applied retroactively.[869] Subsequent to *Deklewa,* the General Counsel took the position that recognition extended prior to 1959 established a section 9(a) relationship.[870] In the General Counsel's view, because section 8(f) was passed in 1959, any relationship established prior to that time would either have been a lawful majority-based section 9(a) relationship or an unlawful minority-based section 8(a)(2) relationship. Moreover, that even if the relationship had been minority-based, the section 10(b) period under the statute would preclude a showing that a section 8(a)(2) relationship had been created at its inception. The General Counsel's position was rejected by the Board in *Brannan Sand & Gravel.*[871] In *Brannan,* the Board held that all construction industry contracts were to be presumed to be section 8(f), even those predating 1959. The Board further rejected the General Counsel's view that section 10(b) would preclude a showing of a minority-based relationship.

The courts have disagreed on whether the Board's retroactive application of *Deklewa* was appropriate.[872]

IX. NOTICE TO TERMINATE OR MODIFY THE LABOR AGREEMENT

A. Notice Requirements Generally

Section 8(d), in defining the duty to bargain collectively, includes notice requirements that must be satisfied prior to termination or modification of a labor contract. Section 8(d)(1) requires that the party desiring termination or modification of the agreement must serve upon the other party to the contract a

[868]*Id.*, 132 LRRM at 1278.

[869]John Deklewa & Sons, *supra* note 857, at 1389, 124 LRRM at 1198.

[870]*See* Brannan Sand & Gravel Co., 289 NLRB 977, 128 LRRM 1249, 1250 (1988).

[871]*Id.*

[872]*Compare* Mesa Verde Constr. Co. v. Laborers, Northern Cal. Dist. Council, 885 F2d 594, 132 LRRM 2461 (CA 9, 1989), *on remand after* 861 F2d 1124, 129 LRRM 3073 (CA 9, 1988) (en banc) *with* NLRB v. W.L. Miller Co., 871 F2d 745, 130 LRRM 3102 (CA 8, 1989).

written notice of the proposed termination or modification 60 days prior to the expiration date of the agreement, or in the event such contract contains no expiration date, 60 days prior to the time it is proposed to make such termination or modification. Section 8(d)(3) provides that the party desiring to terminate or modify the agreement must notify the Federal Mediation and Conciliation Service (FMCS) within 30 days "after such notice of the existence of a dispute"[873] and must simultaneously notify any state or territorial agency established to mediate and conciliate disputes within the state or territory where the dispute occurred, provided no agreement has been reached by that time.[874] Section 8(d)(4) provides that the parties to the labor contract are precluded from striking or locking out for a period of 60 days (1) after the section 8(d)(1) notice is given, or (2) after the expiration date of the contract, whichever occurs later.[875]

In analyzing the interrelationship of these subsections, the Board has held that failure to give the required 30-day notice to federal and state agencies under section 8(d)(3) bars a strike or lockout by the party with the duty to give that notice. The Board also had held, until 1985, that where a party's section 8(d)(3) notice to the FMCS was untimely filed, *both* parties were barred from striking or locking out until 30 days after the untimely notice is filed. In *Painting & Decorating Contractors, Peoria Chapter*,[876] the union notified the multi-employer association more than 60 days prior to the expiration date of the labor agreement that it wished to renegotiate the agreement. However, the union did not file the section 8(d)(3) notice with the FMCS and the appropriate state agency until 19 days before the expiration date. Relying on the union's representation that it had filed a timely section 8(d)(3) notice, the association locked out the unit employees on the expiration date. The Board held that the lockout violated section 8(a)(5). The Board acknowledged that under section 8(d) the union, as the party initially desiring to modify the contract, was obligated to give the 30-day notice to

---

[873]Amax Coal Co. Div. v. NLRB, 614 F2d 872, 103 LRRM 2482 (CA 3, 1980), *rev'd on other grounds*, 453 US 322, 107 LRRM 2769 (1981) (failure to provide written notice to FMCS violative of §8(b)(3), despite FMCS actual knowledge of dispute). *See* Chapter 19, "The Primary Strike," at notes 146–152.

[874]Retail Store Employees Local 322 (Wilhow Corp.), 240 NLRB 1109, 100 LRRM 1384 (1979) (union's failure to provide state agency with notice required under §8(d)(3) held violative of §8(b)(3)).

[875]*See also* discussion *infra* at notes 946–956.

[876]204 NLRB 345, 83 LRRM 1367 (1973), *enforcement denied*, 500 F2d 54, 86 LRRM 2914 (CA 7, 1974).

federal and state mediation services. However, the Board held that the party not obligated to give notice under section 8(d)(3) must also observe a 30-day moratorium following the initiating party's untimely section 8(d)(3) notification before calling a strike or lockout. The Seventh Circuit disagreed. In that court's view, "once the non-initiating party has observed its duty to bargain collectively during the sixty-day period . . . it has fulfilled its duty under §8(d)(3) whether or not the initiating party has met its obligation under §8(d)(3) to notify state and federal mediators."[877]

In *United Artists Communications,*[878] the Board overruled its decision in *Painting & Decorating Contractors, Peoria Chapter*[879] and its progeny, and adopted the view of the Seventh Circuit. The Board now holds that the burden of notifying the mediation services of a dispute under sections 8(d)(3) and (4) rests exclusively with the initiating party and that the initiating party's failure to file such a notice cannot serve to preclude the non-initiating party from undertaking otherwise lawful economic action.

The Board also has ruled that the section 8(d) notice and waiting requirements do not apply to a contract reopening situation in which the employer acts pursuant to the contract and not in modification of it.[880]

In addition to the statutory notice requirements of section 8(d), many labor agreements contain automatic renewal provisions whereby the agreement is automatically renewed

---

[877]*Id.*, 500 F2d at 58. The court rejected the Board's suggestion that an earlier decision, Retail Clerks Local 2819 (Carroll House of Belleville, Inc.) v. NLRB, 265 F2d 814, 43 LRRM 2726 (CADC, 1959), had extended the noninitiating party's duty to bargain collectively beyond the 60-day "cooling off" period commencing with notice to the noninitiating party. In that case, the District of Columbia Circuit had held that the initiating party (there, the union) had violated §8(d)(4) by calling a strike 10 days after giving untimely notice to the federal and state mediators, even though the strike occurred after the 60-day waiting period had passed. In Hooker Chems. & Plastic Co., 224 NLRB 1535, 92 LRRM 1419 (1976), *enforcement denied*, 573 F2d 965, 97 LRRM 3194 (CA 7, 1978), the Board persisted in its position and its order was again denied enforcement by the Seventh Circuit.

[878]274 NLRB 75, 118 LRRM 1353 (1985), *review denied sub nom.* Theatrical Stage Employees v. NLRB, 779 F2d 552, 121 LRRM 2237 (CA 9, 1985), *cert. denied*, 477 US 904, 122 LRRM 2656 (1986). *Accord* Bi-County Wholesale Beverage Distribs. Labor Ass'n, 291 NLRB 466, 130 LRRM 1155 (1988); *cf.* NLRB v. Mar-Len Cabinets, 659 F2d 995, 108 LRRM 2838 (CA 9, 1981), *enforcing in relevant part* 243 NLRB 523, 101 LRRM 1613 (1979), *on remand*, 262 NLRB 1398, 110 LRRM 1515 (1982). In *Mar-Len Cabinets*, the employer unilaterally implemented its bargaining proposals after failing to comply with §8(d)(3). Its mistaken reliance on the union's alleged compliance with the notice requirements was held no defense.

[879]*Supra* note 876.

[880]Schaeff Namco, 280 NLRB 1317, 123 LRRM 1058 (1986).

(usually from year to year) unless one of the parties gives notice (usually more than 60 days) prior to the contract expiration date of its intent to renegotiate a new agreement. The language used in automatic renewal clauses varies. Whether the notice sent to the other party prevents automatic renewal will depend on the specific language used in the contract as well as the language used in the notice. Thus, the Sixth Circuit held that the term of an existing collective bargaining agreement did not expire when the union gave notice of modification, rather than notice of termination.[881] The court stated that the employer must receive clear and explicit notice of termination if the union is to be relieved of its contractual obligations under the existing collective bargaining agreement.

The Board has not followed the Sixth Circuit's view. It has found a violation of section 8(a)(5) where an employer refused to negotiate a new contract on the ground that the prior contract had been automatically renewed because the union's letter indicated a desire to modify rather than terminate the old contract.[882] But when a union fails to comply with the 60-day notice provision of the contract for reopening, participation by the employer in a negotiation meeting with the union does not necessarily constitute a waiver of the notice requirement. In one case the Board found that the employer did not waive its right to notice where it had raised the issue of timeliness at the meeting and had, in addition, asked the Board's regional office for an opinion on the question.[883]

The courts and the Board have shown flexibility in their interpretation of automatic renewal provisions. Typically, a collective agreement requires that written notice of termination or modification be given 60 days prior to the expiration date. In one case,[884] although the employer mailed its notice 61 days prior to contract expiration, it was not actually received by the

---

[881]Office & Professional Employees Local 42 v. Auto Workers Local 174, 523 F2d 783, 90 LRRM 3121 (CA 6, 1975). *Cf.* Kaufman & Broad Home Sys., 607 F2d 1104, 102 LRRM 3033 (CA 5, 1979) (notice to modify prevents automatic extension of agreement). *But see* Oakland Press Co. v. NLRB, 606 F2d 689, 102 LRRM 2537 (CA 6, 1979) (notice to modify sufficient to comply with contractual requirement of notice to terminate).

[882]Associated Gen. Contractors, 190 NLRB 383, 77 LRRM 1210 (1971). *See also* KCW Furniture Co., 247 NLRB 541, 103 LRRM 1194 (1980), *enforced*, 634 F2d 436, 106 LRRM 2112 (CA 9, 1980) (especially if contract clause distinguishes between notice to modify and notice to terminate). *See also* Oakland Press Co. v. NLRB, *supra* note 881.

[883]Sawyer Stores, 190 NLRB 651, 77 LRRM 1434 (1971).

[884]Borman Inv. Co. v. Laundry Workers Local 93, 97 LRRM 2309 (WD Mo, 1977). *See also* Louisville Plate Glass Co., 243 NLRB 1175, 102 LRRM 1108 (1979), *enforced*, 657 F2d 106, 108 LRRM 2716 (CA 6, 1981).

union until 58 days prior to the expiration date. The district court, relying on the Board's decision in *United Electronics Institute,*[885] held that because the notice was delayed by conditions beyond the control of the sender (delay in mails), the expiration notice was effective to prevent automatic renewal of the contract.

In another case the Board held that timely oral notice to the employer of the union's desire to change the terms of the contract sufficed to forestall automatic renewal; accordingly, the employer's subsequent refusal to negotiate violated section 8(a)(5).[886] The Board pointed out[887] that in the absence of a strike or lockout, this issue was purely a contractual matter and the statutory provisions of section 8(d) had no application.

Where a notice of contract termination was not timely received by the employer because it was delayed in the mails due to no fault of the union, the Board rejected the employer's claim that the untimely notice allowed renewal of the collective bargaining agreement.[888] A construction industry employer that had designated an employer's association as its bargaining representative for its 1981–1983 contract with the union prevented the automatic renewal of the agreement by timely notice that it had withdrawn the authority of the association to bargain further on its behalf.[889] The notice requirements of section 8(d) of the Act are not excused by employer unfair labor practices if the strike is an economic one.[890]

Where an employer gave a 60-day contractual notice of contract termination, the failure to provide a timely 30-day notice to the Federal Mediation and Conciliation Service and related state

---

[885]222 NLRB 814, 91 LRRM 1271 (1976).

[886]Jet Line Prods., 229 NLRB 322, 95 LRRM 1075 (1977).

[887]*Id.* (citing United States Gypsum Co., 90 NLRB 964, 26 LRRM 1306 (1950)).

[888]Taft Broadcasting Co., WBRC-TV, 264 NLRB 185, 111 LRRM 1340 (1982), *aff'd*, 712 F2d 1418, 113 LRRM 3816 (CA 11, 1983); *but see* Auto Workers Local 592 v. Sundstrand Corp., 650 F Supp 83, 124 LRRM 2262 (ND Ill, 1986), *later proceeding*, 126 LRRM 3003 (ND Ill, 1987); Southern Cal. Edison, 295 NLRB No. 28, 133 LRRM 1062 (1989).

[889]Electrical Workers (IBEW) Local 532 v. Brink Constr. Co., 825 F2d 207, 126 LRRM 2252 (CA 9, 1987). But where an individual employer signs on to an agreement between the union and an employer association, termination notice between the latter parties will not forestall renewal of the individual agreement unless the individual employer has designated the association as its bargaining representative. C.E.K. Indus. Mechanical Contractors, 295 NLRB No. 70, 131 LRRM 1737 (1989).

[890]Fundacion Educative Ana G. Mendez dba Puerto Rico Junior College, 265 NLRB 72, 111 LRRM 1499 (1982). There the employer unilaterally terminated a well-established practice of evaluating faculty for tenure and promotions. However, the Board determined that, notwithstanding these unilateral acts, the strike was motivated by economic demands and the union was not excused from filing the §8(d) notices.

agencies was held by the Fifth and Second circuits not to extend the contract.[891] These cases were decided under section 301 of the Act.

The Board has recently reaffirmed the principle that the notice requirements of section 8(d) operate wholly independently of any notice requirements that the parties may have agreed to on their own. Parties may not abrogate or waive the section 8(d) notice requirements through their own agreement.[892]

B. Notice Requirements in the Health Care Industry[893]

The National Labor Relations Act was amended in 1974 to cover employees of nonprofit hospitals.[894] The amendments established special procedures for handling labor disputes at "health care institutions." These included special time periods for filing "Section 8(d)" notices and also added a new notice requirement before health care employees would be free to strike or picket.[895]

Section 8(d)(A) requires that the party desiring to terminate or modify a bargaining agreement in the health care industry serve written notice of such intent on the other party at least 90 days before the expiration of the agreement, and give notice to the Federal Mediation and Conciliation Service (FMCS) 60 days prior to the agreement's expiration date. Section 8(d)(B) specifies that in the case of initial contract negotiations "at least thirty days' notice of the existence of a dispute" must be given to the FMCS and any state agency. Upon receiving such notice, the FMCS is required to contact the parties in an effort to achieve a settlement through mediation and conciliation.

In *Affiliated Hospital of San Francisco v. Scearce*[896] a union representing health care employees notified the FMCS more than a

---

[891] Communications Workers v. Southwestern Bell Tel. Co., 713 F2d 1118, 114 LRRM 2302 (CA 5, 1983); Procter & Gamble Indep. Union v. Procter Mfg. Co., 312 F2d 181, 51 LRRM 2752 (CA 2, 1962). *See also* Ottley v. Sheepshead Nursing Home, 688 F2d 883, 111 LRRM 2155 (CA 2, 1982); C.E.K. Indus. Mechanical Contractors, 295 NLRB No. 70, 131 LRRM 1737 (1989).

[892] Geo. C. Christopher & Son, 290 NLRB 472, 131 LRRM 1182 (1988).

[893] *See generally* Veron, *Labor Relations in the Health Care Field Under the 1974 Amendments to the National Labor Relations Act: An Overview and Analysis*, 70 NW. L. REV. 202 (1975); Feheley, *Amendments to the National Labor Relations Act: Health Care Institutions*, 36 OHIO ST. L.J. 235 (1975).

[894] *See* Chapter 5, "The Post-Landrum-Griffin Period."

[895] *See* Chapter 19, "The Primary Strike," at notes 52–57. *See also* Chapter 10, "Representation Proceedings and Elections," at note 188.

[896] 418 F Supp 711, 93 LRRM 2307 (ND Cal, 1976), *aff'd*, 583 F2d 1097, 99 LRRM 3197 (CA 9, 1978).

month before it was required to do so under the statute. The FMCS did not, however, appoint a board of inquiry until 30 days after the last day the union could lawfully have filed its statutory notice. The district court held that the law requires that the board of inquiry be established within 30 days after notice to the FMCS is given, not 30 days after the last day the notice could have been given. The Ninth Circuit affirmed.[897]

If the parties fail to settle the dispute, the employees are not necessarily free to strike. Pursuant to section 8(g), a union is required to give the health care institution a 10-day notice of its intent to strike or picket. In *NLRB v. Electrical Workers (IBEW) Local 388 (Hoffman Co.)*,[898] rejecting the position of the Board, the Seventh Circuit construed the section 8(g) 10-day notice requirement as applying only to unions directing concerted activity at the health care institution itself on behalf of employees of the institution. Thus, the court ruled, the Board was not warranted in finding that a union violated section 8(g) when it picketed an electrical construction contractor on the premises of a hospital without first giving 10 days' notice of intent to picket.

Relying on the *Hoffman* decision, the District of Columbia Circuit, in *Laborers Local 1057 (Mercy Hospital of Laredo) v. NLRB*,[899] refused to enforce a Board order, based on section 8(g), against otherwise lawful reserved-gate picketing by unions representing non–health care employees involved in the renovation of hospital facilities. The court held that Congress had arrived at a fair balance in limiting the section 8(g) notice requirements to the employees of health care institutions to whom the Act's coverage was then being extended and did not intend to restrict the rights already possessed by other employees.[900]

In *Painters Local 452 (Henry C. Beck Co.)*,[901] the Board overruled its prior interpretation of section 8(g) which required prior notice by any labor organization that engaged in concerted activity at the premises of a health care institution even though

---

[897]The Fourth Circuit also holds that the language of the Act is clear in requiring the FMCS to act within 30 days after receiving notice and that nothing in the legislative history points to a contrary interpretation. Sinai Hosp. v. Scearce, 561 F2d 547, 96 LRRM 2355 (CA 4, 1977).

[898]548 F2d 704, 94 LRRM 2536 (CA 7), *cert. denied*, 434 US 837, 96 LRRM 2514 (1977).

[899]567 F2d 1006, 96 LRRM 3160 (CADC, 1977).

[900]*See also* Beck Co., 246 NLRB 970, 103 LRRM 1002 (1979).

[901]246 NLRB 970, 103 LRRM 1002 (1979).

the concerted activity was directed at a non–health care employer present at the health care premises. In so doing the Board adopted the views of the Seventh and District of Columbia circuits[902] that section 8(g) applies only to activity directed at health care institutions.

The Board has held that the section 8(g) 10-day notice requirement has no application to health care employees who had engaged in a concerted work stoppage,[903] nor to a threatened, as contrasted with an actual, strike action against a health care institution.[904] The Board, however, also has held that a union demonstration with informational picket signs was a violation of section 8(g), even though no work stoppage was sought by the union and no disruption occurred.[905] And section 8(g) does apply to informational picketing by a building trades labor organization directed at a health care employer protesting scheduled work on a hospital building expansion program by non–building trades employees.[906]

The Board requires separate compliance with section 8(g) by unions engaging in sympathy striking and picketing. In *Eden Park Management,*[907] three agents of a "sister" union (which did not represent any of the health care institution employees) engaged in sympathy picketing with a union that was on strike against the nursing home. Although the striking union had filed a timely notice, the Board held that the sister union violated section 8(g) by sympathy picketing without filing a separate notice. However, the Board has held, with judicial approval, that the notice requirement of section 8(g) applies only to concerted activities by labor organizations. The Seventh Circuit upheld the

---

[902]NLRB v. Electrical Workers (IBEW) Local 388 (Hoffman Co.), *supra* note 898; Laborers Local 1057 v. NLRB (Mercy Hosp. of Laredo), *supra* note 899.

[903]Montefiore Hosp. & Medical Center v. NLRB, 621 F2d 510, 104 LRRM 2160 (CA 2, 1980); Leisure Lodge Nursing Home, 250 NLRB 912, 105 LRRM 1115 (1980); Villa Care, 249 NLRB 705, 104 LRRM 1274 (1980), *enforcement denied*, 692 F2d 766, 111 LRRM 3063 (CA 9, 1982); Walker Methodist Residence, 227 NLRB 1630, 94 LRRM 1516 (1977).

[904]Retail, Wholesale & Dep't Store Union Dist. 1199-E (Greater Pa. Ave. Nursing Center), 227 NLRB 132, 94 LRRM 1083 (1976).

[905]Retail, Wholesale & Dep't Store Union Dist. 1199 (United Hosps. of Newark), 232 NLRB 443, 96 LRRM 1404 (1977).

[906]Bricklayers Local 40 (Lake Shore Hosp.), 252 NLRB 252, 105 LRRM 1317 (1980); *see also* Sheet Metal Workers Local 324 (Lake Shore Hosp. & Health Related Facility), 254 NLRB 536, 106 LRRM 1140 (1980), where the Board held §8(g) did not apply to informational picketing clearly of a nonunion subcontractor who was performing work on the hospital construction job site.

[907]Service Employees Local 200 (Eden Park Mgmt.), 263 NLRB 400, 111 LRRM 1613 (1982). *See also* Stationary Eng'rs Local 39 (Kaiser Found. Hosps.), 268 NLRB 115, 114 LRRM 1244 (1983), *enforced*, 746 F2d 530, 117 LRRM 2956 (CA 9, 1984).

Board's ruling that section 8(g) does not apply to unauthorized work stoppage by employees in an organized facility.[908] The Board also has held that a strike to protest a health care institution's unfair labor practices is protected and lawful despite the absence of notice.[909]

X. Coalition or Coordinated Bargaining

An important development attributable in some degree to the successful "divide and conquer" tactics used by some employers to gain bargaining leverage in labor negotiations is the increased use by unions of "coalition" or "coordinated" bargaining.[910] The terms "coalition" or "coordinated" bargaining are often interchangeable in popular usage, but there is an important and logical difference between the terms. "Coordinated" bargaining connotes communication and accommodation among different bargaining agents but independent decision making in separate bargaining processes. Such activity is therefore not illegal as such.[911] "Coalition" bargaining, on the other hand, implies a de facto merger of bargaining units, or an effort to achieve that end. Thus, to the extent such a merger is forced on a nonconsenting bargaining partner, a refusal to bargain, by virtue of insistence on a nonmandatory bargaining subject, occurs.

The terms "coordinated" and "coalition" bargaining may refer to the inclusion in a bargaining committee of individuals who are not members of or connected directly with the bargaining unit. These individuals may be members of other unions with which the employer has no other contractual relations.[912] They may also be members of different locals of the same parent union with which the employer has separate agreements. Such

---

[908]East Chicago Rehabilitation Center v. NLRB, 710 F2d 397, 113 LRRM 3241 (CA 7, 1983), *cert. denied*, 465 US 1065, 115 LRRM 2904 (1984).

[909]Washington Heights-West Harlem-Inwood Mental Health Council, 289 NLRB 1122, 131 LRRM 1012 (1988).

[910]*See* General Elec. Co. v. NLRB, 173 NLRB 253, 69 LRRM 1305 (1968), *enforced*, 412 F2d 512, 71 LRRM 2418 (CA 2, 1969). *See also* Chapter 11, "Appropriate Bargaining Units," at note 344.

[911]*See generally* Goldberg, *Coordinated Bargaining Tactics of Unions*, 54 CORNELL L. REV. 897 (1969); Engle, *Coordinated Bargaining: A Snare and a Delusion*, 19 LAB. L.J. 512 (Aug. 1968).

[912]*Supra* note 910. *See* Minnesota Mining & Mfg. Co. v. NLRB, 173 NLRB 275, 69 LRRM 1313 (1968), *enforced*, 415 F2d 174, 72 LRRM 2129 (CA 8, 1969); American Radiator & Standard Sanitary Corp., 155 NLRB 736, 60 LRRM 1385 (1965), *enforcement denied*, 381 F2d 632, 65 LRRM 3071 (CA 6, 1967).

bargaining offers the participating unions the advantage of a united front, more or less, in contract negotiations.

The concept of coordinated or coalition bargaining first gained attention in 1966 when the International Union of Electrical Workers (IUE) formed a coalition with seven other members of the AFL-CIO Industrial Union Department.[913] Their avowed purpose was to develop national goals and to adopt a "coordinated approach" to negotiations with the General Electric Company (GE). In the resulting dispute, *McLeod v. General Electric Co.*,[914] GE representatives walked out of a meeting with the coalition committee, contending that representatives of the seven other unions who were present were not properly a part of the negotiating committee. Both IUE and GE filed unfair labor practice charges. The General Counsel found merit in the union's section 8(a)(5) refusal-to-bargain charge against GE, but dismissed GE's section 8(b)(1)(A) charge that IUE had violated its bargaining duty by insisting that GE deal with the coalition.[915]

The Board found GE guilty of refusing to bargain because its negotiators had walked out of the meeting with the coordinated bargaining committee and had refused to deal with "outsiders."[916] The Second Circuit upheld the Board's order.[917] Addressing itself to the basic issue, "whether a union's inclusion of members of other unions on its bargaining committee justifies an employer's refusal to bargain," the court declared that the "right of employees and the corresponding right of employers . . . to choose whomever they wish to represent them in formal labor negotiations is fundamental to the statutory

---

[913]A similar coalition was formed prior to the 1960 contract negotiations. *See* Cooper, *Boulwarism and the Duty to Bargain in Good Faith*, 20 RUTGERS L. REV. 653, 666 n.41 (1960).

[914]McLeod v. General Elec. Co., 257 F Supp 690, 62 LRRM 2809 (SDNY), *rev'd*, 366 F2d 847, 63 LRRM 2065 (CA 2, 1966), *remanded*, 385 US 533, 64 LRRM 2129 (1967).

[915]The regional director had obtained a temporary injunction from a federal district court under §10(j) restraining the company from refusing to bargain collectively with the IUE negotiating committee. That court ruled that the company's failure to bargain "could not be justified by the conjectural claim that the IUE team was ineluctably bent on 'multi-union bargaining.'" 257 F Supp at 706. The Second Circuit reversed and vacated the injunction without passing on the merits, holding that "[t]he Board has not demonstrated that an injunction is necessary to preserve the status quo or to prevent any irreparable harm." 366 F2d at 850. The Supreme Court granted a stay of the Second Circuit's judgment pending certiorari proceedings, but on certiorari the Court in a per curiam opinion dissolved the stay and set aside the judgment with directions to remand to the district court because the employer and IUE had agreed upon a new collective bargaining contract.

[916]General Elec. Co. v. NLRB, *supra* note 910, at 256.

[917]*Id.*, 412 F2d at 512.

scheme."[918] Although it recognized that the freedom to select representatives was not absolute,[919] the court noted that the infrequency of approved exceptions emphasized the importance of the rule. The court therefore held that, for the employer to prevail in its objections to outsider members of the union negotiating committee, it must sustain the burden of showing a "'clear and present' danger to the collective bargaining process."[920] Finding no such "clear and present danger," the court held that GE was not lawfully entitled to refuse to bargain with the multi-union committee, so long as the committee sought to bargain solely on behalf of the employees who would be covered under the contract being negotiated.

Even prior to the *General Electric* case the Board had declared that an employer could not in good faith refuse to bargain with a union negotiating committee merely because other unions were represented on the committee. In *American Radiator & Standard Sanitary Corp.*[921] the employer was requested by all the unions representing employees at its various plants to bargain jointly. However, the employer declined to meet "with a group not legally certified as the collective bargaining representative."[922] As in *General Electric,* the employer contended that the unions had coalesced for the purpose of compelling companywide bargaining. Relying on its earlier *Standard Oil Co. of Ohio*[923] decision, the Board found that the employer was not relieved of the duty to meet with the duly appointed union committee, even though other unions had members on the committee, since the composi-

---

[918]*Id.* at 516. *See* Prudential Ins. Co. of Am. v. NLRB, 278 F2d 181, 46 LRRM 2026 (CA 3, 1960); NLRB v. Deena Artware, Inc., 198 F2d 645, 30 LRRM 2479 (CA 6, 1952), *cert. denied,* 345 US 906, 31 LRRM 2444 (1953); Pueblo Gas & Fuel Co. v. NLRB, 118 F2d 304, 8 LRRM 902 (CA 10, 1941); Oliver Corp., 74 NLRB 483, 20 LRRM 1183 (1947).

[919]412 F2d at 517 (citing, as exceptions to the general rule: NLRB v. Ladies' Garment Workers (Slate Belt Apparel Contractors' Ass'n), 274 F2d 376, 45 LRRM 2626, 2628 (CA 3, 1960) (ex-union official added to employer committee to "put one over on the union"); NLRB v. Kentucky Utils. Co., 182 F2d 810, 26 LRRM 2287 (CA 6, 1950) ("union negotiator had expressed great personal animosity towards employer"); Bausch & Lomb Optical Co., 108 NLRB 1555, 34 LRRM 1222 (1954) ("union established company in direct competition with employer").

[920]412 F2d at 517.

[921]*Supra* note 912 (court agreed with Board as to right of union to have outsiders present on its negotiating committee, but disagreed as to whether employer had refused to bargain with committee).

[922]*Id.* at 739.

[923]137 NLRB 690, 50 LRRM 1238 (1962), *enforced,* 322 F2d 40, 54 LRRM 2076 (CA 6, 1963) (nonmembers on local union's bargaining committee). *See also* Minnesota Mining & Mfg. Co. v. NLRB, 415 F2d 174, 72 LRRM 2129 (CA 8, 1969); Independent Drugstore Owners of Santa Clara County, 170 NLRB 1699, 69 LRRM 1031 (1968).

tion of the committee was an internal union matter over which the company had no control.

The Board and the courts have consistently followed the rule enunciated in the *Standard Oil, American Radiator,* and *General Electric* cases, regardless of whether the non-local-union committee member was a representative of a labor organization which had a contractual relationship with the employer.[924] However, it was acknowledged even in *General Electric* that a conflict of interest could arise so as to make good-faith bargaining impractical.[925]

An example of such a conflict of interest did occur in *CBS, Inc.,*[926] where the employer (CBS) refused to bargain with a negotiating committee that included a representative of the National Association of Broadcast Engineers and Technicians (NABET). NABET had no contracts with CBS nor did it represent any employees of CBS, but it did represent employees of competitors of CBS. Since CBS planned to reveal confidential trade secrets during negotiations, it contended that the presence of NABET personnel constituted a clear and present danger to the collective bargaining process because CBS would not be able to reveal its confidential business plans under such circumstances. The Board dismissed the refusal-to-bargain charge, and the Second Circuit affirmed. The court concluded that this was a unique situation that justified an exception to the rule that employees are free to choose their own bargaining representatives.[927]

Employer opposition to coordinated or coalition bargaining has focused primarily upon the possible obliteration of "unit" determinations, particularly where separately certified unions represent distinct segments of the company's employees at various locations. A considerable burden falls upon the employer asserting such a position.[928] Employers have argued that this type of bargaining might permit a union to act as bargaining

---

[924]AMF, Inc., 219 NLRB 903, 90 LRRM 1271 (1975); Harley-Davidson Motor Co., 214 NLRB 433, 87 LRRM 1571 (1974); Independent Drugstore Owners of Santa Clara County, *supra* note 923; Roscoe Skipper, Inc., 106 NLRB 1238, 32 LRRM 1658 (1953), *enforced,* 213 F2d 793, 34 LRRM 2315 (CA 5, 1954).

[925]General Elec. Co. v. NLRB, *supra* note 910.

[926]226 NLRB 537, 93 LRRM 1378 (1976), *enforced,* 557 F2d 995, 95 LRRM 2996 (CA 2, 1977).

[927]*Id.,* 557 F2d at 1000.

[928]Indiana & Mich. Elec. Co., 235 NLRB 1128, 98 LRRM 1036 (1978), *enforced,* 599 F2d 185, 101 LRRM 2470 (CA 7, 1979), *cert. denied,* 444 US 1014, 103 LRRM 2143 (1980).

agent for a group of employees for which another union has been certified.[929] In one instance, the District of Columbia Circuit upheld a Board decision that a company could legitimately refuse to meet and bargain at a single time and place on the subject of pension plan benefits for 19 separate units with a union that purported to represent all 19 units.[930] That refusal was not unlawful, even though the employer's pension plans were identical in all 19 units, because the union's demand was an attempt to consolidate the individual groups of employees without following proper Board procedures. Because bargaining-unit modifications are not mandatory bargaining subjects, the Board explained:

> It is well settled that the parties to a collective-bargaining relationship may voluntarily agree—subject to any later determination of appropriateness under Section 9(b) of the Act—to the enlargement or alteration of an existing unit, or to the merger of separate units, theretofore recognized by the parties or found by the Board to be appropriate for the purposes of collective bargaining. But, in the absence of an agreement, neither party may attempt to force upon the other an enlargement, alteration or merger of an established unit or units.[931]

Similarly, the Board has held that a union violated section 8(b)(3) by insisting that identical offers be made to several bargaining units and by conditioning acceptance of an offer to any single unit upon submission of identical offers to all units.[932] In another case, however, the Fourth Circuit agreed with the Board that a union did not violate section 8(b)(3) when it used "pooled voting procedures" with two other locals in rejecting an employer's wage offer. Since the sole purpose of pooling was to maintain common expiration dates, the integrity of the individual units was deemed to be preserved.[933] On the other hand,

---

[929]*See* Benetar, *Coalition Bargaining Under the NLRA*, NYU TWENTIETH ANNUAL CONFERENCE ON LABOR 219 (1968); Abramson, *Coordinated Bargaining by Unions*, *id.* at 231, where arguments both for and against coalition bargaining are advanced.

[930]Oil, Chem. & Atomic Workers v. NLRB (Shell Oil Co.), 486 F2d 1266, 84 LRRM 2581 (CADC, 1973), *denying petition for review of* 194 NLRB 988, 79 LRRM 1130 (1972).

[931]*Id.*, 194 NLRB at 995. *But see* AFL-CIO Joint Negotiating Comm. (Phelps Dodge Corp.) v. NLRB, 459 F2d 374, 79 LRRM 2939 (CA 3), *cert. denied*, 409 US 1059, 81 LRRM 2893 (1972), discussed in Chapter 16, "Subjects of Bargaining," at notes 462–463.

[932]Utility Workers Locals 111, 116, 138, 159, 264, 361, 426, 468, 478, & 492 (Ohio Power Co.), 203 NLRB 230, 83 LRRM 1099 (1973), *enforced*, 490 F2d 1383, 85 LRRM 2944 (CA 6, 1974).

[933]Lynchburg Foundry Co. v. NLRB, 80 LRRM 2415 (CA 4, 1972), *denying petition for review of* 192 NLRB 773, 78 LRRM 1021 (1971). *Cf.* Continental Nut Co., 195 NLRB 841, 79 LRRM 1575 (1972), where a union was found to have engaged in "Boulwarism."

while "group voting, insistence on parallel contract terms for the same or commensurate job classifications, and conditional acceptance of contract proposals do not in themselves constitute illegitimate labor tactics," such tactics "can in context become part of an illegal overall pattern of conduct."[934]

In *Procter & Gamble Manufacturing Co. v. NLRB*,[935] the Fourth Circuit held that an employer violated sections 8(a)(1), (3), and (5) by conduct designed to discourage coordinated bargaining. The employer had four separate plants represented by four different unions. The unions sought to bargain at each plant with a negotiating committee that included employees from the other plants. The employer refused to give vacation time to employees at plants other than that for which the contract was being negotiated. The employer also refused to permit the employees from its other plants onto plant premises for negotiation sessions, or to hold bargaining sessions on weekends. The court held that this conduct had effectively chilled employees' rights to select their own bargaining representatives by preventing or discouraging those representatives from fully participating in negotiations.

XI. BARGAINING DURING THE TERM OF AN EXISTING AGREEMENT

The obligation to bargain collectively is not limited to the negotiation of an agreement. In some instances bargaining can and must be carried on during the term of an existing agreement.[936] In the words of the Supreme Court: "Collective bargaining is a continuing process. Among other things, it involves day to day adjustments in the contract and other working rules, resolution of problems not covered by existing agreements, and the protection of employee rights already secured by contract."[937] The continuing nature of the duty to bargain during

---

[934]Frito-Lay, Inc. v. Teamsters Local 137, 623 F2d 1354, 104 LRRM 2931, 2935 (CA 9), *cert. denied*, 449 US 1013, 105 LRRM 3327 (1980) *and* 449 US 1112, 106 LRRM 2200 (1981).

[935]658 F2d 968, 108 LRRM 2177 (CA 4, 1981), *cert. denied*, 459 US 879, 111 LRRM 2528 (1982). *See also* Teamsters Local 174 v. NLRB (Allied Employers), 723 F2d 966, 115 LRRM 2065 (CADC, 1983).

[936]*See* discussion of waiver, *supra* at notes 741–805. *See generally* Seagle, *Duty of Employer to Bargain in Post-Contract Negotiations*, 51 CORNELL L.Q. 523 (1966); Cox & Dunlop, *The Duty to Bargain Collectively During the Term of an Existing Agreement*, 63 HARV. L. REV. 1097 (1950).

[937]Conley v. Gibson, 355 US 41, 41 LRRM 2089, 2091 (1957). *Accord* NLRB v. Acme Indus. Co., 385 US 432, 64 LRRM 2069 (1967).

the life of a contract was recognized in the early cases of *NLRB v. Sands Manufacturing Co.*[938] and *NLRB v. Highland Park Manufacturing Co.*[939] The court in *Highland Park* articulated the concept that the bargaining agreement provides the "framework" within which the process of collective bargaining may be carried forward. Following *Highland Park,* the Sixth Circuit in *Timken Roller Bearing Co. v. NLRB*[940] ruled that an employer could insist that grievances, including disputes over interpretation of the contract, must be resolved through the contractual grievance and arbitration machinery.

In *NLRB v. Jacobs Manufacturing Co.*[941] the Second Circuit elaborated on the scope of matters open to negotiation during the term of an existing agreement. The court held that, notwithstanding the language in section 8(d) of the Act,[942] an employer is not relieved of the duty to bargain "as to subjects which were neither discussed nor embodied in any of the terms and conditions of the contract."[943] The court's decision was premised

---

[938]306 US 332, 4 LRRM 530, 532 (1939) ("the Act imposes upon the employer the further obligation to meet and bargain with his employees' representatives respecting proposed changes of an existing contract and also to discuss with them its true interpretation . . . ." The same idea was expressed in regard to bargaining under the Railway Labor Act in Rutland Ry. Corp. v. Locomotive Eng'rs, 307 F2d 21, 45, 50 LRRM 2535 (CA 2, 1962), *cert. denied,* 372 US 954, 52 LRRM 2704 (1963) ("clarification through collective bargaining of ambiguous contractual provisions is a most laudable purpose and should be encouraged rather than hampered by the Courts." (dissenting opinion)).

[939]110 F2d 632, 638, 6 LRRM 786 (CA 4, 1940) ("the mere fact that the collective bargaining agreement provides a framework within which the process of collective bargaining may be carried on is of incalculable value in removing the causes of industrial strife").

[940]161 F2d 949, 20 LRRM 2204 (CA 6, 1947). *Accord* NLRB v. Knight Morley Corp., 251 F2d 753, 41 LRRM 2242 (CA 6, 1957), *cert. denied,* 357 US 927, 42 LRRM 2307 (1958). *Cf.* Long Lake Lumber Co., 160 NLRB 1475, 63 LRRM 1160 (1966).

[941]196 F2d 680, 30 LRRM 2098 (CA 2, 1952); *see also* NLRB v. Lion Oil Co., 352 US 282, 39 LRRM 2296 (1957).

[942]The exception provides that the duty to bargain collectively "shall not be construed as requiring either party to discuss or agree to any modification of the terms and conditions contained in a contract for a fixed period, if such modification is to become effective before such terms and conditions can be reopened under the provisions of the contract." Thus, a party may not change terms and conditions of employment governed by contract provisions during the term of the contract, absent consent of the other party. C & S Indus., 158 NLRB 454, 62 LRRM 1043 (1966). *See also* Jones Dairy Farm, 295 NLRB No. 20, 131 LRRM 1497 (1989); Speedrack, Inc., 293 NLRB 1054, 131 LRRM 1347 (1989). The Board had held the unilateral withdrawal of bargaining-unit work during the term of a collective bargaining agreement to be proscribed by §8(d). Park-Ohio Indus., 257 NLRB 413, 107 LRRM 1498 (1981), *enforced,* 702 F2d 624, 112 LRRM 3089 (CA 6, 1983), but this is no longer the law. *See* Chapter 16, "Subjects of Bargaining," at note 58.

[943]196 F2d at 684. The union invoked a contractual wage reopener midway into the contract term. It also requested that the employer take over the entire cost of an existing group insurance plan and establish a pension plan. The employer declined to discuss anything other than wages. When the original contract was negotiated, the union had made similar proposals with respect to the insurance plan but the employer had rejected them. Instead, the parties at that time agreed to certain changes in the cost and benefits of

upon the principle that the general purpose of the Act is to encourage peaceful resolution of industrial disputes through collective bargaining. The court left open, however, the effect on the duty to bargain, if any, of previous discussions where there was no inclusion in the contract of any terms or provisions on the matter. Some cases have indicated that such previous discussion forecloses later bargaining on the subject,[944] while others have been reluctant to hold that one party loses a right merely by talking it over with the other.[945] These issues, and the broader matter of waiver of rights to bargain, are fully addressed in Part VII, A, of this chapter.

Closely related to the *Jacobs Manufacturing* decision are two Supreme Court cases interpreting the modification, notification, and termination provisions of section 8(d).[946] In *Mastro Plastics Corp. v. NLRB*,[947] the Court held that the section 8(d) time requirements apply only to economic strikes, not to strikes in protest of employer unfair labor practices. Since the purpose of an unfair labor practice strike is "not to terminate or modify the

---

the plan. Neither the changes nor the insurance plan itself were mentioned in the contract. The parties had never discussed the establishment of a pension plan. In a three-to-two opinion, the Board found the employer's refusal to discuss a pension plan a violation of §8(a)(5). On the basis of §8(d), however, it found no violation in the refusal to discuss the insurance plan.

Members Houston and Styles, who were in the majority as to pensions but in dissent on the insurance plan, contended that for purposes of §8(d) a matter is "contained in" a contract if it has been "integrated and embodied into a writing." Jacobs Mfg. Co., 94 NLRB 1214, 1217, 28 LRRM 1162 (1951). Since neither insurance nor pensions were mentioned in the contract, those members would have required bargaining on both. Chairman Herzog, whose vote was decisive on both issues, concluded that since pensions were neither "consciously explored" in negotiations nor embodied in the contract, bargaining was required. With regard to the insurance plan, however, Member Herzog was of the view that "rejection of the union's basic proposal, coupled in this particular instance with enhancement of the substantive benefits, constituted a part of the contemporaneous 'bargain' which the parties made when they negotiated the entire . . . contract." *Id.* at 1228. The Second Circuit enforced the Board order as to the pension plan because pensions were "neither discussed nor embodied" in the contract. 196 F2d at 684. The Board's decision with respect to the insurance plan was not appealed.

[944]Timken Roller Bearing Co. v. NLRB, 325 F2d 746, 54 LRRM 2785 (CA 6, 1963), *cert. denied*, 376 US 971, 55 LRRM 2878 (1964) (if a right or benefit for which union desires to bargain during term of existing agreement is one that could be acquired only by virtue of a bargaining agreement, and proposal for such benefit was pressed and rejected during bargaining, failure to include such right or benefit necessarily results in failure to acquire it); United States Steel Corp. v. Nicholas, 229 F2d 396, 37 LRRM 2420 (CA 6), *cert. denied*, 351 US 950, 38 LRRM 2159 (1956) (if existing policy of employer is bargained over in negotiations and contract is silent on a subject because of no agreement, topic was not inadvertently overlooked but was intentionally omitted from contract for its term).

[945]*See* cases *supra* at notes 756–762.

[946]*See* notes 873–909 *supra* and accompanying text.

[947]350 US 270, 37 LRRM 2587 (1956). *See* Chapter 19, "The Primary Strike," at notes 157–161.

contract, but [is] designed instead to protest"[948] an employer's activities, the loss-of-status provisions[949] as well as the section 8(d)(4) prohibition are inapplicable.[950]

In *NLRB v. Lion Oil Co.*[951] the question was posed whether under a contract providing for negotiation and modification at an intermediate date during its term, the union could strike in support of modification demands after the 60-day notice period had elapsed, but prior to the terminal date of the contract. The Supreme Court noted that Congress had recognized a duty to bargain over modifications, and the contract itself contemplated such bargaining. With reasoning similar to that in the *Jacobs* case, the Court said that it would be "anomalous" for Congress to recognize such a duty and at the same time deprive the union of the strike or strike threat.[952] The Court also held that Congress meant "expiration date" to encompass both the final terminal date of the contract and any intermediate dates provided for reopening of terms of the contract.[953]

In *Mine Workers Local 9735 v. NLRB (Westmoreland Coal Co.)*[954] and *Cheney California Lumber Co. v. NLRB*[955] the District of Columbia and Ninth circuits expanded upon *Lion Oil* along the line of the *Jacobs Manufacturing* rule, that is, that the section 8(d) time limits and notice provisions do not apply to strikes during the life of the agreement whose purpose is not to modify the terms of the agreement but rather to obtain terms that the agreement has not settled or has expressly left open. The Ninth

---

[948]350 US at 286.

[949]Section 8(d) reads in part: "Any employee who engages in a strike within [the 60-day period] specified in this subsection . . . shall lose his status as an employee of the employer engaged in the particular labor dispute, for the purposes of sections 8, 9, and 10 of this Act . . . ."

[950]See comment of Senator Ball, 93 CONG. REC. 5,014 (1947), that the provisions of §8(d) are "aimed primarily at protecting the public, as well as the employees, who have been the victims of 'quickie' strikes. I do not think that is taking away any rights of labor . . . ."

[951]*Supra* note 941.

[952]*Id.* at 290–91. The Supreme Court in *Lion Oil* expressly noted agreement. Recently, the Board found that the presence of a no-strike clause will not preclude the use of economic weapons. Specifically, the Board held that "absent clear agreement of the parties to the contrary, the same statutory policies that privilege an employer's unilateral action after impasse on a reopened subject also privilege the collective-bargaining representative's resort to an economic strike over the dispute on that subject, notwithstanding the existence of a no-strike clause." Speedrack, Inc., *supra* note 942, 131 LRRM at 1349; *see also* Hydrologics, Inc., 293 NLRB 1060, 131 LRRM 1350 (1989).

[953]Packinghouse Workers Local 3 (Wilson & Co.) v. NLRB, 210 F2d 325, 33 LRRM 2530 (CA 8, 1954), had held otherwise.

[954]258 F2d 146, 42 LRRM 2320 (CADC, 1958).

[955]319 F2d 375, 53 LRRM 2598 (CA 9, 1963).

Circuit[956] has held that notice need not be given to a state agency under section 8(d)(3) if such agency has no funds for conciliation or mediation. Thus, the union's failure to serve notice on that state agency did not forfeit the employee status of the strikers. The court's rationale was that a completely powerless state agency could not promote collective bargaining; therefore the statute should not be read as requiring a useless act.

Many of the Board and court decisions dealing with the bargaining obligation during the term of an existing contract turn on whether the union has waived its right to bargain over a particular subject, either by virtue of a contractual provision or by reason of its conduct in earlier negotiations.[957]

Other cases involving bargaining during the term of an existing agreement turn on the question of whether the particular subject is or is not a mandatory subject of bargaining.[958] In one case, for example, the Sixth Circuit, in agreement with the Board, held that not only the benefits of an employee health insurance plan, but also the designation of a particular insurance carrier, were mandatory subjects. Hence, the employer who unilaterally terminated its employee health care plan with a particular insurance carrier during the term of the labor contract was held to have violated the Act.[959]

---

[956]Locomotive Firemen (Phelps-Dodge Corp.) v. NLRB, 302 F2d 198, 50 LRRM 2015 (CA 9, 1962). *But cf.* Milk, Ice Cream Drivers & Dairy Employees Local 783 (Cream Top Creamery), 147 NLRB 264, 56 LRRM 1194 (1964).

[957]These matters are fully considered *supra*, Part VII.A. It should be noted that since the Board in Collyer Insulated Wire, 192 NLRB 837, 77 LRRM 1931 (1971), adopted a prearbitration deferral doctrine, many cases involving the question of an employer's right to make a unilateral change during the term of a labor contract have been deferred to contractual grievance-arbitration procedures. *See generally* Chapter 18, "Accommodation of Board Action to the Arbitration Process."

[958]Rockwell Int'l Corp., 260 NLRB 1346, 1347, 109 LRRM 1366 (1982) ("The duty to bargain continues during the existence of a bargaining agreement concerning any mandatory subject of bargaining which has not been specifically covered in the contract . . .").

[959]Golconda Corp., Bastian-Blessing Div. v. NLRB, 474 F2d 49, 82 LRRM 2689 (CA 6, 1973), *enforcing* 195 NLRB 1108, 79 LRRM 1616 (1972), *supplementing* 194 NLRB 609, 79 LRRM 1010 (1971). The court specifically noted, however, that in the particular case before it, it was impossible to separate the benefits from the carrier that provided them, thereby implying that the court might not order reinstatement of the benefits from an insurance carrier in all situations. *See* Chapter 16, "Subjects of Bargaining," at note 115; Standard Fitting Co. v. NLRB, 845 F2d 1311, 128 LRRM 2613 (CA 5, 1988) (failure to bargain over refusal to implement contractual wage increase during term of agreement held violative of §8(a)(5)). *See also* Ford Motor Co. v. NLRB, 441 US 488, 101 LRRM 2222 (1979) (unilateral change in price of cafeteria food during term of agreement violated §8(a)(5)); Keystone Consol. Indus., Keystone Steel & Wire Div. v. NLRB, 606 F2d 171, 102 LRRM 2664 (CA 7, 1979) (unilateral change of administrator of insurance plan during term of contract violated §8(a)(5)). *See* Chapter 16, "Subjects of Bargaining," for a full discussion of mandatory subjects of bargaining.

XII. DUAL EMPLOYER OPERATIONS: THE "DOUBLE-BREASTED" ISSUE

Some unionized employers, particularly in the construction industry, have established separate companies to operate on a nonunion basis. This practice, often referred to as "double breasting," and union reactions to it, have given rise to developments under several sections of the Act, particularly section 8(a)(5), but also sections 8(b)(1), 8(b)(3), 8(b)(4), 8(e), and 301.[960] A leading case, *South Prairie Construction Co. v. Operating Engineers Local 627,*[961] arose under the bargaining provisions of section 8(a)(5). The union alleged that South Prairie and Peter Kiewit Sons' (both subsidiaries of the same parent company) had violated section 8(a)(5) by refusing to apply the collective bargaining agreement between the union and Kiewit to South Prairie's employees. The Board rejected the union's contention that South Prairie and Kiewit constituted a single employer and dismissed the complaint.[962]

On the union's petition for review, the District of Columbia Circuit reversed and found that the companies constituted a single employer. The court relied upon criteria enunciated by the Supreme Court in *Radio & Television Broadcast Technicians Local 1264 v. Broadcast Service of Mobile.*[963] Applying those criteria, the court determined that the facts evidenced "a substantial qualitative degree of integration of operations and common management—one that we are satisfied would not be found in the arms-length relationship existing among unintegrated com-

---

[960]*See* King & LaVaute, *Current Trends in Construction Industry Labor Relations: The Double-Breasted Contractor and the Prehire Contract*, 29 SYRACUSE L. REV. 901 (1978); Bornstein, *Emerging Law of the "Double-Breasted" Operation in the Construction Industry*, 28 LAB. L.J. 77 (1977); Penfield, *The Double-Breasted Operation in the Construction Industry*, 27 LAB. L.J. 89 (1976). *See also* Chapter 28, "Jurisdiction: Coverage of the Act," at notes 144–169.

[961]425 US 800, 92 LRRM 2507 (1976), *aff'g in part and remanding in part sub nom.* Operating Eng'rs Local 627 (Peter Kiewit Sons' Co.) v. NLRB, 518 F2d 1040, 90 LRRM 2321 (CA DC, 1975). *See* Chapter 28, "Jurisdiction: Coverage of the Act," at note 152.

[962]Peter Kiewit Sons' Co., 206 NLRB 562, 84 LRRM 1356 (1973). In cases decided prior to *South Prairie* arising under §8(a)(5), the Board had rejected union claims of single-employer status in connection with "double-breasted" operations similar to those in *South Prairie*. Gerace Constr., 193 NLRB 645, 78 LRRM 1367 (1971); Frank N. Smith Assocs., 194 NLRB 212, 78 LRRM 1603 (1971) (dismissing §8(a)(5) complaints). *Cf.* Carpenters Dist. Council of Houston (Baxter Constr. Co.), 201 NLRB 23, 82 LRRM 1382 (1973) (finding §8(b)(4) violation in picketing of neutral contractor).

[963]380 US 255, 58 LRRM 2545 (1965). *See* Chapter 28, "Jurisdiction: Coverage of the Act," at note 152.

panies."[964] It concluded that the contrary finding of the Board was not warranted by the record of the case.[965]

The Supreme Court affirmed the judgment of the District of Columbia Circuit on the single-employer issue, but held that the court of appeals had acted improperly in deciding that employees of both South Prairie and Kiewit constituted an appropriate bargaining unit, an issue that the Board had not passed upon. Accordingly, that part of the court of appeal's judgment which directed the Board to issue a bargaining order was remanded so that the Board could make the initial determination of the appropriate bargaining-unit issue.

Upon remand, in *Peter Kiewit Sons' Co.*,[966] the Board ruled that the employees of the two subsidiaries constituted two separate bargaining units, and accordingly dismissed the complaint. The Board found particularly relevant the separate bargaining histories (union versus nonunion), an absence of functional integration of operations, differences in the types of work and skills of employees, the extent of decentralization of management and supervision, particularly in regard to labor relations, hiring, discipline, and control of day-to-day operations, and the relatively insignificant extent of interchange and contact between the two groups of employees.

In subsequent cases, the Board has relied upon the criteria used by the circuit court in *South Prairie*. In *Western Union Corp.*[967] the Board did not find a single employer, despite much overlap of corporate officers and significant control by the original corporation over the new corporation's budget and selection of officers and directors. The Board relied heavily on the absence of common control of labor relations. Of the four key elements to a finding of a "single integrated enterprise," namely, common ownership and financial control, common management, interrelation of operations, and integrated control of

[964]518 F2d at 1047.

[965]The court of appeals held, contrary to the Board, that not all of the controlling standards bearing on the single-employer issue must be present in each case in order to find the existence of a single employer. Also, in further disagreement with the Board, the court determined that centralized control of the labor relations of both companies is not a prerequisite for finding that a single employer exists in every case.

[966]231 NLRB 76, 95 LRRM 1510 (1977), *aff'd*, 595 F2d 844, 100 LRRM 2792 (CADC), *cert. denied*, 439 US 827, 99 LRRM 2600 (1978).

[967]224 NLRB 274, 92 LRRM 1443 (1976), *aff'd sub nom.* Telegraph Workers v. NLRB, 571 F2d 665, 97 LRRM 2692 (CADC), *cert. denied*, 439 US 827, 99 LRRM 2600 (1978).

labor relations, the Board found that only common ownership was present.

In *United Constructors*[968] the Board refused to find that union and nonunion contractors constituted a single employer, even though the partners in the "union" firm joined with their sons to form the separate "non-union" company to operate as an open-shop contractor. The Board found significant differences in labor relations between the two companies. It noted that, while both shared office space, office equipment, and the services of a particular individual, rent was paid for those services. There was no evidence, the Board noted, that the "union" employees lost work, which they otherwise would have obtained, to the "non-union" employees.

In *Appalachian Construction,*[969] Appalachian had a collective contract with the Boilermakers Union. A public utility contracted with Appalachian to perform certain maintenance work, which, however, was not performed satisfactorily; therefore the contract was canceled. Appalachian then successfully rebid the contract, specifying that the work would be done by SE-OZ, a nonunion subsidiary of Appalachian. The Board held that it was not faced with a "double-breasted" operation, for this was not an "arms length" subcontracting arrangement. The Board emphasized that (1) daily supervision was the same under both companies, and the supervisors were on Appalachian's payroll; (2) the same person who was both the president of Appalachian and the vice-president of SE-OZ was the officer responsible for both projects; (3) division of profits was determined by the officers of both companies, three out of five of whom were the same; and (4) the project was the first of its kind for SE-OZ—the only difference between Appalachian and SE-OZ working on the project was the absence of union labor. The Board found that the companies were a single integrated employer whose employees constituted a single appropriate bargaining unit and ordered typical remedies for the violations of sections 8(a)(1), (3), and (5).

In *Ellsworth Sheet Metal,*[970] the Board found that two companies constituted a single integrated employer and that a single

---

[968] 233 NLRB 904, 97 LRRM 1409 (1977).
[969] 235 NLRB 685, 98 LRRM 1067 (1978).
[970] 235 NLRB 1273, 98 LRRM 1274 (1978), *enforced*, 603 F2d 214, 103 LRRM 2603 (CA 2, 1979).

bargaining unit of employees was appropriate. Ellsworth, which had a collective bargaining agreement with the Sheet Metal Workers, had established Benchmark as a nonunion company. Benchmark then engaged in the same type of operation as Ellsworth, using Ellsworth's plant and equipment, the same employees, and the same supervisors. The Board held that Benchmark's refusal to work under the collective bargaining agreement which Ellsworth had with the Sheet Metal Workers violated the Act. It specifically found a refusal to bargain in the failure of Benchmark to make payments to certain benefit funds and in its unilateral changing of wage rates without notice or consultation with the union. Make-whole remedies were ordered.

The Board has made similar findings and ordered similar remedies in numerous cases.[971] In *Edward J. White, Inc.*,[972] the ALJ recommended that the respondents be required to restore to a union company bargaining-unit work that had been transferred to a nonunion company. The Board reversed the ALJ as to this remedy, holding that the normal sections 8(a)(1), (3), and (5) remedies were sufficient to redress the unfair labor practices committed. More extensive remedies have been ordered, however, where deemed necessary.[973]

The Board has noted that the "single-employer" rubric "normally applies . . . to situations in which ongoing, nominally distinct businesses are alleged to be one and the same in terms of common control over labor relations, integration of operations,

---

[971] *See, e.g.*, Van-Note Harvey Assocs., 247 NLRB 927, 103 LRRM 1235 (1980); Big Bear Supermarkets No. 3, 239 NLRB 179, 100 LRRM 1067 (1978), *enforced*, 640 F2d 924, 103 LRRM 3120 (CA 9), *cert. denied*, 449 US 919, 105 LRRM 2809 (1980) (franchising context); Lantz, 235 NLRB 994, 100 LRRM 1223 (1978), *enforced*, 607 F2d 290, 102 LRRM 2789 (CA 9, 1979); Safety Elec. Corp., 239 NLRB 40, 99 LRRM 1440 (1978), *enforced*, 620 F2d 311, 108 LRRM 2104 (CA 9, 1980); Don Burgess Constr. Corp., 227 NLRB 765, 95 LRRM 1135 (1977), *enforced*, 596 F2d 378, 101 LRRM 2315 (CA 9), *cert. denied*, 444 US 940, 105 LRRM 2968 (1979).

[972] 237 NLRB 1020, 99 LRRM 1126 (1978).

[973] *E.g.*, Angelus Block Co., 250 NLRB 868, 105 LRRM 1141 (1980). *See also* Lithographers Local 1 v. Stearns & Beale, 812 F2d 763, 124 LRRM 2809 (CA 2, 1987); Teamsters Local 70 v. California Consolidators, 693 F2d 81, 111 LRRM 2785 (CA 9, 1982), *cert. denied*, 469 US 887, 117 LRRM 2571 (1984); Carpenters Local 1846 v. Pratt-Farnsworth, 690 F2d 489, 111 LRRM 2787 (CA 5, 1982), *cert. denied*, 464 US 932, 114 LRRM 2976 (1983), *remanded*, 609 F Supp 1299, 119 LRRM 3529, *supplemented*, 609 F Supp 1302, 119 LRRM 3525 (ED La, 1984); Florida Marble Polishers Health & Welfare Trust Fund v. Edwin M. Green, Inc., 653 F2d 972, 108 LRRM 2308 (CA 5, 1981), *cert. denied*, 456 US 973, 110 LRRM 2320 (1982).

common management, and common ownership."[974] A single-employer finding will not in itself result in the nonunion group of employees being covered by the collective bargaining agreement. Rather, that will depend upon whether the two employee groups constitute an appropriate bargaining unit[975] so that the nonunionized employees are not deprived of their section 7 rights.[976]

The Board and the courts have dealt with an increasing number of cases where the nonunion side of an alleged double-breasted operation was claimed to be the alter ego of the union side. In determining whether one entity is the alter ego of another, the Board considers whether there is "substantially identical management, business purpose, operation, equipment, customers, and supervision, as well as ownership" and a "purpose to evade responsibilities under the Act."[977]

No single one of these alter ego criteria is controlling.[978] The Board has found substantially identical ownership where mem-

---

[974]Gilroy Sheet Metal, 280 NLRB 1075, 123 LRRM 1012, 1012 (1986) (no single-employer finding where union company ceased operations). *See also* Cadet Constr. Co., 287 NLRB 564, 127 LRRM 1148 (1987), *enforced sub nom.* NLRB v. Laborers 1140, 861 F2d 531, 129 LRRM 2973 (CA 8, 1988) (sole proprietorship formed by principal owner of defunct company was not its alter ego where there was 2-year hiatus between company's closing and formation of proprietorship, and other factors militated against finding alter-ego status). *But see* Coastal Cargo Co., 286 NLRB 200, 126 LRRM 1178 (1987) (newly incorporated company was alter ego of another firm that temporarily ceased operations).

[975]Al Bryant, Inc., 260 NLRB 128, 109 LRRM 1284 (1982), *enforced*, 711 F2d 543, 113 LRRM 3690 (CA 3, 1983), *cert. denied*, 464 US 1039, 115 LRRM 2248 (1984); DMR Corp., 258 NLRB 1063, 108 LRRM 1217 (1981), *remanded*, 699 F2d 788, 112 LRRM 3033 (CA 5), *cert. denied*, 464 US 842, 114 LRRM 2568 (1983), *on remand*, 274 NLRB 38, 118 LRRM 1650 (1985), *enforced*, 795 F2d 472, 123 LRRM 2253 (CA 5, 1986); Better Bldg. Supply Corp., 259 NLRB 469, 108 LRRM 1381 (1981), *enforced*, 707 F2d 518, 113 LRRM 3360 (CA 9, 1983), *supplemented*, 283 NLRB 93, 125 LRRM 1165 (1987), *enforced*, 837 F2d 377, 127 LRRM 2393 (CA 9, 1988).

[976]*See* Carpenters Local 1846 v. Pratt-Farnsworth, *supra* note 973. *See also* Chapter 17, "Relation of Board Action to Enforcement of Agreements Under Section 301."

[977]Advance Elec., 268 NLRB 1001, 1003, 115 LRRM 1220 (1984).

[978]*See* Jo-Vin Dress Co., 279 NLRB 525, 123 LRRM 1279 (1986), *enforced*, 819 F2d 1134, 125 LRRM 2615 (CA 3, 1987); Woodline Motor Freight, 278 NLRB 1141, 122 LRRM 1355 (1986), *enforced in part*, 843 F2d 285, 127 LRRM 3260 (CA 8, 1988) (common ownership is not necessary predicate of alter ego status); Rogers Cleaning Contractors, 277 NLRB 482, 121 LRRM 1292 (1985), *enforced*, 813 F2d 795, 125 LRRM 2635 (CA 6, 1987); Samuel Kosoff & Sons, 269 NLRB 424, 429, 116 LRRM 1224 (1984) (alter ego despite separate offices, books, and equipment); Fugazy Continental Corp., 260 NLRB 1225, 109 LRRM 1367 (1982), *enforced*, 817 F2d 979, 125 LRRM 2287 (CA 2, 1987) (no one factor is "sine qua non of alter ego status"). *Cf.* First Class Maintenance Serv., 289 NLRB 484, 128 LRRM 1334 (1988) (no alter ego where substantially identical business purpose, operation, equipment, and customers, but parents were not involved in running son's company even though they "gave" him equipment); Gilroy Sheet Metal, *supra* note 974 (no alter ego where husband and wife separated, and husband formed new company that took over no work of union company that had been owned by husband and wife).

bers of the same family own the companies;[979] supervision where the same method of supervision was utilized, albeit not the same supervisors;[980] customers where the same types of customers were involved;[981] and an intention to evade responsibilities under the Act where the object was to avoid the costs of the labor agreement.[982] A substantially identical business purpose finding will be made if both companies are engaged predominantly, albeit not exclusively, in the same service.[983]

While the Board does not consider it essential that there be an intention to evade responsibilities under the Act in order to find alter ego status,[984] the circuit courts are in disagreement on that point.[985]

---

[979]Advance Elec., *supra* note 977. *Accord* NLRB v. Dane County Dairy, 795 F2d 1313, 122 LRRM 3051 (CA 7, 1986); Haley & Haley, 289 NLRB 649, 128 LRRM 1319, 1322 (1988) (stock of two companies was "concentrated in members of the same family"); Amateyus, Ltd., 280 NLRB 219, 123 LRRM 1341 (1986), *enforced*, 817 F2d 996, 125 LRRM 2329 (CA 2), *cert. denied*, 484 US 925, 126 LRRM 2776 (1987). *See also* Crawford Door Sales Co., 226 NLRB 1144, 94 LRRM 1393 (1976). *Cf.* Superior Export Packing Co., 284 NLRB 1169, 126 LRRM 1040, 1042 (1987), *enforced sub nom.* Meadowlands Hy-Pro Indus. v. NLRB, 845 F2d 1013, 129 LRRM 2528 (CA 3, 1988) (lack of common ownership precluded alter-ego finding: "Board has found such a relationship absent common ownership only where both companies were either wholly owned by members of same family or nearly totally owned by same individual or where the older company continued to maintain substantial control over the business claimed to have been sold to the new company").

[980]NLRB v. Campbell-Harris Elec., 719 F2d 292, 114 LRRM 2881 (CA 8, 1983); Advance Elec., *supra* note 977, at 1003. *Cf.* Haley & Haley, *supra* note 979, 128 LRRM at 1323 (individuals who regularly performed hands-on work could not be said to play significant managerial or supervisory role in alter ego's operation).

[981]Nelson Elec., 241 NLRB 545, 552, 100 LRRM 1588 (1979), *enforced*, 638 F2d 965, 106 LRRM 2393 (CA 6, 1981); *see also* American Pac. Concrete Pipe Co., 262 NLRB 1223, 1226 n.14, 110 LRRM 1540 (1982), *enforced*, 709 F2d 1514, 113 LRRM 2736 (CA 9, 1983).

[982]J.M. Tanaka Constr. v. NLRB, 675 F2d 1029, 110 LRRM 2296 (CA 9, 1982); Haley & Haley, *supra* note 979; Advance Elec., *supra* note 977, at 1004; Samuel Kosoff & Sons, *supra* note 978, at 429. *See supra* note 889.

[983]Haley & Haley, *supra* note 979, 128 LRRM at 1323 (one company hauled logs, the other hauled primarily logs and, additionally, general commodities); Advance Elec., *supra* note 977.

[984]Hiysota Fuel Co., 280 NLRB 763, 123 LRRM 1186 (1986); Gilroy Sheet Metal, *supra* note 974. *But see* Metro Foods, 289 NLRB 1107, 130 LRRM 1390 (1988), where the Board emphasized that the alter ego company was created to avoid the union-contract obligations and get rid of the first company.

[985]*Compare* Goodman Piping Prods. v. NLRB, 741 F2d 10, 117 LRRM 2143, 2144–45 (CA 2), *enforcing* 268 NLRB 1241, 115 LRRM 1319 (1984) *and* NLRB v. Allcoast Transfer, 780 F2d 576, 121 LRRM 2393, 2397 (CA 6, 1986), both finding that intent is not a prerequisite, *with* Penntech Papers v. NLRB, 706 F2d 18, 24, 113 LRRM 2219 (CA 1), *cert. denied*, 464 US 892, 114 LRRM 2648 (1983), Iowa Express Distribution v. NLRB, 739 F2d 1305, 1311, 116 LRRM 3224 (CA 8), *cert. denied*, 469 US 1088, 117 LRRM 3232 (1984) *and* Crest Tankers v. National Maritime Union, 796 F2d 234, 122 LRRM 3237 (CA 8, 1986), holding that unlawful intent is essential.

The Fourth Circuit requires a finding of "some future benefit reasonably accruing from the employer's action," irrespective of intent, in order to find alter-ego status. Alkire v. NLRB, 716 F2d 1014, 114 LRRM 2180, 2184–85 (CA 4, 1983). *Accord* NLRB v. McAllister

Unlike the single-employer analysis, where an alter ego determination is made, there is no requirement of a single appropriate unit in order to apply the labor agreement to the alter ego. Rather, the alter ego is automatically bound to the contract,[986] and the bargaining unit is that described in the contract.[987]

In *A-1 Fire Prevention*,[988] the Board found violations of sections 8(a)(1) and (5) resulting from a unilateral diversion of work from the union company to the nonunion company, notwithstanding its additional finding that it would be inappropriate to extend the bargaining agreement to the nonunion company. The union had been aware that the nonunion company was operating side-by-side with the union company in the same industry. The union also had assented to the common use of employees, and had acquiesced to the "double-breasted" operation during contract negotiations.[989] On remand, the Board concluded that the companies' principal had "disturb[ed] the status quo"[990] by changing work arrangements so as to deliberately divert work from the union company to the nonunion company,[991] and had violated the Act by refusing to bargain over the diversion.[992]

In a different context, the Sixth Circuit has held that an employer may be compelled under section 301 to arbitrate a double-breasted issue under its union contract.[993] The employer, having negotiated contracts with several unions, set up what the union alleged to be sham corporations to operate on a nonunion basis. When it refused to arbitrate whether the new corporations were covered by the union contracts, the unions

---

Bros., 819 F2d 439, 125 LRRM 2566 (CA 4, 1987), *enforcing* 278 LRRM 601, 123 LRRM 1040 (1986). *See supra* note 889.

986Walter N. Yoder & Sons, 270 NLRB 652 n.2, 117 LRRM 1066 (1984), *enforced*, 754 F2d 531, 118 LRRM 2706 (CA 4, 1985); Watt Elec. Co., 273 NLRB 655, 118 LRRM 1352 (1984). *See also* Crest Floors & Plastics, 274 NLRB 1230, 119 LRRM 1202 (1985), *enforced*, 785 F2d 314, 122 LRRM 2368 (CA 9, 1986).

987NLRB v. McAllister Bros., *supra* note 985. *See supra* note 889.

988273 NLRB 964, 118 LRRM 1221 (1984), *on remand from sub nom.* Plumbers & Pipe Fitters Local 669 v. NLRB, 676 F2d 826, 110 LRRM 2125 (CADC, 1982), *supplementing* 250 NLRB 217, 104 LRRM 1370 (1980), *enforced*, 789 F2d 9, 122 LRRM 2139 (CADC, 1986).

989*Id.*, 118 LRRM at 1222. The District of Columbia Circuit had rejected the Board's previous conclusion that such "acquiescence" precluded a finding of a violation. The court stated that the proper standard was not union acquiescence, but rather, whether the union had waived by clear and unmistakable conduct its right to bargain over the employer's transferring work from the bargaining unit. *Id.*

990273 NLRB at 965, 118 LRRM at 1222.

991*Id.* at 966, 118 LRRM at 1224.

992*Id.* at 967, 118 LRRM at 1224.

993Bricklayers Local 6 v. Heminger, Inc., 473 F2d 129, 84 LRRM 2033 (CA 6, 1973).

brought suit to compel arbitration, which the Sixth Circuit granted.[994]

Similarly, a union successfully enforced its agreement with one company against a second company which had been established to operate on a nonunion basis. The district court found that the two companies were sufficiently integrated in operations so as to constitute a single employer and that both were bound by the terms of the collective bargaining agreement.[995] Unions have also tried unsuccessfully to extend contracts to the unorganized parts of double-breasted operations through section 301 suits.[996] In other cases, causes of action against double-breasted operations have withstood motions to dismiss on theories including section 301, the Employee Retirement Income Security Act, and the antitrust laws.[997] Courts have also upheld arbitration of issues arising out of those operations.[998]

But the Board was not precluded from finding single-employer status for purposes of refusal-to-bargain charges by a prior court decision in a section 301 suit holding that the companies were not alter egos.[999] In another section 301 suit, the Fifth Circuit has ruled that the exclusive province of the NLRB to determine appropriate bargaining units does not preclude a judicial determination where neither side has taken the issue

---

[994]*See generally* Steelworkers v. American Mfg. Co., 363 US 564, 46 LRRM 2414 (1960); Chapter 17, "Relation of Board Action to Enforcement of Agreements Under Section 301," at notes 43–49.

[995]Plumbers & Pipe Fitters Local 519 v. Service Plumbing Co., 401 F Supp 1008, 90 LRRM 3127 (SD Fla, 1975). *See also* Land Equip., 248 NLRB 685, 104 LRRM 1100 (1980), *enforced*, 649 F2d 867, 108 LRRM 2175 (CA 9, 1981) (retroactive application of contracts as remedy). A union, however, may waive its right to assert the double-breasted issue. A-1 Fire Protection, 250 NLRB 217, 104 LRRM 1370 (1980).

[996]Florida Marble Polishers Health & Welfare Trust Fund v. Edwin M. Green, Inc., 653 F2d 972, 108 LRRM 2308 (CA 5, 1981), *cert. denied*, 456 US 973, 110 LRRM 2320 (1982); Electrical Workers (IBEW) Local 59 v. Namco Elec., 653 F2d 143, 107 LRRM 3314 (CA 5, 1981).

[997]Garland Coal & Mining Co. v. Mine Workers Dist. 21, 778 F2d 1297, 121 LRRM 2029 (CA 8, 1985); Carpenters Local 1846 v. Pratt-Farnsworth, 690 F2d 489, 111 LRRM 2787 (CA 5, 1982), *cert. denied*, 464 US 932, 114 LRRM 2976 (1983), *remanded*, 609 F Supp 1299, 119 LRRM 3529, *supplemented*, 609 F Supp 1302, 119 LRRM 3525 (ED La, 1984). The court in *Pratt-Farnsworth* decided that a cause of action may be stated under the antitrust laws since the pleadings could be interpreted to allege a restraint on commercial competition rather than an injury to unions or employees. However, in Associated Gen. Contractors of Cal. v. California State Council of Carpenters, 459 US 519, 112 LRRM 2753 (1983), the Supreme Court rejected a similar claim under the antitrust laws.

[998]Gateway Structures v. Carpenters Conference Bd., 779 F2d 485, 121 LRRM 2209 (CA 9, 1985); Cuyahoga Wrecking Corp. v. Laborers Local 210, 644 F Supp 878, 123 LRRM 3192 (WDNY, 1986); R.B. Elec. v. Electrical Workers (IBEW) Local 569, 119 LRRM 2821 (SD Cal, 1985), *aff'd*, 781 F2d 1440, 121 LRRM 3123 (CA 9, 1986).

[999]Penntech Papers v. NLRB, *supra* note 985.

before the Board.[1000] There is, however, authority to the contrary.[1001]

The Board has dealt with the double-breasted issue in other contexts. In one case, the Board dismissed section 8(b)(4)(D) charges against a union, finding that the picketing in question did not have a jurisdictional object but arose from the union's claim to bargaining-unit work and its protest over the allegedly improper transfer of that work to a subsidiary corporation.[1002] The Board has also held that a union's initiation of arbitration procedures in its contract with one employer to obtain an award providing that the contract covered the employees of the employer's nonunion subsidiary, and a subsequent threat to picket the contracting employer to enforce the arbitration award in the union's favor, did not violate sections 8(b)(1)(A), (2), or (3).[1003] In another case, however, a union violated sections 8(e) and 8(b)(3) by insisting on a clause that would have allowed employees it represented to refuse to operate equipment of any employer that had an interest in any nonunion firm doing construction work in the area.[1004]

[1000]Carpenters Local 1846 v. Pratt-Farnsworth, *supra* note 997. *Accord* Operating Eng'rs Local 926 v. Superior Rigging & Erecting Co., 602 F Supp 913, 123 LRRM 3314 (ND Ga, 1984).

[1001]Teamsters Local 70 v. California Consolidators, 693 F2d 81, 111 LRRM 2785 (CA 9, 1982), *cert. denied*, 469 US 887, 117 LRRM 2571 (1984).

[1002]Plumbers & Pipe Fitters Local 36 (Weinheimers, Inc.), 219 NLRB 1016, 90 LRRM 1201 (1975). The union struck the employer with which it had a contract after the employer ceased its own operations as a plumbing contractor and started up two new corporations that engaged in the same kind of work on a nonunion basis. For treatment of jurisdictional disputes generally, see Chapter 25, "Jurisdictional Disputes and Featherbedding." *See also* Iron Workers Local 103 (Higdon Contracting Co.), 216 NLRB 45, 88 LRRM 1067 (1975), *rev'd*, 434 US 335, 97 LRRM 2333 (1978), arising in a §8(b)(7)(C) context. For treatment of organizational and recognitional disputes generally, see Chapter 21, "Picketing for Organization and Recognition."

[1003]Teamsters Local 208 (De Anza Delivery Sys.), 219 NLRB 821, 90 LRRM 1030 (1975). Even though the Board held that the two companies were separate employers, it found that no pressure was brought against the nonunion company and that the arbitration award against the company under contract with the union could not have restrained or coerced the nonunion company or its employees.

[1004]Operating Eng'rs Local 542 (York County Bridge), 216 NLRB 408, 88 LRRM 1405 (1975), *enforced*, 532 F2d 902, 91 LRRM 2976 (CA 3, 1976), *cert. denied*, 429 US 1072, 94 LRRM 2339 (1977). The Board held that the clause violated §8(e) and was not protected by the construction industry proviso because it reached beyond the performance of work at a construction site, and the union was insisting on a nonmandatory subject for bargaining (reasoning that the clause attempted to enlarge its bargaining unit). For treatment of cases under §8(e), see Chapter 24, "Section 8(e): The 'Hot-Cargo' Agreement."

CHAPTER 14

EFFECT OF CHANGE IN BARGAINING REPRESENTATIVE DURING THE TERM OF A COLLECTIVE BARGAINING AGREEMENT

I. CONTEXT IN WHICH THE ISSUE ARISES

This chapter treats the effect of a change of collective bargaining representative during the term of an existing collective bargaining agreement. Such a change which occurs when there is not a bargaining agreement in effect, or when the bargaining agreement is "open," is governed by the ordinary rules applicable to representation procedures.[1] The focus here is whether an unexpired collective bargaining agreement binds the superseding union or the employer.[2]

As a general rule, the existence of a collective bargaining agreement constitutes a bar to an election and to the recognition of a new collective bargaining representative.[3] However, there are situations where the contract does not constitute a bar and a change in bargaining representative may occur notwithstanding the existing agreement. More particularly, the question arises in cases (1) where the existing contract is not a bar to an election by reason of its duration,[4] (2) where there has been a schism in the

[1] *See* Chapter 10, "Representation Proceedings and Elections."

[2] *See* Hale, *Union Affiliations: Examination of the Governing NLRA Standards*, 1983 DET. C.L. REV. 709 (1983) Freidin, *The Board, the "Bar," and the Bargain*, 59 COLUM. L. REV. 61, 82–92 (1959); Comment, *Union Affiliations and Collective Bargaining*, 128 U. PA. L. REV. 430 (1979); Note, *Effect of Pre-Existing Contract on New Bargaining Agent*, 54 COLUM. L. REV. 132 (1954); Note, *Change of Status of a Party to a Collective Bargaining Agreement*, 60 YALE L.J. 1026 (1951).

[3] *See* Chapter 10, "Representation Proceedings and Elections," at notes 119–201.

[4] *E.g.*, American Seating Co., 106 NLRB 250, 32 LRRM 1439 (1953); *see* Chapter 10, "Representation Proceedings and Elections," at notes 127–133.

bargaining representative,[5] or (3) where the contracting union has become defunct[6] or has disclaimed interest in representing the group.[7] Contrasted with these situations are cases where another union, as a result of evolution or reorganization, inherits the powers, assets, and membership, as well as the obligations, of the contracting union.[8]

II. RIGHTS AND OBLIGATIONS OF NEW BARGAINING REPRESENTATIVE AND EMPLOYER UNDER CONTRACT WITH PRIOR REPRESENTATIVE

A. Representation Proceedings

The rules governing the effect of certification of a new bargaining representative on an unexpired agreement have had a checkered history. In early representation cases where an election was directed during the term of a collective bargaining contract, the Board "assumed" that certification of a new union would not affect the validity of any existing collective bargaining agreement.[9] In one case, the Board stated that "[i]t is not our intention to invalidate the contract or to disturb it in any respect. The election which we shall hereinafter direct is for the purpose of determining the identity of the representative which shall administer the contract."[10] The rationale, as later articulated by

---

[5]*E.g.*, Purity Baking Co., 121 NLRB 75, 42 LRRM 1285 (1958); Boston Mach. Works Co., 89 NLRB 59, 25 LRRM 1508 (1950); *see* Chapter 10, "Representation Proceedings and Elections," at note 175.

[6]*E.g.*, Hershey Chocolate Corp., 121 NLRB 901, 42 LRRM 1460 (1958); *cf.* Rocky Mountain Phosphates, 138 NLRB 292, 51 LRRM 1019 (1962) (defunct union superseded by union which secured recognition with authorization cards from majority of employees); *see* Chapter 10, "Representation Proceedings and Elections," at notes 176–180.

[7]*See* Chapter 10, "Representation Proceedings and Elections," at notes 181–183. A union's ability to disclaim its representational status during the term of a collective bargaining agreement is subject to dispute. *Compare* NLRB v. Circle A&W Prods. Co., 647 F2d 924, 107 LRRM 2923 (CA 9), *cert. denied*, 454 US 1054, 108 LRRM 3016 (1981) (disclaimer allowed), Hartz Mountain Corp., 260 NLRB 323, 109 LRRM 1204 (1982), *enforced*, 738 F2d 422, 116 LRRM 3264 (CA 3, 1984), American Sunroof Corp., 243 NLRB 1128, 102 LRRM 1086 (1979) *and* Meat Cutters Local 158 (Eastpoint Seafood Co. Div.), 208 NLRB 58, 85 LRRM 1043 (1973) *with* Toyota Landscape Co. v. Teamsters Local 420, 726 F2d 525, 115 LRRM 2977 (CA 9), *cert. denied*, 469 US 825, 117 LRRM 2551 (1984) (disclaimer not allowed), Estate of Bella Moses, 247 NLRB 144, 103 LRRM 1081 (1980), East Mfg. Corp., 242 NLRB 5, 101 LRRM 1079 (1979) *and* Mack Trucks, 209 NLRB 1003, 85 LRRM 1496 (1974).

[8]*E.g.*, Gate City Optical Co. Div., 175 NLRB 1059, 71 LRRM 1118 (1969); Montgomery Ward & Co., 137 NLRB 346, 50 LRRM 1137 (1962).

[9]Swayne & Hoyt, 2 NLRB 282, 1 LRRM 99 (1936) (dictum); New England Transp. Co., 1 NLRB 130, 1 LRRM 97 (1936) (same).

[10]Register & Tribune Co., 60 NLRB 360, 362, 15 LRRM 233, 234 (1945).

Member Reynolds, was that "neither the employer nor the employee should be enabled by virtue of a proceeding before this Board to discard unilaterally any obligations incurred as a result of their collective bargaining agreement."[11]

In 1950 in *Boston Machine Works*,[12] a schism case, the Board held that it was inappropriate in a representation case to decide the effect of the certification of a new representative upon an existing bargaining agreement and overruled its earlier contrary decisions. The opinion noted that Congress had considered and rejected a proposal to condition certification of a bargaining representative upon the representative's agreement to be bound by any unexpired agreement and reasoned: "[W]e do not believe that this Board should qualify its certification of the employees' bargaining representative by imposing restrictions not to be found in any provision of the Act, and indeed, deliberately omitted therefrom."[13]

While there was some ambiguity in *Boston Machine Works* owing to the Board's refusal to decide the effect of certification on the existing agreement, it is now clear that the Board will not condition certification of a new bargaining representative upon its assumption of any unexpired collective bargaining agreement. Indeed, in later cases the Board has not been reluctant to state, in directing an election, that a new bargaining representative would not be bound by the unexpired contract.[14]

B. Section 8(a)(5) Proceedings: *American Seating*

The Board has also faced the same question—the effect of a newly selected representative upon an existing contract—in a series of unfair labor practice cases.

The earliest of these was *Pacific Greyhound Lines*.[15] The Board had ordered an election despite the existence of an unexpired

---

[11]Boston Mach. Works Co., *supra* note 5, at 61, 25 LRRM at 1510 (dissenting opinion).

[12]*Id.*

[13]*Id.* at 61–62, 25 LRRM 1509–10; *accord* Hershey Chocolate Corp., *supra* note 6, at 909–10, 42 LRRM at 1464 (policy reaffirmed).

[14]*E.g.*, American Sunroof Corp., *supra* note 7 (contracting union disclaimed interest after deauthorization petition filed; Board directed representation election on petition of different union, found unexpired contract no bar because of disclaimer, and refused to condition possible certification on assumption of labor agreement); General Dynamics Corp., 184 NLRB 553, 74 LRRM 1522 (1979) (dictum acknowledging that incumbent union, but not insurgent union, would be bound by unexpired contract for remainder of its term if victorious in representation election).

[15]22 NLRB 111, 6 LRRM 189 (1940).

contract, because the contract had been made with a union that had received unlawful employer assistance.[16] Following certification of the new representative, the employer refused to bargain with the new union. In the ensuing unfair labor practice case, the employer contended that its contract with the predecessor union could not be abrogated either by the employees for whose benefit it was made or by a new representative selected by those employees, a position which the Board rejected.[17]

The Board followed *Pacific Greyhound* when it later rendered the leading decision on this question, *American Seating Co.*[18] There, 2 years after the execution of a 3-year contract between the employer and the United Auto Workers (UAW), the Pattern Makers Union petitioned for an election in a craft unit[19] covered by the UAW contract. In the representation proceeding the Board ruled that the UAW contract constituted no bar to an election since 3-year contracts were not customary in the industry.[20] Thereafter the Pattern Makers Union was certified as the representative of the employees in the unit. The employer, however, insisted that the UAW contract remained generally in effect. In the subsequent unfair labor practice case, the employer maintained that the Pattern Makers Union, as bargaining representative of the craft employees, was required to administer the substantive terms of the existing contract. Relying on traditional common-law agency principles, it contended that the employees, as principals, were bound by the contract executed on their behalf by their agent, and that a mere change in agents could not abrogate the contract. The Pattern Makers Union responded that the unique functions of a statutory collective bargaining representative precluded a blind application of common-law agency principles to the problem.

---

[16]Chapter 8, "Employer Domination and Assistance to Labor Organizations," contains a discussion of employer assistance and domination of labor organizations under §8(a)(2) of the Act.

[17]6 LRRM at 193. In a concurring opinion, Member Smith expressed a different view. He would have allowed abrogation of only those provisions of the contract which were inconsistent with the certification of the new representative, e.g., recognition, a closed shop, and control over administration of the contract. It was his position that provisions covering wages, hours of service, and other working conditions of the covered employees should continue in force.

[18]*Supra* note 4.

[19]For a discussion of craft severance in bargaining units, see Chapter 11, "Appropriate Bargaining Units," at notes 78–101.

[20]The case arose before the Board's ruling that 3-year contracts would be a bar for the entire term regardless of custom in the industry. General Cable Corp., 139 NLRB 1123, 51 LRRM 1444 (1962).

The Board ruled that unless the collective bargaining representative was to be "emasculated" in the exercise of its functions, it must be permitted to negotiate the terms and conditions of employment. The Board thus adopted the general proposition that if an existing contract constitutes no bar to an election, it also is no bar to full bargaining by the new representative.[21] The Board noted that unless the new bargaining representative had the power to negotiate a new agreement, "a great part of the benefit to be derived from the no-bar rule will be dissipated. There is little point in selecting a new bargaining representative which is unable to negotiate new terms and conditions of employment for an extended period of time."[22]

The incumbent union may well find itself in a difficult position because of the *American Seating* rule. Where the signatory union has, for example, entered into a 5-year agreement, it remains bound by the contract even if it wins the election and is certified. If this makes the incumbent organization a "sitting duck" in an election campaign, "it is disadvantaged," the Board reasons, "only because it voluntarily chose to enter into such an agreement knowing that it would not bar an election."[23] In practice, the *American Seating* doctrine operates as a potent deterrent to the negotiation of agreements which do not satisfy the Board's contract-bar rules, particularly agreements for terms longer than 3 years.[24]

In 1973, in *NLRB v. Burns International Security Services*,[25] the Supreme Court conclusively endorsed *American Seating*. The Court cited *American Seating* to support its holding that a successor employer is not bound by a collective bargaining agree-

---

[21]*Accord* Sanders Bus Lines, 256 NLRB 316, 107 LRRM 1260 (1981); American Sunroof Corp., *supra* note 7, at 1129–30, 102 LRRM at 1088.

[22]American Seating Co., *supra* note 4, at 255, 32 LRRM at 1442.

[23]General Dynamics Corp., *supra* note 14, 74 LRRM at 1523. See Chapters 8, "Employer Domination and Assistance to Labor Organizations," and 10, "Representation Proceedings and Elections," for application to decertification petitions and rival union petitions.

[24]General Cable Corp., *supra* note 20.

[25]406 US 272, 284 n.8, 80 LRRM 2225, 2230 n.8 (1972) ("When the union which has signed a collective-bargaining contract is decertified, the succeeding union certified by the Board is not bound by the prior contract, need not administer it and may demand negotiations for a new contract, even if the terms of the old contract have not yet expired").

There had been but little doubt that *American Seating* was authoritative. In Modine Manufacturing Co. v. Machinists, 216 F2d 326, 35 LRRM 2003 (CA 6, 1954), the Court of Appeals for the Sixth Circuit had cast some doubt upon the matter by suggesting in a dictum that only the union-shop and checkoff provisions became inoperative when a new bargaining representative entered the scene, while other provisions of the contract remained in effect to be administered by the newly certified union.

ment negotiated by its predecessors. The Board has subsequently rejected opportunities to impair or question the vitality of *American Seating*.[26]

C. Right of Superseded Contracting Union

The Board and the courts have made clear that no union other than the duly recognized or certified collective bargaining representative retains any rights under a collective bargaining contract.[27] Once a union that is signatory to a contract is decertified or otherwise loses its status as collective bargaining representative, it retains no rights under that contract.[28] This feature of the collective bargaining relationship, which elevates the statutory right to choose a representative over the stability of contract, underscores that the collective bargaining agreement is sui generis. As an exception to this general principle, however, decertified unions have been allowed to process grievances to arbitration where they were asserting rights that arose prior to decertification and there was no successor collective bargaining representative.[29]

III. MERGERS AND TRANSFERS OF AFFILIATION

Different legal issues arise where the successor labor organization is actually a mere continuation of the earlier representative as, for example, following a merger of affiliates of the same national organization or an affiliation by one independent organization with another.[30] Typically, it is a union that finds itself claiming to be a continuation of the earlier organization, thereby

---

[26]*E.g.*, Consolidated Fiberglass Prods., Co., 242 NLRB 10, 101 LRRM 1089 (1979).

[27]National Licorice Co. v. NLRB, 309 US 350, 364–65, 6 LRRM 674, 681–82 (1940); NLRB v. Jones & Laughlin Steel Corp., 301 US 1, 44–45, 1 LRRM 703, 713 (1937). Compare union contract obligations devolving upon a successor employer, discussed in Chapter 15, "Effect of Change in the Employing Unit: Successorship."

[28]Retail Clerks v. Montgomery Ward & Co., 316 F2d 754, 53 LRRM 2069 (CA 7, 1963) (continuation of representational status an "implied condition of the contracts"; court does not reach issue whether contract enforceable by employees or subsequent collective bargaining agent); Modine Mfg. Co. v. Machinists, *supra* note 25 (§301 suit by decertified union to enforce collective bargaining agreement).

[29]Auto Workers v. Telex Computer Prods., 816 F2d 519, 125 LRRM 2163 (CA 10, 1987); United States Gypsum Co. v. Steelworkers, 384 F2d 38, 66 LRRM 2232 (CA 5, 1967), *cert. denied*, 389 US 1042, 67 LRRM 2232 (1968).

[30]For discussion of a successor employer's duty where it is a mere continuance of the predecessor employer, see Chapter 15, "Effect of Change in the Employing Unit: Successorship," at notes 42–49.

seeking to compel the employer to extend recognition to it as the bargaining representative and to honor the existing collective bargaining agreement.[31] The roles may be reversed, however. It may be the employer that claims continuation of the representative's identity to avoid being required to negotiate a new agreement.[32] These situations are the primary focus of this section.

Historically the Board has applied a two-prong test in determining whether to amend a certification to reflect a union's affiliation with another labor organization: (1) whether there has been an adequate opportunity for those affected to participate in, and vote on, the affiliation question (due process); and (2) whether there is substantial continuity between the pre- and postaffiliation union.[33] The same standard has been applied in unfair labor practice cases[34] and in intraunion merger or consolidation cases.[35]

When an employer continues to recognize a changed bargaining representative, it may not challenge the change after expiration of the six-month statute of limitations period prescribed by section 10(b) of the Act.[36]

A. Due Process

Because an affiliation vote concerns the organization and structure of the union and not its representation status, the procedural standards used in Board-conducted representation elections do not apply to affiliation votes.[37] The Board has never specifically defined "adequate due process" although it has char-

---

[31]*E.g.*, New England Foundry Corp., 192 NLRB 785, 78 LRRM 1112 (1971); Hamilton Tool Co., 190 NLRB 571, 77 LRRM 1257 (1971); Universal Tool & Stamping Co., 182 NLRB 254, 74 LRRM 1096 (1970).

[32]Gate City Optical Co. Div., 175 NLRB 1059, 71 LRRM 1118 (1969); Montgomery Ward & Co., 137 NLRB 346, 50 LRRM 1137 (1962).

[33]May Dep't Stores Co., 289 NLRB 661, 128 LRRM 1299 (1988). *See generally* NLRB v. Financial Inst. Employees Local 1182 (Seattle-First Nat'l Bank), 475 US 192, 199, 121 LRRM 2741, 2745 (1986) (review of Board precedent).

[34]NLRB v. Financial Inst. Employees Local 1182 (Seattle-First Nat'l Bank), *supra* note 33, at 200 n.8, 121 LRRM at 2745 n.8; News/Sun Sentinel Co. v. NLRB, 890 F2d 430, 132 LRRM 2988 (CA DC, 1989), *cert. denied*, ___ US ___, 134 LRRM 2536 (1990).

[35]News/Sun Sentinel Co. v. NLRB, *supra* note 34; Retail Clerks Local 428 v. NLRB (Independent Drug Store Owners of Santa Clara County), 528 F2d 1225, 91 LRRM 2001 (CA 9, 1975); Quality Inn Waikiki, 297 NLRB No. 71, 133 LRRM 1078 (1989); Newspapers, Inc., 210 NLRB 8, 86 LRRM 1123 (1974), *enforced*, 515 F2d 334, 89 LRRM 2715 (CA 5, 1975) (division of one local union merged into second local union). The same standard is applied when the representative disaffiliates. Canterbury Villa of Waterford, 282 NLRB 462, 125 LRRM 1027 (1986).

[36]Sewell-Allen Big Star, 294 NLRB No. 6, 133 LRRM 1041 (1989).

[37]Quemetco, Inc., 226 NLRB 1398, 1399, 94 LRRM 1040, 1042 (1976).

acterized this prong of the test as ensuring "democratic process."[38] It has found the due process requirement satisfied where members receive adequate notice of the impending affiliation vote, where there is sufficient opportunity to discuss the affiliation issue, and where the affiliation vote is conducted by secret ballot.[39] But the Board does not require a secret-ballot vote where a regional union merges with a national union and the regional union maintains its organizational structure,[40] nor does it demand these procedural standards where a national union assigns its bargaining rights to affiliated local unions.[41] An affiliation vote may be taken among the entire membership; a unit-by-unit vote is unnecessary.[42] Where it is the parent body that changes its affiliation or merges with another organization, a vote at the local level is not required.[43]

One contested due process issue was whether employees who are in the bargaining unit but are not members of the union are entitled to vote in the balloting over an affiliation or merger. In the *Amoco Production*[44] quartet the Board wavered back and forth on the issue, but eventually overruled earlier decisions and held that due process required the extension of voting rights to nonunion employees. The Board reasoned that the change of a representative's affiliation or identity affects the interests of bargaining-unit members more profoundly than do other decisions, such as strike votes or the election of bargaining committee members, that are customarily regarded as internal union affairs determinable by the members exclusively.[45] Deferring to

---

[38]F.W. Woolworth Co., 285 NLRB 854, 126 LRRM 1139 (1987), *enforced*, 892 F2d 1041, 133 LRRM 2120 (CA 4, 1989).

[39]May Dep't Stores Co., *supra* note 33; Providence Medical Center, 243 NLRB 714, 102 LRRM 1099 (1979); North Elec. Co., 165 NLRB 942, 65 LRRM 1379 (1967). In at least one case the due process requirement was satisfied without a secret-ballot election. Aurelia Osborn Fox Memorial Hosp., 247 NLRB 356, 103 LRRM 1151 (1980).

[40]House of the Good Samaritan, 248 NLRB 539, 103 LRRM 1472 (1980).

[41]Duquesne Light Co., 248 NLRB 1271, 104 LRRM 1043 (1980).

[42]NLRB v. Eastern Conn. Health Servs., 815 F2d 517, 125 LRRM 2332 (CA 2), *cert. denied*, 484 US 845, 126 LRRM 2496 (1987); May Dep't Stores Co., *supra* note 33.

[43]Texas Plastics, 263 NLRB 394, 111 LRRM 1058 (1982).

[44]Amoco Prod. Co., 220 NLRB 861, 90 LRRM 1434 (1975) (nonmembers not entitled to vote), *supplemental decision*, 233 NLRB 158, 97 LRRM 1113 (1977), *second supplemental decision*, 239 NLRB 1195, 100 LRRM 1127 (1979) (reaff'g earlier ruling), *remanded on other grounds*, 613 F2d 107, 103 LRRM 2810 (CA 5, 1980), *third supplemental decision*, 262 NLRB 1240, 110 LRRM 1419 (1982) (overruling earlier decisions and holding nonmembers entitled to vote), *aff'd sub nom.* Oil, Chem. & Atomic Workers Local 4-14 v. NLRB, 721 F2d 150, 114 LRRM 3676 (CA 5, 1983). *Compare* North Elec. Co., *supra* note 39 (voting of members only approved) *with* Jasper Seating Co., 231 NLRB 1025, 96 LRRM 1195 (1977) (voting of members only not approved).

[45]Amoco Prod. Co. (IV), 262 NLRB 1240, 110 LRRM 1419 (1982).

the authority of the Board in such matters, the Fifth Circuit affirmed the Board's decision.[46]

The issue reached the Supreme Court in *NLRB v. Financial Institution Employees Local 1182 (Seattle-First National Bank)*.[47] That case arose when the Board, applying the newly announced rule of *Amoco IV*,[48] upheld the refusal of an employer to bargain with a newly affiliated incumbent representative because nonmembers had not been offered the franchise in the affiliation balloting.[49] The Ninth Circuit rejected the Board's new rule.[50] That court concluded that the Board's prior rule, including the second prong requirement of continuity, adequately protected the statutory interests of all bargaining-unit members and that the *Amoco IV* intrusion into internal union affairs was, accordingly, unauthorized by the Act.

Resolving the conflict in the circuits,[51] the Court fully embraced the reasoning of the Ninth Circuit and rejected the Board's new rule.[52] In the Supreme Court, the Board conceded that the denial of the vote to nonmembers did not raise a question concerning representation but argued that its rule requiring that nonmembers be allowed to vote was nonetheless valid as a reasonable means to protect section 7 rights and to minimize industrial strife. Writing for the unanimous Court, Justice Brennan rejected both arguments: Unless changes in the organization are extensive enough to raise a question concerning its continued representative status, the Board has no authority under the statute either to condone the employer's refusal to bargain or to prescribe changes in the union's internal affairs.[53]

---

[46]Oil, Chem. & Atomic Workers Local 4-14 (Amoco Prod. Co. (IV)) v. NLRB, 721 F2d 150, 114 LRRM 3676 (CA 5, 1983).

[47]*Supra* note 33.

[48]*Supra* note 45.

[49]Seattle-First Nat'l Bank, 265 NLRB 426, 111 LRRM 1637 (1982). The Board vacated an earlier decision which had reached the opposite result. *See* Seattle-First Nat'l Bank, 241 NLRB 751, 100 LRRM 1564 (1979) (amendment of certification granted) *and* 245 NLRB 700, 102 LRRM 1368 (1979) (summary judgment granted).

[50]Financial Inst. Employees Local 1182 v. NLRB (Seattle-First Nat'l Bank), 752 F2d 356, 116 LRRM 3409 (CA 9, 1984), *rehearing denied en banc*, 750 F2d 757, 118 LRRM 2208 (CA 9, 1985).

[51]*Compare* Retail Workers Local 881 v. NLRB (May Dep't Stores Co.), 774 F2d 752, 120 LRRM 2729 (CA 7, 1985) *and* Oil, Chem. & Atomic Workers Local 4-14 (Amoco Prod. Co. (IV)) v. NLRB, *supra* note 46 (accepting position of the Board) *with* NLRB v. Financial Inst. Employees Local 1182 v. NLRB (Seattle-First Nat'l Bank), *supra* note 50 (rejecting the Board's position).

[52]NLRB v. Financial Inst. Employees Local 1182 v. NLRB (Seattle-First Nat'l Bank), *supra* note 33.

[53]*Id.* at 205, 121 LRRM at 2747 ("[n]on-union employees have no voice in the affairs of the union") (quoting NLRB v. Allis-Chalmers Mfg. Co., 388 US 175, 190, 65 LRRM 2449, 2455 (1967)).

The Court noted that the effect of the Board's new rule was to decertify the union even though no question concerning representation had ever been raised or presented to the Board. The argument based on avoidance of industrial strife was also unavailing. Because the employees had not manifested any purpose or desire to reject the union's representation, the Board's rule effectively granted an improper employer veto over internal union decision making which would tend to generate industrial unrest by unnecessarily disturbing settled bargaining relationships. So reasoning, the Court held that the Board had exceeded its authority under the Act.

The Court remarked, however, that the Board retained the authority to order an election when it determined that an affiliation or reorganization was "sufficiently dramatic to alter the union's identity" thereby raising a question concerning representation.[54] A question left open by both the courts and the Board is the extent to which the Board may continue after *Financial Institution Employees* to impose other due process requirements upon internal union affiliation and merger procedures when the agency's processes are invoked, e.g., through a petition for amended certification or a section 8(a)(5) charge.[55]

B. Continuity of Representation

The primary reason for the second prong, requiring substantial continuity in the identity of the bargaining representative, is to open the way for appropriate inquiry where there has been a "'complete loss of the identity of the certified union.'"[56] A major change in the identity of the union raises a question concerning representation and the need for a vote to determine whether the new bargaining representative should be certified. In determining whether such a change has occurred, "[t]he ultimate question is whether the union after affiliation operates in substantially the same way as it did before affiliation."[57]

---

[54]121 LRRM at 2748.

[55]The Court expressly declined to rule on the propriety of the minimal due process prong of the Board's traditional test involving mergers and affiliations. 475 US, at 199 n.6, 121 LRRM at 2745 n.6; News/Sun Sentinel Co. v. NLRB, 890 F2d 430, 132 LRRM 2988, 2991 n.5 (CA DC, 1989), *cert. denied*, ____ US ____, 134 LRRM 2536 (1990); May Dep't Stores Co., 289 NLRB 661, 128 LRRM 1299, 1302 n.16 (1988).

[56]News/Sun Sentinel Co. v. NLRB, *supra* note 55, 132 LRRM at 2990 (quoting Gas Serv. Co., 213 NLRB 932, 933, 87 LRRM 1226, 1227 (1974)).

[57]Seattle-First Nat'l Bank v. NLRB, 892 F2d 792, 133 LRRM 2193, 2199 (CA 9, 1989), *on remand from* NLRB v. Financial Inst. Employees Local 1182, 475 US 192, 121 LRRM 2741 (1986).

While *Financial Institution Employees* may have marked the demise of, or at least a hiatus in, the application of stringent due process analysis, it has breathed new life into the second prong: the inquiry into the continuity of representation. Prior to *Financial Institution Employees,* continuity of representation was admittedly a subordinate inquiry:

> [Continuity of representation] is, of course, a factor to be considered. But where, as here, the employees unanimously elect to affiliate with another union, we are much more concerned with giving effect to the employees' free choice of bargaining representative than with the so-called "continuity of representation" which might be disrupted by such election. For it is the employees' freedom to select a bargaining representative of their choice which is of paramount importance under the Act.[58]

After the Court's decision in *Financial Institution Employees,* the Board, in *Western Commercial Transport,*[59] took a new interest in policing the requirement of continuity of representation. Acknowledging that its renewed interest in the issue was a break from its own previous decisions, the Board overruled inconsistent precedent.[60]

The current test, applied with a new vigor, is whether there is continuity of representation in the "totality of the circumstances."[61] That is, of course, a most malleable standard:

> The Board generally considers a number of factors, including "structure, administration, officers, assets, membership, autonomy, by-laws, size" and looks for changes "in the rights and obligations of the union's leadership and membership, and in the relationships between the putative bargaining agent, its affiliate, and the employer."[62]

The burden of proof is on party seeking to prove discontinuity.[63]

---

[58]Quemetco Inc., 226 NLRB 1398, 1399, 94 LRRM 1040, 1042 (1976).
[59]288 NLRB 214, 127 LRRM 1313 (1988).
[60]*Id.*, 127 LRRM at 1317 n.13.
[61]News/Sun Sentinel Co. v. NLRB, *supra* note 55; Yates Indust., 264 NLRB 1237, 1250, 112 LRRM 1231 (1982).
[62]NLRB v. Insulfab Plastics, 789 F2d 961, 966, 122 LRRM 2105, 2109 (CA 1, 1986) (citations omitted) (quoting NLRB v. Pearl Bookbinding, 517 F2d 1108, 1111–12, 89 LRRM 2614, 2617 (CA 1, 1975); J. Ray McDermott & Co. v. NLRB, 571 F2d 850, 857, 98 LRRM 2191, 2195 (CA 5), *cert. denied,* 439 US 893, 99 LRRM 2657 (1978)). For the Board's own and more detailed description of these same factors, see *Western Commercial Transport, supra* note 59, 127 LRRM at 1316.
[63]Insulfab Plastics, 274 NLRB 817, 821, 119 LRRM 1086 (1985), *enforced,* 789 F2d 961, 122 LRRM 2105 (CA 1, 1986).

In *Western Commercial Transport* itself, notwithstanding a formal affiliation vote, the Board found that the independent's affiliation with a national organization would displace the formerly elected local officers, merge the independent's membership into a much larger organization, and change the identity of those engaged in day-to-day collective bargaining. Most important to the Board was the loss of autonomy of the members of the former independent union. The Board therefore concluded that there was discontinuity of representation, raising a question concerning representation which could only be resolved through a representation proceeding.

Continuity has been found wanting when bargaining, though still to be conducted by members of the former organization, was to be assisted by a representative of the parent body whose signature on any contract was required.[64] There was insufficient continuity where a trusteeship was first imposed by the local's international parent and, after a membership vote, the local was merged into a larger local, thereby losing the ability to select its own officers, conduct its own collective bargaining, and keep its own treasury and office.[65] The Board declined to decide, however, whether the change in representative should be measured from before or after imposition of the trusteeship.

In the unusual circumstance that a predecessor union was a "functioning, viable entity," the Board dismissed a petition to amend certification based upon a membership vote which was conducted after the union's Board of Directors and officers had "repudiated" the planned affiliation leading the Board to believe that there was an insufficient "guaranty of continuity of representation."[66] In the post–*Western Commercial Transport* era the Board has even looked to a union's lack of commitment in honoring the existing agreement as evidence of discontinuity.[67] Since a successor union, properly so-called in this context, is bound to the existing agreement as a matter of law, to say that the judgment of successorship is influenced by the union's willingness to accept the existing contract has a distinctly tautological quality.

Continuity has been found to exist, however, where the structure of the postaffiliation union remains essentially the same and

---

[64]Garlock Equip. Co., 288 NLRB 247, 128 LRRM 1025 (1988).
[65]Quality Inn Waikiki, 297 NLRB No. 71, 133 LRRM 1078 (1989).
[66]Missouri Beef Packers, 175 NLRB 1100, 1101, 71 LRRM 1177, 1179 (1969).
[67]Chas. S. Winner, Inc., 289 NLRB 62, 130 LRRM 1348 (1988).

where that organization through its same officers or representatives continues to have primary responsibility for administering the contract.[68] The merger of a union's parent body with another organization does not break the union's continuity where its relationship with the new organization is virtually the same as its prior relationship with its former parent.[69] A lack of continuity is not established merely because a superior body into which the former independent has merged or affiliated has constitutional authority to review and veto proposed contracts.[70] Nor does a slight diminution in autonomy establish a discontinuity.[71] The mere fact that the unit may have a smaller proportionate overall representation in the new union is not grounds for finding discontinuity.[72]

In analyzing continuity of a union's identity, the legal distinction between a parent body and one of its subordinate locals is material. For example, in *Whisper Soft Mills v. NLRB*,[73] the court held that the employer had not violated section 8(a)(5) by refusing to bargain with the local union when it was the parent body that had been certified as the bargaining representative. Throughout the negotiations, the employer had insisted that the certified international be a signatory, and that continued dealings with the local council were conditioned upon its securing authority to sign on behalf of the international. This was not done, and a strike ultimately ensued over other issues. In reversing the Board's decision, the court stated that the distinction between the local and the international body is significant for purposes of identifying the exclusively authorized bargaining representative.[74] While noting that the international may dele-

---

[68]News/Sun Sentinel Co. v. NLRB, *supra* note 55; (CA DC, 1989); May Dept' Stores Co., *supra* note 55, 128 LRRM at 1303; F.W. Woolworth Co., 285 NLRB 854, 126 LRRM 1139 (1987), *enforced*, 892 F2d 1041, 133 LRRM 2120 (CA 4, 1989); F.W. Woolworth Co., 194 NLRB 1208, 79 LRRM 1255 (1972).

[69]National Posters v. NLRB, 885 F2d 175, 132 LRRM 2502 (CA 4, 1989), *enforcing* 289 NLRB 468, 130 LRRM 1407 (1988).

[70]*Id.*; NLRB v. Insulfab Plastics, *supra* note 62; Seattle-First Nat'l Bank, 290 NLRB 571, 129 LRRM 1020, 1022 (1988), *enforced*, 892 F2d 792, 133 LRRM 2193, 2199 (CA 9, 1989); May Dep't Stores Co., *supra* note 55. *But see* Sun Oil Co. v. NLRB, 576 F2d 553, 556, 98 LRRM 2467, 2469 (CA 3, 1978). The distinction between a right of veto and a requirement of prior approval is not self-evident. *See* text at note 64 *supra*.

[71]May Dep't Stores, *supra* note 55, 128 LRRM at 1303.

[72]F.W. Woolworth Co., *supra* note 68; Montgomery Ward, 188 NLRB 551, 76 LRRM 1364 (1971).

[73]754 F2d 1381, 117 LRRM 2974, *supplemental opinion*, 118 LRRM 3022 (CA 9, 1985), *reversing and vacating* 267 NLRB 813, 114 LRRM 1180 (1983).

[74]The Board had refused to dismiss the complaint on the issue of the international (and not the local council) being the bargaining representative, apparently on a theory of waiver based upon the employer's continuation of negotiations with the council. 267 NLRB at 813 n.2, 114 LRRM at 1181 n.2.

gate its bargaining authority to members of the local, that delegation is a question of agency law. Since the court found that the local had not, under the circumstances, consented to act as the national's agent, the court held that the employer had no duty to bargain with the uncertified local union.[75]

In sum, the Board appears to be at something of a crossroads. Enforcement of an intrusive due process test has been halted by the Supreme Court's reproof in *Financial Institution Employees*[76] that union mergers and affiliations are primarily internal matters. The Board's decisions since *Western Commercial Transport*[77] suggest that despite that reproof, the Board will pursue a closer regulation of these matters using its continuity of representation requirement.

---

[75]*Accord* Auto Workers v. NLRB (Pierce Governor Co.), 394 F2d 757, 67 LRRM 2695 (CA DC), *cert. denied,* 393 US 831, 69 LRRM 2434 (1968).

[76]NLRB v. Financial Inst. Employees Local 1182 (Seattle-First Nat'l Bank), 475 US 192, 205, 121 LRRM 2741, 2747 (1986).

[77]*Supra* note 59; *e.g.,* Quality Inn Waikiki, *supra* note 65; Garlock Equip. Co., *supra* note 64.

Chapter 15

EFFECT OF CHANGE IN THE EMPLOYING UNIT: SUCCESSORSHIP

I. Scope of the Topic

A. Factual Setting

Changes in business ownership have become increasingly common as well as varied in form. Where the seller, or prior employer, is a party to a labor agreement, has a bargaining relationship with a certified or recognized union, or is a respondent in an unfair labor practice proceeding, the question of the legal obligations of a potential new employer to the seller's employees, and to their representative, will inevitably arise. When these obligations are anticipated in a direct sale and purchase of a business, they may be reflected, and their costs allocated, to some extent in the negotiations between seller and buyer. But often such obligations are not anticipated, or the transaction effectuating the change in ownership is less direct, or more complex. And in many instances, it may also be essential to the ownership transaction to evaluate the potential legal obligations in connection with the potential legal rights of the new employer to make changes which correspond to its assessment of the needs of the business to be acquired.

The decisions of the Board and courts balancing these legal obligations and legal rights "across the change in ownership"[1]

[1]John Wiley & Sons v. Livingston, 376 US 543, 551, 55 LRRM 2769 (1964). For a comprehensive discussion of the subject matter of this chapter, see the following commentary: Landau, *Successorship Doctrine, the Courts and Arbitrators: Common Sense or Dollars and Cents?*, 44 U. Miami L. Rev. 403 (1989); George, *Successorship and the Duty to Bargain*, 63 Notre Dame L. Rev. 277 (1988); Murphy, *Successorship and the Forgotten Employee: A Suggested Approach*, NYU Thirty-First Annual Conference on Labor 75 (1978); Henry, *Is There Arbitration After* Burns? *The Resurrection of* John Wiley & Sons, 31 Vand. L.

constitute the law of successorship. The law provides neither a fixed definition of "successor," nor a uniformly accepted set of obligations which flow from the determination that, in certain circumstances, a party is a "successor."[2] Factual circumstances and procedural setting are both significant.

Typically, successorship issues arise in Board proceedings involving alleged unfair labor practices. For the most part, these unfair labor practice cases involve an alleged violation of the new employer's duty to recognize and bargain with the representative of the employees of the former owner.[3] Less frequently, successorship issues arise in grievance-arbitration cases or in section 301 suits in federal court, usually pursuant to a motion by the union to compel arbitration under its contract with the prospective transferor or former employer.[4]

B. A Summary of the Law

The body of successorship law is unusual in two major respects. First, the law is established to an extraordinary extent by decisions of the Supreme Court. Second, these decisions are relatively recent. Only one of the five Supreme Court decisions[5] was rendered prior to 1972, and the scope of that decision has been significantly narrowed. This does not suggest that the law

---

REV. 249 (1978); Donnelley, *Labor Union in Your Client's Business Sale or Acquisition (The Howard Johnson Case & Subsequent Precedent)*, 33 MO. B.J. 33 (1977); Bakaly & Bryan, *Survival of the Bargaining Agreement: The Effect of* Burns, 27 VAND. L. REV. 117 (1974); Benetar, *Successorship Liability Under Labor Agreements*, 1973 WIS. L. REV. 1026; Morris & Gaus, *Successorship and the Collective Bargaining Agreement: Accommodating* Wiley *and* Burns, 59 VA. L. REV. 1359 (1973); Gunther, *The Supreme Court 1971 Term*, 86 HARV. L. REV. 1, 255–56 (1972); Comment, *Successorship Clauses in Collective Bargaining Agreements*, 1979 B.Y.U. L. REV. 99; Comment, *Contractual Successorship: The Impact of* Burns, 40 U. CHI. L. REV. 617 (1973).

[2]Howard Johnson Co. v. Hotel Employees, Detroit Local Joint Executive Bd., 417 US 249, 262 n.9, 86 LRRM 2449 (1974). In cautioning against a fixed definition of "successor," the Court characterized the normal two-step analysis (is the new employer a successor, and if so, is it obligated to bargain (or arbitrate), etc.?) as an artificial division of the question. Thus, the determination that a party is a successor does not lead to a fixed conclusion about the extent to which "successorship" obligations are applicable. However, a two-step analysis is often inescapable because if a party is not a successor, it will usually be unnecessary to consider the extent of its obligations.

[3]Successorship issues also arise in the Board's supplemental or "backpay" proceedings in which the derivative liability of a new employer for the unfair labor practices of the former employer may be litigated. *See* Chapter 31, "NLRB Procedures," at notes 182–183. They may also arise in a Board representation proceeding where a "contract bar" is asserted; *see* Chapter 10, "Representation Proceedings and Elections," at notes 158–160.

[4]*See, e.g.*, John Wiley & Sons v. Livingston, *supra* note 1, discussed *infra* at notes 24–32; Howard Johnson Co. v. Hotel Employees, Detroit Local Joint Executive Bd., *supra* note 2, discussed *infra* at notes 61–69.

[5]John Wiley & Sons v. Livingston, *supra* note 1.

of successorship had not emerged at all, or had been static, before 1972. Rather, it reflects an ongoing synthesis in which many concepts developed by the Board and the circuit courts have been examined and accepted, modified, or rejected in varying measures.

These Supreme Court decisions have been so closely scrutinized by the Board and the lower courts that the phraseology of the opinions has often defined subsequent major issues. The visible role of the lower courts in construing these decisions has stemmed not merely from special procedural considerations inherent in review of both section 301 actions and Board orders but also from the circumstance that most successorship cases involve interpretation not of statutory language "but of Supreme Court pronouncements of the controlling statutory principles . . . ."[6] Thus, the lower courts have tended to take a more independent role in construing the Supreme Court's decisions than they might ordinarily adopt in reviewing Board orders, where the Board itself has construed the statutory provisions of the Act or the Board's own decisions and rules of decision.[7]

These landmark decisions of the Supreme Court are briefly summarized as follows:

The 1964 decision in *John Wiley & Sons v. Livingston*[8] established, in the context of a section 301 action, that certain contractual rights under a labor agreement are not automatically extinguished by the "disappearance" of the contracting employer through merger and that the duty to arbitrate may survive and devolve upon the resultant "new" employer even though the new employer had never signed the contract nor agreed to arbitrate.

---

[6]Machinists (Boeing Co.) v. NLRB, 595 F2d 664, 673 n.41, 98 LRRM 2787 (CA DC, 1978), *cert. denied*, 439 US 1070, 100 LRRM 2268 (1979), where the court stated that in those circumstances "deference to the Board may ordinarily be less appropriate."

[7]This independent role has not been confined to cases in which enforcement of Board orders has been denied; *see, e.g.*, Pacific Hide & Fur Depot v. NLRB, 553 F2d 609, 95 LRRM 2467 (CA 9, 1977); NLRB v. Bausch & Lomb, 526 F2d 817, 90 LRRM 3217 (CA 2, 1975), *denying enforcement in part to* 214 NLRB 338, 88 LRRM 1196 (1974); Pre-Engineered Bldg. Prods., 228 NLRB 841, 96 LRRM 1170 (1977), *enforcement denied*, 603 F2d 134, 101 LRRM 3021 (CA 10, 1979). It has also extended to cases in which Board orders have been enforced or affirmed; *see, e.g.*, Machinists (Boeing Co.) v. NLRB, *supra* note 6; Boeing Co. v. Machinists, 504 F2d 307, 87 LRRM 2865 (CA 5, 1974), *cert. denied*, 421 US 913, 88 LRRM 3456 (1975); NLRB v. Band-Age, Inc., 534 F2d 1, 92 LRRM 2001 (CA 1), *cert. denied*, 429 US 921, 93 LRRM 2570 (1976).

[8]*Supra* note 1.

The 1972 decision in *NLRB v. Burns International Security Services*,[9] an unfair labor practice proceeding, is the centerpiece of contemporary successorship law. The decision resolved two major issues. First, it fixed the fundamental criteria for determining whether a new employer has an obligation to bargain with the representative of its predecessor's employees. (These criteria require comparisons of old and new work forces and old and new employing entities and have become the requisites for determining whether the new employer is a "successor.") Second, it held that a successor's obligation to bargain does not bind it involuntarily to its predecessor's labor agreement.

In 1974, in *Howard Johnson Co. v. Hotel Employees, Detroit Local Joint Executive Board*,[10] the Court held that the criteria which it had established in *Burns* for determining a new employer's bargaining obligation after a change in ownership could not be disregarded in a section 301 action instituted in reliance on *Wiley*.

Earlier that same term (in 1973), in *Golden State Bottling Co. v. NLRB*,[11] the Court held that the duty to remedy unfair labor practices of a predecessor may be imposed upon a successor who takes over a business with knowledge of the unfair labor practices or of the pendency of unfair labor practice proceedings.

Finally, in *NLRB v. Fall River Dyeing & Finishing Corp.*,[12] the Court held in 1987 that transaction forms do not, alone, control a successor's obligation and that the duty to bargain was owed by a new employer who purchased some assets from an effectively defunct predecessor but then pursued much the same business at the same location with much the same work force.

II. HISTORICAL DEVELOPMENT

A. Early Rulings

Although this branch of the law has flowered rather late, its roots are much older and deeper. They date at least to 1939 and follow two general lines of growth.

---

[9]406 US 272, 80 LRRM 2225 (1972).
[10]*Supra* note 2.
[11]414 US 168, 84 LRRM 2839 (1973). *See infra* at notes 416–465.
[12]482 US 27, 125 LRRM 2441 (1987).

The less controversial development concerned employers found to be the *alter ego* of some other or prior employer. As the term suggests, alter ego refers to a situation in which the identity of the employing entities is substantially the same. Thus, the "new employer" might be "merely a disguised continuance of the old employer,"[13] or may have undergone a mere technical change, perhaps to avoid the effect of the labor laws, without any substantial change in ownership or management. In those circumstances the courts have encountered "little difficulty" in holding that the new employer "is in reality the same employer" and subject to similar obligations.[14] The practice of including in Board orders the phrase "successors and assigns" and applying such orders to alter egos was upheld by the Supreme Court in 1945, in *Regal Knitwear v. NLRB*.[15]

As early as 1939, the Board held that, following a nominal change in corporate organization which did not materially alter the nature of the business or the employees, a successor employer was required to bargain with the employees' bargaining agent.[16] The Board continued to hold that the bargaining status of the majority representative remained unchanged when an alteration of business operations did not change the essential attributes of the employment relationship.[17]

These early rulings, however, were not confined to alter ego situations. In several cases in the 1940s, the Board held that a bona fide transferee of a business operation was bound by the certification of the bargaining agent for the unit.[18] The Board's position was that a mere change in ownership did not affect the certification of a bargaining agent in the "employing industry." As early as 1953 the Board drew a prophetic distinction between contract rights and the statutory duty to bargain:

> That the Respondent may not have been bound by [the predecessor's] contract with the Union—indeed that the contract may be construed as specifically rejecting such an obligation—is not controlling. Whether the Respondent was required by the statute to con-

---

[13]Southport Petroleum Co. v. NLRB, 315 US 100, 106, 9 LRRM 411 (1942).

[14]Howard Johnson Co. v. Hotel Employees, Detroit Local Joint Executive Bd., *supra* note 2, at 255.

[15]324 US 9, 15 LRRM 882 (1945).

[16]Charles Cushman Co., 15 NLRB 90, 5 LRRM 113 (1939).

[17]Stonewall Cotton Mills, 80 NLRB 325, 23 LRRM 1085 (1948).

[18]Simmons Eng'g Co., 65 NLRB 1435, 17 LRRM 291 (1946); National Bag Co., 65 NLRB 1078, 17 LRRM 283 (1946), *enforced*, 156 F2d 679 (CA 8, 1946); Syncro Mach. Co., 62 NLRB 985, 16 LRRM 230 (1945); *see also* Johnson Ready Mix Co., 142 NLRB 437, 53 LRRM 1068 (1963).

tinue dealing with the Union as the exclusive representative of its employees is a matter of interpretation of the Act and not of the contract. Though the contract may create private rights and duties enforceable under other laws, so far as this statute is concerned, the obligation to bargain is one neither created nor alterable by private agreement.[19]

Before 1964 the circuit courts were concerned with successorship principally in reviewing Board orders. Section 301 suits to compel arbitration were not approved until 1957[20] and had not been invoked against an unconsenting successor until *Wiley*.[21] Thus, before *Wiley*, the courts held that bargaining orders could be directed against successor employers. In those instances where the courts refused enforcement of Board orders directed at successors, they did not reject the "employing industry" concept of continuity which the Board had adopted.[22] As in the more recent cases, continuity of the work force was a major criterion in determining whether a bargaining obligation would be imposed upon a new employer.[23]

B. *Wiley v. Livingston*

In *Wiley* the Supreme Court required a successor employer to arbitrate grievances pursuant to a prior employer's labor agreement even though the successor had not signed or assumed that agreement or agreed to arbitrate. The Supreme Court's holding represented a substantial departure from ordinary contract law and a commonly held view of the collective bargaining agreement. Previously, a collective agreement was viewed as merely creating personal rights and obligations between the parties who had consented to it.[24]

Wiley arose in 1961, when Interscience, for valid business reasons, was acquired by and merged into a much larger pub-

---

[19]Cruse Motors, 105 NLRB 242, 248, 32 LRRM 1285 (1953).

[20]Textile Workers v. Lincoln Mills, 353 US 448, 40 LRRM 2113 (1957). *See* Chapter 17, "Relation of Board Action to Enforcement of Agreements Under Section 301," at notes 30–41.

[21]John Wiley & Sons v. Livingston, *supra* note 1.

[22]*See, e.g.*, NLRB v. Stepp's Friendly Ford, 338 F2d 833, 57 LRRM 2442 (CA 9, 1964); NLRB v. McFarland, 306 F2d 219, 50 LRRM 2707 (CA 10, 1962); NLRB v. Aluminum Tubular Corp., 299 F2d 595, 49 LRRM 2682 (CA 2, 1962); NLRB v. Auto Vent-Shade, Inc., 276 F2d 303, 45 LRRM 3010 (CA 5, 1960); NLRB v. Alamo White Truck Serv., 273 F2d 238, 45 LRRM 2330 (CA 5, 1959); NLRB v. Lunder Shoe Corp., 211 F2d 284, 33 LRRM 2695 (CA 1, 1954).

[23]*Id.*

[24]*See* Steelworkers v. Reliance Universal, 335 F2d 891, 56 LRRM 2721 (CA 3, 1964).

lishing company, John Wiley & Sons, and Interscience ceased operating as a separate entity. At the time of the merger Wiley's employees (about 300) were not organized, but Interscience had a labor agreement with a union representing 40 of its 80 employees. That agreement did not contain a "successorship clause" purporting to bind the successors and assigns of Interscience,[25] and Wiley did not agree to assume the labor agreement.[26] All but a few of the Interscience employees were retained by Wiley, and they performed essentially the same work on the same products as before the merger.

In discussions before and after the merger, the union contended that it continued to represent the Interscience bargaining-unit employees and that, after the merger, Wiley was obligated to recognize certain rights, such as severance pay, which had "vested" or "accrued" under the Interscience union contract. Wiley claimed that the labor agreement, which had expired a few months after the merger, had terminated for all purposes. When Wiley refused the union's demand that it submit the dispute to arbitration under the Interscience agreement, the union brought a section 301 suit in federal court to compel arbitration.

The holding that Wiley was obligated to arbitrate was phrased by a unanimous Court as follows:

> We hold that the disappearance by merger of a corporate employer which has entered into a collective bargaining agreement with a union does not automatically terminate all rights of the employees covered by the agreement, and that, in appropriate circumstances, present here, the successor employer may be required to arbitrate with the union under the agreement.[27]

There were several expressed limitations to this holding. First, the Court held only that the successor was obligated to arbitrate certain claims which were assertable under provisions of the

---

[25]The absence of a "successorship" or "successors and assigns" clause that would provide that the labor agreement be binding on successors was not a deterrent to finding successorship in *Wiley*. Not even a disclaimer of such obligations was controlling. United States Gypsum Co. v. Steelworkers, 384 F2d 38, 66 LRRM 2232 (CA 5, 1967), *cert. denied*, 389 US 1042, 67 LRRM 2232 (1968); McGuire v. Humble Oil & Ref. Co., 355 F2d 352, 61 LRRM 2410 (CA 2, 1966), *cert. denied*, 384 US 988, 62 LRRM 2339 (1966); Steelworkers v. Reliance Universal, *supra* note 24; Hotel Employees Local Joint Executive Bd., v. Joden, Inc., 262 F Supp 390, 64 LRRM 2113 (D Mass, 1966). By the same token, the presence of a "successors and assigns" clause did not establish successorship in Howard Johnson Co. v. Hotel Employees, Detroit Local Joint Executive Bd., 417 US 249, 86 LRRM 2449 (1974).

[26]The absence of such agreements was deemed immaterial by the Court.

[27]John Wiley & Sons v. Livingston, 376 US 543, 548, 55 LRRM 2769 (1964).

predecessor's contract, and not that any such claim had merit as against Wiley.[28] Second, the Court emphasized that it was not holding that the duty to arbitrate survives in every case in which the ownership or corporate structure of an enterprise is changed, for the Court recognized that there could be cases where "lack of any substantial continuity of identity in the business enterprise before and after the change [in ownership] would make a duty to arbitrate something imposed from without. . . ."[29] The Court did not attempt to define the requisites of continuity, that is, the criteria for successorship, and it declined to express any view about bargaining obligations in an unfair labor practice proceeding. The Court merely concluded that whether rights claimed under the Interscience labor contract, including some rights that assertedly survived the expiration of that contract, could be enforced against Wiley was a question subject to arbitration despite Wiley's lack of consent to arbitrate.

This decision could have been seen as merely a logical extension of the Court's reliance on the role of arbitration as a means of effectuating the national labor policy of avoiding industrial strife, with no major implications for Board proceedings. The Court's opinion, however, was susceptible to a broader reading of the "successor's" liability because, in overcoming the primary hurdle—the contention that the new employer never consented to be bound—the Court declared that "[w]hile the principles of law governing ordinary contracts would not bind to a contract an unconsenting successor to a contracting party, a collective bargaining agreement is not an ordinary contract."[30] It added that a collective bargaining agreement "is not in any real sense the simple product of a consensual relationship."[31] The Court augmented this analytical leap by reference to specific policy considerations, leaving little doubt as to the far-reaching implications of the decision. In terms of policy, it focused upon the need to protect the employees who would not ordinarily participate in the negotiations leading to changes in ownership of businesses. In such negotiations, the interests of the employees would inevitably be incidental to business considerations, the Court stated. Therefore, said the Court, the right of owners to negotiate their

---

[28]In the arbitration that ensued, almost all of the union's claims were rejected. Interscience Encyclopedia, 55 LA 210 (1970).

[29]376 US at 551.

[30]*Id.* at 550.

[31]*Id.*

own terms "must be balanced by some protections to the employees from a sudden change in the employment relationship," and the "transition . . . will . . . be eased and industrial strife avoided if employees' claims continue to be resolved by arbitration . . . ."[32]

1. Impact of *Wiley*: The Courts. Lower courts extended *Wiley* to changes of ownership resulting from a sale of assets. In *Wackenhut Corp. v. Plant Guard Workers*,[33] the Ninth Circuit held that the arbitration clause of a labor agreement "bound" a purchaser of assets who retained most of the predecessor's employees. The Third Circuit, in *Steelworkers v. Reliance Universal*,[34] construed *Wiley* more narrowly than did the Ninth Circuit. Rather than hold a purchaser of assets to an unqualified duty to arbitrate, it held that the arbitrator could decide whether certain provisions in the agreement were binding upon the successor.[35]

The duty to arbitrate was extended, in a Second Circuit decision,[36] to a case in which the new employer had retained only a small fraction of its predecessor's employees. The decision raised questions about the breadth of *Wiley* that were not resolved until the Supreme Court's 1974 decision in *Howard Johnson*.[37]

2. Impact of *Wiley*: The Board. The influence of *Wiley* did not come to fruition at the Board until 1970. In *Wiley*, the court had expressly refused to "suggest any view on the questions surrounding a certified union's claim to continued representative status following a change in ownership . . .",[38] that is, the section 8(a)(5) issue. Thus, the relevance to Board proceedings and the extent to which the Board would be influenced by the reasoning of *Wiley* were at first uncertain. The Board continued to apply its successorship doctrine, and perhaps with more assurance. Until 1970, however, it declined to hold that a successor was bound by the substantive terms of a labor agreement negotiated by its predecessor but not agreed to or assumed by

---

[32]*Id.* at 549.
[33]332 F2d 954, 56 LRRM 2466 (CA 9, 1964).
[34]*Supra* note 24.
[35]In *Wiley*, the Court held that procedural arbitrability is for the arbitrator to decide. John Wiley & Sons v. Livingston, *supra* note 27.
[36]Monroe Sander Corp. v. Livingston, 377 F2d 6, 65 LRRM 2273 (CA 2), *cert. denied*, 389 US 831, 66 LRRM 2308 (1967), *aff'g* 262 F Supp 129, 63 LRRM 2545 (SD NY, 1966).
[37]*Supra* note 25.
[38]376 US at 551.

the successor.[39] The Board did advance one step closer to that view by ruling that whether or not bound by its predecessor's labor agreement, a successor may not institute terms different from the contractual terms without first bargaining with the representative of the predecessor's employees.[40] The Board reasoned that "[i]n this respect, the successor-employer's obligations are the same as those imposed upon employers generally during the period between collective bargaining agreements."[41]

C. The *Burns* Case

Finally, in 1970, the Board fully assimilated *Wiley* to the statutory obligation to bargain. In *William J. Burns International Detective Agency*,[42] the lead case in a series,[43] the Board held that when a business changes hands, absent unusual circumstances, "the national labor policy embodied in the Act requires the successor employer to take over and honor a collective bargaining agreement negotiated on behalf of the employing enterprise by the predecessor."[44]

Burns and the Wackenhut Corporation were competitors in the business of providing plant protection and security services. Both submitted competitive bids to Lockheed Aircraft Corporation for a new contract to replace the expiring contract under which Wackenhut was providing those services. All bidders were apprised of Wackenhut's collective bargaining agreement with the United Plant Guards Union which followed a Board cer-

---

[39]*See* Fed-Mart, 165 NLRB 202, 65 LRRM 1303 (1967) (bargaining ordered, but trial examiner's ruling binding successor to predecessor's contract reversed); Rohlik, Inc., 145 NLRB 1236, 55 LRRM 1130 (1964) (successor ordered to bargain, but Board did not consider effect of predecessor's contract).

[40]Michaud Bus Lines, 171 NLRB 193, 68 LRRM 1033 (1968); Fed-Mart, *supra* note 39; Valleydale Packers, 162 NLRB 1486, 64 LRRM 1212 (1967), *enforced*, 402 F2d 768, 69 LRRM 2622 (CA 5, 1968), *cert. denied*, 396 US 825, 72 LRRM 2431 (1969); Overnite Transp. Co., 157 NLRB 1185, 61 LRRM 1520 (1966), *enforced*, 372 F2d 765, 64 LRRM 2359 (CA 4), *cert. denied*, 389 US 838, 66 LRRM 2307 (1967).

[41]NLRB v. Burns Int'l Sec. Servs., 406 US 272, 272, 80 LRRM 2225 (1972). *See* NLRB v. Katz, 369 US 736, 50 LRRM 2177 (1962), discussed in Chapter 13, "The Duty to Bargain," at notes 73–78.

[42]182 NLRB 348, 74 LRRM 1098 (1970). See text at note 9 *supra*.

[43]The companion cases were Dura Corp., 182 NLRB 360, 74 LRRM 1104 (1970) (presenting the reverse issue: successor employer has right to insist that union adhere to contract it had signed with predecessor employer); Travelodge Corp., 182 NLRB 370, 74 LRRM 1105 (1970) (required degree of continuity in employing enterprise lacking, therefore no violation found); Hackney Iron & Steel Co., 182 NLRB 357, 74 LRRM 1102 (1970) (ordering assumption of predecessor's labor contract upon remand from court of appeals for determination of that issue), *on remand from sub nom.* Chemical Workers v. NLRB, 395 F2d 639, 68 LRRM 2065 (CA DC, 1968).

[44]182 NLRB at 350.

tification approximately 4 months earlier. Burns was awarded the new contract and chose to retain 27 of the 42 guards who had been employed by Wackenhut and represented by the union. In addition, Burns transferred 15 of its own employees from other facilities to Lockheed. The union demanded that Burns recognize it and honor its 3-year term collective bargaining agreement negotiated with Wackenhut. Burns refused both demands, and the union filed unfair labor practice charges.

In holding that Burns was obligated to recognize and bargain with the union, the Board relied upon established precedent. In holding Burns to the substantive terms of Wackenhut's labor agreement, the Board overruled precedent with reasoning that relied upon *Wiley*. Noting that in *Wiley* the Supreme Court had viewed substantial continuity in the employing industry as an essential prerequisite for the survival of a duty to arbitrate, despite a change in ownership, the Board concluded that where the requisite continuity was present in an unfair labor practice proceeding, the policy considerations favoring adherence to existing labor agreements had the same force.

On the employee side of the equation, there was undisputed continuity in the majority of the work force. On the employer side of the equation, the Board found that the business of guarding the Lockheed facility remained essentially unchanged and that the bargaining unit remained appropriate. As for the admonition in section 8(d) that the obligation to bargain "does not compel either party to agree to a proposal or require the making of a concession," the Board held the limitation inapplicable to a successor employer whom it viewed as one who "stands in the shoes of its predecessor."[45]

A major obstacle to the enforcement of that position became apparent later in 1970, when the Supreme Court held in *H.K. Porter Co. v. NLRB*[46] that section 8(d) renders the Board and lower courts powerless to compel an employer or a union to execute or agree to any substantive contractual provision. On this basis, the Second Circuit denied enforcement of that portion of the Board's order in *Burns* requiring an involuntary assumption of the collective bargaining agreement, though it granted

---

[45]*Id.*
[46]397 US 99, 73 LRRM 2561 (1970). *See* Chapter 32, "NLRB Orders and Remedies," at notes 248–250.

enforcement of the bargaining order.[47] The Supreme Court affirmed the Second Circuit, unanimously on the section 8(d) issue, and five-to-four on the bargaining obligation issue.

The factual vehicle which *Burns* presented (and which the Board selected) for a reversal of policy was not a typical successorship situation. That Burns's relationship to Wackenhut was that of a competitor was a persuasive consideration, in the view of four dissenting Supreme Court justices, for holding that Burns had no obligation even to bargain with the union.[48]

D. *Burns*: The Supreme Court's View

1. The Bargaining Obligation. A closely divided Supreme Court sustained the Board's holding that Burns had a duty to bargain with the United Plant Guards. It reaffirmed the view that a mere change in ownership in the employing industry is not such an "unusual circumstance" as to relieve the new employer of an obligation to bargain with its predecessor's employees. The criteria upon which it upheld the bargaining obligation were that the "bargaining unit remained unchanged and a majority of the employees hired by the new employer [were] represented by a recently certified bargaining agent . . . ."[49] On this issue, the Court majority noted that it would have been a "wholly different case" (1) if Burns's operational structure and practices had differed from Wackenhut's so that the bargaining unit was no longer appropriate, or (2) if Burns had exercised its right to assemble a work force, a majority of which, without unlawful discrimination, did not consist of former Wackenhut employees represented by a recently certified union.[50]

The dissenters found unsupportable the Board's assumption that a majority of Burns's employees desired the union as their representative. They also rejected the Board's acceptance of Wackenhut's unit as necessarily appropriate for Burns. The thrust of the dissenting view, however, was that there was insufficient continuity of the enterprise on the employer's side, for the only nexus between Wackenhut and Burns was a "mere naked shifting of a group of employees from one employer to anoth-

---

[47]William J. Burns Int'l Detective Agency v. NLRB, 441 F2d 911, 77 LRRM 2081 (CA 2, 1971), *aff'd sub nom.* Burns Int'l Sec. Servs. v. NLRB, 406 US 272, 80 LRRM 2225 (1972).

[48]NLRB v. Burns Int'l Sec. Servs., *supra* note 41, at 304–5.

[49]*Id.* at 281.

[50]*Id.* at 280 n.5.

er . . . ."[51] The dissent emphasized that Burns, which had succeeded to the service contract only over Wackenhut's opposition, did not acquire a single asset of Wackenhut, either tangible or intangible, by negotiation or transfer. Regarding the expectations of employees that the original employer adhere to its labor agreement, the dissenters would have required that another employing entity perform the contract only when it has succeeded to some asset "by the use of which the employees might have expected the first employer to have performed his contract with them."[52]

2. The Contractual Obligation. The Court unanimously rejected the Board's position that Burns was bound to the terms of Wackenhut's labor agreement, a result which seemed foreshadowed by its then recent holding in *H.K. Porter*.[53] Nonetheless, the Court distinguished *Wiley* on three separate bases. First, on the formal basis of its procedural context and factual setting, the Court noted that (1) *Wiley* arose in a section 301 suit to compel arbitration and not in the context of an unfair labor practice case, and (2) *Wiley* was a narrow holding dealing with a merger occurring against a background of state law which provided that the surviving corporation in a merger was liable for the obligations of the disappearing corporation. (This distinction subsequently proved to be short-lived and controversial.)

The second distinction invoked the same underlying factual consideration that troubled the dissenters on the bargaining obligation; namely, that Wackenhut and Burns were competitors. Thus, unlike *Wiley*, "there was no merger or sale of assets, and there were no dealings whatsoever between Wackenhut and Burns."[54]

In its third distinction, the Court struck a different balance than in *Wiley* in the expression of its views concerning the mandates of federal labor policy. In acknowledging that prevention of industrial strife is an important aim, as was emphasized in *Wiley*, the Court adhered to its view in *H.K. Porter* that Congress had not intended totally to subordinate to that goal the bargaining freedom of employers and unions. While *Wiley* emphasized the possible loss of protection to employees who had no opportunity to participate in the change of ownership transaction,

[51] *Id.* at 304.
[52] *Id.* at 305.
[53] H.K. Porter Co. v. NLRB, *supra* note 46.
[54] NLRB v. Burns Int'l Sec. Servs., *supra* note 41, at 286.

Burns emphasized the countervailing inequities that confronted new employers. Thus, the Court noted, a potential employer might be deterred from taking over a moribund business unless it could make essential changes. "Saddling" the new employer with all of the terms of the old labor contract might, according to the Court, make these changes impossible. Moreover, it noted that a union might be disadvantaged if it made unusual concessions to a failing predecessor employer and later found itself unable to enter into a more favorable contract with an economically strong successor employer. The Court stated:

> The Congressional policy manifested in the Act is to enable the parties to negotiate for any protection either deems appropriate but to allow the balance of bargaining advantage to be set by economic power realities. Strife is bound to occur if the concessions that must be honored do not correspond to the relative economic strength of the parties.[55]

It was thus apparent that a fundamentally different balance of policies separated the result in *Burns* from that in *Wiley*. That difference was little concealed by the *Burns* Court's resort to formal and narrow distinctions.

In the final portion of its opinion the Court held unanimously that Burns was not required to reimburse its employees for unilaterally changing the terms of the Wackenhut labor contract. The Court held that a new employer is ordinarily free to set initial terms and conditions of employment: the Board's pre-*Burns* rule that a new employer must bargain about such changes before imposing them was for the most part overturned.[56] A modicum of vitality was retained by the Court's hedging its position, noting that there may be instances where it is "perfectly clear" that the new employer "plans to retain" the former employees; and in that event, it would be appropriate to "consult" with the bargaining representative.[57] A further note of uncertainty was provided, however, by the caveat that in some situations it would not be clear that a successor has a duty to bargain until it has hired its "full complement" of employees.[58] The Board and lower courts have since wrestled with this issue.[59]

---

[55] *Id.* at 288.
[56] *Id.* at 293–94. *See* cases cited *supra* note 40.
[57] 406 US at 294–95.
[58] *Id.* at 295.
[59] *See* discussion *infra* at notes 77–100 and 248–267.

E. Aftermath of *Burns*

The Court's failure to reconcile the survival of contract rights under *Wiley* with the limitation on the bargaining obligation under *Burns* caused uncertainty and concern. But the possibility of a dual approach to contract and bargaining obligations, based upon the distinction between section 301 actions and unfair labor practice proceedings, persisted for only 2 years.

It was inevitable that *Wiley* and *Burns* would collide, for contract rights and bargaining obligations are not readily divisible, and contracts can themselves lead to bargaining obligations, depending upon the forum chosen.[60] If, for example, under *Wiley*, a new employer were obligated by the preexisting labor agreement to continue the employment of all of the former owner's employees, except those terminated in accordance with the discharge and layoff provisions, its status as a successor (for bargaining purposes as well) was more likely to be assured than if the new employer were free to constitute its own work force. On the other hand, if the new employer were free, under *Burns*, to decide how it would compose its own work force, its own hiring decisions would determine whether there would be the requisite continuity of the work force, and the new employer could independently affect its status as a successor. If a majority of the work force assembled were not holdovers, a union seeking bargaining rights in an unfair labor practice proceeding would be likely to fail. The union's alternative was a section 301 action seeking to compel arbitration of those hiring decisions. That is how the *Howard Johnson*[61] case arose.

F. *Howard Johnson*

Howard Johnson purchased all of the personal property used for a restaurant and motor lodge which it had previously franchised. The predecessor establishment had employed 53 employees. The sellers retained the real property and leased it to Howard Johnson. Howard Johnson commenced operations with 45 employees, of whom only nine were holdovers. The

---

[60] *See* Christensen, *Labor Law Decisions of the United States Supreme Court—October Term, 1973—Addition, Subtraction and Conversation,* ABA LABOR RELATIONS LAW SECTION (1974 Program and Proceedings) 51, 52 (1974).

[61] Howard Johnson Co. v. Hotel Employees, Detroit Local Joint Executive Bd., 417 US 249, 86 LRRM 2449 (1974).

union commenced a section 301 action to compel arbitration on behalf of the former employees who were not hired, with the object of obtaining an arbitration award ordering Howard Johnson to hire them. The former employer conceded that it was required to arbitrate the extent of its liability under the successorship provisions of its labor agreements, but the new employer, Howard Johnson, contested its obligation to arbitrate.

Relying upon *Wiley* rather than *Burns*, the Sixth Circuit ordered Howard Johnson to arbitrate as a successor.[62] The court reasoned that whether or not the new employer could be considered a successor ought not to depend upon the hiring decisions made by the new employer, because it would then be in a position to determine by its own actions whether or not it would become a successor.

Since the result would have differed under *Burns*, had the union filed a refusal-to-bargain charge, the Supreme Court chose not to straddle the two approaches. It reversed the Sixth Circuit, holding that the new employer was not obligated to arbitrate.

The Court first attempted to reconcile its divergent approaches by stating that the reasoning underlying *Burns* must be taken into account in any section 301 suit because

> [i]t would be plainly inconsistent with this view [that the federal common law under section 301 must be fashioned from the policy of national labor laws] to say that the basic policies found controlling in an unfair labor practice context may be disregarded by the courts in a suit under §301, and thus to permit the rights enjoyed by the new employer in a successorship context to depend upon the forum in which the union presses its claim . . . .[63]

While the *Burns* rationale emerged as controlling, the Court did not admit of any irreconcilable conflict between *Wiley* and *Burns*, though it acknowledged that the decisions were "to some extent inconsistent."[64] It distinguished the merger in *Wiley*, in which the former employer had completely "disappeared" and the surviving corporation had hired all the employees of the disappearing entity, from the sale of assets by the predecessor employer in *Howard Johnson*. The latter had remained in existence, retained substantial assets, and even conceded that it was

---

[62]Hotel Employees, Detroit Local Joint Executive Bd. v. Howard Johnson Co., 482 F2d 489, 83 LRRM 2804 (CA 6, 1973).

[63]417 US at 256.

[64]*Id.*

obligated to arbitrate questions concerning its liability resulting from the change in ownership. In a significant footnote, the Court suggested that the union might have sought injunctive relief against the seller prior to sale claiming a breach of the successorship clause in the seller's collective bargaining agreement.[65]

Despite the Court's purported distinguishing of *Wiley*, the "heart of the controversy" was whether the *Burns* case controlled in establishing that a purchaser "had the right not to hire any of the former 'employees,' if it so desired."[66] Once the Court recognized the right of the new employer to operate with its own new work force, considerations of union majority status in *that* work force prevailed in the Court's further conclusion that there was an insufficient continuity in the "identity of the work force across the change of ownership" to require the new employer to arbitrate.[67]

The language the Court used in referring to a "majority" became a source of controversy in subsequent decisions by the Board and lower courts.[68] Nonetheless, the reliance upon majority considerations foreshadowed the declining importance of *Wiley*.[69]

G. *Golden State Bottling Co.*

In *Golden State Bottling Co. v. NLRB*,[70] decided a year before its *Howard Johnson* decision, the Supreme Court approved the Board's existing policy requiring a successor to remedy the unfair labor practices of its predecessor of which it was aware at the time of acquisition. The Court also took the occasion to reaffirm, as a basic policy consideration, the protection of

---

[65]*Id.* at 258 n.3. This possibility, which has been referred to as a "pregnant footnote which . . . falls within the first trimester of gestation" (Christensen, *supra* note 60), would necessitate a balancing of equities as a prerequisite to the granting of injunctive relief. *See* Nursing Home & Hosp. Employees Local 1115 Joint Bd., Fla. Div. v. B&K Invs., 436 F Supp 1203, 96 LRRM 2348 (SD Fla, 1977). *See generally* Chapter 16, "Subjects of Bargaining," at notes 419–421.

[66]417 US at 260, 262.

[67]*Id.* at 263.

[68]*See* discussion *infra* at notes 77–100.

[69]*See* Service Employees Local 47 v. Cleveland Tower Hotel, 606 F2d 684, 102 LRRM 2405 (CA 6, 1979).

[70]414 US 168, 84 LRRM 2839 (1973). *See* Perma Vinyl Corp., 164 NLRB 968, 65 LRRM 1168 (1967), *enforced sub nom.* United States Pipe & Foundry Co. v. NLRB, 398 F2d 544, 68 LRRM 2913 (CA 5, 1968).

employee interests against a sudden change in ownership (citing *Wiley*), and the considerations of majority concepts in establishing continuity (citing *Burns*).

In a potentially significant footnote, the Court pointed out that the general rule of corporate law, that the purchaser of corporate assets is ordinarily not liable for the seller's debts or liabilities unless (1) the purchaser agrees to assume the obligations, (2) the purchaser is a mere continuation of the seller, or (3) the transaction's purpose is to escape liability, is a narrower concept than the labor law doctrine of successorship:

> The refusal to adopt a mode of analysis requiring the Board to distinguish among mergers, consolidations, and purchases of assets is attributable to the fact that, so long as there is a continuity in the "employing industry," the public policies underlying the doctrine will be served by its broad application . . . .[71]

In *Howard Johnson* the Court cited that proposition with approval, but only to show that every rule has its exception and that *Wiley* constituted such an exception, because the merger there occurred against a background of state law embodying the general rule that in a merger the surviving corporation is liable for the obligations of the disappearing corporation.[72] The Board has advanced the view that where the ownership changes arise through a sale of stock, but the former corporation continues to exist, the new corporation may continue to be bound by labor contracts negotiated prior to the sale; and no issue of successorship even arises, because the employing entity has remained the same.[73] In *Clothing Workers v. Ratner Corp.*,[74] the Ninth Circuit, applying similar reasoning, held in a section 301 action that a corporation remained bound by a collective bargaining agreement, though it had become a holding company and had assigned all manufacturing operations to a wholly owned subsidiary.

After *Burns*, and notwithstanding *Howard Johnson*, the principle that a successor may be held to its predecessor's bargaining obligation was well established. However, the precise definition

---

[71]414 US at 182 n.5.

[72]Howard Johnson Co. v. Hotel Employees, Detroit Local Joint Executive Bd., *supra* note 61, at 257.

[73]*See infra* at notes 268–349; TKB Int'l Corp., 240 NLRB 1082, 100 LRRM 1426 (1979); Krupman & Kaplan, *The Stock Purchaser After* Burns: *Must He Buy the Union Contract?*, 31 LAB. L.J. 328 (1980).

[74]602 F2d 1363, 102 LRRM 2571 (CA 9, 1979).

of what constituted a "successor" remained a point of continuing controversy before both the Board and the courts. It was plain enough that successorship turned on a number of related inquiries, all focused upon the degree of continuity between the old and the new employer's business enterprise. These inquiries include (1) whether there is continuity in the work force (the "majority" issue), (2) whether there is continuity in the employing industry, (3) whether there is continuity in the appropriateness of the bargaining unit, and (4) the impact of a hiatus in operations. It was not plain, however, just how these considerations were weighted, either singly or in their various combinations.

H. *Fall River Dyeing*

The fifth and most recent decision of the Supreme Court defining the successorship obligation, *Fall River Dyeing & Finishing Corp. v. NLRB*,[75] supplied much guidance on these questions.

The *Fall River* litigation grew out of the economic collapse of Sterlingwale Industries, which had been in the textile finishing business for many years. After Sterlingwale ceased operations and made an assignment for the benefit of creditors, one of its former employees joined with an officer of a former customer to incorporate Fall River. They intended that Fall River would acquire plant, equipment, and inventory from the creditors or liquidators of Sterlingwale and would hire many of its former employees and supervisors. In September 1982, nine months after Sterlingwale closed, Fall River began operations at the same location performing the same production operations, albeit for a somewhat different clientele, with a work force largely composed of former Sterlingwale employees. In October, while the small work force was still growing, the union that had represented the Sterlingwale employees demanded and was refused recognition.

The union filed unfair labor practice charges, which the Board upheld.[76] The Board reasoned that although the demand for recognition came before Fall River employed a

---

[75]482 US 27, 125 LRRM 2441 (1987).

[76]Fall River Dyeing & Finishing Corp., 272 NLRB 839, 117 LRRM 1436 (1984), *enforced,* 775 F2d 425, 120 LRRM 2825 (CA 1, 1985).

"substantial and representative complement," the demand had been a continuing one which the employer was required to accept in January 1983 once the requisite-size work force had been hired. At that time, a majority of the employees were former Sterlingwale employees. The Board rejected the employer's defense that the former Sterlingwale employees became a minority in the full complement when hiring was completed after January 1983.

The Supreme Court affirmed the Board's rulings in all respects. Agreeing that the Board could properly treat the demand as continuing, and could properly invoke from its representation procedures the settled rule concerning "substantial and representative complement," the Court accepted the presumption that the union continued to enjoy majority status when that complement had been hired. Accordingly, it concluded that the employees had not only a need for, but also the right to, representation during the period of change in the business. Those considerations had to be balanced against the uncertainty and risks that the Board's formulation would cause for the employer in such situations, but the Court agreed with the Board that the balance predominated in favor of representation without unnecessary delay. In this aspect of the decision, one detects a modest resurgence of such policy considerations as continuity of representation and deterrence of industrial strife. Concern for those policies had propelled the Court in *Wiley* and *Golden State*, but in *Burns* and *Howard Johnson* they were subordinated to the efficient movement of capital and other competing interests.

Justice Powell, joined by two other Justices, dissented, emphasizing the absence of any continuity from the business of Sterlingwale to that of Fall River, and the long hiatus in operations. Absent some such connection between the prior and succeeding enterprises, the dissent argued, the similarities of production process and work forces were not a sufficient basis for imposing Sterlingwale's obligation to bargain on Fall River. The dissenters also objected to the Board's use of the substantial complement rule and argued that the obligations of the parties should have been determined only after the full complement was employed so that the rights of all permanent employees might be protected.

III. SUCCESSORSHIP AND THE BARGAINING OBLIGATION

A. Continuity of the Work Force: "The Concept of Majority"

The paramount criterion in determining successorship is the continuity of the work force (i.e., the "majority" issue).[77] In the years following *Burns* and *Howard Johnson*, it became increasingly evident that the concept of majority is multidimensional, that is, "which" majority, "when" was it formed, and "where" did it exist. Not only may the existence of a continued "majority" turn upon the mathematical yardstick used, but as *Fall River Dyeing* confirmed, it may also turn upon the precise time at which it is measured, as well as on a consideration, where applicable, of individual employment decisions.

1. The Applicable Yardstick. Immediately following *Burns* and *Howard Johnson*, there was considerable controversy over "which" majority would be determinative or, viewed another way, which test should be used to determine majority status. This controversy stemmed from the manner in which the phraseology, or formulation, of the test in *Howard Johnson* differed from that in *Burns*.[78] In *Burns*, the Court stated the premise that:

> where the bargaining unit remains unchanged and *a majority of the employees hired by the new employer are represented by a recently certified bargaining agent* there is little basis for faulting the Board's implementation of the express mandates of §8(a)(5) and §9(a) by ordering the employer to bargain with the incumbent union.[79]

---

[77]Fall River Dyeing & Finishing Corp. v. NLRB, *supra* note 75. *See* Nazareth Regional High School v. NLRB, 549 F2d 873, 94 LRRM 2897 (CA 2, 1977), *enforcing in part sub nom.* Roman Catholic Diocese of Brooklyn, 222 NLRB 1052, 91 LRRM 1419 (1976). In Spruce-Up Corp., 209 NLRB 194, 85 LRRM 1426 (1974), the concurring opinion, in reliance upon Goldberg, *The Labor Law Obligations of a Successor Employer,* 63 NW. U.L. REV. 735 (1969), notes that only two cases had been discovered in over a 20-year period in which the Board had found successorship and duty to bargain where a majority of the new employer's work force was not composed of the old employees.

[78]NLRB v. Burns Int'l Sec. Servs., 406 US 272, 80 LRRM 2225 (1972). It is unclear whether the Court intended different tests.

[79]*Id.* at 281, 80 LRRM at 2228 (emphasis added). Although the Court referred to a "certified" bargaining agent, this reference was not deemed to exclude recognized bargaining agents. Eklund's Sweden House Inn, 203 NLRB 413, 83 LRRM 1173 (1973). The reference to certification was framed in terms of the presumption of continued majority stemming from a recent Board election—a presumption with which four dissenters disagreed. While the dissenters disagreed with the majority on the issue of whether Burns was a successor, they nevertheless concurred on the question of the bargaining obligations of a successor.

In *Howard Johnson*, on the other hand, the term "majority" was framed in terms of whether "the successor employer hires a majority of the predecessor's employees. . . ."[80]

In *Burns*, the primary reference point for determining majority status was the new employer's work force, whereas in *Howard Johnson* it was the work force of the predecessor.[81] Not surprisingly, members of the Board expressed differing views of majority status. The initial differences were reflected in a series of divided decisions in which a Board majority held that the appropriate inquiry in determining whether the new employer is a successor is the percentage of the new employer's work force that was previously employed by the predecessor.[82]

The *Burns* test was unequivocally affirmed in the Supreme Court's decision of *Fall River Dyeing*,[83] and there is little indication that the *Howard Johnson* alternative formulation survives.[84]

The Court's decision in *Fall River*, however, has not foreclosed all debate on this issue. The Court stated that if "the new employer makes a conscious decision to maintain generally the same business and *to hire a majority of its employees from the predecessor*, then the bargaining obligation of §8(a)(5) is activated."[85] In discussing when the obligation arises,[86] the Court noted that "the Board with the approval of the Courts of Appeals" followed *Burns* rather than *Howard Johnson*, but concluded by noting that "this issue is not presented in the instant case."[87]

Since 1975, the Board has applied the *Burns* test of majority status without dissent.[88] In no decision since *Burns* has the Board

---

[80]Howard Johnson Co. v. Hotel Employees, Detroit Local Joint Executive Bd., *supra* note 61, at 263, 86 LRRM at 2454.

[81]In neither case was the Court required to consider the possible difference in result stemming from the failure to utilize the same terminology. In *Burns* the number of employees in the new and old employer's work force was identical, and in *Howard Johnson* neither majority test would have been met.

[82]Contract Carrier, 258 NLRB 353, 108 LRRM 1132 (1981) (finding successorship where four of new employer's five employees had worked for predecessor although predecessor employed 10 employees); United Maintenance & Mfg. Co., 214 NLRB 529, 87 LRRM 1469 (1974); Spruce-Up Corp., *supra* note 77. *Cf.* Boeing Co., 214 NLRB 541, 87 LRRM 1461 (1974), *aff'd sub nom.* Machinists v. NLRB, 595 F2d 664, 98 LRRM 2787 (CA DC, 1978), *cert. denied,* 439 US 1070, 100 LRRM 2268 (1979) where the Board addressed the "clear intention" aspect rather than the work-force percentage guideline.

[83]Fall River Dyeing & Finishing Corp. v. NLRB, *supra* note 75, at 41, 125 LRRM at 2446.

[84]*Id.* at 46 n.12, 125 LRRM at 2448 n.12.

[85]*Id.* at 41, 125 LRRM at 2446 (emphasis added).

[86]*Id.* at 48–52, 125 LRRM at 2449–51. *See infra* text accompanying note 108.

[87]*Id.* at 47 n.13, 125 LRRM at 2449 n.13.

[88]*See e.g.*, Ric's Best Auto Painting, 248 NRLB 1028, 104 LRRM 1116 (1980), *enforced,* 652 F2d 64, 108 LRRM 2176 (CA 9, 1981); Bellingham Frozen Foods Div., 237 NLRB 1450, 99 LRRM 1270 (1978), *enforced,* 626 F2d 674, 105 LRRM 2404 (CA 9, 1980), *cert.*

found successorship absent a finding of "majority."[89]

In *G.W. Hunt dba Foremost Foods Distributing*,[90] only four of the new employer's nine employees were part of the predecessor's bargaining unit of six employees. Although all the other relevant factors for successorship appear to have been present, the Board found that because a majority of the new work force was not comprised of the predecessor's employees, the new employer was not a successor. Applying the same rationale, a different result was reached in *Premium Foods*,[91] where the new employer purchased only existing inventory from the predecessor and instituted changes in the scope and direction of the business. Nonetheless, the Board found the new employer to be a successor because five of its eight employees had been part of the predecessor's work force.

In applying the "majority" test, it sometimes becomes critical to ascertain whether an employee of the successor is to be deemed a former employee of the predecessor. In *Stewart Granite Enterprises*,[92] the predecessor, prior to takeover, sharply curtailed its operations and reduced its work force from 33 employees to 10 employees. These 10 employees were retained by

---

denied, 449 US 1125, 106 LRRM 2256 (1981); Roman Catholic Diocese of Brooklyn, 236 NLRB 1, 98 LRRM 1359 (1978), *cert. denied sub nom.* Lay Faculty Ass'n Local 1261 v. Bishop Ford Catholic High School, 450 US 996, 106 LRRM 2816 (1981); Miami Indus. Trucks, 221 NLRB 1223, 91 LRRM 1040 (1975).

[89]*See* Presbyterian Hosp., 285 NLRB 935, 130 LRRM 1196 (1987) (Board corrected ALJ's use of *Howard Johnson* phraseology); Indianapolis Mack Sales & Serv., 272 NLRB 690, 117 LRRM 1395 (1984), *enforcement denied on other grounds*, 802 F2d 280, 123 LRRM 2543 (CA 7, 1986) (Board characterized work force majority as "paramount" and "critical" factor in successorship determination); Sherwood Trucking Co., 270 NLRB 445, 117 LRRM 1175 (1984), *enforcement denied on other grounds*, 775 F2d 744, 120 LRRM 3009 (CA 6, 1985) (majority characterized as "chief consideration"); 221 N. Va. St. dba Silver Spur Casino, 270 NLRB 1067, 116 LRRM 1233 (1984) (Board called majority "keystone" factor in successorship determination). *See also* Hardin's Bakery v. Retail, Wholesale & Dep't Store Union, 877 F2d 1541, 131 LRRM 3252, 3257 (CA 11, 1989), *vacated and reh'g granted*, 893 F2d 1188, 133 LRRM 2608 (CA 11, 1990) (court noted that "continuity of the work force remains the predominant focus of the successorship inquiry").

[90]258 NLRB 1198, 108 LRRM 1216 (1981).

[91]260 NLRB 708, 109 LRRM 1328 (1982), *enforced*, 709 F2d 623, 113 LRRM 3261 (CA 9, 1983).

[92]255 NLRB 569, 107 LRRM 1182 (1981). *See also* Derby Ref. Co., 292 NLRB 1018, 130 LRRM 1353 (1989) (successor employer's employees had been "employed" by predecessor notwithstanding either retirement or refusal of recall from layoff prior to shutdown of operations); Memphis Truck & Trailer, 284 NLRB 900, 126 LRRM 1326 (1987) (interim unemployment held not to have destroyed "continuity of employment"); Mangold Mkts., 280 NLRB 773, 123 LRRM 1303 (1986) (union majority status found where purchaser of single store, which had been part of multistore bargaining unit, hired employees who had little recent work history at particular store and who had left predecessor's employ immediately prior to acquisition or had worked at another store shortly before it terminated operations); Big R Distribs. dba Shoppers Choice, 280 NLRB 1306, 123 LRRM 1254 (1986) (successor's employees had been "employed" by predecessor despite layoff since both had reasonable expectation of recall).

the successor, who subsequently increased its work force to 27 employees. All the additional 17 employees had been employed by the predecessor and had been laid off in the final months before the sale of the plant. The Board, in imposing successorship obligations upon the new employer, "counted" these 17 employees and found that, at all relevant times, the majority of the successor's work force had been employed by the predecessor.

When the predecessor's employees were organized in separate bargaining units, majority status and successorship were determined on an individual unit basis. In *Distillery Workers Local 19 v. Key Wines & Liquors of New Jersey*,[93] a majority of the purchaser's entire work force had worked for the predecessor. However, there was no majority status in the unit of sales employees. The union, which had represented only the sales employees, sued to enforce the contract, arguing that majority status should be measured on the basis of the entire work force. The district court rejected this argument and held that majority status must be measured on a unit basis.

In reviewing Board orders in refusal-to-bargain cases, the courts have not questioned the application of the *Burns* standard.[94] For example, the Court of Appeals for the First Circuit upheld a bargaining order where 35 of the new employer's work force of 37 employees were holdovers, despite the fact that the predecessor had a work force of 250 to 300 employees.[95]

In *NLRB v. Cablevision Systems Development Co.*,[96] the Court of Appeals for the Second Circuit upheld the finding of suc-

---

[93]113 LRRM 3377 (D NJ, 1983). *See also* Base Servs., 296 NLRB No. 23, 132 LRRM 1084 (1989).

[94]Machinists (Boeing Co.) v. NLRB, 595 F2d 664, 98 LRRM 2787 (CA DC, 1978), *cert. denied*, 439 US 1070, 100 LRRM 2268 (1979); NLRB v. Houston Distribution Servs., 573 F2d 260, 98 LRRM 2538 (CA 5, 1978), *enforcing* 227 NLRB 960, 95 LRRM 1100 (1977), *cert. denied*, 439 US 1047, 99 LRRM 3450 (1978); Pacific Hide & Fur Depot v. NLRB, 553 F2d 609, 95 LRRM 2467 (CA 9, 1977); NLRB v. Band-Age, Inc., 532 F2d 1, 92 LRRM 2001 (CA 1), *cert. denied*, 429 US 921, 93 LRRM 2570 (1976); Zim's Foodliner v. NLRB, 495 F2d 1131, 85 LRRM 3019 (CA 7, 1974), *enforcing sub nom.* Parkwood IGA, 201 NLRB 905, 82 LRRM 1682 (1973), *sub nom.* Zim's IGA Foodliner v. NLRB, *cert. denied* 419 US 838, 87 LRRM 2398 (1974); NLRB v. Polytech, Inc., 469 F2d 1226, 81 LRRM 2902 (CA 8, 1972), *enforcing* 186 NLRB 984, 75 LRRM 1491 (1970). Strike replacements subject to being supplanted by unfair labor practice strikers are not counted either way. NLRB v. Fabsteel Co. of La., 587 F2d 689, 100 LRRM 2349 (CA 5, 1979), *enforcing* 231 NLRB 372, 97 LRRM 1104 (1977), *cert. denied*, 442 US 943, 101 LRRM 2556 (1979). On the other hand, employees unlawfully discharged by the predecessor appear to be counted toward the majority in determining whether the subsequent owner is liable, as a successor, for the predecessor's discharges. Bell Co., 243 NLRB 977, 101 LRRM 1572 (1979), *supplementing* 225 NLRB 474, 93 LRRM 1180 (1976), *enforced in part*, 561 F2d 1264, 96 LRRM 2437 (CA 7, 1977). *See generally infra* notes 414–465.

[95]NLRB v. Band-Age, Inc., *supra* note 94.

[96]671 F2d 737, 109 LRRM 3102 (CA 2), *cert. denied*, 459 US 906, 111 LRRM 2608 (1982).

cessorship where continuity of the work force was balanced against corporate changes. In that case, the new employer formed a subsidiary to perform work previously done for it by an independent contractor. Of the subsidiary's 53 employees, 48 were former employees of the independent contractor who performed essentially the same services for the subsidiary as they had previously performed for the independent contractor.

While the *Burns* yardstick has now become established in measuring majority status in unfair labor practice cases, it is unclear which test will be followed in section 301 suits to compel arbitration under a predecessor's labor agreement. The Court of Appeals for the Fifth Circuit, in *Boeing Co. v. Machinists*,[97] concluded that, as in *Howard Johnson*, the number of holdover employees should be measured against the predecessor's work force rather than the successor's:

> As a matter of principle, since the duty to arbitrate arises from an application of the contract between the predecessor employer and his organized employees, the entity whose identity is to be the reference point for judging continuity ought to be the predecessor enterprise.[98]

The court refused to compel arbitration where only 35 percent of the predecessor's employees were hired by Boeing and no tangible assets were transferred to Boeing. In *NLRB v. Band-Age, Inc.*,[99] the Court of Appeals for the First Circuit, in enforcing the Board's order in an unfair labor practice case, applied the *Burns* standard, but indicated its agreement with the Fifth Circuit's view that the *Howard Johnson* yardstick would be applicable in a section 301 suit.

More recent decisions under section 301 have failed to clarify or confirm these earlier holdings.[100]

---

[97]504 F2d 307, 87 LRRM 2865 (CA 5, 1974), *cert. denied*, 421 US 913, 88 LRRM 3456 (1975).

[98]*Id.* at 319, 87 LRRM at 2874.

[99]*Supra* note 94.

[100]*See* Audit Servs. v. Rolfson, 641 F2d 757, 107 LRRM 2586 (CA 9, 1981) (uncertain which majority test applied). *See also* Operating Eng'rs Local 542 v. Evans Asphalt Co., 721 F Supp 73, 132 LRRM 2063 (MD Pa), *aff'd*, 891 F2d 281, 133 LRRM 2072 (CA 3, 1989); (citing *Howard Johnson* and applying *Burns*, the court held asset purchaser not obligated to follow seller's contract); Gigliotti Corp. v. Building & Constr. Trades Council (Philadelphia & Vicinity), 583 F Supp 396, 118 LRRM 2036 (ED Pa, 1984) (merger "survivor" obligated to arbitrate under *Wiley*: no discussion of majority status); Graphic Arts Local 1B v. Martin Podany Assocs., 531 F Supp 169, 109 LRRM 2696 (D Minn., 1982) (applying *John Wiley & Sons v. Livingston*, 376 US 543, 55 LRRM 2769 (1964), the court held purchaser obligated to arbitrate, both majority tests met); *But see* Hardin's Bakery v. Retail, Wholesale, & Dep't Store Union, *supra* note 89.

2. The Appropriate Time for Measuring Majority Status. The work force of the new employer at the time of takeover will frequently be fluid rather than fixed. In such circumstances, it may be inadequate to confine the measurement of majority status to the precise time when, as a transactional matter, the business is acquired.[101] Thus, the dimension of time has become a further significant consideration for measuring majority status.

When the issue first emerged, the Board and circuit courts disagreed on the time for measuring majority status. The Board initially took the position that the critical time for measuring the union's majority status was when the union perfected its demand for recognition.[102] The circuit courts adhered to the view that the critical time for the relevant majority determination was when a "full complement" of employees was hired.[103]

In so holding, the circuit courts focused upon the following dictum in *Burns*:

> Although a successor employer is ordinarily free to set initial terms on which it will hire the employees of a predecessor, there will be instances in which it is perfectly clear that the new employer plans to retain all of the employees in the unit and in which it will be appropriate to have him initially consult with the employees' bargaining representative before he fixes terms. In other situations, however, it may not be clear until the successor employer has hired *his full complement of employees* that he had a duty to bargain with a union, since it will not be evident until then that the bargaining representative represents a majority of the employees in the union as required by §9(a) of the Act . . . .[104]

[101]There may also be instances in which succession may be found to have occurred even prior to the date of actual purchase. In NLRB v. Ethan Allen, Inc., Pine Valley Div., 544 F2d 742, 93 LRRM 2811 (CA 4, 1976), *enforcing in part* 218 NLRB 208, 89 LRRM 1780 (1975), when the sale was delayed by a bankruptcy proceeding against the seller, the new employer began operating the predecessor's plant through a leasing arrangement (with the seller's main creditor) until the sale was consummated some 2 months later. The seller was deemed the successor as of the time when it first took over operation of the plant.

[102]Pacific Hide & Fur Depot v. NLRB, *supra* note 94; Gardena Buena Ventura, 242 NLRB 595, 101 LRRM 1248 (1979), *enforced,* 618 F2d 115, 108 LRRM 2104 (CA 9, 1980); Pre-Engineered Bldg. Prods., 228 NLRB 841, 96 LRRM 1170 (1977), *enforcement denied,* 603 F2d 134, 101 LRRM 3021 (CA 10, 1979).

[103]Pacific Hide & Fur Depot v. NLRB, *supra* note 102; Pre-Engineered Bldg. Prods. *supra* note 102; *see also* NLRB v. Houston Distribution Servs. *supra* note 94 (Fifth Circuit stated its general agreement with "full complement" test but found it not applicable since new employer had unlawfully refused to hire certain of predecessor's employees because of antiunion bias).

[104]NLRB v. Burns Int'l Sec. Servs., 406 US 272, 294–95, 80 LRRM 2225, 2233–34 (1972) (emphasis added).

In *Hudson River Aggregates*,[105] the Board began to retreat from its position relying upon the date of the union's demand for recognition. In that case, the Board referred to a "substantial majority" in a "representative complement" of employees as justifying its refusal to consider an increase from 30 to 40 employees to 90 employees during the six months after the demand. This "substantial and representative complement" test adopted by the Board met with approval in the circuit courts.[106]

The issue reached the Supreme Court in *Fall River Dyeing & Finishing Corp. v. NLRB*.[107] The Court adopted the Board's "substantial and representative complement" rule to determine when the union's majority is to be measured in successorship cases. If the new employer has hired a substantial and representative complement of employees, even though additional employees may later be hired, the new employer has an obligation to bargain with the union if a majority of its employees had been employed by its predecessor. In *Fall River*, the Court explained that the employer will generally "know with tolerable certainty when all its job classifications have been filled or substantially filled, when it has hired a majority of the employees it intends to hire, and when it has begun normal production."[108]

As noted further by the Court, the "substantial and representative complement" rule originated in [connection with] the initial representation elections when, faced with an expanding or contracting workforce, the Board had to determine the appropriate time for an election."[109]

Previously, in *Grico Corp., Aircraft Magnesium Division*,[110] the Board articulated the general standard: "It is well settled that the significant time frame for determining what percentage of a purchaser's employees were former employees of a predecessor

---

[105]246 NLRB 192, 102 LRRM 1524 (1979), *enforced*, 639 F2d 865, 106 LRRM 2313 (CA 2, 1981).

[106]NLRB v. Fall River Dyeing & Finishing Corp., 482 US 27, 125 LRRM 2441 (1987); NLRB v. Jeffries Lithograph Co., 752 F2d 459, 118 LRRM 2681 (CA 9, 1985), *enforcing* 265 NLRB 1499, 112 LRRM 1236 (1982).

[107]*Supra* note 106.

[108]*Id.* at 49–51, 125 LRRM at 2450. *See* Sahara Las Vegas, 284 NLRB 337, 128 LRRM 1085 (1987) (rejecting contention of successor employer, which hired 280 employees of predecessor and 40 others, that it could not determine makeup of regular work force, Board held that purchaser of casino unlawfully delayed recognition of union).

[109]482 US at 50 n.16, 125 LRRM at 2449 n.16 (citing Clement-Blythe Cos., 182 NLRB 502, 74 LRRM 1132 (1970), *enforced*, 77 LRRM 2373 (CA 4, 1971)).

[110]265 NLRB 1344, 1346, 112 LRRM 1147, 1149 (1982), *enforced*, 730 F2d 767, 115 LRRM 3712 (CA 9, 1984) (footnote omitted). *See also* Fall River Dyeing & Finishing Corp. v. NLRB, *supra* note 106.

is when a demand for bargaining has been made and a representative complement of an employer's work force is on the job." Particular applications of the "demand" and the "representative complement" standards raise additional issues which the Board continues to address on a case-by-case basis.

For example, in *Grico*, the Board reemphasized that "a request for bargaining is continuous and need not be repeated."[111] Once a demand has been made, a bargaining obligation will be established if, at any time thereafter, the employees of a predecessor constitute a majority of a representative complement of the new employer's work force.[112] The Supreme Court, in *Fall River*, approved of the Board's "continuing demand" rule.[113]

Under *Burns*, the obligation to bargain can arise even before the new employer begins operations if it is "perfectly clear" that a majority of the new employer's work force will be made up of the predecessor's employees. In *Turnbull Enterprises*,[114] the successor's bargaining obligations were found to arise on the date it acquired the facility pursuant to a bill of sale, even though operations were not commenced until a week later. The ALJ noted that, on the date of the bill of sale, (1) employees were advised of the sale, of their termination, and of their rehire; and (2) the union demanded recognition. Citing the "perfectly clear" test articulated in *Burns*, the Board adopted the ALJ's statement that the bargaining obligation commenced "when the Union made its demand at a time when [the successor] fully realized that its anticipated work force was represented by the Union."[115]

In determining whether a new employer has hired a substantial and representative complement of workers by a given date, the Board and the courts have considered at least five factors, including: (1) whether the job classifications designated for the operation were occupied or substantially so, (2) whether the operation was in normal or substantially normal production, (3) the size of the complement on the date of normal produc-

---

[111]265 NLRB at 1345 n.9, 112 LRRM at 1149 n.9.

[112]*See also* Royal Midtown Chrysler Plymouth, 296 NLRB No. 135, 133 LRRM 1165 (1989); Fremont Ford Sales dba Fremont Ford, 289 NLRB 1290, 131 LRRM 1074 (1988); Cuello Indus. dba Scroll Casual, 278 NLRB 10, 122 LRRM 1264 (1986); Redok Enters., 277 NLRB 1010, 120 LRRM 1337 (1985); General Processing Corp., 263 NLRB 86, 110 LRRM 1479 (1982).

[113]Fall River Dyeing & Finishing Corp. v. NLRB, *supra* note 106, at 52–53, 125 LRRM at 2451.

[114]259 NLRB 934, 109 LRRM 1069 (1982).

[115]*Id.* at 940.

tion, (4) the time expected to elapse before a substantially larger complement would be at work, and (5) the relative certainty of the employer's expected expansion.[116]

The Supreme Court in *Fall River*[117] approved and applied the Board's five-factor analysis and upheld the Board's finding of a substantial and representative complement at a time when the new employer had hired employees in virtually all job classifications, had attained at least 50 percent of full complement, and had reached substantially normal production with a first shift in full operation.[118] In *Fall River*, the Supreme Court noted that in fixing the date at which the bargaining obligation arises, "the significant interest of employees in being represented as soon as possible" may outweigh the objective of maximum employee participation in the selection of a bargaining agent.[119] Subsequent to *Fall River*, in *NLRB v. Cutter Dodge*,[120] the Court of Appeals for the Ninth Circuit also utilized the five-factor analysis to uphold a Board successorship finding.[121]

The Board has held that it is appropriate to delay the bargaining obligation determination where the new employer expects with *reasonable certainty* to *substantially increase* its employee complement within a *relatively short period of time*.[122] All of these factors must be present. For example, even though the new employer opened a new shift and hired additional employees, the appropriate time for measuring majority status was two months

---

[116]Briggs Plumbingware v. NLRB, 877 F2d 1282, 1287, 131 LRRM 2810, 2814 (CA 6, 1989), *enforcing* 286 NLRB 1189, 130 LRRM 1031 (1987); Fall River Dyeing & Finishing Corp. v. NLRB, *supra* note 106; NLRB v. Jeffries Lithograph Co., *supra* note 106; Premium Foods v. NLRB, 709 F2d 623, 628, 113 LRRM 3261, 3264 (1983); Mahoney Foundries, Vermont Foundry Co., Div., 292 NLRB No.108, 131 LRRM 1388 (1989); Good N' Fresh Foods, 287 NLRB 1231, 128 LRRM 1158 (1988); Taylor Stone dba Eastone of Ohio, 277 NLRB 1652, 121 LRRM 1135 (1986).

[117]Fall River Dyeing & Finishing Corp., *supra* note 106, at 49–52, 125 LRRM at 2449–51.

[118]A "substantial and representative complement" need not, however, equate to a majority of the "full complement" work force. *See* NLRB v. Asbury Graphite Mills, 832 F2d 40, 126 LRRM 2900 (CA 3, 1987) (upholding Board's finding that one-third of full complement is "substantial"); NLRB v. Jeffries Lithograph Co., *supra* note 106 (upholding Board's finding that 45 percent constituted "significant share" of eventual complement).

[119]482 US at 49, 125 LRRM at 2450; *see also* Lexington Oil Corp., American Steel Warehousing subsidiary, 283 NLRB 293, 124 LRRM 1395 (1987).

[120]825 F2d 1375, 126 LRRM 2215 (CA 9, 1987).

[121]*Id. See also* NLRB v. Marin Operating dba Clarion Hotel-Marin, 822 F2d 890, 126 LRRM 2078 (CA 9, 1987) (fact that most employees employed on demand date were still serving 90-day probationary period was irrelevant); M.U. Indus., 284 NLRB 388, 125 LRRM 1187 (1987) (fact that new employer was attempting to arrange financing for its business venture at time union made its recognition demand made further expansion of work force speculative and would not defeat successorship finding).

[122]Myers Custom Prods., 278 NLRB 636, 121 LRRM 1209 (1986).

earlier since at that time the plan for expansion was highly uncertain.[123] Similarly, where the new employer was unsuccessful in its desire to hire a significant number of additional registered nurses, the Board found no basis for concluding that the employer's expansion plans were "reasonably certain" to be accomplished within a "relatively short time."[124]

3. Presumption of the Union's Continued Majority Status. Another "majority" consideration is whether the majority status of the *union* transcends the change in ownership of the business. This concerns the question of continued support for the union, as distinct from whether the new employer is a successor.[125]

The Supreme Court in *Fall River* held that, assuming the criteria of successorship are otherwise satisfied, a successor may not escape the presumptions of continued majority status which would have been applicable to its predecessor.[126] Thus, a successor is bound to the same irrebuttable presumption of continued majority status during the year following certification as its predecessor was.[127] Similarly, the same rebuttable presumption of continued majority status following the year of certification obtains.[128] The presumption of continued majority status may be applicable where the successor has taken over only a part

---

[123]Burke-Parsons Bowlby, 288 NLRB 956, 130 LRRM 1322 (1988).

[124]Hospital San Francisco, 293 NLRB 171, 131 LRRM 1344 (1989).

[125]This distinction is demonstrated by the contrasting approaches to "majority" in *Burns* and *Howard Johnson*, discussed *supra* at notes 79–82.

[126]Fall River Dyeing & Finishing Corp. v. NLRB, *supra* note 106; *see also* Briggs Plumbingware v. NLRB, *supra* note 116; Proxy Communications of Manhattan v. NLRB, 873 F2d 552, 131 LRRM 2072 (CA 2, 1989), *enforcing* 290 NLRB 540, 129 LRRM 1175 (1988); Ranch-Way, Inc., 203 NLRB 911, 83 LRRM 1197 (1973), *supplementing* 183 NLRB 1168, 74 LRRM 1389 (1970). *See generally supra* Chapter 10, "Representation Proceedings and Elections," at notes 82–87, and Chapter 12, "Recognition and Withdrawal of Recognition Without an Election," at note 313.

[127]Ranch-Way, Inc., *supra* note 126. *See also* NLRB v. Pepsi-Cola Bottling Co. of Topeka, 613 F2d 267, 103 LRRM 2233 (CA 10, 1980); Springfield Retirement Residence, 235 NLRB 884, 98 LRRM 1091 (1978); Dynamic Mach. Co., 221 NLRB 1140, 91 LRRM 1054 (1975), *aff'd*, 552 F2d 1195, 94 LRRM 3217 (CA 7), *cert. denied*, 434 US 827, 96 LRRM 2513 (1977).

[128]Roman Catholic Diocese of Brooklyn, 222 NLRB 1052, 91 LRRM 1419 (1976), *aff'd sub nom.* Nazareth Regional High School v. NLRB, 549 F2d 873, 94 LRRM 2897 (CA 2, 1977). The rebuttable presumption of continued majority status following the certification year has also been approved in other circuits: *See* NLRB v. Fabsteel Co. of La., 587 F2d 689, 100 LRRM 2349 (CA 5, 1979), *enforcing* 231 NLRB 372, 97 LRRM 1104 (1977), *cert. denied*, 442 US 943, 101 LRRM 2556 (1979); Electrical Workers (IUE) (White-Westinghouse Corp.) v. NLRB, 604 F2d 689, 101 LRRM 2864 (CA DC, 1979), *enforcing* 229 NLRB 667, 96 LRRM 1078 (1977); NLRB v. Band-Age, Inc., 532 F2d 1, 92 LRRM 2001 (CA 1), *cert. denied*, 429 US 921, 93 LRRM 2570 (1976); Paul's Foodliner v. NLRB, 495 F2d 1131, 85 LRRM 3019 (CA 7), *cert. denied sub nom.* Zim's IGA Foodliner v. NLRB, 419 US 838, 87 LRRM 2398 (1974); Valmac Indus., 237 NLRB 992, 99 LRRM 1193 (1978), *enforced*, 599 F2d 246, 101 LRRM 2389 (CA 8, 1979).

of the original bargaining unit.[129] The Board has also applied the presumption where a unit had been created by a merger.[130]

After explaining how the presumptions of majority support apply in nonsuccessorship settings, the Court in *Fall River*, citing *Ray Brooks v. NLRB*,[131] *Terrell Machine Co.*,[132] and *Celanese Corp. of America*,[133] stated:

> The rationale behind the presumptions [of majority support] is particularly pertinent in the successorship situation and so it is understandable that the Court in Burns referred to them. During a transition between employers, a union is in a peculiarly vulnerable position. It has no formal and established bargaining relationship with the new employer, is uncertain about the new employer's plans, and cannot be sure if or when the new employer must bargain with it. While being concerned with the future of its members with the new employer, the union also must protect whatever rights still exist for its members under the collective-bargaining agreement with the predecessor employer. Accordingly, during this unsettling transition period, the union needs the presumptions of majority status to which it is entitled to safeguard its members' rights and to develop a relationship with the successor.[134]

The Court in *Fall River* also indicated[135] that the presumptions of majority support are rebuttable in nature, as articulated by the Board in *Harley-Davidson Transportation Co.*[136] In *Harley-Davidson*, the Board ruled that where a successor employer

---

[129]NLRB v. Fabsteel of La., *supra* note 128 (presumption applied to single plant of multiplant unit purchased by successor because majority support is presumed to be equally distributed through entire original unit); Saks & Co. dba Saks Fifth Ave., 247 NLRB 1047, 103 LRRM 1241 (1980), *enforced in part*, 634 F2d 681, 105 LRRM 3274 (CA 2, 1980) (presumption applied to portion of predecessor's alteration personnel which had been subcontractor of successor for such work). *Contra* W & W Steel Co., 232 NLRB 74, 96 LRRM 1530 (1977), *enforcement denied*, 599 F2d 934, 101 LRRM 2445 (CA 10, 1979) (the union had been certified to represent seven-plant unit and successor had purchased only a single plant; court held successor had established good-faith doubt based on union's multiplant certification and absence of Board election held exclusively at successor's plant). *But see* Electrical Workers (IUE) (White-Westinghouse Corp.) v. NLRB, *supra* note 128 (bargaining order was enforced despite contentions of unit inappropriateness where new employer purchased only five plants of its predecessor's 42 units).

[130]Western Distrib. Co. v. NLRB, 608 F2d 397, 102 LRRM 2510 (CA 10, 1979) *denying enforcement* to 236 NLRB 1224, 98 LRRM 1461 (1978), where the court's rejection of the presumption was focused on a number of considerations.

[131]348 US 96, 35 LRRM 2158 (1954).

[132]173 NLRB 1480, 70 LRRM 1049 (1969), *enforced*, 427 F2d 1088, 73 LRRM 2381 (CA 4), *cert. denied*, 398 US 929, 74 LRRM 2240 (1970).

[133]95 NLRB 664, 28 LRRM 1362 (1951).

[134]482 US at 39, 125 LRRM at 2446 (footnote omitted).

[135]*Id.*, 125 LRRM at 2446–47.

[136]273 NLRB 1531, 118 LRRM 1204 (1985). *See also* Hillhaven Corp., 290 NLRB 258, 131 LRRM 1184 (1988); Briggs Plumbingware v. NLRB, *supra* note 116, at 1288, 131 LRRM at 2814.

voluntarily recognizes a union which has been certified to represent the predecessor's employees for a year or more, the union enjoys only a rebuttable presumption of majority status.[137] Prior to its decision in *Harley-Davidson,* the Board had held that a successor employer whose bargaining obligation was based on voluntary recognition must bargain for a "reasonable time" measured from the time of recognition following the acquisition.[138] In *Fall River,* the Court endorsed the *Harley-Davidson* ruling stating:

> If, during negotiations, a successor questions a union's continuing majority status, the successor "may lawfully withdraw from negotiation at any time following recognition if it can show that the union had in fact lost its majority status at the time of the refusal to bargain or that the refusal to bargain was grounded on a good-faith doubt based on objective factors that the union continued to command majority support."[139]

The Court then suggested that a successor, unsure of a union's continued majority status, could petition the Board for an election.[140] It appears, however, that if the successorship event occurs during the union's "certification year," as was the case in *Burns,* the presumption of majority support will survive the change in employers and will be conclusive.[141]

The Court of Appeals for the Ninth Circuit, in *NLRB v. Joe Costa Trucking, dba Edjo,*[142] has indicated that there are "paired presumptions" of majority support for a union in the successorship context. Not only does the union enjoy a presumption of majority support among employees retained by the successor, but the union also will be presumed to have the support of a ma-

---

[137]*Supra* note 136.

[138]Landmark Int'l Trucks, 257 NLRB 1375, 108 LRRM 1090 (1981), *vacated and remanded,* 699 F2d 815, 112 LRRM 2689 (CA 6, 1983), *on remand,* 272 NLRB 675, 117 LRRM 1314 (1984), *enforcement denied,* 775 F2d 148, 120 LRRM 2865 (CA 6, 1985); Half-Century dba Holiday Inn of Niles, Mich., 241 NLRB 555, 100 LRRM 1547 (1979), *enforcement denied,* 652 F2d 612, 108 LRRM 2597 (CA 6, 1981).

[139]Fall River Dyeing & Finishing Corp. v. NLRB, 482 US 27, 41 n.9, 125 LRRM 2441, 2446 n.9 (1987) (quoting Harley-Davidson Transp. Co., *supra* note 136, at 1531).

[140]Fall River Dyeing & Finishing Corp. v. NLRB, *supra* note 139 (citing NLRB v. Financial Inst. Employees Local 1182 (Seattle-First Nat'l Bank), 475 US 192, 198, 121 LRRM 2741, 2744–45 (1986)).

[141]*See* Fall River, *supra* note 139. The Court strongly suggests that whatever presumption—conclusive or rebuttable—was applicable to the predecessor will also be applicable to the successor whose work force contains a majority of holdover employees. *See also* NLRB v. Jarm Enters. dba Blu-Fountain Manor, 785 F2d 195, 121 LRRM 3105 (CA 7, 1986), *enforcing* 270 NLRB 199, 116 LRRM 1219 (1984) (upholding Board's application to successor of irrebuttable certification year presumption arising out of representation election conducted within 1 year of successor's acquisition).

[142]631 F2d 604, 105 LRRM 3061 (CA 9, 1980), *enforcing* 238 NLRB 1516, 99 LRRM 1719 (1978).

jority of new hires—even though the new hires never worked for the predecessor.[143] In support of the presumption that newly hired employees support the union in the same proportion as did the "original" employees, the court cited two nonsuccessorship cases.[144] The paired presumptions may be overcome by a demonstration that a majority of the holdover employees in fact reject the union (thus implying that a majority of the new hires also reject the union), and the "new hire" presumption can be overcome by a demonstration that the new hires in fact reject the union.[145]

The rebuttable presumption of continued majority status may be overcome, as in nonsuccessor situations, only by a showing of good-faith doubt based upon "objective considerations."[146] The objective factors sufficient to create a good-faith doubt of continued majority status have been the subject of continued Board and court scrutiny. The Board adheres to the rule that a numerical showing of employee membership in, or financial support of, an incumbent union does not conclusively establish the number of employees who continue to desire union representation.[147] Thus, the mere fact that a majority of the holdover employees sought withdrawal cards does not necessarily furnish the successor employer with a good-faith doubt of majority status.[148] Indeed, one of the reasons advanced by the *Fall River*

---

[143]*Id.* at 607, 105 LRRM at 3063. In *Edjo*, a majority of the successor's work force, 21 out of 29, had worked for the predecessor. The successor contended it had evidence that 8 of the 21 holdovers rejected the union, and when those 8 were combined with the 8 new hires, 16 out of 29 employees rejected the union. The Board and the court did not allow the successor to assume that all 8 new hires rejected the union, thus preserving the union's presumed majority support. *But see infra* discussion accompanying note 163.

[144]*Id.* (citing NLRB v. Jim Kelley's Tahoe Nugget, 584 F2d 293, 99 LRRM 2509 (CA 9, 1978), *cert. denied*, 442 US 921, 101 LRRM 2428 (1979) (employer unlawfully refused to bargain; could not show good-faith doubt of union majority); NLRB v. Crimptex, 517 F2d 501, 89 LRRM 2465 (CA 1, 1975) (same)). *See also* NLRB v. Creative Food Design ta Broker, 852 F2d 1295, 128 LRRM 3089 (CA DC, 1988) (once a union is recognized, turnover that occurs after recognition without any other indicia has no legal significance).

[145]NLRB v. Edjo dba Jose Costa Trucking, *supra* note 142.

[146]Virginia Sportswear, 226 NLRB 1296, 94 LRRM 1411 (1976). Comment, *Successor Employer's Obligation to Bargain: Current Problems in the Presumption of a Union's Majority Status*, 8 FORDHAM URB. L.J. 429 (1979–80). See discussion of "objective considerations" in Chapter 12, "Recognition and Withdrawal of Recognition Without an Election," at notes 313–360.

[147]Premium Foods, 260 NLRB 708, 109 LRRM 1328 (1982), *enforced*, 709 F2d 623, 113 LRRM 3261 (CA 9, 1983).

[148]*Id. But see* J&J Drainage Prods. Co., 269 NLRB 1163, 116 LRRM 1386 (1984), where the Board held the successor had sufficient reasonable doubt of continued union majority status when only 6 of 32 unit employees were union members and 1 of 2 stewards at the plant said the employees were not interested in the union; *see also* Landmark Int'l Trucks v. NLRB, 699 F2d 815, 112 LRRM 2689 (CA 6, 1983), *on remand*, 272 NLRB 675, 117 LRRM 1314 (1984), *enforcement denied*, 775 F2d 148, 120 LRRM 2865 (CA 6, 1985) (noting that substantial decline in dues checkoff is most probative evidence of loss of union support).

Court for a presumption of continued majority support is the need to protect the union against the possible inclination of employees "to shun support for their former union, especially if they believe that such support will jeopardize their jobs with the successor . . . ."[149]

Among those considerations which may not, standing alone, constitute a sufficient basis for good-faith doubt are: the failure of a majority of employees hired by the successor to authorize dues checkoffs,[150] the continued solicitation of authorization cards by the union,[151] expressions of employee dissatisfaction with union representation occurring after a successor's unlawful refusal to bargain,[152] crossing a picket line to continue working,[153] a diminished work force,[154] and employee turnover.[155] Nor has the Board found a reasonable good-faith doubt of continued union majority support to have been shown when the

---

[149]Fall River Dyeing & Finishing Corp. v. NLRB, *supra* note 139, at 40, 125 LRRM at 2446.

[150]*See supra* authorities cited in note 146.

[151]Pick-Mt. Laurel Corp., 239 NLRB 1257, 100 LRRM 1236 (1979), *enforcement denied*, 625 F2d 476, 104 LRRM 2703 (CA 3, 1980), *on remand*, 259 NLRB 302, 108 LRRM 1342 (1981).

[152]First Food Ventures, 229 NLRB 1228, 95 LRRM 1241 (1977); Valmac Indus., 237 NLRB 992, 99 LRRM 1193 (1978), *enforced*, 599 F2d 246, 101 LRRM 2389 (CA 8, 1979). *But see* Riverside Produce Co., 242 NLRB 615, 101 LRRM 1371 (1979), where the Board held that the successor employer had a good-faith doubt after four out of six unit employees told the successor they were disenchanted with the union. These conversations took place before the successor's refusal to bargain.

[153]W & W Steel Co., 232 NLRB 74, 96 LRRM 1530 (1977), *enforcement denied*, 599 F2d 934, 101 LRRM 2445 (CA 10, 1979). *See also* First Food Ventures, *supra* note 152.

[154]Nazareth Regional High School v. NLRB, 549 F2d 873, 94 LRRM 2897 (CA 2, 1977), *enforcing in part sub nom.* Roman Catholic Diocese of Brooklyn, 222 NLRB 1052, 91 LRRM 1419 (1976); NLRB v. Band-Age, Inc., 534 F2d 1, 92 LRRM 2001 (CA 1), *cert. denied*, 429 US 921, 93 LRRM 2570 (1976); Gardena Buena Ventura, 242 NLRB 595, 101 LRRM 1248 (1979), *enforced*, 618 F2d 115, 108 LRRM 2104 (CA 9, 1980); Middleboro Fire Apparatus, 234 NLRB 888, 97 LRRM 1384 (1978), *aff'd*, 590 F2d 4, 100 LRRM 2182 (CA 1, 1978) (reduction in unit from 100 employees to 10 employees not a sufficient basis for doubting union's majority status); Dynamic Mach. Co., 221 NLRB 1140, 91 LRRM 1054 (1975), *aff'd*, 552 F2d 1195, 94 LRRM 3217 (CA 7), *cert. denied*, 434 US 827, 96 LRRM 2513 (1977).

[155]Petoskey Geriatric Village, 295 NLRB No. 80, 131 LRRM 1528 (1989); Lockheed Eng'g & Mgmt. Servs. Co., 271 NLRB 119, 116 LRRM 1386 (1984). The rationale for finding that employee turnover is an insufficient basis for doubting the union's continued majority support is the *Laystrom* presumption, which establishes that new employees are presumed to support the union in the same ratio as those whom they have replaced. Laystrom Mfg. Co., 151 NLRB 1482, 58 LRRM 1624 (1965), *enforcement denied on other grounds*, 359 F2d 799, 62 LRRM 2033 (CA 7, 1966). *But see* Western Distrib. Co. v. NLRB, 608 F2d 397, 102 LRRM 2510 (CA 10, 1979), *denying enforcement to* 236 NLRB 1224, 98 LRRM 1461 (1978), where the court rejected a ratio presumption regarding nonholdover employees hired by the new employer, because the union's request to bargain followed only after the ratio had changed substantially. *Accord* Bengal Paving Co., 245 NLRB 1271, 102 LRRM 1374 (1979). *See also* Chapter 12, "Recognition and Withdrawal of Recognition Without an Election," at notes 313–412.

doubt is based upon: the absence of contract or negotiations,[156] the union's failure to appoint a steward,[157] employee statements of disenchantment with the union,[158] or an employee poll of union sentiment conducted by the successor without assurances of nonreprisal.[159]

The Supreme Court in the *Fall River* decision affirmed the Board's finding that a successor may not overcome its unlawful refusal to recognize the union by relying on evidence of lack of employee support obtained after the unlawful refusal occurred. The Court agreed with the court of appeals' observation that "'once it has been determined that an employer has unlawfully withheld recognition of an [sic] employees' bargaining representative, the employer cannot defend against [a] remedial bargaining [order] by pointing to an intervening loss of employee support for the union when such loss of support is a foreseeable consequence of the employer's unfair labor practice.'"[160]

---

[156]Taylor Stone dba Eastone of Ohio, 277 NLRB 1652, 121 LRRM 1135 (1986) (no good-faith doubt despite union's failure to negotiate contract, strike, and 6-month plant close-down); Lockheed Eng'g & Mgmt. Servs. Co., *supra* note 155 (good-faith doubt not supported despite absence of contract and absence of negotiations for a year).

[157]Petoskey Geriatric Village, *supra* note 155 (good-faith doubt not shown by absence of new sign-ups, absence of meetings, and failure to appoint stewards since these are foreseeable consequences of refusal to bargain).

[158]Briggs Plumbingware v. NLRB, 877 F2d 1282, 131 LRRM 2810 (CA 6, 1989), *enforcing* 286 NLRB 1189, 130 LRRM 1031 (1987) (good-faith doubt not supported despite statements by employees of union dissatisfaction, list of employees who revoked prior union authorization cards, and filing of Teamsters election petition); Redok Enters., 277 NLRB 1010, 120 LRRM 1337 (1985) (employee's unverified report that majority of employees no longer supported union insufficient to support good-faith doubt of majority status).

[159]Royal Midtown Chrysler Plymouth, 296 NLRB No. 135, 133 LRRM 1165 (1989) (good-faith doubt not shown by noncategorical employee statements); Roanwell Corp., 293 NLRB 20, 131 LRRM 1234 (1988) (good-faith doubt not supported by successor's poll of union sentiment conducted without assurance of nonreprisal).

[160]Fall River Dyeing & Finishing Corp. v. NLRB, 482 US 27, 53 n.19, 125 LRRM 2441, 2450 n.19 (quoting NLRB v. Fall River Dyeing & Finishing Corp., 775 F2d 425, 433, 120 LRRM 2825 (CA 1, 1985)). *See also* NLRB v. Great Lakes Chem. Corp., Aquabrom Div., 855 F2d 1174, 129 LRRM 2138, *clarified and amended*, 862 F2d 100, 129 LRRM 3140 (CA 6, 1988) (successor could not challenge certified bargaining representative's majority status, despite high turnover since certification 10 years ago and employee filing of decertification petition over 5 years ago, where neither predecessor nor successor employer had once bargained as required; presumption of majority status during first year following certification was still applicable since neither employer had yet attempted to bargain in good faith); Transportation Equip. Servs. dba Bay Area Mack, 293 NLRB 125, 131 LRRM 1777 (1989) (employer received antiunion petition after its rejection of union's demand for recognition and it committed other unfair labor practices); Petoskey Geriatric Village, *supra* note 155 (since predecessor never bargained with union following its certification, certification year had not commenced); Westbridge Manor, 291 NLRB 27, 131 LRRM 1339 (1988), *enforced*, 884 F2d 576, 136 LRRM 3024 (CA 5, 1989) (basis for doubt arose after unlawful refusal to recognize union); Louisiana-Pacific Corp., 283 NLRB 1079, 125 LRRM 1122 (1987), *enforced*, 858 F2d 576, 129 LRRM 2529 (CA 9, 1988);

In the court of appeals' *Fall River* decision, the court noted that had the employees signed the petitions after the employer engaged in lawful bargaining, the successor might have had a basis for withdrawing recognition if the evidence supported a good-faith doubt. This accords with the Board's holding in *Harley-Davidson* that an employee petition submitted after the successor has entered into bargaining with the union supported the employer's good-faith doubt and entitled the employer to withdraw from bargaining.[161]

In *Proxy Communications of Manhattan v. NLRB*,[162] a successor purchased the assets of a struck company and hired the seven nonstrikers and 39 strike replacements who had worked for the seller. The successor was aware that prior to the sale an ALJ had ruled that the seller committed unfair labor practices and that the strike was deemed an unfair labor practice strike. After holding that the successor could *not* make any presumptions regarding whether the nonstrikers *or* the strike replacements supported the union,[163] the Second Circuit held that "the views of the strikers who wish to return to work must be considered in determining whether the union still has majority support."[164] The court commented that the successor could discount the views of the strikers if "the strikers do not request reinstatement after [the successor] has shown its intent to bargain in good faith."[165]

The Board, with approval of the Court of Appeals for the Ninth Circuit, has held that section 10(b) precludes a successor employer from defending against a refusal-to-bargain allegation based upon the alleged unlawful recognition of the union

---

Mediterranean Diner ta Bay Diner, 279 NLRB 538, 123 LRRM 1085 (1986) (because successor knew that predecessor had committed numerous unremedied unfair labor practices which were of such character as to affect union's status and cause employee disaffection, successor was foreclosed from raising majority issue even though certification year had expired).

[161]NLRB v. Fall River Dyeing & Finishing Corp., 775 F2d 425, 433, 120 LRRM 2825, 2828 (CA 1, 1985); Harley-Davidson Transp. Co., 273 NLRB 1531, 118 LRRM 1204 (1985). *See also* Sun Coast Foods, 273 NLRB 1642, 188 LRRM 1389 (1985), *enforcement denied sub nom.* Chemical Workers Local 540 v. NLRB, 107 Lab. Cas. (CCH) ¶10,064 (CA DC, 1986).

[162]873 F2d 552, 131 LRRM 2072 (CA 2, 1989).

[163]*Id.* at 554, 131 LRRM at 2074. *See* Buckley Broadcasting Corp. dba Station KKHI, 284 NLRB 1339, 125 LRRM 1281 (1987) (Board abolished proportionate rule of Pennco, Inc., 250 NLRB 716, 104 LRRM 1473 (1980), *enforced*, 684 F2d 340, 111 LRRM 2821 (CA 6), *cert. denied*, 459 US 994, 111 LRRM 2823 (1982), whereby strike replacements were presumed to support union in same ratio as striking employees). *See also* NLRB v. Curtin Matheson Scientific, 494 US 775, 133 LRRM 3049 (1990) (approving Board's *Buckley Broadcasting* decision, *supra*).

[164]131 LRRM at 2074.

[165]*Id.*

more than six months before the filing of the unfair practice charge.[166]

4. Discriminatory Refusals to Hire Predecessor's Employees. It is well established under *Burns* and *Howard Johnson* that a new employer is free to select its own work force.[167] It is equally clear, however, that in exercising this freedom of selection a new employer may not discriminatorily refuse to hire the employees of its predecessor, either because of their union membership or activities, or because of the desire to avoid having to recognize the union.[168]

In *Fall River*, the Supreme Court reaffirmed its holding in *Burns* that the successor is under no obligation to hire employees of its predecessor, subject, of course, to the stricture that it may not discriminate against union employees in its hiring.[169]

The Board and courts find sections 8(a)(3) and 8(a)(5) violations and impose bargaining orders where, but for the successor's discriminatory refusal to hire the predecessor's employees, the union would have represented a majority of the successor's work force.[170] The Board initially held that there was no

[166]Marin Operating dba Clarion Hotel-Marin, 279 NLRB 481, 123 LRRM 1334 (1986), *enforced*, 822 F2d 890, 126 LRRM 2078 (CA 9, 1987). *But see* Pick-Mt. Laurel Corp., *supra* note 151. *See* Chapter 31, "NLRB Procedures," at notes 126–128, regarding the §10(b) statute of limitations.

[167]NLRB v. Burns Int'l Sec. Servs., 406 US 272, 80 LRRM 2225 (1972); Howard Johnson Co. v. Hotel Employees, Detroit Local Joint Executive Bd., 417 US 249, 86 LRRM 2449 (1974).

[168]Howard Johnson Co. v. Hotel Employees, Detroit Local Joint Executive Bd., *supra* note 167 at 262 n.8, 86 LRRM at 2454 n.8, NLRB v. Foodway of El Paso, 496 F2d 117, 86 LRRM 2809 (CA 5, 1974), *enforcing* 201 NLRB 933, 82 LRRM 1637 (1973); Burns Int'l Sec. Servs., *supra* note 167 at 280 n.5, 80 LRRM at 2228 n.5; Sousa & Sons, 210 NLRB 982, 86 LRRM 1667 (1974). Violations were found in: Kallmann dba Love's Barbeque Restaurant No. 62 v. NLRB, 640 F2d 1094, 107 LRRM 2011 (CA 9, 1981); Mahoney Foundries, Vermont Foundry Co. Div., 292 NLRB 1003, 131 LRRM 1388 (1989); U.S. Marine Corp. & Bayliner Corp., 293 NLRB 669, 131 LRRM 1105 (1989); American Indus. Cleaning Co., 291 NLRB 399, 131 LRRM 1277 (1988); Hudson River Aggregates, 246 NLRB 192, 102 LRRM 1524 (1979), *enforced*, 639 F2d 865, 106 LRRM 2313 (CA 2, 1981); Crawford Container, 234 NLRB 851, 97 LRRM 1338 (1978); Houston Distribution Servs., 227 NLRB 960, 95 LRRM 1100 (1977), *enforced*, 573 F2d 260, 98 LRRM 2538 (CA 5), *cert. denied*, 439 US 1047, 99 LRRM 3450 (1978); Potter's Drug Enters., 233 NLRB 15, 96 LRRM 1450 (1977), *enforced without opinion*, 584 F2d 980, 99 LRRM 3327 (CA 9, 1978); Mason City Dressed Beef, 231 NLRB 735, 97 LRRM 1215 (1977), *enforced in part sub nom.* Packing House & Indus. Servs. v. NLRB, 590 F2d 688, 100 LRRM 2356 (CA 8, 1978).

[169]Fall River Dyeing & Finishing v. NLRB, *supra* note 160, at 39–40, 125 LRRM at 2446.

[170]*See* Mine Workers Local 1329, Dist. 21 v. NLRB (Alpine Constr. Corp.), 812 F2d 741, 124 LRRM 3012 (CA DC, 1987); Food & Commercial Workers Local 152 v. NLRB, 768 F2d 1463, 119 LRRM 3473 (CA DC, 1985), *enforcing in part, denying enforcement in part and remanding sub nom.* Spencer Foods, 268 NLRB 1483, 115 LRRM 1251 (1984); Kallmann dba Love's Barbeque No. 62 v. NLRB, *supra* note 168; NLRB v. Foodway of El Paso, *supra* note 168; Harvard Indus., Elastic Stop Nut Div., 294 NLRB 1102, 131 LRRM 1759 (1989); Systems Mgmt., 292 NLRB 1078, 131 LRRM 1729 (1989); American Golf Corp. dba Seascape Golf Course, 294 NLRB 881, 132 LRRM 1022 (1989); U.S. Marine Corp. &

discrimination where the new employer established valid business reasons for hiring a totally inexperienced work force, a procedure through which it had staffed its other operations in *Inland Container Corp.*[171] Upon remand from the Court of Appeals for the District of Columbia Circuit, however, the Board reversed its holding in light of new evidence that the employer hired only those employees who indicated that they were willing to work in a nonunion environment.[172]

While the successorship context adds a factual dimension, the basic problems of proof in determining whether a discriminatory motive exists remain the same as in other hiring and discharge cases under section 8(a)(3).[173] Thus, efforts by a potential successor to discover from its predecessor the union sympathies of its employees, followed by a refusal to retain employees identified as sympathetic to the union, evidenced a discriminatory motive.[174] Individual employment decisions, when shown to be part of an overall scheme designed to insure that fewer than a majority of the new employer's work force is composed of its predecessor's employees, also may reflect union animus.[175] However, a bona fide restriction prohibiting such hiring contained in a contract with the predecessor may justify the successor's refusal to hire the predecessor's employees, but

---

Bayliner Corp., *supra* note 168; Fremont Ford Sales dba Fremont Ford, 289 NLRB 1290, 131 LRRM 1074 (1988); Superior Export Packing Co., 284 NLRB 1169, 126 LRRM 1040 (1987), *enforced sub nom.* Meadowlands Hy-Pro Indus. v. NLRB, 845 F2d 1013, 129 LRRM 2528 (CA 3, 1988) State Distrib. Co., 282 NLRB 1048, 124 LRRM 1241 (1987); Lexington Oil Corp., American Steel Warehousing subsidiary, 283 NLRB 293, 124 LRRM 1395 (1987); American Press, 280 NLRB 937, 123 LRRM 1064 (1986), *enforced*, 833 F2d 621, 126 LRRM 3131 (CA 6, 1987); Med West Health Care Mgmt. Corp. dba Cedar Falls Health Care Center, 276 NLRB 1300, 120 LRRM 1168 (1985); Tilden Arms Mgmt. Co., 276 NLRB 1111, 120 LRRM 1207 (1985); Sherwood Trucking Co., 270 NLRB 445, 117 LRRM 1175 (1984), *enforcement denied*, 775 F2d 744, 120 LRRM 3009 (CA 6, 1985); Hubacher Cadillac, 267 NLRB 1062, 114 LRRM 1170 (1983), *aff'd mem.*, 760 F2d 275, 119 LRRM 3160 (CA 9, 1985); Hudson River Aggregates, *supra* note 168; Houston Distribution Servs., *supra* note 168; Potter's Drug Enters., *supra* note 168; Greengate Mall, 209 NLRB 37, 85 LRRM 1303 (1974). *See also* Scott v. El Farra Enters. dba Bi-Fair Mkt., 863 F2d 670, 130 LRRM 2160 (CA 9, 1988) (district court erred in denying Board §10(j) relief ordering successor employer to offer employment to predecessor's employees and to bargain with union where regional director had reasonable cause for believing successor engaged in §8(a)(3) discrimination in its hiring of employees).

[171]275 NLRB 378, 119 LRRM 1089 (1985), *supplementing* 267 NLRB 1187, 114 LRRM 1143 (1983), 273 NLRB 1856, 118 LRRM 1384 (1985) *and* 274 NLRB 887, 118 LRRM 1454 (1985).

[172]*Id.*

[173]*See generally* Chapter 7, "Discrimination in Employment."

[174]*Cf.* Sousa & Sons, *supra* note 168. *But see* Big E's Foodland, 242 NLRB 963, 101 LRRM 1422 (1979).

[175]Houston Distribution Servs., *supra* note 168.

the purchaser will not be shielded from a discriminatory refusal to hire where it has been released from such contractual restriction.[176]

Factors tending to show no section 8(a)(3) violation include the failure of a predecessor's employees to file employment applications or to attend employment interviews uniformly required of all potential employees of the new employer.[177] Where the new employer has various locations, a comparison of its hiring procedures is relevant.[178] In some instances, particularly with respect to service contractors, the absence of a discriminatory motive may be supported by a showing that the new employer has, in accordance with its customary practice, staffed its new operation with experienced personnel taken from its other locations.[179] As in other hiring and discharge cases, nondiscriminatory factors such as suitability and availability for employment in the new employer's operations continue to be significant.[180] Similarly, an indication by a predecessor's employee that wage rates or terms of employment inferior to those offered by the predecessor would be unacceptable is an important consideration where the new employer initially plans to offer wage rates or other conditions that are less attractive than its predecessor's.[181]

Application of the six-month time limitation of section 10(b) to the successor's hiring determinations may raise difficult questions. Where the successor notifies an employee of a decision not to rehire in advance of the actual takeover date, the Board has held that the six-month period runs from the date of actual takeover. The Court of Appeals for the Second Circuit, however, treated the date of notification as the beginning of the limitations period.[182]

The new employer may not avoid the consequences of successorship by refusing to hire strikers unlawfully terminated by

---

[176]Greengate Mall, *supra* note 170.

[177]*See* R & L Cartage & Sons, 292 NLRB 530, 131 LRRM 1695 (1989); Vantage Petroleum Corp., 247 NLRB 1492, 103 LRRM 1408 (1980); Houston Distribution Servs., *supra* note 168.

[178]*Cf.* NLRB v. Foodway of El Paso, *supra* note 168.

[179]Industrial Catering Co., 224 NLRB 972, 92 LRRM 1638 (1976); Crotona Serv. Corp., 200 NLRB 738, 82 LRRM 1110 (1972).

[180]*Cf.* Houston Distribution Servs., *supra* note 168.

[181]Vantage Petroleum Corp., *supra* note 177; Crotona Serv. Corp., *supra* note 179.

[182]Nazareth Regional High School v. NLRB, 549 F2d 873, 94 LRRM 2897 (CA 2, 1977), *enforcing in part sub nom.* Roman Catholic Diocese of Brooklyn, 222 NLRB 1052, 91 LRRM 1419 (1976). In *Nazareth*, the court also rejected the Board's finding that a charge filed *before* the notification encompassed the refusal to rehire contained in the notification.

its predecessor and for whom the Board has ordered reinstatement.[183] However, unless the successorship criteria are *otherwise* clearly established, one cannot be certain that a bargaining order will be enforced as an accompaniment to the enforcement of reinstatement orders for discriminatory refusal of employment. Such a bargaining order was refused enforcement in *NLRB v. Tragniew, Inc.*,[184] where the presumption of continued majority was held to have been rebutted, and in *NLRB v. Bausch & Lomb*,[185] where the discriminatees were employed in a peripheral capacity and the appropriateness of the unit was questionable.

B. Continuity of Identity in the Business Enterprise or Employing Industry

The broad test for determining the existence or nonexistence of "successorship," referred to by the Supreme Court in *Howard Johnson*,[186] is the "substantial continuity of identity in the busi-

---

[183]NLRB v. Fabsteel Co. of La., 587 F2d 689, 100 LRRM 2349 (CA 5, 1979), *enforcing* 231 NLRB 372, 97 LRRM 1104 (1977), *cert. denied*, 442 US 943, 101 LRRM 2556 (1979). However, these factors were held not to warrant the issuance of a §10(j) injunction pending the Board's determination of these issues. Crain v. Fabsteel Co. of La., 427 F Supp 316, 94 LRRM 2817 (WD La, 1977). The Board had previously determined that the denial of reinstatement constituted an unfair labor practice and directed that the terminated strikers be reinstated. Mosher Steel Co., 220 NLRB 336, 90 LRRM 1459 (1975), *enforced without opinion*, 532 F2d 1374, 93 LRRM 2018 (CA 5, 1976). However, the facility was sold prior to compliance with the reinstatement order. The new owners hired substantially all of the employees who were on the seller's payroll as of the effective date of the sale. Those employees included replacements for the unfair labor practice strikers. The district court's refusal to issue the temporary injunction was based upon the rationale that until it was established that Fabsteel was a successor and had violated the Act, balancing of the equities militated in favor of preserving the status quo, thereby not requiring the discharge of the replacements to make room for the unfair labor practice strikers. But the Board and the Fifth Circuit subsequently found Fabsteel to be a successor employer and ordered it to reinstate the unfair labor practice strikers. NLRB v. Fabsteel Co. of La., *supra*.

[184]470 F2d 669, 81 LRRM 2336 (CA 9, 1972), *denying enforcement in part sub nom. to* Barrington Plaza & Tragniew, 185 NLRB 962, 75 LRRM 1226 (1970). The ALJ found (1) that when the union was originally accorded recognition it has not established that it represented a majority of the unit employees; (2) that thereafter during a period of approximately 4 years, in which three collective bargaining agreements were negotiated, the union had never made an affirmative showing that it represented an uncoerced majority of the employees in the unit; and (3) that applications for membership cards introduced into evidence at the hearing to demonstrate majority status were tainted by evidence of coercion. *Id.*, 185 NLRB at 970–74, 75 LRRM at 1230. The Ninth Circuit relied on these factual findings by the ALJ in concluding that the presumption of majority status, on which the Board had relied, had been rebutted. *Id.*, 470 F2d at 674–75, 81 LRRM 2339.

[185]526 F2d 817, 90 LRRM 3217 (CA 2, 1975), *denying enforcement in part to* 214 NLRB 338, 88 LRRM 1196 (1974).

[186]Howard Johnson Co. v. Hotel Employees, Detroit Local Joint Executive Bd., *supra* note 167.

ness enterprise." The Board has articulated the test as "substantial continuity of the employing industry."[187] The Board has stated that where a new employer "uses substantially the same facilities and work force to produce the same basic products for essentially the same customers in the same geographic area," it will be regarded as a successor.[188] But when succession is found by the Board, this definition will normally be supplemented by reference to specific criteria applicable to the particular "employing industry."[189]

The criteria which the Board evolved prior to *Burns*, and which it has continued to articulate after *Burns*, include the following:

> Whether (1) there has been a substantial continuity of the same business operations; (2) the new employer uses the same plant; (3) the same or substantially the same work force is employed;

---

[187]Fall River Dyeing & Finishing Corp. v. NLRB, 482 US 27, 125 LRRM 2441 (1987); Gold Kist dba Golden Poultry Co., Agri-International, 271 NLRB 925, 117 LRRM 1127 (1984); Grico Corp., Aircraft Magnesium Div., 265 NLRB 1344, 112 LRRM 1147 (1982), *enforced*, 730 F2d 767, 115 LRRM 3712 (CA 9, 1984); Premium Foods, 260 NLRB 708, 109 LRRM 1328 (1982), *enforced*, 709 F2d 623, 113 LRRM 3261 (CA 9, 1983); Magnolia Manor Nursing Home, 260 NLRB 377, 109 LRRM 1198 (1982); Miami Indus. Trucks, 221 NLRB 1223, 91 LRRM 1040 (1975). *See also* Petoskey Geriatric Village, 295 NLRB No. 80, 131 LRRM 1528 (1989); Hospital San Francisco, 293 NLRB 171, 131 LRRM 1344 (1989); A-1 Schmidlin Plumbing & Heating Co., 284 NLRB 1506, 126 LRRM 1027 (1987); Holiday Inn of Victorville, 284 NLRB 916, 126 LRRM 1203 (1987); Cal-Am Partners, 281 NLRB 170, 124 LRRM 1365 (1986), *enforced*, 819 F2d 1132, 125 LRRM 2615 (CA 3, 1987). In applying this test, the Board has stated that changes effectuated by the new employer may be evaluated to determine whether they constitute "substantial and material changes" in the "employing industry." Woodrich Indus., 246 NLRB 43, 102 LRRM 1407 (1979); Gardena Buena Ventura, 242 NLRB 595, 101 LRRM 1248 (1979), *enforced*, 618 F2d 115, 108 LRRM 2104 (CA 9, 1980).

[188]Valley Nitrogen Producers, 207 NLRB 208, 84 LRRM 1424 (1973); Proxy Communications of Manhattan v. NLRB, 873 F2d 552, 131 LRRM 2072 (CA 2, 1989). *Cf.* Radiant Fashions, 202 NLRB 938, 82 LRRM 1742 (1973).

[189]In Magnolia Manor Nursing Home, *supra* note 187, successorship was found where the location of the nursing facility, the level of care provided, the patients, chief administrator, and the supervisory personnel all remained the same. In Fall River Dyeing & Finishing Corp. v. NLRB, *supra* note 187, the successor conducted a business similar to the predecessor, the same production building was used, and machinery, jobs, and supervision remained the same. In Tilden Arms Mgmt. Co., *supra* note 170, successorship was found where the successor employer, an owner-operator of apartment buildings, provided the same management services, employed the same work force, and used the same supervisors, machinery, equipment, and methods of operation. In Indianapolis Mack Sales & Serv., 272 NLRB 690, 117 LRRM 1335 (1984), *enforcement denied on other grounds*, 802 F2d 280, 123 LRRM 2543 (CA 7, 1986), successorship was found where the employer sold the same brand of trucks, leased the same premises, utilized the same departmental structure, and employed first-line supervisors culled from former branch employees. In State Distrib. Co., 282 NLRB 1048, 124 LRRM 1241 (1987), successorship was found where the employer continued to operate a wine distributorship in the same fashion, and inherited all of the predecessor's suppliers and a large number of its customers. *Compare* Hotel & Restaurant Employees Local 274 (Hospitality Catering ta Warwick Caterers), 282 NLRB 939, 124 LRRM 1250 (1987) (successorship not found where kosher caterer agreed to joint venture with third party and joint venture was nonkosher service).

(4) the same jobs exist under the same working conditions; (5) the same supervisors are employed; (6) the same machinery, equipment, and methods of production are used; and (7) the same product is manufactured or the same services offered.[190]

And in a somewhat more restrictive decision, the Board has suggested that "in order for a successorship to be established there must be an affirmative showing of a purchase, transfer, or takeover of the predecessor's business; and a continuation of that particular operation without a hiatus or significant change with substantially the same employees."[191] At bottom, however, and however described, the enterprise-continuity determination is based upon the totality of circumstances[192] and, thus, requires case-by-case determination.

Notwithstanding its continued reference to a "totality of circumstances" in determining successorship,[193] it has been appar-

---

[190]Border Steel Rolling Mills, 204 NLRB 814, 815, 83 LRRM 1606 (1973); *see also* NLRB v. Great Lakes Chem. Corp., Aquabrom Div., 855 F2d 1174, 129 LRRM 2138, *clarified and amended*, 862 F2d 100, 129 LRRM 3140 (CA 6, 1988); Food & Commercial Workers Local 152 v. NLRB, 768 F2d 1463, 119 LRRM 3473 (CA DC, 1985), *enforcing in part, denying enforcement in part and remanding sub nom.* Spencer Foods, 268 NLRB 1483, 115 LRRM 1251 (1984); NLRB v. Fabsteel Co. of La., *supra* note 183; Dynamic Mach. Co. v. NLRB, 552 F2d 1195, 94 LRRM 3217 (CA 7, 1977), *enforcing* 221 NLRB 1140, 91 LRRM 1054 (1975), *cert. denied*, 434 US 827, 96 LRRM 2513 (1977); A-1 Schmidlin Plumbing & Heating Co., *supra* note 187; Superior Export Packing Co., 284 NLRB 1169, 126 LRRM 1040 (1987); Cencom of Mo., 282 NLRB 253, 123 LRRM 1339 (1986); *see also* Woodrich Indus., *supra* note 187; Alcoholism Servs. of Erie County, 236 NLRB 927, 99 LRRM 1394 (1978); Valmac Indus., 237 NLRB 992, 99 LRRM 1193 (1978), *enforced*, 599 F2d 246, 101 LRRM 2389 (CA 8, 1979); Mondovi Foods Corp., 235 NLRB 1080, 98 LRRM 1102 (1978); Western Distrib. Co., 236 NLRB 1224, 98 LRRM 1461 (1978), *enforcement denied*, 608 F2d 397, 102 LRRM 2510 (CA 10, 1979); Potter's Drug Enters., 233 NLRB 15, 96 LRRM 1450 (1977), *enforced without opinion*, 584 F2d 980, 99 LRRM 3327 (CA 9, 1978); L.A. Beefland, 232 NLRB 1189, 96 LRRM 1481 (1977), *enforced*, 601 F2d 603, 106 LRRM 3076 (CA 9, 1979); Merchants Home Delivery Serv., 230 NLRB 290, 95 LRRM 1357 (1977), *enforcement denied*, 580 F2d 966, 99 LRRM 2291 (CA 9, 1978); C.M.E., Inc., 225 NLRB 514, 92 LRRM 1634 (1976); Miami Indus. Trucks, *supra* note 187. *See also* NLRB v. Jeffries Lithograph Co., 752 F2d 459, 118 LRRM 2681 (CA 9, 1985), *enforcing* 265 NLRB 1499, 112 LRRM 1236 (1982); Premium Foods, *supra* note 187.

[191]Longshoremen (ILA) Baltimore Dist. Council (Rukert Terminals Corp.), 266 NLRB 846, 113 LRRM 1041, 1042 (1983), *enforced*, 764 F2d 234, 119 LRRM 3259 (CA 4, 1985) (holding that there was not successorship where there was no evidence of purchase, transfer, or takeover by alleged successor, nor any evidence that old employer's workers were hired by alleged successor). *See also* Hotel Employees Local 274 (Hospitality Catering ta Warwick Caterers), *supra* note 189 (no successorship found where no transfer of assets, employer not engaged in same business line, and majority of employees not former employees of other company); Williams Motor Transfer, 284 NLRB 1496, 126 LRRM 1030 (1987) (no successorship found where original employees constituted minority, different supervision and working conditions resulted, and new employer did not operate old fleet of trucks); Mine Workers Dist. 23 (Kentucky Lake Dock Co.), 271 NLRB 461, 116 LRRM 1487 (1984) (Board held that employer engaged in "distinct business," and was neither successor nor alter ego).

[192]*See* Fall River Dyeing & Finishing Corp. v. NLRB, *supra* note 187; Hawaii Carpenters Trust Funds v. Waiola Carpenter Shop, 823 F2d 289, 125 LRRM 3442 (CA 9, 1987).

[193]Williams Motor Transfer, *supra* note 191; Premium Foods, *supra* note 187; C.M.E., Inc., *supra* note 190.

ent since *Burns* that the threshold criterion in determining successorship is the continuity of the work force;[194] in no Board decision since *Burns* has a successorship been found absent a finding of "majority."[195] Moreover, once there is a finding of a continued "majority," the primacy of that criterion will ordinarily prevail over particular operational changes made by the new employer.[196]

Yet, "majority" status in the work force will not, standing alone, compel a finding of successorship; for notwithstanding continuity of the employee complement the Board has refused to find successorship where countervailing factors have destroyed the continuity of the employing industry.[197] Thus, where continuity, other than of the work force, consisted primarily of the acquisition of a portion of the customers of a moribund company solicited in competition with other companies, the new employer's operations were viewed as constitut-

---

[194]*See, e.g.*, Operating Eng'rs Local 542 v. Evans Asphalt Co., 721 F Supp 73, 132 LRRM 2063 (MD Pa), *aff'd*, 891 F2d 281, 133 LRRM 2072 (CA 3, 1989); NLRB v. Jeffries Lithograph Co., *supra* note 190; Frank V. & Michael Carlow dba Carlow's, 266 NLRB 305, 112 LRRM 1358 (1983), *enforced*, 738 F2d 423, 116 LRRM 3264 (CA 3, 1984); Homosassa Springs Restaurant, 275 NLRB 1519, 120 LRRM 1051 (1985). Successorship has not been found where, despite the fact the predecessor's business was continued, the majority factor was absent. G.W. Hunt dba Foremost Foods Distrib., 258 NLRB 1198, 108 LRRM 1216 (1981). *See also* M.U. Indus., 284 NLRB 388, 125 LRRM 1187 (1987); Stewart Chevrolet, 262 NLRB 362, 110 LRRM 1313 (1982); General Processing Corp., 263 NLRB 86, 110 LRRM 1479 (1982).

[195]*See* discussion in *supra* note 77. The Board has refrained from making express reference to the primacy of the continuity-of-work-force criterion in articulating its set of criteria, Miami Indus. Trucks, *supra* note 187; or in reviewing a finding of no successorship where a majority was lacking, Industrial Catering Co., *supra* note 179; or in basing its determination of no successorship on other criteria where the question of majority status was clouded, Woodrich Indus., *supra* note 187.

[196]NLRB v. Zayre Corp., 424 F2d 1159, 74 LRRM 2804 (CA 5, 1970). Saks & Co. dba Saks Fifth Ave., 247 NLRB 1047, 103 LRRM 1241 (1980), *enforced in part*, 634 F2d 681, 105 LRRM 3274 (CA 2, 1980); M & H Mach. Co., 243 NLRB 817, 102 LRRM 1038 (1979). Changes will undoubtedly accompany most takeovers; but where there is a large employee complement consisting almost exclusively of holdovers, a basic continuity of the business is indicated—a circumstance which is likely to negate changes that might be more significant in a small work force with a slim majority of holdovers. For example, in *Zayre*, a discount store which had operated autonomously within a small chain was taken over and integrated into a highly centralized large chain. This and numerous internal, marketing, and policy changes raised questions of continued unit appropriateness. However, the Board's decision turned on the large number and overwhelming percentage of holdover employees.

[197]*See* Cagle's Inc., 218 NLRB 603, 89 LRRM 1337 (1975); Co-Op Trucking Co., 209 NLRB 829, 86 LRRM 1242 (1974); Radiant Fashions, *supra* note 188; Atlantic Technical Servs. Corp., 202 NLRB 169, 82 LRRM 1467 (1973), *enforced*, 498 F2d 680, 86 LRRM 2182 (CA DC, 1974); Galis Equip. Co., 194 NLRB 799, 79 LRRM 1073 (1972); Norton Precision, 199 NLRB 1003, 81 LRRM 1585 (1972); Georgetown Stainless Mfg. Corp., 198 NLRB 234, 80 LRRM 1615 (1972); Lincoln Private Police, 189 NLRB 717, 76 LRRM 1727 (1971). Thus, once the "majority" prerequisite has been established, the Board's reference to its inquiry into the "totality" of circumstances becomes more meaningful.

ing an entirely new and independent enterprise, and the "employing industry" was deemed sufficiently fragmented to preclude a finding of successorship.[198]

While there is no single factor that will negate a finding of successorship, the Board has emphasized such combined factors as (1) a long hiatus in the resumption of operations; (2) a difference in location of the resumed operation; (3) a changeover in the supervisory hierarchy; (4) the absence of a carry-over of customers or markets supplied; and (5) a difference in the scale of the operations and the products produced, and in the methods of production.[199] These factors, in various combinations, are sometimes found in circumstances where the change in the employment relationship was not the result of a sale of the business as an ongoing enterprise, and where the employees had no reasonable basis for any expectation that their employment would be resumed at the same location.[200] The existence or nonexistence of such factors may also be relevant to the employees' desires for continued representation.[201]

The Board has found successorship despite a change in some customers and a minor change in operations.[202] Again, a modification of product lines, a significant difference in clientele, and a change in managerial control were deemed not sufficient to negate a finding of successorship where "majority status" in the work force was found.[203] Successorship (or in the alternative, alter ego status) was found where the same individual was principal operator of two enterprises that engaged in the same business with the same employees, supervisors, and customers,

---

[198]*See, e.g.*, Co-Op Trucking Co., *supra* note 197; Lincoln Private Police, *supra* note 197.

[199]*See, e.g.*, Woodrich Indus., *supra* note 187; Radiant Fashions, *supra* note 188 (covenant not to compete); Norton Precision, *supra* note 197; Galis Equip. Co., *supra* note 199.

[200]*See* cases cited in *supra* note 199. *See also* In re Chicago, Milwaukee, St. Paul & Pac. R.R., 658 F2d 1149 (CA 7, 1981), *cert. denied sub nom.* Railway Labor Executives' Ass'n v. Ogilvie, 455 US 1000 (1982) (court refused to impose successorship on noncarrier purchasers of previously abandoned lines of bankrupt railroad or next operators of lines where there was abandonment of specified noncore rail lines, hiatus of operations, and no substantial continuity of work force).

[201]United Maintenance & Mfg. Co., 214 NLRB 529, 87 LRRM 1469 (1974).

[202]Market King, 282 NLRB 876, 124 LRRM 1150 (1987); Contract Carrier, 258 NLRB 353, 108 LRRM 1132 (1981). *See also* NLRB v. Great Lakes Chem. Corp., Aquabrom Div., *supra* note 190 ("simply cosmetic modifications to the physical and organizational structure" or "evolutionary" operational changes which would not affect employees' representational desires are not sufficient to negate successorship finding); NLRB v. South Harlan Coal, 844 F2d 380, 128 LRRM 2182 (CA 6, 1988), *enforcing sub nom.* Croley Coal Corp., 280 NLRB 899, 124 LRRM 1034 (1986) (minor equipment changes did not transform essential nature of operations).

[203]Premium Foods, *supra* note 187; *see also* Food & Commercial Workers Local 152 v. NLRB (Spencer Foods), *supra* note 190.

and there was no hiatus. In finding successorship, the Board held that the work force's expansion and reduction and the predecessor's discharge of all contractual obligations under the Bankruptcy Act were immaterial.[204] Reduction in scale of operations,[205] changes in scope and distribution of operations,[206] changes in business structure,[207] and substantial capital investments and refurbishing of plant and equipment,[208] have all been deemed insufficient in their impact on business operations to negate successorship.

The Board has also stated that it would not confine itself to viewing the facts solely as they existed at the time of transfer, particularly where the new employer's continuation in the same employing industry was a "temporary expedient" and a significant change in the nature of the operations was not only "imminent and certain," but was, in fact, effectuated.[209]

Some appellate court decisions have focused upon the question of "whether there was an 'essential change in the business that would have affected employee attitudes toward representation.'"[210] The Court of Appeals for the Ninth Circuit in *NLRB v.*

---

[204]William B. Allen, 267 NLRB 700, 114 LRRM 1104 (1983), *enforced*, 758 F2d 1145, 118 LRRM 3409 (CA 6, 1985), *cert. denied*, 474 US 1101, 121 LRRM 2368 (1986). *See also* Miner Indus., 285 NLRB 234, 128 LRRM 1104 (1987) (employer that took over bankrupt company's oprations and contracts is successor).

[205]IMS Mfg. Co. v. NLRB, 813 F2d 113, 125 LRRM 2843 (CA 6, 1987); Evans Servs. v. NLRB, 810 F2d 1089, 124 LRRM 2802 (CA 11, 1987); Roanwell Corp., 293 NLRB 20, 131 LRRM 1234 (1988); Homosassa Springs Restaurant, *supra* note 194.

[206]NLRB v. Jeffries Lithograph Co., *supra* note 190. *See also* Harvard Indus., Elastic Stop Nut Div., 294 NLRB 1102, 131 LRRM 1759 (1989); Mario Milevoi, 282 NLRB 779, 125 LRRM 1135 (1987) (superior services not sufficient to necessitate substantial continuity of business operations).

[207]Hardin's Bakery v. Retail, Wholesale & Dep't Store Union, 877 F2d 1541, 131 LRRM 3252 (CA 11, 1989), *vacated and reh'g granted*, 893 F2d 1188, 133 LRRM 2608 (CA 11, 1990); Indianapolis Mack Sales & Serv., *supra* note 189.

[208]NLRB v. Jeffries Lithograph Co., *supra* note 190; El Torito-La Fiesta Restaurants, 295 NLRB No. 56, 131 LRRM 1689 (1989) (successorship found where purchaser closed restaurant temporarily, remodeled, and reopened as different restaurant); P&M Cedar Prods., 284 NLRB 652, 125 LRRM 1367 (1987); Inland Container Corp., 275 NLRB 378, 119 LRRM 1089 (1985), *supplementing* 267 NLRB 1187, 114 LRRM 1143 (1983), 273 NLRB 1856, 118 LRRM 1384 (1985) *and* 274 NLRB 887, 118 LRRM 1454 (1985).

[209]Galis Equip. Co., *supra* note 197. But where subsequent changes were not contemplated at the time, see Valley Nitrogen Producers, 207 NLRB 208, 84 LRRM 1424 (1973). It is unclear whether and how the test of imminency applicable to operational changes will affect consideration of when a "full complement" of employees is assembled by the new employer. *See* discussion *supra* at notes 140–157.

[210]NLRB v. Jeffries Lithograph Co., *supra* note 190, 118 LRRM at 2685 (quoting Premium Foods v. NLRB, 709 F2d 623, 627, 113 LRRM 3261 (CA 9, 1983)). *See also* Fall River Dyeing & Finishing Corp. v. NLRB, 482 US 27, 125 LRRM 2441 (1987); Evans Servs. v. NLRB, *supra* note 205 (management of both companies essentially the same; new employer retained common aspects of business of defunct corporation); IMS Mfg. Co. v. NLRB, *supra* note 205; Food & Commercial Local 152 v. NLRB (Spencer Foods), *supra* note 190.

Jeffries Lithograph Co.,[211] found successorship, despite the expansion of a local operation into a nationwide enterprise, where "day-to-day life" of the production employees remained the same.[212] In *Food & Commercial Workers Local 152 v. NLRB (Spencer Foods)*,[213] the Court of Appeals for the District of Columbia Circuit stated that the appropriate analysis focuses "not on the continuity of the business structure in general, but rather on the particular operations of the business as they affect the members of the relevant bargaining unit."[214]

Finally, in *Fall River*[215] the Supreme Court found that the successor's changes, which included a change in process and a seven-month hiatus between closure by the predecessor and the start-up operations, bore only indirectly upon the employees' working conditions and relationship with the employer and were not sufficient to avoid the finding of a "substantial continuity."

Majority considerations have also been offset by a lack of continuity in the employing industry, where the new employer takes over only a very small segment of the predecessor's bargaining unit in which the employees were previously represented solely by virtue of an accretion into a larger unit by agreement of the parties.[216] Similarly, a bare majority of a greatly reduced bargaining unit, taken over by an employer after a year's hiatus through a management agreement with a trustee in bankruptcy, was deemed insufficient to warrant a finding of successorship.[217]

---

[211]752 F2d 459, 118 LRRM 2681 (CA 9, 1985), *enforcing* 265 NLRB 1499, 112 LRRM 1236 (1982).

[212]*Id.* at 465, 118 LRRM at 2686. Despite the absence of one *Jeffries* factor (supervisors were not the same), one circuit found successorship in Hawaii Carpenters Trust Funds v. Waiola Carpenter Shop, *supra* note 192.

[213]768 F2d 1463, 119 LRRM 3473 (CA DC, 1985), *enforcing in part, denying enforcement in part and remanding sub nom.* Spencer Foods, 268 NLRB 1483, 115 LRRM 1251 (1984).

[214]*Id.* at 1470, 119 LRRM at 3478. *See also* Mine Workers Local 1329, Dist. 21 v. NLRB (Alpine Constr. Corp.), 812 F2d 741, 124 LRRM 3012 (CA DC, 1987).

[215]Fall River Dyeing & Finishing Corp. v. NLRB, *supra* note 210.

[216]Atlantic Technical Servs. Corp., *supra* note 197. *But compare* G.T. & E. Data Servs. Corp., 194 NLRB 719, 79 LRRM 1033 (1971). *See also* Border Steel Rolling Mills, 204 NLRB 814, 83 LRRM 1606 (1973), regarding significance of accretion. *But see* Band-Age, Inc., 217 NLRB 449, 89 LRRM 1522 (1975), *enforced*, 534 F2d 1, 92 LRRM 2001 (CA 1), *cert. denied*, 429 US 921, 93 LRRM 2570 (1976), where a comparable diminution in size of operations, although not of the magnitude of Atlantic Technical Services, did not prevent the finding of successorship where all other relevant factors supported such a finding.

[217]Blazer Indus., 236 NLRB 103, 99 LRRM 1046 (1978); Cagle's Inc., *supra* note 197.

C. Continuity of the Appropriate Bargaining Unit

Bargaining unit changes often accompany a takeover. Some changes may be minor, while others are pervasive. Some may stem from prior planning, while others may be the result of unintended changes in market conditions or customer acceptability. In varying degrees, these changes may affect the appropriateness of the unit.[218] And, as recognized in *Burns*, successorship may depend upon the continued appropriateness of the bargaining unit.[219]

Where a purchaser acquires a predecessor's entire unit intact and keeps the predecessor unit distinct, the continuity of the unchanged unit does not become an issue.[220] But where a purchaser acquires a predecessor's unit intact and attempts to treat it as an accretion to an existing unit, the Board will consider whether the predecessor's unit remains appropriate.[221] In such instances, the purchaser bears "the burden of showing that the historical units are no longer appropriate."[222]

For example, in *Border Steel Rolling Mills*,[223] the Board found no successorship where the predecessor's unit had been integrated into a larger unit and a separate bargaining unit was no longer warranted. There, the Board held that the predecessor's unit was accreted into the succeeding employer's unit.[224] On the

---

[218]*Cf.* NLRB v. Burns Int'l Sec. Servs., 406 US 272, 80 LRRM 2225 (1972).

[219]*Id.* at 280, 80 LRRM at 2228; for discussion of the continued appropriateness of the unit, see Note, *The Bargaining Obligations of Successor Employers*, 88 HARV. L. REV. 759 (1975); Rovins & Rosen, *Labor Law Obligations of Parties to the Sale of a Business*, 25 LAB. L.J. 231, 237–38 (1974).

[220]*See* NLRB v. Winco Petroleum Co., 668 F2d 973, 109 LRRM 2377 (CA 8, 1982) (purchaser of three service stations held to be successor where former three-station unit had retained separate identity within larger organization).

[221]*See* Reliable Trailer & Body, 295 NLRB No. 112, 131 LRRM 1715 (1989) (purchased plant not accretion to purchaser's other plant unit, where purchaser failed to rebut presumption of single plant unit); Armco, Eastern Steel Div., Ashland Works, 279 NLRB 1184, 123 LRRM 1335 (1986), *enforced in part and remanded in part*, 832 F2d 357, 126 LRRM 2961 (CA 6, 1987), *cert. denied*, 486 US 1042, 130 LRRM 2800 (1988) (application of successor's existing union contract to acquired plant as an accretion unlawful; plant retained separate identity).

[222]Indianapolis Mack Sales & Serv., 288 NLRB 1123, 130 LRRM 1240, 1241 (1988).

[223]*Supra* note 216; *cf.* NLRB v. Security-Columbian Banknote Co., 541 F2d 135, 93 LRRM 2049 (CA 3, 1976), where the court likewise held that the new employer was not a successor because the continuity of the appropriate bargaining unit was not maintained. However, the court refused to find that the predecessor's unit was accredited into that of the succeeding employer.

[224]*See also* Indianapolis Mack Sales & Service, *supra* note 222 (predecessor's 16-employee service department and 7-employee parts department were properly consolidated by purchaser, and thus purchaser properly refused to bargain with predecessor union).

other hand, where there is only a moderate expansion in the unit, accretion principles may be operative as a basis for finding a continuity in the employing industry.[225]

In *NLRB v. Winco Petroleum Co.*,[226] a purchaser that consolidated the predecessor's three service stations with four others was held to be a successor. The operations of the new enterprise with respect to the former employees remained the same, and the former three-station unit had retained some degree of separate identity within the larger organization.[227]

As noted above,[228] mere diminution in the size of the unit normally does not present a serious obstacle to a finding of successorship. When, however, the diminution is the result of a severance of geographic or operational facilities or a fragmentation of the employing industry, rather than merely a shrinkage of a discrete unit, the issue is more complex.

Where the new employer acquires only one of a multistore or multiplant unit, successorship will normally be established if the acquired unit is itself an appropriate unit under the Board's traditional criteria.[229] Thus, the purchaser of one of a chain of stores may be a successor if other criteria of continuity are established.[230] Where a purchaser acquired six out of 42 separately certified units, successorship was not negated because the employees of those units were a "distinct, identifiable entity, and they shared a substantial community of interests."[231]

---

[225]*Cf.* Spruce-Up Corp., 209 NLRB 194, 85 LRRM 1426 (1974), *enforced*, 529 F2d 516, 90 LRRM 2525 (CA 4, 1975), where the Board held that the addition of 8 barber shops to the existing 19-shop unit did not destroy the appropriateness of the union's certification.

[226]*Supra* note 220. *See also* Armco, Eastern Steel Div., Ashland Works, *supra* note 221 (application of successor's existing union contract to acquired plant as an accretion unlawful; plant retained separate identity).

[227]*See also* Cencom of Mo., 282 NLRB 253, 123 LRRM 1339 (1986) (successorship found despite consolidations and other changes in job functions).

[228]*See supra* notes 82, 88, 94–95.

[229]This may result from the presumption that a single-plant or single-store unit is appropriate. *See* Stewart Granite Enters., 255 NLRB 569, 107 LRRM 1182 (1981); Zim's Foodliner v. NLRB, 495 F2d 1131, 85 LRRM 3019 (CA 7, 1974), *enforcing sub nom.* Parkwood IGA, 201 NLRB 905, 82 LRRM 1682 (1973), *cert. denied, sub nom.* Zim's IGA Foodliner v. NLRB, 419 US 838, 87 LRRM 2398 (1974). *See also* NLRB v. Fabsteel Co. of La., 587 F2d 689, 100 LRRM 2349 (CA 5, 1979), *enforcing* 231 NLRB 372, 97 LRRM 1104 (1977), *cert. denied*, 442 US 943, 101 LRRM 2556 (1979). *But see* W & W Steel Co., 232 NLRB 74, 96 LRRM 1530 (1977), *enforcement denied*, 599 F2d 934, 101 LRRM 2445 (CA 10, 1979) (certified unit was no longer appropriate). For cases discussing appropriate unit for bargaining upon takeover by a successor, see Good N' Fresh Foods, 287 NLRB 1231, 128 LRRM 1158 (1988); Miles & Sons Trucking Serv., 269 NLRB 7, 115 LRRM 1264 (1984); Eberhard Foods, 269 NLRB 280, 115 LRRM 1224 (1984).

[230]Zim's Foodliner v. NLRB, *supra* note 229.

[231]Electrical Workers (IUE) (White-Westinghouse Corp.) v. NLRB, 604 F2d 689, 696, 101 LRRM 2864, 2867 (CA DC, 1979), *enforcing* 229 NLRB 667, 96 LRRM 1078 (1977).

In situations involving service contracts, where the new employer takes over all of the contract work performed by its predecessor at the same location, the appropriateness of the single location unit ordinarily will be upheld, and the employing industry will be considered intact.[232] However, where the new service employer successfully solicits only a small part of the contract work, sharing services previously performed by the predecessor with other competitors at the same location, the requisite continuity may be lacking or the employing industry may be considered fragmented.[233]

Even within single locations, the recognized or certified unit of the predecessor may not encompass all of the work force, but only one or two distinct segments. Where the new employer has integrated both the operations and the employees involved, the critical question may be whether the bargaining unit remains sufficiently intact to retain its separate identity.[234] On the other hand, the omission of an employee classification from the predecessor's unit usually does not necessarily present a serious challenge to the continued appropriateness of the unit.[235]

In addition, the Board has found that a purchaser was a successor employer where it purchased only a fragment of the original unit, but where the unit fragment, on its own, constituted a separate appropriate unit under the Board's traditional criteria.[236]

In a case presenting difficult issues of successorship, that is, whether the unit remained appropriate and the *Burns* majority test had been met, the Court of Appeals for the Eleventh Circuit held that such issues should be resolved in the first instance by the Board and not by the courts in a contempt proceeding.[237] The basis of the contempt proceedings was a judicially en-

---

[232]NLRB v. Boston-Needham Indus. Cleaning Co., 526 F2d 74, 90 LRRM 3058 (CA 1), *enforcing* 216 NLRB 26, 88 LRRM 1249 (1975).

[233]Nova Servs. Co., 213 NLRB 95, 88 LRRM 1239 (1974). *See also* Co-Op Trucking Co., 209 NLRB 829, 86 LRRM 1242 (1974); Lincoln Private Police, 189 NLRB 717, 76 LRRM 1727 (1971).

[234]NLRB v. Security-Columbian Banknote Co., *supra* note 223.

[235]Springfield Retirement Residence, 235 NLRB 884, 98 LRRM 1091 (1978).

[236]Stewart Granite Enters., *supra* note 229. *See also* discussion of appropriate bargaining unit, *supra* note 207.

[237]Computer Sciences Corp. v. NLRB, 677 F2d 804, 110 LRRM 2642 (CA 11, 1982); *accord* NLRB v. FMG Indus. dba Gamco Indus., 820 F2d 289, 125 LRRM 3013 (CA 9, 1987). *But see* dissenting opinion, 125 LRRM at 3017, stating that notice and hearing on successorship issue are prerequisites to imposing liability on purchaser of business for predecessor's unfair labor practices; however, due process does not require that initial hearing be conducted by NLRB before contempt proceedings commence.

forced bargaining order which had been issued against the predecessor.[238]

D. The Effect of Hiatus

In *Fall River*,[239] the Supreme Court found a 7-month hiatus between the demise of the predecessor and the start-up of the successor not to be determinative of the successorship question. The Court held that such a hiatus is only one factor in the "substantial continuity" calculus and is relevant when there are other indicia of discontinuity.[240] If other factors indicate a continuity between the enterprises, and the hiatus is a normal start-up period, the totality of the circumstances will suggest a successorship situation. Thus, the Board has held that a hiatus between the predecessor's cessation and the successor's commencement of operations is relevant, though not controlling, to a finding of successorship. In *Grico Corp., Aircraft Magnesium Division*,[241] the Board stated: "It is well settled that a hiatus is only material in determining successorship status where there have been other substantial changes in operations."

The Board has further stated that "the significance of a hiatus to successorship status is its effect on the employees' expectations of rehire."[242] Thus, the Board looks at other factors affecting employees' expectations of rehire, including employer pronouncements of its intention to resume operations.[243]

Successorship was found despite a two-month hiatus between closure and resumption of operations where 85 percent of the

---

[238]*See also* NLRB v. Great Lakes Chem. Corp., Aquabrom Div., 855 F2d 1174, 129 LRRM 2138, *clarified and amended*, 862 F2d 100, 129 LRRM 3140 (CA 6, 1988); *cf.* Food & Commercial Workers Local 1529 v. Chambers Big Star No. 52, 124 LRRM 2120 (WD Tenn, 1986) (issue of successorship not deferred to Board in §301 suit); In re Chadbourne Indus., 132 LRRM 2837 (SD NY, 1989) (bankruptcy court, not NLRB, should rule as to successorship status of trustee); In re Goodman, 873 F2d 598, 131 LRRM 2129 (CA 2, 1989) (NLRB, not bankruptcy court, has primary jurisdiction regarding successorship status). *See also* dissenting opinion in NLRB v. FMC Indus. dba Gamco Indus., *supra* note 237.

[239]Fall River Dyeing & Finishing Corp. v. NLRB, 482 US 27, 45, 125 LRRM 2441, 2448 (1987).

[240]*Id.*

[241]265 NLRB 1344, 112 LRRM 1147, 1149 (1982), *enforced*, 730 F2d 767, 115 LRRM 3712 (CA 9, 1984) (successorship despite 4-week hiatus); *see also* RTW Indus., 296 NLRB No. 116, 132 LRRM 1352 (1989) (successorship despite 2-month hiatus).

[242]112 LRRM at 1149.

[243]Food & Commercial Workers Local 152 v. NLRB, 768 F2d 1463, 119 LRRM 3473 (CA DC, 1985), *enforcing in part, denying enforcement in part and remanding sub nom.* Spencer Foods, 268 NLRB 1483, 115 LRRM 1251 (1984); Inland Container Corp., 275 NLRB 378, 119 LRRM 1089 (1985), *supplementing* 267 NLRB 1187, 114 LRRM 1143 (1983), 273 NLRB 1856, 118 LRRM 1384 (1985) *and* 274 NLRB 887, 118 LRRM 1454 (1985); New Stan Dyeing & Finishing Co., 263 NLRB 1050, 111 LRRM 1601 (1982).

employees worked for the predecessor and, at the time of the predecessor's shutdown, employees were told that the plant would reopen soon and they would be recalled.[244] In another case, the Board found successorship despite a 2½-month hiatus, substantial investment in renovations, and a reduction in the number of job classifications, where the hiatus may have been partly attributable to discrimination in hiring.[245] In *Food & Commercial Workers Local 152 v. NLRB (Spencer Foods)*,[246] the Circuit Court for the District of Columbia reversed the Board and found successorship despite a year-and-a-half hiatus. The court found that employer representations and media disclosures caused employees to perceive their status as being temporarily laid off, rather than terminated, employees.

On the other hand, the Board may take the *absence* of a hiatus as a relevant factor in establishing the continuity of the employing enterprise of successorship status.[247]

E. Determining When the Bargaining Obligation Attaches

The bargaining obligation attaches once a successorship exists, that is, once holdover employees constitute a majority of the new, legally sufficient, complement. The underlying question is *when* the successor employer ceases to be free unilaterally to set initial terms and conditions of employment.

Under *Burns* and *Fall River*, the new employer's bargaining obligation does not attach until the majority of the new employee complement is composed of the predecessor's holdover employees. Until that time, the new employer may set initial terms and conditions of employment.[248] Thereafter, on the date when it

---

[244]New-Stan Dyeing & Finishing Co., *supra* note 243.

[245]Inland Container Corp., *supra* note 243.

[246]*Supra* note 243; *see also* Briggs Plumbingware v. NLRB, 877 F2d 1282, 131 LRRM 2810 (CA 6, 1989) (3-month hiatus insufficient evidence of discontinuity).

[247]*See* EPE v. NLRB, 845 F2d 483, 128 LRRM 2246, 2251 (CA 4, 1988) (absence of hiatus was noted); Phillip Wall & Sons, 287 NLRB 1161, 127 LRRM 1312 (1988); Good N' Fresh Foods, *supra* note 229; Big R. Distribs. dba Shoppers Choice, 280 NLRB 1306, 123 LRRM 1254 (1986); Artcraft Ornamental Iron Co., 271 NLRB 829, 117 LRRM 1230 (1984); Sherwood Trucking Co., 270 NLRB 445, 117 LRRM 1175 (1984), *enforcement denied*, 775 F2d 744, 120 LRRM 3009 (CA 6, 1985); William B. Allen, 267 NLRB 700, 114 LRRM 1104 (1983), *enforced*, 758 F2d 1145, 118 LRRM 3409 (CA 6, 1985), *cert. denied*, 474 US 1101, 121 LRRM 2368 (1986); Alpert's, 267 NLRB 159, 113 LRRM 1150 (1983).

[248]The new employer would, of course, be free to offer terms lower or higher than those of its predecessor. Prior to its own decision in William J. Burns, Int'l Detective Agency, 182 NLRB 348, 74 LRRM 1098 (1970), the Board had regarded the obligations of a successor employer in these circumstances as analogous to the obligations of an employer during the period between collective bargaining agreements. Under that approach, it would have

may be determined that the "majority" test has been met, the successor's position is akin to that of an employer confronted with a newly selected bargaining representative.[249] At that juncture, unilateral changes in existing terms become impermissible.[250] However, if the union fails to make a timely request to bargain, the employer may proceed with implementation of its new terms[251] unless such a request by the union would have been futile.[252]

Before a bargaining obligation may attach to a successor, there must be a clear and unequivocal demand by the union to bargain unless such a request would be futile.[253] A valid request to bargain need not, however, be made in any particular form, so long as the request clearly indicates a desire to negotiate and bargain on behalf of the employees in an appropriate unit.[254]

---

been impermissible for the new employer upon takeover to unilaterally establish substantive terms different from those of its predecessor. *See* Valleydale Packers, 162 NLRB 1486, 64 LRRM 1212 (1967), *enforced*, 402 F2d 768, 69 LRRM 2622 (CA 5, 1968). This view was overturned in *Burns*. *See* Machinists (Boeing Co.) v. NLRB, 595 F2d 664, 671 n.32, 98 LRRM 2787, 2791 n.32 (CA DC, 1978), *cert. denied*, 439 US 1070, 100 LRRM 2268 (1979).

[249]Ranch-Way, Inc., 203 NLRB 911, 83 LRRM 1197 (1973), *supplementing* 183 NLRB 1168, 74 LRRM 1389 (1970).

[250]A checkoff provision is regarded as being of contractual origin only, not carrying over as a statutorily defined "existing term" or condition of employment. *See* S-H Food Serv., 199 NLRB 95, 81 LRRM 1181 (1972), *supplementing* 183 NLRB 1216, 74 LRRM 1418 (1970), where the new employer was held not to have violated the duty to bargain when it refused to continue to comply with such a provision. However, unilateral layoff of 50% of the work force was held a refusal to bargain. M & H Mach. Co., 243 NLRB 817, 102 LRRM 1038 (1979). The same was true for other changes without notice to the union, which had demanded bargaining. L.A.X. Medical Clinic, 248 NLRB 861, 104 LRRM 1092 (1980).

[251]Collinge Enters., 210 NLRB 52, 86 LRRM 1086 (1974); *see* Briggs Plumbingware v. NLRB, *supra* note 246 (the concurrence of two events obligates a successor: hiring a substantial and representative complement of predecessor's employees and demand for recognition); Machinists (Boeing Co.) v. NLRB, *supra* note 248, at 675–76, 98 LRRM at 2793, where the court noted that absent a bargaining demand, the new employer can simply institute its hiring terms as the beginning terms of employment, as was done in William J. Burns Int'l Detective Agency, *supra* note 248. The opposite conclusion was reached where the union had not been made aware of the unilateral changes. Pinewood Care Center, 242 NLRB 816, 101 LRRM 1490 (1979).

[252]Armco, Eastern Steel Div., Ashland Works, 279 NLRB 1184, 123 LRRM 1335 (1986), *enforced in part and remanded in part*, 832 F2d 357, 126 LRRM 2961 (CA 6, 1987), *cert. denied*, 486 US 1042, 130 LRRM 2800 (1988) (refusal to bargain violation when successor announced its anticipatory repudiation of its bargaining duty, even though this occurred more than 4 months before union's first official demand for bargaining); Central Am. Airways, 204 NLRB 161, 83 LRRM 1314 (1973). However, where the demand made upon the successor was confined solely to insistence that it execute a labor agreement, it was held not to constitute a proper request for bargaining so as to obligate the successor to bargain. East Belden Corp., 239 NLRB 776, 100 LRRM 1077 (1978); Atlas Graphics, 227 NLRB 136, 94 LRRM 1252 (1976).

[253]*See* Briggs Plumbingware v. NLRB, *supra* note 246; *see also* Armco, Eastern Steel Div., Ashland Works, *supra* note 252.

[254]Al Landers Dump Truck, 192 NLRB 207, 77 LRRM 1729 (1971); *see also* NLRB v. Great Lakes Chem. Corp., Aquabrom Div., *supra* note 238 (continuing demand established by unit's repeated efforts to force predecessor to bargain, despite lack of formal request for 15 months after purchase); Indianapolis Mack Sales & Serv., 288 NLRB 1123,

When a union's request for bargaining has been rejected by the new employer, the demand is continuing and the union is not required to renew the demand later, even if the successor's bargaining obligation was not mature at the time of the original request.[255]

The content of the initial terms offered at the time of hire, as contrasted to those offered or implemented after the bargaining obligation matures, may determine whether the new employer violates section 8(a)(5) by unilaterally changing terms and conditions of employment. The test appears to be whether the unilateral changes were encompassed within the offer or initial terms set forth prior to the time the bargaining obligation ripened.[256]

The major point of controversy as to when the bargaining obligation matures has concerned the exception carved out by the Supreme Court's dictum in *Burns* for "instances in which it is perfectly clear that the new employer plans to retain all of the employees in the unit."[257] In those instances, the Court stated, it will be "appropriate" for the new employer to "initially consult with the employees' bargaining representative before he fixes terms."[258] In some cases since *Burns*, the employer's plans to retain "all of the employees" have been found to be "perfectly clear." Where the offer of employment is unequivocal, or where the new employer has committed itself to hire all of the old unit employees (with no indication at the same time that they would be expected to work under new or different terms), the requirement of initial bargaining has been upheld by the Board with general court approval.[259]

---

130 LRRM 1240 (1988) (demand for bargaining must be made specifically regarding appropriate unit); Trucking Water Air Corp., 276 NLRB 1401, 120 LRRM 1199 (1985) (holding that union agent's request to "discuss the situation" with new employer's president constituted valid bargaining demand). *Cf.* Valu Warehouse Foods, 270 NLRB 316, 116 LRRM 1146 (1984) (holding that new employer did not unlawfully refuse to bargain with union where new employer requested proof of union's claim that it had contract with predecessor).

[255]Fall River Dyeing & Finishing Corp. v. NLRB, *supra* note 239; *but see* Royal Midtown Chrysler Plymouth, 296 NLRB No. 135, 133 LRRM 1165 (1989) (no duty to bargain where demand was made after previous majority status had dissipated).

[256]*See* NLRB v. Dent, 534 F2d 844, 91 LRRM 3007 (CA 9, 1976); NLRB v. Bachrodt Chevrolet Co., 468 F2d 963, 81 LRRM 2244 (CA 7, 1972), *enforcing in part* 186 NLRB 1035, 76 LRRM 1597 (1970); East Belden Corp., *supra* note 252; Central Am. Airways, *supra* note 252; S-H Food Serv., *supra* note 250.

[257]NLRB v. Burns Int'l Sec. Servs., 406 US 272, 294–95, 80 LRRM 2225, 2233 (1972).

[258]*Id.* at 295, 80 LRRM at 2234.

[259]*See* NLRB v. World Evangelism, 656 F2d 1349, 108 LRRM 2573 (CA 9, 1981); Spitzer Akron v. NLRB, 540 F2d 841, 92 LRRM 3007 (CA 6, 1976), *cert. denied*, 429 US 1040, 94

Also, the Board has held that if it is "perfectly clear" that the employer plans to retain a sufficient number of predecessor employees to pass the "majority test," though not "all" the predecessor employees, this also creates a duty to bargain over initial terms.[260]

On the other hand, where the offer of employment is tentative or conditional upon acceptance of the terms offered, the exception requiring initial bargaining has not been applied. In *Spruce-Up Corp.*,[261] the lead case on conditional recruitment, the suc-

---

LRRM 2202 (1977); Howard Johnson Co., 198 NLRB 763, 80 LRRM 1769 (1972), *enforced*, 496 F2d 532, 86 LRRM 2688 (CA 9, 1974). In Nazareth Regional High School v. NLRB, 549 F2d 873, 94 LRRM 2897 (CA 2, 1977), *enforcing in part sub nom.* Roman Catholic Diocese of Brooklyn, 222 NLRB 1052, 91 LRRM 1419 (1976), however, the Court of Appeals for the Second Circuit appeared to consider as crucial the absence of a commitment to retain existing terms rather than an announcement of new terms. The court disagreed with the Board's position, concluding that Spruce-Up Corp., 209 NLRB 194, 85 LRRM 1426 (1974), cannot be limited to the narrow factual circumstance wherein the successor told the union that retention would be on new terms *at the same time* that it promised to rehire the entire unit. "The important consideration in determining whether it is perfectly clear that a successor intends to retain all the employees, is whether they have all been promised reemployment on the existing terms." Nazareth Regional High School, *supra*, at 881, 94 LRRM at 2900. Nevertheless, the Board (and the Ninth Circuit) adheres to its position that the *Burns* exception is operative where the new employer's previously announced plan to retain all predecessor employees is not qualified by any announcement that the new employer clearly intends to establish new conditions of employment. *See, e.g.*, NLRB v. World Evangelism, *supra* (employer must bargain where it did not express intent to modify terms before rehiring); Fremont Ford Sales dba Fremont Ford, 289 NLRB 1290, 131 LRRM 1074 (1988); Sahara Las Vegas, 284 NLRB 337, 128 LRRM 1085 (1987), *enforced*, 886 F2d 1320 (CA 9, 1989) (recognition based on determination of majority status of work force unlawfully delayed until end of 90-day probationary period imposed on predecessor's union employees); Armco, Eastern Steel Div., Ashland Works, *supra* note 252; E G & G Fla., 279 NLRB 444, 123 LRRM 1278 (1986) (Board found that phrase "plans to retain all the employees in the unit" would cover not only situation where successor's plan includes every employee in unit, but also situations where it includes lesser number but still enough to make it evident that union's majority status will continue); Royal Vending Serv., 275 NLRB 1222, 120 LRRM 1044 (1985); Michael J. Malone & Bob Burkheimer dba Sorrento Hotel, 266 NLRB 350, 112 LRRM 1358 (1983); Stewart Granite Enters., 255 NLRB 569, 107 LRRM 1182 (1981); Gardena Buena Ventura, 242 NLRB 595, 101 LRRM 1248 (1979), *enforced*, 618 F2d 115, 108 LRRM 2104 (CA 9, 1980); Joe Costa Trucking Co., 238 NLRB 1516, 99 LRRM 1719 (1978), *enforced sub nom.* NLRB v. Edjo, Inc., 631 F2d 604, 105 LRRM 3061 (CA 9, 1980); Starco Farmers Mkt., 237 NLRB 373, 98 LRRM 1587 (1978); L.A. Beefland, 232 NLRB 1189, 96 LRRM 1481 (1977), *enforced*, 601 F2d 603, 106 LRRM 3076 (CA 9, 1979). In East Belden Corp., *supra* note 252, the same test was applied as of the time the purchaser took control (though it announced that it intended to make changes when escrow closed). In Kallmann dba Love's Barbeque Restaurant No. 62, 245 NLRB 78, 102 LRRM 1546 (1979), *remanded in part*, 640 F2d 1094, 107 LRRM 2011 (CA 9, 1981), the Board applied the same test because it was "perfectly clear" that, but for its union animus, the employer would have hired all of the predecessor's employees. *Accord* Garrison Valley Center, 246 NLRB 700, 102 LRRM 1666 (1979). *See supra* notes 55–56 and accompanying text.

[260]Applebaum Indus., 294 NLRB 981, 133 LRRM 1083 (1989); E G & G Fla., *supra* note 259.

[261]*Supra* note 259. *See also* Machinists (Boeing Co.) v. NLRB, *supra* note 248, at 671 n.32, where the court noted that the decision to retain the former employees was "inseparable' from the decision to "cling" to a scale of lower terms; Ranch-Way, Inc., *supra* note 249; Valley Nitrogen Producers, 207 NLRB 208, 84 LRRM 1424 (1973).

cessor employer expressed a general willingness to hire all of the predecessor's employees, but at the same time indicated that different commission rates would be paid. Since employment depended upon their willingness to accept those terms, and the possibility existed that they would not, the Board majority did not regard it as "perfectly clear" that the employer "planned to retain" all of the predecessor's employees.

In *Spruce-Up* and in other comparable cases,[262] the Board (by divided votes) has generally drawn the line in favor of permitting the new employer to set its initial terms and conditions of employment, on the ground that a new employer would otherwise be reluctant to comment "favorably at all upon employment prospects of old employees for fear he would thereby forfeit his right to unilaterally set initial terms . . . ."[263] The guideline formulated in *Spruce-Up*, which would permit such favorable forecasts, is that

> the caveat in Burns, therefore, should be restricted to circumstances in which the new employer has either actively or, by tacit inference, misled employees into believing they would all be retained without change in their wages, hours, or conditions of employment, or at least to circumstances where the new employer, unlike the Respondent here, has failed to clearly announce its intent to establish a new set of conditions prior to inviting former employees to accept employment.[264]

In *Saks & Co.*,[265] however, a divided Board panel took a limiting view of *Spruce-Up* and decided that (as between affiliated

---

[262]Premium Foods, 260 NLRB 708, 717, 109 LRRM 1328, 1331 (1982), *enforced*, 709 F2d 623, 113 LRRM 3261 (CA 9, 1983). *See also* Holiday Inn of Victorville, 284 NLRB 916, 126 LRRM 1203 (1987); Clair Mfg. Co., 15 A.M.R. §25.052 (Advice Memorandum, 1987); Harbor Cartage, 269 NLRB 927, 116 LRRM 1016 (1984); Half-Century, Inc., 241 NLRB 555, 100 LRRM 1547 (1979); United Maintenance & Mfg. Co., 214 NLRB 529, 536 n.21, 87 LRRM 1469 (1974); Anita Shops, Inc., 211 NLRB 501, 86 LRRM 1347 (1974); Boeing Co., 214 NLRB 541, 87 LRRM 1461 (1974), *aff'd sub nom.* Machinists v. NLRB, 595 F2d 664, 98 LRRM 2787 (CA DC, 1978), *cert. denied*, 439 US 1070, 100 LRRM 2268 (1979). An extensive discussion of the *Spruce-Up* issue is contained in Machinists v. NLRB, *supra*, where the union encouraged the employees of the predecessor to refuse employment at a diminished wage scale.

[263]209 NLRB at 195, 85 LRRM at 1428. The dissenting view is that the possibility of the predecessor's employees' refusal of employment has nothing to do with the "plans" or the intent of the offering employer. The dissenting members in these cases would have found the new employer obligated to bargain "as soon as it manifests an intent to look primarily to the predecessor's unit employees to fill its work force." United Maintenance & Mfg. Co., *supra* note 262, at 536 n.21.

[264]209 NLRB at 195, 85 LRRM at 1428 (footnote omitted). *See* Spitzer Akron v. NLRB, *supra* note 259, where the court found that sufficient evidence existed to establish that the employees were misled by "tacit inference" into believing they would be retained without changes in employment conditions.

[265]Saks & Co. dba Saks Fifth Ave., 247 NLRB 1047, 103 LRRM 1241 (1980), *enforcement denied in part*, 634 F2d 681, 105 LRRM 3274 (CA 2, 1980).

companies, at least) the new employer's immediate interviews with prior employees and reference to their past service credit under a pension plan were sufficient to make it "perfectly clear" that the successor intended to hire all of the predecessor's employees, even though it did not do so. The decision gave little attention to whether employment was conditioned on those employees' acceptance of different terms. The Court of Appeals for the Second Circuit denied enforcement on this point.

In some cases, it may be uncertain whether the new employer has made its hiring plans "perfectly clear" to all, or only to a specific segment, of the predecessor's work force. In one such case, the Board found, and the Court of Appeals for the Ninth Circuit affirmed, that the announced intention to hire encompassed all employees. The Board's bargaining order was enforced even though many of those employees were not hired, and a holdover majority did not exist.[266]

The Board has held that when a successor employer had discriminated against former employees in hiring and it can be inferred that substantially all of the former employees would have been retained absent the unlawful discrimination, the successor employer is not free to set initial terms and conditions of employment without consulting the union.[267]

IV. SUCCESSORSHIP AND THE CONTRACTUAL OBLIGATION

A. The "Alter Ego" Employer

A successor, under *Burns*,[268] is not obligated to assume and is not bound by the substantive provisions of the labor agreement of its predecessor. However, where the new employer is not merely a successor but is the *alter ego* of the predecessor, that is, the former and present employer are, in reality, the same or substantially identical entity, the predecessor's labor contract binds the "new" employer. In making this determination, the Board has stated that it will find an alter ego status "where the

---

[266]Bellingham Frozen Foods v. NLRB, 626 F2d 674, 105 LRRM 2404 (CA 9, 1980), *enforcing in part* 237 NLRB 1450, 99 LRRM 1270 (1978), *cert. denied*, 449 US 1125, 106 LRRM 2256 (1981).

[267]*See supra* notes 170–171 and accompanying text.

[268]NLRB v. Burns Int'l Sec. Servs., supra note 257.

two enterprises have 'substantially identical' management, business purpose, operation, equipment, customers and supervision, as well as ownership."[269]

In successorship cases, the continuity of the employee complement provides the threshold linkage between the old and the new employer. In alter ego cases, the substantial identity of employer ownership and control provides that threshold linkage. Thus, the fact that a new employer is not a successor does not preclude a finding that it is an alter ego.[270] Nor, of course, will a finding that the new employer is not an alter ego preclude a finding that it is a successor.[271]

In business transfer situations, the Board still maintains the established distinction between "successor" employers, who are generally not bound by the terms of the predecessor's agreement with the union but are obligated to bargain with the union, and alter ego employers, who are bound by the substantive terms of the agreement between the predecessor employer and union.[272] Alter ego cases, however, are not limited to situations involving transfer of a business enterprise. Two ostensibly separate employers, both of which continue in business, may be found to be alter egos of one another in appropriate circumstances.[273]

---

[269]Crawford Door Sales Co., 226 NLRB 1144, 94 LRRM 1393 (1976); *see also* Marquis Printing Corp. & Mutual Lithograph Co., 213 NLRB 394, 87 LRRM 1642 (1974). *See also* Chapter 22, "Secondary Strikes and Picketing," at notes 243–257, for discussion of §8(b)(4) implications of the alter ego doctrine.

[270]*See* Schultz Painting & Decorating Co., 202 NLRB 111, 82 LRRM 1680 (1973).

[271]Jersey Juniors, 230 NLRB 329, 95 LRRM 1283 (1977); Bell Co., 243 NLRB 977, 101 LRRM 1572 (1979), *supplementing* 225 NLRB 474, 93 LRRM 1180 (1976), *enforced in part*, 561 F2d 1264, 96 LRRM 2437 (CA 7, 1977), where a divided Board held that the issue of successorship could be litigated on remand even though the General Counsel had relied solely on the theory of alter ego in the original hearing and a finding of alter ego had been rejected by the Court of Appeals for the Seventh Circuit in NLRB v. Bell Co., 561 F2d 1264, 96 LRRM 2437 (CA 7, 1977).

[272]McAllister Bros., 278 NLRB 601, 123 LRRM 1040 (1986), *enforced*, 819 F2d 439, 125 LRRM 2566 (CA 4, 1987); Pinter Bros., 263 NLRB 723, 111 LRRM 1254 (1982); Morton Dev. Corp., 287 NLRB 385, 127 LRRM 1113 (1987), *review granted and remanded sub nom.* Hospital & Health Care Employees Dist. 1199 v. NLRB, 864 F2d 1096, 130 LRRM 2201 (CA 3, 1989) (fundamental changes in nature of operations may justify withdrawal of recognition from incumbent union, even if other alter ego factors are present). For further analysis of alter ego cases, *see* Chapter 13, "The Duty to Bargain," Part XII.

[273]*See, e.g.*, Milford Servs., 294 NLRB 684, 132 LRRM 1079 (1989); Precision Builders, R.S., 296 NLRB No. 15, 132 LRRM 1049 (1989); C.E.K. Indus. Mechanical Contractors, 295 NLRB No. 70, 131 LRRM 1737 (1989); McAllister Bros., *supra* note 272. In addition, where an individual not only owns a corporation, but totally dominates it, and also intermingles corporate and individual assets and liabilities, the Board may conclude that the individual should be deemed the alter ego of the corporation. O'Neill Ltd., 288 NLRB 1354, 129 LRRM 1315 (1988); Weldment Corp. dba Yankee Roller Guide, 275 NLRB 1432, 120 LRRM 1055 (1985); Campo Slacks, 266 NLRB 492, 112 LRRM 1432 (1983).

In addition to being bound by its predecessor's agreement, the alter ego employer has "the same obligation to employees as the original employer."[274] This obligation includes liability for the predecessor's unremedied unfair labor practices[275] and the duty to bargain with the union.[276]

While the effects of an alter ego finding are well settled, the criteria upon which an alter ego finding turns are subject to some variation.

The leading Board decision in the application of alter ego criteria is *Crawford Door Sales Co.*[277] There, a company that sold and installed garage doors was held to be the alter ego of a liquidated company that engaged in the same operation. Both enterprises were wholly owned by members of the same family.[278] Since there were substantially identical managements, business purposes, operations, equipment, customers, and supervision, alter ego status was established. Similarly, where the operations of one enterprise had been transferred to another enterprise, both of which were almost totally owned by the same individual,[279] or by the same parent company,[280] a finding of alter ego status resulted. For example, a nonunion company to which a unionized company had transferred its operations was

---

[274]Custom Mfg. Co., 259 NLRB 614, 109 LRRM 1002 (1981); Shearer dba George C. Shearer Exhibitors Delivery Serv., 262 NLRB 622, 110 LRRM 1337 (1982), *enforced*, 714 F2d 124, 114 LRRM 2976 (CA 3, 1983).

[275]NLRB v. Borg-Warner Corp., 663 F2d 666, 108 LRRM 2862 (CA 6, 1981), *cert. denied*, 457 US 1105, 110 LRRM 2608 (1982).

[276]NLRB v. Tricor Prods., 636 F2d 266, 105 LRRM 3271 (CA 10, 1980). However, pursuant to the principles enunciated in John Deklewa & Sons, 282 NLRB 1375, 124 LRRM 1185 (1987), *enforced sub nom.* Iron Workers Local 3 v. NLRB, 843 F2d 770, 128 LRRM 2020 (CA 3), *cert. denied*, 488 US 889, 129 LRRM 2528 (1988), a nonunion construction company which is the alter ego of a defunct union construction company will not be required to continue a §8(f) relationship beyond the term of the defunct company's last collective bargaining agreement. MIS, 289 NLRB 491, 128 LRRM 1273 (1988). But if the union firm continues to exist, and has not repudiated the §8(f) bargaining relationship, the mere existence of an alter ego company at the time a bargaining agreement is entered into will not be deemed a retroactive repudiation within the meaning of *Deklewa*. William N. Taylor, Inc., 288 NLRB 1049, 129 LRRM 1219 (1988).

[277]*Supra* note 269. For a discussion of related cases involving dual employer operations or the "double-breasted" issue, *see* Chapter 13, "The Duty to Bargain," at notes 960–1004.

[278]Family relationship has been viewed by the Board as a factor in determining common ownership and control. Blake Constr. Co., 245 NLRB 630, 102 LRRM 1471 (1979), *enforcement denied in part*, 663 F2d 272, 108 LRRM 2136 (CA DC, 1981); McDonald's Ready-Mix Concrete & Jim's Ready Mix, 246 NLRB 152, 102 LRRM 1501 (1979); Shield-Pacific, Ltd. & West Haw. Concrete, 245 NLRB 409, 102 LRRM 1497 (1979), *enforced*, 647 F2d 172, 108 LRRM 2176 (CA 9, 1981). *But see* NLRB v. Bell Co., *supra* note 271. However, such relationship is not dispositive, especially where other factors show that the transaction is at arm's length. Joe Costa Trucking Co., *supra* note 259.

[279]P.A. Hayes, Inc., 226 NLRB 230, 94 LRRM 1080 (1976).

[280]Republic Engraving & Designing Co., 236 NLRB 1150, 99 LRRM 1306 (1978).

found to be an alter ego where the same individual owned both companies.[281]

Since *Crawford*, the Board has held that two or more persons or entities are alter egos of one another where they share "substantially identical management, business purpose, operations, equipment, customers and supervision, as well as ownership."[282] The existence or lack of a motive to avoid the labor obligations of one of the two entities is also a factor.[283] Where one entity ceases operations, the lapse of a significant period of time (a hiatus) before a related entity begins operations may militate against alter ego status.[284]

No one factor is determinative, and not all of the above factors must be present.[285] Common ownership is an important element,[286] but the Board has said that common ownership is neither "critical" nor a "necessary predicate."[287] Although com-

---

[281]P.A. Hayes, Inc., *supra* note 279.

[282]Advance Elec., 268 NLRB 1001, 1002, 115 LRRM 1220 (1984). *See also* Milford Servs., *supra* note 273; Ford Bros., 294 NLRB 107, 132 LRRM 1346 (1989); Image Convention Servs., 290 NLRB 422, 129 LRRM 1079 (1988) (applying these criteria and denying alter ego status); Kenmore Contracting, 289 NLRB 336, 128 LRRM 1227 (1988) Unbelievable Fashions, 286 NLRB No. 78, 126 LRRM 1239 (1987) (applying these criteria and finding alter ego status); Denzil S. Alkire, 259 NLRB 1323, 109 LRRM 1107 (1982), *enforcement denied*, 716 F2d 1014, 114 LRRM 2180 (CA 4, 1983); Shellmaker, 265 NLRB 749, 112 LRRM 1072 (1982). *See also* MIS, *supra* note 276 (that two entities occupy same building may indicate alter ego status).

[283]Perma Coatings, 293 NLRB 803, 132 LRRM 1329 (1989) (sincere motivation for creation of new corporation does not preclude alter ego relationship, but absence of union animus generally militates against finding disguised continuance of predecessor); Vainio dba Professional Eye Care, 289 NLRB 738, 131 LRRM 1230 (1988) (no alter ego finding since no showing of antiunion animus); Bufco Corp., 291 NLRB 1015, 130 LRRM 1116 (1988); Image Convention Servs., *supra* note 282; Haley & Haley, 289 NLRB 649, 128 LRRM 1319 (1988), *enforced*, 880 F2d 1147, 132 LRRM 2119 (CA 9, 1989); Continental Radiator Corp., 283 NLRB 234, 124 LRRM 1288 (1987); Market King, 282 NLRB 876, 124 LRRM 1150, 1150 n.3 (1987) (evidence of unlawful antiunion motivation in creation of corporation is relevant, but not essential to finding of alter ego status); Alabama Metal Prods., 280 NLRB 1090, 124 LRRM 1037 (1986); Gilroy Sheet Metal, 280 NLRB 1075, 123 LRRM 1012 (1986); Apex Decorating Co., 275 NLRB 1459, 120 LRRM 1061 (1985); Advance Elec., *supra* note 282.

[284]MIS, *supra* note 276; Cadet Constr. Co., 287 NLRB 564, 127 LRRM 1148 (1987), *enforced sub nom.* NLRB v. Laborers Local 1140, 861 F2d 531, 129 LRRM 2973 (CA 8, 1988).

[285]MIS, *supra* note 276.

[286]*See, e.g.*, Blackberry Creek Trucking, 291 NLRB 474, 131 LRRM 1337 (1988); Superior Export Packing Co., 284 NLRB 1169, 126 LRRM 1040 (1987), *enforced sub nom.* Meadowlands Hy-Pro Indus. v. NLRB, 845 F2d 1013, 129 LRRM 2528 (CA 3, 1988); Clinton Foods, 240 NLRB 1246, 100 LRRM 1416 (1979), *enforcement denied sub nom.* Meat Cutters Local 567 v. NLRB, 663 F2d 223, 106 LRRM 2187 (CA DC, 1980); Crawford Door Sales Co., *supra* note 269.

[287]Bryar Constr. Co., 240 NLRB 102, 104, 100 LRRM 1271 (1979). *See also* Woodline Motor Freight, 278 NLRB 1141, 122 LRRM 1355 (1986), *enforcement granted in part*, 843 F2d 285, 127 LRRM 3260 (CA 8, 1988).

mon ownership is not a prerequisite for an alter ego finding, the Board has pointed out that it has found such a relationship absent common ownership only where both companies were either wholly owned by members of the same family or nearly totally owned by the same individual,[288] or where the older company continued to maintain substantial control over the business claimed to have been sold to the new company.[289]

Family relationships will not result in an alter ego finding absent other indications of alter ego status.[290] Thus, the Board dismissed allegations that a company owned by a husband and wife was the alter ego of their son's company where the parents' participation in the son's company (including the father's 20-percent stock ownership) was insufficient to overcome other evidence establishing that the businesses were operated separately.[291] The Board also rejected alter ego contentions despite family ownership of both companies, where transactions between the two entities were at arm's length and management, customers, and equipment were distinct.[292]

Likewise, no alter ego relationship was established between two partnerships in the general construction business where the first partnership consisted of two coequal partners who later became two of seven coequal partners in the second part-

---

[288]NLRB v. Amateyus dba Volk & Huxley, 817 F2d 996, 125 LRRM 2329 (CA 2), *cert. denied*, 484 US 925, 126 LRRM 2776 (1987); Nelson Elec. v. NLRB, 638 F2d 965, 106 LRRM 2393 (CA 6, 1981); William N. Taylor, Inc., *supra* note 276; Kenmore Contracting, *supra* note 282; Fullerton Transfer & Storage, 291 NLRB 426, 130 LRRM 1456 (1988); Superior Export Packing Co., *supra* note 286.

[289]Superior Export Packing Co., *supra* note 286. *See, e.g.*, McAllister Bros., *supra* note 272 (companies were alter egos despite lack of any common equity ownership, where one company dominated the other through sales and consulting agreements and extensions of credit). *See also* O'Neill Ltd., *supra* note 273 (§10(b) period tolled during fraudulent concealment of alter ego relationship, where one company purported to go out of business, but in fact continued operations through control of an ostensibly independent company); All Kind Quilting, 266 NLRB 1186, 113 LRRM 1129 (1983) (alter ego relationship found between two companies despite lack of common equity ownership).

[290]*E.g.*, Twin Cities Elec., 296 NLRB No. 129, 132 LRRM 1307 (1989).

[291]Victor Valley Heating & Air Conditioning, 267 NLRB 1292, 114 LRRM 1196 (1983); *see also* Oklahoma City E. Express, 281 NLRB 921, 124 LRRM 1107 (1986) (ownership of 19.8% of business by family member by itself is insufficient evidence to support finding of alter ego status).

[292]Friederich Truck Serv., 259 NLRB 1294, 109 LRRM 1112 (1982); *see also* First Class Maintenance Serv., 289 NLRB 484, 128 LRRM 1334 (1988) (son's new nonunion cleaning company, which took over accounts from parents' cleaning company, was nonetheless not alter ego of parents' company, where son had significant business experience, and was independent of, and not financially controlled by, parents or their company); Carpenters Dist. Council of W. Pa. v. W.O. Kessell, Inc., 487 F Supp 54, 107 LRRM 2211 (WD Pa, 1980) (alter ego allegations rejected, despite family's common ownership of two entities, where purchaser of union entity continued to honor collective bargaining agreement). *Cf.* Kenmore Contracting, *supra* note 282.

nership.[293] It was also persuasive that no employees worked for both partnerships at the same time, the business records consistently reflected separate identities, and neither of the two coequal partners played any part in the day-to-day operations of the second partnership.

It is particularly true of alter ego issues that "each case must turn on its own facts."[294] Certain facts may not be probative, however, even if they reflect relationships and practices common to both entities. Thus, in a case where an alter ego relationship was found, the Board specifically disavowed reliance upon the facts that the two enterprises used the services of the same attorney, the same accountant, and the same bank.[295]

The Board's tests for alter ego status are not uniformly accepted by the courts.[296] Different tribunals not only may rely on somewhat different criteria but also may attach different weight to the criteria selected. Thus, in *NLRB v. Bell Co.*,[297] the Court of Appeals for the Seventh Circuit rejected the Board's conclusion that a proprietorship was the alter ego of a corporation, even though the proprietor had formerly been the president of the corporation that had been engaged in a similar business. Noting that the cases relied upon by the Board emphasized common ownership and control, the court concluded that the proprietor was not the prior *owner* of the corporation and there was no evidence that the prior corporate owners owned or controlled the proprietorship. As for the control over the corporation, the court was unwilling to find that the president, who served "at the pleasure of the owners" and whose "authority was subject to restrictions imposed by them,"[298] necessarily controlled the corporation.

---

[293]United Constructors & Goodwin Constr. Co., 233 NLRB 904, 97 LRRM 1409 (1977).

[294]Crawford Door Sales Co., 226 NLRB 1144, 94 LRRM 1393, 1394 (1976). One example concerned a contracting business where a noncontrolling 50% interest was owned by the same person who had previously owned and controlled a liquidated business in the same field. Operationally, the owner, who handled both the "inside" office work and "outside" field operations of the predecessor, confined his role in the new business to that of "outside" operations. Because of markedly divergent labor relations and operational structures, the Board held that he did not constitute an alter ego relationship. John Fender Elec. Co., 244 NLRB 957, 102 LRRM 1398 (1979).

[295]Farmingdale Iron Works, 249 NLRB 98, 98 n.2, 104 LRRM 1210 (1980), *enforced*, 661 F2d 910, 109 LRRM 2360 (CA 2, 1981).

[296]*See, e.g.*, Haley & Haley v. NLRB, 880 F2d 1147, 132 LRRM 2119 (CA 9, 1989); NLRB v. Campbell-Harris Elec., 719 F2d 292, 114 LRRM 2881 (CA 8, 1983) (holding that alter ego finding is based upon substantial identity of ownership, management, business purpose, operation, equipment, customers, and supervision).

[297]561 F2d 1264, 96 LRRM 2437 (CA 7, 1977).

[298]*Id.* at 1268, 96 LRRM at 2439.

In *J.M. Tanaka Construction v. NLRB*,[299] the Court of Appeals for the Ninth Circuit identified "(1) centralized control of labor relations, (2) common management, (3) interrelation of operations, and (4) common ownership and financial control" as factors a court must consider in deciding alter ego questions. In finding an alter ego relationship in *Tanaka* the court concluded that the "most important single factor is centralized control of labor relations,"[300] but also noted that there was "substantially undisputed" evidence that the nonunion company was created for the purpose of avoiding the high cost of dealing with the union.[301]

The Ninth Circuit reiterated the test it used in *Tanaka* in *Haley & Haley v. NLRB*.[302] Although in *Haley & Haley* it acknowledged that the most important single factor in the alter ego analysis is centralized control over labor relations, it emphasized that a threshold determination as to whether both companies are substantially owned and controlled by identical parties must be made in every alter ego case. Under this analysis, the *Haley & Haley* court concluded that Oceanway, a company to which Haley & Haley transferred its assets, was the alter ego of Haley & Haley where the two were owned and controlled by the same parties, the management was identical, there was centralized control over labor relations, and the operations of the two entities were interrelated. In addition, the court found it signifi-

---

[299]675 F2d 1029, 110 LRRM 2296, 2299 (CA 9, 1982), *enforcing* 249 NLRB 238, 104 LRRM 1219 (1980).

[300]*Id.* at 1034, 110 LRRM at 2299. The four factors examined by the *Tanaka* court also comprise the Board's "Single employer" test. *See* Chapter 22, "Secondary Strikes and Picketing," at notes 254–257. Single-employer status alone, however, does not impose one entity's labor contracts on the operations of the other, at least in the absence of an "accretion" or "single appropriate bargaining unit." *See* South Prairie Constr. Co. v. Operating Eng'rs Local 627 (Peter Kiewit Sons' Co.), 425 US 800, 92 LRRM 2507 (1976), *on remand*, 231 NLRB 76, 95 LRRM 1510 (1977); Geo. V. Hamilton, Inc., 289 NLRB 1335, 129 LRRM 1067 (1988); *cf.* Alabama Metal Prods., 280 NLRB 1090, 124 LRRM 1037 (1986). *See also* Chapter 13, "The Duty to Bargain," at notes 960–1004. The Board has acknowledged the interrelated nature of its "single employer" and "alter ego" standards. *See, e.g.*, Las Villas Produce, 279 NLRB 883, 123 LRRM 1124 (1986); Mine Workers Dist. 23 (Kentucky Lake Dock Co.), 271 NLRB 461, 116 LRRM 1487 (1984) (alter ego test may be equated with basic criteria for single-employer finding, but with "more required").

[301]675 F2d at 1035, 110 LRRM at 2300. *See also* Carpenters Local 1478 v. Stevens, 743 F2d 1271, 1276 n.6, 117 LRRM 2023, 2025 n.6 (CA 9, 1984), *cert. denied*, 471 US 1015, 118 LRRM 3344 (1985), where the court noted that the single-employer and alter ego tests are not identical, in that alter ego cases involve the additional determination that "the nonunion entity is a sham attempt to avoid the employer's obligations under the labor agreement."

[302]*Supra* note 296.

cant that Oceanway was activated for purposes of eliminating the high cost of dealing with the union.

The Court of Appeals for the Fourth Circuit, in *Denzil S. Alkire v. NLRB*,[303] reviewed the reaction of other circuit courts to the Board's alter ego decisions. It then applied a two-part test incorporating (1) the general criteria relied upon by the Board, and (2) an analysis of whether the business transfer resulted in, or could reasonably be expected to result in, a benefit to the employer by relieving it of its labor obligations. In *NLRB v. McAllister Brothers*,[304] that court held that while imposition of alter ego status under the *Alkire* test does not hinge on proof of an unlawful employer motive, such a showing will usually satisfy the second part of the *Alkire* test.[305]

There has been some difference of opinion, or at least of terminology, among the circuit courts regarding the significance of unlawful motivation in alter ego cases.

In *Penntech Papers v. NLRB*,[306] the Court of Appeals for the First Circuit held that a court finding that two companies were not alter egos did not collaterally estop the Board from finding that the same two companies constituted a single employer. The court concluded that the "single employer" issue was distinct from that of "alter ego" status, because "unlawful intent or motive are critical inquiries in an alter ego matter which are wholly absent in a single employer analysis."[307]

Citing *Penntech* for the proposition that the focus of the alter ego test is on the existence of an intent to evade labor law obligations, in *Iowa Express Distribution v. NLRB*,[308] the Court of Appeals for the Eighth Circuit enforced a Board alter ego finding.

In *NLRB v. Allcoast Transfer*,[309] the Sixth Circuit enforced a Board alter ego holding, rejecting the company's contention that unlawful motive is a precondition to an alter ego finding. The

---

[303]716 F2d 1014, 114 LLRM 2180 (CA 4, 1983).

[304]819 F2d 439, 125 LRRM 2566 (CA 4, 1987).

[305]*Id.* at 445 n.14, 125 LRRM 2572 n.14.

[306]706 F2d 18, 113 LRRM 2219 (CA 1), *cert. denied*, 464 US 892, 114 LRRM 2648 (1983).

[307]*Id.* at 24, 113 LRRM at 2223.

[308]739 F2d 1305, 116 LRRM 3224 (CA 8), *cert. denied*, 469 US 1088, 117 LRRM 3232 (1984), *reh'g denied*, 470 US 1024 (1985). *See also* Crest Tankers v. National Maritime Union, 796 F2d 234, 122 LRRM 3237 (CA 8, 1986), *aff'd on remand*, 665 F Supp 1431, 126 LRRM 3350 (ED Mo, 1987); NLRB v. Campbell-Harris Elec., 719 F2d 292, 114 LRRM 2881 (CA 8, 1983).

[309]780 F2d 576, 121 LRRM 2393 (CA 6, 1986).

court noted (based on *Penntech* and *Iowa Express*) that the First and Eighth circuits require a showing of intent to evade labor obligations to support an alter ego finding,[310] but declined to adopt this position. Instead, the Sixth Circuit joined the Second Circuit[311] in expressly holding that unlawful motivation is a relevant factor, but not a necessary element in alter ego analysis.

Noting the absence of common ownership (measured by percentage of stock) between a supermarket that closed and one that opened in the same location, the Circuit Court for the District of Columbia affirmed the Board's dismissal of alter ego allegations.[312] Two wholly owned subsidiary companies of the same parent corporation were held to be alter egos by the Sixth Circuit where, although the subsidiary performed different services, there was common ownership and other indicia of alter ego status.[313]

Circuit courts upheld alter ego findings even in the absence of common ownership, however, where the entities in question were subject to a high degree of common operating and financial control and where organizational changes were intended to evade labor obligations.[314]

Some factual settings, such as franchising and bankruptcies, invite a particularly close analysis. Where a franchising transaction was found to be for the purpose of ousting the union from the franchised store, the Board focused upon the retention of financial and operational control by the franchisor. It held that the two enterprises were alter egos although the franchisee (the son of an official of the franchisor) had no ownership or control of the franchisor.[315] On the other hand, in a situation where the

---

[310]Woodline Motor Freight v. NLRB, 843 F2d 285, 127 LRRM 3260 (CA 8, 1988); Crest Tankers v. National Maritime Union, *supra* note 308; Iowa Express Distribution v. NLRB, *supra* note 308; Penntech Papers v. NLRB, *supra* note 306.

[311]Goodman Piping Prods. Co. v. NLRB, 741 F2d 10, 117 LRRM 2143 (CA 2, 1984) (vacating arbitration award which was inconsistent with Board finding that two companies were not alter egos).

[312]Meat Cutters Local 567 v. NLRB, 663 F2d 223, 106 LRRM 2187 (CA DC, 1980), *aff'g in part sub nom.* Clinton Foods, 240 NLRB 1246, 100 LRRM 1416 (1979).

[313]NLRB v. Borg-Warner Corp., 663 F2d 666, 108 LRRM 2862 (CA 6, 1981), *cert. denied,* 457 US 1105, 110 LRRM 2608 (1982). *But see* McAllister Bros., 278 NLRB 601, 123 LRRM 1040 (1986), *enforced,* 819 F2d 439, 125 LRRM 2566 (CA 4, 1987) (holding that where employer exerts substantial degree of control over operations of subsequent employing entity, lack of common ownership does not preclude alter ego status; the Fourth Circuit reasoned that common ownership is not litmus test for alter ego status); *see also* MIS, 289 NLRB 491, 128 LRRM 1273 (1988).

[314]*See, e.g.,* Woodline Motor Freight v. NLRB, *supra* note 310; McAllister Bros., *supra* note 313.

[315]Big Bear Supermarkets No. 3, 239 NLRB 179, 100 LRRM 1067 (1978), *enforced,* 640 F2d 924, 103 LRRM 3120 (CA 9, 1980), *cert. denied,* 449 US 919, 105 LRRM 2809 (1980).

franchise transaction was not considered a sham or a vehicle for ousting the union and where there was no common ownership or control, the Board found no alter ego relationship.[316]

Bankruptcy proceedings raise special issues[317] because trustees, receivers, and debtors-in-possession may be recognized as different "juridical" entities from the debtor under the Bankruptcy Act.[318] Moreover, even if the different "juridical" entities are found to be alter egos, they may not necessarily be bound by the predecessor's labor agreement. Thus, bankruptcy will not prevent an alter ego finding where other countervailing characteristics are present. Corporations that continued the business of a bankrupt company and were operated by the same owner, utilizing the same employees and supervisors, were considered alter egos of the bankrupt company by the Board.[319] It is the obligation of the new entity to assume the debtor's labor agreement, subject to the right of that new entity, in appropriate circumstances, to seek permission of the bankruptcy court to disaffirm the labor agreement.[320] However, even if the labor agreement is disaffirmed, the obligation to bargain may continue. In such circumstances, the alter ego's obligations are similar to those of a successor.[321]

The Second Circuit addressed the interplay between bankruptcy and labor law in *In re Goodman*.[322] The NLRB charged that the named defendants, James Goodman and his wholly owned company, were alter egos of two defunct companies that had committed unfair labor practices and thus had succeeded to their predecessor's labor law liability. Goodman and his wife had

---

[316]Kallmann dba Love's Barbeque Restaurant No. 62, 245 NLRB 78, 102 LRRM 1546 (1979), *remanded*, 640 F2d 1094, 107 LRRM 2011 (CA 9, 1981).

[317]*See generally* discussion of bankruptcy and the NLRA in Chapter 30, "Accommodations to Other Federal Enactments," at notes 100–215.

[318]Bankruptcy Reform Act of 1978, 11 USC §101 et seq. (1988). *See* Oxford Structures, 245 NLRB 1180, 102 LRRM 1477 (1979); Jersey Juniors, 230 NLRB 329, 332, 95 LRRM 1283 (1977) (citing Iron Workers Local 455 v. Kevin Steel Prods., 519 F2d 698, 89 LRRM 3133 (CA 2, 1975); and Teamsters Local 807 v. Bohack Corp., 541 F2d 312, 320, 93 LRRM 2001 (CA 2, 1976), *on remand*, 431 F Supp 646, 95 LRRM 3031 (ED NY, 1977), *aff'd*, 567 F2d 237, 97 LRRM 2275 (CA 2, 1977), *cert. denied*, 439 US 825, 99 LRRM 2600 (1978)).

[319]William B. Allen, 267 NLRB 700, 114 LRRM 1104 (1983), *enforced*, 758 F2d 1145, 118 LRRM 3409 (CA 6, 1985), *cert. denied*, 474 US 1101, 121 LRRM 2368 (1986); *see also* Lewis Canter dba Century Printing Co., 242 NLRB 659, 101 LRRM 1226 (1979), *enforced*, 661 F2d 914, 108 LRRM 2279 (CA 3, 1981) (holding receiver-trustee of bankrupt company was alter ego of company's purchaser). *But see* Wintz Motor Freight, 265 NLRB 922, 112 LRRM 1250 (1982) (holding the United States trustee, which was precluded from acting as trustee in bankruptcy, was not alter ego of company).

[320]*See* Chapter 30, "Accommodations to Other Federal Enactments," at notes 127–173.

[321]*Id.*

[322]873 F2d 598, 131 LRRM 2129 (CA 2, 1989).

each owned one of the companies that ceased operations and filed Chapter 7 bankruptcy petitions. Goodman had also filed for bankruptcy individually and, prior to the close of the companies' bankruptcies, had formed another company.[323] After the NLRB issued its complaint against Goodman and his new company charging that they were alter egos of one of the defunct companies, Goodman and the new company attempted to obtain an order from the bankruptcy court barring the NLRB proceedings on the grounds that Goodman's individual Chapter 7 bankruptcy discharge shielded them from liability for the labor law violations of the predecessor company.[324] The Second Circuit disagreed and held that since the liability of the defendants hinged on whether they were in fact alter egos of their predecessors, the NLRB had primary jurisdiction over the issue and the bankruptcy court lacked jurisdiction to determine this issue of substantive labor law.[325]

Despite the treatment under the Bankruptcy Act, both the debtor-in-possession and the trustee in bankruptcy are normally deemed to be alter egos of debtor employers under the National Labor Relations Act.[326] However, where a trustee has transferred the assets of a declared bankrupt to a successful bidder, the bidder will not be an alter ego unless the requisite criteria are otherwise satisfied.[327] Thus, even if the bidder takes over the same operations at the same location, the absence of common ownership or control or sham transaction will militate against a finding of alter ego status.[328] However, where the original owner-operator continues in the active management and thereafter controls the receiver (e.g., causing a resale to owner-operator's family), the parties will be considered alter egos.[329]

For example, in *NLRB v. Better Building Supply Corp.*,[330] the Court of Appeals for the Ninth Circuit agreed with the Board that a newly formed corporation was liable as an alter ego for an unfair labor practice award against a bankrupt corporation

---

[323]*Id.*
[324]*Id.* at 601, 131 LRRM at 2131.
[325]Id. at 602, 131 LRRM at 2131.
[326]Cagle's, Inc., 218 NLRB 603, 89 LRRM 1337 (1975); Marion Simcox, 178 NLRB 516, 518, 72 LRRM 1183 (1969); *cf.* Oxford Structures, *supra* note 318; Makaha Valley, 241 NLRB 300, 101 LRRM 1040 (1979); Jersey Juniors, *supra* note 318; Airport Limousine Serv., 231 NLRB 932, 96 LRRM 1177 (1977).
[327]Jersey Juniors, *supra* note 318.
[328]*Id.*
[329]Lewis Canter dba Century Printing Co., *supra* note 319.
[330]837 F2d 377, 127 LRRM 2393 (CA 9, 1988).

owned by the same individuals, because debts of a corporation are not discharged in bankruptcy. The owners of the corporations, who had also filed bankruptcy individually and whose debts had been discharged, argued that since the two corporations were alter egos only because of their personal ownership and involvement, the related labor law liabilities should be considered to have been discharged in their personal bankruptcies. The court disagreed, holding that the liability of the bankrupt corporation was assessable directly against the new alter ego corporation.

A partnership also was found to be the alter ego of a bankrupt corporation even though the partnership was owned by father and son whereas the corporation had been owned by the father only, where the partnership did not hire union employees and all aspects of the bankrupt corporation were carried over to the partnership.[331] The filing of a bankruptcy petition and appointment of a debtor-in-possession or trustee does not relieve a company of its obligation to continue to recognize and bargain with an incumbent union.[332] Where, however, the receiver in bankruptcy, rather than the debtor's management, operates the business in a different form with a substantially reduced work force, the Board has declined to find alter ego status.[333]

Bankruptcy also merits special attention because of the Supreme Court's decision in *NLRB v. Bildisco & Bildisco*[334] and the subsequent Bankruptcy Amendments and Federal Judgeship Act of 1984.[335] In cases that arose prior to the Bankruptcy Amendment Act, the Board, relying on *Bildisco,* found that a debtor-in-possession or trustee after the filing of the bankruptcy petition did not commit an unfair labor practice if it unilaterally rejected or modified a collective bargaining agreement before formal approval by the bankruptcy court.[336] For cases arising after July 10, 1984 (the effective date of the Bankruptcy Act Amendments), however, the Board has held that an employer in bankruptcy violates the Act by unilaterally rejecting (or refusing

---

[331]NLRB v. Edward Cooper Painting, 804 F2d 934, 123 LRRM 2905 (CA 6, 1986).

[332]Otten Truck Line, 282 NLRB 494, 124 LRRM 1068 (1986); Superior Installation Co., 267 NLRB 1023, 114 LRRM 1128 (1983).

[333]Blazer Indus., 236 NLRB 103, 99 LRRM 1046 (1978) (the form of business was not deemed as significant as change in supervision and management). *See also* Frank Hennigan, 236 NLRB 1517, 99 LRRM 1272 (1978).

[334]465 US 513, 115 LRRM 2805 (1984).

[335]Pub. L. No. 98-353, §541, 98 Stat. 333, 390–391 (1984), codified in 11 USC §1113.

[336]NLRB v. Edward Cooper Painting, *supra* note 331; San Juan Hotel Corp. dba El San Juan Hotel, 274 NLRB 13, 118 LRRM 1320 (1985).

to execute) a collective bargaining agreement without complying with the procedures provided in 11 U.S.C. §1113,[337] governing an employer's request for relief from its collective bargaining agreement.

Alter ego issues involving criteria from unfair labor practice litigation have also arisen in section 301 contract actions. The issue can arise in an action to compel arbitration, to enforce an arbitration award, or to determine the coverage or extent of coverage of a collective bargaining agreement.[338] One such case held that two nonunion companies were required to abide by the collective bargaining agreement of a third company, their alter ego, and thus were obligated to make payments to a union trust fund.[339]

As just demonstrated, an alter ego question frequently arises in the context of business changes which are alleged to have been undertaken as a subterfuge to avoid bargaining or contractual obligations under the Act. Despite the varied corporate and commercial forms in which business entities may constitute themselves, in cases of alleged subterfuge the test has been whether the newly formed entity is in reality "merely a disguised continuance of the old employer."[340] As in all alter ego cases, the issue is one of substance rather than form. Cosmetic changes, which may serve some legitimate purposes under other statutes, are not determinative.[341] In *Howard Johnson*[342] the Court

---

[337]Image Sys., 285 NLRB 370, 126 LRRM 1129 (1987). *See also* Steelworkers v. Unimet Corp., 842 F2d 879, 127 LRRM 3139 (CA 6), *cert. denied*, 488 U.S. 828, 129 LRRM 2400 (1988). The Bankruptcy Act Amendments of 1984 provide that in order to obtain the bankruptcy court's approval to reject a collective bargaining agreement, a debtor-in-possession must first seek to modify the agreement through bargaining. If bargaining is unsuccessful, rejection will be permitted only if the union's refusal to accept the employer's proposals is "without good cause" and the "balance of the equities clearly favors rejection." 11 USC §1113 (1988).

[338]*See, e.g.* Crest Tankers v. National Maritime Union, 796 F2d 234, 122 LRRM 3237 (CA 8, 1986); Penntech Papers v. NLRB, 706 F2d 18, 113 LRRM 2219 (CA 1), *cert. denied*, 464 US 892, 114 LRRM 2648 (1983). The interrelationship of Board proceedings and court proceedings under §301 is often complex, involving issues of collateral estoppel, res judicata, and the Board's exclusive jurisdiction over representation matters. *See, e.g.*, Teamsters Local 216 v. Granite Rock Co., 851 F2d 1190, 128 LRRM 3060 (CA 9), *cert. denied*, 488 US 986, 129 LRRM 3072 (1988); Culinary Workers Local 226, Local Joint Executive Bd. (Las Vegas) v. Royal Center, 754 F2d 835, 119 LRRM 2958 (CA 9, 1985), *vacated and remanded*, 475 US 1114, 122 LRRM 2079 (1986), *on remand*, 796 F2d 1159, 123 LRRM 2347 (CA 9, 1986), *cert. denied*, 479 US 1033, 124 LRRM 2216 (1987). *Culinary Workers* was vacated and remanded in light of AT&T Technologies v. Communications Workers, 475 US 643, 121 LRRM 3329 (1986).

[339]Developer's Maintenance v. Laborers Health & Welfare Fund, 96 Lab. Cas. (CCH) ¶14,025 (CD Cal, 1982).

[340]Southport Petroleum Co. v. NLRB, 315 US 100, 106, 9 LRRM 411, 413 (1942).

[341]*See, e.g.*, Dee Cee Floor Covering, 232 NLRB 421, 97 LRRM 1072 (1977).

[342]Howard Johnson Co. v. Hotel Employees, Detroit Local Joint Executive Bd., 417 US 249, 86 LRRM 2449 (1974).

expressly stated that changes in corporate forms which involve no more than a "technical change in the structure or identity of the employing entity, frequently to avoid the effect of the labor laws, without any substantial change in its ownership or management"[343] are properly disregarded and the alter ego is subject to all the legal and contractual obligations of the predecessor."[344]

Despite the Board's acceptance of the "disguised continuance" test, its application has not been fully tested. The most obvious example of the subterfuge is where an employer goes entirely out of business for antiunion reasons and another entity in the same line of business is subsequently formed. If there is common ownership and control, the question of alter ego status is clear.[345] On the other hand, it is also well established that an employer may lawfully choose to close its entire business even if motivated by antiunion considerations.[346] Unless it is established that the individuals owning and controlling the liquidated business are sufficiently linked to any new and similar enterprise subsequently formed, alter ego criteria would not be satisfied. However, in *NLRB v. Bell Co.*,[347] the Board's initial finding of alter ego status had been influenced by the union animus of the liquidating employer. The Board had viewed the relationship and transactions between the two entities as not of "arm's-length," and therefore found no complete cessation of the prior business, that is, there was a disguised continuance.[348] But as previously noted, the Court of Appeals for the Seventh Circuit rejected the Board's finding of alter ego status, based on a lack of common ownership and control. The court also acknowledged the prior employer's *Darlington*[349] right to cease business entirely despite antiunion motivations, so that it refused to uphold the alter ego finding on the basis of an antiunion motivation standing alone.

B. The Stock Purchaser

Generally, a change in ownership resulting from a transfer of shares does not raise successorship questions. The Board first

---

[343] *Id.* at 259 n.5, 86 LRRM at 2453 n.5.

[344] *Id.*

[345] *See* Victor Patino, 241 NLRB 774, 100 LRRM 1616 (1979), *enforced*, 642 F2d 456, 108 LRRM 2175 (CA 9, 1981).

[346] Textile Workers v. Darlington Mfg. Co., 380 US 263, 58 LRRM 2657 (1965). *See* Chapter 7, "Discrimination in Employment," at notes 261–266.

[347] 561 F2d 1264, 96 LRRM 2437 (CA 7, 1977).

[348] Bell Co., 243 NLRB 977, 101 LRRM 1572 (1979), *supplementing* 225 NLRB 474, 93 LRRM 1180 (1976), *enforced in part*, 561 F2d 1264, 96 LRRM 2437 (CA 7, 1977).

[349] *Supra* note 346.

articulated its reasons for distinguishing a stock transfer from an assets transfer in its 1979 decision in *TKB International Corp.*[350]

In *TKB*, the Board said that successorship, "contemplates the substitution of one employer for another, where the predecessor employer either terminates its existence, or otherwise ceases to have any relationship to the on-going operations of the successor employer."[351] The Board added that "[o]nce it has been found that this 'break' between predecessor and successor has occurred," it looks to other factors to see "how wide or narrow this disjunction is,"[352] and thus determines the extent of the obligations of the successor. By contrast, a stock transfer, according to the Board, involves "the continuing existence of a legal entity, albeit under new ownership."[353] Thus the Board held that membership in a multi-employer bargaining unit was "assumed by the purchasing entity, or transferee, much in the same way as it assumes the debts, assets, and goodwill of the transferor of the stock."[354]

Previously, the Board, in *Topinka's Country House*,[355] had affirmed, without opinion, an ALJ's decision rejecting application of the *Burns* successorship rationale where a corporation's ownership is changed as a result of a stock transfer.

As the Court of Appeals for the Fourth Circuit has observed in *EPE Inc. v. NLRB*,[356] "the Supreme Court has not had occasion to address the effect of a stock transfer on the labor obligations

---

[350]240 NLRB 1082, 100 LRRM 1426 (1979).

[351]*Id.* at 1083 n.4, 100 LRRM at 1428 n.4.

[352]*Id.*

[353]*Id.; see also, e.g.*, Esmark, Inc. v. NLRB, 887 F2d 739, 750, 132 LRRM 2710, 2720 (CA 7, 1989), *remanding sub nom.* Swift Indep. Corp., 289 NLRB 423, 131 LRRM 1173 (1988); Teamsters Local 249 v. Bill's Trucking, 493 F2d 956, 85 LRRM 2713 (CA 3, 1974); EPE, Inc., 284 NLRB 191, 125 LRRM 1166 (1987), *enforced in part*, 845 F2d 483, 128 LRRM 2246 (CA 4, 1988); Morco, Inc., 258 NLRB 69, 108 LRRM 1126 (1981); Topinka's Country House, 235 NLRB 72, 98 LRRM 1298 (1978), *enforced*, 624 F2d 770, 105 LRRM 3419 (CA 6, 1980); Miller Trucking Serv., 176 NLRB 556, 71 LRRM 1277 (1969), *enforced in part*, 445 F2d 927, 77 LRRM 2964 (CA 10, 1971); *but see* NLRB v. Edjo, Inc., 631 F2d 604, 105 LRRM 3061 (CA 9, 1980) (successorship analysis required corporation with new shareholders to recognize union, but did not require corporation to abide by terms of labor agreement).

[354]240 NLRB at 1085, 100 LRRM at 1430. The Board's description of a transferor's obligations being assumed by a transferee in this stock transfer case is unfortunate, and unnecessarily confusing. It was not the prior *shareholder* who was a member of the multi-employer bargaining unit, but the *corporation* whose shares he owned, and later sold. The Board's holding requiring the corporation whose shares changed hands to remain a member of the multi-employer bargaining unit rested, in fact, on the continuation of the corporate entity. *Id.* at 1083 n.4.

[355]*Supra* note 353.

[356]845 F2d 483, 128 LRRM 2246, 2250 (CA 4, 1988), *enforcing in part* 284 NLRB 191, 125 LRRM 1166 (1987).

of a continuing corporation." The Court's post-*Burns* decision of *Golden State Bottling Co. v. NLRB*[357] suggests in dicta that the form of a corporate transaction is to be minimized for the purpose of the successorship doctrine:

> [T]he refusal to adopt a mode of analysis requiring the Board to distinguish among mergers, consolidations, and purchases of assets is attributable to the fact that, so long as there is a continuity in the "employing industry," the public policies underlying the doctrine will be served by its broad application.[358]

The Court of Appeals for the Fourth Circuit has agreed with the Board that the successorship cases do not apply to a stock transfer, but added this dictum:

> [W]e do not adopt a rule that labor agreements remain in force in every situation where corporate ownership changes through a stock sale. On the contrary, a stock sale could in many cases serve as a vehicle for acquisition of resources that will be used to operate a substantially different enterprise from that conducted by the original owners. This would be the case where a new owner, pursuing the policy endorsed in *Burns,* seeks to breathe new life into a moribund corporation by making substantial changes in its operations. *See* 406 U.S. at 287–88, 92 S.Ct. at 1582. Where the corporate form survives only in name, but an entirely new operation replaces the old, the corporation might not be fairly termed a "continuing" employer in any practical sense. Should substantial changes in an operation indicate that its sale was not a "mere substitution of one owner for another through a stock transfer within the context of an ongoing enterprise," the obligations of the employer may be governed by successorship principles rather than by continued enforcement of an agreement. *See United Food and Commercial Workers v. NLRB,* 768 F2d 1463, 1471 (D.C. Cir. 1985). Indeed, in some cases changes to a business that is acquired through a stock transfer may be so great that the resulting business is not even a "successor." *See Lauer's Furniture Stores, Inc.,* 246 NLRB 360, 102 LRRM 1593 (1979).[359]

Lauer's Furniture Stores,[360] involved a store in serious financial straits. The shares of Lauer were sold to unrelated parties who structured the sale as a stock transfer for the sole purpose of preserving the store's lease. All employees of Lauer were terminated upon the sale of the stock, and one of the new share-

---

[357] 414 US 168, 84 LRRM 2839 (1973). *See* Krupman & Kaplan, *The Stock Purchaser After* Burns*: Must He Buy the Union Contract?,* 31 LAB. L.J. 328 (1980).

[358] 414 US at 182 n.5, 84 LRRM at 2844 n.5.

[359] 845 F2d at 490, 128 LRRM at 2251. *See also* NLRB v. Edjo, Inc., 631 F2d 604, 105 LRRM 3061 (CA 9, 1980) (dicta), *enforcing* Joe Costa Trucking Co., 238 NLRB 1516, 99 LRRM 1719 (1978).

[360] 246 NLRB 360, 102 LRRM 1593 (1979).

holders transferred its own employees to run the store. The ALJ concluded, with Board affirmance, that the general rule obligating corporations to abide by their contracts notwithstanding an ownership change was inapplicable because, other than being a leaseholder, the corporation whose stock was sold ceased operations.[361] While Lauer was found to have violated section 8(a)(5) for refusing to engage in effects bargaining, the shareholder which took over the store, under successorship analysis, was not obligated to recognize Lauer's unions.[362]

The Board applied successorship considerations in *MPE, Inc.*[363] and held that a corporation "which has undergone a complete change of ownership and management, but which has retained essentially the same employees, production process, and location,"[364] was *not* "bound to assume a labor contract of which it was not apprised at the time of the transfer of ownership."[365] The Board apparently placed heavy reliance on the factual conclusion that the stock purchasers were misled by the seller about the existence of a union agreement.

In *Spencer Foods,*[366] the Board held that the traditional successorship criteria was to be applied in determining the bargaining obligations of a corporation whose stock was purchased by a new owner. Prior to the purchase, in the course of bargaining over a new term of a collective bargaining agreement, the employer unsuccessfully sought cost savings, and the operations of the employer were shut down for economic reasons. After the stock of the company was acquired by another corporation, some, but not all, of the employer's plants were reopened after having been closed for 19 months. The Board held that successorship analysis should govern because the nature of the transaction resembled an assets purchase (the purchaser agreed to a stock, rather than assets purchase, solely for tax reasons) and was accompanied by operational changes and a substantial

---

[361] *Id.* at 365.

[362] *Id.*

[363] 226 NLRB 519, 93 LRRM 1325 (1976).

[364] *Id.* at 520, 93 LRRM at 1326–37.

[365] *Id.* at 520, 93 LRRM at 1326. The corporation conceded that it had a duty to recognize and bargain with the union.

[366] 268 NLRB 1483 n.5, 115 LRRM 1251 n.5 (1984), *enforcement denied sub nom.* Food & Commercial Workers Local 152 v. NLRB, 768 F2d 1463, 119 LRRM 3473 (CA DC, 1985). *See also* Mine Workers Local 1329, Dist. 21 v. NLRB (Alpine Constr. Corp.), 812 F2d 741, 124 LRRM 3012 (CA DC, 1987), *vacating and remanding* 276 NLRB 415, 120 LRRM 1158 (1985), where union raised lack of successorship to defend §8(b)(7)(c) charges.

hiatus. The Board concluded that the corporation had no duty to bargain with the union.

In *Food & Commercial Workers Local 152 (Spencer Foods) v. NLRB*,[367] the Court of Appeals for the District of Columbia Circuit reversed the Board's *Spencer Foods* decision. With respect to the sale of stock, the court regarded that form of transaction as relevant, but not determinative. The court acknowledged that in reality a broader form of business reorganization was involved, "and not a mere stock transfer." The court, nonetheless, viewed the "employing industry" as remaining substantially intact, particularly as it "impinged upon union members." While only a small portion of the seller's employees were eventually hired, the court explained that that was attributable to discrimination in restaffing and recall. In *Sterling Processing Corp.*,[368] a 1988 decision involving a company that shut down its plant for 18 months, but whose ownership remained the same, the Board overruled its decision in *Spencer Foods* to the extent it was inconsistent with the decision in *Food & Commercial Workers Local 152*.[369]

Contrary to the Fourth Circuit's suggestion in *EPE, Inc.*[370] that a stock transaction may give rise to application of the successorship doctrine, the Court of Appeals for the Seventh Circuit flatly stated, in *Esmark, Inc. v. NLRB*,[371] "[t]he successorship doctrine is simply inapplicable to a stock sale transaction."

In *Esmark,* a holding corporation decided to make a public offering of part of its holdings. In a complex corporate restructuring prior to the public offering, two plants were isolated at the end of a chain of corporate holdings. Esmark announced, in its prospectus for the public offering, that it intended to renegotiate the labor agreements at the two plants after the public sale of stock.[372] The court agreed with the Board that the public sale of

---

[367]768 F2d 1463, 119 LRRM 3473 (CA DC, 1985), *enforcing in part, denying enforcement in part and remanding in part sub nom.* Spencer Foods, 268 NLRB 1483, 115 LRRM 1251 (1984).

[368]291 NLRB 247, 130 LRRM 1092, 1095 n.9 (1988).

[369]*Id.* The Board noted that "where the employing entity remains the same after a hiatus as it was before, . . . the hiatus, standing alone, does not relieve the [employer] of its bargaining obligations." *Id.* (citing the court's opinion in *Spencer Foods, supra* note 366). A hiatus may, however, allow the employer to unilaterally modify terms and conditions of employment before rehiring employees upon reopening, where the entire prehiatus work force is laid off with no reasonable expectations of recall. Sterling Processing Corp., *supra* note 368.

[370]EPE, Inc. v. NLRB, *supra* note 356, at 489, 128 LRRM at 2250.

[371]*Supra* note 353, at 751.

[372]*Id.* at 751–52.

ownership did not affect the obligations of the corporation owning the plants to abide by the existing agreements,[373] and remanded the case for further consideration of whether the holding company would be separately liable under "alter ego" and other theories which might allow the corporate veil to be pierced.[374]

In addition to holding a corporation to its obligations notwithstanding a change of ownership, the Board may find that a stock purchaser *itself* has successor obligations, and thus is liable for the acts of the corporation whose shares it purchased even though the acts occurred prior to the stock sale. In *Winco Petroleum Co.,*[375] a company merged with Winco 4 weeks after purchasing its stock and was subjected to a bargaining order which was entered against Winco prior to the stock sale, as well as liability for unfair labor practices which occurred prior to the sale.[376] Central to the Board's finding of liability on the part of the stock purchaser were: (1) the purchaser had actual knowledge of Winco's unfair labor practices, (2) there was little or no business interruption, (3) the purchaser continued to operate the enterprise at the same location without substantial change, and (4) the majority of the employees were former employees of Winco.[377] It is doubtful, but not clear, whether the stock purchaser would have been deemed a successor absent its merger with Winco.

The Board may also bind a stock purchaser along with the corporation whose stock was purchased under a single employer analysis. In *Miami Foundry Corp.,*[378] a financially troubled foundry closed its door in midterm of a collective bargaining agreement and laid off all its employees. Fifty-one percent of Miami Foundry stock was purchased nine days later, and a subsidiary of the new majority shareholder began operating the foundry as a nonunion plant. The stock purchaser relied upon *MPE, Inc.*[379] for the argument that Miami, as a newly controlled

---

[373]*Id.*

[374]*Id.* at 752–60.

[375]252 NLRB 1049, 105 LRRM 1506 (1980), *enforced*, 668 F2d 973, 109 LRRM 2377 (CA 8, 1982).

[376]*Id.*

[377]*Id.; compare* Lauer's Furniture Stores, *supra* note 360 (new shareholders found *not* to be alter egos or joint employers).

[378]252 NLRB 2, 105 LRRM 1449 (1980), *enforced*, 682 F2d 587, 111 LRRM 2367 (CA 6, 1982).

[379]*Supra* note 363.

corporation, should be regarded as a successor, noting that the transaction was in the form of a stock sale solely because a tax loss could be taken under the Internal Revenue Code. The Court of Appeals for the Sixth Circuit distinguished *MPE, Inc.*, stating,

> In that case, the Board found at the threshold that the new company completely substituted for the old, and that the old was no longer in existence. . . .
>
> In the case before us . . . . Miami never ceased as a business entity and its obligations under the [collective bargaining] agreement, therefore, never ceased.[380]

Regarding the contention that tax considerations dictated a stock rather than an assets sale, the court declined to hold "that Miami still exists for tax purposes but does not exist for purposes of the labor agreement with Miami workers."[381] The Board, with court affirmance, held Miami, its 51 percent stock purchaser, and the purchaser's operating subsidiary to be a single, integrated enterprise and bound all three entities to honor the collective bargaining agreement.[382]

C. Adoption of Predecessor's Contract

Of course, a successor who assumes or adopts a labor contract is bound by it. The Board has continued its case-by-case approach and has employed a detailed factual analysis in determining whether a successor employer has adopted or assumed the labor contract of its predecessor.[383] While *Burns* established

---

[380]682 F2d at 589, 111 LRRM at 2368.

[381]*Id.*

[382]Miami Foundry Corp., *supra* note 378.

[383]Inland Container Corp., 275 NLRB 378, 119 LRRM 1089 (1985), *supplementing* 267 NLRB 1187, 114 LRRM 1143 (1983), 273 NLRB 1856, 118 LRRM 1384 (1985) *and* 274 NLRB 887, 118 LRRM 1454 (1985); *see also* Haley & Haley v. NLRB, 880 F2d 1147, 132 LRRM 2119, 2121 (CA 9, 1989) (Ninth Circuit stated that "a successor company, unlike an alter ego, is generally not bound by the collective bargaining agreement of its predecessor"); Central States Southeast & Southwest Areas Pension Fund v. PYA Monarch, 851 F2d 780, 784, 9 EB Cases 2650, 2653 (CA 5, 1988) (Fifth Circuit stated that "before completing the asset purchase, . . . [the successor] advised . . . [the union] that it would neither assume the CBA nor accept the obligation to contribute to the . . . Fund"); Martin J. Barry Co., 278 NLRB 393, 121 LRRM 1161, 1162 (1986) (Board reiterated that "under Burns it is clear that a successor employer does not have a statutory bargaining obligation to assume its predecessor's contract with the union"). *See* EPE v. NLRB, 845 F2d 483, 487, 128 LRRM 2246, 2249 (CA 4, 1988) (Fourth Circuit stated that "a continuing unchanged employer remains bound by its obligations, including a collective bargaining agreement . . . [but] a new and different employer that is considered a successor is not bound by its predecessor's agreement"); Wood v. Teamsters Local 406, 807 F2d 493, 124 LRRM 2065 (CA 6, 1986), *cert. denied*, 483 US 1006, 125 LRRM 3064 (1987) (alleged

that a successor may not be bound to an involuntary assumption of the substantive terms of a collective bargaining agreement negotiated by its predecessor, there have been circumstances where the successor has been deemed to have adopted or assumed its predecessor's agreement.[384] Adoption (or assumption) has been found where the successor had not only applied the substantive terms of the agreement but also consulted and negotiated with the union as the bargaining agent for its employees.[385] In such circumstances, the successor's disavowal or refusal in its purchase-sales agreement to adopt the predecessor's labor agreement was viewed as having been abrogated.[386]

Application of the adoption theory has been predicated upon clear evidence of consent, either actual or constructive.[387] The

---

successor, after renouncing predecessor's labor contract, was held not to have assumed that contract, either expressly or impliedly); Steelworkers v. Deutz-Allis Corp., 122 LRRM 2035, 2037 (WD Mo, 1986) (successor was held to have assumed predecessor's labor contract in that successor's pertinent letter to union represented "a clear manifestation of the . . . [successor's] adoption of the contract," and the successor either "knew or had reason to know that the Unions might—indeed, would—accept it as such" (footnote omitted)).

[384]World Evangelism, 248 NLRB 909, 104 LRRM 1096 (1980), *enforced*, 656 F2d 1349, 108 LRRM 2573 (CA 9, 1981); Eklund's Sweden House Inn, 203 NLRB 413, 83 LRRM 1173 (1973); Stockton Door Co., 218 NLRB 1053, 89 LRRM 1428 (1975), *enforced*, 547 F2d 489, 94 LRRM 2288 (CA 9, 1976), *cert. denied*, 434 US 834, 96 LRRM 2513 (1977).

[385]See authorities cited in *supra* note 384. The successor may not condition acceptance of the contract on selective enforcement of certain provisions, even though the union had acquiesced therein with the predecessor. Tasman Sea, 247 NLRB 18, 103 LRRM 1126 (1980).

[386]Eklund's Sweden House Inn, *supra* note 384.

[387]B&K Invs., 248 NLRB 1234, 104 LRRM 1120 (1980); Noriega Indus. dba Pioneer Printers, 201 NLRB 900, 82 LRRM 1396 (1973). *See also* NLRB v. World Evangelism, 656 F2d 1349, 108 LRRM 2573 (CA 9, 1981) (successor was held to have assumed its predecessor's contract by actions which would lead reasonable person to believe that agreement had been reached); Tilden Arms Mgmt. Co., 276 NLRB 1111, 120 LRRM 1207, 1207 (1985) (successor was held bound by predecessor's contract when successor had agreed in contract of sale, "'to accept title to the premises subject to any union service and maintenance contracts'" and did in fact comply with terms and conditions of predecessor's contract); Chaim Babad, Bernard Steinmetz & Emanuel Steinmetz dba J.R.R. Realty Co., 273 NLRB 1523, 118 LRRM 1230 (1985), *enforced*, 785 F2d 46, 121 LRRM 2940, 2943 (CA 2), *cert. denied*, 479 US 830, 123 LRRM 2592 (1986) (Second Circuit, holding that there was "substantial evidence" from which Board could conclude that successor had assumed predecessor's contract, stated that "[i]n determining whether an employer has assumed its predecessor's labor contract, the NLRB is not bound by technical rules of contract law; rather it may adapt those rules to the collective bargaining context"); All State Factors, 205 NLRB 1122, 1127, 84 LRRM 1252 (1973) (ALJ's opinion, affirmed by Board, stated that *Burns* counsels "restraint in applying the adoption theory, absent clear and convincing evidence of consent, either actual or constructive"). *But see* Prime Time Post, 274 NLRB 1496, 119 LRRM 1125 (1985); Food & Commercial Workers Local 1439 (Food City W.), 262 NLRB 309, 110 LRRM 1285 (1982). *See also* In re Goodman, 873 F2d 598, 603, 131 LRRM 2129, 2132 (CA 2, 1989) (Second Circuit stated that board "has expertise in adjudicating successorship issues, and there is an interest in having uniform determinations by a single agency"); NLRB v. St. Mary's Foundry Co., 860 F2d 679, 681, 129 LRRM 2749, 2750 (CA 6, 1988), *enforcing* 284 NLRB 221, 125 LRRM 1146 (1987) (Sixth circuit stated that "a high degree of deference is accorded a finding by the Board

mere continuation of economic benefits prevailing at the time of takeover will not, without more, indicate an adoption of the predecessor's labor agreement. Thus, implementation by the successor of a wage increase provided for in the preexisting labor agreement was not deemed an assumption where the increase was also required by amendments to the minimum wage laws.[388] On the other hand, where a successor has applied both economic and noneconomic provisions of the predecessor's agreement, the Board has found that adoption occurred.[389] Adoption also was found in a section 301 suit to enforce payments to a pension fund where, among other factors, the successor assured the union it would sign the agreement, requested a moratorium on grievances, and also complied with significant contract provisions.[390] A successor that continued to make employee trust fund contributions, as required under the predecessor's labor contract, was held to have assumed the obligation

---

that an employer is liable as a successor employer, since the Board has special expertise in determining this issue").

In NLRB v. Chaim Babad, Bernard Steinmetz & Emanuel Steinmetz dba J.R.R. Realty Co., 785 F2d 46, 50, 121 LRRM 2940, 2942 (CA 2, 1986), a predecessor's labor contract was held to be assumed. Evidence of the assumption included language in the contract for the sale of the business that the labor contract was a permitted encumbrance; assignment of the labor contract to the purchaser at the closing; and, the successor employer's attempting to persuade employee union members to waive their claims.

In NLRB v. Amateyus dba Volk & Huxley, 817 F2d 996, 998, 125 LRRM 2329, 2331 (CA 2), *cert. denied*, 484 US 925, 126 LRRM 2776 (1987), the Second Circuit stated that the Board was "perfectly entitled" to find that the successor had intended to adopt the involved labor contract. The successor did not bargain over initial terms, but it operated in accordance with the terms of that labor contract and gave no indication that it would not adhere to them, but later tried to negotiate modification of the labor contract. *See also* Steelworkers v. Connors Steel Co., 855 F2d 1499, 1507, 129 LRRM 2531, 2537 (CA 11, 1988), *cert. denied sub nom.* Parker v. Connors Steel Co., 490 US 1066, 130 LRRM 2400 (1989), where the Eleventh Circuit held that, after the purchaser had paid benefits for 4 years, the purchaser had "'acted as a successor employer,'" and it was permissible to find that the purchaser "had 'assumed the obligations' under the collective bargaining agreement to pay these benefits."

See also Johnson v. Pullman, 845 F2d 911, 128 LRRM 2361 (CA 11, 1988) (purchaser of plant was not bound by labor contract's successorship clause requiring it to adopt contract or to hire seller's employees, where purchaser was not party to that labor contract).

[388]Virginia Sportswear, 226 NLRB 1296, 1302, 94 LRRM 1411 (1976).

[389]Houshang Vazin dba Super Save, 273 NLRB 20, 29, 118 LRRM 1064 (1984); Ethan Allen, Inc., Pine Valley Div., 218 NLRB 208, 215, 89 LRRM 1780 (1975), *enforced in part*, 544 F2d 742, 93 LRRM 2811 (CA 4, 1976). *See also* Audit Servs. v. Rolfson, 641 F2d 757, 107 LRRM 2586 (CA 9, 1981) (court held that successor that continued to make employee trust fund contributions, as required under predecessor's labor contract, assumed obligation to continue making payments). *But see* Carter dba Bay City Foundry Co. v. CMTA-Molders Health & Welfare Trust, 563 F Supp 244, 116 LRRM 3309 (ND Cal, 1983), *aff'd*, 736 F2d 1310, 116 LRRM 3312 (CA 9, 1984) (court held that successor that was unaware of predecessor's obligation to make employee trust fund contributions, but who made payments to fund upon receiving invoices, had *not* consented to adopting predecessor's obligation).

[390]Teamsters Local 92 v. Strabley Bldg. Supply, 98 LRRM 3025 (ND Ohio, 1978); *accord* Steelworkers v. Deutz-Allis Corp., *supra* note 383.

to continue making the payments.[391] However, one court has held that a successor who was unaware at the time of purchase of the predecessor's contractual obligation to make employee trust fund contributions, but who made payments to the fund upon receiving bills, had not consented to adopting the predecessor's obligation.[392]

A successor that has adopted its predecessor's labor agreement will be required, to the same extent as its predecessor, to bargain about any changes in employment practices, even though they may not be reflected in the agreement.[393]

V. SUCCESSORSHIP AND THE CONTRACT-BAR DOCTRINE

Successorship and contract-bar doctrines[394] each represent an effort to balance competing policies. The successorship rules focus upon the balance between the employees' need for continuity and the new employer's need for flexibility. The contract-bar rules seek to balance the interests of stability in labor relations against the opportunity of employees to select bargaining representatives. Where the doctrines of successorship and contract bar arise in specific cases, these underlying policy considerations present an added dimension to the appropriate

---

[391] Audit Servs. v. Rolfson, *supra* note 389. *See also* Houshang Vazin dba Super Save, *supra* note 389 (successor was held to have violated the Act by failing to make required trust fund contributions). A successor may be obligated to make contributions to union fringe benefits funds based upon hours worked by nonunion employees. Alaska Laborers Trustees v. Construction & Rigging, 644 F Supp 1104, 1105–6 (D Alaska, 1986). *But see* Merrimen v. Paul F. Rost Elec., 861 F2d 135, 129 LRRM 2869 (CA 6, 1988) (Sixth Circuit held that, because of written contract requirement of §302(c)(5)(B), employer could not be held to pension provisions of unsigned labor contract, even if employer voluntarily made payments in accordance with those provisions for a period of time).

[392] Carter dba Bay City Foundry Co. v. CMTA-Molders Health & Welfare Trust, *supra* note 389. *See also* Gariup v. Birchler Ceiling & Interior Co., 777 F2d 370, 120 LRRM 3428, 3431 (CA 7, 1985).

A successor may become obligated to make pension fund contributions by estoppel. Woodward Sand Co. v. Western Conference of Teamsters, 789 F2d 691, 697, 7 EB Cases 1585, 1591 (CA 9, 1986); Operating Eng'rs Pension Trust v. Moine Bros. Excavators, 124 LRRM 2030, 2032 (CD Cal, 1986).

[393] Pepsi Cola Distrib. Co. of Knoxville, 241 NLRB 869, 100 LRRM 1626 (1979), *enforced*, 646 F2d 1173, 107 LRRM 2252 (CA 6, 1981), *cert. denied*, 456 US 936, 109 LRRM 3368 (1982). *See also* Springfield Transit Mgmt., 281 NLRB 72, 123 LRRM 1017 (1986) (successor, under broad assumption of "all labor and other employee contractual obligations" of predecessor, was held to have failed to bargain with union before reducing unilaterally employees' wages).

[394] For a discussion of the contract-bar doctrine generally, see Chapter 10, "Representation Proceedings and Elections," at notes 119–201. *See also* discussion in NLRB v. Burns Int'l 406 US 272, 288 n.8, 290 n.12, 80 LRRM 2225, 2230 n.8, 2232 n.12, in reference to contract bar in decertification situations.

balance. In comparison with the more fully matured contract-bar rules, the contract-bar doctrine in successorship cases is still emerging. Nonetheless, the decisions rendered in contract-bar cases prior to *Burns* are not dissimilar from those arising in comparable fact situations subsequent to *Burns,* though the concepts may become more complex.

Generally, to operate as a bar to a petition filed during its term, a contract must be in writing.[395] If the successor and the incumbent union negotiate and execute a new agreement, this requirement normally will be satisfied. In the event the successor voluntarily assumes the predecessor's preexisting labor agreement rather than entering into a new agreement, the assumption must be expressed in writing in order to operate as a bar.[396] However, where the new employer is substantially "identical" to, or an alter ego of, the prior employer, the contract between the prior employer and the incumbent union may operate as a bar to a petition from an outside union despite the failure of the new employer expressly to assume the contract. For example, where the only changes consisted of the corporate employer's becoming a subsidiary of another corporation and changing its corporate name, the contract was regarded as intact for its unexpired term.[397]

In certain instances, the policies underlying the contract-bar doctrine predominate over successorship considerations. For example, even though a successor employer enters into a written assumption of the predecessor's contract, it will not operate as a bar if it accelerates the termination date so as to reduce the designated period for filing a timely petition.[398] In contrast, successorship policies may prevail where the successor and the incumbent have entered into an agreement which has the effect of extending the expiration date beyond the term of the original agreement between the predecessor and the incumbent union.[399] In this application of its contract-bar rules, the Board has sought to harmonize and accommodate its *premature extension doctrine*[400] with its successorship policies.

---

[395]*See* Chapter 10, "Representation Proceedings and Elections," at note 120.
[396]Trans-American Video, 198 NLRB 1247, 81 LRRM 1162 (1972).
[397]M.B. Farrin Lumber Co., 117 NLRB 575, 39 LRRM 1296 (1957).
[398]Longview Terrace Co., 208 NLRB 699, 85 LRRM 1267 (1974).
[399]Ideal Chevrolet, 198 NLRB 280, 80 LRRM 1599 (1972).
[400]*See* Chapter 10, "Representation Proceedings and Elections," at notes 131 and 196–198.

Under the premature extension doctrine, a contract extended beyond its original expiration date will not bar a petition by other parties which has been timely filed in relation to the original expiration date. However, in *Ideal Chevrolet,*[401] decided shortly after *Burns,* the Board held that a new collective bargaining agreement entered into by the successor and the incumbent union during the unexpired term of the agreement between the predecessor and the incumbent union was a bar to a representation petition for the full term of the new agreement, even though it had been extended beyond the original expiration date of the predecessor's agreement. In refusing to invoke what otherwise would have warranted the application of its premature extension rule, the Board stated: "Were we to find that this new contract is not a bar to the petition . . . we would be discouraging the successor . . . and the incumbent union from creating a new and stable bargaining relationship."[402]

Prior to *Burns,* the Board had reached a similar result in holding that a written "extension agreement" between the successor and the incumbent union barred an otherwise timely decertification petition, where the extension agreement was regarded as a different agreement with new obligations and different starting and expiration dates.[403] In contrast, in another pre-*Burns* case, the Board had invoked its premature extension doctrine and had found no contract bar where it was the predecessor and the incumbent union who had entered into an extension agreement that was subsequently assumed in writing by the successor.[404] In still another case, the Board had also invoked its premature extension doctrine, despite the execution of a "new contract" by the new management, where the only significant change in the ownership or operation was a change in the stock ownership.[405]

Where the successor and the incumbent are permitted to extend a contract "prematurely," contract-bar rules will nonetheless continue to be applicable to the new or extended contract. Thus, the extended agreement may not be a bar to a petition by an outside union or employees for a period in excess

---

[401]*Supra* note 399.
[402]*Id.* at 280.
[403]Chrysler Corp., 153 NLRB 578, 59 LRRM 1529 (1965).
[404]Shop Rite Foods, 162 NLRB 1020, 64 LRRM 1123 (1956). All such cases must now be evaluated in light of NLRB v. Burns, *supra* note 394, and Ranch-Way, 203 NLRB 911, 83 LRRM 1197 (1973), *supplementing* 183 NLRB 1168, 74 LRRM 1389 (1970).
[405]M.B. Farrin Lumber Co., *supra* note 397.

of 3 years.[406] However, a contract in excess of 3 years will bar a petition filed by either of the contracting parties themselves for the duration of the contract.[407]

When a purchaser neither assumes nor extends its predecessor's labor agreement, but commences bargaining with the incumbent union, the purchaser may be confronted with a petition from an outside union prior to the time of execution of the agreement with the incumbent. In such circumstances, the contract-bar principle of *Keller Plastics*,[408] that following lawful recognition the parties may be given a "reasonable" time in which to conclude an agreement undisturbed by challenges to the incumbent's bargaining status, will be applied to a successor.[409] Thus, the successor and the incumbent union normally will be provided with a reasonable period of time in which to conclude an agreement which may extend beyond the expiration date of the predecessor's contract.[410]

Other merger and consolidation cases illustrate additional distinctions which the Board has deemed significant. Where two companies owned by the same employer were consolidated at the location of the second company, the Board held that the labor contract at the latter location served as a bar to an election.[411] But where the merger of two separate employers resulted in a single new unit in which the former employees of both employers were intermingled, the Board held that a prior labor agreement of one of the employers did not bar an election in the single new unit since the Board viewed the merger as resulting in a new operation.[412] Likewise, the Board held that a prior contract did not bar an election where the combined operation of merged employers brought about a fivefold expansion of the number of employees employed by the predecessor whose labor agreement was in question.[413]

---

[406]*Cf.* Ideal Chevrolet, *supra* note 399. *See generally* Chapter 10, "Representation Proceedings and Elections," at note 130.

[407]Montgomery Ward & Co., 137 NLRB 346, 50 LRRM 1137 (1962).

[408]157 NLRB 583, 61 LRRM 1396 (1966). *See* Chapter 10, "Representation Proceedings and Elections," at note 93.

[409]Fed-Mart, 165 NLRB 202, 65 LRRM 1303 (1967); *cf.* Glenn Spooner, 208 NLRB 891, 85 LRRM 1193 (1974), *enforced*, 76 Lab. Cas. (CCH) ¶10,699 (CA 10, 1975) (successor did not know of recognition agreement entered into between predecessor and union just prior to sale).

[410]Ideal Chevrolet, *supra* note 399.

[411]Builders Emporium, 97 NLRB 1113, 29 LRRM 1213 (1952).

[412]L.B. Spear & Co., 106 NLRB 687, 32 LRRM 1535 (1953).

[413]New Jersey Natural Gas Co., 101 NLRB 251, 31 LRRM 1048 (1952). *See also* Panda Terminals, 161 NLRB 1215, 63 LRRM 1419 (1966) (fourfold expansion); Bowman Dairy Co., 123 NLRB 707, 43 LRRM 1519 (1959) (30% of the employees in combined unit had been employed under contract in question).

VI. Liability of Successor for Predecessor's Unfair Labor Practices

A successor employer may become obligated to remedy unfair labor practices committed by its predecessor. Generally, the imposition of such an obligation and its extent will depend upon whether the successor has taken over its predecessor's operations with actual or constructive knowledge of pending unfair labor practice proceedings or outstanding Board orders. Liability has been imposed both where unfair labor practice charges were pending against the predecessor at the time of the transfer[414] and where, although no formal charges had been filed when the transfer occurred, the successor had "notice of the facts and appreciation of the significance of the predecessor's conduct."[415] If it had the required knowledge, joint and several liability may be imposed to remedy the unfair labor practices. This is the teaching of the Supreme Court's *Golden State Bottling*[416] decision. Where those circumstances prevail, the Board

---

[414]Applebaum Indus., 294 NLRB 981, 133 LRRM 1083 (1989); *see* Proxy Communications of Manhattan v. NLRB, 873 F2d 552, 554, 131 LRRM 2072, 2074 (CA 2, 1989), *enforcing* 290 NLRB 540, 129 LRRM 1175 (1988), where the Second Circuit stated that "the NLRB can require Proxy to remedy Federated's unfair labor practices because Proxy is Federated's successor and knew of those practices when it bought the company"; NLRB v. Great Lakes Chem. Corp., Aquabrom Div., 855 F2d 1174, 129 LRRM 2138, *clarified and amended*, 862 F2d 100, 129 LRRM 3140 (CA 6, 1988); NLRB v. Jarm Enters. dba Blu-Fountain Manor, 785 F2d 195, 121 LRRM 3105 (CA 7, 1986), *enforcing* 270 NLRB 199, 116 LRRM 1219 (1984); NLRB v. Winco Petroleum Co., 668 F2d 973, 109 LRRM 2377 (CA 8, 1982). *See also* NLRB v. South Harlan Coal, 844 F2d 380, 385, 128 LRRM 2182, 2187 (CA 6, 1988), where the Sixth Circuit determined that knowledge could be inferred from the circumstances, stating that neither a "denial of any actual knowledge, nor the absence of any other testimony on . . . actual knowledge, precludes this court from upholding the NLRB finding of knowledge of the unfair labor practices." Similarly, a trustee in bankruptcy must remedy the unfair labor practices of the bankrupt. Ohio Container Serv., 277 NLRB 305, 120 LRRM 1279 (1985).

[415]In NLRB v. St. Mary's Foundry Co., 860 F2d 679, 129 LRRM 2749, 2752 (CA 6, 1988), *enforcing* 284 NLRB 221, 125 LRRM 1146 (1987), the same individual was the president of both the predecessor and the successor and was present when the predecessor engaged in its unlawful conduct. The Sixth Circuit held that the purchaser was liable as a successor employer for the predecessor's unfair labor practices, even though formal charges were not filed by the union at the time of the sale, since the purchaser had knowledge that the predecessor was engaging in conduct that could lead to a finding of an unfair labor practice. The Sixth Circuit stated that, "[t]o adopt a bright-line test by holding that a successor employer is liable only in the event charges have been filed, would not serve the remedial purposes of the Act." *Id.*, 129 LRRM at 2752.

[416]Golden State Bottling Co. v. NLRB, 414 US 168, 84 LRRM 2839 (1973). *See generally* Du Ross, *Protecting Employee Remedial Rights Under the* Perma Vinyl *Doctrine,* 39 GEO. WASH. L. REV. 1063, 1089 (1971). By analogy, a successor is also precluded from challenging the appropriateness of a bargaining unit determined in a technical §8(a)(5) proceeding where it had notice of the proceeding. North Am. Soccer League v. NLRB, 613 F2d 1379, 103 LRRM 2976 (CA 5, 1980), *enforcing* 241 NLRB 1225, 101 LRRM 1037 (1979), *cert. denied*, 449 US 899, 105 LRRM 2737 (1980).

now refers to such a successor as a "*Golden State* successor," to distinguish it from a successor found to be an alter ego of the former employer.[417] An officer who is the alter ego of a corporation may even be liable for the corporation's backpay obligation.[418]

The development of the law concerning the liability of "*Golden State* successors" has run an uneven course.[419] It was not settled until the Supreme Court's 1973 *Golden State Bottling*[420] decision that the Board's remedial powers under section 10(c) of the Act included the power to impose such obligations. While the Board has uniformly followed such a policy since 1967, when it decided *Perma Vinyl Corp.*,[421] its position in prior years had been marked by a series of 180-degree turns.

Specifically, in 1944, the Board determined that a bona fide successor was not liable for the unfair labor practices of its predecessor. This position was abandoned in 1947 with the imposition of joint and several liability where the bona fide successor had knowledge of the seller's unfair labor practice at the time of purchase. In 1954, prompted by reversals in two courts of appeal, the Board, in *Symns Grocer Co.*,[422] returned to its 1944 position that the Act does not authorize imposition of responsibility for remedying unfair labor practices on a person who had not engaged in the subject conduct.[423]

Overruling *Symns Grocer* in 1967, the Board held in *Perma Vinyl*[424] that

---

[417]Bell Co., 243 NLRB 977, 101 LRRM 1572 (1979); Victor Patino, 241 NLRB 774, 100 LRRM 1616 (1979), where the new employer is an alter ego.

[418]Carpet City Mechanical Co., 244 NLRB 1031, 102 LRRM 1337 (1979).

[419]This has been unlike the development of the law concerning the liability of alter egos. Historically, the Board, even in its initial years, held with judicial support that an alter ego would be liable for the unfair labor practices of its predecessor. Regal Knitwear Co. v. NLRB, 324 US 9, 15 LRRM 882 (1945) (where such an identity of interests was found, Board orders running to "successors and assigns" of offending employers were upheld by the Supreme Court as early as the 1940s); Southport Petroleum Co. v. NLRB, 315 US 100, 9 LRRM 411 (1942); NLRB v. Hopwood Retinning Co., 104 F2d 302, 4 LRRM 555 (CA 2, 1939), *enforcing* 4 NLRB 922, 1A LRRM 416 (1938). For several propositions, the *Golden State Bottling* decision is also cited with approval in both the majority opinion and the dissenting opinion in Fall River Dyeing & Finishing Corp. v. NLRB, 482 US 27, 125 LRRM 2441 (1987), but both opinions state in effect that the Board's determinations on whether one employer is the successor of another employer are entitled to deference.

[420]Golden State Bottling v. NLRB, *supra* note 416.

[421]164 NLRB 968, 65 LRRM 1168 (1967), *enforced sub nom.* United States Pipe & Foundry Co. v. NLRB, 398 F2d 544, 68 LRRM 2913 (CA 5, 1968).

[422]109 NLRB 346, 34 LRRM 1326 (1954).

[423]Alexander Milburn Co., 78 NLRB 747, 22 LRRM 1249 (1948); South Carolina Granite Co., 58 NLRB 1448, 15 LRRM 122 (1944), *enforced sub nom.* NLRB v. Blair Quarries, Inc., 152 F2d 25, 17 LRRM 683 (CA 4, 1945). *See* Golden State Bottling Co. v. NLRB, *supra* note 416.

[424]*Supra* note 421.

> one who acquires and operates a business of an employer found guilty of unfair labor practices in basically unchanged form under circumstances which charge him with notice of unfair labor practice charges against his predecessor should be held responsible for remedying his predecessor's unlawful conduct.[425]

In *Perma Vinyl,* the Board ordered the purchaser to reinstate and reimburse with back pay four discharged employees. Perma Vinyl had paid backpay to the time of the sale to the purchaser, United States Pipe, but the issue remained as to whether and to what extent United States Pipe was liable for reinstatement of the discharged employees. United States Pipe was not an alter ego of Perma Vinyl; however, it had purchased the assets of Perma Vinyl "with knowledge of the unfair labor proceeding against that company."[426]

Recognizing that United States Pipe was the only employer with the power to reinstate the unlawfully discharged employees, the Board held that United States Pipe had the responsibility for remedying unfair labor practices attached to the business which it had bought and was continuing. The Board relied on the broad reasoning of the Supreme Court in *Wiley*[427] for fashioning this remedy, pointing to the fact that the "employee victims" of unfair labor practices were especially in need of help, for they are "without meaningful remedy when title to the employing business operation changes hands."[428]

In *Golden State Bottling Co. v. NLRB*[429] the Supreme Court adopted the Board's position in *Perma Vinyl* as well as its reasoning. The Court held that where a purchaser with notice of a pending unfair labor practice proceeding is found to have acquired and continued the business without interruption or substantial change in operation, employee complement, or supervisory personnel, it will have joint and several liability for backpay as a consequence of its predecessor's unfair labor practices, and it will be required to offer unlawfully discharged

---

[425]*Id.* at 969; *see* Du Ross, *supra* note 416.

[426]164 NLRB at 968. International Technical Prods. Corp., 249 NLRB 1301, 104 LRRM 1294 (1980), *supplementing* 196 NLRB 523, 80 LRRM 1222 (1972), where backpay liability applied to a successor who had purchased assets "free and clear" in a bankruptcy proceeding (but with knowledge of a predecessor's backpay liability).

[427]John Wiley & Sons v. Livingston, 376 US 543, 55 LRRM 2769 (1964).

[428]164 NLRB at 969.

[429]*Supra* note 416.

employees immediate reinstatement to their former or substantially equivalent positions.[430]

The Court concluded that (1) the Board's discretion under section 10(c) of the Act was broad enough to allow issuance of an order against a successor directing reinstatement with backpay;[431] (2) Rule 65(d) of the Federal Rules of Civil Procedure was not a bar to enforcement of a Board order requiring reinstatement by the successor, because a purchaser with knowledge of an unfair labor practice is in privity with the seller for purposes of the rule; (3) the Board properly balanced the "conflicting legitimate interests of the bona fide successor, the public and the affected employee" in light of the principles set forth in *Wiley*;[432] and (4) the Court's holding did not conflict in any manner with its decision in *Burns*.[433] Thus, the Court highlighted the distinction between the absence of an obligation by the successor to assume the predecessor's labor agreement and the existence of an obligation to remedy its predecessor's unfair labor practices.[434]

Finally, the Court was careful to note as a matter of due process and procedure that prior to any adjudication of its liability, the successor is entitled to notice and a hearing as to "whether it is a successor which is responsible for remedying the predecessor's unfair labor practices" and other facts relevant to the enforcement of the Board's order against it.[435] This cautionary statement was significant because wholly different parties may become involved at different stages of the proceedings,

---

[430]For a detailed discussion of this holding in the context of a new employer's requirement to reinstate strikers who had engaged in an unfair labor practices strike against its predecessor, see NLRB v. Fabsteel Co. of La., 587 F2d 689, 100 LRRM 2349 (CA 5, 1979), *enforcing* 231 NLRB 372, 97 LRRM 1104 (1977), *cert. denied*, 442 US 943, 101 LRRM 2556 (1979).

[431]Section 10(c) grants authority for the Board to require remedial action from "any person named in the complaint" who has engaged in "any such unfair labor practice," but also provides the Board shall have such remedial power "as will effectuate the policies of this Act."

[432]John Wiley & Sons v. Livingston, *supra* note 427. *See also supra* note 416.

[433]NLRB v. Burns Int'l Sec. Servs., 406 US 272, 80 LRRM 2225 (1972). *See also* Golden State Bottling Co. v. NLRB, *supra* note 416.

[434]Although the successor may not be required to assume the labor agreement, liability for payments to pension and health and welfare funds may be imposed where the predecessor was found to have unilaterally discontinued such payments pursuant to an unlawful withdrawal of recognition. Pacific Aggregates, 231 NLRB 214, 96 LRRM 1340 (1977).

[435]Golden State Bottling Co. v. NLRB, *supra* note 416, at 180; NLRB v. East Side Shopper, 498 F2d 1334, 86 LRRM 2817 (CA 6, 1974).

depending upon when the takeover occurs. In subsequent years procedural issues have become prevalent.

Issues concerning a successor's derivative liability may be raised and litigated for the first time at the compliance stage of an unfair labor practice proceeding in a supplementary proceeding.[436] It is not necessary for the Board to initiate a new unfair labor practice proceeding to consider this issue.[437] Nor is the Board required, where a court of appeals has already enforced its initial order, to apply to that court for permission to conduct a supplementary proceeding to determine derivative liability.[438] The circuit courts have been reluctant to permit the Board to litigate "*Golden State* successor" issues initially in contempt proceedings. For example, in *Computer Sciences Corp. v. NLRB*[439] the Board had dispensed with a refusal-to-bargain charge filed against the new employer and instead instituted civil contempt proceedings seeking to hold the new employer in violation of the unfair labor practice order directed at the predecessor. The Court of Appeals for the Eleventh Circuit refused to decide the successorship question as ancillary to the enforcement order and dismissed the contempt petition. The court held that the bona fide dispute over successorship was more appropriately resolved by the Board in the first instance and that the court should resolve a successorship issue in the context of contempt proceedings only if it determines that the issue is a "sham."[440]

---

[436]Coast Delivery Serv., 198 NLRB 1026, 81 LRRM 1417 (1972); *see* NLRB v. C.C.C. Assocs., 306 F2d 534, 50 LRRM 2882 (CA 2, 1962), where the derivative liability of a successor was litigated for the first time after a court *enforced* a Board order for backpay against the predecessor. Since supplementary proceedings are typically concerned with the extent to which backpay may be due, they are frequently designated as "back pay proceedings." *See* discussion in Chapter 31, "NLRB Procedures," at notes 180–183.

[437]*See* authorities cited in *supra* note 436.

[438]*Id*; NLRB v. Royal Palm Ice Co., 201 F2d 667, 31 LRRM 2308 (CA 5, 1953); Home Beneficial Life Ins. Co. v. NLRB, 172 F2d 62, 23 LRRM 2253 (CA 4, 1949); NLRB v. Bird Mach. Co., 174 F2d 404, 24 LRRM 2053 (CA 1, 1949).

[439]677 F2d 804, 110 LRRM 2642 (CA 11, 1982).

[440]*See also* NLRB v. Great Lakes Chem. Corp., Aquabrom Div., 855 F2d 1174, 129 LRRM 2138, 2148, *clarified and amended* 862 F2d 100, 129 LRRM 3140 (CA 6, 1988), where the Sixth Circuit stated that "an employer will not be found in civil contempt of such a bargaining order until a factual determination is made that it is indeed a successor, a principle which this court recognized in remanding the case to the Board to make the initial successorship decision." Although the Ninth Circuit reached a similar conclusion in NLRB v. FMG Indus. dba Gamco Indus., 820 F2d 289, 125 LRRM 3013, 3017 (CA 9, 1987), stating that "[p]olicy considerations . . . dictate that in all but the clearest cases the Board should first resolve the issue," the *Aquabrom* court also held that due process does not require that the initial hearing be conducted by the Board.

Frequently, where the takeover occurs after a Board order issues or after the unfair labor practice hearings have been completed, the compliance stage represents the first occasion for raising issues of derivative liability.[441] Even where there is evidence in the unfair labor practice proceeding, which establishes a foundation for findings as to the relationship between the prior and the present employer, the Board will not impose derivative liability at that initial stage, unless the new employer has been named as a party and afforded a full opportunity to litigate its status in that proceeding. Otherwise, it would not have had its "day in court."[442] Instead, the Board permits its General Counsel to plead and litigate this question during the compliance stage. Thus, even though the principals of the two employers have remained the same and have testified in the underlying unfair labor practices hearing, they may still be afforded a separate day in court, particularly where they testified in their capacities as representatives of the prior employer.[443] Similarly, the Board is reluctant to grant the General Counsel's motion for summary judgment at the compliance stage, if that would deprive a new party of the opportunity to litigate its status in a hearing at that time.[444]

Although the Board has demonstrated a preference for considering issues of derivative liability at the compliance stage,[445] significant controversy has arisen in situations where a new employer was not named as a respondent in the underlying unfair labor practice proceeding despite the General Counsel's awareness of its alter ego status. In 1978 the Board held that

---

[441]NLRB v. C.C.C. Assocs., *supra* note 436; Hot Bagels & Donuts of Staten Island, 244 NLRB 129, 102 LRRM 1163 (1979), *enforced*, 622 F2d 1113, 104 LRRM 2963 (CA 2, 1980); Coast Delivery Serv., *supra* note 436.

[442]George C. Shearer Exhibitors Delivery Serv., 246 NLRB 416, 102 LRRM 1624 (1979), *enforced*, 636 F2d 1210, 108 LRRM 2279 (CA 3, 1980). *See* Marine Mach. Works, 243 NLRB 1081, 101 LRRM 1576 (1979), *enforced*, 635 F2d 522, 106 LRRM 2656 (CA 5, 1981), denying the General Counsel's motion to join an alleged successor in the unfair labor practice proceeding.

[443]*See supra* note 442.

[444]Dews Constr. Corp., 246 NLRB 945, 103 LRRM 1001 (1979), *supplementing* 231 NLRB 182, 95 LRRM 1574 (1977). In unusual circumstances (indisputable evidence of alter ego status and a deliberate scheme to dissipate assets or frustrate the enforcement of backpay liability) a successor's liability was initially determined in a direct contempt proceeding. As noted above, however, absent such factors, the courts have rejected this direct procedure as inappropriate since it undermines the reviewing process and inhibits the Board's role in initially determining all undecided issues.

[445]Southeastern Envelope Co., 246 NLRB 423, 102 LRRM 1567 (1979), *supplementing* 206 NLRB 933, 84 LRRM 1577 (1973).

under those circumstances, even an alter ego employer could not thereafter be held accountable in a backpay proceeding.[446] In the following year, however, a divided Board overruled this position and permitted the General Counsel to litigate the question of derivative liability in a compliance proceeding even though the issue could have been pleaded and litigated in the original unfair labor practice proceeding.[447] In the compliance proceeding, the Board emphasized the finding that the employers were alter egos whose interests "are by definition identical." It therefore concluded that adequate notice had been afforded.[448]

The Board also permitted the General Counsel to litigate for the first time, in a supplementary proceeding, an employer's status as a "*Golden State* successor," even though the employer's status had already been litigated on an alter ego theory in the underlying unfair practice proceeding.[449] The Court of Appeals for the Seventh Circuit, however, rejected the Board's finding that the new employer was an alter ego, but it did not consider the question of its derivative liability as a *Golden State* successor.[450]

When the issue of derivative liability is litigated (generally at the compliance stage), the new employer may raise as defenses, as a threshold matter, that: (1) it is not an alter ego or a successor,[451] (2) it did not possess the knowledge required as a *Golden State* successor,[452] (3) it does not meet the jurisdictional standards of the Board,[453] or (4) the imposition of derivative liability is otherwise inappropriate.[454]

As to the issue of prior knowledge, the Board has placed the burden on the successor to prove lack of knowledge.[455] One obstacle to meeting that burden might be that the successor had, at the time of purchase, obtained an indemnification clause in its sale agreement regarding any obligations incurred as a result of

---

[446]Rose Knitting Mills, 237 NLRB 1382, 99 LRRM 1223 (1978).

[447]Southeastern Envelope Co., *supra* note 445.

[448]*Id.*

[449]Bell Co., 243 NLRB 977, 101 LRRM 1572 (1979) (decision by a divided Board).

[450]NLRB v. Bell Co., 561 F2d 1264, 96 LRRM 2437 (CA 7, 1977).

[451]Dews Constr. Corp., *supra* note 444.

[452]Mansion House Center Mgmt. Corp., 208 NLRB 684, 85 LRRM 1555 (1974).

[453]Northgate Cinema, 233 NLRB 586, 96 LRRM 1598 (1977).

[454]NLRB v. Fabsteel Co. of La., 587 F2d 689, 100 LRRM 2349 (CA 5, 1979), *enforcing* 231 NLRB 372, 97 LRRM 1104 (1977), *cert denied*, 442 US 943, 101 LRRM 2556 (1979). *See* Middle E. Bakery, 243 NLRB 503, 101 LRRM 1507 (1979) (bare assertion of nonsuccessorship as defense after failure to answer complaint is inadequate and untimely).

[455]Mansion House Center Mgmt. Corp., *supra* note 452.

unfair labor practice proceedings against its predecessor.[456] Where, however, there is no face-to-face relationship between the successor and the predecessor, as in a contract-bid situation, prior knowledge may not be as readily available.

A successor also may seek to show that its revenues, unlike its predecessor's, do not meet the Board's jurisdictional standards.[457] Where a full calendar year has not elapsed, the Board will assert jurisdiction on the basis of the income of the predecessor in the previous calendar years based on the projected revenue of the new employer.[458] The basis for rejecting a mutually exclusive test, such as projected revenue, is the concern that a new employer could shield itself from remedies for serious unfair labor practices by a "measured effort" to defeat Board jurisdiction.[459]

In a related context, another defense to liability may be that the purchaser's operations are based upon an independent contractor relationship, rather than the employer-employee relationship that previously existed.[460] In these circumstances, the denial of liability would be based upon the ground that the purchaser is not a successor.[461]

Derivative liability may be imposed upon a parent corporation with respect to unfair labor practices by its subsidiary in certain instances.[462] There, in the case of a bargaining violation, the test is not whether day-to-day labor relations are handled on a local level, but whether the parent corporation has the "present and apparent means" to influence the local negotiations and permits this fact to be traded upon in the local negotiations.[463]

In a collateral development, there is authority for finding that a successor may be required, in a section 301 action, to satisfy an arbitration award arising out of a predecessor's contract, where it had knowledge of the award and expressly assumed the agreement.[464]

Not every unfair labor practice, however, will necessitate a remedial order against a *Golden State* successor. Thus, a suc-

---

[456]Am-Del-Co., Inc. 234 NLRB 1040, 97 LRRM 1419 (1978).
[457]*See generally* Chapter 28, "Jurisdiction: Coverage of the Act," at notes 374–426.
[458]Northgate Cinema, *supra* note 453.
[459]*Id.*
[460]Merchants Home Delivery Serv., 230 NLRB 290, 95 LRRM 1357 (1977).
[461]*Id.*
[462]Royal Typewriter Co. v. NLRB, 533 F2d 1030, 92 LRRM 2013 (CA 8, 1976).
[463]*Id.*
[464]Auto Workers Local 6 v. Saga Foods, 407 F Supp 1247, 91 LRRM 2946 (ND Ill, 1976).

cessor may not be required to remedy a predecessor's unlawful refusal to furnish information to the union, where the information is no longer current and the order against the predecessor suffices as a remedy.[465]

[465]Roman Catholic Diocese of Brooklyn, 222 NLRB 1052, 91 LRRM 1419 (1976), *aff'd sub nom.* Nazareth Regional High School v. NLRB, 549 F2d 873, 94 LRRM 2897 (CA 2, 1977). Nor will a successor to one bargaining unit be required to remedy the unfair labor practices of the predecessor in another unit in which it is not the successor. Bellingham Frozen Foods Div. v. NLRB, 626 F2d 674, 105 LRRM 2404 (CA 9, 1980), *enforcing in part* 237 NLRB 1450, 99 LRRM 1270 (1978), *cert. denied,* 449 US 1125, 106 LRRM 2256 (1981).

Chapter 16

SUBJECTS OF BARGAINING

I. Introduction

This chapter examines the law governing the subject matter of collective bargaining. The Board and the courts have divided bargaining subjects into three discrete categories: mandatory, permissive, and illegal. Sections II and III, *infra,* describe generally the difference between mandatory and permissive bargaining subjects and the consequences of classifying a subject as one or the other. The development of the mandatory and permissive dichotomy is traced through a series of Supreme Court decisions that provide the foundation for analyzing questions involving the dichotomy. Section IV describes in depth mandatory bargaining subjects. Section V describes in depth permissive and illegal bargaining subjects.[1]

II. Historical Background

The law concerning subjects of bargaining has evolved in Board and Supreme Court decisions, with relatively little guidance from the language of the Act or from legislative history. Section 8(5) of the Wagner Act made it an unfair labor practice for an employer "to refuse to bargain collectively with the representatives of his employees, subject to the provisions of section 9(a)." Section 9(a) of the Wagner Act provided that the employees' bargaining representative "shall be the exclusive representative of all the employees . . . for the purpose of collective bargaining in respect of *rates of pay, wages, hours of employ-*

[1]The nature of the duty to bargain in good faith is discussed in Chapter 13, "The Duty to Bargain."

ment, or other conditions of employment."[2] Prior to the Taft-Hartley Act of 1947, this language provided the only statutory guidance concerning subjects for collective bargaining.

In the absence of definitional or restrictive statutory language, the Board, very early, assumed the role of determining what were and were not mandatory bargaining subjects. In 1940, in *Singer Manufacturing Co.*,[3] the Board held that

> [p]aid holidays, vacations, and bonuses constitute an integral part of the earnings and working conditions of the employees and . . . are matters which are generally the subject of collective bargaining . . . . [I]nsistence upon treating such matters as gratuities to be granted and withdrawn at will, constitutes a refusal to bargain . . . .[4]

Following the *Singer* case, the Board held that various integral parts of the employment relationship were embraced by the language of section 9(a).[5] These included discharges,[6] pensions,[7] profit-sharing,[8] work loads and work standards,[9] insurance benefits,[10] the closed and the union shop,[11] subcontracting,[12] shop rules,[13] work schedules,[14] rest periods,[15] and merit increases.[16]

Although Congress amended the Act extensively in 1947, it made no basic change in the legislative framework supporting

---

[2]Emphasis added.

[3]24 NLRB 444, 6 LRRM 405 (1940), *modified on other grounds and enforced,* 119 F2d 131, 8 LRRM 740 (CA 7, 1941).

[4]*Id.* at 470.

[5]Cox & Dunlop, *Regulation of Collective Bargaining by the National Labor Relations Board,* 63 HARV. L. REV. 389, 397–401 (1950).

[6]NLRB v. Bachelder, 120 F2d 574, 8 LRRM 723 (CA 7, 1941).

[7]Inland Steel Co., 77 NLRB 1, 21 LRRM 1310 (1948), *enforced,* 170 F2d 247, 22 LRRM 2506 (CA 7, 1948), *cert. denied,* 336 US 960, 24 LRRM 2019 (1949).

[8]Union Mfg. Co., 76 NLRB 322, 21 LRRM 1187 (1948), *enforced,* 179 F2d 511, 25 LRRM 2302 (CA 5, 1950).

[9]Woodside Cotton Mills Co., 21 NLRB 42, 6 LRRM 68 (1940).

[10]W.W. Cross & Co., 77 NLRB 1162, 22 LRRM 1131 (1948), *enforced,* 174 F2d 875, 24 LRRM 2068 (CA 1, 1949).

[11]Winona Textile Mills, 68 NLRB 702, 18 LRRM 1154 (1946), *enforced,* 160 F2d 201, 19 LRRM 2417 (CA 8, 1947).

[12]Timken Roller Bearing Co., 70 NLRB 500, 18 LRRM 1370 (1946), *enforcement denied on other grounds,* 161 F2d 949, 20 LRRM 2204 (CA 6, 1947); *cf.* Emerson Elec. Mfg. Co., 13 NLRB 448, 4 LRRM 307 (1939).

[13]Timken Roller Bearing Co., *supra* note 12.

[14]Inter-City Advertising Co., 61 NLRB 1377, 1384, 16 LRRM 153 (1945), *enforcement denied on other grounds,* 154 F2d 244, 17 LRRM 916 (CA 4, 1946); Wilson & Co., 19 NLRB 990, 999, 5 LRRM 560 (1940), *enforced,* 115 F2d 759, 7 LRRM 575 (CA 8, 1940); Woodside Cotton Mills Co., *supra* note 9, at 54–55.

[15]National Grinding Wheel Co., 75 NLRB 905, 21 LRRM 1095 (1948).

[16]NLRB v. J.H. Allison & Co., 165 F2d 766, 21 LRRM 2238 (CA 6, 1948), *enforcing* 70 NLRB 377, 18 LRRM 1369 (1946), *cert. denied,* 335 US 814, 22 LRRM 2564 (1948); Aluminum Ore Co. v. NLRB, 131 F2d 485, 11 LRRM 693 (CA 7, 1942), *enforcing* 39 NLRB 1286, 10 LRRM 49 (1942).

the Board's definitions of the subjects of bargaining. With the addition of section 8(d), the phrase "wages, hours of employment, or other conditions of employment," which the Board had construed in the context of section 9(a), became, "wages, hours, and other terms and conditions of employment."[17]

Because Congress did not define substantive bargaining in the Taft-Hartley amendments, the law of collective bargaining[18] has shown a developing pattern of change based upon changes in the economy and society as interpreted by the Board and courts. Justice Stewart, joined by Justices Douglas and Harlan, concurring in the 1964 *Fibreboard* decisions,[19] concluded that

> [t]here was a time when one might have taken the view that the National Labor Relations Act gave the Board and the courts no power to determine the subjects about which the parties must bargain . . . . But too much law has been built upon a contrary assumption for this view any longer to prevail, and I question neither the power of the Court to decide this issue nor the propriety of its doing so.[20]

In 1952, in its first decision on bargaining subjects, *NLRB v. American National Insurance Co.*,[21] the Supreme Court reversed the Board's holding that an employer had violated section 8(a)(5) by making a collective bargaining agreement conditioned on the inclusion of a broad management-rights clause under which certain subjects including promotion, demotion, discharge, discipline, and work schedules, would be nonarbitrable. The Board conceded that the management-rights clause was not unlawful; however, it argued that insistence on such a clause was unlawful because such insistence was a derogation of the

---

[17]The "rates of pay" language of §9(a) was not included in §8(d), apparently because "rates of pay" with "wages" was deemed redundant. Section 9(a)'s "conditions of employment" became "terms and conditions of employment" in §8(d). Taft-Hartley also added §8(b)(3), which made it an unfair labor practice for a labor organization "to refuse to bargain collectively with an employer . . . ."

[18]*See* Section IV *infra*.

[19]Fibreboard Paper Prods. Corp. v. NLRB, 379 US 203, 57 LRRM 2609 (1964). *See* Section IV *infra*, at notes 320–332.

[20]379 US at 219 n.2. Contrast the statement of Senator Walsh, Chairman of the Senate Education and Labor Committee when the Wagner Act was being passed:

> The bill indicates the method and manner in which employees may organize, the method and manner of selecting their representatives or spokesmen, and leads them to the office door of their employer with the legal authority to negotiate for their fellow employees. The bill does not go beyond the office door. It leaves the discussion between the employer and the employee, and the agreements which they may or may not make, voluntary and with that sacredness and solemnity to a voluntary agreement with which both parties to an agreement should be enshrouded.

79 CONG. REC. 7,659 (1935).

[21]343 US 395, 30 LRRM 2147 (1952).

obligation to bargain over conditions of employment. The Court noted that broad management-rights clauses were common in recent collective bargaining agreements, and it viewed the Board's efforts as an unwarranted interference with the collective bargaining process, stating:

> Bargaining for more flexible treatment of [conditions of employment] would be denied employers even though the result may be contrary to common collective bargaining practice in the industry. The Board was not empowered so to disrupt collective bargaining practices. On the contrary, the term "bargain collectively" as used in the act has been considered to absorb and give statutory approval to the philosophy of bargaining as worked out in the labor movement in the United States.[22]

American National was the Court's only major decision on bargaining subjects before *NLRB v. Borg-Warner Corp., Wooster Division*,[23] which established the distinction between mandatory and permissive bargaining subjects—the distinction that governs the law of bargaining subjects today.

III. DEVELOPMENT OF THE DISTINCTION BETWEEN "MANDATORY" AND "PERMISSIVE"

A. *Borg-Warner*—The Basic Principles

The language of the statute (section 8(d)) merely directs bargaining parties to "confer in good faith with respect to wages, hours, and other terms and conditions of employment." From this, the Supreme Court has developed the distinction between *mandatory* bargaining subjects, that is, wages, hours, and other terms and conditions of employment, and *permissive* subjects, that is, nonmandatory subjects that are nevertheless proper bargaining subjects in that they do not conflict with federal or applicable state law. The Court has further refined the definition of mandatory bargaining subjects to include subjects that "vitally affect" employees, including subjects that relate directly to nonemployees, that is, concern individuals or conditions outside the bargaining unit but which nevertheless have a substantial impact on bargaining-unit employees. The Court has also declared that industry collective bargaining practices are "highly relevant" in deciding which subjects are mandatory and that

---

[22]*Id.* at 408.

[23]356 US 342, 42 LRRM 2034 (1958).

Congress intended that the Board, not the courts, should have the primary responsibility for determining which subjects are mandatory. The Court has held that where it is necessary to decide whether certain business decisions are mandatory bargaining subjects the benefits to the collective bargaining process must be balanced against the employer's need for unencumbered decision making in certain areas affecting the employer's business.

In *NLRB v. Borg-Warner Corp., Wooster Division*,[24] decided in 1958, the Supreme Court adopted the Board's analysis, which recognized a distinction between mandatory bargaining subjects and permissive bargaining subjects. The Court reviewed sections 8(a)(5) and 8(d),[25] and reasoned:

> Read together, these provisions establish the obligation of the employer and the representative of its employees to bargain with each other in good faith with respect to wages, hours, and other terms and conditions of employment . . . . The duty is limited to those subjects, and within that area neither party is legally obligated to yield . . . . As to other matters, however, each party is free to bargain or not to bargain, and to agree or not to agree.[26]

The employer, although bargaining in good faith concerning wages, hours, and other terms and conditions of employment, had insisted that any agreement be conditioned on inclusion of (1) a recognition clause granting recognition solely to the local union, even though the international union was the Board-certified bargaining representative, and (2) a "ballot clause" under which a strike could not be conducted over nonarbitrable issues until all bargaining-unit members (union and nonunion) had voted on the company's last offer and which permitted the company, if the offer was rejected, to submit a revised offer within 72 hours for a similar secret ballot. The Court concluded that the recognition clause and the ballot clause were not mandatory bargaining subjects in that they did not concern wages, hours, and other terms and conditions of employment.[27] Agree-

---

[24]*Id.*

[25]The same reasoning is also applicable to §8(b)(3), concerning a union's refusal to bargain. *See generally* Chapters 13, "The Duty to Bargain," and Section IV *infra.*

[26]356 US at 349.

[27]*Id.* at 356–59. The Court had little difficulty finding the recognition clause to be a nonmandatory bargaining subject, stating: "The statute requires the company to bargain with the certified representative of its employees. It is an evasion of that duty to insist that the certified agent not be a party to the collective-bargaining contract." *Id.* at 350.

The ballot-clause analysis, however, was not so easy. The Court, citing *American National Insurance Co., supra* note 21, acknowledged that the employer could have insisted on a no-ing with the Board, the Court held that the employer's insistence on the inclusion of these nonmandatory bargaining subjects was, in effect, a refusal to bargain over the mandatory bargaining subjects, stating:

> The company's good faith has met the requirements of the statute as to the subjects of mandatory bargaining. But that good faith does not license the employer to refuse to enter into agreements on the ground that they do not include some proposal which is not a mandatory subject of bargaining. We agree with the Board that such conduct is, in substance, a refusal to bargain about the subjects that are within the scope of mandatory bargaining. This does not mean that bargaining is to be confined to the statutory subjects. Each of the two controversial clauses is lawful in itself. Each would be enforceable if agreed to by the unions. But it does not follow that, because the company may propose these clauses, it can lawfully insist upon them as a condition to any agreement.[28]

Borg-Warner teaches that a party, regardless of its good faith in bargaining, commits an unfair labor practice when it insists to impasse upon the inclusion of a permissive bargaining subject, that is, a subject outside the scope of "wages, hours, and other terms and conditions of employment."[29]

B. *Pittsburgh Plate Glass*—The "Vitally Affects" Test

In a 1971 decision, *Allied Chemical & Alkali Workers Local 1 v. Pittsburgh Plate Glass Co.*,[30] the Court faced the issue of whether an employer violated section 8(a)(5) by unilaterally modifying, during the term of the contract, a health insurance plan covering retired employees. The case turned on whether the benefits of already-retired employees is a mandatory bargaining subject, since unilateral changes in mandatory bargaining subjects are per se section 8(a)(5) violations.[31] The Board held that changes

---

strike clause because such a clause "regulates the relations between the employer and the employees." 356 US at 350. The ballot clause, however, was not viewed as a "partial 'no-strike' clause" but rather as an attempt to regulate relations "between the employees and their unions." *Id.* It was thus an attempt by "the employer, in effect, to deal with its employees rather than with their statutory representative." *Id.*

[28] *Id.* at 349.

[29] The *Borg-Warner* decision was criticized by commentators in Wollett, *The Borg-Warner Case and the Role of the NLRB in the Bargaining Process,* NYU TWELFTH ANNUAL CONFERENCE ON LABOR 39 (1959); Note, 43 MINN. L. REV. 1225 (1959); Note, 11 STAN L. REV. 188 (1958).

[30] 404 US 157, 78 LRRM 2974 (1971).

[31] *Id.* at 183–88. (In contrast, a unilateral midcontract change relating to a permissive bargaining subject is not an unfair labor practice; the remedy for such a change is to pursue a §301 action or file a grievance under the collective bargaining agreement's grievance-arbitration procedure; if applicable.) *See* NLRB v. Katz, 369 US 736, 50 LRRM 2177 (1962), and discussion in Chapter 13, "The Duty to Bargain," at notes 73–101.

in retired employees' benefits "are embraced by the bargaining obligation and that an employer's unilateral modification of them" constitutes a section 8(a)(5) violation.[32] The Court disagreed.

The Court first rejected the Board's argument that retired employees were employees within the meaning of section 2(3) and that therefore their benefits involved terms and conditions of employment—a mandatory bargaining subject.[33] The Court then addressed the Board's second theory, to wit: Even if retirees are not section 2(3) employees, their benefits "vitally affect" the terms and condition of employment of active employees and are therefore a mandatory bargaining subject. The Court recognized that "matters involving individuals outside the employment relationship, . . . are not wholly excluded [from the mandatory bargaining subjects],[34] citing *Teamsters Local 24 v. Oliver*[35] and *Fibreboard Paper Products Corp. v. NLRB*.[36] The Court accepted the Board's "vitally affects" test but rejected its conclusion that the test was met by retirees' benefits:

> We agree with the Board that the principle of *Oliver* and *Fibreboard* is relevant here; in each case the question is not whether the third-party concern is antagonistic to or compatible with the interest of bargaining-unit employees, but whether it vitally affects the "terms and conditions" of their employment.[37] But we disagree with the Board's assessment of the significance of a change in retirees' benefits to the "terms and conditions of employment" of active employees.[38]

The Court concluded that "[t]he benefits that active workers may reap by including retired employees under the same health

[32]Pittsburgh Plate Glass Co., 177 NLRB 911, 71 LRRM 1433 (1969), *enforcement denied,* 427 F2d 936, 74 LRRM 2425 (CA 6, 1970). *See supra* note 30, at 160.

[33]404 US at 163–76. *See* Chapter 28, "Jurisdiction: Coverage of the Act," at notes 370–373, for a discussion of this issue. In its discussion of §2(3), the Court held that an "established industrial practice" of collective bargaining over retirees' benefits "would not be determinative. Common practice cannot change the law and make into bargaining unit 'employees' those who are not." 404 US at 175–76.

[34]*Id.* at 178.

[35]358 US 283, 43 LRRM 2374 (1959) (federal labor law preempts state antitrust law application to collective bargaining agreement fixing minimum truck leasing payments by employer to lessor-drivers, a mandatory bargaining subject). *See* Section IV *infra,* at notes 168–169, and Chapter 29, "Federal Preemption of State Regulation," at notes 46–50.

[36]*Supra* note 19 (decision to subcontract bargaining-unit work may be a mandatory bargaining subject). *See* Section IV *infra,* at notes 319–332.

[37]The Court added, in a footnote: "This is not to say that application of *Oliver* and *Fibreboard* turns only on the impact of the third-party matter on employee interests. Other considerations such as the effect on the employer's freedom to conduct his business, may be equally important." 404 US at 179 n.19.

[38]*Id.* at 179.

insurance contract are speculative and insubstantial at best."[39] Nevertheless, *Pittsburgh Plate Glass* and its "vitally affects" test provided an avenue for expanding the scope of mandatory bargaining subjects to include issues directly relating to nonemployees or other conditions, so long as a sufficient nexus with the employees' interests can be shown.

C. *Ford Motor Co.*—The Role of the Board and of Industry Bargaining Practices

The Supreme Court's 1979 decision in *Ford Motor Co. v. NLRB*[40] afforded the Court an opportunity to discuss several general considerations regarding the mandatory and permissive dichotomy. The Court agreed with the Board that the employer had violated section 8(a)(5) by unilaterally approving a supplier's increase in the prices charged at the plant cafeteria and vending machines, a mandatory subject of bargaining.[41]

The Court began its analysis by declaring that the Board had primary responsibility for determining which items are mandatory bargaining subjects. The Court traced the legislative history of the Wagner Act of 1935 and the Taft-Hartley Act of 1947, noting congressional rejection of proposals, during the consideration of the Taft-Hartley amendments, to define and limit mandatory bargaining subjects. The Court concluded: "It is . . . evident that Congress made a conscious decision to continue its delegation to the Board of the primary responsibility of marking out the scope of the statutory language and the statutory duty to bargain."[42] The Board's decisions in this area "if reasonably defensible, . . . should not be rejected merely because the courts might prefer another view of the statute."[43] The Court, of course, recognized that there were limits on the Board's discretion in decisions concerning mandatory bargaining subjects.[44]

---

[39] *Id.* at 180.

[40] 441 US 488, 101 LRRM 2222 (1979).

[41] Ford contracted the in-plant food services to a third-party supplier. However, Ford maintained the right to review and approve the quality, quantity, and price of the food.

[42] 441 US at 496.

[43] *Id.* at 497.

[44] Enforcement may be refused where the Board order "has no reasonable basis in law, . . . [is] 'fundamentally inconsistent with the structure of the Act' and an attempt to usurp 'major policy decisions properly made by Congress' [or] . . . 'the Board was moving into a new area of regulation which Congress had not committed it to.'" *Id.*

The Court looked closely at industry practices regarding bargaining over food services and prices and also at the history of bargaining over those subjects at the particular plant. "Although not conclusive," the Court declared, "current industrial practice is highly relevant in construing the phrase 'terms and conditions of employment.'"[45]

The decision is also noteworthy for its breadth. The decision was not limited to the particular facts of the plant in question, that is, a short lunch break, no nearby off-premises alternatives, and a vermin problem discouraging employees from bringing their own food. The Court broadly held that "in-plant food services and prices are 'terms and conditions of employment' subject to mandatory bargaining . . . ."[46]

D. *First National Maintenance Corp.*—The Balancing Test

The Court's 1981 decision in *First National Maintenance Corp. v. NLRB*[47] announced a balancing test regarding the duty to bargain over certain fundamental business decisions. The employer operated a cleaning and maintenance business; it contracted with commercial customers to provide a labor force and supervision in return for reimbursement of its labor costs and payment of a set management fee. Because of a disagreement over a management fee, the employer canceled its contract to provide services for a customer. However, the employer failed to bargain with the union about either the decision to terminate the contract or the effects of the termination on the 35 employees in the bargaining unit, all of whom worked at that customer's facility. The Board held that the employer violated section 8(a)(5) by failing to bargain in each respect. The employer conceded in the court of appeals that its refusal to bargain over the effects of the decision was a violation of section 8(a)(5).[48] The issue before the Supreme Court was whether "an economically-motivated decision to shut down part of a business" is a mandatory bargaining subject.[49]

---

[45]*Id.* at 501.

[46]*Id.* at 504 (Justice Powell concurred in this "bright line" approach, *id.* at 503–4). The Court, however, noted that the decision does not resolve the issue of mandatory bargaining where a plant does not already have in-plant food services. *Id.* at 498 n.10.

[47]452 US 666, 107 LRRM 2705 (1981).

[48]*Id.* at 677 n.15.

[49]*Id.* at 680. The union made no claim that the employer's decision to terminate the contract was based on union animus.

The Court acknowledged that the employer's decision to cancel the contract "had a direct impact on employment, since jobs were inexorably eliminated . . . ."[50] But unlike management decisions that are almost exclusively a matter of concern between employer and employees, the decision to cancel the contract, according to the Court,

> had as its focus only the economic profitability of the contract with [the customer], a concern under these facts wholly apart from the employment relationship. This decision, involving a change in the scope and direction of the enterprise, is akin to the decision whether to be in business at all . . . .[51]

The Court then discussed the policies advanced by the mandatory-bargaining-subject concept and promulgated the following balancing test:

> The concept of mandatory bargaining is premised on the belief that collective discussions backed by the parties' economic weapons will result in decisions that are better for both management and labor and for society as a whole . . . . This will be true, however, only if the subject proposed for discussion is amenable to resolution through the bargaining process. Management must be free from the constraints of the bargaining process to the extent essential for the running of a profitable business . . . . [I]n view of an employer's need for unencumbered decisionmaking, bargaining over management decisions that have a substantial impact on the continued availability of employment should be required only if the benefit, for labor-management relations and the collective bargaining process, outweighs the burden placed on the conduct of the business.[52]

In the circumstances before it, the Court struck the balance in favor of the employer's interest in running a profitable business. The Court's opinion expressly stated that it offered "no view as to . . . plant relocations, sales, other kinds of subcontracting, automation, etc."[53]

The Court stressed, however, that unions have significant input under their right to engage in "effects" bargaining: "[B]argaining over the effects of a decision must be conducted in a meaningful manner and at a meaningful time . . . . [The

---

[50]*Id.* at 677.

[51]*Id.* The Court equated the case to Textile Workers v. Darlington Mfg. Co., 380 US 263, 58 LRRM 2657 (1965). *See* Chapter 7, "Discrimination in Employment," at notes 260–266.

[52]452 US at 678. In adopting the balancing test, the Court made repeated reference to Fibreboard Paper Prods. v. NLRB, 379 US 203, 57 LRRM 2609 (1964), and, especially, to Justice Stewart's concurring opinion.

[53]452 US at 686 n.22.

union] has some control over the effects of the decision and indirectly may ensure that the decision itself is deliberately considered."[54] The Court noted that a union also has section 8(a)(3) protection against "partial closings motivated by anti-union animus."[55] The employer, on the other hand,

> may have great need for speed, flexibility, and secrecy in meeting business opportunities and exigencies. It may face significant tax or securities consequences that hinge on confidentiality, the timing of a plant closing, or a reorganization of the corporate structure. The publicity incident to the normal process of bargaining may injure the possibility of a successful transition or increase the economic damage to the business.[56]

The Court was also concerned that "[l]abeling this type of decision mandatory could afford a union a powerful tool for achieving delay, a power that might be used to thwart management's intentions unrelated to any feasible solution the union might propose."[57] The Court concluded that mandatory bargaining over such decisions would add so little to existing employee rights that the risk of harm to legitimate business interests could not be justified.

E. *Otis Elevator*—The Core of the Business Test

The Board's 1984 decision in *Otis Elevator II*[58] represented a major attempt to formulate an application of *First National Main-*

---

[54] *Id.* at 682.

[55] *See* Chapter 7, "Discrimination in Employment," at notes 265–285.

[56] 452 US at 682–83.

[57] *Id.*

[58] Otis Elevator Co. (II), 269 NLRB 891, 116 LRRM 1075, *correcting* 269 NLRB 891, 115 LRRM 1281 (1984). [**Editor's Note**: In Dubuque Packing Co. (II), 303 NLRB No. 66, 137 LRRM 1185 (1991), the Board overruled *Otis Elevator II* and announced new criteria for determining whether an employer's decision to relocate bargaining-unit work is a mandatory subject. The Board summarized the new standards in these words:

> Initially, the burden is on the General Counsel to establish that the employer's decision involved a relocation of unit work unaccompanied by a basic change in the nature of the employer's operation. [That showing will establish] prima facie that the employer's relocation decision is a mandatory subject of bargaining. . . . [T]he employer may [rebut] by establishing that the work performed at the new location varies significantly from the work performed at the former plant, . . . that the work performed at the former plant is to be discontinued entirely and not moved to the new location, or . . . that the employer's decision involves a change in the scope and direction of the enterprise. Alternatively, the employer may proffer a defense to show by a preponderance of the evidence: (1) that labor costs (direct and/or indirect) was not a factor in the decision or (2) that even if labor costs were a factor in the decision, the union could not have offered labor cost concessions that could have changed the employer's decision to relocate.

Id. 137 LRRM at 1192.]

tenance v. NLRB[59] that would focus upon the reasons underlying the employer's decision, rather than attempting to characterize the transaction. In *Otis,* the employer discontinued its research and development facilities in Mahwah, New Jersey, and consolidated them with operations in East Hartford, Connecticut. The decision was motivated by the employer's determination that its research and development functions overlapped, that its Mahwah facility was outdated, and that technological advances could be enhanced by a consolidation at its newer and larger research center.

Initially, in *Otis Elevator I,*[60] the Board held that the employer unlawfully failed to bargain about its decision. However, the Court of Appeals for the District of Columbia Circuit remanded the case to the Board to reconsider in light of *First National Maintenance.*

In *Otis Elevator II,* the Board was unanimous in holding that the decision to transfer and consolidate operations was not a mandatory subject of bargaining. The majority stated that the critical factor is the "essence of the decision itself, i.e., whether it turns upon . . . labor costs . . . ."[61] Since the decision was found to turn "upon a change in the nature and direction of a significant facet of its business," the majority viewed this as a managerial decision which is at the "core of entrepreneurial control" outside of the scope of section 8(d).[62] On that basis, the majority also concluded that the decision was not amenable to bargaining.

Each of the concurring opinions had a different analytical focus. In Member Zimmerman's opinion, the critical question was whether the employer's decision is "amenable to resolution through collective bargaining."[63]

Member Dennis's opinion set forth a two-step analysis. The first step would require an "amenability" determination: the General Counsel would be required to show that "a factor over which the union has control [was] a significant consideration in the employer's decision." At the second step, the General Counsel would have to prove that the "benefit" (of resolution through the collective bargaining process) outweighs the "burden" on the

---

[59]*Supra* note 47.

[60]Otis Elevator Co. (I), 255 NLRB 235, 106 LRRM 1343 (1981).

[61]*Supra* note 58 at 892.

[62]*Id.,* 115 LRRM at 1281.

[63]*Id.* at 1285. *See* Garwood-Detroit Truck Equip., 274 NLRB 113, 118 LRRM 1417, 1419 (1985).

business that such constraints may impose.[64] "Burden" elements would include the extent of capital commitment; the extent of changes in operation; and the need for speed, flexibility, and confidentiality.

After *Otis Elevator II,* the Board found that a cable company's decision to handle an unusual increase in installation orders through subcontracting "affected the scope of the business and was not a bargainable item."[65] Member Dennis agreed on the basis of her concurring opinion in *Otis.* She found that the impact of the decision on the bargaining relationship was "indirect and attenuated."

IV. Mandatory Subjects of Bargaining

The Act compels collective bargaining[66] with respect to mandatory subjects of bargaining. As the Supreme Court has recognized,[67] mandatory subjects of bargaining are those generally delineated in section 9(a) as "rates of pay, wages, hours of employment, or other conditions of employment," and in section 8(d) as "wages, hours, and other terms and conditions of employment." Congress intended, as the Court indicated in *Ford Motor Co. v. NLRB*[68] that the Board be given "the primary responsibility of marking out the scope of the statutory language and duty to bargain." The scope of collective bargaining, according to the Court, could only be determined after considering prevailing industrial bargaining practices. Because of its special expertise, the Board was thus entrusted with the responsibility of evaluating the dynamics of industrial practice.[69]

The language "rates of pay," and "wages, hours, and other terms and conditions of employment" fixes not only the subjects

---

[64]115 LRRM at 1288. *But cf.* Collateral Control Corp., 288 NLRB 308, 308, 128 LRRM 1097 (1988) (General Counsel does not have burden of showing that decision to subcontract turned on labor costs where "all that is involved is the substitution of one group of workers for another to perform the same task in the same plant under the ultimate control of the same employer").

[65]Ausable Communications, 273 NLRB 1410, 118 LRRM 1295, 1295 (1985). *Accord* Morco Indus., 279 NLRB 762, 122 LRRM 1175 (1986). In Century Air Freight, 284 NLRB 730, 125 LRRM 1237, 1240 (1987), Members Johansen and Babson found it "unnecessary . . . to choose among these tests since . . . the same result is dictated regardless of which test is applied."

[66]Sections 8(a)(5) and 8(b)(3).

[67]NLRB v. Borg-Warner Corp., Wooster Div., 356 US 342, 42 LRRM 2034 (1958). *See* Section III.C, *supra,* for detailed treatment of this case.

[68]441 US 488, 496, 101 LRRM 2222 (1979). *See supra* notes 40–46.

[69]*Id.* at 500 n.12.

about which an employer and a union are compelled by law to bargain, but also those subjects as to which (1) the employer is barred from taking unilateral action and (2) the employee is disabled from making individual agreements with the employer, unless the union waives its right to preempt such unilateral action or individual bargaining.[70] A question concerning the mandatory nature of a subject can arise not only during the negotiation of a collective bargaining agreement but also during the term of an existing agreement. In the latter situation, the question is often whether the right to further bargaining is waived by the existing agreement, and a significant role is played by the Board's deferral policy.[71] When a party's action involves a question as to both the interpretation of a collective bargaining agreement and the legal obligations under the Act, the Board will frequently defer to the arbitration procedures contained in the parties' collective bargaining agreement.[72]

A. Wages

The categories "rates of pay" and "wages" have been given a broad construction by the Board and the courts to cover most of the common forms of compensation for labor performed, as well as most types of agreements designed to protect standards of compensation.

1. In General. Some mandatory subjects falling under the headings of "wages" are so obvious that little discussion is required. Basic hourly rates of pay[73] constitute wages. Despite occasional litigation over piece rates and incentive wage plans,[74] there is no doubt that they are mandatory subjects. Overtime

---

[70]NLRB v. Allis-Chalmers Corp., 601 F2d 870, 102 LRRM 2194 (CA 5, 1979); NLRB v. Katz, 369 US 736, 50 LRRM 2177 (1962). *See* Chapter 13, "The Duty to Bargain," at notes 68–104.

[71]Collyer Insulated Wire, 192 NLRB 837, 77 LRRM 1931 (1971), and related cases discussed in Chapter 18, "Accommodation of Board Action to the Arbitration Process."

[72]*See* Chapter 18, "Accommodation of Board Action to the Arbitration Process," for detailed discussion of the deferral process.

[73]*See, e.g.*, Stewart Granite Enters., 255 NLRB 569, 107 LRRM 1182 (1981); Gray Line, 209 NLRB 88, 85 LRRM 1328 (1974), *enforcement granted in part and denied in part*, 512 F2d 992, 89 LRRM 2192 (CA DC, 1975).

[74]*See* C&S Indus., 158 NLRB 454, 62 LRRM 1043 (1966). Of course, a union may waive a right to compel bargaining over an item of wages, for example, inauguration of an incentive plan during the term of an agreement. Libby, McNeill & Libby, 65 NLRB 873, 17 LRRM 250 (1946). However, such a waiver is not effective if the union has not been presented with the relevant facts prior to the actual implementation of a new wage incentive plan. NLRB v. Crystal Springs Shirt Corp., 637 F2d 399, 106 LRRM 2709 (CA 5, 1981), *enforcing* 245 NLRB 882, 102 LRRM 1404 (1979).

pay[75] is wages. The same is true of shift differentials.[76] Paid holidays,[77] paid vacations,[78] and severance pay,[79] as compensation for services performed, are wages.

2. Specific Forms of Compensation. *a. Bonuses.* Whether a bonus is a mandatory subject of bargaining depends upon whether it is considered "compensation" for services rendered or a "gift." If it is the former, it is a mandatory subject, and the employer may not discontinue it unilaterally. However, if the bonus is a "gift," it is not a mandatory subject. The primary inquiry in making this determination is whether the payment of the bonus has occurred with sufficient regularity to become part of the compensation structure. In addition, the employer's treatment of the bonus as an emolument of employment is meaningful.[80]

The results of this inquiry vary with the factual contexts in which it takes place. The earliest significant court decision[81] approved the Board's holding that an employer must bargain over changes in a Christmas bonus. For years, the employer had paid employees Christmas bonuses equivalent to a percentage of the employees' earnings. When the company installed a retirement plan, it notified the employees that the new plan would cost more than the customary bonus and consequently the amount of the bonus would be changed. The employer refused to bargain

---

[75]*See* Braswell Motor Freight Lines, 141 NLRB 1154, 52 LRRM 1467 (1963); *see also* Care Ambulance dba American Ambulance, 255 NLRB 417, 107 LRRM 1043 (1981), *enforced without opinion,* 692 F2d 702, 111 LRRM 2050 (CA 9, 1982).

[76]B.P. Oil, 256 NLRB 1107, 107 LRRM 1387 (1981), *enforced without opinion,* 681 F2d 804, 109 LRRM 3296 (CA 3, 1982); Smith Cabinet Mfg. Co., 147 NLRB 1506, 56 LRRM 1418 (1964).

[77]Singer Mfg. Co., 24 NLRB 444, 6 LRRM 405 (1940), *modified and enforced,* 119 F2d 131, 8 LRRM 740 (CA 7, 1941).

[78]Jimmy-Richard Co., 210 NLRB 802, 86 LRRM 1591 (1974), *enforced,* 527 F2d 803, 90 LRRM 3258 (CA DC, 1975).

[79]*See* Adams Dairy, Inc., 137 NLRB 815, 50 LRRM 1281 (1962), *modified,* 322 F2d 553, 54 LRRM 2171 (CA 8, 1963), *vacated,* 379 US 644, 58 LRRM 2192 (1965), *on remand,* 350 F2d 108, 60 LRRM 2084 (CA 8, 1965), *cert. denied,* 382 US 1011, 61 LRRM 2192 (1966).

[80]*See, e.g.,* Southern States Distrib., 264 NLRB 1, 111 LRRM 1255 (1982) (finding bonus to be "wages" because employer had paid bonuses every year for 6 years and because, during union campaign, it had distributed letter asking, inter alia, "[d]id you need a union to get your Christmas bonus?"). *See also* Goren Printing Co., 280 NLRB 1120, 123 LRRM 1276 (1986) (employer unlawfully substituted Christmas bonus for contractually mandated performance bonus); Storall Mfg. Co., 275 NLRB 220, 119 NLRB 1132 (1985), *enforced without opinion,* 786 F2d 1169, 122 LRRM 2832 (CA 8, 1986) (employer may neither substitute gift certificate for cash Christmas bonus nor fail to continue to recognize length of service in determining amount of bonus). See discussion of lump sum contract ratification bonuses and their impact on the base rate for purposes of overtime under the Fair Labor Standards Act in Minizza v. Stone Container, 842 F2d 1456, 28 WH Cases 849 (CA 3), *cert. denied,* 488 US 909, 29 WH Cases 1320 (1988).

[81]NLRB v. Niles-Bement-Pond Co., 199 F2d 713, 31 LRRM 2057 (CA 2, 1952).

with the union concerning the new amount of the bonus. The Board held that the bonus was part of "wages" and ordered bargaining. In affirming the Board, the Second Circuit wrote:

> Where, as here, the so-called gifts have been made over a substantial period of time and in amounts that have been based on the respective wages earned by the recipients, the Board was free to treat them as bonuses not economically different from other special kinds of remuneration like pensions, retirement plans, or group insurance, to name but a few, which have been held within the scope of the statutory bargaining requirements.[82]

In contrast, the Eighth Circuit later concluded that a bonus was a gift and not a mandatory subject, based on: (1) absence of consistency or regularity in the practice of awarding bonuses (which had been awarded during only 3 of the 5 prior years); (2) lack of uniformity in the amount of the bonus; and (3) dependence of the payment and the amount of the bonus on the financial condition of the employer.[83]

Where the employer bargains in good faith to impasse before discontinuing a bonus, the Act is not violated.[84] The unilateral discontinuance of a bonus during the term of the contract introduces questions of waiver and of deferral to arbitration. While the Board's *Collyer*[85] principles control the deferral question, the issue of waiver may be independently significant. In *Radioear Corp.*[86] the failure of the union to obtain a "maintenance of standards" clause and the fact that the collective agreement, a first contract, contained a "zipper" clause[87] which did not men-

---

[82]*Id.* at 714.

[83]NLRB v. Wonder State Mfg. Co., 344 F2d 210, 59 LRRM 2065 (CA 8, 1965). These factors have generally been determinative in characterizing a bonus as a gift or as wages. *See* NLRB v. United States Air Conditioning Corp., 336 F2d 275, 57 LRRM 2068 (CA 6, 1964); NLRB v. Citizens Hotel Co., 326 F2d 501, 55 LRRM 2135 (CA 5, 1964); NLRB v. Wheeling Pipe Line, 229 F2d 391, 37 LRRM 2403 (CA 8, 1956); NLRB v. Niles-Bement-Pond Co., *supra* note 81; *cf.* K-D Mfg. Co., 169 NLRB 57, 67 LRRM 1140 (1968), *enforced,* 419 F2d 467, 73 LRRM 2013 (CA 5, 1969); where the Board found that an employer violated the Act by giving Christmas gifts only to non–bargaining-unit employees.

[84]*See e.g.,* Michigan Power Co., 192 NLRB 830, 78 LRRM 1091 (1971).

[85]*Supra* note 71. *See* Chapter 18, "Accommodation of Board Action to the Arbitration Process."

[86]214 NLRB 362, 87 LRRM 1330 (1974), *supplementing* 199 NLRB 1161, 81 LRRM 1402 (1972).

[87]In Columbus & S. Ohio Elec. Co., 270 NLRB 686, 116 LRRM 1148 (1984), *enforced sub nom.* Electrical Workers (IBEW) Local 1466 v. NLRB, 795 F2d 150, 122 LRRM 2948 (CA DC, 1986), the Board held that an integration sentence in a "zipper clause" waived the union's right to bargain over elimination of a 40-year practice of giving a Christmas bonus. In Gayston Corp., 265 NLRB 1, 112 LRRM 1336 (1982), the Board found that a union's agreement to continue existing practices concerning bonuses did not constitute a waiver of its right to bargain over a bonus that the employer unilaterally granted in September, where the employer's usual practice was to grant a bonus at Christmas-time. *Cf.* Southern

tion a Christmas bonus, persuaded a divided Board that the employer did not violate section 8(a)(5) by unilaterally discontinuing a "turkey money" bonus.[88]

When a unilaterally terminated bonus is held to be wages, the Board will usually order its traditional make-whole remedy.[89] In one such case, however, the Eighth Circuit[90] partially reversed a Board determination and held that the employer's good-faith belief that it had the right to withhold bonuses precluded the award of lost bonuses to the employees. The court relied on the fact that the employer made its proposal to discontinue bonuses during negotiations, and the union "harbored and concealed" its objections to this proposal until after the contract had been negotiated.[91]

b. Pensions. The *Inland Steel Co.*[92] decision first raised the question of whether pension benefits are related to productive effort on the part of employees, and thus "wages" within the meaning of the Act. The Board held that pension benefits were "wages," stating:

> There is indeed an inseparable nexus between an employee's current compensation and his future pension benefits . . . . In substance, therefore, the respondent's monetary contribution to the pension plan constitutes an economic enhancement of the employee's money wages. . . . Realistically viewed, this type of wage enhancement or increase, no less than any other, becomes an integral part of the entire wage structure, and the character of the employee representative's interest in it, and the terms of its grant, is

---

Materials Co., 198 NLRB 257, 80 LRRM 1606 (1972), where the contract's "zipper" clause was fraudulently induced by the employer who, during the negotiations, falsely denied that Christmas bonuses had been paid.

[88]The Board had initially deferred to arbitration in accordance with its *Collyer* doctrine. However, after the arbitrator declined to rule on the specific issue upon which the deferral was premised, the Board reconsidered the case. *But see* Radio Tel. Technical School v. NLRB, 488 F2d 457, 84 LRRM 2794 (CA 3, 1973), in which the Board refused to defer to an arbitrator's finding that bonuses were a gift, notwithstanding that they had been paid consistently over many years; the Third Circuit enforced the order finding a §8(a)(5) violation.

[89]*See, e.g.,* John Zink Co. 196 NLRB 942, 80 LRRM 1232 (1972), *enforced in part,* 83 LRRM 3045 (CA 10, 1973). That the withheld bonuses were not easily computed was not a legitimate reason for denying a make-whole remedy. Southern Materials Co., *supra* note 87. *See generally* Chapter 31, "NLRB Procedures."

[90]Century Elec. Motor Co. v. NLRB, 447 F2d 10, 78 LRRM 2042 (CA 8, 1971).

[91]For treatment of unilateral discontinuance of a bonus as a violation of §§8(a)(1) and 8(a)(3), see Tweel Importing Co., 219 NLRB 666, 90 LRRM 1046 (1975); Electro Vector, 220 NLRB 445, 90 LRRM 1241 (1975), *enforcement denied,* 539 F2d 35, 93 LRRM 2021 (CA 9, 1976), *cert. denied,* 434 US 821, 96 LRRM 2512 (1977).

[92]77 NLRB 1, 21 LRRM 1310, (1948), *enforced,* 170 F2d 247, 22 LRRM 2506 (CA 7, 1948), *cert. denied,* 336 US 960, 24 LRRM 2019 (1949). *See also* Pacific Coast Ass'n of Pulp & Paper Mfrs. v. NLRB, 304 F2d 760, 50 LRRM 2626 (CA 9, 1962).

no different than in any other case where a change in the wage structure is effected.[93]

In the same decision, the Board rejected the company's contention that the term "conditions of employment" was limited to the physical conditions under which employees work and did not apply to the terms or conditions under which employment status is offered. In so doing, the Board relied on what it characterized as compelling evidence in the legislative history of the Taft-Hartley amendments that Congress recognized pension and similar welfare plans as falling within the meaning of "wages or other conditions of employment."

As with other mandatory subjects, the duty to bargain with respect to pension plans may be continuous.[94] Accordingly, unilateral effectuation of a pension plan during the term of a collective bargaining agreement which has no provision for pensions violates section 8(a)(5).[95] In *Allied Mills,*[96] the employer urged that it was relieved from such a duty to bargain by the last paragraph of section 8(d).[97] The Board rejected the argument, declaring that section 8(d) was intended to give stability to terms and conditions that have been embodied in a written contract, and that it has no reference to wages, hours, and other terms and conditions of employment that have not been reduced to agreement.

In *John Deklewa & Sons,*[98] the Board held that although a collective bargaining relationship permitted by section 8(f) may

---

[93] 77 NLRB at 4–5.

[94] *See generally* Glanzer, *Impact of ERISA on Collective Bargaining,* 52 ST. JOHN'S REV. 531 (1978).

[95] *See* Stone Boat Yard, 264 NLRB 981, 111 LRRM 1427 (1982), *enforced,* 715 F2d 441, 114 LRRM 2407 (CA 9, 1983), *cert. denied,* 466 US 937, 115 LRRM 3640 (1984).

[96] 82 NLRB 854, 23 LRRM 1632 (1949). *See* Jacobs Mfg. Co., 94 NLRB 1214, 28 LRRM 1162 (1951), *enforced,* 196 F2d 680, 30 LRRM 2098 (CA 2, 1952); Chapter 13, "The Duty to Bargain," at notes 741–755 (Board held employer had duty to bargain over pensions during negotiations conducted under wage reopener in agreement, because contract contained no pension provision and subject matter had not been discussed when previous contract was negotiated; opposite result was reached on health and welfare because this subject had been discussed during prior negotiations). *See also* Wollett, *The Duty to Bargain Over the "Unwritten" Terms and Conditions of Employment,* 36 TEX. L. REV. 863 (1958). *Cf.* McMullans v. Kansas, Okla. & Gulf Ry., 229 F2d 50, 37 LRRM 2363 (CA 10, 1956), for treatment of retirement plan under the Railway Labor Act.

[97] Section 8(d) reads in relevant part:

> [t]he duties so imposed shall not be construed as requiring either party to discuss or agree to any modification of the terms and conditions contained in a contract for a fixed period, if such modification is to become effective before such terms and conditions can be reopened under the provisions of the contract.

[98] 282 NLRB 1375, 124 LRRM 1185 (1987), *enforced sub nom.* Iron Workers Local 3 v. NLRB, 843 F2d 770, 128 LRRM 2020 (CA 3), *cert. denied,* 488 US 889, 129 LRRM 2528 (1988).

not be unilaterally repudiated during its term, such an 8(f) relationship may lawfully be unilaterally repudiated by either party upon the expiration of its term.[99] Thus, an employer's failure to continue to make contractually required payments to fringe benefit funds and its modification of health insurance coverage are in violation of section 8(a)(5) if made prior to the expiration of an 8(f) agreement, but not if made after the expiration and repudiation of such an agreement.[100]

The Board has also made clear that the "written agreement" requirement of section 302(c)(5)(B) of the Labor Management Relations Act of 1947,[101] does not proscribe continued employer contributions to employee benefit trust funds subsequent to the expiration of the collective bargaining agreement.[102]

However, the Supreme Court has ruled that suits to recover such contributions must be brought before the Board. In *Laborers Health & Welfare Trust Fund for Northern California v. Advanced Lightweight Concrete Co.*,[103] the Court held that an action under the Employee Retirement Income Security Act of 1974[104] is limited to the collection of contributions owed during the term of the collective bargaining agreement, and that jurisdiction is vested in the Board to determine whether an employer's unilateral decision to terminate postcontract contributions violates the National Labor Relations Act.

The Court of Appeals for the District of Columbia Circuit considered what type of remedial order is appropriate in the unusual case where an employer unilaterally discontinued pension fund contributions after its contract expired, but thereafter engaged in substantial bargaining with the union after the unlawful unilateral change.[105] The court rejected the Board's make-whole order which required the employer to pay all trust fund contributions provided for in the expired contract from the date of the unilateral change until the employer negotiated a

---

[99]American Thoro-Clean, 283 NLRB 1120, 125 LRRM 1137 (1987).

[100]*Id.* Jack Welsh Co., 284 NLRB 378, 125 LRRM 1222 (1987); Harris Painting, 286 NLRB 642, 126 LRRM 1216 (1987).

[101]29 USC §186(c)(5)(B).

[102]American Distrib. Co., 264 NLRB 1413, 111 LRRM 1344 (1982), *enforced,* 715 F2d 446, 114 LRRM 2402, *amended on denial of reh'g,* 115 LRRM 2046 (CA 9, 1983), *cert. denied,* 466 US 958, 116 LRRM 2096 (1984). *See also* Producers Dairy Delivery v. Western Conference of Teamsters Pension Fund, 654 F2d 625, 108 LRRM 2510 (CA 9, 1981).

[103]484 US 539, 127 LRRM 2657 (1988).

[104]Pub. L. No. 93-496, 88 Stat. 832, 29 USC §1001 et seq. (1988).

[105]NLRB v. Henry Cauthorne ta Cauthorne Trucking, 691 F2d 1023, 111 LRRM 2698 (CA DC, 1982).

new agreement or reached an impasse with the union. The court rejected the presumption that meaningful negotiations are automatically precluded by prior unlawful unilateral practices. The court therefore remanded the case to the Board to consider the duration of the refusal to bargain and to determine whether the parties reached an impasse in those negotiations subsequent to the employer's initial failure to bargain, but prior to the time of the Board's order. In the court's view, reaching impasse in such negotiations would have terminated the employer's remedial liability.

An employer is not obligated to bargain with a union concerning the pension and welfare benefits of former employees who have retired from jobs in the bargaining unit.[106] An employer may nonetheless be obligated under section 301 of the Labor Management Relations Act to continue providing retiree benefits if the recipients have a vested lifetime interest in health and welfare benefits. Several federal courts of appeal have found that there is such an obligation where an expired labor contract demonstrates an intent of the parties that postretirement benefits would continue beyond the life of the agreement.[107] Denial of vested retirement benefits may also expose an employer to liability under the Employment Retirement Income Security Act.[108]

Subsequent to the *Pittsburgh Glass* decision, the Board held in *Titmus Optical Co.*[109] that an employer is not relieved of the obligation to bargain with a union as the representative of its active employees about changes that will affect their benefits after retirement. The employer therefore violated section 8(a)(5) when it unilaterally changed its life insurance plan and advised the union it would no longer pay for insurance premiums on behalf of any employees who retired after a certain date.

---

[106]See discussion of Pittsburgh Plate Glass, *supra* notes 30–39.

[107]*See* Auto Workers v. Yard-Man, Inc., 716 F2d 1476, 114 LRRM 2489 (CA 6, 1983), *cert. denied,* 465 US 1007, 115 LRRM 2448 (1984). *See also* Smith v. ABS Indus., 890 F2d 841, 133 LRRM 2001 (CA 6, 1989); Steelworkers v. Connors Steel Co., 855 F2d 1499, 1504, 129 LRRM 2531 (CA 11, 1988), *cert. denied sub nom.* Parker v. Connors Steel Co., 489 US 1096, 131 LRRM 2400 (1989). *But see* Anderson v. Alpha Portland Indus., 836 F2d 1512 (CA 8, 1988), *cert. denied sub nom.* Anderson v. Slattery Group, 489 US 1051 (1989) (*contra*).

[108]*See, e.g.,* Musto v. American Gen. Corp., 861 F2d 897 (CA 6, 1988), *cert. denied,* 490 US 1020, 10 EB Cases 2328 (1989); Moore v. Metropolitan Life Ins. Co., No. 86 Civ. 2296 (SD NY 1987), *aff'd,* 856 F2d 488 (CA 2, 1988).

[109]205 NLRB 974, 84 LRRM 1245 (1973).

c. Health and Welfare, and Insurance Plans. Group health insurance is clearly a mandatory subject of bargaining.[110] As the First Circuit explained:

> [T]he word "wages" in . . . the Act embraces within its meaning direct and immediate economic benefits flowing from the employment relationship . . . . So construed the word covers a group insurance program for the reason that such a program provides a financial cushion in the event of illness or injury arising outside the scope of employment at less cost than such a cushion could be obtained through contracts of insurance negotiated individually.[111]

Thus a failure to make contractually required payments will generally be a violation of the Act to which economic necessity, cessation of operations, or lack of bad faith will not be a defense.[112]

Although an employer's refusal to negotiate a change in insurance carriers may violate section 8(a)(5),[113] the trend is to analyze whether such a change actually has a substantial impact on terms and conditions of employment. Federal courts of appeal first took this approach. In *Connecticut Light & Power Co. v. NLRB,*[114] the Second Circuit rejected the Board's holding that the selection of a health insurance carrier was a mandatory subject of bargaining. The court found that only where the identity of the carrier itself vitally affects the benefits, coverage, administration, or other terms of the insurance plan does it become a required subject of bargaining. Several other courts, which have held that an employer must bargain over its choice of an insurance carrier, have emphasized that the unilateral change of carrier challenged in those cases adversely affected employee benefits.[115]

---

[110]W.W. Cross & Co. v. NLRB, 174 F2d 875, 24 LRRM 2068 (CA 1, 1949). *See also* Standard Oil Co., 92 NLRB 227, 27 LRRM 1073 (1950) *and* Sylvania Elec. Prods., 127 NLRB 924, 46 LRRM 1127 (1960), *enforcement denied,* 291 F2d 128, 48 LRRM 2313 (CA 1), *cert. denied,* 368 US 926, 49 LRRM 2173 (1961), where the Board found the employer's refusal to furnish data as to the premium cost of a welfare plan to be a refusal to furnish wage data. To the same effect, see Stowe-Woodward, Inc., 123 NLRB 287, 43 LRRM 1415 (1959).

[111]174 F2d at 878.

[112]*See* Xtezo, Inc., 296 NLRB No. 28, 132 LRRM 1078 (1989); Air Convey Indus., 292 NLRB 25, 130 LRRM 1216 (1988).

[113]*See, e.g.,* Master Slack Corp., 230 NLRB 1054, 96 LRRM 1309 (1977), *enforced,* 618 F2d 6, 105 LRRM 2308 (CA 6, 1980).

[114]476 F2d 1079, 82 LRRM 3121 (CA 2, 1973).

[115]*See* Oil, Chem. & Atomic Workers (Kansas Refined Helium Co.) v. NLRB, 547 F2d 575, 92 LRRM 3059 (CA DC, 1976), *cert. denied sub nom.* Angle v. NLRB, 431 US 966, 95 LRRM 2642 (1977) (unilateral change in carrier affected insurance coverage and premiums); Bastian-Blessing v. NLRB, 474 F2d 49, 82 LRRM 2689 (CA 6, 1973) (unilateral change in carrier affected insurance benefits).

The Board has followed this approach. In *Keystone Consolidated Industries, Keystone Steel & Wire Division,*[116] the Board held that an employer violated the Act by unilaterally changing the administrator of a hospital, medical and surgical insurance plan, causing changes in administration and processing of claims as well as some alterations in coverage. But the same employer's change of administrator of its dental expense program was lawful because it did not cause significant such differences.

Decisions in this area often also involve subsidiary questions concerning the waiver of bargaining obligations, application of the *Collyer* doctrine,[117] the duty to furnish information, and the impact of a pending decertification petition. While there are occasions where the employer's past practice and the union's acquiescence will justify unilateral action,[118] there have been cases in which the Board has found unlawful an employer's unilateral discontinuance of employee benefit programs despite the employer's contentions that the union had waived its right to bargain about such termination. For example, in *T.T.P. Corp.,*[119] the Board ruled that a unilaterally established retirement income plan, which had been in effect for 5 years but was neither contained in the collective bargaining agreement between the employer and the union nor discussed during contract negotiations, was a mandatory subject of bargaining. Thus, the employer was under a statutory duty to bargain about its decision to discontinue contributions to the plan, even though the plan document reserved to the employer the right to terminate the plan at any time, as the union knew.

In *Borden, Inc.*[120] a provision reserving to the employer the right to terminate unilaterally an insurance plan was contained in an underlying insurance document. Nonetheless, the Board held that the health, life, and other insurance programs had

---

[116]237 NLRB 763, 99 LRRM 1036 (1978), *enforced in part and remanded,* 606 F2d 171, 102 LRRM 2664 (CA 7, 1979), *modified on reh'g,* 248 NLRB 283, 103 LRRM 1403 (1980), *enforced,* 653 F2d 304, 107 LRRM 3143 (CA 7, 1981). On remand from the Seventh Circuit, the Board rescinded its order that the employer reinstate the original administrator of the hospital, medical, and surgical plan and instead ordered the employer to restore all former benefits and services, to make employees whole for any losses suffered by the unilateral change, and to refrain from revoking or lessening such benefits. *See also* Arno Moccasin Co., 274 NLRB 1515, 119 LRRM 1206 (1985); Clements Wire & Mfg. Co., 257 NLRB 1058, 108 LRRM 1051 (1981).

[117]Collyer Insulated Wire, 192 NLRB 837, 77 LRRM 1931 (1971). *See* Chapter 18, "Accommodation of Board Action to the Arbitration Process."

[118]*See, e.g.,* A-V Corp., 209 NLRB 451, 86 LRRM 1057 (1974).

[119]190 NLRB 240, 77 LRRM 1097 (1971).

[120]196 NLRB 1170, 80 LRRM 1240 (1972).

become a "condition of employment," and there was no clear and unmistakable waiver in the contract of this subject of bargaining. Neither the management-rights clause nor the underlying insurance plan itself was regarded as a waiver. The Board noted that the right of cancellation was contained in the plan, a unilateral document to which the union was not a party. The Board also refused to defer to arbitration since the collective agreement had already expired.[121]

In *Carpenter Sprinkler Corp.*[122] the Board ruled that an employer's substitution of its own pension and health and welfare benefits for benefits provided by an expired contract, when there is no impasse or union waiver of the right to object, violated Section 8(a)(5). But in *O'Malley Lumber Co.*,[123] the Board held that an employer lawfully discontinued monthly payments to the incumbent union's health and welfare fund where the discontinuance was subsequent to an impasse in contract negotiations over the issue of whether the employer's or the union's plan would be used. The Board has similarly held that, where an employer made "diligent and earnest" efforts to engage in bargaining over contract modifications both before and after expiration of its contract and the union continually avoided bargaining, the union waived its right to bargain over the employer's proposed modifications in the contract. Therefore the employer could lawfully implement its proposals, including the discontinuance of its contributions to employee benefit trusts.[124]

Where an employer unlawfully ceased making contributions to the union's health fund and substituted its own plan, the union waived its right to delinquent contributions when it later agreed to accept the new plan and apply it retroactively. Nonetheless, because the initial substitution was unlawful, the Board ordered the employer to make whole any employees who suf-

---

[121]In refusing to defer to arbitration, the Board relied upon its decision in Hilton-Davis Chem. Co., 185 NLRB 241, 75 LRRM 1036 (1970). *But cf.* the Supreme Court's subsequent decision in Nolde Bros. v. Bakery Workers Local 358, 430 US 243, 94 LRRM 2753 (1977), regarding the duty to arbitrate after the expiration of the contract under which a grievance has arisen.

[122]238 NLRB 974, 99 LRRM 1356 (1978), *enforced in part and denied in part*, 605 F2d 60, 102 LRRM 2199 (CA 2, 1979).

[123]234 NLRB 1171, 98 LRRM 1166 (1978).

[124]M & M Bldg. & Elec. Contractors, 262 NLRB 1472, 110 LRRM 1512 (1982). *See also* Gibbs & Cox, 292 NLRB No. 78, 131 LRRM 1425 (1989). *But see* NLRB v. Auto Fast Freight, 793 F2d 1126, 122 LRRM 3058 (CA 9, 1986) (insufficient evidence of union's refusal to bargain).

fered a loss as a result of the unilateral change from the date of substitution to the date of the new agreement.[125]

A unilateral change whereby employees are required to contribute or pay for their own insurance may be violative if it is actually contrary to past practice.[126] However, the unilateral requirement that unit employees pay for their own health insurance may not be contrary to past practice where the employer is simply passing along an unanticipated premium increase which exceeded the dollar maximum the employer had obligated itself to make on behalf of its employees.[127]

In both *A.S. Abell Co.*[128] and *Hearst Corp., Baltimore News American Division,*[129] the Board held the respective employers violated section 8(a)(5) by dealing individually and unilaterally with employees concerning pension and retirement benefits, and by paying employees these benefits in excess of the terms of the collective bargaining agreement. The employers had unilaterally increased retirement benefits to encourage employees to retire because of lack of available work.

Changes in employee benefit programs have resulted in violations of section 8(a)(5) because employers refused to furnish relevant and necessary information to the union upon its request. The Supreme Court in *Katz*[130] acknowledged the inability of the union to know whether the employer's action is in fact a substantial departure from past practice unless there had

---

[125]Arrow Sash & Door Co., 281 NLRB 1108, 123 LRRM 1163 (1986), *supplementing* 276 NLRB 1166, 120 LRRM 1172 (1985).

[126]Garrett Flexible Prods., 276 NLRB 704, 120 LRRM 1124 (1985); Gentzler Tool & Die Corp., 268 NLRB 330, 114 LRRM 1275 (1983), *enforced*, 778 F2d 1211, 121 LRRM 2142 (CA 6, 1985) (employer-paid health and life insurance was part of employees' work compensation).

[127]House of the Good Samaritan, 268 NLRB 236, 114 LRRM 1254 (1983) (before unionization, employer's policy manual had specified dollar maximum for premium payments that employer would make on behalf of its employees. Because this maximum had always exceeded actual premiums, employees had never paid any part of the premium charged by insurance carrier. After unionization, however, employer's insurance carrier unexpectedly raised premiums to amount that exceeded stated maximum). *See also* United Technologies Corp., 278 NLRB 306, 121 LRRM 1156 (1986), where the Board held that an employer did not violate the Act when it failed to bargain with the union before unilaterally implementing a program that gave employees monetary incentives to review their hospital or surgical bills to detect overbilling during the program's 1-year trial period.

[128]230 NLRB 17, 95 LRRM 1284 (1977), *enforced in part and remanded in part*, 590 F2d 554, 100 LRRM 2320 (CA 4), *supplemented*, 243 NLRB 171, 101 LRRM 1381 (1979).

[129]230 NLRB 216, 95 LRRM 1274 (1977), *enforced in part and remanded in part*, 590 F2d 554, 100 LRRM 2320 (CA 4), *supplemented*, 243 NLRB 170, 101 LRRM 1379 (1979).

[130]NLRB v. Katz, 369 US 736, 50 LRRM 2177 (1962). *See* Chapter 13, "The Duty to Bargain," at notes 68–104.

been negotiations with the union.[131] However, in *NLRB v. Milgo Industrial,*[132] the Second Circuit considered the obligation of an employer, during negotiations with a newly certified union, to provide the union a copy of its health plan and information on the cost of its pension plan. In enforcing the Board's bargaining order, the court found that the employer was not obligated to provide a copy of the health plan because it already was available from the insurer, but it affirmed the Board's holding that the employer's refusal to provide cost information on its pension plan violated section 8(a)(5).

The Board has held that a clause in a local agreement requiring the employer to accept preselected employer trustees as its representatives in the administration of the trust fund is a mandatory subject.[133] In addition, the Board has held that an employer's failure to make contractually required fringe benefit fund contributions pursuant to an existing collective bargaining contract for employees it hired as replacements for bargaining-unit members who were engaged in a sympathy strike was a violation of section 8(a)(5).[134]

d. Profit-Sharing Plans. Profit-sharing plans are a form of employee compensation and hence a mandatory subject for bargaining.[135] The Board's decision that a profit-sharing plan is a mandatory subject is consistent with its view that "wages" include almost all emoluments accruing to any employee by reason of the employment relationship.[136]

In *J.P. Stevens & Co.*[137] the Board held that an employer violated section 8(a)(5) by unilaterally shifting the respon-

---

[131]*See* Connecticut Light & Power Co., 220 NLRB 967, 90 LRRM 1307 (1975), *enforced,* 538 F2d 308, 93 LRRM 2336 (CA 2, 1976); L&M Carpet Contractors, 218 NLRB 802, 89 LRRM 1732 (1975).

[132]567 F2d 540, 97 LRRM 2079 (CA 2, 1977), *enforcing* 229 NLRB 25, 96 LRRM 1347 (1977).

[133]*See* Sheet Metal Workers Local 493 (Central Fla. Sheetmetal Contractors Ass'n), 234 NLRB 1238, 97 LRRM 1476 (1978), *aff'd,* 664 F2d 489, 109 LRRM 2638 (CA 5, 1981).

[134]Abbey Medical/Abbey Rents, 264 NLRB 969, 111 LRRM 1683 (1982), *enforced without opinion,* 709 F2d 1514, 113 LRRM 3240 (CA 9, 1983).

[135]Kroger Co. v. NLRB, 401 F2d 682, 69 LRRM 2425 (CA 6, 1968); NLRB v. Black-Clawson Co., 210 F2d 523, 33 LRRM 2567 (CA 6, 1954).

[136]Kroger Co. v. NLRB, 399 F2d 455, 68 LRRM 2731 (CA 6, 1968); Dickten & Masch Mfg. Co., 129 NLRB 112, 46 LRRM 1516 (1960). For example, during the course of an organizing campaign, an employer spokesman indicated to the employees that an existing profit-sharing plan was solely within the discretion of the employer, that the employer would not negotiate with respect to such a plan, and that the plan would be discontinued if the union won the election. This threat to refuse to bargain as to mandatory subject matter was held to be a clear threat of reprisal violative of §8(a)(1). Como Plastics, 143 NLRB 151, 53 LRRM 1278 (1963).

[137]239 NLRB 738, 100 LRRM 1052 (1978), *enforced in part,* 623 F2d 322, 104 LRRM 2573 (CA 4, 1980), *cert. denied,* 449 US 1077, 106 LRRM 2136 (1981).

sibilities for investing the assets of its profit-sharing plan from a corporate trustee to a committee of members of the employer's board of directors. As a profit-sharing plan is a mandatory subject of bargaining, the Board reasoned, so too is the issue of who controls the investment of the plan's assets. The Board reasoned that the loss of the investment expertise of the original trustee could adversely affect the plan.

e. Stock Purchase Plans. In *Richfield Oil Corp.*,[138] the Board decided in 1954 that a stock purchase plan falls within the area of mandatory bargaining.[139] Participation in the plan was open to all regular employees who had completed 1 year of service and who were between the ages of 30 and normal retirement age. Participants contributed a fixed sum from monthly earnings to the plan, and the company made contributions on behalf of participants, ranging from 50 percent to 75 percent of an employee's payments into the plan. The monies were used by the plan's trustees to purchase Richfield common stock. Neither stock nor cash credited to an individual's account was distributable to the individual so long as the participant was a member of the plan. Despite the voluntary nature of the plan, the Board had no difficulty concluding that this stock purchase plan was a form of "wages" and also fell within "other conditions of employment."

Agreeing that stock purchase plans are a mandatory subject of bargaining,[140] the Fourth Circuit nevertheless declined to enforce a Board decision that an employer had not bargained in good faith over a union demand that unit employees be allowed to participate in a stock investment plan.[141] The court noted that the employer had not refused to discuss the plan, was willing to discuss other possible economic alternatives, and had also compromised on other matters which gave its employees benefits they had not previously enjoyed and which resulted in an agreement which the employees ratified.

f. Merit Wage Increases. That an employer has a duty to bargain with respect to merit increases was decided by the Board in

---

[138]110 NLRB 356, 34 LRRM 1658 (1954), *enforced*, 231 F2d 717, 37 LRRM 2327 (CA DC), *cert. denied*, 351 US 909, 37 LRRM 2837 (1956).

[139]*See generally* Hutchinson, *Employee Stock Ownership Plans: A New Tool in the Collective Bargaining Inventory?*, 26 AM. U.L. REV. 536 (1977).

[140]*See, e.g.*, Handleman Co., 283 NLRB 451, 124 LRRM 1369 (1987).

[141]National Steel Corp., Weirton Steel Div. v. NLRB, 689 F2d 504, 111 LRRM 2297 (CA 4, 1982), *denying enforcement to* 259 NLRB 666, 109 LRRM 1004 (1981).

J.H. Allison & Co.[142] The collective bargaining agreement in that case contained a scale of minimum rates. When the employer granted a series of individual wage increases, characterized as "merit increases," the union sought details in order that it might negotiate the matter. The employer refused to supply the requested information on the ground that the granting of merit increases was an exclusive managerial function and not a proper subject for bargaining. The union's request during subsequent contract negotiations to incorporate a clause on merit increases into the contract met with a similar response. The Board held the increases to be an integral part of the wage structure and as such a mandatory subject for bargaining.

In a later case[143] the Board affirmed this conclusion even while acknowledging that it might be difficult or perhaps impossible to establish objective standards for awarding merit increases. On the other hand, where the collective agreement itself contained both a maximum and a minimum rate for each classification as well as a merit rating plan under which each employee was to be reviewed every 4 months, the Board held that the company had no obligation to bargain with the union before putting individual merit increases into effect.[144]

The rationale for holding merit increases to be a mandatory bargaining subject was spelled out by the Fourth Circuit in *NLRB v. Berkley Machine Works*:[145]

> Merit pay where there are a number of employees means more than a gratuity or bonus paid to an occasional employee whom the company wishes to favor on account of his loyalty or efficiency. It means necessarily the formulation and application of standards; and such standards are proper subjects of collective bargaining. Collective bargaining with respect to wages might well be disrupted or become a mere empty form if the control over the wages of individual employees were thus removed from the bargaining area.[146]

In *NLRB v. Katz,*[147] the Supreme Court confirmed the prior opinions of the Board and the lower courts that, under certain

---

[142]70 NLRB 377, 18 LRRM 1369 (1946), *enforced*, 165 F2d 766, 21 LRRM 2238 (CA 6, 1948), *cert. denied*, 335 US 814, 22 LRRM 2564 (1948). *See also* Weston & Brooker Co., 154 NLRB 747, 60 LRRM 1015 (1965), *enforced*, 373 F2d 741, 64 LRRM 2736 (CA 4, 1967); Midwestern Instruments, 133 NLRB 1132, 48 LRRM 1793 (1961).

[143]E.W. Scripps & Co., 94 NLRB 227, 28 LRRM 1033 (1951). *See also* Tide Water Associated Oil Co., 85 NLRB 1096, 24 LRRM 1518 (1949).

[144]General Controls Co., 88 NLRB 1341, 25 LRRM 1475 (1950).

[145]189 F2d 904, 28 LRRM 2176 (CA 4, 1951).

[146]*Id.* at 907.

[147]*Supra* note 130. *See* Chapter 13, "The Duty to Bargain," at notes 68–104.

conditions, merit increases are subject to mandatory bargaining. In *Katz* the merit increases had been granted, without prior notice to the union, to less than half of the employees in the bargaining unit. Concerning the effect of the employer's long-standing practice of granting discretionary merit increases, the Court observed:

> This action . . . must be viewed as tantamount to an outright refusal to negotiate . . . . Whatever might be the case as to so-called "merit raises" which are in fact simply automatic increases to which the employer has already committed himself, the raises here in question were in no sense automatic, but were informed by a large measure of discretion. There simply is no way in such case for a union to know whether or not there has been a substantial departure from past practice, and therefore the union may properly insist that the company negotiate as to the procedures and criteria for determining such increases.[148]

Applying the *Katz* guidelines, the Fifth Circuit defined the burden on an employer who seeks to prove that wage increases during union contract negotiations do not constitute unlawful unilateral action. In *NLRB v. Allis-Chalmers Corp.*[149] the employer had granted increases in wages and benefits to its employees during union contract negotiations. It contended that the increases were in compliance with a periodic survey of wages and benefits and that the increases did not constitute unlawful unilateral action. However, the Fifth Circuit affirmed the Board's holding that the increases were unlawful:

> The employer carries a heavy burden of proving that such adjustments of wages and benefits are purely automatic and pursuant to definite guidelines. The record reflects . . . that the increases were not automatic, in that Allis-Chalmers exercised considerable discretion in determining the timing and amount. Therefore, the union could properly demand bargaining.[150]

Therefore, as in the case of bonuses, the lawfulness of the unilateral grant or discontinuance of merit wage increases depends upon the nature of the past practices—that is, whether "automatic increases to which the employer has already committed himself" or "discretionary" increases.[151] But this broad dis-

---

[148]369 US at 746–47.

[149]601 F2d 870, 102 LRRM 2194 (CA 5, 1979). *Cf.* White v. NLRB, 255 F2d 564, 42 LRRM 2001 (CA 5, 1958), a case antedating *Katz* in which the court set a less severe standard.

[150]601 F2d at 875–76.

[151]NLRB v. Katz, 369 US 736, 907, 50 LRRM 2177 (1962).

tinction has not resulted in a uniform application, and the permissibility of unilateral employer action in respect to merit increases has divided both the Board and the courts.

g. Housing, Meals, Services, and Discounts Supplied by Employer. Generally, the rental of company-owned housing is a mandatory subject of bargaining. The Board's established rule is that employer-provided living accommodations fall within "wages" and "conditions of employment" where the accommodations are an integral part of the employment relations.[152] However, in some situations company housing may be treated as a permissive subject of bargaining. In one such case[153] the Fifth Circuit found that the evidence failed to support a conclusion that the rent charged for company houses was either wages or a condition of employment since the rental arrangement offered no substantial advantage to the employees. The court noted that other adequate housing was available with no transportation problem, that rentals for company housing were comparable to those of the community generally, and that there was no evidence that employees were required to live in the houses.[154]

Nevertheless, "conditions of employment" are not limited to the compulsory aspects of the employer-employee relationship. Predating the housing cases, the Board found company-provided meals to be not only a condition of employment but also wages.[155] Although the company did not expressly require that employees eat on the job, they had no realistic alternative. The Board noted that it had consistently construed "wages" broadly enough to include emoluments supplementary to actual wage rates that accrue to employees from their employment relationship.[156]

Traditionally the NLRB has treated workplace meal prices as a condition of employment. That position was endorsed by the

---

[152]*See* Elgin Standard Brick Mfg. Co., 90 NLRB 1467, 26 LRRM 1343 (1950); Hart Cotton Mills, Inc., 91 NLRB 728, 26 LRRM 1566 (1950), *enforcement denied*, 190 F2d 964, 28 LRRM 2434 (CA 4, 1951).

[153]NLRB v. Bemis Bros. Bag Co., 206 F2d 33, 32 LRRM 2535 (CA 5, 1953).

[154]*Cf.* NLRB Gen. Counsel Admin. Ruling K-209, 37 LRRM 1316 (1956), where the General Counsel refused to issue a complaint on a charge that an employer informed the employees that they must purchase or vacate company houses and that the company refused to discuss the matter with the union.

[155]Weyerhaeuser Timber Co., 87 NLRB 672, 25 LRRM 1163 (1949). *See also* Herman Sausage Co., 122 NLRB 168, 43 LRRM 1090 (1958), *enforced*, 275 F2d 229, 45 LRRM 2829 (CA 5, 1960) (unilateral discontinuance of meal allowance held a §8(a)(5) violation).

[156]*See* Inland Steel Co., 77 NLRB 1, 21 LRRM 1310, *review denied*, 170 F2d 247, 22 LRRM 2506 (CA 7, 1948), *cert. denied*, 336 US 960, 24 LRRM 2019 (1949).

Supreme Court in 1979 in *Ford Motor Co. v. NLRB*.[157] The Seventh Circuit had enforced[158] the Board's order, agreeing that under the facts of the case the employer was obligated to bargain about changes in employee cafeteria and vending machine prices. The Supreme Court relied less on the particular circumstances of the case, for example, the lack of eating alternatives for employees, and more on the reasonableness of the Board's general rule requiring bargaining over in-plant food prices and services. The Board has since held that a paid lunch period is a mandatory subject of bargaining even though only a small fraction of the work force is affected.[159]

Although a new employer normally has the right to announce new terms and conditions of employment, the elimination of free lunches by a successor employer violated section 8(a)(5) where the action was motivated by an intent to reduce support for the union.[160] Free meals were also an issue where they were unilaterally granted, rather than discontinued. In *O'Land, Inc.*,[161] an employer's unilateral grant of free meals to nonstriking employees violated the Act. The alleged reason for the company policy was to reduce violence on the picket line by encouraging nonstrikers to remain on the employer's premises during mealtimes. In the context of the employer's other unlawful unilateral actions and in the absence of notice to the employees that the free meals were a temporary measure for the purpose of protecting the nonstriking employees, the Board held that the unilateral grant of the free meals violated the Act.

Coffee benefits have been an issue in a number of Board cases. In *Chemtronics, Inc.*,[162] the Board held that an employer violated section 8(a)(5) by unilaterally discontinuing its practices of providing employees with coffee and rolls and permitting smoking in the warehouse. On the other hand, in *Weather TEC Corp.*[163] the Board held that a employer's unilateral decision to stop providing transportation and money to purchase coffee and coffee supplies did not violate section 8(a)(5). The Board

---

[157]441 US 488, 101 LRRM 2222 (1979). *See supra* notes 40–46 for a detailed analysis of this case.

[158]Ford Motor Co. v. NLRB, 571 F2d 993, 97 LRRM 3030 (CA 7, 1978).

[159]Van Dorn Plastic Mach. Co., 286 NLRB 1233, 128 LRRM 1265 (1987), *enforced*, 881 F2d 302, 132 LRRM 2200 (CA 6, 1989).

[160]Magnolia Manor Nursing Home, 260 NLRB 377, 109 LRRM 1198 (1982).

[161]206 NLRB 210, 84 LRRM 1378 (1973).

[162]236 NLRB 178, 98 LRRM 1559 (1978).

[163]238 NLRB 1535, 99 LRRM 1709 (1978).

stressed that neither action constituted a "material, substantial and a significant" change from prior practice.[164] The Board also noted that when the union and the employer representatives discussed the change shortly after it had been implemented, the union neither requested that the change be put on the bargaining table nor that the employer revert to its prior policy.

In a variety of other decisions, the Board has defined the term "benefits" to cover various emoluments of employment so that unilateral action concerning such "benefits" has violated section 8(a)(5).[165]

h. Payments and Charges to Nonemployees That Affect Wages of Employees. In two antitrust cases, the Supreme Court held that the concept of "wages" as a mandatory subject of bargaining embraces agreements reasonably designed to protect wage scales, although in form the agreements dealt with "prices" (charged by bands for club dates) or "rental rates" (for leased trucks). In *Musicians v. Carroll*[166] the Court rejected the idea that "the distinction between mandatory and non-mandatory subjects turns on the form of the method taken to protect a wage scale."[167] In *Teamsters Local 24 v. Oliver*[168] the Court held that a state antitrust law could not be enforced to prohibit a clause in a collective bargaining agreement establishing the minimum rental to be paid by signatory carriers to truck drivers owning and driving their own vehicles. The minimum rental provision was a mandatory subject of bargaining because its purpose was

---

[164]*Id.* at 1536.

[165]*See, e.g.*, Seafarers Local 777 (Yellow Cab Co.) v. NLRB, 603 F2d 862, 99 LRRM 2903 (CA DC, 1978), *enforcing in part and denying enforcement in part to* 229 NLRB 1329, 95 LRRM 1249 (1977) (drivers taking their cabs home at night); NLRB v. Central Ill. Pub. Serv. Co., 324 F2d 916, 54 LRRM 2586 (CA 7, 1963) (gas discounts); American Commercial Barge Lines Co., 296 NLRB No. 124, 132 LRRM 1257 (1989) (employees' mode of travel to and from assigned vessels); Donn Prods., 229 NLRB 116, 95 LRRM 1033 (1977), *enforcement granted in part and denied in part*, 613 F2d 162, 103 LRRM 2338 (CA 6), *cert. denied*, 447 US 906, 104 LRRM 2552 (1980) (system to assist employees to obtain personal bank loans); Florida Steel Corp., 231 NLRB 923, 96 LRRM 1173 (1977) (use of credit cards by employees and reimbursement rates for lodging and meal expenses); Master Slack Corp., 230 NLRB 1054, 96 LRRM 1309 (1977), *enforced*, 618 F2d 6, 105 LRRM 2308 (CA 6, 1980) (allowing employees to purchase employer's goods on layaway basis); Eagle Material Handling of N.J., 224 NLRB 1529, 92 LRRM 1571 (1976), *enforced*, 558 F2d 160, 95 LRRM 2934 (CA 3, 1977) (use of company trucks to and from plant); Southland Paper Mills, 161 NLRB 1077, 63 LRRM 1386 (1966) (hunting privilege); Weston & Brooker Co., 154 NLRB 747, 60 LRRM 1015 (1965), *enforced*, 373 F2d 741, 64 LRRM 2736 (CA 4, 1967) (canteen at which employees had been permitted to charge purchases).

[166]391 US 99, 68 LRRM 2230 (1968).

[167]*Id.* at 110. *See* Chapter 30, "Accommodations to Other Federal Enactments," at notes 34–43.

[168]358 US 283, 43 LRRM 2374 (1959). *See* Chapter 29, "Federal Preemption of State Regulation," at notes 46–50.

"to protect the negotiated wage scale against the possible undermining through diminution of the owner's wages for driving which might result from a rental which did not cover his operating costs."[169]

In *Carroll* the Court exempted from federal antitrust regulation the negotiated minimum price lists for orchestra leaders playing club dates. Such minimums were deemed essential to protect the musicians' wage rates. The Court viewed the price floors, including established minimums for orchestra leaders, as "simply a means for coping with the job and wage competition of the leaders to protect the wage scales of musicians who respondents concede are employees on club dates, namely sidemen and subleaders."[170]

3. Effect of Governmental Wage Controls. During the most recent period of overt, federally imposed, wage and price controls,[171] several decisions reinforced the rule that even when subject to such control, wages constitute a mandatory subject of bargaining.[172]

Later, in *National Broadcasting Co.*[173] the Board ruled that a union had not waived its right to bargain over an income savings plan merely because at the outset of negotiations the employer had stated its willingness to comply with the President's suggested, but voluntary, wage guidelines limiting increases to 7 percent. Since the employer had not stated that improvement in benefit levels and wages would have to come from the "same pie" (as defined by the guidelines), the Board held that the employer had not engaged in "package bargaining." Thus, the union's pursuit of certain wage terms did not operate as a waiver of its right to bargain over other benefits, such as the income savings plan.

B. Hours

Writing in an antitrust case, the Supreme Court expressed the bargaining obligation as to hours of employment as follows:

---

[169]358 US at 293–94.

[170]391 US at 109. For a general discussion of the relation of the NLRA to the antitrust laws, see Chapter 30, "Accommodations to Other Federal Enactments."

[171]August 1971–November 1973.

[172]NLRB v. Big Three Indus., 497 F2d 43, 86 LRRM 3031 (CA 5, 1974); Servis Equip. Co., 198 NLRB 266, 80 LRRM 1704 (1972). *See generally* R.W. Kopp, *The Impact of the Phase II Mandatory Pay Controls on Collective Bargaining*, NYU TWENTY-SIXTH ANNUAL CONFERENCE ON LABOR 111 (1973).

[173]252 NLRB 187, 105 LRRM 1304 (1980).

> The particular hours of the day and the particular days of the week during which employees may be required to work are subjects well within the realm of wages, hours, and other terms and conditions of employment about which employers and unions must bargain.[174]

The Board has consistently held that hours, including work schedules and whether there should be Sunday work,[175] are mandatory bargaining subjects. In *Weston & Brooker Co.*[176] the Board held the length of the workday to be a mandatory subject and that an employer's unilateral change constituted a section 8(a)(5) violation.

In certain limited circumstances, the employer may institute changes in hours without bargaining. For example, a unilateral change by an employer did not violate the Act when it caused only minimal inconvenience to the employees.[177] What constitutes minimal inconvenience will depend upon the specific circumstances, however. The Board has upheld the unilateral extension of employees' breaks by 5 minutes where the work had been completed early,[178] but has found that the extension of employees' lunch breaks by 15 minutes was a substantial change in their working conditions that violated section 8(a)(5).[179] In another case the Board found that bargaining over a new rule which required employees to be at their department 5 minutes earlier than had been the past practice was mandatory since it substantially diminished the employees' time for relaxation and refreshment in the cafeteria before starting work.[180]

---

[174]Meat Cutters Locals 189, 262, 320, 546, 571, 638 v. Jewel Tea Co., 381 US 676, 691, 59 LRRM 2376 (1965). For a discussion of the relation of mandatory subjects of bargaining to the antitrust laws, as exemplified by this case and Mine Workers v. Pennington, 381 US 657, 59 LRRM 2369 (1965) (holding that union's agreement with multi employers to impose certain standards relating to mandatory subjects for bargaining on employers outside multi-employers' bargaining unit would fall outside union's exemption from antitrust laws), see Chapter 30, "Accommodations to Other Federal Enactments," at notes 26–33.

[175]Timken Roller Bearing Co., 70 NLRB 500, 18 LRRM 1370 (1946), *enforcement denied on other grounds*, 161 F2d 949, 20 LRRM 2204 (CA 6, 1947); Wilson & Co., 19 NLRB 990, 5 LRRM 560 (1940), *enforced*, 115 F2d 759, 7 LRRM 575 (CA 8, 1940); Woodside Cotton Mills Co., 21 NLRB 42, 6 LRRM 68 (1940).

[176]*Supra* note 165 (citing Homer Gregory Co., 123 NLRB 1842, 44 LRRM 1249 (1959)).

[177]*E.g.*, Oneita Knitting Mills, 205 NLRB 500, 83 LRRM 1670 (1973).

[178]La Mousse, 259 NLRB 37, 108 LRRM 1356 (1981), *enforced without opinion*, 703 F2d 576, 112 LRRM 3168 (CA 9, 1983).

[179]Sertafilm, Atlas Microfilming Div., 267 NLRB 682, 114 LRRM 1120 (1983), *enforced*, 753 F2d 313, 118 LRRM 2628 (CA 3, 1985).

[180]Hedison Mfg. Co., 260 NLRB 590, 109 LRRM 1216 (1982). *See also* Xidex Corp., 297 NLRB No. 9, 132 LRRM 1331 (1989) (employer violated Act by unilaterally changing lunch break from 30-minute unpaid break to 15-minute paid break, even though it had discussed change with union members, including union's sergeant-at-arms, and change was rescinded after very short period). *But see* U.S. Postal Serv., 275 NLRB 360, 119 LRRM

The Board has upheld unilateral changes in working hours in other particular circumstances as well. For example, an employer was able to unilaterally reduce working hours when it had previously provided the union with all the information it used in making the decision and thereafter stood ready to provide the union with explanations or additional data.[181] The Board also held that an employer did not unlawfully engage in a unilateral elimination of a third work shift, where it had notified the union of its proposed change and the union failed to make any reasonable attempt to bargain over the issue.[182]

Absent such extenuation, or a collective agreement authorizing them,[183] unilateral changes in hours violate section 8(a)(5). The District Court for the District of Columbia enjoined an employer, pursuant to section 10(j), from unilaterally reducing the working hours of employees during the pendency of Board proceedings.[184] In *Florida Steel Corp.*,[185] the Board held that the employer acted unlawfully when for a 1-week period it unilaterally imposed a change in hours. In enforcing this part of the Board's order, the Fourth Circuit indicated that regardless of the Company's bad faith, its unilateral action effectively denied the union its opportunity to bargain.

In *Good Hope Industries*,[186] the employer violated section 8(a)(5) by unilaterally adding an "on-call" day to the 4-day workweek. The Board reached this conclusion even though the collective bargaining agreement provided for a 5-day workweek, because (1) a 5-day workweek had not actually been in effect in several years, and (2) the employees had voted to reject the

---

1057 (1985) (employer lawfully began uniform application and enforcement of its established policy of limiting rest breaks to 10 minutes although certain shifts had regularly taken 15-minute breaks and developed established practice as such).

[181]Western Elec. Co., 223 NLRB 86, 92 LRRM 1189 (1976). After the employer provided the union with such information, the union subsequently made only vague and ambiguous requests for information and declined to engage in meaningful bargaining.

[182]K-Mart Corp., 242 NLRB 855, 101 LRRM 1406 (1979), *enforced*, 626 F2d 704, 105 LRRM 2431 (CA 9, 1980).

[183]*E.g.*, Nazareth Literary & Benevolent Inst. dba Saints Mary & Elizabeth Hosp., 282 NLRB 73, 123 LRRM 1297 (1986) (unilateral implementation of "Budget Day" program which frequently reduced employees' scheduled days or hours held lawful, where contract granted employer discretion to "establish, determine and change: shift starting and quitting times, daily and weekly hours of work, and number, time, and length of shifts. . . .").

[184]Humphrey v. Retired Persons Pharmacy, 84 LRRM 2599 (D DC, 1973).

[185]235 NLRB 941, 100 LRRM 1187 (1978), *enforced in part*, 601 F2d 125, 101 LRRM 2671 (CA 4, 1979). *See also* Quality Eng'rd Prods. Co., 267 NLRB 593, 114 LRRM 1100 (1983) (violation where employer unilaterally advanced its employees' usual starting time from 8:00 a.m. to 7:30 a.m., and reduced their workweek from 40 hours to 32 hours).

[186]230 NLRB 1132, 95 LRRM 1518 (1977).

5-day workweek when the employer suggested it before instituting the change.[187] The Board has also found violations where an employer unilaterally eliminated compensatory time-off for Saturday overtime and paid overtime pay instead, thereby effectively converting a voluntary overtime schedule into a mandatory 6-day workweek,[188] and where an employer unilaterally instituted a 7-day, 12-hour shift system of continuous operations in lieu of the prior system of three 8-hour shifts and 5-day-per-week operation expressly provided in the agreement.[189]

An employer may not unilaterally change the work schedule, even advantageously to the employees, for example, where the new schedule would provide employees the opportunity to work on nondaylight premium pay shifts and thereby receive more money.[190]

C. Other Terms and Conditions of Employment

1. In General. Many topics that fall within the phrase "other terms and conditions of employment" are now so clearly recognized to be mandatory subjects of bargaining that no discussion is required. These include: provisions for a grievance procedure[191] and arbitration,[192] layoffs and recalls,[193] dis-

[187] *See also* American Gypsum Co., 285 NLRB 100, 128 LRRM 1105 (1987) (employer violated Act by unilaterally changing employee's weekly work schedule to include extra day, where expired contract required 3 days' notice in work schedules); Technical Careers Insts., 259 NLRB 283, 108 LRRM 1359 (1981) (employer who had official workweek of 39 hours, but who had only required employees to work 35 hours per week, found to have violated the Act by enforcing official workweek policy without bargaining with newly certified union).

[188] Fall River Sav. Bank, 260 NLRB 911, 109 LRRM 1292 (1982). *But see* Blue Cross & Blue Shield (N.J.), 288 NLRB 434, 128 LRRM 1125 (1988) (employer's unilateral implementation of program providing for overtime work at home held lawful, where contract granted employer right to offer or require overtime without limitation).

[189] Kal Kan Foods, 288 NLRB 590, 130 LRRM 1268 (1988); *see also* Rahco, Inc., 265 NLRB 235, 112 LRRM 1398 (1982).

[190] American Oil Co., 238 NLRB 294, 99 LRRM 1253 (1978), *enforced*, 602 F2d 184, 101 LRRM 2981 (CA 8, 1979).

[191] Hughes Tool Co. v. NLRB, 147 F2d 69, 15 LRRM 852 (CA 5, 1945); Bethlehem Steel Co., 136 NLRB 1500, 50 LRRM 1013 (1962), *enforcement denied on other grounds*, 320 F2d 615, 53 LRRM 2878 (CA 3, 1963).

[192] NLRB v. Montgomery Ward & Co., 133 F2d 676, 12 LRRM 508 (CA 9, 1943); NLRB v. Boss Mfg. Co., 118 F2d 187, 8 LRRM 729 (CA 7, 1941).

[193] *See* Hilton Mobile Homes, 155 NLRB 873, 60 LRRM 1411 (1965). *See also* Advertiser's Mfg. Co., 280 NLRB 1185, 124 LRRM 1017 (1986), *enforced*, 823 F2d 1086, 125 LRRM 3024 (CA 7, 1987) (layoffs); Quality Packaging, 265 NLRB 1141, 112 LRRM 1283 (1982) (recall).

charge,[194] workloads,[195] vacations,[196] holidays,[197] sick leave,[198] work rules,[199] use of bulletin boards by unions,[200] change of payment from a weekly salary to an hourly rate,[201] definition of bargaining-unit work,[202] performance of bargaining-unit work by supervisors,[203] employee physical examinations,[204] and duration of the collective bargaining agreement.[205]

---

[194]*See* National Licorice Co. v. NLRB, 309 US 350, 6 LRRM 674 (1940); NLRB v. Bachelder, 120 F2d 574, 8 LRRM 723 (CA 7, 1941). *See also* Michael J. Malone & Bob Burkheimer dba Sorrento Hotel, 266 NLRB 350, 112 LRRM 1358 (1983) (successor employer terminated predecessor's employee complement without prior bargaining).

[195]Beacon Piece Dyeing & Finishing Co., 121 NLRB 953, 42 LRRM 1489 (1958). *See* Little Rock Downtowner, 145 NLRB 1286, 55 LRRM 1156 (1964), *enforced*, 341 F2d 1020, 58 LRRM 2510 (CA 8, 1965) (order to employees to stand at their stations at all times except when on breaks or relief violated §8(a)(5) since there was actual change in work beyond "routine job directions"). In Irvington Motors, Inc., 147 NLRB 565, 56 LRRM 1257 (1964), *enforced*, 343 F2d 759, 58 LRRM 2816 (CA 3, 1965), the Board held the fixing of sales quotas required bargaining; however, the unilateral setting of a requirement that salesmen make five telephone sales calls each day was not so clearly beyond a normal management function as to require notice to and consultation with the union. *Cf.* Little Rock Downtowner, 148 NLRB 717, 57 LRRM 1052, 1053 (1964), where the motel maids were instructed to wash motel room windows every day; the Board held that an employer does not have an obligation to notify and consult the union with respect to matters that fall "within the normal area of day-to-day operating detailed decisions relating to the manner in which work is to be performed."

[196]Great S. Trucking Co. v. NLRB, 127 F2d 180, 10 LRRM 571 (CA 4, 1942).

[197]NLRB v. Sharon Hats, Inc., 289 F2d 628, 48 LRRM 2098 (CA 5, 1961); Bradley Washfountain Co. v. NLRB, 192 F2d 144, 29 LRRM 2064 (CA 7, 1951).

[198]NLRB v. Katz, 369 US 736, 50 LRRM 2177 (1962); *see also* Southern Cal. Edison Co., 284 NLRB 1205, 126 LRRM 1324 (1987), *enforced*, 852 F2d 572 (CA 9, 1988).

[199]NLRB v. Southern Transp., 343 F2d 558, 58 LRRM 2822 (CA 8, 1965); Tower Hosiery Mills, 81 NLRB 658, 23 LRRM 1397 (1949).

[200]NLRB v. Proof Co., 242 F2d 560, 39 LRRM 2608 (CA 7, 1957), *cert. denied*, 355 US 831, 40 LRRM 2680 (1957).

[201]General Motors Corp., 59 NLRB 1143, 15 LRRM 170 (1944).

[202]Almeida Bus Lines, 142 NLRB 445, 53 LRRM 1055 (1963). *See also* Road Sprinkler Fitters Local 669 v. NLRB (A-1 Fire Protection), 676 F2d 826, 110 LRRM 2125 (CA DC, 1982). However, a change in the description of the bargaining unit is not a mandatory subject of bargaining. Newport News Shipbuilding Co. v. NLRB, 602 F2d 73, 101 LRRM 2998 (CA 4, 1979).

[203]Crown Coach Corp., 155 NLRB 625, 60 LRRM 1366 (1965).

[204]Leroy Mach. Co., 147 NLRB 1431, 56 LRRM 1369 (1964), where the Board held that a management-prerogatives clause constituted a union waiver of a right to require the employer to bargain about physical examinations during the term of the existing agreement. *Cf.* Wilburn v. Missouri-Kansas-Texas R.R., 268 SW2d 726 (Tex. Civ. App, 1954) (physical examinations are subject of bargaining under Railway Labor Act).

[205]NLRB v. Yutana Barge Lines, 315 F2d 524, 52 LRRM 2750 (CA 9, 1963); United States Pipe & Foundry Co. v. NLRB, 298 F2d 873, 49 LRRM 2540 (CA 5, 1962). Although a party may generally insist to impasse on mandatory subjects of bargaining, in Sann dba Briarcliff Pavilion for Specialized Care, 260 NLRB 1374, 109 LRRM 1383 (1982), *enforced*, 725 F2d 669, 115 LRRM 2712 (CA 3, 1983), the Board held that an employer's insistence on a contract duration of only 4½ months was an indicium of bad-faith bargaining in the circumstances therein. The question of contract retroactivity is also a mandatory subject of bargaining. Bergen Point Iron Works, 79 NLRB 1073, 22 LRRM 1475 (1948). However, employee ratification of a contract is not. Thus, in NLRB v. Darlington Veneer Co., 236 F2d 85, 38 LRRM 2574 (CA 4, 1956), the Fourth Circuit found a violation of §8(a)(5) in an employer's insistence upon ratification of the contract by secret vote of the employees. *Cf.* NLRB v. Borg-Warner Corp., Wooster Div., 356 US 342, 42 LRRM 2034 (1958); North

2. Specific Terms and Requirements. Some topics of mandatory bargaining that constitute "other terms and conditions of employment" require more than a mere listing. Generally, any genuine and substantive change in "terms and conditions" has been deemed subject to mandatory bargaining, whether the change arose from the promulgation of new terms or from the enforcement of previously unenforced rules. However, both the courts and the Board have recognized exceptions to this rule derived from their efforts to balance employees' and employers' rights and interests.

a. Seniority, Promotions, and Transfers. Seniority, promotions, and transfers have long been recognized as mandatory subjects of bargaining.[206] Seniority is so obviously a condition of employment and so commonly exists under union contracts,[207] that litigation questioning its mandatory status has been minimal. Probationary periods and attendant conditions require bargaining,[208] as do promotions within a bargaining unit.[209] An employer may not unilaterally revoke preferential seniority previously granted informally to union officers and negotiators,[210] nor may it unilaterally abrogate seniority rights upon expiration of a collective agreement establishing these rights. Elimination of such an accrued benefit constitutes a change in a condition of employment.[211] Aptitude testing may not be unilaterally intro-

---

Country Motors, 146 NLRB 671, 55 LRRM 1421 (1964). For further discussion of the subject of ratification, see Part V *infra*, at notes 508–510.

[206]United States Gypsum Co., 94 NLRB 112, 28 LRRM 1015 (1951).

[207]Ford Motor Co. v. Huffman, 345 US 330, 31 LRRM 2548 (1953). *See* Chapter 26, "The Duty of Fair Representation," at notes 293–296.

[208]Oliver Corp., 162 NLRB 813, 64 LRRM 1092 (1967).

[209]Associated Gen. Contractors, Houston Chapter, 143 NLRB 409, 53 LRRM 1299 (1963), *enforced*, 349 F2d 449, 59 LRRM 3013 (CA 5, 1965), *cert. denied*, 382 US 1026, 61 LRRM 2244 (1966). The Board has held that promotion of employees to supervisory positions outside the unit is a mandatory subject when the effect is to transfer bargaining-unit work to nonunit employees. Fry Foods, 241 NLRB 76, 100 LRRM 1513 (1979), *enforced*, 609 F2d 267, 102 LRRM 2894 (CA 6, 1979).

[210]NLRB v. Proof Co., *supra* note 200. It should be noted that preferential seniority to union officers must be limited to layoff and recall. The Board has held that a preferential seniority agreement which is not so limited is presumptively unlawful. Dairylea Coop., 219 NLRB 656, 89 LRRM 1737 (1975), *enforced sub nom.* NLRB v. Teamsters Local 338, 531 F2d 1162, 91 LRRM 2929 (CA 2, 1976). And such superseniority must be confined to union agents who administer the agreement or handle grievances. Gulton Electro-Voice, 266 NLRB 406, 112 LRRM 1361 (1983), *enforced sub nom.* Electrical Workers (IUE) Local 900 v. NLRB, 727 F2d 1184, 115 LRRM 2760 (CA DC, 1984). *See* Chapter 7, "Discrimination in Employment," at notes 369–376. *See also* Note, *Union Steward Superseniority*, 6 N.Y.U. REV. L. & SOC. CHANGE 1 (1976).

[211]NLRB v. Katz, *supra* note 198; Marine & Shipbuilding Workers v. NLRB (Bethlehem Steel Co.), 320 F2d 615, 53 LRRM 2878 (CA 3, 1963). *See also* United States Gypsum Co., *supra* note 206.

duced, and bargaining about such testing is required.[212]

Unilateral changes in seniority[213] or recall policies[214] violate an employer's obligation to bargain in good faith. However, where an employer had unilaterally reclassified an employee to a lower seniority position in order to correct an inequity, the Board found no violation, because the higher position had been granted the employee on a temporary basis, the employee had been paid according to her duties, and the change reflected a longstanding company policy.[215]

Transfer of employees, as a general rule, is a mandatory subject of bargaining.[216] In one case, however, janitorial employees in a university hospital complex were covered by two collective bargaining agreements and belonged to two different local unions. The university laid off all the members of one local and allocated their duties to members of the other local. The laid-off employees could seek work elsewhere or be hired into lower paying jobs under the contract with the retained local. The Board found that this "transfer" of employees to what amounted to a different union was subject to mandatory bargaining.[217] The Seventh Circuit disagreed, however, reasoning that the employer was seeking only to institute a uniform higher standard for cleaning. Since the court found no union animus in the transfers but rather a legitimate business justification, it did not

---

[212]American Gilsonite Co., 121 NLRB 1514, 43 LRRM 1011 (1958), *supplemented*, 122 NLRB 1006, 43 LRRM 1242 (1959).

[213]*See, e.g.*, Johns-Manville Sales Corp., 282 NLRB 182, 123 LRRM 1315 (1986); Schnadig Corp., 265 NLRB 147, 112 LRRM 1331 (1982); MCC Pac. Valves, 244 NLRB 931, 102 LRRM 1183 (1979) (unilateral termination of seniority rights of recalled economic strikers); Longhorn Mach. Works, 205 NLRB 685, 84 LRRM 1307 (1973) (unilateral discontinuation of method of computing seniority).

[214]*See, e.g.*, Schnadig Corp., *supra* note 213; Grand Lodge of Free & Accepted Masons, Masonic Home, 215 NLRB 75, 88 LRRM 1294 (1974), *enforced*, 548 F2d 1276, 94 LRRM 3199 (CA 6, 1977), *cert. denied*, 434 US 822, 96 LRRM 2513 (1978) (refusal to bargain over clause reinstating strikers). *But see* NLRB v. D.H. Farms Co., 481 F2d 830, 83 LRRM 2923 (CA 6, 1973).

[215]Foster Transformer Co., 212 NLRB 936, 87 LRRM 1010 (1974).

[216]*Compare* Union Elec. Co., 196 NLRB 830, 80 LRRM 1110 (1972) *with* Continental Ins. Co. v. NLRB, 495 F2d 44, 86 LRRM 2003 (CA 2, 1974) (unilateral transfer of six employees). *See also, e.g.*, United Technologies Corp., Hamilton Standard Div., 296 NLRB No. 79, 132 LRRM 1240 (1989) (transfer to another location); Otis Elevator Co., 283 NLRB 223, 124 LRRM 1334 (1987) (criteria for transfers); Crest Floors & Plastics dba Pacific Sun, 274 NLRB 1230, 119 LRRM 1202 (1985), *enforced*, 785 F2d 314, 122 LRRM 2368 (CA 9, 1986) (transfer to sister company); San Antonio Portland Cement Co., 277 NLRB 338, 121 LRRM 1234 (1985) (transfer).

[217]University of Chicago, 210 NLRB 190, 86 LRRM 1073 (1974); *see also* Dahl Fish Co., 279 NLRB 1084, 123 LRRM 1322 (1986), *enforced*, 813 F2d 1254, 125 LRRM 3063 (CA DC, 1987).

consider the university's failure to bargain over the transfers a violation of section 8(a)(5).[218]

Promotion of employees within the bargaining unit is a mandatory subject of bargaining.[219] However, promotion of employees to positions outside the bargaining unit is not a mandatory subject.[220]

b. Retirement Eligibility. In the *Inland Steel Co.* case,[221] generally known for its holding that pensions are a mandatory subject for bargaining, the Board and the Seventh Circuit held that an employer must bargain with a union concerning a compulsory retirement age.

In 1986, Congress amended the 1978 Age Discrimination in Employment Act (ADEA)[222] to prohibit compulsory retirement at any age over 40, unless age is a bona fide occupational qualification. In *Air Line Pilots Ass'n v. Trans World Airlines,*[223] both the employer and the union were held liable for violating ADEA by negotiating policies forcing pilots reaching age 60 to retire while permitting pilots disqualified for non-age-based reasons to transfer to flight engineer positions. Elimination of compulsory retirement provisions made illegal by ADEA would not require bargaining, but the elimination of such illegal provisions may result in or be accompanied by other changes in a retirement plan thereby giving rise to a bargaining obligation.[224]

---

[218]University of Chicago v. NLRB, 514 F2d 942, 89 LRRM 2113 (CA 7, 1975). *But see* Newspaper Printing Corp. v. NLRB, 625 F2d 956, 104 LRRM 2432 (CA 10, 1980), *cert. denied,* 450 US 911, 106 LRRM 2512 (1981).

[219]*See, e.g.,* Transit Union v. Donovan, 767 F2d 939, 119 LRRM 3185 (CA DC, 1985), *cert. denied sub nom.* Metropolitan Atlanta Rapid Transit Auth. v. Transit Union, 475 US 1046, 121 LRRM 2792 (1986); Kohler Co., 273 NLRB 1580, 118 LRRM 1236 (1985) (promotions and reclassification of bargaining-unit jobs to nonunit jobs).

[220]*See* Pittsburgh Metal Processing Co., 286 NLRB 734, 128 LRRM 1094 (1987) (no violation of Act when employer failed to bargain over promotion of employees to supervisory positions, where promotions did not have substantial impact on bargaining unit); St. Louis Tel. Employees Credit Union, 273 NLRB 625, 118 LRRM 1079 (1984) (promoting bargaining-unit employees to nonunit supervisory jobs not subject to mandatory bargaining). [**Editor's Note:** A proposal governing the return of supervisors to the unit is a mandatory subject. Remington Arms Co., 298 NLRB No. 35, 134 LRRM 1024 (1990).]

[221]77 NLRB 1, 21 LRRM 1310 (1948), *enforced,* 170 F2d 247, 22 LRRM 2506 (CA 7, 1948), *cert. denied,* 336 US 960, 24 LRRM 2019 (1949).

[222]29 USC §621 et seq. (Supp. III 1979).

[223]713 F2d 940, 114 LRRM 2241 (CA 2, 1983), *aff'd in part and rev'd in part sub nom.* Trans World Airlines v. Thurston, 469 US 111, 36 FEP Cases 977 (1985).

[224]*See* Smith, *Impact of the 1978 ADEA Amendments on Collective Bargaining,* LABOR RELATIONS YEARBOOK—1978, 218 (1979). A change in the compulsory retirement age would not relieve an employer of the obligation to bargain regarding a change in the normal retirement age. Thus, if the normal retirement age were to remain at age 65, a number of issues could arise such as the pension accrual and insurance rights of employees who stay on to work after age 65.

c. Union-Security Provision and Hiring Halls. That a union-shop clause is embraced by "conditions of employment" was recognized prior to *Borg-Warner*.[225] In 1949, the Ninth Circuit held that union security fell within the area of required bargaining.[226] The Third Circuit subsequently held that since union security is a creature of contract, section 8(a)(5) was not violated by an employer who unilaterally ceased giving effect to union-shop and checkoff provisions of a contract upon its expiration.[227]

Under an agency-shop agreement an employee is not required to join the union, but is required to pay to the union an amount equivalent to union dues. Although the Board initially held that an agency shop was not a subject that required bargaining,[228] it later reversed itself.[229] The Sixth Circuit denied enforcement,[230] but the Supreme Court reversed,[231] reasoning that agency-shop proposals impose no burdens in addition to those imposed by union-shop proposals, which are lawful and are a mandatory subject.[232] While agency shop status is a mandatory subject of bargaining, the amount of agency fees assessed by the union is nonmandatory.[233]

---

[225]NLRB v. Borg-Warner Corp., Wooster Div., *supra* note 205. *See supra* notes 23–29.

[226]NLRB v. Andrew Jergens Co., 175 F2d 130, 24 LRRM 2096 (CA 9, 1949), *cert. denied*, 338 US 827, 24 LRRM 2561 (1949). *See also* United States Gypsum Co., *supra* note 206. *Cf.* Vanderbilt Prods. v. NLRB, 297 F2d 833, 49 LRRM 2286 (CA 2, 1961), where the court found that insistence upon an open shop supported a finding of bad-faith bargaining.

[227]Marine & Shipbuilding Workers v. NLRB (Bethlehem Steel Co.), 320 F2d 615, 53 LRRM 2878 (CA 3, 1963), *refusing enforcement to* 136 NLRB 1500, 50 LRRM 1013 (1962). *See also* Tampa Sheet Metal Co., 288 NLRB 322, 129 LRRM 1188 (1988). A union-shop agreement derives its validity from the proviso of §8(a)(3). See Chapter 27, "Union Security." "Checkoff" refers to a system by which an employer deducts union dues from wages upon written authorization by the employee and remits the dues directly to the union. The legality of the checkoff under federal law is governed by §302(c)(4) of the Act which allows payments from an employer to a union "with respect to money deducted from the wages of employees in payment of membership dues in a labor organization: *Provided*, that the employer has received from each employee, on whose account such deductions are made, a written assignment which shall not be irrevocable for a period of more than one year, or beyond the termination date of the applicable collective agreement, whichever occurs sooner . . . ." *See* Presbyterian Hosp., 241 NLRB 996, 101 LRRM 1001 (1979). For a full discussion of the interrelation of contract duration and union-security provisions, see Chapter 27, "Union Security."

[228]General Motors Corp., 130 NLRB 481, 47 LRRM 1306 (1961).

[229]General Motors Corp., 133 NLRB 451, 48 LRRM 1659 (1961).

[230]General Motors Corp. v. NLRB, 303 F2d 428, 50 LRRM 2396 (CA 6, 1962).

[231]NLRB v. General Motors Corp., 373 US 734, 53 LRRM 2313 (1963). *See* Chapter 27, "Union Security," at notes 197–200.

[232]The effect of a right-to-work law which outlaws the agency shop was decided in Retail Clerks Local 1625 v. Schermerhorn, 373 US 746, 53 LRRM 2318 (1963), *aff'd*, 375 US 96, 54 LRRM 2612 (1963). *See* Chapter 27, "Union Security," for a detailed discussion of right-to-work laws.

[233]Service Employees Local 535 (North Bay Dev. Disabilities Servs. dba North Bay Regional Center), 287 NLRB 1223, 127 LRRM 1184 (1988).

A nondiscriminatory referral or hiring hall to be operated by a union is also a mandatory subject for bargaining.[234] The Board has also held that, in the absence of some indication to the contrary, a hiring-hall referral provision would not be presumed to expire with the contract.[235] However, such a provision expired where the contract in which it had been contained had ended years before, after which the union acquiesced for years in the employer's hiring of workers outside the hall.[236]

d. Management Rights and Waiver Clauses. The leading case involving a proposal for a broad management-rights clause is the Supreme Court's decision in *American National Insurance Co.*,[237] which held that an employer's insistence upon a broad management-rights clause covering terms and conditions of employment is not in itself a violation of section 8(a)(5). While the Court held that the Board may not pass judgment upon the desirability of substantive terms of an agreement, it may nevertheless decide whether good-faith requirements of section 8(d) have been met.

The Board views the content of a proposed management-rights clause as one factor in determining whether there is a duty to bargain about the clause. In one case it found that an employer violated section 8(a)(5) by bargaining to impasse on a management-rights clause which would have permitted it to make stenographic transcripts of bargaining sessions.[238] The employer's insistence on the clause was unlawful because the

---

[234]Associated Gen. Contractors, Houston Chapter, 143 NLRB 409, 53 LRRM 1299 (1963), *enforced*, 349 F2d 449, 59 LRRM 3013 (CA 5, 1965), *cert. denied*, 382 US 1026, 61 LRRM 2244 (1966). *Accord* NLRB v. Tom Joyce Floors, Inc., 353 F2d 768, 60 LRRM 2434 (CA 9, 1965). The legality of such a hiring hall was established in Teamsters Local 357 v. NLRB (Los Angeles-Seattle Motor Express), 365 US 667, 47 LRRM 2906 (1961). *See* discussion in Chapter 27, "Union Security," at notes 252–349. *Cf.* Pacific Am. Shipowners Ass'n, 90 NLRB 1099, 26 LRRM 1316 (1950), where a §8(b)(3) charge against a union striking for such a clause was dismissed.

[235]Southwestern Steel & Supply, 276 NLRB 1569, 120 LRRM 1255 (1985), *enforced*, 806 F2d 1111, 123 LRRM 3290 (CA DC, 1986); Southwest Sec. Equip. Corp., 262 NLRB 665, 110 LRRM 1328 (1982), *enforced*, 736 F2d 1332, 116 LRRM 3201 (CA 9, 1984), *cert. denied*, 470 US 1087, 118 LRRM 3040 (1985).

[236]Craft Elec. Co., 293 NLRB 1074, 131 LRRM 1340 (1989).

[237]NLRB v. American Nat'l Ins. Co., 343 US 395, 30 LRRM 2147 (1952). *See* discussion *supra*, at notes 21–22. For cases dealing with management-rights clauses, see Long Lake Lumber Co., 182 NLRB 435, 74 LRRM 1116 (1970); Old Line Life Ins. Co. of Am., 96 NLRB 499, 28 LRRM 1539 (1951). *See also* Chapter 13, "The Duty to Bargain," at notes 285–288.

[238]Water Ass'n, 290 NLRB 838, 129 LRRM 1064 (1988) (audio tape recording); Pennsylvania Tel. Guild, 277 NLRB 501, 120 LRRM 1257 (1985), *enforced*, 799 F2d 84, 123 LRRM 2214 (CA 3, 1986) (tape recorder); Hutchinson Fruit Co., 277 NLRB 497, 120 LRRM 1258 (1985) (same); Quality Engineered Prods. Co., 267 NLRB 593, 114 LRRM 1100 (1983). *See also* Bartlett-Collins Co., 237 NLRB 770, 99 LRRM 1034 (1978), *enforced*, 639 F2d 652, 106 LRRM 2272 (CA 10), *cert. denied*, 452 US 961, 107 LRRM 2768 (1981) (court reporter).

stenographic transcription of bargaining sessions is not a mandatory subject of bargaining.

Although the status of management-rights clause as a mandatory bargaining subject depends on its contents, that is, whether it contains nonmandatory items, more often the contents are only a factor in ascertaining whether the employer has bargained in good faith.[239] In *Preterm, Inc.*,[240] for example, the Board held that a proposal of a broad management-rights clause during contract negotiations did not constitute evidence of a refusal to bargain in good faith,[241] even though the employer submitted its proposal 6 months after negotiations had commenced. The clause provided that the employer's rights under the clause were not reviewable under the grievance or arbitration provisions. The Board held that the employer did not adopt an intransigent position with respect to the proposal and the proposal did not impede the negotiation process.

On the other hand, the Board has held that a rigid and inflexible insistence on a broad management-rights clause, in the context of evidence that the employer is engaged in surface bargaining with no intention of reaching agreement, indicates an unwillingness to bargain in good faith.[242] For example, in *United Contractors*,[243] it found an employer in violation of the Act

---

[239]*See* generally Chapter 13, "The Duty to Bargain."

[240]240 NLRB 654, 100 LRRM 1344 (1979).

[241]*See also* Houston County Elec. Coop., 285 NLRB 1213, 129 LRRM 1337 (1987) (employer did not violate Act by insisting on broad management-rights clause where employer modified clause by withdrawing broad subcontracting language and union never made any counterproposal); Boaz Carpet Yarns, 280 NLRB 40, 122 LRRM 1139 (1986) (adherence to broad management-rights clause not evidence of bad faith where proposal drafted broadly to avoid appearance of waiver of rights, union presented no counterproposal until thirteenth bargaining session, and proposal did not contain no-strike or zipper clauses); Chevron Chem. Co., 261 NLRB 44, 110 LRRM 1005, 1008 (1982), *enforced without opinion sub nom.* Oil, Chem. & Atomic Workers Local 4-447 v. NLRB, 701 F2d 172, 113 LRRM 2112 (CA 5, 1983) (employer did not violate Act by proposing strong management-rights clause where it had manifested its willingness to make concessions during course of bargaining and its proposals were not "harsh, vindictive, or otherwise unreasonable").

[242]*See, e.g.*, Prentice-Hall, 290 NLRB 646, 129 LRRM 1052 (1988) (employer violated §8(a)(5) with proposals, including broad management-rights clause, which rendered substantial portions of proposed contract unenforceable); A-1 King Size Sandwiches, 265 NLRB 850, 112 LRRM 1360 (1982), *enforced*, 732 F2d 872, 116 LRRM 2658 (CA 11), *cert. denied*, 469 US 1035, 117 LRRM 3080 (1984) (employer engaged in surface bargaining where it insisted on management-rights clause that controlled essentially every aspect of employment relationship while it also insisted on very narrow grievance and arbitration clause that excluded disciplinary matters from grievance procedure and no-strike clause that precluded strikes for any reasons, including unfair labor practices).

[243]244 NLRB 72, 102 LRRM 1012 (1979), *enforced*, 631 F2d 735, 108 LRRM 3152 (CA 7, 1980). *See also* Dixie Corp., 105 NLRB 390, 32 LRRM 1259 (1953), distinguishing NLRB v. American Nat'l Ins. Co., *supra* note 237, where an employer who refused to supply relevant data to the union, refused to accept the appropriate bargaining unit, and insisted

where the proposed management-rights clause demanded by the employer would in effect have required the union to yield all bargaining rights on such fundamental items as establishing and enforcing work rules, scheduling of hours and assignment of duties, discipline and discharge of employees, subcontracting of work, and relocation and shutdown of operations. The Board's critical finding was that the employer had no intention of reaching an agreement, evidenced by the fact that the company insisted on a 20-percent wage reduction during the period of widespread inflation without offering any claim of economic necessity.

e. Plant Rules and Discipline. Generally, plant rules are considered subjects of mandatory bargaining, which means that an employer cannot unilaterally implement or change such rules.[244] These include rules pertaining to lunch breaks, absenteeism and tardiness,[245] dress codes,[246] parking regulations,[247] fighting,[248] working on an overtime basis,[249] and safety.[250] Moreover, if the rule affects an employee's continuation of employment, such as a warning and disciplinary system might,[251] it will be a mandatory subject regardless of the

---

on unilateral control of all subjects of bargaining as a condition precedent to agreement also was held in violation of §8(a)(5). And in Stuart Radiator Core Mfg. Co., 173 NLRB 125, 69 LRRM 1243 (1968), an employer who insisted on a detailed management-rights clause which reserved absolute unilateral control of virtually every significant term and condition of employment, coupled with a limitation of grievances and arbitration to the express terms of the contract and a waiver of bargaining, thereby manifested bad faith.

[244]Schraffts Candy Co., 244 NLRB 581, 102 LRRM 1274 (1979); Miller Brewing Co., 166 NLRB 831, 65 LRRM 1649 (1967), *enforced*, 408 F2d 12, 70 LRRM 2907 (CA 9, 1969); Hilton Mobile Homes, 155 NLRB 873, 60 LRRM 1411 (1965), *enforcement denied*, 387 F2d 7, 67 LRRM 2140 (CA 8, 1967).

[245]Murphy Diesel Co. v. NLRB, 454 F2d 303, 78 LRRM 2993 (CA 7, 1971); Kay Fries, Inc., 265 NLRB 1077, 112 LRRM 1377 (1982), *enforced without opinion*, 722 F2d 732, 115 LRRM 2904 (CA 3, 1983) (bereavement leave policy); Production Plated Plastics, 254 NLRB 560, 106 LRRM 1143 (1981) (tardiness rule and lunch and break policies); Kroehler Mfg. Co., 222 NLRB 1269, 91 LRRM 1382 (1976).

[246]Transportation Enters., 240 NLRB 551, 100 LRRM 1330 (1979), *modified in other respects*, 630 F2d 421, 105 LRRM 3168 (CA 5, 1980).

[247]Rudy's Farm Co., 245 NLRB 43, 102 LRRM 1384 (1979).

[248]National Football Players Ass'n v. NLRB, 503 F2d 12, 87 LRRM 2118 (CA 8, 1974).

[249]Colonial Press, 204 NLRB 852, 83 LRRM 1648 (1973), *enforced*, 564 F2d 101, 97 LRRM 2111 (CA 8, 1977).

[250]Boland Marine & Mfg. Co., 225 NLRB 824, 93 LRRM 1346 (1976), *aff'd*, 562 F2d 1259, 96 LRRM 3239 (CA 5, 1977); Pak-Mor Mfg. Co., 241 NLRB 801, 100 LRRM 1630 (1979). *But see* UNC Nuclear Indus., United Nuclear Corp., 268 NLRB 841, 115 LRRM 1111 (1984) (unilateral implementation of oral readiness test of nuclear power plant operators did not violate the Act where it was merely extension of existing training program designed to ensure plant safety). *See infra* at notes 276–284.

[251]In Electri-Flex Co., 228 NLRB 847, 96 LRRM 1361 (1977), *enforced as modified*, 570 F2d 1327, 97 LRRM 2888 (CA 7), *cert. denied*, 439 US 911, 99 LRRM 2743 (1978), the Board found violations of §8(a)(5) where the employer unilaterally instituted and

employer's legitimate reason for its promulgation.[252]

Exceptions to this general proposition have occurred in cases where the change in a plant rule had little or no impact on the employees as a group or on their working conditions.[253] In addition, at least three other situations have at times been treated as exceptions to the general rule.

First, in *Capital Times Co.*,[254] the Board held that an employer providing editorial services for a newspaper was not required to bargain before promulgating a "code of ethics," prohibiting employees from accepting gifts from outsiders occasioned by their employment and requiring employees to disclose outside activities that might constitute conflicts of interest. The Board reasoned that such gifts were not wages since they did not flow from the employer, were not viewed as wages by the union or the employees, and were not compensation for work performed. But in the same case the Board held that a provision in the code for penalties of suspension and discharge was a mandatory subject, because it directly affected employment security.[255]

In *Peerless Publications (Pottstown Mercury)*,[256] the Board adhered to the principles set forth in *Capital Times*, holding that a newspaper could unilaterally promulgate a "code of ethics" forbidding secondary employment that raised a conflict of interest but that the imposition of a penalty for the violation of the "code" triggered a bargaining duty. The Court of Appeals for the District of Columbia Circuit criticized the Board's approach,

---

enforced a written warning system. *See also* Rahco, Inc., 265 NLRB 235, 112 LRRM 1398 (1982) (unilateral institution of highly structured and formalized system of discipline); Robbins Door & Sash Co., 260 NLRB 659, 109 LRRM 1181 (1982) (unilateral institution of stringent disciplinary rules unlawful even if they were instituted to counter employee slowdowns); Lion Uniform, Janesville Apparel Div., 259 NLRB 1141, 109 LRRM 1093 (1982).

[252]Medicenter, Mid-South Hosp., 221 NLRB 670, 90 LRRM 1576 (1975) (polygraph tests). *See also* NFL Mgmt. Council, 203 NLRB 958, 83 LRRM 1203 (1973), *remanded*, 503 F2d 12, 87 LRRM 2118 (CA 8, 1974), *supplemented*, 216 NLRB 423, 88 LRRM 1210 (1975) ("artificial turf" on playing fields was mandatory subject of bargaining).

[253]*See, e.g.*, Pacific Diesel Parts Co., 203 NLRB 820, 83 LRRM 1359 (1973); *cf.* Old Angus, 212 NLRB 539, 86 LRRM 1575 (1974), relying upon the Board's earlier decision in Steel-Fab, Inc., 212 NLRB 363, 86 LRRM 1474 (1974), since overruled by Trading Port, 219 NLRB 298, 89 LRRM 1565 (1975).

[254]223 NLRB 651, 91 LRRM 1481 (1976).

[255]Further refinement of the *Capital Times* decision came in Peerless Publications (Pottstown Mercury), 231 NLRB 244, 95 LRRM 1611 (1977). The *Peerless* employer's code of ethics not only prohibited gifts, but also prohibited employees from engaging in secondary employment if such employment would create a conflict of interest. *Cf.* Capital Times, Co., *supra* note 254, where employees were only required to report secondary employment. The *Peerless* Board determined that the second employment prohibition was not a mandatory subject of bargaining. *See* note 256 *infra*.

[256]*Supra* note 255.

noting that for bargaining purposes the penalty provisions cannot easily be separated from the substantive provisions which they are designed to enforce.[257] Accordingly, the Board was instructed to determine on remand the specific subjects in the "code of ethics" that are mandatorily bargainable.

On remand, the Board reversed its earlier position and concluded that the employer newspaper had unlawfully implemented the Ethics Code unilaterally.[258] The Board stated that such rules may be established unilaterally when they are designed to protect "the core purposes of the enterprise."[259] However, the rules there in question could not be established without bargaining since they were not "narrowly tailored in terms of substance, to meet with particularity only the employer's legitimate and necessary objectives," and were not "appropriately limited in [their] applicability to affected employees to accomplish the necessarily limited objectives."[260] Accordingly, if anything at all remains of the *Capital Times* exception, it is very narrow indeed.

The second exception was made in *Rust Craft Broadcasting*,[261] in which the installation of time clocks without bargaining was held not to be violative of the Act. The Board reasoned that the time clocks were merely a more dependable method of enforcing the employer's longstanding requirement that employees record their time at work, and, therefore, bargaining was not required over this procedural change.[262]

Third, in *Trading Port*,[263] the Board held that an employee-evaluation system utilizing hourly production figures as a guide could be instituted by an employer without affording the union prior opportunity to bargain. The Board based its holding on a principle previously adopted in *Wabash Transformer Corp.*,[264] that management should be granted a substantial degree of

---

[257]Newspaper Guild Local 10 (Greater Philadelphia) v. NLRB (Peerless Publications (Pottstown Mercury)), 636 F2d 550, 105 LRRM 2001 (CA DC, 1980).

[258]Peerless Publications (Pottstown Mercury), 283 NLRB 334, 124 LRRM 1331 (1987).

[259]*Id.* at 335.

[260]*Id.*

[261]225 NLRB 327, 92 LRRM 1576 (1976). *See also* Chef's Pantry, 274 NLRB 775, 119 LRRM 1096 (1985); Care Ambulance dba American Ambulance, 255 NLRB 417, 107 LRRM 1043 (1981), *enforced without opinion*, 692 F2d 762, 111 LRRM 2650 (CA 9, 1982); Moody Chip Corp., 243 NLRB 265, 101 LRRM 1496 (1979); The Bureau of Nat'l Affairs, 235 NLRB 8, 97 LRRM 1447 (1978).

[262]*Supra* note 261. *See also* Nathan Littauer Hosp. Ass'n, 229 NLRB 1122, 95 LRRM 1296 (1977) *and* Cardinal Sys., 259 NLRB 456, 109 LRRM 1005 (1981).

[263]224 NLRB 980, 92 LRRM 1606 (1976).

[264]215 NLRB 546, 88 LRRM 1511 (1974).

flexibility to fashion innovations promoting a more efficient work force.

In addition, as illustrated by *EPE v. NLRB*,[265] unilateral institution of new rules, such as an attendance policy including progressive discipline, can be rendered lawful by a sufficiently broad contractual management-rights clause giving the employer the right to promulgate and to enforce rules of conduct.

f. Drug and Alcohol Testing. In *Johnson-Bateman Co.*,[266] the Board held that testing of "current employees" is a subject of mandatory bargaining. The Board, using the Supreme Court's definition of subjects,[267] opined that mandatory drug- or alcohol-testing programs are "germane to the working environment," are not within the scope of managerial decisions which lie at the core of entrepreneurial control, and therefore are mandatory subjects of bargaining.[268] However, on the same day the Board also held, in *Star Tribune Division*,[269] that an employer may unilaterally institute drug- or alcohol-testing programs designed to screen "job applicants" without violating the Act. The Board reasoned that, since job applicants are not employees within the meaning of the Act, such testing does not "vitally affect" the terms and conditions of employment or the working conditions of the bargaining-unit employees.[270] The Board has subsequently reaffirmed that drug or alcohol testing of job applicants is not a mandatory subject of bargaining.[271]

g. Grievance Procedures and Arbitration. The subjects of grievances and proposals to establish orderly and just methods of presenting grievances are mandatory subjects for collective bargaining.[272] Arbitration clauses are specifically a subject of man-

---

[265]845 F2d 483, 128 LRRM 2246 (CA 4, 1988).

[266]295 NLRB No. 26, 131 LRRM 1393 (1989) (testing of employees who require treatment for injuries received while on the job).

[267]*See* Ford Motor Co. v. NLRB, 441 US 488, 101 LRRM 2222 (1979).

[268]131 LRRM at 1396.

[269]295 NLRB No. 63, 131 LRRM 1404 (1989) (overruling pro tanto Rockwood & Co., 285 NLRB 1114, 128 LRRM 1143 (1987), in which the Board adopted, pro forma in the absence of an exception, the order of the ALJ holding the topic to be mandatory).

[270]131 LRRM at 1407. *See generally* Allied Chemical & Alkali Workers Local 1 v. Pittsburgh Plate Glass Co., 404 US 157, 78 LRRM 2974 (1971) ("vitally affects" test).

[271]*See* RCA Corp., 296 NLRB No. 154, 132 LRRM 1348 (1989); Electric Energy, 296 NLRB No. 76, 132 LRRM 1180 (1989); United Cable Television Corp., 296 NLRB No. 21, 132 LRRM 1058 (1989); GTE Hawaiian Tel. Co., 296 NLRB No. 1, 131 LRRM 1801 (1989).

[272]*See* NLRB v. Independent Stave Co., 591 F2d 443, 100 LRRM 2646 (CA 8, 1979), *cert. denied*, 444 US 829, 102 LRRM 2360 (1979); Electrical Workers (UE) (Star Expansion Indus. Corp.) v. NLRB, 409 F2d 150, 70 LRRM 2529 (CA DC, 1969); NLRB v. Century Cement Mfg. Co., 208 F2d 84, 33 LRRM 2061 (CA 2, 1953); Hughes Tool Co. v. NLRB, 147 F2d 69, 15 LRRM 852 (CA 5, 1945).

datory bargaining.[273]

Two decisions illustrate the controversies that occasionally arise from claims of unilateral alteration of established methods of presenting and resolving grievances. The First Circuit enforced a Board decision holding that an employer violated the Act by not allowing the union to photocopy grievance-related records. This no-photocopy rule was held to have unnecessarily impeded the grievance process, without any legitimate business justification.[274] In another decision, the Board found no violation where the employer refused to permit union representatives access to a telephone to obtain information they believed to be relevant to the grievance under consideration.[275] Although the parties disagreed about whether the union had made telephone calls during the course of other grievance meetings, the Board accepted the determination of the ALJ that the employer had acted in good faith: the parties had already discussed the grievance at some length and the employer believed the information sought by the union was irrelevant and had expressed a willingness to reconvene the meeting at the union's request if the union wished to present any new points.

h. Safety and Health. The contention of some employers that safety regulation is a management function, not subject to negotiation, has been rejected by the Board and the courts. The Fifth Circuit stated it was "inescapable" that "workers, through their chosen representative, should have the right to bargain with the Company in reference to safe work practices."[276] This is also the Board's view. For example, in *Armour Oil Co.*,[277] an employer

---

[273]*See* Electrical Workers (UE) (Star Expansion Indus. Corp.) v. NLRB, *supra* note 272; NLRB v. Davison, 318 F2d 550, 53 LRRM 2462 (CA 4, 1963); NLRB v. Knoxville Publishing Co., 124 F2d 875, 9 LRRM 498 (CA 6, 1942). Regarding the effect of arbitration clauses in expired agreements, see, e.g., Nolde Bros. v. Bakery Workers Local 358, 430 US 243, 94 LRRM 2753 (1977). *See generally* Edwards, *Deferral to Arbitration and Waiver of the Duty to Bargain: A Possible Way Out of Everlasting Confusion at the NLRB*, 46 OHIO ST. L.J. 23 (1985); Note, *Arbitration After Communications Workers: A Diminished Role?*, 100 HARV. L. REV. 1307 (1987).

[274]Communications Workers Local 1051 v. NLRB (AT&T), 644 F2d 923, 106 LRRM 2960 (CA 1, 1981). *See* Champion Parts Rebuilders, Northeast Div. v. NLRB, 717 F2d 845, 114 LRRM 2674 (CA 3, 1983).

[275]E.I. du Pont de Nemours & Co., 259 NLRB 1210, 109 LRRM 1096 (1982).

[276]NLRB v. Gulf Power Co., 384 F2d 822, 66 LRRM 2501, 2502 (CA 5, 1967), *enforcing* 156 NLRB 622, 61 LRRM 1073 (1966). In Fibreboard Paper Prods. Corp. v. NLRB, 379 US 203, 57 LRRM 2609 (1964), the Supreme Court specifically mentioned "safety practices" as a condition of employment in defining the bargaining duty of an employer. *Fibreboard* is discussed *infra* at notes 328–331. *Cf.* Gateway Coal Co. v. Mine Workers, 414 US 368, 85 LRRM 2049 (1974). For discussion of safety-related protests as protected conduct, see Chapter 6, "Interference With Protected Rights," at notes 504–508.

[277]253 NLRB 1104, 106 LRRM 1127 (1981).

who unilaterally replaced trucks driven by its employees with vehicles that were noisier and more difficult to handle and that lacked up-to-date safety equipment violated the Act because the decision resulted in "material, substantial, and significant changes in the drivers' working conditions."[278] In *Winona Industries*[279] an employer who unilaterally promulgated a rule prohibiting employees from wearing "tank tops" at work because it believed that atmospheric formaldehyde could adversely affect exposed skin was found to have violated the Act by refusing to give the union's industrial hygienist access to the worksite in order to investigate the health and safety conditions more fully, to acquire information necessary to assess the validity of the rule, and to prepare for upcoming contract negotiations.[280]

The 1970 Occupational Safety and Health Act (OSHA)[281] guarantees employees a workplace free from recognized hazards that do or could cause death or serious physical harm.[282] These rights may conflict with obligations under a collective bargaining agreement. In a subsequent decision involving an employee who walked off the job rather than continue working under what he considered to be seriously dangerous conditions, the Seventh Circuit said that "the OSHA legislation was intended to create a separate and general right of broad social

---

[278] *Id.* at 1123. Finding that the handling, noise level, and safety equipment of the trucks were conditions of employment, the Board concluded that both the employer's decision to replace the trucks and the effects of that decision were mandatory subjects of bargaining. This was particularly so because the employer's decision was not related to any capital investment or disinvestment program. *See also* Lockheed Shipbuilding & Constr. Co., 273 NLRB 171, 118 LRRM 1283 (1984), *reaff'd in relevant part*, 278 NLRB 18, 121 LRRM 1211 (1986) (unilateral implementation of medical-screening program used to deny employment violates §8(a)(5)).

[279] 257 NLRB 695, 107 LRRM 1605 (1981).

[280] *Id.* The Board held that the information sought concerned health and safety conditions and was relevant to the union's obligation to represent the employees with respect to the terms and conditions of their employment. This approach has since been modified by the Board, which has adopted a balancing test weighing the right of employees to proper representation against an employer's right to control its property and prevent interference with its operations. Holyoke Water Power Co., 273 NLRB 1369, 118 LRRM 1179, *enforced*, 778 F2d 49, 120 LRRM 3487 (CA 1, 1985), *cert. denied*, 477 US 905, 122 LRRM 2656 (1986) (citing similar access balancing test that was first formulated by Supreme Court in NLRB v. Babcock & Wilcox Co., 351 US 105, 38 LRRM 2001 (1956). Applying this new standard, the Board has ruled that an employer unlawfully refused access to a union-appointed industrial hygienist seeking to investigate noise problems. ASARCO, Tennessee Mines Div., 276 NLRB 1367, 120 LRRM 1181 (1985), *enforced in part and denied in part*, 805 F2d 194, 123 LRRM 2985 (CA 6, 1986). In ASARCO, the court of appeals enforced the Board's order requiring access to an accident site and directing the employer to provide photographs which it had taken of the accident site; however, the court denied enforcement of the Board's order entitling the union to the employer's internal accident report.

[281] 29 USC §§651 et seq. (1976).

[282] Whirlpool Corp. v. Marshall, 445 US 1, 8 OSH Cases 1001 (1980).

importance existing beyond the parameters of an individual labor agreement and susceptible of full vindication only in a judicial forum."[283] The Seventh Circuit's broad language in this context, however, may not represent a definitive rule on the power of other forums to consider and resolve safety claims. In *Gateway Coal Co. v. Mine Workers*,[284] for example, a case where a union struck over an employer's decision to reinstate foremen facing criminal charges for falsifying safety records, the Supreme Court ruled that the safety issue was arbitrable under the parties' labor agreement.

i. No-Strike and No-Lockout Clauses. No-strike and no-lockout clauses are considered to be mandatory subjects of bargaining. Thus, an employer or a union may bargain for them to the point of impasse.[285] Such clauses are to be distinguished from the strike-ballot clause held to be a permissive subject of bargaining in *NLRB v. Borg-Warner Corp., Wooster Division*,[286] for the latter relates to the union's internal affairs and the way the union chooses to conduct collective bargaining.

j. Work Assignments. The Board considers a change in work assignments to be a mandatory subject of bargaining, especially when the employer has a prior practice of consulting with employees about work assignments or when changes will significantly affect bargaining-unit work. In these cases, unilateral changes by an employer in particular work assignments are generally unlawful.[287] However, the Board has held that unilateral changes in classifications or duties which are not material, substantial, and significant are not unlawful.[288]

---

[283]Marshall v. N.L. Indus., 618 F2d 1220, 1222 (CA 7, 1980).

[284]*Supra* note 276.

[285]NLRB v. Boss Mfg. Co., 118 F2d 187, 8 LRRM 729 (CA7, 1941); Shell Oil Co., 77 NLRB 1306, 22 LRRM 1158 (1948).

[286]356 US 342, 42 LRRM 2034 (1958).

[287]*E.g.*, St. John's Gen. Hosp. of Allegheny County (ADR Center), 281 NLRB 1163, 124 LRRM 1311 (1986), *enforced*, 825 F2d 740, 125 LRRM 3463 (CA 3, 1987) (employer unlawfully failed to bargain by unilaterally transferring duties from secretaries to nurses' aides within bargaining unit); Engineered Control Sys., 274 NLRB 1308, 119 LRRM 1038 (1985) (employer unlawfully failed to bargain after collective bargaining agreement had expired by unilaterally changing duties of a particular job classification). *But cf.* Charmer Indus., 250 NLRB 293, 104 LRRM 1368 (1980), *enforcement denied sub nom.* Distillery Workers Local 2 v. NLRB, 664 F2d 318, 107 LRRM 3137 (CA 2, 1981), *cert. denied*, 456 US 973, 110 LRRM 2320 (1982), in which the Second Circuit held that the Board, in finding a violative unilateral change, abused its discretion by not deferring to an arbitrator's award. The arbitrator had found, as a matter of contract interpretation, that new payment collection procedures implemented by the employer did not impose a change in work rules. This finding should have been determinative, the court noted, because if no change in working conditions was imposed then no duty to bargain arose.

[288]Alamo Cement Co., 277 NLRB 1031, 121 LRRM 131 (1985).

Such changes, according to the Board, are measured by the extent to which there is a departure from existing terms and conditions of employment.[289] For example, a college violated the Act when it unilaterally changed its past practice of conferring with faculty employees before publishing class schedules for the next school term.[290] Another employer violated section 8(a)(5) by requiring its employees to sign job descriptions where previously the employees' positions had been defined flexibly and all employees had been required to be able to perform all operations.[291] Changing drivers' work assignments from a seniority to a rotation basis without consulting with the union violates the Act.[292] Likewise, an employer violated the Act when it unilaterally changed the dispatching system for its truck drivers.[293]

When an employer promotes employees out of a bargaining unit and into supervisory positions, "the Board draws a sharp distinction based on whether the bargaining unit thereby suffers a significant loss of work."[294] There is generally no duty to bargain where the promotion of employees does not result in the loss of bargaining-unit positions.[295] In contrast, loss of bargaining-unit work due to reassignment of unit members is a mandatory subject of collective bargaining.[296]

The Board has similarly found that an employer cannot unilaterally transfer duties from bargaining-unit employees to a supervisor.[297] In another situation, however, and rather anoma-

---

[289]Southern Cal. Edison Co., 284 NLRB 1205, 126 LRRM 1324 (1987), *enforced*, 852 F2d 572 (CA 9, 1988) (change in temporary work assignment policy for injured workers).

[290]Kendall College, 228 NLRB 1083, 95 LRRM 1094 (1977), *enforced*, 570 F2d 216, 97 LRRM 2878 (CA 7, 1978).

[291]Central Cartage, 236 NLRB 1232, 98 LRRM 1554 (1978), *enforced*, 607 F2d 1007 (CA 7, 1979).

[292]Capital Trucking, 246 NLRB 135, 102 LRRM 1481 (1979).

[293]Long Mile Rubber Co., 245 NLRB 1337, 102 LRRM 1319 (1979) (unilateral changes in dispatching system necessarily affected employee truck drivers' rates of pay, wages, and conditions of employment).

[294]Lutheran Home of Kendallville, Ind., 264 NLRB 525, 525 n.2, 111 LRRM 1654 (1982) (creation of new "supervisor-nursing" job classification to which bargaining-unit members were promoted).

[295]*E.g.*, Pittsburgh Metal Processing Co., 286 NLRB 734, 128 LRRM 1094 (1987); St. Louis Tel. Employees Credit Union, 273 NLRB 625, 118 LRRM 1079 (1984).

[296]Lutheran Home of Kendallville, Ind., *supra* note 294; Fry Foods, 241 NLRB 76, 100 LRRM 1513 (1979), *enforced*, 609 F2d 267, 102 LRRM 2894 (CA 6, 1979); Central Cartage, *supra* note 291; Kendall College, *supra* note 290; *cf.* Kohler Co., 273 NLRB 1580, 118 LRRM 1236 (1985) (unlawful for employer to redefine job description specifically to remove job from bargaining unit.

[297]Gansat, Cincinnati Inquirer Div., 279 NLRB 1023, 122 LRRM 1158 (1986). *See also* Long Island Nursing Home, 297 NLRB No. 5, 132 LRRM 1291 (1989) (transfer of job duties to supervisors and outside contractors).

lously,[298] a proposed contract provision that would give the employer unfettered discretion to remove work from the unit is nonmandatory because it is effectively a proposal to change the scope of the unit.[299]

The issue arises in a difficult manifestation when work newly created by technological change must be assigned by an employer. Where, as a result of automation or other technological change, employees acquire the skills and job duties of a classification excluded from the unit, the employer does not violate the Act by unilaterally removing them from the bargaining unit.[300] It is necessary in addition, however, that the new duties be "sufficiently dissimilar" from those of the remaining bargaining-unit members.[301]

k. No-Discrimination Provisions. Elimination of invidious forms of discrimination in the bargaining unit is a mandatory subject of bargaining[302] and provisions prohibiting discrimination on invidious bases have become commonplace in labor agreements.[303] Such discrimination may be subject to regulation under the provisions of the Act imposing the duty to bargain[304]

---

[298]*See* United Technologies Corp., 292 NLRB 248, 130 LRRM 1445 (1989), *enforced*, 884 F2d 1569, 132 LRRM 3035 (CA 2, 1989) (Board modified order by deleting requirement that employer bargain over nonmandatory subject of inclusion of employees in unit).

[299]Westvaco Corp., 289 NLRB 301, 131 LRRM 1044 (1988). *See* Howard Elec. & Mechanical, 293 NLRB 472, 131 LRRM 1743 (1989) (unilateral removal of apprentices from unit after alleged impasse).

[300]BASF Wyandotte Corp., 276 NLRB 1576, 120 LRRM 1243 (1985).

[301]United Technologies, *supra* note 298 (citing Bay Shipbuilding Corp., 263 NLRB 1133, 111 LRRM 1375 (1982), *enforced*, 721 F2d 187, 114 LRRM 3437 (CA 7, 1983)). *See* Howard Elec. & Mechanical, *supra* note 299.

[302]Jubilee Mfg. Co., 202 NLRB 272, 82 LRRM 1482 (1973), *aff'd sub nom.* Steelworkers v. NLRB, 504 F2d 271, 87 LRRM 3168 (CA DC, 1974). *Cf.* Alexander v. Gardner-Denver Co., 415 US 36, 7 FEP Cases 81 (1974). *See also* Emporium Capwell Co. v. Western Addition Community Org., 420 US 50, 88 LRRM 2660, 2668 (1975) ("The elimination of discrimination and its vestiges is an appropriate subject of bargaining, . . ."). By the same token, the duty to accommodate employees with disabilities imposed by the Americans with Disabilities Act of 1990, 42 USC §12112(b)(5)(A), can be expected to become a mandatory subject and to give rise to difficult problems concerning the duty to bargain during the term of an agreement.

[303]For an example of a provision, *see* Alexander v. Gardner-Denver Co., *supra* note 302.

[304]In Skyline Corp., Nomad Div., 240 NLRB 737, 100 LRRM 1312 (1979), *enforced*, 613 F2d 1328, 103 LRRM 3003 (CA 5, 1980), the Board found that the employer violated §8(a)(5) by conditioning its honoring of a certified union's bargaining request on the employer's receipt of certain statistical information concerning the racial, sexual, and ethnic composition of the union's membership. The Board held that allegations of racial and other types of discrimination by a union are properly cognizable under the duty of fair representation; they must thus be adjudicated under §8(b) of the Act and cannot constitute a defense to a §8(a)(5) proceeding. *See also* NLRB v. Mansion House Center Mgmt. Corp., 473 F2d 471, 82 LRRM 2608 (CA 8, 1973) (refusing enforcement of order to bargain and remanding for inquiry into alleged race discrimination by union); Harris-Teeter Supermarkets, 293 NLRB 743, 131 LRRM 1296 (1989) (employer violated Act by failing to bargain with union before unilaterally implementing sexual harassment policy).

or the duty of fair representation.[305]

l. Change in Operations.[306] When the parties' collective bargaining agreement is silent on the employer's right to make a particular operating change, such a change will be subject to mandatory bargaining if the change has significant impact on employees.[307] For example, in *Columbia Tribune Publishing*[308] the Eighth Circuit upheld the Board's ruling that the employer failed to bargain in good faith regarding a change in the type of machinery used in its business. The employer had changed from the traditional "hot-type" to a new automated process, called "cold-type," in its composing room. The new process resulted in the layoff of half the bargaining unit. The Board found that the employer had violated section 8(a)(5) by failing to bargain in good faith concerning the change.[309]

Where a unilateral change in operations does not have a significant impact on bargaining-unit members, it will not ordinarily violate the Act. For example, a company, subsequent to the commencement of a strike, discontinued the use of electric-eye inspection machines as a result of difficulty in servicing them. No employees lost their jobs because of the action, and the duties of only four employees were changed. The Court of Appeals for the District of Columbia Circuit in *Coca Cola Bottling Works*[310] held the elimination of the machines had no significant

---

[305]*See* Chapter 26, "The Duty of Fair Representation."

[306]*See generally* Ashford & Ayers, *Changes and Opportunities in the Environment for Technology Bargaining*, 62 NOTRE DAME L. REV. 810 (1987); Friedman, *Keeping Big Issues off the Table: The Supreme Court on Entrepreneurial Discretion and the Duty to Bargain*, 37 ME. L. REV. 223 (1985); Zidich, *Robotics in the Workplace: The Employer's Duty to Bargain Over Its Implementation and Effect on the Worker*, 24 SANTA CLARA L. REV. 917 (1984); Morris, *The Role of the NLRB and the Courts in the Collective Bargaining Process: A Fresh Look at Conventional Wisdom and Unconventional Remedies*, 30 VAND. L. REV. 661, 667–76 (1977).

[307]*See, e.g.*, Newspaper Printing Corp. v. NLRB, 625 F2d 956, 104 LRRM 2432 (CA 10, 1980), *cert. denied*, 450 US 911, 106 LRRM 2512 (1981); Bundy Corp., 292 NLRB No. 69, 131 LRRM 1645 (1989); Technicolor Gov't Servs., 271 NLRB 1220, 117 LRRM 1103 (1984).

[308]NLRB v. Columbia Tribune Publishing Co., 495 F2d 1384, 86 LRRM 2078 (CA 8, 1974), *enforcing* 201 NLRB 538, 82 LRRM 1553 (1973). *See also* Newspaper Printing Corp. v. NLRB, *supra* note 307; Island Typographers, 252 NLRB 9, 105 LRRM 1455 (1980), *enforcement denied*, 705 F2d 44, 113 LRRM 2207 (CA 2, 1983).

[309]This decision by the Eighth Circuit may be read as extending the mandatory bargaining requirements of the Supreme Court's decision in Fibreboard Paper Prods. Corp. v. NLRB, 379 US 203, 57 LRRM 2609 (1964), to encompass both automation and technological change. *See infra* note 320.

[310]Retail, Wholesale & Dep't Store Union (Coca-Cola Bottling Works) v. NLRB, 466 F2d 380, 80 LRRM 3244 (CA DC, 1972), *enforcing in part and remanding* 186 NLRB 1050, 75 LRRM 1551 (1970). *See also* Vegas Vic, Inc., 213 NLRB 841, 87 LRRM 1269 (1974), *enforced*, 546 F2d 828, 93 LRRM 3087 (CA 9, 1976) *and* 94 LRRM 2652 (CA 9), *cert. denied*, 434 US 818, 96 LRRM 2512 (1977).

effect on the job of any worker and thus the company was not obligated to submit its decision to collective bargaining.[311]

Even where a change in operations does have a significant impact on employees in the bargaining unit, an employer may make the change if there is clear evidence of waiver of bargaining by the union.[312] The Board generally looks for a clear and unequivocal contractual provision as evidence of waiver.[313]

In *Houston Shopping News Co.*[314] the Board held that an employer violated the Act by unilaterally offering to lease some of its equipment to its unit employees. Member Murphy dissented on the ground that after the offer was made the union failed to protest the making of the offer and participated in the preparation of a response to the offer. The Fifth Circuit refused to enforce the decision for similar reasons, noting that the union had participated in the procedures.[315]

In *Holiday Inn of Benton*,[316] the Board held that the employer violated section 8(a)(5) by failing to notify and bargain with the union representing the employer's waitresses with respect to both its decision to convert its restaurant into a self-service cafeteria and the effects of that decision. In partially enforcing the Board's order, a divided Seventh Circuit found that the restaurant conversion did not constitute an alteration of the "basic operation" within the meaning of that term as applied by the Supreme Court in its *Fibreboard* decision.[317]

In *Metromedia, Inc. v. NLRB*[318] the Eighth Circuit held that the employer violated the Act by failing to negotiate with the union which represented its newsfilm cameramen with respect to the use of portable television cameras.

---

[311]*See also* Westinghouse Elec. Corp., 150 NLRB 1574, 58 LRRM 1257 (1965).

[312]*See, e.g.*, General Elec. Co., 296 NLRB No. 106, 132 LRRM 1312 (1989); Johnson-Bateman Co., 295 NLRB No. 26, 131 LRRM 1393 (1989); Reece Corp., 294 NLRB 448, 131 LRRM 1413 (1989).

[313]Waiver of bargaining rights is treated in detail in Chapter 13, "The Duty to Bargain," text at notes 741–762.

[314]223 NLRB 1133, 92 LRRM 1074 (1976), *enforcement denied*, 554 F2d 739, 95 LRRM 2801 (CA 5, 1977).

[315]*Id.*

[316]237 NLRB 1042, 99 LRRM 1235 (1978), *enforced in relevant part sub nom.* Davis v. NLRB, 617 F2d 1264, 103 LRRM 2965 (CA 7, 1980).

[317]Fibreboard Paper Prods. Corp. v. NLRB, *supra* note 309. See text commencing at note 320 *infra* for discussion of *Fibreboard*.

[318]586 F2d 1182, 99 LRRM 2743 (CA 8, 1978), *enforcing in relevant part* 232 NLRB 486, 96 LRRM 1475 (1977). The employer sought unsuccessfully to defend its failure to bargain on the basis that it had recently agreed to give another union exclusive jurisdiction over the operation of its portable television cameras.

m. Major Business Changes. (1) Subcontracting and Removal of Work From the Bargaining Unit. In 1963, the Board said that with the evolution of the relationship between employers and employees, "new areas may be found which affect 'wages, hours, and other terms and conditions of employment,' and thus the list of mandatory subjects of bargaining quite properly is enlarged."[319] In *Fibreboard Paper Products Corp. v. NLRB*,[320] the Supreme Court said that "while not determinative, it is appropriate to look to industrial bargaining practice in appraising the propriety of including a particular subject within the scope of mandatory bargaining."[321] Such observations on the expandability of the list of mandatory bargaining subjects are especially relevant to developments in the field of subcontracting and other removals of significant work from the bargaining unit.

Two distinct, though closely related, analyses are relevant in this area. Employers may have an obligation to bargain over their decision to subcontract or otherwise remove work from the unit. Even if such a decision itself is not a mandatory subject, however, an employer may have an independent duty to bargain over the effects of such a decision. For many years the Board held that an employer had no duty under section 8(a)(5) to consult with the bargaining representative before deciding to subcontract part of its operation. Thus, in 1949 the Board asserted that it had never held that "an employer may not in good faith . . . change his business structure, [or] sell or contract out a portion of his operation . . . without first consulting the bargaining representative. . . ."[322] However, the Board later developed a rule in subcontracting and related cases that an employer must bargain with the union about the impact and the effects of a decision to subcontract or to make other similar operational changes.[323]

---

[319]Associated Gen. Contractors, Houston Chapter, 143 NLRB 409, 53 LRRM 1299, 1302 (1963), *enforced*, 349 F2d 449, 59 LRRM 3013 (CA 5, 1965), *cert. denied*, 382 US 1026, 61 LRRM 2244 (1966).

[320]Supra note 309.

[321]*Id.* at 211.

[322]Mahoning Mining Co., 61 NLRB 792, 803, 16 LRRM 110 (1945). Unfair labor practice charges in subcontracting cases often involve allegations of violations of §8(a)(3) as well as claims of violations of §8(a)(5). The present discussion is concerned with §8(a)(5). For comprehensive treatment of §8(a)(3), see Chapter 7, "Discrimination in Employment."

[323]*See, e.g.*, Shamrock Dairy, 119 NLRB 998, 41 LRRM 1216 (1957), *modified*, 124 NLRB 494, 44 LRRM 1407 (1959), *enforced*, 280 F2d 665, 46 LRRM 2433 (CA DC), *cert. denied*, 364 US 892, 47 LRRM 2095 (1960); NLRB Gen. Counsel Administrative Ruling 315, 30 LRRM 1102 (1952). *But cf.* NLRB v. Rives Co., 288 F2d 511, 47 LRRM 2766 (CA 5, 1961).

As late as 1961, the Board took the position that the decision to subcontract was not a mandatory subject of bargaining. In its initial opinion in *Fibreboard*,[324] the Board held that an employer's decision to subcontract is not a mandatory bargaining subject because it relates to a "precondition [of employment] necessary to the establishment and continuance of the [employment] relationship from which conditions of employment arise."[325] The Board reasoned that an employer's bargaining obligation does not encompass the issue of whether an employment relationship exists, but, instead, covers terms and conditions of employment after the relationship is established. A decision to subcontract work, the Board concluded, is a basic management decision over which Congress did not intend to compel bargaining.

In 1962 the Board changed its position. In *Town & Country Manufacturing Co.*[326] it announced the rule that an employer violates section 8(a)(5) if it fails to bargain over a decision to subcontract work, even if that decision is based solely on economic considerations. In that case the employer's decision to subcontract was held to be unlawfully motivated by its opposition to the union; however, the Board indicated that the bargaining obligation attached regardless of the employer's motivation:

> The elimination of unit jobs, albeit for economic reasons, is a matter within the statutory phrase "other terms and conditions of employment" and is a mandatory subject of collective bargaining within the meaning of Section 8(a)(5) of the Act.[327]

Shortly thereafter the Board reconsidered and reversed its original decision in *Fibreboard*.[328] Relying on *Town & Country* and the Supreme Court's 1960 decision in *Railroad Telegraphers v. Chicago & North Western Railway*,[329] the Board concluded that

---

[324]Fibreboard Paper Prods. Corp., 130 NLRB 1558, 47 LRRM 1547 (1961), *supplemented*, 138 NLRB 550, 51 LRRM 1101 (1962), *enforced*, 322 F2d 411, 53 LRRM 2666 (CA DC, 1963), *aff'd*, 379 US 203, 57 LRRM 2609 (1964).

[325]*Id.* at 1561.

[326]136 NLRB 1022, 49 LRRM 1918 (1962), *enforced*, 316 F2d 846, 53 LRRM 2054 (CA 5, 1963).

[327]*Id.* at 1027. The Fifth Circuit enforced the Board's decision on the grounds that the company had subcontracted because of antiunion motivation in violation of §8(a)(3). *Supra* note 326.

[328]*Supra* note 324.

[329]362 US 330, 45 LRRM 3104 (1960). The Supreme Court held, interpreting the Railway Labor Act, that a railroad employer was required to bargain over the closing of facilities inasmuch as the action would eliminate jobs. The Board read the decision of the Supreme Court as making it clear that elimination of jobs in the bargaining unit for reasons that were palpably economic was still a "term or condition of employment" over which an employer must first bargain with the union—reasoning which the Board deemed as applicable to the Act.

the employer's failure to bargain over its decision to subcontract maintenance work previously performed by bargaining-unit employees violated section 8(a)(5) of the Act. The Board's order in the second *Fibreboard* decision was enforced by the Court of Appeals for the District of Columbia Circuit,[330] and the Supreme Court affirmed.[331]

In affirming, the Supreme Court held that the decision to subcontract constituted a mandatory subject for bargaining even in the absence of antiunion motivation. Emphasizing the limits of the facts in the case, the Court noted that the company's basic operation did not change as a result of the maintenance subcontract, nor was a capital investment required. Consequently, the company was obligated to bargain over the issue of whether to subcontract the work and, because of its refusal to bargain, the Board was empowered to order the resumption of the plant maintenance operations and reinstatement of the affected employees with backpay so that bargaining could occur as it should have.

Although *Fibreboard* was widely heralded as a case that would resolve broad issues, the actual holding was narrow and limited. The limits of the decision were indicated by the Court:

> We are thus not expanding the scope of mandatory bargaining to hold, as we do now, that the type of "contracting out" involved in this case—the replacement of employees in the existing bargaining unit with those of an independent contractor to do the same work under similar conditions of employment—is a statutory subject of collective bargaining under §8(d). Our decision need not and does not encompass other forms of "contracting out" or "subcontracting" which arise daily in our complex economy.[332]

---

[330]Fibreboard Paper Prods. Corp. v. NLRB, *supra* note 324.

[331]*Id.*

[332]379 US at 215. *Cf.* Teamsters Local 24 v. Oliver, 358 US 283, 43 LRRM 2374 (1959) (contract provisions imposing conditions upon contracting out and leasing of employer's trucks by employees, which governed whether drivers' wages were in fact diminished by arrangements wherby drivers' rentals supposedly covered operating costs, are mandatory subjects of bargaining). Justice Stewart, joined by Justices Douglas and Harlan, concurred in *Fibreboard* because in his view the facts simply involved the substitution of one group of workers for another to perform the same work in the same plant under the ultimate control of the same employer. He stressed that:

> This kind of subcontracting falls short of such larger entrepreneurial questions as what shall be produced, how capital shall be invested in fixed assets, or what the basic scope of the enterprise shall be. In my view, the Court's decision in this case has nothing to do with whether any aspects of those larger issues could under any circumstances be considered subjects of compulsory collective bargaining under the present law.

379 US at 225.

The Board's 1965 decision in *Westinghouse Electric Corp.*[333] provided a comprehensive interpretation of the Supreme Court's *Fibreboard* decision and announced a series of factors that the Board would use to determine whether a particular subcontracting decision necessitated bargaining. Bargaining over the decision to subcontract unit work would generally not be required if (1) the subcontracting is motivated solely by economic reasons, (2) it is the employer's custom to subcontract various kinds of work, (3) no substantial variance is shown in kind or degree from the established past practice of the employer, (4) no significant detriment results to employees in the unit, and (5) the union has had an opportunity to bargain about changes in existing subcontracting practices at general negotiating meetings.[334]

Based on the *Westinghouse* criteria, the Board in 1965 dismissed several complaints over subcontracting practices[335] without giving any precise definition of what constituted a "significant detriment" to employees. Nevertheless, the 1965 dismissals indicated that a decision about subcontracting did not become a mandatory subject on the basis, alone, that most of the work contracted out could have been performed by unit employees,[336] or that unit pay classifications were reduced because of lack of work,[337] or that employees were assigned to work at unskilled jobs.[338] Additionally, the Board has held that an

---

[333]150 NLRB 1574, 58 LRRM 1257 (1965). *Cf.* General Elec. Co., 240 NLRB 703, 100 LRRM 1510 (1979), where the Board upheld the finding of the ALJ that the employer had not violated §8(a)(5) in contracting out carpet cleaning utilizing a steam process, basing his ruling on *Westinghouse* criteria. However, in a concurring opinion, Member Jenkins, who had participated in *Westinghouse*, said the case should have been decided on the basis of the Supreme Court's *Fibreboard* decision since the carpet cleaning fell within the category of "other forms" of subcontracting.

[334]*See* ACF Indus., AMCAR Div. v. NLRB, 596 F2d 1344, 1349, 100 LRRM 3074, 3076 (CA 8, 1979), where the Eighth Circuit commented: "In our view the *Westinghouse* 'guidelines' substantially comport with *Fibreboard* and fairly set forth the factors which should be considered in determining whether an employer has violated the Act by contracting out of work." *See also* ACF Indus., AMCAR Div. v. NLRB, 592 F2d 422, 100 LRRM 2710 (CA 8, 1979). It may not be necessary for all of the *Westinghouse* criteria to be met to avoid the obligation to bargain about the decision to subcontract.

[335]American Oil Co., 155 NLRB 639, 60 LRRM 1369 (1965); American Oil Co., 152 NLRB 56, 59 LRRM 1007 (1965); American Oil Co., 151 NLRB 421, 58 LRRM 1412 (1965); Central Soya Co., 151 NLRB 1691, 58 LRRM 1667 (1965); Superior Coach Corp. 151 NLRB 188, 58 LRRM 1369 (1965); Fafnir Bearing Co., 151 NLRB 332, 58 LRRM 1397 (1965). *See* Note, *Mandatory Subjects of Bargaining, Operational Changes*, 17 U. FLA. L. REV. 109 (1964).

[336]Fafnir Bearing Co., *supra* note 335.

[337]American Oil Co., 155 NLRB 639, 60 LRRM 1369 (1965).

[338]Superior Coach Corp., *supra* note 335.

employer has no duty to bargain over a decision to subcontract work that falls outside the scope of work normally performed by unit employees.[339]

In a later *Westinghouse* case[340] the Board distinguished between provable and speculative impact on employees. The union had charged that unilateral subcontracting by the employer imposed a substantial detrimental effect on the bargaining unit, since employees, who were already on layoff, were not recalled. The union argued that if the subcontracting had not taken place, or had been more limited, certain of the laid-off employees might have returned to gainful employment. The Board rejected this argument since there was no showing that these employees were entitled to recall under the contract, or were available or interested in returning to work. However, in another case where employees were on layoff at the time of the subcontracting, a substantial detrimental impact on the bargaining unit was found.[341] The Board has also held that even without layoffs a substantial detriment is suffered by the bargaining unit when unit work is removed and job classifications are permanently eliminated due to technological advancements.[342]

The Board continued for some time to examine an employer's duty to bargain over subcontracting decisions under the five-part test set forth in *Westinghouse Electric Corp.*[343] In one case, the Board held that an employer did not violate the Act by unilaterally subcontracting the work of a janitor who retired after an illness.[344] It applied the *Westinghouse* factors, placing particular emphasis on the nature and extent of the impact of the employer's decision on unit employees. Because the sub-

---

[339]Central Soya Co., *supra* note 335. In ACF Indus., AMCAR Div., 234 NLRB 1063, 98 LRRM 1287 (1978), *enforced as modified* 596 F2d 1344, 100 LRRM 3074 (CA 8, 1979), an employer that manufactured railroad freight cars unilaterally subcontracted several kinds of work. The Board determined that bargaining over the subcontracting of the work and the rebuilding of certain presses was required under *Fibreboard*, even though bargaining-unit employees had not rebuilt such presses before, since bargaining-unit employees had performed most of the separate elements of rebuilding these presses during routine maintenance. However, the Board determined that other work was properly contracted out without notice to or bargaining with the union because the employees had not done work of a sufficiently similar kind.

[340]Westinghouse Elec. Corp., 153 NLRB 443, 59 LRRM 1355 (1965).

[341]ACF Indus., AMCAR Div. v. NLRB, 596 F2d 1344, 100 LRRM 3074 (CA 8, 1979). "The Board could reasonably infer from these facts that the subcontracting resulted in a loss of reasonably expected work opportunities for men [on layoff] in the bargaining unit." *Id.* at 1350.

[342]Equitable Gas Co., 245 NLRB 260, 102 LRRM 1470 (1979), *enforcement denied*, 637 F2d 980, 106 LRRM 2201 (CA 3, 1981).

[343]*Supra* note 333.

[344]General Elec. Co., 264 NLRB 306, 111 LRRM 1288 (1982).

contracting in question involved only a small portion of one employee's cleaning duties and was therefore de minimis and because it had no demonstrable adverse impact on unit employees, the Board found that the employer's unilateral decision to subcontract was not unlawful. In another case, the Board held that an employer violated the Act by failing to bargain over a decision to transfer bargaining-unit work to the employer's alter ego.[345] In that case, the Board found that the decision to transfer work and the resultant shutdown were not economically motivated. The Board ordered the employer to bargain with the union over the effects of its transfer of the unit work but did not order bargaining over the decision itself since the alter ego had also ceased operations after the transfer. Although the *Westinghouse* test was well established, the courts did not always agree with the results of the Board's application in specific cases.[346]

The Fourth Circuit, in *Mine Workers District 50 v. NLRB (Allied Chemical Corp.)*,[347] held that an employer's duty to bargain over a subcontracting decision varies with the length of time available for implementation of the subcontract. In upholding the Board's dismissal of a refusal-to-bargain charge, the court indicated that full-scale bargaining should not be required in situations where it is necessary for the employer to implement a subcontract immediately. In such cases, according to the court, an employer may satisfy its bargaining obligation by a simple notification to the union and an opportunity for the exchange of ideas. The court explained that the union should not be permitted to stall the decision by insisting on protracted negotiations. After listening to the union's suggestions, the company should be permitted to accept or reject them as its economic judgment dictates. The court thus appeared to be redefining the nature of "impasse" to accommodate its notion of the exigencies of subcontracting decisions.[348] As the court said:

> An employer may be obligated under the compulsion of some circumstances to make subcontracting decisions without delay.

345Whitehall Packing Co., 257 NLRB 193, 107 LRRM 1449 (1981).

346*See, e.g.*, Olinkraft, 252 NLRB 1329, 105 LRRM 1492 (1980), *enforced in part, denied in part and remanded*, 666 F2d 302, 109 LRRM 2573 (CA 5, 1982); Equitable Gas Co., *supra* note 342.

347358 F2d 234, 61 LRRM 2632 (CA 4, 1966). *See also* Puerto Rico Tel. Co. v. NLRB, 359 F2d 983, 62 LRRM 2069 (CA 1, 1966) (finding no adverse impact and rejecting Board determination requiring bargaining).

348*See* Morris, *The Role of the NLRB and the Courts in the Collective Bargaining Process: A Fresh Look at Conventional Wisdom and Unconventional Remedies*, 30 VAND. L. REV. 661, 667–76 (1977).

> Emergencies could arise that require immediate action. The employer's prerogative in this class of cases should be respected without requiring prior bargaining or even notification of the union. However, other contracting decisions may not demand immediate action, and respecting these types of decisions, there may be no practical obstacle in notification of the union, and to affording it an opportunity to be heard.[349]

Where employees have lost significant amounts of overtime or employees have lost their jobs as a result of subcontracting, the Board usually has held that the employer had a duty to bargain about the subcontracting.[350] In such circumstances, the fact that the subcontracting was economically motivated does not excuse the employer from a mandatory duty to notify and bargain with the union about its decision.[351]

A classic example of the difficulty in applying *Fibreboard* is found in the *Adams Dairy*[352] case. Adams Dairy sold milk and dairy products to retail outlets through both driver-salesmen and independent contractors. The company decided to eliminate the use of driver-salesmen and consequently changed its entire distribution system to an independent contractor arrangement. It informed the union of the change and discharged all of its driver-salesmen. The Board ordered reinstatement and backpay. That decision was reversed by the Eighth Circuit.[353] On appeal, the Supreme Court remanded the case to the Eighth Circuit with instructions to reconsider the case in light of its decision in *Fibreboard*.[354] On remand, the Eighth Circuit adhered to its original decision, reasoning as follows: (1) contrary to the situation in *Fibreboard*, the *Adams Dairy* case involved more than just the substitution of one set of employees for another, for the company had changed its basic operating

---

[349]358 F2d at 238. *Cf.* Jersey Farms Milk Serv., 148 NLRB 1392, 57 LRRM 1166 (1964), where the Board found that unilateral subcontracting of bargaining-unit work violated the Act. The Board simply ordered the company to bargain over resumption of operations and any proposed alternatives thereto; it did not order restoration of the status quo ante. See discussion of remedies in Chapter 32, "NLRB Orders and Remedies."

[350]Weston & Brooker Co., 154 NLRB 747, 60 LRRM 1015 (1965), *enforced*, 373 F2d 741, 65 LRRM 2736 (CA 4, 1967).

[351]Key Coal Co., 240 NLRB 1013, 100 LRRM 1444 (1979); Brown Transp. Corp., 140 NLRB 954, 52 LRRM 1151 (1963), *modified as to remedy only*, 334 F2d 243, 56 LRRM 2809 (CA 5, 1964). *See also* ACF Indus., AMCAR Div. v. NLRB, 596 F2d 1344, 100 LRRM 3074 (CA 8, 1979).

[352]Adams Dairy, Inc., 137 NLRB 815, 50 LRRM 1281 (1962), *modified*, 322 F2d 553, 54 LRRM 2171 (CA 8, 1963), vacated, 379 US 644, 58 LRRM 2192 (1965), *on remand*, 350 F2d 108, 60 LRRM 2084 (CA 8, 1965), *cert. denied*, 382 US 1011, 61 LRRM 2192 (1966).

[353]*Id.*

[354]*Id.*

procedure and had liquidated a part of its business; (2) unlike *Fibreboard, Adams Dairy* involved a change in capital structure and a recoupment of capital investment; (3) also contrary to *Fibreboard,* the work done by the independent contractors for *Adams Dairy* was not performed primarily in the Adams plant for the benefit of the dairy; and (4) in *Adams,* unlike *Fibreboard,* the decision to change to distribution by independent contractors was made at a time when the current contract still had 2 years to run and no aura of bad faith appeared to have pervaded the employer's bargaining, as it had appeared in *Fibreboard.*[355]

The *Fibreboard* bargaining obligations have been applied to other types of "contracting out" or "subcontracting" of bargaining-unit work. It has thus been held that an employer violated the duty to bargain about the decision to sublease land requiring substantial reclamation work that resulted from coal mining.[356] Because the employer remained primarily liable on the base lease and received income from the transaction, the Board said that the sublease medium had all "the essential ingredients of basic subcontracting" and could not be regarded purely as a transfer of assets.[357] However, where cargo containers owned by ocean vessel owners were leased to consolidators who loaded cargo into the containers at their off-pier facilities for sea shipment, the Board held that such an arrangement did not constitute subcontracting.[358]

After *Fibreboard,* a decision to subcontract which involved the cessation by the employer of a part of its business operation could necessitate bargaining.[359] During the period between the Supreme Court's 1981 decision in *First National Maintenance Corp. v. NLRB*[360] and the Board's 1984 decision in *Otis Elevator*

---

[355]*Id. But see* Winn-Dixie Stores v. NLRB, 361 F2d 512, 62 LRRM 2218 (CA 5), *cert. denied,* 385 US 935, 63 LRRM 2372 (1966); NLRB v. American Mfg. Co., 351 F2d 74, 60 LRRM 2122 (CA 5, 1965).

[356]Key Coal Co., *supra* note 351.

[357]*Id.* at 1042.

[358]Longshoremen (ILA) (Dolphin Forwarding), 236 NLRB 525, 98 LRRM 1276 (1978), *enforcement denied,* 613 F2d 890, 102 LRRM 2361 (CA DC, 1979), *cert. denied sub nom.* New York Shipping Ass'n v. NLRB, 448 US 906, 104 LRRM 2688 (1980); Longshoremen (ILA) (Consolidated Express), 221 NLRB 956, 90 LRRM 1655 (1975), *enforced,* 537 F2d 706, 92 LRRM 3260 (CA 2, 1976), *cert. denied sub nom.* New York Shipping Ass'n v. NLRB, 429 US 1041, 94 LRRM 2202, *reh'g denied sub nom.* Longshoremen (ILA) v. NLRB, 430 US 911, 94 LRRM 2202 (1977).

[359]*See, e.g.,* NLRB v. Jackson Farmers, Inc., 457 F2d 516, 79 LRRM 2909 (CA 10, 1972); Empire Dental Co., 211 NLRB 860, 87 LRRM 1359 (1974), *enforced,* 538 F2d 337, 93 LRRM 2336 (CA 9, 1976); Florida-Texas Freight, 203 NLRB 509, 83 LRRM 1093 (1973), *enforced,* 489 F2d 1275, 85 LRRM 2845 (CA 6, 1974).

[360]452 US 666, 107 LRRM 2705 (1981). See discussion of balancing test in Section III.D, *supra.*

II,[361] however, an employer's bargaining obligation with respect to a decision to undertake a particular transaction was significantly influenced by the characterization of the transaction as a "partial closing" under *First National Maintenance*, or as a "subcontracting" under *Fibreboard*.[362] Because those categories are not analytically or practically distinct, that approach to the cases was foreordained to end in confusion. For example, in *Marriott Corp., Bob's Big Boy Family Restaurants Division*,[363] an employer unlawfully failed to bargain over its decision to discontinue the shrimp-processing portion of its food-processing operations and to subcontract the work. The employer based its decision on cost and quality control considerations. Acknowledging that the distinction between a partial closing and a subcontracting is "not always readily apparent," the Board found that the employer's decision was a subcontracting decision because the shrimp-processing operation was only one "component part" of the employer's overall food processing operation.[364]

In another case, an employer violated the Act when it unilaterally decided to cease delivering products to its customers with its own trucks.[365] Prior to the change, the employer's own trucking operations had handled only 5 to 10 percent of its total delivery needs, with outside carriers handling the remaining portion of its delivery needs. The employer's decision to have outside carriers make all of its deliveries was based on its desire to cut costs and retrieve the capital invested in its own fleet of trucks. The Board found that the principles of *Fibreboard* rather than *First National Maintenance* controlled because the employer's drivers had been replaced by independent contractors as in *Fibreboard*, and because the employer's operations remained the same after it ceased its own trucking operations—that is, the employer continued to transport products to its customers by way of truck.

The Board's decision in *Otis Elevator II*[366] represented a major attempt to formulate an application of *First National Maintenance*

---

[361]Otis Elevator Co. (II), 269 NLRB 891, 116 LRRM 1075, *correcting* 269 NLRB 891, 115 LRRM 1281 (1984). [**Editor's Note:** In Dubuque Packing Co. (II), 303 NLRB No. 66, 137 LRRM 1185 (1991) the Board overruled *Otis Elevator II*, and announced new critiera for determining whether an employer's decision to relocate bargaining-unit work is a mandatory subject of bargaining.]

[362]Fibreboard Paper Prods. Corp. v. NLRB, 379 US 203, 57 LRRM 2609 (1964).

[363]264 NLRB 1369, 111 LRRM 1354 (1982).

[364]*Id.* at 1371.

[365]Whitehead Bros., 263 NLRB 895, 111 LRRM 1584 (1982).

[366]*Supra* note 361. *See generally* George, *To Bargain or Not to Bargain: A New Chapter in Work Relocation Decisions*, 69 MINN. L. REV. 667 (1985); Susser, *NLRB Restricts Mandatory Bargaining Over Managerial Changes*, 35 LAB. L.J. 415 (1984).

in a way that would focus more fully upon the reasons underlying an employer's decision, rather than attempting to characterize the challenged transaction. That case involved an employer that, for efficiency reasons, had discontinued research and development facilities in New Jersey and consolidated them with other operations in Connecticut. The Board initially held that the employer unlawfully failed to bargain about its decision.[367] However, the Court of Appeals for the District of Columbia Circuit remanded the case to the Board for reconsideration in light of *First National Maintenance*.[368]

On remand the Board unanimously held that the decision to transfer and consolidate operations was not a mandatory subject of bargaining. The decision produced three separate opinions, however, each of which had a different analytical focus.[369] For the majority, the critical factor was whether an employer's decision to change operations "turns upon labor costs." The majority found that since the decision of the employer in *Otis Elevator II* turned instead "upon a change in the nature and direction of a significant facet of its business," the action by the employer was at the "core of entrepreneurial control" and thus not amenable to bargaining. The majority also reasoned that "subcontracting" decisions must be bargained under *Fibreboard*, not because they are properly labeled as subcontracting, "but because in fact the decision turns upon a reduction of labor costs."[370]

On several occasions since, the Board has applied the "labor costs" test from *Otis Elevator II* to determine whether an employer permissibly subcontracted out bargaining-unit work. For example, in *Garwood-Detroit Truck Equipment*[371] the Board found that a decision to subcontract mounting and service work was not a midterm modification in violation of section 8(d) because there was no contract term limiting the employer's decision making regarding subcontracting, and also held that the decision was not a mandatory subject of bargaining where

[367] Otis Elevator Co. (I), 255 NLRB 235, 106 LRRM 1343 (1981).

[368] *Supra* note 360.

[369] For a more detailed discussion of the opinions in *Otis Elevator II*, see Section III. E., *supra*.

[370] *Supra* note 360, 115 LRRM at 1281, 1285.

[371] 274 NLRB 113, 118 LRRM 1417 (1985). *See also* Clinton's Ditch Coop. Co., 274 NLRB 728, 119 LRRM 1065 (1985), *enforcement denied*, 778 F2d 132, 120 LRRM 3562 (CA 2, 1985), *cert. denied sub nom.* Teamsters Local 317 v. Clinton's Ditch Coop. Co., 479 US 814, 123 LRRM 2591 (1986) (employer violated §8(a)(5) by unilaterally subcontracting delivery operation solely to save labor costs); Ausable Communications, 273 NLRB 1410, 118 LRRM 1295, 1295 (1985) (no violation where subcontracting "affected the scope of the business and was not a bargainable item"); *accord* Morco Indus., 279 NLRB 762, 122 LRRM 1175 (1986).

decision making regarding subcontracting, and also held that the decision was not a mandatory subject of bargaining where the essential purpose of the subcontracting "turned not on labor costs but on a significant change in the nature and direction of the Respondent's business."[372] However, the Board has also held that the General Counsel does not have the burden of showing that an employer's decision to subcontract turned on labor costs where "all that is involved is the substitution of one group of workers for another to perform the same task in the same plant under the ultimate control of the same employer."[373] In several cases Board members refused to choose among the alternative tests in *Otis Elevator II*, finding instead that the same result is appropriate regardless of which test is applied.[374]

Subcontracting during a strike has been the subject of considerable litigation. The Ninth Circuit, overruling the Board, has held that an employer need not offer to bargain with a union over the decision and effects of subcontracting bargaining-unit work during a strike.[375] Later, the Board held that an employer need not bargain over subcontracting of bargaining-unit work during a strike if management made the arrangement as a temporary measure adopted to continue business relationships.[376] However in *American Cynamid Co.*[377] the Board held that the employer violated section 8(a)(5) by permanently subcontracting maintenance work and terminating maintenance employees during a strike. The employer had argued that the

[372]274 NLRB at 114–15.

[373]Collateral Control Corp., 288 NLRB 308, 308, 128 LRRM 1097 (1988).

[374]*See, e.g.*, Lapeer Foundry & Mach., 289 NLRB 952, 129 LRRM 1001 (1988); Century Air Freight, 284 NLRB 730, 125 LRRM 1237 (1987). In Food & Commercial Workers Local 150-A v. NLRB (Dubuque Packing Co.), 880 F2d 1422, 132 LRRM 2104 (CA DC, 1989), *remanding* 287 NLRB 499, 130 LRRM 1151 (1987), the Court of Appeals for the District of Columbia Circuit remanded a case for a clearer explanation of the reasoning behind the Board's application of *Otis Elevator II, supra* note 361, to the facts of the case before it. [**Editor's Note**: On remand, the Board overruled *Otis Elevator II; see* **Editor's Note** at *supra* note 361.]

[375]Hawaii Meat Co. v. NLRB, 321 F2d 397, 53 LRRM 2872 (CA 9, 1963).

[376]Empire Terminal Warehouse Co., 151 NLRB 1359, 58 LRRM 1589 (1965), *enforced sub nom.* Teamsters Local 745 v. NLRB, 355 F2d 842, 61 LRRM 2065 (CA DC, 1966).

[377]235 NLRB 1316, 98 LRRM 1429 (1978), *enforced*, 592 F2d 356, 100 LRRM 2640 (CA 7, 1979). *See also* Land Air Delivery, 286 NLRB 1131, 130 LRRM 1015 (1987), *review denied*, 862 F2d 354, 130 LRRM 2118 (CA DC, 1988), *cert. denied*, 493 US 810, 132 LRRM 2623 (1989); Alexander Linn Hosp. Ass'n, 244 NLRB 387, 102 LRRM 1252 (1979), *enforced*, 624 F2d 1090, 106 LRRM 2546 (CA 3, 1980). In Markle Mfg. Co., 239 NLRB 1142, 100 LRRM 1125 (1979), *enforced in part and modified in part*, 623 F2d 1122, 105 LRRM 2500 (CA 5, 1980), refusal by the employer during the course of a strike to furnish the union with requested information concerning its subcontracting practices violated §8(a)(5), even though the Board had determined during the course of its investigation of unfair labor practice charges relating to the employer's subcontracting practices that such practices were consistent with past practice.

Fibreboard doctrine did not apply to strike situations, contending that the strike created an emergency that excused bargaining with respect to its decision to enter into a permanent maintenance subcontract. On review, the Seventh Circuit held that, while the employer during a strike could unilaterally subcontract its maintenance work on a temporary basis, it was illegal to do so on a permanent basis since "no harm" would have emanated from negotiating with the union prior to the decision to permanently subcontract.

In another case, the employer completed a subcontracting arrangement in response to a pending strike threat. The subcontractor required that it be awarded the river-outfitting work at issue for two annual seasons. The Board considered the extended term to be "an economic and business necessity" which did not require prior bargaining.[378] Thus, the temporary subcontracting due to the strike threat could lawfully have an extended life, because the employer's actions were motivated by economic considerations rather than animus toward union representation.

The Board has permitted subcontracting without bargaining during a hiatus between contracts, so long as the subcontracting has been in line with past practice.[379] The Board has also ruled that an employer which had lawfully withdrawn recognition from the incumbent union after expiration of the collective bargaining agreement did not violate section 8(a)(5) by transferring its towing boat operations to chartering companies.[380]

Whether or not there is an obligation to bargain over a decision to contract out or transfer bargaining-unit work, there is a duty to bargain over the effects of such decisions. In *Walter Pape, Inc.*,[381] a dairy products dealer entered into collective bargaining with a union representing its routemen, although prior to the start of the negotiations it had commenced arrangements to have another distributor take over that phase of its operations. The Board concluded that the employer's failure to notify the

---

[378]Elliott River Tours, 246 NLRB 935, 103 LRRM 1095 (1979).

[379]Shell Oil Co., 149 NLRB 283, 287, 57 LRRM 1271 (1964). In a later decision involving another plant of the same employer, Shell Oil Co. 166 NLRB 1064, 65 LRRM 1713 (1967), the Board interpreted a clause in a collective bargaining contract to permit unilateral subcontracting of bargaining-unit work in accordance with past practice.

[380]Upper Miss. Towing Corp., 246 NLRB 262, 102 LRRM 1536 (1979). *See generally* Chapter 12, "Recognition and Withdrawal of Recognition Without an Election."

[381]205 NLRB 719, 84 LRRM 1055 (1973).

union that the route termination was imminent and to bargain as to its effects constituted bad-faith bargaining violative of section 8(a)(5). Although the employer's decision was economically motivated, and most of the drivers had found employment at higher wages, the Board ordered backpay from the date of termination until the employer commenced bargaining as to the effects of the subcontracting.

The unilateral expansion of subcontracting or the alteration in the type of work performed by subcontractors can also violate the Act, depending upon the effects on the bargaining unit. Thus, in *Howmet Corp.*[382] an employer had historically subcontracted portions of its toolroom work. Following union certification, the employer increased the volume of subcontracted work and reassigned other duties, with the result that several employees were laid off. The employer made the decision without giving the union an opportunity to bargain about the decision or its effects. The Board held that the substantial alteration of the subcontracting "in quantity and kind" was a unilateral change in terms and conditions of employment. The employer's failure to bargain as to either the decision or its effects violated section 8(a)(5).[383]

In *Tellespen Petro-Chem Constructors*,[384] the employer failed to notify the union of its decision to subcontract bargaining-unit work; instead, upon determining that its project was behind schedule, it dismissed eight employees and subcontracted that portion of its project. A Board majority held that this action did not violate section 8(a)(5) since the dismissed employees were hired by the subcontractor or by other contractors under the same multi-employer agreement with the same bargaining representative. As the employees merely shifted employers with minimal impact and were protected by the agreement, there was no violation.[385]

Relocation of bargaining-unit work to a different part of an employer's business became a major issue after the Board's 1982

---

[382]197 NLRB 471, 80 LRRM 1555 (1972), *enforced*, 495 F2d 1375, 86 LRRM 2572 (CA 7, 1974). *See also* Torrington Constr. Co., 198 LRRM 1158, 81 LRRM 1102 (1972).

[383]For treatment of similar criteria under the Railway Labor Act, see Japan Air Lines Co. v. Machinists, 389 F Supp 27, 88 LRRM 2910 (SD NY, 1975), *aff'd*, 538 F2d 46, 92 LRRM 3382 (CA 2, 1976).

[384]190 NLRB 433, 77 LRRM 1235 (1971).

[385]Member Brown dissented, stating that the subcontracting was a clear departure from past practice and was thus a matter that should have required bargaining. *See* Webel Feed Mills & Pike Transit Co., 217 NLRB 815, 89 LRRM 1165 (1975) (unilateral de minimis subcontracting). *But see* Ohio Medical Prods., 194 NLRB 1, 78 LRRM 1488 (1971).

decision in *Milwaukee Spring I*.[386] The Board held that the transfer of unit work from a union to a nonunion facility during the term of an existing collective bargaining agreement, for the purpose of reducing labor costs but without the union's consent, constituted a midterm repudiation of the agreement in violation of section 8(d) and sections 8(a)(1), (3), and (5). It was undisputed that the decision was a mandatory subject of bargaining; that the employer had satisfied its obligation to bargain with the union over the decision to relocate; that the decision was economically motivated; and that it was not the result of union animus. Thus, the controversy stemmed from the application of the midterm modification provisions of section 8(d) to midterm relocations, so as to impose the additional requirement upon the employer to obtain the union's consent to the relocation, as distinguished from the general requirement that the employer bargain in good faith to impasse before implementation. In reaching this conclusion, the Board relied upon its earlier, but less visible, decision in *Los Angeles Marine Hardware Co.*,[387] which was enforced by the Ninth Circuit.

Milwaukee Spring II arose when, after significant changes in membership, the Board requested a remand of *Milwaukee Spring I* from the Seventh Circuit.[388] Upon reconsideration, the Board majority reversed its decision and also overruled those portions of *Los Angeles Marine Hardware* that were inconsistent with its reversal.[389] The majority described *Milwaukee Spring I* as a substantial departure from precedent and embraced the view that unless such transfers are prohibited by the labor agreement, an employer is free to take such action if it complies with its bargaining obligations and is not motivated by union animus. As for section 8(d), the Board held that such a relocation is not a midterm modification of terms and conditions of employment within the meaning of that section. The majority explained that the section 8(d) prohibition against midterm modifications applied only to terms "contained in" the bargaining agreement. Since the majority found no provision in the agreement requir-

---

[386]Illinois Coil Spring Co., Milwaukee Spring Div., (I), 265 NLRB 206, 111 LRRM 1486 (1982).

[387]235 NLRB 720, 98 LRRM 1571 (1978), *enforced*, 602 F2d 1302, 102 LRRM 2498 (CA 9, 1979).

[388]Illinois Coil Spring Co. Milwaukee Spring Div., (II) v. NLRB, 718 F2d 1102, 114 LRRM 2376 *and* 116 LRRM 2192 (CA 7, 1983).

[389]Illinois Coil Spring Co., Milwaukee Spring Div., 268 NLRB 601, 115 LRRM 1065 (1984), *aff'd sub nom.* Auto Workers v. NLRB, 765 F2d 175, 119 LRRM 2801 (CA DC, 1985).

ing bargaining-unit work to remain in the same facility (e.g., a work-preservation clause), it held that section 8(d) was not violated. The Board has since indicated that *Milwaukee Spring II* applies with equal force where an employer unilaterally makes a midterm transfer of work from a bargaining unit represented by one union to a unit represented by another union.[390]

In *Brown Co.*,[391] the Board combined the principles set out in *Milwaukee Spring II* and in *Otis Elevator II*, and held that an employer violated section 8(a)(5) when it transferred unit work outside the bargaining unit without obtaining the union's consent in view of the contract's work-preservation clause. The Board first examined and rejected the employer's claim that the contractual provision permitted the transfer of work and found that the employer's actions violated the contract. However, the Board continued, even if the employer unilaterally modified the contract, section 8(d) was violated only if the midterm modification was of a mandatory subject of bargaining.[392] The Board analyzed that question under the guidelines of *Otis Elevator II*, and concluded that because the employer's sole purpose was to reduce labor costs, the work transfer was a mandatory bargaining subject.[393]

(2) Partial Closure, Sale or Merger of Business, or Plant Relocation. The Supreme Court has held that an employer may close its *entire* business for any reason it chooses, including an antiunion motivation. In *Textile Workers v. Darlington Manufacturing Co.*,[394]

---

[390]*See* Dahl Fish Co., 279 NLRB 1084, 123 LRRM 1322 (1986), *enforced*, 813 F2d 1254, 125 LRRM 3063 (CA DC, 1987), indicating that *Milwaukee Spring II* overruled the Board's decision in Boeing Co., 230 NLRB 696, 96 LRRM 1355 (1977), *enforcement denied*, 581 F2d 793, 99 LRRM 2847 (CA 9, 1978). In *Boeing* the Board had held that such a unilateral transfer of work from one unit to another violated the Act. For discussions of other implications of the *Milwaukee Spring II* decision, *see generally* Barton, Milwaukee Spring Division of Illinois Coil Spring Co.: *The Open Road for Employer Relocations of Bargaining Unit Work During the Term of the Collective Bargaining Agreement*, 17 U. TOL. L. REV. 973 (1986); Schwarz, *Section 8(d) of the NLRA and the Duty to Decision-Bargain Over Work Relocation: Some Observations on Management Rights after* Milwaukee Spring II, 36 SYRACUSE L. REV. 1055 (1985).

[391]278 NLRB 783, 121 LRRM 1250 (1986), *aff'd*, 833 F2d 1015, 128 LRRM 2223 (CA 9, 1987), *cert. denied*, 485 US 1039, 128 LRRM 2224 (1988).

[392]This holding was based on the Supreme Court's decision in Allied Chem. & Alkali Workers Local 1 v. Pittsburgh Plate Glass Co., 404 US 157, 185, 78 LRRM 2974 (1971), which held that §8(d) "embraces only mandatory topics of bargaining."

[393]*But see* DeSoto, Inc., 278 NLRB 788, 121 LRRM 1226 (1986), where the Board held that plant closure and transfer of work to other facilities did not violate a contract provision which forbade moving the plant without the union's consent, and therefore did not modify any term contained in the agreement. The Board declined to accept an arbitrator's contrary interpretation of the provision, which the Fourth Circuit had upheld.

[394]380 US 263, 58 LRRM 2657 (1965). *See* discussion in Chapter 7, "Discrimination in Employment," at notes 261–285. *See generally* Wachter & Cohen, *The Law and Economics of*

the Court recognized that a partial closing, intended "to chill unionism," could result in a violation of section 8(a)(3), but left open the question of whether an employer must bargain about an economically motivated decision to close part of its business. In 1981 the Court answered that question in *First National Maintenance Corp. v. NLRB*.[395] It held that while the *effects* of such a decision are subjects for mandatory bargaining,[396] the decision to shut down part of a business for economic reasons is not within section 8(d)'s "terms and conditions of employment."

The Supreme Court's ruling in *First National Maintenance* settled the conflict among the NLRB and the circuit courts on this issue.[397] The Board's position had been that an employer must bargain about an economically motivated decision to close part of its business.[398] In *Ozark Trailers*,[399] the Board reasoned that since the company had based its decision to partially close a plant on its claim of excessive man-hours for production and defective

---

Collective Bargaining: An Introduction and Application to the Problems of Subcontracting, Partial Closure, and Relocation, 136 U. PA. L. REV. 1349 (1988); Roake, *The Spring Has Sprung: The Fate of Plant Relocation as a Mandatory Subject of Bargaining*, 24 SAN DIEGO L. REV. 221 (1987); Lane, *Unfair Labor Practice and Contract Aspects of an Employer's Desire to Close, Partially Close, or Relocate Bargaining Unit Work*, 24 DUQ. L. REV. 285 (1985); Willits, First National Maintenance Corp. v. NLRB—*Employer's Duty to Bargain in Partial Closures*, 7 J. CORP. L. 381 (1982); Moss, *Plant Removal—Labor Law Issues*, 54 CAL. ST. B.J. 42 (1979); Morris, *The Role of the NLRB and the Courts in the Collective Bargaining Process: A Fresh Look at Conventional Wisdom and Unconventional Remedies*, 30 VAND. L. REV. 661 (1977); Comment, *Labor Law-Employer's Duty to Bargain Over a Partial Closure*, 10 RUT. CAM. L.J. 737 (1979); Comment, *Duty to Bargain About Termination of Operations*, 92 HARV. L. REV. 768 (1979).

[395]452 US 666, 107 LRRM 2705 (1981). See discussion of balancing test at Section III.D., *supra*.

[396]There is no dispute that the union must be given a significant opportunity to bargain about these matters of job security as part of the "effects" bargaining mandated by §8(a)(5). *Id.* at 2711. *See also* Brockway Motor Trucks Div. v. NLRB, 582 F2d 720, 99 LRRM 2013 (CA 3, 1978), *denying enforcement to* 230 NLRB 1002, 95 LRRM 1462 (1977).

[397]*Compare* Ozark Trailers, 161 NLRB 561, 63 LRRM 1264 (1966) *with* Brockway Motor Trucks Div. v. NLRB, *supra* note 396; NLRB v. Transmarine Navigation Corp., 380 F2d 933, 65 LRRM 2861 (CA 9, 1967), NLRB v. Adams Dairy, Inc., 350 F2d 108, 60 LRRM 2084 (CA 8, 1965), *cert. denied*, 382 US 1011, 61 LRRM 2192 (1966), NLRB v. Royal Plating & Polishing Co., 350 F2d 191, 60 LRRM 2033 (CA 3, 1965) *and* Thompson Transp. Co., 165 NLRB 746, 65 LRRM 1370 (1967), *enforcement denied*, 406 F2d 698, 70 LRRM 2418 (CA 10, 1969).

[398]*E.g.*, Thompson Transp. Co., *supra* note 397; Drapery Mfg. Co., 170 NLRB 1706, 68 LRRM 1027 (1968). For a discussion of *Darlington* in light of §§8(a)(1) and 8(a)(3), see Chapter 7, "Discrimination in Employment," at notes 261–285. *See also* Fraser & Johnston Co. v. NLRB, 469 F2d 1259, 81 LRRM 2964 (CA 9, 1972); Southeastern Envelope Co., 206 NLRB 933, 84 LRRM 1577 (1973); Regal Aluminum, 190 NLRB 468, 77 LRRM 1303 (1971).

[399]*Supra* note 397. *Accord* Cooper Thermometer Co., 160 NLRB 1902, 63 LRRM 1219 (1966), *enforced in part*, 376 F2d 684, 65 LRRM 2113 (CA 2, 1967), where the Second Circuit upheld the Board's finding of a duty to bargain about transfer of employees to a new location, but refused to enforce parts of the remedy relating to backpay and reinstatement.

workmanship, and since those topics traditionally are subjects of collective bargaining, the entire matter could be submitted to bargaining just as were the labor-cost issues involved in *Fibreboard*.[400] The Board affirmed this position in its 1977 ruling in *Brockway Motor Trucks Div. v. NLRB*,[401] holding that the employer violated the Act because it had not bargained over a partial shutdown decision. The Board noted that there was no showing that the employer's decision to close involved such a "significant investment or withdrawal of capital" as to "affect the scope and ultimate direction of the enterprise," referring to the criteria established in the Board's important decision in *GMC Truck & Coach Div.*[402] The Third Circuit, however, refused to enforce the order, criticizing the Board's per se rule on bargaining over partial closure decisions.[403]

Following *Otis Elevator II*,[404] the Board struggled to apply that precedent in determining whether the decision to relocate is a

---

[400]The Board did not require that the company reopen the closed plant, but it ordered the company to pay back wages to the employees from the date of the decision to close until the date the plant was actually shut down. During this period, employees had been laid off on the basis of seniority.

[401]*Supra* note 396.

[402]191 NLRB 951, 952, 77 LRRM 1537 (1971), *aff'd sub nom.* Auto Workers Local 864 v. NLRB, 470 F2d 422, 81 LRRM 2439 (CA DC, 1972). In that case the Board held that the employer had no duty to bargain over the decision to sell a truck dealership to an owner who would operate it under franchise. The Board explained:

> It appears that the Board has not dealt definitively with the specific question whether the Act imposes a duty to bargain over a decision to *sell* an employing enterprise. We believe, however, that this issue is controlled by the rationale the courts have generally adopted in closely related cases, that decisions such as this, in which a significant investment or withdrawal of capital will affect the scope and ultimate direction of an enterprise, are matters essentially financial and managerial in nature. They thus lie at the very core of entrepreneurial control, and are not the types of subjects which Congress intended to encompass within "rates of pay, wages, hours of employment, or other conditions of employment." Such managerial decisions ofttimes require secrecy as well as the freedom to act quickly and decisively. They also involve subject areas as to which the determinative financial and operational considerations are likely to be unfamiliar to the employees and their representatives.
>
> We therefore disagree with the Trial Examiner here, who found that "[i]n the instant case Respondent made a managerial decision but hardly one lying at the core of the entrepreneurial control." A decision to withdraw capital from a company-operated facility and relinquish operating control to an independent dealership is very much "at the core of entrepreneurial control."
>
> We therefore find that the decision to sell this dealership was not a mandatory subject of bargaining under Section 8(a)(5).

Id., 77 LRRM at 1539 (footnote omitted).
See W.R. Grace & Co., 230 NLRB 617, 95 LRRM 1459 (1977), *enforced as modified*, 571 F2d 279, 98 LRRM 2001 (CA 5, 1978) (no violation for failure to bargain over unilateral decision to close production facility where General Counsel conceded that decision was motivated by legitimate business reasons, but violation of the Act was found for failure to bargain over effects of decision).

[403]*Supra* note 396.

[404]*See* discussion *supra* at notes 361–365.

mandatory subject of bargaining.[405] The Fifth Circuit held that the "labor cost" standard, as applied to a plant relocation, was a reasonably defensible interpretation of the Act in light of the Supreme Court's decision in *First National Maintenance.*[406]

The Fourth Circuit, however, rejected the *Otis II* plurality's labor cost analysis as "flatly inconsistent with *First National Maintenance.*"[407] In reversing a Board holding that an employer is required to bargain over an economically motivated decision to close one of its manufacturing plants, the court reasoned that the Board's labor cost analysis fails to accord sufficient weight to the nature of the decision, that is, whether it involves "a significant change in operations," as mandated by *First National Maintenance.*

Remedies for these violations have been, and are likely to continue to be, among the most difficult that the Board must fashion because of the inevitable economic consequences of efforts to restore the status quo ante.[408] The remedy for a violation where the employer has closed without giving the union notice or an adequate opportunity to bargain has varied with the circumstances. In *Soule Glass & Glazing Co.*[409] the Board ordered the employer to reopen operations, to restore unit work, and to bargain in good faith over any proposed changes in the bargaining unit. The Board found that the inconvenience to the employer in reopening was "relatively slight" because it involved only some movement of trucks and supplies. In *National Family Opinion,*[410] however, where the employer unlawfully failed to bargain over its decision to close a department, the Board did not require the reestablishment of the

---

[405]Inland Steel Container Co., 275 NLRB 929, 119 LRRM 1293 (1985), *review denied sub nom.* Steelworkers Local 2179 v. NLRB, 822 F2d 559, 125 LRRM 3313 (CA 5, 1987). *See also* W. W. Grainger, Inc. v. NLRB, 860 F2d 244, 129 LRRM 2718 (CA 7, 1988); Auto Workers Local 449 v. NLRB (National Metalcrafters), 802 F2d 969, 123 LRRM 2677 (CA 7, 1986) (Board criticized for failure to explicate coherent rationale in finding no violation).

[406]Inland Steel Container Co., *supra* note 405.

[407]Arrow Automotive Indus. v. NLRB, 853 F2d 223, 228, 128 LRRM 3137, 3142 (CA 4, 1988), *denying enforcement of* 284 NLRB 487, 125 LRRM 1188 (1987).

[408]*See* Chapter 32, "NLRB Orders and Remedies," at notes 257–267. The remedy for an unlawful discriminatory plant closure or removal in violation of §8(a)(3) is restoration of the operation unless that would be "unduly burdensome." *See* Chapter 7, "Discrimination in Employment," notes 282–285. *See also* Weather Tamer v. NLRB, 676 F2d 483, 110 LRRM 2573 (CA 11, 1982), *denying enforcement to* 253 NLRB 293, 105 LRRM 1569 (1980) (employer did not violate §§8(a)(3) or (5) by closing plant without bargaining).

[409]246 NLRB 792, 102 LRRM 1693 (1979), *enforcement denied in pertinent part,* 652 F2d 1055, 107 LRRM 2781 (CA 1, 1981).

[410]246 NLRB 521, 102 LRRM 1641 (1979).

discontinued operation, because to do so would have required significant expense and disruption. The Board held that the employer's backpay liability to employees terminated by reason of the discontinued operation would extend from the date of termination until the occurrence of the earliest of four conditions: (1) the parties bargain to agreement on subjects about which the employer is required to bargain; (2) the parties reach a bona fide impasse in bargaining; (3) the failure of the union to request bargaining within 5 days of the issuance of the bargaining order, or to commence negotiations within 5 days of the employer's notice to the union of its desire to bargain; or (4) the subsequent failure of the union to bargain in good faith.

The remedy for an employer's failure to bargain over a decision to close an operation should be contrasted with the more limited remedy provided for an employer's failure to bargain solely with respect to the effects of the decision. For an effects-bargaining violation, the usual remedy is to order backpay starting 5 days after the date of the Board's decision and order and continuing until the occurrence of the earliest of the four conditions listed above, with a minimum of 2 weeks backpay.[411]

In *Smyth Manufacturing Co.*,[412] where the employer had closed its plant and subcontracted the work to a third party without decision bargaining, the Board ordered the employer to resume operations at the closed plant and reinstate the laid-off employees with backpay. The Board justified its order by the fact that the employer's business was thriving and this remedy would not threaten its existence. The Board also reasoned that ordering resumption of discontinued operations amounted simply to directing the employer to resume a course that it had initially regarded as a sound economic venture.

With respect to bargaining over the effects of a decision, the employer's duty to give advance notice to the union will vary with circumstances.[413] In *Chippewa Motor Freight*,[414] the Board found no violation even though the employer gave the union only 2

---

[411]National Car Rental Sys., 252 NLRB 159, 105 LRRM 1263 (1980), *modified and enforced*, 672 F2d 1182, 109 LRRM 2832 (CA 3, 1982); *see also* the discussion in National Family Opinion, *supra* note 410, at 522 n.5.

[412]247 NLRB 1139, 103 LRRM 1432 (1980).

[413]In Metropolitan Teletronics Corp., 279 NLRB 957, 122 LRRM 1107 (1986), *enforced*, 819 F2d 1130, 127 LRRM 2048 (CA 2, 1987), the Board held that the employer's failure to afford the union an opportunity to negotiate over the effects of a plant relocation until after the old plant closed was a violation of its duty to bargain over the effects of the decision to relocate. In dissent, Chairman Dotson argued that the majority had established a per se rule requiring pre-implementation effects bargaining.

[414]261 NLRB 455, 110 LRRM 1140 (1982).

days' advance notice of its decision to close one of its terminals. The Board found that the employer had not made its decision substantially in advance of the 2-day notice and that the employer had engaged in ongoing discussions with the union about its increasing financial difficulties and had based its decision to close the terminal on its financial circumstances, not on any union animus. However, in *NLRB v. National Car Rental System*,[415] a violation was found by the Board and upheld by the Third Circuit. In that case, the employer did not notify the union that it was going to relocate until after it had signed a sales agreement which provided that the employer would discharge or reassign all of its employees within 4 days of signing the agreement. One of the effects about which the employer is required to bargain is employees' rights to transfer to the new location. Because the termination of the employees was presented to the union as a fait accompli, the Board concluded that negotiating attempts by the union over the effect of the closing would have been futile.

Bankruptcy is, of course, a circumstance that may affect the duty to give notice of such decisions for purposes of effects bargaining. In *Yorke v. NLRB*,[416] the Seventh Circuit upheld a Board order imposing upon the trustee-in-bankruptcy the general obligation to bargain over the effects of a closure decision. However, unlike the Board, it concluded that an emergency situation did exist so as to excuse preclosure notification. Nonetheless, the trustee in bankruptcy was still held in violation for failure to subsequently bargain about the effects after the closure occurred.

The First Circuit held, in a case arising under the Railway Labor Act, that an employer is not required to negotiate with a union either about its decision to merge with another company or about the effects of the merger.[417] The court noted that the

---

[415]672 F2d 1182, 109 LRRM 2832 (CA 3, 1982), *enforcing* 252 NLRB 159, 105 LRRM 1263 (1980).

[416]709 F2d 1138, 113 LRRM 3087 (CA 7, 1983), *cert. denied*, 465 US 1023, 115 LRRM 2784 (1984). *See also* Cooper-Jarrett, NLRB Gen. Counsel Advice Memo., Case Nos. 6-CA-15424 and 6-CA-15424-2 (1982) (complaint not issued despite failure to bargain over effects regarding Chapter 11 reorganization where union had not requested bargaining and would have had major role to play in liquidation proceedings as employer's major creditor on creditor's committee).

[417]Machinists Dist. 147 v. Northeast Airlines, 473 F2d 549, 80 LRRM 2197 (CA 1, 1972), *cert. denied*, 409 US 845, 81 LRRM 2390 (1972). For a consideration of the effect of such changes on the rights of the parties under the NLRA, See Chapter 15, "Effect of Change in the Employing Unit: Successorship." *See generally* Coughlin & de Kerckhove, *Labor*

merger did not displace large numbers of workers or deprive them of benefits, the usual justifications for such bargaining.[418]

n. Successorship and "Application of Contract" Clauses. The Board has held that "successorship" clauses and "application of contract" clauses are mandatory subjects of bargaining. In *Mine Workers*[419] the successorship clause required the employer to secure a successor's assumption of collective bargaining agreement obligations before transfer of the business operation, and the application of contract clause required the employer to apply the collective bargaining agreement to employees at all of its coal properties, including those acquired after the effective date of the contract.[420] The Board found (1) the successorship clause would vitally affect the terms and conditions of employment for employees who remained employed at the mine after an employer transfer of ownership, and (2) the application of contract clause vitally affected the terms and conditions of employment by serving to protect the jobs and work standards of bargaining-unit employees through the removal of economic incentives which might encourage the employer to transfer work to other mines under its control. With respect to the successorship clause, the Tenth Circuit enforced the Board's order; but disagreed with the Board on the application of contract clause, holding that it was not a mandatory subject of bargaining.[421] The court stated that the latter clause failed to satisfy

---

Problems in Mergers and Acquisitions, 47 WIS. B. BULL. 29 (Oct. 1974); Abodeely, *The Effect of Reorganization, Merger or Acquisition on the Appropriate Bargaining Unit*, 39 GEO. WASH. L. REV. 488 (1971). *See also* Monongahela Valley Hosp., 248 NLRB 69, 103 LRRM 1393 (1980).

[418]Although the case arose under the Railway Labor Act, the court analyzed cases under the NLRA and considered the impact of the Supreme Court's decision in Fibreboard Paper Prods. Corp. v. NLRB, 379 US 203, 57 LRRM 2609 (1964).

[419]Mine Workers (Lone Star Steel Co.), 231 NLRB 573, 96 LRRM 1083 (1977), *enforcement granted in part, denied in part and remanded*, 639 F2d 545, 104 LRRM 3144 (CA 10, 1980), *cert. denied*, 450 US 911, 106 LRRM 2513 (1981). *See generally* Gaus & Morris, *Successorship and the Collective Bargaining Agreement: Accommodating* Wiley *and* Burns, 59 VA. L. REV. 1359 (Nov. 1973); Comment, *Successorship Clauses in Collective Bargaining Agreements*, 1979 B.Y.U. Rev. 99; Comment, *Defining "Successors" and the Significance of a Successors and Assigns Clause in a Collective Bargaining Agreement*, 49 TUL. L. REV. 644 (1975).

[420]The Board cited Allied Chem. & Alkali Workers Local 1 v. Pittsburgh Plate Glass Co., 404 US 157, 78 LRRM 2974, 2982 (1971), defining a mandatory subject of bargaining as one that settles "an aspect of the relationship between the employer and employees," but also noted that in *Pittsburgh Plate Glass* the court had recognized that a matter involving individuals outside the employment relationship is a mandatory subject of bargaining only if it "vitally affect[s] the 'terms and conditions of [bargaining-unit employees'] employment.'" 404 US at 176, 78 LRRM at 2981 (Emphasis supplied by the court.)

[421]Lone Star Steel Co. v. NLRB, 639 F2d 545, 104 LRRM 3144 (CA 10, 1980).

each portion of the requisite two-prong test in order for a subject involving employees outside the bargaining unit to be a mandatory subject of bargaining: (1) the subject must "vitally affect" terms and conditions or job security of unit employees, and (2) it must represent a direct frontal attack on a problem thought to threaten the basic wage structure established by the collective bargaining agreement. On remand the Board "accepted" the Tenth Circuit's decision as the law of the case. The Board held, accordingly, that the application of contract clause was a nonmandatory subject of bargaining and that the union had violated section 8(b)(3) by striking for that clause.[422]

In *Associated General Contractors,*[423] the Eighth Circuit adopted the Board's view that a "no-conflicting agreement" clause is not a mandatory subject of bargaining. The clause in question would have prevented the union from entering into any collective bargaining agreement with another employer that was more favorable in any respect, unless it offered similarly favorable terms to the signatory party. The court reasoned that there was simply no basis to conclude that such a no-conflicting agreement clause, as distinguished from a "most favored nations" clause, would have vitally affected the wages, hours, and conditions of employment of bargaining-unit employees.

In *Electrical Workers (IBEW) Local 617 (San Mateo National Electrical Contractors Ass'n),*[424] the Board held that a "manpower reciprocal agreement" was a mandatory subject of bargaining because it vitally affected the terms and conditions of employment. The agreement permitted a "traveling employer" to bring in workers from other jurisdictions, but required that for each such worker the employer would hire an additional employee through the local union. In reaching its decision, the Board distinguished *Associated General Contractors of North Dakota v. NLRB*[425] on the basis that the no-conflicting agreement clauses regulated the terms of bargaining between local unions and

---

[422]*See* Mine Workers (Lone Star Steel Co.), 262 NLRB 368, 110 LRRM 1390 (1982), *enforcement granted with order clarified,* 766 F2d 1459, 119 LRRM 3630 (CA 10, 1985).

[423]Associated Gen. Contractors of N.D. v. NLRB, 637 F2d 556, 106 LRRM 2131 (CA 8, 1981), *enforcing* 245 NLRB 328, 102 LRRM 1478 (1979). The clause at issue went beyond the proper purpose of authorizing the revision of the agreement to incorporate concession made by the union to other employers. *See* Dolly Madison Indus., 182 NLRB 1037, 74 LRRM 1230 (1970) ("most favored nation" clause mandatory subject of bargaining).

[424]281 NLRB 1226, 124 LRRM 1301 (1986).

[425]*Supra* note 423.

nonassociation members and did not directly affect wages, hours, and employment conditions of the employees.[426]

o. Arrangements and Conditions for Negotiations. The Board has ruled that the parties must bargain collectively about the preliminary arrangements for negotiations in the same manner they must bargain about substantive terms or conditions of employment. Preliminary arrangements include such matters as scheduling the time, place, length, and agenda of meetings.[427] The Board has stated that "such preliminary matters are just as much a part of the process of collective bargaining as negotiation over wages, hours etc."[428] In *Case, Inc.*,[429] the Board held that an employer with facilities in Kentucky and Tennessee violated the Act by its demand that the union which represented its Kentucky employees meet with the employer in New York or, in the alternative, negotiate by telephone or mail.

Unilateral deviations from established bargaining procedures may violate section 8(a)(5). An employer which unilaterally discontinued such former practices as making its premises available for negotiations, permitting employees to take compensated leave for bargaining purposes,[430] and reimbursing on a per diem arrangement certain travel and lodging expenses for union negotiators committed just such a violation.[431] Con-

---

[426]*Supra* note 424.

[427]*See* Ustad, *Use and Abuse of Ground Rules in Labor Negotiations*, 15 A.F.L.-C.I.O. REV. 102 (1973).

[428]General Elec. Co., 173 NLRB 253, 257, 69 LRRM 1305 (1968), *enforced*, 412 F2d 512, 71 LRRM 2418 (CA 2, 1969). The refusal of the employer to attend scheduled meetings and to deal with preliminary matters where such refusal was based on an improper objection to the composition of the union's committee constituted a violation of §8(a)(5). On review, however, the Second Circuit held that the employer "had an absolute right to refrain from preliminary meetings before the formal notice of reopening [of the contract] and it could condition its agreement to preliminary discussions . . . ." The court thus made a distinction between preliminary and formal bargaining sessions. *Id.*, 412 F2d at 521. See Chapter 13, "The Duty to Bargain," at notes 910–935, for treatment of coalition and coordinated bargaining.

[429]237 NLRB 798, 99 LRRM 1159 (1978), *enforcement granted in part and denied in part sub nom.* NLRB v. Gibraltar Indus., 653 F2d 1091, 107 LRRM 3307 (CA 6, 1981). *See also* Co-Jo dba Clinton Food 4 Less, 288 NLRB 597, 130 LRRM 1441 (1988) (unlawful for employer to insist that union bear all inconvenience and expense of travel to employer's attorney's office located 78 miles from site of employment); Queen Anne Record Sales dba Tower Books, 273 NLRB 671, 118 LRRM 1113 (1984), *enforced without opinion*, 772 F2d 913, 121 LRRM 2048 (CA 9, 1985) (Board denies that it advocates per se approach to deciding where bargaining should take place, but cites with approval cases holding that employer may not refuse to meet at locale near represented employees).

[430]Procter & Gamble Mfg. Co. v. NLRB, 658 F2d 968, 108 LRRM 2177 (CA 4, 1981), *enforcing* 248 NLRB 953, 104 LRRM 1207 (1980), *cert. denied*, 459 US 879, 111 LRRM 2528 (1982).

[431]Midstate Tel. Corp. v. NLRB, 706 F2d 401, 113 LRRM 2213 (CA 2, 1983). The employer in Midstate had entered into a supplemental agreement to reimburse union negotiators for their per diem travel and lodging expenses, but refused to reimburse

versely, the Board has also found that an employer's insistence on negotiating at the plant during regular business hours is lawful, in light of a longstanding practice to that effect and the employer's practice of paying employees for negotiations during working hours.[432]

The Board and the First Circuit have held that, absent union agreement, an employer's insistence that noneconomic issues be discussed and resolved before major economic issues are addressed violates section 8(a)(5).[433]

The constituency of the committee representing either the employer or the union is not a mandatory subject of bargaining, because the law guarantees each party the right to choose its own representatives free of any influence from the other.[434]

The Board and the Fifth Circuit have held that the issue of remuneration of employee-members of the shop committee for time spent in negotiating a collective bargaining agreement is a mandatory subject of bargaining.[435] The Board equated the payment of wages during collective bargaining to the payment of wages during presentation of grievances, and held that the former issue "vitally affect[s]" the relations between an employer and employees and "constitutes an aspect of a relationship between the employer and employees."[436] The Fifth Circuit

---

union negotiators for strike-settlement negotiations conducted after underlying collective bargaining contracts had expired. The Second Circuit held that, even if the supplemental agreement had expired with the collective bargaining contracts, the employer had violated the Act by unilaterally changing the reimbursement scheme which was an existing term or condition of employment. *See also* Dilene Answering Serv., 257 NLRB 284, 107 LRRM 1489 (1981), where the sudden change in communicating bargaining proposals was viewed by the Board as one indicium of ritualistic bad-faith bargaining.

[432]E.I. Du Pont de Nemours & Co., 294 NLRB 563, 131 LRRM 1749 (1989).

[433]South Shore Hosp., 245 NLRB 848, 102 LRRM 1565 (1979), *enforced*, 630 F2d 40, 105 LRRM 2640 (CA 1, 1980), *cert. denied*, 450 US 965, 106 LRRM 2560 (1981); *accord* John Wanamaker, Philadelphia, 279 NLRB 1034, 123 LRRM 1271 (1986). *See also* Plattdeutsche Park Restaurant, 296 NLRB No. 26, 132 LRRM 1109 (1989) (employer's unlawful refusal to sign agreement unless union agreed to drop claims against welfare fund and vacation fund and agreed to termination of previously discharged employee); Meda-Care Ambulance, 285 NLRB 471, 128 LRRM 1276 (1987) (employer's unlawful insistence on union's agreement to "loyalty clause" as condition to future negotiations); Freedom WLNE-TV, 278 NLRB 1293, 122 LRRM 1214 (1986) (employer unlawfully conditioned further movement on union's conducting ratification vote by date certain).

[434]General Elec. Co., *supra* note 428. For general treatment of bargaining conduct required for good-faith bargaining, see Chapter 13, "The Duty to Bargain." *See also* AMF, Inc., 219 NLRB 903, 90 LRRM 1271 (1975). For detailed treatment of the requirements of §8(b)(1)(B) as to union restraining and coercion in the selection of employer representatives, see Chapter 6, "Interference With Protected Rights," at notes 627–651.

[435]Axelson, Inc., 234 NLRB 414, 97 LRRM 1234 (1978), *enforced*, 599 F2d 91, 101 LRRM 3007 (CA 5, 1979). Note that §302 expressly regulates some payments by employers to labor organizations and their agents.

[436]*Id.* at 415. *Cf.* Western Block Co., 229 NLRB 482, 96 LRRM 1415 (1977) (violation of §8(a)(5) where employer unilaterally promulgated policy of charging union for services of employees engaged in union business during working hours).

agreed with this analogy, observing that remuneration benefited all members of the bargaining unit by encouraging the collective bargaining process, thus making it a mandatory subject.[437]

In *Bartlett-Collins Co.*,[438] the Board overruled its prior decisions concerning stenographers at bargaining sessions and held that issues as to the presence of a stenographer during negotiations and the use of a recording device to record those negotiations are permissive rather than mandatory subjects. The Board reasoned that the question of whether a stenographer should be present during negotiations is a 'threshold matter, preliminary and subordinate to substantive negotiations,"[439] and that the Board would be avoiding its statutory responsibility to foster and encourage meaningful negotiations were it to permit a party to stifle negotiations in their inception over such an issue. The Tenth Circuit enforced the Board's order, agreeing that any advantages from stenographic records are outweighed by the disadvantage of allowing a party to insist to impasse upon the presence of a court reporter. The Third Circuit also has approved the Board's position.[440]

V. PERMISSIVE SUBJECTS OF BARGAINING

A. In General

Since the issue first was raised in the early years of the Wagner Act, the Board has consistently held that there are certain subjects about which the parties are free to bargain even though they do not fall within the ambit of "wages, hours, and other terms and conditions of employment," and thus are not mandatory subjects of bargaining.

Among the earliest of these holdings were the cases dealing with the posting of performance bonds or surety bonds that would indemnify a party against breach by the other party. The

---

[437]101 LRRM at 3010.

[438]237 NLRB 770, 99 LRRM 1034 (1978), *enforced*, 639 F2d 652, 106 LRRM 2272 (CA 10), *cert. denied*, 452 US 961, 107 LRRM 2768 (1981); *accord* Nassau Ins. Co., 280 NLRB 878, 124 LRRM 1075 (1986); *see also* Water Ass'n, 290 NLRB 838, 129 LRRM 1064 (1988) (employer's insistence on tape-recording second-step grievance meeting violated §8(a)(5)).

[439]237 NLRB at 773.

[440]Latrobe Steel Corp. v. NLRB, 630 F2d 171, 105 LRRM 2393 (CA 3, 1980), *enforcing in part* 244 NLRB 528, 102 LRRM 1175 (1979), *cert. denied*, 454 US 821, 108 LRRM 2558 (1981).

Board held, as a matter of law, that an employer could not insist that a union post such a bond as a condition precedent to the execution of an agreement.[441]

In none of those cases were the terms "voluntary" or "permissive" subjects of bargaining expressly employed. However, the Board's reasoning demonstrated that it was using that concept. In each case an employer was found guilty of a refusal to bargain because it insisted that agreement on a subject, not itself illegal, was nevertheless a condition precedent to bargaining.

In *Borg-Warner*,[442] distinguishing "permissive" from mandatory subjects, the Supreme Court made it clear that bargaining need not be confined to the subjects mandated by section 8(d). It is lawful for either party to propose for inclusion in a collective bargaining contract any clause addressing any permissive subject of bargaining; the parties may bargain in good faith about that clause, and, if an agreement is reached, may include it in the final contract. But the Court also made it clear that neither party is required to bargain about permissive subjects. The refusal to do so is no violation of section 8(a)(5) or 8(b)(3). And if there has been voluntary bargaining about a permissive subject, refusal either to include the subject in the contract or to agree to a particular resolution of a voluntary subject, is not unlawful. Conversely, a refusal to contract except upon the inclusion of a clause that constitutes a permissive subject is per se (without regard to subjective good or bad faith) a violation of section 8(a)(5) or 8(b)(3) because "such conduct is, in substance, a refusal to bargain about the subjects that are within the scope of mandatory bargaining."[443] In addition, a party's conduct in regard to a permissive subject may be evidence of subjective good or bad faith in bargaining.[444]

Either party may bargain about a permissive topic as if it were a mandatory subject without losing the right, at any time before agreement is reached, to take a firm position that the matter shall not be included in a contract. To sustain a claim of waiver based upon a course of bargaining "would penalize a party to negotiations for endeavoring to reach agreement by consenting to bar-

---

[441]Benson Produce Co., 71 NLRB 888, 19 LRRM 1060 (1946); Scripto Mfg. Co., 36 NLRB 411, 9 LRRM 156 (1941); Interstate S.S. Co., 36 NLRB 1307, 9 LRRM 200 (1941); Jasper Blackburn Prods. Corp., 21 NLRB 1240, 6 LRRM 169 (1940).

[442]NLRB v. Borg-Warner Corp., Wooster Div., 356 US 342, 42 LRRM 2034 (1958). See notes 473–474, *infra*, and accompanying text.

[443]356 US at 349.

[444]Steere Broadcasting Corp., 158 NLRB 487, 62 LRRM 1083 (1966).

gaining upon issues as to which the Act does not require him to bargain."[445]

Applying this principle, the Supreme Court held that when a permissive subject is included in a collective bargaining agreement, that subject is not transformed into a mandatory one even for the term of that agreement.[446] It follows that once a contract has expired a party has no obligation to bargain over a permissive subject even though one or more past contracts contained a provision dealing with that subject.[447]

It must be noted, however, that once a party does agree to a contract which includes a permissive subject, section 8(d) requires the party, upon request, to reduce the agreement to writing.[448]

A party's position at the bargaining table will not be jeopardized by putting forward a package proposal containing both mandatory and permissive items. Thus, in *Nordstrom Inc.*[449] the employer linked a wage proposal with proposals relating to permissive subjects and refused to sign a contract limited to its mandatory proposals. Noting that permissive subjects may have costs that affect the employer's wage proposals, the Board held that the union could not selectively accept portions of the employer's package offer and dismissed the refusal-to-bargain complaint. While a party may not insist to impasse upon permissive proposals, it may alter its mandatory proposals in light of the withdrawal or rejection of the permissive subjects. One party cannot conclude negotiations by agreeing only to those proposals of the other party that comprise mandatory subjects of bargaining unless "all other matters have previously, and independent of the outstanding nonmandatory subject, been agreed upon."[450]

---

[445]Kit Mfg. Co., 150 NLRB 662, 58 LRRM 1140 (1964), *enforced*, 365 F2d 829, 62 LRRM 2856 (CA 9, 1966).

[446]Allied Chem. & Alkali Workers Local 1 v. Pittsburgh Plate Glass Co., 404 US 157, 78 LRRM 2974 (1971). As a consequence, the Court held that unilateral midterm modification of a permissive subject that had been included in the agreement did not constitute an unfair labor practice under the Act. See *supra* at notes 94–117.

[447]*See, e.g.*, Printing Pressmen Local 252 (Columbus) (R.W. Page Corp.), 219 NLRB 268, 89 LRRM 1553 (1975), *enforced*, 543 F2d 1161, 93 LRRM 3055 (CA 5, 1976), discussed at note 498, *infra*.

[448]Associated Bldg. Contractors of Evansville, 143 NLRB 678, 53 LRRM 1395 (1963), *enforced as modified sub nom.* NLRB v. Painters Local 1385, 334 F2d 729, 56 LRRM 2648 (CA 7, 1964). Section 8(d) requires "the execution of a written contract incorporating *any* agreement . . . if requested by either party . . . ." (Emphasis added.)

[449]229 NLRB 601, 96 LRRM 1092 (1977).

[450]*Id.* at 602.

B. Specific Subjects

1. Definition of Bargaining Unit. Whenever bargaining takes place without a prior Board definition of unit, the parties must agree upon the unit to be covered by the contract they negotiate. "The parties cannot bargain meaningfully about wages or hours or conditions of employment unless they know the unit of bargaining."[451] Even when the Board has defined a unit, the parties are free to agree on a negotiated unit different from the certified or recognized unit. In advanced forms of collective bargaining there may be multiple bargaining units applicable to the employees in one certified unit, and one unit may include more than a single certified or recognized unit.[452] In each such instance, the combination of units may be established by voluntary agreement of the parties.[453] The Board accepts as lawful the bargaining units that the parties establish by consensual agreement.[454] Similarly, since there may be several appropriate units applicable to any group of employees,[455] parties are free to agree upon which such unit their contract will cover.

While extensive bargaining about the unit commonly occurs, scope of the unit is not a mandatory subject of bargaining. As noted by the Second Circuit:

> The statute imposes on labor and management alike a duty to bargain in good faith with respect to wages, hours and other conditions of employment. . . . This duty "does not compel either party to agree to a proposal," as Section 8(d) states, "or require the making of a concession," and the Board has no power to settle any of those questions. By way of contrast, it not only has power, but is indeed directed, to decide what is the appropriate bargaining unit in each case.[456]

---

[451]Douds v. Longshoremen (ILA), 241 F2d 278, 39 LRRM 2388, 2391 (CA 2, 1957).

[452]Consensual bargaining patterns may assume many different forms. The actual unit for negotiations may not even coincide with the certified or recognized unit—some issues may be negotiated in local units while other issues may be negotiated in larger units. For example, it is not uncommon for the negotiating unit for pensions to be larger than the negotiating unit for seniority.

[453]See generally discussion of multi-employer bargaining units in Chapter 11, "Appropriate Bargaining Units," and discussion of multilevel bargaining units at notes 393–398 therein.

[454]Radio Corp. of Am., 135 NLRB 980, 49 LRRM 1606 (1962); General Motors Corp., 120 NLRB 1215, 42 LRRM 1143 (1958); Lever Bros. Co., 96 NLRB 448, 28 LRRM 1544 (1951).

[455]*See* Chapter 11, "Appropriate Bargaining Units," at notes 2–4.

[456]Douds v. Longshoremen (ILA), *supra* note 451, at 282.

Where the Board has originally fixed the unit, "it may be altered by agreement of the parties,"[457] but the party seeking to alter the unit may not insist on the alteration to the point of impasse.[458] The Board has approved the voluntary combination into one multiplant unit of several previously certified individual plant units,[459] but insistence to impasse on such a combination is unlawful.[460]

The distinction between mandatory and permissive subjects of bargaining with respect to the scope of the unit is often an elusive one, particularly in coordinated or coalition bargaining.[461] For example, *in AFL-CIO Joint Negotiating Committee (Phelps Dodge Corp.) v. NLRB*,[462] various unions representing a number of units requested bargaining through a joint committee, the aim of which was joint companywide bargaining. When the company refused to participate, the joint negotiating committee instead engaged in separate negotiations at various locations, making identical demands at each. Although the union struck in support of its uniform demands, at no time did it bargain at one location with respect to the wages or employment conditions at other locations. Overruling the Board, the Third Circuit held that even though the uniform simultaneous demands tended to support the union objective of companywide bargaining, a permissive subject, the demands were legitimate mandatory subjects over which the unions could bargain to impasse. "The fact that a demand may have extra-unit effects does not alter its status as a mandatory subject of bargaining."[463]

As a general rule, it is an unfair labor practice for either party to insist that employees be added to or excluded from a certified

---

[457]*Id.*

[458]*See* Canterbury Gardens, 238 NLRB 864, 99 LRRM 1279 (1978); *but see* Salt River Valley Water Users' Ass'n, 204 NLRB 83, 83 LRRM 1536 (1973), *enforced*, 498 F2d 393, 86 LRRM 2873 (CA 9, 1974) (employer violated §8(a)(5) by insisting to impasse upon excluding certain employees from bargaining unit in mistaken belief that they were supervisors). *See also* National Fresh Fruit & Vegetable Co., 227 NLRB 2014, 95 LRRM 1011 (1977), *enforcement denied*, 565 F2d 1331, 97 LRRM 2427 (CA 5, 1978); Retail Clerks Local 588 (Raley's), 224 NLRB 1638, 92 LRRM 1381 (1976), *enforcement denied*, 565 F2d 769, 96 LRRM 2811 (CA DC, 1977).

[459]Radio Corp. of America, *supra* note 454; General Motors Corp., *supra* note 454.

[460]Douds v. Longshoremen (ILA), *supra* note 451; Young & Hay Transp. Co., 214 NLRB 252, 87 LRRM 1319 (1974), *enforced sub nom.* Teamsters Local 54 v. Young & Hay Transp. Co., 522 F2d 562, 90 LRRM 2363 (CA 8, 1975); Longshoremen (ILA) (New York Shipping Ass'n), 118 NLRB 1481, 40 LRRM 1408 (1957), *set aside on other grounds*, 277 F2d 681, 45 LRRM 2551 (CA DC, 1960).

[461]See Chapter 13, "The Duty to Bargain," at notes 910–935.

[462]459 F2d 374, 79 LRRM 2939 (CA 3), *cert. denied*, 409 US 1059, 81 LRRM 2893 (1972).

[463]*Id.* at 378.

unit.[464] Nevertheless, under the unique facts in *Newspaper Production Co. v. NLRB*,[465] the Fifth Circuit affirmed a Board order which allowed a union to bargain to impasse over the scope of the bargaining unit. There a union which represented a unit of skilled photoengravers under a contract about to expire was chosen to represent three general production workers of the same employer. While negotiations concerning the newly represented employees were pending, the photoengravers' contract expired; the union then insisted to the point of striking that the general production workers be included in a single bargaining unit with the photoengravers under one contract. In affirming the Board's conclusion that the union's conduct did not violate section 8(b)(3), the court held that a provision in the expiring photoengravers' contract reflected the parties' intent to include the scope of the bargaining unit among the issues to be resolved at the bargaining table.

The Second Circuit reached a contrary result in *Sperry Rand Corp. v. NLRB*.[466] There, the union attempted to represent certain of the employer's California employees who fell outside a New York bargaining unit. The union had filed a representation petition to represent those workers but lost the election. When the union sought enforcement of an arbitrator's award requiring the company to comply in California with wages and certain other conditions provided by the New York contract, the employer filed charges alleging a violation of section 8(b)(3). The Board dismissed the complaint.[467] In reversing, the court concluded as a matter of law that "regardless of the Union's motive in seeking enforcement of the arbitration award, it committed an unfair labor practice because the subject of the wages and

---

[464]United Technologies Corp., 292 NLRB 248, 130 LRRM 1445 (1989), *aff'd*, 884 F2d 1569, 132 LRRM 3035 (CA 2, 1989); Howard Elec. & Mechanical, 293 NLRB 472, 131 LRRM 1743 (1989); Westvaco Corp., 289 NLRB 301, 131 LRRM 1044 (1988); Facet Enters., 290 NLRB 152, 131 LRRM 1114 (1988); Boston Edison Co., 290 NLRB 549, 129 LRRM 1212 (1988); Boise Cascade Corp., 283 NLRB 462, 124 LRRM 1391 (1987), *enforced*, 860 F2d 471, 129 LRRM 2744 (CA DC, 1988); Bozzuto's, 277 NLRB 977, 120 LRRM 1337 (1985).

[465]503 F2d 821, 87 LRRM 2650 (CA 5, 1974), *enforcing* 205 NLRB 738, 84 LRRM 1186 (1973).

[466]492 F2d 63, 85 LRRM 2521 (CA 2), *cert. denied*, 419 US 831, 87 LRRM 2397 (1974).

[467]Electrical Workers (IUE) Local 445 (Sperry Rand Corp.), 202 NLRB 183, 82 LRRM 1491 (1973). The Board held that no provision of the Act was violated when parties voluntarily agreed that the terms of their collective bargaining agreement would be minimum terms of employment for the employees outside the bargaining unit if the purpose of the agreement was to protect the job security and wage structure of the employees within the unit.

working conditions of the [California] employees was not a *permissible* subject of bargaining at the New York City unit."[468]

Distinguishing a jurisdictional dispute[469] from a question concerning the scope of the bargaining unit, the Board held that an employer lawfully insisted to impasse on excluding employees who typed copy for newly acquired scanner equipment from a unit of composing room employees.[470] The excluded employees also worked in other departments and performed other tasks, and the Board concluded that the employer was not seeking to change the scope of the unit, even though the new scanner equipment would eliminate work previously performed by unit employees.

While clauses concerning the union's jurisdiction or the assignment of work are mandatory subjects of bargaining, the Board scrutinizes such proposed clauses to determine whether they are disguised attempts to change the scope of the unit and, therefore, permissive subjects.[471]

2. Parties to a Collective Bargaining Agreement. The only essential parties to a collective bargaining agreement are the employer or employers of the employees in the unit or units covered by the agreement, or the association to which the employer has delegated bargaining authority, and the certified bargaining representative or other representative of the covered employees.[472] Frequently, additional parties are named. For example: (1) the international union as well as the local, where only the local is certified; (2) the local as well as the international, where only the international is certified; (3) the employer as well as the employer association, where the unit is employer-associa-

---

[468]492 F2d at 69 (emphasis added). "Generally, an employer commits the unfair labor practices of interfering with employees' §7 rights and supporting a union in violation of §8(a)(1) and (a)(2) when it imposes on employees of one unit the contract and bargaining agent of another unit." *Id.* On remand, the Board adopted the Second Circuit's finding. Sperry Rand Corp., 216 NLRB 173, 88 LRRM 1234 (1975), *enforced*, 529 F2d 502, 91 LRRM 2469 (CA 2, 1976).

[469]For treatment of jurisdictional disputes generally, see Chapter 25, "Jurisdictional Disputes and 'Featherbedding.'"

[470]World Publishing Co., 220 NLRB 1065, 90 LRRM 1566 (1975), *review denied sub nom.* Typographical Union Local 190 (Omaha) v. NLRB, 545 F2d 1138, 93 LRRM 3063 (CA 8, 1976). After impasse, the employer unilaterally assigned work on the new equipment to nonunit employees. This, too, was held lawful.

[471]Storer Communications (WJKW-TV-8), 295 NLRB No. 11, 133 LRRM 1024 (1989); Idaho Statesman, 281 NLRB 272, 124 LRRM 1141 (1986), *enforced in part*, 836 F2d 1396, 127 LRRM 2429 (CA DC, 1988); Western Newspaper Publishing Co., 269 NLRB 355, 116 LRRM 1173 (1984).

[472]*E.g.*, a noncertified representative selected by a majority of the employees in an appropriate unit. *See* Chapter 12, "Recognition and Withdrawal of Recognition Without an Election."

tion-wide; (4) the employer association as well as the employer. So long as the parties agree, the law will give effect to their preference; but insistence by either party, to the point of impasse or not signing an otherwise agreed-upon contract unless a given organization or individual other than a required party is added or excluded, is a per se refusal to bargain.

In *Borg-Warner*,[473] the employer insisted that the recognition clause name only the local union as the party to the contract even though the international union was the certified representative. Impasse resulted and the Board held that the employer violated section 8(a)(5). The Supreme Court affirmed, holding:

> The "recognition" clause . . . does not come within the definition of mandatory bargaining. The statute requires the company to bargain with the certified representative of its employees. It is an evasion of that duty to insist that the certified agent not be a party to the collective bargaining contract. The Act does not prohibit the voluntary addition of a party, but that does not authorize the employer to exclude the certified representative from the contract.[474]

An employer may not lawfully insist, as a condition of a contract, that a labor federation be a party to a contract where a local union affiliated with that federation is the certified representative.[475] Similarly, a union is guilty of a refusal to bargain when it refuses to include the employer association where the employer is part of an established multi-employer unit represented by that association.[476]

3. Selection of Bargaining Representative. The selection of a bargaining representative is a permissive subject of bargaining. Accordingly, a union violates not only section 8(b)(1)(B),[477] but also section 8(b)(3), when it insists that the employer designate an association of employers as its bargaining representative, or when it insists that a multi-employer association submit any agreement to the association's national office for approval.[478]

---

[473]NLRB v. Borg-Warner Corp., Wooster Div., 356 US 342, 42 LRRM 2034 (1958).

[474]*Id.* at 350.

[475]NLRB v. Taormina Co., 207 F2d 251, 32 LRRM 2684 (CA 5, 1953), *enforcing* 94 NLRB 884, 28 LRRM 1118 (1951); Standard Generator Co., 90 NLRB 790, 26 LRRM 1285 (1950).

[476]Slate Workers Local 36 (Roofing Contractors Ass'n on S. Cal.), 172 NLRB 2248, 69 LRRM 1300 (1968). *See supra* note 453.

[477]*See* Chapter 6, "Interference With Protected Rights," at notes 627–651.

[478]Electrical Workers (IBEW) Local 428 (National Elec. Contractors Ass'n, Kern County Chapter), 277 NLRB 397, 121 LRRM 1322 (1985); Mine Workers Local 1854 (Amax Coal Co.), 238 NLRB 1583, 99 LRRM 1670 (1978), *enforced in pertinent part*, 614 F2d 872, 103 LRRM 2482 (CA 3, 1980); Retail Clerks Local 770 (Fine's Food Co.), 228 NLRB 1166, 95 LRRM 1062 (1977); Laborers Local 264 (J.J. Dalton), 216 NLRB 40, 88 LRRM 1192 (1975), *enforced sub nom.* NLRB v. Laborers Local 264 (D & G Constr. Co.), 529 F2d 778, 91 LRRM 2209 (CA 8, 1976).

Conversely, an employer violates the Act by insisting to the point of impasse that the union accept a grievance procedure that would not provide for union representation at the first step and would dictate that only an international union representative participate in subsequent steps.[479] An employer may not lawfully refuse to meet with a union negotiating committee simply because it includes a nonemployee.[480]

While an employer may normally insist on bargaining during working hours, the Board has held that an employer violates section 8(a)(5) by refusing to bargain outside working hours, while at the same time refusing to give traveling members of the bargaining committee time off without pay to permit them to participate during working hours.[481] The "travelers" were members of the union negotiating committee at other units, and the Board concluded that the combined actions of the employer unlawfully interfered with the union's selection of its bargaining representatives.

4. Union-Recognition Clause. A union recognition clause is not a mandatory subject of bargaining.[482] Therefore, when an employer intended to phase out a home for the aged in order to relocate elsewhere, it could not insist to impasse on the inclusion of a contract provision that would terminate union recognition upon cessation of operations at the original home.[483] Because a union-recognition clause is not a mandatory subject of bargaining, an employer did not violate section 8(a)(5) when it acquired two new sites and did not adhere to a citywide bargaining-unit provision contained in an expired contract. The employer had not uniformly recognized the union at newly acquired sites during the term of the contract.[484]

5. Performance Bonds, Indemnifications, and Legal Liability Clauses. A performance bond has been consistently

---

[479]Tomco Communications, 220 NLRB 636, 90 LRRM 1321 (1975), *enforcement denied*, 567 F2d 871, 97 LRRM 2660 (CA 9, 1978).

[480]Racine Die Casting Co., 192 NLRB 529, 77 LRRM 1818 (1971).

[481]Indiana & Mich. Elec. Co., 235 NLRB 1128, 98 LRRM 1036 (1978), *reaff'g* 229 NLRB 576, 95 LRRM 1122 (1977), *enforced*, 599 F2d 185, 101 LRRM 2470 (CA 7, 1979), *cert. denied*, 444 US 1014, 103 LRRM 2143 (1980).

[482]NLRB v. Borg-Warner Corp., Wooster Div., *supra* note 473; Jewish Center for the Aged, 220 NLRB 98, 90 LRRM 1222 (1975). *Cf.* Salt River Valley Water Users' Ass'n, *supra* note 458.

[483]Jewish Center for the Aged, *supra* note 482.

[484]Triple A Maintenance Corp., 283 NLRB 44, 124 LRRM 1265 (1987).

treated as a permissive bargaining subject.[485] In *Scripto*,[486] decided under the Wagner Act, the Board found that an employer violated the Act by insisting that the union furnish a bond to indemnify the employer should it be picketed by outside unions. Similarly, a demand, pursued to impasse, regarding indemnification for pressure applied to customers violates the Act.[487] In *C-E Natco/C-E Invalco*,[488] the employer proposed, as part of a memorandum of understanding covering the period between contracts, that the union and its officer post a bond covering damage due to sabotage or vandalism without regard to proof of liability. The Board concluded that although the proposal was a permissive, rather than mandatory, subject of bargaining, the employer did not bargain to impasse or lock out its employees over that issue.

An employer unlawfully insisted to impasse that employees execute a general release as a condition for a severance pay clause. The employer argued that the release "was so intertwined with severance pay as to be a mandatory subject in this context even if not in others." The Board rejected this contention, reasoning that "it would mean that a permissive subject of bargaining would become mandatory whenever it was presented together with a mandatory subject."[489]

A union is guilty of a refusal to bargain if it insists to the point of impasse that the employer furnish a bond for the payment of employees' wages and benefits[490] or to secure performance of

---

[485]NLRB v. Laborers Local 264 (D & G Constr. Co.), 529 F2d 778, 91 LRRM 2209 (CA 8, 1976), *enforcing sub nom.* Laborers Local 264 (J.J. Dalton), 216 NLRB 40, 88 LRRM 1192 (1975); Newberry Equip. Co., 135 NLRB 747, 49 LRRM 1571 (1962); NLRB v. F.M. Reeves & Sons, 273 F2d 710, 45 LRRM 2295 (CA 10, 1959), *adjudicated in contempt*, 47 LRRM 2480 (CA 10), *cert. denied*, 366 US 914, 48 LRRM 2071 (1961).

[486]Scripto Mfg. Co., 36 NLRB 411, 9 LRRM 156 (1941).

[487]Arlington Asphalt Co., 136 NLRB 742, 49 LRRM 1831 (1962), *enforced*, 318 F2d 550, 53 LRRM 2462 (CA 4, 1963).

[488]272 NLRB 502, 117 LRRM 1265 (1984), *supplemented*, 282 NLRB 314, 123 LRRM 1332 (1986). *See also* Ashe Brick Co., 280 NLRB 1383, 123 LRRM 1023 (1986) (subject of compensation for damages to company's property is permissive).

[489]Borden, Chem. Div., Thermoplastic Prods., 279 NLRB 396, 123 LRRM 1239 (1986) (distinguishing Sea Bay Manor Home for Adults, 253 NLRB 739, 106 LRRM 1010 (1980)). *See* Stamford Bd. of Educ. v. Stamford Educ. Ass'n, 697 F2d 70, 112 LRRM 2605, 30 FEP Cases 1379 (CA 2, 1982) (provision in collective bargaining agreement in which union agreed to hold employer harmless for any judgments, costs, and fees incurred in defending sex discrimination claim was contrary to public policy expressed in Title VII, and, therefore, void).

[490]Excello Dry Wall Co., 145 NLRB 663, 55 LRRM 1015 (1963). *See also* NLRB v. Frost-Whited Co., American Compress Warehouse Div., 350 F2d 365, 59 LRRM 2739 (CA 5, 1965), *cert. denied*, 382 US 982, 61 LRRM 2147 (1966). *Cf.* Bricklayers Local 3 (Associated

the contract.[491]

In *Radiator Specialty Co.*,[492] the Board held that a clause subjecting a union to liability for violation of a no-strike clause is a permissive subject of bargaining. The Fourth Circuit disagreed; it held such clause to be entirely different from an indemnity requirement and therefore a mandatory subject.[493] The court viewed the clause as simply stating what the law provides. In a case which arose before the enactment of section 301, the Board held that an employer violated the Act by insisting, as a condition to execution of an agreement, that the union register with a state court in order to make it amenable to any suit that might be brought thereafter by the employer.[494]

6. Administrative Expense Funds. The Board has held, with the approval of the Eighth Circuit, that a union violates section 8(b)(3) by insisting to impasse on a contract provision that would require the employer to contribute to a fund created to ensure that the employer pays for the cost of administering various employee fringe benefit funds.[495] The nexus between the means by which the administrative expenses would be paid and the ultimate provision of the fringe benefits to employees was deemed insufficient to make the fund a mandatory subject of bargaining.

7. Interest Arbitration and Bi-Level Bargaining. The Board has consistently held that clauses in which a party agrees to use interest arbitration to settle a future contract are permissive and not mandatory subjects of bargaining. In *Mechanical Contractors Ass'n of Newburgh*,[496] the parties had agreed in successive con-

---

Gen. Contractors, Eastern Wash. Builders Chapter), 162 NLRB 476, 64 LRRM 1085 (1966), *enforced*, 405 F2d 469, 69 LRRM 2944 (CA 9, 1968) (union may not insist on penalty clause calling for reimbursement to union for dues and initiation fees lost as result of improper subcontracting).

[491]Painters Local 164, 1010, 1287 v. NLRB (Cheatham Painting Co.), 293 F2d 133, 48 LRRM 2060 (CA DC), *cert. denied*, 368 US 824, 48 LRRM 3110 (1961).

[492]143 NLRB 350, 53 LRRM 1319 (1963), *enforced in part*, 336 F2d 495, 57 LRRM 2097 (CA 4, 1964). *See* North Carolina Furniture, 121 NLRB 41, 42 LRRM 1271 (1958). *See also* Covington Furniture Mfg. Co., 212 NLRB 214, 87 LRRM 1505 (1974), *enforced*, 514 F2d 995, 89 LRRM 3024 (CA 6, 1975), where the Board held that an employer could not insist upon union agreement to indemnify the employer against any threats, coercion, harassment, or intimidation of employees who were not union members. In Hall Tank Co., 214 NLRB 995, 88 LRRM 1208 (1974), the Board held unlawful an employer's insistence upon an indemnification clause as the quid pro quo for a grievance and arbitration provision.

[493]Radiator Specialty Co. v. NLRB, 336 F2d 495, 57 LRRM 2097 (CA 4, 1964).

[494]Dalton Tel. Co., 82 NLRB 1001, 24 LRRM 1001 (1949), *enforced*, 187 F2d 811, 27 LRRM 2503 (CA 5), *cert. denied*, 342 US 824, 28 LRRM 2625 (1951).

[495]Laborers Local 264 (D & G Constr. Co.), *supra* note 485.

[496]202 NLRB 1, 82 LRRM 1438 (1973).

tracts that an Industrial Relations Council (IRC) composed of members selected by the international union and the employer association would resolve outstanding bargaining issues. The union objected to the IRC's decision to include the clause in the next contract, and the ALJ agreed that the employer's insistence violated section 8(a)(5). The Board distinguished the IRC clause from traditional interest arbitration clauses because the IRC clause merely created a bi-level bargaining system and did not represent an irretrievable surrender of economic weapons.[497] Having found that the clause merely extended the bargaining process to a higher level of authority and that no impasse could be reached until this higher level had deadlocked, the Board found it unnecessary to decide whether an IRC clause was a nonmandatory subject of bargaining.

In *Printing Pressman Local 252 (Columbus) (R.W. Page Corp.)*,[498] the Board decided that an interest-arbitration clause is a permissive subject of bargaining. The Fifth Circuit agreed. The prior collective bargaining contracts, including the one in effect during the negotiations, had contained interest-arbitration clauses under which deadlocked bargaining issues were to be resolved through tripartite arbitration. Unlike *Mechanical Contractors Ass'n of Newburgh*, this case dealt with a true interest-arbitration clause upon which the union insisted to impasse, thereby violating section 8(b)(3). Thus, parties may voluntarily agree upon an interest-arbitration clause without violating the Act, but neither party may insist to impasse on its inclusion.

Subsequently, in *Plumbers & Pipefitters Local 387 (Mechanical Contractors Ass'n of Iowa)*,[499] the Board held that an IRC clause was a permissive subject of bargaining upon which a party could not insist to impasse. Unlike *Mechanical Contractors Ass'n of Newburgh*, the IRC had not reached a unanimous decision perpetuating the clause. In subsequent local negotiations, the union refused to accept an IRC clause in the successor contract. The Board adopted, without discussion, the ALJ's conclusion that

---

[497]The Board found that the procedures of the IRC differed from arbitration in that (1) the IRC panel was composed of interested parties in equal number; (2) the IRC's decisions were made only after the immediate parties to the negotiations had deadlocked; (3) the IRC's decision had to be unanimous; and (4) if the IRC panel could not reach a unanimous decision, the parties could resort to economic weapons.

[498]219 NLRB 268, 89 LRRM 1553 (1975), *enforced*, 543 F2d 1161, 93 LRRM 3055 (CA 5, 1976). *See* Chapter 18, "Accommodation of Board Action to the Arbitration Process," at notes 167–168.

[499]266 NLRB 129, 112 LRRM 1365 (1983). *See also* Electrical Workers (IBEW) Local 194 (Cahn Elec. Co.), 285 NLRB 328, 128 LRRM 1024 (1987).

the clause created an interest-arbitration mechanism, which would clearly render it nonmandatory. However, even if the IRC constituted "collective bargaining at a different level by a different set of negotiators," the clause was permissive only. So construed, the clause would be an attempt to dictate the composition of a party's negotiating team, a subject that is clearly permissive rather than mandatory.

Because interest arbitration is not a mandatory subject of bargaining and is strictly a creature of contract, an employer does not violate the Act by repudiating an interest-arbitration clause. Instead, the union must sue to compel arbitration or to enforce the award.[500] It is well established that a party may not use an existing interest-arbitration clause to perpetuate that clause; otherwise, "a party, having once agreed to the provision, may find itself locked into that procedure for as long as the bargaining relationship endures."[501] The Fifth Circuit explained that such a result would have the effect of binding the parties to forgo use of economic weapons in support of bargaining positions.[502] The Ninth Circuit has refused to enforce an arbitration award that reimposed the interest-arbitration clause in the successor contract.[503] In so holding, the court distinguished an earlier decision enforcing an ex parte award reimposing an interest arbitration clause in a successor contract on the ground that the employer's defenses were barred by its failure to move to vacate the award.[504] Similarly, the Eighth Circuit refused to enforce an ex parte award that renewed the

---

[500]Electrical Workers (IBEW) Local 113 (Collier Elec. Co.), 296 NLRB No. 144, 132 LRRM 1297 (1989) (union does not violate §8(b)(3) by suing to enforce interest-arbitration award where contract arguably binds employer to arbitrate, even where employer has withdrawn from multi-employer association whose contract governs arbitration); Tampa Sheet Metal Co., 288 NLRB 322, 129 LRRM 1188 (1988). *But see* Electronic Reproduction Serv. Corp., 213 NLRB 758, 87 LRRM 1211 (1974) (refusal to sign and apply contract settled by valid arbitration was §8(a)(5) repudiation of obligation to recognize and bargain with union). [**Editor's Note:** *See* Sheet Metal Workers Local 9 (Concord Metal), 301 NLRB No. 32, 136 LRRM 1338 (1991) *and* Sheet Metal Workers Local 20 (Baylor Heating and Air Conditioning), 301 NLRB No. 29, 137 LRRM 1175 (1991), for application of *Collier Elec.* to relationships established pursuant to §8(f).]

[501]Printing Pressmen Local 252 (Columbus) (R.W. Page Corp.), *supra* note 498, 543 F2d at 1169. *See* Connecticut Light & Power Co., 220 NLRB 967, 90 LRRM 1307 (1975), *enforced*, 538 F2d 308, 93 LRRM 2336 (CA 2, 1976); Pic Walsh Freight Co., 216 NLRB 627, 89 LRRM 1268 (1975); L&M Carpet Contractors, 218 NLRB 802, 89 LRRM 1732 (1975).

[502]NLRB v. Milgo Indus., 567 F2d 540, 97 LRRM 2079 (CA 2, 1977), *enforcing* 229 NLRB 25, 96 LRRM 1347 (1977).

[503]American Metal Prods. v. Sheet Metal Workers Local 104, 794 F2d 1452, 123 LRRM 2824 (CA 9, 1986).

[504]Sheet Metal Workers Local 252 v. Standard Sheet Metal, 699 F2d 481, 112 LRRM 2878 (CA 9, 1983).

interest-arbitration clause, the only point of contention between the parties in negotiation.[505] The circuit court reasoned that the union's insistence upon an interest-arbitration clause in a new contract would be an unfair labor practice, and that an award renewing such an interest-arbitration clause is thus unenforceable. The court did note, however, that once included in contracts, interest-arbitration clauses are generally enforceable.[506]

8. Internal Union Affairs. Mandatory subjects of bargaining concern relations between the employer and the employees, not between the union and the employees. An employer may request bargaining about internal union matters but may not insist to impasse over such proposals.

Thus, an employer may not insist upon a clause providing that nonunion employees shall have a right to participate in and vote at union meetings.[507] Nor may it insist upon a clause requiring a strike vote among employees before a strike occurs,[508] or upon employee ratification as a condition precedent to execution of a collective bargaining agreement,[509] or making further concessions.[510] Nor can an employer rely upon a tie vote to disavow an agreement negotiated with the union's leadership.[511] Nevertheless, in an Advice Memorandum, the General Counsel refused to issue a complaint where the employer insisted that the union honor an agreement to permit nonmembers to vote on the ratification of the contract. Recognizing that this demand was a nonmandatory subject of bargaining that could not have been advanced to impasse, the General Counsel reasoned that the union had acquiesced in the demand and could not evade its agreement with the employer.[512] The Board has ruled, how-

---

[505]Sheet Metal Workers Local 14 v. Aldrich Air Conditioning, 717 F2d 456, 114 LRRM 2657 (CA 8, 1983).

[506]Sheet Metal Workers Local 206 v. R.K. Burner Sheet Metal, 859 F2d 758, 129 LRRM 2866 (CA 9, 1988); *Id. See* Hotel Employees Local 703 v. Williams, 752 F2d 1476, 118 LRRM 2600 (CA 9, 1985) (interest arbitration directed after contract expiration where contract provided for interest arbitration only of wages and fringe benefits).

[507]NLRB v. Corsicana Cotton Mills, 178 F2d 344, 347, 24 LRRM 2494 (CA 5, 1949).

[508]*Id. See* Borg-Warner Corp., Wooster Div., 356 US 342, 42 LRRM 2034 (1958).

[509]Houchens Mkt. v. NLRB, 375 F2d 208, 64 LRRM 2647 (CA 6, 1967), *enforcing* 155 NLRB 729, 60 LRRM 1384 (1965); Movers & Warehousemen's Ass'n, 224 NLRB 356, 92 LRRM 1236 (1976), *enforced*, 550 F2d 962, 94 LRRM 2795 (CA 4, 1977).

[510]Zayre Dep't Stores, 289 NLRB 1183, 131 LRRM 1238 (1988); Freedom WLNE-TV, 278 NLRB 1293, 122 LRRM 1214 (1986); Borden, Chem. Div., Thermoplastic Prods., 279 NLRB 396, 123 LRRM 1239 (1986).

[511]NLRB v. Newtown Corp., 819 F2d 677, 125 LRRM 2629 (CA 6, 1987), *enforcing* 280 NLRB 350, 122 LRRM 1227 (1986).

[512]Nichols Homeshield, Amsco Div., NLRB Gen. Counsel Advice Memo., Case No. 18-CA-8439, 114 LRRM 1287 (1983).

ever, that an employer cannot deal directly with represented employees because the union refused to permit nonmembers to vote on the ratification of a contract.[513]

Similarly, a clause providing that the contract should become void if the percentage of employees paying their dues by checkoff dropped below 50 was held to be a permissive subject of bargaining.[514] Clauses that require the union to provide withdrawal cards to any employee who might be transferred out of the unit,[515] or that require that all shop stewards be chosen from particular classifications of employees are permissive.[516] The Board found an employer guilty of violating section 8(a)(5) by refusing to bargain unless the certified union was qualified pursuant to pertinent state law to engage in business as a labor union[517] and submitted an affidavit certifying that none of its officers was affiliated with the Communist Party.[518]

Similarly, an employer violates section 8(a)(5) when it insists to the point of impasse that a union withdraw fines previously imposed upon employees who, in violation of a union rule, had crossed picket lines during a strike,[519] or that any change in the union's constitution, bylaws, or affiliation would invalidate the contract.[520]

The Board has also ruled that the amount of an agency fee to be paid by employees who did not wish to become union members was not a mandatory subject of bargaining. Thus, a union did not unlawfully refuse to provide information concerning its revenues and expenditures to the employer.[521]

---

[513]Standard Fittings Co., 285 NLRB 285, 127 LRRM 1064 (1987), *enforced*, 845 F2d 1311, 128 LRRM 2613 (CA 5, 1988).

[514]NLRB v. Darlington Veneer Co., 236 F2d 85, 38 LRRM 2574 (CA 4, 1956) *Cf.* Bethlehem Steel, 133 NLRB 1400, 49 LRRM 1018 (1961) (indicating that it would be unlawful for employer to insist upon clause requiring individual signatures on grievances).

[515]NLRB v. Superior Fireproof Door & Sash Co., 289 F2d 713, 47 LRRM 2816 (CA 2, 1961).

[516]*Id.*

[517]Herron Yarn Mills, 160 NLRB 629, 63 LRRM 1022 (1966). *See also* NLRB v. Dalton Tel. Co., 82 NLRB 1001, 24 LRRM 1001 (1949), *enforced*, 187 F2d 811, 27 LRRM 2503 (CA 5), *cert. denied*, 342 US 824, 28 LRRM 2625 (1951).

[518]Herron Yarn Mills, *supra* note 517.

[519]Universal Oil Prods. Co. v. NLRB, 445 F2d 155, 77 LRRM 2005 (CA 7, 1971); Nordstrom, Inc., 229 NLRB 601, 96 LRRM 1092 (1977).

[520]Betra Mfg. Co., 233 NLRB 1126, 97 LRRM 1005 (1977), *enforced*, 624 F2d 192, 106 LRRM 2365 (CA 9, 1980), *cert. denied sub nom.* Thomas v. NLRB, 450 US 996, 106 LRRM 2817 (1981).

[521]Service Employees Local 535 (North Bay Regional Center), 287 NLRB 1223, 127 LRRM 1184 (1988).

9. Union Label. Although unions have long contended that the union label is sufficiently related to wages, hours, and conditions of employment for it to be a mandatory subject of bargaining, the Board rejects this view and holds that it is permissive. In *Kit Mfg. Co.*,[522] the Board noted that whatever economic advantage use of the label may afford an employer, and whatever impact it may have on the salability of its product, "its relation to wages, hours or other terms or conditions of employment is at best remote and speculative."[523] Nevertheless, an agreement that the contract contain a union "bug" is binding. Thus, a union did not refuse to bargain in good faith when it refused to execute a contract which, in violation of such an agreement, did not contain the "bug."[524]

10. Industry Promotion Funds. An industry promotion fund is a permissive subject for bargaining, and a union violates section 8(b)(3) by insisting to impasse on the adoption of a clause requiring employer contribution to such fund.

In the *Daelyte Service* case,[525] a member of a multi-employer bargaining unit refused to sign a contract negotiated by its employer association and the union, claiming that the clause requiring it to contribute to a promotion fund was illegal. The employer filed a refusal-to-bargain charge against the union, alleging that its conduct in demanding such a clause violated section 8(b)(3). Dismissing the complaint, the Board held that neither the demand by the union nor the acquiescence by the multi-employer group was unlawful. Since the parties had mutually agreed to the clause, there was no necessity for the Board to decide whether the subject was mandatory or permissive.

Shortly thereafter, in the *Mill Floor* case,[526] the Board squarely

---

[522]150 NLRB 662, 58 LRRM 1140 (1964), *enforced*, 365 F2d 829, 62 LRRM 2856 (CA 9, 1966).

[523]*Id.* at 662 n.1.

[524]Electrical Workers (IBEW) Local 1464 (Kansas City Power & Light Co.), 275 NLRB 1504, 120 LRRM 1057 (1985), *supplementing* 275 NLRB 557, 119 LRRM 1147 (1985). In the earlier case, the Board had held that the employer's refusal to have the contract printed with a "bug" was a peripheral matter which would not justify the union's refusal to sign the contract.

[525]Building Serv. Employees Local 139 (Daelyte Serv. Co.), 126 NLRB 63, 45 LRRM 1275 (1960).

[526]Carpenters Local 2265 (Mill Floor Covering), 136 NLRB 769, 49 LRRM 1842 (1962), *enforced*, 317 F2d 269, 53 LRRM 2311 (CA 6, 1963).

decided the issue. There, the union insisted to impasse on the following clause:

> Each employer agrees to contribute one (1¢) cent per hour for each hour worked by each Employee covered by this Agreement to [a] Promotional Fund. . . . A uniform collection machinery will be established to collect the contributions due under this section.[527]

The Board found the fund to be a permissive subject and the union's insistence upon it a violation of section 8(b)(3). The Board considered the industry promotion fund "to be outside the employment relationship . . . ," concerned "rather with the relationship of employers to one another, or, like advertising, with the relationship of an employer to the consuming public."[528]

Upon the expiration of a contract requiring contributions to such a fund, an employer may lawfully cease contributing to the fund without negotiating to impasse.[529] Even where the employer unlawfully repudiates the contract, the Board will not require the employer to make delinquent payments to an industry promotion fund.[530]

11. Employees Excluded From Coverage of the Act: Supervisors and Agricultural Labor.[531] Although the Act is not applicable to supervisors or to agricultural labor, the Board has held that the parties may bargain about such categories of employees. But a party may not insist, to the point of refusing to sign a contract applicable to employees covered by the Act, that the contract cover supervisors[532] or agricultural labor.[533] Furthermore, an employer is not obligated to bargain about the

---

[527]*Id.* at 776.

[528]*Id.* at 771.

[529]Big D Serv. Co., 267 NLRB No. 25, 113 LRRM 1144 (1983). *See also* Sheet Metal Workers Local 206 v. West Coast Sheet Metal Co., 660 F Supp 1500, 125 LRRM 3201 (SD Cal, 1987).

[530]Service Art Co., 291 NLRB 234, 131 LRRM 1280 (1988), *enforced*, 872 F2d 1027 (CA 6, 1989); American Thoro-Clean, 283 NLRB 1107, 125 LRRM 1115 (1987), *supplemented*, 283 NLRB 1120, 125 LRRM 1137 (1987); Carthage Sheet Metal Co., 286 NLRB 1249, 129 LRRM 1053 (1987).

[531]See Chapter 28, "Coverage of the Act," at notes 213–245 and 279–289, for a discussion of supervisors and agricultural laborers, respectively.

[532]NLRB v. Retail Clerks Local 648 (Safeway Stores), 203 F2d 165, 31 LRRM 2606 (CA 9, 1953), adjudging union in contempt for insisting on bargaining for supervisory employees in violation of a consent decree enforcing Safeway Stores, 96 NLRB 581, 28 LRRM 1554 (1951), *cert. denied sub nom.* NLRB v. Retail Clerks Local 648, 348 US 839, 34 LRRM 2898 (1954); Plumbers & Pipefitters S. Cal. Dist. Council 16 (Aero Plumbing Co.), 167 NLRB 1004, 66 LRRM 1233 (1967), *enforced*, 449 F2d 668, 78 LRRM 2260 (CA 9, 1971).

[533]Mine Workers Dist. 50 (Central Soya Co.), 142 NLRB 930, 53 LRRM 1178 (1963).

promotion of employees to supervisory positions where the promotions do not eliminate unit classifications and do not have a substantial impact on the bargaining unit.[534]

12. Settlement of Unfair Labor Practice Charges. Neither party is compelled to negotiate with the other about the settlement of unfair labor practice charges filed with the Board.[535] Thus, if a party demands that charges against it be withdrawn as a condition to negotiating,[536] or if it seeks to condition wage increases upon the withdrawal of charges against it,[537] it violates the Act. Similarly, when one party insists to impasse that the other party abandon litigation[538] or withdraw a grievance for which the union is seeking arbitration, a violation occurs.[539]

In *Reichhold Chemicals*,[540] the Board held that a proposed waiver of the right to file unfair labor practice charges if the employer disciplined or replaced illegal strikers was a permissive subject of bargaining. Insistence to impasse on such a waiver was, accordingly, a violation of section 8(a)(5). In a prior decision involving the same parties, the Board had held that the

---

[534]Pittsburgh Metal Processing Co., 286 NLRB 734, 128 LRRM 1094 (1987).

[535]John Wanamaker Philadelphia, 279 NLRB 1034, 123 LRRM 1271 (1986); Griffin Inns, 229 NLRB 199, 95 LRRM 1072 (1977); Electrical Workers (IBEW) Local 1229 (Jefferson Standard Broadcasting Co.), 94 NLRB 1507, 28 LRRM 1215 (1951). *See also* Litton Indus. v. NLRB, 533 F2d 1030, 92 LRRM 2013 (CA 8, 1976), *enforcing* 209 NLRB 1006, 85 LRRM 1501 (1974), where the court enforced a Board order finding that an employer violated §8(a)(5) by conditioning bargaining upon withdrawal of unfair labor practice charges and upon a 60-day extension on the expiring contract. *But see* Star Mfg. Co. v. NLRB, 536 F2d 1192, 92 LRRM 3179 (CA 7, 1976), *enforcing in part* 220 NLRB 582, 90 LRRM 1360 (1975), where the Seventh Circuit sustained the employer's good-faith doubt of the union's majority status and found that the employer's insistence upon the withdrawal of unfair labor practice charges before the commencement of bargaining did not violate the Act; Carlsen Porsche Audi, 266 NLRB 141, 112 LRRM 1319 (1983) (no insistence to impasse).

[536]Stackpole Components Co., 232 NLRB 723, 96 LRRM 1324 (1977); Perry Publications, Inc., 151 NLRB 1030, 58 LRRM 1561 (1965); Ohio Car & Truck Leasing, 149 NLRB 1423, 58 LRRM 1008 (1964); Silby-Dolcourt Chem. Indus., 145 NLRB 1348, 55 LRRM 1160 (1964); Kit Mfg. Co., 142 NLRB 957, 53 LRRM 1178 (1963), *enforced in part*, 335 F2d 166, 56 LRRM 2988 (CA 9, 1964), *cert. denied*, 380 US 910, 58 LRRM 2496 (1965).

[537]Butcher Boy Refrigerator Door Co., 127 NLRB 1360, 46 LRRM 1192 (1960), *enforced*, 290 F2d 22, 48 LRRM 2058 (CA 7, 1961).

[538]NLRB v. Carpenters Local 964 (Contractors & Suppliers Ass'n of Rockland County, N.Y.), 447 F2d 643, 78 LRRM 2167 (CA 2, 1971) (union was found to have violated §8(b)(3) by insisting that employer association with which it was negotiating abandon litigation concerning management of trust fund and agree to employ as trustees of trust fund only employers of Carpenters); Stackpole Components Co., *supra* note 536; Peerless Food Prods., 231 NLRB 530, 96 LRRM 1048 (1977).

[539]Inner City Broadcasting Corp., 270 NLRB 1230, 116 LRRM 1347 (1984); Good GMC, 267 NLRB 583, 114 LRRM 1033 (1983); B.C. Studios, Inc., 217 NLRB 307, 89 LRRM 1126 (1975) (employer violates §8(a)(5) by conditioning continued bargaining on union's withdrawal from arbitration of grievance relating to backpay wage claim on behalf of certain employees).

[540]288 NLRB 69, 127 LRRM 1265 (1988), *supplementing* 277 NLRB 639, 120 LRRM 1339 (1985).

waiver of the right to file charges was a mandatory subject of bargaining because it was "merely derivative of the waiver of the right to strike."[541] Reversing itself on reconsideration, the Board reasoned that an in futuro waiver of Board access is "contrary to a fundamental policy of the Act and is unrelated to terms and conditions of employment."[542]

In *Plattdeutsche Park Restaurant*,[543] an employer violated section 8(a)(5) by refusing to sign a contract unless the union withdrew suits filed to collect delinquent trust fund contributions and agreed to the unlawful discharge of an employee.

13. Transcript of Negotiations. The use of a stenographer or recording device in negotiation is a permissive subject.[544] Extending this principle, the Board held that a party could not insist upon the continuation of a past practice of recording grievance sessions[545] or other contractually required meetings.[546] The recording of arbitration proceedings, however, is a mandatory subject of bargaining. The Board reasons that arbitration is a quasi-adjudicatory proceeding not necessarily concerned with the encouragement of the free and open discussion so vital to collective bargaining.[547]

14. Miscellaneous. In *Western Massachusetts Electric Co. v. NLRB*,[548] the First Circuit, denying enforcement of a Board order, ruled that an employer did not violate the Act by refusing to furnish information relating to a decision to subcontract where the decision itself was not a mandatory subject of bargaining. Had the decision fallen in the mandatory bargaining category, then the demand for information would have been presumptively relevant.

---

[541]*Id.*, 277 NLRB at 640.

[542]*Id.*, 288 NLRB at 71.

[543]296 NLRB No. 26, 132 LRRM 1109 (1989).

[544]Bartlett-Collins Co., 237 NLRB 770, 99 LRRM 1034 (1978), *enforced*, 639 F2d 652, 106 LRRM 2272 (CA 10, 1981).

[545]Water Ass'n, 290 NLRB 838, 129 LRRM 1064 (1988); Pennsylvania Tel. Guild (Bell Tel. Co. of Pa.), 277 NLRB 501, 120 LRRM 1257 (1985), *enforced*, 799 F2d 84, 123 LRRM 2214 (CA 3, 1986); Hutchinson Fruit Co., 277 NLRB 497, 120 LRRM 1258 (1985).

[546]Bakery Workers Local 455 (Nabisco Brands, Chuckles Div.), 272 NLRB 1362, 118 LRRM 1007 (1984).

[547]Communications Workers (Chesapeake & Potomac Tel. Co.), 280 NLRB 78, 124 LRRM 1009 (1986), *enforced*, 818 F2d 29, 125 LRRM 2352 (CA 4, 1987).

[548]573 F2d 101, 98 LRRM 2851 (CA 1, 1978), *denying enforcement to sub nom.* Connecticut Light & Power Co., 229 NLRB 1032, 96 LRRM 1348 (1977). [**Editor's Note:** In Dubuque Packing Co. (II), 303 NLRB No. 66, 137 LRRM 1185 (1991), the Board noted, but did not decide, the question of whether a request for information relating to work relocation must be honored even if the decision is not a mandatory subject.]

In *Salvation Army of Massachusetts, Dorchester Day Care Center,*[549] the Board held that the employer unlawfully conditioned its attendance at bargaining sessions upon the union's agreement to contract provisions that recognized the employer's "ecclesiastical or religious mission." Similarly, a loyalty clause requiring the employees and their representatives to use their best efforts to promote the employer's interests was not a mandatory subject of bargaining.[550]

In *Harvstone Manufacturing Corp.,*[551] the Board considered the question of whether an employer could insist to impasse upon the elimination of cost-of-living adjustments which had not yet been paid under an expired contract. The Board viewed the adjustments as an accrued benefit that had been already bargained. Accordingly, the modification of that benefit was a permissive subject of bargaining upon which one party could not insist. It distinguished the accrued benefit from current or future benefits which would be mandatory subjects. Similarly, in *Public Service Electric & Gas Co.,*[552] the Board held unlawful an employer's conditioning of a successor agreement on the union's "consent" to the abrogation of a retroactivity clause in the expired contract.

In *United Technologies Corp.,*[553] the Board held that union proposals to control the use of student/employees in the summer was permissive where the summer employees were not included in the bargaining unit and the union disclaimed any interest in representing them. The Board concluded that the summer employees did not "vitally affect" unit employees because there was no claim that unit employees lost any work opportunities. Thus, the Board viewed the existence and continuation of the summer program itself as discretionary.

---

[549]271 NLRB 195, 116 LRRM 1410 (1984), *enforced,* 763 F2d 1, 119 LRRM 2587 (CA 1, 1985).

[550]Meda-Care Ambulance, 285 NLRB 471, 128 LRRM 1276 (1987).

[551]272 NLRB 939, 117 LRRM 1447 (1984), *enforcement denied,* 785 F2d 570, 121 LRRM 3371 (CA 7), *cert. denied sub nom.* Electrical Workers (IBEW) Local 134 v. Harvstone Mfg. Corp., 479 US 821, 123 LRRM 2591 (1986). The court denied enforcement on the ground that neither the contractually enforceable duty to pay the cost-of-living adjustments nor the employees' right to receive the adjustments arose during the life of the contract.

[552]280 NLRB 429, 123 LRRM 1314 (1986), *enforced without opinion,* 815 F2d 695, 125 LRRM 2152 (CA 3, 1987). *See also* R.E.C. Corp., 296 NLRB No. 163, 132 LRRM 1268 (1989) (provision retroactively accepting prior unilateral midterm modification is permissive).

[553]274 NLRB 1069, 118 LRRM 1556 (1985), *enforced sub nom.* NLRB v. United Technologies Corp., Pratt & Whitney Air Craft Div., 789 F2d 121, 122 LRRM 2250 (CA 2, 1986).

VI. ILLEGAL SUBJECTS OF BARGAINING

A. Relationship to Duty to Bargain

Neither party may require that the other agree to contract provisions that are unlawful under the Act.[554] In 1948 the Board stated:

> [W]hat the Act does not merit is the insistence, as a condition precedent to entering into a collective bargaining agreement, that the other party to the negotiations agree to a provision or take some action which is unlawful or inconsistent with the basic policy of the Act. Compliance with the Act's requirement of collective bargaining cannot be made dependent upon the acceptance of provisions in the agreement which, by their terms or in their effectuation, are repugnant to the Act's specific language or basic policy.[555]

Insistence upon an illegal provision thus violates the duty to bargain. Two prominent types of clauses that violate specific provisions of the Act are "closed shop" clauses (or other illegal union-security clauses), prohibited by sections 8(a)(3) and 8(b)(2),[556] and "hot-cargo" clauses, prohibited by section 8(e).[557] The relationship between illegal clauses and the duty to bargain has been defined as follows:

> Neither party may require that the other agree to contact provisions which are unlawful. And when . . . one of the parties creates a bargaining impasse by insisting, not in good faith, that the other agree to an unlawful condition of employment, that party has violated its statutory duty to bargain.[558]

---

[554]Meat Cutters Local 421 (Great Atl. & Pac. Tea Co.), 81 NLRB 1052, 23 LRRM 1464 (1949); National Maritime Union (Texas Co.), 78 NLRB 971, 22 LRRM 1289 (1948), *enforced*, 175 F2d 686, 24 LRRM 2268 (CA 2, 1949), *cert. denied*, 338 US 954, 25 LRRM 2395 (1950). *Cf.* concurring opinion of Mr. Justice Harlan in NLRB v. Borg-Warner Corp., Wooster Div., 356 US 342, 360, 42 LRRM 2034 (1958), where he said that "[o]f course an employer or union cannot insist upon a clause which would be illegal under the Act's provisions."

[555]National Maritime Union (Texas Co.), *supra* note 554, at 981–82.

[556]*See generally* Chapter 27, "Union Security."

[557]*See generally* Chapter 24, "Section 8(e): The 'Hot-Cargo' Agreement."

[558]Meat Cutters Local 421 (Great Atl. & Pac. Tea Co.), *supra* note 554, at 1061, in which the Board found a union's insistence upon an illegal union-security clause to be a violation of §8(b)(3) as well as §8(b)(2). *Note:* The primary emphasis in this part is upon those decisions dealing with illegal subjects of bargaining that are not included within a specific substantive area. For detailed discussion of decisions dealing with illegal "hiring-hall" or "closed-shop" clauses, see Chapter 27, "Union Security;" for "hot-cargo" provisions, see Chapter 24, "Section 8(e): The 'Hot-Cargo' Agreement"; for contractual violation of the duty of fair representation, including violations based on race, see Chapter 26, "The Duty of Fair Representation"; and for the effect that the inclusion of certain illegal provisions has upon the "contract-bar" doctrine, see Chapter 10, "Representation Proceedings and Elections."

Illegal subject cases generally arise in a context of other indicia of bad faith including the insistence upon such proposals to impasse. No decision has been found holding that the Act is violated merely by the proposal of an illegal subject, and in at least one case, the Board has declined so to hold.[559] If the proposal of an illegal subject of bargaining is a violation of sections 8(a)(5) or 8(b)(3) only when pressed to the point of impasse, the distinction between illegal subjects and permissive rights might seem at first to be of little significance. The import of the distinction lies elsewhere. Although a party may not insist on a permissive subject to the point of impasse, such a subject may by mutual approval of the parties be incorporated in the agreement. But an illegal subject may never be properly included in the agreement.[560]

It is less clear, however, whether the Act is violated by insistence on a provision that is legal under the Act but illegal under state law. In one case,[561] the Board considered a union's insistence upon the inclusion of any agency-shop clause claimed by the company and General Counsel to be illegal under the Arizona constitution and right-to-work statutes. The General Counsel's motion for summary judgment was denied by the Board by a vote of four-to-one. Two majority members could not determine the meaning of the clause with sufficient clarity to pass on its legality without an evidentiary hearing, while the two others stated that there was no authoritative state court opinion on the legality of such agency-shop agreements in Arizona.[562]

B. Specific Illegal Subjects

Although there are few decisions defining what constitute illegal subjects of bargaining, some guidelines are available. A

---

[559]Sheet Metal Workers Local 91 (Schebler Co.), 294 NLRB 766, 131 LRRM 1609 (1989). *See* text *infra* at note 590. As a practical matter, it is not likely that a party receiving the illegal request would file an unfair practice charge when the other party merely presents the illegal subject and does not press for its inclusion in the contract.

[560]Honolulu Star-Bulletin, 123 NLRB 395, 43 LRRM 1449 (1959), *enforcement denied on other grounds*, 274 F2d 567, 45 LRRM 2184 (CA DC, 1959).

[561]Steelworkers Local 4102 (Capital Foundry), 199 NLRB 153, 81 LRRM 1188 (1972).

[562]One member dissented, as he was persuaded that the agency-shop clause in question violated the Arizona constitution and statutes and that insistence upon its inclusion in the contract and a strike in furtherance thereof violated §8(b)(3). *See* Chapter 27, "Union Security," at notes 223–251, and Chapter 29, "Federal Preemption of State Regulation," at notes 322–337.

provision for a closed shop,[563] or for a hiring hall giving preference to union members,[564] and a "hot-cargo" clause in violation of section 8(e)[565] are commonly recognized illegal subjects of bargaining. Additionally, a union breaches its duty to bargain in good faith under section 8(b)(3) when it demands a contract provision that is inconsistent with the duty of fair representation owed by the union to the employees.[566] A proposal that requires separation of employees on the basis of race is an unlawful subject of bargaining.[567]

If a union seeks to have its rules and regulations incorporated in an agreement with an employer, a rule or regulation requiring discrimination in favor of union members must be excluded since it would violate the Act.[568] But the rule in question must explicitly call for illegal conduct to support a finding of violation.[569]

Since an employer's insistence that it have a contractual right to discharge employees for "union activity" is held to be a violation of section 8(a)(5),[570] such a contractual clause would undoubtedly be an illegal bargaining subject. And, since an employer's grant of a 20-year seniority credit to strikers who return to work during a strike has been held to be inherently discriminatory,[571] it should follow that such a superseniority plan is an illegal topic for bargaining.[572]

---

[563]Penello v. Mine Workers, 88 F Supp 935, 25 LRRM 2368 (D. DC, 1950); Honolulu Star-Bulletin, *supra* note 560. *See generally* Chapter 27, "Union Security." *See* Comment *Subjects Included Within Management's Duty to Bargain Collectively*, 26 LA. L. REV. 630 (1966).

[564]NLRB v. National Maritime Union (Texas Co.), *supra* note 554. *See* Chapter 27, "Union Security," for a discussion of hiring-hall agreements.

[565]Lithographers Local 17 (Graphic Arts Employers Ass'n), 130 NLRB 985, 47 LRRM 1374 (1961), *enforced*, 309 F2d 31, 51 LRRM 2093 (CA 9, 1962), *cert. denied*, 372 US 943, 52 LRRM 2673 (1963). *See also* Lithographers Local 78 (Employing Lithographers of Greater Miami), 130 NLRB 968, 47 LRRM 1380 (1961), *enforced*, 301 F2d 20, 49 LRRM 2869 (CA 5, 1962), and Chapter 24, "Section 8(e): The 'Hot-Cargo' Agreement."

[566]Longshoremen (ILA) Local 1367 (Galveston Maritime Ass'n), 148 NLRB 897, 57 LRRM 1083 (1964). *See* Chapter 26, "The Duty of Fair Representation."

[567]Hughes Tool Co., 147 NLRB 1573, 56 LRRM 1289 (1964). *See* Chapter 26, "The Duty of Fair Representation."

[568]NLRB v. News Syndicate Co., 365 US 695, 47 LRRM 2916 (1961).

[569]*Id.* at 699–700 (citing NLRB v. News Syndicate Co., 279 F2d 323, 46 LRRM 2295 (CA 2, 1960)).

[570]Gay Paree Undergarment Co., 91 NLRB 1363, 27 LRRM 1006 (1950).

[571]NLRB v. Erie Resistor Corp., 373 US 221, 53 LRRM 2121 (1963). *See* Chapter 7, "Discrimination in Employment," at notes 88–94.

[572]*See* Great Lakes Carbon Corp. v. NLRB, 360 F2d 19, 62 LRRM 2088 (CA 4, 1966), holding that a negotiated contract provision giving superseniority to replacements for striking employees was unlawful on its face and must be eliminated from the contract. *But cf.* Philip Carey Mfg. Co. v. NLRB, 331 F2d 720, 55 LRRM 2821 (CA 6, 1964), *cert. denied*, 379 US 888, 57 LRRM 2307 (1964).

The federal antitrust statutes[573] may also determine the illegality of certain subjects of bargaining. As the Supreme Court declared in *Mine Workers v. Pennington*:[574] [A]n agreement resulting from union-employer negotiations" is not "automatically exempt from Sherman Act scrutiny simply because the negotiations involve a compulsory subject of bargaining. . . . [T]here are limits to what a union or an employer may offer or extract in the name of wages," so that antitrust laws are violated when a union agrees "with one set of employers to impose a wage scale on other bargaining units."[575]

Insistence upon a tripartite arbitration panel to resolve work jurisdiction disputes when the management representatives are neither chosen nor designated by the employer violates the Act.[576] The union's good-faith but mistaken belief that the demand was legal and hence a mandatory subject of bargaining is not a defense to a charge of refusal to bargain.[577]

An employer may nevertheless be required to bargain with a newly certified union prior to eliminating practices in which its supervisors had traditionally acquiesced, even though these practices may entail violations of law. For example, in *Evening News Publishing Co.*,[578] the company and its employees had for many years engaged in various questionable overtime and reimbursement practices. In 1970 the company was purchased. Although the new management became aware of these practices, it took no steps to eliminate them until almost a year after the union had been certified. When the union protested the company's announced intention to discontinue the questionable practices, the company went through the formality of discussing the matter but at no time seriously considered changing its intention.[579] The company argued, inter alia, that it had not

---

[573]15 USC §§1–7, 12–27 (1964). *See generally* Chapter 29, "Federal Preemption of State Regulation."

[574]Mine Workers v. Pennington, 381 US 657, 59 LRRM 2369 (1965).

[575]*Id.* at 664–65. For a detailed discussion of *Pennington*, see Chapter 30, "Accommodations to Other Federal Enactments," at notes 26–33.

[576]Associated Gen. Contractors, Evansville Chapter v. NLRB, 465 F2d 327, 80 LRRM 3157 (CA 7, 1972), *cert. denied*, 409 US 1108, 82 LRRM 2139 (1973). The court reversed the Board's finding that the union demand did not violate §8(b)(1)(B) by restraining or coercing the association "in the selection of [its] representatives for the purpose of . . . the adjustment of grievances. . . ." *Id.* at 331. The Board did not petition for certiorari and subsequently applied the law of the case. Associated Gen. Contractors, Evansville Chapter, 200 NLRB 77, 81 LRRM 1557 (1972).

[577]465 F2d at 334.

[578]196 NLRB 530, 80 LRRM 1230 (1972).

[579]Although at one point after the practices had already been discontinued, the company proposed a general monetary increase to compensate employees for their losses in exchange for the union's concession of its union security clause. *Id.* at 535.

been obligated to bargain over the abrogation of immoral and illegal payment practices. Rejecting the argument, the Board declined to "pass a moral judgment on a practice joined in by employer representatives as well as by the employees."[580]

An employer violated section 8(a)(5) by insisting to impasse that the union acquiesce in its unlawful recognition of another union in another unit.[581]

In *NLRB v. Longshoremen (ILWU) Local 13 (Pacific Maritime Ass'n)*,[582] the Ninth Circuit enforced a Board decision that a union violated section 8(b)(3) by insisting to impasse on a hiring program giving preference for class B referrals to persons with 100 hours of longshoremen experience and requiring sponsorship for class A referrals. The court considered the union's background of past discrimination and held that insisting to impasse on these "illegal demands" violated the Act.

A union also violated section 8(b)(3) by insisting on the inclusion of a contract provision requiring the employer to pay an additional five cents an hour to union stewards, ostensibly for the purpose of reimbursing them for expenses incurred in administering the contract.[583] The Board ruled that the clause was presumptively unlawful because it conferred benefits exclusively on the union steward and because no evidence established the necessity for the payment.

An employer violated section 8(a)(5) by insisting on a strike settlement agreement in which it would reinstate striking employees only if the union guaranteed in writing that the employees would return to work for a specific period of time and would waive substantial legal rights of the employees.[584]

In *Chicago District Council of Carpenters (Polk Bros.)*,[585] the Board held that a union's insistence upon the inclusion of sub-

---

[580]*Id.* The Board said that even if the payments were not properly reported for tax purposes, that would still not abrogate the employer's duty to negotiate with the union prior to discontinuing them.

[581]Newspaper Agency Corp., 201 NLRB 480, 82 LRRM 1509 (1973), *aff'd sub nom.* Graphic Arts v. NLRB, 505 F2d 335, 86 LRRM 3234 (CA DC, 1974).

[582]549 F2d 1346, 95 LRRM 2215 (CA 9, 1977), *enforcing* 210 NLRB 952, 86 LRRM 1716 (1974), *cert. denied*, 434 US 922, 96 LRRM 2747 (1977).

[583]Teamsters Local 20 (Seaway Food Town), 235 NLRB 1554, 98 LRRM 1233 (1978).

[584]American Cyanamid Co., 235 NLRB 1316, 98 LRRM 1429 (1978), *enforced*, 592 F2d 356, 100 LRRM 2640 (CA 7, 1979).

[585]275 NLRB 294, 119 LRRM 1114 (1985). The General Counsel issued a complaint and obtained an injunction against the enforcement of a work-preservation clause designed to combat double-breasting where the union and nonunion companies had different job sites. D'Amico v. Painters Dist. 51 (Manganaro Corp. of Md.), 120 LRRM 3473 (D Md, 1985).

contracting restrictions prohibited by section 8(e) of the Act, as a condition of consummating any collective bargaining agreement, violated section 8(b)(3). Exceptions pursuant to the construction industry proviso to section 8(e) were unavailing, since the employer's carpet installation operations did not qualify it as an employer in the construction industry.

The Board in *BASF Wyandotte Corp.*,[586] rejected a company's claim that various privileges that it had previously granted the union (such as use of office space and equipment) violated section 302 of the Labor Management Relations Act, and were, therefore, illegal subjects of bargaining that could be unilaterally discontinued. The Board concluded that the withdrawn privileges were not illegal under section 302 and were otherwise mandatory subjects of bargaining.

A clause making a contract terminable at will is repugnant to the basic policy of the Act.[587] Absent lawful or reasonable economic justification, insistence to impasse on such a clause violates the Act.

In a case arising under Title VII, the Second Circuit held that a "hold harmless" clause relating to sex discrimination was void as against public policy.[588] Similarly, the Board held that an employer unlawfully demanded the modification of provisions in a court-approved Title VII settlement agreement that had been incorporated into their contract.[589] The settlement agreement had a 5-year term which had not yet expired.

But a union that proposed a clause unlawful under section 8(e) in response to an employer's midterm request for wage

---

586 274 NLRB 978, 119 LRRM 1035 (1985), *enforced*, 798 F2d 849, 123 LRRM 2320 (CA 5, 1986). The changes instituted included the following: (1) requiring the union to cease using an office, including office furnishings and telephone, previously provided by the company to the union for the purpose of conducting union business concerning bargaining-unit employees; (2) requiring the union to cease using the company's copying machine; (3) ceasing to provide the chairman of the union's workmen's committee with 4 hours of paid time each workday for conducting union business on company property; (4) ceasing to pay union committeemen and the chairman of the workmen's committee for working time spent meeting with employees to discuss grievances and complaints; (5) requiring the chairman and committeemen to obtain the permission of the company manager of human resources (as well as their own supervisors) before engaging in union business. *See also* BASF Wyandotte Corp. v. Chemical Workers Local 227, 791 F2d 1046, 122 LRRM 2750 (CA 2, 1986); Independent Stave Co., 278 NLRB 593, 122 LRRM 1104 (1986).

587 Massillon Hosp. Ass'n dba Massillon Community Hosp., 282 NLRB 675, 124 LRRM 1125 (1987).

588 Stamford Bd. of Educ. v. Stamford Educ. Ass'n, 697 F2d 70, 112 LRRM 2605, 30 FEP Cases 1379 (CA 2, 1982).

589 Chesapeake Plywood, 294 NLRB 201, 133 LRRM 1013 (1989).

cost reductions did not violate section 8(b)(3).[590] Because the union proposed the "integrity clause" in voluntary midcontract bargaining and because the union's proposal could have been modified to result in a lawful clause, the Board found that the union's insistence on the clause was not unlawful.

---

[590]Sheet Metal Workers Local 91 (Schebler Co.), 294 NLRB 766, 131 LRRM 1609 (1989).

Part V

ARBITRATION AND THE ACT

CHAPTER 17

RELATION OF BOARD ACTION TO ENFORCEMENT OF AGREEMENTS UNDER SECTION 301

I. INTRODUCTION

Collective bargaining generally results in a collective bargaining contract.[1] This chapter explores the relation of Board action to the enforcement of the contract.[2] The question of accommodating Board action to the arbitration process is reserved for the following chapter.[3] The present chapter is concerned with

---

[1]"The Act contemplates the making of contracts with labor organizations. That is the manifest objective in providing for collective bargaining." Consolidated Edison v. NLRB, 305 US 197, 236, 3 LRRM 645, 656 (1938).

[2]For bibliographic materials, see the following: St. Antoine, *Judicial Review of Labor Arbitration Awards: A Second Look at* Enterprise Wheel *and Its Progeny*, 75 MICH. L. REV. 1137 (1977); Feller, *The Coming End of Arbitration's Golden Age*, in ARBITRATION—1976, Proceedings of the 29th Annual Meeting, National Academy of Arbitrators, 97 (B. Dennis & G. Somers eds. 1976); Feller, *A General Theory of the Collective Bargaining Agreement*, 61 CALIF. L. REV. 663 (1973); Summers, *Collective Agreements and the Law of Contracts*, 78 YALE L.J. 525 (1969); Meltzer, *Ruminations About Ideology, Law, and Labor Arbitration*, in THE ARBITRATOR, THE NLRB, AND THE COURTS, Proceedings of the 20th Annual Meeting, National Academy of Arbitrators, 1 (D. Jones ed. 1967) (also 34 U. CHI. L. REV. 545 (1967)); Sovern, *Section 301 and the Primary Jurisdiction of the NLRB*, 76 HARV. L. REV. 529 (1963); Feldesman, *Section 301 and the National Labor Relations Act*, 30 TENN. L. REV. 16 (1962); Aaron, *On First Looking Into the* Lincoln Mills *Decision*, in ARBITRATION AND THE LAW, Proceedings of the 12th Annual Meeting, National Academy of Arbitrators, 1 (J. McKelvey ed. 1959); Jenkins, *The Impact of* Lincoln Mills *on the National Labor Relations Board*, 6 UCLA L. REV. 355 (1959); Cox, *The Legal Nature of Collective Bargaining Agreements*, 57 MICH. L. REV. 1 (1958); Dunau, *Contractual Prohibition of Unfair Labor Practices: Jurisdictional Problems*, 57 COLUM. L. REV. 52 (1957); Bunn, Lincoln Mills *and the Jurisdiction to Enforce Collective Bargaining Agreements*, 43 VA. L. REV. 1247 (1957); Feinsinger, *Enforcement of Labor Agreements—A New Era in Collective Bargaining*, 43 VA. L. REV. 1261 (1957); Cox, *Rights Under a Labor Agreement*, 69 HARV. L. REV. 601 (1956); Wollett & Wellington, *Federalism and Breach of the Labor Agreement*, 7 STAN. L. REV. 445 (1955); Note, *Section 301(a) and the Federal Common Law of Labor Agreements*, 75 YALE L.J. 877 (1966); Comment, *The Emergent Federal Common Law of Labor Contracts: A Survey of the Law Under Section 301*, 28 U. CHI. L. REV. 707 (1961).

[3]Contracts usually contain agreements to arbitrate. Hence, many cases in this chapter which bear upon the interpretation of contracts by the Board will also involve arbitration.

the Board's practice and jurisdiction in relation to the collective bargaining agreement. It presents the statutory source of this jurisdiction, compares it with the jurisdiction of the courts under section 301,[4] and broadly analyzes the problems faced by the Board in interpreting a contract between an employer and a labor organization. In presenting the statutory source of section 301 jurisdiction, however, this chapter (in Part III, *infra*) treats extensively the parallel development of the law arising in section 301 actions under collective bargaining agreements, even though such law does not derive directly from the provisions of the National Labor Relations Act.

II. SECTION 10(a) POWER OF THE BOARD

Under section 10(a) of the Act, "[t]he Board is empowered . . . to prevent any person from engaging in any unfair labor practice . . . . This power shall not be affected by any other means of adjustment or prevention that has been or may be established by agreement, law, or otherwise . . . ."[5]

Prior to 1947, the same section read: "This power shall be exclusive, and shall not be affected by any other means of adjustment . . . ." In the Taft-Hartley amendments, the exclusivity of the Board's power to remedy unfair labor practices was modified by striking the words "shall be exclusive, and" and by adding a proviso. The amended section empowers the Board to cede jurisdiction to a state or territorial agency under certain conditions,[6] but the Board has never concluded a cession agreement with a state agency.[7]

However, the cases are treated here only because of their relation to general contractual problems.

[4]This chapter does not attempt full coverage of §301. Since this section is not part of the NLRA, it falls outside the direct scope of this treatise.

[5]See generally Chapters 31, "NLRB Procedures," and 32, "NLRB Orders and Remedies," for discussion of NLRB procedures, orders, and remedies.

[6]The proviso was drafted in response to the decision of the Supreme Court in Bethlehem Steel Co. v. New York Labor Bd., 330 US 767, 19 LRRM 2499 (1947). *See* S. REP. No. 105, 80th Cong., 1st Sess. 26, pt. 2 (1947); Street, Elec. Ry. & Motor Coach Employees v. Wisconsin Employment Relations Bd., 340 US 383, 397, 27 LRRM 2385 (1951); Algoma Plywood Co. v. Wisconsin Employment Relations Bd., 336 US 301, 313, 23 LRRM 2402 (1949). The *Bethlehem Steel* case had left a "doubt whether a state board could act, either after a formal cession by the National Board or upon a declination of jurisdiction 'for budgetary or other reasons.'" Guss v. Utah Labor Relations Bd., 353 US 1, 8, 39 LRRM 2567, 2570 (1957). The proviso to §10(a) "is the exclusive means whereby States may be enabled to act concerning the matters which Congress has entrusted to the National Labor Relations Board." *Id.* at 9, 39 LRRM at 2570.

[7]*See* Chapter 29, "Federal Preemption of State Regulation," at notes 343–344.

Under section 10, the Board has plenary jurisdiction over the adjudication of unfair labor practices, except where it cedes jurisdiction as provided in section 10(a) or declines jurisdiction as provided in section 14(c). The Act does not expressly prevent the Board from resolving questions of contract interpretation when necessary to the exercise of its jurisdiction over unfair labor practice charges, and it is settled that the Board possesses such authority.[8]

III. SCOPE AND PURPOSE OF SECTION 301

A. Background and Legislative History

1. Background. The Wagner Act of 1935[9] was directed at protecting employees' self-organization rights and, toward that goal, made unlawful employer practices that interfered with the employees' right to organize. The Wagner Act did not impose restrictions on union practices. Unions were often further insulated by the prevailing theory that they were not legal entities; thus, in many states they could not be sued directly for failure to honor their contractual obligations.[10] By the mid-1940s, the political climate had changed, and, in addition, the massive union organizing drives of the 1930s had produced ongoing collective bargaining in almost every major industry.[11]

The Taft-Hartley Act of 1947 imposed restrictions on union practices, including the section 8(b)(3) prohibition against refusing to bargain with employers.[12] It also sought to make collective bargaining agreements more readily enforceable at law. Section 301[13] was enacted to give the federal courts power to enforce collective bargaining agreements in suits by and against labor organizations.

---

[8]NLRB v. C & C Plywood Corp., 385 US 421, 64 LRRM 2065 (1967), discussed at notes 286–293, *infra*.

[9]*See* Chapters 1, "Historical Background of the Wagner Act," and 2, "The Wagner Act Period."

[10]*See* Pullman Standard Car Mfg. v. Steelworkers Local 2928, 152 F2d 493, 17 LRRM 624 (CA 7, 1945).

[11]*See* Cox, *Some Aspects of the Labor Management Relations Act, 1947*, 61 HARV. L. REV. 274, 277 (1947). *See* Chapter 3, "The Taft-Hartley Changes."

[12]Cox, *supra* note 11.

[13]61 Stat. 156 (1947), 29 USC §185 (1988).

2. Legislative History. Section 301(a) of the Labor Management Relations Act provides:[14]

> Suits for violation of contracts between an employer and a labor organization representing employees in an industry affecting commerce as defined in this Act, or between any such labor organizations, may be brought in any district court of the United States having jurisdiction of the parties, without respect to the amount in controversy or without regard to the citizenship of the parties.[15]

As early as 1943, Congress had considered questions of union responsibility under a collective bargaining agreement.[16] In 1946 Congress passed a bill making voluntary associations suable in the federal courts;[17] this bill was vetoed by the President.[18] In the 80th Congress, bills were introduced to make

---

[14]A summary of the legislative history of §301 is given in the appendix to Justice Frankfurter's dissenting opinion in Textile Workers v. Lincoln Mills, 353 US 448, 485, 40 LRRM 2113 (1957). It is also discussed in Westinghouse Salaried Employees v. Westinghouse Elec. Corp., 348 US 437, 35 LRRM 2643 (1955) (Frankfurter, J.), and in the majority opinion of *Lincoln Mills*. In spite of the judicial reliance on that legislative history, one court has described it as "extremely fragmentary." McCarroll v. Carpenters Dist. Council of Los Angeles County, 49 Cal2d 45, 58, 315 P2d 322, 329, 40 LRRM 2709 (1957). *See also* Chapter 3, "The Taft-Hartley Changes."

[15]61 Stat. 156 (1947), 29 USC §185 (1988). The discussion in this chapter is limited to application of §301 to collective bargaining agreements. However, that section has been held applicable to an expanding array of other agreements, including: (1) union constitutions, Plumbers & Pipe Fitters Local 334 v. Plumbers & Pipe Fitters, 452 US 615, 107 LRRM 2715 (1981); Boilermakers v. Olympic Plating Indus., 870 F2d 1085, 130 LRRM 3001 (CA 6, 1989); Boilermakers v. Cement Workers Local Lodge D111, 858 F2d 1559, 129 LRRM 2810 (CA 11, 1988), *cert. denied*, 490 US 1047, 131 LRRM 2200 (1989); Machinists Dist. 94, Local 1484 v. Longshoremen (ILWU) Local 13, 781 F2d 685, 121 LRRM 2837 (CA 9, 1986); Trail v. Teamsters, 542 F2d 961, 93 LRRM 3076 (CA 6, 1976); Hotel Employees Local 400 v. Svacek, 431 F2d 705, 75 LRRM 2427 (CA 9, 1970); (2) jurisdictional agreements and Article XX of the AFL-CIO constitution, Machinists Dist. 94, Local 1484 v. Longshoremen (ILWU) Local 13, *supra*; Santos v. Carpenters Dist. Council of New York & Vicinity, 547 F2d 197, 199 n.1, 94 LRRM 2244, 2245 n.1 (CA 2, 1977); Drywall Tapers & Pointers Local 1974 v. Plasterers & Cement Masons Local 60, 537 F2d 669, 92 LRRM 3203 (CA 2, 1976); (3) merger agreements between two unions, Boilermakers v. Cement Workers Local D111, *supra*; Boilermakers v. Szoke, 128 LRRM 2496 (ED Pa, 1987), *aff'd*, 835 F2d 283, 128 LRRM 2567 (CA 3, 1987); and (4) an international's action to enforce a trusteeship, Boilermakers v. Boilermakers Local 714, 845 F2d 687, 128 LRRM 2259 (CA 7, 1988). *See, generally*, Note, *Applying the "Contracts Between Labor Organizations" Clause of Taft-Hartley Section 301: A Plea for Restraint*, 69 YALE L.J. 299 (1959). Section 301 has been held not to extend to: (1) internal union-employee agreements, Distler v. Mine Workers, 711 F2d 76, 113 LRRM 3588 (CA 7, 1983); (2) agreements between a company and a union not comprised of that company's employees, Marine Eng'rs Dist. 2 v. Grand Bassa Tankers, 663 F2d 392, 108 LRRM 2873 (CA 2, 1981), *but see* Retail Clerks Locals 128 & 633 v. Lion Dry Goods, 369 US 17, 49 LRRM 2670 (1962); or (3) guaranty agreements between a contractor and subcontractor, Xaros v. US Fidelity & Guaranty Co., 820 F2d 1176, 125 LRRM 3119 (CA 11, 1987).

[16]*E.g.*, H.R. 1781, 78th Cong., 1st Sess. (1943) (federal incorporations); S. 1641, 79th Cong., 1st Sess. (1945) (sanctions for contract violators); S. 1656, 79th Cong., 1st Sess. (1945) (cause of action for strikes in violation of contract); S. 55, 80th Cong., 1st Sess. (1947) (federal jurisdiction); S. 937, 80th Cong., 1st Sess. (1947) (federal labor courts).

[17]*See* S. REP. No. 1177, 79th Cong., 2d Sess., pt. 2, at 3–4, 10–14 (1946).

[18]H. R. DOC. NO. 651, 79th Cong., 2d Sess. (1946).

collective bargaining contracts mutually enforceable.[19] It was in this same Congress that the Taft-Hartley Act was adopted, including section 301. This section has raised multitudinous issues of interpretation, preemption, and jurisdiction—many of which have a bearing on the Board's power to interpret a collective bargaining contract.

Congress sought in section 301 to add stability to labor relations by providing a means to enforce agreements between unions and employers. The Senate report stated that "[s]tatutory recognition of the collective agreement as a valid, binding, and enforceable contract is a logical and necessary step. It will promote a higher degree of responsibility upon the parties to such agreements, and will thereby promote industrial peace."[20]

The Senate bill contained a proposal to make a breach of contract an unfair labor practice. This was deleted in conference on the ground that "[o]nce the parties have made a collective bargaining contract the enforcement of that contract should be left to the law and not to the National Labor Relations Board."[21]

B. A Source of Federal Substantive Law

The first major issue in litigation based on section 301 was whether this section authorized the application of federal substantive law or whether it was simply procedural. In *Westinghouse Salaried Employees v. Westinghouse Electric Corp.*[22] a divided Supreme Court refused to permit a union to recover wages owed to individual employees which had allegedly been withheld in violation of a collective bargaining agreement. There was no majority opinion, although six justices in three opinions concurred that the section did not permit a union to enforce what was said to be a personal right of the employees.[23] The opinions discussed several issues which had attended prior litigation over

---

[19]H. R. 3020, 80th Cong., 1st Sess., §302 (1947); S. 1126, 80th Cong., 1st Sess., §301 (1947).

[20]S. REP. NO. 105, 80th Cong., 1st Sess. 17–18 (1947).

[21]H.R. CONF. REP. NO. 510, 80th Cong., 1st Sess. 42 (1947). *See* C & C Plywood, 148 NLRB 414, 57 LRRM 1015 (1964); *see also* Chapter 18, "Accommodation of Board Action to the Arbitration Process," at notes 23–27.

[22]*Supra* note 14.

[23]*Id.* at 439–61 (Frankfurter, Burton & Minton, J.J.): *id.* at 461 (Warren, C.J., Clark, J.); *id.* at 464 (Reed, J.). These rights are variously characterized as "peculiar to the individual benefit which is their subject matter," *id.* at 460; "uniquely personal," *id.* at 461; and arising "from separate hiring contracts between the employer and the employee," *id.* at 464.

section 301[24] but did not resolve them. The Court's plurality opinion, written by Justice Frankfurter, concluded that the language of the statute and the legislative history indicated that the section was "a mere procedural provision"[25] which did not create any substantive federal law to govern the enforcement of collective bargaining agreements.[26] Therefore, Justice Frankfurter found it difficult to sustain the view that suits under section 301 involved a federal question; and he also noted that such suits were not based on diversity of citizenship. Accordingly, a serious question was posed as to whether there was any constitutional basis for the exercise of jurisdiction by federal courts over suits under section 301. To avoid that issue and the difficulties which he believed would be presented by any attempt to elaborate a "federal common law" to govern the enforcement of collective bargaining agreements, Justice Frankfurter concluded that, whether or not the applicable substantive law (federal or state) recognized a right in a union to vindicate individual causes of action, "Congress did not intend to burden the federal courts" with such suits.[27]

Justice Douglas's dissent stated that Congress "created federal sanctions for collective bargaining agreements, made cases and controversies concerning them justiciable questions for the federal courts, and permitted those courts to fashion from the federal statute, from state law, or from other germane sources, federal rules for the construction and interpretation of those collective bargaining agreements."[28] In addition, the dissenters would have held that the union had standing to bring the suit.[29]

The basic constitutional question of *Westinghouse* was settled in the watershed case of *Textile Workers v. Lincoln Mills*.[30] The union had brought an action under section 301 for specific enforcement of an agreement to arbitrate. The Supreme Court, in an opinion written by Justice Douglas, declared that an agreement

---

[24]Does §301 give to the federal courts jurisdiction to apply state law? Is such a grant of jurisdiction in conflict with Article III, §2, of the Constitution? Does §301 create a federal substantive law? Or may the federal courts apply state law under a theory of "protective jurisdiction"? For relevant cases, *see id.* at 452 nn. 25 & 26. *See also* Textile Workers v. Lincoln Mills, *supra* note 14, at 450–51 nn. 1 & 2.

[25]348 US at 449.

[26]*Id.* at 459.

[27]*Id.*

[28]*Id.* at 465 (Black and Douglas, J.J.)

[29]*Id.*

[30]*Supra* note 14. Two companion cases were also decided: Goodall-Sanford, Inc. v. Textile Workers Local 1802, 353 US 550, 40 LRRM 2118 (1957); General Elec. Co. v. Elec. Workers (UE) Local 205, 353 US 547, 40 LRRM 2119 (1957).

to arbitrate is a "quid pro quo" for a no-strike agreement. Section 301 was viewed as expressing a federal policy that "federal courts should enforce these agreements . . . and that industrial peace can be best obtained only in this way."[31] The Court then held that "the substantive law to apply in suits under §301(a) is federal law, which the courts must fashion from the policy of our national labor laws."[32] It thus rejected the theory that section 301 is not itself a source of substantive law and is merely jurisdictional.

The Court charted the course of a new common law of the collective bargaining agreement. Although some substantive law could be found in the Labor Management Relations Act, Justice Douglas noted that

> [o]ther problems will lie in the penumbra of express statutory mandates. Some will lack express statutory sanctions but will be solved by looking at the policy of the legislation and fashioning a remedy that will effectuate that policy. The range of judicial inventiveness will be determined by the nature of the problem . . . . Federal interpretation of the federal law will govern, not state law.[33]

Nevertheless, state law "if compatible with the purpose of §301, may be resorted to in order to find the rule that will best effectuate the federal policy."[34] Such state law, however, is "not . . . an independent source of private rights."[35] Since federal law was at issue, the Court found no constitutional impediment; a case arising under section 301 is a case arising under the laws of the United States. "It is not uncommon for federal courts to fashion federal law where federal rights are concerned."[36] The Court then concluded that the unenforceability at common law of an executory promise to arbitrate future disputes was no barrier to the enforcement of such a promise under section 301.[37] It concluded, as well, that the federal courts had jurisdiction to enforce such a promise despite the strictures of the Norris-La Guardia Act.[38] The Court held that the employer should be ordered to arbitrate the claim presented by the union.

---

[31] 353 US at 455.
[32] *Id.* at 456.
[33] *Id.* at 457.
[34] *Id.*
[35] *Id.*
[36] *Id.*
[37] *Id.*
[38] *Id.* at 458. *See infra* at notes 160–281.

Although *Lincoln Mills* distinguished *Westinghouse*, it also undermined its rationale.[39] Thus it was no great surprise when in 1962, in *Smith v. Evening News Ass'n*,[40] the Supreme Court finally announced the demise of *Westinghouse*. At the same time, it held that under section 301 an individual employee, as well as a union, has a right to sue for the breach of a collective bargaining agreement.[41]

C. The *Steelworkers Trilogy*

From its inception, the new common law of the collective bargaining agreement featured the promotion of grievance arbitration as its centerpiece. In 1960 the Supreme Court enshrined that centerpiece in three protective decisions known as the *Steelworkers Trilogy*:[42] *American Manufacturing*,[43] *Warrior & Gulf*,[44] and *Enterprise Wheel*.[45] Justice Douglas was again the author of the Court's opinions.

In *American Manufacturing* the Court acted to discourage judicial intervention into the merits of the grievance prior to submission to arbitration. The case involved an employee who settled a worker's compensation action in which his physician had expressed the opinion that the employee's injury had rendered him permanently partially disabled. The employer relied on that opinion as the basis for refusing the grievant's claim to reinstatement and for its own refusal to arbitrate the grievance. The district court held the employee was estopped because of his settlement in the worker's compensation action. The Sixth Circuit affirmed[46] because, in its view, the grievance was frivolous, patently baseless, and thus not subject to arbitration.

---

[39]Even after *Lincoln Mills*, some courts continued to deny unions the right to sue for employee wages. *See, e.g.*, Machinists Local 2040 v. Servel, Inc., 268 F2d 692, 44 LRRM 2340 (CA 7, 1959).

[40]371 US 195, 199, 51 LRRM 2646 (1962).

[41]*But cf.* Republic Steel Corp. v. Maddox, 379 US 650, 58 LRRM 2193 (1965), requiring exhaustion of contractual grievance remedies before an action can be brought under §301. *See* Chapter 26, "The Duty of Fair Representation," at notes 45–64.

[42]For comprehensive analysis of the *Steelworkers Trilogy* and discussion of its progeny, see Morris, *Twenty Years of* Trilogy: *A Celebration*, in DECISIONAL THINKING OF ARBITRATORS AND JUDGES, Proceedings of the 33d Annual Meeting, National Academy of Arbitrators, 331 (J. Stern & B. Dennis eds. 1980).

[43]Steelworkers v. American Mfg. Co., 363 US 564, 46 LRRM 2414 (1960).

[44]Steelworkers v. Warrior & Gulf Navigation Co., 363 US 574, 46 LRRM 2416 (1960).

[45]Steelworkers v. Enterprise Wheel & Car Corp., 363 US 593, 46 LRRM 2423 (1960).

[46]Steelworkers v. American Mfg. Co., 264 F2d 624, 43 LRRM 2757 (CA 6, 1959).

The Supreme Court reversed, thereby rejecting application of the then popular *Cutler-Hammer*[47] doctrine. In *Cutler-Hammer* the New York courts had denied arbitration when "the meaning of the provision of the contract sought to be arbitrated" was deemed by the court to be "beyond dispute."[48] The Supreme Court recognized that even frivolous cases could be arbitrated if the subject matter was arbitrable: "Whether the moving party is right or wrong is a question of contract interpretation for the arbitrator."[49] It was not the function of the courts to construe a collective bargaining provision that was subject to arbitration. Rather, when parties had promised to arbitrate their disputes about the meaning and application of an agreement, the courts were to enforce that promise by sending the parties to the arbitrator.

The second *Trilogy* case was *Warrior & Gulf*,[50] where the union sought to compel the employer to arbitrate a dispute over the contracting out of maintenance work.[51] The employer relied on a provision in the collective agreement which stated that issues that were "strictly a function of management" were not arbitrable. The case thus concerned the question of *substantive arbitrability*.[52] Although the Supreme Court recognized that this was an issue to be determined by the court, it was to be determined with deference to the central role of arbitration under the collective agreement. Accordingly, the Court announced a *presumption of arbitrability*:

> An order to arbitrate the particular grievance should not be denied unless it may be said with positive assurance that the arbitration clause is not susceptible of an interpretation that covers the asserted dispute. Doubts should be resolved in favor of coverage.[53]

In *Enterprise Wheel*,[54] the third *Trilogy* case, the Court established a very deferential standard of judicial review of the

---

[47]In re Cutler-Hammer, Inc., 271 App. Div. 917, 67 NYS2d 317, *aff'd*, 297 NYS2d 519, 74 NE2d 464, 20 LRRM 2445 (1947).

[48]*Id.* at 918.

[49]363 US at 568.

[50]*Supra* note 44.

[51]*Cf.* Fibreboard Paper Prods. Corp. v. NLRB, 379 US 203, 57 LRRM 2609 (1964); Chapter 16, "Subjects of Bargaining," at notes 319–332.

[52]*Cf.* John Wiley & Sons v. Livingston, 376 US 543, 55 LRRM 2769 (1964), where the Court ruled that the determination of *procedural arbitrability* was properly the function of the arbitrator.

[53]363 US at 582–83.

[54]*Supra* note 45.

arbitrator's award. The case involved the discharge of several employees who had engaged in a work stoppage in protest of the discharge of a fellow employee. The arbitrator had found that although the work stoppage was improper, the discharges were not justified under the agreement. He therefore modified the discipline to a 10-day suspension.

The Fourth Circuit denied enforcement of the arbitrator's remedy on the ground that the backpay award for time subsequent to the expiration of the contract was unenforceable.[55]

It was the Supreme Court's view, as expressed in all the *Trilogy* opinions, that the parties had contracted for the arbitrator's judgment and the courts were not to reject that judgment merely because they disagreed with the interpretation of the arbitrator.[56] Accordingly,

> [t]he labor arbitrator's source of law is not confined to the express provisions of the contract as the industrial common law—the practices of the industry and the shop—is equally a part of the collective bargaining agreement, although not expressed in it.[57]

As the Court noted in a later case, the arbitrator was the "proctor"[58] of the parties' bargain. Consistent with that concept of the arbitrator's highly independent role, the Court in *Enterprise Wheel* approved the arbitrator's award and generally defined the limits of judicial review of an arbitrator's interpretation of the collective agreement. The respective roles of arbitrator and court were spelled out in the following language:

> [The] arbitrator is confined to interpretation and application of the collective bargaining agreement; he does not sit to dispense his own brand of industrial justice. He may of course look for guidance from many sources, yet his award is legitimate only so long as it draws its essence from the collective bargaining agreement. When the arbitrator's words manifest an infidelity to this obligation, courts have no choice but to refuse enforcement of the award.[59]

The court expressly declined to accept a standard of review that would require an arbitrator to apply the "correct principles of law to the interpretation of the collective bargaining agreement," because

---

[55]Steelworkers v. Enterprise Wheel & Car Corp., 269 F2d 327, 44 LRRM 2349 (CA 4, 1959).

[56]*Supra* note 44 at 578.

[57]*Id.* at 581–82.

[58]Alexander v. Gardner-Denver Co., 415 US 36, 53, 7 FEP Cases 81 (1974).

[59]*Supra* note 45, at 597.

> acceptance of this view would require courts . . . to review the merits of every construction of the contract [making] meaningless the provisions that the arbitrator's decision is final . . . . It is the arbitrator's construction which was bargained for; and so far as the arbitrator's decision concerns construction of the contract, the courts have no business overruling him because their interpretation of the contract is different from his.[60]

The strong presumption of arbitrability first announced in *American Manufacturing* and *Warrior & Gulf* was reaffirmed by the Supreme Court in *AT&T Technologies v. Communications Workers*.[61] In that case the union demanded arbitration of a dispute over layoffs. The employer refused, asserting that its decision that there was a lack of work necessitating layoffs was not arbitrable. The Seventh Circuit affirmed an order directing the employer to arbitrate, but directed the parties to submit to the arbitrator the issue of arbitrability.[62] The Supreme Court vacated and remanded. The Court first validated the presumption established in the *Trilogy* cases:

> [W]here the contract contains an arbitration clause, there is a presumption of arbitrability in the sense that "[a]n order to arbitrate the particular grievance should not be denied unless it may be said with positive assurance that the arbitration clause is not susceptible of an interpretation that covers the asserted dispute. Doubts should be resolved in favor of coverage."[63]

The Supreme Court found the presumption particularly applicable where the arbitration clause is broad.[64] In the absence of any express provision excluding a particular grievance from arbitration, only the most forceful evidence of a purpose to exclude the claim from arbitration will prevail.[65] The unanimous Court vacated and remanded, however, directing that the court, and not the arbitrator, must make the threshold determination that the dispute is arbitrable.[66] The circuit courts have

---

[60]*Id.* at 598–99.

[61]475 US 643, 121 LRRM 3329 (1986).

[62]Communications Workers v. Western Elec. Co., 751 F2d 203, 118 LRRM 2121 (CA 7, 1984).

[63]121 LRRM at 3332 (quoting Steelworkers v. Warrior & Gulf Navigation Co., *supra* note 44, at 582–83, 46 LRRM at 2419–20).

[64]121 LRRM at 3332.

[65]*Id.*

[66]On remand, the employer was ordered to arbitrate, Communications Workers v. AT&T Technologies, 125 LRRM 2085 (ND Ill, 1987).

enforced the strong presumption of arbitrability reaffirmed in *AT&T*,[67] and have done so in a wide variety of cases.[68]

Similarly, in *Paperworkers v. Misco, Inc.*,[69] the Supreme Court reaffirmed the narrow scope of judicial review of arbitration awards that was established in *Enterprise Wheel.* Reversing a court of appeals decision that had overturned an arbitrator's award, the Court held:

> [A]s long as the arbitrator is even arguably construing or applying the contract and acting within the scope of his authority, that a court is convinced he committed serious error does not suffice to overturn his decision.[70]

In *Misco,* the Court also reaffirmed the narrow base for overturning an arbitration decision on grounds of public policy, emphasizing its prior requirement that to justify judicial intervention, the decision must contravene "some explicit public policy" that is "well-defined and dominant," and is to be ascertained by reference to the laws and legal precedents and not from general considerations of supposed public interest.[71] Following *Misco,* the courts of appeal have diverged in their interpretation of the requirements for meeting the "public policy"

---

[67]*See, e.g.*, Sheet Metal Workers Local 20 v. Baylor Heating & Air Conditioning, 877 F2d 547, 131 LRRM 2838 (CA 7, 1989); Typographical Union Local 16 (Chicago) v. Chicago Newspaper Publishers' Ass'n, 853 F2d 506, 129 LRRM 2732 (CA 7, 1988); Teamsters Local 70 v. Interstate Distrib. Co., 832 F2d 507, 126 LRRM 3127 (CA 9, 1987); Communications Workers v. Michigan Bell Tel. Co., 820 F2d 189, 125 LRRM 2934 (CA 6, 1987); Bechtel Constr. v. Laborers, 812 F2d 750, 124 LRRM 2785 (CA 1, 1987); Pitta v. Hotel Ass'n of New York City, 806 F2d 419, 124 LRRM 2109 (CA 2, 1986). *But see* Contra Costa Legal Assistance Workers v. Contra Costa Legal Servs. Found., 878 F2d 329, 131 LRRM 2934 (CA 9, 1989); Oil, Chem. & Atomic Workers Local 7-1 v. Amoco Oil Co., 883 F2d 581, 132 LRRM 2283 (CA 7, 1989) (contracting out unit work not arbitrable); Pennsylvania Power Co. v. Electrical Workers (IBEW) Local 272, 886 F2d 46, 132 LRRM 2388 (CA 3, 1989) (setting wage rate for new job not arbitrable); Teamsters Local 315 v. Union Oil Co. of Cal., 856 F2d 1307, 129 LRRM 2249 (CA 9, 1988), *cert. denied*, 488 US 1043, 130 LRRM 2584 (1989).

[68]*See, e.g.*, Mine Workers Local 1545 v. Inland Steel Co., 876 F2d 1288, 131 LRRM 2693 (CA 7, 1989) (prior awards not given prospective effect); McKinstry Co. v. Sheet Metal Workers Local 16, 859 F2d 1382, 129 LRRM 2781 (CA 9, 1988) (third-party beneficiary's demand for arbitration); Eberle Tanning Co. v. Food & Commercial Workers Section 63L, 682 F2d 430, 110 LRRM 3136 (CA 3, 1982) (enforcing arbitration of employer's grievance); Mine Workers Dist. 5 v. Consolidated Coal Co., 666 F2d 806, 109 LRRM 2001 (CA 3, 1981) (determining application of prior settlement to new dispute).

[69]484 US 29, 126 LRRM 3113 (1987).

[70]*Id.*, 126 LRRM at 3117.

[71]*Id.* at 3119 (quoting W.R. Grace & Co. v. Rubber Workers Local 759, 461 US 757, 766, 113 LRRM 2641 (1983)). In *Misco*, the 5th Circuit refused to enforce an award directing reinstatement of an employee for alleged possession of marijuana on company property. The circuit court referred to a "public policy" against operation of dangerous machinery by drug-impaired persons, Misco, Inc. v. Paperworkers, 768 F2d 739, 743, 120 LRRM 2119 (CA 5, 1985). The Supreme Court was unanimous in reversing.

exception.[72] *Misco's* reaffirmation of the limited judicial review of arbitration awards has not precluded courts from vacating awards because arbitrators have exceeded their contractual authority,[73] frequently on grounds that appear to invoke public policy.[74]

Under certain limited circumstances, the conduct of a party during litigation has been found to preclude it from asserting the arbitrability of the underlying dispute as a defense to the action.[75]

D. Jurisdiction of the Courts: State and Federal

The jurisdiction of the courts under section 301 was clarified in *Charles Dowd Box Co. v. Courtney*[76] and in *Teamsters Local 174 v. Lucas Flour Co.*[77] In the first of these cases the Court held that state courts have concurrent jurisdiction with the federal courts

---

[72]*Compare* Delta Airlines v. Air Line Pilots, 861 F2d 665, 130 LRRM 2014 (CA 11, 1988), *cert. denied*, 493 US 871, 132 LRRM 2623 (1989) (vacating award reinstating pilot discharged for reporting to work and flying employer's airplane while intoxicated *and* Georgia Power Co. v. Electrical Workers (IBEW) Local 84, 707 F Supp 531, 130 LRRM 2419 (ND Ga, 1989) (vacating award reinstating employee discharged for drug use) *with* Northwest Airlines v. Air Line Pilots, 808 F2d 76, 124 LRRM 2300 (CA DC, 1986), *cert. denied*, 486 US 1014, 128 LRRM 2296 (1988) (upholding reinstatement of pilot discharged for intoxication) *and* Bechtel Constr. v. Laborers Dist. Council, 130 LRRM 2749 (ED Pa), *aff'd*, 865 F2d 249, 130 LRRM 2856 (CA 3, 1988), *cert. denied*, 489 US 1017, 130 LRRM 2856 (1989) (affirming award reinstating employee discharged for drug use). *See also* Stead Motors of Walnut Creek v. Machinists Lodge 1173, 886 F2d 1200, 132 LRRM 2689 (CA 9, 1989) (en banc) (reversing denial of enforcement of award of reinstatement); Communications Workers v. Southeastern Elec. Coop., 882 F2d 467, 132 LRRM 2381 (CA 10, 1989) (enforcing award reinstating employee discharged for sexual assault of customer); Crafts Precision Indus. v. Machinists Lodge 1836, 889 F2d 1184, 132 LRRM 3044 (CA 1, 1989) (enforcing award of reinstatement).

[73]Allen v. Allied Plant Maintenance Co., 881 F2d 291, 132 LRRM 2021 (CA 6, 1989); Geo. A. Hormel & Co. v. Food & Commercial Workers Local 9, 879 F2d 347, 131 LRRM 3018 (CA 8, 1989); Container Prods. v. Steelworkers, 873 F2d 818, 131 LRRM 2623 (CA 5, 1989); Electrical Workers (IBEW) Local 429 v. Toshiba Am., 879 F2d 208, 131 LRRM 2921 (CA 6, 1989).

[74]*See, e.g.*, Georgia-Pacific Corp. v. Paperworkers Local 27, 864 F2d 940, 130 LRRM 2208 (CA 1, 1988); Bruno's v. Food & Commercial Workers Local 1657, 858 F2d 1529, 129 LRRM 2815 (CA 11, 1988); Scott Paper Co., S.D. Warren Co. Div. v. Paperworkers Local 1069, 845 F2d 3, 128 LRRM 2175 (CA 1), *cert. denied*, 488 US 992, 129 LRRM 3072 (1988).

[75]*E.g.*, Jones Motor Co. v. Teamsters Local 633, 671 F2d 38, 109 LRRM 2793 (CA 1, 1982), *cert. denied*, 459 US 943 (1982) (union admitted jurisdiction, engaged in discovery, and moved for summary judgment); Hardline Elec. v. Electrical Workers (IBEW) Local 1547, 680 F2d 622, 110 LRRM 3041 (CA 9, 1982), *cert. denied*, 459 US 1170, 112 LRRM 2456 (1983) (employer asserted arbitrability but made no attempt to arbitrate or seek prompt stay pending arbitration); California Trucking Ass'n v. Teamsters Local 70, 679 F2d 1275, 108 LRRM 2955 (CA 9, 1981), *cert. denied*, 459 US 970, 111 LRRM 2744 (1982) (union repudiated contract directly before court); Reid Burton Constr. v. Carpenters Dist. Council of S. Cal., 535 F2d 598, 602–4, 92 LRRM 2321, 2323–25 (CA 10, 1976), *cert. denied*, 449 US 824, 105 LRRM 2657 (1980) (same).

[76]368 US 502, 49 LRRM 2619 (1962).

[77]369 US 95, 49 LRRM 2717 (1962).

over suits brought under section 301. In affirming the Supreme Judicial Court of Massachusetts, the Supreme Court held that section 301 does not divest the state courts of jurisdiction, but rather was meant to supplement state jurisdiction. Section 301 provides that suits of the kind described "may" be brought in the federal district courts, not that they must be.[78] The Court noted that "nothing in the concept of our federal system prevents state courts from enforcing rights created by federal law."[79]

In *Lucas Flour* the Court made clear, however, that federal law prevails in the substantive interpretation of labor contracts. Where local laws are incompatible with the principles of federal labor law, the former must give way to the latter.[80] In stressing the need for uniform law in cases arising under section 301, the Court noted that "the existence of possibly conflicting legal concepts might substantially impede the parties' willingness to agree to contract terms for final arbitral or judicial resolution of disputes."[81] The Court concluded that "in enacting Section 301 Congress intended doctrines of federal labor law uniformly to prevail over inconsistent local rules."[82]

E. Jurisdiction of the Courts: Preemption

As noted, *Lincoln Mills* established the jurisdiction of the courts to enforce collective bargaining agreements. Under the doctrine of federal preemption,[83] in matters arguably subject to section 7 or section 8 of the Act, "the States as well as the federal courts must defer to the exclusive competence of the National Labor Relations Board."[84] Nevertheless, a series of cases decided by the Supreme Court in 1962[85] securely established that the state and federal courts have jurisdiction over suits arising under collective bargaining contracts by virtue of sec-

---

[78]368 US at 506.

[79]*Id.* at 507.

[80]369 US at 104.

[81]*Id.*

[82]*Id.*

[83]*See* Chapter 29, "Federal Preemption of State Regulation," at notes 227–273, for a more detailed discussion of §301 and preemption. See also the discussion of preemption in fair representation cases in Chapter 26, "The Duty of Fair Representation," at notes 139–161.

[84]Building Trades Council (San Diego) v. Garmon, 359 US 236, 245, 43 LRRM 2838 (1959). *See* Chapter 29, "Federal Preemption of State Regulation," at notes 70–100.

[85]Smith v. Evening News Ass'n, 371 US 195, 51 LRRM 2646 (1962); Sinclair Ref. Co. v. Atkinson, 370 US 195, 50 LRRM 2420 (1962); Teamsters Local 174 v. Lucas Flour Co., *supra* note 77; Charles Dowd Box Co. v. Courtney, *supra* note 76.

tion 301, even though the conduct involved is arguably subject to the provisions of the NLRA.[86]

Conversely, in *Smith v. Evening News Ass'n*,[87] the Court expressly held that "[t]he authority of the Board to deal with an unfair labor practice which also violates a collective bargaining contract is not displaced by §301, but it is not exclusive and does not destroy the jurisdiction of the courts under §301."[88] That holding was reaffirmed in 1974 in *William E. Arnold Co. v. Carpenters District Council of Jacksonville & Vicinity*.[89]

The extensive preemption of conflicting state and federal regulation by this overlapping jurisdiction of the Board and the courts is dealt with elsewhere.[90]

F. Overlapping Jurisdiction: Conflict or Accommodation?

1. Federal and State Courts. *a. Concurrent Jurisdiction.* State and federal courts have concurrent jurisdiction in section 301 suits. Therefore "[i]t is implicit . . . that 'diversities and conflicts' may occur, no less among the courts of the . . . federal circuits, than among the courts of the several States . . . ."[91] It is the function of the Supreme Court "to resolve and accommodate such diversities"[92] under one federal law.

Lucas Flour[93] established the preeminence of federal law, which previously had been considered or applied by only a few of the state courts that had assumed jurisdiction in section 301 suits.[94] The Court reemphasized that "the subject matter of §301(a) 'is peculiarly one that calls for uniform law.' . . . The possibility that individual contract terms might have different

---

[86]Prior to these decisions, some courts had opted for the exclusive jurisdiction of the NLRB. *See, e.g.*, Chemical Workers v. Olin Mathieson Chem. Corp., 202 F Supp 363, 49 LRRM 2646 (SD Ill, 1962); Doll & Toy Workers v. Metal Polishers, 180 F Supp 280, 45 LRRM 2567 (SD Cal, 1960).

[87]*Supra* note 85.

[88]*Id.* at 197. The arguments in favor of the exercise of concurrent jurisdiction by the courts are thoroughly analyzed in Sovern, *Section 301 and the Primary Jurisdiction of the NLRB*, 76 Harv. L. Rev. 529 (1963).

[89]417 US 12, 86 LRRM 2212 (1974), and *infra* at notes 276–281.

[90]See Chapter 29, "Federal Preemption of State Regulation," concerning preemption of conflicting state regulation, and Chapter 30, "Accommodations to Other Federal Enactments," for treatment of conflicting federal regulation.

[91]Charles Dowd Box Co. v. Courtney, *supra* note 76, at 514, 49 LRRM at 2623.

[92]*Id.*

[93]Teamsters Local 174 v. Lucas Flour Co., *supra* note 77.

[94]*See, e.g.*, Machinists Local Lodge 774 v. Cessna Aircraft Co., 186 Kan 569, 352 P2d 420, 46 LRRM 2459 (1960); McCarroll v. Carpenters, Dist. Council of Los Angeles, 49 Cal2d 45, 60, 315 P2d 322, 330, 40 LRRM 2709, 2715 (1957), *cert. denied*, 355 US 932, 41 LRRM 2431 (1958).

meaning under state and federal law would inevitably exert a disruptive influence upon both the negotiation and administration of collective agreements."[95]

State courts exercising concurrent jurisdiction in section 301 suits must therefore apply federal substantive law.[96] The application of federal law cannot be evaded by artful pleading; a claim which is, in essence, a section 301 action, but is brought under diversity jurisdiction will be refashioned by the court thus requiring the utilization of federal law.[97]

b. Statutes of Limitations. In *DelCostello v. Teamsters*,[98] the Supreme Court decided that the applicable statute of limitations in a section 301 action should be derived from federal law. The Court found that an employee's hybrid action against both the employer (for violation of the collective bargaining contract) and the union (for breach of duty of fair representation) had no close analogy in state law, but rather presented an array of interests similar to those balanced by Congress in establishing the limitations period of section 10(b) of the Act.[99] Accordingly, the 6-month period of limitations prescribed in section 10(b) was applied. The *DelCostello* rule has since been applied to other hybrid actions.[100] But the *DelCostello* rule was inapplicable, and the state limitation on contract actions was invoked, where an employer repudiated all of its obligations under a collective

---

[95]369 US at 103.

[96]*See* Rubber Workers Local 1075 v. Rubber Workers, 716 F2d 182, 189, 114 LRRM 2614, (CA 3, 1983); Fraser v. James, 655 F Supp 1073, 1076 (D VI, 1987).

[97]*See* Marzuki v. AT&T Technologies, 878 F2d 203, 207, 131 LRRM 2941, 2945 (CA 7, 1989); Evans v. Einhorn, 855 F2d 1245, 1255, 129 LRRM 2094, 2102-02 (CA 7, 1988); Oglesby v. RCA Corp., 752 F2d 272, 118 LRRM 2203 (CA 7, 1985); Majewski v. B'nai B'rith Int'l, 232 App. DC 162, 721 F2d 823, 114 LRRM 3297, *amended*, 115 LRRM 2065 (CA DC, 1983); St. James v. Scot Lad Foods, 652 F Supp 1228, 1231–32, 125 LRRM 3498, 3500–1 (ND Ill, 1987); Turner v. General Motors Corp., 112 LRRM 2420 (ED Mich, 1982).

[98]462 US 151, 113 LRRM 2737 (1983). *See also* Chapter 26, "The Duty of Fair Representation."

[99]29 USC §160(b) (1988).

[100]*See* Alcorn v. Burlington N. R.R., 878 F2d 1105, 131 LRRM 3069 (CA 8, 1989); Communications Workers v. Western Elec. Co., 860 F2d 1137, 129 LRRM 2933 (CA 1, 1988); Adams v. Budd Co., 846 F2d 428, 128 LRRM 2387 (CA 7, 1988), *cert. denied*, 488 US 1008, 130 LRRM 2192 (1989); Wozniak v. Auto Workers Local 897, 842 F2d 633, 128 LRRM 2264 (CA 2, 1988); Pejic v. Hughes Helicopters, 840 F2d 667 (CA 9, 1988); Chrysler Workers Ass'n v. Chrysler Corp., 834 F2d 573, 126 LRRM 3223 (CA 6, 1987), *cert. denied*, 486 US 1033, 128 LRRM 2568 (1988); Metz v. Tootsie Roll Indus., 715 F2d 299, 114 LRRM 2340 (CA 7, 1983), *cert. denied*, 464 US 1070, 115 LRRM 2360 (1984); Ernst v. Indiana Bell Tel. Co., 717 F2d 1036, 114 LRRM 2740 (CA 7, 1983), *cert. denied*, 464 US 1041, 115 LRRM 2248 (1984); Perez v. Dana Corp., 718 F2d 581, 114 LRRM 2814 (CA 3, 1983); Benson v. General Motors Corp., 716 F2d 862, 114 LRRM 2919 (CA 11, 1983); McLinn v. Boeing Co., 715 F Supp 1024, 133 LRRM 2539 (D Kan, 1989); Machinists v. Caribe Gen. Elec. Prods., 718 F Supp 115 (D PR, 1989); Helms v. Yellow Freight Sys., 721 F Supp 277 (D Kan, 1989); Mallack v. Teamsters Local 805, 690 F Supp 276 (SD NY, 1988). *See also* Chapter 26, "The Duty of Fair Representation."

bargaining agreement, including the duty to arbitrate, even though the union had acquiesced in the repudiation.[101]

In *West v. Conrail*,[102] the Supreme Court held that *DelCostello* requires the filing, but not the service, of a complaint in a hybrid action within the 6-month limitation period.[103] Courts have struggled over when the 6-month limitation period commenced to run[104] and under what circumstances it will be tolled.[105] As a general rule, the employee's right to bring suit accrues when the employee knows, or should have known, of the union's breach.[106] The limitations period of a section 301 suit is not tolled by pursuit of a Board action.[107] But, the limitations period is tolled by an employee's good-faith attempt to rectify the contract breach, prior to suit, including the pursuit of internal union remedies, even if the pursuit ultimately proves futile.[108]

---

[101]Garcia v. Eidal Int'l Corp., 808 F2d 717, 124 LRRM 2195, 2196 (CA 10, 1986), *cert. denied*, 484 US 827, 126 LRRM 2495 (1987); O'Hare v. General Marine Transp. Corp., 740 F2d 160, 168, 117 LRRM 2038, 2044 (CA 2, 1984), *cert. denied*, 469 US 1212, 118 LRRM 2576 (1985) (*DelCostello* "cannot reasonably be expanded to all section 301 claims . . . which might also have established an unfair labor practice charge"). *Accord* Trustees of Wyoming Laborers Health & Welfare Plan v. Morgen & Osgood Constr. Co., 850 F2d 613 (CA 10, 1988); Cabarga-Cruz v. Fundacion Educativa Ana G. Mendez, 822 F2d 188, 125 LRRM 3163 (CA 1, 1987).

[102]481 US 35, 124 LRRM 3137 (1987).

[103]*Id. See also* Celeryvale Transp. v. M.W. Kellogg Co., 822 F2d 16 (CA 6, 1987); Cange v. Stotler & Co., 826 F2d 581, 599 (CA 7, 1987) (interpreting *West* to hold that Federal Rules of Civil Procedure govern where there is inconsistent state law dealing with commencement of hybrid actions). *But see* Winkels v. George A. Hormel & Co., 874 F2d 567, 569, 131 LRRM 2338, 2339–40 (CA 8, 1989) (*West* "simply cannot be read to require the imposition of federal procedural rules when the hybrid action is initiated in state court").

[104]Dement v. Richmond, Fredericksburg & Potomac R.R., 845 F2d 451, 128 LRRM 2235 (CA 4, 1988); Bonds v. Coca-Cola Co., 806 F2d 1324, 123 LRRM 3284 (CA 7, 1986); King v. New York Tel. Co., 785 F2d 31, 121 LRRM 2758 (CA 2, 1986); Adkins v. Electrical Workers (IUE), 769 F2d 330, 119 LRRM 3594 (CA 6, 1985); Samples v. Ryder Truck Lines, 755 F2d 881, 118 LRRM 3233 (CA 11, 1985); Lewis v. Laborers Local 100, 750 F2d 1368, 118 LRRM 2146 (CA 7, 1984). In an action under Title VII of the Civil Rights Act of 1964, the Supreme Court held, in an action for injury caused by changes in a seniority system, that the limitations period began to run when the changes were adopted, rather than when the complainant became affected by them. Lorance v. AT&T Technologies, 490 US 900 (1989). The 1991 Civil Rights Act amended the statute to effectively overrule that decision. *See* 42 USC §2000e-5(e)(2).

[105]Ghartey v. St. John's Queens Hosp., 869 F2d 160, 130 LRRM 2816 (CA 2, 1989); Davis v. Smith's Transfer, 841 F2d 139, 127 LRRM 2845 (CA 6, 1988); Trent v. Bolger, 837 F2d 657, 127 LRRM 2505 (CA 4, 1988); Galindo v. Stoody Co., 793 F2d 1502, 123 LRRM 2705 (CA 9, 1986); Sevako v. Anchor Motor Freight Co., 792 F2d 570, 122 LRRM 3316 (CA 6, 1986); Hill v. Georgia Power Co., 786 F2d 1071, 122 LRRM 2779 (CA 11, 1986).

[106]*See, e.g.*, Bartels v. Sports Arena Employees Local 137, 838 F2d 101, 127 LRRM 2497 (CA 3, 1988); Chrysler Workers Ass'n v. Chrysler Corp., *supra* note 100; Samples v. Ryder Truck Lines, *supra* note 104.

[107]Kolomick v. Steelworkers Dist. 8, 762 F2d 354, 119 LRRM 2393 (CA 4, 1985); Nicely v. United States Steel Corp., 574 F Supp 184, 114 LRRM 3566 (WD Pa, 1983), *aff'd*, 813 F2d 398, 124 LRRM 2952 (CA 3), *cert, denied*, 484 US 825 (1987); Martin v. Adams Distribution Servs., 114 LRRM 3562 (WD Mo, 1983).

[108]Frandsen v. Railway Clerks, 782 F2d 674, 684, 121 LRRM 2465 (CA 7, 1986). *See also* Trent v. Bolger, *supra* note 105, at 659; Adkins v. Electrical Workers (IUE), *supra* note 104.

DelCostello left unsettled the applicability of the 6-month limitations period to section 301 actions not conjoined with an action for breach of duty of fair representation. The Court cited, but did not overrule, *Auto Workers v. Hoosier Cardinal Corp.*,[109] which had applied a 6-year state limitation period to the standard union section 301 action against an employer for breach of contract. In *DelCostello*, however, Justice Brennan suggested that the continued applicability of *Hoosier Cardinal* was an open question.[110]

At least six circuits, citing the utility of prompt resolution, have ruled that the same considerations articulated in *DelCostello* require the application of the 6-month period to actions to compel arbitration.[111] However, five circuits (including three that apply the 6-month period in actions to compel arbitration) have applied an analogous state limitation period to actions to enforce, modify, or vacate arbitration awards.[112]

The First and Sixth circuits have applied analogous state limitation periods to section 301 actions by employees against their employers for breach of collective bargaining agreements.[113] But the Second Circuit has applied the 6-month period to an employee action brought under section 301 against the union only for breach of the duty of fair representation.[114] In *Electrical Workers (IBEW) v. Hechler*,[115] the Supreme Court

---

[109]383 US 696, 61 LRRM 2545 (1966).

[110]462 US at 158–59 n.12.

[111]Communications Workers v. Western Elec. Co., *supra* note 100; Teamsters Local 174 v. Trick & Murray, Inc., 828 F2d 1418, 126 LRRM 2736 (CA 9, 1987); Associated Brick Mason Contractors of Greater N.Y. v. Harrington, 820 F2d 31, 125 LRRM 2648 (CA 2, 1987); McCreedy v. Auto Workers Local 971, 809 F2d 1232, 124 LRRM 2508 (CA 6, 1987); Machinists Local 1688 v. Allied Prods. Corp., 786 F2d 1561, 122 LRRM 2264 (CA 11, 1986); Teamsters Local 315 v. Great W. Chem. Co., 781 F2d 764, 121 LRRM 2666 (CA 9, 1986); Westinghouse Indep. Salaried Unions v. Westinghouse Elec. Corp., 736 F2d 896, 116 LRRM 2732 (CA 3, 1984). *But see* Elevator Constructors v. Home Elevator Co., 798 F2d 222, 123 LRRM 2355 (CA 7, 1986).

[112]Operating Eng'rs Local 150 v. Centor Contractors, 831 F2d 1309, 126 LRRM 2548 (CA 7, 1987); Postal Workers v. U.S. Postal Serv., 823 F2d 466, 126 LRRM 2263 (CA 11, 1987); Champion Int'l Corp. v. Paperworkers, 779 F2d 328, 121 LRRM 2449 (CA 6, 1985); Plumbers & Pipe Fitters Pension Fund Local 130 v. Domas Mechanical Contractors, 778 F2d 1266, 121 LRRM 2146 (CA 7, 1985); Carpenters Local 1020 v. FMC Corp., 724 F2d 815, 115 LRRM 2582 (CA 9, 1984); Electrical Workers (IUE) v. Ingram Mfg. Co., 715 F2d 886, 888, 114 LRRM 3083, 3085, *reh'g denied*, 720 F2d 677 (CA 5, 1983), *cert. denied*, 466 US 928, 115 LRRM 3416 (1984). *See also* Posadas de P.R. Assocs. v. Asociacion de Empleados de Casino de P.R., 873 F2d 479, 131 LRRM 2223 (CA 1, 1989).

[113]Cabarga-Cruz v. Fundacion Educativa Ana G. Mendez, *supra* note 101; Apponi v. Sunshine Biscuits, 809 F2d 1210, 124 LRRM 2494 (CA 6, 1987), *cert. denied*, 484 US 820, 126 LRRM 2495 (1987).

[114]Eatz v. Electrical Workers (IBEW) Local 3, DME Unit, 794 F2d 29, 122 LRRM 2953 (CA 2, 1986); *see also* Legutko v. Teamsters Local 816, 853 F2d 1046, 128 LRRM 3228 (CA 2, 1988) (6-month limitation applies to §301 claims brought by member against union for breach of constitution and against employer for contract breach).

[115]481 US 851, 125 LRRM 2353 (1987).

remanded the case for determination of the applicability of *DelCostello* to an employee's claim of breach of a contract to which she claimed she was a third-party beneficiary. On remand, the Eleventh Circuit applied the state limitations period for breach of contract.[116]

In *Reed v. Transportation Union*,[117] the Supreme Court declined to apply the *DelCostello* rule to free speech and assembly claims brought by union members against their unions under section 101(a)(2) of the LMRDA. The Court applied the state general personal injury limitations period, but left open whether *DelCostello* might apply to those Title I claims that most directly relate to collective bargaining.[118] Finally, in suits by unions or pension fund trustees against employers for breach of the collective bargaining agreement, two circuits have applied the state statute of limitations for breach of contract.[119]

2. The Board and the Courts. The Supreme Court recognized that the exercise of concurrent jurisdiction by the Board and the courts might raise "serious problems," but it preferred to face these problems as they occur.[120] In its amicus brief in *Smith v. Evening News*, the Board expressed the view that concurrent jurisdiction in this area would actually promote the purposes of the LMRA.[121] Furthermore, the Board has declined to exercise its own jurisdiction when it believes that the federal labor policy is better served by leaving the parties to other procedures.[122] As pointed out in *Charles Dowd Box*, Congress

[116]Hechler v. Electrical Workers (IBEW), 834 F2d 942, 127 LRRM 2135 (CA 11, 1987); *see also* Sams v. Food & Commercial Workers, 866 F2d 1380, 130 LRRM 2805 (CA 11, 1989).

[117]488 US 319, 130 LRRM 2137 (1989).

[118]*Id.*, 130 LRRM at 2142 n.6. *See also* Hester v. Operating Eng'rs Local 660, 878 F2d 1309, 132 LRRM 2011 (CA 11, 1989) (state statute of limitations applied where member claimed that union breached duty of fair representation and violated safeguards against improper disciplinary actions). *But see* Clift v. Auto Workers, 881 F2d 408, 412, 132 LRRM 2123, 2126–27 (CA 7, 1989) ("[a]lthough the claims in this particular case bear upon formation of the collective bargaining agreement, this alone is insufficient under *Reed* to compel the application of a federal limitations period").

[119]Elevator Constructors v. Home Elevator Co., *supra* note 111; O'Hare v. General Marine Transp. Corp., *supra* note 101.

[120]Smith v. Evening News Ass'n, 371 US 195, 197–98, 51 LRRM 2646 (1962).

[121]*Id.* at 197 n.6.

[122]See discussion of the *Spielberg* and *Collyer* doctrines in Chapter 18, "Accommodation of Board Action to the Arbitration Process." Spielberg Mfg. Co., 112 NLRB 1080, 36 LRRM 1152 (1955); Collyer Insulated Wire, 192 NLRB 837, 77 LRRM 1931 (1971). In reaffirming the jurisdiction of the courts over §301 suits involving alleged unfair labor practices, the Supreme Court, in *William E. Arnold*, referred to the Board's policy "to refrain from exercising jurisdiction in respect of disputed conduct arguably both an unfair labor practice and a contract violation when . . . the parties have voluntarily established by contract a binding settlement procedure." William E. Arnold Co. v. Carpenters Dist. Council of Jacksonville & Vicinity, 417 US 12, 16, 86 LRRM 2212 (1974) (citing, inter alia, Collyer Insulated Wire, *supra*).

"deliberately chose to leave the enforcement of collective bargaining agreements 'to the usual process of the law.'"[123] But the Court has also held, in the clearest terms, that enforcement of a contract by a court does not affect the jurisdiction of the Board to remedy unfair labor practices.[124] Thus, while the Court may assure uniformity of legal principle by reason of final review, the overlap of jurisdiction presents the risk that the Board and a court will render contradictory decisions. Some inconsistency may be the price of prompt and efficient enforcement of contract rights.[125]

The concurrent jurisdiction of the Board and the courts requires the courts to decide whether they should exercise their jurisdiction over questions within the primary jurisdiction of the Board.[126] Some issues which are litigable in a section 301 action are, nevertheless, near the core of the exclusive jurisdiction of the Board to resolve representational and unfair labor practice disputes under the Act. On such issues, the courts may, and often do, decline to act.[127] These include a union's majority status;[128] the employer's duty to bargain;[129] an appropriate bargaining unit;[130] employer coercion of employees to force

---

[123]Charles Dowd Box Co. v. Courtney, 368 US 502, 513, 49 LRRM 2619 (1962).

[124]Smith v. Evening News Ass'n, *supra* note 120, at 197. *See also* Dunau, *Contractual Prohibition of Unfair Labor Practices: Jurisdictional Problems*, 57 COLUM. L. REV. 52 (1957).

[125]*See* Sovern, *Section 301 and the Primary Jurisdiction of the NLRB*, 76 HARV. L. REV. 529 (1963).

[126]Parker v. Connors Steel Co., 855 F2d 1510, 129 LRRM 2539 (CA 11, 1988), *cert. denied*, 490 US 1066, 131 LRRM 2400 (1989); Brown v. Keystone Consol. Indus., 680 F Supp 1212, 127 LRRM 2934 (ND Ill, 1988); Operating Eng'rs Local 926 v. Superior Rigging & Erecting Co., 602 F Supp 913, 123 LRRM 3314 (ND Ga, 1984).

[127]*See generally* Chapter 30, "Accommodation to Other Federal Enactments."

[128]Mo-Kan Teamsters Pension Fund v. Creason, 716 F2d 772, 115 LRRM 2130 (CA 10, 1983), *cert. denied*, 464 US 1045, 115 LRRM 2712 (1984); Glaziers Local 767 v. Custom Auto Glass Distribs., 689 F2d 1339, 111 LRRM 2665 (CA 9, 1982) (employer estopped from asserting in §301 action defense, that union did not enjoy majority support when agreement was executed because that issue should be presented to and decided by Board); Health & Welfare Plan v. Associated Wrecking Co., 638 F2d 1128, 106 LRRM 2257 (CA 8, 1981), *cert. denied*, 461 US 926, 113 LRRM 2448 (1983); Hotel Employees Local 355 v. Pier 66 Co., 599 F Supp 761, 118 LRRM 3133 (SD Fla, 1985); Retail Drug Employees' Welfare Trust Fund v. Hemmat, 98 Lab. Cas. (CCH) ¶10,409 (WD Wash, 1983). *But see* Butchers Local 498 v. SDC Inv., 631 F Supp 1001, 122 LRRM 2146 (ED Cal, 1986).

[129]Serrano v. Jones & Laughlin Steel Co., 790 F2d 1279, 122 LRRM 2297 (CA 6, 1986); Morello v. Federal Barge Lines, 746 F2d 1347, 117 LRRM 2877 (CA 8, 1984); Parker v. Connors Steel Co., *supra* note 126; Lexington Cartage Co. v. Teamsters, 713 F2d 194, 113 LRRM 3781 (CA 6, 1983).

[130]Boilermakers v. Olympic Plating Indus., 870 F2d 1085, 130 LRRM 3001 (CA 6, 1989); Clothing & Textile Workers v. Facetglas, Inc., 845 F2d 1250, 128 LRRM 2252 (CA 4, 1988); Teamsters Local 682 v. Bussen Quarries, 849 F2d 1123, 129 LRRM 2287 (CA 8, 1988); Teamsters Local 70 v. California Consolidators, 693 F2d 81, 111 LRRM 2785 (CA 9, 1982), *cert. denied*, 469 US 887, 117 LRRM 2571 (1984); Electrical Workers (IBEW) Local

ratification of a collective bargaining agreement;[131] employer discrimination against employees;[132] a validity of settlement agreements ending an employment dispute;[133] union successorship;[134] an employer's duty to make pension and other fund contributions;[135] an employer's duty to maintain the status quo after expiration of a contract during negotiations for a new contract;[136] and a union's internal dealings with its members.[137]

The primary jurisdiction of the Board does not deprive the courts of jurisdiction, rather, it raises prudential concerns about whether to exercise it. As the Supreme Court held in *Kaiser Steel Corp. v. Mullins*,[138] courts have the jurisdiction and the obligation to determine the legality of a particular contract provision where illegality under the Act is raised as a defense. The Court held that the exclusive primary jurisdiction of the Board to

---

204 v. Iowa Elec. Light & Power Co., 668 F2d 413, 109 LRRM 2305 (CA 8, 1982); Yellow Freight Sys. v. Machinists Local 701, 684 F2d 526, 111 LRRM 2140 (CA 7, 1982); King Coal Co. v. Mine Workers, 530 F Supp 517, 110 LRRM 2786 (ND Ala, 1982). *See also* South Prairie Constr. Co. v. Operating Eng'rs Local 627, 425 US 800, 92 LRRM 2507 (1976) (vacating and remanding bargaining-unit determination by circuit court where none had been made by Board).

[131]Casaneda v. Dura-Vent Corp., 648 F2d 612, 107 LRRM 3179 (CA 9, 1981).

[132]Ethridge v. Harbor House Restaurant, 861 F2d 1389, 130 LRRM 2001 (CA 9, 1988); Buscemi v. McDonnell Douglas Corp., 736 F2d 1348, 116 LRRM 3197 (CA 9, 1984); Stephens v. Roadway Express Co., 119 LRRM 2312 (ND Ga, 1982).

[133]Alabama By-Products Corp. v. Mine Workers Local 1288, 109 LRRM 2427 (ND Ala, 1981) (settlement in which employee was given 20-day suspension rather than discharge in return for promise to foreswear certain union offices); Clothing & Textile Workers v. Standard-Coosa-Thatcher Carpet Yarn Div., 516 F Supp 1078, 110 LRRM 2276 (ND Ala, 1981).

[134]Teamsters Local 807 v. Brink's, 744 F2d 283, 117 LRRM 2306 (CA 2, 1984); Oil, Chem. & Atomic Workers v. Standard Oil of Ind., 529 F Supp 184, 109 LRRM 3010 (ND Ill, 1981).

[135]Laborers Health & Welfare Trust Fund for N. Cal. v. Advanced Lightweight Concrete Co., 484 US 539, 127 LRRM 2657 (1988) (no jurisdiction under ERISA over claim that refusal to make postcontract contributions to fund; after contract expiration, such claims involve issues under §8(a)(5) of the Act and must be presented to Board); *see also* U.A. 198 Health & Welfare, Educ. & Pension Funds v. Rester Refrigeration Serv., 790 F2d 423, 122 LRRM 2457 (CA 5, 1986), *cert. denied*, 485 US 904, 127 LRRM 2912 (1988); Electrical Workers (IBEW) Local 22 v. Nanco Elec., 790 F2d 59, 122 LRRM 2826 (CA 8, 1986); Waggoner v. Dallaire, 767 F2d 589, 119 LRRM 3553 (CA 9, 1985), *cert. denied*, 475 US 1064, 121 LRRM 2992 (1986); Auto Workers v. Facet Enters., 601 F Supp 292, 119 LRRM 2981 (ED Mich, 1984). *But see* Pipe Fitters Health & Welfare Trust v. Waldo R., Inc., 872 F2d 815, 131 LRRM 2105 (CA 8), *cert. denied*, 493 US 977, 132 LRRM 2960 (1989).

[136]Cement Masons Health & Welfare Trust Fund for N. Cal. v. Kirkwood-Bly, 692 F2d 641, 111 LRRM 3041 (CA 9, 1982), *aff'g* 520 F Supp 942, 111 LRRM 3038 (ND Cal, 1981). *See also* Johnson v. Pullman, Inc. 845 F2d 911, 128 LRRM 2361 (CA 11, 1988) (claims under expired agreement are within Board's exclusive jurisdiction); Laborers Health & Welfare Trust Fund for N. Cal. v. Hess Concrete Constr. Co., 594 F Supp 273, 117 LRRM 2816 (ND Cal, 1984).

[137]Hays v. National Elec. Contractors Ass'n, 629 F Supp 87, 121 LRRM 2363 (ND Cal, 1984), *aff'd*, 781 F2d 1321, 121 LRRM 2663 (CA 9, 1986) (Board has exclusive jurisdiction over claim that union unfairly applied hiring-hall rule). *See also* cases cited at note 161, *infra*.

[138]455 US 72, 109 LRRM 2268 (1982).

resolve unfair labor practice issues did not preclude judicial determination of the issue since "a court must reach the merits of an illegality defense in order to determine whether the contract clause at issue has any legal effect in the first place."[139] Similarly, in *Communications Workers v. Beck*,[140] the Supreme Court held that courts have jurisdiction to hear employees' claims that a union's agency fees violated their First Amendment and fair representation rights, although the union's defense asserted the validity of the fees under section 8(a)(3) of the Act.

Where signatory and nonsignatory contractors brought an action claiming a repudiation of a prehire agreement, at least one court has held that the Board's primary jurisdiction does not bar the assertion of jurisdiction.[141] A duty of fair representation claim is exempt from preemption under *Vaca v. Sipes*,[142] even when it is joined with related claims against an employer.[143]

The risk of conflicting results, or the occurrence of them, has produced a range of responses in the courts. One circuit has ruled that the possibility of conflicting decisions entitled the Board to intervene of right in a section 301 action.[144] Another has suggested, in affirming a judgment in a section 301 action, that if the Board should thereafter render a conflicting order, the district court could reconsider the issuance of injunctive relief on motion by one of the parties.[145] The Ninth Circuit, however, has ruled that a judicial decision granting the rescis-

---

[139]*Id.* at 84, 109 LRRM at 2273. *See also* Electrical Workers (IBEW) Local 481 v. Sign-Craft, Inc., 864 F2d 499, 130 LRRM 2198 (CA 7, 1988); Typographical Union No. 16 (Chicago) v. Chicago Sun-Times, 860 F2d 1420, 129 LRRM 2948 (CA 7, 1988); Mack Trucks, Inc. v. Auto Workers, 856 F2d 579, 129 LRRM 2338 (CA 3, 1988), *cert. denied*, 489 US 1054, 130 LRRM 2656 (1989); Plumbers & Pipe Fitters Local 72 v. John Payne Co., 850 F2d 1535, 128 LRRM 3213 (CA 11, 1988); Courier-Citizen Co. v. Graphic Arts Local 11, 702 F2d 273, 112 LRRM 3122 (CA 1, 1983); Chicago Area Vending Employers Ass'n v. Teamsters Local 761, 564 F Supp 1186, 116 LRRM 2667 (ND Ill, 1983). *Compare* Teamsters Local 302 v. Vevoda, 772 F2d 530, 120 LRRM 2785 (CA 9, 1985), *cert. denied*, 475 US 1036, 121 LRRM 3432 (1986) *with* Glaziers Local 767 v. Custom Auto Glass Distribs., *supra* note 128.

[140]487 US 735, 128 LRRM 2729 (1988). *But see* In re Goodman, 873 F2d 598, 131 LRRM 2129 (CA 2, 1989); Parker v. Connors Steel Co., *supra* note 126, at 1517, 129 LRRM at 2543–44 ("the primary jurisdiction rationale has the greatest validity when a party has sought redress for his claims from the NLRB and in the face of an adverse decision the claims are restructured as state law claims and pursued in state court").

[141]Gateway Structures v. Carpenters Local 46 (N. Cal. Counties Conference Bd.), 681 F Supp 1437, 128 LRRM 2945 (ND Cal, 1987).

[142]386 US 171, 64 LRRM 2369 (1967).

[143]Breininger v. Sheet Metal Workers Local 6, 493 US 67, 132 LRRM 3001 (1989).

[144]Newport News Shipbuilding & Dry Dock Co. v. Peninsula Shipbuilders Ass'n, 646 F2d 117, 107 LRRM 2085 (CA 4, 1981).

[145]Bell Prod. Eng'rs Ass'n v. Textron, 688 F2d 997, 998 n.1, 111 LRRM 2773 (CA 5, 1982).

sion of a labor agreement invalidated the subsequent Board finding of a section 8(a)(5) violation premised on the continued existence of the contract, and the court refused to enforce the Board's order.[146] The court said "the Board cannot breathe new life into that which has expired by judicial decree."[147]

The court in *Pratt-Farnsworth*[148] noted that where an issue is concurrently presented to the Board and a district court, the latter should consider staying the action pending Board determination as a matter of "comity" or "deference" to the Board's expertise.[149] If the court does not stay or dismiss proceedings, the possibility of inconsistent rulings arises and the issue is committed to the sound discretion of the trial court.[150] Four circuits have held that courts have jurisdiction under section 301 to resolve even representational issues underlying a contract claim, at least when those issues are not pending before the Board.[151]

Several courts have held that where an employer is involved in bankruptcy proceedings, concurrent Board proceedings on

---

[146]NLRB v. Heyman, 541 F2d 796, 92 LRRM 3603 (CA 9, 1976).

[147]*Id.* at 800. Judge, now Justice, Kennedy concurred, observing that the concurrent jurisdiction should cause either forum to give some collateral estoppel effect to a prior final order of the other. *Id.* at 802.

[148]Carpenters Local 1846 v. Pratt-Farnsworth, *amended,* 112 LRRM 2525, 690 F2d 489, 111 LRRM 2787, (CA 5, 1982), *cert. denied,* 464 US 932, 114 LRRM 2976 (1983).

[149]*Id.*, 111 LRRM at 2804–5 & n.11, and 112 LRRM at 2525. *See also* American Commercial Barge Lines Co. v. Seafarers, 730 F2d 327, 116 LRRM 2201 (CA 5, 1984) (doctrine of primary jurisdiction supports court's deferral of employer's claim for injunction against strikes seeking to compel contributions to employee benefit trust funds).

[150]Sheet Metal Workers Local 252 v. Standard Sheet Metal, 699 F2d 481, 112 LRRM 2878 (CA 9, 1983); Northern Cal. Dist. Council of Hod Carriers v. Opinski dba E.J. Opinski Bldg. Contractor, 673 F2d 1074, 110 LRRM 2205 (CA 9, 1982) (district court should have stayed proceedings); Food & Commercial Workers Local 400 v. Marval Poultry Co., 128 LRRM 2383 (WD Va, 1986) (staying §302 claim). *But see* Postal Workers v. U.S. Postal Serv., 766 F2d 715, 119 LRRM 3448 (CA 2, 1985), *cert. denied,* 475 US 1046, 121 LRRM 2792 (1986) (neither pendency of discharged postal worker's unfair labor practice charge before Board nor review procedures under Civil Service Reform Act deprive district court of jurisdiction to enjoin Postal Service from discharging employee pending arbitrator's decision).

[151]Communications Workers v. U.S. W. Direct, 847 F2d 1475, 128 LRRM 2698 (CA 10, 1988); Plumbers & Pipe Fitters Local 72 v. John Payne Co., *supra* note 139; Rozay's Transfer v. Teamsters Local 208, 850 F2d 1321, 128 LRRM 2955 (CA 9, 1988), *cert. denied,* 490 US 1030, 130 LRRM 3208 (1989); Trustees of Iron Workers Fund v. A&P Steel, 812 F2d 1518, 124 LRRM 2878 (CA 10, 1987); Carpenters Local 2247 v. Endicott Enters., 806 F2d 918, 124 LRRM 2265 (CA 9, 1986), *cert. denied,* 484 US 850, 126 LRRM 2496 (1987); Carpenters Local 1694 v. W.T. Galliher & Bros., 787 F2d 953, 122 LRRM 2063 (CA 4, 1986); John S. Griffith Constr. Co. v. Carpenters, 785 F2d 706, 121 LRRM 3385 (CA 9, 1986). *See also* LAWI/CSA Consolidators dba Consolidators Handling Co. v. Teamsters Local 63, 849 F2d 1236, 128 LRRM 2968 (CA 9, 1988). *But see* Boilermakers v. Olympic Plating Indus., 870 F2d 1085, 130 LRRM 3001 (CA 6, 1989); Teamsters Local 682 v. Bussen Quarries, 849 F2d 1123, 129 LRRM 2287 (CA 8, 1988); Clothing & Textile Workers v. Facetglas, Inc., 845 F2d 1250, 128 LRRM 2252 (CA 4, 1988).

unfair labor practice charges should not be enjoined, particularly if the assets of the employer are not thereby threatened[152] or if the proceeding relates primarily to a governmental or public policy interest, rather than to a pecuniary interest in the debtor's property.[153]

A federal district court has jurisdiction under section 301 to entertain a breach of contract action, even if the dispute arises in an industry over which the Board has declined to exercise jurisdiction.[154] Similarly, the refusal of the General Counsel or a regional director to issue a complaint[155] is generally unreviewable but not a bar to a section 301 action.[156]

Findings by the Board in unfair labor practice cases may bar subsequent section 301 suits by application of the doctrine of collateral estoppel.[157] Some courts, however, have refused to be bound by Board findings, asserting that to make such determinations conclusive "goes beyond settled principles by affording to a discretionary administrative decision the weight ordinarily reserved to a final judgment entered by a court of competent jurisdiction."[158] Cases in which collateral estoppel is sought to be applied must be analyzed carefully to ensure that the issues are

---

[152]In re Goodman, *supra* note 140; NLRB v. Edward Cooper Painting, Inc., 804 F2d 934, 123 LRRM 2905 (CA 6, 1986); NLRB v. Evans Plumbing Co., 639 F2d 291, 106 LRRM 3059 (CA 5, 1981); Armour Oil Co. v. NLRB, Region 32, 120 LRRM 3006 (CD Cal, 1985); In re Nicholas, Inc., 55 BR 212, 121 LRRM 2579 (Bankr D NJ, 1985); In re Rath Packing Co., 38 BR 552, 116 LRRM 2039 (Bankr ND Iowa, 1984); In re Tucker Freight Lines, 115 LRRM 2202 (Bankr WD Mich. 1983); *but see* NLRB v. Superior Forwarding, 762 F2d 695, 119 LRRM 2619 (CA 8, 1985).

[153]NLRB v. Edward Cooper Painting, Inc., *supra* note 152.

[154]Electrical Workers (IBEW) Local 481 v. Sign-Craft, Inc., *supra* note 139; Richards v. Electrical Workers (IBEW) Local 134, 790 F2d 633, 122 LRRM 2380 (CA 7, 1986); Pari-Mutuel Clerks of La. Local 328 v. Fair Grounds Corp., 703 F2d 913, 113 LRRM 2201 (CA 5), *cert. denied*, 464 US 846, 114 LRRM 2568 (1983); Electrical Workers (IBEW) Local 1501 v. American Totalisator Co., 529 F Supp 419, 109 LRRM 2585 (D Md, 1982). *But see* Retail, Wholesale & Dep't Store Union Local 310 v. NLRB (Scioto Downs), 745 F2d 358, 117 LRRM 2576 (CA 6, 1984) (district court does not have jurisdiction to determine "whether unfair labor practice has been committed" and if so, to remedy same, when Board declines to assert jurisdiction over horseracing industry). *See* Chapter 28, "Jurisdiction: Coverage of the Act."

[155]Lithographers Local 1 v. Stearns & Beale, 812 F2d 763, 124 LRRM 2809 (CA 2, 1987); Courier-Citizen Co. v. Graphic Arts Local 11, *supra* note 139.

[156]New York Racing Ass'n v. NLRB, 708 F2d 46, 113 LRRM 2746 (CA 2), *cert. denied*, 464 US 914, 114 LRRM 2776 (1983).

[157]Weed v. East Tex. Motor Freight Lines, 592 F Supp 713, 114 LRRM 3449, 3450 (ND Tex, 1983); Edward D. Sultan Co. v. Teamsters Local 427, 95 LRRM 3081 (D Haw, 1977). *See also* Chapter 22, "Handbilling and Consumer Picketing," as to application of collateral estoppel principles to §303 suits.

[158]Painters Local 257 v. Johnson Indus. Painting Contractors, 448 NE2d 1307, 115 LRRM 2437, 2439 (Mass App Ct), *review denied*, 453 NE2d 1231 (1983). *See also* Toyota Landscape Co. v. Teamsters Local 420, 726 F2d 525, 115 LRRM 2977 (CA 9), *cert. denied*, 469 US 825, 117 LRRM 2551 (1984) (district court has section 301 jurisdiction despite dismissal of unfair labor practice action by Board); Bricklayers, Metropolitan Detroit Dist. Council v. J.E. Hoetger & Co., 672 F2d 580, 109 LRRM 3073 (CA 6, 1982).

in fact identical since the widely differing contexts of labor law and contractual interpretation may require that different legal conclusions be reached from the same set of facts.[159]

IV. Injunctions in Aid of Arbitration: Section 301 Versus Norris-LaGuardia

A. From *Sinclair Refining* to *Boys Markets*

Section 301 cannot be read in isolation from section 4 of the Norris-LaGuardia Act.[160] This section deprives the federal

---

[159]Olchowik v. Sheet Metal Workers, 875 F2d 555, 131 LRRM 2475 (CA 6, 1989) (NLRB's finding that union's expulsion of member constituted unfair labor practice and that union's oral charges against member were afterthoughts, did not preclude litigation of issues in member's action alleging that his expulsion violated his rights under LMRDA); Pantex Towing Corp. v. Glidewell, 763 F2d 1241, 119 LRRM 3137 (CA 11, 1985) (employer alleged that union and union agent intentionally interfered with company's operations, engaged in tortious conduct, and coerced employees; collateral estoppel does not preclude court from relitigating prior determination by Board that union-initiated work stoppage was protected concerted activity under LMRA); O'Hare v. General Marine Transp. Corp., 740 F2d 160, 117 LRRM 2038 (CA 2, 1984), *cert. denied*, 469 US 1212, 118 LRRM 2576 (1985) (court of appeals' prior holding that various unfair labor practice charges arising from attempted repudiation of contract was time-barred does not present res judicata bar to trust fund's action under §301 to recover unpaid pension and insurance contributions pursuant to contract, even though two actions involve same case of operative facts); Quinn v. DiGiulian, 739 F2d 637, 116 LRRM 3321 (CA DC, 1984) (court has jurisdiction over union member's claim that union and officers unlawfully refused to accept dues, suspended him, and instructed other members not to work with him because he ran for union office, even though member already had won Board ruling on essentially same facts); Penntech Papers v. NLRB, 706 F2d 18, 113 LRRM 2219 (CA 1), *cert. denied*, 464 US 892, 114 LRRM 2648 (1983) (collateral estoppel does not preclude Board from finding that parent company and two subsidiaries are "single employer" despite federal district court's conclusion under "alter ego" analysis that parent was not bound by contract; two questions are conceptually distinct); Glaziers Local 767 v. Custom Auto Glass Distribs., 689 F2d 1339, 111 LRRM 2665 (CA 9, 1982); Hudson-Berlind v. Teamsters Local 807, 597 F Supp 1282, 119 LRRM 3599 (ED NY, 1984) (Board finding that employer was not employer of drivers who were discharged and that union therefore illegally picketed collaterally estops union from claiming that employer illegally discharged drivers).

[160]29 USC §104 (1964). For a history of these developments, see Chapters 1, "Historical Background of the Wagner Act," 2, "The Wagner Act Period," 3, "The Taft-Hartley Changes," and 4, "The Landrum-Griffin Changes." For bibliographical material see the following: Cantor, Buffalo Forge *and Injunctions Against Employer Breaches of Collective Bargaining Agreements*, 1980 WIS. L. REV. 247 (1980); Fried, *Injunctions Against Sympathy Strikes: In Defense of* Buffalo Forge, 54 N.Y.U. L. REV. 289 (1979); Cohen, *Strikes and Injunctions: The* Buffalo Forge *Case*, NYU THIRTIETH ANNUAL CONFERENCE ON LABOR 171 (1977); Lowden & Flaherty, *Sympathy Strikes, Arbitration Policy and the Enforceability of No-Strike Agreements—An Analysis of* Buffalo Forge, 45 GEO. WASH. L. REV. 633 (1977); Smith, *Supreme Court,* Boys Markets *Labor Injunctions and Sympathy Work Stoppages*, 44 U CHI. L. REV. 321 (1977); Axelrod, *The Application of the* Boys Markets *Decision in the Federal Courts*, 16 B.C. INDUS. & COM. L. REV. 893 (1975); Comment, *Injunctions May Issue Against Labor Unions to End Strike Over Safety Disputes Despite Absence of a No-Strike Clause in Collective Bargaining Agreements*, 63 GEO. L.J. 275 (1974); Gould, *On Labor Injunctions, Unions, and the Judges: The* Boys Markets *Case*, 1970 SUP. CT. REV. 215 (1970); Note,

courts of jurisdiction to issue injunctions that would prohibit certain specified acts in connection with a labor dispute.[161] *Lincoln Mills* rejected the argument that Norris-LaGuardia withdrew from the courts jurisdiction to compel arbitration.[162] But in *Sinclair Refining Co. v. Atkinson*[163] the Supreme Court held that no-strike clauses in collective bargaining agreements were not specifically enforceable in the federal courts because section 301 had not diminished the force of the federal anti-injunction legislation.

The effect of the ruling in *Sinclair Refining* was compounded by the Supreme Court's subsequent decision in *Avco Corp.*,[164] which held that a suit brought in a state court under section 301 to enforce a no-strike clause was removable to the federal courts. Taken together, *Sinclair Refining* and *Avco* severely limited the availability of injunctions against strikes in breach of contract. Injunction suits filed in state court could be removed to federal court, where no injunction could be issued.[165]

Prospective Boys Markets *Injunctions*, 90 HARV. L. REV. 790 (1977); Note, *Prospective Injunctions and Federal Labor Law Policy: Of Future Strikes, Arbitration, and Equity*, 52 NOTRE DAME L. REV. 790 (1976). *See also* materials cited in *supra* note 2.

[161]The specified acts are numerous and are phrased in broad terms. Consequently the question seldom arises whether a particular act sought to be enjoined is outside the ambit of §4. That question did arise, however, in Bituminous Coal Operators Ass'n v. Mine Workers, 585 F2d 586, 99 LRRM 2612 (CA 3, 1978), where an employers' association sought an injunction enforcing an international union's alleged contractual obligation to ensure compliance by its members with the implied no-strike pledge in the collective bargaining agreement. Although the requested injunction would not by its terms have prohibited strikes or picketing, the court held §4 to be applicable, stating: "We do not hold that in a Section 301 suit an injunction would never be available to enforce a collateral, contractual undertaking not subject to arbitration, for conceivably some such contractual undertaking might not involve the activities protected by Section 4. But we do hold that where, as here, the real objective of the injunction sought is to prevent work stoppages and picketing, Section 4 applies." *Id.* at 594. Several cases have presented the question whether §4 applies to a strike called to further a union's political goals. The Supreme Court has resolved all doubts and has held that §4 applies in such cases. Jacksonville Bulk Terminals v. Longshoremen (ILA), 457 US 702, 110 LRRM 2665 (1982); *cf. also* Longshoremen (ILA) v. Allied Int'l, 456 US 212, 110 LRRM 2001 (1982); Chapter 22, "Handbilling and Consumer Picketing," Part IV.

[162]Textile Workers v. Lincoln Mills, 353 US 448, 457–59, 40 LRRM 2113 (1957).

[163]370 US 195, 50 LRRM 2420 (1962).

[164]Avco Corp. v. Machinists Aero Lodge 735, 390 US 557, 67 LRRM 2881 (1968).

[165]Both *Sinclair* and *Avco* left unclear whether state courts could issue injunctions. *See* Avco Corp. v. Machinists Aero Lodge 735, *supra* note 164, at 560 n.2; *cf.* Railroad Trainmen v. Jacksonville Terminal Co., 394 US 369, 382 n.18, 70 LRRM 2961 (1969). *See also* Summers, *Labor Law Decisions of the Supreme Court, 1961 Term*, in ABA LABOR RELATIONS LAW SECTION PROCEEDINGS 51, 63 (1962). For further discussion, see *infra* at notes 278–279.

Nothwithstanding *Sinclair* and *Avco*, both state and federal courts often entered orders enforcing arbitration awards requiring the cessation of a strike. *See, e.g.*, New Orleans S.S. Ass'n v. Longshoremen (ILA) Local 1418, 389 F2d 369, 67 LRRM 2430 (CA 5), *cert. denied*, 393 US 828, 69 LRRM 2434 (1968); Philadelphia Marine Trade Terminal Ass'n v. Longshoremen (ILA) Local 1291, 365 F2d 295, 62 LRRM 2791 (CA 3, 1966), *rev'd on other grounds*, 389 US 64, 66 LRRM 2433 (1967); Ruppert v. Egelhofer, 3 NY2d 576, 148 NE2d

The decision in *Sinclair Refining* was controversial,[166] and it remained the law for only 8 years. In *Boys Markets v. Retail Clerks Local 770*[167] the Supreme Court concluded in light of its consequences that *Sinclair* had been improvidently decided. Dividing five-to-two, the Court reversed *Sinclair*, holding that strikes in breach of contract concerning matters that are subject to a mandatory grievance arbitration procedure can be enjoined by the federal courts.[168]

B. The *Boys Markets* Injunction

1. The Prerequisites for Issuance of Injunctive Relief. *a. In General.* Asserting that Norris-LaGuardia does not bar the granting of injunctive relief in all cases, the *Boys Markets* majority nonetheless emphasized the narrowness of its holding.[169] The Court said it was dealing only with the situation where a contract contains a "mandatory grievance adjustment or arbitration procedure." Even then, the Court stated, injunctive relief is not appropriate in every case "as a matter of course."[170] The Court

---

129 (1958). *See generally* M. Bernstein, PRIVATE DISPUTE SETTLEMENT 601–40 (1968); Note, *Circumventing Norris-LaGuardia with Arbitration Clauses*, 44 NOTRE DAME L. REV. 431 (1969).

[166]*See Report of Special* Atkinson-Sinclair *Committee*, in ABA LABOR RELATIONS LAW SECTION PROCEEDINGS 226 (1963). The neutral members of the "Special *Atkinson-Sinclair* Committee" recommended that *Sinclair* be overruled to permit injunctions against breach-of contract strikes, but only where the dispute underlying the strike is arbitrable. *Id.* at 241–42.

[167]398 US 235, 74 LRRM 2257 (1970).

[168]Justice Black, joined by Justice White, dissented, observing that nothing had changed since 1962 except "the membership of the Court and the personal view of one Justice." Justice Stewart, the Justice to whom he referred, explained in a concurring opinion, quoting the late Justice Frankfurter, that "[w]isdom too often never comes, and so one ought not to reject it merely because it comes late." *Id.* at 255.

[169]*Id.* at 253.

[170]*Id.* at 253–54. In addition to §4, other sections of Norris-LaGuardia impose limitations on the issuance of injunctions which may be applicable in §301 suits brought to enforce no-strike obligations. For example, §9 (29 USC §109 (1970)), provides that "every restraining order or injunction granted in a case involving or growing out of a labor dispute shall include only a prohibition of such specific act or acts as may be expressly complained of in the . . . complaint . . . and as shall be expressly included in [the] findings of fact made and filed by the court . . . ." This section has been applied to limit the availability of broad, prospective injunctive relief in *Boys Markets* cases. *See infra* at notes 225–228. In addition, §7 (29 USC §107 (1970)), specifies several procedural and evidentiary requirements to be followed by the courts in issuing injunctions in labor disputes. The courts have generally held that the Norris-LaGuardia §7 requirements are applicable in *Boys Markets* cases consistent with the policies of §301. *See* United States v. Cunningham, 599 F2d 120, 126 n.12, 101 LRRM 2508 (CA 6, 1979); Celotex Corp. v. Oil, Chem. & Atomic Workers, 516 F2d 242, 89 LRRM 2372 (CA 3, 1975); Hoh v. Pepsico, Inc., 491 F2d 556, 85 LRRM 2517 (CA 2, 1974); United States Steel Corp. v. Mine Workers, 456 F2d 483, 79 LRRM 2518 (CA 3), *cert. denied*, 408 US 923, 80 LRRM 2855 (1972); Typographical Union No. 18 (Detroit) v. Detroit Newspaper Publishers Ass'n 471 F2d

adopted the prerequisites for injunctive relief which had been set forth in Justice Brennan's *Sinclair* dissent. Those prerequisites are as follows:

> A District Court entertaining an action under §301 may not grant injunctive relief against concerted activity unless and until it decides that the case is one in which an injunction would be appropriate despite the Norris-LaGuardia Act. When a strike is sought to be enjoined because it is over a grievance which both parties are contractually bound to arbitrate, the District Court may issue no injunctive order until it first holds that the contract *does* have the effect; and the employer should be ordered to arbitrate, as a condition of his obtaining an injunction against the strike. Beyond this, the District Court must, of course, consider whether issuance of an injunction would be warranted under ordinary principles of equity—whether breaches are occurring and will continue, or have been threatened and will be committed; whether they have caused or will cause irreparable injury to the employer; and whether the employer will suffer more from its denial of an injunction than will the union from its issuance.[171]

These several prerequisites to injunctive relief will be treated in turn in the following sections. In general, however, the courts have required full compliance with the requirements, refusing, for example, to enjoin a refusal to remain in a relationship of employment,[172] or to construe the Bankruptcy Reform act as an

---

872, 82 LRRM 2332 (CA 6, 1972), *cert. denied*, 411 US 967, 83 LRRM 2039 (1973). *Cf.* Associated Gen. Contractors of Ill. v. Teamsters, Illinois Conference, 486 F2d 972, 975–76, n.8, 84 LRRM 2555 (CA 7, 1973). The Supreme Court has not addressed the question of the applicability of these various Norris-LaGuardia requirements in *Boys Markets* cases. In Granny Goose Foods v. Teamsters Local 70, 415 US 423, 445 n.19, 85 LRRM 2481 (1974), the Court reserved decision on whether a temporary restraining order issued under *Boys Markets* is subject to the 5-day limit contained in §7 of Norris-LaGuardia. There is a split in the circuits as to one important question in this area: whether a party's liability for injury caused by the grant of an injunction is limited to the amount it posted pursuant to the requirement of §7. *Compare* Typographical Union No. 16 (Chicago) v. Chicago Newspaper Publishers' Ass'n, 620 F2d 602, 605, 103 LRRM 2957, 2960 (CA 7, 1980) *and* Ladies' Garment Workers v. Donnelly Garment Co., 147 F2d 246, 15 LRRM 923 (CA 8), *cert. denied*, 325 US 852, 16 LRRM 917 (1945) *with* United States Steel Corp. v. Mine Workers, *supra*.

With respect to the applicability of the *Boys Markets* concept to disputes which are subject to the Railway Labor Act, see Trans Int'l Airlines v. Teamsters Local 2707, 650 F2d 949, 103 LRRM 2669 (CA 9, 1980), *cert. denied*, 449 US 1110, 106 LRRM 2200 (1981). The classic Railway Labor Act case allowing an injunction over a grievance subject to statutory arbitration was Railroad Trainmen v. Chicago River & Ind. R.R., 353 US 30, 39 LRRM 2578 (1957), which the Supreme Court in Sinclair Ref. Co. v. Atkinson, *supra* note 163, had refused to follow by analogy.

[171]398 US at 254 (quoting Sinclair Ref. Co. v. Atkinson, *supra* note 163, at 228) (emphasis in original).

[172]Heheman v. E.W. Scripps Co., 661 F2d 1115, 108 LRRM 2736 (CA 6, 1981), *cert. denied*, 456 US 991, 110 LRRM 2440 (1982); *see also* Powell v. National Football League, 678 F Supp 777, 128 LRRM 3119 (D Minn, 1988).

exception to Norris-LaGuardia.[173]

b. Strike in Breach of a Contract. The principles enunciated in the *Sinclair* dissent and adopted by the *Boys Markets* majority emphasize that no injunction may issue against a strike unless the court first finds that the strike[174] is in breach of a no-strike clause. However, an express no-strike clause is not a prerequisite to a *Boys Markets* injunction. In *Lucas Flour*[175] the Supreme Court had held that where a dispute is arbitrable under the contract, the union ordinarily should be considered to have obligated itself not to strike over that dispute. This implied obligation served as the basis for the issuance of a *Boys Markets* injunction in *Gateway Coal Co. v. Mine Workers District 4, Local 6330*.[176] The contract in *Gateway* did not contain a no-strike provision. The Supreme Court nonetheless held that absent an explicit expression of a contrary intention, an agreement to arbitrate should be construed, even in the absence of a no-strike clause, as giving rise to a no-strike obligation which is "coterminous" with the arbiration clause.[177]

The rule articulated in *Lucas Flour* and *Gateway Coal* is one of contract interpretation, and a no-strike obligation will not be implied from an arbitration clause where to do so would be inconsistent with the manifest intent of the parties.[178] In vir-

---

[173]Elsinore Shore Assocs. v. Hotel Employees Local 54, 820 F2d 62, 125 LRRM 2690 (CA 3, 1987); Crowe & Assocs. v. Bricklayers Local 2, 713 F2d 211, 114 LRRM 2024 (CA 6, 1983); Petrusch dba B & L Distribution Center v. Teamsters Local 317, 108 LRRM 2608 (ND NY, 1981), *aff'd*, 667 F2d 297, 109 LRRM 2197 (CA 2, 1981), *cert. denied*, 456 US 974, 109 LRRM 3184 (1982).

[174]Various courts have held that there need not be a showing of an actual strike before relief may be granted. In National Rejectors Indus. Div. v. Steelworkers Local 6178, 562 F2d 1069, 96 LRRM 2120 (CA 8, 1977), *cert. denied*, 435 US 923, 97 LRRM 3040 (1978), an injunction was issued when the employer's plant was reduced to 70% of normal productiv ity primarily as a result of the suspension of numerous employees following a concerted refusal of employees to abide by six new work rules. *See also* Avco Corp. v. Auto Workers Local 787, 459 F2d 968, 974, 80 LRRM 2290 (CA 3, 1972), where the court enjoined a concerted refusal to work overtime. However, an *implied* no-strike obligation will not ordinarily be construed to reach such conduct. *See* note 178, *infra*.

[175]Teamsters Local 174 v. Lucas Flour Co., 369 US 95, 49 LRRM 2717 (1962).

[176]414 US 368, 85 LRRM 2049 (1974).

[177]*Id.* at 382.

[178]Prior to *Gateway Coal*, the Supreme Court had cautioned against linking no-strike obligations to arbitration provisions in every situation. *See* Drake Bakeries v. Bakery Workers Local 50, 370 US 254, 261, 50 LRRM 2440 (1962). Justice Black argued in his *Lucas Flour* dissent that since employers regularly bargain for express no-strike clauses, the absence of such an express clause may indicate that the parties have considered and rejected its inclusion. 369 US at 109–10. After *Lucas Flour*, however, most courts have found that a no-strike obligation should be implied from an arbitration clause; but some courts have refused to draw such an inference where it would have been inconsistent with the parties' bargaining history. *See, e.g.*, Rochester Tel. Corp. v. Communications Workers, 78 LRRM 2213 (WD NY, 1971), *rev'd on other grounds*, 456 F2d 1057, 79 LRRM 2770 (CA 2,

tually all cases, however, the courts have found it appropriate to infer the existence of a no-strike obligation with respect to matters that the parties are contractually bound to arbitrate.[179] Where the obligation not to strike is inferred from the inclusion of a mandatory grievance procedure in the contract, it extends only to the completion of the arbitration process. Absent an express provision in the contract, the court will not presume an agreement not to strike pending judicial enforcement of the arbitrator's award.[180]

Express no-strike clauses also raise questions of interpretation. In particular, where a contract contains a broadly worded nostrike clause but expressly excludes certain types of disputes from the no-strike obligation, the court must decide whether the dispute sought to be enjoined is covered by the general no-strike clause or falls within one of the exclusions. In such a case, the Sixth Circuit ruled that "[w]here the union has expressly reserved its right to strike over certain issues, a *Boys Markets* injunction should not issue unless it clearly appears to the trial judge that the dispute which underlies the strike is subject to a no-strike obligation."[181] Where the exception to the no-strike provision is conditioned on the determination of an underlying dispute, the court must determine whether the exception may be relied upon before the underlying dispute is resolved in arbitration.[182]

1972). Similarly, where the parties have bargained for an express no-strike clause narrower than the arbitration provisions, a broader no-strike obligation is not ordinarily implied. *See* NLRB v. State Elec. Serv., 477 F2d 749, 82 LRRM 3154 (CA 5,), *cert. denied*, 414 US 911, 84 LRRM 2458 (1973). It has been held that an arbitration clause does not give rise to an implied "no-slowdown" obligation. Jessop Steel Co. v. Steelworkers Local 1141, 428 F Supp 172, 94 LRRM 3089 (WD Pa, 1977).

[179]The Seventh Circuit found a no-strike promise in Eaton Corp. v. Machinists, 580 F2d 254, 258, 99 LRRM 2042 (CA 7, 1978), even though the contract provided that "nothing contained in this agreement is to be construed as abrogating the union's right to strike." The court relied on other contractual language requiring the exhaustion of the grievance and arbitration procedure and banning strikes pending arbitration. The court considered this unusual set of provisions to constitute an express no-strike clause notwithstanding the disclaimer. *But see* Carbon Fuel Co. v. Mine Workers, 444 US 212, 102 LRRM 3017 (1979) (in light of negotiating history and lack of proof of union ratification or condonation of wildcat strike, arbitration clause did not imply obligation of union to use "best efforts" to end strike).

[180]Skokie Valley Beverage Co. v. Teamsters Local 744, 563 F Supp 460 (ND Ill, 1983).

[181]Waller Bros. Stone Co. v. Steelworkers Dist. 23, 620 F2d 132, 137, 104 LRRM 2168, 2171 (CA 6, 1980); Roadway Express v. Teamsters Local 515, 642 F Supp 116, 122 LRRM 3155 (ND Ga, 1986); National Wrecking Co. v. Kumerow, 606 F Supp 374 (ND Ill, 1985); Maiers Motor Freight v. Teamsters Local 299, 113 LRRM 2822, 2825 (ED Mich, 1982).

[182]Local Cartage Ass'n of Greater St. Louis v. Teamsters Local 600, 574 F Supp 1573 (Ed Mo, 1983).

A variety of employee activities may violate a no-strike clause, including a work slowdown,[183] a concerted refusal to work overtime,[184] and a concerted exercise of individual rights under a contract.[185]

A nonsignatory employer (e.g., an alleged successor) may not be enjoined from hiring nonunion employees pending arbitration, at least "absent a judicial determination that the two corporations are alter egos or a singular employer . . . ."[186] Similarly, a court should enforce a no-strike clause at the behest of a putative alter ego only after determining that it is bound by the contract. When arbitration of the alleged alter ego status is pending, injunctive relief must await an arbitrator's determination.[187]

c. Strike Over an Arbitrable Dispute. Since the object of a *Boys Markets* injunction is to aid the arbitration process, in order to be enjoined a strike must be "over a grievance which both parties are contractually bound to arbitrate."[188] In *Boys Markets* the union struck over a demand that supervisory employees cease performing bargaining-unit work, a dispute clearly "over" a grievance subject to the arbitration clause of the contract. By contrast, in *Buffalo Forge Co. v. Steelworkers*[189] the strike at issue was a sympathy strike in support of a sister union. Although the issue of whether the no-strike clause in the contract barred such sympathy strikes was subject to the grievance machinery, the strike itself "was not *over* any dispute between the Union and the employer that was even remotely subject to the arbitration provisions of the contract." Thus, "[t]he strike had neither the pur

---

[183]National Elevator Indus. v. Elevator Constructors, 776 F2d 374, 120 LRRM 3187 (CA 1, 1985) (declining to follow Jessop Steel Co. v. Steelworkers Local 1141, *supra* note 178) (slowdown not prohibited by no-strike clause); *see also* Otis Elevator Co. v. Elevator Constructors Local 1, 684 F Supp 80, 128 LRRM 3124 (SD NY, 1988).

[184]National Elevator Indus. v. Elevator Constructors, *supra* note 183 (union enjoined from refusing to work overtime); *cf.* Elevator Mfrs. Ass'n of N.Y. v. Elevator Constructors Local 1, 689 F2d 382, 111 LRRM 2631 (CA 2, 1982) (refusal to sign up for overtime).

[185]Catalytic, Inc. v. Monmouth & Ocean County Bldg. Trades Council, 829 F2d 430, 126 LRRM 2425 (CA 3, 1987), *cert. denied sub nom.* Operating Eng'rs Local 825 v. Catalytic, Inc., 485 US 1020, 128 LRRM 2144 (1988) (work stoppage caused by handbilling over work assignment dispute); Otis Elevator Co. v. Elevator Constructors Local 1, *supra* note 183 (shutting off of beepers); Wireless Cable of N.Y. v. Electrical Workers (IBEW) Local 3, 127 LRRM 2046 (SD NY, 1987) (work stoppage caused by refusal to reinstate employee pending grievance).

[186]Service Employees Local 47 v. Commercial Property Servs., 755 F2d 499, 118 LRRM 2786, 2790 (CA 6), *cert. denied*, 474 US 850, 120 LRRM 2632 (1985).

[187]Tudor Fashions v. Romney, 634 F Supp 297, 123 LRRM 2049 (SD NY, 1986).

[188]Boys Markets v. Retail Clerks Local 770, 398 US 235, 254, 74 LRRM 2257 (1970).

[189]428 US 397, 92 LRRM 3032 (1976). *See infra* at notes 233–234.

pose nor the effect of denying or evading an obligation to arbitrate"[190] and therefore could not be enjoined.

In *Jacksonville Bulk Terminals v. Longshoremen (ILA)*,[191] the Supreme Court declined the invitation to overrule or modify *Buffalo Forge*. The case arose out of the ILA's boycott, in protest of the Soviet invasion of Afghanistan, of cargo bound for the Soviet Union. After finding the Norris-LaGuardia Act applicable to "politically motivated" work stoppages, the Court held that no *Boys Markets* injunction was available:

> *Buffalo Forge* makes it clear that a *Boys Markets* injunction pending arbitration should not issue unless the dispute underlying the work stoppage is arbitrable. The rationale of *Buffalo Forge* compels the conclusion that the Union's work stoppage, called to protest the invasion of Afghanistan by the Soviet Union, may not be enjoined pending the arbitrator's decision on whether the work stoppage violates the no-strike clause in the collective-bargaining agreement. The underlying dispute, whether viewed as an expression of the Union's "moral outrage" at Soviet military policy or as an expression of sympathy for the people of Afghanistan, is plainly not arbitrable under the collective-bargaining agreement.[192]

The Court added:

> . . . Indeed, the question whether striking over a nonarbitrable issue violates other provisions of the collective bargaining agreement may itself be an arbitrable dispute. The fact remains, however, that the strike itself was not over an arbitrable dispute and therefore may not be enjoined pending the arbitrator's ruling on the legality of the strike under the collective barginging agreement.[193]

Suits for injunctions against wildcat strikes often run afoul of the requirement of arbitrability.[194] *Complete Auto Transit v. Reis*[195] involved a wildcat strike that had not been precipitated by any dispute with the employer, but rather by differences

---

[190]428 US at 407–8 (emphasis in original).

[191]457 US 702, 110 LRRM 2665 (1982). *See also* Hampton Roads Shipping Ass'n v. Longshoremen (ILA), 631 F2d 282, 105 LRRM 2506 (CA 4, 1980), *cert. denied*, 458 US 1105, 110 LRRM 2744 (1982).

[192]457 US at 722.

[193]*Id.* See Chapter 1, "Historical Background of the Wagner Act," at notes 72–79 for historical treatment of the Norris-LaGuardia Act. *See* notes 233–242 *infra* regarding the applicability of that Act in sympathy strike situations.

[194]*E.g.*, Automobile Transp. v. Ferdnance, 420 F Supp 75, 92 LRRM 3610 (ED Mich, 1976).

[195]641 F2d 1110, 103 LRRM 2722 (CA 6, 1980), *aff'd on other grounds*, 451 US 401, 107 LRRM 2145 (1981). The Supreme Court expressly reserved decision on this issue. *Id.* at 404–5 & n.4. *See also* Jacksonville Bulk Terminals v. Longshoremen (ILA), *supra* note 191, 110 LRRM at 2673 n.22.

between the union members and the union. The lower court denied injunctive relief, relying on *Buffalo Forge*, finding that the strike was not over an arbitrable dispute. Thereafter, the union and its members settled their dispute, but the strike continued over the employer's refusal to grant amnesty to the strikers. The employer again moved for injunctive relief, and the lower court again refused to issue an injunction. The Sixth Circuit reversed, finding that the work stoppage which had begun over a dispute that was not subject to arbitration had continued because of a dispute that *was* arbitrable—the amnesty issue. Accordingly, the new dispute fell within the ambit of *Boys Markets*.[196]

In *Gateway Coal Co. v. Mine Workers District 4, Local 6330*[197] the Supreme Court announced that the presumption of arbitrability announced in the *Steelworkers Trilogy* cases[198] should be applied in *Boys Markets* cases.[199] A dispute is deemed to be not arbitrable where the contract clearly gives one party the right to make a unilateral decision on the issue,[200] or where the Board has rendered a decision on the matter in dispute.[201] Some courts have held that each issue covered by the injunction must be shown to be arbitrable or the entire injunction will be struck down.[202]

---

[196]Boys Markets v. Retail Clerks Local 770, *supra* note 188. *See also* Coordinating Comm. Steel Cos. v. Steelworkers, 436 F Supp 208, 95 LRRM 3257 (WD Pa, 1977) (refusing to enjoin strike over putatively "local" issues where parties had agreed upon binding interest arbitration as substitute for right to strike or lockout as to all "national," but not "local," issues which parties could not resolve at bargaining table).

[197]414 US 368, 85 LRRM 2049 (1974).

[198]*See* text *supra* at notes 43–60.

[199]*See also* National Rejectors Indus. Div. v. Steelworkers Local 6178, 562 F2d 1069, 96 LRRM 2120 (CA 8, 1977), *cert. denied*, 435 US 923, 97 LRRM 3040 (1978). *But see* Matson Plastering Co. v. Plasterers Local 295, 633 F2d 1037, 106 LRRM 2129 (CA 9, 1980), *cert. denied*, 454 US 816, 108 LRRM 2559 (1981) (where it is not clear that strike is over arbitrable issue and is in violation of no-strike clause, district court has no jurisdiction to enjoin strike activity pending arbitrator's decision).

The presumption of arbitrability in *Boys Markets* cases is important, for the choice of a standard for determining what issues are arbitrable may determine whether an injunction issues. *See* Axelrod, *The Application of the* Boys Markets *Decision in the Federal Courts*, 16 B.C. INDUS. & COM. L. REV. 893, 914–19 (1975).

[200]Auto Workers v. Lester Eng'g Co., 718 F2d 818, 114 LRRM 2783 (CA 6, 1983).

[201]King Coal Co. v. Mine Workers, 530 F Supp 517, 110 LRRM 2786 (ND Ala, 1982). *Cf.* South Carolina Stevedores Ass'n v. Longshoremen (ILA) Local 1422, 765 F2d 422, 119 LRRM 3112 (CA 4, 1985) (properly issued injunction dissolved; arbitral ruling under national master contract precluded arbitration under local agreement).

[202]Hardline Elec. v. Electrical Workers (IBEW) Local 1547, 680 F2d 622, 110 LRRM 3041 (CA 9, 1982), *cert. denied*, 459 US 1170, 112 LRRM 2456 (1983); Fein Container Corp. v. Steel Metal Fabricators Local 810, 694 F Supp 1001 (D NJ, 1986). *But see* Elsinore Shore Assocs. v. Hotel Employees Local 54, 820 F2d 62, 125 LRRM 2690 (CA 3, 1987) (injunction upheld compelling arbitration, struck down as to prohibiting work stoppage, where dispute was partly arbitrable).

Once it is found that the dispute is subject to an arbitration procedure, the court may not enjoin the strike unless the employer is willing to arbitrate the underlying dispute.[203] In *Jacksonville Maritime Ass'n v. Longshoremen (ILA) Local 1408-A*,[204] however, the Fifth Circuit rejected the union's contention that the employer must both allege and *prove* its willingness to arbitrate an admittedly arbitrable issue before an injunction could properly issue. The court stated that it would not accept such a "procedural nicety" absent a clear directive from the Supreme Court.[205] On the other hand, some district courts have held that an employer must affirmatively pursue arbitration in order to prevail in a request for injunctive relief.[206] In any event, an attempt to avoid arbitration while at the same time seeking injunctive relief would not satisfy the *Boys Markets* prerequisites.[207]

Mutuality of access to arbitration by the employer and the union is not a prerequisite to enjoining a strike. In *Eaton Corp. v. Machinists*[208] the Seventh Circuit rejected the union's claim that an injunction could not issue since the employer had no "obligation" to initiate a grievance and take it to arbitration. The court held that *Boys Markets* does not require that both parties have the right to initiate arbitration, but only that both parties be bound to arbitrate if the union elects to pursue that remedy.[209]

Where the arbitration obligation has expired or terminated, a *Boys Markets* injunction is inappropriate.[210] Moreover, *Boys Mar-*

---

[203]Indeed, the court must order arbitration of the dispute prior to the issuance of the injunction. See discussion *infra* at notes 222–224.

[204]571 F2d 319, 98 LRRM 2184 (CA 5, 1978).

[205]*Id.* at 324.

[206]United Parcel Serv. (N.Y.) v. Teamsters Local 804, 698 F2d 100, 112 LRRM 2648 (CA 2, 1983); Restaurant Assocs. Indus. v. Hotel Employees Local 71, 78 LRRM 2559 (ED NY, 1971); Elevator Mfrs. Ass'n of N.Y. v. Elevator Constructors Local 1, 331 F Supp 165, 78 LRRM 2215 (SD NY, 1971).

[207]Chief Freight Lines Co. v. Teamsters Local 886, 514 F2d 572, 89 LRRM 2044, 2051 (CA 10, 1975). *See* Laborers Local 120 v. Shumaker Bros. Indus., 113 LRRM 3358 (SD Ind, 1983) (injunction denied where strike protested employer's refusal to pay wages ordered by arbitrator and no-strike claused excluded strikes over wage claims). *But cf.* Anheuser-Busch v. Teamsters Local 133, 477 F Supp 742, 102 LRRM 2990 (ED Mo, 1979) (injunction issued despite union's contention that dispute had already been arbitrated and employer was refusing to comply with award).

[208]580 F2d 254, 99 LRRM 2042 (CA 7, 1978).

[209]*Id.; see also* Steelworkers v. Fort Pitt Steel Casting Div., 598 F2d 1273, 101 LRRM 2406 (CA 3, 1979); Avco Corp. v. Auto Workers Local 787, 459 F2d 968, 80 LRRM 2290 (CA 3, 1972).

[210]National Mine Serv. Co. v. Steelworkers Local 8016, 385 F Supp 856, 87 LRRM 3288 (ND WVa, 1974), *aff'd per curiam,* 510 F2d 966, 88 LRRM 2847 (CA 4, 1975) (contract properly terminated by union); A.S. Abell Co. v. Typographical Union No. 12 (Baltimore), 85 LRRM 2368 (D Md, 1974) (contract expired). *Cf.* Newspaper Guild Local 52 (Northern Cal.) v. Sacramento Union, 856 F2d 1381, 129 LRRM 2361 (CA 9, 1988); Purex

kets applies only where the collective bargaining agreement contains a "mandatory" grievance adjustment or arbitration procedure, that is, one which requires that contract disputes be settled by the grievance-arbitration procedure and allows the union to invoke the procedure without the employer's further consent.[211] Finally, an arbitration clause, unlike a no-strike clause, must be expressly agreed upon by the parties; an arbitration clause will not be implied from other contractual commitments.[212]

d. Irreparable Injury and the Balance of Equities. In *Boys Markets* the Court cautioned the lower courts not to grant injunctive relief unless warranted under ordinary principles of equity. These require determination of whether the alleged contract breaches "have caused or will cause irreparable injury to the employer; and whether the employer will suffer more from the denial of an injunction than will the union from its issuance."[213] The courts have usually found irreparable injury[214] and that the equities favored the employer.[215] Often the courts have simply

---

Corp. v. Teamsters Local 618, 705 F2d 274, 112 LRRM 3433 (CA 8, 1983) (arbitration clause limited to employee grievances cannot be read to render contract termination clause arbitrable). *But see* Catalytic, Inc. v. Building Trades Council (Monmouth & Ocean County), 829 F2d 430, 126 LRRM 2425 (CA 3, 1987), *cert. denied sub nom.* Operating Eng'rs Local 825 v. Catalytic, Inc., 485 US 1020, 128 LRRM 2144 (1988) (upholding injunction against work stoppage based on implied extension of expired contract). *See also* Elsinore Shore Assocs. v. Hotel Employees Local 54, *supra* note 202 (no injunction of strike over wage demand during bargaining under reopener). However, the obligation to arbitrate does not necessarily terminate with the expiration of the contract. *See* Nolde Bros. v. Bakery Workers Local 358, 430 US 243, 94 LRRM 2753 (1977).

[211] *See* Boys Markets v. Retail Clerks Local 770, 398 US 235, 253, 74 LRRM 2257 (1970). Provisions requiring mutual consent for submission to arbitration cannot support a *Boys Markets* injunction, for *Boys Markets* applies only to institutionalized, mutually binding, arbitration procedures and not to ad hoc arrangements. *See* Associated Gen. Contractors of Ill. v. Teamsters, Illinois Conference, 454 F2d 1324, 79 LRRM 2555 (CA 7, 1972); Womeldorf, Inc. v. Teamsters Local 220, 369 F Supp 901, 87 LRRM 2316 (WD Pa, 1974). On the other hand, a contract stating that a party "may" invoke arbitration, rather than stating that it *must* do so, will support injunctive relief. Steelworkers v. Fort Pitt Steel Casting Div., *supra* note 209, 101 LRRM at 2410.

[212] *See* Lynchburg Foundry Co. v. Pattern Makers, 597 F2d 384, 101 LRRM 2047 (CA 4, 1979); Operating Eng'rs Local 675 v. Trumbull Corp., 93 LRRM 2337 (SD Fla, 1976).

[213] 398 US at 254. Earlier in its opinion the Court remarked that "an award of damages after a dispute has been settled is no substitute for an immediate halt to an illegal strike." *Id.* at 248. This statement, however, concerned whether injunctive relief should be available under any circumstances; it does not undercut the requirement that an employer must prove irreparable injury in the particular case in order to obtain an injunction. *See* Granny Goose Foods v. Teamsters, Local 70, 415 US 423, 441–42, 85 LRRM 2481 (1974).

[214] *See, e.g.*, Jacksonville Maritime Ass'n v. Longshoremen, (ILA) Local 1408-A, *supra* note 204; General Bldg. Contractors Ass'n v. Operating Eng'rs Locals 542, 542-A, 542-B, 371 F Supp 1130, 86 LRRM 2677 (ED Pa, 1974).

[215] *See, e.g.*, Gateway Coal Co. v. Mine Workers Dist. 4, Local 6330, *supra* note 197. Western Publishing Co. v. Graphic Arts Local 254, 522 F2d 530, 90 LRRM 2257 (CA 7,

stated, without discussion, that the employer would suffer more from the denial of an injunction than the union would from a grant of relief.[216] In thus striking the balance in favor of the employer, however, the courts have often required the employer to take certain actions pending arbitration,[217] which in effect may grant the union complete or partial relief pending arbitration.[218]

There have been very few cases in which courts have denied injunctive relief solely on general equity grounds.[219] In one such case, *Anheuser-Busch, Inc. v. Teamsters Local 633*,[220] the First Circuit held that a district court abused its discretion by enjoining a strike brought on by an employer's disciplining of brewery employees for wearing "tank top" shirts. While the dispute over the employer's right to prohibit the wearing of such shirts was concededly subject to the grievance-arbitration procedures of the contract, the First Circuit stated: "[A]n employer cannot be permitted to qualify for injunctive relief simply by responding to minor employee infractions in a way that brings serious and irreparable damage upon himself by causing a shutdown . . . ."[221] The controversy was whether the employees would continue to wear tank-top shirts pending submission to arbitration, and the employer's expected injury if they did could

---

1975), *cert. denied,* 423 US 1088, 91 LRRM 2195 (1976). On the issue of the relative equities between the employer and the union, decisions involving union efforts to obtain "status quo" injunctions, discussed *infra* at notes 247–271, are instructive.

[216]*See, e.g.,* Edward L. Nezelek, Inc. v. Teamsters Local 294, 342 F Supp 507, 80 LRRM 3459 (ND NY, 1972).

[217]*E.g.,* Hanna Mining Corp. v. Steelworkers, 464 F2d 565, 80 LRRM 3268 (CA 8, 1972) (per curiam).

[218]*E.g.,* Gateway Coal v. Mine Workers Dist. 4, Local 6330, 414 US 368, 85 LRRM 2049 (1974) (termination of two foremen who violated safety rules; district court, in issuing *Boys Markets* injunction, ordered employer to suspend two foremen pending arbitration); Hanna Mining Corp. v. Steelworkers, *supra* note 217. *Cf. infra* at notes 247–252.

[219]*See, e.g.,* Anheuser-Busch, Inc. v. Teamsters Local 633, 511 F2d 1097, 88 LRRM 2785 (CA 1), *cert. denied,* 423 US 875, 90 LRRM 2744 (1975); North Am. Coal Corp. v. Mine Workers Local 2262, 497 F2d 459, 86 LRRM 2339 (CA 6, 1974); Greater N.Y. Health Care Facilities Ass'n v. Ottley, 499 F Supp 279, 106 LRRM 2181 (SD NY, 1980) (court dissolved preliminary injunction due to employer association's inequitable conduct in engineering lockout at one facility and failing to meet obligations with regard to health plan payments; court had originally struck balance of equities in favor of employer association, relying heavily on possible injury to nursing home patients, Greater N.Y. Health Care Facilities Ass'n v. Ottley, 493 F Supp 612, 106 LRRM 2169 (SD NY, 1980)).

[220]*Supra* note 219.

[221]*Id.* at 1099. *Anheuser-Busch* was distinguished in an Eighth Circuit decision, where the court affirmed a district court's issuance of a *Boys Markets* injunction, stating: "[The company] did not bring about the disruption itself by insisting upon enforcement of minor work rules. The company was willing to, and did in fact suspend enforcement of its rules pending resolution of the underlying dispute through arbitration." National Rejectors Indus. Div. v. Steelworkers Local 6178, 562 F2d 1069, 1077, 96 LRRM 2120 (CA 8, 1977), *cert. denied,* 435 US 923, 97 LRRM 3040 (1978).

not be deemed either irreparable or greater than that to the union from issuance of an injunction.

e. Employer Ordered to Arbitrate. As stated in *Boys Markets,* "the employer should be ordered to arbitrate as a condition of his obtaining an injunction against [a] strike."[222] The Second Circuit, in *Teamsters Local 807 v. Bohack Corp.,*[223] set aside a *Boys Markets* injunction because of the failure of the district court to order arbitration of the underlying dispute. The district court had relied on the fact that the employer had earlier filed for bankruptcy and was operating under the jurisdiction of the bankruptcy court. The Second Circuit ruled that a bankruptcy action does not necessarily immunize an employer from strikes, and that bankruptcy does not relax *Boys Markets* requirements.[224]

f. Limitations on Prospective Relief; Mootness. Ordinarily, *Boys Markets* injunctions against strikes will be granted only where the strike is occurring or is imminent. In some cases, however, employers have sought and received prospective injunctive relief, that is, injunctions prohibiting future strikes over events that have not yet occurred. Three circuits have affirmed prospective injunctions in situations where there was a pattern of past strike violations deemed likely to continue if not enjoined.[225] Four other circuits have reversed prospective injunctions where there was insufficient proof of a pattern of past violations and where the injunctions were broadly framed to encompass strikes on issues over which the union had never

---

[222]*Supra* note 211, at 254; *accord* Teamsters Local 807 v. Bohack Corp., 541 F2d 312, 93 LRRM 2001 (CA 2, 1976), *cert. denied,* 439 US 825, 99 LRRM 2600 (1978); Emery Air Freight Corp. v. Teamsters Local 295, 449 F2d 586, 78 LRRM 2466 (CA 2, 1971), *cert. denied,* 405 US 1066, 79 LRRM 3092 (1972).

[223]*Supra* note 222.

[224]For a discussion of the relation of bankruptcy to NLRB action, see Chapter 30, "Accommodations to Other Federal Enactments," at notes 102–215.

[225]United Parcel Serv. (N.Y.) v. Teamsters Local 804, *supra* note 206 (demonstrated pattern of strikes in breach of contract). *Compare* Old Ben Coal Corp. v. Mine Workers Local 1487 (II), 500 F2d 950, 87 LRRM 2078 (CA 7, 1974) (injunction prohibiting "strikes resulting from any differences or local trouble which parties are contractually obligated to arbitrate," *Id.* at 951, where local union had engaged in 25 strikes in breach of a no-strike clause over 3½-year period) *with* Old Ben Coal Corp. v. Mine Workers Local 1487 (I), 457 F2d 162, 79 LRRM 2845 (CA 7, 1972) (broad prospective relief earlier held inappropriate). *See* Peabody Coal Co. v. Mine Workers Local 1670, 416 F Supp 485, 93 LRRM 2532 (ED Ill, 1976) (district court applies *Old Ben (II)* and issued broad prospective injunctive relief where local union had engaged in 37 strikes over arbitrable issues during 4½-year period). C F & I Steel Corp. v. Mine Workers, 507 F2d 170, 87 LRRM 3197 (CA 10, 1974) (injunction limited to future strikes over employee discharges, employee suspensions, and work assignments—issues over which union had proclivity for striking).

previously struck.[226] The Seventh Circuit affirmed a prospective injunction prohibiting "strikes resulting . . . from any differences or local troubles which the parties [are contractually] obligated to arbitrate. . . ."[227] In direct disagreement, the Fifth Circuit held that such a broad injunction is prohibited by section 9 of the Norris-LaGuardia Act and violates federal labor policy.[228]

Questions of prospective injunctive relief under *Boys Markets* are sometimes addressed as mootness questions. In *Kentucky West Virginia Gas Co. v. Oil, Chem. & Atomic Workers Local 3-510*[229] the union gave strike notice over the discharge of an employee, alleging it was entitled to strike under the contract. The strike did not materialize, the strike notice was later withdrawn, and the underlying dispute was submitted to binding arbitration. Holding that the employer's request for injunctive relief against the threatened strike was moot, the Sixth Circuit observed: "There is no indication that the union will direct that a strike be commenced in the near future . . . . Thus, the threat of a strike over the . . . discharge is certainly not a 'continuing and brooding presence.'"[230] The case was not moot, however, as to the union's contention that it had the right to strike over discharges which were arbitrable and the court ordered the union to submit that question to arbitration.[231]

In *Donovan Construction Co. v. Laborers Local 383*[232] the Ninth Circuit held that the entry of a permanent injunction was appro-

---

[226]Latas Libby's v. Steelworkers, 609 F2d 25, 102 LRRM 2796 (CA 1, 1979); United States Steel Corp. v. Mine Workers, 534 F2d 1063, 91 LRRM 3031 (CA 3, 1976); *see* Pittsburgh-Des Moines Steel Co. v. Steelworkers, 633 F2d 302, 105 LRRM 2198 (CA 3, 1980); Bituminous Coal Operators' Ass'n v. Mine Workers, 585 F2d 586, 99 LRRM 2612 (CA 3, 1978); Southern Ohio Coal Co. v. Mine Workers Local 1957, 551 F2d 695, 94 LRRM 2609 (CA 6), *cert. denied,* 434 US 876, 96 LRRM 2512 (1977); United States Steel Corp. v. Mine Workers, 519 F2d 1236, 90 LRRM 2539 (CA 5, 1975).

[227]Old Ben Coal Corp. v. Mine Workers Local 1487 (II), *supra* note 225, 87 LRRM at 2079. *Cf.* Latas Libby's v. Steelworkers, *supra* note 226, where the court stated in dictum: "[W]e do not say that repeated violations of a no-strike covenant never warrant broad prospective relief . . . ." *Id.* at 31–32.

[228]United States Steel Corp. v. Mine Workers, 519 F2d 1236, 1247 n.21, 90 LRRM 2539 (CA 5, 1975). The court discussed its disagreement with the Seventh Circuit's second *Old Ben* decision; *accord* Drummond Co. v. Mine Workers Dist. 20, 598 F2d 381, 101 LRRM 2754 (CA 5, 1979) (court reaffirmed its *United States Steel Corp.* holding and reserved decision on whether narrower prospective injunction can ever be appropriate).

[229]549 F2d 407, 94 LRRM 2652 (CA 6, 1977).

[230]*Id.* at 411.

[231]*See also* Cedar Coal Co. v. Mine Workers, 560 F2d 1153, 95 LRRM 3015 (CA 4, 1977), *cert. denied,* 434 US 1047, 97 LRRM 2441 (1978).

[232]533 F2d 481, 92 LRRM 2068 (CA 9, 1976). *See also* Jacksonville Bulk Terminals v. Longshoremen (ILA), 457 US 702, 704 n.1, 110 LRRM 2665 (1982), rejecting a mootness assertion on the grounds that the issue of whether the ceased conduct violates the agreement remained and the work stoppage could resume at any time.

priate and not moot even though the underlying jurisdictional dispute had gone to arbitration and both parties were acceding to the arbitrator's decision. The court held that a party could not moot an injunction action arising from its own misconduct simply by ceasing the challenged acts. Where a "convincing" showing is made of a reasonable apprehension of recurrence, an injunction operating prospectively is appropriate. At the same time, the appellate court found the district court's injunction too broad; the order should not have gone beyond enjoining any future strike similar to that which had occurred.

2. Sympathy Strikes Not Enjoinable: *Buffalo Forge*. The Supreme Court's 1976 decision in *Buffalo Forge Co. v. Steelworkers*[233] held that sympathy strikes were not enjoinable under *Boys Markets* because they are not "over" issues that the striking union is obligated to arbitrate, that is, the underlying dispute is typically between another union and the employer. *Buffalo Forge* arose when production and maintenance (P&M) employees refused to cross a picket line established by office and technical (O&T) employees working for the same employer. The P&M and O&T employees were represented in separate bargaining units by separate Steelworkers locals. The O&T strike was in support of bargaining demands for an initial collective bargaining agreement for the O&T unit. The collective bargaining agreement in effect between the employer and the striking P&M local contained broad no-strike and arbitration clauses. The parties agreed that the issue of whether the no-strike clause prohibited sympathy strikes was arbitrable. The employer sought an injunction pending arbitration of *that* issue.

The Supreme Court held that the case was governed by Norris-LaGuardia:

> *Boys Markets* plainly does not control this case . . . . The strike was not *over* any dispute between the Union and the employer that was even remotely subject to the arbitration provisions of the contract. The strike at issue was a sympathy strike in support of sister unions negotiating with the employer; neither its causes nor the issue underlying it was subject to the settlement procedures provided by the contracts between the employer and respondents. The strike had neither the purpose nor the effect of denying or evading an obligation to arbitrate or of depriving the employer of its bargain.[234]

---

[233]428 US 397, 92 LRRM 3032 (1976).
[234]*Id.* at 407–8.

The Court made clear that an injunction would not be appropriate simply because the sympathy strike allegedly violated the contract: "[T]he Court has never indicated that the courts may enjoin actual or threatened contract violations despite the Norris-LaGuardia Act."[235] It noted that such a rule would conflict with the congressional intent of the Taft-Hartley Act, as illustrated by Congress' specific rejection of a proposal that the Norris-LaGuardia Act's prohibition against labor-dispute injunctions be lifted to allow for federal court injunctive enforcement of collective bargaining agreements. Under a contrary rule, moreover, the courts would be called upon to resolve disputed issues of contract interpretation even though the parties had bargained for arbitral interpretation, thereby depriving the parties of the benefit of their bargain.[236] The Supreme Court refused to extend *Boys Markets* beyond its "narrow" holding, allowing for injunctive relief against strikes only where the underlying dispute is subject to a mandatory arbitration obligation.[237] The Court thus insisted, consistent with the *Steelworkers Trilogy,* that the arbitrator—not the district court—be the primary interpreter of the collective bargaining agreement in disputes the parties have agreed to arbitrate.

The circuit courts have developed fairly consistent criteria for applying *Buffalo Forge.* Sympathy strikes will not be enjoined absent proof that the sympathy strikers have joined in the primary strike and are, in effect, seeking for themselves the concessions on arbitrable issues sought by the primary strikers.[238]

---

[235]*Id.* at 409.

[236]An employer might obtain injunctive relief, however, even if the underlying dispute is not arbitrable, by submitting to arbitration the issue of whether the strike violates the no-strike clause and obtaining enforcement of a favorable arbitration award, which could include injunctive relief and/or damages. *See, e.g.,* New Orleans S.S. Ass'n v. Longshoremen (ILA) Local 1218, 626 F2d 455, 105 LRRM 2539 (CA 5, 1980), *aff'd sub nom.* Jacksonville Bulk Terminals v. Longshoremen (ILA), 457 US 702, 110 LRRM 2665 (1982), and cases cited at note 165 *supra.* In *Jacksonville Bulk Terminals,* the Supreme Court expressly noted that an arbitrator's decision finding the strike to be in violation of a no-strike clause was enforceable by an injunction. The Court also noted that a damage action under §301 was available for the breach of the no-strike clause even though a *Boys Markets* injunction was not available. *See infra* note 237.

[237]*Boys Markets* and *Buffalo Forge* relate only to injunctive relief; a union that strikes over an issue that is not subject to mandatory arbitration may still be held liable in monetary damages where the strike is in violation of a no-strike clause. *See, e.g.,* Iowa Beef Processors v. Meat Cutters, 597 F2d 1138, 101 LRRM 2235 (CA 8), *cert. denied,* 444 US 84, 102 LRRM 2440 (1979) (union held liable for damages resulting from sympathy strike in breach of no-strike clause); Note, *Damage Remedies for Sympathy Strikes After* Buffalo Forge, 78 COLUM. L. REV. 1164 (1978).

[238]Zeigler Coal Co. v. Mine Workers Local 1870, 566 F2d 582, 96 LRRM 3360 (CA 7, 1977), *cert. denied,* 436 US 912, 98 LRRM 2349 (1978); Cedar Coal Co. v. Mine Workers, *supra* note 231; Southern Ohio Coal Co. v. Mine Workers Local 1957, *supra* note 226.

Using that test, the Seventh Circuit narrowly confined an injunction, stating "that, if the defendants' strike were simply an extension of the illegal . . . wildcat, this would be a paradigm case for a *Boys Markets* injunction. [But] the defendants were [not] adopting the grievances and goals of the [other] local as their own and thus striking 'over' a matter subject to arbitration."[239] The Fourth Circuit, however, distinguished *Buffalo Forge* and held a strike enjoinable where a union sought to compel a concession on an arbitrable issue to a sister union involving the same employer, same location, same bargaining unit, and same contract, under circumstances that would increase the union's chances of obtaining the same benefit as its sister union.[240] The union, in effect, had made the cause of the sister union "its own."[241] But in the same case the court refused to distinguish *Buffalo Forge* where a union had engaged in a sympathy strike in support of a sister local's efforts to obtain a concession on an arbitrable issue from another employer, since the sympathy strikers there were not seeking a concession on an arbitrable issue from their own employer. The determinative issue is thus whether the sympathy strikers are merely expressing solidarity with another group of employees or are attempting to obtain for themselves a concession on an arbitrable issue.[242]

3. Safety Strikes. In *Gateway Coal Co. v. Mine Workers District 4, Local 6330*[243] the Supreme Court concluded that the "'presumption of arbitrability' announced in the *Steelworkers* trilogy applies to safety disputes."[244] However, the Court also concluded that

> a work stoppage called solely to protect employees from immediate danger is authorized by [section 502 of the Taft-Hartley Act] and cannot be the basis for either a damages award or a *Boys Markets* injunction . . . . [A] union seeking to justify a contractually prohibited work stoppage under Section 502 must present "ascertainable,

[239]Zeigler Coal Co. v. Mine Workers Local 1870, *supra* note 238, at 585. This decision closely parallels the Sixth Circuit's decision in Southern Ohio Coal Co. v. Mine Workers, *supra* note 226, both as to facts and law. The Sixth Circuit stressed that the focus is whether the sympathy strike is over an arbitrable issue, not whether the primary strikers are striking over an arbitrable issue.

[240]Cedar Coal Co. v. Mine Workers, *supra* note 231.

[241]*Id.* at 1172.

[242]The line between solidarity and adoption of a grievance as one's own can be a nice one. In the cases discussed *supra,* the Sixth and Seventh circuits apparently required direct proof that the sympathy strikers were seeking concessions for themselves. The Fourth Circuit, however, was willing, at least in part, to infer adoption of a sister local's grievance from the close identity of the two unions.

[243]414 US 368, 85 LRRM 2049 (1974).

[244]*Id.* at 379. See discussion *supra* at note 53.

objective evidence supporting its conclusion that an abnormally dangerous condition for work exists."[245]

Absent such evidence, *Boys Markets* is fully applicable.[246]

4. Injunctions Against Employers to Preserve the Status Quo. In *Locomotive Engineers v. Missouri-Kansas-Texas Railroad Co. (MKT)*[247] the Supreme Court held that a district court may require an employer to restore the status quo as the price of obtaining a strike injunction under the Railway Labor Act.[248] The case arose after the railroad substituted diesel locomotives for its shorter range steam locomotives and issued a set of "General Orders" doubling the length of the railroad's runs, thereby eliminating the jobs of several employees and requiring the relocation of others. When the unions threatened to strike, the railroad submitted the dispute to the National Railroad Adjustment Board (NRAB) and sought an injunction in federal court against the strike pending decision by the Board. The district court granted the injunction, but upon condition that the railroad either (1) restore the situation that existed prior to the General Orders, or (2) pay the affected employees the wages they would have received had the orders not been issued.

The Supreme Court upheld the jurisdiction of the district court to impose the conditions.[249] The Court rejected the employer's theory "that the conditions imposed by the District Court constituted a preliminary decision on the merits of the parties' dispute and therefore encroached upon the jurisdiction of the [NRAB]."[250] On the contrary, the Court concluded, the conditions imposed by the district court were "designed not only to promote the interests of justice, but also to preserve the jurisdiction of the [NRAB]."[251] The rationale was the following:

---

[245]414 US at 385–87 (quoting the dissenting opinion in the court of appeals, Gateway Coal Co. v. Mine Workers Dist. 4, Local 6330, 466 F2d 1157, 1162, 80 LRRM 3153 (CA 3, 1972)).

[246]In Gateway Coal Co. v. Mine Workers Dist. 4, Local 6330, 80 LRRM 2633 (WD Pa, 1971), *aff'd,* 414 US 368, 85 LRRM 2049 (1974), the district court enjoined the strike and also ordered the employer to take safety precautions pending arbitration. *See* note 218 *supra. But see* Irvin H. Whitehouse & Sons Co. v. NLRB, 659 F2d 830, 108 LRRM 2578 (CA 7, 1981) (rejecting Board's determination that strike was protected by §502; court relied in part on broad arbitration clause which was read to prohibit safety strikes).

[247]363 US 528, 46 LRRM 2429 (1960).

[248]Injunctions against strikes over grievance issues ("minor disputes") under the RLA had been approved by the Supreme Court as early as 1957. Railroad Trainmen v. Chicago River & Ind. R.R., 353 US 30, 39 LRRM 2578 (1957).

[249]363 US at 531–32.

[250]*Id.* at 532.

[251]*Id.* at 534.

> The dispute out of which the judicial controversy arose does not merely concern rates of pay or job assignments, but rather involves the discharge of employees from positions long held and the dislocation of others from their homes. From the point of view of these employees, the critical point in the dispute may be when the change is made, for, by the time of the frequently long-delayed [NRAB] decision, it might well be impossible to make them whole in any realistic sense. If this be so, the action of the district judge, rather than defeating the [NRAB's] jurisdiction, would operate to *preserve* that jurisdiction by preventing injury so irreparable that a decision of the [NRAB] in the unions' favor would be but an empty victory.[252]

Although *MKT* involved the Railway Labor Act, the principles discussed in *MKT* apply as well to contracts executed under the Taft-Hartley Act which contain arbitration clauses.[253]

The post–*Boys Markets* circuit court decisions are generally in harmony regarding the criteria for restraining an employer's actions pending arbitration. The determinative factor is whether injunctive relief is necessary to protect the arbitration process itself, as where an employer's actions prior to an arbitrator's ruling would have the effect of undercutting the arbitrator's ability to render an effective award.[254] As the Fourth

---

[252]*Id.* (emphasis added). *MKT* involved conditions imposed on an employer as the price of a strike injunction. But subsequent cases have established that in certain circumstances, an injunction requiring an employer to restore the status quo pending arbitration can be entered even when no injunction against the union is sought or obtained by the employer. See cases cited in note 254, *infra.*

[253]*See, e.g.*, Gateway Coal Co. v. Mine Workers Dist. 4, Local 6330, *supra* note 246, in which the Supreme Court approvingly noted this feature of the injunction entered by the district court.

[254]*See* Industrial Workers (Gulf Coast) (NIWU) v. Exxon Corp., 712 F2d 161, 114 LRRM 2016 (CA 5, 1983); Auto Workers v. Dana Corp., 679 F2d 634, 110 LRRM 2519 (CA 6, 1982), *dismissed as moot due to intervening settlement,* 697 F2d 718, 112 LRRM 2457 (CA 6, 1983); Machinists Local Lodge 1266 v. Panoramic Corp., 668 F2d 276, 109 LRRM 2169 (CA 7, 1981). *See also* Nursing Home & Hosp. Union 434 v. Sky Vue Terrace, 759 F2d 1094, 119 LRRM 2097 (CA 3, 1985); Postal Workers v. Bolger, 621 F2d 615, 104 LRRM 2341 (CA 4, 1980); Typographical Union No. 16 (Chicago) v. Chicago Newspaper Publishers' Ass'n, 620 F2d 602, 103 LRRM 2957 (CA 7, 1980); Steelworkers v. Fort Pitt Steel Casting Div., 598 F2d 1273, 101 LRRM 2406 (CA 3, 1979) (employer enjoined, pending arbitration, from ceasing health plan payments even though contract had expired); Teamsters Local 71 v. Akers Motor Lines, 582 F2d 1336, 99 LRRM 2601 (CA 4, 1978), *cert. denied,* 440 US 929, 100 LRRM 2687 (1979); Transit Union Div. 1384 v. Greyhound Lines (II), 550 F2d 1237, 95 LRRM 2097 (CA 9), *cert. denied,* 434 US 837, 96 LRRM 2514 (1977); Lever Bros. Co. v. Chemical Workers Local 217, 554 F2d 115, 95 LRRM 2438 (CA 4, 1976); Auto Workers v. Exide Corp., 688 F Supp 174, 130 LRRM 2405 (ED Pa), *aff'd,* 857 F2d 1464, 134 LRRM 3200 (CA 3, 1988); Wireless Cable of N.Y. v. Electrical Workers (IBEW) Local 3, 127 LRRM 2046 (SD NY, 1987); Oil, Chem. & Atomic Workers v. Texaco Ref. & Mktg., 660 F Supp 1350, 125 LRRM 3127 (D Del, 1987); Ladies' Garment Workers v. Bali Co., 649 F Supp 1083, 123 LRRM 3210 (D PR, 1986), *appeal dismissed,* 815 F2d 691 (CA 1, 1987).

Circuit stated in *Lever Brothers Co. v. Chemical Workers Local 217*:[255]

> An injunction to preserve the *status quo* pending arbitration may be issued either against a company or against a union in an appropriate *Boys Markets* case where it is necessary to prevent conduct by the party enjoined from rendering the arbitral process a hollow formality in those instances where, as here, the arbitral award when rendered could not return the parties substantially to the *status quo ante.*[256]

The Ninth Circuit has held that a status quo injunction may also be appropriate in cases where the employer has agreed to maintain the status quo pending arbitration as a quid pro quo for the union's agreement not to strike.[257] In such cases, the courts would be enforcing the parties' quid pro quos—the union's no-strike obligation and the employer's status quo obligation—pending disposition of the underlying arbitrable dispute. The Seventh and Sixth circuits have held that contractual status quo obligations do not warrant injunctive relief in cases where an arbitrator could grant appropriate relief and effectively restore the status quo ante.[258]

Injunctions pending arbitration have been granted where the employer intended to implement a major business change that threatened to present the union and the arbitrator with a fait accompli. For example, injunctions have issued in favor of unions in cases where the employer intended to close a plant and move production elsewhere,[259] close down an ancillary part of

---

[255]*Supra* note 254.

[256]*Id.* at 123.

[257]Transit Union Div. 1384 v. Greyhound Lines (II), *supra* note 254. In Transit Union Div. 1384 v. Greyhound Lines (I), 529 F2d 1073, 91 LRRM 2456 (CA 9, 1976), the court enjoined work-schedule changes pending arbitration on general equity principles. The Supreme Court, in Greyhound Lines v. Transit Union Div. 1384, 429 US 807, 807, 93 LRRM 2362 (1976), vacated judgment and remanded the case "for further consideration in light of *Buffalo Forge.*" On remand, the Ninth Circuit held injunctive relief was inappropriate because the work-schedule changes would not frustrate and interfere with the arbitral process, and Greyhound did not commit itself to maintaining the status quo pending arbitration, Transit Union Div. 1384 v. Greyhound Lines (II), *supra. Accord* Postal Workers, Seattle, Wash., Local v. U.S. Postal Serv., 101 LRRM 2565 (WD Wash, 1979) (implementation of no-smoking rule enjoined where collective bargaining agreement had status quo provisions regarding working conditions).

[258]Typographical Union No. 16 (Chicago) v. Chicago Newspaper Publishers' Ass'n, *supra* note 254; Typographical Union No. 18 (Detroit) v. Detroit Newspaper Publishers Ass'n, 471 F2d 872, 82 LRRM 2332 (CA 6, 1972), *cert. denied,* 411 US 967, 83 LRRM 2039 (1973).

[259]Teamsters Local 71 v. Akers Motor Lines, *supra* note 254; Lever Bros. Co. v. Chemical Workers Local 217, *supra* note 254 (union relied on contract clause requiring employer to give union "due consideration" before assigning work to outside contractors); Ladies' Garment Workers v. Bali Co., *supra* note 254; Teamsters Local 961 v. Graves

its operations,[260] or liquidate assets at a time when grievances involving potential monetary liability were pending.[261] On the other hand, employers have generally prevailed in cases involving methods of operations that had been changed but where the change could be reversed if so ordered by an arbitrator and the work force would remain intact during the interim period.[262]

As in strike injunctions against unions, injunctions pending arbitration against employers are to be issued only in accordance with traditional principles of equity, including a showing of irreparable injury, that the potential harm to the employer should an injunction issue does not clearly outweigh the potential harm to the union should an injunction not issue, and that the union has a reasonable likelihood of success on the merits.[263]

Truck Line, 502 F Supp 1292, 106 LRRM 2233 (D Colo, 1980). *But cf.* Hoh v. Pepsico, Inc., 491 F2d 556, 85 LRRM 2517 (CA 2, 1974) (court refused to enjoin brewery closing where, inter alia, the union's contractual grievance was extremely weak, balance of equities strongly favored employer, and Norris-LaGuardia Act procedures were not followed. *See also* Nursing Home & Hosp. Employees Local 1115, Fla. Div. v. B & K Invs., 96 LRRM 2353 (SD Fla, 1977) (purchaser of nursing home enjoined from reselling home pending arbitration concerning purchaser's contractual obligations as successor).

[260]Bakery Drivers Local 802 v. S. B. Thomas, Inc., 99 LRRM 2253 (ED NY, 1978) (closing down delivery of baked goods to restaurants); Koster Bakeries v. Teamsters Local 802, 97 LRRM 2806 (SD NY, 1977) (bakery enjoined pending arbitration from eliminating its bread delivery routes).

[261]Teamsters Local 71 v. Akers Motor Lines, *supra* note 254.

[262]Postal Workers v. Bolger, *supra* note 254; Typographical Union No. 16 (Chicago) v. Chicago Newspaper Publishers' Ass'n, *supra* note 254. Typographical Union No. 18 (Detroit) v. Detroit Newspaper Publishers Ass'n, *supra* note 258. In Mail Handlers v. Postal Workers, 103 LRRM 3107 (D Neb, 1978), the Postal Service was enjoined, pending arbitration, from reducing staff at a post office where the displaced employees would have to transfer, with their families, hundreds of miles away, thereby imposing a serious hardship and an obstacle to restoring the status quo should the arbitrator rule in the union's favor.

[263]*See, e.g.*, Independent Oil & Chem. Workers of Quincy v. Procter & Gamble Mfg. Co., 864 F2d 927, 130 LRRM 2311 (CA 1, 1988) (injunction denied); Morton v. Beyer, 822 F2d 364 (CA 3, 1987) (reduction in wages not irreparable harm); Nursing Home & Hosp. Union 434 v. Sky Vue Terrace, *supra* note 254 (injunction granted); Food & Commercial Workers Local 626 v. Kroger Co., 778 F2d 1171, 120 LRRM 3550 (CA 6, 1985), *cert. denied,* 479 US 815, 123 LRRM 2591 (1986) (injunction denied; no irreparable harm); Lever Bros. Co. v. Chemical Workers Local 217, *supra* note 254 (injunction granted); Consolidated Freightways Corp. v. Highway Truckdrivers Local 107, No. 87-1493 (ED Pa, 6/24/87) (1987 WESTLAW 12756) (same); Food & Commercial Workers Local 17a v. Superior's Brand Meats, 656 F Supp 746 (ND Ohio, 1987) (injunction denied); Stevens Shipping & Terminal Co. v. Longshoremen (ILA) Local 1422, 121 LRRM 3227 (D SC, 1985) (injunction granted; immediate and irreparable injury found); Electrical Workers (UE) v. Simpson Mfg. Co., 115 LRRM 2149 (ND Cal, 1983) (injunction granted); Mine Workers Local 1110 v. Consolidation Coal Co., 531 F Supp 734, 112 LRRM 2259 (ND WVa, 1982) (injunction granted; balance of equities favors employees where employer's refusal to allow individual employees to testify or be present at grievance procedures would render arbitration "hollow formality"); Auto Workers v. Lester Eng'g Co., 575 F Supp 797, 110 LRRM 2285 (ND Ohio, 1982) (injunction denied; no likelihood of success on merits; damages adequate remedy; granting injunction would cause irreparable harm to interests of others and would not serve public interest); Teamsters Local 705 v. Almarc Mfg., 553 F Supp 1170, 112 LRRM 2236 (ND Ill, 1982), *motion to suspend denied,* 112 LRRM 2368 (CA 7,

The element of irreparable injury is especially important in cases where the injunction is premised on the rationale of preserving the arbitration process, that is, maintaining the status quo where the employer's action threatens to present the union and the arbitrator with a fait accompli.

Employer action that threatens permanent loss of employment[264] or accrued benefits may constitute irreparable injury. While this typically involves relocation or closing of the entire plant,[265] changes in business practice that threaten the employment of individuals within a continuing operation are also covered.[266] Changes in work conditions and employee benefits can

---

1982); Dresser Indus., Dresser Clark Div. v. Steelworkers Local 4601, 110 LRRM 2661 (WD NY, 1981) (injunction denied; no likelihood of success on merits); Food & Commercial Workers Local 692 v. Pantry Pride, 522 F Supp 1009, 109 LRRM 2009 (D Md, 1981) (no likelihood of success on merits); Greater N.Y. Health Care Facilities Ass'n v. Ottley, 499 F Supp 279, 106 LRRM 2181 (SD NY, 1980) (preliminary injunction vacated; where it appears employer has engineered lockout of union employees and has failed to live up to obligation to fund hospital benefits, "balance of the equities" supports ending of injunction prohibiting strikes). *But see* Machinists Local Lodge 1266 v. Panoramic Corp., *supra* note 254, 109 LRRM at 2175 (grant of injunction affirmed despite district court's failure to require union to establish likelihood of prevailing on merits; court held that where failure to enjoin employer's action would leave arbitrator with no real power to award adequate remedy, party seeking injunction need only establish "that the position he will espouse in arbitration is sufficiently sound to prevent the arbitration from being a futile endeavor") (citing Lawe v. Newman, 689 F2d 378, 111 LRRM 2591 (CA 2, 1982) (denial of injunction affirmed; standard for granting preliminary injunction in Second Circuit requires "a showing of (a) irreparable harm and (b) either (1) likelihood of success on the merits or (2) sufficiently serious questions going to the merits to make them a fair ground for litigation and a balance of hardships tipping decidedly toward the party requesting the preliminary relief." *Id.*, 111 LRRM at 2592); Teamsters Local 71 v. Akers Motor Lines, *supra* note 254; Transamerica Delaval v. Steelworkers, 109 LRRM 3064 (SD Tex, 1982)).

[264]Machinists Local Lodge 1266 v. Panoramic Corp., *supra* note 254; Auto Workers v. Goodyear Aerospace Corp., 656 F Supp 1283 (ND Ohio, 1986) (sale to successor); Electrical Workers' (UE) v. Simpson Mfg. Co., *supra* note 263 (company relocation enjoined in light of likely difficulty that largely Latino employees not fluent in English will have in finding another job); Transamerica Delaval v. Steelworkers, *supra* note 263 (discharged employee reinstated pending outcome of litigation; safety hazards at employee's new job presented threats to his health and life that could cause irreparable harm); Typographical Union No. 101 (Columbia) v. Evening Star Newspaper Co., 100 LRRM 2394, 2396 (D DC, 1978) (newspaper closing). In several cases, courts have denied injunctions against plant closings or relocation where employers could respond in money damages or reinstatement. *See* Aluminum Workers Local 215 v. Consolidated Aluminum Corp., 696 F2d 437, 112 LRRM 2299 (CA 6, 1982) (possible repossession, foreclosure, or injury to credit status of laid-off employees not type of harm that threatens integrity of arbitral process); Retail, Wholesale & Dep't Store Union Local 1034 v. Doxsee Food Corp., 650 F Supp 861, 124 LRRM 2752 (D Del, 1986); Hotel Employees Local 274 v. Westin Bellevue Stratford, 633 F Supp 869, 122 LRRM 3111 (ED Pa, 1986); Auto Workers Local 645 v. General Motors Assembly Div., 112 LRRM 3344 (CD Cal, 1982). *But see* Food & Commercial Workers Local 692 v. Pantry Pride, *supra* note 263 (loss of medical insurance pending arbitration was held to be not irreparable).

[265]*See* cases cited *supra* note 259.

[266]Locomotive Eng'rs v. Missouri-Kansas-Texas R.R., 363 US 528, 46 LRRM 2429 (1960); Transamerica Delaval v. Steelworkers, *supra* note 263; Bakery Drivers Local 802 v. S.B. Thomas, Inc., *supra* note 260.

satisfy the requirement of irreparable injury.[267] But, a nonsignatory employer (e.g., an alleged successor) may not be enjoined from hiring nonunion employees pending arbitration, at least "absent a judicial determination that two corporations are alter egos or a singular employer . . . ."[268] Unions seeking to enjoin employers' unilateral implementation of drug testing programs generally have been denied injunctive relief based on the absence of irreparable harm.[269]

The element concerning likelihood of success on the merits has been modified by some courts so as to avoid unnecessary judicial interpretation of the contract, in accordance with the Supreme Court's admonitions in *Buffalo Forge*.[270] According to the Fourth Circuit, "'a plaintiff . . . need only establish that the position he will espouse in arbitration is sufficiently sound to prevent the arbitration from being a futile endeavor.'"[271]

In addition to requiring that injunctions against employers meet traditional equitable standards, some courts have applied the Norris-LaGuardia Act to requests for injunctive relief under *Boys Markets*. The procedural requirements of section 7—including live testimony in an open court with an opportunity for cross-examination—are the most frequently applied.[272]

---

[267]Mine Workers Local 1110 v. Consolidation Coal Co., *supra* note 263 (change in vacation policy); Postal Workers Oakland Local v. U.S. Postal Serv., 107 LRRM 2943 (ND Cal, 1981) (employer's removal of rest bars from work station enjoined; removal might force retirement).

[268]Service Employees Local 47 v. Commercial Property Servs., 755 F2d 499, 118 LRRM 2786, 2790 (CA 6), *cert. denied*, 474 US 850, 120 LRRM 2632 (1985). *But see* Steelworkers v Connors Steel Co., 847 F2d 707, 128 LRRM 2807 (CA 11, 1988) (parent of bankrupt subsidiary enjoined from terminating benefits, based on finding of alter ego status).

[269]Oil, Chem. & Atomic Workers Local 2-124 v. Amoco Oil Co., (Casper Refinery, Wyo.), 651 F Supp 1, 123 LRRM 3104 (D Wyo, 1986); Oil, Chem. & Atomic Workers Local 6-10 v. Amoco Oil Co., 653 F Supp 300, 123 LRRM 2934 (D ND, 1986); Electrical Workers (IBEW) Local 1900 v. Potomac Elec. Power Co., 634 F Supp 642, 121 LRRM 3287 (D DC, 1986). *But see* Stove Workers v. Weyerhaeuser Paper Co., 650 F Supp 431, 126 LRRM 2184 (SD Ill, 1986) (enjoining implementation of drug and alcohol testing program pending arbitration).

[270]Teamsters Local 71 v. Akers Motor Lines, *supra* note 254; Lever Bros. Co. v. Chemical Workers Local 217, *supra* note 254; Transit Union Div. 1384 v. Greyhound Lines (I), *supra* note 257 (principle not affected by Supreme Court vacation and remand or decision in *Greyhound (II)); see* Bakery Drivers Local 802 v. S. B. Thomas, Inc., *supra* note 260. In Hoh v. Pepsico, Inc., *supra* note 259, a pre–*Buffalo Forge* case, the Second Circuit held that the *Steelworker Trilogy* presumption of arbitrability does not apply to the "likelihood of success on merits" test. The court cautioned trial court judges "to exercise the sound discretion of the chancellor." *Id.* at 561. The court concluded by noting the inequity of an injunction where the grievance "although arguably arbitrable is plainly without merit." *Id.*

[271]Teamsters Local 71 v. Akers Motor Lines, *supra* note 254, at 1342, 99 LRRM at 2605 (quoting, in part, Lever Bros. Co. v. Chemical Workers Local 217, *supra* note 254, at 120).

[272]Utility Workers Local 246 v. Southern Cal. Edison Co., 852 F2d 1083, 129 LRRM 2077 (CA 9, 1988); Telegraph Workers v. Western Union, 771 F2d 699, 120 LRRM 2403

Other courts have affirmed strict application of the section 8 requirement that the party seeking the injunction make "every reasonable effort" to settle the dispute,[273] the section 9 mandate that the injunction be drawn with specificity,[274] and the section 6 requirement that union officers can be held liable for its members' acts only upon clear proof of participation, authorization, or ratification of such acts.[275]

C. Injunction Suits in State Courts

In *William E. Arnold Co. v. Carpenters District Council of Jacksonville & Vicinity*[276] the Supreme Court rejected a claim that state court jurisdiction over collective bargaining disputes should be limited to claims for damages rather than injunctive relief. But the Court has never resolved the question of whether a state court is obligated to mirror the result that would obtain in the federal courts.[277]

In *Avco Corp. v. Machinists, Aero Lodge 735*,[278] a pre–*Boys Markets* decision, the Supreme Court held that section 301 suits brought in state courts are removable.[279] *Avco* left unanswered

---

(CA 3, 1985); United Parcel Serv. (N.Y.) v. Teamsters Local 804, 698 F2d 100, 112 LRRM 2648 (CA 2, 1983); Auto Workers Local 155 v. LaSalle Mach. Tool, 696 F2d 452, 112 LRRM 2199 (CA 6, 1982); Northern Stevedoring & Handling Corp. v. Longshoremen (ILWU) Local 60, 685 F2d 344, 111 LRRM 2245 (CA 9, 1982); Dresser Indus., Dresser Clark Div. v. Steelworkers Local 4601, *supra* note 263; Service Employees Local 250 v. Ralph K. Davies Medical Center, 110 LRRM 2964 (ND Cal, 1982). *But see* Machinists Local Lodge 1266 v. Panoramic Corp., *supra* note 254 (full evidentiary hearing should normally be required, but failure to have one will not be grounds for vacating injunction where facts on which injunction was based were undisputed, time was of the essence, and employer had been offered opportunity for hearing but had declined it); Teamsters Local 705 v. Almarc Mfg., *supra* note 263 (no reference to Norris-LaGuardia Act; court merely made specific findings of fact and conclusions of law required by §52(a) of the Federal Rules of Civil Procedure).

[273]United Parcel Serv. (N.Y.) v. Teamsters Local 804, *supra* note 272 ("every reasonable effort" does not require prior demand for arbitration when such demand has little chance of inducing settlement of dispute before entry of injunction).

[274]*Id.*; Service Employees Local 250 v. Ralph K. Davies Medical Center, *supra* note 272.

[275]Dresser Indus., Dresser Clark Div. v. Steelworkers Local 4601, *supra* note 272.

[276]417 US 12, 86 LRRM 2212 (1974).

[277]The question was left open in Avco Corp. v. Machinists Aero Lodge 735, 390 US 557, 560 n.2, 67 LRRM 2881 (1968). Since many states have their own "little Norris-LaGuardia statutes," this question does not frequently arise.

[278]*Supra* note 277.

[279]This rule was extended to removal of state administrative proceedings in Martin v. Schwerman Trucking Co., 446 F Supp 1130, 97 LRRM 3177 (ED Wis, 1978). One federal court has held that a §301 suit to compel arbitration is removable even where the collective bargaining agreement provided that neither party would seek to remove such an action. Carillo v. Hospital Employees Local 1115, 441 F Supp 619, 96 LRRM 3196 (SD NY, 1977). The court noted that because federal law would apply even in the state court action, it would be a waste of judicial resources to remand the case to state court.

the question of the effect of removal upon an existing state court injunction. The answer was supplied in *Granny Goose Foods v. Teamsters Local 70.*[280] Upon removal to a federal court, an ex parte temporary restraining order issued by a state court remains in force under state law, but in no event longer than the period of time provided by Rule 65(b) of the Federal Rules of Civil Procedure measured from the date of removal.[281]

V. NLRB INTERPRETATION OF THE COLLECTIVE BARGAINING AGREEMENT

The Board's role in interpreting labor agreements diminished since its adoption in 1971 of the prearbitral deferral policy of *Collyer Insulated Wire.*[282] However, where deferral to arbitration is not appropriate under the *Collyer* doctrine, or where the parties either have not agreed to a grievance-arbitration procedure in their contract or have declined to utilize an existing grievance-arbitration procedure, the Board has occasion to interpret the labor contract in connection with its unfair labor practice jurisdiction. The Board may also be required to construe contract provisions in other circumstances, as in determining whether a contract meets the criteria of the contract-bar doctrine. The discussion that follows deals with the Board's statutory authority to interpret labor agreements and the application of that authority.

---

[280]415 US 423, 85 LRRM 2481 (1974).

[281]Prior to *Granny Goose,* there was uncertainty regarding how long a state court injunction or restraining order remained in effect after removal. The uncertainty was caused by the apparent conflict between 28 USC §1450 (which provides, in essence, that state court injunctions or restraining orders upon removal remain in force until dissolved by the federal court) and Rule 65(b) of the Federal Rules of Civil Procedure (which provides, in essence, that temporary restraining orders expire within 10 days unless extended). In *Granny Goose* the Supreme Court accommodated these two provisions, stating:

> We can find no indication that Congress intended §1450 as an exception to its broader, longstanding policy of restricting the duration of *ex parte* restraining orders. The underlying purpose of §1450—ensuring that no lapse in a state court temporary restraining order will occur simply by removing the case to federal court—and the policies reflected in Rule 65(b) can easily be accommodated by applying the following rule: An *ex parte* temporary restraining order issued by a state court prior to removal remains in force after removal no longer than it would have remained in effect under state law, but in no event does the order remain in force longer than the time limitations imposed by Rule 65(b) . . . .

Id. at 439–40.

[282]192 NLRB 837, 77 LRRM 1931 (1971). For detailed discussion of the *Collyer* deferral doctrine and its development since 1971, see Chapter 18, "Accommodation of Board Action to the Arbitration Process."

A. Statutory Authority to Interpret Agreements

A contract violation is not of itself an unfair labor practice.[283] In early decisions, the Supreme Court recognized that the Board has jurisdiction over contract disputes to the extent necessary to resolve unfair labor practice charges.[284] With the emergence of section 301 and the developing of a federal common law governing interpretation of collective bargaining agreements,[285] however, the Court was again faced with the issue of the Board's jurisdiction to construe a contract. The Board's general authority so to do was affirmed in *NLRB v. C & C Plywood Corp.*[286]

The contract in that case authorized the employer "'to pay a premium rate over and above the contractual classified wage rate to reward any particular employee for some special fitness, skill, aptitude or the like.'"[287] Relying on this provision, the employer unilaterally established an incentive pay scale for all employees in a category of jobs. The Board found that the contract did not authorize this action and the employer therefore violated section 8(a)(5) by its unilateral conduct.[288] The Ninth Circuit held the Board acted without jurisdiction: "[S]ince it has no jurisdiction to enforce collective bargaining agreements as such, both reason and policy dictate that adjudication of disputes, as to the scope of contractual rights and obligations, be by tribunals empowered to compel compliance with them."[289]

The Supreme Court reversed. It held that the Board did "no more than merely enforce a statutory right" and that the Board's interpretation of the agreement went no further than to determine that the union had not agreed to give up the statutory safeguards.[290] The Court said that legislative history, precedent,

---

[283]*E.g.*, Mine Workers v. NLRB (Boone County Coal Corp.), 257 F2d 211, 214–15, 42 LRRM 2264 (CA DC, 1958); Independent Petroleum Workers v. Esso Standard Oil Co., 235 F2d 401, 405, 38 LRRM 2307 (CA 3, 1956); NLRB v. Pennwoven, Inc., 194 F2d 521, 524, 29 LRRM 2307 (CA 3, 1952). *See* Chapter 18, "Accommodation of Board Action to the Arbitration Process," at note 23.

[284]*E.g.*, J. I. Case v. NLRB, 321 US 332, 340, 14 LRRM 501 (1944); *accord* Sbicca, Inc., 30 NLRB 60, 72, 8 LRRM 33 (1941). *See* Dunau, *Contractual Prohibition of Unfair Labor Practices: Jurisdictional Problems*, 57 COLUM. L. REV. 52, 58, 72–74 (1957). *Cf.* Carey v. Westinghouse Elec. Corp., 375 US 261, 55 LRRM 2042 (1964).

[285]*See supra* at notes 22–41.

[286]385 US 421, 64 LRRM 2065 (1967). *See* Chapter 18, "Accommodation of Board Action to the Arbitration Process," at notes 23–27.

[287]*Id.* at 423 (qutoing contract).

[288]C & C Plywood, 148 NLRB 414, 57 LRRM 1015 (1964).'

[289]NLRB v. C & C Plywood, 351 F2d 224, 227–28, 60 LRRM 2137 (CA 9, 1965). The contract in question did not provide for binding arbitration, although that omission does not now affect the sweep of the decision. *See infra* note 292.

[290]385 US at 428.

and the interest of efficient administration all led to the conclusion that the Board does not exceed its jurisdiction when it construes a labor agreement where necessary to decide an unfair labor practice case.[291] The Court also noted that the contract in question did not have an arbitration clause, and therefore the Board's policy of deferring to arbitration was not involved.[292] *C & C Plywood* established that the Board's jurisdiction under section 10(a) is not displaced because relief may also be available under section 301 or because the Board must interpret the contract in order to decide the unfair labor practice issue.[293] The circuits disagree, at least to some extent, over the degree of deference they owe to the Board's interpretation of collective bargaining agreements. Some decisions defer when interpretation is necessary to the adjudication of unfair labor practice charges, is reasonable, and is not inconsistent with the Act.[294] Others extend less deference to the Board's interpretations.[295]

B. Cases Where the Board Interprets Contract Provisions

In *C & C Plywood,* a contract provision was asserted as a defense to an unfair labor practice charge. There are other ways

---

[291]*Id.* at 430. The Court cited Mastro Plastics Corp. v. NLRB, 350 US 270, 37 LRRM 2587 (1956), where the Court approved the Board's construction of a no-strike clause in order to resolve §§8(a)(1), (2), and (3) charges. *See* Chapter 19, "The Primary Strike," at note 85 and notes 157–161.

[292]The Board's policy of deferral to arbitration is a matter of discretion, rather than an issue of Board jurisdiction. "There is no question that the Board is not precluded from adjudicating unfair labor practice charges even though they might have been the subject of an arbitration proceeding and award." International Harvester Co., 138 NLRB 923, 925, 51 LRRM 1155 (1962). The Supreme Court's decisions are in accord. *See* NLRB v. Acme Indus. Co., 385 US 432, 64 LRRM 2069 (1967); Carey v. Westinghouse Elec. Corp., *supra* note 284. See also text accompanying notes 121–124, *supra*. Board policy regarding deferral to the arbitral process is discussed in detail in Chapter 18, "Accommodation of Board Action to the Arbitration Process."

[293]*Accord* NLRB v. Strong, 393 US 357, 70 LRRM 2100 (1969); NLRB v. Great Dane Trailers, 388 US 26, 30-31 n.7, 65 LRRM 2465 (1967); Carey v. Westinghouse Elec. Corp., *supra* note 284; Smith v. Evening News Ass'n, 371 US 195, 197, 51 LRRM 2646 (1962). See also text accompanying notes 121–124, *supra*.

[294]Electrical Workers (IBEW) Local 1392 v. NLRB (Indiana & Mich. Elec. Co.), 786 F2d 733, 121 LRRM 3259 (CA 6, 1986); Molders & Allied Workers Local 164 v. NLRB (Pacific Steel Casting Co.), 765 F2d 858, 860, 119 LRRM 3311 (CA 9, 1985).

[295]Manchester Health Center dba Crestfield Convalescent Home v. NLRB, 861 F2d 50, 129 LRRM 2849 (CA 2, 1988); Electrical Workers (IBEW) Local 1395 v. NLRB (Indianapolis Power & Light Co.), 797 F2d 1027, 1030, 122 LRRM 3265 (CA DC, 1986) (deference extended to factual findings bearing on intent but not to ultimate legal conclusions attached to words and conduct); Mission Marine, Pacemaker Yacht Co. Div. v. NLRB, 663 F2d 455, 458, 108 LRRM 2817 (CA 3, 1981) (courts owe no particular deference to Board on matters of contract interpretation); Irvin H. Whitehouse & Sons Co., v. NLRB, 659 F2d 830, 833, 108 LRRM 2578 (CA 7, 1981), (courts not obligated to defer to Board but this court generally exercises deference because of Board's expertise).

in which issues of contract interpretation may be relevant to the Board's jurisdiction over unfair labor practices and representation proceedings. For example, a collective bargaining agreement may incorporate an affirmative statutory obligation. In such cases, the Board may resolve the question even though the decision about the unfair labor practice is pro tanto a resolution of the contract question. In addition, the Act makes certain contractual arrangements illegal, for example, section 8(a)(3) prohibits closed-shop agreements and section 8(e) bars hot-cargo clauses. In such cases, the Board must measure the contract by the statutory standard to test its legality. Thus, issues of contract interpretation arise in many forms in the Board's exercise of its jurisdiction over unfair labor practices.

This discussion provides a broad description of categories of cases in which the Board has interpreted, and sometimes invalidated, collective bargaining agreements or clauses. These subjects are analyzed in depth elsewhere in this treatise. Discussion here is limited to the identification of categories in which contract interpretation questions frequently arise at the Board.

1. Interpretation of Lawful Contract Clauses. Questions of contract interpretation frequently arise in section 8(a)(5) or 8(b)(3) cases involving the duty to bargain, especially as it relates to changes in employment conditions or bargaining activity during the life of the contract.[296] Successorship issues also frequently require resort to and interpretation of the applicable agreement.[297]

Cases harmonizing individual rights under section 7 of the Act with collective obligations under bargaining agreements require the Board often to determine the extent to which a union has waived or restricted individual rights by contract, and whether such waivers or restrictions are lawful.[298] Section 8(a)(3) cases involving employee discipline or discharge may implicate contract interpretation questions where the employer asserts that the conduct of the employee involved violated the applicable collective bargaining agreement, or that the action complained of was consistent with contract provisions, past practice, and arbitration decisions and therefore was not motivated by union animus.[299] Unions may become party to

---

[296]See Chapter 13, "The Duty to Bargain," at notes 741–805.
[297]*See generally* Chapter 15, "Effect of Change in the Employing Unit: Successorship."
[298]*See, e.g.*, Chapter 13, "The Duty to Bargain," at notes 741–805.
[299]*See generally* Chapter 7, "Discrimination in Employment."

such cases and assert contractually based defenses to charges under section 8(b)(1)(A) or 8(b)(2).[300]

The Board and the Courts have repeatedly been called upon to construe and then address the validity of contract clauses in cases asserting violations of sections 8(a)(2) and 8(b)(1) involving such matters as superseniority and discrimination in favor of union members of specific unions.[301]

Parties will frequently support their positions in work assignment disputes under section 8(b)(4)(D) by reference to applicable contract language and past practice under an agreement.[302] Similar contract interpretation issues arise in various representational cases, where the Board may have to construe the recognition clause to determine the scope of existing bargaining units[303] or evaluate a contract for purposes of determining the applicability of the contract-bar doctrine.[304]

2. Interpretation to Determine Whether Express Statutory Prohibitions Have Been Violated. The Act specifically prohibits certain types of contractual arrangements. The Board is often faced with construing contract language in light of the statutory language and applicable case law. Union-security arrangements,[305] hot-cargo clauses,[306] and featherbedding clauses[307] fit into this catcgory.

---

[300]*Id.*
[301]*See generally* Chapter 8, "Employer Domination and Assistance to Labor Organizations."
[302]*See generally* Chapter 25, "Jurisdictional Disputes and 'Featherbedding.'"
[303]*See* Chapter 10, "Representation Proceedings and Elections," at notes 202–218.
[304]*Id.*
[305]*See generally* Chapter 27, "Union Security."
[306]*See generally* Chapter 24, "Section 8(e): The 'Hot-Cargo' Agreement."
[307]*See generally* Chapter 25, "Jurisdictional Disputes and 'Featherbedding.'"

CHAPTER 18

ACCOMMODATION OF BOARD ACTION TO THE ARBITRATION PROCESS

I. INTRODUCTION AND HISTORICAL DEVELOPMENT[1]

A. Arbitration and the Courts

In contemporary American labor law the arbitration process is the primary mechanism for resolving disputes arising under collective bargaining agreements. As the Supreme Court has explained, the grievance-arbitration procedure is

> the very heart of the system of industrial self-government. Arbitration is the means of solving the unforeseeable by molding a system

---

[1]Literature on this subject has been extensive. Bibliographical materials include the following: R. Covington, ARBITRATORS AND THE BOARD: A REVISED RELATIONSHIP (1978); M. Trotta, ARBITRATION OF LABOR-MANAGEMENT DISPUTES 132–48 (1974); Sherman, *The Role and Rights of the Individual in Labor Arbitration*, 15 WM. MITCHELL L. REV. 379 (1989); Lees, *To Arbitrate or Not to Arbitrate: Who Decides?*, 39 LAB. L.J. 418 (1988); St. Antoine, *Deferral to Arbitration and Use of External Law in Arbitration*, 10 INDUS. REL. L.J. 19 (1988); Gates & Elder, Olin *Must Not and Will Not Survive*, 38 LAB. L.J. 723 (1987); Henkel & Kelly, *Deferral to Arbitration After* Olin *and* United Technologies: *Has the NLRB Gone Too Far?*, 43 WASH. & LEE L.R. 37 (1986); Mack & Bernstein, *NLRB Deferral to the Arbitration Process: The Arbitrator's Demanding Role*, 40 ARB. J. 33 (Sept, 1985); Morris, *NLRB Deferral to the Arbitration Process: The Arbitrator's Awesome Responsibility*, 7 INDUS. REL. L.J. 290 (1985); Moses, *Deferral to Arbitration in Individual Rights Cases: A Re-Examination of* Spielberg, 51 TENN. L. REV. 187 (1984); Vacura, *Arbitration and NLRB Deferral: From* Spielberg *to* Suburban Motor Freight *and Beyond*, 20 WILLAMETTE L.J. 785 (1984); Alleyne, *Arbitration and the NLRB: The Nature of the Deferral Beast*, 4 INDUS. REL. L.J. 587 (1981); Harper, *Union Waiver of Employee Rights Under the NLRA: Part II, A Fresh Approach to Board Deferral to Arbitration*, 4 INDUS. REL. L.J. 680 (1981); Truesdale, *Is* Spielberg *Dead?*, NYU THIRTY-FIRST ANNUAL CONFERENCE ON LABOR 47 (1978); Hardin, *NLRB Jurisdiction: New Accommodations to Alternative Forums*, LABOR LAW DEVELOPMENTS 1974 (Twentieth Annual Institute on Labor Law, Southwestern Legal Foundation), 211 (1974); Teple, *NLRB Policy of Deferral to Arbitration*, 5 U. TOL. L. REV. 5 (1974); Getman, Collyer Insulated Wire: *A Case of Misplaced Modesty*, 49 IND. L.J. 57 (1973); Zimmer, *Wired for* Collyer: *Rationalizing NLRB and Arbitration Jurisdiction*, 48 IND. L.J. 141 (1973); Miller, *Deferral to Arbitration—Temperance or Abstinence?*, 7 GA. L. REV. 595 (1973); Nash, Wilder, & Banof, *Development of the* Collyer *Deferral Doctrine*, 27 VAND. L. REV. 23 (1973); Murphy & Sterlacci, *Review of the National Labor Relations Board's Deferral Policy*, 42 FORDHAM L. REV. 291 (1973); Isaacson & Zifchak, *Agency Deferral to Private Arbitration of Employment*

> of private law for all the problems which may arise and to provide for all their solution in a way which will generally accord with the variant needs and desires of the parties. The processing of disputes through the grievance machinery is actually a vehicle by which meaning and content is given to the collective bargaining agreement.
>
> . . . The grievance procedure is, in other words, a part of the continuous collective bargaining process.[2]

Initially there was some doubt as to whether executory agreements to arbitrate grievances under labor contracts were enforceable. At common law, judicial process could not be invoked to compel compliance with an arbitration clause as to a dispute that was not in being when the agreement was executed.[3] After

---

Disputes, 73 COLUM. L. REV. 1383 (1973); Hilbert, *NLRB and Arbitration: The Impact of* Collyer Insulated Wire, 6 GA. L. REV. 522 (1972); Menard, *National Labor Relations Board—No Longer a Threat to the Arbitral Process?*, 23 LAB. L.J. 140 (1972); Anderson, *NLRB and Private Arbitration: Should* Collyer *Be Extended to Employee Discipline Cases?*, 13 B.C. INDUS. & COM. L. REV. 1460 (1972); Schatzki, *Earliest Returns From the NLRB's New Deferral Policy in* Collyer Insulated Wire, NYU TWENTY-FIFTH ANNUAL CONFERENCE ON LABOR 97 (1972); Anderson. *Concurrent Jurisdiction—NLRB and Private Arbitration: A Pragmatic Analysis*, 12 B.C. INDUS. & COM. L. REV. 179 (1970); Peck, *Accommodation and Conflict Among Tribunals: Whatever Happened to Preemption?*, LABOR LAW DEVELOPMENTS 1969 (Fifteenth Annual Institute on Labor Law, Southwestern Legal Foundation) 121 (1969); Bond, *The Concurrence Conundrum: The Overlapping Jurisdicture of Arbitration and the National Labor Relations Board*, 12 S. CAL. L. REV. 42 (1968); Brown, *The National Labor Policy, the NLRB and Arbitration*, in DEVELOPMENTS IN AMERICAN AND FOREIGN ARBITRATION (Proceedings of the Twenty-First Annual Meeting, National Academy of Arbitrators) 83 (1968); Cushman, *Arbitration and the Duty to Bargain*, 1967 WIS. L. REV. 612 (1967); Rothschild, *Arbitration and the National Labor Relations Board: An Examination of Preferences and Prejudices and Their Relevance*, 28 OHIO ST. L.J. 195 (1967); Ordman, *Arbitration and the NLRB—A Second Look*, in THE ARBITRATOR, THE NLRB, AND THE COURTS (Proceedings of the Twentieth Annual Meeting, National Academy of Arbitrators) 47 (1967); Dunau, *Contractual Prohibition of Unfair Labor Practices: Jurisdictional Problems*, 57 COLUM. L. REV. 52 (1967); Seitz, *Grievance Arbitration and the National Labor Policy*, NYU EIGHTEENTH ANNUAL CONFERENCE ON LABOR 201 (1966); Lesnick, *Arbitration as a Limit on the Discretion of Management, Union, and NLRB: The Year's Major Developments*, NYU EIGHTEENTH ANNUAL CONFERENCE ON LABOR 7 (1966); Moss, *Arbitration and the NLRB's Jurisdiction*, NYU SEVENTEENTH ANNUAL CONFERENCE ON LABOR 65 (1965); Harris, *The National Labor Relations Board and Arbitration—The Battle of Concurrent Jurisdiction*, 16 SYRACUSE L. REV. 545 (1965); McCulloch, *The Arbitration Issue in NLRB Decisions*, 19 ARB. J. 134 (1964); McCulloch, *Arbitration and/or the NLRB*, 18 ARB. J. 3 (1963); Christensen, *Arbitration, Section 301, and the National Labor Relations Act*, 37 N.Y.U. L. REV. 411 (1962); Cummings, *NLRB Jurisdiction and Labor Arbitration: "Uniformity" vs. "Industrial Peace,"* 12 LAB. L.J. 425 (1961); Levitt, *Interrelationships in the Interpretation of Collective Bargaining Agreements*, 10 LAB. L.J. 484 (1959); Samoff, *The NLRB and Arbitration: Conflicting or Compatible Currents*, 9 LAB. L.J. 689 (1958); Note, *NLRB and Deference to Arbitration*, 77 YALE L.J. 1191 (1968); Note, *Employers' Duty to Supply Economic Data for Collective Bargaining*, 57 COLUM. L. REV. 112 (1957). See also bibliographical references cited in relevant footnotes throughout this chapter, particularly in note 62, *infra*.

[2]Steelworkers v. Warrior & Gulf Navigation Co., 363 US 574, 581, 46 LRRM 2416, 2419 (1960). *See* Chapter 17, "Relation of Board Action to Enforcement of Agreements Under Section 301," at notes 50–53.

[3]*See, e.g.*, Red Cross Line v. Atlantic Fruit Co., 264 US 109, 125 (1924); F. Elkouri & E. Elkouri, HOW ARBITRATION WORKS 39–41 (4th ed. 1985).

passage of the United States Arbitration Act of 1935,[4] some federal courts relied on that statute to specifically enforce arbitration agreements in collective bargaining contracts. It is still unclear, however, whether that Act applies to disputes under collective agreements. Section 1 of that Act, which defines its scope, specifically provides: "[N]othing herein contained shall apply to contracts of employment of seamen, railroad employees, or any other class of workers engaged in foreign or interstate commerce."[5] There is a split of authority as to whether this exclusion concerns only individual contracts of employment or is also applicable to collective bargaining contracts. The courts which have found the Federal Arbitration Act applicable to collective agreements have generally theorized that the term "contracts of employment" in section 1 refers only to individual transactions rather than union-negotiated agreements.[6] But other courts have interpreted section 1 to exclude coverage for labor agreements if the workers subject to the contract are in any way "engaged" in interstate commerce.[7] However, the issue of statutory coverage under the Arbitration Act became virtually moot following the Supreme Court's holding in *Textile Workers v. Lincoln Mills*.[8] As previously noted,[9] the Court held that section 301[10] not only authorized federal courts to assume jurisdiction over suits for specific performance of agreements to arbitrate, but also mandated that the substantive law to be applied in such suits would be federal law, to be fashioned by the courts from the policy underlying national labor legislation. Rejecting

---

[4]9 USC §§1–14 (1988).

[5]9 USC §1 (1988).

[6]Electrical Workers (UE) Local 205 v. General Elec. Co., 233 F2d 85, 98, 38 LRRM 2019 (CA 1, 1956), *aff'd on other grounds*, 353 US 547, 40 LRRM 2119 (1957); *see* Machinists Local 967 v. General Elec. Co., 406 F2d 1046, 70 LRRM 2477 (CA 2, 1969); Retail, Wholesale & Dept. Store Union Local 19 v. Buckeye Cotton Oil Co., 236 F2d 776, 781, 38 LRRM 2590 (CA 6, 1956); Signal-Stat Corp. v. Electrical Workers (UE) Local 475, 235 F2d 298, 302, 38 LRRM 2378 (CA 2, 1956), *cert. denied*, 354 US 911, 40 LRRM 2200 (1957); *cf.* Erving v. Virginia Squires Basketball Club, 468 F2d 1064 (CA 2, 1972) (exclusionary clause in §1 applied only to those actually in transportation industry).

[7]These courts interpret "engaged" broadly to include workers involved in production industries as well as employees involved in transportation industries. Electrical Workers (UE) v. Miller Metal Prods., 215 F2d 221, 34 LRRM 2731 (CA 4, 1954); Pennsylvania Greyhound Lines v. Street, Elec. Ry. & Motor Coach Employees, 193 F2d 327, 30 LRRM 2310 (CA 3, 1951); Textile Workers v. Cone Mills Corp., 166 F Supp 654, 43 LRRM 2012 (MD NC, 1958).

[8]353 US 448, 40 LRRM 2113 (1957).

[9]*See* Chapter 17, "Relation of Board Action to the Enforcement of Agreements Under Section 301," at notes 30–39.

[10]29 USC §185(a) (1988).

an argument that the Norris-LaGuardia Act[11] would bar an injunction, the Court granted specific performance of an obligation to arbitrate a grievance dispute.

Thereafter, in the *Steelworkers Trilogy*,[12] the Supreme Court defined the relationship between the courts' section 301 authority and the arbitration process. These landmark cases established the following general propositions: (1) The function of the court is limited "to ascertaining whether the party seeking arbitration is making a claim which on its face is governed by the contract."[13] (2) All doubts as to the coverage of the arbitration clause should be resolved in favor of arbitration.[14] (3) An arbitrator's award, although it must draw its essence from the collective bargaining agreement, must be enforced by the courts even if the arbitrator's interpretation of the contract is ambiguous or would differ from the court's decision on the merits of the dispute.[15] The Court found support for such deference to arbitration both in legislative history[16] and in sections 201 and 203(d) of the Labor Management Relations Act, which provide that final adjustment by a method agreed upon by the parties is the desirable method of settling grievance disputes arising from collective bargaining agreements.[17]

When a party refuses to arbitrate, however, the courts must determine whether the parties have agreed to arbitrate the particular issue.[18] Since arbitration is a voluntary undertaking, parties cannot be required to arbitrate matters not included in their agreement. However, the courts have broadly interpreted

---

[11]29 USC §104 (1988).

[12]Steelworkers v. American Mfg. Co., 363 US 564, 46 LRRM 2414 (1960); Steelworkers v. Warrior & Gulf Navigation Co., *supra* note 2; Steelworkers v. Enterprise Wheel & Car Corp., 363 US 593, 46 LRRM 2423 (1960). *See* Chapter 17, "Relation of Board Action to Enforcement of Agreements Under Section 301," at notes 42–59.

[13]Steelworkers v. American Mfg. Co., *supra* note 12 at 568. The Court rejected the notion that a court could decide the merits of a grievance under the guise of a decision on arbitrability, and expressly disapproved of such cases, particularly Machinists Dist. 15 v. Cutler-Hammer, Inc., 271 AD 917, 67 NYS2d 317, 19 LRRM 2232, *aff'd*, 297 NY 519, 74 NE2d 464, 20 LRRM 2445 (1947).

[14]Steelworkers v. Warrior & Gulf Navigation Co., *supra* note 2.

[15]Steelworkers v. Enterprise Wheel & Car Corp., *supra* note 12.

[16]*See* Textile Workers v. Lincoln Mills, *supra* note 8.

[17]29 USC §§171, 173(d) (1988).

[18]AT&T Technologies v. Communications Workers, 475 US 643, 121 LRRM 3329 (1986); Nolde Bros. v. Bakery & Confectionery Workers Local 358, 430 US 243, 94 LRRM 2753 (1977); Gateway Coal Co. v. Mine Workers Dist. 4, Local 6330, 414 US 368, 85 LRRM 2049 (1974); John Wiley & Sons v. Livingston, 376 US 543, 55 LRRM 2769 (1964); Steelworkers v. Warrior & Gulf Navigation Co., *supra* note 2.

arbitration clauses to include most contractual disputes.[19] Judicial development under section 301 resolved most questions of conflict between arbitration and the courts in favor of the arbitral process.[20]

B. Jurisdiction of the NLRB Over Arbitral Matters

Acts by an employer or a union may generate claims of rights under both the labor agreement and the Act. Typical examples of such claims include: (1) A union's claim that the discipline or discharge of an employee is both a violation of the "just cause" clause in the labor contract and a violation of sections 8(a)(1) and 8(a)(3); (2) a union's claim that an employer's unilateral change in wages or working conditions not only violates provisions of the contract but also the employer's duty to bargain under section 8(a)(5); (3) an employer's claim, in response to a union's demand under Section 8(a)(5) for information to process a grievance, that the union has contractually waived any right to such information.[21] In these instances, where provisions of the collective bargaining agreement and sections of the National Labor Relations Act both apply, two questions arise: (1) Does the Board have jurisdiction under the Act when the parties by contract have provided a means to resolve all contractual disputes and, if so, (2) can the Board nevertheless withhold its jurisdiction by either honoring the award of an arbitrator who has decided the contractual dispute, or by declining to act prior to an arbitral decision?

Section 10(a) of the Act establishes the Board's authority: "The Board is empowered . . . to prevent any person from engaging in any unfair labor practice . . . . *This power shall not be affected by any other means of adjustment or prevention that has been or may be established by agreement*, law, or otherwise."[22] Thus, on its face, the Board's statutory authority is paramount.

---

[19]For a discussion of the construction to be placed upon typical arbitration clauses, see F. Elkouri & E. Elkouri, *supra* note 3, at 212–221; Cox, *Reflections Upon Labor Arbitration*, 72 HARV. L. REV. 1482, 1507–10 (1959). For an example of the difficulty in narrowing the scope of arbitration, see Electrical Workers (IUE) v. General Elec. Co., 407 F2d 253, 70 LRRM 2082 (CA 2, 1968), *cert. denied*, 395 US 904, 71 LRRM 2254 (1969); Electrical Workers (IUE) v. General Elec. Co., 332 F2d 485, 56 LRRM 2289 (CA 2), *cert. denied*, 379 US 928, 57 LRRM 2608 (1964).

[20]See authorities cited in note 1 of Chapter 17, "Relation of Board Action to Enforcement of Agreements Under Section 301."

[21]*See infra* at notes 145–199.

[22]Emphasis added.

In *NLRB v. C & C Plywood Corp.*[23] the Supreme Court rejected the notion that the Board lacked jurisdiction over alleged unfair labor practices solely because the dispute might also involve interpretation of terms in the collective agreement. The Court said that the Taft-Hartley Congress's failure to include an amendment to give the NLRB unfair labor practice jurisdiction over contract violations[24] was to insure that the Board would not have a "generalized power to determine the rights of parties under all collective agreements [which] would have been a step toward governmental regulation of the terms of those agreements."[25] The Court held that in determining whether or not the employer had violated its duty to bargain, the Board would not be imposing its views as to the meaning of the collective bargaining agreement; rather, it would "merely enforce a statutory right which Congress considered necessary to allow labor and management to get on with the process of reaching fair terms and conditions of employment."[26] Accordingly, the Court concluded that "the Board, in necessarily construing a labor agreement to decide this unfair labor practice case, has not exceeded the jurisdiction laid out for it by Congress."[27] However, as the Court was careful to point out, the collective bargaining agreement in that case contained no arbitration clause. Thus, although the Supreme Court held that the Board had the power to interpret a contract enforceable under section 301, the issue remained whether the Board had the authority to interpret a contract that included an applicable arbitration clause.

The cases that introduced this problem, a series of circuit court decisions in the early 1960s, dealt with the right to information. In *Sinclair Refining Co. v. NLRB*[28] the Fifth Circuit refused to require the production of data which the union and

---

[23]385 US 421, 64 LRRM 2065 (1967). See discussion in Chapter 17, "Relation of Board Action to Enforcement of Agreements Under Section 301," at notes 286–295.

[24]One early version of the Senate bill contained the following provision: "§8(a) It shall be an unfair labor practice for an employer . . . (b) to violate the terms of a collective bargaining agreement or the terms of an agreement to submit a labor dispute to arbitration. . . ." Section 8(b)(5) would have placed a similar limit on unions. S. 1126, 80th Cong., 1st Sess., *reprinted in* 1 LEGISLATIVE HISTORY OF THE LABOR MANAGEMENT RELATIONS ACT, 1947 109–111, 114 (1948); *see also* S. REP. NO. 105, 80th Cong., 1st Sess. 20–21, 23 (1947). A similar proposal was contained in the House bill. H.R. REP. NO. 245, 80th Cong., 1st Sess. 21 (1947). These sections were deleted from the bills in the House-Senate Conference. H.R CONF. REP. NO. 510, 80th Cong., 1st Sess. 42 (1947).

[25]385 US at 427.

[26]*Id.* at 428.

[27]*Id. See* note 34, *infra.*

[28]306 F2d 569, 50 LRRM 2830 (CA 5, 1962), *denying enforcement to* 132 NLRB 1660, 48 LRRM 1544 (1961).

the Board considered relevant to a demotion grievance. Relying on the *Steelworkers Trilogy*, the court said that the Board had improperly adjudicated the underlying grievance under the guise of determining the relevance of the data sought.[29] In *Timken Roller Bearing Co. v. NLRB*,[30] the Sixth Circuit granted enforcement of a Board order to furnish information relevant to a grievance, but only because the court concluded that the issue of the duty to furnish information was not subject to arbitration under the terms of the collective bargaining agreement. In *Square D Co. v. NLRB*[31] the Ninth Circuit refused enforcement of a Board order requiring an employer to furnish information relevant to an incentive plan grievance. The employer had argued that matters related to the incentive plan were not grievable, and, therefore, it had no obligation to furnish information. The court recognized primary jurisdiction in the arbitral process, stating: "In the absence of an arbitrator's decision on this issue [grievability] the Board *had no power* to determine that the Company committed unfair labor practices. . . ."[32]

Meanwhile, the Supreme Court addressed the issue of the Board's power versus the arbitral process. In its 1964 decision of *Carey v. Westinghouse Electric Corp.*,[33] the Court held that parties may resort to arbitration to resolve jurisdictional disputes even when such disputes could also be placed before the Board in a section 8(b)(4)(D) case or in a section 9 unit-clarification proceeding. In so holding, the Court noted the Board's adoption of discretionary, nonjurisdictional deference to arbitration awards. The Court acknowledged the Board's authority in such matters of concurrent jurisdiction, stating: "Should the Board disagree with the arbiter . . . , the Board's ruling would, of course, take precedence; and if the employer's action had been in accord with that ruling it would not be liable for damages under §301."[34]

---

[29]The Board had in fact interpreted the contract and had decided the extent of management prerogative, concluding that the union had not waived its right to dispute the claim of lack of work.

[30]325 F2d 746, 54 LRRM 2785 (CA 6, 1963), *cert. denied*, 376 US 971, 55 LRRM 2878 (1964).

[31]332 F2d 360, 56 LRRM 2147 (CA 9, 1964).

[32]*Id.* at 366 (emphasis added).

[33]375 US 261, 55 LRRM 2042 (1964).

[34]*Id.* at 272. *See also infra* at notes 328–331. In its 1967 decision in NLRB v. C & C Plywood, *supra* note 23, which involved a contract that did not provide for binding arbitration, the Court held that the Board has jurisdiction to resolve disputed contractual issues to the extent necessary to reach an unfair labor practice issue.

In its 1967 decision in *NLRB v. Acme Industrial Co.*[35] the Supreme Court held that the Board has jurisdiction over cases involving the duty to furnish information relevant to grievances, even though the underlying grievances involve contract disputes subject to binding arbitration. In so holding, the Court disagreed with the approach taken by the circuit courts in *Sinclair Refining Co., Timken Roller Bearing,* and *Square D Co.*[36] The Court began its analysis by rejecting a mechanical application to the Board's role of the *Steelworkers Trilogy* court-versus-arbitration accommodation, saying: "The relationship of the Board to the arbitration process is of a quite different order."[37] It noted that, unlike the courts, the Board has the section 10(a) power to prevent unfair labor practices, and this power is not affected by private means of adjustment. "Thus, to view the *Steelworkers* decisions as automatically requiring the Board in this case to defer to the primary determination of an arbitrator is to overlook important distinctions between those cases and this one."[38] The Court did not discuss the extent to which the Board could resolve disputed grievances in connection with its unfair labor practice jurisdiction. Instead, it simply observed that the Board, in ordering the employer to provide information to the union, was not deciding the merits of contract grievances—rather, it was aiding the arbitral process by enabling the parties to sift out unmeritorious claims.

Finally, in its 1969 decision in *NLRB v. Strong Roofing & Insulating Co.*,[39] the Court held that the Board, having found that an employer violated section 8(a)(5) by refusing to execute a contract negotiated by its employer association, has the power to order the employer to make payments of fringe benefits as required by the contract. The Court rejected the argument that an order for payment of fringe benefits could only be obtained through the contract's grievance-arbitration procedure:

> [The Board's] authority to [remedy unfair labor practices] is not "affected by any other means of adjustment or prevention that has

---

[35]385 US 432, 64 LRRM 2069 (1967). (*C & C Plywood* and *Acme* were decided on the same day; Justice Stewart wrote both opinions.) The Seventh Circuit below had adopted the reasoning of Sinclair Ref. Co., *supra* note 28, and had denied enforcement of the Board's order.

[36]*See* notes 28–32 *supra*.

[37]385 US at 436 (citing Carey v. Westinghouse Elec. Corp., *supra* note 33).

[38]*Id.* at 437.

[39]393 US 357, 70 LRRM 2100 (1969).

> been or may be established by agreement, law or otherwise . . . ." §10(a). . . . Hence, it has been made clear that in some circumstances the authority of the Board and the law of contract are overlapping, concurrent regimes, neither pre-empting the other. . . . [T]he Board may proscribe conduct which is an unfair labor practice even though it is also a breach of contract remediable as such by arbitration and in the courts. . . . It may also, if necessary to adjudicate an unfair labor practice, interpret and give effect to the terms of a collective bargaining contract.[40]

Justice Douglas, in a lone dissent, argued that the fringe-benefit issue should be decided by arbitrators, not the Board, a tribunal "alien to the system envisioned by *Lincoln Mills*."[41]

By this series of decisions, the Supreme Court has ruled unmistakably that the Board's power in unfair labor practice and representation cases is not subordinate to or dependent upon the arbitral process. Accordingly, the Board and courts have concentrated their attentions upon the circumstances under which the Board, *as a matter of discretion*, should defer to the arbitral process.

Although the Board has unreservedly held that it has jurisdiction to determine unfair labor practices that may also be covered under the grievance procedures of a collective bargaining agreement, it has long ruled that it may choose not to exercise that jurisdiction where it overlaps arbitral jurisdiction. In *International Harvester Co.*[42] an employee alleged that the union had violated sections 8(b)(1)(A) and 8(b)(2) and that the employer had violated sections 8(a)(1) and 8(a)(3) by requiring the employee's discharge for failing to pay union membership dues during the term of a valid union-security agreement. An arbitrator, however, had determined the issue adversely to the employee. Although the Board deferred to the arbitrator's decision, it emphasized this caveat:

> There is no question that the Board is not precluded from adjudicating unfair labor practice charges even though they might have been the subject of an arbitration proceeding and award. Section 10(a) of the Act expressly makes this plain, and the courts have uniformly so

---

[40] *Id.* at 360–61. *Accord, e.g.*, Los Angeles Marine Hardware Co. v. NLRB, 602 F2d 1302, 102 LRRM 2498 (CA 9, 1979); Morrison-Knudsen v. NLRB, 418 F2d 203, 72 LRRM 2460 (CA 9, 1969).

[41] 393 US at 366. Justice Black, concurring, would have remanded the case to the Board to consider whether the fringe-benefit issue should be submitted to arbitration. *Id.* at 362.

[42] 138 NLRB 923, 51 LRRM 1155 (1962), *enforced sub nom.* Ramsey v. NLRB, 327 F2d 784, 55 LRRM 2441 (CA 7), *cert. denied*, 377 US 1003, 56 LRRM 2544 (1964).

held. However, it is equally well-established that the Board has considerable discretion to respect an arbitration award and decline to exercise its authority over alleged unfair labor practices if to do so will serve the fundamental aims of the Act.[43]

C. From *Spielberg* to *Collyer*

The Board has developed standards for exercising its discretionary authority. Its *Spielberg*[44] standards, adopted in 1955, apply to cases where an arbitral award has already been rendered. Its *Collyer*[45] standards, adopted in 1971, apply to cases where the Board defers to the arbitral machinery before an arbitral award has been rendered, subject to possible Board review of the ultimate award under *Spielberg* standards. *Spielberg* and *Collyer* have received wide acceptance by the reviewing courts.

1. The *Spielberg* Rationale. In the early days of the Act the Board was reluctant to accommodate itself to the decision of any other tribunal. Even where an arbitrator had ordered discriminatorily discharged employees to be reinstated, the Board, relying on section 10(a), refused to recognize the award and independently examined the charged conduct to ascertain whether there had been any violation of the Act.[46] Occasionally, however, a trial examiner would honor an arbitration award because the examiner felt it would effectuate the policies of the Act.[47] But it was not until 1955, in *Spielberg Manufacturing Co.*,[48] that the Board set forth specific criteria for deferral to arbitration awards.

---

[43]*Id.* at 925–26; this language was cited with approval by the Supreme Court in Carey v. Westinghouse Elec. Corp., *supra* note 33, at 271.

[44]Spielberg Mfg. Co., 112 NLRB 1080, 36 LRRM 1152 (1955). *See infra* at notes 218–361.

[45]Collyer Insulated Wire, 192 NLRB 837, 77 LRRM 1931 (1971).

[46]*E.g.*, Rieke Metal Prods. Corp., 40 NLRB 867, 10 LRRM 82 (1942).

[47]*E.g.*, Paramount Pictures, 79 NLRB 557, 576, 22 LRRM 1428 (1948). The trial examiner relied upon Timken Roller Bearing Co., 70 NLRB 500, 18 LRRM 1370 (1946), *enforcement denied*, 161 F2d 949, 20 LRRM 2204 (CA 6, 1947), where the Board had dismissed part of a refusal-to-bargain complaint initiated by a union that had simultaneously invoked the Board's processes and the grievance machinery in its contract and had lost the arbitral decision. The Board said in *Timken*: "It is evident that the Union has concurrently utilized two forums for the purpose of litigating the matter here in dispute. . . . [I]t would not comport with the sound exercise of our administrative discretion to permit the Union to seek redress under the Act after having initiated arbitration proceedings which, at the Union's request, resulted in a determination upon the merits." *Id.* at 501. The Boaord's theory in *Timken* appeared to have been that the union had made an election of remedies, rather than that the arbitrator's opinion was entitled to any weight.

[48]*Supra* note 44.

In *Spielberg* the parties had agreed, as part of a strike settlement, to arbitrate the employer's refusal to reinstate four strikers accused of picket-line misconduct. When the arbitration panel denied them reinstatement, the employees filed an unfair labor practice charge. The Board decided to accept the decision of the arbitration panel as the basis for finding that the employer had not violated the Act.[49] In dismissing the complaint, the Board promulgated a three-pronged test for determining when to defer: (1) that the proceedings be fair and regular, (2) that all parties agree to be bound, and (3) that the decision not be repugnant to the purpose and policies of the Act.[50] If these criteria are met, deferral is deemed appropriate.[51]

The rationale of *Spielberg* was elucidated in *International Harvester Co.*,[52] where the Board stated:

> The Act . . . is primarily designed to promote industrial peace and stability by encouraging the practice and procedure of collective bargaining. Experience has demonstrated that collective-bargaining agreements that provide for final and binding arbitration of grievances and disputes arising thereunder, as a "substitute for industrial strife," contribute significantly to the attainment of this statutory objective. . . .
>
> . . .
>
> If complete effectuation of the Federal policy is to be achieved, . . . the Board . . . should give hospitable acceptance to the arbitral process as "part and parcel of the collective bargaining process itself," and voluntarily withhold its undoubted authority to adjudicate alleged unfair labor practice charges involving the same subject matter, unless it clearly appears that the arbitration proceedings were tainted by fraud, collusion, unfairness, or serious procedural irregularities or that the award was clearly repugnant to the purposes and policies of the Act.[53]

Since its *Spielberg* decision the Board has added a fourth and rather variably administered criterion: that the issue involved in the unfair labor practice case must have been presented to and

---

[49]The Board noted that it would not "necessarily decide the issue of alleged strike misconduct as the arbitration panel did." *Id.* at 1082.

[50]A fourth test was added later. *See infra* at note 54 and notes 222–237.

[51]Spielberg Mfg. Co., *supra* note 44, at 1082. Additional standards applied by the courts are discussed *infra* at notes 370–414.

[52]*Supra* note 42.

[53]*Id.* at 926–27. The Supreme Court quoted this language with approval in Carey v. Westinghouse Elec. Corp., *supra* note 33, at 271.

considered by the arbitrator, or at least that the contrary not be evident.[54]

2. The *Collyer* Rationale. In some areas of labor law, parties are required to utilize and sometimes fully exhaust grievance-arbitration machinery before being permitted to use another forum.[55] But there has never been a rigid exhaustion requirement for access to the NLRB. Prior to its 1971 *Collyer* decision, the Board usually found that failure to use an available grievance procedure was not a bar to the processing of a charge. First in *Merrimack Manufacturing Co.*[56] and then in succeeding cases,[57] the Board consistently settled disputes involving charges of discrimination. Its position was less consistent in cases involving refusal to bargain.[58] However, in its 1963 decision in *Dubo Manufacturing Corp.*[59] the Board held that it would defer action pending completion of the grievance-arbitration process where the dispute was already being handled within that process.

Collyer Insulated Wire[60] marked a watershed in the accommodation of Board authority to the parties' private arbitral machinery. Although the Board had occasionally dismissed

---

[54]Raytheon Co., 140 NLRB 883, 52 LRRM 1129 (1963), *set aside on other grounds*, 326 F2d 471, 55 LRRM 2101 (CA 1, 1964). The Board has fluctuated on the question of who must prove what to satisfy this criterion. *Compare* Suburban Motor Freight, 247 NLRB 146, 103 LRRM 1113 (1980) *with* Olin Corp., 268 NLRB 573, 115 LRRM 1056 (1984) (overruling *Suburban Motor Freight*). *See infra* notes 258–263.

[55]*See, e.g.*, Republic Steel Corp. v. Maddox, 379 US 650, 58 LRRM 2193 (1965). *See also* Drake Bakeries v. Bakery Workers Local 50, 370 US 254, 50 LRRM 2440 (1962).

[56]31 NLRB 900, 8 LRRM 170 (1941).

[57]*See, e.g.*, Flasco Mfg. Co., 162 NLRB 611, 64 LRRM 1077 (1967); Woodlawn Farm Dairy Co., 162 NLRB 48, 63 LRRM 1495 (1966); Operating Eng'rs Local 701 (Peter Kiewit Sons' Co.), 152 NLRB 49, 59 LRRM 1009 (1965); Plumbers & Pipe Fitters Local 469 (Associated Plumbing, Heating & Piping Contractors of Ariz.), 149 NLRB 39, 57 LRRM 1257 (1964); Electric Motors & Specialties, 149 NLRB 131, 57 LRRM 1258 (1964); Aerodex, Inc., 149 NLRB 192, 57 LRRM 1261 (1964); National Screen Prods. Co., 147 NLRB 746, 56 LRRM 1274 (1964); Lummus Co., 142 NLRB 517, 53 LRRM 1072 (1963); Todd Shipyards Corp., 98 NLRB 814, 29 LRRM 1422 (1952); General Elec. X-Ray Corp., 76 NLRB 64, 21 LRRM 1150 (1948); Marlboro Cotton Mills, 53 NLRB 965, 13 LRRM 142 (1943); Walt Disney Prods., 48 NLRB 892, 12 LRRM 146 (1943), *enforced as modified*, 146 F2d 44, 15 LRRM 691 (CA 9, 1944), *cert. denied*, 324 US 877, 16 LRRM 918 (1945).

[58]Board Member Brown would have deferred almost every decision until a grievance had been processed. *See, e.g.*, Aetna Bearing Co., 152 NLRB 845, 59 LRRM 1258 (1965); Flintkote Co., 149 NLRB 1561, 57 LRRM 1477 (1964); Thor Power Tool Co., 148 NLRB 1379, 1382, 57 LRRM 1161 (1964), *enforced*, 351 F2d 584, 60 LRRM 2237 (CA 7, 1965).

[59]142 NLRB 431, 53 LRRM 1070 (1963) (§8(a)(3) case). The resulting arbitration award in *Dubo* was thereafter disregarded, however, since the arbitration panel had not considered the allegation of discrimination. Dubo Mfg. Corp., 148 NLRB 1114, 57 LRRM 1111 (1964), *enforced*, 353 F2d 157, 60 LRRM 2373 (CA 6, 1965). *See also infra* at note 117.

[60]*Supra* note 45.

complaints in unfair labor practice cases because the issue was subject to resolution under the parties' grievance-arbitration procedures,[61] it was not until *Collyer* that a definite system of prearbitral referral was adopted. *Collyer* involved a section 8(a)(5) charge of failure to bargain. A plurality of Chairman Miller and Member Kennedy wrote the Board's decision; Member Brown concurred, urging deferral in an even broader range of cases. Members Fanning and Jenkins, in separate opinions, strongly dissented.[62]

In *Collyer* the employer contended that the union's section 8(a)(5) charge, alleging unilateral changes in conditions of employment, should be deferred to the grievance-arbitration procedure of the parties' labor contract. The Board majority ruled that the Board should and would defer to existing grievance-arbitration procedures prior to either party's invocation of those procedures. In support of that result, the plurality opinion emphasized that: (1) The dispute arose "within the confines of a long and productive collective bargaining relationship," and there was no claim of "enmity by Respondent to employees' exercise of protected rights";[63] (2) "Respondent . . . credibly asserted its willingness to resort to arbitration under a clause providing for arbitration in a very broad range of disputes and unquestionably broad enough to embrace 'the dispute before

---

[61]*E.g.*, Jos. Schlitz Brewing Co., 175 NLRB 141, 70 LRRM 1472 (1969). Just a few months before *Collyer* the Board refused to defer §§8(a)(3) and (5) issues to existing grievance-arbitration procedures, in Curtis Mfg. Co., 189 NLRB 192, 77 LRRM 1220 (1971).

[62]*Collyer* has also been widely debated outside the Board. *See, e.g.*, Getman, *Labor Arbitration & Dispute Resolution*, 88 YALE L.J. 916 (1979); Christensen, *Private Judges, Public Rights: The Role of Arbitration in the Enforcement of the National Labor Relations Act*, in THE FUTURE OF LABOR ARBITRATION IN AMERICA (J. Correge, V. Hughes & M. Stone, eds.) 49 (1976); Nash, *Board Referral to Arbitration and* Alexander v. Gardner-Denver: *Some Preliminary Observations*, 25 LAB. L.J. 259 (1974); Teple, *Deferral to Arbitration: Implications of NLRB Policy*, 29 ARB. J. 65 (1974); Zimmer, *Wired for* Collyer: *Rationalizing NLRB and Arbitration Jurisdiction*, 48 IND. L.J. 141 (1973); Getman, Collyer Insulated Wire: *A Case of Misplaced Modesty*, 49 IND. L.J. 57 (1973); Belkin, *Are Arbitrators Qualified to Decide Unfair Labor Practice Cases?*, 24 LAB. L.J. 818 (1973); Schatzki, *NLRB Resolution of Contract Disputes Under Section 8(a)(5)*, 50 TEX. L. REV. 225 (1972); Johannesen & Smith, Collyer: *Open Sesame to Deferral*, 23 LAB. L.J. 723 (1972); Menard, *The NLRB—No Longer A Threat to the Arbitral Process?*, 23 LAB. L.J. 140 (1972); Atleson, *Disciplinary Discharges, Arbitration, and NLRB Deference*, 20 BUFFALO L. REV. 355 (1971); Note, *Labor Law—Arbitration—Announcement of Deferral Policy*, 17 ST. LOUIS U.L.J. 411 (1973); Note, *The NLRB's Arbitration Deferral Policy Under* Collyer: *The Impact of* National Radio Co., 53 B.U.L. REV. 711 (1973); Note, *NLRB—Jurisdiction—Standards for Deferral to Arbitration Where No Award Has Been Issued*, 41 FORDHAM L. REV. 1975 (1972); Note, *Labor Law—NLRB Unfair Labor Practice Jurisdiction and Arbitration—Effect of Deferring to Arbitration Prior to Issuance of Award*, 18 WAYNE L. REV. 1191 (1972).

[63]Collyer Insulated Wire, *supra* note 45, at 842.

the Board'";[64] and (3) the contract and its meaning lay at the center of the dispute.[65]

The Board's plurality opinion rested on broad foundations: (1) that the courts have recognized a national policy of encouraging resolution of labor disputes through the grievance-arbitration machinery; (2) that it is in keeping with the statutory policy, expressed in section 203(d) of the LMRA to encourage the parties to resolve disputes through the "method agreed upon by the parties"; (3) and further, that "disputes such as these can better be resolved by arbitrators with special skill and experience in deciding matters arising under established bargaining relationships than by the application by this Board of a particular provision of our statute."[66]

Concluding that it would be consistent "with the fundamental objectives of federal law to require the parties here to honor their contractual obligations rather than, by casting this dispute in statutory terms, to ignore their agreed-upon procedures,"[67] the Board ordered the complaint dismissed. But to protect the statutory rights of the charging party, the Board also retained jurisdiction

> solely for the purpose of entertaining an appropriate and timely motion for further consideration upon a proper showing that either (a) the dispute has not, with reasonable promptness after the issuance of this decision, either been resolved by amicable settlement in the grievance procedure or submitted promptly to arbitration, or (b) the grievance or arbitration procedures have not been fair and regular or have reached a result which is repugnant to the Act.[68]

Member Brown, concurring, supported a broader concept of deferral, emphasizing one reason in particular:

> The scope, both in function and utilization, of grievance arbitration is by itself sufficient reason to consider deferring to that process. The grievance-arbitration process is one of the most important tools

[64] *Id.*
[65] *Id.*
[66] *Id.* at 839.
[67] *Id.* at 843.
[68] *Id.* The Board has rescinded deferral of a complaint where the dispute was not submitted to arbitration with "reasonable promptness" after the deferral decision. Typographical Union No. 101 (Columbia) (Washington Post Co.), 220 NLRB 1173, 90 LRRM 1523 (1975); Typographical Union No. 101 (Columbia) (Byron S. Adams Printing), 219 NLRB 88, 90 LRRM 1008 (1975).

> of collective bargaining, and the *raison d'etre* of the National Labor Relations Act is to encourage collective bargaining.[69]

He asserted his willingness to defer in cases alleging violations of sections 8(a)(1) and (a)(3), as well as in section 8(a)(5) cases such as *Collyer.*

Member Fanning argued in dissent that "[t]he majority's insistence that the parties' statutory rights cannot be adjudicated in this case except through the authority of an arbitrator verges on the practice of compulsory arbitration."[70] He contended, inter alia, that arbitrators are generally "loath to intrude into the area of public rights or national labor policy."[71] He concluded that it was "inappropriate . . . to cede our jurisdiction in all cases involving arbitration to a tribunal that may, and often does, provide only a partial remedy."[72]

Member Jenkins added that the majority opinion was a "complete reversal of Board precedent" and warned that the Board's protection would be unavailable in those situations where "unfair labor practices . . . involve in part, and perhaps distantly, the interpretation of a contract provision."[73]

In *National Radio Co.*,[74] the *Collyer* deferral policy was materially expanded to cover charges under sections 8(a)(1) and (3). Member Penello joined Chairman Miller and Member Kennedy to form the majority; Members Fanning and Jenkins continued to dissent. The complaint in *National Radio* alleged that the employer violated section 8(a)(5) by unilaterally changing the conditions under which union representatives were allowed to process grievances on company time and also violated section 8(a)(3) by discharging a union steward for refusal to obey the new rules. While acknowledging that *Collyer* involved essentially a question of contract interpretation and that the sec-

---

[69]192 NLRB at 844.

[70]*Id.* at 847. Chairman Miller and Member Kennedy responded that they were not compelling any party to do anything which they had not agreed to do in their labor contract. *Id.*

[71]*Id.* at 849.

[72]*Id.* at 850.

[73]*Id.*

[74]198 NLRB 527, 80 LRRM 1718 (1972). Newly appointed Member Penello had already joined Chairman Miller saying of the scope of *Collyer*: "The Board will apply the *Collyer* rule where two basic conditions have been met: (1) the disputed issues are, in fact, issues susceptible of resolution under the operation of the grievance machinery agreed to by the parties, and (2) there is no reason for us to believe that use of that machinery by the parties could not or would not resolve such issues in a manner compatible with the purposes of the Act." Eastman Broadcasting Co., 199 NLRB 434, 437, 81 LRRM 1257 (1972).

tion 8(a)(3) allegation at hand presented an unalloyed, statutory issue, the Board majority reversed the ALJ and withheld decision of the dispute: "[t]he crucial determinant is . . . the reasonableness of the assumption that the arbitration procedure will resolve this dispute in a manner consistent with the standards of *Spielberg*."[75] Deferral was grounded on several factors: the vast experience of arbitrators in regularly dealing with the issue of "just cause" for discharge or discipline, the increasing case load before the Board, a recognition that the arbitration procedure is a therapeutic experience which may strengthen the relationship between the union and the employer (suggesting that Board intervention might be an unsettling force), and a belief that the union would be strongly motivated to protect the rights of employees who were engaged in activities on behalf of the union.[76] While the discharge of the union steward might have suggested union animus by the employer, the majority did not find a history of union animus such as to preclude deferral.

The dissenting members strongly objected to this extension of *Collyer* policy to discriminatory discharge cases. They stated:

> Statutory protection against discrimination on the job because of engaging in, or refraining from, union activity is an *individual* right, unlike the union or group right to be protected from unilateral changes in the collective-bargaining agreement. Because it is granted by the statute to individuals, it cannot be reduced, altered or displaced by any agreement between the employer and the union.[77]

They noted the Board's mandate to protect public rights, especially individual rights, and questioned the competence of arbitrators to deal with the statutory question of discrimination, because arbitrators would lack the Board's investigative and legal resources and its capabilities and expertise in handling statutory issues. They were concerned about an arbitrator finding that an employer had some cause for discipline or discharge, but without consideration of the statutory issues.[78]

---

[75]198 NLRB at 531, 80 LRRM at 1723.
[76]*Id.*
[77]*Id.* at 1724 (emphasis in original).
[78]They stated: "In many, and perhaps most, discharge cases, a good reason may exist for firing the employee; if so, the arbitration inquiry ends there, and the employee is out of a job. The Act, however, requires that the employee be protected against discharge for union reasons, even though there may be a different and good reason for his discharge. Consequently the Board in nearly every discriminatory discharge case examines the evidence and the circumstances in order to determine whether the "good" reason was the real reason or a pretext for firing the employee." *Id.* at 534, 80 LRRM at 1725. *See generally* Chapter 7, "Discrimination in Employment."

The arbitrator in *National Radio* held the arbitration award in abeyance while the Board considered the case. Subsequently he found that the discharge had not been motivated by union animus and was lawful.[79] The union then[80] filed a motion with the Board asserting that the arbitrator had failed to dispose of all of the statutory issues raised by the complaint and that he had reached a decision repugnant to the Act. A divided Board dismissed the request for further consideration.[81] Although the arbitrator had not directly ruled on the section 8(a)(5) issue with respect to the employer's imposition of the new reporting requirement, the Board observed that the union had not initially asked the arbitrator to resolve that issue and subsequently it did not avail itself of the opportunity to expand the scope of the arbitration procedure to include the issue. Dissenting Member Fanning viewed the decision as a violation of the majority's promise to consider such issues in its retention of jurisdiction under the *Collyer* policy.[82]

In 1977, after changes in its membership, the Board announced in *General American Transportation Corp.*[83] that it would begin restricting the deferral of cases under *Collyer* to those cases alleging violations of sections 8(a)(5) and 8(b)(3). Previously, the Board had applied *Collyer* when prearbitral deferral request was timely raised[84] in cases alleging a wide variety of statutory violations of sections 8(a)(1),[85] 8(a)(3),[86]

---

[79]National Radio Co., 60 LA 78 (1973). The arbitrator, Professor Archibald Cox, found that the grievant had a duty to abide by the rule and to file a grievance.

[80]The Board's order had retained jurisdiction, as is typical of all *Collyer*-type orders. *See* note 68 *supra*.

[81]National Radio Co., 205 NLRB 1179, 84 LRRM 1105 (1973).

[82]*Id.* at 1181.

[83]228 NLRB 808, 94 LRRM 1483 (1977). *See infra* at notes 102–103.

[84]The Board will not defer to prospective arbitration unless the issue of deferral is raised during or before the unfair labor practice hearing. Cutten Supermarket, 220 NLRB 507, 90 LRRM 1250 (1975); Duchess Furniture, 220 NLRB 13, 90 LRRM 1160 (1975); Erie Strayer Co., 213 NLRB 344, 87 LRRM 1162 (1974); Asbestos Workers Local 22 (Rosendahl, Inc.), 212 NLRB 913, 87 LRRM 1604 (1974); Operating Eng'rs Local 9 (Fountain Sand & Gravel Co.), 210 NLRB 129, 86 LRRM 1303 (1974); Redco Constr. Corp., 206 NLRB 150, 84 LRRM 1205 (1973); Asko, Inc., 202 NLRB 330, 83 LRRM 1498 (1973); *but see* Norfolk, Portsmouth Wholesale Beer Distribs. Ass'n, 196 NLRB 1150, 80 LRRM 1235 (1972) (Member Fanning, dissenting, argued that the parties had not raised deferral either at the hearing or in their briefs). *Cf.* Alameda County Ass'n for Mentally Retarded, 255 NLRB 603, 107 LRRM 1001 (1981) (respondent did not assert deferral as an affirmative defense). *See* notes 119–120 and 211 *infra*.

[85]Todd Shipyards Corp., 203 NLRB 114, 83 LRRM 1104 (1973). The General Counsel's Revised Guidelines on *Collyer* (*infra* note 209) indicate that §8(a)(2) cases may be appropriate for deferral.

[86]Bell Tel. Co., 214 NLRB 980, 87 LRRM 1542 (1974).

8(a)(5),[87] 8(b)(1)(A),[88] 8(b)(1)(B),[89] 8(b)(2),[90] and 8(b)(3).[91] However, the Board had also refused to defer in many other types of cases. Its determination whether to defer revolved around the same factors relied upon by the Board majority to justify the deferral in *Collyer*: (1) existence of a stable collective bargaining relationship, (2) respondent's willingness to arbitrate the arbitrable issue, and (3) determination of whether the contract and its meaning are central to the dispute.[92]

In 1984, in *United Technologies Corp.*,[93] after further changes in membership, the Board again expanded prearbitral deferral. Overruling its 1977 decision in *General American*, the Board resumed deferral under the *Collyer* doctrine of cases alleging violations of sections 8(a)(1) and (3) and 8(b)(1)(A) and (2).

3. *Collyer* in the Reviewing Courts. The appellate courts quickly approved and enforced the *Collyer* doctrine as originally announced.[94] As early as 1975, the Second Circuit declared that

---

[87]Granite City Steel Co., 211 NLRB 880, 87 LRRM 1006 (1974); National Heat & Power Corp., 201 NLRB 1019, 82 LRRM 1436 (1973); Great Coastal Express, 196 NLRB 871, 80 LRRM 1097 (1972); Coppus Eng'g Corp., 195 NLRB 595, 79 LRRM 1449 (1972).

[88]Teamsters Local 70 (Nabisco, Inc.), 198 NLRB 552, 80 LRRM 1727 (1972), *aff'd*, 479 F2d 770, 83 LRRM 2612 (CA 2, 1973).

[89]Typographical Union No. 101 (Columbia) (Washington Post Co.), 207 NLRB 831, 85 LRRM 1018 (1973), Typographical Union No. 12 (Baltimore) (A. S. Abell Co.), 201 NLRB 120, 82 LRRM 1127 (1973); Mailers Union No. 36 (Houston Chronicle), 199 NLRB 804, 81 LRRM 1310 (1972).

[90]Newspaper Guild of Brockton (Enterprise Publishing Co.), 201 NLRB 793, 82 LRRM 1337 (1973), *aff'd*, 493 F2d 1024, 85 LRRM 2746 (CA 1, 1974).

[91]Teamsters Local 70 (Nabisco, Inc.), *supra* note 88.

[92]In Typographical Union No. 101 (Columbia) (Washington Post Co.), 220 NLRB 1173, 90 LRRM 1523 (1975), Member Penello, on the one hand, and Members Fanning and Jenkins, on the other, debated the meaning of available statistics reflecting the Board's *Collyer* experience. Member Penello argued that *Collyer* has "encourage[d] unions and employers to pursue collective bargaining solutions," noting that during the period between May 1973 and April 1974 the regional offices had tentatively dismissed 511 cases under *Collyer*. Members Fanning and Jenkins thought "it perhaps more likely that the cases were simply dropped because of lack of financial or other ability to pursue them, thus leaving unremedied whatever statutory violations may have occurred." *Id.* at 1175.

[93]268 NLRB 557, 115 LRRM 1049 (1984); *see infra* at notes 106–116.

[94]Electrical Workers (IBEW) Local 2188 (Western Elec. Co.) v. NLRB, 494 F2d 1087, 85 LRRM 2576 (CA DC), *cert. denied*, 419 US 835, 87 LRRM 2398 (1974); Associated Press v. NLRB, 492 F2d 662, 85 LRRM 2440 (CA DC, 1974) (listing in its footnote the six courts that have given "apparent approval" to *Collyer* without directly passing on it); Provision House Workers Local 274 (Urban N. Patman, Inc.) v. NLRB, 493 F2d 1249, 85 LRRM 2863, 2863 (CA 9), *cert. denied*, 419 US 828, 87 LRRM 2397 (1974) (deferral appropriate even though "characterization of the dispute as one involving interpretation of a contract, rather than existence of the contract, is not wholly free from doubt"); T.I.M.E.-DC, Inc. v. NLRB, 504 F2d 294, 87 LRRM 2853 (CA 5, 1974); NLRB v. Railway, Airlines, & S.S. Clerks (Yellow Cab Co. of Tampa), 498 F2d 1105, 86 LRRM 3199 (CA 5, 1974); NLRB v. Lithographers Local 271 (United States Playing Card Co.), 495 F2d 763, 86 LRRM 2655 (CA 6, 1974); Enterprise Publishing Co. v. NLRB, 493 F2d 1024 (CA 1, 1974); Nabisco, Inc. v. NLRB, 479 F2d 770, 83 LRRM 2612 (CA 2, 1973).

"the validity of the *Collyer* doctrine is no longer seriously in doubt."[95] In a dictum in *William E. Arnold Co. v. Carpenters District Council of Jacksonville & Vicinity*,[96] the Supreme Court stated that the Board's *Collyer* doctrine "harmonizes" with Congress' expressed concern that voluntary dispute-resolution procedures be used to resolve labor-management disputes under a labor contract.[97] The courts have also upheld the Board's refusal to defer under *Collyer*.[98]

The Court of Appeals for the District of Columbia Circuit placed some limitations on its approval of *Collyer*. That court stated that deferral may not be appropriate (1) if arbitration would impose an undue financial burden on one of the parties, or (2) if it prevents an orderly exposition of the legal issue, such as where successive ad hoc arbitrations produce no consistent rule.[99]

When the Board in *National Radio Co.*[100] expanded *Collyer* to include section 8(a)(3) violations, the Second Circuit accepted the Board's position, agreeing that arbitration was appropriate where that process is likely to resolve the dispute between the parties.[101] [*See* **Editor's Note** below.]

---

[95]Machinists Lodges 700, 743, 1746 (United Aircraft Corp.) v. NLRB, 525 F2d 237, 239, 90 LRRM 2922 (CA 2, 1975).

[96]417 US 12, 16, 86 LRRM 2212 (1974). *See* Chapter 17, "Relation of Board Action to Enforcement of Agreements Under Section 301," at notes 88 and 276, and Chapter 29, "Federal Preemption of State Regulation," at note 304.

[97]In Machinists Lodges 700, 743, 1746 (United Aircraft Corp.). v. NLRB, *supra* note 95, the Second Circuit noted: "The Supreme Court has since added further authority to the policy by quoting favorably from the Board's reasoning in the Collyer decision in William E. Arnold Co. v. Carpenters. . . ." *Id.* at 239. *See also* Printing Pressmen Local 252 (Columbus) (R. W. Page Corp.), 219 NLRB 268, 89 LRRM 1553 (1975), *enforced*, 543 F2d 1161, 93 LRRM 3055 (CA 5, 1976).

[98]NLRB v. Railway, Airlines & S.S. Clerks (Yellow Cab Co. of Tampa), *supra* note 94; NLRB v. Lithographers Local 271 (United States Playing Card Co.), *supra* note 94, 86 LRRM at 2656 (refusal to defer was not abuse of Board's discretion even though "it might have been better to defer the issues . . . to arbitration"). *See* T.I.M.E.-DC, Inc. v. NLRB, *supra* note 94, 87 LRRM at 2860 (neither *Spielberg* nor *Collyer* are applicable where grievance proceedings "are not even-handed").

[99]Electrical Workers (IBEW) Local 2188 (Western Elec. Co.) v. NLRB, *supra* note 94.

[100]198 NLRB 527, 80 LRRM 1718 (1972).

[101]Machinists Lodges 700, 743, 1746 (United Aircraft Corp.) v. NLRB, *supra* note 95. [**Editor's Note:** In Hammontree v. NLRB, 925 F2d 1486, 136 LRRM 2478 (CA DC, 1991), the Court of Appeals for the District of Columbia Circuit, sitting en banc, upheld the Board's policy of deferring a broad range of statutory issues to arbitration, including issues arising under sections 8(a)(3) and 8(b)(1)(A). Judge Wald, writing for the majority, rested the decision on the discretion of the Board to exercise its jurisdiction or not in the service of the broad policies of the Act. Concurring, Judge Edwards suggested the additional justification that unions have the capacity under the Act to waive section 7 rights of represented employees in exchange for roughly equivalent contractual rights.]

D. Contractions and Expansions of *Collyer* Deferral Policy

1. Restricting the Deferral Practices: *General American Transportation.* In 1977, in two cases decided on the same day, the Board effectively overruled the *National Radio* expansion of the *Collyer* doctrine, while affirming the validity of *Collyer* in its original scope.

In *General American Transportation Corp.*,[102] after changes in membership, the Board overruled *National Radio. General American* involved an allegedly discriminatory discharge in violation of sections 8(a)(1) and (3). Members Fanning and Jenkins reasserted their disapproval of deferring the adjudication of statutory rights; Chairman Murphy, concurring, reasoned that *Collyer* deferral should apply only to sections 8(a)(5) and 8(b)(3) complaints where "the dispute is principally between the contracting parties—the employer and the union—[and] the principal issue is whether the complained-of conduct is permitted by the parties' contract."[103] She viewed such issues as "eminently suited to the arbitral process," which would ordinarily also resolve the unfair labor practice issue.

In the second case, *Roy Robinson, Inc.*,[104] Chairman Murphy joined Members Penello and Walther, the dissenters in *General American*, to reaffirm the Board's original *Collyer* policy in failure-to-bargain cases—essentially relying on the rationale contained in the original decision.

Shortly after those decisions, the General Counsel issued a policy memorandum[105] indicating that deferral was to be applied in the future only to charges of violations of sections 8(a)(5) and 8(b)(3) which meet "the traditional *Collyer* test."

2. Expanding the Deferral Practice: *United Technologies.* In 1984, in *United Technologies Corp.*,[106] the Board overruled the 6-year-old deferral policy of *General American Transportation Corp.*[107] The majority recited numerous policy considerations in favor of deferral—factors which it believed the Board had ignored in *General American* when it "emasculated the Board's

---

[102]*Supra* note 83.
[103]*Id.* at 810.
[104]228 NLRB 828, 94 LRRM 1471 (1977).
[105]NLRB Gen. Counsel Memo., No. 77-58 (May 25, 1977), *Regional Office Handling of* Collyer *Issues in Light of the Board's Decision in* General American Transportation Corp., LABOR RELATIONS YEARBOOK—1977 320 (1978).
[106]*Supra* note 93.
[107]228 NLRB 808, 94 LRRM 1483 (1977).

deferral policy."[108] *United Technologies* involved allegations that an employee was threatened with discipline in violation of section 8(a)(1). The employer denied any such violation and asked that the dispute be deferred to the grievance-arbitration provisions of the parties' collective bargaining agreement. The ALJ declined to defer based on *General American.* The Board decided to overrule *General American* and defer the case to arbitration. In support of its return to the liberal deferral standards of *Collyer* and *National Radio Co.*[109] the Board noted the "abundantly clear" congressional intent that "final adjustment by a method agreed upon by the parties is hereby declared to be the desirable method for settlement of grievance disputes arising over the application or interpretation of an existing collective-bargaining agreement."[110]

The Board noted its 1943 decision in *Consolidated Aircraft Corp.*[111] wherein it eschewed the "role of policing collective contracts between employers and the labor organizations by attempting to decide whether disputes as to the meaning and administration of such contracts constitute unfair labor practices under the Act."[112] The Board noted its "limited resources" and its policy of encouraging parties to resolve disputes through collectively bargained mechanisms, instead of demanding Board adjudication of the innumerable disputes which arise in the day-to-day relationship between employees and their employer.[113] Finally, the Board reemphasized the factors underlying the *Collyer* deferral doctrine:

> The dispute arose within the confines of a long and productive collective bargaining relationship; there was no claim of employer animosity to the employees' exercise of protected rights; the parties' contract provided for arbitration in a very broad range of disputes; the arbitration clause clearly encompassed the dispute at issue; the employer had asserted its willingness to utilize arbitration to resolve the dispute; and the dispute was eminently well suited to resolution by arbitration.[114]

In referring the matter to arbitration in *United Technologies* the Board retained jurisdiction pending acceptable resolution of the

---

[108]268 NLRB at 559.

[109]*Supra* note 100.

[110]268 NLRB at 558 (quoting 29 USC §173(d) (1976)).

[111]47 NLRB 694, 12 LRRM 44 (1943), *enforced in pertinent part,* 141 F2d 785, 14 LRRM 553 (CA 9, 1944).

[112]268 NLRB at 558.

[113]United Aircraft Corp., 204 NLRB 879, 880, 83 LRRM 1411 (1973), *enforced sub nom.* Machinists Lodges 700, 743, 1746 v. NLRB, 525 F2d 237, 90 LRRM 2922 (CA 2, 1975).

[114]268 NLRB at 558.

case consistent with the *Spielberg* standards. The Board remarked of its decision that "[i]t is merely the prudent exercise of restraint, a postponement of the use of the Board's process to give the parties' own dispute resolution machinery a chance to succeed."[115] Since the decision of *United Technologies*, the Board has followed the broader deferral standard there embraced.[116]

E. The Board's *Dubo* Deferral Policy

Long before *Collyer* and *National Radio*, the Board ruled in *Dubo Manufacturing Corp.*[117] that deferral of a section 8(a)(3) allegation was appropriate pending completion of the grievance-arbitration procedure, provided the dispute had already been submitted to that procedure. In practice, continuation of the Board's *Dubo* policy moderated the impact of the Board's contraction of *Collyer* during the years when *General American Transportation Corp.*[118] supplied the controlling rule. A charging party alleging discrimination under section 8(a)(3) who had grievance-arbitration machinery available under which to seek a remedy, could avoid deferral under *General American*; but, under the Board's *Dubo* policy, the party could avoid deferral only at the price of forgoing its use of the grievance-arbitration machinery.[119] In one case, however, *Youngstown Sheet & Tube*

[115] *Id.* at 560.

[116] *See* Editor's Note, *supra* note 101.

[117] 142 NLRB 431, 53 LRRM 1070 (1963). *See also infra* at notes 209–217.

[118] *Supra* note 107. The General Counsel's memorandum, *supra* note 105, following *General American Transportation Corp.*, states: "[T]he GAT [*General American Transportation*] decision merely broaden(s) the area of nondeferral under *Collyer*. In cases to which the *GAT* policy applies, charging parties will no longer be 'forced,' on pain of dismissal, to pursue the grievance-arbitration procedure. But even in such cases, if the charging party is in the grievance-arbitration channel and *voluntarily* elects to stay there, after having been apprised of his 'entitlement' under *GAT* to a General Counsel or Board determination, there is nothing in *GAT* that suggests that his case cannot be deferred under *Dubo* so long as he opts to continue in that channel. To the contrary, former Chairman Murphy's concurring opinion in *GAT* suggests that such deferral would be appropriate. Consequently *Dubo* will be applied to all non-*Collyer* cases, including those which are non-*Collyer* because of the *GAT* policy." *Supra* note 105, at 322.

[119] On May 14, 1979, the General Counsel issued another memorandum on the subject entitled *Procedures for Application of the* Dubo *Policy to Pending Charges*, NLRB Gen. Counsel Memo., No. 79-36. It emphasized that the *General American Transportation* decision did not undermine the validity of *Dubo* referrals. Thus, while "individual" charges might no longer be subject to a *Collyer*-type deferral, they would be subject to a *Dubo* deferral "provided that the individual and the charging union are voluntarily pursuing the matter through the grievance-arbitration machinery." Where the individual and the charging union, therefore, are given the opportunity to choose between arbitration and the Board processes, and they have chosen arbitration, the case will be deferred. The memo provides, however, that there should not be a deferral where the individual and the charging union choose to drop the grievance. At that point the

Co.,[120] the Board refused to defer under *Dubo* even though the dispute had already reached the third step of the contractual grievance procedure. The charging party had not been informed of its right to a Board determination, the grievance had not yet been submitted to arbitration, and the Board noted there was no certainty that it would be.[121]

Since *United Technologies* restored the broad scope of Board deferral, the General Counsel has deferred under the *Collyer* and *Dubo* doctrines, applying the substantive law indicated by the Board's articulation of its deferral policies.[122]

II. PREARBITRAL DEFERRAL: APPLYING THE *COLLYER* DOCTRINE

A. The Parties' Relationship

Where there is no stable collective bargaining relationship, or where the respondent's conduct indicates a rejection of collective bargaining and the organizational rights of employees, the Board will ordinarily not defer under *Collyer*.[123] However, where there is "effective dispute-solving machinery available, and if the combination of past and present alleged misconduct does not appear to be of such character as to render the use of

---

regional office will proceed to a merit determination. The General Counsel's revised guidelines also suggest that at three specified stages during the course of the investigation of the charge the regional office should inquire regarding respondent's willingness to arbitrate. *See also* NLRB Gen. Counsel Memo., No. 81-39 (July 17, 1981), opting in favor of deferral as to the open question of *Dubo* deferral where the individual abandons a grievance although the union continues to process it. *See* Ball Corp., 257 NLRB 971, 108 LRRM 1021 (1981) (Board declined to defer to contractual grievance procedure where union had processed discharge grievance through third step but decided not to proceed to arbitration or to file unfair labor practice charge).

[120]235 NLRB 572, 98 LRRM 1347 (1978). *See also* National Rejectors Indus., 234 NLRB 251, 97 LRRM 1142 (1978) (no deferral where submission of dispute to arbitration was not voluntary but was compelled by court order).

[121]The General Counsel's 1979 memorandum, *supra* note 119, which was issued after the *Youngstown* decision, stressed that the regional offices should "fully and effectively" apprise the individual and the union of the options available and the consequences of each option. For example, if the grievance is dropped in reliance upon the Board's processes and the Board decides that the charge is not meritorious, the charging party may be left with no means of redress.

[122]*See* General Counsel's guideline memorandum concerning United Technologies Corporation, "NLRB General Counsel on Deferral Doctrine," LABOR RELATIONS YEARBOOK—1984 344 (1985).

[123]Mountain States Constr. Co., 203 NLRB 1085, 83 LRRM 1208 (1973); *see* Meilman Food Indus., 234 NLRB 698, 97 LRRM 1372 (1978), *aff'd sub nom.* Meat Cutters Local 304 v. NLRB, 593 F2d 1370, 108 LRRM 2174 (CA DC, 1979); AMF, Inc., 219 NLRB 903, 909, 90 LRRM 1271 (1975); Capitol Roof & Supply Co., 217 NLRB 1004, 89 LRRM 1191 (1975); Westinghouse Learning Corp., 211 NLRB 19, 86 LRRM 1709 (1974). *See also* note 127 *infra*.

the machinery unpromising or futile," the Board will apply its "usual deferral policies."[124] But regardless of the parties' prior collective bargaining relationship, certain conduct standing by itself may be so egregious as to prevent the Board from deferring to prospective arbitration. Thus, the Board has not deferred where the unfair labor practice charge alleges that the employer's conduct was in retaliation or reprisal for an employee's resort to the grievance procedure or otherwise "strikes at the foundation of that grievance and arbitration mechanism upon which [the Board has] relied in the formulation of [the] *Collyer* doctrine."[125] The Board has deferred to existing arbitration awards under *Spielberg*, however, rejecting claims that the employer acted in reprisal against the grievant for processing grievances.[126]

Where the conduct of the respondent constituted a rejection of collective bargaining principles or organizational rights of employees, the Board has usually refused to defer.[127] Thus, where an employer interfered with the use of the grievance-arbitration procedure, prearbitral deferral was denied.[128] And

---

[124]United Aircraft Corp., *supra* note 113, at 879; Packerland Packing Co., 216 NLRB 841, 88 LRRM 1488 (1975).

[125]North Shore Publishing Co., 206 NLRB 42, 84 LRRM 1165 (1973) (quoting from Joseph T. Ryerson & Sons, 199 NLRB 461, 467, 81 LRRM 1261 (1972)). *See also* Eldorado Club, 220 NLRB 183, 90 LRRM 1373 (1975); Whirlpool Corp., 216 NLRB 183, 88 LRRM 1329 (1975); Morrison-Knudsen Co., 213 NLRB 280, 87 LRRM 1655 (1974), *enforced*, 521 F2d 1404, 90 LRRM 3074 (CA 8, 1975); Independent Stave Co., 208 NLRB 233, 85 LRRM 1394 (1974) (a separate ground for refusing to defer was allegation in complaint that respondent had attempted to hinder access to Board's processes); *contra* U.S. Postal Serv., 210 NLRB 560, 86 LRRM 1222 (1974).

[126]Adolph Coors Co., 208 NLRB 676, 85 LRRM 1127 (1974); Gulf States Asphalt Co., 200 NLRB 938, 82 LRRM 1008 (1972); Superior Motor Transp. Co., 200 NLRB 892, 82 LRRM 1083 (1972); Terminal Transp. Co., 185 NLRB 672, 75 LRRM 1130 (1970).

[127]Edward J. White, Inc., 237 NLRB 1020, 99 LRRM 1126 (1978) (employer's unilateral changes in working conditions and refusal to bargain); Helvetia Sugar Coop., 234 NLRB 638, 98 LRRM 1290 (1978) (refusal to bargain with certified union and unilateral change of certain terms and conditions of employment); Los Angeles Marine Hardware, 235 NLRB 720, 98 LRRM 1571 (1978), *enforced*, 602 F2d 1302, 102 LRRM 2498 (CA 9, 1979) (employer repudiated collective bargaining agreement with union); Texaco, Inc., 233 NLRB 375, 96 LRRM 1534 (1977) (employer dealt directly with employees over change in starting times); Fairfield Nursing Home, 228 NLRB 1208, 96 LRRM 1180 (1977) (employer refused to pay wage increases and holiday benefits provided for in collective agreement); Ram Constr. Co., 228 NLRB 769, 95 LRRM 1125 (1977) (employer pressured employees to accept practice inconsistent with labor contract and retaliated against employees when they attempted to assert their contractual rights); Anaconda Co., 224 NLRB 1041, 93 LRRM 1139 (1976), *enforced*, 99 LRRM 2634 (CA 9, 1978) (employer's refusal to apply contract to employment site constituted repudiation of bargaining relationship); F.S. Wiley Co., 224 NLRB 1170, 92 LRRM 1589 (1976) (employer's conditioning of employment on nonmembership in union interfered with organizational rights).

[128]St. Joseph's Hosp. (Our Lady of Providence Unit), 233 NLRB 1116, 97 LRRM 1212 (1977); U.S. Postal Serv., 228 NLRB 1235, 94 LRRM 1728 (1977); Nissan Motor Corp.,

if the parties at the prospective arbitration hearing will not protect or actively support the charging party's interests or, for some reason, will be hostile to the charging party or its cause, the Board will refuse to defer.[129] Similarly, it also refused to defer where the union had been decertified and therefore might not have been interested in pursuing the grievance.[130]

B. The Parties' Willingness to Arbitrate and Arbitrability

Deferral under *Collyer* is not available to parties who are unwilling to arbitrate or are unwilling to waive the procedural defense that the grievance was not timely filed.[131]

Deferral is also generally denied where the Board concludes that the issue involved is not, at least arguably, covered by the contract and its arbitration provision.[132]

---

226 NLRB 397, 93 LRRM 1249 (1976) (employer suspended union committeeman for processing grievances); Wabash Asphalt Co., 224 NLRB 820, 93 LRRM 1254 (1976) (employer refused to hire employees referred from hiring hall because of their previous use of grievance system).

[129] Iron Workers Local 433 (Associated Gen. Contractors of Cal.), 228 NLRB 1420, 96 LRRM 1125 (1977), *enforced*, 600 F2d 770, 101 LRRM 3119 (CA 9, 1979), *cert. denied*, 445 US 915, 103 LRRM 2669 (1980); Electrical Workers (IBEW) Local 367 (Gary Billcheck), 230 NLRB 86, 96 LRRM 1182 (1977), *enforced*, 578 F2d 1375, 99 LRRM 2633 (CA 3, 1978), *cert. denied*, 439 US 1070, 100 LRRM 2268 (1979); United Parcel Serv., 228 NLRB 1060, 96 LRRM 1288 (1977); Operating Eng'rs Local 18 (S. J. Groves & Sons Co.), 227 NLRB 1477, 94 LRRM 1336 (1977); Teamsters Local 70 (Lucky Stores, Inc.), 226 NLRB 205, 93 LRRM 1245 (1976), *enforcement modified on other grounds*, 580 F2d 1053, 99 LRRM 2634 (CA 9, 1978); Plumbers & Pipe Fitters Local 725 (Powers Regulator Co.), 225 NLRB 138, 93 LRRM 1045 (1976), *enforced*, 512 F2d 550, 98 LRRM 2475 (CA 5, 1978); Electrical Workers (IBEW) Local 675 (S & M Elec. Co.), 223 NLRB 1499, 92 LRRM 1207 (1976), *enforced*, 559 F2d 1208, 96 LRRM 2106 (CA 3, 1977); Western Exterminator Co., 223 NLRB 1270, 92 LRRM 1161 (1976), *enforcement denied on other grounds*, 565 F2d 1114, 97 LRRM 2187 (CA 9, 1977); Columbian Corrugated Container Corp., 226 NLRB 147, 93 LRRM 1232 (1976); Machinists Lodge 1129 (Sunbeam Corp.), 219 NLRB 1019, 90 LRRM 1040 (1975); General Motors Corp., 218 NLRB 472, 89 LRRM 1891 (1975); United States Steel Corp., 216 NLRB 874, 88 LRRM 1649 (1975); U.S. Postal Serv., 215 NLRB 488, 88 LRRM 1099 (1974); Standard Fruit & S.S. Co., 211 NLRB 121, 87 LRRM 1134 (1974); Seafarers (Sea-Land Serv.), 207 NLRB 958, 85 LRRM 1177 (1973); Laborers Local 207 (A & E Constr. Co.), 206 NLRB 902, 84 LRRM 1474 (1973); Fleet Carrier Corp., 201 NLRB 227, 82 LRRM 1178 (1973); Machinists Lodge 68 (West Winds), 205 NLRB 132, 84 LRRM 1030 (1973), *vacated on other grounds sub nom.* Kling v. NLRB, 503 F2d 1044, 88 LRRM 2385 (CA 9, 1975); Pauley Paving Co., 200 NLRB 861, 82 LRRM 1005 (1972), *enforced*, 85 LRRM 2594 (CA 4, 1974); Kansas Meat Packers, 198 NLRB 543, 80 LRRM 1743 (1972).

[130] Seng Co., 205 NLRB 200, 83 LRRM 1577 (1973).

[131] U.S. Postal Serv., 225 NLRB 220, 93 LRRM 1089 (1976); Pilot Freight Carriers, 224 NLRB 341, 92 LRRM 1338 (1976).

[132] Western Mass. Elec. Co., 228 NLRB 607, 95 LRRM 1605 (1977), *enforcement denied on other grounds*, 573 F2d 101, 98 LRRM 2851 (CA 1, 1978); Teamsters Local 70 (Lucky Stores, Inc.), *supra* note 129; Operating Eng'rs Local 400 (Hilde Constr. Co.), 225 NLRB 596, 92 LRRM 1494 (1976), *aff'd* 561 F2d 1021, 95 LRRM 3010 (CA DC, 1977); Graphic Arts Local 277 (S & M Rotogravure Serv.), 222 NLRB 280, 91 LRRM 1139 (1976); Raymond Int'l, 218 NLRB 202, 89 LRRM 1461 (1975); Graphic Arts Local 277 (S & M

Where some, though not all, of the unfair labor practice allegations can be dealt with in arbitration, the Board has indicated that deferral may not be appropriate. In *Sheet Metal Workers Local 17 (George Koch Sons)*[133] it explained:

> Where an entire dispute can adequately be disposed of under the grievance and arbitration machinery, we are favorably inclined toward permitting the parties to do so. One of our reasons for so doing is to avoid litigating the same issues in a multiplicity of forums. But [where] we must perforce determine a part of the dispute, there is far less compelling reason for not permitting the entire dispute to be resolved in a single proceeding.[134]

Of course, should the Board find that no arbitration agreement exists, it will not defer.[135] And if the ultimate decision maker has been involved in the events giving rise to the grievance, deferral will not be allowed.[136] Deferral has also been denied where respondent's conduct limited access to the contractual grievance-arbitration procedures.[137]

Where a final and binding procedure does not exist, the Board will not defer.[138] Two cases have suggested that expiration of

---

Rotogravure Serv.), 219 NLRB 1053, 90 LRRM 1081 (1975); Operating Eng'rs Local 428 (Mercury Constructors), 216 NLRB 580, 88 LRRM 1354 (1975); Southwestern Bell Tel. Co., 198 NLRB 569, 80 LRRM 1711 (1972), *remanded in light of arbitration award sub nom.* Communications Workers v. NLRB, 86 LRRM 3247 (CA DC, 1973); Norfolk, Portsmouth Wholesale Beer Distribs. Ass'n, 196 NLRB 1150, 80 LRRM 1235 (1972).

[133] 199 NLRB 166, 81 LRRM 1195 (1972), *enforced*, 502 F2d 1159, 85 LRRM 2548 (CA 1, 1974).

[134] *Id.* at 168.

[135] Atlas Tack Corp., 226 NLRB 222, 93 LRRM 1236 (1976), *enforced*, 559 F2d 1201, 96 LRRM 2660 (CA 1, 1977).

[136] Westinghouse Elec. Corp., 206 NLRB 812, 84 LRRM 1580 (1973), *enforcement denied*, 506 F2d 668, 87 LRRM 2686 (CA 4, 1974); National Football League, 203 NLRB 958, 83 LRRM 1203 (1973), *remanded*, 503 F2d 12, 87 LRRM 2118 (CA 8, 1974).

[137] Teamsters Local 46 (Guinness-Harp Corp.), 236 NLRB 1160, 98 LRRM 1523 (1978) (dispute between employer and union over existence of collective bargaining agreement found likely to inhibit access to grievance-arbitration procedures); Edward J. White, Inc., *supra* note 127 (issues concerning respondent's unilateral changes and its refusal to bargain could not be resolved through existing contractual grievance procedure).

[138] Wheeler Constr. Co., 219 NLRB 541, 90 LRRM 1173 (1975); Machinists Dist. 10 (Ladish Co.), 200 NLRB 1159, 82 LRRM 1081 (1972); Tulsa-Whisenhunt Funeral Homes, 195 NLRB 106, 79 LRRM 1265 (1972) (arbitration could only be invoked by agreement of both parties); *see* Harley-Davidson Motor Co., 214 NLRB 433, 87 LRRM 1571 (1974) (suggesting deferral inappropriate where dispute arose after expiration of labor contract and no arbitration procedure existed at that time); *cf.* Columbus & S. Ohio Elec. Co., 205 NLRB 187, 83 LRRM 1558 (1973); *see* Communications Workers (Western Elec. Co.), 204 NLRB 782, 83 LRRM 1583 (1973) (Board reluctant to defer where contract did not specify means for employer to file grievance); Great Scott Supermarkets, 206 NLRB 447, 84 LRRM 1563 (1973) (Board adopted pro forma ALJ's conclusion that neither *Collyer* nor *Spielberg* permitted dismissal of complaint without reservation of jurisdiction pending outcome of arbitration solely because union during grievance proceedings had decided not to seek arbitration).

the labor contract can be another factor precluding deferral.[139]

Even though the final step in the grievance procedure is a bipartite panel and not conventional arbitration, the Board may nevertheless defer.[140] And a union's inability to undertake the cost of arbitration because of its financial condition does not necessarily preclude deferral where the dispute meets *Collyer* deferral prerequisites.[141]

Deferral to arbitration is only available to those who are parties to the agreement to arbitrate. Many violations of the Act (e.g., secondary boycott cases) involve persons who are not parties to the labor contract in issue. The Board will not defer to arbitration where all of the interested parties in the unfair labor practice case cannot participate in the arbitration proceeding.[142] Another example involved a nonunion company which had repudiated the union contracts of two other employers owned by the same company. The issues arising from the repudiation and the remedies applicable to it were deemed outside the scope of the arbitrator's authority, and the Board did not defer.[143] Deferral will also be denied if a respondent refuses unconditionally to promise to proceed to arbitration.[144]

---

[139]Meilman Food Indus., *supra* note 123; Sahara-Tahoe Corp., 229 NLRB 1094, 96 LRRM 1583 (1977), *enforced*, 581 F2d 767, 99 LRRM 2837 (CA 9, 1978), *cert. denied*, 442 US 917, 101 LRRM 2428 (1979).

[140]Teamsters Local 70 (Nabisco, Inc.), 198 NLRB 552, 80 LRRM 1727 (1972), *aff'd*, 479 F2d 770, 83 LRRM 2612 (CA 2, 1973).

[141]Croatian Fraternal Union, 232 NLRB 1010, 97 LRRM 1209 (1977). *But see* Electrical Workers (IBEW) Local 2188 (Western Elec. Co.) v. NLRB, 494 F2d 1087, 85 LRRM 2576 (CA DC), *cert. denied*, 419 US 835, 87 LRRM 2398 (1974).

[142]Masters, Mates & Pilots (Seatrain Lines), 220 NLRB 164, 90 LRRM 1691 (1975); Fenix & Scisson, Inc., 207 NLRB 752, 85 LRRM 1380 (1973), *enforced*, 506 F2d 1404, 87 LRRM 3276 (CA 7, 1974) (validity of agreement under §8(f)); Machinists Dist. 10 (Ladish Co.), *supra* note 138; Boilermakers Local 92 (Bigge Drayage Co.), 197 NLRB 281, 80 LRRM 1382 (1972) (§8(e) case).

[143]Frank Naccarato Constr. Co. & Tacoma Framing Co., 233 NLRB 1394, 97 LRRM 1060 (1977). In Consolidation Coal Co., 253 NLRB 789, 106 LRRM 1013 (1980), *enforcement denied*, 669 F2d 482, 109 LRRM 2452 (CA 7, 1982), involving Board rejection of an employer argument that an unfair labor practice charge should have been deferred to the parties' grievance and arbitration procedure, the Board enforced an ALJ decision requiring the employer to sign a written agreement embodying the terms of an absentee policy negotiated with the union. Application of *Collyer* was refused on two separate grounds: (1) the dispute involved the fundamental existence of an agreement between the parties, as opposed to a dispute concerning the interpretation of an agreement; and (2) the respondent employer had not raised the issue of deferral at any time before the filing of its exceptions to the ALJ decision.

[144]Columbus Foundries, 229 NLRB 34, 95 LRRM 1090 (1977).

C. Whether the Dispute Centers on the Collective Bargaining Agreement

1. Matters Incidentally Related to the Collective Bargaining Agreement. *Collyer* emphasized that prearbitral deferral is appropriate where the underlying dispute before the Board centers on the interpretation or application of the collective bargaining contract.[145] As the Board stated in an early *Collyerized* case, "when . . . the alleged unfair labor practices are . . . intimately entwined with matters of contractual interpretation, it would . . . effectuate the policies of the act to remit the parties in the first instance to the procedures they have devised for determining the meaning of their agreement."[146] Notwithstanding that concept, the Board has refused to defer on certain issues that fall within the scope of its own primary jurisdiction, although they might arguably also touch upon the contractual relations between the employer and the union. One such area is the clarification of or accretion to a bargaining unit. For example, where a union has filed a grievance claiming that its collective bargaining agreement requires coverage of additional employees, the Board has generally refused deferral.[147]

One such case was *Marion Power Shovel Co.*[148] The employer had extensively reorganized operation of its plant where the employees had been represented by two different unions. After the reorganization, both unions claimed to represent certain additional employees; the employer filed a section 9(b) unit-clarification petition with the Board seeking a determination that only a single bargaining unit was appropriate. One union objected to the petition on grounds that the representation questions were properly subjects of grievances which it had filed under a current arbitration clause. Considering the matter pri-

---

[145]*See* text *supra* note 45.

[146]Teamsters Local 70 (Nabisco, Inc.), *supra* note 140, at 554. In Standard Oil Co., 254 NLRB 32, 106 LRRM 1271 (1981), the Board deferred where the employer had unilaterally offered employees free comprehensive medical examinations; the employer based its action on a contractual clause which made employee physical condition a factor in assignment of work.

[147]Massachusetts Elec. Co., 248 NLRB 155, 103 LRRM 1404 (1980); Retail Clerks Local 588 (Raley's), 224 NLRB 1638, 92 LRRM 1381 (1976), *enforcement denied on other grounds*, 565 F2d 769, 96 LRRM 2811 (CA DC, 1977); Fort Tryon Nursing Home, 223 NLRB 769, 92 LRRM 1132 (1976); Hershey Foods Corp., 208 NLRB 452, 85 LRRM 1312 (1974), *enforced*, 506 F2d 1052, 90 LRRM 2890 (CA 3, 1974); Germantown Dev. Co., 207 NLRB 586, 84 LRRM 1495 (1973); Combustion Eng'g, 195 NLRB 909, 79 LRRM 1577 (1972).

[148]230 NLRB 576, 95 LRRM 1339 (1977).

marily a question of unit appropriateness, the Board refused to defer to the arbitration process. It stated: "The determination of questions of representation, accretion and appropriate unit do not depend upon contract interpretation but involve the application of the statutory policy, standards, and criteria. These are matters for decision of the Board rather than an arbitrator."[149] The primary issues in such cases are not limited to contractual intent of the parties to a collective bargaining agreement; instead, they include the organizational rights of employees under section 7 and the Board's section 9 determination of the appropriate bargaining unit.

Moreover, unit-accretion cases often involve competing labor organizations seeking to include workers under their respective collective bargaining agreements.[150] If the Board were to defer such disputes to arbitration, the possibility of dual arbitration proceedings and conflicting awards would arise.[151] In such cases unit-clarification proceedings are more appropriate for resolution of the dispute than arbitration. All parties can fully participate in the Board proceeding, and the problems of litigation, expense, and delay arising from the enforcement of ex parte arbitration awards may be avoided.[152]

The Board has also refused to defer, despite *Collyer*, in cases regarding employee rights protected under section 7 which either would not fall under provisions of a collective bargaining agreement or would be inadequately protected under the contract.[153] In *United States Steel Corp.*[154] the employer, under its rule banning all distribution of literature anywhere on company premises, refused to allow two employees to distribute literature,

---

[149] *Id.*, 95 LRRM at 1341–42.

[150] *See, e.g.*, Pacific Northwest Bell Tel. Co., 207 NLRB 1, 84 LRRM 1398 (1973); Crown Cork & Seal Co., 203 NLRB 171, 83 LRRM 1088 (1973).

[151] *But cf.* Carey v. Westinghouse Elec. Corp., 375 US 261, 55 LRRM 2042 (1964). *See also infra* at notes 169–170.

[152] Crown Cork & Seal Co., *supra* note 150.

[153] Chrysler Corp., 242 NLRB 577, 101 LRRM 1268 (1979) (intraunion attempts by employees to convince employees not to ratify collective bargaining agreement); Potter Elec. Co., 237 NLRB 1289, 99 LRRM 1248 (1978), *enforcement modified on other grounds*, 600 F2d 120, 101 LRRM 2378 (CA 8, 1979) (discharged employees denied rights to union representation under §8(a)(1)); Youngstown Sheet & Tube Co., 235 NLRB 572, 98 LRRM 1347 (1978) (suspension for refusal to perform unsafe work violates §8(a)(1)); Iron Workers Local 433 (Associated Gen. Contractors of Cal.), 228 NLRB 1420, 96 LRRM 1125 (1977), *enforced*, 600 F2d 770, 101 LRRM 3119 (CA 9, 1979), *cert. denied*, 445 US 915, 103 LRRM 2669 (1980) (union threats and violations of hiring-hall procedure under §§8(b)(1)(A) and 8(b)(2)); McLean Trucking Co., 231 NLRB 706, 96 LRRM 1302 (1977) (discharge of employee for seeking union representation regarding a disciplinary suspension violated §8(a)(1)).

[154] 223 NLRB 1246, 92 LRRM 1158 (1976).

a practice that the Board found to be protected under section 7 of the Act.[155] It refused to defer to the parties' grievance-arbitration mechanism since there was no assurance that section 7 rights of the employees were covered by the contract, saying:

> Both the Board and the courts have consistently held that, under *Collyer*, deferral of consideration by the Board is dependent on the express language of the contract. Note that nowhere in this . . . agreement are there any provisions relating to distribution of Section 7 literature. The authority of the arbitrator is limited to those matters explicitly contained in the contract. Thus, it can be readily seen that there is no authority invested in an arbitrator to hear or decide matters not covered in the contract.[156]

Similarly, in *Joseph T. Ryerson & Sons*,[157] an employer violated section 8(a)(1) by threatening an employee-union official for his participation in the filing of a grievance. The Board refused to defer to the collective bargaining agreement because it did not appear that the threat, which was unaccompanied by any discipline or other change in the employee's employment status, could form the basis for a contractual grievance, though it was unlawful under section 8(a)(1). Furthermore, there was no showing that an arbitrator would have any authority under the contract to remedy the company's interference with the employee's performance of grievance functions.

The Board has also refused to defer to grievance arbitration the allegation that an employer interfered with the processing of unfair labor practice charges in violation of section 8(a)(4).[158] In *McKinley Transport*,[159] an employee claimed that he had been discharged for filing unfair labor practice charges. The Board noted that questions concerning alleged interference with access to its processes were "solely within the Board's province to

---

[155]*See* NLRB v. Magnavox Co., 415 US 322, 85 LRRM 2475 (1974), and Chapter 6, "Interference With Protected Rights," at notes 192–198.

[156]223 NLRB at 1247.

[157]199 NLRB 461, 81 LRRM 1261 (1972); *see also* Native Textiles, 246 NLRB 228, 102 LRRM 1456 (1979) (employer interfered with fundamental §7 right of employees to designate their representatives by refusing to meet with union representative for purpose of processing grievances).

[158]M & B Contracting Corp., 245 NLRB 1215, 102 LRRM 1564 (1979), *enforced*, 653 F2d 245, 107 LRRM 3135 (CA 6, 1981); U.S. Postal Serv., 227 NLRB 1828, 94 LRRM 1685 (1977); Houston Chronicle Publishing Co., 227 NLRB 1829, 94 LRRM 1639 (1977) (employer threatened to sue employee and union for expenses incurred when employee filed unfair labor practice charge instead of utilizing contractual grievance process); Diversified Indus., 208 NLRB 223, 85 LRRM 1394 (1974).

[159]219 NLRB 1148, 90 LRRM 1195 (1975).

decide."[160] Because it was the Board's duty to maintain free access to and prohibit interference with its processes, such allegations could "not . . . be delegated to the parties or exclusively subject to collective bargaining."[161]

The Board has also refused prearbitral deferral where the issue concerns more a question of law—that is, an interpretation of statutory rights or duties under the Act—than a matter of contractual interpretation, or where there would be some doubt as to whether the arbitrator could or would consider the statutory issue.[162] In *Atlas Tack Corp.*[163] the Board found that an employer's alleged unilateral change of working conditions could not be deferred to a grievance procedure since the propriety of the employer's action turned on whether an impasse had occurred during negotiations, and there was no arbitration procedure in effect covering that period.

Similarly, in *Ernst Construction Division*,[164] an employer sought to defer to arbitration its action in laying off an employee. The employee, who had been reinstated by an earlier NLRB order, had filed both a grievance and an unfair labor practice charge over the layoff. Although the arbitrator could have resolved the contractual issues, deferral was inappropriate because the arbitrator would not be able to determine whether the company had abided by the Board's prior order. Compliance with a previous Board order was deemed "a matter clearly inappropriate for determination by an arbitrator."[165]

The need for interpretation of the Act has also been the basis for refusal to defer cases involving definition of mandatory subjects of bargaining[166] or the contest of rival unions to represent employees. In *Printing Pressmen Local 252 (Columbus)*[167] a

---

[160]*Id.* at 1151.

[161]*Id.*

[162]In U.S. Postal Serv., 239 NLRB 97, 99 LRRM 1515 (1978), the employer moved for a summary judgment asserting that a postal employee's §§8(a)(1) and 8(a)(3) charges involving claims of employment discrimination should be deferred to administrative procedures of the Civil Service Commission, based on the Board's policy in Dubo Mfg. Corp., 142 NLRB 431, 53 LRRM 1070 (1963). The Board overruled the motion and ordered a hearing on the substantive issues.

[163]226 NLRB 222, 93 LRRM 1236 (1976), *enforced*, 559 F2d 1201, 96 LRRM 2660 (CA 1, 1977).

[164]217 NLRB 1069, 89 LRRM 1233 (1975).

[165]*Id.*

[166]*See generally* Chapter 16, "Subjects of Bargaining."

[167]Printing Pressmen Local 252 (Columbus) (R. W. Page Corp.), 219 NLRB 268, 89 LRRM 1553 (1975). *See* Chapter 16, "Subjects of Bargaining," at note 498. *See also* Anaconda Co., 224 NLRB 1041, 93 LRRM 1139 (1976), *enforced*, 99 LRRM 2634 (CA 9, 1978); Electrical Workers (IUE) Local 742 (Randall Bearings, Inc.), 213 NLRB 824, 87 LRRM 1272 (1974), *enforced*, 519 F2d 815, 90 LRRM 2747 (CA 6, 1975); Communications Workers (Western Elec. Co.), 204 NLRB 782, 83 LRRM 1583 (1973).

union had insisted during negotiations on the continuation of an interest-arbitration clause from the previous collective bargaining agreement. It also demanded, under the interest-arbitration obligation contained in the prior contract, that the company arbitrate the inclusion of the clause in the new agreement. The Board refused deferral because the dispositive issues were whether the proposed clause of the new agreement was a mandatory subject of bargaining under the Act and, if not, whether the union had bargained to impasse on the matter in violation of section 8(b)(3). "The questions presented are therefore not ones of contract interpretation but of statutory obligation. They are legal questions concerning the . . . Act which are within the special competence of the Board rather than of an arbitrator."[168]

In rival union situations two or more unions may claim to represent the employees of an employer under existing contractual provisions.[169] In such cases the Board finds arbitration inappropriate because one union is attacking the validity of another labor organization's contract with the employer.[170] The Board considers such issues to be difficult, if not impossible, for an arbitrator to resolve to finality, for they may require that an arbitrator declare invalid the very contract from which the arbitrator's authority is derived. And more important, a rival union will lack standing to attack the propriety of another union's contract under the latter's grievance-arbitration procedure. In such cases, the Board generally exercises its authority to determine whether a collective bargaining agreement is valid, thus insuring uniformity of interpretation despite the contention that the underlying dispute is arbitrable.

Finally, even where there is language in the contract upon which the dispute may be centered, the nature of the conduct involved in the dispute, or the language of the contract itself, may affect the Board's decision on whether to defer.[171] Where

---

[168]219 NLRB at 270.

[169]*E.g.*, Fenix & Scisson, Inc., 207 NLRB 752, 85 LRRM 1380 (1973), *enforced*, 506 F2d 1404, 87 LRRM 3276 (CA 7, 1974); Scottex Corp., 200 NLRB 446, 82 LRRM 1287 (1972).

[170]*But cf.*, under the Railway Labor Act, Transportation-Communication Employees v. Union Pac. R.R., 385 US 157, 63 LRRM 2481 (1966).

[171]The Board has refused to defer because, at least in part, there was no language in the contract upon which the underlying dispute could be resolved. Keystone Steel & Wire Div., 217 NLRB 995, 89 LRRM 1192 (1975); Longshoremen (ILWU) Local 6 (Associated Food Stores), 210 NLRB 666, 86 LRRM 1534 (1974), *enforced*, 220 NLRB No. 123, 90 LRRM 1363 (1975); Bio-Science Laboratories, 209 NLRB 796, 85 LRRM

the contract language on its face is illegal,[172] or where it may compel the arbitrator to reach a result inconsistent with the policy of the Act, the Board does not defer.[173] In one case the Board declined to defer to arbitration where the respondent's argument construing the contract language to justify its conduct was deemed "patently erroneous."[174] Where the Board has considered the contract language unambiguous and, therefore, that the special competence of an arbitrator is not needed to interpret the contract,[175] or where violation of the contract has seemed so clear to the Board that there could be no contrary interpretation by an arbitrator,[176] the Board has decided the case. And where the respondent's conduct did not create even a prima facie case of breach of either the contract or the Act, the Board has refused to defer.[177]

2. Discharge and Discipline Cases. Undoubtedly the most controversial and inconsistent application of the Board's deferral principal has concerned actions taken against an employee who allegedly violates sections 8(a)(3) or 8(b)(2) and at the same time allegedly violates a "just cause" provision in a collective bargaining agreement. The Board's initial decision deferring in such cases, *National Radio Co.*,[178] established a policy that the Board abandoned in *General American Transportation Corp.*[179] then resurrected in *United Technologies Corp.*,[180] as discussed above.[181]

1568 (1974); Lithographers Local 271 (United States Playing Card Co.), 204 NLRB 418, 83 LRRM 1459 (1973), *enforced*, 495 F2d 763, 86 LRRM 2655 (CA 6, 1974); *see* Teamsters Local 85 (Tyler Bros. Drayage Co.), 206 NLRB 500, 84 LRRM 1641 (1973).

[172]Electrical Workers (IBEW) Local 901 (Ernest P. Breaux Elec. Co.), 220 NLRB 1236, 90 LRRM 1439 (1975) (§8(b)(1)(B) case where contract reserved right of union to discipline members, including supervisors); Operating Eng'rs Local 701 (Associated Gen. Contractors), 216 NLRB 233, 88 LRRM 1243 (1975), *enforced*, 578 F2d 841, 99 LRRM 2333 (CA 9, 1978) (§8(e) case).

[173]*See* Masters, Mates & Pilots (Seatrain Lines), 220 NLRB 164, 90 LRRM 1691 (1975) (submitting clause that violates §8(e) to arbitrator for enforcement may compound violation of Act); Operating Eng'rs Local 701 (Associated Gen. Contractors), *supra* note 172.

[174]Harley-Davidson Motor Co., 214 NLRB 433, 87 LRRM 1571 (1974).

[175]Oak Cliff-Golman Baking Co., 202 NLRB 614, 82 LRRM 1688 (1973).

[176]Struthers Wells Corp., 245 NLRB 1170, 102 LRRM 1484 (1979), *enforced*, 636 F2d 1210, 107 LRRM 2599 (CA 3, 1980), *cert. denied*, 452 US 916, 107 LRRM 2632 (1981); Meilman Food Indus., 234 NLRB 698, 97 LRRM 1372 (1978), *aff'd sub nom.* Meat Cutters Local 304 v. NLRB, 593 F2d 1370, 108 LRRM 2174 (CA DC, 1979).

[177]National Football League, 203 NLRB 958, 83 LRRM 1203 (1973), *remanded*, 503 F2d 12, 87 LRRM 2118 (CA 8, 1974).

[178]198 NLRB 527, 80 LRRM 1718 (1972).

[179]228 NLRB 808, 94 LRRM 1483 (1977).

[180]268 NLRB 557, 115 LRRM 1049 (1984).

[181]*Supra* at notes 93–106.

In practice, the differential treatment of cases arising under sections 8(a)(5) and 8(b)(3), on the one hand, and of those arising under sections 8(a)(1), 8(a)(3), 8(b)(1)(A), and 8(b)(2), on the other, was not always clear. Many cases involved issues of both employee discrimination and refusal to bargain. For example, in *Northeast Oklahoma City Manufacturing Co.*[182] the employer allegedly violated section 8(a)(5) by failing timely to pay contractual bonuses under a collective bargaining agreement. It was further alleged that the employer later violated sections 8(a)(3) and (1) when it discharged 12 employees who struck over the failure to make the timely payments. But the Board reversed the ALJ's decision to defer. In its view the alleged delinquencies in bonus payments involved both private contractual rights under section 8(a)(5) and "also the quite separate rights of employees to engage in conduct ostensibly coming within the protection of Section 7 of the Act . . . ."[183] Accordingly, said the Board, where the violation of a respondent's duty to bargain is "inextricably related" to violations of employees' section 7 rights, deferral is improper.[184]

Another reason proffered by the Board for its refusal under *General American* to defer in cases involving allegations of both failure to bargain and denial of employees' rights under section 7 is that in cases alleging both types of violations it would unduly fragment the proceeding to defer only the alleged violation of the duty to bargain.[185]

3. Matters Involving the Contract: Unilateral Action. Prior to the Board's decision in *Collyer*,[186] there was some question whether an offer to arbitrate conduct that amounted to unilateral action would be an adequate defense to a refusal-to bargain charge. Some commentators suggested that "[d]uring the term of a collective bargaining agreement an offer to follow the contract grievance procedure satisfies any duty to bargain collectively with respect to a matter to which the contract grievance procedure may apply."[187] Under that approach, if an

---

[182]230 NLRB 135, 95 LRRM 1276 (1977).
[183]*Id.* at 135.
[184]*See also* National Rejectors Indus., 234 NLRB 251, 97 LRRM 1142, 1143–44 (1978), *cert. denied sub nom.* Steelworkers v. National Rejectors Indus., 435 US 923, 97 LRRM 3040 (1978); Meilman Food Indus., *supra* note 176.
[185]Meilman Food Indus., *supra* note 176; Texaco, Inc., 233 NLRB 375, 96 LRRM 1534 (1977).
[186]Collyer Insulated Wire, 192 NLRB 837, 77 LRRM 1931 (1971).
[187]Cox & Dunlop, *The Duty to Bargain Collectively During the Term of an Existing Agreement*, 63 HARV. L. REV. 1097, 1101 (1950); *see also* Peck, *Accommodation and Conflict Among*

employer should appeal to contractual arbitration in response to a protest concerning its unilateral act, the Board should look not to the whole contract but only to the meaning of the arbitration clause. Its function, similar to that of the courts,[188] would be to determine "arbitrability." Beyond that, it would abstain from interfering in the parties' contractual relationship. Although the relation of the Board to the arbitral process is different in several important respects from that of the courts,[189] in the situation of unilateral action the Board would recognize that the parties have bargained for arbitration and that the arbitral procedure is "continued bargaining." Thus, the Board would avoid deciding the merits of the dispute and would instead determine only arbitrability.

Support for this abstention position stems from some of the Board's early decisions, such as *McDonnell Aircraft Corp.*[190] The contract there spelled out job specifications, provided for a grievance procedure, and included a management-rights clause. When the employer unilaterally assigned certain employees to clerical work which was being performed by others, the union filed a grievance. The contractual procedure was followed through the third step; but instead of going to the fourth step, which was arbitration, the union filed an unfair labor practice charge alleging violation of the employer's duty to bargain. The Board recognized that the employer's unilateral act "gave rise to a dispute over the interpretation and administration of the

---

Tribunals: Whatever Happened to Preemption?, LABOR LAW DEVELOPMENTS 1969 (Fifteenth Annual Institute on Labor Law, Southwestern Legal Foundation) 121 (1969); Hanley, *The NLRB and the Arbitration Process: Conflict or Accommodation?*, LABOR LAW DEVELOPMENTS 1968 (Fourteenth Annual Institute on Labor Law, Southwestern Legal Foundation) 151 (1968); Note, *The NLRB and Deference to Arbitration*, 77 YALE L.J. 1191, 1210–18 (1968).

[188]*See generally* Chapter 17, "Subjects of Bargaining," at notes 42–52.

[189]*See* NLRB v. Acme Indus. Co., 385 US 432, 64 LRRM 2069 (1967); Carey v. Westinghouse Elec. Corp., 375 US 261, 55 LRRM 2042 (1964).

[190]109 NLRB 930, 34 LRRM 1472 (1954). This decision followed Board holdings in Consolidated Aircraft Corp., 47 NLRB 694, 12 LRRM 44 (1943), *enforced as modified*, 141 F2d 785, 14 LRRM 533 (CA 9, 1944) and Crown Zellerbach Corp., 95 NLRB 753, 28 LRRM 1357 (1951), that the Board would refrain from deciding any question of contract interpretation that was capable of being resolved under a contractual grievance-arbitration procedure. *See also* National Dairy Prods. Corp., 126 NLRB 434, 45 LRRM 1332 (1960) (Board dismissed dispute over arbitrability of subcontracting issue); United Tel. of the W., 112 NLRB 779, 36 LRRM 1097 (1955) (disputes arising out of parties' conflicting contract interpretations should not be resolved by the Board because it does not effectuate the Act for the Board to police contracts); Timken Roller Bearing Co., 70 NLRB 500, 18 LRRM 1370 (1946), *enforcement denied*, 161 F2d 949, 20 LRRM 2204 (CA 6, 1947) (union electing to pursue grievance process cannot do so when dissatisfied employees file §8(a)(5) charge).

agreement,"[191] but said that the employer satisfied its obligation to bargain by treating the union's complaint as a grievance and by showing its willingness to process the grievance under the contractual procedure. The Board thus dismissed the complaint.

On its face, the holding of *Collyer*[192] would seem to lend support to the concept that an employer satisfies its duty to bargain when it simply offers to arbitrate unilateral actions taken without discussion with the union. In *Collyer*, the Board dismissed the complaint because the subject matter of the dispute—pay rate and job changes—could have been settled by the parties' contractual grievance procedure. But in *Collyer*, unlike *McDonnell Aircraft* and *National Dairy Products Corp.*,[193] the Board looked at factors other than mere arbitrability of the dispute. It held that deferral was appropriate, despite the unilateral change in working conditions and pay rates, because the arbitral interpretation of the contract would resolve both the unfair labor practice issue and the contract-interpretation issue. The meaning of the contract was perceived as the very heart of the dispute, however, since the employer would violate its duty to bargain only if it did not have the right under the contract to take the action.

Cases subsequent to *Collyer* have reenforced this approach: the Board will not confine itself simply to determining the arbitrability of a contractual dispute, and the mere offer to resolve issues involving unilateral conduct through grievance procedures will not necessarily satisfy a party's duty to bargain. The decision of *Alfred M. Lewis, Inc.*,[194] illustrates the point. There the company had unilaterally established production quota systems with disciplinary sanctions for nonfulfillment. The union arbitrated two grievances over the matter, losing both. While a third grievance was pending, it filed refusal-to-bargain charges under section 8(a)(5). The Board looked to the merits of the dispute and refused to defer either to the two prior

---

[191] 109 NLRB at 934.

[192] Collyer Insulated Wire, *supra* note 186. *Accord* Jos. Schlitz Brewing Co., 175 NLRB 141, 70 LRRM 1472 (1969); Vickers, Inc., 153 NLRB 561, 59 LRRM 1516 (1965); Flintkote Co., 149 NLRB 1561, 57 LRRM 1477 (1964); Bemis Bros. Bag Co., 143 NLRB 1311, 53 LRRM 1489 (1963); Montgomery Ward & Co., 137 NLRB 418, 50 LRRM 1162 (1962).

[193] *Supra* note 190.

[194] 229 NLRB 757, 95 LRRM 1216 (1977), *enforced in pertinent part*, 587 F2d 403, 99 LRRM 2841 (CA 9, 1978).

arbitral awards or to the pending grievance, because regardless of the contractual claims the unilateral action was clearly a violation of "well-established Board precedent."[195] On appeal, the employer argued that it had fulfilled its duty to bargain by following the grievance procedure, which was in itself a bargaining mechanism. The Ninth Circuit rejected that theory, noting that the grievance procedure was inadequate because the arbitrators' prior decisions had violated clear principles of labor law under the Act. The court also observed:

> An essential aspect of the Union's role in collective bargaining is its right to be consulted by the employer about mandatory subjects of bargaining and to make comments, objections, or suggestions to the employer before action is taken. This is a practical mechanism to insure the stability of industrial relations . . . . It would wholly undercut the duty to bargain if the employer were allowed to act with reference to a mandatory bargaining subject and then simply defend its actions in a later arbitration hearing.[196]

In *Texaco, Inc.*[197] the Board noted other circumstances where deferral was deemed inappropriate as to an employer's unilateral change of working conditions. There the employer had changed the employees' hours of starting work, without consulting the union, and then requested the employees to withdraw their premium pay grievance concerning the change in work schedules. Since there was evidence that the employer would not comply with an arbitrator's award concerning the unilateral change, and since the employer had engaged in direct dealings with the employees concerning their grievances, thereby separately violating section 8(a)(5), the Board refused deferral. It noted that even if an arbitrator were to find the unilateral changes in the work schedule improper and hold that they must be discussed with the union, it is not likely that the arbitrator would adequately remedy the employer's misconduct in dealing

---

[195]*Id.*

[196]*Id.*, 587 F2d at 408. *See* NLRB Gen. Counsel Report, Second Quarter, 1980, LABOR RELATIONS YEARBOOK—1980 303–6 (1981), discussing a case where deferral to an arbitration award was declined and a complaint was issued regarding an employer's unilateral promulgation of a new rule for employee absences. *Cf.* Keebler Co., 75 LA 975 (1980), where in a *Collyer–Dubo* case, the arbitrator found the employer's unilateral issuance of absenteeism rules to be a violation of the recognition clause in the collective bargaining agreement; thereupon, deferring to the arbitrator's award, the regional director dismissed the union's charge of refusal to bargain under §8(a)(5). *But cf.* Pet, Inc., Bakery Div., 264 NLRB 1288, 111 LRRM 1495 (1982), *enforced sub nom.* Bakery Workers Local 25 v. NLRB, 730 F2d 812, 115 LRRM 3390 (CA DC, 1984). *See* note 300, *infra.*

[197]*Supra* note 185.

directly with the employees. The Board also took into account potential future misconduct, that is, that the employer would disregard the arbitration award and continue to violate its bargaining obligation. In such a situation, a Board order rather than an arbitrator's award seemed the more appropriate remedy. Thus, in cases where the Board determines that an arbitrator cannot adequately remedy alleged violations of the duty to bargain, it will not defer.

The Board has declined to defer to arbitration in cases of union unilateral conduct. In *Western Electric Co.*,[198] shortly after the signing of a collective bargaining agreement, a union allegedly violated sections 8(b)(3) and 8(d) of the Act when it engaged in a strike in order to secure modification of the contract. The union contended that the propriety of its unilateral action (i.e., the strike) should be determined by arbitration and not by the Board. The Board decided that before deferring to arbitration it must first determine the similarity of the issues to be addressed by the Board and the arbitrators. It determined that the issues before it as to the propriety of the strike would be whether the union had complied with the statutory notice requirements of section 8(d) and whether the purpose of the strike was to achieve a modification of the agreement; the issue before the arbitrator, on the other hand, would be whether there was a breach of the no-strike clause, and this issue would not depend upon notice requirements or improper purpose to achieve a modification. Since "the necessary parallelism of the arbitrable issue and the statutory issue [did] not exist,"[199] the Board refused to defer to the arbitration mechanism of the contract. The Board also noted that the union's conduct was not a mere breach of the collective agreement but amounted to a repudiation of that agreement. Additionally, it was unclear to the Board whether the strike issue was arbitrable, since the contract did not expressly provide that the employer could invoke the arbitration clause.

4. Demands for Information. Cases involving an alleged refusal by an employer to furnish information needed by a union for use in a grievance proceeding have also been excluded

---

[198]Communications Workers (Western Elec. Co.), 204 NLRB 782, 83 LRRM 1583 (1973).

[199]*Id.*, 83 LRRM at 1586.

from *Collyer* deferral.[200] The reason for the exception is that the obligation to provide such information is derived from statutory duties independent of the labor contract, as the Supreme Court held in *NLRB v. Acme Industrial Co.*[201] In one case, however, the Board determined that there was specific language in the collective agreement concerning the obligation to furnish information, and that such procedure provided a "quick and fair means" to resolve the dispute, and deferred to the arbitral process notwithstanding *Acme*.[202] But where a contract is silent on the subject or does not contain a clear and effective waiver of the union's right to information, the Board does not defer.[203] The Board views deferral in "duty to furnish information" cases as inappropriate for the additional reason that such refusal to furnish relevant information constitutes interference with the very grievance procedure to which the employer is attempting to defer.[204] "[A]n employer is not obliged to furnish any information the union may request, but the Board has determined that such information as is relevant and reasonably necessary for the union to discharge its bargaining obligation on behalf of the employees it represents must be provided."[205] The standard for determining the relevancy of requested information is liberal and it is only necessary to establish "the probability that the desired information is relevant, and that it would be of use to the union in carrying out its statutory duties and responsibilities."[206]

In *American National Can Co.*[207] the Board, applying its refusal-to-furnish-information principles to an employer's refusal to grant the union access to its plant, determined that deferral would be inappropriate. The employer refused to grant union representatives access to its manufacturing plant to

---

[200]NLRB v. Davol, Inc., 597 F2d 782, 101 LRRM 2242 (CA 1, 1979); St. Joseph's Hosp. (Our Lady of Providence Unit), 233 NLRB 1116, 97 LRRM 1212 (1977); A. O. Smith Corp., 223 NLRB 838, 92 LRRM 1160 (1976); Worcester Polytechnic Inst., 213 NLRB 306, 87 LRRM 1616 (1974).

[201]*Supra* note 189. *See* Chapter 13, "The Duty to Bargain," at notes 450–657.

[202]United Aircraft Corp., 204 NLRB 879, 83 LRRM 1411 (1973), *aff'd sub nom.* Machinists Lodges 700, 743, 1746 v. NLRB, 525 F2d 237, 90 LRRM 2922 (CA 2, 1975).

[203]American Standard, 203 NLRB 1132, 83 LRRM 1245 (1973); *see also* Worcester Polytechnic Inst., *supra* note 200.

[204]St. Joseph's Hosp. (Our Lady of Providence Unit), *supra* note 200; A. O. Smith Corp., *supra* note 200.

[205]E.I. du Pont de Nemours & Co., 271 NLRB 1245, 1247, 117 LRRM 1111 (1984); *see also* Stephen Oderwald, Inc., 284 NLRB 277, 126 LRRM 1359 (1987).

[206]NLRB v. Acme Industrial Co., *supra* note 189, at 437; *see also* Leland Stanford Junior Univ., 262 NLRB 136, 110 LRRM 1275 (1982), *enforced*, 715 F2d 473, 114 LRRM 2444 (CA 9, 1983).

[207]293 NLRB 901, 131 LRRM 1153 (1989).

monitor temperature levels in conjunction with a heat-relief grievance. In refusing to defer the case to arbitration, the Board noted "the principles applied by the Board in refusing to defer requests-for-information cases to contractual grievance-arbitration provisions are equally applicable to the question whether to defer requests-for-access-to-obtain information cases."[208]

D. The Board's Continuing Role in *Collyer* and *Dubo* Deferral Cases

When a case is deferred on the authority of *Collyer* the Board retains jurisdiction solely for the purpose of entertaining a motion (1) that the dispute has not been promptly settled or arbitrated, or (2) that the arbitration has failed to meet *Spielberg* standards. The General Counsel is responsible for the administration of these requirements where cases are deferred without issuance of a complaint.[209] Upon a determination that a case is properly deferrable under *Collyer*, the General Counsel, through the regional director, notifies both the charged and charging parties that Board deferral is conditioned upon the prompt submission of the dispute to an arbitrator.[210] The General Counsel enforces the deferral decision by notifying the charged party that absent a prompt submission of the dispute to an arbitrator, deferral will be rescinded, the case will be further

---

[208]*Id.*, 131 LRRM at 1156.

[209]*See* "First Questions From *Collyer*," speech delivered by General Counsel Nash, LABOR RELATIONS YEARBOOK—1971 151 (1971). Eastman Broadcasting Co., 199 NLRB 434, 437, 81 LRRM 1257 (1972). General Counsel Nash issued three informational memoranda regarding *Collyer: Arbitration Deferral Policy Under* Collyer (Feb. 28, 1972) (*see* LABOR RELATIONS YEARBOOK—1972 258 (1973)); *Arbitration Deferral Policy Under* Collyer—*Revised Guidelines* (May 10, 1973); and Collyer *Deferral in Disputes Over Refusal to Furnish Information* (Dec. 18, 1973). In his *Revised Guidelines* memorandum, *supra*, he stated that according to Board decisions, "deferral may . . . be appropriate where the dispute raises issues of law and is not dependent upon interpretation of ambiguous contract provisions." *See* Peerless Pressed Metal Corp., 198 NLRB 561, 80 LRRM 1708 (1972).

The Board rarely has the opportunity to review the General Counsel's guidelines on how *Collyer* will be interpreted. This is because the Board has no means to review a decision by the General Counsel to defer and to refuse to issue a complaint. *See* Chapter 31, "NLRB Procedures," at note 133. It is only when the General Counsel has refused to defer and has issued a complaint that the Board has the opportunity to review the General Counsel's interpretation of *Collyer*. National Radio Co., 205 NLRB 1179, 84 LRRM 1105 (1973), illustrates the Board's reconsideration of a case that had been originally deferred under the *Collyer* doctrine. Another reported case of Board reconsideration after *Collyerization* is U.S. Postal Serv., 241 NLRB 1253, 101 LRRM 1074 (1979).

[210]*See* General Counsel's guidelines, *Arbitration Deferral Policy Under* Collyer—*Revised Guidelines*, *supra* note 209, at 44–45.

processed by the General Counsel, and a subsequent attempt by the charged party to seek deferral will be considered belated and will be opposed by the General Counsel.[211] In addition, the charging party is notified that its unwillingness to submit the dispute to an arbitrator will result in dismissal of its charge.[212]

After the Board's *General American Transportation Corp.* decision,[213] the General Counsel applied the *Collyer* doctrine to cases raising violations of sections 8(a)(5) and 8(b)(3).[214] However, since *United Technologies* broadened the scope of Board deferral, the General Counsel has continued to defer under the *Collyer* and *Dubo* doctrines to cases raising violations of sections 8(a)(1), (3), and (5) and 8(b)(1)(A), (2), and (3).[215] While *Collyer* policy requires a charging party to choose arbitration, where it is available, as the forum for the resolution of its dispute, *Dubo* policy requires that the charging party choose either the Board or arbitration as the forum for resolution of the dispute.[216] Upon a determination that the issues raised by the unfair labor practice charge are presently or could be the subject of a grievance, the General Counsel notifies the charging party that it must choose its forum. If the charging party wishes the General Counsel to issue a complaint and vindicate statutory rights, then it must withdraw from the grievance-arbitration procedure and not take any action inconsistent with that withdrawal. If the charging party wishes to remain within the grievance-arbitration procedure, then the General Counsel will defer pending resolution of the dispute in that procedure. As in a *Collyer* deferral, the

---

[211] *Id.* at 43. However, there is a substantial unresolved issue of whether the Board will accept the General Counsel's position that a charged party's offer to arbitrate is belated as long as the offer comes no later than at the time of the unfair labor practice hearing. *See* cases cited in note 84 *supra.* In Jack Thompson Oldsmobile, Inc., 256 NLRB 24, 107 LRRM 1166 (1981), *enforcement granted in part and denied in part*, 684 F2d 458, 110 LRRM 3368 (CA 7, 1982), where there was no deferral, the Board noted that the respondent did not raise the issue of deferral until after the unfair labor practice hearing and, therefore, the issue was not fully litigated (deferral was deemed inappropriate for the further reason of a §8(a)(3) allegation in the case).

[212] General Counsel's revised guidelines, at 45.

[213] 228 NLRB 808, 94 LRRM 1483 (1977).

[214] *See* Gen. Counsel Memo., No. 77-58 (May 25, 1977), *Regional Office Handling of* Collyer *Issues in Light of the Board's Decision in* General American Transportation Corp., LABOR RELATIONS YEARBOOK—1977 320 (1978).

[215] *Id. See* Gen. Counsel Memo., No. 79-36, *Procedures for Application of the* Dubo *Policy to Pending Charges* (May 14, 1979); General Counsel's guideline memorandum concerning United Technologies Corporation, "NLRB General Counsel on Deferral Doctrine," LABOR RELATIONS YEARBOOK—1984 344 (1985).

[216] *See* discussion *supra* at notes 117–122.

General Counsel will review the arbitration award or the settlement of the grievance under *Spielberg* standards.[217]

III. POSTARBITRAL DEFERRAL: APPLYING THE *SPIELBERG* STANDARDS

Where the subject of an unfair labor practice has been decided in an arbitration proceeding, the Board continues to determine deference to the arbitration award under its *Spielberg*[218] doctrine. Under *Spielberg* and its progeny there are four standards that must be satisfied before the Board will defer to the decision of the arbitral tribunal: (1) the unfair labor practice issue must have been presented to and considered by the arbitral tribunal;[219] (2) the arbitral proceedings must "appear to have been fair and regular"; (3) all parties to the arbitral proceedings must have "agreed to be bound"; and (4) the decision of the arbitral tribunal must not be "clearly repugnant to the purposes and policies of the Act."[220]

There are some cases where the Board does not defer under *Spielberg* because of the nature of the issue presented. These special situations—principally cases involving section 8(a)(2) charges and representation issues—are discussed in a later section of this chapter.[221] The conventional *Spielberg* standards are considered immediately below.

---

[217]*See* Gen. Counsel Memo., No. 79-36, *supra* note 215. For an example of such review, see Keebler Co., 75 LA 975 (1980).

[218]Spielberg Mfg. Co., 112 NLRB 1080, 36 LRRM 1152 (1955). *See supra* at notes 44–54. Two earlier cases that served as forerunners of the doctrine were Wertheimer Stores Corp., 107 NLRB 1434, 33 LRRM 1398 (1954), and Monsanto Chem. Co., 97 NLRB 517, 29 LRRM 1126 (1951), *enforced*, 205 F2d 763, 32 LRRM 2435 (CA 8, 1953).

[219]This standard was spelled out some years after *Spielberg* in Raytheon Co., 140 NLRB 883, 52 LRRM 1129 (1963), *set aside on other grounds*, 326 F2d 471, 55 LRRM 2101 (CA 1, 1964). However, in Olin Corp., 268 NLRB 573, 115 LRRM 1056 (1984), the Board significantly relaxed this requirement. *See infra*, notes 257–270. *See also* Monsanto Chem. Co., 130 NLRB 1097, 47 LRRM 1451 (1961). The other three standards were spelled out in Spielberg Mfg. Co., *supra* note 218.

[220]See Truesdale, *Is* Spielberg *Dead?*, NYU THIRTY-FIRST ANNUAL Conference on Labor 47 (1978), which illustrated that throughout the period of debate on and following the *General American Transportation* shrinkage of the *Collyer* doctrine, the Board continued to apply *Spielberg* standards. By refusing to issue a complaint, the General Counsel routinely screens out most of the *Spielberg*-type cases. Complaints are issued only when the General Counsel concludes that *Spielberg* deferral should not take place.

[221]*See infra* at notes 384–408.

A. The Issue Under the Act Was Presented and Considered in Arbitration

In its earliest formulation of *Spielberg* standards, the Board would not defer to an award unless the unfair labor practice issue had been both presented to and considered by the arbitrator.[222] This position was illustrated by the Board's early holdings in *Ford Motor Co.*[223] and *Monsanto Chemical Co.*[224] In *Ford* the Board refused to give weight to an award where the unfair labor practice issue had never been presented to the umpire. The case concerned employees who had participated in or instigated a work stoppage during the term of the existing contract. The Board noted that the arbitrator "did not have before him, nor did he pass upon the question, now presented to the Board, whether [the employer] had the legal right to suspend [the employees] . . . ."[225]

In *Monsanto* the Board refused to recognize an award upholding the discharge of an employee. Although the issue of whether the employee had been illegally discharged for union activity was presented to the arbitrator, he did not pass upon it. In refusing to defer, the Board stated that "[i]t manifestly could not encourage the voluntary settlement of disputes or effectuate the policies and purposes of the Act to give binding effect . . . to an arbitration award which does not purport to resolve the unfair labor practice issue . . . which is the very issue the Board is called upon to decide. . . ."[226]

In 1974, in *Electronic Reproduction Service Corp.*,[227] the Board made a major shift in emphasis, expanding the role of the

---

[222]Hawkins v. NLRB, 358 F2d 281, 61 LRRM 2622 (CA 7, 1966), *denial of petition to set aside* Mitchell Transp., 152 NLRB 122, 59 LRRM 1028 (1965); Dubo Mfg. Corp., 142 NLRB 431, 53 LRRM 1070 (1963). Precision Fittings, 141 NLRB 1034, 52 LRRM 1443 (1963) (trial examiner's report); Raytheon Co., *supra* note 219; Electrical Workers (IBEW) Local 340 (Walsh Constr. Co.), 131 NLRB 260, 48 LRRM 1022 (1961); Ford Motor Co., 131 NLRB 1462, 48 LRRM 1280 (1961); Hamilton-Scheu & Walsh Shoe Co., 80 NLRB 1496, 23 LRRM 1263 (1948). These cases, in which a discriminatory reason for a discharge had been masked behind a lawful reason, are frequently referred to as "pretext" cases. *See generally* Chapter 7, "Discrimination in Employment." *See also* McCulloch, *The Arbitration Issue in NLRB Decisions*, 19 ARB. J. 134, 137–38 (1964); McCulloch, *Arbitration and/or the NLRB*, 18 ARB. J. 3, 9 (1963); Comment, 38 U. COLO. L. REV. 363, 372–73 (1966).

[223]*Supra* note 222.

[224]*Supra* note 219.

[225]131 NLRB at 1462–63. *Accord* Raytheon Co., *supra* note 219; La Prensa, Inc., 131 NLRB 527, 48 LRRM 1076 (1961).

[226]130 NLRB at 1099.

[227]213 NLRB 758, 87 LRRM 1211 (1974).

arbitral tribunal under the postarbitral *Spielberg* review standards. The union in *Electronic Reproduction* had decided at the arbitration hearing involving the discharge of certain employees that it would not present evidence to the arbitrator in support of its belief that the discharges were discriminatory under the Act. Prior to *Electronic Reproduction*, as noted above, the Board had held that it would not defer under *Spielberg* unless the unfair labor practice issue before the Board was both presented to and considered by the arbitrator.[228] In *Electronic Reproduction* the Board reversed those earlier rulings (insofar as discharge and discipline cases were involved), stating:

> [W]e believe the better application of the underlying principles of *Collyer* and *Spielberg* to be that we should give full effect to arbitration awards dealing with discipline and discharge cases, under *Spielberg*, except when unusual circumstances are shown which demonstrate that there were bona fide reasons, other than a mere desire on the part of one party to try the same set of facts before two forums, which caused the failure to introduce such evidence at the arbitration proceeding.[229]

The Board indicated, however, that the principle of *Electronic Reproduction*, which was designed in part to avoid "piecemeal litigation," would not be appropriate where the arbitrator specifically declined to pass on "statutory" issues or where the parties by agreement excluded "statutory" issues from the arbitration. Otherwise, for the purpose of *Spielberg* deferral, it would be presumed that the arbitrator had considered the issue of whether the discharge or discipline of the grievant (usually the charging party) was for pretextual reasons, unless there was a bona fide reason for the arbitrator not to receive evidence concerning the theory of pretextual discharge or unless the arbitrator refused or was prohibited from considering that theory.[230]

The *Electronic Reproduction* approach prevailed until 1980, when, after changes in membership, the Board expressly over-

---

[228]In Yourga Trucking, 197 NLRB 928, 80 LRRM 1498 (1972), the Board held that the party seeking deferral under *Spielberg* had the burden of demonstrating that the statutory issue had been presented in the arbitration proceeding. *See also* John Sexton & Co. Div., 213 NLRB 798, 87 LRRM 1241 (1974) (*accord*).

[229]213 NLRB at 762.

[230]*Id.* Dissenting Members Fanning and Jenkins stated that the majority's holding "means, of course, that the Board for all practical purposes will no longer decide any part of a case which has been or could have been decided by an arbitrator who has issued an award." *Id.*, 87 LRRM at 1219.

ruled it in *Suburban Motor Freight*.[231] The charging party in *Suburban* had been reinstated by an arbitral "Joint Grievance Committee," then fired again for a rule infraction. The committee again ordered his reinstatement, but with a 60-day suspension. He later filed an unfair labor practice charge alleging that the discharges had been motivated by employer reaction to his complaints to the union about certain employer practices. These allegations had not been presented to the joint committee. The Board declined to defer. Conceding that the rule of *Electronic Reproduction* encouraged settlement under contract procedures—thereby reducing multiple litigation—the Board nevertheless concluded that the rule delegated too much of the Board's responsibility to protect section 7 rights. The majority stated:

> [W]e will no longer honor the results of an arbitration proceeding under *Spielberg* unless the unfair labor practice issue before the Board was both presented to and considered by the arbitrator. In accord with the rule formerly stated in *Airco Industrial Gases* [Pacific Division, 195 NLRB 676, 79 LRRM 1497 (1972)], we will give no deference to an arbitration award which bears no indication that the arbitrator ruled on the statutory issue of discrimination in determining the propriety of an employer's disciplinary actions. In like accord with the corollary rule stated in *Yourga Trucking* [197 NLRB 928, 80 LRRM 1498 (1972)], we shall impose on the party seeking Board deferral to an arbitration award the burden to prove that the issue of discrimination was litigated before the arbitrator.[232]

Even before *Suburban Motor Freight*, the Board in many cases had continued to refuse to defer where an arbitrator had not considered the unfair labor practice issue.[233] In *Teamsters Local 46 (Port Distributing Co.)*[234] the union had unilaterally halted its practice of not enforcing the union-security clause with respect

---

[231]247 NLRB 146, 103 LRRM 1113 (1980) (Chairman Fanning and Members Jenkins and Truesdale as the majority and Member Penello dissenting). *See* Propoco, Inc., 263 NLRB 136, 110 LRRM 1496 (1982), *aff'd*, 742 F2d 1438, 118 LRRM 2966 (CA 2, 1983), discussed at notes 252–256, *infra*.

[232]247 NLRB at 147. *See also supra* at note 228.

[233]*E.g.*, in Kroger Co., 226 NLRB 512, 93 LRRM 1315 (1976), the arbitrator had noted that an issue was raised about the employer's failure to furnish information relevant to the grievance, but he did not rule on the matter, leaving it for disposition as part of compliance with his backpay award against the employer; the Board treated this as a failure to resolve the unfair labor practice issue, holding that the arbitrator's resolution did not provide assurance against future violations of the statute. *See also* Ad Art, Inc., 238 NLRB 1124, 99 LRRM 1626 (1978), *enforced*, 645 F2d 669, 107 LRRM 3292 (CA 9, 1981); Davol, Inc., 237 NLRB 431, 99 LRRM 1011, (1978), *enforced*, 597 F2d 782 (CA 1, 1979).

[234]236 NLRB 1175, 98 LRRM 1519 (1978).

to casual employees. When the union sought arbitration to enforce its new application of the union-security clause, the employer filed an unfair labor practice charge alleging violations of sections 8(b)(1)(A) and 8(b)(2), which charges were deferred under the *Collyer* doctrine. The arbitrator then found that in spite of a long contrary practice, clear contract language supported the union's position. Citing its decision in *Alfred M. Lewis, Inc.*,[235] the Board refused to defer because the arbitrator had not addressed the unfair labor practice issue. The Board then found the arbitrator's conclusion contrary to Board law.

In January 1984, at the same time that the Board extended prearbitral deferral by overruling *General American Transportation Corp.*,[236] the Board overruled *Suburban Motor Freight* and eased its standards of postarbitral deferral under *Spielberg*. In *Olin Corp.*[237] the Board held that an arbitrator has adequately considered an alleged unfair labor practice if (1) the contractual issue is factually parallel to the unfair labor practice issue, and (2) the arbitrator was presented generally with the facts relevant to resolving the unfair labor practice.

Determining the extent to which the unfair labor practice issue must have been presented to and considered by the arbitration tribunal in order to satisfy the Board's requirement for deferral is not easy. As the following cases demonstrate, the Board's assessment of arbitration awards and its decisions whether to defer have been characterized by a notable lack of consistency. The cases present a variety of fact patterns which, nevertheless, provide a general sense of the Board's oscillations in this area.

1. The Standard of Arbitral Review: What, and How Thoroughly, the Arbitrator Considered. In *Kansas City Star Co.*,[238] a case decided before *Suburban Motor Freight*,[239] employees were discharged for engaging in a wildcat strike; the next day the employer rescinded the collective bargaining agreement and refused to rehire the employees, who had offered to return. Without passing on the legality of the rescission, an arbitrator upheld the discharges (except for two employees who had not

---

[235] 229 NLRB 757, 95 LRRM 1216 (1977), *enforced in pertinent part*, 587 F2d 403, 99 LRRM 2841 (CA 9, 1978).

[236] 228 NLRB 808, 94 LRRM 1483 (1977).

[237] *Supra* note 219.

[238] 236 NLRB 866, 98 LRRM 1320 (1978).

[239] *Supra* note 231.

refused to work). A divided Board dismissed the complaint, relying on *Spielberg*,[240] but expressly declining to rely on *Electronic Reproduction Service Corp.*,[241] thus casting some doubt on its continued vitality.

Did that imply that *Spielberg* deferral was appropriate when an arbitrator failed or declined to "assume" the role of the Board and directly and expressly make rulings on unfair labor practices? The Board suggested an answer in *Atlantic Steel Co.*[242] There the arbitrator had sustained the discharge of an employee who had been terminated for his past record of discipline and for publicly calling his foreman derogatory names. At the arbitration hearing, the grievant claimed that he had been harassed by the foreman for circulating an employee petition concerning certain benefits. The Board's ALJ refused to defer on the grounds that the arbitrator had not decided the underlying unfair labor practice and that the arbitrator's conclusion was not consistent with Board precedent. The Board disagreed. Deferring to the arbitrator's award and dismissing the complaint, the Board stated:

> Must the arbitrator actually discuss the unfair labor practice, or is it sufficient that he or she considered all of the evidence relevant to the unfair labor practice in determining whether the discharge was lawful under the contract? . . . [W]hile it may be preferable for the arbitrator to pass on the unfair labor practice directly, the Board generally has not required that he or she do so. Rather, it is necessary only that the arbitrator has considered all of the evidence relevant to the unfair labor practice in reaching his or her decision.[243]

---

[240]Member Truesdale, in a concurring opinion which was embraced by the majority, stated:

> "[W]hile the arbitrator did not pass on the legality of the rescission, he was required to rule on every factual and legal question necessary to the resolution of this issue, since the legality of rescission as a self-help remedy available to respondent turns on whether respondent could legally discharge the strikers, and whether the strike was legal. Both of these issues were considered fully by the arbitrator in the context of the pending unfair labor practices. . . . Thus, my decision to concur rests on the unique relationship between the issues decided and the one omitted—since all of the factual and legal findings necessary to the resolution of the 8(a)(5) allegation concerning rescission were also necessary to a determination of the legality of the discharges. These issues were vigorously litigated before the arbitrator, and he reached his decision on the basis of the full record. No more is required." 236 NLRB at 869.

[241]*Supra* note 227. In Atlantic Steel Co., 245 NLRB 814, 102 LRRM 1247 (1979), *infra* at notes 242–243, the Board noted that deferral had been appropriate on the rescission issue in *Kansas City Star* because the arbitrator's findings were "both complete and comprehensive and factually parallel to the unfair labor practice question." 245 NLRB at 815.

[242]*Supra* note 241.

[243]*Id.* at 815. *See infra* at notes 252–256.

2. The Board's Application of *Suburban Motor Freight*. The Board remained sharply divided on deferral after *Suburban Motor Freight*,[244] and its decisions reflected the intensity of the differences. In the cases decided immediately following *Suburban*, it appeared that comprehensive and express consideration of the unfair labor practice issue by the arbitrator was not a requisite for deferral. However by mid–1982, as indicated by the decision in *Propoco, Inc.*,[245] the Board's approach had become more demanding of both the arbitrator and the parties as to the kind of arbitral record and consideration that would be required for deferral.

In *Bay Shipbuilding Co.*[246] the employer unilaterally changed its welfare benefit program from an insured program with one carrier to a self-insured program with another carrier. The collective bargaining agreement stated that the existing insurance coverage was to continue during the term of the agreement. The arbitrator decided that the term "coverage" meant welfare benefits and that these had not been changed by the employer; therefore there was no violation of the collective bargaining agreement. In a section 8(a)(5) proceeding the Board deferred to the arbitrator's decision, even though his award stated that he had not considered the unilateral action an unfair labor practice issue. The Board deemed his holding that the contract permitted the change as necessarily a ruling that there was no unfair labor practice.[247]

In *Chemical Leaman Tank Lines*[248] a truck driver was discharged for refusing to drive a truck with a defective spring assembly. The truck was loaded with nitrogen. The collective bargaining agreement stated that equipment must not be taken out in an unsafe condition. A joint labor-management arbitration panel denied the grievance. The ALJ found that the stat-

---

[244]*Supra* note 231.
[245]*Supra* note 231.
[246]251 NLRB 809, 105 LRRM 1376 (1980).
[247]Concurring Member Truesdale saw the case as similar to *Atlantic Steel Co., supra* note 241, where it was not necessary for the arbitrator to expressly rule on the unfair labor practice because he considered the related facts and decided the underlying issue. Dissenting Member Jenkins noted that *Suburban Motor Freight* explicitly stated that the facts relating to the unfair labor practice must be *both* presented to and considered by the arbitrator, and that in unfair labor practice cases involving a change of carrier, the Board considers such matters as the financial stability of the successor carrier and comparability of service being provided; there was no evidence that these factors had been presented to the arbitrator. *Id.*
[248]251 NLRB 1058, 105 LRRM 1276 (1980).

utory issue—whether the employee had been engaged in protected concerted activity based on reasonable safety considerations—had not been presented to nor considered by the arbitration panel. The panel, which had made no written findings, had considered only the safety clause. The Board deferred, applying the approach used in *Atlantic Steel Co.*,[249] to conclude that the arbitration panel had necessarily considered facts parallel to those needed to decide the unfair labor practice charge.

In *Magnetics International*,[250] however, the Board refused to defer to an arbitration award that had upheld the disciplinary suspension and discharge of a union steward for activity that the Board deemed to be protected. The Board noted that the "arbitrator considered only the contractual constraints upon the Respondent, not the statutory."[251]

In 1982, in *Propoco, Inc.*,[252] following further changes in membership, the still-divided Board reaffirmed and tightened the *Suburban Motor Freight*[253] doctrine. A cleaning service company discharged an employee who wrote and signed a complaint letter also signed by nine other employees. The grievant was fired after she refused to apologize for writing the letter. In arbitration, the union attorney submitted no evidence as to whether the discharge was an unfair labor practice; his only contention was that the discharge was discriminatory in view of the failure of the employer to impose discipline on any of the other letter signers. Although a copy of the NLRB complaint was submitted to the arbitrator, he indicated that he did not consider the complaint to be before him. However, he did conclude that the grievant was not discharged because of union activity or any other conduct protected by the Act, and that the discharge was for just cause.

The Board majority found that the latter statement was merely gratuitous and that the unfair labor practice issue had

---

[249]*Supra* note 241.

[250]254 NLRB 520, 106 LRRM 1133 (1981), *enforced*, 699 F2d 806, 112 LRRM 2658 (CA 6, 1983).

[251]*Id.* at 522. *See also* Triple A Mach. Shop, 245 NLRB 136, 102 LRRM 1559, 1561 (1979), where the arbitrator failed to pass on statutory issues involved in the discharge of employees for strike misconduct. Concluding that the arbitrator had "in effect, rendered 'compromise awards.'" the Board refused to defer.

[252]263 NLRB 136, 110 LRRM 1496 (1982), *aff'd*, 742 F2d 1438, 118 LRRM 2966 (CA 2, 1983).

[253]247 NLRB 146, 103 LRRM 1113 (1980). *But cf.* Pet, Inc., Bakery Div., 264 NLRB 1288, 111 LRRM 1495 (1982), *enforced sub nom.* Bakery Workers Local 25 v. NLRB, 730 F2d 812, 115 LRRM 3390 (CA DC, 1984).

neither been presented to nor considered by the arbitrator. The Board accordingly declined to defer to the arbitration award. In reaffirming *Suburban*, the Board made clear that a grievant could elect not to present the unfair labor practice issue to the arbitrator.[254] It stated:

> A grievant may choose to challenge disciplinary action solely on the ground that discipline invoked for the stated offense was inconsistent with the employer's past practice or otherwise violated contractual provisions unrelated to the Act. The election to proceed in the contractually created arbitration forum provides no basis, in and of itself, for depriving an alleged discriminatee of the statutorily created forum for adjudication of unfair labor practice charges.[255]

The dissenters would have deferred to the arbitrator's award, contending that it met all of the *Spielberg* standards. Chairman Van de Water used the occasion to charge that the *Suburban Motor Freight* doctrine departed from sound deferral policy:

> The arbitral forum is the one selected through collective bargaining by the parties to resolve their disputes and once that forum has been invoked the grievant should be required to raise any statutory issues before the arbitrator or be precluded from subsequently raising them before the Board.[256]

3. The Board Abandons *Suburban Motor Freight*: Factual Parallelism Under *Olin*. The dissent in *Propoco, Inc.*,[257] eventually prevailed over the majority opinion, and the Board overruled *Suburban Motor Freight* and adopted more lenient postarbitral deferral standards. *Olin Corp.*[258] involved the discharge of a local union's president for participating in and

---

[254]According to the majority, a "single litigation requirement might actually discourage resort to contractual grievance and arbitration proceedings." 110 LRRM at 1498.

[255]110 LRRM at 1498. The decision also commented, in response to criticism by Chairman Van de Water, on the matter of how thoroughly the statutory issue must be presented: "This problem, to the extent that it exists, will be no greater in the context of arbitration proceedings than when presented in the context of summary judgment proceedings, motions for reconsideration, or unfair labor practice proceedings relevant to conduct not specifically alleged as unlawful in the complaint." *Id.* And in response to Member Hunter's criticism that the decision requires litigation of the unfair labor practice issue in exactly the same manner as if it were before the Board, the majority stated: "Other than in *Spielberg* itself, the Board has imposed no special rules concerning the manner in which such an issue can be litigated in arbitration proceedings." *Id.* at 1499 n.8.

[256]*Id.* at 1503. The Chairman also wrote: "Absent evidence to the contrary, the Board should be willing to assume that arbitrators have considered the issue presented to them, including any unfair labor practice issue." *Id.*

[257]*Supra* note 252.

[258]268 NLRB 573, 115 LRRM 1056 (1984).

failing to prevent a "sick-out." The collective bargaining agreement affirmatively required union officers not to participate in and to try to stop strikes when they occurred. The discharged employee grieved and the arbitrator upheld the discharge under the contract. In the unfair labor practice proceeding, the ALJ refused to defer to the arbitration award because it was limited to interpretation of the contract and the arbitrator did not explicitly refer to the statutory rights and the waiver questions raised before the Board. On the merits, however, the ALJ upheld the discharge.

Rejecting the ALJ's analysis, the Board overruled *Suburban Motor Freight* noting that "it hardly needs repeating that national policy strongly favors the voluntary arbitration of disputes."[259] The Board announced the following standard for deferral to arbitration awards:

> We would find that an arbitrator has adequately considered the unfair labor practice if (1) the contractual issue is factually parallel to the unfair labor practice issue, and (2) the arbitrator was presented generally with the facts relevant to resolving the unfair labor practice. In this respect, differences, if any, between the contractual and statutory standards of review should be weighed by the Board as part of its determination under the *Spielberg* standards of whether an award is "clearly repugnant" to the Act. And, with regard to the inquiry into the "clearly repugnant" standard, we would not require an arbitrator's award to be totally consistent with Board precedent. Unless the award is "palpably wrong," i.e., unless the arbitrator's decision is not susceptible to an interpretation consistent with the Act, we will defer.[260]

The Board placed the burden of proof on the party objecting to deferral. "We would require that the party seeking to have the Board reject deferral and consider the merits of a given case show that the above standards for deferral have not been met. Thus, the party seeking to have the Board ignore the determination of an arbitrator has the burden of affirmatively demonstrating the defects in the arbitral process or award."[261] The Board concluded that it would fulfill its statutory obligation of assuring protection of employee rights by reviewing arbitral awards to insure they are not inconsistent with nor clearly repugnant to the NLRA.

---

[259] *Id.* at 574.
[260] *Id.*
[261] *Id.*

Considering the case before it, the Board found that there was no evidence that the statutory and contractual issues were factually dissimilar or that facts generally relevant to the unfair labor practice question were not presented to the arbitrator. Additionally, the Board held that the arbitrator's award was not clearly repugnant to the Act.

The Board has applied its liberalized version of *Spielberg* deferral in subsequent cases.[262] The application of the *Olin* standard of factual parallelism demonstrates that the Board no longer requires explicit consideration of statutory issues or legal standards by an arbitrator before it will defer to an arbitral award.[263] Rather, the Board will, at this stage of the deferral inquiry, examine only the question of whether the arbitrator considered the factual issues that also would be considered in the unfair labor practice case,[264] on the basis of an adequate factual record.[265]

The Board applied the *Olin* factual parallelism standard in *Anderson Sand & Gravel Co.*[266] Two employees were discharged for striking in breach of contract. A joint union-employer committee considered and upheld the discharges. The Board deferred to that determination, emphasizing that the contractual "no-strike" issue was factually parallel to the unfair labor practice issue of whether the employee's statutory right had been waived by the no-strike clause. The Board found that the facts about the strike and the contract had been generally presented and that the General Counsel had not proved that important facts were left out. Although the law on waiver of section 7 rights was not

---

[262] Dennison Nat'l Co., 296 NLRB No. 22, 132 LRRM 1076 (1989); American Broadcasting Co., 290 NLRB 86, 131 LRRM 1252 (1988); Ohio Edison Co., 274 NLRB 874, 118 LRRM 1429 (1985).

[263] In Olin Corp., *supra* note 258, the Board indicated that the problem of comparing contractual and statutory legal standards to determine whether an arbitration award is an adequate statutory resolution of the unfair labor practice claim will be considered under that part of the *Spielberg* test that examines whether the award is "clearly repugnant" to the policies of the Act. *See also* Anderson Sand & Gravel Co., Anderson Prestress Div., 277 NLRB 1204, 121 LRRM 1069 (1985) (Board requires deferral although arbitration panel did not receive submission on law or refer to unfair labor practice issue in its award). *But see* Dick Gidron Cadillac, 287 NLRB 1107, 128 LRRM 1142 (1988) (no deferral where statutory issue not considered); M & G Convoy, 287 NLRB 1140, 130 LRRM 1150 (1988).

[264] National Linen Serv., 293 NLRB No. 122, 131 LRRM 1233 (1989) (no deferral to grievance when it did not resolve issues raised in complaint); Ryder/P.I.E. Nationwide, 278 NLRB 713, 122 LRRM 1264 (1986), *enforcement denied on other grounds*, 810 F2d 502, 124 LRRM 3024 (CA 5, 1987).

[265] Donald Browne, 278 NLRB 103, 121 LRRM 1121 (1986); Anderson Sand & Gravel Co., Anderson Prestress Div., *supra* note 263.

[266] Anderson Sand & Gravel Co., Anderson Prestress Div., *supra* note 263.

before the arbitration panel, the Board said that this was not a proper objection under the factual parallelism test of *Olin*. Finally, the Board noted that the award was not clearly repugnant to the purposes and policies of the Act. That the General Counsel or the Board might decide the contractual issues differently from the arbitration panel does not warrant refusing to defer to the award.[267]

In *Reichhold Chemicals*,[268] the company converted three union employees to supervisory positions and the union argued that bargaining-unit work had been removed in violation of the contract. The Board held that deferral was required even though the arbitrator refused to consider the unfair labor practice issue, because the contract and statutory issues were factually parallel.

In *Martin Redi-Mix*,[269] the Board noted that, while factual issues under the contract and the statutory claims must be factually parallel, it is not a necessary predicate to deferral that an award explicitly address the unfair labor practice claim. In *Aces Mechanical Corp.*[270] the Board refused to defer on the basis that the prearbitration contractual issues and postarbitration statutory issues were not factually parallel. After a steward was discharged, the employer conditioned reinstatement on the steward's agreement to relinquish his office as steward. Deferral was inappropriate because the facts concerning the alleged unlawful reinstatement occurred after the date of discharge and were not considered by the arbitration panel in upholding the discharge. The Second Circuit denied enforcement of the Board's order, however, because the arbitrators had been presented with evidence of the steward's reinstatement and their decision effectively decided the issue.

4. Deferral to Joint Committee Awards. The Board has stated that, consistent with the Act's policy of permitting parties to resolve their disputes in the manner which they deem best, it will consider the decisions of joint union-employer committees to be similar to those of other arbitral tribunals. The Board will defer to resolution of grievances made by such joint committees, just as it does to formal arbitration awards, as long as the *Spielberg*

---

[267]*Id.*
[268]275 NLRB 1414, 120 LRRM 1037 (1985).
[269]274 NLRB 559, 118 LRRM 1425 (1985).
[270]NLRB v. Aces Mechanical Corp., 837 F2d 570, 127 LRRM 2513 (CA 2, 1988), *denying enforcement of* 282 NLRB 928, 124 LRRM 1145 (1987).

standards are met.[271] "Where . . . the parties have found that the machinery which they have created for the amicable resolution of their disputes has adequately served its purpose, we shall accept such a resolution absent evidence of irregularity, collusion or inadequate provisions for the taking of testimony."[272] The Board so ruled and deferred to a joint committee award despite testimony that members of the joint committee had given the grievant and his witness a tongue-lashing.[273] Moreover, the Supreme Court has given its approval of such committee decisions.[274] However, in *Herman Brothers*,[275] the Board refused to defer because the arbitration proceedings were not deemed fair and regular, thus failing the *Spielberg* standards. The arbitration panel consisted of union and management representatives, both of whose interest appeared aligned against the charging party grievant.

B. Fair and Regular Proceedings

1. The Arbitral Procedure. The Board's criteria for fairness and regularity are intended to establish minimum due-process-type standards for the conduct of arbitration proceedings. Thus, deferral has been denied where evidence was deliberately withheld from the arbitrator,[276] where the grievant was given insufficient time to prepare,[277] or was not afforded an opportunity to confront witnesses,[278] or to cross-examine them.[279] Abrasive

---

[271]Ryder Truck Lines, 287 NLRB 806, 127 LRRM 1283 (1987), *on remand from* 786 F2d 1516, 122 LRRM 2084 (CA 11, 1986); Carolina Freight Carriers Corp., 281 NLRB 440, 123 LRRM 1342 (1986); Ryder/P.I.E. Nationwide, *supra* note 264; Alpha Beta Co., 273 NLRB 1546, 118 LRRM 1202 (1985), *aff'd sub nom.* Mahon v. NLRB, 808 F2d 1342, 124 LRRM 2762 (CA 9, 1987); Terminal Transp. Co., 185 NLRB 672, 75 LRRM 1130 (1970); Modern Motor Express, 149 NLRB 1507, 58 LRRM 1005 (1964). *See* Comment, *Concurrent Jurisdiction of Arbitrators and the NLRB*, 38 U. COLO. L. REV. 363, 376 (1966).

[272]Denver-Chicago Trucking Co., 132 NLRB 1416, 48 LRRM 1524, 1526 (1961).

[273]*Id.*

[274]Teamsters Local 89 v. Riss & Co., 372 US 517, 52 LRRM 2623 (1963).

[275]Herman Bros. v. NLRB, 658 F2d 201, 108 LRRM 2327 (CA 3, 1981), *enforcing* 252 NLRB 848, 105 LRRM 1374 (1980).

[276]Precision Fittings, 141 NLRB 1034, 52 LRRM 1443 (1963).

[277]Gateway Transp. Co., 137 NLRB 1763, 50 LRRM 1495 (1962) (grievant was pressed to arbitration 2 days after notice). *But cf.* Raytheon Co. v. NLRB, 326 F2d 471, 55 LRRM 2101 (CA 1, 1964), where the Board refused to honor an award because, among other reasons, the grievant was not granted a requested continuance. The court said: "[W]e cannot think the Board would have expected us to rule it unfair if a trial examiner, rather than an arbitrator, had refused to grant a further continuance on this record." *Id.* at 473.

[278]Honolulu Star-Bulletin, 123 NLRB 395, 43 LRRM 1449, *enforcement denied on other grounds*, 274 F2d 567, 45 LRRM 2184 (CA DC, 1959) (trial examiner's decision).

[279]Versi Craft Corp., 227 NLRB 877, 94 LRRM 1207 (1977).

demeanor by the arbitrator, however, has not prevented deferral.[280]

The Board declined to defer where the union did not present any evidence on the grievant's behalf.[281] And deferral was not granted where one of the parties affected by the award was not represented in the arbitration proceeding.[282]

Arbitration which is held before discipline is made effective does not preclude deferral, as in a case where the collective bargaining agreement required the employer to continue employees on the payroll until the dispute was resolved by an arbitrator.[283]

2. Hostility of the Tribunal or Union Representative Toward the Grievant. Where the arbitrator may be predisposed against the grievant, deferral to the award will not result. This situation has occasionally occurred under contracts where the machinery provides for final judgment by a joint labor-management committee and where one or more of the committee members may have reason to rule against the grievant regardless of the merits of the dispute. In *Roadway Express*,[284] for example, the grievant was the leader of the opposition to incumbent union officials and was also well known for his attacks upon the employing industry; the Board refused to honor an award that was adverse to him.[285] Also, the Board will not defer to an

---

[280]In Denver-Chicago Trucking Co., *supra* note 272, the Board deferred to a joint committee award despite testimony that members of the joint committee had given the grievant and his witnesses a tongue-lashing. In U.S. Postal Serv., 241 NLRB 1253, 101 LRRM 1074 (1979), the charging party sought the Board's decision after the arbitrator's award had been handed down. A Board majority refused. The dissenting members would have found the procedure irregular because of the arbitrator's alleged shouting and abusive comments (directed toward the charging party, her counsel, and her witnesses) and because of his refusal to proceed with the arbitration unless the charging party's counsel returned a certain document to respondent.

[281]General Iron Corp., 218 NLRB 707, 89 LRRM 1788 (1975) (Board also noted that no interpreter was available at arbitration, although grievant did not speak English).

[282]Retail Clerks Local 324 (Esgro, Inc.), 206 NLRB 931, 84 LRRM 1431 (1973).

[283]American Bakeries Co., 249 NLRB 1249, 104 LRRM 1305 (1980). The arbitrator permitted the discharge of two of six employees charged with a work stoppage for refusing to work overtime; the two were union stewards whom the arbitrator found to be instigators.

[284]145 NLRB 513, 54 LRRM 1419 (1963).

[285]Likewise, in Youngstown Cartage Co., 146 NLRB 305, 55 LRRM 1301 (1964), it refused to honor such an award where the grievant had been a dissident within the union. In Mason & Dixon Lines, 237 NLRB 6, 98 LRRM 1540 (1978), union officials on the grievance committee had opposed the dissident faction of which the grievant was a member, and the union official who represented the grievant before the grievance committee had not discussed the case with him prior to the hearing; deferral was refused. However, it did not take such a strong showing for the Board to refuse to defer to a joint labor-management committee in Brown Co., 243 NLRB 769, 101 LRRM 1608 (1979), *aff'd in pertinent part*, 663 F2d 1078, 109 LRRM 2663 (CA 9, 1981).

arbitration award where the charging party's interests could not have been properly represented because of the representative's hostility.[286]

C. Agreement of All Parties to Be Bound

The *Spielberg* requirement that all parties agree to be bound by the award has received little attention; usually all parties, by virtue of the collective bargaining agreement, have explicitly agreed to be bound by the contractual arbitral procedure. There have been only a few cases concerning this standard. The Board refused to give effect to an arbitration award in *Hershey Chocolate Corp.*[287] where none of the employees involved had agreed to be bound by the award. The Board held that the award was "contrary to law."

The Board deferred to an arbitration procedure under a labor contract which did not contain specific language stating that the procedure was final and binding in *Champlin Petroleum Co.*[288] The Board pointed out, however, that "it is reasonable to infer that [such finality] was the intention of the parties. Otherwise, the arbitral procedure would be illusory, and resort thereto an exercise in futility."[289]

Where a lessee was not a party to the arbitration proceeding which had been initiated by the union to enforce a subcontracting clause against the lessee's operations, the Board did not defer.[290] And where a successor-employer was not a party to the bargaining agreement nor to the arbitration proceeding, the Board would not defer.[291]

---

[286]Longshoremen (ILWU) Local 27 (Morris R. Bond), 205 NLRB 1141, 84 LRRM 1546 (1973), *enforced*, 514 F2d 481, 89 LRRM 2113 (CA 9, 1975). *See also* Russ Togs, Inc., 253 NLRB 767, 106 LRRM 1067 (1980).

[287]129 NLRB 1052, 47 LRRM 1130 (1960), *enforcement denied on other grounds*, 297 F2d 286, 49 LRRM 2173 (CA 3, 1961) (there was also an element of adverse relation between union and charging parties). *See* Edward Axel Roffman Assocs., 147 NLRB 717, 56 LRRM 1268 (1964) (employer withdrew from arbitration following arbitrator's ruling that matter was arbitrable; trial examiner ruled: "Despite Respondent's voluntary withdrawal . . . the arbitration proceedings . . . appear to have been fair and regular.") In T.I.M.E.-DC, Inc., 215 NLRB 1175, 93 LRRM 1270 (1976), the Board declined to defer to an award assigning contested work to one union where the union which claimed the work was not party to the arbitration.

[288]201 NLRB 83, 82 LRRM 1388 (1973).

[289]*Id.* at 90.

[290]Federated Dep't Stores, 235 NLRB 711, 97 LRRM 1556 (1978).

[291]Retail, Wholesale & Dep't Store Union Dist. 1199E (Greater Pa. Ave. Nursing Center), 238 NLRB 9, 99 LRRM 1194 (1978), *remanded sub nom.* Hospital & Health Care Employees v. NLRB, 613 F2d 1102, 103 LRRM 2001 (CA DC, 1979); the court disagreed on this and other points on which the Board had relied.

Dicta in *Great Scott Supermarkets*[292] suggest that the *Spielberg* reference to agreement of the "parties" to be bound does not refer to individual discriminatees but to the union and the employer.[293]

D. The Award Is Not Repugnant to the Policies of the Act

In *Kansas City Star*,[294] Member Truesdale used the decision to express his strong support of *Spielberg* policy and to suggest the Board's proper reviewing role under that policy. He likened the Board's role to that of a reviewing court—which should avoid de novo weighing of the evidence. Commending the majority in the case, he said:

> The majority reviews the record evidence, sees no irregularities in the proceedings and no facial errors in the arbitrator's factual findings, and then examines the arbitrator's legal conclusion to see if, on the facts he has found, it is consistent with Board law. Finding that it is, and that the arbitrator actually considered Board Law in ruling on all of the discharges . . . the majority defers to the arbitrator's decision. This approach is more consistent not only with past *Spielberg* decisions, but also with the strong labor policy which favors voluntary arbitration.[295]

He criticized the dissenters for refusing to defer to part of the arbitrator's award, charging that they had conducted an exhaustive de novo review in which they had substituted "their judgment for that of the arbitrator."[296]

In *Atlantic Steel Co.*,[297] as previously noted, the Board deferred to an arbitral award, finding that it was not repugnant to the Act because "the arbitrator thoroughly considered all of the evidence and made factual findings that are clearly supported by the evidence." And significantly, he "considered the factors

---

[292]206 NLRB 447, 452–53, 84 LRRM 1563 (1973) (ALJ's decision).

[293]"[T]here should not be a broad rule that deferral under *Collyer* can be vetoed by the Charging Party or alleged discriminatees who were not parties to the contract." 206 NLRB at 452. "[T]he policy . . . should be that where the individuals object to arbitration because the interest of their bargaining representative is adverse to the individual's interest, deferral to arbitration should not be had." *Id.* at 453.

[294]Kansas City Star Co., 236 NLRB 866, 98 LRRM 1320 (1978).

[295]*Id.* at 869.

[296]*Id.* at 868. The dissenters reviewed the evidence and the award in great detail, agreeing with the arbitrator in part and disagreeing in part, relying on Banyard v. NLRB, 505 F2d 342, 345, 87 LRRM 2001 (CA DC, 1974), to the effect that the *Spielberg* doctrine is appropriately applied "only where the resolution of the contractual issues is congruent with the resolution of the statutory unfair labor practice issues." *See infra* at note 370.

[297]245 NLRB 814, 102 LRRM 1247 (1979).

which the Board considers. . . ."[298] Member Penello, concurring, rejected the suggestion that conformity of the award to Board precedent was an essential predicate to deferral.[299]

Ultimately, in *Inland Steel Co.*[300] the Board ruled authoritatively that "[t]he test of repugnancy under Spielberg is not whether the Board would have reached the same results as an arbitrator, but whether the arbitrator's award is palpably wrong as a matter of law."[301] That standard of scrutiny was emphatically reaffirmed by the Board in *Olin Corp.*,[302] where the Board defined "palpably wrong" as "not susceptible to an interpretation consistent with the Act."[303]

In *Max Factor & Co.*[304] the Board stated that it would not defer to an arbitration award rendered *after* an ALJ's decision has been issued.

The Board has refused to defer to arbitration awards that have failed to apply, have misapplied, or should not have attempted to apply certain key principles embodied in the Act. The following cases illustrate the types of awards that have been found repugnant under various Boards' views of the Act.

The Board has often refused to defer in cases involving the infringement of protected rights of individual employees. The Board thus has refused to defer to arbitration awards: where the discharge of an employee was based partly on the employee's refusal to be questioned without union representation;[305] where the arbitrator had upheld the discharge of an employee based in part on the employee's use of the contract grievance pro-

---

[298]*Id.* at 816.

[299]In his view, his colleagues " 'adopted' [the award] as if the arbitrator were some sort of unofficial administrative law judge. Deferral under such a standard furthers neither the aim nor the efficient administration of the Act but encourages full litigation before the Board of deferrable disputes." *Id.* at 817. *See also* Babcock & Wilcox Co., 249 NLRB 739, 104 LRRM 1199 (1980), *enforced,* 697 F2d 724, 112 LRRM 2713 (CA 6, 1983), and Member Penello's dissent therein; Pincus Bros., Inc.-Maxwell, 237 NLRB 1063, 99 LRRM 1099 (1978) (refusing deferral and declining to rule on record comprised only of arbitration award), 241 NLRB 805, 100 LRRM 1630 (1979), *enforcement denied,* 620 F2d 367, 104 LRRM 2001 (CA 3, 1980) (because of Board's failure to apply its own *Spielberg* standards). In NLRB v. Wilson Freight Co., 604 F2d 712, 102 LRRM 2269 (CA 1, 1979), *denying enforcement to* 234 NLRB 844, 97 LRRM 1412 (1978), *cert. denied,* 445 US 962, 103 LRRM 3082 (1980), the First Circuit held the Board must defer to some of the factual issues decided by the arbitral tribunal. *See infra* at notes 376–377 and 381.

[300]263 NLRB 1091, 111 LRRM 1193 (1982).

[301]*Id.*, 111 LRRM at 1193.

[302]268 NLRB 573, 115 LRRM 1056 (1984).

[303]*Id.* at 574. See *supra* notes 257–270.

[304]239 NLRB 804, 100 LRRM 1023 (1978), *enforced,* 640 F2d 197, 105 LRRM 2765 (CA 9, 1980), *cert. denied,* 451 US 983, 107 LRRM 2384 (1981).

[305]Illinois Bell Tel. Co., 221 NLRB 159, 91 LRRM 1116 (1975). *See* Chapter 6, "Interference With Protected Rights," at notes 454–503.

cedure;[306] where part of the arbitrator's award required the employee to waive future rights under section 7 of the Act;[307] and where the arbitration award upheld discharge or discipline based upon verbal abuse of an employer in the course of an employee's exercise of section 7 rights.[308]

In *Pincus Brothers, Inc.-Maxwell*[309] deferral to an award was refused where the Board found that the discharged employee had been engaged in protected section 7 activities. However, the Third Circuit reversed that decision, holding that the Board had abused its discretion by applying the wrong standard. The court said that since the employee's "conduct was arguably unprotected," the arbitration award upholding his discharge should have prevailed: "Where there are two arguable interpretations of an arbitration award, one permissible and one impermissible, the Board must defer to the decision rendered by the arbitrator."[310]

Awards that impair employee right of access to NLRB process are deemed repugnant to the Act. Thus, the Board refused to defer where the arbitrator's award involved a waiver by the employee of his right to file an unfair labor practice charge,[311] and where an arbitrator upheld a discharge for disloyalty to the employer when the disloyalty consisted of seeking Board assistance in the dispute between the grievant and the employer.[312]

In cases since *Olin*, the Board has deferred to arbitration awards not fully consistent with Board precedent on the unfair

---

[306]Sea-Land Serv., 240 NLRB 1146, 100 LRRM 1406 (1979); Shippers Dispatch, 223 NLRB 439, 92 LRRM 1252 (1976).

[307]Ford Motor Co. (Rouge Complex), 233 NLRB 698, 96 LRRM 1513 (1977).

[308]Union Fork & Hoe Co., 241 NLRB 907, 101 LRRM 1014 (1979); Ad Art, Inc., 238 NLRB 1124, 99 LRRM 1626 (1978), *enforced*, 645 F2d 669, 107 LRRM 3292 (CA 9, 1981); Clara Barton Terrace Convalescent Center, 225 NLRB 1028, 92 LRRM 1621 (1976); Hawaiian Hauling Serv., 219 NLRB 765, 90 LRRM 1011 (1975), *enforced*, 545 F2d 674, 93 LRRM 2952 (CA 9, 1976); Dreis & Krump Mfg. Co., 221 NLRB 309, 90 LRRM 1647 (1975), *enforced*, 544 F2d 320, 93 LRRM 2739 (CA 7, 1976). But the Board upheld an award sustaining a discharge for verbal abuse where the unprotected language was not found to be related to the processing of a grievance. Atlantic Steel Co., *supra* note 297. *See also* AMF Voit, Inc., 223 NLRB 363, 92 LRRM 1335 (1976).

[309]*Supra* note 299.

[310]*Id.*, 620 F2d at 368.

[311]Douglas Aircraft Co., 234 NLRB 578, 97 LRRM 1242 (1978), *enforcement denied*, 609 F2d 352, 102 LRRM 2811 (CA 9, 1979); Super Valu Stores, 228 NLRB 1254, 95 LRRM 1444 (1977); Texaco, Inc., 233 NLRB 375, 96 LRRM 1534 (1977).

[312]Virginia-Carolina Freight Lines, 155 NLRB 447, 60 LRRM 1331 (1965).

labor practice claim.[313] The Board has deferred in cases involving claims of discrimination for the exercise of section 7 rights,[314] refusal-to-bargain charges,[315] an alleged *Weingarten* violation,[316] an alleged hot-cargo clause,[317] and alleged discrimination under section 8(a)(3).[318]

U.S. Postal Service[319] illustrates the Board's willingness to defer to arbitration awards not fully consistent with Board precedent. Following an alleged *Weingarten* violation, the employee was reinstated by an arbitrator, but without backpay. The arbitrator specifically found that the employee had waived her right to a steward's presence at her disciplinary interview even though the employer did not tell her of her option to forego the interview. Although the Act requires either compliance with *Weingarten* or a meaningful waiver, the Board held that the arbitrator's failure

---

[313]*See, e.g.*, Martin Redi-Mix, 274 NLRB 559, 118 LRRM 1425 (1985); United Parcel Serv., 274 NLRB 667, 118 LRRM 1414 (1985), *enforcement denied*, 785 F2d 807, 121 LRRM 3349 (CA 9, 1986); Cone Mills Corp., White Oat Plant, 273 NLRB 1515, 118 LRRM 1197 (1985); U.S. Postal Serv., 275 NLRB 430, 119 LRRM 1153 (1985); Anderson Sand & Gravel Co., Anderson Prestress Div., 277 NLRB 1204, 121 LRRM 1069 (1985); Teamsters Joint Bd. (Anheuser-Busch), 272 NLRB 763, 121 LRRM 1050 (1985) (deferral proper where arbitrator's award not totally consistent with Board precedent concerning lawful seniority provision under §§8(b)(1)(A) and 8(b)(2)); West Penn Power Co., 274 NLRB 1160, 118 LRRM 1529 (1985) (deferral proper where arbitrator levied harsher punishment on union representatives for not attempting to stop work stoppage; decision was not clearly repugnant under Metropolitan Edison Co. v. NLRB, 460 US 693, 112 LRRM 3265 (1983)); Altoona Hosp., 270 NLRB 1179, 116 LRRM 1276 (1984); Louis G. Freeman Co., 270 NLRB 80, 117 LRRM 1047 (1984); *but cf.* Chevron U.S.A., 275 NLRB 949, 119 LRRM 1238 (1985) (deferral proper where arbitrator upheld discipline of employees for engaging in sympathy strike; arbitrator's decision not clearly repugnant under Board's new standard enunciated in Indianapolis Power & Light Co., 273 NLRB 1715, 118 LRRM 1201 (1985)) On review, the court reversed, holding that retroactive invocations of *Indianapolis Power & Light* were unjustified, Oil, Chem. & Atomic Workers Local 1-547 v. NLRB (Chevron, USA) 842 F2d 1141, 127 LRRM 3164 (CA 9, 1988); John Morrell & Co., 270 NLRB 1, 116 LRRM 1177 (1984), *aff'd*, 770 F2d 1400, 120 LRRM 2342 (CA 6, 1985) (deferral improper where union did not waive union steward's §7 rights under Metropolitan Edison Co. v. NLRB, *supra*, and arbitrator held that employer could discipline union steward more severely than other employees).

[314]*See, e.g.*, Altoona Hosp., *supra* note 313 (Board deferred to award that balanced employer's need for confidentiality and employee's need to investigate her grievances); Anderson Sand & Gravel Co., Anderson Prestress Div., *supra* note 313 (Board deferred to award concerning discharge of wildcat strikers); Texaco, 279 NLRB 1259, 122 LRRM 1129 (1986) (Board deferred to award concerning suspension and discharge of employees for alleged strike misconduct).

[315]*See, e.g.*, Badger Meter, 272 NLRB 824, 117 LRRM 1358 (1984) (Board deferred to arbitral decision that subcontracting was permitted under contract).

[316]NLRB v. J. Weingarten, Inc., 420 US 251, 88 LRRM 2689 (1975); Altoona Hosp., *supra* note 313.

[317]Liquid Carbonic Corp., 277 NLRB 851, 121 LRRM 1116 (1985).

[318]U.S. Postal Serv., 288 NLRB 500, 128 LRRM 1078 (1988).

[319]*Supra* note 313.

to apply a technical requirement, while inconsistent with Board precedent, was not "repugnant to the policies of the Act."[320]

Despite the *Olin* expansion of deferral practice, the Board has declined in numerous cases to defer to arbitration awards found to be clearly repugnant to the policies of the Act.[321]

IV. OTHER FACTORS AFFECTING THE BOARD'S POSTARBITRAL DEFERRAL POLICY

There are a number of specific types of cases involving arbitral awards and other final settlements between parties in which the Board may choose not to apply its *Spielberg* deferral policy.

A. Representation Cases

For many years the "leading case" dealing with the Board's deference to arbitral awards in representation cases was *Raley's, Inc.*[322] In *Raley's* the issue before the arbitrator was whether certain employees were covered by the contract between the parties to the arbitration proceeding. The arbitrator held that they were. Thereafter, a rival union filed a petition with the Board seeking representation of the employees in question. At the Board hearing, the union which had prevailed in arbitration intervened, contending that its contract with the employer covered the employees in question, that the petition was therefore not timely filed with respect to the contract, and that the contract

---

[320] *Id.*

[321] Manitowoc Eng'g Co., 291 NLRB 915, 130 LRRM 1072, 1074 (1988) (refusal to defer to award involving unlawful seniority provisions "because it is not susceptible to an interpretation consistent with the Act"); U.S. Postal Serv., 290 NLRB 120, 129 LRRM 1043 (1988) (pattern of hostile conduct fundamentally at odds with the Act and policy behind deferral—arbitration procedure had been ineffective); MIS, 289 NLRB 491, 128 LRRM 1273 (1988) (arbitrator's decision palpably wrong where it fails to take into consideration change in NLRB law); Sherwood Diversified Servs., Federated Answering Serv. Div., 288 NLRB 341, 128 LRRM 1162 (1988); Earl C. Smith, Inc., 278 NLRB 664, 121 LRRM 1255 (1986) (award which directed employer merely to comply with subsequent contract as remedy for previous contract violation palpably wrong); Garland Coal & Mining Co., 276 NLRB 963, 120 LRRM 1159 (1985) (no deferral to arbitration award upholding discipline of union official for refusal to follow employer's order when employee was acting in his capacity as union official); John Morrell & Co., *supra* note 313 (refusal to defer to arbitration award upholding discipline of union official for failure to end strike when no-strike clause did not give union explicit duty of ending unauthorized work stoppages).

[322] 143 NLRB 256, 53 LRRM 1347 (1963).

should act as a bar.[323] Agreeing with the intervenor, the Board dismissed the petition, holding that:

> The same considerations which moved the Board to honor arbitration awards in unfair labor practice cases are equally persuasive to a similar acceptance of the arbitral process in a representation proceeding such as the instant one. Thus, where, as here, a question of contract interpretation is in issue . . . and an award has already been rendered which meets Board requirements applicable to arbitration awards, we think that it would further the underlying objectives of the Act to promote industrial peace and stability to give effect thereto."[324]

Following the approach which it had used in *International Harvester Co.*,[325] the Board disposed of the argument that the petitioner had not been represented before the arbitrator: "[w]hile the petitioner was not a party to the arbitration . . . its position was vigorously defended by the Employer. . . ."[326]

The Supreme Court's decision the following year in *Carey v. Westinghouse Electric Corp.*,[327] reinforced the Board's approach in *Raley's*. There the Court held a dispute to be arbitrable whether viewed as a representation or as a work-assignment dispute, notwithstanding that the Board also had jurisdiction over the matter.[328] The Court's order bound only the employer and one of the two unions involved in the dispute. Nevertheless, since arbitration might have resolved the dispute, the Court required the parties to abide by the contractual agreement to arbitrate.

The further history of *Carey v. Westinghouse* is enlightening. When the case was submitted to arbitration the arbitrator partially agreed with the grieving union, ordering the company to recognize the Electrical Workers (IUE) as the collective bargaining representative of certain specified employees.[329] His deci-

---

[323]*See generally* Chapter 10, "Representation Proceedings and Elections," at notes 119–201.

[324]143 NLRB at 258–59.

[325]138 NLRB 923, 51 LRRM 1155 (1962), *enforced sub nom.* Ramsey v. NLRB, 327 F2d 784, 55 LRRM 2441 (CA 7), *cert. denied*, 377 US 1003, 56 LRRM 2544 (1964).

[326]143 NLRB at 260 n.17. *But see* Hotel Employers Ass'n, 159 NLRB 143, 148 n.7, 62 LRRM 1215 (1966); Hamilton-Scheu & Walsh Shoe Co., 80 NLRB 1496, 23 LRRM 1263 (1948).

[327]375 US 261, 55 LRRM 2042 (1964).

[328]*See* Raley's, Inc., *supra* note 322, at 259 n.13. For the view that the Board's jurisdiction in this field should be exclusive, see Feinberg, *The Arbitrator's Responsibility Under the Taft Hartley Act*, 18 ARB. J. 77, 86 (1963); Cummings, *NLRB Jurisdiction and Labor Arbitration: "Uniformity" v. "Industrial Peace,"* 12 LAB. L.J. 425, 433 (1961).

[329]Westinghouse Elec. Corp., 45 LA 161 (1965).

sion, in effect, divided the employees between two collective bargaining units based on salary criteria. But when the Board considered the case, it retreated perceptibly from *Raley's*, refusing to defer to the arbitrator's award.[330] It stated:

> Here . . . the ultimate issue of representation could not be decided by the Arbitrator on the basis of his interpreting the contract under which he was authorized to act, but could only be resolved by utilization of Board criteria for making unit determinations. In such cases, the Arbitrator's award must clearly reflect the use of and be consonant with Board standards. In this case apparently not all the evidence concerning all these standards was available to the arbitrator for his consideration and appraisal, and his award reflects this deficiency.[331]

Almost immediately, the Board began placing limits on *Raley's*. Initially these limits were considered under the *Spielberg* criterion of whether the arbitral award was in keeping with and therefore not repugnant to the Act.[332] But by 1974, in *Hershey Foods Corp.*,[333] the Board explicitly suggested that it would not defer to an arbitral award in a representation matter. In response to the argument that the arbitration award had made a final and binding determination of the issue, the Board stated: "The short answer to that contention is that to do so would be contrary to controlling Board precedent."[334] Finding that prevailing Board law did not warrant deferral, it held that the respondent union's claim, which alleged an accretion to the unit, must be examined on its merits. *Raley's* was distinguished as standing for the proposition that the Board would defer only when the question before both it and the arbitral tribunal was solely one of contract interpretation.

The Board's broad expression in *Raley's, Inc.*[335] regarding accommodation to arbitral awards involving representation issues has thus been slowly abandoned, despite meager explicit reference to *Raley's*. Thus, by 1975, in *Commonwealth Gas Co.*,[336] the Board declared without citation: "[I]t is well established that

---

[330]Westinghouse Elec. Corp., 162 NLRB 768, 64 LRRM 1082 (1967).
[331]*Id.* at 771.
[332]Westinghouse Elec. Corp., *supra* note 330. The initial limitations appear in Warm Springs Lumber Co., 181 NLRB 600, 73 LRRM 1429 (1970); Hotel Employers Ass'n, *supra* note 326.
[333]208 NLRB 452, 85 LRRM 1312 (1974), *enforced*, 506 F2d 1052, 90 LRRM 2890 (CA 3, 1974).
[334]*Id.* at 457.
[335]*Supra* note 322.
[336]218 NLRB 857, 858, 89 LRRM 1613 (1975).

the Board will not defer to arbitration or an arbitration award concerning representation issues such as the ones involved herein as opposed to questions of contract interpretation." Circuit Judge Friendly cogently commented: "We do not think it profitable to engage in lengthy discussion of decisions, notably *Raley's*. . . . [T]he Board seems to have become rather disenchanted with *Raley's*."[337]

In representation cases, regardless of *Collyer* and *Dubo*, the Board will normally proceed and not wait for an arbitrator to render an award. As to existing awards, as noted, its policy is rarely to defer.[338]

B. Certain Unfair Labor Practices: Sections 8(a)(2) and 8(a)(4)

The Board has declined to defer to arbitration awards involving section 8(a)(2) (unlawful assistance to a union) and section 8(a)(4) (discrimination for filing NLRB charges or giving testimony). In *Servair, Inc.*[339] the employer admitted that it had violated section 8(a)(2) by assisting the Operating Engineers in an election which the Teamsters lost. Shortly after the election a Teamster supporter was discharged, as were 19 employees who stopped work in protest over his discharge. An arbitrator found most of the discharges to be for cause. The ALJ would not defer to the award because the arbitrator had considered the discharges solely with reference to section 8(a)(3) of the Act, without taking into account the section 8(a)(2) unlawful assistance charges. He thus found violations of sections 8(a)(1), (2), and (3)

---

[337]Long Island College Hosp. v. NLRB, 566 F2d 833, 845 n.5, 96 LRRM 3119 (CA 2, 1977).

[338]*See* Libby, McNeill & Libby, 159 NLRB 677, 62 LRRM 1276 (1966) (suit to compel arbitration stayed pending Board decision); Humble Oil & Ref. Co., 153 NLRB 1361, 1363, 59 LRRM 1632 (1965) ("[Union's] contractual right to arbitrate disputes . . . does not preclude the Board from determining a question concerning the appropriateness of unit"); Standard Register Co., 146 NLRB 1042, 56 LRRM 1003 (1964); Savage Arms Corp., 144 NLRB 1323, 1324, 54 LRRM 1253 (1963). The Second Circuit subsequently reversed a district court order compelling arbitration of the same issues involved in the *Humble* Board case, *supra*, on the ground that the Board had effectively decided all of the issues. McGuire v. Humble Oil & Ref. Co., 355 F2d 352, 61 LRRM 2410 (CA 2), *cert. denied*, 384 US 988, 62 LRRM 2339 (1966). *But see* A. Seltzer & Co. v. Livingston, 253 F Supp 509, 61 LRRM 2581 (SD NY, 1966) (arbitration with one union not stayed, despite company's contract with another union for same unit and pendency of representation petition); *cf.* Electrical Workers (IBEW) Local 51 v. Illinois Power Co., 357 F2d 916, 61 LRRM 2613 (CA 7), *cert. denied*, 387 US 850, 63 LRRM 2235 (1966).

[339]236 NLRB 1278, 99 LRRM 1259 (1978), *enforced in part*, 607 F2d 258, 102 LRRM 2705 (CA 9, 1979). *See infra* at notes 378–379 for subsequent history of the case.

and ordered reinstatement of the strikers. The Board affirmed, declaring that arbitration was not appropriate in this case because the discharges were "so closely intertwined with, and indeed, a part of, the 8(a)(2) allegations, which types of allegations never have been and cannot be delegated to an arbitrator . . . .[340] The Ninth Circuit, however, showed little patience with the Board's putting the case in a special category because of the section 8(a)(2) violations; it therefore denied enforcement with respect to reinstatement of the strikers because of the Board's failure to follow its own *Spielberg* standards.[341] The court viewed the issue as a factual one—whether the motive for the discharge was unlawful—an issue that the arbitrator had resolved in favor of the employer. The court noted that if the motive had been unlawful, there would be little difference in characterizing the action as a violation of section 8(a)(2) as well as of section 8(a)(3).

In a case involving a charge of section 8(a)(4) violation, *Filmation Associates,*[342] the Board stated:

> The prohibition expressed in Section 8(a)(4) against discharging or otherwise discriminating against an employee because he has filed charges or given testimony under the Act is a fundamental guarantee to employees that they may invoke or participate in the investigative procedures of this Board without fear of reprisal and is clearly required in order to safeguard the integrity of the Board's processes. In our view the duty to preserve the Board's processes from abuse is a function of this Board and may not be delegated to the parties or to an Arbitrator. Accordingly, as we conclude that issues involving Section 8(a)(4) of the Act are solely within the Board's province to decide we will not apply the *Spielberg* doctrine to such issues.[343]

C. Work-Assignment Disputes—Deferral by Statute

Section 10(k) is the only section of the Act specifically authorizing the Board to stay its hand if the parties can demonstrate that they have an agreed-upon means of settling their dispute. In relevant part, this section provides:

---

[340] 102 LRRM at 2707.

[341] *See also infra* at notes 370–408.

[342] 227 NLRB 1721, 94 LRRM 1470 (1977).

[343] *Id.* at 1721. *Accord* Art Steel of Cal., 256 NLRB 816, 107 LRRM 1325 (1981). *See* NLRB v. Wilson Freight Co., 604 F2d 712, 102 LRRM 2269 (CA 1, 1979), *cert. denied,* 445 US 962, 103 LRRM 3082 (1980), where the court noted but did not comment on *Filmation*; it did not deny enforcement because of the Board's failure to defer to the arbitral award as such, but declared that the Board was bound to defer to some of the factual issues decided in arbitration. *See infra* at notes 376–377.

> Whenever it is charged that any person has engaged in an unfair labor practice within the meaning of paragraphs (4)(D) of Section 8(b), the Board is empowered and directed to hear and determine the dispute out of which such unfair labor practice shall have arisen, unless . . . the parties to such dispute submit to the Board satisfactory evidence that they have . . . agreed upon methods for the voluntary adjustment of the dispute.

This is obviously a different kind of deferral from that involved in *Spielberg* and *Collyer.* If an agreed-upon method for voluntary adjustment of the dispute exists, the Board lacks jurisdiction to consider the dispute—whether before or after the voluntary adjustment occurs. This subject is covered elsewhere in detail.[344] In quashing a notice of hearing, the Board stated in *Mine Workers Local 1269 (Ritchey Trucking)*:[345]

> The *Spielberg* deferral criteria are inapplicable to our assessment of a jurisdictional dispute settlement mechanism because Section 10(k) provides that the existence of an agreed-upon method deprives the Board of jurisdiction to determine the dispute. This is in direct contrast to the *Spielberg* situation where the Board, in its discretion, declines to exercise its jurisdiction and defers to an arbitration decision. The issue before us, therefore, is whether or not all parties to the dispute have agreed to be bound to a method for settlement of the dispute.[346]

The Board's requirement that all of the parties to the dispute must be bound by the agreed-upon method for adjustment has been approved by the Supreme Court.[347] Where all parties are not so bound and an arbitral decision has been rendered, the question then becomes not one of deferral, but to what degree the Board will give weight to the arbitral award in arriving at its own decision.[348]

D. Settlement or Other Disposition Under a Grievance Procedure Short of an Arbitral Award

Many grievances are resolved by the parties short of arbitration. Will the Board defer to the parties' settlement or other

---

[344] *See generally* Chapter 25, "Jurisdictional Disputes and 'Featherbedding.'"

[345] 241 NLRB 231, 100 LRRM 1496 (1979).

[346] *Id.* at 232.

[347] NLRB v. Plasterers & Cement Masons Local 79, 404 US 116, 78 LRRM 2897 (1971). *See* Chapter 25, "Jurisdictional Disputes and 'Featherbedding,'" at note 71.

[348] Newspaper & Mail Deliverers of N.Y. & Vicinity v. News Syndicate Co., 141 NLRB 578, 52 LRRM 1339 (1963); *see also* McLeod v. Newspaper & Mail Deliverers of N.Y. & Vicinity, 209 F2d 434, 51 LRRM 2292 (SD NY, 1962). *See* Chapter 25, "Jurisdictional Disputes and 'Featherbedding'" at notes 93–133.

nonimposed disposition of the grievance? While the Board has not explicitly stated that it will apply *Spielberg* standards to grievance settlements, the rationale for doing so is, simply, that the opposite policy would require that every grievance involving a potential unfair labor practice charge would have to be taken to arbitration whenever a party desired that the Board defer. This would be a result contrary to the underlying purposes of *Collyer* and *Spielberg*: the encouragement of private dispute resolution and the reduction of litigation.[349]

1. Voluntary Grievance Settlements. In *Central Cartage Co.*,[350] a 1973 case, the grievant-employee had filed a charge with the Board and in due course the ALJ issued a decision, under *Collyer*, deferring consideration to the arbitral process. The matter was then privately settled. Subsequently, the General Counsel requested that the Board consider the original charge. The Board declined, asserting not only that all of the issues involved had been considered and resolved, but also that none of the parties directly involved had challenged the terms of the settlement. And in *Coca-Cola Bottling Co. of Los Angeles*[351] the Board held that an employer had not violated section 8(a)(1) by entering into a private settlement in which the employee had agreed to withdraw his claim with the Board in exchange for a reduction of his discipline. The Board rejected the argument that deferral was inappropriate because it deprived the employee of his right to use the Board's processes. It found instead that the agreement was the product of negotiations in which both sides had compromised.

In *Super Value Xenia*,[352] however, the Board refused deferral to the result reached in Step 4 of a bipartite grievance procedure, because the employee-grievants had not been present at the meeting, no testimony had been taken, and no transcript was available.

In spite of the *Central Cartage* and *Coca-Cola* cases, the Board on several occasions has indicated that it will not defer to private settlements. For example, in *Laredo Packing Co.*[353] the Board

---

[349]See NLRB Gen. Counsel Memo., No. 81-39 (July 17, 1981), which implicitly recognizes this point. The memo deals generally with *Dubo* deferral where the aggrieved individual has chosen not to use the contract grievance procedure but the union is pursuing the issue on its own through that procedure. Dubo Mfg. Corp., 142 NLRB 431, 53 LRRM 1070 (1963).

[350]206 NLRB 337, 84 LRRM 1273 (1973).

[351]243 NLRB 501, 101 LRRM 1456 (1979).

[352]228 NLRB 1254, 95 LRRM 1444 (1977). There were other reasons for refusing to defer.

[353]254 NLRB 1, 106 LRRM 1350 (1981).

declined to defer to a grievance settlement that resulted in withdrawal of a reprimand, for the stated reason that the grievance was settled short of arbitration. In *Owens-Corning Fiberglas Co.*[354] a union steward was singled out by the employer from a group of employees who had been drinking on duty and was discharged because the employer expected the union steward to meet a higher standard of conduct. An informal settlement was reached during the grievance procedure, reducing the penalty to an 11-day suspension without pay. The Board declined to defer on the grounds that the settlement agreement had been "entered into by the parties without the Board's participation or approval"[355] and also because the settlement clearly did not consider the section 8(a)(3) aspect of the case. The Board has also indicated that it will not apply *Spielberg* to awards reached short of arbitration because in such cases there is no award by an impartial tribunal.[356]

In *Ford Motor Co. (Rouge Complex)*[357] the charging parties had been disciplined for distributing literature at the plant; their grievances were adjusted at an early stage of the grievance procedure and were not submitted to arbitration. In rejecting the employer's request for deferral under *Spielberg* to this final and binding resolution through the contractual grievance machinery, the Board cited its decision in *Whirlpool*[358] and *Pontiac Motor Division*,[359] indicating that it would not defer to grievance settlements. It also noted that, in any event, the settlement was repugnant to the Act.[360]

In *Roadway Express*,[361] the Board refused to defer to the voluntary settlement of the discharge of an employee for engaging in union activities. The Board noted that the legality of the dis-

---

[354]236 NLRB 479, 98 LRRM 1234 (1978).

[355]*Id.* at 479.

[356]*See* U.S. Postal Serv., 237 NLRB 117, 99 LRRM 1431 (1978) (ALJ stated that *Spielberg* was inapplicable because grievance was settled short of arbitration); General Motors, Pontiac Motors Div., 132 NLRB 413, 48 LRRM 1368 (1961) (noting absence of arbitral award to review). *See also* Whirlpool Corp., 216 NLRB 183, 88 LRRM 1329 (1975).

[357]233 NLRB 698, 96 LRRM 1513 (1977).

[358]Whirlpool Corp., *supra* note 356.

[359]General Motors, Pontiac Motors Div., *supra* note 356. The grievance settlement required the waiver by the charging parties of their rights to distribute literature in the future.

[360]*See generally supra* at notes 294–321.

[361]246 NLRB 174, 102 LRRM 1391 (1979), *supplemented in* 250 NLRB 393, 104 LRRM 1349 (1980), *enforcement denied,* 647 F2d 415, 107 LRRM 2155 (CA 4, 1981). *See also* Alpha Beta Co., 273 NLRB 1546, 118 LRRM 1202 (1985), *aff'd sub nom.* Mahon v. NLRB, 808 F2d 1342, 124 LRRM 2762 (CA 9, 1987) (deferral to bipartite settlement where employees had agreed).

charge had not been discussed, and that the employee was dissatisfied with the settlement, which included reinstatement but no backpay. The Board split, the plurality asserting that although the Board has discretion to defer to a private settlement that has been voluntarily arrived at by the parties, covers all pertinent issues, and effectuates the policies of the Act, deferral was inappropriate in this instance. The Fourth Circuit reversed. That court found insufficient evidence to support the Board's findings—the validity of the discharge had been considered and the employee-grievant had knowingly agreed to the settlement.

2. Grievances Dropped by the Union. In *Electric Motors & Specialties*,[362] grievances had been processed through several steps of the grievance procedure but not to arbitration. The employer argued that since its contract provided that where arbitration was not requested a grievance would be deemed abandoned, the Board's *Spielberg* rule should be applicable just as if the matter had been fully arbitrated. The Board rejected this argument.[363] *Whirlpool Corp.*[364] involved a similar situation. A terminated employee, after having his grievance processed by the union, filed an unfair labor practice charge. The regional director had initially deferred to the grievance procedure under *Collyer*; but later, after the employee complained that the union had failed to take his case to arbitration, a complaint was issued. Deferral was refused because "[i]t is undisputed that the full range of the mechanism for the determination of the dispute has not been utilized and there is no award that may be examined for conformity with *Spielberg* requirements.[365]

E. Failure to Abide by an Arbitral Award

Failure of a respondent to comply with an arbitration award may be a factor in the Board's determination whether to defer or whether to issue a formal Board order.

In *Malrite of Wisconsin*,[366] the collective bargaining contract provided that the employer was to assign only one person to a

---

[362] 149 NLRB 131, 57 LRRM 1258 (1964).

[363] *See also* General Motors, Pontiac Motors Div., *supra* note 356; Dant & Russell, 92 NLRB 307, 27 LRRM 1088 (1950), *set aside on other grounds*, 195 F2d 299, 29 LRRM 2585 (CA 9, 1952), *rev'd*, 344 US 375, 31 LRRM 2303 (1953), *enforced*, 207 F2d 165, 32 LRRM 2740 (CA 9, 1953) (trial examiner's decision).

[364] *Supra* note 356.

[365] *Id.* at 186 (from ALJ decision). *See also* NLRB v. Maxwell dba Pioneer Concrete Co., 637 F2d 698, 106 LRRM 2387 (CA 9, 1981), *enforcing* 241 NLRB 264, 101 LRRM 1012 (1979).

[366] 198 NLRB 241, 80 LRRM 1593 (1972), *enforced sub nom.* Electrical Workers (IBEW) Local 1715 v. NLRB, 494 F2d 1136, 85 LRRM 2823 (CA DC, 1974).

given classification. Ignoring the union and soliciting written consents from individual employees, the employer nevertheless assigned additional employees to the classification. An arbitrator then held that the action violated the agreement, and he directed the employer to cease assigning more than one person to the classification. When the employer refused to comply, the union filed refusal-to-bargain charges with the NLRB rather than seeking court enforcement of the arbitration award. The Board, deferring to the award under *Spielberg* principles, dismissed the complaint. The majority opinion noted that "direct court enforcement of arbitrator's awards can provide more prompt and effective action" than can the various steps of the Board's unfair labor practice procedures.[367] Two years later, however, in *Electronic Reproduction Service Corp.*[368] the Board distinguished *Malrite*. The employer refused to accept an interest arbitration award establishing various terms of a new agreement. The Board held that there should be no deferral with respect to the employer's alleged violation of section 8(a)(5). The Board distinguished this situation, which involved arbitration of new terms of the contract, from the situation in *Malrite*, which involved application of a negotiated term of the contract:

> In these circumstances, in which respondents in effect have repudiated the Collective Bargaining process, judicial enforcement of the arbitrator's Award will not serve to remedy the unfair labor practices and the desirability of encouraging resort to arbitration must yield to the Board's duty to protect the bargaining process. This can be done . . . only by an effective Board Order. . . ."[369]

V. Response of the Reviewing Court to the Board's Deferral Standards

As reflected throughout this chapter, the appellate courts have approved the Board's general approach on deferring to arbitration awards, both as to the *Collyer* prearbitral doctrine and the *Spielberg* standards. In specific cases, however, the courts

---

[367]*Id.*, 80 LRRM at 1594.

[368]213 NLRB 758, 87 LRRM 1211 (1974), on a point presumably not affected by the Board's later overruling of the more controversial aspect of the case in Suburban Motor Freight, 247 NLRB 146, 103 LRRM 1113 (1980). *But see* Electrical Workers (IBEW) Local 113 (Collier Elec. Co.), 296 NLRB No. 144, 132 LRRM 1297, 1301 (1989) ("interest arbitration [is] a permissive subject of bargaining and thus it is not an unfair labor practice to repudiate such a provision"). *See* Chapter 16, "Subjects of Bargaining," at notes 500–505.

[369]213 NLRB at 759.

have frequently disagreed with the Board in the implementation of both *Collyer* and *Spielberg*.

In their early decisions following *Collyer*, several reviewing courts pressed the Board toward a narrow deferral policy. In 1974 the Court of Appeals for the District of Columbia Circuit, in *Banyard v. NLRB*,[370] announced two additions to the *Spielberg* requirements for deferral. The court reversed the Board's decision to defer because of the failure of the arbitral tribunals to consider section 8(a)(1) issues, adding that *Spielberg* applies only if the arbitral tribunal "clearly decided the issue on which it is later urged that the Board should give deference, and . . . the arbitral tribunal decided an issue within its competence."[371]

The Ninth Circuit, in *Stepenson (Fikse Brothers) v. NLRB*,[372] approved similar requirements. These cautious approvals of limited deferral were reflected in caution at the Board, as evidenced by the overruling of *Electronic Reproduction Service Corp.*[373] in *Suburban Motor Freight*.[374] The restoration, in *Olin Corp.*,[375]of a broader deferral practice at the Board has presented another round of similar questions to the courts, as is more fully considered below.

The Board was also criticized in the courts for too cautious a deferral policy. In *NLRB v. Wilson Freight Co.*[376] the First Circuit denied enforcement in a case where the Board had refused to defer to an award of a labor-management joint board which had sustained the discharge of a union steward. The court charged that "the Board exceeded its authority to the extent it redecided in [the grievant's] favor factual matters determined by the arbitrators. . . ."[377]

Servair, Inc. v. NLRB,[378] previously noted, was another case where the Ninth Circuit refused to enforce parts of a Board

---

[370]Banyard v. NLRB, 505 F2d 342, 87 LRRM 2001 (CA DC, 1974), *remanding* 202 NLRB 710, 82 LRRM 1652 (1973) *and* 203 NLRB 157, 83 LRRM 1149 (1973), *supplemented by* 216 NLRB 925, 88 LRRM 1649 (1975).

[371]*Id.* at 343.

[372]550 F2d 535, 94 LRRM 3224 (CA 9, 1977), *remanding* 220 NLRB 1301, 90 LRRM 1354 (1975).

[373]*Supra* note 368.

[374]*Supra* note 368.

[375]268 NLRB 573, 115 LRRM 1056 (1984).

[376]604 F2d 712, 102 LRRM 2269 (CA 1, 1979), *cert. denied*, 445 US 962, 103 LRRM 3082 (1980).

[377]*Id.* at 722.

[378]236 NLRB 1278, 99 LRRM 1259 (1978), *enforced in part and remanded*, 607 F2d 258, 102 LRRM 2705 (CA 9, 1979), *opinion withdrawn and case remanded*, 624 F2d 92, 105 LRRM 2649 (CA 9, 1980). *See supra* at notes 339–341.

order which had found that 19 employees, who had walked off the job, were discharged in violation of section 8(a)(2). The Board acknowledged that the arbitrator had before him the issue of the legality of the discharge under section 8(a)(3). In the court's view: "The Board simply chose to proceed on the basis of 8(a)(2) in addition to 8(a)(3). That choice does not justify ignoring the arbitration award,[379] which had upheld the discharges. The court subsequently withdrew its opinion and simply instructed the Board to reconsider its decision under the *Spielberg* standards.

Again, in *Douglas Aircraft Co. v. NLRB*,[380] the Ninth Circuit criticized the Board for failing to defer to an arbitral award which had denied a grievant backpay on each of two grounds. One ground was his abusive and uncivil conduct, the other his rejection of a grievance settlement conditioned on his withdrawing his NLRB charge. The court agreed that the second reason for denying backpay was violative of the Act. Nevertheless, because the arbitrator, in clarifying his award, had stated there was no evidence that the discharge was for protected activities and that abusive conduct was independently sufficient to deny backpay, the court concluded that the Board should have deferred.

Less than a year later, the Third Circuit, in *NLRB v. Pincus Brothers, Inc.,-Maxwell*,[381] cited *Douglas Aircraft* with approval in refusing to enforce an order in which the Board had failed to defer to an arbitral award.

In *Hospital & Health Care Employees v. NLRB*,[382] the Court of Appeals for the District of Columbia Circuit held that the Board is required to give an adequate explanation of its refusal to defer to an arbitral award. The court recognized that the Board's construction of the contract, even when different from that of the arbitrator, is entitled to precedence unless arbitrary or capricious. "Nonetheless," said the court, "it is important that disputants continue to be attracted to arbitration for resolution of differences that are susceptible to arbitration."[383] The dis-

---

[379] 102 LRRM at 2709.

[380] 609 F2d 352, 102 LRRM 2811 (CA 9, 1979), *denying enforcement to* 238 NLRB 668, 99 LRRM 1274 (1978).

[381] 620 F2d 367, 104 LRRM 2001 (CA 3, 1980), *cert. denied*, 451 US 983, 107 LRRM 2384 (1981).

[382] 613 F2d 1102, 103 LRRM 2001 (CA DC, 1979).

[383] *Id.* at 1109.

pute concerned contracting out of work, about which the court said that

> before the Board reached a result contrary to the Arbitrator, it should have spoken directly and fully to the issue [to be] decided. . . .
>
> . . .
>
> . . . [W]hatever the final result, the Board should explicitly discuss the implications of the collective bargaining agreement as interpreted by the arbitrator, both because adequate review of the Board's decision cannot be completed without a full explanation of its reasoning and because the respect due the arbitral process requires as much.[384]

After *Suburban Motor Freight*[385] several courts commented favorably on the Board's policy in *Suburban* or enforced orders where the Board denied deference to arbitral awards.[386]

In *St. Luke's Memorial Hospital v. NLRB*[387] the Seventh Circuit agreed with the Board's refusal to defer to an arbitral award where the arbitrator had been selected by a dubious process and where the award did not reflect an appreciation of Board policy or clearly adjudicate the unfair labor practice issues.

In *NLRB v. Max Factor & Co.*[388] the Sixth Circuit enforced an order where the Board had declined to defer to an arbitration award, asserting that the Board's duty to prevent unfair labor practices outweighs the policy of encouraging arbitration.

In three decisions, the Third Circuit enforced Board orders in cases in which deferral had been refused: *NLRB v. General Warehouse Corp.*,[389] *Hammermill Paper Co. v. NLRB*,[390] and *Herman Brothers v. NLRB*.[391]

The Ninth Circuit, in upholding the Board's refusal to defer to an arbitration award in *Ad Art, Inc.*,[392] presented its conception of the abuse-of-discretion test applicable to the Board in deferral cases, saying: "The Board only abuses its wide discre-

---

[384]*Id.*

[385]*Supra* note 368.

[386]*But see* Fournelle v. NLRB, 670 F2d 331, 109 LRRM 2441 (CA DC, 1982).

[387]623 F2d 1173, 104 LRRM 2788 (CA 7, 1980), *enforcing* 240 NLRB 1180, 100 LRRM 1393 (1979).

[388]640 F2d 197, 105 LRRM 2765 (CA 9, 1980), *enforcing* 239 NLRB 804, 100 LRRM 1023 (1978), *cert. denied*, 451 US 983, 107 LRRM 2384 (1981).

[389]643 F2d 965, 106 LRRM 2729 (CA 3, 1981), *enforcing* 247 NLRB 1073, 103 LRRM 1294 (1980).

[390]658 F2d 155, 108 LRRM 2001 (CA 3, 1981), *enforcing* 252 NLRB 1236, 105 LRRM 1409 (1980), *cert. denied*, 460 US 1080, 112 LRRM 3448 (1983).

[391]658 F2d 201, 108 LRRM 2327 (CA 3, 1981), *enforcing* 252 NLRB 848, 105 LRRM 1374 (1980).

[392]238 NLRB 1124, 99 LRRM 1626 (1978), *enforced*, 645 F2d 669, 107 LRRM 3292 (CA 9, 1981).

tion if it fails to follow its own deferral standards or if the standards themselves are invalid."[393]

However, rejecting the Board's refusal to defer in *Fournelle v. NLRB*,[394] the Court of Appeals for the District of Columbia Circuit ruled that the Board "was not free . . . to substitute its own interpretation of the contract" for a permanent umpire's authoritative construction of a no-strike clause to impose a higher duty on union officials to obey its requirements.[395] In *Distillery Workers Local 2 (Charmer Industries) v. NLRB*,[396] the Second Circuit held that the Board had abused its discretion in declining to defer to an arbitrator's award that had found a unilateral change in sales procedure for liquor salesmen not to be a change in work rules under the collective agreement—a determination that the court said was necessarily dispositive of the section 8(a)(5) statutory issue. The Ninth Circuit, in refusing enforcement in *Albertson's, Inc. v. NLRB*,[397] charged that the Board had failed to consider evidence that the grievant would have been fired for incompetence despite any union activity on her part.

The Board majority in *Olin Corp.*[398] read the courts of appeals' decisions approving *Suburban Motor Freight* as holding only that "*Suburban* fell within the Board's 'wide discretion'; the decisions do not find that the *Suburban* standards are the only ones consistent with the statute."[399]

However, some conflict persists among the circuits. While approval has been expressed by the Fifth,[400] Sixth,[401] Ninth,[402]

---

[393]*Id.*, 645 F2d at 675.

[394]*Supra* note 386. *See also* Szewczuga v. NLRB, 686 F2d 962, 110 LRRM 3289 (CA DC, 1982), *cert. denied*, 460 US 1098, 113 LRRM 2112 (1983) (failure to raise *Spielberg* deferral issue before the Board precludes its assertion before reviewing court); Metropolitan Edison Co. v. NLRB, 663 F2d 478, 108 LRRM 3020 (CA 3, 1981), *aff'd on other grounds*, 460 US 693, 112 LRRM 3265 (1983) (refusing to rule on application of *Spielberg* standards because arbitration award had not been issued on facts of case).

[395]670 F2d at 345.

[396]664 F2d 318, 107 LRRM 3137 (CA 2, 1981), *denying enforcement to* 250 NLRB 293, 104 LRRM 1368 (1980), *cert. denied*, 456 US 973, 110 LRRM 2320 (1982).

[397]661 F2d 939, 108 LRRM 2714 (CA 9, 1981), *rev'g and remanding* 252 NLRB 529, 105 LRRM 1443 (1980).

[398]268 NLRB 573, 115 LRRM 1056 (1984).

[399]*Id.* at 575.

[400]NLRB v. Ryder/P.I.E. Nationwide, 810 F2d 502, 506, 124 LRRM 3024, 3027 (CA 5, 1987).

[401]Wheeling-Pittsburgh Steel Corp., 821 F2d 342, 125 LRRM 2824 (CA 6, 1987); Lewis v. NLRB, 779 F2d 12, 120 LRRM 3559 (CA 6, 1985).

[402]Garcia v. NLRB, 785 F2d 807, 809–10, 121 LRRM 3349, 3351–52 (CA 9, 1986); *but see* Oil, Chem. & Atomic Workers Local 1-547 v. NLRB (Chevron, USA), 842 F2d 1141,

Tenth,[403] and District of Columbia[404] circuits for the Board's new deferral standards, the Eleventh Circuit[405] has criticized them as inadequate to protect employee statutory rights. The Ninth Circuit decisions,[406] while accepting the deferral standard, reversed the Board's decision in each case upon other grounds. The Second Circuit has twice specifically reserved judgment on the question of whether the *Olin* standards sufficiently protect employee rights under the Act.[407]

VI. *COLLYER* AND *SPIELBERG* EVALUATED

The full impact of the *Collyer, Spielberg,* and *Dubo* doctrines is difficult to perceive because so many of the basic decisions applying those doctrines are made by the General Counsel through regional offices—decisions as to whether to defer to an arbitral award, to issue a complaint, to pursue or encourage settlement, or to recommend withdrawal or dismissal of a charge. These relatively informal and unpublished decisions, which give meaning to the doctrines, defy quantification. Only a small portion of the cases in which deferral takes place result in reported decisions. The regional offices will not issue a complaint on a charge otherwise meritorious if the subject matter of the dispute has resulted in an arbitral award which the regional office views as meeting *Spielberg* requisites. Thus, it is at the regional office level, where charges originate, that the real effect of *Spielberg* in avoiding litigation of the same dispute in two forums occurs. When a case in which the respondent is seeking deferral to an arbitration award results in a reported Board decision,

---

1146, 127 LRRM 3164, 3169 (CA 9, 1988); Mahon v. NLRB, 808 F2d 1342, 1345, 124 LRRM 2762, 2764–65 (CA 9, 1987).

[403]NLRB v. Babcock & Wilcox Co., 736 F2d 1410, 116 LRRM 2748 (CA 10, 1984). *But cf.* Harberson v. NLRB, 810 F2d 977, 984, 125 LRRM 2667, 2672 (CA 10, 1987) (court did not address issue of appropriateness of *Olin* standard, but remanded to Board for articulation of reasons for deferring to arbitrator's award).

[404]Bakery Workers Local 25 v. NLRB (Pet, Inc.), 730 F2d 812, 816, 115 LRRM 3390, 3393 (CA DC, 1984). *But cf.* Darr v. NLRB, 801 F2d 1404, 1408–9, 123 LRRM 2548, 2551–52 (CA DC, 1986) (remanding case to the Board for articulation of general theory on deference and how deferral policy applies to particular case). [**Editor's Note:** In Hammontree v. NLRB, 925 F2d 1486, 136 LRRM 2478 (CA DC, 1991), the Court of Appeals for the District of Columbia Circuit, sitting en banc, expressly approved the Board's adoption of the *Olin* standards. *See supra* note 101, **Editor's Note.**]

[405]Taylor v. NLRB, 786 F2d 1516, 122 LRRM 2084 (CA 11, 1986).

[406]*See* note 402, *supra.*

[407]NLRB v. Aces Mechanical Corp., 837 F2d 570, 127 LRRM 2513 (CA 2, 1988) (criticizing the Board for nonapplication of *Olin* standards); Nevins v. NLRB, 796 F2d 14, 18 n.1, 122 LRRM 3147, 3151 n.1 (CA 2, 1986) (remanding case to the Board after finding *Olin* standards were improperly applied).

ordinarily it will have been fully litigated for a second time before the Board—even in those cases where the Board ultimately decides to defer to the arbitral award.

Some of the arguments supporting *Collyer* are the following: (1) avoidance of litigation of the same dispute in two forums—the arbitration tribunal and the Board; (2) the national labor policy favoring the use of private dispute-resolution machinery agreed upon by the parties: (3) "the societal rewards of arbitration outweigh a need for uniformity of result or a correct resolution of the dispute in every case";[408] (4) the desirability of limiting government intervention into labor disputes; (5) the reduction in demands upon the limited resources of the National Labor Relations Board; (6) the more expeditious resolution of disputes under grievance-arbitration machinery; (7) the usual finality attached to arbitration awards; and (8) through *Spielberg* review, the Board can still act, after the arbitration award, to maintain adequate protection of statutory rights.

Some of the arguments on the other side are the following: (1) only the Board has the investigative and legal resources and the knowledge and expertise to process complaints concerning violations of the statute; (2) arbitrators frequently lack the competence or willingness to deal with statutory violations; (3) often the contractual and statutory issues are not congruent, causing the arbitral authority to leave statutory issues unresolved; (4) the inability of an arbitrator to provide an effective remedy at times, particularly for continuing violations; (5) the greater difficulty posed for the Board in protecting statutory rights if it must await the outcome of the arbitral process, and evidence is no longer fresh; (6) the delay that may occur in providing a necessary statutory remedy; and (7) the possible antipathy or unenthusiastic response by the union to an individual's claim of statutory violations.

The *Spielberg* doctrine itself has not been seriously challenged. However, some of the arguments used against *Collyer* are also arguments against any form of deferral. The 1980 Board decisions in *Suburban Motor Freight*[409] and *General American Transportation Corp.*[410] indicated a significant contraction of the deferral

---

[408]Judge Rosenn in the lead opinion in NLRB v. Pincus Bros., Inc.-Maxwell, 620 F2d 367, 374, 104 LRRM 2001 (CA 3, 1980).

[409]*See supra* note 231.

[410]*See supra* note 83.

policy. The overruling of these cases in 1984 by *Olin Corp.*[411] and *United Technologies*[412] promises broader, more liberal use of the deferral doctrine.[413]

Present standards of arbitration review provide significant pressures on the side of deferral. In particular the burden is on the party "seeking to have the Board reject deferral and consider the merits of a given case [to] show that the . . . standards for deferral have not been met. Thus, the party seeking to have the Board ignore the determination of an arbitrator has the burden of affirmatively demonstrating the defects in the arbitral process or award."[414]

---

[411]*See supra* note 258.
[412]*See supra* note 106.
[413]Liberal deferral is not without its critics. *See, e.g.,* dissents in Olin and United Technologies, *supra* notes 258 and 106.
[414]Olin Corp., *supra* note 398, at 574. *See supra* notes 258–261.